Schroeder's Collectible
TOYS
Antique to Modern
Price Guide

Second Edition

Edited by Sharon and Bob Huxford

COLLECTOR BOOKS

A Division of Schroeder Publishing Co., Inc.

The current values in this book should be used only as a guide. They are not intended to set prices, which vary from one section of the country to another. Auction prices as well as dealer prices vary greatly and are affected by condition as well as demand. Neither the Editors nor the Publisher assumes responsibility for any losses that might be incurred as a result of consulting this guide.

Searching For A Publisher?

We are always looking for knowledgeable people considered to be experts within their fields. If you feel that there is a real need for a book on your collectible subject and have a large comprehensive collection, contact us.

On The Cover:
Early child's carousel horse, 37", wood with cast-iron handle and mounts, upholstered seat, $120.00.
Charlie McCarthy hand puppet, Ideal, 1930s, 10", mint, $375.00.
American Flyer Engine, Ives cars train set, ca 1920s, cast iron windup engine #12, $225.00.
Railton gas powered racer, 17", near mint, $2,700.00.
Walt Disney's Mousketeer Annette paper dolls, Whitman Publishing Co., 1958, near mint, $50.00. *Courtesy of Beth Summers.*
Mysto Magic Set, Gilbert, 1920s, near mint in excellent box, $450.00.
Charmin' Cathy, auburn, with glasses and tag, $110.00. *Courtesy of Kathy Lewis.*

Editorial Staff:
Editors: Sharon and Bob Huxford
Research and Editorial Assistants: Michael Drollinger, Nancy Drollinger, Steve Drollinger, Linda Holycross, Donna Newnum, Loretta Woodrow
Cover Design: Beth Summers
Layout: Terri Stalions, Beth Ray, Michelle Dowling

Additional copies of this book may be ordered from:

COLLECTOR BOOKS
P.O. Box 3009
Paducah, Kentucky 42002-3009

@$17.95. Add $2.00 for postage and handling.

Copyright: Schroeder Publishing Co., Inc. 1996

Introduction

It seems that every decade will have an area of concentrated excitement when it comes to the antiques and collectibles marketplace. What Depression Glass was to the late sixties, Fiesta to the seventies, and cookie jars were to the eighties, toys are to the nineties. No one even vaguely involved in the field can have missed all the excitement toys have stirred up among many, many collectors. There are huge toy shows nationwide; scores of newsletters, magazines and trade papers that deal exclusively with toys; cataloged toy auctions with wonderful color photographs and several hundred lots each; and more and more toy collector's guides are appearing in the book stores each week.

If you've been using *Schroeder's Antiques Price Guide*, you know that we try very hard not to omit categories where we find even a minor amount of market activity — being collectors ourselves, we know how frustrating it can be when you are unable to find any information on an item in question. But that book is limited to a specific number of pages, and as we watched the toy market explosion taking place, we realized that if we were to do it justice, we would have to publish a companion guide devoted entirely to toys. And following the same convictions, we decided that rather than to try to zero in on only the larger, more active fields, we'd try to represent toys of all kinds, from the 19th century up to today. This is the format we chose to pursue.

Our concept is unique in the collectibles field. Though we designed the book first and foremost to be a price guide, we wanted to make it a buying/selling guide as well. So we took many of our descriptions and values from the 'toys for sale' lists of dealers and collectors around the country. In each of those listings we included a dealer's code, so that if you were looking for the particular model kit (or whatever) that (S5) had to offer, you'd be able to match his code with his name and address in the 'Dealer's Codes' section and simply drop him a line or call him to see if it were still available. Our experiment seems to have been successful. Feedback from the first edition indicates that many of our original sellers did very well, making productive contacts with collectors who not only purchased items from them on their initial call but left requests for other merchandise they were looking for as well.

Our first edition contained almost 24,000 listings, but even at that we realized that when it comes to the toy market, that only began to scratch the surface. Our second edition is just as large, and virtually all of our material is fresh. The few categories that were repeated in their entirety from the first edition generally are those that were already complete or as nearly complete as we or our advisors could make them. But even those have been checked to make sure that values are still current and our information up to date.

We found that organizing toys was mind-boggling. Collectors were quick to tell us that generally toys can't be sorted by manufacturer. So we had to devise a sort that would not only be easy to use but one that our staff could work with. With this in mind, we kept our categories very broad and general. On the whole this worked very well, but we found that the character section was so large (4,000 lines) it overwhelmed our character advisors, and we were embarrassed to send the printouts to them. So even though our original approach may still be the most user-friendly, we pulled out several groups of collectibles and genres and made them their own categories. But you'll find 'See Alsos' in bold, cross-references within the description lines, and a detailed index to help you locate the items you're looking for with ease.

What we want to stress is that our values are not meant to set prices. Some of them are prices realized at auction; you'll be able to recognize these by the 'A' at the end of the description line. The listings that have neither the 'A' code or the dealer code mentioned above were either sent to us for publication by very knowledgeable collectors who specialize in those specific types of toys or were originally dealer coded but altered at the suggestion of an advisor who felt that the stated price might be misleading (in which case, the dealer's code was removed). There are so many factors that bear on the market that for us to attempt to set prices is not only presumptuous, it's ludicrous. The foremost of these factors is the attitude of the individual collector — his personal view of the hobby. We've interviewed several by telephone; everyone has his own opinion. While some view auction prices as useless, others regard them as actual selling prices and prefer them to asking prices. And the dealer who needs to keep turning his merchandise over to be able to replenish and freshen his stock will of necessity sell at lower prices than a collector who will buy an item and wait for the most opportune time to turn it over for maximum profit. So we ask simply that you arrive at your own evaluations based on the information we've provided.

We hope you enjoy our book and that you'll be able to learn by using it. We don't presume to present it as the last word on toys or their values — there are many specialized books by authors who are able to devote an entire publication to one subject, covering it from 'A' to 'Z,' and when we're aware that such a text book exists, we'll recommend it in our narratives. If you have suggestions that you think will improve our format, let us hear from you — we value your input. Until next time — happy hunting! May you find that mint-in-the-box #1 Barbie or if you prefer that rare mechanical bank that has managed to so far elude you. But even if you never do, we hope that you'll find a generous measure of happiness and success, a treasure now and then, and new friends on every journey.

The Editors

Advisory Board

The editors and staff take this opportunity to express our sincere gratitude and appreciation to each person who has contributed their time and knowledge to help us. We've found toys to be *by far* the largest, most involved field of collecting we've ever tried to analyze, but we will have to admit, it's great fun! We've been editing general price guides for almost fifteen years now, and before ever attempting the first one, we realized there was only one way we would presume to publish such a guide. And that would be to first enlist the help of knowledgeable collectors around the country who specialized in specific areas. Last year we had nearly 80; this year we have 120, and we're still looking for help in several areas. Generally the advisors are listed following each category's narrative, so if we have mentioned no one and you feel that you are qualified to advise us, have the time and would be willing to help us out with that subject, please contact us. We'd love to have you on our advisory board. (We want to stress that even if an advisor is credited in a category narrative, that person is in no way responsible for errors. Errors are our responsibility.) Even if we currently list an advisor for your subject, contact us so that we'll have your name on file should that person need to be replaced. This of course happens from time to time due to their interests changing or because they find they no longer have the time.

While some advisors sent us listings and prices, others provided background information and photographs, checked printouts or simply answered our questions. All are listed below. Each name is followed by their code, see the section called *Dealer and Collector Codes* for an explanation of how these are used in the listings.

Geneva Addy (A5)
Diane Albert (T6)
Sally and Stan Alekna (A1)
Jane Anderson (A2)
Aquarius Antiques (A3)
Pamela E. Apkarian-Russel (H9)
Bob Armstrong (A4)
Richard Belyski (B1)
Larry Blodget (B2)
Bojo (B3)
Dick Borgerding (B4)
Sue and Marty Bunis (B11)
Danny Bynum (B7)
Bill Campbell (10)
Casey's Collectible Corner (C1)
Brad Cassidy (C13)
Mark Chase and Michael Kelly (C2)
Arlan Coffman (C4)
Joel Cohen (C12)
Cotswold Collectibles (C6)
Marilyn Cooper (C9)
Cynthia's Country Store (C14)
Rosalind Cranor (C15)
Allen Day (D1)
Marl Davidson (D2)
Larry DeAngelo (D3)
Doug Dezso (D6)
Donna and Ron Donnelly (D7)
George Downes (D8)

Allan Edwards (E3)
Paul Fink (F3)
Mike and Kurt Fredericks (F4)
Steve Fisch (F7)
Lee Garmon
Carol Karbowiak Gilbert (G6)
Mark Giles (G2)
Bill Hamburg (H1)
Don Hamm (H10)
George Hardy (H3)
Ellen and Jerry Harnish (H4)
Roger Inouye (I1)
Terri Ivers (I2)
Ilene Kayne (K3)
Trina and Randy Kubeck (K1)
David Kolodny-Nagy (K2)
Roger Nazeley (N4)
Tom Lastrapes (L4)
Kathy and Don Lewis (L6)
Val and Mark Macaluso (M1)
Bill Mekalian (M4)
John McKenna (M2)
Steven Meltzer (M9)
Lucky Meisenheimer (M3)
Gary Mosholder (G1)
Judith Mosholder (M7)
Natural Way (N1)
Roger Nazeley (N4)
Dawn Parrish (P2)

Judy Posner (P6)
Diane Patalano (P8)
Sheri and John Pavone (P3)
Pat and Bill Poe (P10)
Gary Pollastro (P5)
John Rammacher (S5)
Jim Rash (R3)
Robert Reeves (R4)
Charlie Reynolds (R5)
Craig Reid (R9)
David E. Richter (R1)
David Riddle (R6)
Scott Smiles (S10)
Irwin Stern (S3)
Bill Stillman (S6)
Nate Stoller (S7)
Steve Santi (S8)
Cindy Sabulis (S14)
Jon Thurmond (T1)
Richard Trautwein (T3)
Marcie and Bob Tubbs (T5)
Judy and Art Turner (H8)
Marci Van Ausdall (V2)
Norm Vigue (V1)
Randy Welch (W4)
Dan Wells (W1)
Henri Yunes (Y1)

Acknowledgments

A very special thank you to the dealers of The Old Tyme Toy Mall in James Dean's hometown, Fairmount, Indiana. We visited them for several days this spring and photographed hundreds of items from their booths. If you're passing through the area, it's a stop you should make.

Besides our advisory board, several more people helped us in various ways, perhaps offering advice or sending material or photographs. We want to acknowledge their assistance and express our appreciation to them as well. And if your name should be here and isn't, we do apologize and hope you'll forgive us. The omission was unintentional.

Stanley A. and Robert S. Block (B8)
Joyce Bee
Kim Bordner
Glen Brady
Bill Bruegman (T2)
Ken Clee (C3)
Kent Comstock
Gordy Dutt (D9)
Dunbar Gallery (D10)
Gary Haisley
Alan Hunter
Dave Hutzley

Dana Johnson Enterprises (J3)
Mike's General Store (M5)
The Mouse Man Ink (M8)
Gary Metz (M10)
Philip Norman (N2)
Olde Tyme Toy Mall (O1)
Parkway Furniture & Gift Shop (P1)
Hank Quant
James Raush
Mike Rosco
S&E Sales
Lloyd White

How to Use This Book

Concept. Our design for this book is two-fold. Primarily it is a market report compiled from many sources, meant to be studied and digested by our readers, who can then better arrive at their own conclusion regarding prices. Were you to ask ten active toy dealers for their opinion as to the value of a specific toy, you would no doubt get ten different answers, and who's to say which is correct? Quite simply, there are too many variables to consider. Condition is certainly subjective, prices vary from one area of the country to another, and probably the most important factor is how you personally view the market — how much you're willing to pay and at what price you're willing to sell. So use this as a guide along with your observations at toy shows, flea markets, toy auctions and elsewhere to arrive at an evaluation that satisfies you personally.

The second function of this book is to put buyers in touch with sellers who deal in the type of toys they want to purchase. Around the first of the year, we contacted dealers allover the country asking them to send us their 'for sale' lists and permission to use them as sources for some of our listings, which we coded so as to identify the dealer from whose inventory list the price and description were taken. Even though much of their merchandise will have sold since we entered our data early last spring, many of them tell us that they often get similar or even the same items in over and over, so if you see something listed you're interested in buying, don't hesitate to call any of them. Remember, though, they're not tied down to the price quoted in the book, since their asking price is many times influenced by what they've had to pay to restock their shelves. Let us know how well this concept works out for you.

Toys are listed by name. Every effort has been made to list a toy by the name as it appears on the original box. There have been very few exceptions made, and then only if the collector-given name is more recognizable. For instance, if we listed 'To-Night Amos 'n' Andy in Person' (as the name appears on the box lid), very few would recognize the toy as the Amos 'n' Andy Walkers. But these exceptions are few.

Descriptions and sizes may vary. When we were entering data, we often found the same toy had sold through more than one auction gallery or was listed in several dealer lists. So the same toy will often be described in various ways, but we left descriptions just as we found them, since there is usually something to be gleaned from each variation. We chose to leave duplicate lines in when various conditions were represented so that you could better understand the impact of condition on value. Depending on the source and who was doing the measuring, we found that the size of a given toy might vary by an inch or more. Not having the toy to measure ourselves, we had to leave dimensions just as they were given in auction catalogs or dealer lists.

Lines are coded as to source. Each line that represents an auction-realized price will be coded 'A' at the end, just before the price. Other letter/number codes identify the dealer who sent us that information. These codes are explained later on.

As we said before, collectors have various viewpoints regarding auction results. You will have to decide for yourself. Some feel they're too high to be used to establish prices while others prefer them to 'asking' prices that can sometimes be speculative. We must have entered about 8,000 auction values, and here is what we found to be true: the really volatile area is in the realm of character collectibles from the '40s, '50s, and '60s — exactly where there is most interest, most collector activity and hot competition when the bidding starts. But for the most part, auction prices were not far out of line with accepted values. Many times, compared to the general market place, toys in less-than-excellent condition actually sold under 'book.' Because the average auction-consigned toy is in especially good condition and many times even retains its original box, it will naturally bring higher prices than the norm. And auctions often offer the harder-to-find, more unusual items. Without taking these factors into consideration, prices may seem high, when in reality, they may not be at all. Prices may be driven up by high reserves, but not all galleries have reserves. Whatever your view, you'll be able to recognize and consider the source of the values we quote and factor that into your personal evaluation.

Categories that have priority. Obviously there are thousands of toys that would work as well in one category as they would in another, depending on the preference of the collector. For instance, a Mary Poppins game would appeal to a games collector just as readily as it would to someone who bought character-related toys of all kinds. The same would be true of many other types of toys. We tried to make our decisions sensibly and keep our sorts simple. But to avoid sending our character advisors such huge printouts, we felt that it would be best to pull out specific items and genres to create specific categories, thereby reducing the size of the character category itself. We'll guide you to those specialized categories with cross-references and 'See Alsos.' If all else fails, refer to the index. It's as detailed as we know how to make it.

These categories have precedence over Character:

Action Figures	Marx
Battery-Operated Toys (also specific manufacturers)	Model Kits
Books	Nodders
Bubble Bath Containers	Paper Dolls
Celebrity Dolls	Pez Dispensers
Character and Promotional Drinking Glasses	Pin-Back Buttons
Character Clocks and Watches	Plastic Figures
Chein	Playsets
Coloring, Activity and Paint Books	Puppets
Corgi	Puzzles
Dakins	Records
Disney	Snow Domes
Dolls, Celebrity	Sports Collectibles
Fisher-Price	Toothbrush Holders
Games	View-Master
Guns	Western
Halloween Costumes	Windups, Friction and Other Mechanicals
Lunch Boxes	

Price Ranges. Once in awhile, you'll find a listing that gives a price range. These result from our having found varying prices for the same item. We've taken a mid-range — less than the highest, a little over the lowest — if the original range was too wide to really be helpful. If the range is still coded 'A' for auction, all the prices we averaged were auction-realized prices.

Condition, how it affects value, how to judge it. The importance of condition can't be stressed enough. Unless a toy is exceptionally rare, it must be very good or better to really have much collector value. But here's where the problem comes in: though each step downward on the grading scale drastically decreases a toy's value, as the old saying goes, 'beauty is in the eye of the beholder.' What is acceptable wear and damage to one individual may be regarded by another as entirely too much. Criteria used to judge condition even varies from one auction company to the next, so we had to attempt to sort them all out and arrive at some sort of standardization. Please be sure to read and comprehend what the description is telling you about condition; otherwise you can easily be mislead. Auction galleries often describe missing parts, repairs and paint touch-ups, summing up overall appearance in the condition code. When losses and repairs were noted in the catalog, we noted them as well. Remember that a toy even in mint restored condition is never worth as much as one in mint original condition. And even though a toy may be rated 'otherwise EX' after losses and repairs are noted, it won't be worth as much as one with original paint and parts in excellent condition. Keep this in mind when you use our listings to evaluate your holdings.

These are the conditions codes we have used throughout the book and their definitions as we have applied them:

M — mint. Unplayed with, brand new, flawless.
NM — near mint. Appears brand new except on very close inspection.
EX — excellent. Has minimal wear, very minor chips and rubs, a few light scratches.
VG — very good. Played with, loss of gloss, noticeable problems, several scratches.
G — good. Some rust, considerable wear and paint loss, well used.
P — poor. Generally unacceptable except for a filler.

Because we do not use a three-level pricing structure as many of you are used to and may prefer, we offer this table to help you arrive at values for toys in conditions other than those that we give you. If you know the value of a toy in excellent condition and would like to find an approximate value for it in near mint condition, for instance, just run your finger down the column under 'EX' until you find the approximate price we've listed (or one that easily factors into it), then over to the column headed 'NM.' We'll just go to $100.00, but other values will be easy to figure by addition or multiplication. Even though at auction toys in very good to excellent condition sometimes bring only half as much as a mint condition toy, the collectors we interviewed told us that this was not true of the general market place. Our percentages are simply an average based on their suggestions.

G	VG	EX	NM	M
40/50%	55/65%	70/80%	85/90%	100%
5.00	6.00	7.50	9.00	10.00
7.50	9.00	11.00	12.50	15.00
10.00	12.00	15.00	18.00	20.00
12.00	15.00	18.00	22.00	25.00
14.00	18.00	22.50	26.00	30.00
18.00	25.00	30.00	35.00	40.00
22.50	30.00	37.50	45.00	50.00
27.00	35.00	45.00	52.00	60.00
32.00	42.00	52.00	62.00	70.00
34.00	45.00	55.00	65.00	75.00
35.00	48.00	60.00	70.00	80.00
40.00	55.00	68.00	80.00	90.00
45.00	60.00	75.00	90.00	100.00

Condition and value of original boxes and packaging. When no box or packaging is referred to in the line or in the narrative, assume that the quoted price is for the toy only. Please read the narratives! In some categories (Corgi, for instance), all values are given for items mint and in original boxes. Conditions for boxes (etc.) are in parenthesis immediately following the condition code for the toy itself. In fact, any information within parenthesis at that point in the line will refer to packaging. Collector interest in boxes began several years ago, and today many people will pay very high prices for them, depending on scarcity, desirability and condition. The more colorful, graphically pleasing boxes are favored, and those with images of well-known characters are especially sought-after. Just how valuable is a box? Again, this is very subjective to the individual. We asked this question to several top collectors around the country, and the answers they gave us ranged from 20% to 100% above mint-no-box prices.

Advertising. You'll notice display ads throughout the book. We hope you will contact these advertisers if they deal in the type of merchandise you're looking for. If you'd like your ad to appear in our next edition, please refer to the advertising rate chart in the back of the book for information.

Listing of Standard Abbreviations

These abbreviations have been used throughout this book in order to provide you with the most detailed descriptions possible in the limited space available. No periods are used after initials or abbreviations. When two dimensions are given, height is noted first. When only one measurement is given, it will be the greater — height if the toy is vertical, length if it is horizontal. (Remember that in the case of duplicate listings representing various conditions, we found that sizes often varied as much as an inch or more.)

Am	American	MIP	mint in package
att	attributed to	mk	marked
bl	blue	MOC	mint on card
blk	black	MOT	mint on tree
brn	brown	NM	near mint
bsk	bisque	NP	nickel plated
c	copyright	NRFB	never removed from box
ca	circa	NRFP	never removed from package
cb	cardboard	orig	original
CI	cast iron	o/w	otherwise
compo	composition	P	poor
dbl	double	Pat	patented
dk	dark	pc	piece
dtd	dated	pg, pgs	page, pages
ea	each	pk	pink
emb	embossed	pkg	package
EX	excellent	pnt	paint, painted
F	fine	prof	professional
fr	frame, framed	rfn	refinished
ft, ftd	foot, footed	rnd	round
G	good	rpl	replaced
gr	green	rpr	repaired
hdl	handle, handled	rpt	repainted
hdw	hardware	rstr	restored
illus	illustrated, illustration	sq	square
inscr	inscribed	sz	size
jtd	jointed	turq	turquoise
litho	lithographed	unmk	unmarked
lt	light, lightly	VG	very good
M	mint	wht	white
MBP	mint in bubble pack	w/	with
mc	multicolored	w/up	windup
MIB	mint in box	yel	yellow

Action Figures

Back in 1964, Barbie dolls had taken the feminine side of the toy market by storm. Hasbro took a risky step in an attempt to target the male side. Their answer to the Barbie craze was GI Joe. Since no self-respecting boy would admit to playing with dolls, Hasbro called their boy dolls 'action figures,' and to the surprise of many, they were phenomenally successful. Both Barbie and GI Joe were realistically modeled (at least GI Joe was) and posable 12" vinyl dolls that their makers clothed and accessorized to the hilt. Their unprecedented successes spawned a giant industry with scores of manufacturers issuing one 'action' figure after another, many in series. Other sizes were eventually made in addition to the 12" dolls. Some are 8" to 9", others 6", and many are the 3¾" figures that have been favored in recent years.

This is one of the fastest growing areas of toy collecting today. Manufacturers of action figures are now targeting the collector market as well as the kids themselves, simply because the adult market is so active.

Beware of condition! Original packaging is extremely important. In fact, when it comes to the recent issues, loose, played-with examples are seldom worth more than a few dollars. Remember, if no box is mentioned, values are for loose (unpackaged) dolls.

Advisors: George Downs (D8), Robert Reeves (R3), Best of the West.

See also Barbie Dolls; Celebrity Dolls; Character, TV and Movie Collectibles; GI Joe; Star Trek; Star Wars.

A-Team, figure, Hannibal Smith, Galoob, 1983, MOC (minor shelf wear), H4..$12.00

A-Team, figure, Murdock, Galoob, 1983, MOC, from $15.00 to $18.00.

A-Team, figure, Templeton Peck (Face), Galoob, 1983, MOC, from $15.00 to $18.00.

Action Jackson, outfit, Aussie Marine #1101, Mego, 1972, EX (orig box), H4 ....$8.00
Action Jackson, outfit, Baseball #1115, Mego, 1972, EX (orig box), H4..$8.00
Action Jackson, outfit, Rescue Squad #1107, Mego, 1972, MIB, H4 ....$10.00
Action Jackson, outfit, Ski Patrol #1105, Mego, 1972, EX+ (orig box), H4 ....$8.00
Action Jackson, outfit, Snow Mobile #1112, Mego, 1972, MIB, H4 ....$10.00
Action Jackson, outfit, Surf & Scuba #1118, Mego, 1972, MIB, H4 ....$10.00
Action Man, see GI Joe category

Adventures of Indiana Jones, figure, Kenner, 12", MIB, $225.00.

Adventures of Indiana Jones, accessory, Desert Convoy Truck, Kenner, 1982-83, MIB, H4..$35.00

Adventures of Indiana Jones, accessory, Map Room Adventure set, Kenner, 1982-83, MIB, D8 ....$35.00

Adventures of Indiana Jones, figure, Belloq, Kenner, 1982-83, ceremonial robe, mail-in figure, MIB, H4 ....$9.00

Adventures of Indiana Jones, figure, Cairo Swordsman, Kenner, 1982-83, missing sword, EX+, H4................................$5.00

Adventures of Indiana Jones, figure, German Mechanic, Kenner, 1982-83, MOC, H4 ....$24.00

Adventures of Indiana Jones, figure, Indiana Jones, Kenner, 1982-83, MOC, D8 ....$125.00

Adventures of Indiana Jones, figure, Toht or Cairo Swordsman, Kenner, 1982-83, MOC, D8, ea $12.00

American West, figure, Buffalo Bill, Mego, 1973-75, 8", M (NM box)..$40.00

Archies, figure, Archie, Marx, 1975, 9", MOC, H4..........$35.00

Archies, figure, Jughead, Marx, 1975, 9", MOC, H4 ....$35.00

Batman, accessory, Batmobile, Toy Biz, 1989, NRFB, H4 ....$50.00

Batman, accessory, Batwing, Toy Biz, 1989, NRFB, H4 ...$45.00

Batman, figure, Batman, Kid Biz (Toy Biz, Australia), 1989, MOC, H4..$70.00

Batman, see also Dark Knight

Battlestar Galactica, accessory, Colonial Stellar Probe, Mattel, 1978, M (NM box), H4..$29.00

Battlestar Galactica, figure, Daggit, Mattel, 1978, 3¾", EX+, H4..$15.00

Battlestar Galactica, figure, Impervious Leader, Mattel, 1978, 3¾", MOC $12.00

Battlestar Galactica, figure, Lucifer, Mattel, 1978, 3¾", EX+, H4..$18.00

Best of the West, accessory, buckboard wagon, Marx, 1965-76, complete, MIB, R4..$60.00

Best of the West, accessory, Circle X Ranch, Marx, 1965-76, MIB, R4 ....$75.00

Best of the West, accessory, covered wagon, Marx, 1965-76, MIB, R4 ....$60.00

Best of the West, accessory, Fort Apache playset, Marx, 1965-76, MIB, R4 ....$100.00

Best of the West, accessory, Indian Teepee playset, Marx, 1965-76, MIB, R4 ....$85.00

Best of the West, accessory, Johnny West Jeep Camping set, Marx, 1965-76, complete, R4..................................$100.00

Best of the West, accessory, Johnny West Ranch Carry-All, Marx, 1965-76, MIB, R4 ....$50.00

Best of the West, buffalo, Marx, 1965-76, complete, MIB, R4 ....$150.00

Best of the West, buffalo, Marx, 1965-76, EX, H4............$50.00

Best of the West, dog, Flick or Flack, Marx, 1965-76, MIB, R4, ea $80.00

Best of the West, dog, German Shepherd or Brittany Spaniel, Marx, 1965-76, EX, H4, ea...$40.00

Best of the West, figure, Black Bart, Marx, 1965-76, 11½", no accessories, NM, S2 ....$55.00

Best of the West, figure, Captain Maddox, Marx, 1965-76, MIB, R4..$85.00

Battlestar Galactica, Cylon Raider, Mattel, MIB, $45.00.

Battlestar Galactica, figure, Adama, Apollo or Starbuck, Mattel, 1978, 3¾", MOC, ea..................................$20.00

Battlestar Galactica, figure, Cylon Centurian, Mattel, 1978, 3¾", silver, w/weapon, EX+, H4.................................$14.00

Battlestar Galactica, figure, Cylon Centurian, Mattel, 1978, 12", VG, H4 ....$20.00

Battlestar Galactica, figure, Cylon Commander, Mattel, 1978, 3¾", gold, w/weapon, EX+, H4 ....$18.00

Best of the West, figure, Chief Cherokee, Marx, NM (EX box), H4, $50.00.

Best of the West, figure, Fighting Eagle, Marx, 1965-76, molded gr body (rare), w/most accessories, EX, H4 ....$125.00

Best of the West, figure, General Custer, Marx, 1965-76, NM (EX box), H4 ....$80.00

Best of the West, figure, Geronimo, Marx, 1965-76, missing yel headband (EX box), H4....................................$75.00

Best of the West, figure, Geronimo, Marx, 1965-76, molded orange body (rare), w/accessories still sealed in plastic, H4..$80.00

Best of the West, figure, Jamie West, Marx, 1965-76, MIB, R4 ....$40.00

Best of the West, figures, Jane West, MIB, $50.00; Tom Maddox, Marx, 1967, 12", MIB, $85.00.

Best of the West, figure, Janice West, Marx, 1965-76, MIB, R4..$40.00

Best of the West, figure, Jay West, Marx, 1965-76, w/most accessories, H4 ....$26.00

Best of the West, figure, Jeb Gibson, Marx, 1965-76, MIB, R4, minimum value..$40.00

Best of the West, figure, Johnny West, Marx, 1965-76, complete w/all accessories, EX, H4 ....$39.00

Best of the West, figure, Johnny West, Marx, 1965-76, M (NM box), H4..$65.00

Best of the West, figure, Josie West, Marx, 1965-76, MIB, R4.$40.00

Best of the West, figure, Princess Wildflower, Marx, 1965-76, NM (worn & taped box), H4 ....$50.00

Best of the West, figure, Sam Cobra, Marx, 1965-76, complete w/all accessories, EX, H4 ....$49.00

Best of the West, figure, Sam Cobra, Marx, 1965-76, M in sealed plastic bag (NM box), H4 ....$110.00

Best of the West, figure, Sam Cobra, Marx, 1965-76, NM (rpr box), H4..$95.00

Best of the West, figure, Sam Cobra, Marx, 1965-76, no accessories, G, H4 ....$20.00

Best of the West, figure, Sheriff Garrett, Marx, 1965-76, MIB, R4...$125.00

Best of the West, figure, Zeb Zachary, Marx, 1965-76, MIB, R4, minimum value...$150.00

Best of the West, figure set, Chief Cherokee w/horse, Marx, 1965-76, EX, S2..$125.00

Best of the West, figure set, Jane West & Flame, Marx, 1965-76, EX (EX box), H4 ....$110.00

Best of the West, figure set, Johnny West & Geronimo w/Buckskin, Marx, 1965-76, complete, VG (VG box), H4..$200.00

Best of the West, figure set, Johnny West & Thunderbolt, Marx, 1965-76, EX (EX box), H4......................................$110.00

Best of the West, horse, Buckskin, Marx, 1965-76, MIB, R4..$60.00

Best of the West, horse, Comanche, Marx, 1965-76, NMIB (w/Fort Apache Fighters, end flap tears), H4..........$125.00

Best of the West, horse, Comanche, Marx, 1965-76, w/accessories, EX+, H4..$49.00

Best of the West, horse, Flame, Marx, 1965-76, MIB, R4..$50.00

Best of the West, horse, Pancho, Marx, 1965-76, M (NM box), H4 ....$60.00

Best of the West, horse, Thunderbolt, Marx, tan version, MIB, from $40.00 to $50.00.

Best of the West, horse, Thunderbolt, Marx, 1965-76, blk version, NMIB, H4 ....$70.00

Big Jim, accessory, Big Jim's PACK boat, Mattel, 1973-76, blk, incomplete, VG, J5 ....$25.00

Big Jim, accessory, Big Jim's PACK Corvette, Mattel, 1973-76, blk, incomplete, VG, J5...$25.00

Big Jim, accessory, case, Mattel, 1973-76, color photo on vinyl, VG, J5..$25.00

Big Jim, accessory, Pro Sports Gear, Mattel, 1973-76, G (no insert in box), H4 ....$18.00

Big Jim, accessory, raft, Mattel, 1973-76, w/oars, VG, H4..$8.00

Big Jim, accessory, Safari Jeep, Mattel, 1973-76, w/accessories, 19", M (NM box), T2 ....$59.00

Big Jim, accessory, Sports Camper, Mattel, 1973-76, w/most accessories, EX, H4 ....$10.00

Big Jim, accessory, US Olympic Ski Run, Mattel, 1973-76, complete w/instructions, NM (EX+ box), T2 ....$29.00

Big Jim, accessory, walkie-talkies, Mattel, 1973-76, diecut parachute becomes antenna, EX (orig box), J5 ....$35.00

Big Jim, figure, Baron Fangg, Mattel, MIB, $40.00.

Big Jim, figure, Big Jack, Mattel, 1973-76, MIB, H4 ....$39.00

Big Jim, figure, Big Jim, Mattel, 1973-76, in Eagle outfit w/accessories & eagle, H4 ....$22.00

Big Jim, figure, Big Jim, Mattel, 1973-76, in basketball outfit w/ball, EX, H4 ....$20.00

Big Jim, figure, Big Jim, Mattel, 1973-76, in cowboy outfit, EX, H4 ....$22.00

Big Jim, figure, Big Jim, Mattel, 1973-76, in football pants & shirt, EX+, H4 ....$18.00

Big Jim, figure, Big Jim's PACK Zorak, Mattel, 1973-76, w/pants & boots, EX+, H4 ....$28.00

Big Jim, figure, Big Josh, Mattel, 1973-76, in commando outfit w/accessories, EX+, H4 ....$22.00

Big Jim, outfit, Action Adventure Basketball #8854 or Skin Diving #8855, Mattel, 1973-76, MOC, H4, ea $10.00

Big Jim, outfit, arctic explorer, Mattel, 1973-76, jacket, pants, boots, snowshoes & rifle, EX, H4 ....$7.00

Big Jim, outfit, scuba diver, Mattel, 1973-76, tanks, flippers & mask, MOC, H4 ....$10.00

Big Jim (European), figure, Big Jim Commander, Deluxe; Astros; Vector; Baron Fangg; NRFB, H4, ea $40.00

Big Jim (European), figure, Dr Alec, Deluxe; w/accessory vehicle, NRFB, H4 ....$50.00

Big Jim (European), figure, Professor Obb Overlord, Kendo Outfit; Big Jim Explorer; NRFB, H4, ea, from $25 to $30.00

Big Jim (European), outfit, Attack Vehicle Driver, NRFB, H4 ....$12.00

Big Jim (European), outfit, Communications Agent, NRFB, H4 ....$12.00

Big Jim (European), outfit, Equestrian #9922, bl window box set, NRFB, H4 ....$15.00

Big Jim/James Bond (European), figure, Big Jim Agent, Karate outfit NRFB, H4 ....$35.00

Big Jim/James Bond (European), figure, Big Jim Agent 004, 6 exchangeable faces & disguises, NRFB, H4 ....$40.00

Big Jim/James Bond (European), figure, Commando Jeff or Air Ace, NRFB, H4, ea $50.00

Big Jim/Space Series (European), figure, Captain Laser, NRFB, H4 ....$79.00

Big Jim/Western Series (European), figure, Frescia Rugiada, female Indian, NRFB, H4 ....$70.00

Bionic Woman, accessory, Bionic Beauty Salon, Kenner, 1976-77, MIB $20.00

Bionic Woman, figure, Fembot, Kenner, 1976-77, 12", MIB $80.00

Bionic Woman, figure, Jaime Sommers, Kenner, 1976-77, 12", in bl outfit w/shoes, EX, S2 ....$20.00

Bionic Woman, outfit, Floral Delight, Kenner, 1976-77, MOC, T1 ....$6.00

Bionic Woman, outfit, Gold Evening Dress, Kenner, 1976-77, MOC, T1 ....$6.00

Black Hole, figure, Charles Pizer, Dan Holland, Dr Alex Durant, Hans Reinhardt, Kate McRae, Mego, 1980, 12", MIB, J5, ea $35.00

Bonanza, accessory, 4-in-1 Wagon, Am Character, 1966, w/all accessories, NM $50.00

Bonanza, box for Hoss figure, Am Character, 1966, VG, J2 ....$60.00

Bonanza, box for Little Joe figure, Am Character, 1966, VG, J2 ....$65.00

Bonanza, figure, Ben Cartwright, Am Character, 1966, complete w/accessories, M, H4 ....$75.00

Bonanza, figure, Hoss, American Character, 1966, 8", EX (EX box), $100.00.

Bonanza, figure set, Ben Cartwright w/horse, Am Character, 1966, MIB $180.00

Bonanza, figure set, Hoss w/horse, Am Character, 1966, MIB (orig display box w/stables), S2 ....$170.00

Bonanza, figure set, Little Joe w/horse, Am Character, 1966, w/all accessories except pistol, VG, H4......................$99.00

Bonanza, horse, Am Character, 1966, blk & wht saddle, for 9" figure, VG, H4 ....$25.00

Bonanza, horse, Am Character, 1966, no accessories, H4 .$12.00

Bonanza, mountain lion, Am Character, 1966, EX, H4 ...$15.00

Bruce Lee, figure, Lar-Go, 1983, 6", w/bo stick, MOC $45.00

Bruce Lee, figure, Lar-Go, 1983, w/nunchaku, M (NM box), T2 ....$35.00

Buck Rogers, figure, Ardella, Draco or Draconian Guard, Mego, 1979, 3¾", MOC, ea..$15.00

Buck Rogers, figure, Buck Rogers, Mego 1979, 12", NRFB ..$50.00

Buck Rogers, figure, Dr Heur, Mego, 1979, 12", MIB, J5 .$35.00

Buck Rogers, figure, Dr Heur, Mego, 1979, 12", NRFB $50.00

Buck Rogers, figure, Draco, Mego, 1979, 12", EX (orig box) .$30.00

Buck Rogers, figure, Draco, Mego, 1979, 12", NRFB........$50.00

Buck Rogers, figure, Draco, Mego, 1979, 3¾", EX, H4 ....$3.00

Buck Rogers, figure, Draconian Guard, Mego, 1979, 12", NRFB $75.00

Buck Rogers, figure, Killer Kane, Mego, 1979, 12", MIB, J5 ....$35.00

Buck Rogers, figure, Tiger Man, Mego, 1979, 12", NRFB..$75.00

Buck Rogers, figure, Twiki, Mego, 1979, 3¾", MOC (sealed) $40.00

Captain Action, accessory, Action Boy boomerang, Ideal, 1966-68, EX+, D8 ....$35.00

Captain Action, accessory, Captain Action laser rifle, Ideal, 1966-68, EX, H4 ....$18.00

Captain Action, accessory, Directional Communicator, Ideal, 1966-68, M, M5 ....$95.00

Captain Action, accessory, Flash Gordon helmet, Ideal, 1966-68, VG, H4 ....$15.00

Captain Action, accessory, Green Hornet mask, gas mask, jacket or pants, Ideal, 1966-68, EX, H4, ea...........................$75.00

Captain Action, accessory, jet mortar, Ideal, 1966-68, NM, M5..$115.00

Captain Action, accessory, Phantom belt w/holster, Ideal, 1966-68, EX, H4 ....$12.00

Captain Action, accessory, Sgt Fury mask w/beard, Ideal, 1966-68, EX, H4 ....$15.00

Captain Action, accessory, Spiderman belt, Ideal, 1966-68, EX, H4 ....$40.00

Captain Action, accessory, Steve Canyon helmet w/oxygen mask, Ideal, 1966-68, EX, H4 ....$20.00

Captain Action, accessory, Steve Canyon parachute & harness, Ideal, 1966-68, EX, S2 ....$75.00

Captain Action, accessory, Superman Kryptonite, Ideal, 1966-68, EX, H4 ....$14.00

Captain Action, accessory, Survival Kit, Ideal, 1966-68, complete, NM, S2 ....$150.00

Captain Action, accessory, Weapons Arsenal, Ideal, 1966-68, NM, M5 ....$170.00

Captain Action, accessory, Weapons Arsenal, Ideal, 1966-68, EX, S2 ....$130.00

Captain Action, figure, Action Boy, Ideal, 1967, w/accessories, EX, H4 ....$325.00

Captain Action, figures, Ideal: Captain Action, EX (original box), $200.00; Buck Rogers, NM, $465.00; Lone Ranger, EX, $270.00; Aquaman, EX+, $255.00; Tonto, NM+, M5, $560.00.

Captain Action, figure, Aquaman, Ideal, 1966-68, w/flasher ring, EX+, M5 ....$255.00

Captain Action, figure, Buck Rogers, Ideal, 1966-68, w/flasher ring, NM, M5..$465.00

Captain Action, figure, Dr Evil, Ideal, 1966-68, w/lab coat only, NM, M5 ....$185.00

Captain Action, figure, Ideal, 1966-68, EX+ (VG+ box), M5...$210.00

Captain Action, figure, Ideal, 1966-68, orig outfit, G, H4 ....$175.00

Captain Action, figure, Lone Ranger, Ideal, 1966-68, w/flasher ring, EX, M5 ....$270.00

Captain Action, figure, Tonto, Ideal, 1966-68, w/eagle & 4 arrows, flasher ring, NM, M5 ....$560.00

Captain Action, outfit, Aquaman, Ideal, 1966-68, EX, H4..$95.00

Captain Action, outfit, Batman, Ideal, 1966-68, EX $140.00

Captain Action, outfit, Captain Action jumpsuit w/emblem, Ideal, 1966-68, VG, H4...$15.00

Captain Action, outfit, Captain America, Ideal, 1966-68, w/accessories, EX, H4 ....$100.00

Captain Action, outfit, Captain America body suit, Ideal, 1966-68, EX+, T1 ....$45.00

Captain Action, outfit, Dr Evil shirt & pants, Ideal, 1966-68, EX, H4 ....$75.00

Captain Action, outfit, Tonto shirt, Ideal, 1966-68, EX, H4..$25.00

Captain Action, panther, Ideal, 1966-68, EX+, D8..........$45.00

Charlie's Angels, see Celebrity Dolls

CHiPs, figure, Ponch, Mego, 8", MOC $25.00

Clash of the Titans, figure, Kraken Monster, Mattel, EX, H4...$65.00

Comic Action Heroes, figure, Batman, Mego, 1975-78, 3¾", w/rope & base, EX, H4 ....$14.00

Comic Action Heroes, figure, Captain America, Mego, 1975-78, 3¾", w/shield & base, EX, H4 ....$25.00

Comic Action Heroes, figure, Joker, Mego, 1975-78, 3¾", no accessories o/w EX, H4 ....$12.00

Comic Action Heroes, figure, Penguin, Mego, 1975-78, 3¾", w/umbrella & base, EX, H4 ....$25.00

Comic Action Heroes, figure, Robin, Mego, 1975-78, 3¾", w/Batrope & base, EX, H4...$25.00

Comic Action Heroes, figure, Spiderman, Mego, 1975-78, 3¾", no accessories or base o/w EX, H4 ....$14.00

Crash Dummies, figure, Pitstop, premium item, only available in Canada, MOC $20.00

Crash Dummies, figure, Vince or Larry, MOC, D8, ea $18.00

Dark Knight, accessory, Batcycle or Jokercycle, Kenner, 1990, MOC, D8, ea $18.00

Dark Knight, figure, Shadow Wing, Wall Scaler, Iron Winch, Crime Attack, Tec Shield or Bruce Wayne, Kenner, 1990, MOC, D8, ea $15.00

Dark Knight, figure, Sky Escape Joker, Kenner, 1990, MOC, D8 ....$25.00

Dark Knight, figure, Thunderwhip or Power Wing, Kenner, 1990, MOC, D8, ea $28.00

DC Comics Super Heroes, figure, Lex Luthor, Toy Biz, MOC, $12.00.

Defenders of the Earth, figure, Phantom, Galoob, 1986, MOC, D8 ....$18.00

Defenders of the Earth, figure, Lothar, Galoob, MOC, O1, $30.00.

Dino-Riders, figure set, Nova on Demon, Tyco, 1989-90, MOC, T1 ....$5.00

Dino-Riders, figure set, Orion on Six-Gill, Tyco, 1989-90, MOC, T1 ....$5.00

Dukes of Hazzard, figure, Bo, Mego, 8", MOC, $25.00.

Dukes of Hazzard, figure, Boss Hogg, Mego, 1981, 8", M (NM card), H4 ....$19.00

Dukes of Hazzard, figure, Daisy Duke, Mego, 1981, 8", M (EX card) $28.00

Dukes of Hazzard, figure, Daisy Duke, Mego, 3¾", MOC, $35.00.

Dukes of Hazzard, figure, Luke Duke, Mego, 1981, 8", MOC, H4..............................$19.00

Dune, figure, Sardaukar Warrior, LJN, 1984, MOC, T1 ....$25.00

Evel Knievel, accessory, King of Stuntman Arctic Explorer set, Ideal, 1970s, MOC, T1 ....$35.00

Evel Knievel, accessory, Precision Miniature Dragster, Ideal, 1970s, M (EX box), J5 ....$25.00

Evel Knievel, accessory, stunt show vinyl case & accessories, Ideal, 1970s, EX, J5 ....$35.00

Evel Knievel, figure, Derry Darling, Ideal, 1970s, w/motorcycle, VG (orig box), J5 ....$25.00

Evel Knievel, figure, Evel Knievel, Ideal, 1970s, on motorcycle, MIB, S2 ....$65.00

Flash Gordon, figure set, includes Flash, Lizard Woman, Ming, Thun & Dr Zarkon, Mattel, 1979, 3¾", complete, H4 ....$50.00

Happy Days, accessory, car, Mego, 1978, for 8" figures, NMIB, C1..$99.00

Happy Days, accessory, Fonzie's Garage playset, Mego, 1978, NMIB, C1 ....$169.00

Happy Days, figure, Fonzie, Mego, 1978, 8", MOC, J2 .....$35.00

Honey West, accessory, Gilbert, complete with binoculars, pistol, shoes and glasses, MIP, $40.00.

Honey West, figure, Gilbert, 1965, 12", EX, H4 ....$89.00

Indiana Jones, see Adventures of Indiana Jones

James Bond, accessory, pool table set, Gilbert, 1965, MOC, D8 .$45.00

James Bond, figure, Goldfinger, Odd Job or Bond in scuba gear, Gilbert, 1965, MOC, ea $25.00

James Bond, figure, M, Dr No, Largo or Domino, Gilbert, 1965, MOC, S2, ea $20.00

Johnny West, see Best of the West

Karate Kid, accessory, Competition Center, Remco, 1986, w/mat, arena & referee, MIB, S2 ....$35.00

Legend of the Lone Ranger, figure, Butch Cavendish, Gabriel, 1982, 9½", MIB..$90.00

Legend of the Lone Ranger, figure, Lone Ranger, Gabriel, 1982, 9½", MIB..$75.00

Legend of the Lone Ranger, figure, Tonto, Gabriel, 1982, 9½", MIB..$60.00

Legend of the Lone Ranger, horse, Scout, Gabriel, 1982, M (EX card), S2 ....$25.00

Lone Ranger (Rides Again), accessory, Apache Buffalo Hunt or Tribal Powwow, Gabriel, 1979, MIB, ea $60.00

Lone Ranger (Rides Again), accessory, Carson City Bank or Missing Mountain Climber, Gabriel, 1979, M (worn box), ea..$55.00

Lone Ranger (Rides Again), accessory, Hopi Medicine Man or Mysterious Prospector, Gabriel, 1979, M (worn box), ea $60.00

Lone Ranger (Rides Again), accessory, Kidnappers, Gabriel, 1979, MIB..$95.00

Lone Ranger (Rides Again), accessory, Lost Cavalry Patrol, Gabriel, 1979, MIB, C3 ....$50.00

M*A*S*H, accessory, Headquarters, Tri-Star, MOC, J2 .$20.00

M*A*S*H, accessory, jeep, Tri-Star, includes 3¾" figure, 1982, NMIB, C1 ....$31.00

M*A*S*H, figure, Hawkeye, Hotlips or BJ, Tri-Star, lg, MOC, ea..$40.00

M*A*S*H, figure, Klinger, Tri-Star, 3¾", MOC, T1.......$12.00

Mad Monster, figure, The Dreadful Dracula, Mego, 1974, 8", EX, H4 ....$65.00

Mad Monster, figure, The Horrible Mummy, Mego, 1974, VG, O1 ....$30.00

Mad Monster, figure, The Monster Frankenstein, Mego, 1974, 8", EX, H4..$35.00

Major Matt Mason, accessories, Uni-Tred Space Hauler, MIB, $65.00; Star Seeker, MIB, $100.00; Uni-Tred and Space Bubble, MIB, $160.00; Space Bubble, MIB, $70.00; Astro Trac, MIB, $85.00; Space Crawler, MIB, M5, $70.00.

Major Matt Mason, accessory, binoculars or movie camera, Mattel, 1966-68, EX, H4, ea, from $7 to..............................$8.00

Major Matt Mason, accessory, carrying case, Mattel, 1966-68, NM, J5 ....$20.00

Major Matt Mason, accessory, Cat Trak, Mattel, 1966-68, red or wht, EX, H4, ea..$10.00

Major Matt Mason, accessory, crescent wrench, hammer or screwdriver, Mattel, 1966-68, EX, H4, ea, from $5 to..$7.00

Major Matt Mason, accessory, Decontamination Rifle, Mattel, 1966-68, w/tanks, EX, H4..$10.00

Major Matt Mason, accessory, Firebolt Space Cannon, Mattel, 1966-68, G, H4..$18.00

Major Matt Mason, accessory, Gamma Ray Guard Pack, Mattel, 1966-68, MOC, D8..$95.00

Major Matt Mason, accessory, Jet Pack, Mattel, 1966-68, w/belt, no string, EX, H4 ....$8.00

Major Matt Mason, accessory, Laser Rifle, Mattel, 1966-68, minor chrome wear, H4..................................$10.00

Major Matt Mason, accessory, Radiation Detector, Mattel, 1966-68, includes hand-held device & Geiger counter, EX, H4 ....$10.00

Major Matt Mason, accessory, Space Glider Plane, Mattel, 1966-68, VG, H4 ....$28.00

Major Matt Mason, accessory, Space Shelter Pack, Mattel, 1966-68, MOC, D8..................................$95.00

Major Matt Mason, accessory, Space Sled, Mattel, 1966-68, EX, H4 ....$10.00

Major Matt Mason, accessory, Space Travel Pack, Mattel, 1966-68, MOC, D8..................................$95.00

Major Matt Mason, accessory, Star Seeker, Mattel, 1966-68, EX+ (EX+ box), M5..................................$75.00

Major Matt Mason, accessory, Supernaut Power Limbs Pack, Mattel, 1966-68, MOC, D8..................................$95.00

Major Matt Mason, accessory, Talking Command Console, Mattel, 1966-68, working, J6..................................$110.00

Major Matt Mason, accessory, walkie-talkie, Mattel, 1966-68, EX, H4 ....$10.00

Major Matt Mason, figure, Callisto Alien, Mattel, 1966-68, EX, H4 ....$50.00

Major Matt Mason, figure, Captain Laser, Mattel, 1966-68, w/helmet & backpack only, non-working, H4..................................$45.00

Major Matt Mason, figure, Matt Mason, Mattel, 1966-68, w/helmet, EX, H4 ....$45.00

Major Matt Mason, figure, Scorpio, Mattel, 1966-68, EX, H4 ....$290.00

Major Matt Mason, figure, Sgt Storm, Mattel, 1966-68, w/helmet, EX, H4 ....$55.00

Man From UNCLE, figure, Illya Kuryakin, Gilbert, 1965, 12", no accessories or paperwork, EX (EX box), H4..................................$89.00

Man From UNCLE, figure, Napoleon Solo, Gilbert, 1965, 12", w/badge, NMIB, M5..................................$215.00

Man From UNCLE, outfit, wht tux w/short-sleeved shirt, Gilbert, 1965, H4..................................$9.00

Marvel Super Heroes, figure, Aquaman, Toy Biz, MOC ..$25.00

Marvel Super Heroes, figure, Captain America, Toy Biz, MOC..................................$18.00

Marvel Super Heroes, figure, Daredevil, Toy Biz, MOC...$65.00

Marvel Super Heroes, figure, Dr Doom, Toy Biz, MOC, S2.$50.00

Marvel Super Heroes, figure, Dr Octopus, Toy Biz, MOC.$12.00

Marvel Super Heroes, figure, Flash, Toy Biz, MOC..........$12.00

Marvel Super Heroes, figure, Green Goblin, Toy Biz, w/lever, MOC..................................$65.00

Marvel Super Heroes, figure, Green Lantern, Toy Biz, MOC..................................$25.00

Marvel Super Heroes, figure, Hawkman, Toy Biz, MOC..$25.00

Marvel Super Heroes, figure, Incredible Hulk, Toy Biz, 15", MIB $60.00

Marvel Super Heroes, figure, Spiderman, Toy Biz, 15", MIB..................................$50.00

Marvel Super Heroes, figure, Thor, Toy Biz, 1st edition, w/short hammer, MOC..................................$55.00

Marvel Super Heroes, figure, Venom, Toy Biz, 15", MIB .$50.00

Marvel Super Heroes Secret Wars, accessory, Tower of Doom, Mattel, 1984, MIB (sealed), S2 ....$85.00

Marvel Super Heroes Secret Wars, figure, Captain America and His Secret Shield, Mattel, MOC, from $20.00 to $25.00.

Marvel Super Heroes Secret Wars, figure, Captain America, Mattel, 1984, M(EX card)..................................$15.00

Marvel Super Heroes Secret Wars, figure, Daredevil, Mattel, 1984, MOC, D8..................................$30.00

Marvel Super Heroes Secret Wars, figure, Falcon, Mattel, 1984, MOC, D8..................................$55.00

Marvel Super Heroes Secret Wars, figure, Kang, Mattel, 1984, MOC, D8..................................$65.00

Marvel Super Heroes Secret Wars, figure, Kang, Mattel, 1984, EX+, D8..................................$5.00

Marvel Super Heroes Secret Wars, figure, Spiderman, Mattel, 1984, red, MOC, D8..................................$35.00

Marvel Super Heroes Secret Wars, figure, Spiderman, Mattel, 1984, blk, MOC, D8..................................$55.00

Masters of the Universe, figure, Extender, Mattel, 1985, w/accessories & comic book, EX+, H4..................................$10.00

Masters of the Universe, figure, Grizzlor, Mattel, 1986, w/accessories & comic book, EX+, H4..................................$9.00

Masters of the Universe, figure, Man-at-Arms, Mattel, 1981, w/accessories & comic book, EX+, H4..................................$5.00

Masters of the Universe, figure, Mantenna, Mattel, 1984, w/accessories, EX+, H4..................................$8.00

Masters of the Universe, figure, Ram Man, Mattel, 1982, w/accessories & comic book, EX+, H4..................................$5.00

Masters of the Universe, figure, Rio Blast, Mattel, 1985, w/accessories & comic book, EX+, H4..................................$10.00

Masters of the Universe, figure, Stonedar, Mattel, 1985, w/accessories & comic book, EX+, H4..................................$5.00

Masters of the Universe, figure, Sy-Klone, Mattel, 1984, w/accessories & comic book, EX+, H4..................................$7.00

Masters of the Universe, figure, Webstor, Mattel, 1981, w/accessories & comic book, EX+, H4..................................$7.00

Micronaut, figure set, includes Repto, Membros & Antron, Mego, 1977, complete, H4..................................$60.00

Mini-Monster, accessory, playcase for 3½" figures, Remco, 1983, M, H4...$18.00

Moonraker, figure, Holly, Mego, 1979, 12½", fully jtd, magnetic mouth, EX+ (EX box), A $72.00

Moonraker, figure, Jaws, Mego, 1979, 12½", fully jtd w/magnetic mouth, scarce, EX (VG+ box), A $175.00

Mork & Mindy, accessory, 4-Wheel Drive Truck, Mattel, 1970s, for 9" figures, M (dented box), J5 ....$25.00

Muhammad Ali, figure, Mego, 1976, 8", w/boxing action, MOC, S2...$150.00

Noble Knights, accessory, Gold Knight's horse armor, Marx, 1968-72, 12", sealed..$65.00

Noble Knights, accessory, Silver Knight's instruction sheet, Marx, 1968-72 ....$35.00

Noble Knights, figure, Sir Gordon the Gold Knight, Marx, 1968-72, missing part of bow & 5 of 6 arrows, H4.....$65.00

Noble Knights, figure, Sir Stuart the Silver Knight, Marx, 1968-72, VG $90.00

Noble Knights, horse, Bravo, Marx, 1968-72, NMIB, H4 .$99.00

Noble Knights, horse, Valor, Marx, 1968-72, NMIB, H4 ....$135.00

Official Scout High Adventure, accessory, Avalanche on Blizzard Ridge set, Kenner, 1974, EX, H4 ....$25.00

Official Scout High Adventure, accessory, Balloon Race to Devil's Canyon set, Kenner, 1974, M (EX box), H4 .$35.00

Official Scout High Adventure, accessory, Danger at Snake River set, Kenner, 1974, EX, H4 ....$20.00

Official Scout High Adventure, accessory, Lost in the High Country set, Kenner, 1974, EX, H4 ....$18.00

Official Scout High Adventure, accessory, metal detector, Kenner, 1974, EX, H4 ....$8.00

Official Scout High Adventure, accessory, Pathfinder Jeep & Trailer set, Kenner, 1974, VG (VG box), H4............$45.00

Official Scout High Adventure, accessory, Search for the Spanish Galleon set, Kenner, 1974, EX, H4 ....$20.00

Official Scout High Adventure, accessory, Warning From Thunderhead Weather Station, Kenner, 1974, MIB (lt wear), H4..$28.00

Official Scout High Adventure, figure, Bob Scout, Kenner, 1974, orig outfit, EX+, H4..$26.00

Official Scout High Adventure, figure, Craig Cub Scout, Kenner, 1974, orig outfit, EX+, H4.................................$18.00

Official Scout High Adventure, figure, Steve Scout, Kenner, 1974, in wht T-shirt & shorts, EX+, H4 ....$22.00

Official World's Greatest Super Heroes, accessory, Batcage, Mego, 1972-78, VG (orig box), I2 ....$32.00

Official World's Greatest Super Heroes, accessory, Batmobile, Mego 1972-78, VG, H4...$45.00

Official World's Greatest Super Heroes, figure, Batgirl, Mego, 1972-78, 8", complete w/outfit, EX, S2 ....$95.00

Official World's Greatest Super Heroes, figure, Batman, Mego, 1972-78, 8", removable cowl, complete, EX, H4 .....$125.00

Official World's Greatest Super Heroes, figure, Batman, Mego, 1972-78, 12", NRFB, H4 ....$90.00

Official World's Greatest Super Heroes, figure, Captain America, Mego, 1972-78, 8", complete w/accessories, M, I2 ......$80.00

Official World's Greatest Super Heroes, figure, Catwoman, Mego, 1972-78, 8", no gloves, EX+, D8 ....$85.00

Official World's Greatest Super Heroes, figure, Conan, Mego, 1972-78, 8", MOC, H4...$280.00

Official World's Greatest Super Heroes, figure, Conan, Mego, 1972-78, 8", EX, H4..$99.00

Official World's Greatest Super Heroes, figure, Falcon, Mego, 1972-78, 8", MIB, H4..$129.00

Official World's Greatest Super Heroes, figure, Falcon, Mego, 1972-78, 8", minor pnt wear, H4................................$30.00

Official World's Greatest Super Heroes, figure, Fist-Fighting Batman, Mego, 1975, 8", MIB, S9 ....$325.00

Official World's Greatest Super Heroes, figure, Green Arrow, Mego, 1972-78, 8", EX, O1.....................................$90.00

Official World's Greatest Super Heroes, figure, Green Goblin, Mego, 1972-78, 8", MIB...$250.00

Official World's Greatest Super Heroes, figure, Green Goblin, Mego, 1972-78, 8", NM (EX box), O1, $225.00.

Official World's Greatest Super Heroes, figure, Green Goblin, Mego, 1972-78, 8", missing purse o/w EX, H4 ....$45.00

Official World's Greatest Super Heroes, figure, Human Torch, Mego 1972-78, 8", MOC...$60.00

Official World's Greatest Super Heroes, figure, Human Torch, Mego, 1972-78, 8", NM (EX+ box), D8 ....$150.00

Official World's Greatest Super Heroes, figure, Incredible Hulk, Mego, 1972-78, 8", MOC, S2.................................$35.00

Official World's Greatest Super Heroes, figure, Incredible Hulk, Mego, 1978, 12", EX, S2...$30.00

Official World's Greatest Super Heroes, figure, Invisible Woman, Mego, 1972-78, 8", EX, H4 ....$30.00

Official World's Greatest Super Heroes, figure, Ironman, Mego, 1972-78, 8", M (NM box), H4................................$129.00

Official World's Greatest Super Heroes, figure, Joker, Mego, 1972-78, 8", complete w/outfit, NM, S2 ....$75.00

Official World's Greatest Super Heroes, figure, Lizard, Mego, 1972-88, 8", MOC, H4..$149.00

Official World's Greatest Super Heroes, figure, Lizard, Mego, 1972-78, 8", no jacket o/w EX, H4............................$45.00

Official World's Greatest Super Heroes, figure, Mr Mxyzptlk, Mego, 1972-78, 8", M (shelf-worn box), H4..............$60.00

Official World's Greatest Super Heroes, figure, My Mxyzptlk, w/smirk, Mego, 1972-78, 8", M (opened Kresge card), H4..$99.00

Official World's Greatest Super Heroes, figure, Penguin, Mego, 1972-78, 8", M (shelf-worn box), H4........................$65.00

Official World's Greatest Super Heroes, figure, Riddler, Mego, 1972-78, 8", EX+, D8..$95.00

Official World's Greatest Super Heroes, figure, Robin, Mego, 1972-78, 8", complete w/outfit, M (NM card), S2.....$85.00

Official World's Greatest Super Heroes, figure, Robin, Mego, 1972-78, 8", VG, H4..$25.00

Official World's Greatest Super Heroes, figure, Shazam, Mego, 1972-78, 8", EX+ (EX box), D8..............................$150.00

Official World's Greatest Super Heroes, figure, Spiderman, Mego, 1972-78, 8", MOC, H4....................................$20.00

Official World's Greatest Super Heroes, figure, Spiderman, Mego, 1972-78, 12", EX, W2....................................$85.00

Official World's Greatest Super Heroes, figure, Thing, Mego, 1972-78, 8", M (NM box), H4 ....$90.00

Official World's Greatest Super Heroes, figure, Thor, Mego, 1972-78, 8", missing helmet, hammer, wrist bands o/w VG, H4 ....$35.00

Official World's Greatest Super Heroes, figure, Thor, Mego, 1972-78, 8", touch up/rpt hammer handle o/w EX, H4.........$85.00

Official World's Greatest Super Heroes, figure, Wonder Woman, Mego, 1972-78, 8", MIB, H4....................................$245.00

One Million BC, figure, Grok, Mego, 1976, 8", MOC, H4.$39.00

One Million BC, figure, Orm, Mego, 1976, 8", M (EX card), H4...$39.00

One Million BC, figure, Trag, Mego, 1976, 8", MOC, H4..$39.00

Over the Top, figure, Lincoln Hawks, LewCo, 1986, 8", MOC, S2 ....$25.00

Pee Wee's Playhouse, figure, King of Cartoons, Matchbox, 1988, MOC, J6...$18.00

Pee Wee's Playhouse, figure, Miss Yvonne, Matchbox, 1988, 6", MOC, H4..$15.00

Pee Wee's Playhouse, figure, Reba, Matchbox, 1988, 6", MOC, H4..$20.00

Pee Wee's Playhouse, figure, Ricardo, Matchbox, 1988, 6", MOC, H4..$20.00

Peter Pan, figure, Captain Hook, Sears, 1988-89, MOC, D8..$9.00

Planet of the Apes, accessory, catapult & wagon, Mego, 1973-75, NMIB, S2..$55.00

Planet of the Apes, accessory, Fortress playset, Mego, 1973-75, G (EX box), H4 ....$85.00

Planet of the Apes, accessory, throne, Mego, 1973-75, MIB, S2 ....$50.00

Planet of the Apes, accessory, Village playset, Mego, 1973-75, complete & unused (EX box), D9..............................$49.00

Planet of the Apes, figure, Alan Verdon, Mego, 1973-75, 8", EX, H4 ....$30.00

Planet of the Apes, figure, Astro, Mego, 1973-75, EX, S2 ....$35.00

Planet of the Apes, figure, Cornelius, Mego, 1973-75, 8", EX, H4..$28.00

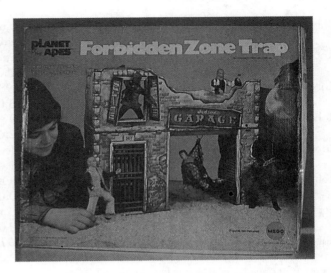

Planet of the Apes, accessory, Forbidden Zone Trap playset, Mego, MIB, $50.00.

Planet of the Apes, figure, Dr Zaius, Mego, 1973-75, 8", no vest o/w EX, H4..$28.00

Planet of the Apes, figure, General Urko, Mego, 1973-75, 8", no accessories or boots o/w EX, H4 ....$25.00

Planet of the Apes, figure, General Ursus, Mego, 1973-75, 8", missing knife o/w EX, H4 ....$40.00

Planet of the Apes, figure, Peter Burke, Mego, 1973-75, 8", EX, H4 ....$30.00

Planet of the Apes, figure, Soldier Ape, Mego, 1973-75, 8", w/all accessories & gloves, H4.....................................$55.00

Planet of the Apes, figure, Soldier Ape, Mego, 1973-75, 8", no accessories o/w EX, H4.....................................$30.00

Planet of the Apes, figure, Zira, Mego, 1973-75, 8", w/all accessories, NM, I2..$35.00

Planet of the Apes, horse, Stallion, Mego, 1973-75, MIB, H4 ....$95.00

Police Academy, accessory, Precinct Police Station, Kenner, 1989, MIB, S2..$55.00

Police Academy, figure, Eugene Tackleberry, Kingpin or Mahoney, Kenner, 1989, MOC, T1, ea.......................$5.00

Police Academy, figure, Larvelle Jones or Sky Glidin' Zed, Kenner, 1989, MOC, D8, ea $9.00

Rambo, figure, Rambo, Coleco, w/motorized battle action, 7", MIB, S2..$25.00

Real Ghosbusters, figure, Terror Tongue, Nasty Neck, Terrible Teeth or Ecto 3, Kenner, 1986-90, MOC, D8, ea........$8.00

Robin Hood, Prince of Thieves, figure, Akeem, Kenner, 1991, MOC..$10.00

Robin Hood, Prince of Thieves, figure, Crossbow or Longbow Robin Hood (orig head), Kenner 1991, MOC, S2, ea.$20.00

Robin Hood, Prince of Thieves, figure, Dark Knight, Kenner, 1991, MOC..$15.00

Robin Hood, Prince of Thieves, figure, Friar Tuck, Kenner, 1991, MOC..$25.00

Robin Hood & His Merry Men, figure, Friar Tuck, Mego, 1974, 8", missing sandle, NMIB, S2 ....$40.00

RoboCop, figure, RoboCop, China (unlicensed), 12", NRFB (box shows cop getting out of car), H4 ....$50.00

RoboCop, figure, Talking RoboCop, Taiwan (unlicensed), not sold in US, MIB, H4.....................................$99.00

RoboCop & Ultra Police, accessory, Robo-Copter, Kenner, 1989-90, MIB..$50.00

RoboCop & Ultra Police, accessory, Robo-Cycle, Kenner, 1989-90, MIB, S2..$25.00

RoboCop & Ultra Police, figure, Anne Lewis, Kenner, 1989-90, MOC, D8...$12.00

RoboCop & Ultra Police, figure, Dr McNamara, Chainsaw, Headhunter or Nitro, Kenner, 1989-90, MOC, D8, ea...........$9.00

Robotech, figure, Robotech Master, Matchbox, 1985, MOC, H4...$10.00

Rocky, figure, Hulk Hogan as Thunderlips, United Artists Corp, 1983, 8", MOC, H4...................................$30.00

Rookies, figures, Chris, Willie, Mike & Terry, LJN, 1973, w/accessories, set of 4, 9", MOC, H4......................$80.00

Secret Wars, see Marvel Super Heroes Secret Wars

Shogun Warriors, accessory, Bazoler action vehicle, Mattel, 1979-80, EX, J2..$15.00

Shogun Warriors, figure, Mazinga, Mattel, 1979-80, EX, K2..$30.00

Six Million Dollar Man, accessory, Critical Assignment Arms, Kenner, 1975-77, M (NM box), H4.......................$19.00

Six Million Dollar Man, accessory, OSI Headquarters, Kenner, 1975-77, labels applied, NMIB, S2.....................$65.00

Six Million Dollar Man, figure, Oscar Goldman, Kenner, 1975-77, w/exploding briefcase, EX, S2.....................$25.00

Six Million Dollar Man, figure, Steve Austin, Kenner, 1975-77, w/equipment & accessories, EX+, H4.................$29.00

Six Million Dollar Man, figure, Steve Austin w/Bionic Grip, Kenner, 1977, MIB, S2..................................$95.00

Space: 1999, figure, Commander Koenig, Mattel, 1976-77, 9", EX, H4..$15.00

Space: 1999, figure, Dr Russell, Mattel, 1976-77, 3¾", EX, H4...$18.00

Space: 1999, figure, Professor Bergman, Mattel, 1976-77, 9", EX, H4...$20.00

StarCom, figure, Torvek or Von Dar, Coleco, MOC, S2, ea..$10.00

Starsky and Hutch, figure, Chopper, Mego, 8", MOC, $25.00.

Starsky & Hutch, figure, Capt Dobey, Mego, 1976, 8", MOC, H4..$29.00

Starsky & Hutch, figure, Huggy Bear, Mego, 1976, rare, MOC, S2...$85.00

Starsky & Hutch, figure, Starsky or Hutch, Mego, 1976, MOC, ea...$30.00

Steve Scout, see Official Scout High Adventure

Super Heroes, see Official World's Greatest Super Heroes

Super Naturals, figure, Hooter Heroic, Mr Lucky or See-Thru Heroic Ghostling, Tonka, 1986, MOC, T1, ea...........$5.00

Super Pirates, figure, Black Beard, Mego, 1974, 8", complete w/accessories, NM, I2.............................$50.00

Super Powers, accessory, Batmobile, Kenner, 1984-86, for 5" figures, NMIB.....................................$75.00

Super Powers, accessory, Darkseid Destroyer playset, Kenner, 1984-86, MIB (sealed), D9.........................$39.00

Super Powers, accessory, Delta Probe One, Kenner, 1984-86, MIB, H4..$20.00

Super Powers, accessory, Lex Soar-7, Kenner, 1984-86, MIB, H4...$10.00

Super Powers, figure, Batman, Kenner, 1984-86, MOC, S2...$50.00

Super Powers, figure, Brainiac, Kenner, 1984-86, complete, H4...$10.00

Super Powers, figure, Cyclotron, Kenner, 1984-86, MOC, H4...$60.00

Super Powers, figure, Darkseid, Kenner, 1984-86, M (worn/dented card), H5......................................$14.00

Super Powers, figure, Desaad, Kenner, 1984-86, MOC, H4..$20.00

Super Powers, figure, Flash, Kenner, 1984-86, complete, H4...$3.00

Super Powers, figure, Flash, Kenner, 1984-86, MOC........$15.00

Super Powers, figure, Kalibak, Kenner, 1984-86, MOC, H4...$10.00

Super Powers, figure, Mr Freeze, Kenner, 1984-86, MOC, H4...$70.00

Super Powers, figure, Mr Miracle, Kenner, 1984-86, MOC, H4...$130.00

Super Powers, figure, Orion, Kenner, 1984-86, MOC......$55.00

Super Powers, figure, Samurai, Kenner, 1984-86, MOC, H4...$85.00

Super Powers, figure, Tyr, Kenner, 1984-86, MOC, H4...$60.00

Swamp Thing, figure, Snap Up or Snare Arm, Kenner, 1990-91, MOC, T1, ea..$10.00

SWAT, figure set w/playset, LJN, 1975-76, 5 figures w/accessories, desk & chair, walkie-talkies, barricades, etc, H4...$125.00

Tarzan King of the Apes, figure, Kala the Ape, Dakin, 1984, MOC, S2...$30.00

Tarzan King of the Apes, figure, Tarzan, Dakin, 1984, 7", MOC...$30.00

Teenage Mutant Ninja Turtles, figure, Ace Duck, Playmates, 1988-91, w/pop-up display, MOC, D8....................$55.00

Teenage Mutant Ninja Turtles, figure, April O'Neil, Playmates, 1988-91, orig 1st issue, no stripe, EX+, H4..............$100.00

Teenage Mutant Ninja Turtles, figure, April O'Neil, Playmates, 1988-91, orig 1st issue, no stripe, MOC, S2............$175.00

Teenage Mutant Ninja Turtles, figure, April O'Neil, Playmates, 1988-91, 2nd issue, bl stripe, MOC, S2................$50.00

Teenage Mutant Ninja Turtles, figure, April O'Neil w/Channel 6 News van, Playmates, 1988-91, w/gr outfit, MIB, S2 ..**$55.00**

Teenage Mutant Ninja Turtles, figure, Foot Soldier, Playmates, 1988-91, orig, MOC, S2 ....**$25.00**

Teenage Mutant Ninja Turtles, figure, Krang, Playmates, 1988-91, orig issue, MOC, S2 ....**$20.00**

Teenage Mutant Ninja Turtles, figure, Leatherhead, Playmates, 1988-91, orig issue, MOC..**$50.00**

Teenage Mutant Ninja Turtles, figure, Ray Fillet, Playmates, 1988-91, color-changing issue (recalled), MOC........**$25.00**

Teenage Mutant Ninja Turtles, figure, Tattoo, w/decal applied, rare, MOC, S2 ....**$65.00**

Terminator II, figure, Blaster T-1000, Techo Punch, Power Arm, Secret Weapon or Damage Repair, Kenner, 1991, MOC, D8, ea..**$9.00**

Terminator II, figure, John Connor, Kenner, 1991, MOC, D8 ..**$15.00**

Terminator II, figure, Terminator II, limited video offer when movie came out, 11", EX, H4 ....**$25.00**

Uncanny X-Men, see X-Men

Universal Studio's Creature, figure, Remco, 1980, MOC (sunburst glow card), H4 ....**$16.00**

Universal Studio's Dracula, figure, Remco, 1980, 3½", MOC, H4..**$16.00**

Vikings, figure, Erik, Marx, no accessories, EX, H4 ....**$30.00**

Vikings, figure, Erik, Marx, w/accessories, H4 ....**$99.00**

Vikings, figure, Odin, Marx, complete, EX, H4 ....**$99.00**

Vikings, horse, dk brn w/jtd head & neck, also has wheels, w/armor, VG, H4 ....**$60.00**

Waltons, accessory, Country Store, Mego, 1976, MIB **$75.00**

Waltons, accessory, Farmhouse, Mego, 1976, MIB........**$100.00**

Waltons, figure set, John Boy & Mary Ellen, Mamma & Daddy or Grandpa & Grandma, Mego, 1976, 8", MIB, ea pr.....**$75.00**

Welcome Back Kotter, accessory, Classroom playset, Mattel, 1976, MIP **$45.00**

Welcome Back Kotter, figure, Mr Kotter, Barbarino, Horshack, Washington or Epstein, Mattel, 1976, 8", MOC, ea..**$25.00**

Willow, figure, Nookmaar Warrior or Airk Thaughbauer, Tonka, 1988, MOC, T1, ea. **$5.00**

Wizard of Oz, figure, Tin Woodsman, Mego, 1974, 8", MIB, from $20.00 to $35.00.

Wizard of Oz, accessory, Emerald City playset, Mego, 1974, MIB, H4 ....**$95.00**

Wizard of Oz, accessory, Witch's Castle playset, Sears exclusive, sealed & NM (no box), H4 ....**$450.00**

Wizard of Oz, figure, Cowardly Lion, Mego, 1974, 8", MIB, H4 ....**$28.00**

Wizard of Oz, figure, Dorothy, Mego, 1974, 8", MIB, H4 .**$28.00**

Wizard of Oz, figure, Glinda, Mego, 1974, 8", MIB, H4 ...**$30.00**

Wizard of Oz, figure, Scarecrow, Mego, 1974, 8", missing diploma o/w MIB, H4 ....**$20.00**

Wizard of Oz, figure, Tin Woodsman, Mego, 1974, 8", MIB, H4 ....**$20.00**

Wizard of Oz, figure, Wicked Witch, Mego, 1974, 8", MIB, $60.00.

Wizard of Oz, figure, Wicked Witch, Mego, 1974, 8", MIB, H4 ....**$60.00**

Wizard of Oz, figure, Wizard, Multi-Toy, 1988, 12", MIB, H4..**$30.00**

Wonder Woman, figure, Steve Trevor, Mego, 1976, 12", NRFB, H4 ....**$80.00**

Wonder Woman, figure, Wonder Woman in Diana Prince outfit, Mego, 1976, 12", NMIB, I2 ....**$35.00**

World's Greatest Super Knights, figure, Ivanhoe, Mego, 1975-76, 8", missing shield & lance o/w EX, H4.................**$35.00**

World's Greatest Super Knights, figure, King Arthur, Mego, 1975-76, 8", missing crown o/w EX, H4....................**$45.00**

World's Greatest Super Knights, figure, Sir Lancelot, Mego, 1975-76, 8", missing shield o/w EX, H4 ....**$45.00**

WWF, World Wrestling Federation, figure, Andre the Giant, Hasbro, 1990, MOC **$100.00**

WWF, World Wrestling Federation, figure, Bam Bam Bigelow, Brett Hart, Undertaker or Mr Perfect, MOC (red), D8, ea...**$15.00**

WWF, World Wrestling Federation, figure, Big Boss Man, Greg Valentine or Undertaker, MOC (bl), D8, ea, from $12 to..**$15.00**

WWF, World Wrestling Federation, figure, Big John Studd, Mr Wonderful or Bruno Sammartino, LJN, MOC, D8, ea .**$50.00**

WWF, World Wrestling Federation, figure, Bobby the Brain, Johnny Hart or Yard Dog Mason, LJN, MOC, D8, ea .$35.00

WWF, World Wrestling Federation, figure, Brutus, MOC (purple), D8 ....$10.00

WWF, World Wrestling Federation, figure, Brutus, MOC (striped), D8...$25.00

WWF, World Wrestling Federation, figure, Captain Lou Albano, Hasbro, 1990, VG, H4................................$12.00

WWF, World Wrestling Federation, figure, Classie Freddi Blassie, Roddy Piper, Mr Fugi or Mean Gene, LJN, MOC, D8, ea $35.00

WWF, World Wrestling Federation, figure, Cowboy Bob, Magnificent Murati or Brutis Beefcake, LJN, MOC, D8, ea...$60.00

WWF, World Wrestling Federation, figure, Doink the Clown, Rick Steiner or Scott Steiner, MOC (purple), D8, ea, from $12 to $14.00

WWF, World Wrestling Federation, figure, Earthquake, Typhoon or Ultimate Warrior, MOC (bl), D9, ea $25.00

WWF, World Wrestling Federation, figure, Fred Balassie, Hasbro, 1990, w/cane, VG, H4................................$12.00

WWF, World Wrestling Federation, figure, Hercules Hernandez or Elizabeth, LJN, MOC, D8, ea................................$70.00

WWF, World Wrestling Federation, figure, Hillbilly Jim, Hasbro, 1990, w/hat, VG, H4...$12.00

WWF, World Wrestling Federation, figure, Hulk Hogan, Hasbro, 1990, w/championship belt, VG, H4 ....$15.00

WWF, World Wrestling Federation, figure, Hulk Hogan, MOC, D8...$20.00

WWF, World Wrestling Federation, figure, Jake the Snake, Roddy Piper, LJN, MOC (bl), D8, ea.........................$20.00

WWF, World Wrestling Federation, figure, Nailz, Komala, Shawn Michaels, Owen Hart or Crush, MOC (yel), D8, ea...$20.00

WWF, World Wrestling Federation, figure, Nikolai Volkoff, Ron Shiek or Hillbilly Jim, LJN, MOC, D8, ea.........$25.00

WWF, World Wrestling Federation, figure, Randy Macho Man, Special Delivery Jones or Johnny Valient, LJN, MOC, D8, ea...$40.00

WWF, World Wrestling Federation, figure, Razor Ramone, MOC (yel), D8 ....$35.00

WWF, World Wrestling Federation, figure, Ted Arcidi, Rick Steamboat, Greg Valentine or Terry Fink, LJN, MOC, D8, ea...$60.00

WWF, World Wrestling Federation, figure, Texas Tornado or Sgt Slaughter, MOC (bl), D8, ea $20.00

WWF, World Wrestling Federation, figure, WWF Referee, LJN, 1980s, MOC, D8...$75.00

WWF, World Wrestling Federation, figure, Yoko Zumo, MOC (red), D8 ....$25.00

X-Men, figure, Apocalypse or Archangel, Toy Biz, MOC, D8, ea...$12.00

X-Men, figure, Banshee, Toy Biz, 1st edition, MOC, D8 .$12.00

X-Men, figure, Cannonball, Toy Biz, purple outfit, MOC, D8..$12.00

X-Men, figure, Colossus, Toy Biz, 1st edition, MOC........$20.00

X-Men, figure, Cyclops, Toy Biz, 1st or 2nd edition, MOC ..$12.00

X-Men, figure, Iceman, Toy Biz, 1st edition, MOC..........$35.00

X-Men, figure, Storm, Toy Biz, 1st edition, MOC...........$35.00

X-Men, figure, Wolverine II, Toy Biz, MOC $18.00

Zorro, figure, Amigo, Gabriel, 1981, MOC, S2................$20.00

Zorro, figure, Zorro, Gabriel, 1981, MOC, S2.................$20.00

Activity Sets

Activity sets that were once enjoyed by so many as children — the Silly Putty, the Creepy Crawlers, and those Mr. Potato Heads — are finding their way back to some of those same kids, now grown up, more or less, and especially the earlier editions are carrying pretty respectable price tags when they can be found complete or reasonably so. The first Thingmaker/Creepy Crawler (Mattel, 1964) in excellent but played-with condition will sell for about $65.00 to $75.00.

Advisor: Jon Thurmond (T1).

See also Character, TV and Movie Collectibles; Coloring, Activity and Paint Books; Disney; Playsets; Western.

Adams' Hocus-Pocus Magic Set, SS Adams, 1962, rabbit in top hat on box lid, complete & unused, NM (EX box) ...$85.00

Adams' Real Magic Set, SS Adams, performing magician on box lid, EX (G box), A...$150.00

Animal Stencils, Milton Bradley, ca 1930, EX (orig box) .$50.00

Beads To String, Parker Bros, ca 1930, EX (orig box) $20.00

Creeple Peeple Thingmaker, Mattel, 1965, M (VG box), from $35.00 to $45.00.

Creeple Peeple Thingmaker, Mattel, M (M box), from $50 to $55.00

Creepy Crawlers, Giant, Mattel, 1968, w/molds & goop, MIB (sealed), from $75 to...$85.00

Creepy Crawlers, 1st series, Mattel, 1964, w/oven & 2 full bottles of goop, VG (VG box), from $65 to...................$75.00

Creepy Crawlers II, Mattel, 1978, w/mold & 4 bottles of goop, 2 molds missing o/w NMIB, S2 ....$45.00

Dinosaur Foto-Fun Printing Kit, Fun Bilt/KFS, 1958, print on paper or cloth, unused $24.00

Doozies, Kenner, 1961, circular styrofoam stacking sections & Vac-U-Form facial pcs, forms totem poles, M............$35.00

Ernest Sewell Young Magician's Table, British, instructions on inside lid, complete, EX..$165.00

Favorite Funnies Printing Set, FAS, 1930s, features Dick Tracy, BO Plenty, Orphan Annie, etc, complete, unused, MIB...$50.00

Fright Factory, Mattel, 1966, w/molds & accessories, EX (EX box) $60.00

Funnies Kasting Kit, Playstone, 1936, rubber mold set includes Harold Teen, Chester Gump & 3 others, EX+ (G box), A $75.00

Great Foodini Magic Set, Pressman, NMIB, J2 ....$100.00

Incredible Edibles (Kooky Kakes) Thingmaker Set, NMIB, J2 ....$50.00

Johnny Toymaker Starter Set, Topper Toys, MIB (sealed)..$65.00

Little Country Doctor Kit, Transogram, 1945, VG+ $30.00

Magic Dots for Little Tots, Milton Bradley, 1907, 5 picture boards, hundreds of colored dots, EX (EX box), P3 ..$25.00

Mandrake, Transogram, 1949, EX $65.00

Microscope, Porter Microcroft, 1956, NM (orig wooden box) $50.00

Mr Potato Head Cooky Cumber Set, missing a few pcs, G (VG box), H4...$25.00

Mr Potato Head Frenchy Fry Set, very rare, few pcs missing, VG (VG box) $50.00

Mr Potato Head Oscar Orange Set, VG............................$35.00

Mr Tricko Magic Set, Remco, 1960s, EX (VG box), J5....$25.00

Mysto Magic Exhibition Set, Gilbert, 1938, complete w/tricks & instructions, EX+ (EX box), A $87.00

Mysto Magic Exhibition Set, Gilbert #21/2, 1938, complete, EX+ (EX box), A $314.00

Mysto Magic Set, early, contains magic apparatus & several tricks, complete, EX, from $350 to..........................$400.00

Mysto Magic Set #2, AC Gilbert, w/all tricks, instruction book, wand, makeup, moustache & poster, M (EX+ box), A..$270.00

Picture Stamp & Printing Set, Fulton, Series #18, late 1920s, 2 pads (lg & sm), 2 letter-printing blocks, EX (EX box), P3...$45.00

Shrunken Head Apple Sculpture Set, features Vincent Price on cover, MIB (sealed), J6..$35.00

Spud-ettes the Potato Head Pets, Hasbro, 1950s, VG $35.00

Strange Change Machine, Mattel, EX+ $75.00

Super Thingmaker, Mattel, NM......................................$125.00

Thingmaker Skeleton Mold, EX..$10.00

Thingmaker Skeleton Maker Pak, Mattel, MOC $75.00

Topper Monster Maker, M, from $60 to $75.00

Vac-U-Form Mold Set, Mattel, 1960s, EX (EX box)........$85.00

Mr. and Mrs. Potato Head and Pets, Hasbro, MIB, O1, $55.00.

Young Gardener, Revell, 1950s, complete with van and gardening tools, NM (VG box), $35.00 to $50.00.

Mr. Potato Head, West Germany, 1950s, missing 1 of 21 pieces, EX, A, $85.00.

Zenith TV Premium Magic Set #919A, NRFB, A, $100.00.

Advertising

The assortment of advertising memorabilia geared toward children is vast — plush and cloth dolls, banks, games, puzzles, trucks, radios, watches and much, much more. And considering the popularity of advertising memorabilia in general, when you add to it the crossover interest from the realm of toys, you have a real winning combination! Just remember to check for condition very carefully; signs of play wear are common. Think twice about investing much money in soiled items, especially cloth or plush dolls. Stains are often impossible to remove.

For more information we recommend *Zany Characters of the Ad World* by Mary Jane Lamphier; *Advertising Character Collectibles* by Warren Dotz; *Advertising Dolls Identification & Value Guide* by Joleen Ashman Robison and Kay Sellers; *Huxford's Collectible Advertising* by Sharon and Bob Huxford; *Pepsi-Cola Collectibles, Vols I, II, and III*, by Bill Vehling and Michael Hunt; and *Collectible Coca-Cola Toy Trucks* by Gael de Courtivron.

Advisors: Jim Rash (R3), advertising dolls and plastic cereal premiums; Larry Blodget (B2), Post Cereal cars.

See also Bubble Bath Containers; Character, TV and Movie Collectibles; Dakins; Disney; Fast-Food Collectibles; Halloween Costumes; Pin-Back Buttons; Premiums; Radios; Telephones; and other specific categories.

AC Spark Plugs, figure, National Products, 1950s, winking & smiling horse atop wheeled bathtub, pot metal, 4", EX, A **$95.00**

Actigall, squeeze toy, Gall Bladder Doll, Summit, 1989, plastic, 4", R3 ....**$20.00**

Actigall, squeeze toy, Gall Bladder Doll, Summit, 1989, plastic, 8", R3 ....**$30.00**

Admiral Appliance, bank, George Washington-type figure, 1980s, vinyl, 7", MIB, H4 ....**$20.00**

Alka-Seltzer, bank, Speedy figure, 1960s, vinyl, 5½", R3 ....**$250.00**

Alka-Seltzer, squeeze toy, Speedy figure, 1960s, vinyl, 8", R3 ....**$500.00**

Allied Van Lines, doll, Buddy Lee, in full uniform w/hat, EX, A **$300.00**

Alpo, figure, Dan the Dog, plush w/collar, D4 ....**$10.00**

American Dental Association, comic book, Casper the Friendly Dentist, 1967, 16 pgs, 5x7", M, T2 ....**$12.00**

American Savings, bank, figural pig, transparent bl & wearing hat, 4½", NM, S2 ....**$15.00**

Apple Jacks, ring, HR Puff 'n Stuf, EX **$60.00**

Aquafresh Toothpaste, Wet Watch, MIP **$10.00**

Aunt Jemima, see Black Americana category

Baby Ruth, doll, Hasbro, 1971, beanbag body, VG, R3 ....**$30.00**

Ballard Biscuits, bank, NM **$20.00**

Banker's Sytstems Inc, bank, Crunch Bird on nest, 1980, vinyl, 6", R3 ....**$25.00**

Baskin Robbins, figure, bendable PVC spoon w/arms & legs, labeled Baskin Robbins on back, 5", M, H4 ....**$8.00**

Bazooka Bubble Gum, car, The Atom w/driver, NM, J2 ..**$20.00**

Bear Brand Hosiery, dolls, painted oilcloth bears, 9½", $135.00 each.

Beech-Nut Gum, figure, Fruit Stripe Gum Man, Multiple Products, 1967, bendable wire arms & legs, 7½", VG, R3 ....**$150.00**

Big Boy, bank, Big Boy figure, 1970s, chubby, vinyl, MIB, H4 ....**$29.00**

Big Boy, bank, Big Boy figure, 1970s, slender, vinyl, M, H4 ..**$35.00**

Big Boy, bank, Big Boy figure, 1973, head turns, vinyl, 9", EX+ **$20.00**

Big Boy, bank, Big Boy figure, 1994, vinyl, 10", M (in plastic bag), H4 ....**$14.00**

Big Boy, wristwatch, Marc's, early, non-working o/w EX, J2 .**$40.00**

Blue Bonnet Margarine, hand puppet, Butter Cup, EX, O1 ..**$15.00**

Boo Berry, see General Mills

Borax, scale model of 20 mule team, M (in orig shipping box), H4 ....**$30.00**

Borden, board game, Elsie & Her Family, 1941, NMIB, J2 .**$130.00**

Borden, doll, Elsie, plush w/rubber face, EX, O1 ....**$40.00**

Borden, doll, Elsie the Cow, plush, jointed shoulders, 13", NM in box marked Krueger, $325.00.

Borden, doll, Elsie the Cow, USA, velveteen w/pnt features, jtd shoulders, bl pinafore w/daisy trim & Elsie, 13", EX, A..$325.00

Borden, figure, Elsie the Cow, bendable PVC, 3½", M, H4..$20.00

Borden, pin, Elsie the Cow, plastic, 1¾", $75.00.

Bosco, bank/jar, figural top & spout, 1960s, EX, S2..........$30.00

Bubble Yum, bank, EX....................................$15.00

Buddy L, bank, Easy Saver, 1970s, red metal cash register, 6", EX, S2..$35.00

Buster Brown, bank, No Parents Allowed, 1980s, 11", R3..$40.00

Buster Brown, Moon Mission Agent Wrist Decoder, 1950s, w/secret compartment & sm decoder book, EX, H4..$75.00

Buster Brown & Tige, ring, C10............................$27.00

Buster Brown Shoes, figure, standing bsk figure of Buster w/jtd arms, 1920s, 4", EX, A..............................$110.00

Buster Brown Shoes, magic slate, 1950s-60s shoe store giveaway, M, S2..$20.00

Buster Brown Shoes, whistle, prewar Japan, Buster standing w/arms at side, blow through feet, pnt bsk, 2¾", NM+, A..$187.00

Buster Brown Stockings, paint box, scarce, MIB, A.......$215.00

Buster Brown Stockings, paint box, 1902, scarce, VG, A.$94.00

Buster Brown, see also Games category

C&H Sugar, doll, Hawaiian Girl, stuffed cloth, MIP, H4...$9.00

Calumet Baking Powder, bank, tin-can shape w/paper litho label, litho tin 'Thank You' child atop can, 7½", G, A..$75.00

Campbell's Soup, doll, ca 1900, cloth & compo, w/up, 7½", VG+, M5..$425.00

Campbell's Soup, squeeze toy, Campbell Boy or Girl, 1974, 10", R3, ea..$30.00

Campbell's Wizard of O's, figure, 1970s, 6½", EX, S2.......$40.00

Cap'n Crunch, bank, Cap'n Crunch figure, 1975, molded vinyl, 7½", EX, from $35 to..................................$50.00

Cap'n Crunch, bank, Cap'n Crunch figure, 1975, molded vinyl, 7½", trap missing, chips around coin slot, G, H4.......$10.00

Cap'n Crunch, bank, Jean LaFoote figure, 1975, molded vinyl, 7½", M, R3..$90.00

Cap'n Crunch, cars, 1974, 3 different, M, R3..................$10.00

Cap'n Crunch, coloring book, Whitman, 1968, few pgs colored o/w EX, I2..$9.00

Cap'n Crunch, game figures, 1974, 3 different, M, R3, ea..$5.00

Cap'n Crunch, Sea Cycle, mail-order premium, M (in shipping bag), H4..$35.00

Cap'n Crunch, treasure chest, EX, S2..........................$85.00

Caravelle Candy Bar, figure, Caravelle Candy Man, 1967, bendable wire arms, R3..................................$150.00

Champion Autoparts, figure, MIP..............................$15.00

Chesty Potato Chips, squeeze toy, Chesty Boy, 1958, vinyl, R3..$500.00

Chiffon Margarine, doll, Mother Nature, stuffed cloth wearing dress, yarn hair, MIP, H4..............................$29.00

Chips Ahoy, figure, vinyl cookie, 4", EX, H4..................$10.00

Chocks Vitamins, doll, Chocks Man, stuffed cloth, 20", VG, H4..$22.00

Chore Boy, doll, Chore Girl, stuffed cloth, minor discoloration, H4..$12.00

Chore Boy, figure, 1991, vinyl w/yel sponge base & gray pan for hat, 6", M, R3..................................$30.00

Chrysler, bank, Mr Fleet figure, 1973, vinyl, 9", R3.......$350.00

Chuck E Cheese, bank, vinyl, NM, T1..........................$25.00

Clark Candy Bar, squeeze toy, Clark boy holding candy bar, 1960s, vinyl, 8½", M, R3..............................$200.00

Coca-Cola, bank, 1950s, red vending machine w/wht lettering, coin slot at top, EX, A..............................$65.00

Coca-Cola, bank/dispenser, Linemar, litho tin w/4 plastic glasses & stopper, 9", EX+ (VG+ box), A..................$445.00

Coca-Cola, car, red & wht Ford style w/allover advertising, wht-wall tires, friction, NM (in orig window box), A.....$250.00

Coca-Cola, doll, Buddy Lee, in full uniform w/logoed hat, EX+, A..$650.00

Coca-Cola, games, 1940s, game box w/checkers, dominos, cribbage board, 2 decks of cards & score pad, EX+ (G+ box), A..$130.00

Coca-Cola, Playtown Hot Dog & Hamburger Stand, ca 1950s, stand w/accessories, wood, metal & plaster, NM (NM box), A..$325.00

Coca-Cola, record carrier, Hi-Fi Club, holds 45-rpm records, w/index, NM, M5..................................$30.00

Coca-Cola, Toy Town Cutout, dtd 1927, cut-out town w/vehicles on 10x15" heavy paper, EX+, A..................$104.00

Coca-Cola, tractor & trailer, Buddy L, 1989, MIB, S2.....$30.00

Coca-Cola, truck, Big Wheel, battery-op, NM (EX+ box), M5..$50.00

Coca-Cola, truck, Buddy L, 1989, 5", MIB, S2.................$20.00

Coca-Cola, truck, Buddy L #5426, 1960, 1st version of the yel metal Ford-style dbl-decker w/wraparound bumper, NMIB, A..$550.00

Coca-Cola, truck, Buddy L #5546, ca 1956, yel metal International dbl-decker, NMIB, A..................................$725.00

Coca-Cola, truck, Buddy L #5646, ca 1957, yel metal GMC dbl-decker w/loading ramp & orig cases, NMIB, A........$600.00

Coca-Cola, truck, Budgie, 1950s, bright yel diecast w/various decals, 5¼", EX+, A..................................$170.00

Coca-Cola, truck, Lincoln Toys, Canada, 18" long, M5, blocks: $10.00 each; truck and blocks: $800.00.

Coca-Cola, truck, Marx, 1954, red & yel pressed steel w/decals, 6 plastic cases, 12½", EX, A $281.00

Coca-Cola, truck, Marx #991, ca 1951, yel metal cab & stake bed w/Sprite boy logo on side panel, NMIB, A $625.00

Coca-Cola, truck, Marx #991, ca 1953, rare gray metal cab, Sprite boy logo on side of stake bed, NMIB, A........$900.00

Coca-Cola, truck, Marx/Canadian, ca 1950, red plastic Ford style w/center divider, 6 orig cases, NM, A..............$525.00

Coca-Cola, truck, Marx/US, ca 1950, yel plastic Ford-style dbl-decker w/5 orig cases, scarce, NM, A $375.00

Coca-Cola, truck, Metalcraft #171, ca 1932, A-frame cargo bed w/10 orig bottles, rubber tires, EX+, A.....................$775.00

Coca-Cola, truck, Smith-Miller, 1979, red GMC dbl-decker w/6 cases of gr bottles, stamped 2 of 50, rare, w/orig box, A $1,700.00

Coca-Cola, Volkswagen Truck, Tippco, Germany, 1950s, 9", MIB, D10, $950.00.

Coco Puffs, Sonny Cards, 2x1½" animal rummy cards, cereal box prize, 1970s, EX, J5 ....$10.00

Cocoa Puffs, bank, plastic, deposit coin & music plays, mail-in premium, MIB, S2 ....$25.00

Comfort Inn, figure, Choice-a-saurus, EX, H4 ....$8.00

Continental Bank, coloring book, 1968, used, EX, J6.......$15.00

Count Chocula, see General Mills

Cracker Jack, prize, 1920s, miniature drawing book w/tracing paper, EX $110.00

Cracker Jack, prize, 1928, Birds We Know miniature book, EX...$75.00

Cracker Jack, prize, 1931, tin sled, 2", EX........................$39.00

Cracker Jack, prize, 1937, tin helicopter w/yel rotor, wood stick, 2⅝", EX $24.00

Cracker Jack, prize, 1939, iron-on transfer of sports figure, EX...$18.00

Cracker Jack, prize, 1946, magic game book, erasable slate series of 13, EX, ea..$27.00

Cracker Jack, prize, 1949, aluminum clicker, pear shape, EX..$32.00

Cracker Jack, prize, 1949, miniature coloring book of animals, EX..$35.00

Cracker Jack, prize, 1950-53, plastic tube-shaped whistle w/animals on top, 1 of 6, 1⅜", EX $6.50

Cracker Jack, prize, 1954, plastic dog w/hollow base, series of 10, EX, ea. $4.50

Cracker Jack, prize, 1964 to recent, pinball game, plastic, EX..$5.00

Curad, bank, Taped Crusader figure, 1975, vinyl, 7½", R3..$35.00

Curity, doll, Dydee Bear, plush w/cloth diaper, H4 ....$15.00

Curity, doll, Miss Curity (nurse), 1950s, hard plastic w/rooted hair on vinyl head, cloth uniform, 17", EX+..............$80.00

Del Monte, bank, Del Monte Big Top Bonanza, 1985, clown on base, 28", H4...$14.00

Dr Miles Medicines, booklet advertising medicines along w/magic tricks throughout, ca 1910, 5x6", EX+.........$15.00

Dutch Boy Paints, hand puppet, 1950s, 12", NM $30.00

Eight O'Clock Coffee, bank, 1940s, 5", EX.....................$45.00

Elsie the Cow, see Borden

Energizer Batteries, Christmas ornaments, set of 4 Bunnies, premiums w/battery purchase, MIP $10.00

Energizer Batteries, figure, plush Bunny, mail-in premium, 24", MIB, S2..$125.00

Energizer Batteries, figure, plush Bunny in Santa hat, Christmas store display, 36", M, S2.......................................$250.00

Energizer Batteries, flashlight, Energizer Bunny, 1991, squeezable vinyl, 4", MOC, H4 ....$10.00

Eskimo Pie, doll, Eskimo Pie Man, newer, stuffed cloth w/name on jacket, 15", EX, H4 ....$8.00

Esso Oil, bank, Esso Drop figure, 1992, wht plastic w/bl & red chest logo, 7", EX, R3 ....$60.00

Esso Oil, bank, Esso Tiger figure, vinyl, 9", NM, T1........$35.00

Esso Oil, doll, Esso Tiger, stuffed cloth, EX, H4................$12.00

Esso Oil, figure, Esso Tiger, walks by battery-op remote while holding flower bouquet, plush w/vinyl head, 11", NM, A...$270.00

Eveready Batteries, bank, blk cat w/decal, 1981, vinyl, 8½" long, VG, R3..$10.00

Facit, figure, Facit Man, 1960s, PVC, 4", R3....................$25.00

Famous Footwear, figure, soft-bodied spider, 8", NM, T1 ....$10.00

Fanny Farmer Candies, truck, Japan, red & wht litho tin w/blk rubber tires, ...For Boys & Girls, friction, 8½", EX, A..$88.00

Farmer Jack Supermarkets, bank, Farmer Jack figure, 1986, vinyl, 7", EX, R3..$30.00

Farmer's Brand, doll, Farmer Boy, printed and stuffed cloth, 14", EX, $185.00.

Fig Newtons, cookie figure w/jtd arms, Nabisco, 1983, EX, H4..............$10.00

Florida Oranges, squeeze toy, Florida Orange Bird, 1974, vinyl, 6", EX, R3 ....$15.00

Franken Berry, see General Mills

Franklin Life Insurance Co, doll, Ben Franklin, stuffed cloth, some discoloration, G, H4 ....$8.00

Frito Lay, coloring book, Frito Kid Circus, 1950s, rare, EX (orig pkg) $45.00

Frito Lay, pencil topper, Frito Bandito, 1968, yel figure, premium, 2", NM, S2..............$35.00

Frito Lay, pencil topper, Muncha Bunch, 1970, red cowboy-like figure, premium, 1⅝", MIP, S2 ....$30.00

Frito Lay, pencil topper, WC Fritos, 1970, red figure, premium, 1¾", MIP, S2..............$25.00

Fruit Brute, see General Mills

Fruit Roll-Ups, figure, Rollupo the Wizard, bendable, 6", EX, H4..............$12.00

General Jeans, see Miller's Outpost

General Mills, beach bag, Monster Cereal printed on both sides, 1973, unused, M..............$60.00

General Mills, biplanes, 1972, Redberry or Grapefellow, M, R3, ea..............$50.00

General Mills, cars, Monster, 3 different, plastic, M, R3, ea $10.00

General Mills, cars, Wacky Racers, 1969, 3 different, M, R3, ea..............$40.00

General Mills, coloring book, Monster Cereal, 1973, mail-in premium, NM $75.00

General Mills, decal, Boo Berry rub-on, MIP..............$15.00

General Mills, eraser, memo pad & crayons w/General Mills characters, MIP, H4 ....$6.00

General Mills, figures, Franken Berry or Count Chocula, plastic, 2", M, R3, ea..............$12.00

General Mills, magnets, Franken Berry, Boo Berry & Count Chocula, 1980s, set of 3, MOC, S2 ....$25.00

General Mills, pencil set, Count Chocula & friends, 1983, 4-pc set, MIP, S2..............$35.00

General Mills, squeeze toy, Boo Berry, 1978, 7½", M, R3..$60.00

General Mills, squeeze toy, Count Chocula, 1978, 8", NM/M, J2/R3, from $40 to $60.00

General Mills, squeeze toy, Franken Berry, 1978, 8", EX, R3..............$60.00

General Mills, squeeze toy, Fruit Brute, 1978, 8", EX, R3.$60.00

General Mills, squeeze toy, Trix Rabbit, 1978, 8½", EX, R3..............$30.00

General Mills, yo-yo, Big 'G,' bl plastic w/wht lettering, premium, EX, S2..............$20.00

Gerber, doll, Gerber Baby, 17", MIB, I2..............$78.00

Gerber, squeeze toy, girl wearing dress & apron which reads I'm a Gerber Kid, 1985, vinyl, 8", EX, H4..............$10.00

Good Humor, squeeze toy, Good Humor Bar w/bite missing, 1975, soft vinyl, 8", rare, M, R3 ....$450.00

Good Humor, truck, Linemar, 1950s, wht tin w/driver in open cab, logoed sides, friction, 4", NM (EX box), A $408.00

Goodrich Silvertown Tires, wrecking truck, sheet metal, red cab, logo on bed, blk rubber tires, 12", EX (worn box), A..$625.00

Goodyear, riding toy, Goodyear Blimp, 20", EX, S2 ....$30.00

Grandma's Cookies, bank, 1970s, hard plastic, M, R3......$35.00

Green Giant, doll, Little Sprout, plush w/cloth outfit & gr felt leaf hair, 12", EX, H4..............$18.00

Green Giant, figure, Jolly Green Giant, 1975, vinyl w/swivel waist, 9½", EX+, A $55.00

Green Giant, figure, Little Sprout, vinyl, EX+ $15.00

Green Giant, figure, Little Sprout, vinyl, M (in orig opened mailer bag), H4..............$18.00

Greyhound Bus, bank, Jimson, late 1960s, plastic, 10", S2 .$40.00

Gulf, doll, right foot stamped King Cole, in full uniform w/hat, VG+, A..............$350.00

Gulf Publishing, figure, hard-hat worker, brass, NM, T1..$95.00

Hamburger Helper, clock, figural Helping Hand, plastic, MIB, S2 ....$55.00

Hamburger Helper, doll, Helping Hand, plush, VG, H4 ..$15.00

Hartz Mountain, figure, cat or dog, 1974, plastic, premium, M, R3, ea $30.00

Hawaiian Punch, watch, features Punchy, new old stock .$65.00

Heinz, delivery truck, Dinky, Heinz 57 Varieties & can of baked beans on side, yel & red, 5½", EX, A $120.00

Heinz, delivery truck, Metalcraft, sheet metal w/Heinz 57 logo & product names, wht w/blk rubber tires, 12", EX, A..$475.00

Heinz, figure, Heinz Ketchup Ant, bendable PVC, 4½", M, H4 ....$10.00

Heinz, talking alarm clock, Aristocrat Tomato in dapper attire behind logo-shaped clock on rnd base, 9½", MIB, R3..$150.00

Hershey, Hersheykins, ea w/heads shaped like a Hershey's Kiss & holding a different candy bar, PVC, 3", H4, ea........$4.00

Honecombs, glow-in-the-dark monster heads, Frankenstein or Mummy, assembled, EX, ea $12.00

Honeycombs, spoon hangers, Baloo, Mowgli or King Louie, 1960s, EX, ea..............$12.00

Honeywell Co, doll, Allergy Annie, stuffed cloth w/weepy eyes & holding flower, unmk, 14", H4..............$15.00

Hood Dairy, squeeze toy, vinyl Hood Dairyman figure, 1981, M, R3..............$60.00

Howard Johnson's, bank, replica of orig restaurant, 1950s, plastic, VG, H4 ....$39.00

Humble Oil, see Esso Oil

Hush Puppies Shoes, squeeze toy, Hush Puppy, 1956, vinyl, EX, R3 ....$15.00

Husky Dog Food, bank, actual can w/label, NM, T1 ....$5.00

Icee, bank, Icee Bear figure, 1974, plastic, 8", EX, R3 ......$25.00

Indian Gum, ring, emb design of Indian chief in headdress on front w/Indian symbols on sides, silvered metal, NM, A $140.00

Ivory Soap, bank, wht plastic pig figure wearing bl shirt w/message Save w/Ivory, VG, H4..$29.00

Jack Frost, doll, stuffed cloth w/name on breast pocket, scarf & hat w/ball on top, 16", EX, H4 ....$12.00

Jell-O, kite, 1950s, promo item, EX, J5 ....$15.00

Jerry's Restaurants, flasher ring, 1960s, H4 ....$12.00

Jiffy Peanut Butter, periscope, w/Jiffy Kangaroo, NM, T1 ..$12.00

Keds, decoder/yo-yo toy, 1960s, premium, MIP, J5 ....$15.00

Keebler, backpack, features Ernie the Elf, EX+ $15.00

Keebler, bank, Ernie the Elf, ceramic, 8", M, S2 ....$45.00

Kellogg's, Baking Soda PT Boat, MIB, J2 ....$32.00

Kellogg's, Baseball Game ring, C10 ....$150.00

Kellogg's, canteen, features Snap! Crackle! & Pop!, w/assembly instructions, 4½" dia, H4 ....$5.00

Kellogg's, cereal bowl, features Tony the Tiger on side of bowl w/figural paws for base, 1981, plastic, 5" dia, EX, D2 .$15.00

Kellogg's, Crazy Cars, snap-together hard plastic w/screw, 1969, unassembled, 2", M, T2 ....$12.00

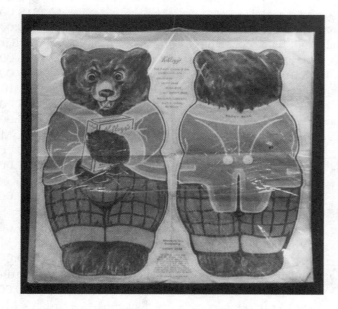

Kellogg's, doll, Daddy Bear, 1925, printed cloth, uncut, 14½", M, $125.00.

Kellogg's, doll, Sweet Heart Corn figure, 1981, vinyl w/cloth clothes, mail-in premium, 9", EX, H4 ....$25.00

Kellogg's, doll, Tony the Tiger, 1960s, stuffed cloth, 13", EX, H4..$25.00

Kellogg's, figure, Pop!, 1974, pnt soft vinyl w/swivel head, 7", EX, J2/T2, from $24 to..$30.00

Kellogg's, figures, Uncle Sam, English Bobbie, Royal Guard or Little Red Riding Hood, 1969, wood w/felt, 3"-4", H4, ea $10.00

Kellogg's, friction toy, Snap!, Talbot Toys, 1984, MOC (bubble slightly opened), H4 ....$18.00

Kellogg's, friction toy, Tucan Sam, 1984, 2½", NM $15.00

Kellogg's, lunch box, features Snap!, Crackle! & Pop!, premium, NM, S2..$85.00

Kellogg's, magic color card featuring Snap!, Crackle! & Pop!, 1933, EX (EX envelope), J2......................................$70.00

Kellogg's, painter's cap, features Snap!, Crackle! & Pop!, 1983, VG, S2 ....$20.00

Kellogg's, plane, Dick Dastardly, 1969, M, R3 ....$40.00

Kellogg's, push puppet, Crackle figural, NM, T1 ....$15.00

Kellogg's, ramp walker, Cornelius Sugarcoat, 1963, M, R3 ..$90.00

Kellogg's, slide-tile puzzle, Dig'em, Toucan Sam or Tony the Tiger, NM, S2, ea $25.00

Kellogg's, slide-tile puzzle, Snap!, Crackle!, Pop!, 1979, light fading o/w VG, S2 ....$20.00

Kellogg's, Swoppets, Huck, Yogi, Boo-Boo, Mr Jinks, Toni the Tiger & Pixie Mouse, 1959, M, R3, ea......................$25.00

Kellogg's, Toolie Birds, 1969, 8 different, M, R3, ea........$22.00

Kellogg's Pop Tarts, bank, Milton the Toaster, 1980, plastic & paper, 5", missing decal, EX+, R3..............................$80.00

Kellogg's Pop Tarts, stencil plates, features several Kellogg's characters w/Pop Tarts box w/offer on back, 1970s, H4 ....$25.00

Kentucky Fried Chicken, bank, Colonel Sanders figure w/bucket of chicken, 1970, plastic, 10", EX..............................$25.00

Kentucky Fried Chicken, bank, Colonel Sanders figure w/cane, 1965, wht plastic w/blk trim, 13", pnt wear $35.00

Kentucky Fried Chicken, nodder, Colonel Sanders, 1964, plastic, R3..$75.00

King Vitamin, hologram ring w/secret compartment, C10 .$150.00

Kit Cereal, ring, Rocket to the Moon, w/1 rocket & instruction booklet, M (orig mailer), C10 ....$775.00

Kool-Aid, basketball figure, PVC, rare, MIP....................$10.00

Kool-Aid, doll, Kool-Aid Kid, 1989, vinyl, 12½", NM.....$20.00

Kool-Aid, drinking straws, 2 figural, 1985, MOC, S2.......$20.00

Kool-Aid, figure, walker, minor pnt wear, missing counterbalance coin o/w VG, H4 ....$39.00

Kraft, bank, Chees-a-saurus Rex figure, 1992, 7", NM, R3 .$20.00

Kraft, squeeze toy, vegetable salad person, 1968, vinyl, M, R3 ..$200.00

Kraft Macaroni & Cheese, figure, Cheese-a-saurus Surfer, Roller Skater or Baseball Player, plastic, 5¼", M, ea $10.00

Lady Luck Casino, figure, Mad Money (court jester), vinyl, 3", NM $5.00

Lemon Pledge, doll, stuffed cloth, EX, H4 ....$12.00

Life 'O' Wheat Breakfast Food, circus & animals, ca 1910, 9" cut-out tent w/12 animals & acts, rare premium, NM, A $90.00

Lifesavers, figure, Multi-Products, 1967, bendable, VG, R3 .$150.00

Lucky Charms, doll, 1960s, stuffed cloth, EX, H4............$28.00

Lucky Charms, figure, Springy, 1960s, red, cereal box prize, 2", EX, J5 ....$25.00

Lysol-Hinds-Etiquet, jack-in-the-box, cube pops up to feature The Lucy Show which advertises Lysol, non-working, VG, A $150.00

M&M's, candy dipsenser, Plain or Peanut figures, 10", MIB, S2, ea...$25.00

M&M's, figures, rubber, set of 4, 3", M, S2 ....$20.00

M&M's, figures, set of 4 bears w/different T-shirts, 2½", M, S2 ....$25.00

Magic Chef, bank, figural, 1960s, vinyl, 7½", NM............$20.00

Mattel, dolls, Matty Mattel & Sister Belle, 1960s, EX, S2, pr $65.00

Mayflower, truck, 1960-70s, yellow plastic with red lettering, 14", M (watermarked box), $20.00.

Maypo, bank, Marky Maypo figure, 1960s, vinyl, 9", EX, R3 .$40.00

McColl's Peanut Butter, bank, ceramic, 6", NM, M5 ....$20.00

Meadow Gold Butter, truck, Metalcraft, Beatrice logo on door, yel-pnt sheet metal, electric lights, 13", G, A $425.00

Meow Mix, pet squeak toy, cat figure, 1975, 5", VG, R3..$40.00

Michelin, figure, Michelin Man w/hands on hips, 1980s, wht hollow plastic, 12", EX+ $50.00

Mid-America Federal Savings Bank, bank, vinyl eagle figure holding pot of gold, 9", EX, H4 ....$30.00

Midgetoys, salesman's sample, cb box w/2 layers of 18 diecast vehicles, complete w/ad inserts, 2½" to 9", MIB, A..$335.00

Miller's Outpost, bank, General Jeans figure, 1979, hard plastic, 8½", EX, R3 ....$45.00

Mr Clean, doll, NM, J2 ....$135.00

Mr Clean, figure, 1961, vinyl, 8½", EX+, A......................$75.00

Mr Softee Ice Cream, parlor ring w/Official club membership kit & certificate for iron-on transfer, EX, H4...................$40.00

Nabisco, bowl hanger, Buffalo Bee, 1963, M, R3..............$10.00

Nabisco, bowl hangers, Jungle Book, 1967, 6 different, R3, ea $10.00

Nabisco, bowl hangers, Winnie the Pooh, 1966, 7 different, M, R3, ea $6.00

Nabisco, see also Fig Newtons

Nabisco Spoonsize Shredded Wheat, figures, Crunchy or Munchy Spoonmen, 1966, M, R3, ea $40.00

Natural Gas, bank, Genie bobbin' head, 8", NM, $225.00.

Nestlé Chocolate, doll, Chocolate Swiss Man in shorts, 12", M (in mailer bag), H4 ....$16.00

Nestlé Cookie Mix, alarm clock, brn cookie w/gold bells, 1970s, EX, J5 ....$45.00

Nestlé Quik, bank, hot cocoa container w/drawings of gold coins & the US Mint, 1980s, NM, S2 ....$5.00

Nestlé Quik, drink shaker, bird figure, Rarity, 1950s-60, EX, S2 ....$65.00

Nestlé Quik, drink shaker, man w/hat, Rarity, 1950s-60, some pnt loss o/w VG, S2 ....$45.00

Nestlé Quik, figure, Quik Bunny, 1991, bendable, 6", H4.$12.00

Old Dutch Cleanser, pull toy, Hubley, 1932, depicts girl chasing dirt, pnt CI, 8⅝", EX, A....................................$5,500.00

Oscar Mayer, bank, Wienermobile, EX, H4......................$18.00

Oscar Mayer, ring, features Oscar the Chef, plastic, H4...$12.00

Oscar Mayer, Weinermobile, late 1980s, mail-in premium, 12", MIB, S2 ....$45.00

Paas, figure, duck or chicken, 1979, EX, R3, ea $15.00

Pappy Parker Chicken House Restaurant, figure, Pappy Parker, 1973, brn vinyl, 6", VG+, H4..................................$45.00

Penzoil, truck, ladder on roof, plastic, 8½", VG+, A $50.00

Pepsi-Cola, Truck, Buddy L, wood and masonite, green paint, 15¾", with pressed steel hand truck, EX, $800.00.

Pepsi-Cola, truck, Marx, 1940s, wht plastic cab, tin bed lithoed w/carrying cases, wood wheels, scarce, EX+, A........$185.00

Pepsi-Cola, truck, Marx, 1948, wht plastic w/5 decals, open bed holds bottles, 11", EX, A $240.00

Pepsi-Cola, truck, Nylint, ca 1950s, metal w/various logos in open divided cargo bed w/enclosed top & back, 16", EX+, A $400.00

Pepsi-Cola, truck, Nylint, steel w/snub-nosed cab & various logos in open cargo bays, wht-wall tires, 16", EX, A $195.00

Pepsi-Cola, water pistol, 1989, can shape, MOC, S2........$20.00

Pepto Bismal, bank, 24-Hour Bug figure, soft plastic, 7½", EX, H4 ....$70.00

PF Flyers, Treasure Hunt Spyglass, 1970s, 7" cb telescope w/plastic lens, color illus of a treasure map, EX, J5 ....$15.00

Philgas, doll, Buddy Lee in full uniform, no hat, EX+, A..$350.00

Pillsbury, bank, slot in top, lid comes off, tin, few scratches, 4", A3 ....$15.00

Pillsbury, book bag, Goofy Grape/Poppin' Fresh, 1969, very scarce..$75.00

Pillsbury, doll, Poppin' Fresh, stuffed cloth, EX, H4 ....$14.00

Pillsbury, doll, Poppin' Fresh, terry cloth, G, O1 ....$25.00

Pillsbury, figure, Popper (little boy), Poppie (little girl) or Bub Bun (baby), vinyl, NM, S2, ea $25.00

Pillsbury, figure, Poppin' Fresh, vinyl, G, O1 ....$15.00

Pillsbury, finger puppet, Biscuit the Cat, vinyl, rare, EX, S2 ....$35.00

Pillsbury, finger puppet, Flapjack the Dog, vinyl, EX, S2 .$55.00

Pillsbury, finger puppet, Grandma, vinyl, EX, S2..............$50.00

Pillsbury, finger puppet, Poppin' Fresh, vinyl, 3½", VG+, H4...$10.00

Pillsbury, iron-on transfer, Rudy the Tutti Frutti, ca 1960s, M (orig mailing envelope), T2...................................$15.00

Pillsbury, pillow, Funny Face & Choo-Choo Cherry, 1970, M, ea $45.00

Pillsbury, playhouse w/figures, vinyl, M (in shipping box), H4 ....$250.00

Pillsbury, school box, features Poppin' Fresh, w/pencils, eraser, etc, EX..$95.00

Planters, bank, Mr Peanut, 1950s, on rnd blk base, molded plastic, 8½", NM..$15.00

Planters, coloring book, Famous Men, 1930s, EX $35.00

Planters, coloring book, Presidents, 1950s, EX.................$10.00

Planters, coloring book, Presidents, 1977, EX $5.00

Planters, coloring book, 50 states, 1960s, EX $5.00

Planters, costume, Mr Peanut, 1960s, gold plastic w/emb letters, EX $500.00

Planters, doll, Mr Peanut, Chase Bag Co, 1967, stuffed cloth, 18" or 20", NM (in mailer bag), ea............................$20.00

Planters, figure, Mr Peanut, jtd wood w/blk arms & legs, wht hands & bl hat mk Mr Peanut on band, 9", NM $200.00

Planters, figure, Mr Peanut, 1991, bendable PVC, 6", H4 .$10.00

Planters, figure, Mr Peanut, plastic, 8½", $15.00.

Planters, puzzle, Just Nuts About You, 1970s, MIB..........$25.00

Poll Parrot Shoes, flasher ring, clown image, EX, J2 ....$45.00

Pops-Rite Popcorn, doll, stuffed cloth, 12", M (in mailer envelope), H4..$20.00

Popsicle, bicycle license plate, early 1980s, in-pack premium, M, S2...$10.00

Popsicle, Mystery Musical Truck, Mattel, 1955, plastic, w/Popsicle Pete Gift premium flyer, 11", NM+ (EX+ box), A $420.00

Post Cereals, ambulance, F&F Mold, 1957 Ford Fire Chief's, NM, B2, ea, from $5 to $10.00

Post Cereals, car, F&F Mold, 1950 Ford, NM, B2, from $20 to $75.00

Post Cereals, car, F&F Mold, 1951 Ford, NM, B2, from $50 to $200.00

Post Cereals, car, F&F Mold, 1954, Mercury Convertible, NM, B2, from $50 to $200.00

Post Cereals, car, F&F Mold, 1954 Ford, NM, B2, from $20 to $35.00

Post Cereals, car, F&F Mold, 1954 Mercury (other closed cars), NM, B2, from $25 to $50.00

Post Cereals, car, F&F Mold, 1954 Mercury XM, NM, B2, from $15 to $30.00

Post Cereals, car, F&F Mold, 1954 T-Bird, NM, B2, from $75 to $150.00

Post Cereals, car, F&F Mold, 1955 Ford, all, NM, B2, ea, from $5 to $15.00

Post Cereals, car, F&F Mold, 1957 Ford Fire Chief's, NM, B2, from $5 to...$10.00

Post Cereals, car, F&F Mold, 1957 Ford Victoria, Sunliner or Custom, NM, B2, ea, from $25 to $75.00

Post Cereals, car, F&F Mold, 1960 Plymouth, all except red, NM, B2, ea, from $10 to..............................$20.00

Post Cereals, car, F&F Mold, 1960 Plymouth, red, NM, B2, from $75 to...$150.00

Post Cereals, car, F&F Mold, 1961 T-Bird, all except roadster, NM, B2, ea, from $5 to $15.00

Post Cereals, car, F&F Mold, 1966 Mustang, all, NM, B2, ea, from $3 to...$5.00

Post Cereals, car, F&F Mold, 1967 Mercury Cougar, NM, B2, from $2 to...$5.00

Post Cereals, car, F&F Mold, 1969 Mercury, all, NM, B2, ea from $10 to...$15.00

Post Cereals, truck, F&F Mold, 1956 Ford Tractor-Trailer, NM, B2, from $10 to $15.00

Purina Dog Chow, train car, HO scale, mail-in premium, M, S2...$10.00

Quaker, Quangaroo Gyrocycle, 1973, M, R3 ....$25.00

Quaker, Quangaroo Simon Says, 1974, plastic, M, R3 .....$90.00

Quaker, Quisp Gyrocycle, 1973, M, R3 ....$30.00

Quaker, Quisp Unicycle, 1971, M, R3 ....$60.00

Raid Bug, remote control, 1 of 3000 made, very rare, EX, H4...$590.00

Raid Bug, w/up, 5", missing antenna & w/up key o/w EX, H4...$60.00

Ralston, belt buckle, metal, NM, T1 ....$15.00

Ralston, figures, Cookie Crisp Cop, Crook or Sonic Hedgehog, 1990, M, R3, ea...................................$5.00

Ralston, Flying Casper, 1972, M, R3 ....$50.00

Ralston, Freakies boats, 1974, 7 different, plastic, M, R3, ea.$30.00

Ralston, Freakies cars, 1974, 7 different, plastic, M, R3, ea..$3.00

Ralston, Freakies figures, 1972, 7 different, plastic, M, R3, ea $10.00

Ralston, Major Moonstone buggy, 1975, 5 different, M, R3, ea $40.00

Ralston, ramp walkers, Cecil the Computer, Grins, Smiles, Giggles or Laughs, 1976, M, R3, ea $20.00

Ralston, squeeze toy, chuckwagon, 1975, vinyl, 8" long, NM, T1 ....$37.50

Ray-O-Vac, flashlight, Captain Ray-O-Vac in early spacesuit, 1952, w/scarce game book, NM (EX box), A $215.00

RCA, bank, TV Joe, 1960, figure w/RCA Tubes & Silverama logos on gray uniform & hat w/blk trim, plastic, 5", M, R3 ....$50.00

ReaLemon, figure, lemon w/arms & legs, PVC, 2", EX, H4 .$8.00

Red Goose, ring, glow-in-the-dark w/secret compartment, NM, C10 ....$150.00

Reddy Kilowatt, figure, 1960s, glow-in-the-dark, MOC (in orig mailer box), H4 ....$195.00

Reddy Kilowatt, figure, 1961, hard plastic, 5", M, R3 .....$125.00

Royal Gelatin, bank, King Royal figure, 1970s, vinyl, 10", M, R3 ....$250.00

Sargento Cheeses, doll, plush mouse w/vinyl hands & face, EX, H4 ....$15.00

Seaman's Savings Bank, bank, early, figural, NM, J2 ....$45.00

Sears, flasher ring, flashes from Santa Claus to 'Sears Has Everything' w/trees, S2 ....$20.00

Seven-Up, see 7-Up at end of listings

Shell, game, Stop & Go, unpunched, 1936, NM, J2 ....$45.00

Shell, gas station, W Germany, 1950s, station w/red flat roof & yel lithoed pumps, friction tanker & car, 5½", NM, A $250.00

Shell, truck, Ertl, metal & plastic super tanker, gas station promotion, 19", NMIB, S2 ....$55.00

Shell, truck, Metalcraft, pnt sheet metal, red cab, 8 cans of oil in yel bed, 12", EX, A $500.00

Shell Oil, truck, Tootsietoy, diecast tanker, NM, T1 ....$75.00

Sinclair Oil, dinosaurs, 4 different, obtained w/ea 8-gal fillup, MIP (bag w/header card), ea..$15.00

Slush Puppy, doll, plush dog wearing bl shirt w/letter 'S' & bl cap, EX, H4 ....$15.00

Smokey Bear, see US Forest Service

Spam, bank, M $10.00

Star Brand Shoes, race car premium, lithographed tin, wheels turn, 8½", G/VG, $400.00.

Star Brand Shoes, race car, litho tin, flat fold-together car w/turning wheels, premium, 8½", VG-, A $400.00

Star-Kist, doll, Charlie Tuna, plush, 15", MIP, D4 ....$15.00

Star-Kist, doll, talking stuffed Charlie Tuna, 1969, 14", non-working o/w EX, H4 ....$25.00

Star-Kist, inflatable Charlie Tuna, 1980, EX, H4 ....$20.00

Star-Kist, lamp, Charlie figure, EX, T1 ....$50.00

Star-Kist, necklace, gold-tone metal w/charm of Charlie Tuna on anchor, 1970, 1¼", EX, J5 ....$10.00

Star-Kist, pin, rhinestone Charlie Tuna w/anchor, M, D4 ....$10.00

Star-Kist, squeeze toy, Charlie Tuna figure, 1973, 7", NM, A $50.00

Sugar Crisp Cereal, doll, Sugar Bear, plush wearing bl turtleneck shirt, 5", VG, H4 ....$3.00

Sugar Crisp Cereal, doll, Sugar Bear, plush wearing Hawaiian or bl shirt, NM, S2, ea $10.00

Sugar Crisp Cereal, figure, Sugar Bear, plastic w/clip on back, 2", H4 ....$3.00

Sugar Crisp Cereal, watch, features Sugar Bear, 1970s, rpl band (?), clean & bright but non-working, J5 ....$45.00

Swiss Miss Chocolate, doll, Swiss Miss, 1978, stuffed, cloth clothes & apron, braided yarn hair, 17", MIP, H4 .....$30.00

Talon Zipper Co, doll, bear w/jackhammer, plush w/rubber hands, '42' on hat, w/zipper & lock tag, 7", EX+ (EX box), A $176.00

Tang, figures, Tang Lips, rubber, 3-pc set, 2", S2 ....$15.00

Tastee Freeze, doll, plastic w/cloth dress & chest banner reading Miss Tastee Freeze, 8", EX, H4 ....$20.00

Teddy Grahams, yo-yo, plastic, M, D4 ....$2.00

Teddy Ruxpin, store display, Teddy w/stage & background, VG, S2 ....$225.00

Texaco, doll, cheerleader, vinyl w/movable arms & legs, red & wht outfit, complete w/accessories, 11½", MIB, A $70.00

Texaco, hat, Fire Chief, EX, J2 ....$50.00

Tony's Pizza, squeeze toy, Mr Tony, 1974, vinyl, 9", EX+ $50.00

Toys R Us, bank, figural Baby Gee bust, plastic, 6", NM, S2 ....$30.00

Toys R Us, figure, Geoffrey Giraffe, 1986, foam w/removable clothing, M, S2 ....$45.00

Toys R Us, jack-in-the-box, Geoffrey Giraffe, Mattel, VG, S2 ....$45.00

Travel Lodge, doll, Sleepy Bear, plush, NM, T1 ....$35.00

Trix Cereal, see General Mills

United Airlines, coloring book, Whitman, 1969, J5 ....$20.00

US Forest Service, doll, Smokey Bear, Ideal, stuffed, w/badge, 18", no hat, VG $30.00

US Forest Service, doll, Smokey Bear, Knickerbocker, 1972, stuffed cotton, 6", EX (EX box), D9 ....$18.00

US Forest Service, doll, Smokey Bear, 1985, plush w/cloth hat, 6", M $20.00

US Forest Service, doll, Woodsy Owl, Knickerbocker, 1972, stuffed cloth, Give A Hoot Don't Pollute! 6½", MIB.$25.00

Waldorf Lager, truck, Metalcraft, Forest City Brewery on door, wht-pnt sheet metal, 8 wooden barrels in bed, 13", G, A $2,100.00

Woodsy Owl, see US Forest Service

Zenith, Magic Set #919A, see Activity Sets category

Zeppelin, cookie box, Novelty Candy Co, 1926, diecut cb zeppelin above image of 3 children, 4", EX+, A $75.00

Westinghouse, doll, Lotta Light Mazda Lamp Girl, original uncut printed cloth, 17", $85.00.

7-Up, figure, Fresh-Up Freddie, Canadian, stuffed cloth body w/rubber head, 15", G, M5 ....$50.00
7-Up, figure, Spot, 1988, bendable, 5", MOC, S2.............$25.00
7-Up, wristwatch, 1980s, blk band, 1" dia, EX, J5.............$45.00

Aeronautical

Toy manufacturers seemed to take the cautious approach toward testing the waters with aeronautical toys, and it was well into the second decade of the 20th century before some of the European toy makers took the initiative. The earlier models were bulky and basically inert, but by the fifties, Japanese manufacturers were turning out battery-operated replicas with wonderful details that advanced with whirring motors and flashing lights.

Advisor: Dan Wells (W1).

See also Battery Operated; Cast Iron, Airplanes; Model Kits; Windups, Friction and Other Mechanicals.

Air France Transantlantic Airplane, red lithographed tin, 4 self-propelled motors and front wheels, battery-operated front light, 23½" wingspan, NM, A, $3,700.00.

Air Express Plane, Girard, litho tin, rachet mechanism makes noise as toy is pushed, 9", EX-, A $240.00
Air France Travel Agent Airplane, cast aluminum, 29", NM, M5...$350.00
Air Mail Helicopter, KO, battery-op, pilot moves head & arms, 2 spinning rotors, 10", NM (EX box) $175.00
Air Mail Plane, Keystone, late 1920s, red tri-motor w/red wings, 24", G-, A...$546.00
Air Mail Plane, Keystone, star in circle on wingtips, 24", A...$900.00
Airplane w/Automatic Turn Over Propellers, Linemar, battery-op, 19", some denting, G (orig box), A....................$125.00

Airways Express Air Mail, Girard, 1920s-30s, tin and celluloid, 13" long, EX, A, $300.00.

Airport Service Helicopter, Alps, battery-op, twin plastic rotors & canopy, 13", won't move o/w working, VG, A $30.00
American Ace Glider, USA, Pat Mar 15, 1927, cloth on light framework, 32" long, G, A $200.00
Army Bomber, silver pnt & litho tin tri-motor w/gr detachable wings, 26½", crazing on wings, several bends, G, A...$140.00
Autogiro Plane, Wyandotte, self-propelling rotor blades, red & yel pnt sheet metal, 10", EX (EX box), A................$650.00
B-61 Buzz Bomber, Alps, friction, tin w/rubber nose cone, mk USAF on wings & GM-544 on tail fin, 12", EX+ (EX box), A $410.00

BAC (Vickers) VC 10, Marusyo, 1960s, plane marked BOAC, blue and white tin, friction, 16" wingspan, MIB, D10, $275.00.

Biplane, Kingsbury, sheet metal w/CI pilot, rpl rubber tires, 16", EX, A $650.00

Biplane, Rico/Spain, 1950s, battery-op, advances as prop spins & makes engine noise, lights flash, 12", NM (EX box), A...$975.00

Boeing Stratocruiser, Wyandotte, red w/navy wings, pressed steel w/metal props, wood wheels, 13" wingspan, NM (G box), A...$416.00

Boeing 707, Daiya, friction, silver w/red & bl trim, 10½" wingspan, NM (EX box), A $95.00

Boeing 747 Jet Plane, Hong Kong, 1970, MIB, R7 ....$75.00

Bulldog T-360, S&E/Japan, battery-op, red & yel tin w/pilot in open cockpit, working prop & lights, 15", EX, A $355.00

Cessna 310, friction, wht & bl w/name & NO 37979 on wing, metal props spin, 12" wingspan, VG, A $201.00

Citroen DS19, 1960s, Bandai, friction, red-pnt tin w/bl interior, NP trim, 8", EX-, A $40.00

Curtiss Jenny Trainer, S&E/Japan, red lithographed tin biplane, friction, MIB, A, $214.00.

D-Olaf Bomb-Dropping Airplane, Tipp, litho tin, 4 lead cap bombs hang from wings, WWII German markings, 10", VG+, A...$935.00

Douglas Sky Rocket, Bandai, friction, wht needle-nose jet w/detailed pilot, Navy decals, 11", EX+, (EX box), A .$115.00

Eagle Air Scout Airplane, Marx, litho tin, eagles depicted on wings, propeller spins when toy is pulled, 25½", EX-, A $575.00

Elegant Miniatures Aircraft Set, Marx, military, commercial & space vehicles, diecast, rare, MIB, A.........................$350.00

Empire Express, silver w/red wings, tail prop turns when pushed, pnt & litho heavy gauge tin, 17", pnt loss, G-, A $60.00

EPL-1 Zeppelin, 1907, 7½", 2 rpl tabs, 2 missing o/w EX+, M5...$450.00

F-104 Jet Fighter, ASC, friction, mk US Air Force, litho tin w/pilot under plastic dome, 13", EX+ (EX+ box), A ..$150.00

F-104A Lockheed Jet, KO, friction, gray needle-nosed jet w/red rubber rockets, USAF decals, 11", NM (EX box), A.$146.00

F-105 Fighter Plane, Asahi, friction, sparker, blk litho tin, 8½", G, A $65.00

Fighter Plane, KO, battery-op, stop-&-go & other actions, bombs under wings are battery boxes, 10½", M (EX box), A...$451.00

Flapping Wing Plane, Fischer, ca 1910, wings flap & rear prop spins, w/pilot, tin w/spoked balloon tires, 10", EX+, A $2,000.00

Flying Tiger, TN, battery-op, silver plane w/red latters advances as props spin, tail section opens as light goes on, 14", MIB, A $276.00

Flying-Wonder Plane, Arnold, lithographed tin, 10" wingspan, M (worn box), D10, $135.00.

Frog Interceptor, England, aluminum single prop w/bull's-eye insignias, 12" wingspan, VG (VG box), A $100.00

FU-572 Jet Fighter, Y, 1950s, friction, cutouts in fuselage shows sparking action, 6½", NM, A $68.00

Globe Master C124 Troop Carrier, Bandai, red, wht & bl metal w/plastic props, friction, 17" wingspan, EX+ (EX box), A $365.00

Graf Zeppelin DLZ 127, German, litho tin, 15", VG, A .$600.00

Grumman F9F-5 Panther Jet, Navy VF-127, friction, working compass in cockpit w/tin pilot under dome, rare, 12", EX, A $351.00

Gyrocopter, Occupied Japan, 1940s, tin with hand-painted details and spinning blades, key-wind, 4½" long, NM (EX box), A, $185.00.

Helibus Helicopter, Arnold, EX (orig box), W5 ....$225.00

Helicopter w/Piston Action, friction, litho tin, silver w/moving pistons in plastic nose, 10½", VG (orig box), A $30.00

Hiller Hornet Helicopter, TN, friction, litho tin, metal blades, hinged rudder, 10", EX (orig box), A $110.00

Hindenburg Zeppelin, Tipp, litho tin w/celluloid props, on/off switch, 11", rpl blades, EX, A $825.00

Hi-Wing Monoplane, England, 1930s, advances on tin balloon tires, windup, 17" wingspan, EX, A, $300.00.

HX 131 Plane, Boycraft, metal, 3-prop, 26½", orig pnt & decals w/minor rust, A $675.00

Intercontinental KLM Jet, VEB, mostly tin, friction, 14", NM (EX box), A $75.00

Lockheed Plane, Marusan, litho tin, red, blk & yel, 3-prop, 14", bad rust on wing tip, non-working, G-, M5 ....$600.00

Lockheed Sirius, w/lights, 22", rstr, A.........................$400.00

Lockheed Starfire FA-882, friction w/sparking action, litho tin, red & blk, G, A..$85.00

Lockhead Starfire FA-982, ET/Japan, lithographed tin, 18½" wingspan, sparking action incomplete, A, $85.00.

Lufthansa Jet Boeing 727, MT, friction w/battery-op flashing engine lights & noise, NM (EX box), A $75.00

Monoplane, Wyandotte, blk & yel pressed steel, 7", scratches, G, A $40.00

Navy Cougar Jet, Y, friction w/lever-activated wings w/6 rockets, wht, red & navy, detailed pilot, 8½", EX, A.............$182.00

Navy Demon Jet, TN/Japan, friction w/battery-op lights, 8", NM, A $111.00

Navy Fighter #467, Hubley, diecast w/retractable red wings & landing gear, plastic cockpit, 9" wingspan, NM (EX box), A $250.00

Navy Fighter Bomber #495, Hubley, cast metal w/sliding canopy, retractable gear, etc, 10", EX (VG+ box), A $148.00

Navy Scorpion Jet, Y, friction w/lever-activated folding wings, detailed pilot, 8½", EX+, A.....................................$233.00

Pan Am China Clipper, Wyandotte, red- & wht-pnt pressed steel w/brass engines & NP props, 9", minor scratches o/w EX, A $275.00

Pan Am DC-8 Jet Plane, H, friction, tin w/rubber engines & tires, 7½", NM (EX+ box), A $95.00

Pan Am Douglas DC-7C World Airways Plane, TN, battery-op, remote control, 19", EX (EX box), A.......................$470.00

Pan Am Jet, 1980s, 12", MIB, S2 ....$35.00

Pan Am Super-7 Clipper, box only, 1950s, litho cb w/Clipper image, 18", EX+, A......................................$83.00

Pan American Airlines, Japan, 1950s, lithographed tin, friction, 7½" wingspan, MIB, D10, $75.00.

Passenger Biplane, Meccano, pressed steel, constructed from building kit, bl & wht w/decal, 14", EX, A $385.00

Pioneer Air Express Airplane, Marx, 1920s, silver & bl litho tin, Indian chief depicted on wings, 25", VG/EX, A......$630.00

Piper Aztec, ATC, friction, litho tin, red & wht, 3 tin passengers, 18", missing tail wheel & 1 blade, VG, A..........$45.00

Right Plane Monoplane, Scheible, lt bl, red & yel w/belt-driven propeller, 29", scratches o/w VG, A..........................$525.00

Spirit of St Louis Airplane, HTTC, lithographed tin with plastic spinning prop, X-2 Ryan NYP on tail fin, 12" long, scarce, NM (VG box), from $400.00 to $550.00.

Single-Engine Army Scout, Steelcraft, 23", EX, A.........$400.00

Spirit of St Louis, inscribed, NP steel construction w/wood wheels, 11½" wingspan, EX, A...............................$191.00

Starfire FA-985 Jet, Y, cutouts in fuselage show sparking action, tin w/lithoed pilot & co-pilot, 8½", NM, A $105.00

Tomcat F-14A Jet Fighter, Son Al Toys, battery-op, tin & plastic, blinking lights & sound, 13", EX (EX box), A $63.00

TWA DC-7C Airplane, Yonezawa, 1960s, battery-op, tin, 23" wingspan, broken props, sm dents, bent tail, G $200.00

TWA 727 Jet Plane, friction, wht tin w/red trim, 14", NM (EX box), A..$60.00

Twin-Engine, Wyandotte, gr-pnt pressed steel w/NP props, 9½", minor scratches o/w VG, A $70.00

Twin-Engine, Wyandotte, gr-pnt pressed steel w/yel wings, NP props, 5¼", pnt chips & scratches, G, A $20.00

United Airlines DC-7, friction, litho tin, mk Main Liner, props spin when activated, 11", EX+ (EX+ box), A $248.00

United Airlines Plane, 1950s-60s, friction, litho tin, 7" long, NM, S2...$45.00

USAF Air Transport, Wyandotte, silver-colored pressed steel w/metal props, decals, 13" wingspan, NM (VG box), A...$416.00

USAF BK-02VF Jet, Tomiyama, blk & red, 17", EX+, M5..$110.00

USAF FG-761 Jet, ASG, friction, red & wht tin w/pilot lithoed in cockpit, 15", EX, A $125.00

U.S. Air Force Fighter Plane, black and red lithographed tin with plastic nose cone, friction, 19" wingspan, VG, A, $150.00.

USAF Fighter, friction, bl & red litho tin, rotating prop, 8", EX (orig box), A...$100.00

USAF Jet Bomber Squadron, Payton, set of 5 plastic jets, ea 5½", MIB, A...$50.00

USAF Jet Plane, Japan, 1950s, battery-op, 39 men in action poses on unpunched sheet, 13", NM (VG box), A..$225.00

USAF Strato-Jet, battery-op, advances w/blinking red lights, 11" wingspan, EX+ (EX+ box), A $160.00

USAF Transport Helicopter, TN, friction, spinning front & rear blades, flying horse images, EX+ (EX box), A $160.00

Viscount Air Liner, Tomiyama, battery-op, silver & red tin & plastic, walking stewardess, 19", EX (G box), A......$350.00

XF-160 Plane, TN, 1950, battery-op, NM, R7.................$85.00

Zeppelin, att Orobr, litho tin, yel w/red detailing, 10", VG+, A...$685.00

Automobiles and Other Vehicle Replicas

Listed here are the model vehicles (most of which were made in Japan during the 1950s and '60s) that were designed to realistically represent the muscle cars, station wagons, convertibles, budget models, and luxury cars that were actually being shown concurrently on showroom floors and dealer's lots all over the country. Most were made of tin, many were friction powered, some were battery operated. In our descriptions, all are tin unless noted otherwise.

When at all possible, we've listed the toys by the names assigned to them by the manufacturer, just as they appear on the original boxes. Because of this, you'll find some of the same models listed by slightly different names. All vehicles are painted or painted and lithographed tin unless noted.

Advisors: Nancy and Jim Schaut (A3).

See also Promotional Cars; specific manufacturers.

Alpha Romeo, Asahi, friction, red, 6½", EX+ (EX+ box), A $150.00

Aston-Martin Secret Agent's Car, Gilbert, with plastic figures, battery-operated lights and sound, 11¼", MIB, A, $250.00.

Austin A50 Cambridge, 1950s, friction, wht & maroon w/red interior, 8", non-working, G-, A $200.00

Austin Healey 100 Six Coupe #706, Bandai, friction, lt gr w/blk top, 8", NM (EX+ box), A $443.00

Avanti Coupe, 1960s, Bandai, gold 2-door w/red interior, 8", VG- (torn orig box), A...$150.00

BMW Isetta, Indian Head, friction, yel & red, 4¾", scarce sz, NM (EX+ box), A...$333.00

BMW Turbo #12, Alps, battery-op, red, yel & blk plastic w/headlights & sound, 11", MIB, A $85.00

BMW 1500, 1960s, Ichiko, friction, bl, 8½", NM (NM box), A...$125.00

Buick, 1953, Marusan, friction, lt bl, EX, A....................$175.00

Buick, 1956, Japan, battery-op, red, 7½", non-working, VG (torn box), A $35.00

Buick, 1959, Cragstan, battery-op, remote control, red & yel, 12", NM (rpr box), A $150.00

Buick Riviera Scenicruiser Station Wagon, 1971, Asahi, friction, wht w/bl-tinted windows, 14¾", EX, A $60.00

Buick Sedan, 1963, TN, friction, red w/bl interior, 15¾", EX, A...$350.00

Buick Convertible, 1958, Japan, cream with red and cream interior, 6", MIB, $165.00.

Buick Sedan Postal Car, 1949, US Zone Germany, friction, hand-painted and detailed composition driver, whitewall tires, 11", MIB, from $750.00 to $900.00.

Buick Special, 1961, Ichiko, friction, wht & gr w/red & bl interior, NP trim, 8", EX (separation to box), A............$120.00

Buick Special, 1963, Japan, battery-op, yel w/blk vinyl top, red & wht interior, NP trim, 11½", NMIB, A $95.00

Buick Station Wagon, 1958, Bandai, friction, 2-tone brn w/bl interior, 8", VG-, A $20.00

Cadillac, Plaything, battery-op, dk gr & cream w/gold-tone lights, plastic steering wheel, 9¾", MIB, A..............$310.00

Cadillac, 1954, Gama/W Germany, friction, bl 4-door w/litho interior, chrome trim, wht-wall tires, 12½", EX+, A $575.00

Cadillac Convertible, 1959, Bandai, friction, black 4-door with red interior, 11½", EX (torn original box), A, $285.00.

Cadillac Convertible, Bandai, friction, purple 4-door w/gr interior, 12", no steering, VG (torn box), A $180.00

Cadillac Convertible, Bandai, friction, wht w/red interior, NP trim, brake lever on dash, 8", G, A $25.00

Cadillac Convertible, 1950, Bandai, battery-op, working horn & lights, 10½", EX+, R7..$175.00

Cadillac Convertible, 1959, Bandai, friction, blk 4-door w/red interior, 11½", EX (torn box), A..............................$285.00

Cadillac Convertible, 1959, Bandai, friction, red 4-door w/gr interior, 11½", VG+, A...$150.00

Cadillac Convertible (Kingsize), 1970, Iway/Korea, MIB, R7 ....$100.00

Cadillac Convertible, Schuco, silver plastic with red interior, buttons on console control direction, 11½", EX (G box), A, $245.00.

Cadillac Eldorado, friction, red w/red interior, NP trim, 10½", NM (orig box), A $180.00

Cadillac Electromobile, TN, friction, blk 4-door convertible w/gr & yel interior, 13", EX- (VG box), A $800.00

Cadillac Sedan, friction, bl w/front & rear plates, 9½", EX (EX box), A...$180.00

Cadillac Sedan, 1959, Bandai, friction, gold w/gr interior, NP trim, 11", VG, A $85.00

Cadillac Sedan, 1959, Bandai, friction, wht w/bl & gray interior, NP trim, 8", minor scratches & dents, G, A $35.00

Cadillac Sedan, 1960, Bandai, wht w/pk & wht interior, NP trim, 11", EX, A $75.00

Cadillac Sedan, Marusan, friction, black with blue and white interior, 12", non-working, G+, A, $200.00.

Chevrolet Bel Air Station Wagon, 1961, ATC, friction, gr & wht w/plastic windshield & windows, 10", EX (EX box), A...$495.00

Chevrolet Camaro, Bandai, battery-op, red w/bl interior, clear plastic hood w/light-up engine, fan works, 13", EX, A $130.00

Chevrolet Camaro, 1967, Taiyo, friction, red w/red interior, NP trim, 9¾", EX (orig box), A..........................$100.00

Chevrolet Camaro Z-29, 1970, Taiyo, battery-op, bl & wht w/NP trim, 10", non-working, VG (orig box), A.......$45.00

Chevrolet Convertible, 1958, Bandai, friction, red & orange w/yel interior, NP trim, 8", VG (G box), A.............$150.00

Chevrolet Corvair, 1960, friction, bl w/wht roof, plastic windshield, blk tires w/wht hubcaps, 9", NM+ (EX box), A $150.00

Chevrolet Corvair, 1962, Bandai, friction, red w/plastic windows, 8½", NM (VG box), A $154.00

Chevrolet Corvair Sedan, 1961, Bandai, friction, red w/checked interior, 8", VG+, A $55.00

Chevrolet Corvette, Yonezawa, friction, red w/silver top, NP trim panels, 9½", G, A $210.00

Chevrolet Corvette Convertible, Bandai, battery-op, red, operating gear shift, 8", non-working, EX (orig box), A.$140.00

Chevrolet Corvette Convertible, 1962, Japan, red with black top, 8", NM, D10, $150.00.

Chevrolet Corvette Sting Ray, 1964, Japan, friction, 7", M, D10, $225.00.

Chevrolet Nomad Station Wagon, 1958, Japan, blue with white top, 6", MIB, $250.00.

Chevrolet Impala, 1960s, friction, yel & red w/red & wht interior, NP trim, 7½", non-working, G, A $40.00

Chevrolet Impala, 1962, Bandai, friction, yel w/gr & wht interior, NP trim, 11", G-, A $55.00

Chevrolet Impala Convertible, friction, red w/orange interior, opening doors, 8", EX (orig box), A.........................$170.00

Chevrolet Pickup Truck, SSS, friction, bl & wht w/gr interior, 7", VG- (bent box), A $150.00

Chevrolet Sport Coupe, 1959, friction, gr & red w/wht & gr interior, NP hubcaps, 7", G+ (torn box), A..............$65.00

Chevrolet Station Wagon, 1956, Bandai, friction, lift up & pull rear window & gate, engine noise, 9¾", NM (EX box), A $331.00

Chrysler Imperial, Bandai, friction, cream 2-door w/red top, 8", EX (orig box), A...$215.00

Chrysler Imperial, 1960, Bandai, friction, wht w/red top, plastic windshield & taillights, 8¼", NM+ (EX+ box), A ..$225.00

Chrysler Imperial, 1960, Bandai, friction, cream 2-door with red top, 8", EX (original box), A, $215.00.

Chrysler Valiant Sedan, Bandai #736, friction, red, 8¼", EX+, (VG box), A $92.00

Citroen DS-19, Bandai, friction, gr w/cream top, 8", VG+, A...$125.00

Edsel Convertible, 1958, Haji, friction, turq w/red & wht interior, 11", windshield missing, VG-, A $450.00

Edsel Station Wagon, 1958, TN, friction, red, blk & wht w/NP trim, pop-up rear window, 10½", M $350.00

Edsel Station Wagon, 1958, Japan, friction, red, black and white, working tailgate & pop-up rear window, 10½", VG/EX, from $200.00 to $250.00.

Ferrari #1, Bandai, friction, red w/NP trim, 8½", windshield & steering wheel missing, G+, A $200.00

Ferrari #3, 1960s, Bandai, friction, yel w/NP trim, 8½", EX, A $300.00

Ferrari Berlinetta 250 Le Mans, Asahi, friction, red w/racing logos, 10½", EX+ (EX box), A $150.00

Ferrari Berlinetta 250 Le Mans, ATC, battery-op, red w/engine lithoed on trunk, engine noise, 11", NM (EX+ box), A $210.00

Ford Convertible, 1956, Haji, green with green and cream interior, 7¾", rare, MIB, from $750.00 to $1,000.00.

Ford Convertible, 1956, Haji, friction, gr w/gr & cream interior, 7¾", VG+ (VG box), A $400.00

Ford Convertible, 1956, Haji, friction, red w/yel & bl interior, trunk opens, back seat folds, 12", G, A $300.00

Ford Country Squire Station Wagon, friction, red & wht, 10", EX (EX+ box), A $92.00

Ford Fairlane, 1958, Ichiko, friction, pk & orange w/orange interior, NP trim, 12", VG-, A $425.00

Ford Custom Ranch Wagon, Bandai, friction, yellow with black top, red interior, opening tailgate, 12", G+ (VG box), A, $300.00.

Ford Delivery Sedan, Japan, friction, yellow and black with lift-up rear window, Standard Coffee advertising on side, 11½", G, $500.00.

Ford Fairlane, 1959, ATC, friction, cream & red 2-door w/lt gr interior, 7½", VG (orig box), A $75.00

Ford Fairlane Sports Coupe, 1964, Haji, Scale Model Car Series, maroon w/tan litho interior, 9", EX- (orig box), A....$55.00

Ford Fairlane Station Wagon, 1957, Bandai, friction, 2-tone gr w/red & wht interior, 12", missing tailgate window, VG, A $180.00

Ford Fairlane 500 Skyliner, Cragstan, battery-op, remote control, retractable roof, 11", EX (EX box), A $350.00

Ford Fairlane, 1956, Yonezawa, friction, 2-tone blue with green interior, 12¼", MIB, from $900.00 to $1,200.00.

Ford Falcon, 1961, Bandai, friction, 8¼", NM (EX+ box), A..$92.00

Ford Galaxie Retractable Hardtop, 1958, friction, red & cream w/plaid interior, lever-op roof, 11", EX, A $45.00

Ford Galaxie 500 Yellow Cab, Toymaster, 9¼", EX (VG+ box), A $108.00

Ford GT, Bandai, bump-&-go action w/motor sound & flashing light, yel tin, 10", NM (VG box), A $94.00

Ford Model-A Van Truck, Bandai, Express Delivery on panel, opening rear doors, 6½", NM (orig box), A $65.00

Ford Mustang, 1965, Bandai, battery-op, blk & red w/blk interior, 11", VG (orig box), A...........................$50.00

Ford Mustang GT, friction, 16", EX (orig box), A..........$250.00

Ford Mustang GT, 1966, AMF/USA, red plastic, battery-op lights, hood lifts to show V-8 engine, 16", rare, NM (EX box), A..$125.00

Ford Mustang Race Car, 1970, Daishin, battery-op, EX, R7..$25.00

Ford Pickup Truck, friction, 10½", EX (orig box), A $225.00

Ford Ranchero, Bandai, friction, orange & bl, working tailgate, 12", VG, A..$300.00

Ford Ranchero, 1957, Bandai, friction, rare orange & gr, 12", missing windshield, bumper & window, G+, A.......$250.00

Ford Sedan, 1950s, Japan, battery-op, red w/NP hubcaps, Electro Car mk on box, 7½", G+ (orig box), A.....................$30.00

Ford Skyliner Retractable Top, 1958, TN, battery-op, 9", NM (EX box), A..$290.00

Ford Station Wagon, 1957, friction, red w/bl top, opening tailgate, 7½", VG (orig box), A..............................$125.00

Ford T-Bird, 1956, TN, friction, gr & red w/lavender interior, lift-off plexiglass top, 8", VG (torn box), A...............$60.00

Ford T-Bird, 1960, Bandai, friction, red & wht w/bl interior, NP trim, 8", non-working, EX (box punctured), A..........$80.00

Ford T-Bird, 1961, Bandai, brn & beige w/yel interior, NP trim, 8", EX, A...$50.00

Ford T-Bird, 1962, Yonezawa, battery-op, wht over red w/red & wht interior, NP trim, 11", EX (orig box), A...........$300.00

Ford T-Bird, 1964, Bandai, friction, blk & red w/yel interior, NP trim, 11", VG, A......................................$50.00

Ford T-Bird Hardtop, 1963, Yonezawa, battery-op, red w/red & wht interior, trunk & hood open, 11", VG, A.........$160.00

Ford Woody Station Wagon, 1950s style, friction, gr w/litho wood-grain sides, NP trim, 7", EX, A.......................$150.00

GMC Stake-Bed Truck, friction, NMIB, A......................$65.00

Jaguar XK 150, Bandai, friction, pnt & litho tin, bl w/wht top, red & tan interior, 9½", VG-, A $165.00

Jaguar 3.4, Bandai, friction, pnt & litho tin 1950s style, red & yel interior, blk tonneau, 8", EX, A $170.00

Lincoln Capri Sedan, 1953, Yonezawa, friction, wht & bl w/orange interior, NP trim, 12", missing windows, G+, A..........$700.00

Lincoln Continental Mark III, Bandai, friction, Model Auto Series decal on underside, red w/blk top, 11", EX, A $186.00

Lincoln Continental Mark V Convertible, Japan, battery-op, remote control, 12", NM (G- box), A $500.00

Lincoln Station Wagon, 1958, Rosko, friction, wht over gr, 9", VG (taped orig box), A...............................$70.00

Lincoln Zephyr Sedan, 1936, Skoglund & Olson, aluminum, blk w/wht rubber tires, 9¼", scarce, EX, A....................$400.00

Lotus Elan, Bandai, friction, red with black top, detailed lithographed interior, black rubber tires with fancy hubs, 8¼", NM (EX+ box), A, $100.00.

Mercedes Convertible Model 5720 Elektro, Schuco, battery-op, remote control, forward & reverse gears, 9¾", NM, A..$1,550.00

Mercedes Police Car, Samshin, battery-op, silver & blk w/NP trim, 9", EX (orig box), A...$375.00

Mercedes SL Coupe, 1950s, Bandai, friction, silver-tone w/blk top, plastic windshield, 8½", MIB, A $200.00

Mercedes-Benz Taxi, 1963, Bandai, battery-operated, painted and lithographed tin, black with flashing lights, door opens, 10¼", EX, working, A, $90.00.

Mercedes Z80 SL, Schuco, battery-op, 4-speed w/reverse, 11", missing cable to hand-held steering wheel, EX+ (VG box), M5..$495.00

Mercedes 219 Convertible, 1960s, Bandai, friction, lime gr w/red & yel interior, NP trim, 8", VG, A $110.00

Mercedes 219 Sedan, Bandai, friction, red w/red & yel interior, 9", VG- (orig box), A...$275.00

Mercedes 220-S, SSS, friction, blk w/wht-wall tires, 12", EX, A..$181.00

Mercedes 230-SL, 1960s, Alps, battery-op, blk & red w/red & wht interior, NP trim, 10", EX (orig box), A...........$200.00

Mercedes 230-SL Elektro-Fernlenk, Schuco #5307, battery-op, remote control, w/dashboard key, 10", NM (EX box), A..$2,000.00

Mercedes 250-SE, 1960s, Ichiko, battery-op, dk red pnt w/red & tan interior, 13", EX (orig box), A...........................$120.00

Mercedes 300-SE, Chiku, friction, plastic wheels & hubcaps, 24", MIB, A..$90.00

Mercedes 300-SE, Ichiko, friction, silver w/bl & silver interior, 23½", NM (orig box), A..$70.00

Mercedes 300-SL, 1950s, friction, blk w/gr interior, NP trim, 9", VG, A...$190.00

Mercedes 300-SL #4 Race Car, Bandai, friction, red, bl & yel w/orange & bl interior, NP trim, VG, A..................$300.00

Mercedez 230-SL, ATC, friction, red, plastic windshield & steering wheel, 11", NM, A.....................................$135.00

Mercury, 1953, Japan, battery-op, gray, 9¾", EX (orig box), A $275.00

Mercury Special Racer, Asahi, litho tin, red, yel & orange, 7½", non-working, G, A $85.00

MG, 1954, Bandai, friction, lime gr w/plaid interior, 11", NM (orig box), A..$475.00

MG, 1955, SSS, 1950s, friction, cream & bl w/red seat, flip-down windshield, 6", NM (VG box), A $122.00

MG Magnette Convertible, Bandai, friction, 2-tone gr w/gray & red interior, 8½", VG (orig box), A ...$375.00

MG Magnette Convertible, 1960s, Bandai, friction, red & wht w/silver & red interior, NP trim, 8½", G, A $190.00

MG Roadster, Doepke, red pnt cast aluminum w/plastic seats & working steering wheel, 15½", pnt chips, VG, A $120.00

MGA Roadster, Bandai, battery-op, wht pnt & litho tin w/operating gear shift, 8", non-working, VG (orig box), A.$350.00

MGA Sports Roadster, Lincoln, battery-op, remote control, 7", EX (EX box), A $275.00

Oldsmobile, ATC, friction, bl 2-door w/lithoed headlights & side trim, 13", EX, A...$480.00

Oldsmobile, 1958, ATC, friction, blk & orange w/red & wht interior, NP trim, 12", 2 hubcaps missing, G, A $190.00

Oldsmobile Toronado, 1966, Bandai, gold w/pk interior, NP trim, engine noise, 11", VG, A.............................$30.00

Oldsmobile 98, 1961, Ichiko, friction, lt bl & bl w/red & wht interior, NP trim, 13", windshield missing, G, A.......$65.00

Plymouth Fury Convertible, 1957, Bandai, friction, bl & wht w/yel & gr interior, NP trim, 8", G, A $100.00

Plymouth Station Wagon, 1961, Ichiko, friction, red & wht w/red & wht interior, NP trim, 12", G, A................$200.00

Plymouth Valiant Sedan, 1961, Bandai #813, friction, gr, 8½", NM (EX box), A $166.00

Pontiac Grand Prix Racer, Bandai, battery-op, remote control, 11", non-working o/w VG, A $45.00

Porsche Rally Car, 1960s, TPS, battery-operated, red with blue and brown interior, 9¾", EX (torn and faded box), A, $85.00.

Porsche Rally Racer, 1960s, gr w/yel & bl stripes, red interior, #37 on side, STP logo, 11", VG, A $60.00

Porsche 7500 Electro-Matic, Distler, battery-op, gr, w/shift lever, off/on key, 10", non-working, VG (G-box), A $220.00

Porsche 911, 1960, Bandai, battery-op, remote control, realistic motor sound, 10", MIB; A $105.00

Porsche 911R, Schuco, battery-op, red & yel plastic w/tinted windows, forward & reverse action, 10", NM (EX box), A $149.00

Porsche 935, 1970, Taiwan, battery-op, MIB, R7 ....$50.00

Rambler Classic Station Wagon, 1961, Bandai, friction, 8¼", EX+ (VG box), A $92.00

Rambler Convertible, Yonezawa, friction, bl, No 1 emb on front plate, 8½", EX+ (VG box), A $190.00

Renault Dauphine, Bandai, friction, off-wht w/gray interior, 8", no hubcaps, non-working, G (orig box),A................$65.00

Renault Sedan, 1950s, Yonezawa, friction, bl w/gr interior, 7½", VG, A..$150.00

Rolls-Royce, Bandai, friction, red & wht, 11", EX, A $550.00

Rolls-Royce, 1960s, friction, wht & bl w/gr interior, 8½", EX, A..$90.00

Rolls-Royce Silver Coupe, 1950s, Bandai, friction, blk w/yel interior, NP trim, 12", VG-, A...............................$160.00

SAAB Sedan, Bandai, friction, blk w/red & wht interior, 7½", EX (orig box), A...$290.00

Studebaker Packard Convertible, Schuco, battery-op, remote control (missing), 11", rpr fender (torn box), A......$500.00

Toyota Corolla 1100 Deluxe, TT, friction, bl w/plastic windows, 19½", M (EX+ box), A...$224.00

Triumph TR-2 Roadster, Bandai, friction, red w/red & wht interior, NP trim, folding windshield, 8", VG, A...........$140.00

Triumph TR-3, Bandai, International Gear Shift Car Series, battery-operated, silver, 8", EX (original box), A, $95.00.

Triumph TR-4, Bandai, battery-op, remote control, red & wht w/brn interior, 8", VG (VG box), A $75.00

Valiant Convertible, Yonezawa, friction, red, working windshield wipers, 9", EX+ (VG box), A $213.00

Volkswagen Ambulance, TN, battery-op, remote control, wht, 5½", EX (orig box), A..$90.00

Volkswagen Beetle, US Zone, pnt & litho tin, blk, split rear window, 7", VG, A...$230.00

Volkswagen Bus, Bandai, friction/battery-op, red & wht w/red interior, NP trim, 9½", non-working, rust/pitting, G, A $110.00

Volkswagen Bus, 1950s, Tipp, gray, red & blk w/red & wht interior, sliding roof, 9", VG (G box), A $575.00

Volkswagen Car, 1970, Hong Kong, battery-op, remote control, MIB, R7 ....$50.00

Volkswagen Convertible, Bandai, battery-op, remote control, plastic driver, 7", EX (orig box), A............................$50.00

Volkswagen Fire Truck, Bandai, friction, red w/yel interior , 7¾", VG, A..$120.00

Volkswagen Karman Ghia, 1960s, Bandai, friction, blk w/red & wht interior, 7", EX (orig box), A $140.00

Volkswagen Milk Truck, 1950s, Tipp, wht & bl w/NP trim, 9", non-working, VG, A $240.00

Volkswagen Pickup Truck, 1960s, Bandai, battery-op, bl w/NP trim, 7¾", NM (orig box), A.....................................$160.00

Volkswagen Sedan (Kingsize), Bandai, battery-op, red w/NP trim, see-through engine compartment, 15", VG (orig box), A.....................................$275.00

Volkswagen 1200 Sedan, Indian Head, friction, bl, 7", NM (EX+ box), A.....................................$167.00

Volkswagen 1500 Sedan, friction, blk w/red & wht interior, 7", EX (orig box), A.....................................$110.00

Volkswagen 1600, 1961, Yonezawa, battery-op, lighted rear end, opening hood, trunk & door, 13½", non-working, G, A.....................................$90.00

Volvo Amazon, 1960s, Bandai, friction, 2-tone gr w/yel & bl interior, 8", G, A.....................................$165.00

Volvo Sedan, friction, blk 2-door w/bl interior, 7½", VG (orig box), A.....................................$425.00

Banks

The impact of condition on the value of a bank cannot be overrated. Cast-iron banks in near-mint condition with very little paint wear and all original parts are seldom found, and might bring twice as much (if the bank is especially rare, up to five times as much) as one in average, very good original condition with no restoration and no repairs. Overpainting and replacement parts (even screws) have a very negative effect on value. Mechanicals dominate the market, and some of the hard-to-find banks in outstanding, near-mint condition may exceed $20,000.00! (Here's a few examples: Girl Skipping Rope, Calamity, Mikado, and Jonah and the Whale.) Still banks are widely collected as well, with more than 3,000 varieties having been documented. Beware of modern reproductions, especially mechanicals. Watch for paint that is too bright and castings that do not fit together well.

For more information we recommend *The Dictionary of Still Banks* by Long and Pitman; *The Penny Bank Book* by Moore; *The Bank Book* by Norman; and *Penny Lane* by Davidson.

Advisor: Diane Patalano (P8).

See also Advertising; Battery-Operated; Character, TV and Movie Collectibles; Disney; Diecast Collector Banks; Reynolds Toys; Rock 'n Roll; Santa; Western.

MECHANICAL BANKS

Acrobat Bank, Book of Knowledge, pnt CI, 9", EX, A...$130.00

Always Did 'Spise a Mule, Book of Knowledge, 1950s, w/jockey, EX.....................................$350.00

Always Did 'Spise a Mule, J&E Stevens, pnt CI, boy on bench, 10" base, EX+, A.....................................$1,725.00

Always Did 'Spise a Mule, J&E Stevens, pnt CI, boy on bench, 10" base, VG, A.....................................$863.00

Always Did 'Spise a Mule, J&E Stevens, pnt CI, w/jockey, 10" base, EX.....................................$1,800.00

Always Did 'Spise a Mule, J&E Stevens, pnt CI, w/jockey, 10" base, VG, A.....................................$625.00

Artillery Bank, Book of Knowledge, 1950s, soldier shoots coin from mortar into fortress, EX.....................................$350.00

Artillery Bank, J&E Stevens, pnt CI, soldier shoots coin from mortar into fortress, 9" base, G, A, from $675 to.....$900.00

Artillery Bank, Shepard Hardware, nickel-plated cast iron, soldier shoots coin from mortar into fortress, EX, from $2,000.00 to $2,200.00.

Artillery Bank, Shepard Hardware, NP CI, soldier shoots coins from mortar into fortress, 8", missing trap, G, A.....$500.00

Bad Accident, J&E Stevens, pnt CI, boy darts in front of Black man on mule cart, 10" base, EX, A.....................................$3,220.00

Bad Accident, J&E Stevens, pnt CI, boy darts in front of Black man on mule cart, 10" base, rpl figure, some rpt, G, A.....................................$525.00

Bill-E-Grin, J&E Stevens, pnt CI bust, sticks out tongue & rolls eyes, 4¼", trap missing, G, A.....................................$475.00

Bill-E-Grin, J&E Stevens, pnt CI bust, sticks out tongue & rolls eyes, 4¼", EX.....................................$2,500.00

Billy Goat, J&E Stevens, CI, goat on filigreed base, 5½", rare, G, A.....................................$1,725.00

Bird in House, Germany, 1950s, tin, w/up, NMIB..........$150.00

Bird on Roof, J&E Stevens, CI, 4³⁄₁₆" base, EX, A.......$1,725.00

Bird on Roof, J&E Stevens, CI, 4³⁄₁₆" base, VG, A......$1,380.00

Birdie Putt, Utexiqual/Richard's Toys, 1st in series of 4, EX..$375.00

Black Minstrel, Germany, gr, blk & yel litho tin, Black man's face w/open mouth above verse, curved top, 7", VG, A....$350.00

Boy Milking Cow, Book of Knowledge, 1950s, CI, EX...$450.00

Boy Milking Cow, 1970s, CI, EX.....................................$125.00

Boy on Trapeze, J Barton & Smith, pnt CI, 5" base, EX+, A.....................................$3,450.00

Boy Scout Camp, J&E Stevens, pnt CI, 9⅞" base, EX+, A....$6,900.00

Boy Scout Camp, J&E Stevens, pnt CI, 9⅞" base, rpl flag & arm, G, A...$1,840.00

Buddy Bank, Marx, litho tin, boy tilts arm to flip coin into glass jar, 4½", few scratches o/w EX, A............................$110.00

Bulldog, Book of Knowledge, 1950s, CI, place coin on nose, pull tail & coin is swallowed, EX....................................$350.00

Bulldog, J&E Stevens, pnt CI dog w/glass eyes snaps coin from nose, 7½", trap missing, G, A................................$375.00

Bulldog Savings Bank, Ives Blakeslee & Co, blk-pnt CI w/gold accents, dog takes coin from man's hand, w/up, 9", EX, A...$4,400.00

Butting Buffalo, Kyser & Rex, pnt CI, buffalo butts boy up tree trunk w/raccoon atop, 7¾" base, rpl trap o/w EX+, A..........$5,175.00

Butting Goat, Judd Mfg, CI, goat springs forward & deposits coin into tree trunk, 4¾" base, G, A........................$196.00

Butting Goat, Judd Mfg, CI, goat springs forward & deposits coin into tree trunk, 4¾" base, EX+, A....................$460.00

Cabin Bank, Book of Knowledge, 1950s, CI, EX...........$325.00

Cabin Bank, J&E Stevens, pnt CI, Black man standing at door of slant-roof cabin, 3⅝", few scratches & chips o/w VG, A..$600.00

Calamity, J&E Stevens, pnt CI, 3 football players on base, 7½" base, EX-, A..$19,550.00

Cat & Mouse, Book of Knowledge, 1950s, cat jumps over ball as mouse goes between legs, EX...................................$375.00

Cat & Mouse (Cat Balancing), J&E Stevens, pnt CI, 5⅜" base, EX, A...$2,530.00

Cat Boat, pnt CI boat on base w/life preserver on side, sheet metal sail swings into cat 'yachtsman,' 13", VG+, A...$80.00

Century of Progress (Copy of Sears Building), Arcade, Chicago World's Fair, 1934, pnt CI, 7", G-, A.......................$350.00

Chief Big Moon, J&E Stevens, painted cast iron, Indian seated in front of tepee faces frog, oblong base, 10", NM, D10, from $4,000.00 to $5,000.00.

Chief Big Moon, J&E Stevens, pnt CI, Indian seated in front of tepee faces frog on oblong base, 10", VG, A........$1,955.00

Circus Bank, Shepard Hardware, pnt CI, clown on horse cart in center ring, 9" dia, rpl crank, EX+, A................$14,950.00

Clown Bank, Chein, 1930s, litho tin clown bust, press lever & tongue comes out to receive coin, no hat, 5¼", VG, A..$55.00

Clown Bank, Chein, 1930s, litho tin clown bust, press lever & tongue comes out to receive coin, 5¼", EX+, A........$97.00

Clown on Globe, J&E Stevens, pnt CI, 9", EX+.........$4,500.00

Clown on Globe, J&E Stevens, pnt CI, 9", G, A........$2,070.00

Clown on Globe, J&E Stevens, pnt CI, 9", slight fading o/w NM, A..$5,175.00

Creedmore Bank, J&E Stevens, pnt CI, man shoots coin into tree trunk, 10" base, G, A, from $400 to..................$500.00

Cresent Cash Register, J&E Stevens, CI, put coin into slot, depress lever & bell rings, 6", EX, A, from $475 to .$550.00

Cross-Legged Minstrel Bank, L Levy Co, litho & pnt tin, Black man in top hat & striped pants on rnd base, 7", VG, A........$425.00

Darktown Battery Bank, J&E Stevens, pnt CI, 3 baseball players on rectangular base, 10", rpr, VG, A....................$1,600.00

Darktown Battery Bank, J&E Stevens, pnt CI, 3 baseball players on rectangular base, 10", EX+.................................$4,500.00

Dentist, J&E Stevens, pnt CI, dentist ready to pull Black man's tooth, ftd base, 9½", minor rpt, EX, A.................$16,100.00

Drunken Scotsman, pnt cast metal, portly figure nods head when coin is deposited, 8", G, A.................................$45.00

Eagle & Eaglets, J&E Stevens, pnt CI, 6¾" oval base, EX+, A, from $1,610 to...$2,000.00

Eagle & Eaglets, J&E Stevens, pnt CI, 6¾" oval base, G, A..$475.00

Eagle & Eaglets, J&E Stevens, pnt CI, 6¾" oval base, slight pnt wear, non-working bellows o/w VG, A...................$725.00

Elephant & Three Clowns, J&E Stevens, pnt CI, elephant on drum w/performing clowns, 5½", lacking pnt, P, A .$575.00

Elephant w/Howdah, Enterprise Mfg, pnt CI & wood, man pops out when elephant puts coin in mouth, 7", non-working, G+, A..$250.00

Elephant w/Howdah, Hubley, gray-pnt CI, put coin on trunk, pull tail & trunk rises & deposits coin, 8", VG+, A .$750.00

Ferris Wheel, Hubley, w/CI gondolas, wind & deposit coin, coin drops to activate Ferris wheel, 22", EX+, A..........$6,900.00

Fortune Teller Savings Bank, Baumgarten & Co, CI combination safe, paper fortunes appear in window, VG+, A, from $450 to..$575.00

Frankenstein's Hand Bank, TN/Japan, place coin at door of tin house, door opens to reveal hand that drags coin in, MIB, A...$175.00

Frog Bank (Two Frogs), J&E Stevens, pnt CI, sm frog on back flips coin into lg frog's mouth, 8¾" base, M, A $1,450.00

Frog on Round Base, J&E Stevens, yel, gr & red-pnt CI, hole in top of base, 4½", pnt wear, G, A..............................$500.00

Girl Skipping Rope, J&E Stevens, pnt CI, girl in yel dress, 8⅛" base, NM, A...$48,300.00

Golfer, John Wright Toys of Pennsylvania, MIB............$325.00

Guided Missile Bank, Astro Mfg, 1950, silver metal rocket shape, coin flies into nose cone, 11", NM (EX box), A.........$90.00

Hall's Excelsior Bank, J&E Stevens, pnt CI building w/teller in cupola, 5", EX...$1,250.00

Hall's Excelsior Bank, J&E Stevens, pnt CI building w/teller in cupola, 5", pnt chips, trap missing, G-, A................$375.00

Home Bank, Morrison, red brick litho tin building w/gr roof showing teller at window, 6", some spotting, G+, A .$85.00

Home Bank, painted cast iron, NM, D10, $2,200.00.

Leap Frog Bank, Shepard Hardware, Pat 1891, painted cast iron, EX, D10, from $6,000.00 to $8,000.00.

Home Town Battery, Book of Knowledge, 1950s, CI, EX...$375.00

Humpty Dumpty, Book of Knowledge, 1950s, pnt CI, clown bust, EX...$375.00

Humpty Dumpty, Shepard Hardware, pnt CI, clown bust, EX+...$2,800.00

Humpty Dumpty, Shepard Hardware, pnt CI, clown bust, P, A..$200.00

Humpty Dumpty, Shepard Hardware, pnt CI, clown bust, VG $1,100.00

Humpty Dumpty, Shepard Hardware, pnt CI, clown bust, 7½", G-, A..$150.00

Indian Shooting Bear, Book of Knowledge, 1950s, EX...$400.00

Indian Shooting Bear, J&E Stevens, pnt CI, brn bear, 10½" base, some feathers missing, damage to base, G, A..$625.00

Indian Shooting Bear, J&E Stevens, pnt CI, wht bear, 10½" base, VG+...$2,000.00

John Deere Blacksmith, CI, blacksmith deposits coin into anvil w/hammer, EX color, from $1,200 to....................$1,500.00

Jolly 'N' Bank, blk-pnt CI bust of Black man w/straight bow, octagonal wood base, 6¾", rpt, G, A..........................$40.00

Jolly 'N' Bank, J&E Stevens, blk-pnt CI bust of Black man w/red-pnt lips & wht teeth, 7", G, A $425.00

Jolly 'N' Bank, John Harper & Co/English, pnt CI bust of Black man in wht top hat, 7½", G, A $140.00

Jolly 'N' Bank, Starkies/English, pnt aluminum bust of Black man, 5¼" pnt chips, G, A..$75.00

Jolly 'N' Bank, Sydenham & McOustra/English, pnt CI bust of Black man, rnd holes in back of head & base, 5¼", G, A...........$75.00

Jolly Sambo Bank, possibly Harper, blk-pnt CI bust of Black man w/red-pnt lips & wht teeth, 7", minor pnt wear o/w VG, A..$200.00

Jonah & the Whale, Book of Knowledge, 1950s, pnt CI, EX $350.00

Jonah & the Whale, Shepard Hardware, pnt CI, 10¼" base, VG, A, from $1,955 to..$2,760.00

Jonah & the Whale, 1970s, pnt CI, EX $125.00

Juke Box (Select-O-Matic), Haji Toys of Japan, 1950s, tin, mechanical w/up, actually plays, VG $250.00

Leap Frog Bank, Book of Knowledge, 1950s, CI, boy hops over another, EX...$375.00

Leap Frog Bank, Shepard Hardware, pnt CI, 5", trap missing & no spring, pnt chips, G from $1,800 to.................$2,000.00

Liberty Bell, 1960s, pnt CI, insert coin & bell rings, EX...$275.00

Lion & 2 Monkeys, Kyser & Rex, 1883, VG+, from $2,000 to $2,200.00

Little Moe, Chamberlin and Hill, England, Pat 1931, painted cast iron, NM, D10, $2,450.00.

Little Moe Bank, pnt CI bust of Black man w/1 arm tipping hat & 1 arm putting coin into mouth, 5½", VG, from $650 to...$800.00

Magician, J&E Stevens, pnt CI, magician at table on stepped base, 4", EX, A from $4,000 to...........................$6,500.00

Magician, 1970s, EX...$125.00

Mammy & Child, Kyser & Rex, pnt CI, gr dress version, 7½", VG, A..$6,000.00

Mammy & Child, Kyser & Rex, pnt CI, red dress version, EX, from $4,800 to..$5,200.00

Mammy & Child, Kyser & Rex, pnt CI, red dress version, 7½", NM, A...$10,350.00

Mammy & Child, Kyser & Rex, pnt CI, yel dress version, 7½", G, A...$1,350.00

Mason, John Wright of Pennsylvania, 1960s, CI, scarce, EX $995.00

Mason, Shepard Hardware, pnt CI, 2 bricklayers on base, EX, minimum value $8,500.00

Mason, Shepard Hardware, pnt CI, 2 bricklayers on rare red base, faded, G, A $1,955.00

Mason, Taiwan, 1960s, coin goes through brick wall as mason raises & lowers brick & trough, hard to find............$675.00

Milking Cow, J&E Stevens, pnt CI, reddish brn cow on thin 9¾" base, EX+, A $4,600.00

Monkey & Coconut, J&E Stevens, CI, monkey on 5" rectangular base deposits coin into coconut, EX, A, from $1,150 to.......$1,600.00

Monkey & Coconut, J&E Stevens, CI, monkey on 5" rectangular base deposits coin into coconut, NM, A $2,900.00

Monkey Bank, Hubley, pnt CI, monkey leaps to deposit coin in organ held by man, 8¾" base, new trap, some rpt, G, A .$95.00

Monkey Tipping Hat, Chein, red, yel & brn litho tin dressed monkey on base mk Thank You, 5", minor scratches o/w VG, A $50.00

Monkey w/Coin in Stomach, SS&SD Tallman, japanned CI, very rare, EX+, A $3,220.00

Monkey w/Tray, Germany, brn tin monkey w/tray sitting atop litho tin monkey cage, 6½", some wear, G, A $190.00

Motor Bank (Trolly Car), Kyser & Rex Co, CI, 4", EX, A .$4,370.00

Mule Entering Barn, J&E Stevens, pnt CI, mule kicks legs & flips coin into barn, dog exits, 8½" base, VG+, A.........$1,265.00

Mule Entering Barn, J&E Stevens, pnt CI, mule kicks legs & flips coin into barn, dog exits, 8½" base, G, A.........$575.00

Mule Entering Barn, J&E Stevens, pnt CI, mule kicks legs & flips coin into barn, dog exits, 8½" base, EX.........$1,600.00

New Bank, J&E Stevens, pnt CI, building on footed base, 9½", G, A $575.00

North Pole Bank, J&E Stevens, pnt CI, flag pops out of of globe on base depicting expedition, 4" base, rare, EX, A........$2,530.00

North Pole Bank, J&E Stevens, 2nd casting, pnt CI, flag pops out of globe on base depicting expedition, 6¾", EX, A.$1,100.00

Novelty Bank, J&E Stevens, pnt CI building w/bank teller inside, 6¼", pnt chips, VG, A $750.00

Octagonal Fort, pnt CI, cannon facing fort on oblong base, 11¼", rare, EX, A $3,450.00

Olympic Colosseum, John Wright Toys for US Olympic Committee, runner deposits coin into Olympic flame, EX ..$1,500.00

Organ Bank w/Cat & Dog, Kyser & Rex, pnt CI, dog & cat atop crank organ turn & monkey drops coin, 7½", VG, A $750.00

Organ Bank w/Cat & Dog, Kyser & Rex, 7½", EX......$1,500.00

Organ Bank w/Monkey, Kyser & Rex, pnt CI, monkey on organ tips hat when coin is deposited, 6½", G-, A $200.00

Organ Bank w/Monkey (Medium), Kyser & Rex, pnt CI, monkey atop crank organ, 5¾", EX, A...........................$748.00

Organ Bank w/Monkey (Miniature), Kyser & Rex, pnt CI, monkey atop crank organ, EX $775.00

Owl, J&E Stevens, NP CI, deposit coin & owl turns head, 7½", some pnt chips & wear, head sticks o/w VG, A.......$350.00

Owl, Kilgore Mfg, CI, slot in head, deposit coin & eyes roll, 6", EX, A $483.00

Paddy the Pig, CI, 1970s...$95.00

Patronize the Blind Man & His Dog, J&E Stevens, pnt CI, dog deposits coin, 5¾", rpr base, dog rpl, pnt chips, G+, A $1,700.00

Pelican Bank (Arab), J&E Stevens, pnt CI, pelican opens mouth to expose figure, 8", VG, A $525.00

Pelican Bank (Mammy), Trenton Lock & Hardware, japanned CI, pelican opens mouth to expose pnt figure, 8", EX+, A $4,025.00

Penny Pineapple, Am, 1960s, pnt CI pineapple w/face & arms, commemorating Hawaii entering the Union, 1 of 500, VG, A..$100.00

Penny Pineapple, Am, 1960s, pnt CI pineapple w/face & arms, commemorating Hawaii entering the Union, 1 of 500, NM $595.00

Pig in Highchair, J&E Stevens, NP CI, deposit coin in mouth & his tongue moves upward, G, A $500.00

Pistol Bank, Richard Elliot Co, sheet metal gun shape, 5½", G-, A $150.00

Presto Bank, Kyser & Rex, red & brn pnt CI building, 4½", pnt chips, G, A $220.00

Professor Pug Frogs Great Bicycle Feat, J&E Stevens, pnt CI, 10" base, rpr to frog & base o/w EX, A......................$2,990.00

Punch & Judy, Shepard Hardward, pnt CI, 2 figures in puppet theater, G, A from $725 to......................................$850.00

Punch & Judy, Shepard Hardware, pnt CI, 2 figures in puppet theater, EX, A, from $3,450 to $4,500.00

Punch & Judy Money Box, English, litho tin, 2 figures in puppet theater, VG (end flap missing from box), A............$120.00

Rabbit in Cabbage, Kilgore Mfg, pnt CI, 4⅛" base, VG, A.$700.00

Reclining Chinaman, J&E Stevens, pnt CI, yel pants, put coin in pocket, press lever, hand reveals cards, 9", G, A....$1,300.00

Rocket Bank, Duro Mold, 1950, silver-tone metal, place coin, push button & coin flies into nose, 8", MIB, A $245.00

Rooster Bank, Kyser & Rex, pnt CI, drop coin in rooster's tail & head moves, 6¼", rpt head, VG, A $190.00

Santa Claus, Shepard Hardware, pnt CI, Santa on beveled base deposits coin into chimney, 4⅛" base, G, A.........$1,380.00

Santa Claus at Chimney, John Wright Toys, 1960s, CI, EX .$595.00

Shoot-A-B'ar, 1950s, CI, Davy Crockett shoots coin in bear's mouth, scarce, EX..$495.00

Southern Comfort, 1950s, CI, soldier shoots coin into bottle, EX...$95.00

Speaking Dog, J&E Stevens, pnt CI, girl seated in front of dog, NM $2,400.00

Speaking Dog, J&E Stevens, 1880s, painted cast iron, blue dress, EX, D10, $1,950.00.

Speaking Dog, Shepard Hardware, pnt CI, girl seated in front of dog, maroon base, G-, A..................................$299.00

Speaking Dog, Shepard Hardware, pnt CI, girl seated in front of dog, EX+, A..$1,800.00

Speaking Dog, Shepard Hardware, pnt CI, girl seated in front of dog, G, A, from $525 to $600.00

Squirrel & Tree Stump, Mechanical Novelty Works, CI, 6¾" base, non-working lever, G, A.............................$1,265.00

Standing Rabbit, Lockwood Mfg, pnt CI, dk brn & gold rabbit on rnd stepped base, 6", 1 ear not working, G, A $325.00

Strike Bowling, Utexiqual/Richard's Toys, 3rd in series of 4, EX...$475.00

Stump Speaker, Shepard Hardware, pnt CI, Black man w/satchel on sq base, some rpt & new push rod, VG, A..........$850.00

Stump Speaker, Shepard Hardware, pnt CI, Black man w/satchel on sq base, rpl satchel, hat & base, chips, G, A.......$500.00

Stump Speaker, Shepard Hardware, pnt CI, Black man w/satchel on sq base, NM..$8,500.00

Sweet Thrift Bank, red litho tin tall booth w/arched top & glass window, dispenses candy in drawer, 6", worn, G-, A.$75.00

Tabby Bank, pnt CI, cat sitting atop egg on pedestal watching chick's head when coin is dropped, 4½", chips, G, A...$225.00

Tammany Bank, J&E Stevens, pnt CI, man seated in chair, hand deposits coin into pocket, pnt chips, G, A.....$270.00

Tammany Bank, J&E Stevens, pnt CI, man seated in chair, hand deposits coin into pocket, EX, from $675 to...$750.00

Tammany Bank, 1970s, CI..$95.00

Teddy & the Bear, Book of Knowledge, 1950s, CI, EX ..$350.00

Teddy & the Bear, J&E Stevens, pnt CI, man shoots coin into tree trunk, bear pops up, 10⅛" base, G-, A, from $850 to $1,200.00

Teddy & the Bear, J&E Stevens, pnt CI, man shoots coin into tree trunk, bear pops up, 10⅛" base, VG, M11.....$2,000.00

Teddy & the Bear, Taiwan, CI, EX....................................$150.00

Tennis Players, John Wright, pnt CI, Billie Jean King 'serves' coin over net, 10¾", VG, A $40.00

Toad on Stump, J&E Stevens, 1880, VG.......................$750.00

Trick Dog, Hubley, 1920s, painted cast iron, black & white dog, clown in black and yellow, 8¾", plain blue base, EX+, D10, minimum value $650.00.

Trick Dog, Hubley, pnt CI, blk & wht dog & clown in blk & yel, solid bl base, VG, A $300.00

Trick Dog, Hubley, pnt CI, dog leaps through clown's hoop & deposits coin in barrel, 6-part base, EX, A............$1,100.00

Trick Dog, Hubley, pnt CI, dog leaps through clown's hoop & deposits coin in barrel, 6-part base, no trap, G, A ...$300.00

Trick Dog, Hubley, pnt CI, dog leaps through clown's hoop & deposits coin in barrel, 6-part base, no trap, VG, A .$725.00

Trick Pony, Shepard Hardware, pnt CI, red base, EX+ ..$2,800.00

Trick Pony, Shepard Hardware, pnt CI, rpl tail, G, A ...$325.00

Trick Pony, Shepard Hardware, pnt CI, VG+, A........$1,650.00

Two Frogs, J&E Stevens, 1882, CI, EX.......................$4,800.00

Uncle Sam, Book of Knowledge, 1950s, CI, bl shirt, wht pants w/red stripes, red base, EX $550.00

Uncle Sam, CI, 1970, EX...$125.00

Uncle Sam, Shepard Hardware, 1886, CI, NM, from $3,800 to..$4,000.00

Uncle Tom (Star & Lapel), Kyser & Rex, pnt CI bust, 5¼", rpl trap, G-, A $250.00

Uncle Tom (Star & No Lapel), Kyser & Rex, pnt CI bust, 5⅛", shirt rpt, G, A $200.00

US & Spain, Book of Knowledge, 1950s, CI, EX $350.00

US & Spain, J&E Stevens, pnt CI, cannon on wall facing ship's mast, 8⅜" base, rpl mast, G, A $978.00

Watch Dog Safe, J&E Stevens, pnt CI, blk combination safe w/gold relief, 5¾", some pnt chips & scratches o/w VG+, A...$300.00

Watch Dog Safe, J&E Stevens, pnt CI, blk combination safe w/gold relief, 5¾", no bellows, some pnt wear & rust, G+, A...$100.00

Weeden's Plantation Darky Saving Bank, pnt & emb tin, 2 minstrels on cabin platform, 5½", key missing, pnt loss, G, A $450.00

Wild West, 1950s, cast metal, single gun shoots at cowboy, EX..$95.00

William Tell, Book of Knowledge, 1950s, CI $350.00

William Tell, Classic Iron, 1960s, CI, EX......................$275.00

William Tell, J&E Stevens, CI, EX $1,250.00

William Tell, J&E Stevens, pnt CI, G+, A $600.00

Wireless Bank, J Hugo Mfg, pnt CI & litho tin building, deposits coin at sound of hands clapping, battery-op, 5", G, A $45.00

World's Fair, J&E Stevens, pnt CI, Indian offers Columbus peace pipe, 8½" base, G, A...................................$633.00

World's Fair, J&E Stevens, pnt CI, Indian offers Columbus peace pipe, 8½" base, NM..................................$4,500.00

Zoo Bank, Kyser & Rex, pnt CI, red & gr lion & tiger appear when monkey's head is pushed into window, 4¼", VG, A $1,250.00

REGISTERING BANKS

Ben Franklin Thrift Bank, tin litho, shape of cash register, VG $250.00

Lucky Savings Banks, Am Can Co, litho tin cash register shape w/center lever, bell rings, 5", VG+, A......................$35.00

Park-O-Meter, Zell, 1950s, plastic parking meter that automatically registers money, MIB, J5 ....$35.00

STILL BANKS

Abe Lincoln Glass Bottle, 1930s, removable tin cap, VG .$65.00

All-American Mail Box Bank, Superior Stationary, 1950s, red, wht & bl 4-legged mailbox shape, steel, 9", MIB.....$155.00

Armored Car, Callen Manufacturing Comp (US), metal, EX...$48.00

Baseball Player, AC Williams, 1920s, painted cast iron, gold with red cap, EX, D10, $450.00.

Boo Belly Bear, striped shirt w/bl pants, place coin in mouth & belly grows, NMIB..$25.00

Brooklyn Savings Bank, porcelain, architectural copy of the actual bank, metal coin trap o/w EX $65.00

Burgler Proof House Safe, Stevens, plated CI combination safe w/ornate reliefs, 6", some wear o/w VG+, A.............$15.00

Buster Brown & Tige, pnt CI, 5¼", EX, A......................$220.00

Century of Progress, CI building w/center tower, 7", G, A $800.00

Circus Elephant, 1950s, on pedestal tub, EX....................$95.00

City Bank w/Crown, pnt CI Victorian bank building, 5½", rpt, VG, A..$175.00

Clown, AC Williams, 1908, painted cast iron, blue with red cap, gold trim, NM, D10, $300.00.

Clown w/Crooked Hat, 1950s, CI................................$125.00

Columbia Bank, Kenton, wht-pnt CI sq building w/ornate dome top, repro combination trap, 7¼", VG+, A $325.00

Columbia Bank, Kenton, wht-pnt CI sq building w/ornate dome top, 5¾", VG, A $110.00

Dreadnought, England, CI, depicts battleship, handshake & Union Jacks, 7", some pnt wear o/w VG, A.............$350.00

Early American Combination Safe, 1950s, blk metal, real combination lock & throw bolt, 4½", VG $65.00

Early American Combination Safe, 1950s, blk metal, real combination lock & throw bolt, 6", VG+.........................$95.00

Elephant, Arcade, 1910-32, trunk curled under, pnt CI, 4½", VG+, A..$44.00

Elephant, USA, CI, 6", heavy pnt loss o/w VG, A $35.00

Elephant w/Howdah, Williams, pnt CI, gold w/red harness, 6½", EX..$150.00

Elephant w/Howdah, 1970s, CI, EX.............................$75.00

Empire State Building (w/image of Statue of Liberty), 1950s, CI, side coin slot & key lock trap $95.00

Every Copper Helps, Chamberlin & Hill/English, natural brass finish, 6", EX, A...$160.00

Farmer Pig, ceramic, bl pants, red shirt & blk hat.............$48.00

Fez, maroon pnt CI Shriner's fez, 1½", few sm chips o/w VG, A...$10.00

Fidelity Trust Vault with Lord Fauntleroy, T. Barton Smith, 1890, painted cast iron, EX, D10, $850.00.

Fido, Hubley, pnt CI, blk & wht puppy w/head slightly cocked & ears flared out, 4¾", few pnt chips o/w VG, A.......$35.00

Flying Saucer Bank, Duro Mold, 1950s, diecast saucer on globe w/names of planets on windows, 5", EX (EX box), A .$162.00

Foxy Grandpa, pnt CI figure in silver suit & bowler hat standing w/hands on hips, 5½", pnt chips & scratches, G, A...$80.00

George Washington, CI, standing figure, VG...................$75.00

Girl w/Parasol, pnt CI figure in wht flowered dress & bonnet holding bl parasol, 7½", pnt chips & wear, G, A.......$35.00

Gladiator Bank, red & blk CI building w/statue on cupola, 9¼", G+, A..$650.00

Globe on Arc, Grey Iron, 1900-03, pnt CI, 5¼", EX, from $285 to..$400.00

Golliwog, standing, pnt CI, red & bl, 6½", dull pnt, rust, G, A...$220.00

Grandma & Grandpa, porcelain, 'Save For Retirement,' both hold hat upside down for donation, pr $75.00

Happy Days Barrel Bank, Chein, 1930s, sq key trap lock .$75.00

Horse, Arcade, 1910-32, pnt CI, Beauty emb on 1 side, 4¾", VG, A $55.00

Horseshoe, Arcade, gold-finished CI & wire mesh, 2-sided horseshoe w/horse head in profile, 3¼", VG, A.........$30.00

Independence Hall Tower, Enterprise Mfg, bronze-finished CI, 8¾", wear to finish o/w VG, A $400.00

Independence Hall Tower, Enterprise Mfg, pnt CI, bell rings, 9¼", some pnt wear o/w VG, A $525.00

Indian, Hubley, pnt CI, Indian standing w/tomahawk & hand over forehead peering, 6¼", VG, A $350.00

Indian, 1960s, cast wht metal, headdress & hatchet, slot in back of head $65.00

Kitten, wht-pnt CI kitten w/pink bow in upright sitting position, 7", pnt chips, G, A..$30.00

Lincoln, Penn Manufacturing Co of California, 1940s, hand-painted, hatchet & saw stuck in log, NMIB $375.00

Lion (Standing), John Wright Toys of Pennsylvania, 1960s, CI..$65.00

Log Cabin, Chein, ca 1935, Black banjo player & dancing girl lithoed on front of tin cabin, 3", rare, EX, A $300.00

Lost Dog, pnt CI, blk seated dog, 5½", VG, A................$450.00

Mail Box, 1950s, tin, miniature, NMIB $65.00

Maine Battleship, Grey Iron Co, CI, 6½", missing trap, G, A $250.00

Mammy, CI figure in bl w/silver apron standing w/hand on hip & holding spoon, 5¾", pnt chips & rust, G-, A.........$50.00

Mammy, CI figure in red dress & wht apron w/hands on hips, 5¼", pnt chips & rust on base o/w VG, A $150.00

Mammy, CI figure in red dress & wht apron w/hands on hips, 5¼", EX+, A $300.00

Merry-Go-Round, Grey Iron Co, 1920s, pnt CI, 4½", VG+, A $397.00

Pistol Packing Pirate, 1930s, wht metal, key trap lock......$95.00

Policeman, bl-pnt CI figure standing w/hand on hip & cradling nightstick in crook of arm, 5¾", G-, A $50.00

Prancing Horse, 1930s, CI, gold pnt, 4½", VG, from $95 to..$150.00

Prancing Horse on Pebbled Base, USA, pnt CI, 7½", sm amount of copper pnt remaining o/w VG, A............................$64.00

Presto Bank, pnt CI building w/knobed dome, 4", EX....$200.00

Punch and Canine Cop, English, 1920s, lithographed tin, M, D10, $250.00.

Punch & Judy, litho & emb tin, scenes on 4 sides of theater w/hinged roof, 2¾", VG, from $210 to....................$300.00

Reindeer, AC Williams, 1920s, sm, VG..........................$45.00

Retriever Dog, 1920s, CI, pack on back, blk, EX $95.00

Riverboat, wht-pnt CI side-wheeler w/gr paddle boxes & red trim, 7½", pnt chips & loss, G, A............................$150.00

Roller Safe, Kyser & Rex, 1882, CI, EX- $215.00

Safe, Kenton, plated CI & steel w/cut-out filigree design, 2¾", wear to pnt & plating, G, A $20.00

Mystic Radio, Kenton, 1920s, painted cast iron, EX, D10, $225.00.

Santa with Tree, Hubley, painted cast iron, 6", NM, D10, minimum value, $650.00.

New England Church, wht-pnt CI w/gr roof, front steeple entrance, 7½", pnt chips, G+, A $85.00

Notre Dame Trinket Box, CI, hinged lid & cloth lining..$125.00

Old Lady Who Lived in a Shoe, yel shoe, bl roof, children poking heads out of windows......................................$95.00

Oriental Camel, gold-pnt CI, w/calf on rockers, 5⅜", pnt wear, G+, A..$325.00

Save for a Rainy Day, 1930s, litho tin w/children, key lock coin trap, EX..$150.00

Seaman's Sailor Savings, 1940s, wht porcelain w/metal coin trap, VG $65.00

Seated Cat, hand-painted blk & yel ceramic, right paw raised, 6", slot in back of head, G $24.00
Seated Kitty, Hubley, 1930s, CI, 4¾", EX......................$150.00
Seated Pig, AC Williams, 1910-34, CI, 4½", VG+, A $44.00
Seated Pig, John Wright of Pennsylvania, CI, EX $95.00
Sharecropper, blk w/gold pnt CI figure in hat standing w/hands in pockets, 5¼", pnt chips, rust & wear, G-, A $55.00
Transvaal Money Box, English, maroon-pnt CI portly figure in top hat & smoking pipe, 6", few pnt chips o/w VG, A $125.00
Trolley, gold-pnt CI w/coin slot on side of roof, 4½", G, A..$150.00
US Capitol Trinket Box, CI, hinged lid & cloth lining, EX $95.00
Victorian House, Stevens, gold-pnt CI, twin chimneys, 4½", rpt, VG+, A..$150.00
Windmill, Japan, litho tin, blades spin, NMIB, A $65.00
Wise Pig, Hubley, 1930s, CI, NM $350.00

Wise Pig, Hubley, 1930s, painted cast iron, 6⅝", EX, D10, $150.00.

WWI Tank, pnt CI, 5¾", no pnt, G, A $45.00
WWI Tank, US made, tin, mc litho, EX+.......................$175.00
Young Negro, AL/English, pnt CI bust, 4½", traces only of orig pnt, G, A...$65.00

Barbie and Friends

No one could argue the fact that vintage Barbies are holding their own as one of the hottest areas of toy collecting on today's market. Barbie was first introduced in 1959, and since then her face has changed three times. Her hair has been restyled over and over, she's been blond and brunette, and it's varied in length from above her shoulders to the tips of her toes. She's worn high-fashion designer clothing and pedal pushers. She's been everything from an astronaut to a veterinarian, and no matter what her changing lifestyle required, Mattel (her 'maker') has provided it for her.

Though even Barbie items from recent years are bought and sold with fervor, those made before 1970 are the most sought

after. You'll need to do lots of studying and comparisons to learn to distinguish one Barbie from another, but it will pay off in terms of making wise investments. There are several books available; we recommend them all: *The Wonder of Barbie* and *The World of Barbie Dolls* by Paris and Susan Manos; *The Collector's Encyclopedia of Barbie Dolls and Collectibles* by Sibyl DeWein and Joan Ashabraner; *The Story of Barbie* by Kitturah B. Westenhouser; and *Barbie Fashion, Vol. 1, 1959-1967,* by Sarah Sink Eames.

Remember that unless the box is mentioned in the line (orig box, MIB, MIP, NRFB, etc.), values are given for loose items. As a general rule, a mint-in-box doll is worth twice as much as one mint, no box. The same doll, played with and in only good condition, is worth half as much (or even less).

Advisor: Marl Davidson (D2).

DOLLS

Allan, 1964, pnt red hair, nude, straight legs, VG, A.......$30.00
Allan, 1964, pnt red hair, orig bl shorts & striped jacket, straight legs, MIB (no liner), D2 ....$125.00
Angie 'N Tangie, Pretty Pairs, 1970, NRFB, A $225.00
Barbie, #1, 1958-59, blond hair, MIB, D2 ....$4,500.00
Barbie, #1, 1958-59, blond hair, orig swimsuit, shoes & hoop earrings, NM, D2...$2,995.00
Barbie, #1, 1958-59, brunette hair, orig swimsuit, shoes & hoop earrings, EX, D2 ....$2,500.00

Barbie, #1, redhead prototype, 1 of a kind, from the Marl Davidson collection, minimum value $50,000.00.

Photo courtesy of Marl Davidson.

Barbie, #3, 1960, blond hair, MIB, D2.........................$1,300.00
Barbie, #3, 1960, blond hair, orig swimsuit, NM, D2 .....$995.00
Barbie, #3, 1960, blond hair loosely retied, nude, straight legs, G, A..$350.00

Barbie, #3, 1960, brunette hair, MIB, D2 ....$1,400.00

Barbie, #3, 1960, brunette hair, orig swimsuit, M, D2 ....$795.00

Barbie, American Beauty Queen, 1991 department store special, NRFB, D2 ....$20.00

Barbie, American Girl, 1965, titian hair, bendable legs, MIB, D2 ....$850.00

Barbie, American Girl, 1965, titian hair, orig 1-pc swimsuit, bendable legs, NM, A................................$270.00

Barbie, American Girl (side part), 1964, blond hair, NRFB, D2..$3,995.00

Barbie, Animal Lovin', 1988, MIB, D2 ....$12.00

Barbie, Army, 1989, MIB, D2..$15.00

Barbie, Astronaut, 1985, orig outfit, gear & helmet, NM, A $20.00

Barbie, Blue Rhapsody, 1986, 1st in series, some loose glitter on gown o/w NM, A....................................$120.00

Barbie, Bubble-Cut, 1961, blond hair, MIB, D2 ....$295.00

Barbie, Bubble-Cut, 1961, blond hair, orig pk & wht swimsuit, EX+, D2 ....$125.00

Barbie, Bubble-Cut, 1964, blond hair, no lipstick, wearing Resort outfit, straight legs, G, A................................$65.00

Barbie, Bubble-Cut, 1964, titian hair, wearing Garden Party dress, straight legs, G, A $40.00

Barbie, Bubble-Cut, 1969, brunette hair, wearing Mood for Music outfit, straight legs, G, A $55.00

Barbie, Canadian, International series, 1987, NRFB, A...$38.00

Barbie, Busy w/Holdin' Hands, 1971, $195.00.

Barbie, Color Magic, 1966, blond hair, NRFB, D2 .....$2,500.00

Barbie, Color Magic, 1966, blond hair, orig 1-pc checked swimsuit & headband, bendable legs, NM, A..................$280.00

Barbie, Color Magic, 1966, brunette hair, coral lips, orig 1-pc checked swimsuit & headband, bendable legs, NRFB, D2 ....$3,250.00

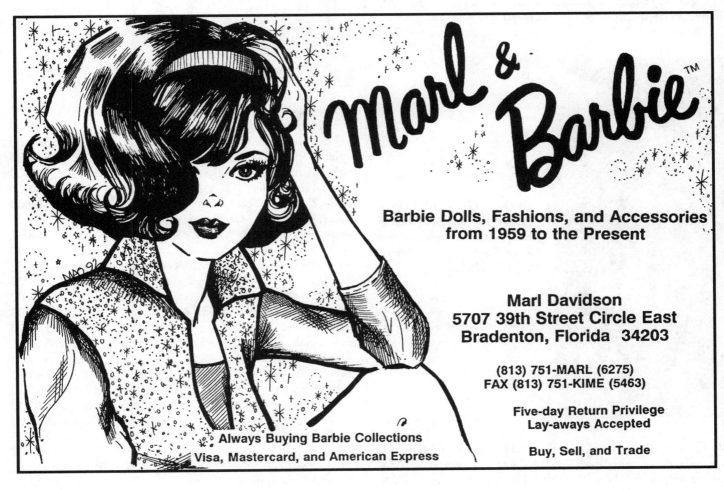

Barbie, Color Magic, 1966, brunette hair, orig 1-pc checked swimsuit & headband, bendable legs, NM, D2 ....$800.00

Barbie, Color Magic, 1966, titian hair, in Stripes Away outfit, EX+, D2 ....$800.00

Barbie, Crystal Rhapsody, 1992, 1st in Presidential Porcelain Collection, MIB, A $210.00

Barbie, Cute 'N Cool, Target, 1991, NRFB, D2 ....$45.00

Barbie, Desert Storm, 1992 department store special, NRFB, D2...$20.00

Barbie, Dream Date, 1982, MIB, D2 ....$15.00

Barbie, Empress Bride, Bob Mackie, 1992, MIB, D2.......$650.00

Barbie, Enchanted Evening, 1987, porcelain, MIB, A....$170.00

Barbie, Eskimo, International series, 1990, NRFB, A.......$20.00

Barbie, Evening Elegance, JC Penney, 1990, NRFB, D2 ..$75.00

Barbie, Evening Splendor, JC Penney, 1992, MIB, D2.....$20.00

Barbie, Fashion Queen, 1963, molded brunette hair, orig swimsuit & turban, w/3 wigs, VG+, D2 ....$120.00

Barbie, Fashion Queen, 1963, molded brunette hair, orig swimsuit & turban, w/3 wigs & stand, NRFB, D2............$195.00

Barbie, Gay Parisienne, 1991, porcelain, NMIB, A........$120.00

Barbie, German, International series, 1986, NRFB, A $65.00

Barbie, Gold Medal, 1975, blond hair, orig swimsuit & medal, bendable legs, NMIB, A $50.00

Barbie, Gold Sensation, 1993, missing stand, shoes & certificate o/w MIB, A $140.00

Barbie, Golden Greetings, FAO Schwarz, 1989 department store special, MIB, A...$175.00

Barbie, Golden Greetings, FAO Schwarz, 1989 department store special, NRFB, D2 ....$195.00

Barbie, Icelandic, International series, 1986, NRFB, A....$65.00

Barbie, Japanese, International series, 1984, orig outfit, NM, A $65.00

Barbie, Live Action, 1971, blond hair, orig 2-pc outfit w/fringe, rooted eyelashes, bendable arms & legs, NM, A........$55.00

Barbie, Living, 1970, brunette hair, nude, rooted eyelashes, bendable arms & legs, VG, A $55.00

Barbie, Miss, 1964, pnt hair w/orange band, NRFB, D2 .$1,350.00

Barbie, Miss, 1964, pnt hair w/orange band, orig swimsuit, sleep eyes, bendable legs, no wigs, G, A..........................$150.00

Barbie, Montgomery Wards, 1971, rare, NRFB (pk window box), D2..$995.00

Barbie, Neptune Fantasy, Bob Mackie, 1992, MIB, D2 ..$650.00

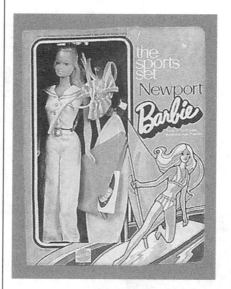

Barbie, Newport Barbie Sport Set, #7807, 1974, NRFB, $95.00.

Barbie, Growin' Pretty Hair, 1st edition, blond hair with hair pieces and accessories, pink dress, NRFB, $295.00.

Barbie, Night Sensation, FAO Schwarz, 1991, NRFB, A ..$85.00

Barbie, Party Sensation, 1990, MIB, D2...........................$15.00

Barbie, Pepsi Spirit, 1989, NRFB, A $45.00

Barbie, Perfume Pretty, 1987, NRFB, A...........................$15.00

Barbie, Peruvian, International series, 1985, NRFB, A $48.00

Barbie, Pink Jubilee, Wal-Mart, 1987, MIB, D2 ....$30.00

Barbie, Platinum, Bob Mackie, 1991, MIB, A $300.00

Barbie, Quick Curl Miss America, 1972, NRFB, D2 ....$65.00

Barbie, Radiant in Red, 1992 department store special, NRFB, D2...$60.00

Barbie, Roller Skating, 1980 department store special, NRFB, D2...$25.00

Barbie, Royal, 1979, NRFB, A $120.00

Barbie, Scottish, 1990, NRFB, A.....................................$25.00

Barbie, Silken Flame, 1992, porcelain, NMIB, A $120.00

Barbie, Solo in the Spotlight, 1990, porcelain w/microphone, NMIB, A..$80.00

Barbie, Southern Belle, 1993, MIB, D2...........................$40.00

Barbie, Starlight Splendor, Bob Mackie, 1991, MIB, D2.$695.00

Barbie, Sterling Wishes, Spiegel, 1991, MIB, D2.............$70.00

Barbie, Superstar in the Spotlight, 1977, MIB, D2 ....$30.00

Barbie, Sweet 16, Canadian, 1973, NRFB, A $35.00

Barbie, Swirl Ponytail, 1964, blond hair, MIB, D2 ....$595.00

Barbie, Swirl Ponytail, 1964, blond hair, orig 1-pc red swimsuit, straight legs, snags in swimsuit o/w NM, A..............$200.00

Barbie, Growin' Pretty Hair, 1972, 2nd edition, blond hair, orig maxi dress, rooted eyelashes, bendable legs, NM, A ..$70.00

Barbie, Happy Holidays, 1988, MIB, D2 ....$495.00

Barbie, Talking, 1969, blond hair, orig 3-pc swimsuit & wrist tag, M, D2 ....$150.00

Barbie, Talking, 1969, brunette hair, NRFB, D2 ....$295.00

Barbie, Talking, 1970, blond hair, orig gold & wht outfit, NRFB, D2 ....$325.00

Barbie, Talking, 1970, brunette hair, orig gold & wht outfit, rare, NRFB, D2 ....$300.00

Barbie, Twist 'N Turn, 1967, brunette hair, orig swimsuit & wrist tag, M, D2 ....$250.00

Barbie, Twist 'N Turn, 1968, titian hair, orig checked swimsuit, NRFB, D2 ....$650.00

Barbie, Twist 'N Turn, 1969, brunette hair, orig swimsuit, MIB, D2 ....$495.00

Barbie, Twist 'N Turn, 1970, titian hair, NRFB, D2 ......$495.00

Barbie, Walk Lively Miss America, 1972, brunette hair, orig gown & crown, rooted eyelashes, bendable legs, NM, A $50.00

Barbie, Wedding Day, 1989, porcelain, w/stand & bouquet, NM, A $150.00

Barbie, Western Fun, 1989 department store special, NRFB, D2 ....$25.00

Barbie, Winter Fantasy, FAO Schwarz, 1990 department store special, NRFB, D2 ....$295.00

Brad, New Talking, 1971, NRFB, D2 ....$135.00

Cara, Quick Curl, 1975, orig outfit, shoes & necklace, NM, D2 ....$30.00

Casey, Twist 'N Turn, 1967, brunette hair, orig 1-pc swimsuit, rooted eyelashes, bendable legs, G, A $60.00

Casey, 1975, blond hair, nude, straight legs, NMIP, A.....$60.00

Christie, Sunsational Malibu, 1981 department store special, NRFB, D2 ....$20.00

Christie, Talking, 1970, orig 3-pc leatherette outfit, NRFB, D2 ....$195.00

Christie, Twist 'N Turn, 1970, orig pk & yel swimsuit, NRFB, D2 ....$250.00

Courtney, Teen Time, 1988 department store special, NRFB, D2 ....$20.00

Fluff, Living, 1971, NRFB, D2 ....$150.00

Francie, Twist 'N Turn, 1966, #966, brunette hair, bendable legs, rooted eyelashes, 1-piece outfit, MIB, $195.00.

Francie, Busy, 1972, blond hair, orig jeans, shirt & brn belt, bendable arms & legs, missing hair ribbon, NM, A ...$95.00

Francie, Hair Happenin's, 1970, blond hair, nude, rooted eyelashes, twist waist & bendable legs, NM, A $85.00

Francie, Quick Curl, 1973, brunette hair, nude, twist waist, bendable legs, G, A..$13.00

Francie, 1966, blond hair, bendable legs, NM, D2 ....$125.00

Francie, 1966, blond hair, straight legs, MIB, D2 ....$450.00

Francie, 1975, brunette hair, orig 1-pc bl swimsuit, straight legs, NMIP, A $65.00

Jamie, Walking, 1970, titian hair, wearing Furry Friends outfit, M, D2 ....$350.00

Kelley, Quick Curl, 1973, titian hair, orig dress w/polka-dot & plaid pattern, bendable legs, NM, A $45.00

Kelley, Yellowstone, 1974, long titian hair, suntan skin, nude, twist waist, bendable legs, NM, A $80.00

Ken, Busy, 1972, pnt brn hair, orig shirt, pants & belt, bendable arms & legs, NM, A...$35.00

Ken, Busy Talking, #1196, 1972, painted brown hair, molded teeth, jointed thumb, bendable arms and legs, NRFB, A, $100.00.

Ken, Busy Talking, 1972, pnt hair, orig outfit & accessories, M, D2...$50.00

Ken, Dance Club, 1989 department store special, NRFB, D2 ....$20.00

Ken, Dream Date, 1982 department store special, NRFB, D2 ....$25.00

Ken, Free Moving, 1975, pnt hair, orig outfit & accessories, EX+, D2 ....$35.00

Ken, Live Action, 1971, pnt brn hair, orig pants, shirt & fringe vest, NM, A $35.00

Ken, Malibu, 1970s, pnt hair, wearing Sea Scene outfit, EX, D2 ....$25.00

Ken, Rappin' Rockin, 1991 department store special, NRFB, D2 ....$15.00

Ken, Spanish Talking, 1969, pnt hair, NRFB, D2 ....$95.00

Ken, Sparkle Surprise, 1991, MIB, D2 ....$10.00

Ken, Sunset Malibu, 1970, NRFB, D2 ....$35.00

Ken, Supersport, Canadian, 1982, MIB, D2.....................$10.00

Ken, Walk Lively, 1971, pnt hair, orig bl shirt & plaid pants, M, D2..$50.00

Ken, 1961, flocked blond hair, nude, straight legs, NM, A.$65.00

Ken, 1961, flocked blond hair, straight legs, NRFB, D2.$350.00

Ken, 1961, flocked brunette hair, straight legs, NRFB, D2 .$350.00

Ken, 1962, pnt blond hair, nude, straight legs, NM, A.....$35.00

Ken, 1962, pnt blond hair, straight legs, MIB, D2 ....$125.00

Ken, 30th Anniversary, 1991, porcelain, A $95.00

Kevin, Cool Tops, 1990 department store special, NRFB, D2..$15.00

Lori 'N Rori, Pretty Pairs, NRFB, D2 ....$250.00

Midge, 1963, blond hair, orig swimsuit, straight legs, EX+, D2..$85.00

Midge, 1963, brunette hair, straight legs, NRFB, D2......$275.00

Midge, 1963, titian hair, nude, straight legs, EX, D2 ....$75.00

Midge, 1963, titian hair, orig swimsuit, straight legs, MIB, D2..$150.00

Midge, 1964, blond hair in orig set, wearing Candy Striper Volunteer outfit, straight legs, VG, A................................$65.00

Midge, 1965, blond hair, orig swimsuit & ribbon, bendable legs, NM, D2..$250.00

Midge, 1965, titian hair, bendable legs, MIB, D2 ....$550.00

Midge, 1988, Cool Times, titian hair, all original, MIB, $25.00.

Midge, 30th Anniversary, 1992, missing shoes & certificate o/w MIB, A...$65.00

Nan 'N Fran, Pretty Pairs, NRFB, D2 ....$250.00

PJ, Live Action, 1971, blond hair w/braided sections & beaded ties, nude, rooted eyelashes, bendable arms & legs, G, A..$25.00

PJ, Twist 'N Turn, 1970, blond hair, nude, rooted eyelashes, bendable legs, G, A...$20.00

PJ, Twist 'N Turn, 1970, NRFB, D2 ....$250.00

Ricky, 1965, NRFB, D2...$195.00

Skipper, Dramatic Living, rare 2-pc yel swimsuit, w/orange skooter, NRFB, D2 ....$295.00

Skipper, Homecoming Queen, 1988 department store special, NRFB, D2..$20.00

Skipper, Horse Lovin', 1982, MIB, D2 ....$15.00

Skipper, Living, 1970, blond hair, wearing newer bl satin gown, rooted eyelashes, bendable arms & legs, NM, A........$25.00

Skipper, Poseable, NRFP, D2 ....$40.00

Skipper, Twist 'N Turn, 1968, brunette hair, orig turq & pk swimsuit, NRFB, D2..$295.00

Skipper, Twist 'N Turn, 1968, titian hair, orig turq & pk swimsuit, EX+, D2 ....$85.00

Skipper, Twist 'N Turn, 1969, blond hair, pk & red checked sun suit, rare, NRFB, D2...$395.00

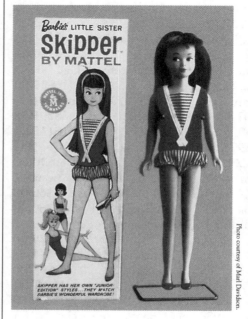

Skipper, 1963, titian hair, original nautical-style swimsuit, straight legs, with stand, NM, $100.00.

Photo courtesy of Marl Davidson.

Skipper, 1965, blond hair, orig nautical-style swimsuit, bendable legs, NM, D2..$75.00

Skipper, 1965, titian hair, orig nautical-style swimsuit, bendable legs, NRFB, D2 ....$395.00

Skipper, 1970, reissue, blond hair, straight legs, rare, no wrist tag o/w M, D2...$300.00

Skipper, 1970, reissue, brunette hair, straight legs, rare, NRFB, D2 ....$500.00

Skooter, 1965, blond hair, straight legs, NRFB, D2........$235.00

Skooter, 1965, blond hair retied on sides, wearing Lots of Lace dress, straight legs, VG, A $25.00

Skooter, 1965, titian hair, straight legs, rpl bows o/w MIB, D2..$125.00

Stacey, Talking, 1967, red hair, orig 2-pc swimsuit, NRFB, D2 .$350.00

Stacey, Twist 'N Turn, 1968, blond hair, NRFB, D2......$500.00

Stacey, Twist 'N Turn, 1968, blond hair, wearing Harem M-M outfit, rooted eyelashes, bendable legs, NM, A..........$95.00

Stacey, Twist 'N Turn, 1969, titian hair in orig set, orig 1-pc swimsuit, rooted eyelashes, bendable legs, M, A......$135.00

Steffie, Busy, 1972, brunette hair, orig print dress & accessories, bl spots on legs o/w M, D2...$65.00

Steffie, Walk Lively, 1972, brunette hair, nude, rooted eyelashes, bendable legs, VG, A..................$30.00

Steffie, Walk Lively, 1972, brunette hair, wearing Party Line dress, rooted eyelashes, bendable legs, M, D2 ....$175.00

Tutti, 1966, blond or brunette hair, NRFB, D2 ....$150.00

CASES

Barbie's Playhouse Pavillion, #2914, Europe, 1978, plastic 2-room carrying case, NRFB, D2 ....$65.00

Ken, 1961, lavender, orig tag, NM, D2 ....$15.00

Miss Barbie, 1963, blk patent leather w/zipper closure, no mirror o/w EX, D2 ....$95.00

Skipper & Scooter, 1965, yel, oblong, VG, D2................$10.00

Tutti, German, 1974, orange, orig manufacturer's note inside, NM, D2 ....$50.00

CLOTHING AND ACCESSORIES

After Five, Barbie, #934, complete, EX+, D2....................$50.00

All That Jazz, Barbie, #1848, missing gold belt, NM, D2.$110.00

American Airline Stewardess, Barbie, #984, complete, NM, D2.............$75.00

Arabian Nights, Barbie, #874, missing earrings, bracelet & lamp, G, D2 ....$50.00

Arabian Nights, Ken, #774, complete, rpl gr gem o/w NM, D2.............$50.00

Army & Airforce, Ken, #797, complete, NM, A $40.00

At Ease Fashion Pak, Ken & Allan, 1964-67, complete w/jeans & red & wht striped shirt, MOC, D2 ....$35.00

Ballerina, Barbie, #989, missing crown & poster, EX, D2.$25.00

Ballet Class, Skipper, #1905, complete, M, D2 ....$50.00

Barbie Baby-Sits, #953, 1st edition, complete, M, D2 ....$150.00

Barbie Baby-Sits, #953, 2nd edition, complete, M, D2...$225.00

Benefit Performance, Barbie, #1667, complete, EX+, D2 ..$325.00

Best Foot Forward Fashion Pak, Ken & Allan, 1964-67, complete w/6 pairs of shoes & socks, MOC, D2 ....$75.00

Best Man, Ken, #1425, NRFB, D2 ....$1,200.00

Big Business, Ken, #1434, NRFB, D2 ....$35.00

Bold Gold, Ken, #1436, complete, M, D2 ....$25.00

Bridal Brocade, Barbie, #3417, complete, G, A $35.00

Bride's Dream, Barbie, #947, complete, EX+, D2 ....$65.00

Buckaroo Blues, Francie, #3449, 1970, NRFB (worn), A, $60.00.

Busy Gal, Barbie, #981, complete, G-, A $45.00

Busy Gal, Barbie, #981, complete, NM, D2 ....$145.00

Campus Corduroys, Ken, #1410, NRFB, D2 ....$50.00

Campus Hero, Ken, #770, complete, M, D2 ....$25.00

Campus Hero, Ken, #770, NRFB, D2 ....$95.00

Candy Striper Volunteer, Barbie, #889, complete, NM, D2..$225.00

Check the Slacks Fashion Pak, Skipper, 1970, complete w/slacks & shoes, MOC, D2 ....$12.00

Checkmates, Francie, #1259, complete, M, D2 ....$65.00

Cheerful Chef Fashion Pak, Ken & Allan, 1964-67, complete w/hat, apron & utensils, MOC, D2 ....$95.00

Cheerleader, Barbie, #876, complete, NM, D2 ....$75.00

Cinderella, Barbie, #872, missing booklet o/w complete, EX+, D2 ....$175.00

College Student, Ken, #1416, rare, complete, M, D2 .....$265.00

Color Coordinates Fashion Pak, Barbie & Midge, #1832, 1964-65, complete w/5 purses & matching shoes, MOC, D2 .....$65.00

Concert in the Park, Francie, #1256, missing purse, M, D2 ..$40.00

Day at the Fair, Skipper, #1911, complete, M, D2...........$95.00

Denim Wrap, Barbie, #1476, complete, M, D2.................$25.00

Denims On, Francie, #1290, complete, NM, A $55.00

Disc Dater, Barbie, #1633, complete, NM, D2 ....$150.00

Dogs 'N Duds, Barbie, #1613, complete, M, D2 ....$150.00

Dr Ken, #793, complete, NM, A $25.00

Dream Team, Barbie, #3427, complete, NM+, D2 ....$50.00

Dreamy Pink, Barbie, #1857, complete, NM, D2.............$25.00

Drum Major, Ken, #775, NRFB, D2................................$150.00

Easter Parade, Barbie, #971, replica hat, complete, NM, D2 ....,$895.00

Enchanted Evening, Barbie, #983, complete, EX, D2 ....$150.00

Evening Gala, Barbie, #1660, complete, G, D2 ....$75.00

Evening Splendour, Barbie, #961, complete, NM, D2....$125.00

Evening Splendour, Barbie, #961, complete, VG, A $35.00

Fab Fur, Barbie, #1493, complete, EX, D2 ....$95.00

Fashion Add-On Hair Originals, Barbie, #2457, 1978, hair pcs & accessories, MOC, D2 ....$10.00

Fashion Editor, Barbie, #1635, complete, M, D2 ....$250.00

Fashion Shiner, Barbie, #1691, complete, M, D2 ....$95.00

Floating Gardens, Barbie, #1696, complete, NM, D2.....$250.00

Flower Girl, Skipper, #1904, NRFB, D2 ....$125.00

Flower Wower, Barbie, #1453, NRFB, D2 ....$60.00

Fun on Ice, Ken, #791, NRFB, D2.................................$95.00

Fun Shine, Barbie, #3480, NRFB, D2 ....$175.00

Furry-Go-Round, Francie, #1296, complete, EX+, D2 ...$295.00

Garden Party, Barbie, #931, EX, D2 ....$50.00

Garden Wedding, Barbie, #1658, complete, NM, D2 ....$195.00

Goin' Bowling, Ken, #1403, NRFB, D2 ....$65.00

Goin' Huntin', Ken, #1409, complete, VG, A.................$30.00

Goin' Sleddin', Skipper, #3475, NRFB, D2 ....$65.00

Golden Elegance, Barbie, #992, coat only, EX, D2..........$25.00

Golden Girl, Barbie, #911, complete, NM, D2................$55.00

Golden Glory, Barbie, #1645, complete, M, D2 ....$250.00

Golfing Greats, Barbie, #3413, NRFB, D2 ....$150.00

Graduation, Barbie, #945, missing diploma, EX, D2.........$15.00

Graduation, Ken, #795, gown only, EX, D2 ....$5.00

Groovin' Gauchos, Barbie, #1057, NRFB, D2 ....$250.00

Guinevere, Barbie, #873, shoes missing o/w complete, EX, D2....................$65.00

Hair Happening, Barbie, #2267, 1978, head & wig set from Europe, MOC, D2..$20.00
Happy Go Pink, Barbie, #1868, complete, M, D2 ....$75.00
Holiday Dance, Barbie, #1639, complete, M, D2 ....$375.00
Horray for Leather, Barbie, #1477, NRFB, D2..................$75.00
Ice Cream 'N Cake, Skipper, #1970, complete, M, D2.....$45.00
Icebreaker, Barbie, #942, complete, EX, D2......................$35.00
Important Investments, Barbie, #1482, NRFB, D2...........$75.00
In Training, Ken, #780, complete, M, D2..........................$15.00
International Fair, Barbie, #1653, complete, EX, D2 .....$150.00
Invitation to Tea, Barbie, #1632, complete, M, D2........$250.00
Japanese Real Silk Kimono, Barbie, 1965, complete, rare, M, D2 ....$1,200.00
Jump Into Lace, Barbie, #1823, complete, NM, D2..........$45.00
Ken in Switzerland, #776, complete, NM, A $55.00
Kitty Capers, Barbie, #1061, NRFB, D2 ....$575.00
Knitting Pretty, Barbie, #957, pk, complete, rare, NM, D2 ....$250.00
Lace Caper, Barbie, #1791, complete, VG, A $15.00
Lemon Fluff, Skipper, #1749, NRFB, D2 ....$40.00
Let's Dance, Barbie, #978, missing jewelry, NM, D2 ....$45.00
Let's Explore, Ricky, #1506, NRFB, D2 ....$75.00
Lights Out, Ricky, #1501, NRFB, D2................................$50.00
Little Bow Pink, Barbie, #1483, dress only, EX, D2 ....$15.00
Little Leaguer, Ricky, #1504, NRFB, D2...........................$75.00
Little Miss Midi, Skipper, #3468, NRFB, D2 ....$35.00
London Tour, Barbie, #1661, complete, VG, A $30.00
Long on Leather, Francie, #1769, missing scarf & boots, M, D2 ....$25.00
Loungin' Around Fashion Pak, Ken & Allan, 1964-67, complete w/shorts & paisley shirt, MOC, D2 ....$25.00
Lounging Lovelies, Skipper, #1930, complete, NM, D2 ...$40.00
Madras Mod, Barbie, #3485, complete, NM, D2 ....$40.00
Masquerade, Barbie, #944, missing invitation, EX+, D2 ..$65.00
Masquerade, Ken, #794, NRFB, D2 ....$85.00
Midi Marvelous, Barbie, #1870, complete, G, A $25.00

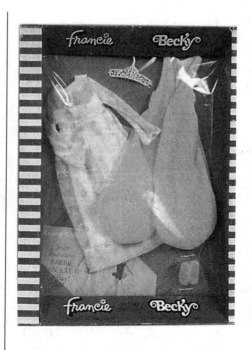

Midi Duet, Francie, #3451, 1970, NRFB (worn/small tear), A, $80.00.

Midi Mood, Barbie, #3407, MOC, D2 ....$50.00
Midnight Blue, Barbie, #1617, complete, EX+, D2 ....$200.00
Miss Astronaut, Barbie, #1641, complete, M, D2...........$495.00
Mood for Music, Barbie, #940, missing jewelry, NM, D2 .$70.00
Movie Date, Barbie, #933, complete, EX, D2 ....$20.00
Mr Astronaut, Ken, #1415, complete, G, A $115.00
Nifty Knickers, Skipper, #3291, MOC, D2 ....$45.00
Night Lighter, Barbie, #3423, complete, M, D2...............$50.00
Night Scene, Ken, #1496, NRFB, D2................................$40.00
Nightly Negligee, Barbie, #965, complete, EX+, D2.........$25.00
Now Wow, Barbie, #1853, missing hose, NM, D2............$35.00
O-Boy Corduroy, Barbie, #3486, NRFB, D2 ....$95.00
Off to Bed, Ken, #1413, complete, M, D2........................$95.00
On the Avenue, Barbie, #1644, complete, VG, D2........$150.00
Outdoor Casuals, Skipper, #1915, NRFB, D2 ....$95.00
Pajama Pow, Barbie, #1806, jumpsuit & shoes only, NM, D2 ....$50.00
Party Date, Barbie, #958, complete, EX, D2 ....$50.00
Peachy Fleecy, Barbie, #915, feather missing on hat, NM, D2 ....$45.00
Peasant Pleasant, Barbie, #3482, NRFB, D2 ....$125.00
Pink Fantasy, Barbie, #1754, complete, M, D2 ....$70.00
Pink Sparkle, Barbie, #1440, complete, EX+, D2 ....$50.00
Plantation Belle, Barbie, #966, complete, NM, D2 ....$175.00
Play Ball, Ken, #792, NRFB, D2.......................................$75.00
Poncho Put Ons, Barbie, #3411, complete, M, D2 ....$65.00
Poodle Parade, Barbie, #1643, complete, G, A...............$250.00
Pretty as a Picture, Barbie, #1652, complete, M, D2 ......$195.00
Pretty Power, Barbie, #1863, complete, G, D2.................$20.00
Quick Changes, Skipper, #1962, MOC, D2......................$95.00
Quick Shift, Francie, #1244, complete, NM, A $60.00
Red Flare, Barbie, #939, complete, EX+, D2....................$50.00
Registered Nurse, Barbie, #991, complete, NM, EX, D2 ..$75.00
Roller Skate Date, Ken, #1405, complete, M, D2.............$40.00
Rovin' Reporter, Ken, #1417, complete, M, D2 ....$150.00
Ruffles 'N Swirls, Barbie, #1783, NRFB, D2 ....$60.00

Masquerade, Skipper, #3471, 1970, NRFB, $95.00.

Sailor, Ken, #796, complete, G, A $33.00
Satin 'N Rose, Barbie, #1611, complete, M, D2 ....$125.00
Saturday Night Date, Ken, #786, NRFB, D2 ....$125.00
Saturday Show, Ricky, #1502, NRFB, D2......................$50.00
Sea Worthy, Barbie, #1872, tie missing from dress, NM, A...$43.00
Senior Prom, Barbie, #951, complete, M, D2 ....$85.00
Shift Into Knit, Barbie, #1478, NRFB, D2.......................$60.00
Shoes for Sports Fashion Pak, Ken & Brad, 1964-67, complete, MOC, D2 ....$7.00

Silver Polish, Barbie and Stacey, #1492, 1967, NRFB (slightly worn), A, $75.00.

Singing in the Shower, Barbie, #988, complete, NM, D2..$40.00
Skate Mates, Barbie, #1793, costume only, NM, D2 ....$8.00
Ski Queen, Barbie, #948, complete, NM, D2 ....$65.00
Ski Scene, Barbie, #1797, complete, VG, A $35.00
Ski Scene, Barbie, #1797, NRFB, D2 ....$90.00
Skin Diver, Ken, #1406, complete, EX, D2......................$15.00
Sleeping Beauty, Barbie, #1636, complete, VG, D2 ....$40.00
Slumber Party, Barbie, #1642, complete, M, D2.............$150.00

Smart Switch, Barbie and Francie, #1776, 1967, very rare, NRFB, $375.00.

Solo in the Spotlight, Barbie, #982, complete, EX+, D2.$150.00
Sophisticated Lady, Barbie, #993, complete, NM, D2....$140.00
Sorority Meeting, Barbie, #937, complete, NM, A $28.00
Special Date, Ken, #1401, MOC, D2 ....$95.00
Sport Shorts, Ken, #783, NRFB, D2.................................$55.00
Stormy Weather, Barbie, #949, complete, M, D2 ....$35.00

Striped Types, Francie and Casey, #1243, 1969, NRFB (worn/taped), A, $55.00.

Studio Tour, Barbie, #1690, complete, NM, D2 ....$85.00
Suburban Shopper, Barbie, #969, complete, NM, D2.......$90.00
Summer Number, Francie, #3454, NRFB, D2 ....$125.00
Sunday Suit, Ricky, #1503, NRFB, D2..............................$50.00
Sunday Visit, Barbie, #1675, complete, EX, D2............$150.00
Sunny Pastels, Skipper, #1910, NRFB, D2 ....$95.00
Sunny Slacks, Francie, #1761, NRFB, D2..........................$45.00
Sweater Girl, Barbie, #976, missing booklet, NM, D2......$55.00
Swirly Q, Barbie, #1822, dress only, NM, D2 ....$25.00
Tangerine Scene, Barbie, #1451, skirt only, M, D2 ....$5.00
Teeter Timers, Skipper, #3467, NRFB, D2.......................$30.00
Tennis Anyone, Barbie, #941, complete, M, D2 ....$45.00
Tennis Tunic, Francie, #1221, NRFB, D2 ....$50.00
Tenterrific, Francie, #1211, complete, EX, D2 ....$75.00
Terry Togs, Ken, #784, NRFB, D2 ....$65.00
Top It Off Fashion Pak, Ken & Allan, 1964-67, complete w/6 hats, MOC, D2 ....$50.00
Touchdown, Ken, #799, complete, EX, D2......................$35.00
Town Togs, Skipper, #1922, complete, M, D2...................$65.00
Travel Togethers, Barbie, #1688, complete, NM, D2 ....$55.00
TV's Good Tonight, Ken, #1419, NRFB, D2 ....$125.00
Twice as Nice, Skipper, #1735, orange, rare, MOC, D2...$65.00
Twilight Twinkle, Francie, #3459, NRFB, D2 ....$195.00
Vacation Time, Barbie, #1623, complete, NM, D2 ....$75.00
Velvet 'N Lace, Skipper, #1948, NRFB, D2 ....$150.00
Velvet Ventures, Barbie, #1488, MOC, D2 ....$85.00
Vested Interest, Francie, #1224, NRFB, D2 ....$50.00
Victory Dance, Ken, #1411, NRFB, D2 ....$125.00
Waltz in Velvet, Francie, #1768, complete, M, D2 ....$125.00

Weekenders, Barbie, #1815, NRFB, D2 ....$895.00
White Magic, Barbie, #1607, complete, NM, A $55.00
Wild 'N Wooly, Francie, #1218, NRFB, D2 ....$110.00
Winter Holiday, Barbie, #975, complete, NM, D2 ....$60.00

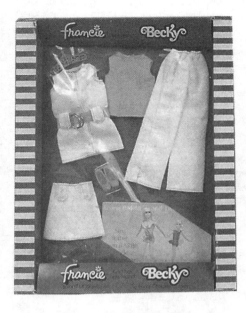

With-It-Whites, Francie, 1970, NRFB (worn), A, $50.00.

Yachtsman, Ken, #789, NRFB, D2 ....$95.00
Zokko, Barbie, #1820, complete, VG, A $28.00

FURNITURE AND ROOMS

Barbie Room-Fulls Country Kitchen, #7407, 1974, NRFB, D2, $50.00.

Barbie Bath 'N Beauty Place, #9056, Sears Exclusive, 1975, NRFB, D2 ....$10.00
Barbie Bedroom Accents, grandfather clock, #2372, 1985, NRFB, D2...$8.00

Barbie Bedroom Accents, mirror, 1985, NRFB, D2 ....$5.00
Barbie Dream Canopy Bed, #5641, 1987, NRFB, D2 ....$15.00
Barbie Dream Furniture, sofa & coffee table, #2474, 1978, M (worn box), D2 ....$10.00
Barbie Dream Furniture, vanity & stool, #2469, 1978, NRFB, D2..$15.00
Barbie Dream House Finishing Touches, bedroom set, #3768, MOC, D2 ....$6.00
Barbie Dream House Finishing Touches, living room set, #3769, 1981, MOC, D2 ....$6.00
Barbie Kitchen Accents, microwave, #2373, 1985, NRFB, D2 ....$10.00
Barbie Light Up Vanity, #5847, Europe, 1982, NRFB, D2 .$20.00
Barbie Living Room Set, 1983, wht wicker, NRFB, D2....$20.00

Barbie Room-Fulls Firelight Living Room, #7406, 1975-76, NRFB, D2, $50.00.

Barbie Room-Fulls Studio Bedroom, #7405, 1974, NRFB, D2 ....$50.00
Barbie's Electronic Piano, #5085, 1981, battery-op, NRFB, D2 ....$35.00
Barbie's Step 'N Style Boutique, 1988, NRFB, D2............$10.00
Barbie's Suzy Goose Wardrobe, #463, 1963, MIB, D2....$125.00
Barbie Townhouse, #7825, 1975, 3 floors w/elevator, NRFB, D2...$50.00
Musical Rocking Chair, #31191, Sears Exclusive, 1973, MIB, D2 ....$25.00
Skipper's Dream Room, #4094, 1964, NRFB, D2 ....$600.00
Skipper's Jeweled Bed, Suzy Goose, 1965, MIB, D2 ....$150.00
Skipper's Jeweled Vanity, Suzy Goose, 1965, NRFB, D2.$250.00
Skipper's Jeweled Wardrobe, Suzy Goose, 1963, NM, D2 .$50.00
Skipper's 2-in-1 Bedroom, #9282, 1975, NRFB, D2 ....$95.00
Superstar Barbie Piano Concert, 1990, NRFB, D2 ....$25.00
Tutti & Todd's Dutch Bedroom Set, 1964, M, D2 ....$800.00
Tutti's Playhouse, 1965, complete, NM, D2 ....$50.00

GIFT SETS

Ballerina on Tour, 1976, MIB, A $90.00

Barbie & Ken Campin' Out, #4984, 1983, MIB, D2.........$50.00

Barbie Action Accent, #1585, rare, missing workout rope o/w M, D2...$95.00

Barbie Around the Clock, 1963, complete w/brunette bubble-cut Barbie & 3 outfits, NMIB, A $4,300.00

Barbie Color Magic Doll & Costume Set, #1043, 1965, MIB, D2 ....$4,500.00

Barbie Dance Club, #4917, 1989, MIB, D2.......................$50.00

Barbie Denim Fun, #4893, 1989, MIB, D2......................$50.00

Barbie Dream Wardrobe, #3331, 1991, MIB, D2 ....$20.00

Barbie Foaming Beauty Bath, 1960s, MIB, A $135.00

Barbie for President, #3722, 1992, MIB, D2 ....$35.00

Barbie Sharin' Sisters, #5716, 1991, MIB, D2 ....$35.00

Dance Magic Barbie & Ken, #5409, 1990, MIB, D2.........$45.00

Disney Barbie & Friends, Toys R Us, 1991, MIB, A.........$70.00

Francie and Her Swingin' Separates, #1042, 1966, NRFB, $550.00.

Francie Rise & Shine, #1194, 1971, MIB, D2 ....$995.00

Happy Birthday Barbie, 1984, MIB, D2 ....$40.00

Midge's Ensemble, #1012, straight-legged brunette, rare, NRFB, $1,300.00.

My First Barbie Deluxe Fashion Set, #2483, 1991, MIB, D2 ....$12.00

Pink & Pretty Barbie Modeling Set, #5239, 1981, MIB, D2 ....$45.00

Pose 'N Play Skipper & Her Swing-a-Rounder Gym, #1179, 1971, MIB, D2 ....$195.00

Tennis Star Barbie & Ken, #7801, 1988, MIB, D2 ....$35.00

Tutti Walking My Dolly, NRFB, D2................................$450.00

Vacation Sensation, #1675, 1988, MIB, D2....................$35.00

Western Fun Barbie, #5408, 1990, MIB, D2 ....$65.00

VEHICLES

Airplane, Barbie & Ken, Irwin, 1963, rare, replica nose cone & missing steering wheel o/w EX, D2 ....$500.00

Austin Healy, Irwin, 1962, orange w/aqua interior, NMIB, A $185.00

Barbie Goin' Boating, #7738, Sears Exclusive, 1973, NM, D2 ....$50.00

Barbie Going Camping Set, with Breezy Buggy and Tent Trailer, #8669, 1973-75, NRFB, $25.00.

Classy Corvette, #9612, 1976, NRFB, $35.00.

Country Camper, #4994, 1970, NMIB, D2......................$35.00

Dream Carriage w/Dapple Gray Horses, Europe, 1982, MIB (seperate boxes), D2 ....$125.00

Dune Buggy, Barbie & Ken & All Their Friends, #5908, 1970, NRFB, D2 ....$300.00

Ferrari, #3136, 1987, red, MIB, D2..................................$50.00

Ferrari, #3564, 1988, wht, MIB, D2.................................$50.00

Mercedes, 1963, gr, NMIB, D2......................................$150.00

Skipper's Motorbike, 1989, MIB, D2 ....$5.00

Star Cycle, #2149, 1978, MIB, D2 ....$20.00

Sun 'N Fun Buggy, #1158, 1970, orange, MIB, D2 ....$75.00

Super Corvette, #1291, 1979, remote control, NRFB, D2.$75.00

Ten Speeder, #7777, 1973, MIB, D2 ....$15.00

Travelin' Trailer, #5489, 1982, NRFB, D2......................$25.00
1957 Belair Chevy, 1989, aqua, 1st edition, M, D2 ....$50.00
1957 Belair Chevy, 1989, aqua, 1st edition, NRFB, D2....$75.00

MISCELLANEOUS

Autograph Book, Barbie, 1961, unused, M, D2 ....$95.00
Barbie Gold Medal Jewelry, necklace & ring or bracelet & ring,
    #8059, 1975, MOC, D2...$15.00

Barbie Travel Case, 1961, M, $35.00.

Book, Barbie's Easy as Pie Cookbook, Random House, 1964, M,
    D2 ....$110.00
Book, Barbie's Fashion Success, Random House, 1962, M,
    D2 ....$50.00
Book, Barbie's New York Summer, Random House, 1962, EX,
    D2 ....$30.00

**Comic Book, Barbie
and Ken, 1962, M, min-
imum value $95.00.**

Book, Portrait of Skipper, 1964, NM, D2..........................$15.00
Booklet, Skipper, Skooter & Ricky, D2 ....$8.00
Booklet, World of Barbie, D2 ....$30.00
Booklet, World of Barbie Fashions by Mattel, D2 ....$10.00
Box, Barbie #1, 1958-59, G-, D2.....................................$100.00
Box, Beautiful Bride Barbie, 1976, NM, D2......................$15.00
Box, Bubble-Cut Barbie w/titian hair, 1964, VG, D2.......$75.00
Box, Dramatic New Living Barbie, 1969, G, G2 ....$25.00
Box, Dramatic New Living Barbie, 1969, NM, J2............$70.00
Box, Gold Medal Barbie, 1974, EX, D2.............................$8.00

Box, Ponytail Barbie #3, blond hair, 1960, EX, D2..........$45.00
Box, Ricky, 1965, G, D2..$35.00
Box, Spanish Talking Barbie, 1967, missing end flap o/w VG,
    D2 ....$15.00
Brush & Comb, I'm Into Barbie, Avon, 1989, EX, D2 .....$10.00
Coin Purse, Skipper, 1964, bl, EX, D2 ....$30.00
Colorforms, Barbie Dream House, 1979, complete, M,
    D2 ....$12.00
Colorforms, Western Barbie, #657, 1982, NRFB, D2 ....$5.00
Coloring Book, see Coloring, Activity and Paint Books category
Dress-Up Set, Western Barbie, #635, 1981, NRFB, D2 ....$15.00
Jewelry Box, 1963, red, EX, D2...$25.00
Lotion, Barbie, 1961, box features Barbie #1 dressed in Sweater
    Girl outfit, MIB, D2 ....$100.00
Magazine, Barbie, Fall 1988, D2 ....$5.00
Magazine, Barbie, Winter 1985, D2 ....$5.00
Magazine, February Barbie Talk, 1972, special Valentine issue,
    D2 ....$15.00
Magazine, World of Barbie, 1964, features Barbie in Sophisti-
    cated Lady outfit, 1st & only issue, NM, D2 ....$85.00
Medallion, Barbie's 30th Anniversary, 2" coin in plastic case,
    Barbie logo on velvet bag, NM, A..............................$20.00
Paper Dolls, see Paper Dolls category
Pattern, Hootenanny, Sew-Free #1707, NRFB, D2 ....$75.00
Pattern, McCall's #7545, girls' nightgown & robe w/matching
    Barbie doll costume, M, D2 ....$25.00
Pattern, Sorority Tea, Sew-Free #1703, NRFB, D2 ....$75.00
Pillow Case, 1991, features Barbie, M, D2..........................$5.00
Playset, Backyard Patio, 1986, NRFB, D2.........................$15.00
Playset, Barbie Loves McDonald's, #5559, 1982, MIB, D2 .$65.00
Playset, Barbie Pool Party, #7795, 1973, NRFB, D2 ....$25.00
Playset, Barbie's Great Shapes Workout Center, 1984, NRFB,
    D2..$20.00
Playset, Barbie's Olympic Ski Village, #7412, 1974, NRFB,
    D2 ....$45.00
Playset, Western Fun Campin', 1990, NRFB, D2 ....$20.00

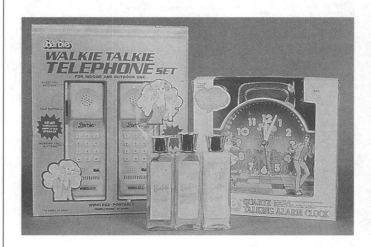

**Walkie Talkie Telephone Set, Nasta, NRFB, $15.00;
Bubbling Milk Bath, Cologne and Lotion, gold plastic lids
with paper labels, 1961, G, set of 3, $195.00; Quartz
Talking Alarm Clock, Janex Corp., #8120, 1983, NRFB,
$15.00.**

Posters, 1974, set of 10 miniature posters to color, NM, D2 ..$5.00
Powder Puff Mitt, Barbie, 1961, MIB, D2 ....$125.00
Radio, Superstar Barbie, 1980, NRFB, D2 ....$10.00
Record Tote, 1961, blk w/paper sleeves for record storage, G, A $45.00
Tea Set, Barbie's 25th Anniversary, 1984, NM, D2 ....$75.00
Tea Set, Barbie Sweet 16, #682, 1973, EX, D2 ....$15.00
Wallet, Skipper in Masquerade, 1964, bl, EX, D2............$30.00

Battery Operated

From the standpoint of being visually entertaining, nothing can compare with the battery-operated toy. Most (probably as much as 95%) were made in Japan from the forties through the sixties, though some were distributed by American companies — Marx, Ideal, and Daisy, for instance — who often sold them under their own names. So even if they're marked, sometimes it's just about impossible to identify the actual manufacturer. Though batteries had been used to power trains and provide simple illumination in earlier toys, the Japanese toys could smoke, walk, talk, drink, play instruments, blow soap bubbles, and do just about anything else humanly possible to dream up and engineer. Generally, the more antics the toy performs, the more collectible it is. Rarity is important as well, but first and foremost to consider is condition. Because of their complex mechanisms, many will no longer work. Children often stopped them in midcycle, rubber hoses and bellows aged and cracked, and leaking batteries caused them to corrode, so very few have survived to the present intact and in good enough condition to interest a collector. Though it's sometimes possible to have them repaired, unless you can buy them cheap enough to allow for the extra expense involved, it is probably better to wait on a better example. Original boxes are a definite plus in assessing the value of a battery-op and can be counted on to add from 30% to 50% (and up), depending on the box's condition, of course, as well as the toy's age and rarity.

We have made every attempt to list these toys by the name as it appears on the original box. Some will sound very similar. Many toys were reissued with only minor changes and subsequently renamed. For more information we recommend *Collecting Toys* by Richard O'Brien (Books Americana).

Advisor: Tom Lastrapes (L4).

See also Aeronautical; Automobiles and Other Vehicle Replicas; Boats; Marx; Robots and Space Toys.

Accordion Bear, Alps, plush bear w/microphone plays accordion & sways while eyes light up, 11", NM (EX box), A.$925.00
Accordion Player Hobo, Alps, seated hobo plays accordion while plush monkey plays cymbals, MIB, L4 ....$525.00
Acrobat Cycle, TJ-503, spins & does wheelies w/engine noise & flashing headlight, plastic, 9½", MIB, A $70.00
Air Mail Helicopter, KO, mystery action w/spinning rotors & rotor sounds, MIB, L4..$225.00
Aircraft Carrier, Hong Kong, 1970, plastic, MIB, R7 ....$55.00
American Cars Set, Bandai, pnt & litho tin, bl Stingray, red Mustang, 7", G+ (torn box), A $140.00

Andy Gard Electric ICBM Interceptor #351, 1950s, fires missiles, orange plastic, remote control, 14", MIB $125.00
Anti-Aircraft Jeep, K, advances as gun revolves & fires, litho tin, 9½", needs new flint o/w NM (EX+ box), A $204.00
Antique Gooney Car, Alps, 1960s, 4 actions, MIB $150.00
Armored Truck, Andy Gard, 1940s-early 50s, yel, red & blk plastic w/coin slot, remote control, 7", MIB, A $121.00
Army Radio Jeep, Linemar, 1950s, 4 actions, 7", NM $160.00
Army Tank, Daiya, brn litho tin, 8½", no guns, I2 ....$75.00
Arthur A-Go-Go Drummer, Alps, mop-haired figure beats light-up drum & sways, 9½", EX+ (EX box), A................$645.00
Astrodog, Snoopy look-alike, MIB, T1 ....$175.00
Atom Motorcycle, Modern Toys, rolls forward, stops & driver dismounts & climbs aboard, tin, 12", EX, A $475.00
Atom Submarine, turns & fires 8 deck-mounted missiles, remote control, NMIB, W5 ....$275.00
Automatic Train Station & Rubber Track, Cragstan, train runs & stops as conductor moves on platform, 9", scarce, MIB, A $187.00
Backfiring Hot Rod, Revell, 1950, push remote-control plunger w/caps to backfire, red & yel plastic, M (EX box), A .$180.00
Ball-Blowing Clown, TN, ball stays suspended in air as clown wanders around, litho tin w/cloth outfit, NM (NM box)..$425.00
Ball-Playing Bear, w/detachable umbrella, 5 celluloid balls & duck, rare, MIB, L4..$875.00
Ball-Playing Dog, Linemar, hits ball w/racket, eyes roll, tin & plush, 9", EX (NM box) $195.00
Balloon Bear, Alps, plush bear sits on litho tin footstool & blows balloon, 11", EX (G box), A................................$75.00
Balloon Bunny, Y, walks, rings bell & makes sounds, remote control, MIB, L4...$275.00
Balloon Vendor, Japan, 1961, clown w/balloons & bell, tin, cloth & vinyl, 11", EX (EX box)..............................$170.00
Barbeque Rotisserie, Japan, 1950s style, insert chicken over grill, w/utensils & towel, tin, 7½", NMIB $120.00
Barber Bear, Linemar, plush & litho tin, 11", NM (EX box)..$525.00
Barney Bear the Drummer Boy, Alps, beats drum while eyes light up, remote control, MIB, L4 ....$200.00
Bartender w/Revolving Eyes, cloth-dressed figure w/shaker & martini glass behind litho tin bar, 12", MIB $100.00
Batmobile, Alps, 1966, bump-&-go action, light-up machine gun w/sound & flashing rear engine lights, 11", rare, EX, A..$702.00
Batmobile, Richman Toys, Limited Edition, remote control w/independent suspension, 21", MIB, S2................$400.00
Batmobile, Taiwan, bump-&-go action w/lights & sound, litho tin w/vinyl-headed Batman & Robin, 11", NM (NM box), A $256.00
Batmobile, Toy Biz, 1989, radio controlled, MIB, S2 ....$95.00
Battleship, Hong Kong, 1970, plastic, MIB, R7 ....$55.00
Bear the Magician, Y, standing bear lowers & raises hat revealing various items, rare, NMIB, L4........................$3,500.00
Beauty Parlor Bear, S&E, beautician bear works on bear client in chair, 10", NM (EX box), A $975.00
Beechcraft, TN, tin plane advances as plastic props spin, lithoed w/pilot & female passenger, EX (EX box), A..........$125.00

Beethoven the Piano Playing Dog, TN, dog plays piano & moves head, plush & litho tin, 8½", scarce, NM (EX box), A $267.00

Begging Puppy, Y, 1960s, G..$25.00

Big John Chimpee Chief, Alps, 1960, MIB, R7.............$120.00

Big Ring Circus Truck, MT, brightly lithoed bump-&-go truck w/clown driver ringing bell, MIB, L4 ....$575.00

Billy & Betsy Jolly Riding in Their Old-Fashion Car, Craftoy, 3 actions, M (EX box) $295.00

Bimbo the Drumming Clown, Cragstan, advances & beats drum, remote control, litho tin, MIB $595.00

Black Knight, unauthorized Batmobile w/figures, Alps, gun appears from hood & fires, 11½", rare, EX (EX box), A..$1,025.00

Blacksmith Bear, 1950s, 6 actions, 9½", MIB $400.00

Blinky the Xylophone Clown, Amico, walks & plays w/moving head & light-up eyes, remote control, 10", EX (VG box), A $395.00

Blushing Cowboy, Y, 1960s, 4 actions, NM....................$125.00

Blushing Willie, Y, 1960, 10", EX, R7...............................$60.00

Blushing Willie, Y, 1960, 10", NM, R7..............................$80.00

Bongo Monkey, Alps, seated monkey plays bongos, MIB, L4 ....$200.00

Bouncing Army Jeep, MT, 1950s, 4 actions, NM...........$125.00

Brave Eagle, Japan, cloth-dressed Indian w/vinyl face & hands plays tin drum, 12", non-working, VG (torn box), A .$25.00

Brave Eagle, Japan, cloth-dressed Indian w/vinyl face & hands plays tin drum, 12", MIB $125.00

Broadway Trolley, MT, 1950s, litho tin, EX $95.00

Bubble Blowing Boy, Y, bends forward & puts bubble maker in pan, litho tin, 7½", scarce, NM (EX box), A...........$259.00

Bubble Blowing Elephant, Y, trunk blows bubbles, plush-covered w/litho tin base, 7", MIB $125.00

Bubble Blowing Kangaroo, MT, mother on base lowers wire into pan as baby in pouch turns head, litho tin, 9", EX+, A...$141.00

Bubble Blowing Lion, MT, blows bubbles & head moves, light-up eyes, litho tin, 7", NM (EX box), A...................$171.00

Bubble Blowing Monkey, Alps, 1959, plush monkey dips wand in solution & blows bubbles, eyes light, 10", NM (EX+ box), A..$165.00

Bubble Blowing Musician, Y, man in suit & hat dips trumpet in cup & blows bubbles, tin platform, M (EX box), A.$286.00

Bubble Blowing Musician, Y, man in suit & hat dips trumpet in cup & blows bubbles, tin platform, EX, A $115.00

Bubble Blowing Popeye, Linemar, arm raises & pipe lights, mc litho tin figure on yel & bl base, 12", EX (orig box)...........$1,050.00

Bullfighter & Bull, MIB, S2...$175.00

Bunny the Magician, Alps, clothed plush bunny sways & tips hat while performimg card trick, 13", EX+ (EX box), A...$433.00

Busy Cook, Hong Kong, 1970, NMIB, R7 ....$15.00

Busy Housekeeper, Alps, 2 versions w/rabbit or bear cleaning w/lighted vaccuum, MIB, L4, ea.............................$425.00

Busy Secretary, Linemar, 1950s, 7 actions, mc litho tin & pnt rubber head, NM $250.00

Captain Blushwell, Y, hat bounces, pours drink, blushes & eyes roll, tin, vinyl & cloth, 11", MIB $165.00

Car & House Trailer, Japan, red car pulls red & wht trailer w/pull-out canopy, 16½", VG, A $160.00

Cat 'N Carrier, Cragstan, 1970, remote control, MIB, R7.$35.00

Cement Mixer, TN, pnt & litho tin, orange & yel w/bl mixer, 10", parts missing, non-working, G, A $75.00

Champion Happy Plane, TPS, mc litho tin & plastic, 9", NM, A $100.00

Champion Motorcyclist, MT, Howdy Doody look-alike mounts & dismounts motorcycle, rare, MIB, L4 ....$1,800.00

Champion Weight Lifter, YM, 1960, clothed plush monkey lifts barbells, face turns red, 10", MIB, R7.......................$135.00

Charlie the Drumming Clown, Alps, plays drums & cymbals, head moves and nose lights up, tin and plastic, 9", EX+ (EX box), A, $130.00.

Charlie Weaver Bartender, TN, makes drink, smacks lips while face turns red & ears smoke, 12", NM (EX box), A..$125.00

Chef Cook, Yonezawa, chef chews & flips omelet as he sways, cloth, vinyl & litho tin, 10", EX+ (EX+ box), A $232.00

Chippy the Chipmunk, Alps, 1950s, 12", MIB..............$250.00

Circus Jet, TN, jet circles & trigger fires machine gun, litho tin, minor scuffs on hdl o/w EX (EX box), A $121.00

Circus Lion, VIA, plush lion sits on tin pedestal w/carpet that activates actions, 10", NM (EX box), A $450.00

City Bus Line Bus, red w/wht roof, 14", NM, M5 ....$180.00

Climbing Donald Duck on His Friction Fire Engine, Linemar, Pluto driving & Mickey at rear, 18", VG+ (EX box), A $1,500.00

Climbing Linesman, TPS, scurries up & down 3-section pole, w/helmet light, 5", EX+ (EX box), A......................$606.00

Clown Carnival Bumper Car, Japan, erratic action w/lights & sound, litho tin, 10", EX+, A $363.00

Cola Drinking Bear, Alps, 1950s, 3 actions, EX................$65.00

Cola Drinking Bear, Alps, 1950s, 3 actions, rare yel version, NMIB..$185.00

Comic Jumping Jeep w/Music, Alps, 1970s, plastic & litho tin, EX (EX box) $275.00

Comic Tank, Tomy, brightly lithoed tank w/moving eyes & mystery action, MIB, L4 ....$250.00

Communication Truck, metal, sends Morse code, NMIB, L5 ....$375.00

Computer Truck, Eldon, futuristic truck w/programable driving pattern, MIB, L4..$100.00

Coney Island Rocket Ride, Alps, 1950s, spins w/ringing bell & flashing lights, litho tin, 14", rare, MIB, A...........$1,000.00

Cragstan Bullfighter, TN, 1950s, litho tin, EX $95.00

Cragstan Crapshooter, Y, man in visor holding dice cup &' money stands before table, 9¼", M (worn box), A..$125.00

Cragstan Crapshooting Monkey, NMIB, M5 ....$90.00

Cragstan Dodge-Em Tricky Action Game, 2 bumper cars w/child drivers navigate enclosure until 1 escapes, EX (EX box), A...$71.00

Cragstan Dog Shuttling Train Set, Y, vinyl dog engineer in tin engine travels track & performs, NM (EX box), A .$254.00

Cragstan One-Armed Bandit, Y, 1960s, MIB $275.00

Cragstan Playboy, seated man in blk cloth tux & top hat pours a drink, 5¼", EX, A $100.00

Cragstan Roulette Man, Japan, 1950s, NM (NM box), S9 ....$275.00

Cragstan Telly Bear, S&E, dial phone for 6 actions, plush, cloth & litho tin, 9", EX+ (VG+ box), A $325.00

Cragstan Two-Gun Sheriff, Y, 1950s, 5 actions, EX (G box)...$200.00

Cragstan 732 Mountain Cable Car, operates w/rubber-coated wires, 'Scenic Mountain Tours...,' 7", NM (EX+ box), A...$165.00

Custom 'T' Ford Hot Rod, Alps, advances & shakes as engine lights & smoke comes from radiator, 10", NM (M box), A...$135.00

Cycling Daddy, Bandai, vinyl figure in cloth clothes rides tricycle, 10", NM (EX+ box), A.....................................$150.00

Dancing Dan, Bell Mfg, 1940s, Black man does the jig in front of lamppost, plastic, 15", NMIB, A $280.00

Dancing Merry Chimp, CK/Japan, performs 16 combined actions, plush & litho tin, MIB.................................$325.00

Dandy Happy Drumming Pup, Alps, seated plush dog plays drums, light-up eyes, 9", EX+ (EX box) $190.00

Dennis the Menace Playing Xylophone, Rosko, 1950s, 3 actions, MIB, from $250 to..$350.00

Dentist Bear, S&E, plush bear using lighted drill on patient who lifts cup & spits into pan, 10", NM (EX+ box), A...$750.00

Desert Patrol Jeep, MT, travels w/spinning action, ack-ack gun fires sound & swivels, tin & vinyl, 11", M (EX+ box), A...$176.00

Dice Throwing Monkey, Alps, 1960, MIB, R7 ....$100.00

Dick Tracy Police Car, Linemar, gr w/roof light, remote control, litho tin, 8½", EX+ (EX box), A............................$403.00

Diesel Locomotive, FYT/Taiwan, 1975, MIB, R7 ....$40.00

Dinosaur (Jiras), Bullmark/Japan, tin & vinyl, 11", NM (EX box), A...$500.00

Disney Acrobats, Linemar, 3 different versions w/Mickey, Pluto or Donald, rare, 9", MIB, L4, ea $875.00

Dolly Seamstress, TN, embroidering action & moving head, light-up eyes, tin & plastic, MIB..............................$395.00

Donald Duck Acrobat, see Disney Acrobats

Donald Duck Piston Race Car, TN/WDP, spinning action w/flashing lights & pistons, plastic, 9", MIB, A.......$141.00

Doodle the Poodle, Mego/Japan, 1960, MIB, R7 ....$75.00

Dozo the Steaming Clown, Rosko, sweeps floor & steam comes out of his hat & coat, litho tin w/cloth outfit, MIB.$425.00

Drinkers Savings Bank, J, place coin on bar, fellow lifts mug, coin shoots across bar into cash register, 10", NM, A...$150.00

Drinking Bear, Alps, 1970, MIB, R7 ....$80.00

Drinking Captain, S&E, 1950, MIB, R7 ....$180.00

Drinking Licking Cat, TN, pours & drinks from cup, plush, plastic & litho tin, MIB..$325.00

Drinking Monkey (orangutan version), Alps, seated plush monkey pours drink, head moves, eyes light, 10", NM (G box), A...$150.00

Drumming Bear, Y, walks & plays drum w/lighted eyes, rare, 12½", NMIB, L4..$1,600.00

Dump Tractor N-65, Trademark KDP Made in Japan, 1950s, forward and reverse action, rear bed dumps, orange and black lithographed tin, 8", MIB, A, $116.00.

Dump Truck, Bandai, 1960, MIB, R7 ....$125.00

Earthworm Cement Mixer, Hong Kong, 1970, MIB, R7 ..$20.00

El Toro, tin matador waves red cape & moves side-to-side in front of snorting plush bull, 9", NMIB, A................$230.00

Electric Open Car, KKK, gear shift controls forward & reverse action, yel w/blk rubber tires, tin, 7", NM (EX box), A...$100.00

Expert Motor Cyclist, MT/Japan, rider dismounts and remounts, working headlight, tin, 11", EX+ (torn box), $1,250.00.

Fairy Land Train #0741, Daiya, 1950s, 3 actions, NM $70.00

Feeding Bird Watcher, Linemar, 3 baby birds shriek to get fed, plush nest in litho tin tree, MIB...............................$525.00

Filling Station w/Studebaker, Distler, litho tin Shell station w/attached hose & plastic Studebaker, NM (EX+ box), A.................$270.00

Fire Bird III, Alps, futuristic car travels with bump-&-go action, flashing lights and engine noise, 11½", EX (VG+ box), A, $475.00.

Fire Boat, Japan, remote control, red & wht litho tin, 11", EX (orig box), A $65.00

Fire Chief Car, Cragstan #650, red Buick w/siren sound & flashing light, remote control, 6½", NM (EX box), A $62.00

Fire Chief Car, TN, advances w/bump-&-go action as fireman turns siren hdl, hood light flashes, 10", NM (EX box), A $220.00

Fire Department Motorcycle Patrol, TN, fireman on red tin cycle advances w/clanging noise, working headlight, 10", NM, A $425.00

Fire Engine, Hong Kong, 1970, MIB, R7 .... $35.00

Fishing Bear's Bank, Wonderful Toys/Japan, w/3 tin fish & coin, rare, MIB, L4 .... $3,200.00

Fishing Polar Bear, Alps, plush bear pulls fish out of pond, throws it in basket & laughs, tin base, 10", NM (EX box), A $300.00

Flippity Flyer, Mego/Japan, 1970, MIB, R7 .... $100.00

Flutterbirds, Alps, 2 birds fly up & down above birdhouse as 1 chirps in door, litho tin & plush, 27", EX+ (EX box), A $418.00

Flying Circus, Tomiyama, 3 bears swing above net, 3rd bear transfers magnetically, 17", scarce, NM (EX box), A $851.00

Flying Dutchman, Remco, orig box, T1 .... $125.00

Frankenstein Monster, TN, sways as arms move, pants fall as he blushes, tin, vinyl & cloth, 13", NM (EX+ box), A .$300.00

Frankie the Roller Skating Monkey, Alps, skates forward & backward, remote control, 12", M (EX box), A $245.00

Frankie the Roller Skating Monkey, Alps, 12", EX (orig box), T1 .... $185.00

Fred & Barney Car, AHI, 1974, very rare, NM, S2 .... $175.00

Fred Flintstone's Bedrock Band, Alps, 1962, 4 actions, litho tin, NMIB $1,500.00

Friendly Bartender, Amico/Taiwan, 1970, MIB $25.00

Funland Cup Ride, Sonsco, EX, S9 .... $200.00

Funland Cup Ride, Sonsco, kids w/vinyl heads spin around in cups as they rotate w/bell noise, M (EX box), from $300 to $375.00

G-Man Patrol Car, Linemar, early blk & wht police car, remote control, 8½", MIB, A $484.00

Galloping Horse & Rider, Cragstan, gallops along w/hoof beat noise, 12", NM (EX+ box) $275.00

General Patton Tank M-107, Daiya, litho tin, remote control, 7", MIB, L4 .... $275.00

Gino the Neopolitan Balloon Blower, Rosko, man rings bell & blows up 'balloons' (bubbles), MIB, L4 .... $225.00

GM Jalopy Car, Easton/Taiwan, 1975, MIB, R7 .... $30.00

Godzilla, walks, opens mouth & roars, MIB, S2 .... $150.00

Golden Jubilee Car, TN, 1950s, 4 actions, NM $185.00

Good-Time Charlie, MT, 1960, NM, R7 .... $110.00

Gorilla, TN/Japan, remote control, 9½", NMIB, M5 ..... $340.00

Grand-Pa Panda Bear, MT, plush panda in rocking chair eats popcorn & eyes light, MIB, L4 .... $475.00

Grandpa Bear, Alps, bear rocks in chair, smokes pipe & reads book, MIB, L4 .... $475.00

Grandpa Car, Y, red tin car goes w/rattling noise & smoke, side lamps light, 10", NM (EX box) $150.00

Grandpa Classic Car, TN, 1950, MIB, R7 .... $100.00

Great Eagle Machine Gun, MT, 1950, MIB, R7 .... $125.00

Green Hornet Secret Service Car, ASC, bump-&-go action w/lights & gun sound, tin w/vinyl half-figure driver, 11", EX, A $545.00

Greyhound Scenicruiser Bus, forward & reverse action, litho tin, 7¼", non-working, G, A $40.00

Gypsy Fortune Teller, Ichida, 1950s, insert coin & she moves crystal ball, nods, raises arm & card appears, 10", MIB $1,500.00

Happy Band Trio, MT, plush dog, rabbit & bear playing instruments on litho tin stage w/cb backdrop, 11", NM (NM box), A $259.00

Happy Naughty Chimp, Daishin, 1960, MIB, R7 .... $125.00

Happy Plane, TPS, mk Champion, advances in erratic pattern w/spinning prop, 10" wingspan, EX+ (EX box), A ..$184.00

Happy Santa, Alps, beats bass drum and rings bell, light-up hat needs bulb, tin, cloth and vinyl, 11½", EX (VG+ box), A, $200.00.

Happy Santa, RF/Japan, seated Santa w/lighted eyes, MIB, L4 .... $375.00

Happy Santa, Zawa/Japan, Santa stands & sits on chimney while ringing bell, MIB, L4 .... $495.00

Happy the Clown Puppet Show, Yonezawa, tin clown w/cloth outfit operates tin & wood marionette, 10", EX (NM box), A $277.00

Happy the Clown Violinist, Alps, rocks while playing violin, celluloid face, 10", NM (EX box)............................$775.00

High Jinks at the Circus Clown, Alps, 6 actions w/performing monkey, MIB, L4..$425.00

Highway Drive, TN, mc litho tin, 15", control panel detached, non-working, G (orig box), A $85.00

Highway Patrol Car, Bandai, mystery bump-&-go action w/rotating sirens & dome light, litho tin, 11", MIB, A $110.00

Highway Patrol Cycle, MT/Japan, advances with loud noise as headlight goes on, officer dismounts, lithographed tin, 12", NM (EX box), A, $650.00.

Hoopy the Fishing Duck, Alps, plush & tin duck pulls fish out of pond, quacks & eyes light up, 10", NM (EX box), A.$443.00

Hoot-Hoot Locomotive, MT/Hong Kong, 1970, MIB, R7 .$40.00

Hoppity Hare, Alps, 1983, MIB, R7............................$40.00

Hot Rod Limousine, Alps, 1960s, 4 actions, NMIB $350.00

Hot Rod, TN/Japan, driver steers and engine shakes, lithographed tin, 10½", non-working otherwise EX (original box), A, $180.00.

Hot Rod Racer, Bandai, litho tin & plastic, bl, 10", non-working, G+ (orig box), A $55.00

Hot Rod T Ford, Alps, 1950, MIB, R7..........................$295.00

Hungry Baby Bear, Yonezawa, mama gives baby a bottle, when pulled away she cries, plush & tin, 9", EX+, M5......$165.00

Hungry Baby Bear, Yonezawa, mama gives baby a bottle, when pulled away she cries, plush & tin, 9", NMIB..........$300.00

Hungry Hound Dog, Y, 1950s, 6 actions, rare, EX..........$225.00

Hy-Que the Amazing Monkey, TN, 6 actions, litho tin w/cloth outfit, 6½", MIB, S2 ....$450.00

Ice Cream Baby Bear, MT, cloth bear in chair dips spoon into bowl & simulates chewing action, 9", rare, EX (EX box), A $650.00

Indian Drummer, seated Indian in full headdress & cloth clothes beats on drum, 12", VG+, A..................................$80.00

International Fork Lift, Japan, bump-&-go action w/working fork lift, litho tin, 7½", VG, A..............................$110.00

Interplanetary Rocket, Y, Japan, litho tin & plastic, rises w/lights & sound, 14½", EX (VG box), A $160.00

James Bond Aston Martin DB5, Gilbert/Japan, pnt tin, gray, working lights, machine guns & shield, 11", EX, A..$200.00

Japanese Bullet Train, MT, litho tin train w/8-pc plastic track, 9", MIB, L4 ....$175.00

Jolly Bear the Drummer Boy, K, 7", NMIB....................$250.00

Jolly Chimp, Daishin, cloth-dressed plush monkey w/vinyl hands & feet bangs cymbals, 10½", non-working o/w EX, A .$50.00

Jolly Peanut Vendor, TN, plush bear pushes litho tin peanut cart w/lights & smoking action, 8½", EX (EX+ box)......$350.00

Jolly Santa on Snow, Alps, Santa in cloth suit skis or roller skates, remote control, 12", NM (EX box), A $265.00

Jolly Santa on Snow, Alps, Santa on removable skis, MIB, L4..$375.00

Jumbo the Bubble Blowing Elephant, Yonezawa, 1950, plush elephant puts head in cup & blows bubbles, 7", EX (EX box), A $125.00

Jumbo the Bubble Blowing Elephant, Yonezawa, 1950, plush elephant puts head in cup & blows bubbles, 7", VG (EX box), A $90.00

Jumping Funny Frog, CK, 1970, MIB, R7 ....$50.00

Jungle Jumbo, Japan, elephant advances then stops & howls while hunter shoots, remote control, 10", NM (EX+ box), A $314.00

Jungle Trio, Linemar, 2 monkeys & elephant on pedestal playing instruments, litho tin, vinyl & rubber, 8", EX $575.00

Kissing Couple, Ichida, bump-&-go car rolls as bird spins & chirps on hood, figures turn heads, 10", EX (VG+ box), A ..$220.00

K55 Electric Tractor, MT, red tin dozer-type vehicle w/driver travels forward & reverse, 7", NM (M box), A........$120.00

Ladder Fire Engine, Asahi, forward & reverse action, litho tin, remote control, 8", MIB, A $105.00

Lady Pup Tending Her Garden, Cragstan, 1950s, 5 actions, litho tin & cloth, 8", NM..$250.00

Linus Lovable Lion, Illco/Hong Kong, 1970, MIB, R7 .....$40.00

Lite-O-Wheel Go Kart, Japan, 10", NMIB, A $125.00

Loop Plane, Japan, loops or flies straight, gun fires sound, red, wht & bl, litho tin w/pilot, remote control, MIB, A $226.00

Loop the Loop Monkey, TN, 1960, MIB $125.00

Love Beetle Volkswagen, Taiyo, litho tin, NP trim, lighted rear window, 10", VG (stained box), A $100.00

Lunar Captain, TN, Japan, plastic & litho tin, pivoting capsule, non-working, 12½", EX (EX box), A......................$110.00

M-48 Tank, litho tin, 8", NM (damaged lid o/w VG box), A..$35.00

Mac the Turtle w/Barrel, Y, Mac pushes barrel as his legs move & face turns red, 9", EX (EX box), A........................$175.00

Magic Bulldozer, TN, 1950s, 3 actions, MIB $175.00

Magic Man, Marusan, litho tin clown in cloth outfit smokes pipe & tips his hat, 11", EX (EX box), A..........................$400.00

Magic Snowman, MT, shakes his head & air comes out of top hat & balances ball, light-up eyes, 11", EX (EX box), A $220.00

Major Tootie, Alps, plays drum, 14", MIB, L4................$250.00

Mambo the Drumming Elephant, Alps, 1950, NM, R7 ....$140.00

Mambo the Drumming Panda Bear, Taiwan, 1970, EX, R7 ....$25.00

Maxwell Coffee-Loving Bear, TN, plush bear holds coffeepot that lights up & smokes, litho tin base, 11", EX (EX box), A $180.00

McGregor, TN, 1960, seated Scotsman puffs smoking cigar, stands & closes eyes, tin & vinyl, 12", EX, R7.........$125.00

McGregor, TN, 1960, seated Scotsman puffs smoking cigar, stands & closes eyes, tin & vinyl, 12", NM (EX box) $175.00

Mercedes Police Car, Schuco, pnt & litho tin, gr w/wht top mk Polizei, 8½", bl light does not work, EX A...............$400.00

Merry-Go-Round, TN, carnival truck hauling merry-go-round, spins forward & reverse, remote control, NM (VG+ box), A $477.00

Mexicalli Pete, Alps, tin monkey in cloth clothes moves head while playing bongo drums, 10", EX+, A $90.00

Mickey Mouse Acrobat, see Disney Acrobats

Mickey Mouse Club Dance-A-Tune, WDP, blow kazoo & Mickey dances on stage, plastic, 7", MIB, A............$160.00

Mickey Mouse Melody Railroad, Frankonia/WDP, 1967, characters navigate as songs play, scarce, NM (EX box), A...$1,500.00

Mickey the Drummer, Japan, 1950s, head moves while drumming, tin w/cloth clothes & lighted glass eyes, 11½", NM, A $850.00

Mickey the Magician, Linemar/WDP, Mickey points to top hat & chick appears, tin w/cloth outfit, 11", NM (EX box), A $2,050.00

Mighty Mike the Barbell Lifter Bear, K, lifts light-up barbells overhead, plush & litho tin, 12", EX (VG box), A ..$275.00

Mini-Car Transporter, Sears/mk Made in Japan, remote control w/6 different actions, plastic, 15½", NM (EX box), A $135.00

Miss Friday the Typist, TN, girl types & bell rings, litho tin, 8", EX (EX box) $200.00

Monkees GTO, pnt tin, red w/4 plastic Monkees figures, 12", non-working, G+, A $275.00

Monkey on a Picnic (no hat version), Alps, plush monkey eats banana & drinks, belly swells, 10", EX (VG box), A.$265.00

Monkey on a Picnic (w/hat version), Alps, plush monkey eats banana & drinks, belly swells, 10", NM (EX box), A.$425.00

Monkey Playing Guitar, G, S2 ....$165.00

Monkey the Shoe Maker, TN, seated monkey smokes pipe & hammers on shoe, rare, MIB, L4 ....$775.00

Mother Goose, Cragstan/Japan, 1950, EX, R7................$100.00

Motion-ettes, see Universal Studios Motion-ettes

Mr Fox the Magician, Y, scarce bubble-blowing version of fox that points & moves head while lifting hat, NM (EX box), A $525.00

Mr Gori Gorilla, Alps, 1960, NM, R7............................$40.00

Mr MacPooch Taking a Walk & Smoking His Pipe, Cragstan, plush & litho tin w/fabric clothes, remote control, MIB $250.00

Mr Magoo Car, Hubley, steers, rocks, rattles & rolls, w/removable top, MIB, L4..$475.00

Mumbo Jumbo the Hawaiian Drummer, Alps, 1960s, 3 actions, NM..$150.00

Musical Cadillac, Japan, 9", NM, M5 ....$250.00

Musical Clown, TN, plays London Bridge on xylophone, NMIB, L4 ....$775.00

Musical Marching Bear, Alps, plush tin bear w/cloth pants marches while beating drum & blowing horn, 11", MIB..$675.00

Musical Showboat, Japan, hammers hit xylophone & play 'Oh Suzanna' as paddle-wheeler advances, 13½", NM (EX+ box), A...$201.00

NAR Television Truck, Linemar, advances w/stop-&-go action as cameramen swing side-to-side on top, 11", EX+ (EX+ box), A...$604.00

NBC Television Truck, Y, 1950s, tin w/cameraman on top, TV screen on side lights up & shows parade, 8", VG, A..$525.00

News Service Car, TPS/Japan, marked Porsche on trunk, advances on two wheels as it turns, lithographed tin with plastic figure on roof, 9½", EX+ (EX box), A, $525.00.

Non-Stop Boat, Y, litho tin boat changes directions in water, MIB, L4..$375.00

Nosey the Sniffing Dog, Mego/Japan, 1972, MIB, R7 ......$50.00

Nutty Mad Indian, standing cloth-dressed Indian beats war drum, 14", NMIB, A..$95.00

Nutty Nibs, Linemar, native w/lg earrings flips nuts into mouth as eyes move, litho tin, 12", EX (VG box), A $1,300.00

Ol' Sleepy Head Rip, Y, bird on headboard chirps as Rip sits up in bed, opens eyes & yawns, 9", NM (EX box), A...$425.00

Old Tyme Town Car, SH, 1950, NM..............................$95.00

Overland Express Train, TN, bump-&-go action w/whistle sound, litho tin, 16½", MIB, A $116.00

Overland Stagecoach, MT, galloping action & sound w/driver holding reins, litho tin & plastic, 18", NM (NM box) $175.00

Papa Bear, SAN/Japan, plush bear walks & smokes pipe, 8½", discolored & non-working remote, 8½", G (taped box), A $45.00

Pat O'Neill the Fun Loving Irishman, TN, hold flame to glass cigar tip to start many actions, 11", rare, NM (EX box), A...$600.00

Patrol Auto-Tricycle, TN/Japan, bump-and-go action with lights and sound, lithographed tin and plastic, 10", EX (torn box), A, $450.00.

Pelican w/Fish in Mouth, Y, 1960s, 4 actions, EX $90.00

Pet Turtle, Alps, advances w/head moving in & out of shell, pull-string action, litho tin, 7", EX+ (EX box), A ...$132.00

Pete the Talking Parrot, TN, parrot perched on tree branch repeats messages, 17", EX+, M5 ....$375.00

Peter the Drumming Rabbit, Cragstan, walks & plays drum, light-up eyes, pk plush w/fabric trousers, remote control, MIB...$195.00

Phantom Raider, Ideal, 1963, NMIB $200.00

Picnic Bunny, Alps, pours carrot juice into cup & drinks it, NMIB, M5 ....$75.00

Piggy Cook, Y, pig w/hat flips egg in frying pan, MIB, L4..$300.00

Pinkee the Farmer Truck, Japan, litho tin, 9", non-working, G, A $65.00

Pinky the Clown, Alps, cloth & vinyl clown blows whistle as he balances ball on nose & juggles, 10½", EX+ (VG box), A $347.00

Pinocchio, Rosco, plays London Bridge, tin figure w/vinyl head on litho tin base, MIB $325.00

Pioneer Bulldozer w/Sand Loader, Japan, litho tin, orange, 17", tread rpr on dozer, accessory missing, VG, A $55.00

Pistol Pete, Marusan, litho tin & cloth, 11", EX (EX box)..$250.00

Piston Silver Express, Tai-Fong/Taiwan, 1970, M, R7 .....$40.00

Pluto Acrobat, see Disney Acrobats

Polar Bear, Alps, 1980, MIB, R7 ....$60.00

Police Car, Linemar, forward & reverse action w/flashing siren & sound, remote control, 8½", NMIB, A $297.00

Police Car, Y, 1970, plastic, NM, R7 ....$30.00

Police Command Car, Yanoman Toys, stop-&-go action w/machine gun sound & flashing lights, tin, 13½", VG (VG box), A $110.00

Police Convertible, Daiya, mystery action w/siren & flashing light, tin w/2 celluloid figures, 13½", VG (VG box), A $110.00

Police Jeep, TN, features steering action, headlights & siren sound, MIB $395.00

Pop Corn (sic) Vendor, TN, litho tin duck pushes cart & corn pops, 7½", scarce, EX (EX box), A...........................$412.00

Popcorn Vendor, S&E/Cragstan, plush bear pedals litho tin cart while umbrella spins & popcorn pops, 8", EX (EX box) $475.00

Popeye in Rowboat, Linemar, remote control, missing 1 oar, 10", A, $5,500.00.

Porsche, Bandai, 1967, stop-&-go w/rotating fan, wht w/bl & orange interior, 10", VG+ (orig box), A..................$160.00

Power Shovel, Alps, moves, digs & turns, red, remote control, 9", some actions not working o/w EX (torn box), A..$65.00

Pretty Peggy Parrot, Rosko Toy, light-up eyes & squawking sound w/movable head & tail, plush & tin, 12", NM (EX box), A...$219.00

Professor Owl, Y/Japan, turns while chirping and raises pointer to chalkboard, complete with two disks, 8½", NM (EX box), A, $575.00.

Rabbits & Carriage, S&E, mama rabbit pushes baby rabbit in buggy, w/tin butterfly, MIB, L4 ....$475.00

Race Car #2, Tippco/Germany, 1930s, yellow and black tin, 13½", NM, D10, $2,800.00.

Race Car #4 (Indianapolis Special), Tomiyama, advances w/motor sound, gold, lighted, 14½", rusted, G+, A.$225.00

Radar Tank, Japan, 1960s, advances w/non-fall action, litho tin, NM (EX box), A $370.00

Railroad Hand Car, KDP, men work hdls & car goes around rubber cable laid out in any shape, 9", NM (EX box), A...$205.00

Reading Bear, Alps, 1950s, 5 actions, 9", EX $175.00

Real Sound Police Car, Alps, non-stop action w/siren & flashing light, litho tin, 11½", MIB, A $110.00

Reversible Race Car, Hong Kong, 1970, NM, R7.............$35.00

Rock 'N Roll Hot Rod, TN, bump-&-go action w/driver turning head, lights flash, litho tin, 7½", EX (G box), A.....$461.00

Rock 'N Roll Monkey, Alps, cloth-faced monkey plays guitar, sways & stomps foot, 12", NM (EX+ box), A..........$250.00

Rocking Grandpa, smokes pipe while rocking in chair, EX, S2 ....$175.00

Roger Rabbit Bobber, Epoch, moves w/sound, 15", MIB .$800.00

Roll-Over Rover, Taiwan, 1970, MIB, R7 ....$30.00

Royal Cub, S&E, mama bear pushes baby bear in buggy w/6 other actions, MIB, L4 ....$475.00

Russian Taxi, Ichiko, litho tin, bl w/red interior, 9", EX, A $225.00

Sally the Seal, Alps, 1981, MIB, R7.............................$50.00

Sam the Shaving Man, Plaything, vinyl head moves & lights up to show beard, powders face, shaves, 12", NM (EX+ box), A $250.00

Sand Buggy, Hong Kong, 1970, MIB.............................$60.00

Santa Copter, Illco, advances w/non-fall action, sound & whirling blade, litho tin w/vinyl Santa, 9", M (NM box) $150.00

Santa Copter, MT, 1960, missing propeller o/w MIB, R7.$100.00

Santa in Sleigh, Modern Toys, litho tin & plastic w/lights & sound effects, 17", EX $200.00

Santa on Scooter, Modern Toys, bump-&-go action w/clanging bell & flashing lights, litho tin & vinyl, MIB..........$125.00

Santa Ringing Bell, Japan, 1950s, head moves side-to-side & eyes flash, plush, vinyl & litho tin, 13½", EX, A.....$110.00

Shaking Classic Car, Japan, 1960, MIB $125.00

Shoe Shine Joe w/Lighted Pipe, TN, plush monkey turns boot in hand as he buffs it, tin base, 9", NM (EX box), A ...$160.00

Shooting Gallery Roaring Gorilla, MT, gorilla raises arms & roars w/lighted eyes, MIB, L4 ....$475.00

Shutter Bug, TN, advances & takes pictures, litho tin, MIB...$695.00

Shuttle Train w/Coal Loader, Tomiyama, climbs track, deposits coal & reverses, tin, 36", non-working, EX (EX box), A...$168.00

Shuttling Dog Train, Cragstan/Japan, 1950, EX, R7 ......$100.00

Silver Mountain Express, MT, 1960, MIB, R7.................$50.00

Ski Lift, Alps, goes to end of cable & changes direction, 7", NM, M5 ....$150.00

Skipping Monkey, TN, 1960s, 2 actions, NMIB.............$100.00

Sleeping Baby Bear, Y, bear stretches, yawns & rises from bed when clock rings, plush & litho tin, MIB $345.00

Smokey the Bear, Marusan, puffs on pipe while walking w/shovel, plush w/tin shoes & hat, cloth pants, 9", NM (G box), A...$285.00

Smokey the Bear Jeep, TN, forward & reverse action w/flashing light & siren sound, litho tin, rare, MIB.............$1,200.00

Smoking & Shoe-Shining Panda Bear, Alps, seated panda shines shoes & smokes pipe, EX, L4.............................$165.00

Smoking Bear in Rocking Chair, plush, 9", EX, A............$75.00

Smoking Bunny, SAN, walks & lifts lighted pipe to mouth & blows smoke, tin & cloth, 9", MIB.........................$250.00

Smoking Grandpa, Japan, 1950, VG+, R7.....................$165.00

Smoking Popeye, Linemar, pipe lights up as he smokes, lithographed tin, 8½", NM (NM box), A, $1,750.00.

Smoking Volkswagen, Japan, pnt tin w/plastic trim, see-thru lighted engine compartment, 10½", EX (orig box), A...$80.00

Smoky Joe Auto, Marusan, litho tin, red driver w/vinyl head smoking light-up pipe, 8½", VG+, A $70.00

Snake Charmer, Linemar, snake charmer plays flute as snake wiggles out of smoking basket, litho tin, 7", M (EX box), A...$550.00

Sneezing Bear, Linemar, plush bear sneezes & brings tissue to his nose, eyes light up, tin base, 9", EX (EX box), A.....$440.00

Snorkel Pumper Fire Engine, Bandai, 1970, MIB, R7 ....$100.00

Snowmobile, Bandai, bl, red & gr, remote control, tin & plastic, 9½", EX (orig box), A $150.00

Spad Stunt Plane, TPS, roll-over action, red, litho tin & plastic, 9", non-working, G, A...$50.00

Spanking Bear, Linemar, mama bear spanks baby & he cries & kicks, litho tin & plush, 10", NM (EX box) $575.00

Sparky the Seal, MT, seal walks & balances ball in stream of air above nose, plush over tin, 8", MIB, A....................$130.00

Spin-A-Disk Monkey, S&E, seated monkey in hat spins yo-yo-like disk, MIB, L4 ....$375.00

SSN 571 Nautilus, SAN, 1950s, forward & reverse action w/spinning prop & deck lights, 12", scarce, NM+ (EX+ box), A...$316.00

Stagecoach, litho tin w/plastic horses, 20", VG+, W5 ....$200.00

Stick-Shift Bulldozer, Imco/Hong Kong, 1975, MIB, R7..$35.00

Strange Explorer, DSK, lg gorilla on underplate lifts tank & flips it over, light flashes in cockpit, 8", NM, A.............$170.00

Strutting My Fair Dancer, Haji, dances in place, litho tin & vinyl, MIB...$250.00

Strutting Sam, Japan, dances in place, lithographed tin, 11", M (G box), A, $475.00.

Telephone Bear, MT/Japan, plush bear on lithographed tin chair, picks up phone and makes chattering sound, 9½", NM (EX+ box), A, $260.00; Chef Cook, Yonezawa/Japan, chef chews and flips omelet as he sways, cloth, vinyl and lithographed tin, 10", EX+ (EX+ box), A, $230.00.

Stunt Plane, TPS, 1960, NM $175.00
Sunbeam Jeep, KKK, travels forward & backward, litho tin w/3 full-figure soldiers, 10" long, NM (EX box), A $225.00
Super Control Anti-Craft Jeep, S&E, w/removable turret, programable driving pattern, MIB, L4 ....$350.00
Supreme Blender, Red Box/Hong Kong, 1976, MIB, R7 ..$35.00
Surry Jeep, TN, tin driver w/articulated arms drives cloth-canopied Jeep w/bump-&-go action, lights work, 11", NM, A $175.00
Suzie the Cashier Bear, Linemar, clothed plush bear moves head side to side as she hits cash register, 9", EX, A.........$725.00
Taxi Cab, Y, bump-&-go action as dashboard meter changes fare, passenger door opens, flashing roof light, 9", EX (EX box), A $100.00
Teddy Bear Swing, Yonezawa, plush bear flips forward & backward on litho tin bar, 13", scarce, EX (VG+ box) ...$375.00
Teddy Go Kart, Alps, plush-over-tin bear walks & pulls tin cart, growls, 9", scarce, NM (EX box), A $254.00
Teddy the Artist, Yonezawa, put crayon in hand & insert template, Teddy simulates drawing an animal, 9", EX (G box), A..$315.00
Teddy the Artist, Yonezawa, put crayon in hand & insert template, Teddy simulates drawing an animal, 9", MIB .$500.00

Teddy the Drummer, Alps, 1970, MIB, R7 ....$75.00
Telephone Rabbit, MT, sits in rocking chair & picks up phone, plush & litho tin, MIB $285.00
Tom & Jerry Helicopter, MT, bump-&-go action w/spinning rotor blade, EX, L4 ....$325.00
Tom & Jerry Locomotive, MT, bump-&-go action w/ringing bell, litho tin w/vinyl figures, 9", NM (EX box), A .$276.00
Toyland Parade, DY/Taiwan, 1970, MIB, R7...................$60.00
Traveler Bear, K, tin & plush bear walks while holding suitcase & cane, eyes blink, 8", EX+ (EX box) $275.00
Tric-Cycling Clown, Cragstan/Japan, moves on unicycle as he holds up lighted balls, 12", scarce, EX+ (EX box) ...$775.00
Trumpet Playing Monkey, Cragstan, plush & litho tin, M (NM box)...$275.00
Tugboat, Marusan, 1950s, advances & puffs out smoke, litho tin, 13", EX (VG box), A...$140.00
Tumbling Buggy, Taiwan, 1970, NMIB, R7.......................$15.00
Twin Train Set #372, Woodhaven, 1950s, train travels around track w/city theme, old store stock, MIB, A $175.00

Teddy the Balloon Blowing Bear, Alps, stomps feet and blows balloon, eyes light up, lithographed tin and plush, 11", VG (box panels torn), A, $65.00.

Twin Racing Cars, Japan, lithographed tin, remote control, NMIB, D10, $500.00.

Twin Western Railroad Set, Woodhaven, 1950s, train travels around track w/western theme, old store stock, MIB, A..$260.00

Two-Gun Sheriff, w/moving eyes, G, S2........................$135.00

Universal Studios Motion-ettes, Wolf Man, dbl arm movement & head turns, eyes glow & makes horror sound, M (NM box), P3..$50.00

Vacation Set, Bandai, wht Chevy pulls red, wht & bl trailer w/pull-out canopy, 17¼", non-working o/w EX (EX box), A..$140.00

Vacationer Cabin Cruiser w/Outboard Motor, Linemar, 12½", circuit in boat not working, VG+ (orig box), A......$120.00

Volkswagen Fire Chief Car, Illco, 1970, MIB, R7 ....$50.00

Wacky Droopy Snoopy Dog, EX+ (NM box), T1.............$35.00

Walking Bear w/Xylophone, Linemar, eyes light up, plush & tin, 10", rare, VG+ (EX box), A $525.00

Walking Gorilla, MT, remote control, rare, NMIB, L4..$1,600.00

Walking Knight in Armor, MT, litho tin, remote control, rare, NMIB $3,200.00

Walking Penguin, MT, advances w/flapping wings, light-up eyes, plush & litho tin, remote control, 9", EX, A $141.00

Warpath Willie, Hong Kong, 1970, MIB, R7 ....$65.00

Western Bad Man at Red Gulch Bar, MT/Japan, outlaw takes drink from bartender then fires gun, 10", EX+ (EX+ box), A, $575.00.

Western Bad Man at Red Gulch Bar, Japan, outlaw takes drink from bartender then fires gun, EX+..........................$375.00

Western Road Roller, TM, litho tin, red, bubble-blowing plastic stack, 9¾", EX-, A $75.00

Western Style Music Box, Linemar, plastic cowboy w/gun dances in front of tin music hall, NM (EX box), A $201.00

Whirly Twirly Rocket Ride, Alps, rockets spin w/flashing lights & bell noise, litho tin, battery-op, 13", EX+, A $322.00

Whistling Showboat, MT, 1950, whistles w/bump-&-go action, detachable smokestacks, MIB, L4 ....$250.00

Wild West Rodeo Bubbling Bull, Linemar, cowboy on bull that dips nose in water & blows bubbles, 7", NM (EX box), A ...$251.00

Windy the Juggling Elephant, TN, waves feet while spinning umbrella or blows ball, plush & tin, 10½", NM (EX box), A $235.00

Wolfman, see Universal Studios Motion-ettes

World Champion Cyclist, MT, cycle advances w/noise & stops, driver lifts leg to simulate dismount, 11", NM+ (EX box), A..$1,101.00

Worried Mother Duck, Japan, she quacks & advances, stops to see if baby is following, litho tin, 10", EX (EX box), A..$171.00

Yellow Cab, Linemar, forward & reverse action w/siren sound, remote control, 7½", NM (EX box), A $168.00

Yo-Yo Car, Japan, lighted wheels, 9½", NMIB, A $200.00

Zoom Speedboat, Japan, visible engine w/moving piston, litho tin, 11", non-working, EX (torn box), A $90.00

Bicycles, Tricycles and Motorbikes

The most interesting of the vintage bicycles are those made from 1920 into the 1960s, though a few even later models are collectible as well. Some from the fifties were very futuristic and styled with sweeping Art Deco lines, others had wonderful features such as built-in radios and brake lights, and some were decked out with saddle bags and holsters to appeal to fans of Hoppy, Gene and other western heroes. Watch for reproductions.

Condition is everything when evaluating bicycles, and one worth $2,500.00 in excellent or better condition might be worth as little as $50.00 in unrestored, poor condition. But here are a few values to suggest a range.

Advisor: Richard Trautwein (T3).

AMF's Batman, 1972, 20", EX, J2 ....$200.00

Bowden Spacelander 600D, boy's, lt bl futuristic fiberglass body w/wht-wall tires, A...$3,100.00

Columbia, girl's, turq, 20", orig condition, A $50.00

Columbia #46, 1894, girl's, front brake & coaster pegs on forks, wooden chain guard & rear fender, Christy seat, rstr, A..$1,100.00

Columbia Airider Twinbar, boy's, orig brn pnt & decals, chrome fenders, blk-wall tires, storage compartment, 24", VG, A..$1,700.00

Columbia Deluxe, 1948, boy's, red & cream springer w/front fender light, orig condition $560.00

Columbia Five-Star, ca 1988 reproduction, boy's, gr & wht w/chrome fender headlight, wht-wall tires...............$500.00

Columbia Five-Star American, boy's, 26", orig condition, A $65.00

Columbia Special, boy's, orig blk & wht pnt w/red trim, wht-wall tires, fender headlight, clock/speedometer, 26", A..$1,450.00

Columbia Three-Star, 1954, girl's, w/springer tank, rear carrier, front fender torpedo light & wht-walls, rstr (?), A ..$300.00

Columbia-Westfield Vicking, ca 1948, boy's, w/tank, crossbar handlebars, torpedo light & rear carrier, A.............$200.00

Dayton Streamliner, boy's, med gr w/chrome chain guard, wht-wall tires, 26", extremely rare, A..........................$5,200.00

Elgin Robin, boy's, orig red pnt w/wht trim, wht-wall tires, fender headlight, horn on tank w/emb lettering, 26", G, A $3,300.00

Elgin Skylark, Sears, ca 1937, girl's, bl w/rear carrier & roller speedometer, VG+, A $3,000.00

Evinrude, boy's, red streamline body w/decals & pinstripe, wht-wall tires, fender headlight, 26", very rare, rstr, A .$4,200.00

Firestone Super Cruiser, 1953, boy's, red & maroon w/wht-walls, rstr, A $1,050.00

Firestone Twin Flex, Dayton, orig condition, A..........$1,300.00

Gene Autry, girl's, orig brn & cream pnt w/chrome-studded fenders & chain guard, blk-wall tires, handlebar horn, 24", A $800.00

Girard, girl's, wooden rear fender & chain guard, stenciled fr, leather grips & Sager saddle seat, A $300.00

Harley-Davidson, boy's, orig red pnt except fenders & chain guard, lg handlebars, A...$550.00

Harley-Davidson #520, ca 1920, boy's juvenile, thumb bell, rear-wheel kickstand, 20", rstr, A $1,000.00

Hartford, ca 1893, girl's, hard tires, orig decal on steering neck, rstr, A $3,000.00

Hawthorne girl's bike by Wards, green and cream with yellow pinstripe, balloon tires, restored, A, $250.00.

Hawthorne, Montgomery Wards, ca 1947, boy's, w/springer, tank, headlight, speedometer & wht-walls, orig condition, A $550.00

Hawthorne 'Zep,' ca 1938, boy's, tank w/rear carrier, orig condition, A $2,100.00

Hawthorne V-71 Victory, girl's, rstr, A $150.00

Huffy (Dayton) Twin-Flex, boy's, dk bl & cream w/blk-wall tires, fender headlight, 26", rstr, A $1,500.00

J.C. Higgins boy's bike, red and white with yellow pinstripes, balloon tires, restored, A, $330.00.

JC Higgins, 1951, boy's, blk, orig condition, A.................$75.00

Kirk Co Yale Shaft Drive, boy's, blk body w/no fender guards, blk-wall tires on wood rims, older rstr, 28", A $750.00

Mercury Quad, gr 4-seater w/yel trim, no fender or chain guards, winged foot diecut nameplate, rstr, A...................$2,900.00

Monarch, boy's, orig maroon & cream pnt w/chrome fender headlight, wht-wall tires, tank horn, 24", M, A.......$425.00

Monarch, ca 1898, boy's, shaft-drive, pneumatic, rstr, A..$650.00

Monarch Super Deluxe, girl's, rear carrier, front fender light, 26", orig condition, A..$275.00

Norwood #6, ca 1896, boy's, wood rims, rstr, A..............$550.00

Roadmaster Luxury Liner, boy's, w/tank, rear carrier & wht-walls, amateur rstr, A..$225.00

Roadmaster Luxury Liner, girl's, orig metallic turq pnt w/chrome fenders, wht-wall tires, spring fork, 26", A.............$500.00

Rollfast, boy's, gray & brn w/wht-wall tires, horn & lights, spring fork, 26", A..$1,000.00

Rollfast Hopalong Cassidy, boy's, blk w/wht trim & chrome studs, wht-wall tires, fender headlight, 26", rstr, A...$1,700.00

Rollfast Hopalong Cassidy, 1950, girl's, saddle seat w/holster & gun, chrome studs, wht-walls, 26", orig condition, A..$1,650.00

Schwinn boy's bike, red and black with white pinstripes, balloon tires, horn and headlight, restored, A, $330.00.

Schwinn Auto Cycle, ca 1940, boy's, maroon & cream w/tank & rear carrier, front fender light & wht-walls, rstr (?), A...$900.00

Schwinn Black Phantom, boy's, 26", rstr, A $850.00

Schwinn Black Phantom, girl's, 26", rstr, A...................$400.00

Schwinn Green Phantom, ca 1951, boy's, w/tank & rear carrier, front fender light, wht-walls, orig condition, A.......$500.00

Schwinn Hornet, boy's, wht-walls, orig condition, A.....$200.00

Schwinn MK IV, 1958, boy's, red w/tank horn, orig condition, A $100.00

Schwinn Panther, ca 1958, boy's, metallic gold w/2-tone seat, front & rear carriers, complete & orig condition, M, A...$150.00

Schwinn Panther, 1952, boy's, bl & aqua, orig condition, A $650.00

Schwinn Red Phantom, boy's, red w/chrome fenders, wht-wall tires, front hand brake, spring fork, 26", rstr, A....$1,500.00

Schwinn Starlet, 1955, girl's, gr & cream, orig condition, A $175.00

Sears Elgin Bluebird, mid-1930s, boy's, bl w/red trim, wht-wall tires, built-in speedometer, rstr, A $8,500.00

Shelby Airflo, boy's, red w/bl trim, wht-wall tires, 26", rstr, A $200.00

Shelby Streamline, 1953, girl's, bl & wht springer w/rear carrier, Delta triple light, orig condition, A $200.00

Shelby Super Air Flow, ca 1939, boy's, w/rare promotional chain guard, rstr, A................$8,000.00

Sherrell Classic, ca 1984, futuristic design w/wht tires, never ridden, A................$1,150.00

Silver King Flo Cycle #MO 37, boy's, aluminum w/combination horn & headlight, wht-wall tires, speedometer, 24", rstr, A................$1,200.00

Victor, 1891, boy's, cushion tire safety, orig condition, A...$1,350.00

Waverly, Indiana Cycle, boy's, w/bike meter, thumb bell & headlamp, rstr, A................$275.00

Western Flyer Twin Flex, Daton, ca 1938, boy's, w/rear carrier & front fender light, orig condition, A $1,300.00

Western Flyer X53, blk & gold, orig condition, A..........$450.00

Wolf-American Duplex Tandem, 3-wheeled bl side-by-side 2-seater w/dbl handlebars, blk-wall tires, very rare, rstr, A................$4,700.00

MOTORBIKES

Monarch Super-Twin, ca 1949, orig blk pnt w/red-orange trim, chrome fender headlight, fender-attached kickstand, EX+, A................$3,200.00

Speed Bike, Metal Specialties, ca 1930, orig red pnt, rear wheel kickstand, 12" pneumatic tires w/red spokes, G, A..$850.00

Whizzer Sportsman, red w/wht pinstripe, chrome tank, carrier & trim, wht-wall tires, 2-tone windshield, 20", rstr, A................$5,000.00

TRICYCLES

Clipper Tricycle, cast-iron chassis with padded wood seat, early, VG, A, $250.00.

Ferbo, blk body w/bicycle chain, no fenders, 12" wide-spoked front wheel, G, A $225.00

Grendon Pioneer, orig red pnt, no fenders, 19½" wide-spoked front wheel, G, A $375.00

Grendon Pioneer w/Sidecar, ca 1928, lt gr w/fenders, windshield & red fold-down top on sidecar, 44", rstr, A $2,300.00

Murry, Airflow Jr, pnt pressed steel, red, streamlined, steel seat, 17½", pnt chips & scratches, G, A................$200.00

Stream Line, Art Deco design w/orig red pnt & wht pin-stripe, pneumatic tires, built-in headlight, 18" front wheel, A $650.00

Wood & Wrought Iron, 19th century, straight handlebar, wide-spoked wooden wheels, very rare, A $450.00

Black Americana

Black subjects were commonly depicted in children's toys as long ago as the late 1870s. Among the most widely collected today are the fine windup toys made both here and in Germany. Early cloth and later composition and vinyl dolls are favorites of many; others enjoy ceramic figurines. Many factors enter into evaluating Black Americana, especially in regard to the handmade dolls and toys, since quality is subjective to individual standards. Because of this you may find wide ranges in dealers' asking prices. In order to better understand this field of collecting, we recommend *Black Collectibles Sold in America* by P.J. Gibbs.

Advisor: Judy Posner (P6).

See also Battery-Operated Toys; Schoenhut; Windups, Friction and Other Mechanicals.

Book, Children's Stories That Never Grow Old, Reilly & Britton, 1908, 19 stories, 312 pgs, EX, P6 ....$95.00

Book, Little Black Sambo, David McKay Publishing, 1937, hardcover, color illus every other pg, EX, P6 ....$125.00

Book, Little Black Sambo Children's Book, Rand McNally, 1937, 64 pgs, EX, P6 ....$95.00

Book, Little Brown Koko's Pets & Playmates, 1959, 96 pgs, EX $55.00

Book, Meg & Moe, Lothrop, Lee & Shepard, 1938, hardcover, w/dust jacket, EX, P6 ....$125.00

Book, Old Uncle Ned, by Stephen Foster, 1880s, illus GW Brenneman, rare, tape rpr, P6 ....$175.00

Book, Pink Laffins Coontown & Other Comedy & Fun, ca 1900, 64 pgs of ethnic jokes, stories & illus, scarce, VG $75.00

Book, Rastus Augustus Explains Evolution, by BH Shadduck, 1928, 1st edition, 32 pgs, P6................$85.00

Book, Samantha Among the Colored Folks, Kemble, 1894, EX $125.00

Book, Uncle Remus Stories, Joel Chandler Harris, Saalfield, 1934, stories w/color illus, EX................$95.00

Book, Uncle Tom's Cabin, Harriet Beecher Stowe, colorful illus of Eva running to Topsy on cover, NM, A $60.00

Book, Uncle Tom's Cabin, Young Folks Edition, Donahue, Uncle Tom & Eva on cover, illus, NM................$85.00

Crap Shooter, 1930s, tan-skinned celluloid boy w/red shorts strikes pose as dice come up, P6 ....$45.00

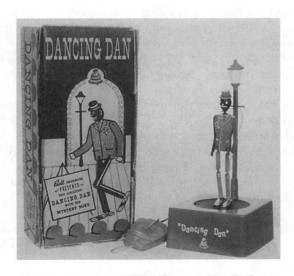

Dancing Dan, Bell Products, colored plastic figure moves to sound activation through microphone, EX (original box), A, $225.00.

Dancing Sambo Magic Trick, jtd cb figure, 1940s, M (NM envelope) $45.00

Dice Toy, Alco/Britian, activate plunger to spin laughing head & dice, 2" dia, NM, A $121.00

Doll, Aunt Jemima, 1940s, colorful oilcloth, brn skin tone, 12", EX, P6 ....$90.00

Doll, Beatrice Wright, ca 1967, hard plastic w/dk brn skin & rooted long straight hair, 18", EX...........................$145.00

Doll, Beloved Belindy, Knickerbocker, 1965, cloth, 14", EX, P6 ....$500.00

Doll, Japan, celluloid, fully jointed, $290.00.

Photo courtesy of Continental Hobby House

Doll, Tag-Along (Sambo's tiger), stuffed plush, w/orig tag, 10", NM+, A $100.00

Doll, Topsy-Turvy, Bruckner, 1901, stuffed fabric, skirt missing, 12" $175.00

Doll, 1900-30s, blk-pnt bsk body w/jtd arms & legs, molded & pnt features, 3 tufts of hair form pigtails, 6", G $95.00

Figures, Amos 'N Andy, Correll & Godson, 1930, jtd wood, 6", NM, pr $450.00

Five Jolly Darkies, WS Reed, litho paper on wood, 5 caricature panels move up & down w/crank & rod, 9", no crank, G, A $300.00

Game, Alabama Coon, G, (21" box), $175.00.

Game, Basket Ball, Russell, 1929, try to get ball into basket held by Black man, 7x5", EX (EX box) $200.00

Game, Black Man Bagatelle, German, 1880s, try to put wht balls in mouth for teeth, 2½" dia, NM $100.00

Game, Black Woman Bagatelle, German, 1880s, try to put balls in mouth for teeth, 2½" dia, NM $100.00

Game, Jav-Lin, All-Fir, 1931, target game, scarce, EX, A, $140.00.

Game, Little Black Sambo, Cadaco-Ellis, 1945, missing 4 markers & spinner o/w VG $85.00

Game, Minstrel Sam, 1920s, spin trumpet in right spot, 3¾" dia, NMIB...$150.00

Game, Snake Eyes, 1957, dice & 50 illus cards, last Black game mfg in US, MIB $95.00

Game, The Game of Sambo, Parker Bros, ca 1915, toss rings on Sambo's pipe, 10", rare, NMIB (minor edge rpr) $400.00

Jazz Band, Mayfair Novelty, 1920s, 12 paper litho marching band figures on card, ea 2½", MOC, A $40.00

Mask, Mammy, late 1930s-early '40s, pnt pressed canvas w/conton top cover, exaggerated features, NM...................$25.00

Pull Toy, George Pal, complete w/Jasper from Jasper & the Watermelons, EX, P6 ....$275.00

Puppet, Black Policeman, Childcraft, 1968, rubber, 10", M..$30.00

Puppet, Clippo Presents Lucifer, marionette, Effanbee, wood and composition, box marked FAO Schwarz, 14", EX (G box), $650.00.

Puppet, Black Roy Rogers, 1950s, hand puppet w/cloth body & pnt vinyl face, 8", EX....................................$65.00
Puppet, compo Black boy in red & wht checked shirt w/peach-colored bibs & wht hat, wooden base, 14½", torn/soiled $150.00

Swingin' Sam the Saxaphone Man, German, 1920s, litho tin squeeze toy, 1920s, 6", EX, $425.00.

Boats

Though some commercially made boats date as far back as the late 1800s, they were produced on a much larger scale during WWI and the decade that followed and again during the years that spanned WWII. Some were scaled-down models of battleships measuring nearly three feet in length. While a few were actually seaworthy, many were designed with small wheels to be pulled along the carpet or out of doors on dry land. Others were motor-driven windups, and later a few were even battery operated. Some of the larger manufacturers were Bing (Germany), Dent (Pennsylvania), Orkin Craft (California), Liberty Playthings (New York), and Arnold (West Germany).

Advisors: Richard Trautwein (T3); Dick Borgerding (B4)
See also Cast Iron, Boats; Battery-Operated Toys; Tootsietoys; Windups, Friction and Other Mechanicals; and other specific manufacturers.

Airboat, Bing, pnt tin, gr & yel, w/driver, w/up, 8", EX, A..$525.00

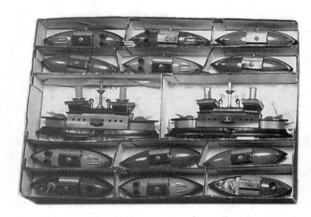

Armada, Hess, deluxe set of 14 boats consisting of 2 battleships, cruisers, etc., litho tin windups, M (original box), A, $3,400.00.

Battleship, Bing, pnt tin, dk bl & gray, removable twin stack, clockwork, NM, 19½", A $2,990.00
Battleship, Bing, pnt tin, 2-tone gray hull & superstructure w/brn deck, 4 stacks & 8 guns, w/up, 28", pnt chips, G, A .$1,100.00

Battleship Constitution, Orkin, minor restoration, 35" long, D10, $2,500.00.

Battleship, Fleischmann, pnt tin, gray & brn, intricate superstructure, 21", rstr, loose crane, pnt chips o/w VG+, A..$2,400.00

Battleship, France, pnt tin, 2-tone gray w/red trim, single oscillating engine & propeller, CI wheels, 31", VG, A.....$9,500.00

Battleship, Orkin, pnt tin & wood, cream, gr & red overpnt, 5 guns, 2 stacks & screws, w/up, 30", G+, A............$1,100.00

Battleship, Orkin, pnt tin & wood w/gr & gray hull, blk superstructure, w/up, 25", pnt wear on hull & guns, G, A..$425.00

Battleship, Orobr/Germany, litho tin w/single mast, paper flag, 16 guns, 2 funnels & 2 lifeboats, 11¼", EX, A.........$800.00

Battleship (Third Series), Marklin, pnt tin, 2-tone gray, 22 guns, 2 masts & 6 lifeboats, etc, w/up, 28", EX, A.........$7,700.00

Battleship Dreadnaught, Marklin, 1st series, pnt tin, red, wht & gray, 13 brass cannons, w/up, 42", rstr, EX, A $21,000.00

Battleship New York, Marklin, ca 1910, pnt tin, 2 stacks & single mast, 28", EX (orig wooden box), A..............$33,350.00

Battleship New York, Marklin, pnt tin, gray & red, 2 stacks & masts, 4 lifeboats, cannons, 36", EX, A..............$32,200.00

Battleship Oregon, Converse, early 20th century, litho tin & wood, 2 American flags, 17½", G, A $518.00

Battleship Schwaben, Marklin, pnt tin, red & wht w/gold trim, 5 guns, 2 lifeboats on davits, live steam, 16", EX, A $15,000.00

Battleship St Vincent, tin floor-type w/2 masts & twin stacks, 6 turrets, w/up, non-working o/w EX, A $185.00

Boat and Motor, Langcraft, wooden, battery-operated, 12", MIB, D10, $150.00.

Cabin Cruiser Miss America, mav be Orkin or Seaworthy, 1930s, 18", NM, D10, $500.00.

Cabin Cruiser, Orkin, pnt tin, cream & red hull w/cream & mahogany superstructure, 32", some parts missing, G+, A...$450.00

Cabin Cruiser, Orkin, w/up, 32", EX, B4......................$1,750.00

Cabin Cruiser, Orkin, 31", some pnt loss, EX, A............$550.00

Carrier, Liberty Playthings, w/up, 27", EX, B4................$650.00

Cruiser, Bing, pnt tin, gray & blk, 4 stacks, w/up, 24", VG+, A...$1,000.00

Cruiser, Bing, pnt tin, gray & red, 4 stacks, w/up, 23", pnt chips, scuffs o/w VG, A $1,200.00

Cruiser, Marklin/Germany, pnt tin, blk & brn hull w/gray superstructure, 16½", power plant & mast missing, G+, A $3,000.00

Destroyer, Liberty Playthings, 4 stacks, w/up, 27", EX, B4 ....$350.00

Destroyer, Orkin, 25", EX-, A.................................$1,500.00

Destroyer #3012, Ives, pnt tin, 2-tone gray, 2 masts & stacks, w/up, 13", non-working, VG, A................................$500.00

Destroyer Taku, tin floor type w/twin stacks, single gun fore & aft, w/up, 9½", G+, A $100.00

Dingy, Orkin, w/up, 22", EX, B4 ....$300.00

Ferryboat, Bing, maroon & gray pnt & stenciled side-wheeler w/hinged roof & 2 stacks, w/up, 16", 1 stack missing, G+, A $525.00

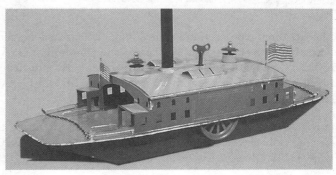

Ferryboat, Bing, hand-painted and stenciled, tin double side-wheeler with 2 ventilator shafts, 1 large stack in center, windup, 16" long, EX, A, $1,400.00.

Fireboat, Liberty Playthings, w/up, 22", EX, B4 ....$350.00

Fireboat, pnt tin, red, blk & tan, lg bell, w/up key in single stack, 8", rstr, A $275.00

Fireboat, pnt tin, red & wht, hose reel & deck boiler, pumps water, 12", some pnt flaking & missing figure o/w VG, A...$750.00

Flotilla, Hess, pnt tin battleship & 3 sm escorts linked by rods, w/up, 19", rods missing, few scratches o/w EX, A $280.00

Flotilla, Hess, pnt tin battleship & 4 sm escorts linked by rods, w/up, EX (G box), A $900.00

Flotilla, Japan, pnt wood, red & wht battleship w/4 sm escorts, 8" w/2" escorts, A...$50.00

Flying Boat, Fleischmann, pnt tin, operates when on water or when hanging, 18", rpt, VG+, A $5,100.00

Freighter, French, pnt tin, red & blk hull w/gr & wht deck & superstructure, rear deck hatch lifts, w/up, 26", G, A $900.00

Freighter, Liberty Playthings, w/up, 27", EX, B4.............$425.00

Gunboat, att Carette, pnt tin w/8 guns & 3 stacks, 16", missing 1 stack, rudder wheel broken, G, A $800.00

Gunboat, Bing, gray tin hull w/gun-firing mechanism, w/up, pnt loss, 19", G, A $1,600.00

Gunboat, Bing, pnt tin, gray hull w/cream & red superstructure, w/up, 16½", VG+, A...$700.00

Gunboat, Bing, pnt tin, single stack, 16½", pnt chips, G, A $300.00

Gunboat, Bing, pnt tin, twin stacks, w/up, 15½", rpt, G+, A $450.00

Gunboat, Bing, painted tin, cream & gray, articulated captain holding binoculars, windup, 9½", paint chips on hull, VG, A, $300.00; Gunboat Kasuga, Bing, painted tin, gray, gun-firing and rudder-turning mechanism, windup, 20", VG, A, $1,000.00.

Gunboat, Bing, 2-tone gray w/single mast, 2 stacks, cap-firing & steering mechanism, w/up, 16", pnt chips, VG+, A .$850.00

Gunboat, blk, olive & wht w/tan deck, single gun, w/up, 7½", rpt, A $65.00

Gunboat, Carette, litho tin floor type w/flywheel above deck, single stack, friction, 10", stack rpl, pnt chips, G+, A $150.00

Gunboat, Carette, pnt tin, cream & wht, 3 stacks & single mast, single gun fore & aft, 11", VG, A............................$575.00

Gunboat, Carette, pnt tin, pale gr & wht, single deck gun, w/up, 7", pnt loss, G, A $200.00

Gunboat, Carette, pnt tin, red, cream & wht, single gun, mast & stack, 7½", rstr, A $225.00

Gunboat, Carette, pnt tin, red & blk & tan w/gr upper deck, guns fore & aft, w/up, 13", missing mast, pnt chips, EX, A $475.00

Gunboat, Carette, pnt tin, red & wht, guns mounted fore & aft, 12", rpt deck, new masts, 12", VG, A $550.00

Gunboat, Carette, pnt tin, 2-tone gray, gun-firing mechanism, w/up, 19", G, A $1,600.00

Gunboat, Orkin, pnt tin, gray & gr, 1 deck gun, w/up, 16", scratches o/w VG, A..$220.00

Gunboat, pnt tin, 2-tone gray w/red trim, 2 stacks, w/up, 15", non-working, rpt o/w VG, A $400.00

Gunboat #3012, Ives, pnt tin, gray, 2-masted w/2 deck guns & stacks, w/up, 13", pnt chips, weak gun barrel o/w VG, A...$350.00

Gunboat Bantam, France, pnt tin w/cast anchors, sm guns, spring-loaded turret guns & rocket launcher, w/up, 27", VG, A..$650.00

Gunboat Kasuga, Bing, pnt tin, gray, gun-firing & rudder mechanism, w/up, 20", some rust & wear, VG, A.........$1,000.00

Launch, Germany, pnt tin, red & wht hull w/tan deck, wht superstructure & canopy, w/up, 17", pnt chips, scratches, VG, A $500.00

Le Raceret, Jouet, bl w/driver & flag, tin, 7", NMIB, A .$920.00

Marsh Craft, Ernst Plank/Germany, pnt tin, 2 floating chambers flank steering wheel w/2 paddle wheels, 10½", A.**$2,400.00**

Ocean Liner, Arnold (?), pnt tin, red, blk & wht, 2 stacks, w/up, 9½", rpt, pnt chips, VG, A $210.00

Ocean Liner, Bing, pnt tin, red, bl & wht, 4 stacks, w/up, 8", EX, A $350.00

Ocean Liner, Bing, pnt tin, red, wht & blk, 3 stacks & masts, 4 ventilators, etc, w/up, 40", upper deck rstr, EX, A.**$6,000.00**

Ocean Liner, Bing, pnt tin, red & wht hull w/litho superstructure, w/up, 6½", 1 tab & rudder missing, G-, A $70.00

Ocean Liner, blk-pnt wood hull w/red-pnt tin superstructure that lifts for rubber-band drive, 14", VG, A...............$55.00

Ocean Liner, Carette, pnt tin, blk, red & wht hull, 4 stacks, w/up, 13½", non-working, rpt, G, A $350.00

Ocean Liner, Carette, pnt tin, red, wht & blk, 3 stacks, w/up, 9½", partial rpt, some touchups, G, A......................$290.00

Ocean Liner, Carette, pnt tin, red & wht, twin screws, 4 stacks, w/up, 15", missing lifeboats, pnt loss, G+, A $850.00

Ocean Liner, Carette (?), pnt tin w/stenciled portholes, red, wht & tan, 1 stack, 32", EX, A................................**$6,900.00**

Ocean Liner Carmania, Germany, painted tin, windup, 2 stacks, 6 lifeboats, 24", G, A, $1,850.00.

Ocean Liner, Fleischmann, pnt tin w/wht superstructure on red & bl hull, twin stacks, w/up, 13", pnt chips, VG+, A $850.00

Ocean Liner, Fleischmann, rpt tin, red & blk w/wht deck, w/up, 13", G, A..$450.00

Ocean Liner, Fleischmann (?), pnt tin, cream & red w/3 gray stacks, w/up, 10½", rpt, VG, A $250.00

Ocean Liner Carmania, German, 2 stacks, 6 lifeboats, 24", rpt hull, broken rail, needs rpr, G, A........................$1,850.00

Ocean Liner Kronprinz Wilhelm, Marklin, pnt tin, 4 stacks, 2 masts, 37", appears EX, A $23,000.00

Ocean Liner Libertania, Liberty Playthings, w/up, 27", EX, B4 ....$800.00

Ocean Liner Queen Mary, rpt tin, red & blk w/wht deck, 3 stacks, w/up, G-, A $400.00

Ocean Liner Rhein, Marklin, pnt tin, red, wht & blk, 2 masts, dbl stacks, 16 lifeboats, etc, w/up, 26½", EX, A .$17,000.00

Outboard, Orkin, w/up, 22", EX, B4............................$900.00

Paddle-Wheeler, Carette, pnt tin, red & wht side-wheeler w/tan deck, 2 stacks, w/up, 7½", rstr, A $400.00

Paddle-Wheeler, Carette, pnt tin, red & wht side-wheeler w/twin stacks & forward wheel house, w/up, 7¾", rpt, EX, A $550.00

Paddle-Wheeler, Falck, red & wht tin w/ornate mermaid figurehead, single stack, 2 sm spoked side-wheels, w/up, 9", EX, A $825.00

Paddle-Wheeler, Fallows, early, red, wht & bl emb tin side-wheeler on cast spoke wheels, 8½", rpt, pnt wear, VG+, A $500.00

Paddle-Wheeler, Fleischmann, pnt tin, red & wht w/brn deck, twin stacks, w/up, 8½", non-working, deck detached, G, A...$300.00

Paddle-Wheeler, NY Ferry Co, Reed, late 19th century, paper litho, missing 1 wheel o/w EX, A...........................$3,738.00

Paddle-Wheeler, pnt tin, red & wht hull on side-wheeler w/lithoed superstructure, w/up, 8¼", non-working, G, A...$425.00

Paddle-Wheeler New York, Marklin, painted tin, red and white side-wheeler with 2 masts & stacks, 5 lead figures, original wheels, 19½", replaced lifeboats & masts, minor repairs, A, $47,000.00.

Patrol Boat Kasuga, Bing, pnt tin, 2-tone gray w/2 blk stacks & red trim, 2-gun turret, 20", rpt Japanese flag, EX, A...$1,000.00

Patrol Boat U-25, France, pnt tin w/brass fitting, electric drive, 21", hatch access cover rpl, pnt chips, G+, A..........$120.00

Patrol Boat V22, Canot JRD/France, pnt tin, gray, removable deck, 13", missing rudder, deck gun & ventilator o/w VG, A $120.00

Riverboat, Bing, pnt tin, red & blk hull, early electric motor powered by battery, 13", rpl canopy, pnt loss, VG, A...$475.00

Riverboat, Bing, pnt tin, red & wht w/cast-metal captain, w/up, 20", pnt chips, G+, A...$2,200.00

Riverboat, Carette, pnt tin, cream & red, flat metal figure, under canopy, w/up, 22", non-working, pnt chips, G+, A $1,300.00

Riverboat, Carette, pnt tin, w/sailors, 7½", pnt loss, VG, A $750.00

Riverboat Queen Mary, Marusan, litho tin, puffs smoke, 12", non-working, EX (orig box), A $160.00

Runabout, Orkin, w/up, 22", EX, B4 ....$450.00

Sailboat, Lutz, ca 1900, pnt tin, bl-gr & brn hull w/red & cream interior, 16", EX, A $1,035.00

Sailboat, pnt tin, red & wht, w/cloth sails & propeller, w/up, 9", very rare, pnt chips o/w VG, A $1,500.00

Sea Plane, Liberty Playthings, w/up, 21", EX, B4...........$400.00

Sea Scooter, Liberty Playthings, w/up, 14", EX, B4 ....$225.00

Side-Wheeler Atlantic, Althof Bergmann, painted tin, 2 stacks, 10", NM, D10, $4,500.00.

Skipper, Orkin, w/up, 22", EX, B4..................................$300.00

Speedboat, Bing, gray & wht tin live steamer w/red & gold trim, 19", missing burner, pnt chips o/w VG, A............$1,000.00

Speedboat, Japan, red & bl tin hull w/plated deck fittings, battery-op headlights, 17", non-working, VG, A..........$300.00

Speedboat, Jep/France, pnt tin, bl & wht, cast-metal driver, w/up, 14", pnt loss, G, A $150.00

Speedboat, Liberty Playthings, w/outboard motor, w/up, 16", EX, B4...$175.00

Speedboat, Liberty Playthings, w/twin cockpit, w/up, 14", EX, B4...$225.00

Speedboat, Lindstrom, 18", NM, D10, $750.00.

Speedboat, Lionel, pnt tin, red & cream, opening hatch, 2 compo drivers in forward cockpit, w/up, 17", VG, A $450.00

Speedboat, pnt tin w/brass boiler & oscillating cylinder, 25", rpl cover, missing burner, pnt chips o/w VG, A............$625.00

Speedboat (Jet-Putt-Putt), Alden Novelty, pnt tin w/impulse steam power, 9", G+ (G box), A $95.00

Speedboat (Tic-Toc), Abbey/Germany, 2-tone pnt tin w/wht stripe, driver in aft cockpit, 9", G (G box), A............$80.00

Speedboat #44, Lionel, pnt tin, gr & wht w/litho mahogany deck, 2 compo drivers at stern, w/up, 17", non-working, VG+, A..$600.00

Speedboat Allen Lee-N7, pnt tin, gr & blk, compo figures in forward cockpit, w/up, 17", G-, A................................$275.00

Speedboat Flying Yankee, gr & natural wood hull, heavy duty w/up motor & cable-rigged steering, 20", VG, A.....$220.00

Speedboat Miss America, Mengel Playthings, varnished wood w/brass trim, w/up, 14", VG+, A.............................$350.00

Speedboat Miss Liberty, Japan, pnt tin, red & gray w/brass boiler & single oscillating engine, 14", VG, A.................$325.00

Speedboat Pollywog, Boucher, red-pnt wood hull w/covered aluminum deck, live steam power plant, 24½", EX, A.$550.00

Speedboat Vixen, Ives, pnt tin, gr & wht w/tan deck, open cockpit w/seating, w/up, 13", pnt chips, VG+, A............$925.00

Speedboat Whiz, Boucher, pnt tin, gr & wht hull w/tan deck & brass engine cover, w/up, 21", pnt chips, G, A........$425.00

Speedster, Orkin, w/up, 27", EX, B4.........................$850.00

Sportster, Liberty Playthings, w/up, 16", EX, B4.............$150.00

Steam Launch, Bing, pnt tin, red & blk w/cream canopy, brass boiler & turbine wheel, 13", rpl canopy & stack, VG, A..$950.00

Steam Launch, Bing, tin w/cream-pnt superstructure on red & blk hull, turbine wheel, 20", rpl canopy & stack o/w VG, A..$1,700.00

Steam Launch, Carette, pnt tin, red & wht hull w/cream deck, brass boiler & oscillating engine, 22", rpl canopy, G+, A..$1,450.00

Steam Launch, France, copper & blk-pnt brass hull w/horizontal brass boiler & oscillating engine, 11", rpt, G, A..$2,200.00

Steam Launch, Planck/Germany, pnt brass hull w/brass boiler & oscillating engine, 10½", burner missing, G, A.......$160.00

Steam Launch, Planck/Germany, pnt tin, red & wht w/brass boiler, oscillating engine, 10½", G+, A...................$375.00

Steam Launch, pnt tin, gray w/brass boiler, oscillating engine, burner integral w/hull, 16½", rpt, pnt chips, G, A...$450.00

Steam Launch, pnt tin, red & wht hull, horizontal brass boiler & oscillating engine, 10", burner incomplete, G, A....$200.00

Steam Launch, Schoener, pnt tin, red & wht w/brass hull, vertical boiler & oscillating engine, 10", rpt, wear o/w VG, A..$300.00

Steam Launch, Union Mfg, polished brass open hull w/sm horizontal boiler & oscillating engine, 9½", VG, A.......$300.00

Steam Launch, Union Mfg, polished brass w/boiler & tin burner, oscillating cylinder, 13", EX (EX wood box), A...$1,450.00

Steam Launch, Union Mfg, polished brass w/boiler & tin burner, oscillating cylinder, 13", VG, A...............................$450.00

Steam Launch, Weeden, pnt tin, gray hull w/tin boiler & oscillating engine, burner integral w/hull, 14½", VG, A.$400.00

Steam Launch, Weeden, pnt tin w/brass boiler, 14½", VG (G box), A..$1,050.00

Steamboat America, Weeden, pnt copper, red & blk, oscillating engine, removable ventilated deck, 25", pnt chips, VG, A..$7,500.00

Steamship, Raduiquet (?), tin w/wood deck, oscillating cylinder, brass boiler, 2 masts, 3 stacks, 20", G+, A................$600.00

Steamship, red, blk & cream tin, 2-masted w/3 stacks, w/up key in center stack, 11", rstr, EX, A...........................$325.00

Steamship Chicago, Ives, red & blk tin w/tan decks & stacks, wht superstructure, twin stacks, 11", G, A..............$200.00

Submarine, Bing, early model, pnt tin, gray w/red stripe, single flag fore & aft, w/up, 10¼", pnt chips, VG, A.........$190.00

Submarine, Bing, gray-pnt tin w/bl turret, w/firing cannon & fanciful periscope, w/up, 17", VG, A......................$450.00

Submarine, Bing, later model, pnt tin, gray w/red stripe, w/up, 8½", few pnt chips o/w VG, A................................$75.00

Submarine, Bing, pnt tin, blk & gray, single flag, w/up, 8½", non-working, major pnt loss, G-, A.........................$65.00

Submarine, Marklin, pnt tin, olive gr, fixed diving planes, w/up, 12", EX, A..$550.00

Submarine, Marklin, pnt tin, olive gr & gray, w/up, 14", no diving planes, some deck fittings missing o/w VG, A...$900.00

Submarine, pnt tin, blk & gray w/cream deck, aft flag, 11½", rpr, minor pnt chips, o/w VG+, A.............................$110.00

Submarine, Wolverine, olive & red litho tin w/adjustable planes, w/up, 12½", EX, A.....................................$50.00

Submarine (Nautilus), San Jo Pan, pnt tin, dk bl & wht w/lighted ventilator towers, battery-op, 16", VG+, A..................$95.00

Submarine (U-Boat), Marklin, pnt tin plate, w/periscope & lifeboat, clockwork mechanism, 30", appears EX, A.$8,625.00

Submarine (Unda-Wunda), Sutcliffe/England, pnt tin, red & gray, w/up, 9", rubber cork deteriorated o/w EX (VG box), A..$85.00

Submarine #09, gray-pnt tin w/unusual propulsion system, 20", handrails damaged, pnt chips, dents, G+, A............$250.00

Submarine Au Nain Bleu, France, gray-pnt steel, electrically powered w/clockwork diving controls, 25½", VG+, A..$260.00

Submarine Au-Tom-A-Ton, Am, pnt & litho tin w/crackle-finished gray hull, run by compressed air, 13", G+, A..$100.00

Submarine G-150, early, pnt tin & wood w/movable planes & rudder, w/up, 11", pnt loss on wood, G, A...............$160.00

Submarine Sea Wolf (Atomic), Sutcliffe, red, yel & gold tin, w/up, 10", scarce, MIB, A.....................................$151.00

Tanker Esso, Fleischmann, red & blk tin hull, 2-masted, single stack, w/up, 19½", rpl masts, pnt chips, G+, A........$500.00

Tender, Orkin, w/up, 30", EX, B4..............................$1,150.00

Torpedo Boat, Carette, pnt tin, brn & blk, 2-masted w/2 deck guns & 3 stacks, w/up, 15½", non-working, G+, A .$550.00

Torpedo Boat, France, gray-pnt tin w/2 torpedo tubes in bow, w/up, 19", pnt chips, VG, A...............................$1,500.00

Torpedo Boat, Germany, pnt tin, red & bl, 4 stacks & 3 swivel guns, 2 lifeboats, 1 mast & adjustable rudder, 28", EX, A..$5,500.00

Torpedo Boat, Liberty Playthings, w/up, 25", EX, B4.....$300.00

Torpedo Boat, Marklin, blk-pnt tin w/red bottom, 4 stacks, single mast, 5 torpedo guns, etc, 22¾", EX, A...........$4,200.00

Tourboat Liberty, Liberty Playthings, varnished wood hull w/brass cabin & litho tin canopy, w/up, 17", G, A..$200.00

Tugboat, Ives, red & blk tin hull w/tan deck & brn superstructure, 2-masted, single stack, 10½", G+, A...............$525.00

Tugboat, 2-tone gr-pnt pressed steel w/polished trim, rstr, non-working, EX, A..$2,100.00

Tugboat & Scow, Liberty Playthings, w/up, 24", EX, B4.$150.00

Tugboat w/Water Gun, Bing, pnt tin, red & wht, adjustable rudder & searchlight, single stack, w/up, 12½", M, A..$1,000.00

Tugboat, Buddy L, 2-tone green-painted pressed steel with polished trim, restored, 28", non-working, EX, A, $2,100.00.

US Merchant Marine, Ives, 2-tone gray tin w/tan & wht super-
    structure, w/up, 12", non-working, VG, A..............$575.00
Warship HMS Resolution, Marklin, pnt tin, gray w/red & blk, 2
    tacks & masts, 10 cannons, 36", EX, A $14,950.00
Water Taxi, Orkin, w/up, 30", EX, B4 ....$800.00
Yacht Viking, Hornby/England, red-pnt tin hull w/yel deck
    & cabin, pnt tin sail, w/up, 17", rpl mast, pnt chips, G,
    A..$190.00

Books

Books have always captured and fired the imagination of children, and today books from every era are being collected. No longer is it just the beautifully illustrated Victorian examples or first editions of books written by well-known children's authors, but more modern books as well.

One of the first classics to achieve unprecedented success was *The Wizard of Oz* by author L. Frank Baum — such success, in fact, that far from his original intentions, it became a series. Even after Baum's death, other authors wrote Oz books until the decade of the 1960s, for a total of more than forty different titles. Other early authors were Beatrix Potter, Kate Greenaway, Palmer Cox (who invented the Brownies), and Johnny Gruelle (creator of Raggedy Ann and Andy). All were acomplished illustrators as well.

Everyone remembers a special series of books they grew up with, the Hardy Boys, Nancy Drew Mysteries, Tarzan — there were countless others. And though these are becoming very collectible today, there were many editions of each and most are very easy to find. Generally the last few in any series will be most difficult to locate, since fewer were printed than the earlier stories which were likely to have been reprinted many times. As is true of any type of book, first editions or the earliest printing will have more collector value.

Big Little Books came along in 1933 and until edged out by the comic book format in the mid-1950s sold in huge volumes, first for a dime and never more than 20¢ a copy. They were printed by Whitman, Saalfield, Goldsmith, Van Wiseman, Lynn, and World Syndicate, and all stuck to Whitman's original format — thick hand-sized sagas of adventure, the right-hand page with an exciting cartoon, well illustated and contrived so as to bring the text on the left alive. The first hero to be immortalized in this arena was Dick Tracy, but many more were to follow. Some of the more collectible today feature well-known characters like G-Men, Tarzan, Flash Gordon, Little Orphan Annie, Mickey Mouse, and Western heroes by the dozens.

Little Golden Books were first published in 1942, by Western Publishing Co. Inc. The earliest had spines of blue paper that were later replaced with gold foil. Until the 1970s the books were numbered from 1 to 600, while later books had no numerical order. The most valuable are those with dust jackets from the early forties or books with paper dolls and activities. The three primary series of books are Regular (1-600), Disney (1-140), and Activity (1-52). Books with the blue or gold paper spine (not foil) often sell at $8.00 to $15.00. Dust jackets alone are worth $20.00 and up in good condition. Paper doll books are generally valued at about $30.00 to $35.00, and stories about TV Western heroes at $12.00 to $18.00. First editions of the 25¢ and 29¢ cover price books can be identified by a code (either on the title page or the last page); '1/A' indicates a first edition while a number '/Z' will refer to the twenty-sixth printing. Condition is important but subjective to personal standards. For more information we recommend *Collecting Little Golden Books, Vols I and II*, by Steve Santi (S8). The second edition also includes information on Wonder and Elf books.

Advisors: Ron and Donna Donnelly (D7), Big Little Books; Joel Cohen (C12), Disney Pop-Up Books; Ilene Kayne (K3), Little Golden Books and Wonder Books.

See also Black Americana; Coloring, Activity and Paint Books; Rock 'n Roll.

BIG LITTLE BOOKS

Ace Drummond, Captain Eddie Rickenbacker, #1177, 1935,
    EX+ $20.00
Adventure in Outer Space, 1968, VG, S2 ....$15.00
Allen Pike of the Parachute Squad, #1481, 1941, VG......$15.00
Andy Panda & the Mad Dog Mystery, Walter Lantz, 1947,
    G $10.00
Bonanza, The Bubble Gum Kid, 1967, NM, C1 ....$18.00
Brad Turner in Trans-Atlantic Flight, #1425, 1939, EX+ .$22.00
Buccaneers, 1958, G..$3.50
Buck Jones & the Two-Gun Kid, G $18.00
Buck Jones in the Fighting Rangers, 1936, VG................$30.00
Buck Rogers in the 25th Century AD, 1933, Cocomalt pre-
    mium, EX $60.00
Bullet Benton, 1939, EX....................................$12.00
Clyde Beatty, the Daredevil Lion & Tiger Tamer, 1938,
    VG $15.00
Cowboy Lingo, Whitman #1457, 1938, VG $14.00
Cowboy Stories, 1933, premium, G............................$10.00
Daniel Boone, World, 1934, bl cloth, NM......................$14.50
Detective Higgins of the Rocket Squad, #1484, VG $20.00
Dick Tracy Encounters Facey, 1967, G $7.50
Dick Tracy Solves the Penfield Mystery, 1934, 1st edition,
    VG..$28.00
Don O'Dare Finds War, Whitman #1438, 1940, VG $7.50
Don Winslow of the Navy Vs the Scorpion Gang, #1419, 1938,
    G $10.00

Donald Duck & the Fabulous Diamond Fountain, 1967, G.**$5.00**
Donald Duck & the Fabulous Diamond Fountain, 1967, EX **$10.00**
Donald Duck & the Mystery of the Double X, 1949, EX+..**$45.00**
Down Cartridge Creek, Pinto Shane, 1938, G **$10.00**
Fantastic Four in the House of Horrors, 1968, VG **$3.50**
Flash Gordon & the Tournaments of Mongo, #1171, 1937, 1st edition, EX...**$60.00**

Flash Gordon and the Water World of Mongo, 1930, EX, $50.00; Jungle Jim and the Vampire Woman, EX, $45.00; Zane Grey's King of the Royal Mounted Gets His Man, #1452, 1938, EX+, $30.00.

Flash Gordon & the Witch Queen of Mongo, 1936, EX+.**$70.00**
Flying the Sky Clipper w/Winsie Atkins, #1108, 1936, 1st edition, EX...**$28.00**
Foreign Spies, Doctor Doom & the Ghost Submarine, 1939, G..**$16.00**
Frank Buck Presents Ted Towers Animal Master, #1175, 1935, VG **$22.00**
G-Man on the Crime Trail, 1938, NM, J2.......................**$35.00**
Gene Autry & Bandits of Silver Tip, 1949, EX **$15.00**
Gene Autry & Raiders of the Range, 1946, EX **$25.00**
Gene Autry & the Gun-Smoke Reckoning, D8 ....**$35.00**
Gene Autry in Law of the Range, 1939, G+ **$32.00**
Ghost Trip to Treasure Island, 1967, worn cover, G, S2 ....**$5.00**
Giant Trouble, 1968, G, S2...**$10.00**
House of Horrors, 1968, VG, S2.....................................**$10.00**
Jack Armstrong & the Ivory Treasure, 1937, VG **$10.00**
Jungle Jim, #1138, 1936, EX **$45.00**
Junior Nebb on the Diamond Bar Ranch, 1938, VG **$8.50**
Lady & the Tramp, 1955, VG, J5 ....**$10.00**
Lassie & the Shabby Sheik, 1968, VG, S2......................**$10.00**
Li'l Abner in New York, #1198, 1936, EX+ **$35.00**
Little Annie Rooney & the Orphan House, #1117, 1936, 1st edition, EX...**$24.00**
Little Men (movie version), 1934, G-..............................**$15.00**
Little Orphan Annie & Punjab the Wizard, 1935, G.......**$15.00**
Little Orphan Annie & Sandy, 1933, 300 pgs, G.............**$18.00**
Little Orphan Annie & the Ghost Gang, 1936, G...........**$15.00**
Lone Ranger & the Black Shirt Highway Man, 1939, VG **$30.00**
Lone Ranger & the Red Renegades, 1939, VG.................**$25.00**
Lone Ranger & the Secret Weapon, 1939, G **$20.00**
Man From UNCLE & the Calcutta Affair, 1934, G...........**$9.50**
Men of the Mounted, #755, 1st edition, 1934, Cocomalt premium, EX **$25.00**

Mickey Mouse & Bobo the Elephant, 1935, EX, A **$40.00**

Mickey Mouse and Pluto the Racer, 1936, VG, A, $44.00; Mickey Mouse and the Sacred Jewel, 1936, VG, A, $35.00; Mickey Mouse Runs His Own Newspaper, 1937, EX, A, $75.00.

Mickey Mouse & the Dude Ranch Bandits, 1943, VG, A.**$35.00**
Mickey Mouse Bellboy Detective, 1945, EX+, A..............**$75.00**
Mickey Mouse in the Race for Riches, 1938, VG, A **$45.00**
Mickey Mouse in the World of Tomorrow, 1948, EX+, A..**$65.00**
Mickey Mouse Mystery at Disneyland, #5770, 1975, NM ..**$8.00**
Mickey Mouse on Sky Island, 1941, EX+, A.....................**$55.00**
Mickey's Dog Pluto, Whitman, 1943, EX, A **$30.00**
Oswald the Rabbit Plays G-Man, Walter Lantz, 1937, G.**$20.00**
Popeye in Puddleburg, 1934, G **$18.50**
Powder Smoke Range, 1937, G- **$15.00**
Prairie Bill & the Covered Wagon, #758, 1934, VG+......**$25.00**
Red Barry Ace Detective, #1157, G+...............................**$18.00**
Red Ryder & the Squaw-Tooth Rustlers, 1946, EX, A **$21.00**
Red Ryder Acting Sheriff, 1949, G- **$15.00**
Rex Beach's Jaragu of the Jungle, 1937, G **$7.50**
Road Runner & the Lost Road Runner Mine, 1974, VG ...**$3.50**
Roy Rogers & the Mystery of the Lazy M, 1948, VG- **$12.50**
Roy Rogers at Crossed Feathers Ranch, 1945, VG **$18.00**
Roy Rogers King of the Cowboys, 1953, VG, J5 ....**$10.00**
Scrappy, 1934, EX...**$20.00**
Secret Agent X-9, 1936, EX **$40.00**
Shootin' Sheriffs of the Wild West, 1936, VG **$12.00**
Skeezix in Africa, #1112, 1934, 1st edition, EX...............**$21.00**
Skyroads w/Hurricane Hawk, 1936, VG **$18.00**
SOS Coast Guard, #1191, 1936, G **$15.00**

Snow White and the Seven Dwarfs, #1460, 1938, VG, $20.00.

Steve Hunter of the US Coast Guard, 1942, EX, J5 ....$15.00
Tailspin Tommy & the Sky Bandits, 1938, VG...............$12.50
Tarzan Escapes, #1182, NM..$90.00
Tarzan of the Apes, #744, 1933, G...$25.00
Tarzan Twins, #770, 1935, VG $47.00
Texas Kid, 1937, VG $15.00

Texas Ranger, VG, $35.00; *Radio Patrol Trailing the Safeblowers*, #1173, 1937, VG, $35.00.

Tom Mix & the Hoard of Montezuma, 1937, G..............$15.00
Tom Mix in the Range War, #1166, 1937, VG $18.50
Tom Swift & His Magnetic Silencer, 1941, scarce, G......$15.00
Uncle Sam's Sky Defenders, 1941, EX, J5.........................$15.00
Wells Fargo, 1938, G-..$18.00
Will Rogers, Saalfield #1096, 1935, G $12.50
Windy Wayne & His Flying Wing, 1942, VG.................$10.00
Winning of the Old Northwest, World, 1934, NM..........$25.00
Woody Woodpecker & the Meteor Menace, 1967, NM, S2 ....$15.00

BIG GOLDEN BOOKS

Adventures of Mr Toad, Disney, 1949, VG $20.00
Aristocats, Disney, 1970, EX $10.00
Bambi, Disney, 1972, VG $3.00
Frosty the Snowman, 1979, VG $3.00
Lassie Finds a Way, 1957, VG $8.00
Mickey Mouse in Hideaway Island, Disney, 1980, VG.......$6.00
Quick Draw McGraw, 1961, M $20.00
Snow White & the Seven Dwarfs, Disney, 1952, VG $7.00
Surpise Package, Disney, 1948, VG...................................$12.00
True Story of Smokey the Bear, 1971, VG $10.00
Yogi Bear, a Christmas Visit, 1961, EX $15.00

LITTLE GOLDEN BOOKS

Alice in Wonderland, #D16, 1st edition, VG-EX, K3 ......$10.00
All My Chickens, #200-67, A edition, VG-EX, K3 ....$5.00
Alvin's Daydreams, #107-73, MCMXC edition, VG-EX, K3..$5.00
Animals' Christmas Eve, #154, 1st edition, VG-EX, K3.....$2.00
Aristocats, #D122, 1st edition, VG-EX, K3 ....$12.00
Bambi, #D90, 36th edition, VG-EX, K3............................$4.00

Bambi, Walt Disney, #7, 1948, NM, $12.00.

Bedtime Stories, #2, 7th edition, bl spine, 42 pgs, VG-EX, K3..$16.00
Big Bird's Red Book, #157, 3rd edition, VG-EX, K3..........$3.00
Big Bird Visits Navajo Country, #108-68, A edition, VG-EX, K3..$5.00
Bongo, #D9, E edition, VG-EX, K3..................................$10.00
Bouncy Baby Bunny Finds His Bed, #129, 1st edition, VG-EX, K3..$9.00
Brave Eagle, #294, B edition, VG-EX, K3 ....$7.00
Bugs Bunny, #72, B edition, VG-EX, K3............................$6.00
Bugs Bunny & the Indians, #120, C edition, VG-EX, K3..$12.00
Bugs Bunny at the County Fair, #164, A edition, VG-EX, K3..$12.00
Bugs Bunny Gets a Job, #136, 1st edition, VG-EX, K3.....$14.00
Bunny Book, #215, C edition, VG-EX, K3 ....$2.00
Casper & Friends Boo-o-s on First, #107-85, 1992 edition, VG-EX, K3..$6.00
Chip 'N Dale, #105-78, A edition, VG-EX, K3 ....$6.00
Chip Chip, #28, E edition, VG-EX, K3..............................$8.00
Christmas Story, #158, A edition, peach background, VG-EX, K3..$12.00
Christmas Story, #158, E edition, peach background, VG-EX, K3..$9.00
Christmas Story, #158, 12th edition, wht background, VG-EX, K3..$2.00

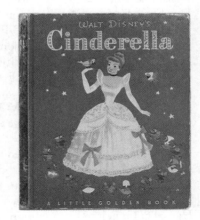

Cinderella, Walt Disney, #13, 1950, NM, $12.00.

Circus Time, #31, I edition, VG-EX, K3 ....$20.00
Color Kittens (w/Color Kitten card game), #202-38, 17th edition, VG-EX, K3 ....$20.00

Colors Are Nice, #496, 8th edition, VG-EX, K3 ....$3.00

Cookie Monster & the Cookie Tree, # 159, 3rd edition, VG-EX, K3 ....$6.00

Counting Rhymes, #12, E edition, VG-EX, K3.................$10.00

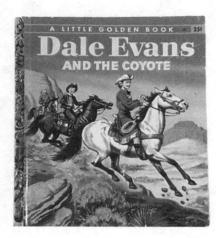

Dale Evans and the Coyote, #253, 1956, M, $18.00.

Dale Evans & the Lost Gold Mine, #213, A edition, VG-EX, K3 ....$18.00

Davy Crockett, #D45, A edition, VG-EX, K3 ....$12.00

Disneyland Parade w/Donald Duck, #D123, 2nd edition, VG-EX, K3 ....$8.00

Donald Duck & the Witch Next Door, #D127, 7th edition, VG-EX, K3 ....$4.00

Donald Duck & the Witch Next Door, #102-44, Q edition, VG-EX, K3 ....$2.00

Donald Duck Instant Millionaire, #102-44, H edition, VG-EX, K3 ....$3.00

Donald Duck's Toy Train, #D18, 14th edition, VG-EX, K3 ....$6.00

Donald Duck's Toy Sail Boat, #D40, E edition, VG-EX, K3.$10.00

Duck & His Friends, #81, A edition, VG-EX, K3 ....$8.00

Duck & His Friends, #81, 6th edition, VG-EX, K3 ....$4.00

Fairy Tales, #9, F edition, VG-EX, K3 ....$12.00

Favorite Nursery Tales, #D125, 5th edition, VG-EX, K3 ...$2.50

First Bible Stories, #198, A edition, VG-EX, K3 ....$22.00

Five Little Firemen, #64, F edition, 42 pgs, VG-EX, K3...$12.00

Flying Car, #D96, A edition, VG-EX, K3 ....$12.00

Four Little Kittens, #322, C edition, VG-EX, K3...............$9.00

Frosty the Snowman, #142, A edition, G, K3 ....$7.00

Frosty the Snowman, #142, E edition, bl cover, VG-EX, K3 ....$4.50

Fuzzy Duckling, #78, C edition, VG-EX, K3.....................$9.00

Garfield & the Cat Show, #110-85, MCMXCI edition, VG-EX, K3 ....$3.00

Golden Book of Birds, #13, 4th edition, VG-EX, K3........$12.00

Golden Sleepy Book, #46, E edition, VG-EX, K3.............$14.00

Grandpa Bunny, #D21, A edition, VG-EX, K3 ....$24.00

Hansel & Gretel, #17, G edition, VG-EX, K3 ....$13.00

Hansel & Gretel, #217, A edition, VG-EX, K3 ....$10.00

How To Tell Time, #285, E edition, VG-EX, K3 ....$12.00

Howdy Doody & Clarabell, #121, A edition, VG-EX, K3.$18.00

Howdy Doody Circus, #99, B edition, VG-EX, K3 ....$16.00

Hymns, #34, C edition, VG-EX, K3.................................$12.00

Hymns, #34, H edition, VG-EX, K3.................................$9.00

I Have a Secret, #495, A edition, K3 ....$22.00

I'm an Indian Today, #425, A edition, K3 ....$14.00

I Think About God, #111, 6th edition, VG-EX, K3..........$5.00

J Fred Muggs, #234, A edition, VG-EX, K3 ....$20.00

Johnny Appleseed, #D11, D edition, VG-EX, K3............$14.00

Jolly Barnyard, #67, 13th edition, VG-EX, K3 ....$2.00

Kermit Save the Swamp, #111-84, A edition, VG-EX, K3.$6.00

Lady, #D103, 8th edition, VG-EX, K3 ....$5.00

Lady & the Tramp, #105-55, D edition, VG-EX, K3 ....$4.00

Let's Go Shopping w/Peter & Penny, #33, B edition, VG-EX, K3...$15.00

Little Golden Book of Poetry, 1st edition, VG-EX, K3 ....$15.00

Little Red Hen, #6, 5th edition, bl spine, 42 pgs, VG-EX, K3 ....$16.00

Little Red Riding Hood, #300-65, MCMXCII edition, illus by Joe Evers, VG-EX, K3 ....$4.00

Little Red Riding Hood, #42, W edition, 24 pgs, VG-EX, K3 ....$12.00

Little Trapper, #79, B edition, 28 pgs, VG-EX, K3 ....$12.00

Lively Little Rabbit, #15, 4th edition, bl binding, VG-EX, K3 ....$18.00

Magic Next Door, #106, 4th edition, VG-EX, K3 ....$6.00

Mannie the Donkey, #D75, A edition, VG-EX, K3.........$10.00

Mary Poppins, #D113, B edition, VG-EX, K3...................$10.00

Mickey Mouse's Picnic, Walt Disney, #15, 1949, EX, $15.00.

Mister Ed, #483, A edition, VG-EX, K3 ....$17.00

Mother Goose, #4, 2nd edition (wartime), bl spine, 24 pgs, VG-EX, K5 ....$20.00

My Home #115, 4th edition, VG-EX, K3...........................$3.00

My Little Golden Picture Dictionary, #90, A edition, VG-EX, K3 ....$15.00

My Little Golden Picture Dictionary, #90, D edition, VG-EX, K3 ....$6.00

National Velvet, #431, A edition, VG-EX, K3................$10.00

New Baby, #41, G edition, VG-EX, K3............................$15.00

Night Before Christmas, #20, D edition, Santa on roof cover, gilt, VG-EX, K3 ....$10.00

Night Before Christmas, #20, F edition, gr cover, VG-EX, K3..$7.00

Night Before Christmas, #20, 1st edition, reindeer cover, bl spine, VG-EX, K3 ....$23.00

Night Before Christmas, #20, 31st edition, red cover, VG-EX, K3 ....$1.50

Noah's Ark, #109, 4th edition, VG-EX, K3 ....$4.00

Nursery Tales, #14, 3rd edition, bl binding, VG-EX, K3 ..$18.00

Pete's Dragon, #105-44, I edition, VG-EX, K3 ....$3.00

Peter & the Wolf, #D5, I edition, no gold spine, VG-EX, K3..$8.00

Peter & the Wolf (Mickey Mouse Club book), #D56, A edition, VG-EX, K3..$15.00

Peter Pan & Wendy, #D110, 20th edition, VG-EX, K3 .....$3.00

Pinocchio, #D8, L edition, VG-EX, K3..........................$10.00

Pluto Pup Goes to Sea, #D 30, A edition, VG-EX, K3 .....$12.00

Porky Pig & Bugs Bunny — Just Like Magic, #146, 4th edition, VG-EX, K3..$4.00

Prayers for Children, #5, S edition, VG-EX, K3 ....$10.00

Prince & the Pauper, #105-71, A edition VG-EX, K3........$3.00

Raggedy Ann & Andy Help Santa Claus, #156, 2nd edition, VG-EX, K3..$4.00

Rin-Tin-Tin & the Lost Indian, #276, A edition, VG-EX, K3$12.00

Robin Hood, #D126, 1st edition, VG-EX, K3 ....$12.00

Robin Hood, #D48, A edition, VG-EX, K3 ....$10.00

Santa's Toy Shop, #D16, A edition, K3 ....$12.00

Scuffy the Tugboat, #30, 2nd edition, VG-EX, K3 ....$20.00

Seven Little Postmen, #504, 5th edition, VG-EX, K3......$10.00

Seven Sneezes, #51, A edition, VG-EX, K3....................$18.00

Seven Sneezes, #51, C edition, VG-EX, K3....................$12.00

Sleeping Beauty, #104-56, E edition, VG-EX, K3.............$2.00

Sleeping Beauty & the Good Fairies, #D71, A edition, VG-EX, K3..$14.00

Sorcerer's Apprentice, #100-79, A edition, K3 ....$6.00

Story of Jesus, #27, D edition, VG-EX, K3 ....$12.00

Surprise for Mickey Mouse, #D105, 2nd edition, VG-EX, K3..$4.00

Swiss Family Robinson, #D95, A edition, VG-EX, K3 .....$12.00

Tawny Scrawny Lion, #138, 8th edition, VG-EX, K3 ....$5.00

Three Bears, #47, D edition, 42 pgs, VG-EX, K3..............$14.00

Three Bears, #47, 38th edition, VG-EX, K3 ....$8.00

Three Little Pigs, #D10, L edition, K3 ....$8.00

Three Little Pigs, #D78, 40th edition, VG-EX, K3 ....$3.00

Thumper, #D119, B edition, VG-EX, K3.........................$15.00

Toby Tyler, #D87, B edition, VG-EX, K3.........................$10.00

Tom & Jerry Christmas, #197, A edition, VG-EX, K3 .....$12.00

Tom & Jerry Christmas, #197, F edition, VG-EX, K3 ....$6.00

Uncle Remus, #D6, D edition, VG-EX, K3.........................$6.00

Uncle Wiggily, #148, A edition, VG-EX, K3 ....$14.00

Very Busy Barbie, #107-90, A edition, VG-EX, K3 ....$6.00

What Am I?, #58, B edition, VG-EX, K3..........................$10.00

Winnie the Pooh/Honey Tree, #D116, B edition, VG-EX, K3 .$7.00

Winnie the Pooh/Honey Tree, #D116, 23rd edition, VG-EX, K3 ....$2.00

Woodsy Owl, #107, 2nd edition, VG-EX, K3 ....$6.00

Woody Woodpecker Takes a Trip, #445, A edition, VG-EX, K3 ....$9.00

Woody Woodpecker Takes a Trip, 3rd edition, VG-EX, K3..$4.00

Words, #45, 42nd edition, VG-EX, K3...............................$3.00

Zorro, #D68, B edition, VG-EX, K3 ....$13.00

POP-UP BOOKS

Christmas Time in Action, 1949, 20 pgs of stories, poems & songs w/6 pop-ups, illus by Tilley, NM, A $121.00

Dick Tracy, Capture of Boris Arson, **Pleasure Books, 1937, 3 pop-ups of Tracy in action scenes, complete, EX, $350.00.**

Flash Gordon, Tournament of Death, Pleasure Books, 1935, 3 pop-ups, Alex Raymond art, EX+, $475.00.

Flintstones & the Unhappy Rich Man, England, 1974, 4 pop-ups, scarce, NM, A...$60.00

Fold-Away Nativity Book, Garden City Books, 1951, illus by Catherine Barnes, NM $75.00

Goldilocks & the Three Bears, Blue Ribbon, 1934, 8x9", VG .$200.00

Hector Protector & As I Went Over the Water, Maurice Sendak, Harper, 1965, M (NM dust jacket) $75.00

Honey Bears & Their Forest Friends, Modern Promotions, 1984, 6 pop-ups, M...$7.00

Hopalong Cassidy & Lucky at the Double-X Ranch, Garden City, 1950, 2 pop-ups, 11", M, A...............................$85.00

Huckleberry Hound & the Dog-Cat, 1974, EX+, C1 ....$21.00

Jolly Jump-Ups' Vacation Trip, McLoughlin Bros, 1952, 6 pop-ups, VG+..$40.00

Jolly Jump-Ups & Their New House, McLoughlin Bros, 1939, NM...$175.00

Jolly Jump-Ups Mother Goose Book, McLoughlin Bros, 1944, NM...$175.00

Little Mermaid, Disney, 1st edition, 6 pop-ups, M...........$15.00

Little Orphan Annie & Jumbo the Circus Elephant, Blue Ribbon Pleasure Books, 1935, 3 pop-ups, VG+.............$300.00

Mickey Mouse, Blue Ribbon, 1933, 3 pop-ups, EX+, A .$263.00

Mickey Mouse, Blue Ribbon, 1933, 3 pop-ups, G, A......$100.00

Mickey Mouse in King Arthur's Court, English version, 1930s, 4 full-color pop-ups, hardbound, VG+.......................$475.00

Mickey Mouse Presents His Silly Symphonies, Blue Ribbon, 1933, Babes in the Woods/King Neptune, 3 pop-ups, VG ..$575.00

Mother Goose, Blue Ribbon, 1934, 3 pop-ups, illus by Harold Lentz, 9½x8", VG...$250.00

New Adventures of Tarzan, Pleasure, 1935, 3 pop-ups, 9", EX+ $425.00

Old-Fashioned Garden, 1987, 4 pop-ups, EX...................$15.00

Peter Pan, Hallmark, ca 1965, 4 pop-ups, illus by Bob Brackman, VG+ (VG+ dust jacket) $35.00

Pinocchio, Blue Ribbon, 1932, 4 pop-ups, hardbound, EX+, A..$244.00

Pinocchio, Granddreams Limited, 1991, 6 pop-ups, NM .$12.50

Pop-Up Minnie Mouse, Blue Ribbon, 1933, 3 pop-ups, 27 pgs, EX+, A...$275.00

Puss-In-Boots, Blue Ribbon, 1934, blk & wht illus, scarce, minor wear o/w EX, A..$195.00

Santa Claus Storyland, 3-D snow on cover, hardbound, 18 pgs, MIB, A...$95.00

Photo courtesy of Joel Cohen.

Snow White, **French version by Hachette, Walt Disney, 1930s, rare, $1,200.00.**

Storyland Pop-Up Book, Hallmark, 5 pop-ups, NM.........$12.50

Tim Tyler in the Jungle, Pleasure Books, 1935, 3 pop-ups, hardbound, EX+, A $245.00

Tim Tyler in the Jungle, Pleasure Books, 1935, 3 pop-ups, hardbound, VG, A..$138.00

Very Far Away, Maurice Sendak, Harper, 1957, M (NM dust jacket)...$125.00

Visit to the Haunted House, 1992, 5 pop-ups, EX $12.50

Who Framed Roger Rabbit, Budget Books, Australia, hardbound, M, D1..$75.00

Wind in the Willows, 1983, 1st edition, 4 pop-ups, M.....$25.00

Wizard of Oz, Hallmark, 1976, 22 pgs, scarce, NM, A......$53.00

TELL-A-TALE

Bedknobs & Broomsticks, 1971, EX $6.00

Big Little Kitty, 1953, M..$7.00

Buffy & the New Girl, 1969, EX.......................................$6.00

Donald Duck in Frontierland, Disney, 1957, EX................$6.00

Gingerbread Man, 1976, EX+, P3.....................................$5.00

Hiding Place, 1971, EX..$2.00

Horse for Charlie, 1970, EX...$4.50

Hungry Lion, EX $5.00

Land of the Lost & the Dinosaur Adventure, 1975, EX......$4.00

Lassie & the Firefighters, 1968, EX...................................$6.00

Lassie & the Kittens, 1956, NM $8.00

Mary Poppins, Disney, 1964, NM.....................................$6.00

Mother Goose, 1958, EX...$7.00

Nancy & Sluggo in the Big Surprise, 1974, M $8.00

Peter Pan & the Tiger, Disney, 1976, M............................$5.00

Rinty & Pals for Rusty, 1957, EX.....................................$5.00

Rudolph the Red-Nosed Reindeer, 1980, M $5.00

Scooby Doo at the Zoo, 1974, EX, P3 ....$4.00

Slowpoke at the Circus, 1973, VG+...................................$2.00

Smokey Bear Saves the Forest, 1971, EX...........................$5.00

Swiss Family Duck, 1964, EX, P3.......................................$4.00

Three Bears, 1960, NM..$5.00

Tweety & Sylvester Picnic Problems, 1970, EX, P3............$4.00

Uncle Wiggily & the Alligator, 1953, VG+ $5.00

Woody Woodpecker & a Peck of Trouble, 1951, EX.........$5.00

Zoo Friends Are at Our School Today, 1979, EX...............$3.00

WHITMAN

Annette Funicello & the Mystery at Moonstone, TV Authorized Edition, 1962, NM, C1..$15.00

Annie Oakley, TV Authorized Edition, 1957, NM, C1 ...$20.00

Beverly Hillbillies, Saga of Wildcat Creek, **1963, EX+, O1, $10.00.**

Big Valley (from TV series), EX (w/dust jacket)................$4.00

Bonanza, Killer Lion, 1966, EX, P3 ....$8.00

Bonanza, TV Authorized Edition, 1977, NM, C1............$18.00

Buffy (Family Affair) Finds a Star, TV Authorized Edition, 1970, NM, C1 ....$20.00

Cheyenne & Lost Gold of Lion Park, TV Authorized Edition #27, 1958, Clint Walker photo cover, NM, C1........$18.00

Dick Tracy, Chester Gould, 1943, hardbound, EX+ (w/dust jacket), P3..$25.00

Donald Duck, Linette, 1935, Donald's 1st book, illus, 14 pgs, EX+, A...$190.00

Donald Duck & the Wishing Star Story Book, 1952, hardbound, EX+, T2...$18.00

Dr Kildare Assigned to Trouble, TV Authorized Edition, 1963, NM, C1 ....$13.00

Dragnet, TV Authorized Edition, 1957, NM, C1 ....$19.00

F-Troop, Great Indian Uprising, 1967, VG, D9.................$6.00

F-Troop, TV Authorized Edition, EX, D8.................$12.00

Flintstones & Dino, Tip-Top Tale, 1961, EX.................$7.50

Flipper, Mystery of the Black Schooner, 1966, EX+, P3...$10.00

Gene Autry & the Ghost Riders, hardbound, D8.............$15.00

Gingerbread Man, 1944, Fuzzy Wuzzy series, M (NM dust
   jacket) $75.00

Green Hornet & the Case of the Disappearing Doctor, TV
   Authorized Edition, 1966, NM, C1.............................$36.00

Hawaii Five-O, The Octopus Caper, 1971, NM, C1 ....$17.50

Invaders, TV Authorized Edition, 1967, NM, C1............$14.00

Lassie Rescue in the Storm, Cozy-Corner series, 1951, EX+,
   T2..$24.00

Lone Ranger & the War Horse, Cozy-Corner series, 1951, NM,
   C1..$30.00

Lucy & the Madcap Mystery, 1963, NM, C1 ....$19.00

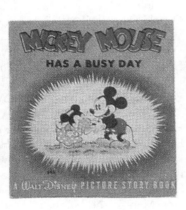

Mickey Mouse Has a Busy Day, Walt Disney Enterprises, 1937, EX, A, $75.00.

Miss Sniff the Fuzzy Cat, 1945, Fuzzy Wuzzy series, NM (EX+
   dust jacket) $75.00

Mission Impossible, Priceless Particle, 1969, EX+, P3 ......$10.00

Mission Impossible, The Money Explosion, TV Authorized Edi-
   tion, 1970, NM, C1 ....$17.00

Mod Squad, Assignment: The Hideout, 1970, hardbound, minor
   surface & edge wear o/w EX, D9..................................$6.00

Munsters & the Great Camera Caper, EX+, I2 ....$12.00

Munsters Last Resort, 1965, EX, H4.................................$16.00

Patrick the Fuzziest Bunny, 1946, Fuzzy Wuzzy series, NM .$30.00

Patty Duke, Mystery Mansion, 1964, EX+, P3 ....$10.00

Real McCoys, TV Authorized Edition, NM, C1...............$17.00

Rifleman, TV Authorized Edition, 1959, color hardbound, NM,
   T2..$24.00

Story of Our Gang, Romping Through the Hal Roach Come-
   dies, 1929, hardbound, EX, A......................................$60.00

Uncle Scrooge Rainbow Runaway, 1965, hardbound, EX+, T2..$18.00

Voyage to the Bottom of the Sea, TV Authorized Edition, 1965,
   hardbound, EX+, C1...$21.00

Voyage to the Bottom of the Sea, TV Authorized Edition, 1965,
   water stained, G, S2 ....$5.00

Walt Disney's Silly Symphony, WDE, 1937, Mickey's Magic
   Hat/Cookie Carnival, 4 illus pgs w/script, EX, A.......$88.00

Waltons, TV Authorized Edition, 1975, NM, C1.............$14.50

Wyatt Earp, Whitman, 1956, EX (w/dust jacket) $7.00

Zorro, 1958, hardbound, EX, D9 ....$10.00

WONDER BOOKS

Alvin's Lost Voice, #824, 1963, EX........................$6.00

Billy & His Steamroller, #557, 1951, EX...................$5.50

Brave Little Duck, #777, 1953, NM $2.50

Brave Little Steam Shovel, #555, 1951, EX $5.00

Child's Garden of Verses, #704, 1958, EX...................$3.00

Come & See the Rainbow, #743, 1960, M..................$5.00

Cozy Little Farm, #749, 1946, EX..........................$2.50

Felix the Cat, #665, 1953, EX $10.00

Gandy Goose, #695, 1957, NM $10.00

Giraffe Who Went to School, #551, 1951, NM.................$6.00

Heckle & Jeckle, #694, 1957, NM.........................$7.00

Heidi, #532, 1950, NM $5.00

Hungry Little Bunny, #531, 1950, M........................$5.00

It's a Lovely Day, #632, 1956, EX.........................$4.50

Little Garage Man, #744, 1960, M..........................$4.00

Little Train that Saved the Day, #571, 1952, EX+ $4.00

Merry Christmas Mr Snowman, #818, 1951, EX.................$4.50

Mother Goose, #501, 1946, EX...........................$5.50

Peter Rabbit & Reddy Fox, #611, 1954, NM $5.00

Rattle-Rattle Train, #655, 1974, NM.......................$4.00

Romper Room Safety Book, #854, 1974, M $3.50

Sleeping Beauty, #635, 1956, M $4.00

Tom Corbett Trip to the Moon, #713, 1953, NM $9.00

Tuggy the Tugboat, #696, 1958, NM $4.00

Who Lives on the Farm, #518, 1949, EX....................$6.00

Wonder Book of Bible Stories, #577, 1951, NM.................$5.00

Wonder Book of Christmas, #575, 1951, M.....................$7.00

MISCELLANEOUS

Adventures of a Brownie, Miss Murlock, Altemus, ca 1900, picture pasted on gray cloth, G+, S12............................$15.00

Adventures of Holly Hobbie, Delacorte, 1980, 1st edition, 261
   pgs, EX (VG+ dust jacket)..$25.00

Alice All-By-Herself, Elizabeth Coatsworth, Macmillan, 1937, 1st
   edition, illus by Marguerite De Angeli, 181 pgs, NM...$40.00

Amazing Spiderman, Lancer Books, 1966, paperback, minor yellowing to pgs o/w EX, D9...$13.00

Arabian Nights, World, 1924, illus by Frances Brundage, gilt
   cloth, VG $25.00

Bambi's Children, Bobbs Merrill, 1939, 1st American edition,
   315 pgs, VG+ (G dust jacket) $35.00

Big Book of Animal Stories, Kenosha, 1946, 118 pgs, EX+ (EX
   dust jacket) $25.00

Billy Whiskers in the South, Frances Montgomery, Saalfield,
   1917, 6 color plates, 148 pgs, G.................................$55.00

Bird Children, Elizabeth Gordon, Volland, 40th edition, illus by
   MT Ross, pictorial boards, 95 pgs, VG, S12...............$35.00

Black Stallion Revolts, Walter Farley, Random House, 1953, 1st
   edition, 305 pgs, VG (G+ dust jacket)........................$25.00

Bomba the Jungle Boy & the Swamp of Death, Ron Rockwood,
   1929, VG+, I2...$16.00

Boy Scouts of the Air in the Northern Wilds, Chicago, 1912, 1st
   edition, pictorial cloth, VG......................................$12.50

Boys' Book of Sports & Outdoor Life, Maurice Thompson, Century, 1886, 1st edition, illus, 352 pgs, VG, S12........$150.00

Bozo Helps Dinky Toot the Horn, McGraw-Hill, 1964, cb pgs, EX+, C1 ....$16.00

Bozo Meets the Silly Sea Serpent, Saalfield, 1961, NM......$8.00

Brady Bunch, Adventure on the High Seas, 1973, paperback, NM, C1 ....$15.00

Brady Bunch, The New York Mystery, 1970s, paperback, EX, J5 ....$10.00

Buffalo Bill, D'Aulaire & Parin, Doubleday, 1952, 1st edition, color boards, 40 pgs, VG (VG dust jacket), S12......$125.00

Buster Brown, book, Buster Brown's Latest Frolics, Cupples & Leon, 1906, paperback, 21 pgs, VG+, A $125.00

Buster Brown, book, Buster Brown the Fun Maker, RF Outcault, 1912, 29 pgs, scarce, EX, A $303.00

Candy Land, McLoughlin Little Color Classics, 1928, illus by Hildegard, 30 pgs, G+, S12..$25.00

Charlie McCarthy, ...So Help Me, Mr. Bergen, Grosset & Dunlap, 1938, EX, $30.00.

Charlotte's Web, EB White, Harper & Bros, 1952, 1st edition, illus by Garth Williams, 184 pgs, VG $85.00

Charlotte's Web, EB White, Harper & Bros, 1952, M (NM dust jacket) $150.00

Cheery Scarecrow, Johnny Gruelle, Donohue, 1929, VG (VG dust jacket), S12 ....$65.00

Child's Book of Bible Stories, Jane Werner, 1944, 1st edition, illus by Masha, 54 pgs, VG (VG dust jacket)............$20.00

Child's Garden of Verses, Oxford University Press, 1947, 1st edition, illus by Tasha Tudor, F (VG dust jacket)........$185.00

Child's Garden of Verses, Robert L Stevenson, Garden City, 1942, illus by Pelagie Doane, VG (VG dust jacket), S12 ....$75.00

Child's Geography of the World, Appleton, revised edition, 1951, tan cloth, 451 pgs, VG (VG dust jacket), S12.$20.00

Children's Stories in American History, London, 1886, 1st edition, gilt emb leather, 356 pgs, EX $35.00

Chitty-Chitty Bang-Bang, Ian Fleming, 1972, 3rd printing, paperback, EX, P3 ....$3.00

Christmas Book, Norman Rockwell, Abrams, 1977, 1st edition, wht boards, 222 pgs, VG (VG pictorial dust jacket), S12..$15.00

Christmas Stories, Story Lady Series, 1920, 2nd edition, illus by Frederic Richardson, 94 pgs, VG+ (G dust jacket), S12...$40.00

Cinderella's Ball Gown, Tiny Golden Books/Walt Disney Collection #9, early 1980s, M, S2 ....$5.00

Cornelli, Johanna Spyri, Lippincott, 1920, illus by Maria L Kirk, blk emb cloth, pictorial end papers, 275 pgs, VG, S12 .$15.00

Cotton in My Sack, Lippincott, 1949, 1st edition, illus by Lois Lenski, 191 pgs, VG...$50.00

Country ABC, Oxford University Press, ca 1940, hardbound, 52 pgs, VG $30.00

Curious George Flies a Kite, 1958, paperback, VG, P3.......$4.00

Curious George Gets a Medal, 1957, paperback, EX, P3 ....$5.00

Dark Shadows, In a Funny Vein, 1969-70, paperback, NM, C1 ....$18.00

Dick & Jane & Our New Friends, Scott Foresman, 1946, 191 pgs, VG+ $48.00

Dionne Years, Pierre Berton, Toronto, 3rd printing, 232 pgs, VG (VG dust jacket) $10.00

Discovery 64: Let's Discover Cats Story Book, Saalfield, 1964, 20 pgs, NM, T2 ....$8.00

Doctor Dolittle's Garden, Hugh Lofting, Stokes, 1927, 1st edition, 237 pgs, VG+ $75.00

Donald Duck Book, 1935, blk & wht illus w/1 color plate, hardbound, EX+, A..$146.00

Donald's Lucky Day, Walt Disney, 1939, illus, EX+, A....$98.00

Dopey & the Wicked Witch, Tiny Golden Books/Walt Disney Collection #10, early 1980s, M, S2 ....$5.00

Eddie & the Fire Engine, New York, 1949, 1st edition, illus by Carolyn Haywood, 189 pgs, VG $5.00

Fairy Stories, Merrill, 1953, color illus, 10x13", EX+, T2.$20.00

Felix Et Riri, French volume by Hachette, 1933, illus by Pat Sullivan, cloth-bound pictorial wrapper, NM, A..........$103.00

Fighting Man of Mars, Edgar Rice Burroughs, illus by Hugh Hutton, 319 pgs, VG (VG dust jacket), S12 ....$50.00

First Men to the Moon, Holt, 1960, 1st edition, illus by Fred Freeman, 96 pgs, VG+ (G+ dust jacket), S12............$25.00

Flicka's Friend, Mary O'Hara, 1982, 284 pgs, NM (NM dust jacket) $10.00

Gidget, Bantam, 1957, Sandra Dee photo cover, VG, D9 ..$3.00

Gidget Goes Hawaiian, Bantam, 1961, Deborah Walley head shot on cover, EX+, D9 ....$6.00

Girl From UNCLE, Birds of a Feather Affair, Signet, 1966, Stephanie Powers on cover, EX, D9 ....$6.00

Good Grief, Pharos, 1989, 1st edition, illus by Charles M Schulz, 256 pgs, EX+ (EX+ dust jacket) $10.00

Heidi, Johanna Spyri, Lippincott, 1919, illus by Maria Kirk, 14 color plates, 319 pgs, VG...$65.00

Jack & the Beanstalk, Duenewald Printing, 1944, mechanical w/pull tabs, NM $60.00

Jetsons' Sunday Afternoon on the Moon, Durabook, 1972, NM, C1...$15.00

Jo's Boys, Louisa May Alcott, Roberts Bros, 1886, 1st edition, VG+ $125.00

Jolly Old Shadow Man, Gertrude Kay, Volland, 1st edition, 1920, pictorial boards, VG, S12 ....$40.00

Laddie, Evelyn Whitaker, Altemus, 1903, illus by Bradley & Brill, pk, gr & blk emb on orange cloth, VG, S12 .....$10.00

Laugh-In, paperback, EX, J2 ....$10.00

Little Red Engine Gets a Name, Faber & Faber, ca 1940, 32 pgs, VG (VG dust jacket) $15.00

Little Red Hen, Macmillan, 1928, illus by Elmer Hader, VG+...$30.00

Little Workers ABC, McLoughlin Bros, 1901, 1st edition, ea letter chromolithograph illus, G+, S12 ....$290.00

Littlest Rebel, Random House, 1939, Shirley Temple Edition, movie photos, 214 pgs, VG (G+ dust jacket), S12 ....$25.00

Lone Ranger Hi-Yo Silver Story Book, 1938, lg, C10 ....$325.00

Lost in Space, Pyramid, 1967, paperback, VG+, C1 ....$15.00

Luck of the Ducks (Donald Duck), 1969, hardbound, VG, S2 ....$15.00

Maggie Simpson's Alphabet Book, Counting Book, Book of Colors & Shapes & Book of Animals, Harper, set of 4, M, K1 ....$18.00

Man Who Was Magic, Paul Gallico, New York, 1966, 1st edition, VG (VG dust jacket) $10.00

Mary Poppins Come Back, Reynal & Hitchcock, 1935, 1st American edition, illus by Mary Shepard, 268-pg, VG (dust jacket) $50.00

Mickey Fait Du Camping, 1933, features French Disney comic strips, hardbound, 32 pgs, EX+, A $65.00

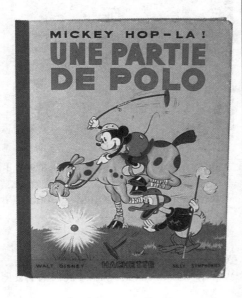

Mickey Mouse, Une Partie De Polo, French edition by Hachette, Walt Disney, rare, $1,500.00.

Mickey Mouse Fire Brigade, British, 1936, illus, hardbound, EX, A $80.00

Mickey Mouse Stories, Walt Disney Studios, 1937, blk & wht illus, EX, A..$72.00

Mickey Mouse Story Book, McKay, 1931, blk & wht illus, 62 pgs, 8", EX, A...$70.00

Mickey's New Car, Tiny Golden Books/Walt Disney Collection #4, early 1980s, M, S2.................................$5.00

Mother Carey's Chickens, Kate Douglas Wiggin, Houghton, 1st edition, 1911, illus by Alice B Stephens, 356 pgs, VG, S12 ....$25.00

Mother Goose, Franklin Watts, 1965, 1st American edition, 80 pgs, VG (VG dust jacket)............................$30.00

Mother Goose, Her Best-Known Rhymes, Saalfield, 1st edition, 1933, illus by Fern Bisel Peat, VG (G+ dust jacket), S12..$55.00

Mother Goose Story Book, Winston Easy-To-Read Story Books, 1920, photo pasted on cover, 96 pgs, VG (G dust jacket), S12..$30.00

Munsters, 1964, paperback, EX+, C1 ....$27.00

Muppet Show Bill, Jim Henson, Random House, 1982, 1st edition, 29 pgs, NM $8.00

My Pets, World, 1929, Mammoth series, 200 pgs, pictorial boards, EX (G dust jacket) $25.00

Neverending Story, Michael Ende, Doubleday, 1983, 1st edition, 396 pgs, NM (VG+ dust jacket)....................$40.00

Night Before Christmas, Clement Moore, Lippincott, 1st American edition, illus by Rackham, NM (G+ dust jacket) $185.00

Nobody's Perfect Charlie Brown, Fawcett, 1969, paperback, EX+, P3 ....$5.00

Old Old Tales Retold, Volland, 1923, 1st Volland edition, illus by Frederick Richardson, G, S12.................$55.00

Our Old Nursery Rhymes, 1911, H Willebeek LeMair illus, EX, P3 ....$40.00

Pablo the Penguin Takes a Trip, Tiny Golden Books/Walt Disney Collection #6, early 1980s, M, S2.................$5.00

Pan & His Pipes & Other Tales for Children, Victor Talking Machine Co, 1916, 10 stories, 80 pgs, VG, S12.........$15.00

Peter the Goat, David McKay, 1940, illus by Diana Thorne, VG (G dust jacket)..$25.00

Pets, McClure Phillips, 1906, 1st edition, illus by AB Frost, cream cloth, 47 pgs, VG, S12...........................$35.00

Pew Wee's Playhouse, Big Top Pee Wee, M, S2 ....$15.00

Porky Pig's Duck Hunt, Saalfield, 1938, 12 pgs, VG, A .$198.00

Puss in Boots, Macmillan, 1937, illus by Frank Dobias, NM $30.00

Raggedy Ann & Andy & the Nice Fat Policeman, 1st edition, 1942, illus by Worth Gruelle, 95 pgs, VG, S12..........$50.00

Raggedy Ann in Cookie Land, Johnny Gruelle, Volland, 1931, 1st edition, 95 pgs, VG $85.00

Raggedy Ann's Wishing Pebble, Johnny Gruelle, Volland, 25th edition, 1925, G-, $20.00.

Red Feather, Grosset & Dunlap, Little Indian Series, 1934, 126 pgs, VG+ (G dust jacket), S12 ....$35.00

Rescuers Save a Penny, Tiny Golden Books/Walt Disney Collection #2, early 1980s, M, S2 ....$5.00

Rip Van Winkle, Washington Irving, Abingdon, 1969, 40 pgs, VG+ (VG dust jacket).....................................$10.00

Roy Rogers Adventures No 3, Dean, hardbound, VG, A .$30.00

Runaway Robot Book, Scholastic Book Services, 1965, paperback, VG+, T2......................................$12.00

Scooby Doo & the Case of the Counterfeit Money, Rand McNally, 1976, hardbound, EX+, P3 ....$5.00

Simpsons Poster Book, Button-Up, includes 8 different tear-out posters, 11½x16½", M, K1......................$5.00

Sleepy-Time Stories, Putnam, 16th printing, illus by Maud Humphrey, gilt & blk on gold cloth, 177 pgs, VG, S12 ....$35.00

Smitty at the Ballgame, Cupples & Leon, 1929, features Smitty w/Babe Ruth, hardbound, some wear, A......................$135.00

Snuggy Bedtime Stories, Stokes, 1906, 1st edition, Christmas Stocking Series, 126 pgs, G, S12 ....$45.00

Starsky & Hutch, Volume 1 or 2, VG, paperback, S2, ea...$7.50

Stories for Little Curly Locks, Dutton, 1885, illus, picture pasted on gr cloth, VG, S12 ....$30.00

Stuart Little, Harper & Bros, 1945, 1st edition, illus by Garth Williams, 131 pgs, VG......................$75.00

Sunbonnet Babies in Mother Goose Land, Eulalie Grover, Rand McNally, 1928, later printing, 115 pgs, G+ $60.00

Supergirl Storybook, GP Putnam's Sons, 1984, color photos from the movie, EX, D9......................$3.00

Swiss Family Robinson, T.H. Robinson illustrator, Garden City, EX, $27.50.

Tall Book of Fairy Tales, Harper, 1947, illus by William Sharp, 124 pgs, VG (G+ dust jacket), S12 ....$20.00

Tarzan of the Apes, Grosset & Dunlap, 1927, red cloth, 392 pgs, VG (G+ dust jacket illus by Fred J Arting), S12 ....$75.00

Teddy Bear & Other Songs, AA Milne, Dutton, 1926, 1st American edition, illus by EH Shepard, w/music, G+ (G dust jacket) $75.00

Television Book of Hopalong Cassidy & His Young Friend Danny, Bonnie Book, 1950, moving pictures on cover, NM+, A $55.00

Three Little Pigs, David McKay, illus by John R Neill, VG+ .$45.00

Three Little Pigs Fool a Wolf, Tiny Golden Books/Walt Disney Collection #7, M, S2......................$5.00

Tin Soldier, McLoughlin Bros, 1945, full-pg illus, 36 pgs, EX, (VG dust jacket) $10.00

Tiny Golden Book Library, 1980, 12 books in figural bookcase box, M, S2......................$35.00

Tortoise & the Hare, 1935, hardbound, VG, J5......................$25.00

Treasure Book of Best Stories, Saalfield, 1939, illus, hardbound, EX+, P3......................$25.00

Treasure Things, Volland, 1st edition, 1922, 35 pgs, VG, S12......................$45.00

Tucked-In Tales, Rand McNally, 1939, illus by Clarence Biers, VG......................$20.00

Uncle Wiggily's Woodland Games, Howard Garis, 1922, 3 stories, color illus by Lang Cambell, hardbound, scarce, EX, A .$45.00

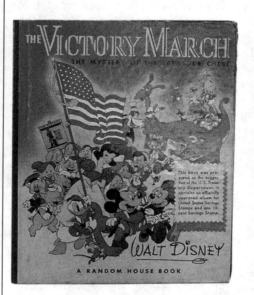

The Victory March, The Mystery of the Treasure Chest, Walt Disney, Random House, movable features on pages, 1942, C12, $575.00.

Walt Disney's Living Desert, Simon & Schuster, 1954, illus from movie, 124 pgs, VG $10.00

Water Babies, Charles Kingsley, London, 8 color plates, 246 pgs, NM......................$75.00

White Sparrow, Macmillan, 1933, 1st edition, illus by Lynd Ward, 46 pgs, VG (G dust jacket)......................$45.00

Wizard of Oz, 1950, hardbound, VG, S2......................$25.00

Woody Woodpecker, Xerox Pub, 1971, softbound, EX, P3..$4.00

Breyer

Breyer collecting seems to be growing in popularity, and though the horses dominate the market, the company also made dogs, cats, farm animals, wildlife figures, dolls, and tack and accessories such as barns for their models. They've been in continuous production since the 1950s, all strikingly beautiful and lifelike in both modeling and color. Earlier models were glossy, but since 1968 a matte finish has been used, though glossy and semi-glossy colors are now being re-introduced, especially in special runs. (A special run of Family Arabians was done in the glossy finish in 1988.) Condition and rarity are the most important worth-assessing factors.

Advisor: Carol Karbowiak Gilbert (G6) (author of several Breyer articles and a book that will be released in 1996).

Action American Appaloosa Stock Horse Foal #238, 1987-88, EX......................$4.00

Adios #50, matte bay, VG $25.00
Appaloosa Stock Horse Foal #238, 1984-86, EX..............$15.00
Appaloosa Stock Horse Stallion #232, 1981-87, VG $16.00

Bear Cub, #308, brown-faced version, 1967-73, 5", $25.00; Bear, #306 (mother bear), brown-faced version, 1967-73, 11", $35.00.

Bitsy Breyer & Quarter Horse Western Set #105, 1983-87, EX $10.00
Black Angus Bull #72, glossy, 1958-95, EX......................$30.00
Bloodhound #325, matte brn, EX................................$100.00
Brahma Bull #70, glossy, 1958-95, EX.........................$30.00
Brighty (burro) #375, matte gray, EX.........................$30.00
Bucking Bronco #190, matte blk, VG $45.00
Cips #116, matte bay pinto, VG...............................$30.00
Donkey #81, matte silver gray, EX $15.00
Elephant #391, matte gray, EX................................$15.00
Family Arabian Foal #9, glossy alabaster, VG $15.00
Family Arabian Stallion #4, lt chestnut, EX $15.00
Family Arabian Stallion #7, glossy alabaster, VG $20.00
Family Arabian Stallion #8, glossy alabaster, VG $25.00
Fighting Stallion #33, matte orange palomino, VG..........$80.00
Foundation Stallion #64, matte blk, EX........................$25.00
Grazing Foal #151, blk, EX....................................$50.00
Grazing Mare #143, matte palomino, VG.......................$40.00
Hanoverian #58, matte bay, VG $40.00
Hobo w/stand #625, matte buckskin, EX $40.00
Jasper Hog #355, matte gray & wht, EX.......................$10.00
Jumping Horse 'Stonewall' #300, jumping over wall, 1965-88, EX...$29.00
Kelso #601, 1988, MIB $29.00
Lady Phase #40, 1976-85, VG+..................................$25.00
Lassie #66, matte brn & wht, VG..............................$90.00
Legionario III Famous Andalusian #68, 1982, MIB..........$25.00
Lying Down Foal #166, buckskin, 1966-74, EX $35.00
Lying Foal #165, matte blk appaloosa, VG $15.00
Lying Foal #166, matte buckskin, VG..........................$35.00
Lying Foal #167, matte red roan, VG..........................$80.00
Lying Unicorn #245, matte alabaster, VG $25.00
Man O' War #47, 1967-95, EX..................................$16.00
Modernistic Doe #102, matte gold, VG $90.00

Morganglanz #59, matte sorrel, VG, ...$25.00
Mother Bear #306, 1967-73, EX................................$35.00
Mustang #87, matte buckskin, VG $25.00
Old Timer #205, gray gelding w/harness, blinders & hat, glossy, EX...$25.00
Pony of the Americas, matte leopard appaloosa (6-spot version), VG $40.00
Prancing Arabian Stallion #812, lt chestnut, 1988, MIB $31.00
Prong Antelope #310, matte brn, EX $90.00
Proud Arabian Foal #15, glossy bay, old mold, VG...........$40.00
Proud Arabian Mare #215, 1972-88, EX $22.00
Racehorse #36, w/saddle, glossy chestnut, VG.................$80.00
Rearing Stallion #183, matte palomino, VG $20.00
Rin-Tin-Tin #64, matte brn & wht, VG.........................$90.00
Running Foal #131, matte lt smoky gray, VG..................$40.00
Running Mare #124, matte bay, EX $45.00
Stock Horse Foal #224, matte buckskin, EX $18.00
Stretch Morgan #48, matte blk, VG............................$25.00
Suckling Foal from set #3155, matte lt chestnut, 1973-85, EX $23.00
Texas Longhorn Bull #75, 1961-89 (no model made in 1962), EX...$23.00
Touch of Class #420, matte bay, VG...........................$24.00

Trakehner, #54, 1979-84, semi-gloss and matte variations, $30.00.

Unicorn #210, matte alabaster, VG $35.00
Western Horse #56, orange palomino w/tack, VG $55.00
Western Prancer #115, 1961-63, EX $50.00
Yellow Mount #51, 1970-87, EX $30.00

Bubble Bath Containers

Since back in the 1960s when the Colgate-Palmolive Company produced the first Soaky, hundreds of different characters and variations have been marketed, bought on demand of the kids who saw these characters day to day on TV by parents willing to try anything that might make bathtime more appealing.

Purex made their Bubble Club characters, and Avon and others followed suit. Most Soaky bottles came with detachable heads made of brittle plastic which cracked easily. Purex bottles were made of a softer plastic but tended to loose their paint. Remember, value is affected to a great extent by condition.

Advisor: Jon Thurmond (T1).

Alvin (Chipmunks), 1960s, on stack of books, VG..........$15.00
Baloo, EX, O1, from $15 to $25.00
Bamm-Bamm, VG, O1 ....$25.00
Bambi, EX $30.00
Barney Rubble, 1976, empty, MIB $25.00
Batman, Avon, MIB $25.00
Batman, Soaky, VG, O1 ....$50.00
Beatles, Paul McCartney, G $75.00
Beatles, Paul McCartney, VG $85.00
Beatles, Ringo Starr, EX, O1 ....$110.00

Bozo the Clown, VG, O1, from $20.00 to $28.00.

Broom Hilda, VG..$35.00
Brutus, VG $45.00
Bugs Bunny, Colgate-Palmolive, rubber, 8", missing plug o/w NM, C1 ....$27.00
Bugs Bunny, leaning against egg, VG........................$15.00
Bugs Bunny, w/striped scarf, VG, from $10 to............$15.00
Bugs Bunny, wearing tux, 50th Anniversary, M $10.00
Bullwinkle, 1960s, M $35.00
Casper the Friendly Ghost, VG, from $30 to $35.00
Cecil, 1950, bright gr, 8", NM+, from $30 to..............$35.00
Cinderella, 1960s, movable arms, bl dress, NM, from $30 to $35.00
Creature From the Black Lagoon, NM $95.00
Deputy Dawg, EX, from $20 to $25.00
Dick Tracy, minor pnt wear....................................$35.00
Donald Duck, VG, O1 ....$20.00
Donald Duck, 1960s, 1-pc version, NM $20.00
Dopey, VG, from $20 to $25.00
Dum Dum, VG, from $20 to.....................................$25.00
Elmer Fudd, VG $25.00

Felix the Cat, red, VG $35.00
Frankenstein, VG, O1, from $80 to...........................$85.00
Fred Flintstone, VG, O1 ....$20.00
Girl Mousketeer, VG $30.00

Goofy, Colgate Soaky, M on original cardboard base, O1, $40.00.

Goofy, VG, O1, from $12 to.....................................$18.00
Gumby, Perma Toy, No More Tears, 1987, 9½", M (sealed), S2..$20.00
Jiminy Cricket, VG..$15.00
King Louie, VG $25.00
Linus, Avon, 1970s, some pnt wear, G, S2 ....$15.00
Lippy the Lion, Purex, 1960s, EX $55.00
Mickey Mouse, band leader, VG $20.00
Mickey Mouse, w/red shirt, VG................................$20.00
Mighty Mouse, Colgate-Palmolive, VG $20.00
Mighty Mouse, full body, 1963, VG..........................$25.00
Mighty Mouse, 1965, VG $25.00
Morocco Mole, VG..$20.00
Mr Jinx w/Pixie & Dixie, Colgate-Palmolive, 1963, Mr Jinx hugs Pixie & Dixie, 10", NM $25.00
Mr Magoo, VG, O1, from $20 to...............................$26.00
Mummy, VG $125.00
Mush Mouse, EX, from $45 to $50.00
Muskie, 1960s, red & yel, VG $25.00
Pebbles, VG, O1 ....$25.00
Peter Potamus, Purex, NM $20.00
Peter Potomus, Purex, w/orig paper tag, M................$25.00
Pinocchio, Amway, 1973, EX, from $15 to $20.00
Pinocchio, Soaky, 1960s, NM+ $20.00
Pokey (Gumby's friend), 1987, M (sealed), S2 ....$20.00
Popeye, Soaky, 1960s, EX $30.00
Porky Pig, VG $20.00
Princess Leia, see Star Wars category
Punkin' Puss, EX..$35.00
Punkin' Puss, full, w/tag, M....................................$50.00
Quick Draw McGraw, VG..$35.00
Ricochet Rabbit, VG $50.00
Robin (Batman), 9¾", VG.......................................$75.00
Robot, gold, VG, O1...$12.00

Rocky Squirrel, 1960s, M, from $25 to $30.00
R2-D2, see Star Wars category
Sailor, Avon, VG, O1 ....$10.00
Santa Claus, VG, from $8 to $15.00
Secret Squirrel, EX $45.00
Simon (Chipmunk), VG, O1 ....$20.00
Slimer (Ghostbusters), Ducair, 1988, M (sealed) $15.00
Smokey the Bear, 9", EX $25.00
Smokey the Bear, 9", VG $18.00
Snoopy, Avon, retains orig label, 5½", EX $10.00
Snow White, VG $25.00
Speedy Gonzales, bl & brn, VG, O1 ....$25.00
Spouty the Whale, w/orig paper tag, M $25.00
Squiddly Diddly (purple octopus), VG $50.00

Superman, Avon, 1978, 8", NM, S2, minimum value $35.00.

Superman, Soaky, VG $30.00
Tennessee Tuxedo, 1960s, EX $20.00
Tennessee Tuxedo, 1960s, VG, O1 ....$10.00
Theodore Chipmunk, VG, O1 ....$20.00
Thumper, VG $25.00
Top Cat, 1960s, standing on garbage can, yel, EX $30.00
Top Cat, 1960s, standing on garbage can, yel, NM, C1 ...$45.00
Touche Turtle, Purex, 1960s, M $35.00
Tweety Bird, on cage, VG $25.00
Tweety Bird, on stump, VG $25.00
Wendy Witch, minor pnt wear o/w EX $35.00
Wolf, VG, O1 ....$45.00
Wolfman, VG, O1, from $75 to $95.00
Woody Woodpecker, VG, O1, from $15 to $25.00
Yakky Doodle Duck, 1976, full, MIP, S2 ....$35.00
Yakky Doodle Duck, 1976, w/orig paper tag, M $25.00
Yogi Bear, VG $25.00

Buddy L

First produced in 1921, Buddy L toys have escalated in value over the past few years until now early models in good original condition (or restored, for that matter) often bring prices well into the four figures when they hit the auction block. The business was started by Fred Lundahl, founder of Moline Pressed Steel Co., who at first designed toys for his young son, Buddy. They were advertised as being 'Guaranteed Indestructible,' and indeed they were so sturdy and well built that they just about were. Until wartime caused a steel shortage, they were made of heavy gauge pressed steel. Many were based on actual truck models; some were ride-ons, capable of supporting a grownup's weight. Fire trucks with hydraulically activated water towers and hoisting towers that actually worked kept little boys entertained for hours. After the war, the quality of Buddy Ls began to decline, and wood was used to some extent. Condition is everything. Remember that unless the work is done by a professional restorer, overpainting and amateur repairs do nothing to enhance the value of a toy in poor condition. Professional restorations may be expensive, but they may be viable alternatives when compared to the extremely high prices we're seeing today. In the listings that follow, toys are all pressed steel unless noted.

See also Advertising; Boats.

AIRPLANES

Catapult Airplane, orange & blk w/decal, 2-door hangar, lever opens door & catapults 7" plane, EX $900.00
Double Airplane Hangar #5010, 1930-31, tan w/dbl-hinged doors & red trim, 20¼", VG $358.00
Monocoupe w/Hangar #2007, 1930-31, bl w/orange wings, decal on fuselage, dbl doors, 12¼", G $715.00

CARS AND BUSSES

Bonnet Bus, olive gr w/gold trim, doors open, solid body, 29", pnt chips & wear, A $2,200.00
Convertible #471, wood w/maroon pnt, wood wheels, NP hubcaps & headlights, trunk opens, top retracts, 18¾", G $220.00
Convertible #499, wood w/metallic bl pnt, Bakelite wheels, NP grille & electric lights, ivory roof retracts, 18", VG.$825.00
Express Bus #209 Coach, gr w/all decals, 29", some corrosion, VG $2,900.00
Flivver Roadster, blk w/spoked balloon tires, orig decal, 11", dull old partial rpt, G, A $525.00
Greyhound Bus #481, wood w/ivory, bl & gray pnt, wood wheels w/chrome hubcaps, metal trim, 18¼", G $550.00
Greyhound Bus #855, w/up w/battery-op light, bl & wht, door opens, bell rings, 16½", VG (orig box) $325.00
Long Distance Bus, orig gr now has gr rpt, steers & doors open, 28½", G- $1,450.00
Scarab #211, 1941, red w/plated bumper, headlights & hood trim, decals on sides, unpowered, 10½", M $495.00
Station Wagon, pnt wood & paper-covered plywood 'Woody' type, 18½", windshield rpl, other pcs touched up, G-, A $90.00
Town & Country Convertible, pnt & varnished wood w/flip-back wood top, 18½", door hdls missing, scratches, G, A $75.00

CONSTRUCTION

Concrete Mixer, gray, working cranks, brass spigot on tanks, 14½", pnt loss & rust, G, A $450.00

Contractor's Dump Truck, 1920s, 11", minor pnt wear o/w EX $1,150.00

Derrick #240, 1921-32, red on spoked CI blk base, 13" w/20" boom, needs restringing, G $550.00

Dredge on Treads, blk & red, 33", sides of treads sanded for rpt, minor rust & scratches o/w VG, A $3,800.00

Hoisting Tower #350, dk gr w/red, gold & blk decals, crank mechanism lowers chute, w/3 adjustable chutes, 38", EX+ $1,265.00

Pile Driver Car, black with red roof, paint loss, areas of rust, 18", G, A, $2,300.00; Improved Shovel, steam shovel on treads, black and red paint, 21", VG, A, $3,700.00.

Road Roller, steam type, gr & red w/some NP, 18½", steering broke, wht pnt spots on side, G, A $2,000.00

Sand Loader, dk gr & blk, chained mechanism, 18", pnt chips, minor rust on bucket & wheels o/w VG, A $210.00

Sand Screener, buckets on chain deposit dirt in hopper w/screen hand crank, 4 CI wheels, 22x24", pnt loss & wear, G $500.00

Steam Shovel #2205, 1930s, blk w/maroon roof, 24", mechanism needs rpr o/w VG+ $500.00

Traveling Overhead Crane, blk & red rpt, 45", pitting & scratches, G, A $950.00

Trench Digger, yel & red, working cranks, 19", rpt treads & rpl gears, VG, A $3,200.00

Wheeled Dredge, blk w/red roof, 32", pnt loss & pitting, no bucket, G, A $190.00

Wrecking Crane, blk w/red roof, 36", rstr, VG+, A........$575.00

FIREFIGHTING

Aerial Ladder Truck, red w/crank-type boom mechanism, 38", rstr, EX+, A $425.00

Aerial Ladder Truck, red w/hydraulic mechanism, 26", overall pitting, G-, A $210.00

Aerial Ladder Truck, 1935, open, 4-prong expanding ladder can be raised & lowered, turning front wheels, 37", EX $1,000.00

Aerial Ladder Truck Rider #27, 1933-34, red w/rubber tires, spring-powered mechanism, 29½", VG $1,210.00

Fire Chief Car, wood with metal bell, headlights and grille, ca 1940s, 18", VG, $700.00.

Fire Engine, red, 23", rust & wear, G-, A $600.00

Fire Hose & Water Pumper Truck, w/2 ladders & finger-actuated pump, 12", unused, rare, NM (G box), A $300.00

Fire Pumper #205A-B, 1929, red w/solid wheels, professional rstr, 23⅜", M......................................$1,705.00

Fire Truck, 1928, w/hose reel & 2 ladders, turning front wheels, bell & railings, all orig, 26" $1,265.00

Fire Water Tower, reaches 36" when activated hydraulically, grille belt, disk wheels, 46", VG......................$3,680.00

Ladder Truck, pnt wood, red & yel, extension ladder, 20", pnt chips o/w VG, A $130.00

Ladder Truck, swinging wrecker boom, 4 ladders, 25", pnt loss & rust, G-, A..$625.00

Water Tank Truck, bl cab w/red chassis & gr tank, rubber tires, steers & doors open, spigot works, 24", parts missing, G $575.00

OUTDOOR TRAINS

Ballast Car, blk, side opening doors, 21½", missing 1 coupler o/w VG, A $1,000.00

Boxcar, red, 21", no couplers, pnt chips & rust, G-, A ...$225.00

Boxcar, red, 21", no couplers o/w EX, A $950.00

Caboose, New Haven, red, 8 wheels, 19", rpl coupler, rust & pnt chips, G, A $650.00

Construction Car, red, tipping 4-wheel car, 10½", couplers damaged, decal fading & rust, G, A..........................$1,350.00

Flat Car, blk, 21", decal flaking o/w VG, A $800.00

Flat Car, red rpt, 20", rpl couplers o/w VG, A $110.00

Hopper Car, blk, 20½", minor decal loss o/w EX, A....$1,950.00

Improved Shovel, red & blk w/NP shovel, 21", rust, no couplers, G, A..$2,800.00

Locomotive & Tender, pnt steam-type 4-6-2 w/8-wheel tender, 33½", broken coupler o/w VG, A..........................$450.00

Locomotive & Tender, steam type, 43", VG, A $750.00

Overhead Car, blk & red, 45", areas of rpt & scratches o/w VG, A..$1,200.00

Passenger Coach #208, lt gr w/gold trim, dual rear wheels, steers & doors open, 29⅛", EX...............................$5,720.00

Round House #80, 1929-32, made for industrial train, dk gr w/decals, 3 bays, 1 side open, G- $110.00

Union Pacific Railroad, engine, tender & tanker, 59", rpt, few parts missing o/w G-VG $500.00

TRUCKS AND VANS

Air Force Missile Interceptor #5547, bl w/plastic launcher & missiles, 15", EX+ (EX box), A $220.00

Air Mail Truck #2004J, 1930-32, red w/blk cab, dual rear tires, headlights, sm pnt chips, EX $3,520.00

Air Mail Truck #68502, blk cab, red chassis, enclosed body, Firestone tires on red wheels, 22", P $660.00

Army Truck, olive drab w/silver grille, wood wheels, Army on cloth canopy, emb mks on sides, 17¼", EX...............................$130.00

Army Truck #342, wood, dk olive w/decal on hood, blk wheels w/red hubcaps, yel headlights, 12⅞", M (G box).....$250.00

Artillery Unit Half Track Truck, dk olive w/plated grille, plastic wheels, cannon w/spring mechanism, 13", NM.......$265.00

Baggage Truck #203B, 1927-29, blk cab w/red chassis & wheels, yel stake sides, 25⅞", worn wheel bushings, VG-.$2,090.00

Butterfingers/Baby Ruth, 1930s, yel & gr tractor, 2 yel & red trailers (9½x12"), G- $600.00

Circus Truck, Zoo-A-Rama, bl, plastic animals revolve in cage as truck advances, 'B' on hubcaps, 18", NM (EX box), A $270.00

Circus Truck #484, wood, red & yel cab, mc circus wagon, Bakelite wheels, decals w/animals, 24", MIB...............$1,815.00

City Dray #439, yel w/gr trim, electric headlights, IH-type grille, orig hand truck, 19⅜", EX $715.00

Coal Truck, missing part of chute, bent axle, needs rstr, rpt, 12x25½" $650.00

Contractor's Dump Truck, 1920s, dark green paint, red trim on wheels, 13", EX+, D10, $1,150.00.

Dairy Truck #2002J, 1930s, blk cab, gr stake sides, front bumper, rubber tires w/rear duals, doors open, 24", G $2,200.00

Delivery Truck, blk cab, dk gr body & red chassis, steers, 24½", 1 door missing o/w VG $325.00

Dump Truck, blk & red, open cab type w/cable rachet dump mechanism, 25", scratches & pitting, G-, A............$240.00

Dump Truck, brn & yel, yel grille, orange dump bed, decals on sides, 17¼", VG- $94.00

Dump Truck #201A, blk w/red chassis, hydraulic dump mechanism, 24", pitting & dents, G-, A...............................$850.00

Dump Truck #434, 1935, yel cab & chassis, red bed, NP grille, electric headlights, decals & emb mks, 19½", VG+ ..$195.00

Dump Truck #902 Rider, 1948, Type II, bl & wht, red wheels & rubber tread, 25⅞", bent axle, missing seat & hdl, VG...............................$825.00

Dump Truck Rider #34, orange, hydraulic mechanism, 20", EX, M5...............................$100.00

Dump Truck, 1930s, dark green with red bed and wheel trim, 22", EX, D10, $1,950.00.

Emergency Auto Wrecker #3317, bright yel w/red & gr decals, 12½", EX+ (EX+ box), A...............................$330.00

Express Line Van, gr & blk w/wht tires, 25", rstr, EX, A...$425.00

Express Truck, blk w/open cab & bed, drop tailgate, 24½", bent front axle, partial rpt, rear fenders detached, G, A..$300.00

Express Truck Tractor & Trailer #34, 1933, red & gr, electric headlights, complete w/orig batteries, 23⅝", EX+ ...$330.00

Flivver Pickup, blk Model T w/balloon tires, 12", pnt loss & rust, steering damaged, left front wheel detached, G-, A ..$425.00

Ford Model-T Roadster Pickup, blk w/silver & red spoke wheels, 12", EX, A...............................$800.00

Huckster Model-T Truck, working steering, 14½", right axle bent, lt pnt loss & rust, G $1,350.00

Ice Truck, blk w/yel bed, ice blocks & tongs, new canvas cover, 26", rstr, EX, A $600.00

Ice Wagon #12 Rider, blk cab w/yel body, red bumpers & wheels, removable saddle, decals, ice block, 27", no tongs, G.$990.00

International Dairy Transport, red & wht w/rubber tires, tandem trailer w/removable door, 25", G-, A $375.00

Little Elf Pickup, 1923-28, blk & red w/wood van body, missing radiator & ornament, worn pnt, sm, A...............................$1,155.00

Lumber Truck, blk & red, 24", missing 2 side panels & tailgate rail, pnt chips, VG, A $2,500.00

Mail Truck, blk body w/lt gr cage, red chassis, steers, 24½", 1 rear door missing, G...............................$275.00

Maintenance Truck #450, 1952, gr & gray, Telephone Maintenance decals, hard rubber tires, trailer/poles, NM (VG box) ...$935.00

Market Truck, wht & orange, plated grille, dummy headlights, Bakelite wheels (1 rpl), missing divider, 21⅝", EX....$66.00

McCormick-Deering Red Baby Express Truck, 1923, spoked aluminum wheels, decals, rpl fenders, 24", G............$2,310.00

Merry-Go-Round Truck, pnt body, wood & plastic revolving carousel, sm scratches, 12½", G...............................$55.00

Milk Truck, wood w/fiberboard sides, blk & red pnt, Buddy L Milk Farms decals, sliding doors, sm chips, 13⅛", VG...............................$465.00

Model-T Produce Truck, blk & maroon, full rooftop, turning front wheels, 14", rstr, M, A..................$1,150.00

Moving Van #366, 1945, wood, orange & blk, decals on sides & hood, 27⅝", sm pnt chips, 1 rpl hubcap, VG-..........$150.00

Moving Van #413, 1950s, red cab w/plated grille, removable cream van w/gray roof & decals, rubber tires, 20", VG+ $176.00

Oil Tanker, mid-1920s, blk w/red trim, orig pnt, 26", 90% decals, dents in rear fender, tap resoldered, no straps, A $1,150.00

Pickup Truck, 1920s, green with red trim on wheels, 12", EX, D10, $1,350.00.

Railway Express, milk ad on side, 22", EX, A $700.00

REA Railway Express Van #5532, gr, VG $125.00

Riding Academy Horse Van, late 1950s, missing horses & clear plastic dome, EX+..$60.00

Shell Pickup & Delivery, ca 1940s, yellow with Shell decals, plated grille, with Shell can bank, 13", EX, D10, $350.00.

Shell Pickup & Delivery, ca 1940s, yel w/Shell decals, plated grille, w/Shell can bank, 13", VG.............................$240.00

Speedster Rider, 1932, red w/NP IH-style grille, electric headlights, 18¾", missing saddle, EX $303.00

Supermarket Delivery Truck, wht, open truck w/mini grocery bags, 13", NM, A $300.00

Supermarket Delivery Truck, wht, open truck w/mini grocery bags, 13", pnt chips o/w VG, A $100.00

Tank Truck, gr & blk w/wht balloon tires, 25½", rstr, EX, A $600.00

Texaco Tanker, red w/plastic wheels, 24", pnt chips & wear, G, A $70.00

Truck, #803 Rider, 1945, bl & wht, dummy headlights, rubber tires w/duals, missing saddle, 23", EX $825.00

Truck, Jr Series, 1930s, closed cab, opening doors, headlights, rubber tires, closed box body, 22", total rpt, A $650.00

Truck, 1920s, blk w/logo stickers, made for peddling fruits/veggies, open bed w/top & side stakes, 14", EX..........$2,800.00

Truck #51 Rider, 1935, red w/NP grille, electric headlights, Bakelite wheels, 24½", missing saddle, rpl axle, G $1,100.00

Van Freight Carriers Cab & Trailer, red & cream w/blk rubber tires, 20", MIB, A $375.00

Wrecker, blk open cab w/red chassis, hook & crane, 12x25½", labels partially torn o/w EX...................................$1,700.00

Wrecker, late '40s, lt yel & brn, NP grille, dummy headlights, stamped & emb mks, blk wheels w/yel centers, G-....$99.00

Wrecker, red & bl cab, wht bed, blk wooden tires, orig rope & hook on hoist, 18", EX, A $210.00

Wrecker, 1933-34, red & wht w/blk & red rubber tires, sq cab, 2-tone radiator, electric headlights, 27", scarce, EX, A...$1,890.00

Wrecker #358, Type I, wood, brn & gr w/yel headlights & hubcaps, decals, w/hook, 17¾", missing crank hdl, VG+...$165.00

Wrecker #358, Type III, 1945, wood, brn & turq w/yel lights & hubcaps, orig tow hook, 18", split but complete, VG...$110.00

Building Blocks and Construction Toys

Toy building sets were popular with children well before television worked its mesmerizing influence on young minds; in fact, some were made as early as the end of the eighteenth century. Important manfacturers include Milton Bradley, Joel Ellis, Charles M. Crandall, William S. Tower, W.S. Read, Ives Manufacturing Corporation, S.L. Hill, Frank Hornby (Meccano), A.C. Gilbert Brothers, The Toy Tinkers, Gebruder Bing, R. Bliss, S.F. Fischer, Carl Brandt Jr., and F. Ad. Richter (see Richter Anchor Stone Building Sets). Whether made of wood, paper, metal, glass, or 'stone,' these toys are highly prized today for their profusion of historical, educational, artistic, and creative features.

Richter's Anchor (Union) Stone Building Blocks were the most popular building toy at the beginning of the twentieth century. As early as 1880, they were patented in both Germany and the USA. Though the company produced more than 600 different sets, only their New Series is commonly found today (these are listed below). Their blocks remained popular until WWI, and Anchor sets were one of the first toys to achieve international 'brand name' acceptance. They were produced both as basic sets and supplement sets (identified by letters A, B, C, or D) which increased a basic set to a higher level. There were dozens of stone block competitors, though none were very successful. During WWI the trade name Anchor was lost to A.C. Gilbert (Connecticut) who produced Anchor blocks for a short time. Richter responded by using the new trade name 'Union' or 'Stone Buiilding Blocks,' sets considered today to be Anchor blocks despite the lack of the Richter's Anchor trademark. The A.C. Gilbert Company also produced the famous Erector sets which were made from about 1913 through the late 1950s.

Note: Values for Richter's blocks are for sets in very good condition.

Advisors: Arlan Coffman (C4); George Hardy (H3), Richter's Building Blocks.

American Bricks, #715, sm set, EX, T1 ....$35.00
American Bricks, #725, lg set, EX, T1 ....$50.00
Block City, #B-150, sq box style, complete, EX, T1 ....$35.00
Capsela 400, motorized building toy, J6 ....$42.00
Dux, W Germany, Auto Dux 612, plastic & metal VW, blister
    packed, EX (orig box), A...$40.00

Erector #1, AC Gilbert, 1913, complete, EX, $550.00.

Erector, #4, 1938, EX (cb box), A.................................$120.00
Erector, #4½, 1935, EX (red tin box), A $55.00
Erector, #6½, EX, A $50.00
Erector, #7½, pressed steel, builds many different trucks, 28",
    w/instructions, EX (orig box), M5 ....$975.00
Erector, #8½, very clean, A $40.00
Erector, #8½, w/whistle, NMIB..$400.00
Erector, #10053, Rocket Launcher Set, A $40.00
Erector, Cape Canaveral, 1950s, w/instructions, EX (metal box),
    T1..$95.00
Erector, Cape Canaveral, 1960s, EX+(metal box), T1 ....$65.00
Erector, Powerline Set, w/motors, EX (orig box), T1 ....$35.00
Gothic Structures, SF Fisher, Germany, wooden building blocks,
    MIB, A $80.00
Halsam American Skyline, construction set, M (EX box), J6..$42.00
International Airports, girder & panel set, J5 ....$55.00

Kenner, Girder & Panel Set, sq cube, 1970s, VG, T1 ......$25.00
Lincoln Logs, JL Wright, 1930, dbl set, NMIB $90.00
Lincoln Logs, 1923, EX (EX box), J2 ....$50.00

Log Cabin Playhouse, Joel Ellis, Springfield, Vermont, ca 1865, wood with metal reinforcing bars, complete, EX, $750.00.

Meccano, Aeroplane Constructor, tin set complete w/instructions to
    build 3 prewar planes, 11" wingspan, M (EX+ box) ...$1,200.00
MT, Construction Electric Automobile, unassembled Volkswa-
    gen, tin, battery-op, 4½", EX+ (EX+ box), A..........$281.00
Schoenhut, Skyline Builder Kit #654, engine house, A ...$25.00
Wankel Rotary Engine, kit, MIB (sealed), J6....................$16.00

RICHTER ANCHOR STONE BUILDING SETS

DS, Set #E3, w/metal parts & roof stones, H3 ....$45.00
DS, Set #3A, w/metal parts & roof stones, H3................$50.00
DS, Set #5, w/metal parts & roof stones, H3 ....$100.00
DS, Set #5A, w/metal parts & roof stones, H3 ....$150.00
DS, Set #7, w/metal parts & roof stones, H3 ....$250.00
DS, Set #7A, w/metal parts & roof stones, H3 ....$175.00
DS, Set #9A, w/metal parts & roof stones, H3 ....$250.00
DS, Set #11, w/metal parts & roof stones, H3 ....$675.00
DS, Set #11A, w/metal parts & roof stones, H3 ....$300.00
DS, Set #13A, w/metal parts & roof stones, H3 ....$325.00
DS, Set #15, w/metal parts & roof stones, H3 ....$1,300.00
DS, Set #15A, w/metal parts & roof stones, H3 ....$475.00
DS, Set #17A, w/metal parts & roof stones, H3 ....$475.00
DS, Set #19A, w/metal parts & roof stones, H3 ....$900.00
DS, Set #21A, w/metal parts & roof stones, H3 ....$975.00
DS, Set #23A, w/metal parts & roof stones, H3 ....$750.00
DS, Set #25A, w/metal parts & roof stones, H3 ....$1,300.00
DS, Set #27, w/metal parts & roof stones, H3 ....$5,000.00
Fortress Set #402, H3...$90.00
Fortress Set #402A, H3...$115.00
Fortress Set #404, H3...$200.00
Fortress Set #404A, H3...$275.00
Fortress Set #406, H3...$400.00
Fortress Set #406A, H3 ....$400.00
Fortress Set #408, H3...$800.00
Fortress Set #408A, H3...$800.00
Fortress Set #410, H3..$1,600.00
Fortress Set #410A, H3...$750.00
Fortress Set #412A, H3...$1,300.00

Fortress Set #414, H3 ....$3,650.00
GK-NF, Set #6, H3...$120.00
GK-NF, Set #6a, H3...$100.00
GK-NF, Set #8, H3...$220.00
GK-NF, Set #8A, H5..$100.00
GK-NF, Set #10, H3...$300.00
GK-NF, Set #10A, H3...$120.00
GK-NF, Set #12, H3...$500.00
GK-NF, Set #12A, H3...$195.00
GK-NF, Set #14A, H3...$200.00
GK-NF, Set #16, H3...$800.00
GK-NF, Set #16A, H3...$240.00
GK-NF, Set #18A, H3...$375.00
GK-NF, Set #20, H3 ....$1,400.00
GK-NF, Set #20A, H3...$450.00
GK-NF, Set #22A, H3...$450.00
GK-NF, Set #24A, H3...$500.00
GK-NF, Set #26A, H3...$1,125.00
GK-NF, Set #28, H3 ....$3,875.00
GK-NF, Set #28A, H3...$1,000.00
GK-NF, Set #30A, H3...$1,125.00
GK-NF, Set #32B, H3...$1,600.00
GK-NF, Set #34, H3 ....$6,000.00
GK-NK, Great-Castle, H3 ....$9,950.00
KK-NF, Set #5, H3 ....$45.00
KK-NF, Set #5A, H3 ....$55.00
KK-NF, Set #7, H3 ....$100.00
KK-NF, Set #7A, H3 ....$90.00
KK-NF, Set #9A, H3 ....$100.00
KK-NF, Set #11, H3 ....$275.00
KK-NF, Set #11A, H3 ....$275.00
KK-NF, Set #13A, H3 ....$300.00
KK-NF, Set #15A, H3 ....$450.00
KK-NF, Set #17A, H3 ....$750.00
KK-NF, Set #19A, H3 ....$1,500.00
KK-NF, Set #21, H3 ....$3,500.00
Modern House & Country House Set #206, H3 ....$600.00
Modern House & Country House Set #208, H3 ....$600.00
Modern House & Country House Set #210, H3 ....$600.00
Modern House & Country House Set #301, H3 ....$300.00
Modern House & Country House Set #301A, H3 ....$500.00
Modern House & Country House Set #303, H3 ....$800.00
Modern House & Country House Set #303A, H3 ......$2,000.00
Modern House & Country House Set #305, H3 ....$2,500.00
Neue Reihe, Set #102, H3 ....$75.00
Neue Reihe, Set #104, H3 ....$100.00
Neue Reihe, Set #106, H3 ....$150.00
Neue Reihe, Set #108, H3 ....$240.00
Neue Reihe, Set #110, H3 ....$425.00
Neue Reihe, Set #112, H3 ....$500.00
Neue Reihe, Set #114, H3 ....$800.00
Neue Reihe, Set #116, H3 ....$1,325.00

California Raisins

The California Raisins made their first TV commercials in

the fall of 1986. The first four PVC figures were introduced in 1987, the same year Hardee's issued similar but smaller figures, and three 5½" Bendees became available on the retail market. In 1988 twenty-one more Raisins were made for retail as well as promotional efforts in grocery stores. Four were graduates identical to the original four characters except standing on yellow pedestals and wearing blue graduation caps with yellow tassels. Hardee's increased their line by six.

In 1989 they starred in two movies: *Meet the Raisins* and *The California Raisins — Sold Out*, and eight additional characters were joined in figurine production by five of their fruit and vegetable friends from the movies. Hardee's latest release was in 1991, when they added still four more. All Raisins issued for retail sales and promotions in 1987 and 1988 (including Hardee's) are dated with the year of production (usually on the bottom of one foot). Of those released for retail sales in 1989, only the Beach Scene characters are dated, and these are actually dated 1988. Hardee's 1991 series are also undated. For more information, see *The Flea Market Trader, Revised Tenth Edition*, by Sharon and Bob Huxford.

Advisor: Larry DeAngelo (D3).

Beach Theme Edition, Girl Sitting on Sand, mk 1988 CALRAB, w/boom box & gr shoes, M $15.00

Photo courtesy of Larry DeAngelo.

Beach Theme Edition, Hula Girl, marked 1988 CALRAB, white gloves and yellow shoes, M, $15.00.

Beach Theme Edition, Male in Beach Chair, mk 1988 CALRAB, orange sandals & sunglasses, M................$17.00
Beach Theme Edition, Male w/Surfboard, mk 1988 CALRAB, wht gloves & yel sandals, M $15.00
Bendees, flat bodies, set of 3, M..$45.00
Christmas Issue, Candy Cane, mk 1988 CALRAB, gr glasses, red sneakers, holding candy cane, M $9.00
Christmas Issue, Santa, mk 1988 CALRAB, red cap, gr sneakers, M $9.00
First Commercial Issue, Guitar, mk 1988 CALRAB, red guitar, M $8.00
First Commercial Issue, Singer, mk 1988 CALRAB, microphone in left hand not connected to face, M $5.00
First Commercial Issue, Sunglasses 1, mk 1988 CALRAB, aqua glasses glued on, eyes visible, M..............................$16.00

First Commercial Issue, Sunglasses 2, mk 1988 CALRAB, aqua sunglasses molded on, eyes can't be seen, M $6.00

First Commercial Issue, Winky, mk 1988 CALRAB, winking, right hand in hitchhike position, M...........................$5.00

First Key Chains, Hands, mk 1987 CALRAB, both hands up, thumbs touch head, M..$7.00

First Key Chains, Microphone, mk 1987 CALRAB, right hand points up, microphone in left hand, M.........................$7.00

First Key Chains, Saxophone, mk 1987 CALRAB, gold sax, no hat, M...$7.00

First Key Chains, Sunglasses, mk 1987 CALRAB, orange glasses, index fingers touch face, M......................................$7.00

Graduate Key Chains, Hands, mk 1988 CALRAB Lic Applause Lic, both hands up, thumbs touch head, M.................$25.00

Graduate Key Chains, Microphone, mk 1988 CALRAB Lic Applause Lic, right hand points, left hand holds microphone, M...$25.00

Graduate Key Chains, Saxophone, mk 1988 CALRAB Lic Applause Lic, gold sax, no hat, M $25.00

Graduate Key Chains, Sunglasses, mk 1988 CALRAB Lic Applause Lic, orange glasses, index fingers touch face, M $25.00

Graduates From First Commercial Issue, Conga Dancer, mk 1988 CALRAB w/Clamation on bottom of yel plastic base, bl shoes, M...$35.00

Graduates From First Commercial Issue, Singer, mk 1988 CALRAB w/Clamation on bottom of yel plastic base, M..$35.00

Graduates From Post Raisin Bran Issue, Hands, mk 1988 CALRAB w/Clamation on bottom of yel plastic base, M..$35.00

Graduates From Post Raisin Bran Issue, Saxophone, mk 1988 CALRAB w/Clamation on bottom of yel base, M.....$35.00

Graduates From Post Raisin Bran Issue, Sunglasses, mk 1988 CALRAB w/Clamation on bottom of yel base, M.....$35.00

Hardee's 1st Promotion, Hands, mk 1987 CALRAB, both hands up, thumbs touch head, sm, M.....................................$3.00

Hardee's 1st Promotion, Microphone, mk 1987 CALRAB, right hand points up, microphone in left hand, sm, M.........$3.00

Hardee's 1st Promotion, Saxophone, mk 1987 CALRAB, gold sax, no hat, sm, M...$3.00

Hardee's 1st Promotion, Sunglasses, mk 1987 CALRAB, orange glasses, index fingers touch face, sm, M......................$3.00

Hardee's 2nd Promotion, Captain Toonz, mk Mfg Applause Inc 1988, bl boom box, yel glasses & sneakers, sm, M........$5.00

Hardee's 2nd Promotion, FF Strings, mk Mfg Applause Inc 1988, bl guitar, orange sneakers, sm, M...................................$5.00

Hardee's 2nd Promotion, Rollin' Rollo, mk Mfg Applause Inc 1988, roller skates, yel sneakers & hat mk H, sm, M ...$5.00

Hardee's 2nd Promotion, SB Stuntz, mk Mfg Applause Inc 1988, yel skateboard, bl sneakers, sm, M $5.00

Hardee's 2nd Promotion, Trumpy Trunote, mk Mfg Applause Inc 1988, w/trumpet, bl sneakers, sm, M $5.00

Hardee's 2nd Promotion, Waves Weaver, mk Mfg Applause Inc 1988, yel surfboard, red glasses & sneakers, sm, M.......$5.00

Hardee's 4th Promotion, Alotta Stile, mk 1992 CALRAB-Applause, shopping bags & violet heels, MIP (w/trading card) $15.00

Hardee's 4th Promotion, Alotta Stile, w/radio, M $7.00

Hardee's 4th Promotion, Anita Break, mk 1992 CALRAB-Applause, w/boom box & pk boots, MIP (w/trading card) $15.00

Hardee's 4th Promotion, Anita Break, w/shopping bags, M..$7.00

Hardee's 4th Promotion, Benny, mk 1992 CALRAB-Applause, w/bowling ball & bag, MIP (w/trading card) $15.00

Hardee's 4th Promotion, Benny, w/bowling ball, M $7.00

Hardee's 4th Promotion, Buster, mk 1992 CALRAB-Applause, blk & yel sneakers & skateboard, MIP (w/trading card)..$15.00

Hardee's 4th Promotion, Buster, w/skateboard, M $7.00

Meet the Raisins 1st Edition, Banana White, mk Clamation-Applause, issued May 1989, yel dress, M....................$15.00

Meet the Raisins 1st Edition, Lick Broccoli, mk Claymation-Applause, issued May 1989, gr & blk, red & orange guitar, M..$12.00

Meet the Raisins 1st Edition, Piano, mk CALRAB-Applause, issued May 1989, red hair, bl piano, gr sneakers, M...$15.00

Meet the Raisins 1st Edition, Rudy Bagaman, mk Clamation Applause, vegetable cigar, purple shirt, fliplops, M ...$15.00

Meet the Raisins 2nd Edition, AC, mk CALRAB-Applause, issued Sept 1989, 'Gimme-5' pose, tall pompadour, red sneakers, M $95.00

Meet the Raisins 2nd Edition, Cecil Thyme, mk Clamation-Applause, issued Sept 1989, orange carrot-like, M $85.00

Meet the Raisins 2nd Edition, Leonard Limabean, marked Clamation-Applause, issued September 1989, purple coat, blue hat, M, $85.00.

Meet the Raisins 2nd Edition, Mom, mk CALRAB-Applause, issued Sept 1989, yel hair, pk apron, M......................$85.00

Post Raisin Bran Issue, Hands, mk 1987 CALRAB, left hand points up, right hand points down, M $4.00

Post Raisin Bran Issue, Microphone, mk 1987 CALRAB, right hand in fist, microphone in left hand, M $4.00

Post Raisin Bran Issue, Saxophone, mk 1987 CALRAB, inside of sax pnt blk, M $4.00

Post Raisin Bran Issue, Sunglasses, mk 1987 CALRAB, orange glasses, right hand points up, left hand points down, M .$4.00

Sandwich Music Box, Hands, mk 1987 CALRAB, both hands out to side w/fingers pointing, M $25.00

Sandwich Music Box, Mircophone, mk 1987 CALRAB, both hands out as if to hug, M $25.00

Sandwich Music Box, Sunglasses, mk 1987 CALRAB, both hands out as if to hug, M $25.00

Second Commercial Issue, Bass Player, mk 1988 CALRAB-Applause, gray slippers, MIP (w/application to join fan club) $20.00

Second Commercial Issue, Drummer, mk 1988 CALRAB-Applause, w/blk hat w/yel feather, MIP (w/application to join fan club) $12.00

Second Commerical Issue, Girl w/Tambourine, Ms Delicious, mk 1988 CALRAB-Applause, yel shoes, holding tambourine, M $15.00

Second Key Chains, Hip Band Hip Guitarist (Hendrix), mk 1988 CALRAB-Applause, headband, yel guitar, sm, M...$25.00

Second Key Chains, Hip Band Microphone-Female, mk 1988 CALRAB-Applause, yel shoes & bracelet, sm, M $20.00

Second Key Chains, Hip Band Microphone-Male, mk 1988 CALRAB-Applause, left hand extended w/open palm, sm, M..$20.00

Second Key Chains, Hip Band Saxophone, mk 1988 CALRAB-Applause, blk beret, bl eyelids, sm, M $20.00

Special Edition, Michael, mk Lic By Applause Lic, silver microphone, stud belt, M..$20.00

Special Lovers Issue, Female, mk 1988 CALRAB-Applause, issued Oct 1988, holding Be Mine heart, M $8.00

Special Lovers Issue, Male, mk 1988 CALRAB-Applause, issued Oct 1988, holding I'm Yours heart, M $8.00

Special Raisin Club Issue, Tambourine Female, mk 1988 CALRAB-Applause, gr shoes & bracelet, tambourine held down, M...$15.00

Third Commercial Issue, Hip Band Hip Guitarist (Hendrix), mk 1988 CALRAB-Applause, headband, yel guitar, M ..$25.00

Third Commercial Issue, Hip Band Microphone-Female, mk 1988 CALRAB-Applause, yel shoes & bracelet, M.....$9.00

Third Commercial Issue, Hip Band Microphone-Male, mk 1988 CALRAB-Applause, left hand extended w/open palm, M...$9.00

Third Commercial Issue, Hip Band Saxophone, mk 1988 CALRAB-Applause, blk beret, bl eyelids, M.............$15.00

Unknown Promotion, Blue Surfboard, marked 1987 CALRAB, same as Sunglasses, but board in right hand, not connected to foot, M, $50.00.

Photo courtesy of Larry DeAngelo.

Unknown Promotion, Blue Surfboard, mk 1988 CALRAB, same as 1987 issue but w/vertical board connected to right foot, M $35.00

MISCELLANEOUS

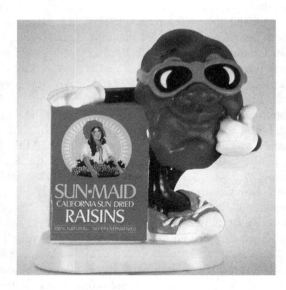

Bank, Sun Maid Raisin in orange sunglasses and sneakers stands beside box, marked 1987 CALRAB, 7½", $25.00.

Backpack, turq w/3 girls on stage, MIP, S2 ....$55.00

Big Red Box, w/figure, crayons, games, etc, Sunmaid mail-in premium, rare, MIB (sealed), S2 ....$175.00

Board Game, cb fold-out board w/dice & figures, etc, Post Rasin Bran premium, M...$25.00

Bookmarkers, set of 10, D3 ....$25.00

Chalkboard, w/either Jazz Band or Beach Scene, 16½", M (sealed), S2, ea...$35.00

Clay Factory Mold & Paint Set, M (worn box), S2 ....$30.00

Coin Purse, unlicensed, figural, w/or w/out sunglasses, EX, S2, ea $20.00

Colorforms, 1987, MIB $15.00

Coloring or Children's Books, 4 different, S2, ea.............$20.00

Comic Books, #1 or #2, MIP, S2, ea.................................$30.00

Computer Game, IBM 'DOS,' The Raisins Get Kidnapped, MIB, D3...$25.00

Corkboard, w/either Jazz Band or Beach Scene, 11", M (sealed), S2, ea...$25.00

Display Box, for Christmas figures, M, S2 ....$55.00

Display Box, for Michael Jackson figures, M, S2 ....$75.00

Display Box, for stickers, w/some stickers & book (partially filled), S2 ....$30.00

Display Box, top only, for At the Beach plush figures, M, S2 ....$25.00

Display Figure, Vac-U-Form, lg pink stage w/bl drapes, NM, D3/S2 ....$150.00

Flicker Cards, set of 4, M, S2...$25.00

Kite, octopus style, 6½", MIP, S2 ....$35.00

Lapel Pins, set of 3, MOC, S2 ....$100.00

Mask, AC, unlicensed, full head, rare, S2 ....$150.00

Mirror Clip-On Figure, unlicensed, S2............................$35.00
Painter's Cap, EX, S2..$25.00
Photo & Autograph Album for School Friends, 8" sq, rare, S2 ....$50.00
Poster, California Raisin Band, 22x28", M, D3..................$8.00
Radio, figural, AM-FM, MIB, D3, from $150 to.............$175.00
Refrigerator Magnets, mk 1988 CALRAB-Applause, set of 4, M..$60.00
Seat Shirt, super-sz T-shirt that covers car seat or lounge chair, rare, MIB, S2..$75.00
Stadium Cups, set of 3, Tiny Good Bite, Justin X Grape & Ben Inda Sun, M, D3...$10.00
Stickers, puffy type, MIP, S2 ....$10.00

Video, Meet the Raisins, Atlantic Video, MIB, $30.00.

Wall Clock, wristwatch shape, aqua, 36", NM, S2 ....$95.00
Watch, flip-top, female figure w/yel shoes & tambourine, MIP, S2..$75.00
Watch, flip-top, male singer w/hands raised, MIP, S2 ......$60.00
Watch, flip-top, male w/fingers pointing inward, MIP, S2 .$60.00
Watch, w/interchangable band, includes bumper sticker & newsletter, fan club premium, M (orig mailer), S2..$150.00
Welcome Mat, woven type w/Jazz band, rare, M, S2 ......$115.00

Candy Containers

As early as 1876, candy manufacturers used figural glass containers to package their candy. They found the idea so successful that they continued to use them until the 1960s. The major producers of these glass containers were Westmoreland, West Bros., Victory Glass, J.H. Millstein, J.C. Crosetti, L.E. Smith, and Jack and T.H. Stough. Some of the most collectible and sought after today are the character-related figurals such as Amos 'n Andy, Barney Google, Santa Claus, and Jackie Coogan, but there are other rare examples that have been known to command prices of $1,000.00 and more. Some of these are Black Cat for Luck, Black Cat Sitting, Quick Firer Cannon (with original carriage), and Mr. Rabbit with Hat (that books for $1,800.00

even in worn paint). There are many reproductions; know your dealer. For a listing of these reproductions, refer to *Schroeder's Antiques Price Guide* by Sharon and Bob Huxford.

'L' numbers in the listings that follow refer to *An Album of Candy Containers, Vols 1 and 2,* by Jennie Long; 'E&A' numbers correlate with *The Compleat American Glass Candy Containers Handbook* by Eikelberner and Agadjanian, revised by Adele Bowden.

Advisor: Doug Dezso (D6).

For other types of candy containers, see Halloween; Pez Dispensers; Santa Claus.

Airplane, Spirit of Goodwill, 5" long, EX, $165.00.

Airplane, US Army B-51, w/wings, L#591........................$50.00
Alarm Clock, #11, L #549..$110.00
Auto w/Tassels #1, L #360 (E&A #64)..........................$250.00
Bear on Circus Tub, orig blades, L #1 (E&A #83).........$375.00
Bird Cage, L #230..$150.00
Bottle, Round Nurser, L #70 (E&A #549)......................$20.00
Candlestick, L #201..$300.00
Candy Cane, Mercury Glass, L #613 ....$80.00
Car, Electric Coupe #1, L #354 (E&A #49).....................$60.00
Car, Long Hood Coupe #3, L #359 (E&A #51) $110.00
Chicken in Sagging Basket, L #8.................................$75.00
Chicken on Round Base, L #1 (E&A #146), from $250 to ..$300.00
Decorettes, L #655...$125.00
Dirgible, Los Angeles, L #322 ....$175.00
Dog w/Top Hat, L #480 (E&A #194-2) $25.00
Fire Engine, bl glass, L #381 (E&A #218-1) $100.00
Fish, L #34...$400.00
Gas Pump, L #316 (E&A #240)...................................$225.00
Glass House, top closure, L #512...............................$200.00
Happifat, Borgfeldt, pnt glass fat boy on tin drum-like base w/coin slot, 4½", VG, A...$250.00
Hot Doggie, clear w/pnt, L #14 (E&A #320).................$465.00
Ice Truck, L #458, all orig $700.00
Jack-O'-Lantern, blk cat, L #158 (E&A #349-1)...........$450.00
Jackie Coogan, #1, G pnt, L #90 (E&A #345) $1,200.00
Kewpie by Barrel, Borgfeldt, 20% orig pnt on glass, 3", VG, A...$50.00
Lantern, Barn Type #1, L #177....................................$95.00
Lantern, K-600, L #187 (E&A #445)..............................$22.50
Lantern, oval panels, L #570 ....$30.00

Little Express, L #405 ....$350.00
Locomotive, 888, single window w/closure, E&A #481....$25.00
Lynne Doll Nurser, L #72 (E&A #550) $32.00
Naked Child, Victory Glass, L #94................................$65.00
Pencil, L #263 (E&A #567) $58.00
Poodle Dog, glass head, L #471...................................$15.00
Pumpkin Head Witch, L #265 (E&A #594)...................$550.00
Rabbit Begging, orig pnt, closure, L #50 (E&A #611)......$82.50
Rabbit Crouching, L #41 (E&A #615), EX pnt.............$105.00

Rabbit Mother and Daughter, worn paint, $1,200.00.

Photo courtesy of Doug Dezso.

Rabbit Running on Log, gold pnt, L #42 (E&A #603)...$200.00
Santa by Chimney #672, unfinished clear glass, 3½", VG ..$300.00
Santa Claus, banded coat, L #97 (E&A #669) $200.00
Scotty, Dog, L #17 (E&A #184) $15.00

Soldier, khaki uniform, worn original paint, 5½", G, A, $1,000.00.

Telephone, Victory Glass #1, L #298 (E&A #746-1).....$200.00
Valise, L #220 ....$450.00

Wagon or Stagecoach, L #441.......................................$125.00
Wheelbarrow, w/closure, L #391 (E&A #350) $100.00
Windmill, shaker top, orig blades, L #445 ....$250.00

Cast Iron

Realistically modeled and carefully detailed cast-iron toys enjoyed their heyday from about the turn of the century (some companies began production a little earlier) until about the 1940s when they were gradually edged out by lighter weight toys that were less costly to produce and to ship. (Some of the cast irons were more than 20" in length and very heavy.) Many were vehicles faithfully patterned after actual models seen on city streets at the time. Horse-drawn carriages were phased out when motorized vehicles came into use.

Some of the larger manufacturers were Arcade (Illinois), who by the 1920s was recognized as a leader in the industry; Dent (Pennsylvania); Hubley (Pennsylvania) and Kenton (Ohio). In the 1940s Kenton came out with a few horse-drawn toys which are collectible in their own right, but naturally much less valuable than the older ones. In addition to those already noted, there were many minor makers; you will see them mentioned in the listings.

For more detailed information on these companies, we recommend *Collecting Toys* by Richard O'Brien (Books Americana).

Advisor: John McKenna (M2).

See also Pull and Push Toys.

AIRPLANES

Air Force Fighter, Arcade, 1941, bl w/wooden wheels, steel wings & propeller, 6", M, A $275.00
Airmail, Kenton, bl w/NP motor, wheels & propeller, 7" wingspan, minor pnt chips o/w VG, A $475.00
Airmail, Kenton, gr w/NP wheels & propeller, 6¼", EX, A $350.00
Airmail, Kenton, gr w/NP wheels & propeller, 9½", VG, A .$1,850.00
America, Hubley, gray w/blk rubber tires, NP propellers rotate, w/clicker, 13", EX, A....................................$4,200.00
Bremen, Hubley, gr w/NP wheels, propellers & pilots, 7", VG, A $1,100.00
Do-X, Hubley, bl & red w/rubber tires, 6 propellers over wings, 4¾", EX, A..$375.00
Fokker Plane (salesman's sample), Vindex, 1929, gr & red w/NP props & wheels, 9½", M, A..............................$24,000.00
Ford Cabin Aeroplane, Dent, gr w/NP wheels & propellers, 11¼", M, A..$6,000.00
Friendship, Hubley, yel w/wht rubber tires, NP propellers, w/clicker, 10¾", EX, A..$9,000.00
Gremen, Hubley, 7½", some pnt wear, G, A $400.00
H-21 American Eagle, Hubley, 1960, red & bl pnt, MIB, R7..$100.00
H-21 American Eagle, Hubley, 1960, yel & orange pnt, EX+, R7..$45.00
Lindy, Hubley, gray w/blk rubber tires, NP rotating propellers, 10¾", EX, A $2,200.00

Lindy NR-211, Hubley, red & blk w/rubber tires, NP propeller, VG, A...$7,000.00

Lucky Boy Glider, Dent, NP, 4¼", rare, NM, A.............$600.00

Monocoupe, Arcade, ca 1928, orange and black with white rubber tires, steel wings, nickel-plated propeller, original decal, 12" wingspan, EX, D10, $1,850.00.

Monocoupe, Arcade, ca 1929, gr w/NP wheels & propeller, 5½", scarce, EX, A $475.00

Sea Gull, Kilgore, orange w/NP wheels & propeller, 8", EX, A $1,300.00

Sea Gull Flying Boat, Kilgore, bl fuselage & cream wings, NP single engine mounted above wings, 8" wingspan, VG, A.....$525.00

Tat, Kilgore, red & yel w/NP wheels & propeller, NM, A.$7,500.00

Travel Air Mystery Plane, Kilgore, bl w/NP wheels & propeller, 5⅝", EX, A..$450.00

BOATS

Battleship, red & wht w/yel decks, 14", rpl masts & cannons, G+, A $350.00

Battleship, silver pnt, on wheels, 6½", worn pnt, gun missing, G+, A $50.00

Battleship, wht hull & mustard-colored superstructure, 20", rpl mast, some pnt loss, G, A $1,000.00

Gunboat, Conestoga Mfg, 'Big Bang' ship fires carbide charge, 9½", rpl stack, G+, A.....................................$65.00

Oarsmen in Racing Scull, US Hardware, w/4 articulated crew members, 8½", rpt oars, pitted & bent o/w VG, A ..$650.00

Oarsmen in Racing Scull, US Hardware, 9 men in gr & tan scull on ornate wheels, 15", VG, A..............................$5,500.00

Paddleboat Puritan, wht side-wheeler w/red trim, movable beam, 11", pnt chips, G, A................................$500.00

Showboat, Arcade, 1929, red, gr & wht rpt w/rubber tires & bell, w/anchor, 10⅝", VG, A.............................$525.00

CIRCUS AND ACCESSORIES

Circus Wagon, Arcade, 1920s, horse-drawn, w/teddy bank, 16", EX $750.00

Ferris Wheel, Hubley, 6 gondolas w/2 riders in each, rpt, 14" dia..$200.00

Overland Circus Band Wagon, 1920s, red wagon w/4 band members pulled by 2 wht horses w/riders, 16½", pnt chips, G, A .$270.00

Overland Circus Cage Wagon with Bear, Kenton, 1930s, red wagon with gold trim and yellow wheels pulled by 2 white horses, white bear in cage, 14", NM, D10, $450.00.

Overland Circus Truck, Kenton, 1925, yel w/pnt wheels, w/driver & hippo, 7¼", EX, A $1,300.00

Overland Circus Wagon, Kenton, 1930s, red pnt calliope wagon pulled by 2 wht horses, 2 figures, 12½", EX, A $575.00

Royal Circus Cage w/Bear, Hubley, red & wht cage w/sliding door, driver atop, 2 wht horses, some chips, 13"......$485.00

Royal Circus Cage w/Lions, Hubley, gray & red cage w/2 lions, driver atop, 16", worn, A $1,900.00

CONSTRUCTION

Austin Roll-A-Plane, Arcade, 1928, NP driver, side cylinder & roller, red spoke wheels, 7½", G, A...........................$450.00

Buckeye Ditch Digger, Kenton, ca 1930, red & gr w/NP crank, digger & wheels, chain drive, 9", EX, A $875.00

Fairfield Ditch Digger, Kenton, red & gr w/wht rubber tires, chain drive, 9½", EX, A $2,700.00

Galion Master Road Roller, Kenton, red w/NP wheels & wood roller, 7", EX, A $400.00

Huber Steam Roller, orange w/pnt driver, NP wheels & front roller, 7¾", EX+, A..$403.00

Jaeger Cement Mixer, Kenton, 1935, gr & red w/NP operating pcs, blk rubber tires, 7", M......................................$600.00

Jaeger Cement Mixer Truck, Kenton, gr w/wht rubber tires, NP cylinder & pulley, 9", EX, A $2,400.00

Jaeger Cement Mixer Truck, Kenton, red w/wht rubber tires, NP cylinder & pulley, 7⅜", NM, A $2,400.00

Mack Cement Mixer, Dent, brass pattern w/wht rubber tires, 11¼", extremely rare, EX, A $20,000.00

Mack Hoist Truck, Arcade, 1932, red & gr w/wht rubber tires, integral driver, orig label, 11⅜", VG, A $1,700.00

Mack Ingersoll Rand Air Compressor Truck, red & gr w/NP spoke wheels, C-style cab w/driver, 8", rare, fr rpr, VG, A $2,900.00

P&H Power Excavator, Vindex, gr & red w/yel logo, shovel dumps by hand chain, 10½", scarce, NM, A $7,500.00

Panama Steam Shovel, Hubley, bl & silver, 8⅝", EX $1,000.00

Panama Steam Shovel Truck, Hubley, red & gr rpt w/wht rubber tires, NP shovel, 12", EX.......................................$1,200.00

Road Roller, Hubley, 1930s, gr & red w/NP driver, 7¾", rare, EX, A $550.00

Road Sweeper, Dent, 1930s, gr & red w/orig brush & gear-driven mechanism, 1 of 2 known, 7¾", EX, A.................$3,700.00

Steam Shovel Truck, Hubley, gray & red w/wht rubber tires, NP shovel, w/driver, 8¼", EX.......................................$475.00

Steam Shovel Truck, Hubley, red & gr w/NP spoke wheels & shovel, 6¾", G, A $275.00

Steam Shovel Truck, Hubley, red & gr w/wht rubber tires, NP shovel, w/driver, 9¾", EX $500.00

Steam Shovel Truck, Hubley, red rpt w/NP wheels & shovel, 4", EX, A $220.00

FIREFIGHTING

Ahrens-Fox Fire Engine, Hubley, red w/spoke wheels, 3½", VG, A $350.00

Ahrens-Fox Fire Engine, Hubley, red w/wht rubber tires, 4½", EX, A $200.00

Ahrens-Fox Ladder Truck, Hubley, red w/wht rubber tires, NP engine & removable driver, 11", NM, A $7,700.00

Ahrens-Fox Ladder Truck, Hubley, red w/wht rubber tires, 6¾", NM, A $550.00

Fire Chief Car, Arcade, 1941, red w/blk rubber tires, Fire Chief stenciled on roof, 5⅝", VG, A...............................$240.00

Fire Chief Car, Dent, red w/yel spoke wheels, open tiller, separate driver, 5", EX, A $250.00

Fire Patrol Truck, Hubley, 1920s, bl w/red spoke wheels, integral driver w/3 firemen in back, 7½", VG, A $600.00

Fire Patrol Truck, Kenton, red w/wht rubber tires, orig driver & 3 firemen, 9", EX, A $1,400.00

Fire Pumper, Arcade, 1920s, red w/NP wheels, integral driver, orig decal, 6¾", NM, A $475.00

Fire Truck, Hubley, red w/yel spoke wheels, integral driver, 5½", pnt chips o/w VG, A...$50.00

Ladder Truck, Arcade, red & yel w/blk rubber tires, pnt driver & fireman in back, 15¾", EX, A $1,050.00

Ladder Truck, Graham, 1933, red snap-apart model w/wht rubber tires, 5", EX, A...$250.00

Ladder Truck, Hubley, red w/NP grille & ladders, wht rubber tires, 6", pnt chips & scratches o/w VG, A $100.00

Ladder Truck, Hubley, 1929, red w/NP tires & driver, 13", NM, A $950.00

Ladder Truck, Kenton, gr w/wht rubber tires, full-figure driver, 9", VG, A...$800.00

Ladder Truck, Carpenter, 1880s, red and black with black and cream articulated horses, 24", EX, D10, $2,850.00.

Ladder Truck, red & blk w/NP grille & bell, wht rubber tires, w/driver & passenger, 6", rpl ladders & pnt chips, G, A $100.00

Mack Ladder Truck, Arcade, red & yel w/NP spoke wheels & driver, 17¾", EX, A...$2,600.00

HORSE-DRAWN

Chester Gump Cart, Arcade, yel wicker design cart w/spoke wheels pulled by 1 horse, w/driver, 7½", pnt worn, G, A.........$250.00

Delivery Wagon #5, Kenton, gr wagon w/driver pulled by 2 horses, 15", heavy pnt wear, G, A $110.00

Doctor's Cart, Carpenter, red cart w/spoke wheels pulled by wht horse, 10", rpl flat figure & bench, G, A $75.00

Dumping Coal Wagon, Ives, gray wagon w/red wheels & Black driver pulled by brn mule, 13", chips & scratches o/w VG, A $725.00

Farm Wagon, Arcade, 1939, red w/gr chassis, 2 gray horses & separate driver, rubber tires, 10¾", NM, A $950.00

Fire Pumper, Hubley, ca 1948, red w/yel wheels, w/driver, 1 wht & 2 blk horses, 10", EX, A $105.00

Fire Pumper, NP engine w/3 pnt horses & single driver, 19", G, A $900.00

Fire Pumper, Wilkins, bronze-finished pumper on red wagon pulled by 2 detachable horses, 2 firemen, 18", some chips, A $3,450.00

Fire Wagon, Wilkins, tank w/2 ladders on wagon pulled by 2 detachable horses, 2 firemen, 19", pnt chips, A ...$3,220.00

Fire Wagon w/Hose Reel, Wilkins, reel on base w/4 heart-shaped spoke wheels, w/driver & 2 detachable horses, 16", VG, A...$2,415.00

Hansom Cab, bl cab w/yel spoke wheels pulled by wht horse, driver in red & lady passenger in yel, 16", VG, A ...$250.00

Hansom Cab, Pratt & Letchworth, 1890s, blk & yel cab pulled by brn horse, driver has movable arms, 11", G, A ...$450.00

Hansom Cab, Wilkins, blk cab w/yel wheels pulled by blk horse, no figure, 10½", pnt chips, G, A $55.00

Ladder Truck, Hubley, ca 1948, red w/yel tin ladders & wheels, 2 firemen, 1 wht & 2 blk horses, 17", NM, A..........$220.00

Milk Wagon, wht wagon w/driver pulled by blk horse, 10", pnt chips & wear o/w VG, A $75.00

Panama Wagon, Wilkins, red w/2 blk horses, orig driver, 19", G, A...$475.00

Sand & Gravel Wagon, gr & red wagon w/driver pulled by blk & wht horses, 15", pnt chips & wear, G, A $110.00

Sand & Gravel Wagon, red wagon w/gr wheels pulled by blk horse, no figure, 10½", VG, A $65.00

Surrey, Hubley, maroon carriage w/red spoke wheels pulled by 1 blk horse & 1 NP, w/driver & lady passenger, 14", VG, A $250.00

MOTOR VEHICLES

Note: Description lines for generic vehicles may simply begin with 'Bus,' 'Coupe,' or 'Motorcycle,' for example. But more busses will be listed as 'Coach Bus,' 'Coast-To-Coast,' 'Greyhound,' 'Interurban,' 'Mack,' or 'Public Service' (and there are other instances); coupes may be listed under 'Ford,' 'Packard,' or some other specific car company; and lines describing motorcycles might be also start 'Armored,' 'Excelsior-Henderson,' 'Delivery,' 'Policeman,' 'Harley-Davidson,' and so on. Look under 'Yellow Cab' or 'Checker Cab' and other cab companies for additional 'Taxi Cab' descriptions. We often gave any lettering or logo on the vehicle priority when we entered descriptions, so with this in mind, you should have a good idea where to look for your particular toy. Body styles (Double-Decker Bus, Cape-Top Roadster, etc.) were also given priority.

American Car & Foundry Bus, Arcade, 1927, orange w/wht rubber tires, orig hood ornament, 11⅜", scarce, VG, A $2,600.00

American Oil Co Gasoline Truck, Dent, red w/gold lettering & trim, NP wheels, 10½", old factory stock, NM, A ...$850.00

Armored Motorcycle, Hubley, red w/blk rubber tires, separate driver, passenger & shield, 8½", VG, A $1,550.00

Army Tank, Arcade, 1937, camouflage finish w/rubber tread, crank-operated gun shoots steel balls, 7½", MIB, A .$2,200.00

Auto Dump Truck, Dent, 1920s, red w/silver & yel spoke wheels, separate NP driver, 8", EX, A....................$1,800.00

Bell Telephone Truck, Hubley, gr w/spoke wheels, C-style cab, no driver, 3¾", G, A $160.00

Bell Telephone Truck, Hubley, gr w/spoke wheels, C-style cab w/driver, 5¼", G, A $240.00

Bell Telephone Truck, Hubley, gr w/spoke wheels, C-style cab w/driver, sheet metal cover, 2 ladders & tools, 7", NM, A $1,200.00

Bell Telephone Truck, Hubley, gr w/wht rubber tires, C-style cab, no driver, 3", VG, A $220.00

Bell Telephone Truck, olive gr w/gold trim, NP spoke wheels, 7", VG+, A $400.00

Blue Bird Cab, Arcade, 1927, bl & wht w/NP wheels, 5¼", G, A $625.00

Blue Streak Roadster, Kilgore, bl & yel w/red seat, wht rubber tires, mounting pads on dashboard, 6", scarce, EX, A $500.00

Borden's Milk Truck, Hubley, wht w/wht rubber tires, 3⅝", NM, A $450.00

Breyer's Ice Cream Delivery Van, Dent, 1932, orange w/rpt NP wheels, w/driver, movable doors on 1 side, EX, A .$2,100.00

Brinks Express Van, Arcade, 1932, red w/wht rubber tires, rear door opens & locks, 11¾", rare, EX, A $20,000.00

Buick Coupe, Arcade, 1927, lt gr w/wht rubber tires, NP driver, 8½", VG, A $4,000.00

Buick Deluxe Sedan, Arcade, 1927, lt gr w/wht rubber tires, NP driver, 8½", VG, A $4,300.00

Buick Deluxe Sedan, Arcade, 1927, red w/NP spoke wheels & driver, retains orig sticker, 8½", rare, EX, A.........$4,000.00

Buick Deluxe Sedan, Arcade, 1927, yel w/wht rubber tires, NP driver, retains orig sticker, 8½", rare, EX, A.........$7,700.00

Bus, Arcade, mk Santa Fe Trailways on top, red & cream w/NP front & rear grille, wht rubber tires, 9", EX, A $1,500.00

Bus Line Bus, Dent, brass pattern, 7½", EX, A $600.00

Bus Line Bus, Dent, yel, pnt wheels, 8⅜", scarce, VG, A....$550.00

Cape-Top Roadster, Hubley, ca 1920, gray w/red spoke wheels, separate driver, 7¼", EX, A $900.00

Car & Trailer, Arcade, red car w/wht rubber tires pulls gr trailer w/blk tires, 6½", VG, A...$110.00

Car Carrier, Arcade, Model A truck and trailer, green truck with red bed hauls 1 green and 3 red cars, all have nickel-plated wheels, 24½" long, EX, $4,000.00.

Car Carrier, Arcade, 1932, red truck w/NP wheels carries 3 Ford sedans, 24½", VG, A...$2,500.00

Car Carrier, Arcade, 1939, gr truck w/blk rubber tires carries 2 cars & 2 trucks on trailer, 11⅜", VG+, A $475.00

Car Carrier, Arcade, 1939, gr truck w/blk rubber tires carries 2 cars & 2 trucks on trailer, 15⅜", EX+, A..............$1,300.00

Car Carrier, Hubley, 1932, red truck w/NP wheels carries 3 bl integral Buicks on trailer, 10", EX, A $1,650.00

Car Carrier, Hubley, 1938, red truck w/wht rubber tires carries 4 cars on trailer, 10", NM, A $475.00

Checker Cab, Freidag, 1920s, blk w/checker design, riveted driver, 4536 license plate, w/spare tire, 7½", EX, A $4,000.00

Chevrolet Coupe, 1925-28, gray and black with white rubber tires, 8¼", NM, $2,200.00.

Chevrolet Sedan, Arcade, 1928, single-stripe version, dk bl & blk w/wht rubber tires, 8", NM, A $8,000.00

Chevrolet Sedan, Arcade, 1928, single-stripe version, gr & blk w/NP tires, 8", G, A...$950.00

Chevrolet Sedan, Arcade, 1930, dk bl & blk w/NP tires, 8¼", EX, A $2,900.00

Chevrolet Stake Truck, blk & lt gray pnt w/chrome driver, pnt wht-wall tires, 9¼", EX+, A $750.00

Chevrolet Stake Truck, Freidag, 1925, gray & blk w/spoke wheels, 4 barrels in bed, 7⅝", VG, A....................$1,200.00

Chevrolet Superior Roadster, Arcade, 1925, blk w/spoke wheels & NP driver, 7", NM, A $2,300.00

Chevrolet Superior Touring Car, Arcade, 1925, NP spoke wheels & driver, 7", G, A.......................................$800.00

Chevrolet Utility Stake Truck, Arcade, 1925, gray & blk w/spoke wheels, NP driver, 9", EX, A $950.00

Chrysler Airflow, Hubley, tan w/NP grille & bumpers, wht rubber tires, 8", G, A...$600.00

Chrysler Airflow, Hubley, 1934, silver w/wht rubber tires, NP grille & bumpers, electric headlights, 8", NM, A.$3,100.00

Chrysler Airflow Roadster, Hubley, 1935, bl w/wht rubber tires, NP grille & bumpers, electric lights, 7", EX, A $1,100.00

Chrysler Airflow Sedan, Hubley, red with nickel-plated grille and bumpers, white rubber tires, 6½", NM, $650.00.

City Ambulance, Arcade, 1932, bl w/wht rubber tires, 6", EX, A $700.00

City Ambulance, Arcade, 1932, bl w/wht rubber tires, 8", EX, A $650.00

Coach Bus, Dent, 1925, lt gr w/NP wheels & rpt hubcaps, 7⅝", scarce, EX, A $1,300.00

Coach Bus, Freidag, bl w/NP wheels, 8⅞", rare, G, A $675.00

Coal Truck, Hubley, red w/NP spoke wheels, open cab w/driver, 6⅝", NM, A..$1,100.00

Coal Truck, Kenton, red & gr w/wht rubber tires, integral driver, dump mechanism missing o/w EX, A.....................$1,050.00

Coast-To-Coast Bus, Dent, brass pattern, 15½", EX, A..$2,900.00

Coupe, Freidag, 1924, blk w/pnt spoke wheels, driver in window, 5¾", VG, A..$425.00

Coupe, Hubley, 1928, pnt wheels, integral driver, 6⅝", spare tire missing o/w VG, A $210.00

Coupe, Hubley, 1928, pnt wheels, integral driver, 8⅛", spare tire missing o/w VG, A $500.00

Coupe, Kilgore, ca 1922, bl w/NP wheels, 2 spring-mounted passengers, 6¼", G, A $275.00

Cross Country Bus, Arcade, 1937, blk & wht w/wht rubber tires, Shortline stenciled on roof, 7½", NM, A $2,200.00

Delivery Cycle, Say It w/Flowers, Hubley, 1933, bl w/blk rubber tires, w/clicker, 10½", EX, A................................$18,000.00

Delivery Cycle, uniformed driver on 3-wheeler w/fenced cargo bed, NP wheels, 6½", VG, A...............................$600.00

Delivery Cycle, Vindex, orange w/blk rubber tires, NP handlebars, full-figure driver, 9", EX, A...........................$5,000.00

Delivery Truck, Arcade, lt gr w/wht rubber tires, 8⅜", rare, EX, A...$5,500.00

Delivery Truck, Hubley, 1920s, gr pnt, open bed, 8½", scarce, G, A..$425.00

Dodge Coupe, Arcade, 1922, bl & blk w/spoke wheels, NP driver, removable spare tire, 8¾", EX, A $3,700.00

Double-Decker Bus, AC Williams, yel w/NP wheels, 7¾", G, A...$210.00

Double-Decker Bus, Arcade, 1929, gr w/blk rubber tires, 3 NP passengers on top deck, orig decal, 8", EX, A $675.00

Double-Decker Bus, Arcade, 1929, gr w/wht rubber tires, NP driver, orig decal, 8", VG, A $550.00

Double-Decker Bus, Arcade, 1929, red w/wht rubber tires, NP driver, 8", NM, A...$1,050.00

Double-Decker Bus, Arcade, 1936, gr w/blk rubber tires, 8⅛", EX, A...$1,200.00

Double-Decker Bus, Chicago Motor Coach, Arcade, 13½", VG, A...$2,200.00

Double-Decker Bus, Kenton, red & gr w/wht rubber tires, 4 figures on top deck, 11¾", EX, A $1,900.00

Double-Decker Bus, Kenton, w/3 figures, 10", touchup o/w EX, A $900.00

Dump Truck, Hubley, green with red bed, nickel-plated wheels, 9", EX, $1,500.00.

Dump Truck Trailer, Arcade, 1931, gr & red w/NP wheels, optional pup trailer, 20½", VG, A......................$1,550.00

Elgin Street Sweeper, Hubley, silver w/full-figure driver, many moving parts, 8¾", EX, A $3,900.00

Excelsior-Henderson Police Motorcycle w/Sidecar, Vindex, gr w/rubber tires, salesman's sample w/orig pull cord, NM, A...$7,500.00

Express Stake Truck, Kilgore, bl, gr & yel snap-apart model w/wht rubber tires, 5⅝", NM, A............................$425.00

Express Trailer, Arcade, 1929, orange w/spoke wheels, separate driver, orig label, 7½", EX, A $850.00

Express Truck, Arcade, 1929, gr w/wht rubber tires, NP driver, 8½", VG, A $1,650.00

Fageol Bus, AC Williams, 1926, bl & red w/passengers in windows, solid nickel wheels, 7⅛", VG, A $250.00

Fageol Bus, Arcade, red & gold w/solid nickel wheels, 7¾", EX, A $310.00

Fageol Bus, Arcade, red w/NP wheels, gold trim, 8", rpt, rpl front wheels, VG, A $55.00

Fageol Safety Coach, Arcade, lt bl w/blk rubber tires, 12", rpt, EX, A $375.00

Ford Aviation Semi Tanker, Kilgore, 1931, red & tan w/NP spoke wheels, 12¼", EX, A $4,200.00

Ford Coupe, AC Williams, 1934, red & bl snap-apart model w/wht rubber tires, NP grille, 6¾", EX, A................$750.00

Ford Coupe, AC Williams, 1936, lt gr w/wht rubber tires, 4½", EX, A $450.00

Ford Coupe, Arcade, 1925, blk w/NP spoke wheels & driver, 6½", NM, A..$550.00

Ford Coupe, Arcade, 1927, red w/NP spoke wheels & driver, 6¾", EX, A..$325.00

Ford Coupe, Champion Hardware, red w/side mounts & NP wheels, 7½", EX, A $375.00

Ford Dump Truck, Arcade, 1929, gr & red w/NP spoke wheels, 7¼", VG, A..$425.00

Ford Model A, AC Williams, gr w/wht rubber tires, 5¼", NM $400.00

Ford Model A Car Carrier, gr truck w/NP wheels carries 4 cars on trailer, 21½", rare, EX, A $3,400.00

Ford Model A Coupe w/Rumble Seat, Arcade, 1928, orange w/NP wheels & driver, 6½", EX $600.00

Ford Model A Coupe w/Rumble Seat, Arcade, 1928, red w/wht rubber tires, NP driver, 6½", VG.....................$550.00

Ford Model A Express Truck, AC Williams, red w/NP winch & wht rubber tires, 7", VG, A $275.00

Ford Model A Stake Truck, AC Williams, bl w/NP spoke wheels, 7", EX, A $260.00

Ford Model A Stake Truck, Arcade, gr w/NP spoke wheels, 7", G, A..$190.00

Ford Model A Wrecker, Arcade, gr w/wht rubber tires, orig sticker, 7", NM $600.00

Ford Model A Wrecker, Arcade, red & gr w/NP spoke wheels, separate boom, 7", VG, A $550.00

Ford Model A Wrecker, Hubley, red snap-apart model w/rubber tires & dual side mounts, NP hook, 6¾", VG, A.....$300.00

Ford Model T Coupe, AC Williams, bl w/NP spoke wheels, 6", G, A..$180.00

Ford Model T Coupe, Arcade, 1922, blk w/NP spoke wheels & driver, 6½", EX, A $325.00

Ford Model T Dump Truck, Arcade, 1927, blk & gray w/NP spoke wheels, spring release beside seat dumps box, 8", EX $1,750.00

Ford Model T Express Truck, AC Williams, red & blk w/simulated wood body, spoke wheels, 7", G, A $275.00

Ford Model T Express Truck, Arcade, 1920s, blk w/NP spoke wheels & driver, 8⅜", G, A............................$500.00

Ford Model T Stake Truck, North & Judd, mk Anchor Truck Co, blk & gray w/NP spoke wheels & driver, 8¾", G, A..$2,100.00

Ford Model T Touring Car, Arcade, blk w/NP spoke wheels & driver, 6¼", VG, A......................................$400.00

Ford Model T w/Center Door, Arcade, 1924, blk w/NP spoke wheels & driver, 6½", EX $650.00

Ford Model T Wrecker, Arcade, 1927, wht w/NP wheels & drivers, stenciled sides, 10⅝", rare, VG, A $1,250.00

Ford Sedan, Arcade, 1924, bl w/NP spoke wheels & driver, 6½", VG, A..$375.00

Ford Sedan, Arcade, 1924, gr w/NP spoke wheels & driver, 6½", NM, A $1,200.00

Ford Semi Gas Tanker, AC Williams, 1930s, bl w/NP wheels, 7", VG, A..$275.00

Ford Semi Trailer, AC Williams, red w/NP spoke wheels, Coast-To-Coast Carriage Co on door, 10⅛", EX, A..........$600.00

Ford Stake-Body Truck, Arcade, 1928, blk w/NP spoke wheels & driver, 9", EX....................................$1,100.00

Ford Touring Car, Arcade, 1923, blk w/NP spoke wheels & driver, 6½", NM, A $425.00

Freeman's Dairy Truck, Dent, red w/wht rubber tires, pnt figure, Best By Taste emb on side, 5½", VG, A $600.00

Futuristic Sedan, AC Williams, red w/wht rubber tires, 8½", scarce, EX, A $400.00

Gas & Oil Truck, Kenton, red & gr w/pnt wheels, C-style cab, separate driver, 11¼", VG, A...............................$1,650.00

Gasoline Truck, AC Williams, 1936, red Packard-style w/wht rubber tires, raised gold lettering, 6¾", NM............$450.00

Gasoline Truck, Skoglund & Olson, red & silver w/dbl rear wheels, 10½", EX, A...$2,200.00

Greyhound Bus, Arcade, ca 1936, green with yellow details, white rubber tires, 7½", EX, D10, $650.00.

Greyhound Bus, Arcade, bl, cream & yel w/NP front & rear grille, blk rubber tires, 9", EX, A $450.00

Greyhound Bus, Arcade, bl & wht w/blk rubber tires, traces of orig label, 9", EX, A..$350.00

Greyhound Bus, Arcade, bl & wht w/NP front & rear grille, wht rubber tires, 9", EX, A $425.00

Ford Model T Doctor's Coupe, red with nickel-plated driver and wheels, 7", EX, D10, $1,450.00.

Greyhound Bus, Arcade, mk Coast-to-Coast, bl & wht w/blk rubber tires, 9", EX, A $425.00

Greyhound Bus, Arcade, mk Great Lakes 1936 Expo, bl & wht w/wht rubber tires, 6¾", NM, A...............................$850.00

Greyhound Bus, Arcade, mk Great Lakes 1936 Expo, bl & wht w/wht rubber tires, 10¾", VG, A...............................$650.00

Greyhound Bus, Arcade, mk 1933 Century of Progress, bl & wht w/wht rubber tires, 5⅝", NM, A...............................$350.00

Greyhound Bus, Arcade, mk 1933 Century of Progress, bl & wht w/wht rubber tires, 10⅜", NMIB, A........................$850.00

Greyhound Bus, Arcade, mk 1933 Century of Progress, bl & wht w/wht rubber tires, 14¼", EX, A $575.00

Greyhound Bus, Arcade, mk 1934 Century of Progress, bl & wht w/blk rubber tires, 11⅝", EX, A.............................$375.00

Greyhound Bus, Arcade, mk 1939 NY World's Fair, bl, wht & red w/blk rubber tires, orig decal, 8¼", NMIB, A $800.00

Greyhound Bus, Arcade, mk 1939 NY World's Fair, bl & wht w/wht rubber tires, orig decal, 6¾", NM, A $425.00

Greyhound Bus, Kenton, mk 1933 Century of Progress, bl w/wht rubber tires, 10⅞", VG $2,500.00

Harley-Davidson Motorcycle, Hubley, bl w/NP spoke wheels, full-figure driver, dual headlights, 7", EX, A.........$1,400.00

Harley-Davidson Motorcycle, Hubley, olive green with white rubber tires, integral driver, 5¼", EX, $450.00.

Harley-Davidson Motorcycle, Hubley, orange w/blk rubber tires, full-figure driver, 9", rare, G+, A $3,400.00

Harley-Davidson Motorcycle w/Police Sidecar, Hubley, red & bl w/wht rubber tires, orig driver & passenger, 5", EX, A..$850.00

International Delivery Truck, Arcade, 1932, 2-tone bl w/yel stripe, wht rubber tires, NP driver, 9½", very scarce, NM, A...$10,000.00

International Dump Truck, Arcade, 1936, gr w/red chassis, wht rubber tires, NP radiator, lights & bumper, 10", EX, A...$2,000.00

International Pick-Up Truck, Arcade, 1941, bright yel w/blk rubber tires, 9¼", NM, A $1,300.00

International Red Baby Dump Truck, Arcade, 1922, red w/rpt spoke wheels, 10½", EX....................................$750.00

International Red Baby Dump Truck, Arcade, 1923, red w/wht rubber tires, NP driver & winch, 10½", NM $1,250.00

International Stake Truck, Arcade, 1936, gr w/wht rubber tires, NP radiator, lights & bumper, 11⅞", EX, A $1,800.00

International Stake Truck, Arcade, 1937, yel w/NP radiator, lights & bumper, cab-over-engine type, 9¼", NM, A $1,450.00

International Stake Truck, Arcade, 1941, red w/wht rubber tires, 11⅛", NMIB, A..$3,000.00

International Wrecker, Arcade, 1940, red & yel w/blk rubber tires, sheet-metal chassis, 13", EX, A $750.00

Interurban Bus, Dent, metallic rpt w/wht rubber tires, 9", VG, A $400.00

Interurban Bus, Dent, orange w/NP wheels, retains factory sample tag, 6", NM, A $550.00

Lifesaver Truck, Hubley, no pnt, w/orig tag, 4¼", rare, G-, A $425.00

Limousine, Hubley, 1920s, silver w/red spoke wheels, 7", VG, A $160.00

Lincoln Touring Car, AC Williams, 1924, red w/spoke wheels, 7", EX, A...$325.00

Lincoln Zephyr Sedan & House Trailer, Hubley, red w/wht rubber tires, NP grille & bumpers, 13½", NM, A $2,400.00

Live Stock Truck, lt bl & maroon pnt w/Live Stock on stake sides, chrome wheels, ca 1925, 8", EX+, A $920.00

Lubrite Gasoline Mack Truck, Arcade, bl w/NP spoke wheels, 13", G $1,750.00

Mack Bus #6, Arcade, red & wht w/NP wheels, driver & side mount, 13", extremely rare, EX, A $15,000.00

Mack Contractors Truck, Dent, brass pattern w/wht rubber tires, C-style cab, 10¾", scarce, EX, A...........................$1,200.00

Mack Dump Truck, Arcade, 1928, bl w/gold & wht trim, spoke wheels, NP T-bar, Bulldog... decal, 12", EX, A $1,700.00

Mack Dump Truck, Arcade, 1928, orange w/NP spoke wheels & driver, 8¼", EX, A...$1,250.00

Mack Dump Truck, Arcade, 1928, red w/gold & wht trim, spoke wheels, NP T-bar, Bulldog... decal, 12", EX, A $1,500.00

Mack Dump Truck, Arcade, 1931, red w/spoke wheels, scissor dump, 8¼", rpl driver, VG $1,450.00

Mack Dump Truck, Arcade, 1932, red & yel w/wht rubber tires, NP driver, side dump, 8½", VG, A $2,100.00

Mack Dump Truck, Champion, 1930, red & gr w/wht rubber tires, C-style cab, 7¾", VG.......................................$225.00

Mack Dump Truck, Hubley, red & gr w/spoke wheels, C-style cab w/integral driver, 6¾", EX, A $625.00

Mack Dump Truck, Hubley, 1933, bl w/NP spoke wheels, C-style cab w/driver, 6¾", NM, A $1,350.00

Mack Dump Truck, Hubley, 1933, gr & red w/wht rubber tires, C-style cab w/driver, 6¾", VG, A $325.00

Mack Dump Truck, Hubley, 1933, gray w/red spoke wheels, C-style cab w/driver, 6¾", rpr chassis, G, A................$350.00

Mack Dump Truck, Kenton, 1920s, red & gr w/yel spoke wheels, C-style cab, movable tailgate, 15½", VG, A $2,400.00

Mack Gasoline Truck, Arcade, 1929, bl w/NP wheels & driver, tanker holds water, screw-on cap, 12½", VG $1,750.00

Mack Gasoline Truck, Arcade, 1929, red w/NP wheels & driver, tanker holds water, screw-on cap, 12½", G $1,450.00

Mack Gasoline Truck, Champion, red w/NP wheels, C-style cab, 8", NM, A...$750.00

Mack Gasoline Truck, Hubley, orange w/NP spoke wheels, C-style cab w/driver, 8¾", VG, A $1,150.00

Mack Ice Truck, Arcade, red w/wht rubber tires, integral driver, w/ice cubes & tongs, 6¾", EX, A $475.00

Mack Ice Truck, Arcade, 1927, blue with nickel-plated wheels and driver, with ice cube and tongs, 8½", EX, D10, $1,750.00.

Mack Ice Truck, Arcade, 1932, bl w/gold trim, NP wheels & driver, w/ice cube & tongs, 8", tailgate missing o/w EX, A......$850.00

Mack Ice Truck, Hubley, bl rpt w/NP spoke wheels, integral driver, w/ice cube & tongs, 6¾", EX, A $270.00

Mack Stake Truck, AC Williams, red w/wht rubber tires, C-style cab, 4¾", VG $175.00

Mack Stake Truck, Arcade, 1929, red w/NP spoke wheels & driver, dual rear wheels, 10½", rpl rear stake o/w EX, A.................................$2,300.00

Mack Stake Truck, Champion, red w/wht rubber tires, C-style cab, 7½", EX, A $375.00

Merchants Delivery Van, Hubley, yel w/NP wheels, 6", VG, A..$600.00

Motor Express Van, 1938, Art Deco style w/cab-over-engine design, gr, silver & red, 2-pc, 7⅜", VG, A $250.00

Motorcycle, Hubley, gr w/blk rubber tires, removable driver, 4 cylinders, 9", VG, from $975 to $1,300.00

Motorcycle, Hubley, red w/blk rubber tires, removable driver, 4 cylinders, 9", EX, from $1,275 to $1,700.00

Motorcycle w/Sidecar, Champion, bl & red w/wht rubber tires, 6", VG, from $280 to.................................$375.00

Motorcycle w/Sidecar, Champion, red w/wht rubber tires, 5⅛", VG, from $245 to $330.00

Motorcycle w/Sidecar, Hubley, bl w/NP sidecar & passenger, 4", NM, from $210 to.................................$280.00

Motorcycle w/Sidecar, Hubley, red w/blk rubber tires, separate driver & passenger, 8½", VG, from $1,000 to $1,350.00

Motorcycle w/Sidecar, Kilgore, red & bl w/NP spoke wheels, full-figure driver, 5¾", EX, from $775 to.................$900.00

Motorcycle w/Sidecar, Kilgore, red & orange w/spoke wheels, no passenger, 4⅝", VG, from $195 to...........................$275.00

Moving Van, AC Williams, red w/NP spoke wheels, 4¾", VG, A..$320.00

Moving Van, Arcade, 1929, wht & red w/wht rubber tires & dual side mounts, rear doors open, 13", EX, A ...$11,000.00

New York World's Fair Sight-Seeing Vehicle, car pulls trailer w/seats, 7", G, A..........................$135.00

Nu Car Transport, Hubley, 1932, red truck w/blk rubber tires carries 4 vehicles, 17¼", EX, A $1,550.00

Oldsmobile Coach, Vindex, 1929, red w/NP spoke wheels, 8", rare, VG, A.................................$4,500.00

Oldsmobile Sedan, Vindex, 1929, red w/NP spoke wheels, salesman's sample w/orig decal, 8", M, A...................$15,000.00

Packard Club Sedan, Vindex, 1929, salesman's sample w/attached tag, rare, NM $1,500.00

Packard Moving Van, Rekberger, 1922, gr w/NP driver, David Warehouses advertising on sides, 7¼", scarce, NM, A.....................................$4,700.00

Packard Straight Eight, Hubley, red & blk w/NP figure & engine block, hood & doors open, 11½", rare, EX, A....$16,000.00

Panel Van, Champion, red w/wht rubber tires, 7¾", EX, A..$800.00

Parlor Coach, Arcade, yel w/NP wheels, 9¼", NM, A.$1,700.00

Pennsylvania Independent Oil Co Mack Truck, Arcade, red w/NP spoke wheels, 13", rpl side rails o/w EX, A.$2,600.00

Pennsylvania Rapid Transit Bus, Arcade, gr & yel w/wht rubber tires & side mount, 13", VG, A $3,500.00

Pickwick Nite Coach, Kenton, gr & yel rpt w/wht rubber tires, 7½", EX, A...................................$650.00

Pickwick Nite Coach, Kenton, gr & yel w/NP wheels, front end & exhaust, 9½", EX, A...................................$3,200.00

Plymouth Tow Truck, Arcade, 1930s, NP bumper & grille, Plymouth on door, orig tires, 4½", EX, A $320.00

Police Motorcycle, AC Williams, orange w/wht rubber tires, integral driver, 7", EX, A..........................$600.00

Police Motorcycle, Champion, bl w/NP spoke wheels, integral driver, 7", VG, A..........................$400.00

Police Motorcycle, Champion, bl w/wht rubber tires, integral driver, 7", VG, A..........................$170.00

Police Motorcycle, Globe, 1930s, red w/integral driver in bl uniform, 8¼", EX, A..........................$2,100.00

Police Motorcycle, Hubley, 1938, gr w/blk rubber tires, integral driver, 6⅜", M, A..........................$525.00

Police Motorcycle and Sidecar, Champion, red and blue with white rubber tires, integral police figures, 7½", EX, D10, $1,100.00.

Police Motorcycle w/Sidecar, Globe, 1930s, red w/integral driver in blk uniform, 8¼", G, A $950.00

Police Patrol Truck, Kenton, red w/wht rubber tires, 4 reproduction figures, 9", VG, A..........................$190.00

Pontiac Roadster, Kilgore, wht & red rpt w/NP wheels, bumpers, grille & side lights, 10½", EX, A $1,350.00

Pontiac Sedan, Arcade, gr 4-door w/NP grille, blk rubber tires, 6¼", G, A..........................$375.00

Pontiac Stake Truck, Arcade, red w/NP grille & wht rubber tires, 6⅛", worn tires o/w EX, A $525.00

Popeye Motorcycle, see Character Collectibles category

Public Service Bus, Dent, brass pattern w/NP wheels, 13¾", EX, A $3,600.00

Public Service Bus, Dent, yel w/gr roof, NP & pnt wheels, 13¾", NM, A $5,700.00

Racer, AC Williams, bl w/wht rubber tires, 2 passengers, 7⅛", EX, A $650.00

Racer, AC Williams, 1930s, bl w/NP spoke wheels, integral driver, 6¼", EX, A $475.00

Racer, AC Williams, 1930s, gr w/wht rubber tires, NP driver, 8½", VG+, A $375.00

Racer, Arcade, 1920s, blk w/gold spoke wheels, NP driver, 7¾", NM, A $750.00

Racer, Arcade, 1932, bl w/NP wheels, pnt driver & passenger, 5½", G, A $145.00

Racer, Arcade, 1932, red w/NP wheels, exhaust, driver & passenger, 6⅝", G, A $400.00

Racer, Arcade, 1932, red w/NP wheels, pnt driver & passenger, 5½", VG, A $250.00

Racer, Champion, 1930s, red w/NP wheels, separate driver, 8½", G, A $250.00

Racer, Champion, 1935, gr & red w/wht rubber tires, 7½", rpl front tires, G, A $325.00

Racer, Freidag, 1930s, bl w/NP wheels, driver & passenger, 6½", rare, G, A $650.00

Racer, Hubley, bl w/silver pistons, wht rubber tires & NP driver, 7¼", EX, A $350.00

Racer, Hubley, 1930s, red highlights w/spoke wheels, features 12 moving cylinders, separate driver, 10⅜", G, A $1,600.00

Racer, Hubley, 1932, yel w/wht rubber tires, separate driver, 6¼", EX, A $250.00

Racer, Kenton, silver w/red spoke wheels, separate driver & steering wheel, 7", VG, A $190.00

Racer, Kenton, 1920s, red w/NP spoke wheels & driver, gas tank behind seat, 6¼", G, A $170.00

Racer, Kilgore, red rocket-type w/wht rubber tires, snap-apart model, 6½", VG, A $160.00

Racer #1, Hubley, red rpt w/NP wheels, separate driver, 7¾", EX, A $220.00

Racer #5, Arcade, 1936, red w/wht rubber tires, 7¾", VG, A $400.00

Racer #5, Hubley, 1930s, gr w/yel & wht wheels, hood opens, 9⅜", VG, A $2,200.00

Racer #5, Hubley, 1930s, silver & red w/blk rubber tires, features opening hood & clicker, 9½", VG, A $2,100.00

Racer #8, Hubley, silver & red w/wht rubber tires, 7", old store stock, M, A $700.00

Racer #9, Arcade, 1932, red w/NP wheels, exhaust, driver & passenger, 7¾", VG, A $1,600.00

Racer #9, Arcade, 1932, yel w/NP wheels, exhaust, driver & passenger, 7¾", VG, A $1,800.00

Reo Coupe w/Rumble Seat, Arcade, 1931, yel w/NP wheels, driver & grille, side mounts on both sides, 9", EX ..$4,500.00

Roadster, Freidag, 1922, bl w/spoke wheels, 9¼", VG, A .$700.00

Roadster, Kilgore, red w/NP wheels & driver, 4⅛", VG, A ..$225.00

Roadster, Kilgore, red w/NP wheels & driver, 6¼", EX, A ..$450.00

Roadster, Open; Globe, bl w/blk rubber tires, separate NP driver & children in rumble seat, 11½", VG, A $750.00

Roadster, Open; Kilgore, 1928, yel w/NP wheels & driver, 6⅛", EX, A $500.00

Scania-Vabis Bus, Skoglund & Olson, red w/wht rubber tires, 10½", rare, EX, A $2,900.00

Sedan, AC Williams, 1932, blk & yel snap-apart model w/wht rubber tires, 8", EX, A $375.00

Sedan, AC Williams, 1936, red & bl w/wht rubber tires, NP grille, 7", fr cracked in 4 spots o/w EX, A $100.00

Sedan, Dent, brass pattern, 6¼", EX, A $475.00

Sedan, Dent, 1930, bl w/NP wheels & rear mount, 7⅝", EX+, A $475.00

Sedan, Hubley, bl, NP grille & bumpers, 7¼", G+, A $275.00

Sedan, Iron Art, 1950s, jutting headlights & radiator cap, 6", EX, A $76.00

Sedan, Kenton, 1923, red w/pnt spoke wheels, separate driver, 10", M, A $6,000.00

Sedan w/Landau Top, Kenton, gr w/NP wheels, 5¼", rare, EX, A $325.00

Seeing New York Bus, Kenton, 1911, mc rpt, Mama Katzenjammer & other comic character as passengers, 11", rstr, A .$3,500.00

Semi Trailer Truck, Arcade, 1933, red & yel w/rubber tires, 7⅛", VG, A $400.00

Special Delivery Motorcycle, Kilgore, yellow with white rubber tires, 4½", EX, $450.00.

Stake Truck, Arcade, 1929, bl w/spoke wheels, orig label, 7", NM, A $700.00

Stake Truck, Arcade, 1929, gr w/NP wheels & driver, removable tailgate, 8½", G, A $1,100.00

Stake Truck, orange & blk w/6 wht rubber tires, 5¼", rpl spring, G, A $85.00

Standard Oil Semi Tanker, Kenton, 1933, red w/wht rubber tires, NP driver & grille, 12½", EX, A $3,500.00

Steam Pumper, red w/wht rubber tires, integral driver, NP boiler & pump trim, 4½", VG, A $130.00

Studebaker Ice Truck, Arcade, 1938, red w/wht rubber tires, NP radiator, lights & bumper, 6¾", EX, A $500.00

Taxi Cab, Arcade, bl w/NP wheels & driver, 9", rare color, EX, A $6,000.00

Taxi Cab, Arcade, blk & wht, w/driver, Business Man's Cab stenciled on roof, 8", NM, A $10,000.00

Taxi Cab, Arcade, 1923, brn & wht w/NP wheels & driver, 9", rpl radiator screen o/w EX, A $2,200.00

Taxi Cab, Freidag, 1920s, blk w/red diamond design, riveted driver, 4536 license plate, w/spare tire, 7½", VG, A $2,400.00

Taxi Cab, Hubley, orange & blk w/wht rubber tires, separate driver, chassis & luggage rack, 8", VG, A $900.00

Taxi Cab, Kenton, red, wht & blk w/wht wheels, 8½", rare, EX, A $4,000.00

Taxi-Type Sedan, Hubley, red w/yel spoke wheels, 5½", several pnt chips, G, A $95.00

Texaco Delivery Truck, Hubley, ca 1935, red with black lettering, nickel-plated bumper, white rubber tires, 7½", NM, D10, $750.00.

Texaco Semi Gas Tanker, Kenton, 1933, red w/wht rubber tires, 9", EX, A $1,100.00

Touring Car, Open; Dent, gr w/red spoke wheels, NP driver & passenger, 12", EX, A $875.00

Touring Car, Open; Dent, red rpt w/spoke wheels, NP driver & passenger, 9¼", EX, A $450.00

Toy-Town Bus, Kilgore, bl w/NP wheels, 7¾", scarce, G, A .$525.00

Toy-Town Delivery Van, Kilgore, red w/NP wheels, 6", VG, A $750.00

Tractor Train, Arcade, 1939, mk New York World's Fair, bl & red, w/driver, 7½", NMIB, A $750.00

Transcontinental Bus, Vindex, 1929, gr & yel w/NP wheels, integral roof rack, salesman's sample, 12", rare, M, A $18,000.00

Truck, Freidag, 1920s, orange w/spoke wheels, integral driver, flat bed, 7½", rpt, EX, A $350.00

Truck, Freidag, 1920s, red & orange w/spoke wheels, integral driver, 8⅜", G, A $750.00

Truck Set, AC Williams, red, bl & gr w/NP wheels, complete w/gas truck, stake truck & trailer, EX (rpr box top), A $325.00

Truck w/3 Tandem Trailers, Kenton, trailers mk Ice, Speed & Coal, red truck w/NP wheels, 19", EX, A $1,350.00

Valley View Dairy Truck, Dent, bl w/wht rubber tires, pnt figure, Guernsey A Milk emb on side, 8", old store stock, A $1,000.00

Water Tower Truck, Kenton, red & bl w/pnt wheels, separate driver, 11½", VG+, A $850.00

White Bus #6, Arcade, bl w/wht rubber tires & side mount, NP driver, 13", G, A...$3,700.00

White Delivery Van, Arcade, 1929, gr w/NP driver, David Warehouses advertising on sides, 13", 1 of 4 known, NM, A $22,000.00

White Dump Truck, Arcade, 1929, red & blk w/wht rubber tires, NP driver, 11½", rare, EX, A $23,000.00

White Moving Van, Arcade, 1929, brass pattern w/wht rubber tires, 13⅝", extremely rare, EX, A $5,700.00

Woody Station Wagon, Hubley, bl & blk snap-apart model w/wht rubber tires, 5", VG, A $300.00

World's Fair Tour Bus, Arcade, bl & wht w/NP grille, graphics, 5½", G, A...$85.00

Wrecker, Arcade, red w/wht rubber tires, NP winch, 5½", VG, A $95.00

Wrecker, Arcade, 1929, red w/pnt wheels, NP driver, Red Baby & International Harvester stenciled on sides, 12", EX, A...$2,400.00

Wrecker, Dent, w/wrecking gear, bronze w/wht rubber tires, 11½", EX, A..$900.00

Wrecker Car, Kenton, 1927, red & yel w/pnt wheels & driver, 9½", scarce, EX, A...$2,400.00

Yellow Baby Dump Truck, Arcade, 1923, orange w/NP wheels, driver & winch, 10½", EX, A $1,550.00

Yellow Cab, Arcade, blk & orange w/NP wheels, telephone numbers on wheels, 5¼", scarce, EX, A $850.00

Yellow Cab, Arcade, orange & blk w/NP wheels & driver, 8", EX, A..$1,200.00

Yellow Cab, Arcade, 1927, blk & yel w/pnt wheels, 5¼", EX, A...$700.00

Yellow Cab, Arcade, 1933-34 Ford, 4-door, Century of Progress Chicago 1933 on roof, nickel-plated grille, white rubber tires, 6½", EX, $1,450.00.

Yellow Cab, Arcade, 1941, blk rubber tires, 4½", NM, A..$550.00

Yellow Cab, Arcade, 1941, yel w/blk rubber tires & working clicker, separate driver & passenger, 8¼", M, A...$1,500.00

Yellow Cab, Hubley, pnt wheels, 8¼", EX, A $950.00

Yellow Cab Panel Delivery Truck, Arcade, yel & blk w/wht tires & side mount for spare, 8½", rare, NM, A $10,500.00

5-Ton Stake Truck, Hubley, 1920s, gr w/yel spoke wheels, full-figure driver, open cab, 16½", rpt, EX, A $850.00

5-Ton Stake Truck, Hubley, 1920s, yel w/red spoke wheels, full-figure driver, open cab, lift-up gate, 16½", VG, A..$1,050.00

MISCELLANEOUS

Baby Carriage, Kilgore, pnt w/NP hood, push hdl & wheels, 4⅞", EX, A...$450.00

Bobsled, 2 riders, 4¾", EX, A $350.00

Boy in Wagon, bl w/NP wheels, 3½", VG, A $220.00

Boy Surfer, Hubley, boy in red Jantzen swimwear mk Beach Patrol, orig pull-string & clicker, 7½", NM, A...**$14,000.00**

Covered Wagon Trailer, Arcade, brass pattern, 6½", EX, A **$475.00**

Express Wagon, Champion, red pnt w/NP wheels, 7½", EX, A **$110.00**

Gas Pump, Arcade, 6½", EX, A......................................**$750.00**

Grasshopper, Hubley, gr w/NP rear legs that move when bug is pulled, 4½", VG, A **$200.00**

Landing of Columbus, J&E Stevens, free-standing figure of Columbus w/articulated bell, 7¼", VG, A **$650.00**

Lighthouse, Mason Davis, 12", VG, A **$75.00**

Pony Blimp, Kenton, 1930, G, A **$125.00**

Pullman Railplane, Arcade, red pnt, stenciled roof, rubber tires, 5", NM, A...**$260.00**

Sign, National Highway 41, ca 1930, cream, yellow and red with black details, 5½", EX, $350.00.

Tools, Arcade, NP hammer, shovel, pick, etc, approximately 2" ea, set of 10, S9...**$100.00**

Catalogs

In any area of collecting, old catalogs are a wonderful source for information. Toy collectors value buyers' catalogs, those from toy fairs, and Christmas 'wish books.' Montgomery Ward issued their first Christmas catalog in 1932, and Sears followed a year later. When they can be found, these 'first editions' in excellent condition are valued at a minimum of $200.00 each. Even later issues may sell for upwards of $75.00, since it's those from the 1950s and 1960s that contain the toys that are now so collectible.

Advisor: Bill Mekalian (M4)

AC Gilbert Toys, 1958, EX, J2 ....**$40.00**

AMF Juvenile Wheel Goods, 1971, 28 pgs, EX, M4 ....**$8.00**

Aurora Games, 1973, 22 pgs, EX, M4 ....**$10.00**

Aurora Hobby Kits, 1974, 30 pgs, EX, M4 ....**$10.00**

Aurora Toys, 1972, 6 pgs, EX, M4 ....**$5.00**

Bachmann Hobby Catalog, 1973, 30 pgs, EX, M4 ....**$12.50**

Beacon Auto Stores Toy Carnival, 1957-58, 24 pgs, VG+, A **$46.00**

Beckley Ralston Co, 1913, bicycle & motorcycle equipment, over 275 pgs, A **$30.00**

Breyer Animal Creations, 1976, 10 pgs, EX, M4 ....**$10.00**

Buddy L, folding brochure, 1930, 2-sided color sheet w/mailing envelope & letter, fold marks, EX, A **$250.00**

Buddy L New Fun World, 1968, w/price list, 28 pgs, EX, M4 ....**$40.00**

Buddy L Train Sets, 1976, 4 pgs, EX, M4 ....**$25.00**

Butler Bros Christmas, 1927, 662 pgs, EX **$90.00**

CG Good, 1973, 6 pgs, EX, M4 ....**$5.00**

Chicago Skates, 1935, blk & wht/color, w/price list, EX ..**$20.00**

Child Guidance Platt & Munk Tinkertoy, 1972, 32 pgs, EX, M4 ....**$20.00**

Chilton Toys, 1975, w/price list, 14 pgs, EX, M4 ....**$8.00**

Coleco Toys, Games & Sporting Goods, 1972, 52 pgs, EX, M4..**$10.00**

Colorforms, 1973, 28 pgs, EX, M4 ....**$5.00**

Corgi Toys, 1966, 48 pgs, EX+ **$65.00**

Creative Playthings, 1976, 24 pgs, EX, M4 ....**$10.00**

Davis Grabowski Toy Imports, 1976, w/price list, 44 pgs, EX, M4 ....**$20.00**

Eagle Fall & Winter, 1975, 12 pgs, EX, M4.......................**$5.00**

Edward K Tryon Co Toys & Sporting Goods, 1950, blk & wht w/some color, price list, G+, A **$15.00**

Effanbee Dolls That Touch Your Heart, 1972, 12 pgs, EX, M4 ....**$10.00**

Ertl Model Kits, 1973, 6 pgs, EX, M4 ....**$10.00**

F.A.O. Schwarz Christmas, 1959, includes Steiff, Fisher-Price, Playsets, large plastic sets, Schuco, Dinky, Matchbox and more, 8x11" with 96 pages, EX+, A, $35.00.

Fisher-Price, 1960, pocket-sz, EX, M4 ....**$18.00**

Fisher-Price, 1974, w/price list, 22 pgs, EX, M4 ....**$45.00**

Fisher-Price Toys Make Learning Fun, 1968, 24 pgs, EX, M4 ....**$50.00**

Gabriel, 1975, features The Lone Ranger, 6 pgs, EX, M4 ...**$5.00**

Gabriel Learning Toys & Games, 1976, 24 pgs, EX, M4 ..**$20.00**

George H Bowman Miniature Cooking Sets, 1929, blk & wht w/color cover, w/price list & mailer, EX, A **$20.00**

Golden Press (Fall), 1967, 36 pgs, EX, M4 ....**$25.00**

Hasbro, 1976, w/price list, 54 pgs, EX, M4 ....**$75.00**

Hasbro, 1993, GI Joe & WWF Wrestling, M....................**$35.00**

Hasbro Dolls, 1972, 16 pgs, EX, M4 ....**$25.00**

Hot Wheels, 1968, NM, M5..**$38.00**

Hot Wheels Collector's Catalog, 1969, M, J2 ....**$18.00**

Hub Cycle Co, 1919, cycles & velocipedes, blk & wht, EX, A **$40.00**

Hubley, 1970, w/price list, 30 pgs, EX, M4 ....**$12.50**

Ideal, 1976, features Evel Knievel, w/price list, 84 pgs, EX, M4 ....$38.00

Indian Bicycles & Children's Vehicles, ca 1920, 33 pgs, NM, A $125.00

Ives Toys, 1920s, color cover, black and white inside pages, EX, A, $50.00.

Ives Trains, 1930s, mc cover w/blk & wht illus, EX..........$50.00

Kenner, 1976, Six Million Dollar Man, 98 pgs, EX, M4...$50.00

Kilgore Cast-Iron Toys, 1930s, color, w/price list, EX, A .$225.00

Knickerbocker, 1972, features Raggedy Ann & Andy, w/price list, 24 pgs, EX, M4 ....$32.00

Kusan Toys, 1968, w/price list, 14 pgs, EX, M4.................$12.50

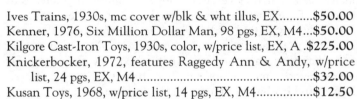
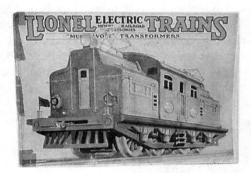

Lionel Trains, 1927, full color, variety of trains and parts, 46 pages, 8½x11", VG, A, $35.00.

Marshall Field, 1969, reprint, 35 pgs, M............................$20.00

Marx Toys, 1972, w/price list, 72 pgs, EX, M4 ....$50.00

Marx Toys Springtime, 1976, 20 pgs, EX, M4...................$35.00

Matchbox, pocket-sz, VG, W1 ....$75.00

Matchbox, 1968, pocket-sz, NM, W1 ....$10.00

Matchbox, 1984, Japanese, pocket-sz, NM+, W1 ....$10.00

Matchbox Dealer Catalog, 1978, NM+, W1.....................$22.50

Matchbox Dealer Catalog, 1983, NM, W1 ....$9.00

Matchbox Miniature Scale Models, 1970, 26 pgs, EX, M4 .$68.00

Mattel Big Jim PACK Brochure, 1975, 4 pgs, EX, M4......$12.50

Mattel Games, Crafts & Hobbies, 1971, 1st proof, 30 pgs, EX, M4 ....$75.00

Mattel Quick Reference Guide, 1971, 64 pgs, EX, M4 .....$18.00

Mego, 1974, w/Superstars (Super Heroes), 34 pgs, EX, M4 ..$125.00

Mego, 1976, w/Cher & Our Gang, 60 pgs, EX, M4 ....$125.00

Mego, 1979, 25th Anniversary, NM $95.00

Milton Bradley Games & Puzzles, 1970, 58 pgs, EX, M4 ..$25.00

Milton Bradley TV Promo Brochure, 1976, red, wht & bl cover, 4 pgs, EX, M4 ....$8.00

Montgomery Ward Christmas Catalog, 1955, features Davy Crockett, Lone Ranger, etc, 256 pgs, EX, A $122.00

Montgomery Wards Christmas Catalog, 1974, NM, J2 ....$30.00

Murry Bicycles, 1973, w/price list, 18 pgs, EX, M4..............$5.00

Ny-Lint, 1967, 14 pgs, EX, M4 ....$18.00

Ohio Art, 1970, The World of Toys, w/price list, 16 pgs, EX, M4 ....$12.50

Parker Bros Buyer's Guide, 1972, 12 pgs, EX, M4 ....$12.50

Parker Bros Games & Toys, 1976, w/price list, 40 pgs, EX, M4 ....$40.00

Playskool, 1960, pocket-sz, EX, M4 ....$50.00

Playskool, 1968, w/Lincoln Log insert, 48 pgs, EX, M4 ....$50.00

Pressman Toy Factory, 1876, 22 pgs, EX, M4 ....$5.00

Ranger Bicycles, 1921, blk & wht & color illus, EX $55.00

Remington Bicycles, 1893, EX..$195.00

Revell Model Kits, 1969, w/price list, 24 pgs, EX, M4 ......$38.00

Santa's Plaything, 1961, features 296 items w/32 color photos, EX, A $39.00

Schoenhut, 1912, wood dolls, blk & wht, EX, A $35.00

Schwinn Dealer, 1947, bl cover, A $60.00

Schwinn Parts, 1950s, A $10.00

Sears Christmas Catalog, 1946, 242 pgs, EX $85.00

Sears Christmas Catalog, 1958, features several Roy Rogers items, 439 pgs, EX, A..$83.00

Sears Christmas Mailer, 1934, images of Buck Rogers, Mickey Mouse Ingersoll watch & Shirley Temple doll, 32 pgs, VG+ $55.00

Sears Christmas Wish Book, 1975, 616 pgs, NM..............$45.00

Spiegel Christmas Catalog, 1959, 404 pgs, EX.................$85.00

Star Bicycles & Tricycles, 1887, 35 pgs, EX....................$180.00

Steiff, 1950s, 16 pgs, EX+ $45.00

Steiff's New Items for Easter '74, 6 pgs, EX, M4..............$20.00

Structo, 1922, color & blk & wht, w/price list, G+, A...$230.00

Structo, 1956, pocket-sz, EX, M4 ....$10.00

Structo Empire Builders, 1920s, color & blk & wht, VG, A.$130.00

Structo Model Building Kits & Supplies, 1915, blk & wht, G+, A $110.00

Tin Toys 1945-75 Color Reference Book, Michael Buhler, 1978, features Marx, Chein, Arnold, etc, 76 pgs, NM, A....$77.00

Tinker Toys & Games, 1920, color, w/price list & mailer, minor creases, EX, A $25.00

Tonka, 1973, pocket-sz, EX, M4...$12.50

Tonka Toys Price Guide, 1962, pocket-sz, EX, M4...........$18.00

Tootsietoy, 1976, 100th Anniversary, J5 ....$25.00

Topper Toys, 1971, 98 pgs, EX, M4....................................$18.00

Tyco HO Scale Electric Trains, 1971, w/price list, 30 pgs, EX, M4 ....$12.50

View-Master Stereo Pictures, 1973, w/price list, 26 pgs, EX, M4 ....$70.00

Vogue Dolls, 1974, w/price list, 10 pgs, EX, M4................$12.50
Wonder Sells Happiness, 1971, 8 pgs, EX, M4..................$10.00

Celebrities and Personalities

From the early days of the silver screen we remember Charlie Chaplin whose mute antics managed to express very eloquently his intent, the slap-stick comedy of Laurel and Hardy, and many other film stars equally as popular. During the thirties there was Shirley Temple and the Three Stooges, whose careers spanned more than a decade; and from the fifties, Hollywood's golden era, came stars like Marilyn Monroe and Clark Gable. Retail merchants, true to their calling, deluged the market with memorabilia of all types — toys, paper dolls, jewelry, books, records, etc. Even today's movie and TV icons — Madonna and Michael Jackson, for example — are represented at the retail level by a vast assortment of merchandise. Many of their fans zero in on their favorites and are able to build an interesting and comprehensive collection around them.

See also Books; Celebrity Dolls; Coloring, Activity and Paint Books; Paper Dolls; Records; Rock 'n Roll; Sports Collectibles; Western.

Arthur Godfrey, ring, yel plastic w/photo, EX $15.00
Arthur Godfrey, ukulele & song book, NMIB $15.00
Charlie Chaplin, crib toy, ca 1930, Chaplin standing in famous pose, hole in hat for string, 3½", NM......................$150.00
Charlie Chaplin, music box, Enesco, 4" figure on revolving base, 1989, MIB $38.00
Charlie Chaplin, T-shirt, gray w/blk silhouette of Charlie & his name, lg, M, S2 ....$20.00
Elvira, belt w/removable dagger, 1986, MOC, J2 ....$20.00
Elvira, cassette tape w/narration of spooky sounds, MOC, S2..$20.00
Elvira, earrings, MOC, M4..$5.00
Elvira, Macabre Makeup Crayons, Imagineering, 1990, MOC, S2...$25.00
Elvira, Midnight Kiss Lip Color, 1990, M, S2 ....$25.00
Elvira, Nightmare Nail Enamel, Imagineering, 1990, M, S2..$25.00
Elvira, play eyelashes, very colorful, MOC, H4..................$5.00
Elvira, press-on nails, 1993, MOC, S2 ....$25.00
Jackie Coogan, figure, 1920s, orange & gr celluloid w/hands in pockets, 5½", EX, J5..$85.00
Jackie Coogan, figure, 1920s, wht chalk, w/hands in suspenders, Jackie Coogan the Kid mk on base, VB, J5 ....$85.00
Jackie Coogan, pencil case, 1920s, yel litho tin picturing the 'kid,' 2x8" long, VG, J5...$15.00
Jackie Coogan, Tom Sawyer Paint Set Standard Solophone Mfg, 1931, unused, NMIB...$95.00
Laurel & Hardy, bank, Stan Laurel or Oliver Hardy figures, Play Pal, 1974, vinyl, 7½", EX, ea $45.00
Laurel & Hardy, figure, Stan Laurel, Parks, 1962, hollow plastic in striped gown, blk shoes & surgeon's light, 5", M ...$55.00
Laurel & Hardy, light-up drawing desk, Lakeside, 1962, rare, NM, S2 ....$175.00
Laurel & Hardy, sticker board, 1983, w/vinyl stickers, 8x10", MIP, S2 ....$20.00

Lucille Ball & Bob Hope, writing tablet, 1960s, color cover, M $35.00
Marilyn Monroe, figure, Presents, from How To Marry a Millionaire, PVC, 3¾", MIB, S2 ....$10.00
Marilyn Monroe, figure, Royal Orleans, from How To Marry a Millionaire, ceramic, 4", M, S2 ....$35.00
Milton Berle, ring, 1950s, gold-tone metal, NM..............$15.00
Mr T, jewelry set, Imperial, 15 pcs MOC (sealed) $15.00
Mr T, key case & wallet set, Big T's Enterprises, MO........$7.50
Mr T, puzzle, figural Mr T, Illco, MIB $15.00
Mr T, rubber stamp, bust image, 1983, MOC, S2 ....$15.00
Pinky Lee, paint set, 1950s, complete, NM (EX+ box), S2 .$49.00
Pinky Lee, shoelaces, 1952, bright pk w/gold accents, MIP, T2...$18.00
Rock Hudson, writing tablet, 1950s, color photo w/facsimile autograph, 8x11", unused, NM+ $20.00
Tommy Steele, guitar, Selcol, pictures Tommy playing guitar, 22", rare, EX, A...$150.00
Tony Curtis, writing table, 1950s, M..............................$20.00

Celebrity Dolls

Celebrity and character dolls have been widely collected for many years, but they've lately shown a significant increase in demand. Except for the rarer examples, most of these dolls are still fairly easy to find at doll shows, toy auctions, and flea markets, and the majority are priced under $100.00. These are the dolls that bring back memories of childhood TV shows, popular songs, favorite movies and familiar characters. Mego, Mattel, Remco and Hasbro are among the largest manufacturers.

Condition is a very important worth-assessing factor, and if the doll is still in the original box, so much the better! Should the box be unopened (NRFB), the value is further enhanced. Using mint as a standard, add 50% for the same doll mint in the box and 75% if it has never been taken out. On the other hand, values of dolls in only good or poorer condition drop at a rapid pace.

Advisor: Henri Yunes (Y1).

See also Action Figures.

Photo courtesy of Henri Yunes.

Ben Casey M.D. (Vince Edwards), Bing Crosby Productions, 1962, 11½", MIB, $350.00.

Beatles (George Harrison), Remco, w/instrument, VG, R2.$45.00

Beatles (John Lennon), Remco, w/instrument, VG, R2.$125.00

Beatles (Paul McCartney), Remco, w/o instrument, VG, R2...$30.00

Beatles (Ringo Starr), Remco, w/instrument, VG, R2......$75.00

Beatles (Ringo Starr), Remco, w/o instrument, VG, R2...$25.00

Beverly Johnson, see Real Models Collection

Boy George, LJN, plush, 14", NMIB $50.00

Boy George, LJN, 1984, 11½", scarce, MIB, O1, $125.00.

Brook Shields, LJN, 1982, in prom dress, 11½", rare, MIB .$100.00

Brook Shields, LJN, 1982, regular version, MIB $30.00

Brook Shields, LJN, 1983, suntan version, 11½", MIB.....$50.00

Captain & Tennile, Mego, 1970s, 12", MIB, ea $35.00

Charlie's Angels (Cheryl Ladd as Kris), Hasbro, 1977, 8½", MOC...$35.00

Charlie's Angels (Farrah Fawcett as Jill), Hasbro, 1977, 8½", MOC...$35.00

Charlie's Angels (Jaclyn Smith as Kelly), Hasbro, 1977, 8½", MOC...$35.00

Charlie's Angels (Kate Jackson as Sabrina), Hasbro, 1977, 8½", MOC, J2 ....$35.00

Cher, see Sonny & Cher

Cheryl Tiegs, see Real Models Collection

Christie Brinkley, see Real Models Collection

Dave Clark Five, Remco, 1964, features lg Dave w/other sm members, complete set, M (torn box), A.................$180.00

Diana Ross, Mego, 1977, 12", NRFB $125.00

Diana Ross of the Supremes, Ideal, 1969, 19", rare, MIB..$150.00

Dolly Parton, Eegee, 1980, red pantsuit, 11½", NRFB......$45.00

Dolly Parton, Eegee, 1987, cowgirl outfit, 11½", NRFB ...$60.00

Donnie & Marie Osmond, Mattel, 1978, 12", M (together in box), C1 ....$69.00

Dorothy Hamill, Olympic, Ideal, 1977, 11½", NRFB $75.00

Dr Dolittle (Rex Harrison), Mattel, 1967, 6", MIB, A $25.00

Dr Kildare (Richard Chamberlin), Metro-Goldwyn Mayer, 1962, 11½", rare, MIB $350.00

Elizabeth Taylor, Butterfield-8, Tri-Star Dolls, 1982, 11½", NRFB..$125.00

Elvis Presley, Graceland, 1982, in any of 6 outfits, 11½", NRFB, ea..$70.00

Florence Griffith Joiner (Flo-Jo), LJN, 1989, Olympic gold medal runner, 11½", NRFB $35.00

Flying Nun (Sally Field), Hasbro, 1967, 12", NRFB.......$200.00

Gone With the Wind (Clark Gable as Rhett Butler), World Dolls, 1980, 1st edition, 12", NRFB $65.00

Gone With the Wind (Vivian Leigh as Scarlett), World Dolls, 1980, 1st edition, 12", NRFB..................................$65.00

Groucho Marx, Effanbee, 1983, Legends series, 17", M....$45.00

Hardy Boys (Parker Stevenson as Frank Hardy), Kenner, 12", NRFB $45.00

Hardy Boys (Shaun Cassidy as Joe Hardy), Kenner, 12", NRFB $45.00

Home Alone (Macaully Caulkin as Kevin), makes screaming sounds, MIB, T1...$20.00

I Love Lucy (Desi Arnez as Ricky Ricardo), Applause, 1988, 17", MIB...$40.00

I Love Lucy (Desi Arnez as Ricky Ricardo), Hamilton Presents, 1991, vinyl, w/stand, 15½", MIB..................$30.00

I Love Lucy (Lucille Ball as Lucy Ricardo), 1950s, stuffed cloth, I Love Lucy on apron, NM $200.00

Jackie Coogan, Kamkin, 1925, reddish-blond mohair wig, missing shoes, 19", EX, A $978.00

Joe Namath, Mego, 1970, 11½", rare, MIB, $300.00.

Photo courtesy of Henri Yunes.

Julia (Diahann Carroll), Mattel, 1969, in nurse's outfit, 11½", MIB...$140.00

Julia (Diahann Carroll), Mattel, 1969, metallic jumpsuit, talker, 11½", MIB $200.00

Kiss (Ace Frehley), Mego, 1978, 12", NRFB $125.00

Kiss (Gene Simmons), Mego, 1978, 12", NRFB.............$125.00

Kiss (Paul Stanley), Mego, 1978, 12", NM (damaged box), H4 ....$99.00

Kiss (Peter Criss), Mego, 1978, 12", NRFB....................$125.00

Laurel & Hardy, Knickerbocker 1965, cloth w/vinyl heads, 9", VG, S2, pr..$65.00

Laverne & Shirley (Michael McKean as Lenny & David L Lander as Squiggy), Mego, 1977, 12", NRFB, pr............$190.00

Laverne & Shirley (Penny Marshall as Laverne & Cindy Williams as Shirley), Mego, 1977, 12", NRFB, pr ...$125.00

Mae West, Effanbee, Great Legends series, MIB $120.00

Marilyn Monroe, Tri-Star, 1982, in any outfit, NRFB, ea .$75.00

Mary Poppins (Julie Andrews), Horsman, 1964, 10", NRFB ..$50.00

Monkees Show Biz Baby (Davy Jones), Hasbro, 1967, no shoes or belt, B3 ....$49.00

Monkees Show Biz Baby (Micky Dolenz), Hasbro, 1967, complete w/clothing, shoes & belt, EX, B3 ....$78.00

Monkees Show Biz Baby (Mike Nesmith), Hasbro, 1967, complete w/clothing, shoes & belt, EX, B3 ....$78.00

Monkees Show Biz Baby (Peter Tork), Hasbro, 1967, complete w/clothing, shoes & belt, EX, B3 ....$78.00

Munsters (Al Lewis as Grandpa), Remco #1821, 1964, 6", NMIB...$190.00

Munsters (Fred Gwynne as Herman Munster), Remco #1820, 1964, MIB...$150.00

Munsters (Yvonne De Carlo as Lilly Munster), Remco #1822, 1964, MIB $45.00

OJ Simpson, Shindana, 1975, 9½", VG, S2 ....$75.00

Police Woman (Angie Dickenson as Pepper Martin), Horsman, 1976, 9", MIB, H4 ....$45.00

Police Woman (Angie Dickenson as Pepper Martin), Horsman, 1976, 9", EX, J5...$20.00

Sonny & Cher (Cher), Mego, 1977, Growing Hair, 12", NRFB...$80.00

Sonny & Cher (Cher), Mego, 1976, pk dress, 12", NRFB.$45.00

Sonny & Cher (Sonny Bono), Mego, 1976, 12", NRFB...$80.00

Three Stooges, Collins, 1982, stuffed cloth w/life-like hair, set of 3, ea 13", MOC, A....................................$138.00

Vanna White, Shopping Club in Spain, 11½", MIB, S2 ..$35.00

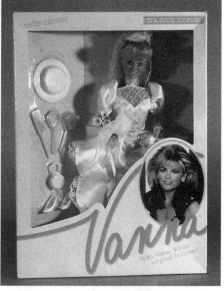

Vanna White, in wedding dress, Totsy Toys, 1990 Limited Edition, rare, MIB, $100.00.

Photo courtesy of Henri Yunes.

Wayne Gretsky, Mattel, 1980, 12", M (EX- box), M5 ...$130.00

Wizard of Oz (Judy Garland as Dorothy), Effanbee, 1984, Great Legends series, MIB $125.00

Cereal Boxes

This is an area of collecting that attracts crossover interest from fans of advertising as well as character-related toys. What makes a cereal box interesting? Look for Batman, Huckleberry Hound, or a well-known sports figure like Larry Bird or Roger Marris on the front or back. Boxes don't have to be old to be collectible, but the basic law of supply and demand dictates that the older ones are going to be expensive! After all, who saved cereal boxes from 1910? By chance if Grandma did, the 1910 Corn Flakes box with a printed-on baseball game could get her $750.00. Unless you're not concerned with bugs, it will probably be best to empty the box and very carefully pull apart the glued flaps. Then you can store it flat. Be sure to save any prize that might have been packed inside. Unless noted, our values are for boxes in mint condition, whether full or folded.

Advisor: Jon Thurmond (T1).

Princess Diana and Prince Charles, Goldberger, 1982 Wedding, MIB, $160.00 for the pair.

Photo courtesy of Henri Yunes.

Real Models Collection (Beverly Johnson), Matchbox #54613, 1989, 11½", MIB....................................$35.00

Real Models Collection (Cheryl Tiegs), Matchbox #54612, 1989, 11½", NRFB..................................$35.00

Real Models Collection (Christie Brinkley), Matchbox #54611, 1989, 11½", NRFB..................................$35.00

Redd Foxx, Shindana, 1976, stuffed cloth, 2-sided image, MIB $35.00

Redd Foxx, Shindana, 1977, stuffed cloth, talker, MIB....$45.00

Rocky (Sylvester Stallone), Phoenix Toys, 1986, 16", NRFB..$15.00

Batman Cereal, 1990, M $7.50

Cap'n Crunch, 1990, Bike Wheel Rattler, T1 ....$3.00

Cap'n Crunch Berries, 1990, Magic Puppets, T1 ....$4.00

Cheerios, 1986, free Nestle Quik offer, T1......................$4.00

Cheerios, 1987, free M&M's inside, T1............................$3.00

Cocoa Pebbles, 1991, Bedrock Cave Games offer, T1 ....$5.00

Cocoa Puffs, 1950s, aircraft carrier & jet launcher cutout on back, VG $65.00

Franken Berry Cereal, 1974, EX, from $85 to $100.00

Franken Berry Cereal, 1985, free Wacky Wafers, T1 ....$5.00

Fruit Loops, 1987, free Garfield padlock offer, T1...............$4.00

GI Joe, Ralston, 1980s, pictures GI Joe, NM, J5 ....$35.00

Grape Nuts Flakes, 1960s, Mickey Mantle on front, baseball cards on back, complete, EX $225.00

Honey-Nut Cheerios, 1990, Magic Motion Sticker, T1 .....$3.00

Hot Wheels Cereal, 1990, Win Super Chargers, T1.........$10.00

Jetsons Cereal, 1990, free Lunar Launcher, T1 ....$5.00

Kellogg's All Stars, 1960, Huckleberry Hound cutouts on back, EX+ $125.00

Kellogg's Cocoa Krispies, 1981, free Sneaky Squeaker, T1 .$5.00

Kellogg's Cocoa Krispies, 1986, free Hot Wheels offer, T1 ..$10.00

Kellogg's Corn Flakes, Corny & Friend in Another Tall-Up Tale, back only, EX, J2...$30.00

Kellogg's Corn Flakes, Make-up Mask, back only, EX $10.00

Kellogg's Corn Flakes, 1960s, Huckleberry Hound on front, Yogi Bear driving car on back, EX $125.00

Kellogg's Corn Flakes, 1961, Huckleberry Hound & Quick Draw McGraw masks on front, EX..$85.00

Kellogg's Corn Flakes, 1961, Yogi Bear Birthday, EX+...$125.00

Kellogg's Corn Flakes, 1970s, Fernando Valenzuela on front, Spalding baseball offer on back, NM, T2 ....$29.00

Kellogg's Corn Flakes, 1973, biography scenes of Clara Barton, EX, J2 ....$45.00

Kellogg's OK's, 1960s, Yogi Bear, box front only, EX, from $20 to $25.00

Kellogg's OK's, 1962, Yogi Bear on front, NM $250.00

Kellogg's OK's Snack Pack, 1960s, Brawny on front, VG.$25.00

Kellogg's Raisin Bran, 1984, free bumper stickers, T1.........$5.00

Kellogg's Rice Krispies, Canadian, Snap!, Crackle! & Pop! on front, Annie Oakley doll offer on back, NM $95.00

Kellogg's Rice Krispies, Pitch & Hit Baseball Game, front & back only, EX, J2..$40.00

Kellogg's Rice Krispies, 1950, mk Bob Smith, features Howdy Doody on front, scarce, EX, from $250 to...............$300.00

Kellogg's Rice Krispies, 1960s, Woody Woodpecker's Message Contest, EX, from $85 to..$100.00

Kellogg's Rice Krispies Snack Pack, 1960s, Snap! Crackle! & Pop! on front, VG...$25.00

Kellogg's Sugar Smacks, Canadian, 1958, Smaxey the Seal, ring offer on back, NM $225.00

Kellogg's Super Pops, 1950s, Andy Devine as Jingles on front, 3-D cut-out scene on back, EX $165.00

Kix, 1951, rodeo cattle chute cutout on box, uncut, M, J2 ..$60.00

Lucky Charms, 1st box, front & back only, EX, J2 ....$50.00

Nabisco Klondike Pete's Crunchy Nuggets Rice Cereal, 1974, w/stick-on premium offer, M $100.00

Nabisco Rice Honey's, 1964, Winnie the Pooh on front & back, EX+ $125.00

Nabisco Shreddies Whole Wheat, Canadian, 1960s, treasure map offer, M...$65.00

Post Alpha-Bits, 1960s, mailman on front delivers letters, missing parts of flaps, G $100.00

Post Sugar Crisp, 1950s, Sugar Bear's Playhouse, entire box designed as playhouse, EX $225.00

Post Toasties, 1934, 1-pc w/back & 2 side panels featuring 'Mickey Out West,' cowboy Mickey on horse & Pluto, EX, M8 ....$40.00

Post Toasties, 1934, 1-pc w/back & 2 side panels featuring the Disney Silly Symphonies characters, EX, M8 ....$35.00

Post Toasties, 1935, Mickey Mouse Band Concert, back only, VG+ $35.00

Post 40% Bran Flakes, Li'l Abner & Dogpatch characters on back, VG $125.00

Quaker Oats, Canadian, black and white photo of Roy Rogers and Trigger advertising free photo for 2 box tops, scarce, VG+, A, $215.00.

Quaker Pettijohns Rolled Whole Wheat, EX, J2 ....$30.00

Quaker Puffed Rice, Sgt Preston picture to color on back, unused, M $150.00

Quaker Puffed Wheat, features Shirley Temple, dated 1939, EX, minimum value, $300.00.

Ranger Joe Wheat Honnies, 1950s, Ranger Joe on front, airfield cutout on back, EX $225.00

Sir Grapefellow Cereal, 1973, glider plane offer on back, NM $100.00

Super Golden Crisp, 1992, free Chinese yo-yo offer, T1 ....$4.00

Wheaties, 1950s, 10x12" Bambi Fun Mask on back, VG, J5.$15.00

Wheaties, 1980s, Jerry Rice on front, M $12.00

Wheaties, 1990, Michael Jordan, unused file copy, M, T2 .$12.00

Character and Promotional Drinking Glasses

Once given away by fast-food chains and gas stations, a few years ago, you could find these at garage sales everywhere for a dime or even less. Then, when it became obvious to collectors that these glass giveaways were being replaced by plastic, as is always the case when we realize no more (of anything) will be forthcoming, we all decided we wanted them. Since many were character-related and part of a series, we felt the need to begin to organize these garage-sale castaways, building sets and completing series. Out of the thousands available, the better ones are those with super heroes, sports stars, old movie stars, Star Trek, and Disney and Walter Lantz cartoon characters. Pass up those whose colors are worn and faded. Unless another condition or material is indicated in the description, values are for glass tumblers in mint condition. Cups are plastic unless noted otherwise.

There are some terms used in our listings that may be confusing if you're not familiar with this collecting field. 'Brockway' style tumblers are thick and heavy, and they taper at the bottom. 'Federal' is thinner, and top and diameters are equal.

Advisors: Mark E. Chase (C2) and Michael J. Kelly, authors of *Collectible Drinking Glasses* (Collector Books, 1995). See also Clubs, Newsletters and Other Publications.

Alice in Wonderland, Canadian (Secma), sm juice, set of 6, A $37.00
Alice in Wonderland, Wonderful World of Disney, WDP/Pepsi, A $14.00
Andy Panda & Miranda, Walter Lantz, 5⅝", A.............$21.00
Aquaman, Super Heroes, DC Comics/Pepsi, 1978, 6¼", A ..$8.00
Archie Bunker for President, goblet, Arby's, 4 characters in yel on gr, lg, A $10.00

Archies, Mr Weatherby Drops In, Welch's, 1974, 4¼", $5.00.

Bambi, Wonderful World of Disney, WDP/Pepsi $18.00
Batman, Super Heroes Series, DC Comics/Pepsi, 1976, A .$19.00
Batman, Ultramar/Pepsi, Canadian, set of 6, A $25.00
Beaky Buzzard, Warner Bros/Pepsi, Federal, wht letters, 1973, 16-oz, A $5.00

Beauregard, Taco Villa/Pepsi, 1979, A $8.00
Big Baby Huey, Harvey Cartoons/Pepsi, shows action, 5", A ..$6.00
Big Baby Huey, Harvey Cartoons/Pepsi, 16-oz, A.............$18.00
Big Bad Wolf, Disney, 1930s, 4¾", A.............................$147.00
Big Boy, 3⅝", A..$18.00
Big Boy, 50th Anniversary, A..$9.00
Big Yella, Kellogg's, 1977, 4½" $8.00
Boris & Natasha, PAT Ward/Pepsi, 16-oz, A.....................$18.00
Boris Badenov, PAT Ward/Pepsi, 12-oz, A.......................$11.00
Bugs Bunny, Warner Bros/Pepsi, Brockway, logo under name, 16-oz, A..$10.00
Bugs Bunny, Warner Bros/Pepsi, Federal, logo under name, 15-oz, A $12.00
Bugs Bunny, Warner Bros/Pepsi, Federal, wht letters, 1973, 16-oz, A $10.00

Bugs Bunny, What's Up Doc, Welch's, 1973, 4½", $5.00.

Bugs Bunny, 50th Birthday, Canadian, 1990, shows action, set of 4, A $11.00
Bugs Bunny & Marvin w/Ray Gun, Warner Bros, 1976, A...$34.00
Bugs Bunny in Diving for Carrots, Looney Tunes Adventure Series, Arby's, 1988, 5⅝", A.......................................$19.00
Bullwinkle, PAT Ward/Pepsi, blk letters, 16-oz, A...........$16.00
Bullwinkle Crosses the Delaware, Arby's, 1976, 16-oz, A..$17.00
Buzz Buzzard & Space Mouse, Walter Lantz, 5⅝", A........$23.00
Captain America & the Falcon, Super Heroes, Marvel Comics/7 Eleven, 5½" $20.00

Captain Crook, Collector Series, McDonald's, 12-oz, A $4.00

Captain Crook, McDonaldland Action Series, 1977, EX, P3 ....$5.00

Care Bears, Friend Bear or Good Luck Bear, Pizza Hut/Pepsi, A $11.00

Casper & Nightmare's Midnight Ride, Arby's, 1976, 12-oz, A..$15.00

Casper & The Haunted House, Harvey Cartoons/Pepsi, 12-oz, A..$6.00

Charles Dickens, red characters w/wht script at bottom, 4¾", MIB, A..$15.00

Chilly Willy, Walter Lantz, 16-oz, A $31.00

Chilly Willy & Smedly, Walter Lantz, wht letters, 5⅝", A..$27.00

Christmas Carol, Subway/Pepsi, set of 4, A $20.00

Cinderella, Fairy Good & Kind..., red, yel & bl, 5¼", A ..$10.00

Cinderella, gr & yel, 4⅝", rare color combination, A, from $12 to..$15.00

Cinderella, red, yel & bl, 4⅝", complete set of 8, A $62.00

Clarabelle Cow, Disney, 1930s, 4⅜", A.........................$39.00

Cool Cat, Warner Bros/Pepsi, Federal, logo under name, 1973, 15-oz, A..$26.00

Cool Cat & Beaky, flying kite, Warner Bros, 1976, A........$6.00

Cuddles & Oswald, Walter Lantz, 5⅝", A $28.00

Daffy Duck, Warner Bros/Pepsi, Federal, wht letters, 16-oz, A..$5.00

Daffy Duck & Porky Pig, w/cooking pot & Ladle, Warner Bros, 1976, slight imaging problems, A..............................$29.00

Daffy Duck in Jungle Jitters, Looney Tunes Adventure Series, Arby's, 1988, 5⅝", A $19.00

Daisy, Picnic Series, WDP/Pepsi, 1979, A $2.00

Davy Crockett, Walt Disney, 4¼", $12.00.

Detroit Redwings, Burr & Klima, Little Caesar's Pizza, 1988, A..$8.00

Detroit Tigers, Rozena, Trammell & Johnson, Little Caesar's Pizza, 1984, A...$5.00

Dinosaur, Monster March, Sea World/Pepsi/Pizza Hut, set of 4, A..$15.00

Disney Classic Tumbler, Burger King, M, C3, complete set of 8 ....$29.00

Donald Duck, Hook's Drugs, 1984, A $26.00

Donald Duck, Picnic Series, WDP/Pepsi, 1979, A.............$8.00

Droopy, MGM/Pepsi, wht letters, 1975, A.......................$15.00

Dudley Do-Right, PAT Ward/Pepsi, 16-oz, A, from $11 to ..$17.00

Dynomutt, Hanna-Barbera/Pepsi, 1977, 6¼", A..............$29.00

Elmer Fudd, Pepsi, Brockway, 1973, 6¼", $5.00.

Elmer Fudd, Warner Bros/Pepsi, Federal, blk letters, 16-oz, A $4.00

Empire Strikes Back, Boba Fett, Burger King, M..................$3.00

Empire Strikes Back, C-3PO, Burger King, NM..................$4.00

Empire Strikes Back, Darth Vader, Burger King, 1980, NM ..$4.00

Empire Strikes Back, R2-D2, Burger King, 1980, NM $4.00

Ernest, Soft Batch Reminds Me of Cookies..., Keebler, 1984, A $8.00

Fantastic Four, Super Heroes, Marvel Comics/7 Eleven, 1977, 5½" $20.00

Flash, Super Heroes, DC Comics/Pepsi, 1978, 6¼", A $10.00

Flintstones, Hanna-Barbera/Pepsi, 1977, 6¼", A..............$26.00

Flintstones, Welch's, face in bottom, 4", NM, I2 ....$8.00

Frawley, Taco Villa/Pepsi, 1979, A....................................$9.00

Garfield, Home James, McDonald's, set of 4, A................$24.00

Ghostbusters, Sunoco, Canadian, 1989, set of 6, A $37.00

Ghostbusters, w/No Ghost logo, NM $5.00

Goofy, Mickey's Christmas Carol, WDP/Coca-Cola, 1982, 6⅛", A $11.00

Goonies, Sloth & Goonies, Godfather's Pizza/Coca-Cola, 1985, 5⅝", A $5.00

Great Muppet Caper, McDonald's, 1981, 6", EX, P3 ....$3.00

Green Lantern, Super Heroes Moon Series, Pepsi, 1976, A..$11.00

Grimace, Collector Series, McDonald's, 12-oz, A $11.00

Gulliver's Travels, Snoop, Paramount, 1939, 4½", A $15.00

Happy Days, Fonz (portrait), Dr Pepper, A $15.00

Happy Days, Fonz on motorcycle, Dr Pepper, A $22.00

Happy Days, Joanie, Dr Pepper, A...................................$10.00

Happy Days, Ralph, Dr Pepper, A $10.00

Happy Days, Richie, Dr Pepper, A $8.00

Holly Hobbie, Christmas, Coca-Cola, 1977, numbered set of 4, A $15.00

Holly Hobbie, Christmas, Coca-Cola, 1981, set of 3, A...$10.00

Holly Hobbie, Happy Talk, Coca-Cola, set of 6, A $10.00

Holly Hobbie, Simple Pleasures, Coca-Cola, set of 6, A ..$21.00

Holly Hobbie, Start Each Day in a Happy Way, bl girl, MIB, A $3.00

Holly Hobbie, 12 Days of Christmas, Coca-Cola, 1979, numbered set of 4, A...$17.00

Horace & Clarabelle, Happy Birthday Mickey, 1978, A ..$21.00

Hot Stuff, Harvey Cartoons, button bottom, A................$23.00

Hot Stuff, Harvey Cartoons/Pepsi, blk letters, 16-oz, A ...$15.00

Howard the Duck, Super Heroes, Marvel Comics/7 Eleven, 1977, 5½" $20.00

Howdy Doody, Welch's, 1950s, Here Comes Music for the Doodyville Circus, NM, C1...................................$24.00

Howdy Doody, Welch's, 1950s, set of 4 different, M, A ...$60.00

Huckleberry Hound & Yogi Bear, Hanna-Barbera/Pepsi, 1977, 6¼", A..$27.00

Incredible Hulk, Super Heroes, 7 Eleven/Pepsi, 1977, A..$25.00

Indiana Jones & the Temple of Doom, Wendy's/7-Up, 1984, 4 different, 5¾", A, ea..$9.00

Indianapolis 500, 1951, from $16 to................................$18.00

James Bond, View to a Kill, 007 Collector Series, 4", A...$14.00

Jim Bowie, fighting Indian, red, gr & wht on clear, A......$25.00

Jiminy Cricket, Musical Notes, Disney, Canadian, 4⅝", A..$8.00

Josie & the Pussycats, Hanna-Barbera/Pepsi, 1977, 6¼", A, from $23 to $28.00

Julius Irving, Taco Villa/Pepsi, 1979, from $10 to $15.00

Jungle Book, Bagheera, Pepsi...$75.00

Jungle Book, Balou, Pepsi $70.00

Jungle Book, Mowgli, Pepsi, M, I2 ....$60.00

Jungle Book, Shere Kahn, Pepsi $65.00

Keebler's, 135th Anniversary, 1988, A..............................$8.00

Lady & the Tramp, Wonderful World of Disney, WDP/Pepsi, A $25.00

Lampwick, orange, 4¾", A..$22.00

Lazlo, Taco Villa/Pepsi, 1979 ....$12.00

Li'l Abner, Al Capp, 1949, blk on clear, 4¾" $25.00

Li'l Abner, Sneaky Pete's Hot Dogs, 1975 ....$75.00

Li'l Abner & Daisy Mae, Kickapoo Joy Juice, Al Capp, 1977, A $21.00

Little Lulu, Alvin, MH Buell, A..$60.00

Little Orphan Annie, Sunday Funnies, Pepsi, A................$9.00

Little Orphan Annie & Sandy, Swensen's, 1982, A $5.00

Lou Gerhig, United Oil/Pepsi, A.....................................$10.00

Mickey, Donald & Goofy, American on Parade, Coca-Cola, A $2.00

Mickey Mouse, All-Star Parade, Disney, 4½", A $17.00

Mickey Mouse, Happy Birthday, 50 Years of Magic, WDP/Coca-Cola, A...$6.00

Mickey Mouse Club, set of 5, A $30.00

Mickey Mouse Club Filmstrip, set of 4, A $45.00

Mighty Mouse, Pepsi-Cola, Brockway, 16-oz, A............$500.00

Minnie Mouse, Picnic Series, WDP/Pepsi, 1979, A............$7.00

Monopoly, Just Visiting, Arby's, 1985, A.........................$10.00

Moon Mullins, Sunday Funnies, 1976, 5⅝", A $10.00

Mortimer, Taco Villa, 1979..$12.00

Mr Peabody, PAT Ward/Pepsi, blk letters, 16-oz, A.........$14.00

Mumbly, Hanna-Barbera/Pepsi, 1977, A...........................$20.00

Natasha, PAT Ward/Pepsi, 12-oz, A $9.00

National Flag Foundation, Grand Union, pedestal foot, A ..$3.00

National Flag Foundation, Serapis, pedestal foot, A $5.00

National Flag Foundation, The Green Mountains, Coca-Cola, 1976, A $4.00

NFL, Browns, Mobil, dbl bands, 5½", A............................$4.00

NFL, Burger Chef, smoked glass, 1979, 5⅝", A................$5.00

NFL, Celtics World Championship, Mobil, 4", A $3.00

NFL, Cowboys, Mobil, single bands, 5½", A......................$6.00

NFL, Redskins Helmet, Mobil, frosted, 4", A....................$3.00

Night Before Christmas, Pepsi, 1982, set of 4, A $12.00

Noid, Avoid the Noid Sports Series, Domino's Pizza, A.....$4.00

Nursery Rhymes, A Frog He Would a Wooing Go..., Hazel Atlas, ribbed, A $10.00

Nursery Rhymes, Jack & Jill, pk, A $3.00

Nursery Rhymes, Peter Piper, bl & wht, A........................$5.00

Nursery Rhymes, Pussy Cat, Pussy Cat..., Hazel Atlas, ribbed, A..$11.00

Nutcracker Suite, McDonald's, 1990, set of 4, A.............$16.00

Ohio Indian, pitcher, frosted glass, $32.00; with 2 matching 6½" tumblers featuring Tecumseh and Prophet (from a set of 8), frosted glass, $7.50 each.

Oklahoma Indians, Hen-Toh, 8 different, 6½", ea..............$8.00

Olive Oyl, Popeye's Fried Chicken, 1978, A $20.00

Pancho, Pepsi, Brockway, 16-oz, A...................................$7.00

Pappy Yokum, Sneaky Pete's Hot Dogs, 1975, A..............$50.00

Paul Revere, Heritage Collector Series, Coca-Cola, 1976, A .$3.00

Penguin, Super Heroes Moon Series, Pepsi, 1976, A, from $20 to $25.00

Pepe Le Peu, Warner Bros/Pepsi, Federal, blk letters, 16-oz, A $7.00

Petunia Pig, Warner Bros/Pepsi, Federal, wht letters, 1973, 16-oz, A $6.00

Pierre the Bear, LK, 1977, set of 4, A $8.00

Pierre the Bear, LK, 1978-79, set of 4, A..........................$12.00

Pinocchio, Musical Notes, Disney, red, 4¾", A $12.00

Pinocchio, Wonderful World of Disney, WDP/Pepsi, A ..$25.00

Pittsburgh Steelers, Alltime Greatest Steelers, McDonald's, 1982, numbered set of 4, A...............................$20.00

Pittsburgh Steelers, Andy Russell, Brockway, 1976, 6¼", A....$9.00

Pittsburgh Steelers, Ray Mansfield, Brockway, 1976, 6¼", A $9.00

Pittsburgh Steelers, 1990, Hall of Fame, set of 4, C11 .....$20.00

Pittsburgh Steelers Superbowl #14, McDonald's, set of 4, A $20.00

Pluto, Disney, 1930s, 4⅜", A $36.00

Pluto, 1971-72 Walt Disney World souvenir, $6.00.

Popeye, Popeye's Fried Chicken 10th Anniversary, Pepsi, A $11.00

Popeye & Oscar, mk King Features Syndicate, 1933, Popeye on 1 side & Oscar on the other, 5", EX+ $65.00

Popeye & Swee' Pea, mk King Features Syndicate, 1933, Popeye on 1 side & Swee' Pea on the other, 5" $65.00

Porky Pig, Warner Bros/Pepsi, Brockway, logo under name, 16-oz, A, from $6 to $7.00

Porky Pig, Warner Bros/Pepsi, Federal, wht letters, 1973, 16-oz, A $6.00

Porky Pig, Warner Bros/Pepsi, logo under name, 15-oz, A .$12.00

Rescuers, Brutus & Nero, WDP/Pepsi, 1977, A $18.00

Rescuers, Penny, WDP/Pepsi, 1977, A.............................$14.00

Return of the Jedi, Darth Vader & Luke Skywalker, Burger King, 1983, NM...$3.00

Return of the Jedi, Emperor's Throne Room, Burger King, 1983, NM...$3.00

Return of the Jedi, Ewok Village, Burger King, 1983, NM .$3.00

Return of the Jedi, Han Solo, Burger King, 1983, NM $3.00

Return of the Jedi, Han Solo/Tatooine Desert, Burger King, 1983, NM...$3.00

Return of the Jedi, Jaba the Hut, Burger King, 1983, NM ..$3.00

Return of the Jedi, Leia Organa, Burger King, 1983, NM...$3.00

Richie Rich, Harvey Cartoons/Pepsi, A...........................$21.00

Road Runner, Warner Bros/Pepsi, Brockway, 16-oz, A $10.00

Road Runner, Warner Bros/Pepsi, Federal, 1973, 15-oz, A..$25.00

Roberto Clemente, United Oil/Pepsi, A...........................$14.00

Robin, Super Heroes Moon Series, Pepsi, 1976, A $11.00

Rocky, Pepsi, 1970s, shows action, M $9.00

Rocky in the Dawn's Early Light, Arby's, 1976, 12-oz, A.$15.00

Rocky Squirrel, PAT Ward/Pepsi, wht or blk letters, 16-oz .$15.00

Sad Sack, Harvey Cartoons, A $34.00

Scooby Doo, Hanna-Barbera/Pepsi, 1977, 6¼", A, from $15 to...$26.00

Shazam, Super Heroes Series, Pepsi, 1978, NM, D9 ....$10.00

Sigmund, Taco Villa, 1979...$12.00

Sleeping Beauty, Good Fairies Bestow Their Gifts, 1958, EX, I2 ....$20.00

Sleeping Beauty, Samson (Prince Phillip's horse), A, from $12 to $15.00

Sleeping Beauty, WDP, 1958, set of 5 ea w/different characters, 5", M, A $70.00

Slow Poke, Warner Bros/Pepsi, Brockway, blk letters.......$40.00

Snidely Whiplash, PAT Ward/Pepsi, wht letters, 16-oz, A..$11.00

Snow White, Wonderful World of Disney, WDP/Pepsi, A..$28.00

Snow White & the Seven Dwarfs, 1939, set of 8, 4½", M .$180.00

Speedy Gonzales, Warner Bros/Pepsi, Federal, wht letters, 16-oz, A $4.00

Spiderman, Super Heroes, Marvel Comics/7 Eleven, 1977, 5½", A $40.00

Spike, MGM/Pepsi, wht letters, 1975, A $19.00

Star Trek, Captain James Kirk, Dr Pepper, 1976, A $25.00

Star Trek III: Search for Spock, Taco Bell, 1984, set of 4, A $11.00

Star Trek the Motion Picture, Decker & Ilia, Coca-Cola, 1980, NM, I2 ....$22.00

Supergirl, Super Hero Moon Series, Pepsi, 1976, A, from $10 to $15.00

Superman, ...Uses X-Ray Vision, Pepsi, 1964, red & gray, 5⅝", A $48.00

Superman, breaking chains, Pepsi, 1978, 6", A $7.00

Superman, Pepsi, 1971, 4", A $7.00

Superman, saving bus, Pepsi, 1964, bl & pk, 5⅝", A $23.00

Superman the Movie, DC Comics/Pepsi, 1978, set of 6, A..$21.00

Superman the Movie, Kal-el Comes to Earth, DC Comics/Pepsi, 1978, 5⅝", A $5.00

Superman the Movie, Lois Lane Is Saved by Her Hero, DC Comics/Pepsi, 1978, 5⅝", A $11.00

Swee' Pea, Popeye's Pals, Popeye's Famous Fried Chicken/Pepsi, 1979, A $28.00

Sylvester, Pepsi, 1973, 6½", $5.00.

Sylvester, Warner Bros/Pepsi, Brockway, logo under name, 16-oz, A $8.00

Sylvester, Warner Bros/Pepsi, Federal, blk letters, 16-oz, A..**$9.00**

Sylvester, Warner Bros/Pepsi, Federal, logo under name, 16-oz, A **$15.00**

Sylvester, Warner Bros/Pepsi, Federal, wht letters, 16-oz, A ..**$4.00**

Sylvester & Tweety in Anchors Away, Looney Tunes Adventure Series, Arby's, 1988, 6", A **$20.00**

Tasmanian Devil, Warner Bros/Pepsi, Brockway, wht letters, 16-oz, A..**$15.00**

Terry & the Pirates, Sunday Funnies, Pepsi, A **$8.00**

Thor, Super Heroes, Marvel Comics/7 Eleven, 1977, 5½", A **$20.00**

Tom Mix, 1930s, photo & signature on cobalt glass, fluted, 4", extremely rare, NM+, A **$95.00**

Tom Sawyer, Classics, Libbey, 3¼", A **$7.00**

Toucan Sam, Kellogg's, 1977, 4½", $8.00.

Tweety Bird, Marriott's Great America, 1975, 4⅝", A.....**$18.00**

Tweety Bird, Warner Bros/Pepsi, 1973, 5-oz, A...............**$18.00**

Twelve Days of Christmas, Pepsi, Brockway, 16-oz, set of 12, A **$36.00**

Ty Cobb, United Oil/Pepsi, A..**$15.00**

Underdog, phone booth, Walter Lantz, 12-oz, A..............**$11.00**

Wally Walrus, Walter Lantz, A..**$48.00**

Wally Walrus & Homer Pigeon, Walter Lantz, 5⅝", A....**$31.00**

Wendy, Harvey Cartoons/Pepsi, wht letters, 16-oz, A......**$21.00**

Wile E Coyote, Marriott's Great America, 1975, 4⅝", A.**$23.00**

Wile E Coyote, Warner Bros/Pepsi, Federal, wht letters, 16-oz, A..**$4.00**

Wile E Coyote, Warner Bros/Pepsi, Federal, 15-oz, A **$9.00**

Winnie the Pooh & Friends, chasing butterfly, Sears, A..**$11.00**

Winnie the Pooh for President, Sears, A **$16.00**

Wizard of Id, Arby's, 1983, 6 different, A, ea....................**$10.00**

Wizard of Oz, Cowardly Lion, S&C Co, yel, wavy, 5", A.**$10.00**

Wizard of Oz, Denslow highball, gr Oz logo, A..................**$8.00**

Wizard of Oz, Dorothy, S&C Co, pk, wavy, 5", A............**$10.00**

Wizard of Oz, Glinda, S&C Co, pk, fluted, 5", A..............**$18.00**

Wizard of Oz, Scarecrow, Land of Ahs Series, Kentucky Fried Chicken, 1984, A **$25.00**

Wizard of Oz, Tin Woodman, S&C Co, gr, plain, 5", A ..**$11.00**

Wizard of Oz, Wicked Witch of the West, S&C Co, fluted bottom, 5", A **$33.00**

Wizard of Oz, Winkies, S&C Co, starburst on bottom, fluted, 5", A **$26.00**

Wizard of Oz, Wizard, S&C Co, pk, plain, 5", A..............**$11.00**

Wizard of Oz, Wizard, wavy, 5", A **$10.00**

Wizard of Oz, 50th Anniversary, Whataburger, 1989, A....**$4.00**

Wonder Woman, Super Heroes/Pepsi, 1978, 6¼", EX........**$8.00**

Wonder Woman, Super Heroes/Pepsi, 1978, 6¼", G, I2 ....**$3.00**

Woody Woodpecker, Knothead & Splinter, Walter Lantz, wht letters, 5⅝", A **$21.00**

Woody Woodpecker, Walter Lantz, wht letters, 16-oz, A ..**$14.00**

Yogi Bear, w/picnic basket, Hanna-Barbera, 1983, A.......**$18.00**

Yosemite Sam, Warner Bros/Pepsi, Federal, blk letters, 16-oz, A **$6.00**

101 Dalmatians, Wonderful World of Disney, WDP/Pepsi, A **$11.00**

CHARACTER AND PROMOTIONAL PLASTIC CUPS

Babar's Magic Show, Arthur, Babar or Rataxes, Arby's, M, P10, ea **$5.00**

Batman, McDonald's, 1992, M, P10, ea...........................**$3.00**

Batman & Robin, 1966, insulated, rare, VG, S2..............**$45.00**

Beatles Love Song, 1970s, EX..**$25.00**

Captain Scarlet, Pizza Hut (Europe), complete set of 4, M, C3 ....**$32.00**

Conehead, Subway, M, S2...**$10.00**

Elvira, glow-in-the-dark, premium, M, S2........................**$25.00**

Max Headroom, M, S2 ....**$20.00**

Planet of the Apes, EX, S2 ....**$15.00**

Rocketeer, Pizza Hut, 1991, M, P10 ....**$5.00**

Spaceship, rocket ship shape w/removable nose cone, clear plastic w/spaceship graphics, 7½", EX, D9 ....**$5.00**

Star Trek Next Generation, Pizza Hut (Europe), complete set of 4, M, C3 ....**$35.00**

Super Heroes, Burger King, Batman, Superman, Wonder Woman & Darkseid, set of 4, H4 ....**$39.00**

Who Framed Roger Rabbit, McDonald's, 32-oz.................**$5.00**

CHARACTER AND PROMOTIONAL MUGS

Bamm-Bamm, Flintstones Vitamin premium, 1972, NM, C1...**$14.00**

Bart Simpson, infant's travel mug, Binky, wht plastic w/dbl hdl, yel leak-proof lid, M, K1 ....**$6.00**

Batman, 1960s, opaque wht, H4.....................................**$12.00**

Batman Returns, Applause, 1991, figural ceramic, MIB, H4.**$12.00**

Billy Bob, Showbiz Pizza Place......................................**$2.00**

Bob Hope, figural ceramic, NM......................................**$35.00**

Bugs Bunny, Marriott's Great America, milk glass, pedestal foot, 1975, 5½", A **$10.00**

Capt Midnight, Beetleware, 1955-57, C10 ....**$38.00**

Cindy Bear, Arby's, Yogi & Friends Series, M, P10 ....**$5.00**

Dick Tracy, Applause, A...**$5.00**

Dino, Flintstones Vitamin premium, 1972, plastic, VG, S2 .**$25.00**

Felix the Cat, Skansen, 1991, yel ceramic w/6 illus, MIB, C1 .**$31.00**

Frostie Root Beer, portrait of old bearded man w/red earmuffs, 6", A **$7.00**

Garfield, I'd Like Mornings Better..., McDonald's, A.........**$6.00**

Garfield, I'm Easy To Get Along With..., McDonald's, 1987, C11 ....$2.00

Garfield, Use Your Friends Wisely..., McDonald's, 1987, C11 .$2.00

Gone for the Morning, McDonald's, A $3.00

Grimace, McDonald's, purple, 1993, M, P10 ....$5.00

Howdy Doody, Sipmug, Kagran/Doodlings Inc, NM (EX box), A $135.00

Jiminy Cricket, lt bl plastic w/flasher eyes, 4", NM, D9....$10.00

Lazy Smurf, ceramic, 1982, A $4.00

Lemon Yellow, 1969, figural funny face, NM, S2 ....$25.00

Looney Tunes, Kentucky Fried Chicken, complete set of 4, M, C3..$29.00

Marvin the Martian, M, D4...$12.00

Mickey Mouse, plastic ice cream cone, S1 ....$10.00

Mitzi, Showbiz Pizza Place, A $2.00

Nervous Coffee, Freed Novelty Inc, 1950s, turq plastic w/battery-op vibrator, M (EX+ box), T2 ....$20.00

Nestle Quik, figural Bunny head, NM..............................$6.00

Nestle Quik, wht ceramic w/saying on back & Bunny in 17 different poses on front, M, S2 ....$15.00

Pebbles Flintstone, Flintstones Vitamin premium, 1972, NM, C1..$14.00

Pittsburgh Steelers, 50th Anniversary, Arby's/Dr Pepper, A..$3.00

Popeye, King Features, comic strip, 1980, 3½", VG $5.00

Rainbow Brite on Parade, 1983 ....$6.00

Return of the Jedi, 1983, Leia, Ewok, C-3PO, R2-D2 & Wicket, plastic, EX, S2 ....$10.00

Rocketeer, Applause, MIB, H10......................................$15.00

Ronald McDonald, plastic, 3½", A $5.00

Smokey the Bear, milk glass $14.00

Snoopy, Allergic to Mornings, EX, O1...............................$5.00

Snoopy, Christmas 1976, NM, O1 ....$20.00

Snoopy, w/root beer mug, A&W, mail-order promotion, 6", MIB, A $19.00

Star Trek, Captain Kirk, Hamilton, ceramic, M (NM box), P9 ....$20.00

Star Wars, Yoda & Luke, Hamilton, ceramic, MIB, P9 ....$20.00

Superman, in flight, milk glass, 1971, M, C1 ....$29.00

Toucan Sam, plastic w/feet, Kellogg's premium, 1981, NM.$8.00

Woody Woodpecker, wood grain w/emb face on both sides, 1970s premium, G, S2 ....$20.00

Character Clocks and Watches

Clocks and watches whose dials depict favorite sports and TV stars have been manufactured with the kids in mind since the 1930s, when Ingersoll made both a clock and a wristwatch featuring Mickey Mouse. The #1 Mickey wristwatch came in the now-famous orange box illustrated with a variety of Disney characters. The watch itself featured a second hand with three revolving Mickey figures. It was available with either a metal or leather band. Babe Ruth stared on an Exacta Time watch in 1949, and the original box contained not only the watch but a baseball with a facsimilie signature.

Collectors prize the boxes about as highly as they do the watches. Many were well illustrated and colorful, but most were promptly thrown away, so they're hard to find today. Be sure you buy only watches in very good condition. Rust, fading, scratches or other signs of wear sharply devaluate a clock or a watch. Hundreds have been produced, and if you're going to collect them, you'll need to study *Comic Character Clocks and Watches* by Howard S. Brenner (Books Americana) for more information.

Advisor: Bill Campbell (C10).

See also Advertising; California Raisins.

CLOCKS

Batman Talking Alarm Clock, Janex, 1974, 3-D figures of Robin in Batmobile & Batman by dial w/Bat emblem, EX+, J2 ....$65.00

Batman Talking Alarm Clock, Janex, 1974, 3-D figures of Robin in Batmobile & Batman by dial w/Bat emblem, MIB, A $116.00

Betty Boop Alarm Clock, Betty, Koko & Bimbo w/nodding head for second hand on rnd dial, MIB, A $80.00

Big Bird Alarm Clock, Bradley, 1970s, VG, J5 ....$35.00

Bugs Bunny Alarm Clock, Ingraham, 1940s, VG, J5 ....$65.00

Bugs Bunny Talking Alarm Clock, Janex TW, full-figure Bugs Bunny beside face, plastic, battery-op, 7", NM $35.00

Cinderella Alarm Clock, Bradley/WDP Phinney-Walker, full-figure Cinderella w/glowing slipper in center, rare, MIB, A...$110.00

Cookie Monster Alarm Clock, Bradley, 1970s, VG, J5 ....$35.00

Donald Duck Alarm Clock, Bayard/France, 1960s, Donald figure keeps time, chrome fr, wht base, 4½" dia, M (EX box), A...$205.00

Donald Duck Alarm Clock, Forestville/WDP, Donald dancing w/glow-in-the-dark hands on dial, hexagonal, rare, MIB, A...$172.00

Felix the Cat Alarm Clock, image of Felix & mouse w/nodding head as second hand on rnd dial, MIB, A................$100.00

Hopalong Cassidy Alarm Clock, US Time, 1950, Hoppy riding Topper on dial, Hopalong Cassidy in raised letters on base, EX, $200.00.

Howdy Doody Talking Alarm Clock, 1974, EX+, J2........$95.00

Masters of the Universe Talking Alarm Clock, NM (EX box), O1 ....$28.50

Mickey Mouse & Goofy Alarm Clock, Bradley/WDP, 1960s, full figures in center, 4½" dia, EX+.................................$100.00

Mickey Mouse & Pluto Alarm Clock, Bradley/WDP, 1950s-60s, 2-bell, Mickey in nightcap & Pluto sleeping, scarce, NM $150.00

Mickey Mouse Alarm Clock, Bayard/France, 1960s, Mickey figure keeps time, chrome fr, red base, 4½" dia, M (EX box), A $190.00

Mickey Mouse Alarm Clock, Bayard/France, 1960s, Mickey figure keeps time, chrome fr, red base, 4½" dia, M (VG box), A $135.00

Mickey Mouse Alarm Clock, British Ingersoll, 1933, Mickey's hands keep time, red metal fr (rpt), 4", rare, NM, A .$448.00

Mickey Mouse Boutique Alarm Clock, Bradley/WDP, 2-bell, full-figure Mickey emb on bl dial, oval, scarce, MIB, A $140.00

Mickey Mouse Electric Wall Clock, 1970s, figure of Mickey w/hands indicating time, red metal case, VG, S2 ......$75.00

Mickey Mouse Pendulum Clock, French, 1933, diecut Mickey atop heart-shaped fr, red & blk, 8", rare, EX+, A $468.00

Mighty Mouse Alarm Clock, Japan, 2-bell, Mighty Mouse's arms keep time on rnd dial, scarce, EX+, A $100.00

Miss Piggy Alarm Clock, Times, w/picture inset, electric, EX, S2 ....$55.00

Pluto Alarm Clock, Bayard, 1964, second hand w/star moves Pluto's head back & forth, 4½" dia, NM, A...............$175.00

Raggedy Ann & Andy Talking Alarm Clock, HK Janex, I Love You lettered in heart on face, plastic, battery-op, 7", EX+, A...$50.00

Ronald McDonald Alarm Clock, metal fr w/Ronald on dial, MIB, S2 ....$35.00

Ronald McDonald Alarm Clock, tilted head pose, M, C11.$40.00

Roy Rogers and Trigger Alarm Clock, Ingraham, 1950s, desert scene with Roy and Trigger, galloping motion ticks off seconds, 4" square, NM+ (EX+ box), $400.00.

Roy Rogers & Trigger Alarm Clock, 1950s, Trigger rears as clock ticks, EX, S9.................................$185.00

Roy Rogers & Trigger 40-Hour Alarm Clock, box only, pictures Roy riding Trigger on front, NM, A $147.00

R2-D2 & C-3PO Talking Alarm Clock, MIB, H4...........$65.00

Strawberry Shortcake Alarm Clock, Elgin/Bradley, full figure on rnd dial, bobbing head for second-hand movement, MIB, A $80.00

Three Little Pigs Alarm Clock, Ingersoll, 1934, Three Little Pigs surround lg image of Big Bad Wolf, 4" dia, VG, A ..$355.00

Thundercats Talking Alarm Clock, rare, NM $75.00

Underdog Alarm Clock, Leonardo/Germany, octagon shape w/Underdogs arms telling time, 3" dia, MIB (scarce box), A $147.00

Winnie the Pooh Alarm Clock, Bradley/WDP, Winnie's arms keep time, plastic & metal w/button on top, 3" sq, NM+ $50.00

Woody's (Woodpecker) Cafe Alarm Clock, Hong Kong, 2nd issue, tree trunk & Woody rocking w/second hand, 4½" dia, EX, A $111.00

Woody Woodpecker Alarm Clock, Columbia, 1959, 1st issue, Woody in chef's outfit ticks off seconds, 5" dia, NM, A $225.00

POCKET WATCHES

Babe Ruth, Exacta Time, 1950s, numbers surround Babe w/2 bats in ball diamond, name across chest, 1⅞" dia, EX+, A $450.00

Buck Rogers 25th Century, Dille, 1930s, working, 2" dia, EX, A $650.00

Dan Dare, Ingersoll/Great Britain, 1950s, dial shows space scene w/spaceship & gun ticking off seconds, M (EX box), A $785.00

Dan Dare, 1950s, Dan Dare shoots monster, Eagle logo on back, NM, A $330.00

Fred Flintstone, Swiss Made, 1973, numbers surround full figure flanked by name & Yabba Dabba Doo!, 2" dia, NM, A $409.00

Hopalong Cassidy, unmarked, 1950s, chrome case, black dial with white numbers surrounding Hoppy's image and name, 2" diameter, EX+, $90.00.

Hopalong Cassidy, US Time, 1950, 1¾" dial w/Hoppy encased in blk metal, orig rope attachment, EX, A.......................$400.00

Mickey Mouse, British Ingersoll, 1930s, chubby Mickey w/enamel hands on celluloid dial, 4" dia, rare, NM, A...............$771.00

Mickey Mouse, mk Foreign-Ingersoll, 1930s, lg Mickey w/3 sm Mickeys in disk that ticks off seconds, very rare, NM+, A...$1,026.00

Mickey Mouse, WD Co, full-figure Mickey displayed on dial w/metal case, 2" dia, NM, A.....................................$90.00

Mickey Mouse, WDP/USA, Mickey's arms keep time, NP case, 2" dia, EX+, A...$100.00

Mickey Mouse & Goofy, Bradley/WDP, both characters on dial w/metal case, 2" dia, NM, A.......................................$143.00

Mighty Mouse, NP, shows Mighty Mouse flexing his muscles, 1⅞" dia, EX+, A $100.00

Roy Rogers, Bradley, 1959, lg image of Roy w/sm image of Roy on rearing Trigger in background, EX, A.................$300.00

Three Little Pigs, Ingersoll, 1934, wolf's eye moves ticking off seconds, fob chain w/glass button showing Mickey, NM, A $625.00

Three Stooges, mk FTCC, Moe pulling Curly's tooth out w/pliers, NP case, 2" dia, EX, A...$75.00

WRISTWATCHES

Alice in Wonderland, 1950s-60s, full-figure Alice on sq base, MIB, A..$180.00

Babe Ruth, Exacta Time, 1950s, Official Sports Watch of Champions, expansion band, NM+ (EX+ baseball pkg), A...$1,300.00

Baby Sinclair (Dinosaurs TV Show), MOC, S2 ....$20.00

Barbie Fashion Watch, MOC, S2.....................................$25.00

Bart Simpson, Aye Carumba or Bart Man, MOC, S2, ea...$30.00

Batman (1st Movie), Batman or Joker glow-in-the-dark graphics, S2, ea $30.00

Big Bad Wolf, Ingersoll, 1934, prominent image of Big Bad Wolf w/Three Little Pigs, metal band, 1" dia, rare, NM, A .$770.00

Bronco Western Watch, Gilbert, 1950s, mounted on silver-tone saddle attached by stirrup clips, MIB $100.00

Bugs Bunny, Warner, 1951, full-figure Bugs keeping time w/carrots on rnd dial, NM+ (no top o/w EX box), A.......$415.00

Buzz Corey Space Patrol, US Time, 1950, shows military & standard time, includes working compass, NM (EX+ box), A $750.00

Captain Marvel, Fawcett, 1948, Captain Marvel holding plane on rnd dial, name in script, 1¼" dia, M (EX+ box), A...$825.00

Captain Planet, digital, girl's or boy's, MOC, S2, ea.........$20.00

Captain Planet, flip-top, girl's or boy's, S2, ea $30.00

Chucky (Child's Play Movie), flip-top, MOC, S2 ....$100.00

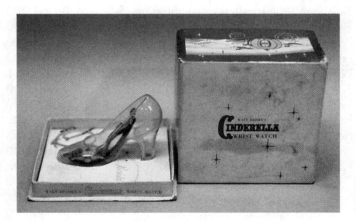

Cinderella, American, 1950s, Walt Disney, watch with blue band rests in slipper, MIB, D10, $450.00.

Daffy Duck, 1980s, hologram showing Daffy wearing LA Dogers uniform, MOC, S2..$30.00

Dale Evans, Bradley, 1951, rectangular, full-figure Dale on dial, gray band, NM+ (EX box bottom), A.....................$164.00

Dale Evans, Bradley, 1951, rectangular w/Dale & Buttercup surrounded by horseshoe, M (EX+ box), A $315.00

Dale Evans, Ingraham, 1951, rectangular w/Dale & Buttercup surrounded by horseshoe, expansion band, NM+ (EX box), A...$205.00

Dark Wing Duck, Disney, flip-top, MOC, S2 ....$20.00

Darth Vader, Texas Instruments, EX, S2 ....$100.00

Darth Vader, w/torso & Tie Fighter & X-wing as hands, 1 of 7,500 made, MIB, S2...$250.00

Davy Crockett, 1954, w/orig powder horn w/leather strap, ¾" dia, NM (orig box w/insert) $300.00

Dick Tracy, New Haven, ca 1947, rectangular w/Dick Tracy on dial, lt brn band, EX (EX box), A $350.00

Dick Tracy, New Haven, ca 1947, rectangular w/Dick Tracy on dial, lt brn band, appears unused, NM+ (EX box), A .$450.00

Dick Tracy, New Haven, 1951, Tracy w/snub-nosed gun ticking off seconds, leather band, scarce version, NM+ (EX+ box), A...$650.00

Dick Tracy (Movie), radio watch, MOC, S2 ....$25.00

Dukes of Hazzard, Unisonic, 1981, General Lee on dial, MIB, C1...$45.00

Elvis, Koral, 1992, man's or lady's digital w/Elvis postage stamp on dial, blk band, NRFB, H4, ea $15.00

Flash Gordon Star Watch, 1979, MOC, J2 ....$20.00

Fred Flintstone & Dino, Lewco, 1968, figural, MIP, S2....$20.00

Gene Autry Champion, Wilane, 1948, Gene's face on round dial, western-style leather band, 1¼" diameter, NM+ (EX box), A, $600.00.

George Jetson & Astro Dog, digital, figural, MOC, S2.....$25.00

GI Joe Combat Watch, Gilbert, 1965, w/compass, sighting lenses & standard/military time dial, MIB $250.00

Goofy, Helbros, 1972, arms w/wht gloves revolve in reverse, w/orig instructions, band & cover, MIB, A $552.00

Gumby, Lewco, figural, MOC, S2 ....$15.00

Honeymooners, 1980s, features Jackie Gleason, premium from Showtime to promote The Lost Episodes, EX (in mailer), J5.....$45.00

Hopalong Cassidy, US Time, ca 1950, Hoppy on 1" dia dial, blk leather band w/silkscreened cactus & horseshoes, MIB, A............$580.00

Hopalong Cassidy, 1950s, bust of Hoppy on dial, blk leather band, inscr Good Luck From Hoppy, EX, A $75.00

Howdy Doody, Ingraham, 1954, rnd dial w/Howdy characters, blk band, 1" dia, unused, MIB (M cb stand-up display), A $850.00

Howdy Doody, Ingraham, 1954, rnd dial w/Howdy characters, red band, 1" dia, unused, NM (EX cb stand-up display), A $657.00

Itchy & Scratchy Show, Big-Time Enterprises, 5-function quartz, adjustable strap, plastic band, w/battery, MIP, K1, ea $20.00

James Bond 007 Spy Watch, Gilbert, 1965, w/secret sighting lenses & world time guide, MIB, A...........................$256.00

Jessica Rabbit, Disney, legs move w/second hand, discontinued due to poor design (wound counterclockwise), M, D1 ....$300.00

Jetsons, Lewco, figural, MOC, S2.....................................$20.00

Joe Carioca, US Time/WDP, 1953, Birthday series, dial shows Joe w/hands keeping time, yel leather band, EX (EX box), A $320.00

Judy Jetson, Lewco, figural flip-top, MOC, S2 ....$35.00

Knight Rider, Larami, KITT on dial, MOC, C1 ....$23.00

Li'l Abner, New Haven, 1947, rnd dial w/bust image, American flag ticks off seconds, leather band, NM (EX+ box), A..$435.00

Li'l Abner, New Haven, 1947, rnd dial w/bust image, mule's head ticks off seconds, leather band, M (EX+ box) $435.00

Little Orphan Annie, New Haven, ca 1950, rectangular w/full-figure Annie on face, lt brn band, EX (EX box), A $235.00

Little Orphan Annie, New Haven/New Syndicate, 1930s, pk band w/Annie & Sandy on rectangular face, EX+ (EX box), A...$273.00

Little Rascals, 1986, features Buckwheat on band, MIB.$125.00

Lone Ranger, New Haven, 1940, rectangular w/Lone Ranger on Silver, Hi-Yo Silver in script, leather band, NM (G box), A $215.00

Marshmallow Man (Ghostbusters), flip-top, MOC, S2 ....$20.00

Mary Marvel, Fawcett, 1948, Mary Marvel in action pose on rnd face, red band, working, very scarce, M (EX+ box), A .$375.00

Max Headroom, wht cartoon-like illus, MOC, S2............$65.00

Max Headroom, yel TV-shaped pop-up w/flicker screen showing Max, MOC, S2 ....$65.00

Mickey Mouse, Bradley, 1970s, full figure on rnd face, leather band, EX+ (EX+ box)...$75.00

Mickey Mouse, Ingersoll, ca 1948, Mickey on dial, orig red band, NM (EX+ box w/insert & orig price tag), A............$305.00

Mickey Mouse, Ingersoll, 1930s, Mickey's arms keep time, red suede band, scarce, EX, A $125.00

Mickey Mouse, Kelton, 1946, first postwar Mickey watch, gold-tone on rectangular dial with Mickey's head, tan band, unused, M, A, $242.00.

Mickey Mouse Top Hat De Luxe, Ingersoll, 1938, Walt Disney Enterprises, boy's version, yellow-gloved hands keep time, with original insert, MIB, from $1,500.00 to $2,000.00.

Mickey Mouse, Ingersoll, 1930s, tiny Mickeys circle as second hand moves, chain-link band, EX+ (scarce box), A.$523.00

Mickey Mouse, Ingersoll, 1933, box only, some wear, insert missing, A $199.00

Mickey Mouse, Ingersoll, 1947, Deluxe version, Mickey's yel-gloved hands keep time, orig instructions & tag, MIB, A $460.00

Mickey Mouse, Vantage, 1970s, Disneyland above full figure & name on rnd face w/cloth band, 1½" dia, EX+ (VG box), A..$88.00

Mickey Mouse, WPD, 1954, Mickey on face, red band, mk Mouseketeers on box, complete w/cb Mickey figure, EX (EX box), A..$350.00

Mickey Mouse Mouseketeers, US Time/WDP, 1955, dial w/Mickey using hands to keep time, red band, EX (EX display box), A...$225.00

No-Ghost (Ghostbusters), figural flip-top, S2..................$15.00

Pee Wee Herman, flip-top, MIP, S2.................................$65.00

Pinocchio, flip-top, Disney, MOC, S2 ....$20.00

Pokey (Gumby), digital figure, MOC, S2.........................$35.00

Popeye, New Haven, 1936, Popeye & friends around dial, A $400.00

Rocketeer, Fossil, MIB, J2 ....$220.00

Roger Rabbit, Shiraka, set of 4, MIB, w/display, D1 ....$500.00

Roy Rogers, Bradley, 1950s, Roy & Trigger on rnd dial, EX (EX pop-up box), A $350.00

Roy Rogers, Ingraham, 1951, rectangular dial w/Roy on rearing Trigger, NM+ (EX box), A $266.00

Simpsons, Nelsonics, LCD 5-function, plastic, several styles, MIP, K1, ea $15.00

Slimer (Ghostbusters), figural flip-top, M, S2...................$20.00

Snow White, US Time, 1950s, 3-quarter image of Snow White on rnd dial, engraved, leather strap, 1" dia, VG+, A .$20.00

Spock (Star Trek), Lewco, figural, MIP, S2 ....$95.00

Sta-Puft (Ghostbusters), M, S2 ....$15.00

Star Wars, Bradley, musical, MIB, S2 ....$125.00

Superman, New Haven, 1939, rectangular dial with half-figure image of Superman and name, leather band, NM, $350.00.

Superman, New Haven, 1948, rectangular dial w/full-figure Superman, blk leather band, NM+ (EX+ box), A...$800.00
Sylvester & Tweety Bird, figural flip-top, MOC, S2.........$40.00
Tasmanian Devil, Fantasma, limited edition, 3-D laser hologram, MOC, S2..$60.00

Tom Corbett Space Cadet, Ingraham, 1951, Tom and spaceship on round dial, spaceship and planet silkscreened on band, NM+ (EX+ box), A, $1,200.00.

Tom Corbett, Ingraham, 1951, Tom & spaceship on rnd dial, spaceship & planet silkscreened on band, EX....................................$350.00
Who Framed Roger Rabbit?, Disney Channel promotion, M, D1 ....$100.00
Wonder Woman Superhero, 1977, MIB, J5....................$120.00
Zorro, US Time/WDP, 1957, blk dial w/Zorro in script, orig blk leather band, w/hat display, unused, MIB, A...........$311.00
Zorro, US Time/WDP, 1957, blk dial w/Zorro in script, orig blk leather band, w/hat display, EX (EX box), A...........$227.00

Character, TV and Movie Collectibles

To the baby boomers who grew up glued to the TV set and addicted to Saturday matinees, the faces they saw on the screen

were as familiar to them as family. Just about any character you could name has been promoted through retail merchandising to some extent; depending on the popularity they attain, exposure may continue for weeks, months, even years. It's no wonder, then, that the secondary market abounds with these items or that there is such wide-spread collector interest. For more information, we recommend *Character Toys and Collectibles, Vols I and II*, by David Longest, and *Cartoon Friends of the Baby Boom Era* by Bill Bruegman.

Note: Though most characters are listed by their own names, some will be found under the title of the group, movie, comic strip, or dominant character they're commonly identified with. The Joker, for instance, will be found in the Batman listings.

Advisors: Jerry and Ellen Harnish (H4); Trina and Randy Kubeck (K1), The Simpsons; Norm Vigue (V1); TV Collector (T6); Alan Edwards (E3); Casey's Collectible Corner (C1); Bill Stillman (S6), Wizard of Oz.

See also Action Figures; Battery-Operated; Books; Celebrity Dolls; Chein; Character Clocks and Watches; Coloring, Activity and Paint Books; Dakins; Disney; Fisher-Price; Games; Guns; Halloween Costumes; Lunch Boxes; Marx; Model Kits; Paper Dolls; Pin-Back Buttons; Plastic Figures; Paper Dolls; Playsets; Puppets; Puzzles; Records; Toothbrush Holders; View-Master; Western; Windups, Friction and Other Mechanicals.

A-Team, Colorforms Adventure Set, 1983, EX...............$15.00
A-Team, Mr T, see Celebrities category
A-Team, race car set, NMIB, S2 ....$85.00
Addams Family, bank, Thing figure, Filmways, 1964, MIB.$125.00
Addams Family, candy tubes w/finger puppets, 1993, 3 different, M, S2, ea $10.00
Addams Family, Colorforms Cartoon Kit, 1965, MIB....$175.00
Addams Family, dolls, Morticia & Gomez, AB Productions, 1993, stuffed cloth, Sat morning cartoon series, 22", M, H4, pr $40.00
Addams Family, gumball machine, w/1" plastic figures of Gomez, Morticia, Uncle Fester & Lurch, rare, EX, H4...........$25.00
Airwolf, uzi dart gun & target, mini set, MOC.................$10.00
Alf, bank, 1988, figural bust, plastic, 6½", VG.................$12.00
Alf, Crayon-By-Number Set, 1987, MIB, S2 ....$10.00
Alf, doll, plush, 16", MIB..$20.00
Alf, figure, clips on rear-view mirror, M...........................$10.00
Alfred E Neuman, figure, Concepts Plus, 1988, bendable, 9", MIP, K1 ....$8.00
Alvin & the Chipmunks, bank, Alvin figure, 1980s, vinyl, EX..$12.00
Alvin & the Chipmunks, camera, Del Monte premium, florescent gr, NM, S2 ....$15.00
Alvin & the Chipmunks, doll, Alvin, stuffed talker, 24", EX, S1 ....$25.00
Alvin & the Chipmunks, doll, Alvin, 1983, stuffed talker, 18", NM, S1..$25.00
Alvin & the Chipmunks, toothbrush, battery-op, VG $12.00
Andy Gump, bank, Toy Doctor, dtd 1980, pnt CI, Andy on bench reading paper w/boy standing behind, 4½", EX, A $30.00
Andy Panda (Woody Woodpecker), ring w/emb figure, NM, S2...$20.00

Annie, doll set w/limo, Annie, Daddy Warbucks, Punjab, Miss Hannigan & Molly, Knickerbocker, 1982, ea MIB, H4.**$75.00**

Annie, motion lamp, from 1982 movie, MIB, S1 ....**$75.00**

Annie, see also Little Orphan Annie

Aquaman, figure, Bend-n-Flex, Mego, 6", NM, H4 ....**$15.00**

Archie, Band of Musical Instruments Set, Emenee, 1960s, w/cb picture record, missing slide trombone, VG, J5..........**$45.00**

Archie, figure, Jesco, bendable, 6", MIP, K1 ....**$6.00**

Archies, Fuzzy Face (magnetic drawing picture), Ja-Ru, 1987, features Mr Weatherbee, MOC, S2...............................**$7.50**

Archies, record, 1960s, cut out from Post cereal box, EX, J5...**$15.00**

Archies, tattoos, Topps, 1969, tattoo sheet & gum in unopened 2x4" wrapper, M, T2...**$20.00**

Astro Boy, change purse, shaped like Astro Boy's face w/zippered closure, plastic, NM, C1..**$18.00**

Astro Boy, nodder, 1980s, lg plush figure w/flame design on boots, spring head, w/orig tag, M, C1.............................**$27.00**

Astro Boy, squirt gun, M, H4...**$12.00**

Astro Boy, tattoo wrapper, Topps, 1960s, scarce, M, T2 ..**$40.00**

Atom Ant, magic slate, Watkins, 1967, M **$40.00**

Attack of the Killer Tomatoes, figures, PVC, set of 4, M, S2 ....**$20.00**

Babba Louie, bank, 1976, figural fun bath, w/tag, M **$15.00**

Baby Snooks, Flexy doll, Ideal, 1940, NM, A **$200.00**

Baby Snookums, figurine, Germany, 1920s, grinning boy seated w/legs spread on mk base, bsk, 3", EX+, A **$61.00**

Back to the Future, Delorean car, remote control, MIB, S2.**$125.00**

Bamm-Bamm, see Flintstones

Banana Splits, doll, Bingo, lightly faded, S2 ....**$45.00**

Banana Splits, figure, Drooper (Dakin-like), MIP, H4 .....**$89.00**

Banana Splits, figure, Snorky, (Dakin-like), tail missing, H4...**$39.00**

Banana Splits, Kut-Up Kit, Larami, 1973, w/scissors & stencils, M (NM card), C1 ....**$29.00**

Banana Splits, pillow doll, Kellogg's premium, 1960s, stuffed cloth, 10", EX, J5 ....**$35.00**

Barney Rubble, see Flintstones

Batman, bank, Batman bust, Mego, 1974, plastic, 8", M ..**$60.00**

Batman, bank, Batman bust, Mego, 1974, plastic, 8", no trap o/w VG, M5 ....**$20.00**

Batman, bank, Penguin bust, Mego, 1974, plastic, 8", no trap o/w VG+, M5 ....**$15.00**

Batman, belt, Lee, 1982, w/tag, elastic, child-sz, M, S2 ....**$15.00**

Batman, bicycle license plate, Marx, 1976, MIP..............**$20.00**

Batman, bicycle siren, Empire, 1970s, M (VG box), J5 ....**$10.00**

Batman, binoculars & telescope, Henry Gordy, 1988, MOC, S2...**$10.00**

Batman, book bag/carry-all (Batman Returns), illus, M, S2.**$20.00**

Batman, bowl, 1966, plastic w/color picture of the Joker in center, 5" dia, EX, J5...**$10.00**

Batman, candy containers, DC Comics, 1989, plastic Batman heads, set of 3, 2½", M, A..**$20.00**

Batman, chair (Batman Returns), inflatable Penguin, Play Time, 1991, MIB, S2...**$35.00**

Batman, charm bracelet, 1966, 8", MOC, M5 ....**$50.00**

Batman, Chute, CDC, 1966, official Batman figure w/27" chute, NMOC, D9...**$37.00**

Batman, comb, 1960s, red in wht pouch w/insignia, G, S2..**$20.00**

Batman, Crime Fighter Set, 1988, handcuffs, compass, etc, MOC...**$20.00**

Batman, doll (1st movie), Applause, cloth & vinyl, w/tag, 13"...**$30.00**

Batman, figure, Batman (Ultimate), Kenner, 15", MIB....**$40.00**

Batman, figure, Hong Kong, early 1970s, yel rubber, 6", NM, S2...**$15.00**

Batman, figure, Joker, Presents, w/stand, 15", M...............**$35.00**

Batman, flasher ring, 1960s, flashes from Batmobile to Batcopter, EX...**$25.00**

Batman, frisbee (1st movie), logoed, MOC, S2.................**$10.00**

Batman, helmet, Ideal/NPPI, 1966, bl vinyl w/cb Batman face, 12", NM (NM pkg), A **$193.00**

Batman, belt, Morris, 1966, EX/NM, $20.00.

Batman, helmet & cowl, Ideal, 1966, plastic, child-sz, lg, EX, S2 ....$175.00

Batman, lamp, 1970s, vinyl Batman & cave base, VG, S2 .$85.00

Batman, makeup kit (1st movie), MIB (photo of Jack Nickolson as the Joker on box)..$25.00

Batman, night light, 1966, M, S2 ....$15.00

Batman, pencil sharpener, Batman figure, Janex, 1970s, battery-op, EX, S2 ....$75.00

Batman, pencil sharpener, Robin, 1970s, puffy vinyl, MIP, S2 ....$10.00

Batman, pinups, color, 11x14", MIP (sealed), J2 ....$30.00

Batman, Play-Doh Set, Kenner, 1990, w/all the Batman characters, MIB, S2 ....$20.00

Batman, playsuit, Kabaya, 1989, w/cape, cowl & belt, M (in sm box), S2...$35.00

Batman, pogo stick, 1970s, lg plastic bust, VG, S2 ....$150.00

Batman, Projector Gun, Toy Biz, 1989, MIB, S2 ....$35.00

Batman, Race Set (Batman Returns), w/cars & track, limited edition, S2...$85.00

Batman, ring, 1960s, from gumball machine, rubber, NM.$20.00

Batman, snow-cone cup, 1960s, 5½", M, M5 ....$4.00

Batman, store display (1st movie), features 3-D Vac-U-Form Batman head & cape, 31", MIB, S2 ....$95.00

Batman, sunglasses, 1960s, w/sticker, VG, J5 ....$15.00

Batman, Superpowers Stain-Painting Set, Craft, MIB (sealed), C1...$18.00

Batman, T-shirt, Batman, 1989, front w/Batman & Batmobile, back w/logo, extra lg, M, S2 ....$20.00

Batman, T-shirt, Joker, 1989, cartoon version, M, S2 ......$20.00

Batman, wallpaper, 1966, repeated design of Batman, Robin & the Batmobile, unused roll, EX, J5 ....$195.00

Batman, Water Bopper Blow-Up, features the Joker, 1989, MIP, S2 ....$20.00

Batman & Robin, flicker ring, 1970s, changes from Batman to Robin, sm, M, S2 ....$20.00

Batman & Robin, key ring, 1966, inset picture of both, MIP, S2...$25.00

Batman & Robin, pencil case, National Periodical, 1976, EX, S2...$25.00

Batman & Robin, placemats, 1960s, figural vinyl, NM, J5, pr...$65.00

Batman & Robin, poster, 1966, glow-in-the-dark, 16x12", MIP, S2...$95.00

Batman & Robin, walkie-talkies, National Prod, 1973, litho tin & plastic, battery-op, NRFB, A $105.00

Beany & Cecil, carrying case, 1961, rnd red vinyl w/hdl, NM...$35.00

Beany & Cecil, doll, Cecil, talker, rare, NM $170.00

Beany & Cecil, jack-in-the-box, Mattel, NM...................$65.00

Ben Casey, Deluxe Hospital Set, Transogram, 1950s, medicine chest w/doctor's bag, MIB...$95.00

Ben Casey, playsuit, 1950s, cloth shirt, pants & mask w/doctor props, NM (EX box), J5...$45.00

Betty Boop, doll, Fleischer Studios label, compo w/side-glancing pnt eyes, molded blk dress, high-heeled feet, 12", VG $650.00

Betty Boop, figure, Fleischer Studios/Japan, 1930s, pnt bsk, 3", VG, S9 ....$145.00

Betty Boop, figure, Fleischer Studios/Japan, 1930s, pnt bsk, 3", NM, A $260.00

Betty Boop, figure, NJ Croce, 1988, bendable, 7½", MIP, K1 .$7.00

Betty Boop Tea Set, lustre ware, 1930s, 15-piece, MIB, $495.00.

Betty Rubble, see Flintstones

Beverly Hillbillies, Ugly Mugly Color Slide Strips, Remco, 1968, Jethro Strikes Oil & A Picnic, 2 3-D strips, NM, C1 ..$31.00

Bewitched, tablet, 1964, color cast photo cover, 8x10", unused, M..$35.00

Big Bird, see Sesame Street

Bimbo (Betty Boop's dog), figure, Fleischer Studios, molded & jtd wood in gr & blk, 9", EX, A................................$525.00

Bimbo (Betty Boop's dog), figure, Fleischer Studios/Japan, pnt bsk, 3½", EX, A $100.00

BJ & the Bear, Pontiac Trans Am, JRU, 1981, 1/64 scale, MOC...$15.00

Blondie, Comic Construction Set, KFS, 1934, complete w/unpunched characters, scarce, NM (EX+ box), A.$160.00

Blondie, figures, 8 different, bl plastic, EX, H4 ....$80.00

Blondie, paint box, 1952, tin, features various characters painting a portrait of Blondie, NM, A...............................$25.00

Blondie, paint set, Am Crayon, 1946, tin box, EX $15.00

Bonanza, see Western category

Bonny Braids, see Dick Tracy

Bonzo, figure, prewar Japan, celluloid w/pnt features, jtd arms & legs, 9", EX, A $850.00

Bozo the Clown, bank, Larry Harmons, 1987, bust figure, MIP, S2...$25.00

Bozo the Clown, doll, full-figure talker, EX $75.00

Bozo the Clown, doll, Knickerbocker, Bend 'Em, 9", NMIP, J2...$28.00

Bozo the Clown, doll, Mattel, talker, working, EX+, J2 ...$70.00

Bozo the Clown, figure, Jesco, bendable, 6", MIP, K1.........$4.00

Bozo the Clown, gumball dispenser, 1987, figural, 2¾", MOC $10.00

Bozo the Clown, inflatable toy, Ideal, 1960s, vinyl w/Bozo's head on a log, mk 'Ride-a-log' on side, EX, J5 ....$25.00

Bozo the Clown, kazoo, Ja-ru, 1990, figural, 5½", MOC, S2...$10.00

Bozo the Clown, membership kit, 1972, w/patch & card, MOC $12.00

Bozo the Clown, pencil sharpener, wall-type, VG $50.00

Bozo the Clown, squirting watch, Ja-Ru, 1990, figural, MOC $25.00

Bozo the Clown, sticker board, 1983, w/vinyl sticker sheet, 8x10", MIP, S2...$20.00

Brother Juniper, plate, Shafford, cartoon on milk glass, Publisher's Syndicate, 1958, set of 5, 4", NM, T2 ....$50.00

Brownies, figure, Chinaman, papier-mache head & body w/molded & pnt maroon coat, 8½", EX, A..............$425.00

Brownies, figure, papier-mache head, hat & body, pnt eyes, in gr jacket, bow tie, yel vest, ochre pants, 9", EX, A $450.00

Brownies, figure, Policeman, from Nine-Pin set, litho paper, 12½", EX+, A $140.00

Buck Rogers, Chemical Laboratory, Gropper Mfg, 1930s, complete with glass vials, chemicals in illustrated containers, utensils and instruction booklet, NM (EX+ box with illustrated insert), A, $2,175.00.

Buck Rogers, microphones, hand-held, set of 2, VG, O1 .$95.00

Buck Rogers, pail, head shape, EX, J2 ....$25.00

Buck Rogers, Space Glasses, Norton-Honer, 1950s, bright plastic binoculars w/strap, NM (EX box), A $110.00

Buck Rogers, Star Fighter Command Center, Mego, 1979, MIB (sealed), C1..$75.00

Buck Rogers, walkie-talkies, Remco, w/moving decoder disk & Buck Rogers certificate, EX (EX box), A.................$140.00

Buck Rogers & Twiki, Deluxe Communications Set, H-G Toys, 1970s, walkie-talkies, belt, watch, decoder & robot, NRFB, H4 ....$30.00

Bucky O'Hare, Toad Double-Bubble Vehicle or Toad Croaker Vehicle, MIB, ea $20.00

Bugs Bunny, birthday candle, w/50th-Anniversary picture, 4½", MOC, S2...$5.00

Bugs Bunny, doll, Mattel, 1971, talker, stuffed body, arms & legs w/plastic head & ears, NM, H4 ....$35.00

Bugs Bunny, figure, Applause, bendable, 7", MIP, K1........$4.00

Bugs Bunny, figure, Applause, 1991, as Los Angeles Dodger, bendable, 3½", MIP, K1.......................................$4.25

Bugs Bunny, figure, Evan K Shaw, ca 1940, posed in wide stance eating carrot w/hand on hip, ceramic, 9", EX+, A $160.00

Bugs Bunny, figure, 50th Anniversary, limited edition, plush wearing gold tux, 16", MIB, S2.............................$75.00

Bugs Bunny, gumball dispenser, 1989, Bugs w/carrot on tree stump, miniature, MOC, S2 ....$10.00

Bugs Bunny, party pack, 50th Anniversary, w/8 ea cups, plates, napkins, etc, MIP, S2..$10.00

Bugs Bunny, pencil hugger, Applause, 1990, w/American or National League team logo, 2", MIP, K1, ea $2.25

Bugs Bunny, pencil sharpener, w/Porky Pig, 1970s, puffy vinyl, 3½", MIP, S2..$8.00

Bugs Bunny, pencil sharpener, ca 1970, 'Eh, Sharpen Up, Doc!' on green base, battery-operated, M, $35.00.

Bugs Bunny, plate, Bugs holding carrot w/Elmer Fudd, Daffy Duck & Porky Pig, EX, S2...$20.00

Bugs Bunny, radio/electric toothbrush holder, figural, no brushes o/w EX, I2 ....$26.00

Bugs Bunny, tattoos, Topps, 1971, tattoo sheet & gum in unopened 1½x3½" wrapper, NM $20.00

Bugs Bunny, wallet, 1981, girl's, cloth w/Bugs imprinted on front, EX, S2 ....$15.00

Bullwinkle, bank, plastic, 12", EX, A $65.00

Bullwinkle, false teeth, Larami, 1971, 4x5½", MOC (color photo card) $20.00

Bullwinkle, figure, Japan, 1960, 6", MIB, A.....................$92.00

Bullwinkle, figure, Jesco, bendable, 7", MIP, K1 ....$5.00

Bullwinkle, figure, Wham-O, 1972, bendable, MOC $45.00

Bullwinkle, jewelry hanger, 1960s, gold metal w/suction cup on back of head, EX, J5...$10.00

Bullwinkle, Spelling & Counting Board, Larami, 1969, MOC (EX card), C1...$21.00

Bullwinkle, ukulele, 1969, NMOC, J2 ....$25.00

Buster Brown & Tige, see Advertising category

Cabbage Patch Kids, bank, baby wrapped in bl towel, vinyl, VG, S2 ....$20.00

Cabbage Patch Kids, bank, Black girl w/pigtails holding piggy bank, 6½", EX, S2 ....$25.00

Cabbage Patch Kids, bank, girl w/brn hair & purple dress, EX, S2 ....$25.00

Cabbage Patch Kids, cassette player, 1983, EX, I2 ....$9.00

Cabbage Patch Kids, puffy stickers, Diamond Toymakers, 1983, sheet of 22, MIP, S2..$15.00

Captain America, figure, Just Toys, bendable, 6", MIP, K1 ..$5.00

Captain America, gumball machine, figural (Secret Wars), NMIB, S2...$45.00

Captain America, playset, Toy Biz, 1990, w/chest plate, mask & shield, MIB, S2 ....$50.00

Captain Kangaroo, doll, Mr Green Jeans, Child Guidance, 1976, plush, NMIB, S2 ....$55.00

Captain Kangaroo, magic slate, E Fairchild Corp, 1960s, w/stylus, old store stock, M $25.00

Captain Kangaroo, party dress, RKA Inc, 1966, paper dress illus w/all of the characters, child-sz, unused, scarce, M $50.00

Captain Kangaroo, toy milk bottles, Jak Pak, 1977, w/8 plastic bottles, MOC, S2 ....$20.00

Captain Kid, pirate outfit, Carnell, ca 1950, complete with 9½" flintlock cap pistol, plastic sabre, leather belt with embossed coins, and bandana, unused, NM (EX box), A, $135.00.

Captain Marvel, punch-out figure to assemble, Ski Jump or Flying, NM (in orig envelope), ea....................$18.00

Captain Planet, Planeteer Power Ring, Tiger, 1991, w/light & sound, MOC, S2 ....$20.00

Casper the Friendly Ghost, bank, ceramic, Casper holding money sack, emb USA, 8", NM, A..............$335.00

Casper the Friendly Ghost, costume, pajama, NMIB, J2 ..$35.00

Casper the Friendly Ghost, doll, Knickerbocker, 1970s, plush, musical, w/faded cap & shirt, VG, S2 ....$30.00

Casper the Friendly Ghost, doll, Mattel, talker, 15", VG, I2 .$70.00

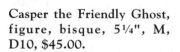

Casper the Friendly Ghost, figure, bisque, 5¼", M, D10, $45.00.

Casper the Friendly Ghost, figure, Mattel, 1971, talker w/oversized head & pull string, 4", NM, C1 ....$81.00

Casper the Friendly Ghost, figure, Sutton, 1972, vinyl, 6¾", EX, S2 ....$75.00

Casper the Friendly Ghost, jack-in-the-box, Mattel, EX ..$85.00

Casper the Friendly Ghost, lamp shade, Harvey Famous Cartoons, features Casper & friends on merry-go-round, M, A....$51.00

Charlie Brown, see Peanuts

Charlie McCarthy, gum wrapper, Bergen's Better Bubble Gum, EX, J2 ....$15.00

Charlie McCarthy, lapel pin, figural, M, J2....................$25.00

Charlie McCarthy, spoon, figural, M, M9 ....$25.00

Charlie McCarthy, talking birthday card, early, unused, M, J2 ....$80.00

Charlie's Angels, Colorforms, 1978, MIB $60.00

Charlie's Angels, necklace, Fleetwood, 1977, M (NM card), C1 ....$27.00

Child's Play, doll, Chucky, newest version w/short hair & faded denim, 12", S2 ....$15.00

Child's Play, doll, Chucky, 12", M, S2 ....$20.00

Child's Play, doll, Chucky, 18", M, S2 ....$30.00

Child's Play, doll, Chucky, 24", M, S2 ....$40.00

Child's Play III, doll, Chucky, 1991, video store promo, 12", M, S2 ....$50.00

Chilly Willy, doll, Walter Lantz, 1959, plush, VG, S2 .....$25.00

Chilly Willy, figure, 1970s, ceramic, 9", EX, S2................$25.00

Chilly Willy, ring, yel plastic w/blk emb figure, premium, NM, S2 ....$20.00

CHiPs, binoculars, MIB..$20.00

CHiPs, Colorforms, 1981, MIB, C1................................$15.00

CHiPs, Emergency Medical Kit, MIB..............................$30.00

CHiPs, motorcycle, Fleetwood, w/removable rider, 1981, MOC, C1 ....$23.00

Clarabell, see Howdy Doody

Close Encounters of the Third Kind, postcard book, T1 ..$15.00

Cookie Monster, see Sesame Street

Cosby Show, scrapbook w/photos & bios of cast members, Starbooks, 1986, VG $8.00

Curious George, doll, Knickerbocker, stuffed, 14", S1 ......$15.00

Daffy Duck, bank, Great America Exclusive, 1977, vinyl figure, 7¼", M $18.00

Daffy Duck, candle holder, Looney Tunes, 1980, pnt bsk, M, J2 ....$35.00

Daffy Duck, figure, Applause, bendable, 5", MIP..............$18.00

Daffy Duck, figure, 1970s, wire, 2½", EX, J5 ....$10.00

Daffy Duck & Pepe Le Peu, placemat, Pepsi, plastic w/graphics, 1976, unused, NM..$4.00

Dennis the Menace, crash helmet, Ideal, 1950s, unused, NMIB $60.00

Dennis the Menace, doll, 14", MIB................................$125.00

Dennis the Menace, figure, 1970s, vinyl, 7", EX, J5..........$20.00

Deputy Dawg, bagatelle game, Imperial Toy, 1978, NM, T2 ..$8.00

Dick Tracy, Candid Camera, Seymour Sales, 1940s-50s, blk plastic w/Graf 50mm lens, EX+, C1 ....$72.00

Dick Tracy, Christmas tree lights, Mutual, 1950s, 7 sockets, EX (EX box), A $85.00

Dick Tracy, Crayon-By-Numbers Coloring Set, Transogram, 1954, 44 cards & 16 crayons, scarce, MIB................$95.00

Dick Tracy, figure, Bonny Braids, Charmore, 1951, rubber, 1¼", EX (on display card), A $45.00

Dick Tracy, Braces for Smart Boys and Girls, complete with suspenders, badge, whistle and magnifying glass, M (NM box), A, $90.00.

Dick Tracy, figure (from movie), Breathless Mahoney, resin, 1 of 5,000 made, 7", S2 ....$135.00

Dick Tracy, figure (from movie), Dick Tracy, resin, 1 of 5,000, 7", MIB, S2 ....$135.00

Dick Tracy, films, Acme, 1948, In Movie Style #2, #3 & #4, ea film comes in own box displayed in lg box, NM (EX box) $85.00

Dick Tracy, magnifying glass, Laramie, 1979, MOC...........$5.00

Dick Tracy, movie viewer, Acme, 1955, plastic viewer & 2 films, EX+ (NM card) $48.00

Dick Tracy, washing machine, features Sparkle Plenty, plays tune This Is the Way We Wash Our Clothes, tin, 13", EX, A $150.00

Dick Tracy, 2-transistor radio receiver, Tribune, 1961, litho tin & plastic, w/shoulder holster, 4½", MIB $85.00

Dick Tracy, 2-Way Wrist Radios, transmits up to ½ mile, plastic, MIB $70.00

Dilly Dally, see Howdy Doody

Dinky Duck, magic slate, Lowe, 1952, w/wood stylus, unused, NM $20.00

Dr Dolittle, jack-in-the-box, litho tin, NM $65.00

Dr Dolittle, Magic Set, Remco, 1967, M (EX box), J5 .....$20.00

Dr Kildare, medical kit, Hasbro, NMIB...........................$40.00

Dr Kildare, nodder, MGM, early 1960s, pnt compo figure w/spring-mounted head, 7", EX...............................$150.00

Dr Kildare, Pencil-By-Number Color Set, Standard Toykraft, 1962, 9x13", EX+, T2 ....$39.00

Dr Suess, book holder, Cat in the Hat figure, NM, S2 .....$20.00

Dr Suess, doll, Cat in the Hat, 1970, talker, 26"...........$150.00

Dr Suess, doll, Dr Duess, 1970, talker, rare, S2 ....$125.00

Dr Suess, doll, Fedwick (moose), 1983, plush, 20", NM ..$40.00

Dr Suess, doll, Grinch, Coleco, 1983, How the Grinch Stole Christmas, 24", rare, NM $125.00

Dr Suess, doll, Horton (elephant), 1983, plush, 15", NM..$50.00

Dracula, bank, Japan, ceramic, 7", NM, J2 ....$45.00

Dracula, bank, Japan, 1960s, hand grabs coin, battery-op, EX (EX box), S2 ....$95.00

Dracula, doll, Presents, M..$20.00

Dracula, figure, Just Toys, 60th-Anniversary edition, bendable, 6", MIP, K1 ....$5.00

Dracula, figure, Presents, 1992, vinyl w/cloth cape, rarest of 4 monster figures, M (in plastic bag & box), H4...........$70.00

Drooper, see Banana Splits

Dudley Do-Right, dinner set, Libbey/Arrowhead, character illus on plastic plate & bowl w/plain plastic cup, MIB......$65.00

Dudley Do-Right, figure, Jesco, 1991, bendable, 5½", MIP, K1 ....$5.00

Dudley Do-Right, figure, Wham-O, 1972, bendable, MOC, S2 ....$20.00

Dudley Do-Right, magic slate, Saalfield, 1970, lift-up erasable film on cb, wood stylus, 8x12", VG+, T2 ....$20.00

Dukes of Hazzard, bowl, plate & cup set, Deka Plastics, 1982, MIB..$20.00

Dukes of Hazzard, cars, Ertl, 1/64th scale, set of 4, NMIB..$40.00

Dukes of Hazzard, Colorforms, 1981, EX.......................$30.00

Dukes of Hazzard, General Lee Wrist Racer, Knickerbocker, 1983, EX...$18.00

Dukes of Hazzard, shoelaces, LJN, 1981, 40", M $15.00

Dukes of Hazzard, tray, MIP...$40.00

Elmer Fudd, figure, as Detroit Tiger, Applause, 1991, bendable, 3½", MIP, K1 ....$4.25

Elmer Fudd, figure, Japan, 1975, pnt ceramic, 4¼", M......$30.00

Emergency, Paramedic Kit, Fleetwood, 1975, 7-pc, MOC.$35.00

ET, bike, w/Elliot, friction, MOC...................................$18.00

ET, book & record set, MIP..$8.00

ET, bowl, plate & mug, MIB $18.00

ET, calendar, 1983, EX..$5.00

ET, Colorforms, dress-up set, ET in girl's clothing, M (sealed) $15.00

ET, Colorforms, regular set, M $12.00

ET, doll, in bl outfit, 8", MIB $20.00

ET, doll, talker, MIB...$22.00

ET, iron-on transfer, triangular w/cloud & rainbow graphics, M $5.00

ET, light-up finger, tip lights up, MOC............................$8.00

ET, night light, vinyl figure, 8", MIB $15.00

ET, pool toy, inflatable ET, MIB.....................................$15.00

ET, pop-up spaceship, MOC...$12.00

ET, ruler, 3-D flasher, plastic, 6", NM $5.00

ET, scooter, Coleco, 1983, G..$25.00

ET, toothbrush, figural, battery-op, M (in window box) ..$15.00

ET, toy talking phone, 1982, speaks 6 different messages, MIB $30.00

ET, TV tray, little girl kissing ET on nose, M (sealed) $8.00

Fall Guy, break-apart truck, Fleetwood, 1981, friction, MOC..$18.00

Farrah Fawcett, styling & makeup head, MIB.................$150.00

Felix the Cat, bop bag, Dartmore, 1950s, red & wht w/weighted bottom, 11" $48.00

Felix the Cat, charm, English, 1920s, emb brass, 1", NM .$60.00

Felix the Cat, dexterity puzzle, Felix traps silver mouse, metal & glass, 2" dia, EX, A..$100.00

Felix the Cat, doll, stuffed felt w/glass eyes, unmk, 12", EX, A $125.00

Felix the Cat, drum, prewar Spain, red, yel & bl metal w/images of Felix playing drums & other characters, 5", EX+, A....$216.00

Felix the Cat, figure, Applause, 1988, bendable, 6", MIP, K1 ..**$6.00**
Felix the Cat, figure, hollow bsk, eyes move, 6½", EX+, A.**$450.00**
Felix the Cat, figure, prewar Japan, upright w/lg grin & 'jiggle' eyes, celluloid, 6¾", very rare, NM **$275.00**

Felix the Cat, figure, Nifty, jointed and painted wood, 5", M, D10, $525.00.

Felix the Cat, figure, 1930s, walking pose w/hands behind back on platform, lead w/pnt features, 2½", EX **$110.00**
Felix the Cat, flasher ring, Vari-Vue, 1960s-70s, M **$25.00**
Felix the Cat, jigger toy, pnt wood, 11", pnt loss to hands & head, complete & orig, A...**$175.00**
Felix the Cat, rattle/whistle, shows Happy Hooligan on reverse, litho tin, 4", NM, A **$175.00**
Felix the Cat, school crayons, 1930s, EX (EX box) **$40.00**
Felix the Cat, trinket box, chrome over brass w/raised image of Felix on lid, 2" dia, EX+ **$185.00**

Flash Gordon, casting set, Home Foundry Co, 1934, lead figure mold set complete with paints, lead, utensils, molds and brushes, NM (EX box with Alex Raymond graphics), A, $1,000.00.

Flash Gordon, Christmas tree lights, box of 8, EX..........**$150.00**
Flash Gordon, kite, graphic of Flash's head, wrapped in paper tube, EX, J5 ....**$45.00**
Flash Gordon, magazine, Strange Adventure, 1936, features Flash in The Masters of Mars, scarce, G, A **$168.00**
Flash Gordon, medals & insignia, Larami, 1978, set of 5, M (NM card) **$5.00**
Flash Gordon, Pistol Lite, Ja-Ru, 1981, MOC **$15.00**

Flash Gordon, printing set, M Shimmel & Sons, early 1970s, rubber stamps, M (EX+ card) **$15.00**
Flash Gordon, tray, 1979, full-color image of Flash battling lizards, 17½", EX, D9 ....**$8.00**
Flintstones, bank, Bedrock Savings, 1979, litho tin, no stopper o/w EX..**$15.00**
Flintstones, bank, Fred bust, 1986, vinyl, VG.................**$10.00**
Flintstones, bank, Pebbles riding Dino, 1960s, vinyl, 13", very rare, NM..**$35.00**
Flintstones, bar of soap, Roclar, 1976, unused, M (in wrapper), T2 ....**$8.00**
Flintstones, Bedrock Airplane (Flintstone kids vehicle), Coleco, 1986, MIB, S2 ....**$30.00**
Flintstones, bicycle license plate, features Fred, Gordy, 1979, plastic, MOC **$10.00**
Flintstones, bicycle license plate, features Pebbles & Bamm-Bamm, Gordy, 1979, MOC **$10.00**
Flintstones, bubble pipe, Fred figure, S2.......................**$15.00**
Flintstones, bubble pipe, Pebbles figure, EX, S2............**$15.00**
Flintstones, Colorforms, 1972, MIB.............................**$15.00**
Flintstones, cradle, 1963, red plastic w/Pebbles graphics, 17", MIB, A **$100.00**
Flintstones, doll, Bamm-Bamm, Ideal, 12", VG, S2.........**$35.00**
Flintstones, doll, Barney, Knickerbocker, 1977, stuffed, M..**$18.00**
Flintstones, doll, Dino, plush, M **$15.00**
Flintstones, doll, Fred, Knickerbocker, 6", MIB, C1 ....**$17.00**
Flintstones, doll, Fred, 1960s, plush & vinyl w/gr hair & cloth outfit, EX, S2..**$100.00**
Flintstones, doll, Pebbles, Mighty Star, 1982, stuffed body w/vinyl head & limbs, 12", MIB.............................**$20.00**
Flintstones, doll, Pebbles, wrapped in blanket, EX **$75.00**
Flintstones, figure, Fred, 1960s, wood figure w/rope arms, cloth caveman outfit & oversized boxing gloves, 6", EX+ ..**$75.00**
Flintstones, figure, Fred, 1960s-70s, hard plastic, 6", EX, S2.**$20.00**
Flintstones, figure, Fred or Barney, TV Tinykins, pnt hard plastic, 2", M **$18.00**
Flintstones, magazine, Jack & Jill, March 1963, Pebbles — The Flintstones' New Baby w/cutouts, NM, T2 ....**$12.00**
Flintstones, Make-A-Pillow, graphics of all characters, material only, NM, S2 ....**$10.00**
Flintstones, Milk & Juice Bar, Transogram, 1960s, squeeze vinyl dispensers & liquid pours into cups, NM (VG box), A **$185.00**
Flintstones, night light, Barney, Electroid, 1979, MOC **$8.00**
Flintstones, Play Set, Marx/Hanna-Barbera, 1961, 6 pnt plastic figures, supermarket background, NM (EX window box)..**$145.00**
Flintstones, puffy magnets, 1978, set of 8, 4", M..............**$18.00**
Flintstones, puffy stickers, Fred or Wilma, 1977, 6", MIP, ea .**$5.00**
Flintstones, rubber stamp kit, 1989, 4 stamps & ink pad, M (sealed) **$8.00**
Flintstones, squeeze toy, Fred figure, Sanitoy, 1979, soft rubber, 9", EX...**$28.00**
Flintstones, toy phone, 1960s, red & wht w/bone-shaped receiver, paper litho under dial shows 5 characters, rare, MIB..**$185.00**
Flintstones, Tuck-Away Holster Set, Hanna-Barbera, 1961, 3" metal cap gun w/Wilma pictured on holster, M (EX box), A..**$35.00**

Flintstones, stroller, Ideal/Hanna-Barbera, 1963, bright yellow plastic Dino, pull rope attached to nose, 18½" long, EX+, A, $320.00.

Flintstones, Wonder Whiskers (magnetic drawing toy), Gordy, 1988, put the whiskers on Fred, H4..............................$3.00

Flip the Frog, figure, 1930s, bsk, 3½", EX, A $275.00

Flipper, comb, ca 1966, figural, bl plastic, M $18.00

Flying Nun, flying figure, Rayline Products, 1970, plastic w/attaching propeller blade device, 5", NRFB...........$75.00

Flying Nun, picture for needlepoint, orange fr, EX...........$25.00

Frankenstein, bank, TN/Japan, place coin at door of tin house, push down & door opens to hand that drags coin in, MIB, A $175.00

Frankenstein, door hanger, rubber & plastic plaque laughs w/eye contact, battery-op, 8", MIB, A...................................$45.00

Frankenstein, figure, AHI/Azark, 1974, bendable rubber, 5", G, H4 ....$15.00

Frankenstein, figure, Imperial, 1986, hard rubber, movable head & arms, EX+ (orig plastic wrapper)..............................$8.00

Frankenstein, figure, Just Toys, 60th-Anniversary edition, bendable, 6", MIP, K1...$5.00

Frankenstein, figure, Remco, 1980, glow-in-the-dark, M (EX card), S2..$20.00

Frankenstein, figure, Russ Berrie, plastic, gr & dk bl w/touch of red, 1½", D9 ....$9.00

Frankenstein, figure, 1980s, rubber, 6", MIC, J5 ....$10.00

Frankenstein, Glow Silly Putty, Larami, 1979, MOC.......$12.00

Frankenstein, grab bag, Best Plastic, 1963, color illus Frankie, Dracula & King Kong, 3x7", NM............................$40.00

Frankenstein, iron-on transfers, Wangs, 1990, Spooky Scenes, MIB $5.00

Freddy Krueger, see Friday the 13th or Nightmare on Elm Street

Friday the 13th, doll, Freddy Krueger, talker, MIB $35.00

Friday the 13th, light-up hockey mask, video store promo, EX, S2..$175.00

G-Man, hairbrush, child's, 1930s, M, J2...........................$45.00

Garfield, doll, Mattel, 1983, talker w/moving eyes, EX, S2..$75.00

Garfield, school kit, 1980s, complete w/pencil pouch & accessories, MIP, S2 ....$15.00

Garfield, shoelace locks, 1989, figural, MOC, S2 ....$10.00

Garrison's Gorillas, Paint-By-Number Set, Saalfield, 1964, 2 canvases w/10 vials of oil pnts, MIB (sealed)..............$50.00

Ghostbusters, cartoon gift set, MIB, S2............................$20.00

Ghostbusters, Ecto Plasm Goop, full container, M (sealed), S2 ....$20.00

Ghostbusters, Ecto 500 Race Car, MIB, S2......................$35.00

Ghostbusters, Ecto-Blaster, shoots foam bullets, MIB, S2..$85.00

Ghostbusters, Ecto-Bomber, MIB, S2................................$85.00

Ghostbusters, Ecto-Headphones, very rare, MIB, S2 ....$85.00

Ghostbusters, Ecto-1 Ambulance, NMIB, S2 ....$85.00

Ghostbusters, figure, Sta-Puft, 1984, vinyl, NM, S2 ....$20.00

Ghostbusters, figures, Slimer, Japan, 2 different, resin, S2, ea...$50.00

Ghostbusters, Ghost Extinguisher Squirt Gun, shaped like fire extinguisher, MOC, S2..$20.00

Ghostbusters, Ghost Nabber, Kenner, 1986, shoot/snag wand & 3 cloth ghosts, MIB, S2 ....$85.00

Ghostbusters, Ghost Spooker, electronic modulator changes voice to sound like ghosts, MIB, S2 ....$75.00

Ghostbusters, Ghost Sweeper, MIB, S2 ....$25.00

Ghostbusters, Ghost Trap, MIB, S2 ....$55.00

Ghostbusters, Grab-A-Meter, Kenner, 1986, w/grab claws, missle & launcher, MIB, S2.......................................$50.00

Ghostbusters, Nutrona Blaster, Kenner, 1986, w/spinning Nutrona ray, MIB, S2 ....$75.00

Ghostbusters, plaster molding set, features Sta-Puft & other characters, w/molds & pnt, MIB, S2 ....$30.00

Ghostbusters, Shrinky Dinks, MIB....................................$25.00

Ghostbusters, tray, 1986, M, S2...$30.00

Ghostbusters, Water Zapper, rare, MIB, S2 ....$85.00

Ghostbusters, wind sock, extemely rare, MIP, S2 ....$40.00

Gilligan's Island, tablet, 1965, Gilligan & Skipper color photo cover, unused, M..$35.00

Godzilla, figure, 1985, friction, 3", rare, MOC, S2...........$35.00

Gone With the Wind, brooch, Lux Soap, C10...............$125.00

Great Grape Ape, iron-on transfer, 1976, 4¼", M $10.00

Green Hornet, flasher rings, Vari-Vue, 1960s, set of 12, M..$250.00

Green Hornet, hat & mask, Arlington/Greenway, 1966, blk felt w/decal & orig tag, attached mask, NM..................$175.00

Green Hornet, magic slate, 1960s, graphics of Green Hornet & Kato in action, VG, J5..$45.00

Green Hornet, ring, w/emblem, M, J2....................................$45.00

Green Hornet & Kato, masks, Arlington Hats/Greenway, 1966, plastic, unused, NM (EX+ card)..............................$300.00

Green Lantern, glow-in-the-dark ring, plastic, premium, M, S2 ....$35.00

Gremlins, backpacks, Gizmo or Stripe, 3 different, w/tags, M, S2, ea..$35.00

Gremlins, ball & dart set, MIP, S2 ....$65.00

Gremlins, belt, 1984, Gizmo & Stripe on elastic belt w/Gizmo on rnd buckle, w/tag, M, S2..$20.00

Gremlins, figure, Gizmo, vinyl, 6", MIB..............................$40.00

Gremlins, figure, Stripe, LJN, 1984, vinyl, 12", MIB, D4 .$45.00

Gremlins, gum dispenser, Stripe figure, rare, MOC, S2 ....$50.00

Gremlins, Magic Catch Mits, baseball-type gloves w/velcro ball, MIB, S2..$65.00

Gremlins, night light, Gizmo figure, MOC, S2 ....$25.00

Gremlins, Shrinky Dinks, 1984, MIB, S2.............................$25.00

Gremlins, Water Hatchers, Gizmo & Stripe, LJN, 1990, w/storage pod, add water & watch them grow, MOC, S2 ...$25.00

Grouch or Grover, see Sesame Street

Gumby, doll, stuffed, w/plastic eyes & felt features, 22", S1.$18.00

Gumby, figure, Applause, 1989, as baseball player, bendable, 5", MIP, K1 ....$5.00

Gumby, figure, Applause, 1989, as surfer, bendable, 5", MIP, K1 ....$5.00

Gumby, figure, Applause, 1989, bendable, 5", MIP, K1......$4.00

Gumby, figure, Playskool, 1988, bendable, 6", MIP, K1......$4.00

Gumby, figure, Pokey, Jesco, bendable, 10", MIP, K1.......$12.00

Gumby, figure, Pokey, Jesco, bendable, 6", MIP, K1...........$4.00

Gumby, figure, Pokey, Lakeside, 1965, orange rubber, vending machine premium, 2x2", M, T2....................................$6.00

Gumby, figures, Gumby or Pokey, 1980s, foam, 15", MIB, S2, ea $55.00

Gumby, jeep, Lakeside, 1965, missing windshield, G (VG box), H4 ....$18.00

Gumby, Cowboy Adventure Costume, Lakeside, 1965, MOC, $12.00.

Gumby, outfits, Astronaut, Cowboy, Fireman or Knight Adventure Costume Set, Lakeside, 1965, MOC, H4, ea......$12.00

Gumby, paddle ball, MIP, S2...$10.00

Gumby, Shrinky Dinks, 1988, MIB, S2..............................$20.00

Happy Days, Colorforms, The Fonz, 1976, MIB $20.00

Happy Days, Flip-A-Knot, National Marketing, 1977, MIP ..$20.00

Happy Days, guitar, 1976, plastic w/color photo of the Fonz, Richie & Potsy, 20", EX, J5.......................................$25.00

Happy Days, viewer, Larami, 1980, features Fonz & rest of cast, MIC...$18.00

Happy Hooligan, figure, prewar Germany, pnt bsk in classic garb, 7½", very scarce, NM, A $240.00

Happy Hooligan, nesting figure, wood, 6½", VG, A.........$30.00

Hardy Boys, record player, Vanity Fair, 1978, features Shawn Cassidy & Parker Stevenson, NM......................$125.00

Harry & the Hendersons, figure, Just Toys, bendable, 7", MIP, K1 ....$5.00

Hawaii Five-O, binoculars, Larami, MIB, $25.00.

He-Man, see Masters of the Universe

Heckle & Jeckle, bagatelle game, Imperial Toy, 1978, NM, T2...$8.00

Heckle & Jeckle, magic slate, Lowe, 1952, EX+, T2 ....$18.00

Herman & Katnip, Deep View Paint Set, Pressman, 1961, 11x14" 3-D picture w/6 colors, bowl & brush, M (NM box), T2...$59.00

Hogan's Heroes, writing tablet, 1960s, unused, NM, C1 ..$33.00

Hokey Wolf, tablet, 1961, 8x11", EX+..............................$15.00

Honeymooners, slide-tile puzzle, Roalex, 1956, plastic w/images of all characters, 6½", rare, EX (EX card), A $190.00

Hong Kong Phooey, iron-on transfer, 1976, M, S2..........$20.00

Hopperoo, doll, Hanna-Barbera/Germany, 1960s, gr head w/gold on gr cloth body, felt hands, NM, C1 ....$90.00

Howdy Doody, baby rattle, Clarabell, Stahlwood/Kagran, pnt vinyl face atop suction-cup rattle, NM (EX box), A............$176.00

Howdy Doody, baby rattle, Howdy, Stahlwood/Kagran, pnt vinyl face atop suction-cup rattle, EX (EX box), A $145.00

Howdy Doody, Bandage Strips, Kagran, 1950s, complete w/36 bandages & color photo, NM (NM box), A $56.00

Howdy Doody, bank, Clarabell figure, NBC Straco, flocked w/vinyl base, MIP $15.00

Howdy Doody, bank, Howdy figure, NBC Straco, flocked w/vinyl base, MIP $15.00

Howdy Doody, bank, Phineas T Bluster figure, NBC Straco, flocked w/vinyl base, 7", MIP $15.00

Howdy Doody, carrying case, w/Mr Bluster, Kagran, 1953, Welch's Grape Juice Doodyville Village series, cb, 5", NM, A $436.00

Howdy Doody, Coloring Set, Kagran, 1950s, 3 lg & 3 sm follow-the-number drawings w/12 colored pencils, EX (EX box), A $648.00

Howdy Doody, curtains, 1950s, single panel w/repeated pattern of Howdy & friends, 83", NM, A $209.00

Howdy Doody, doll, Goldberger, stuffed w/vinyl head, movable jaw, dressed w/leather-like boots, 12", VG.................$65.00

Howdy Doody, earmuffs, unmk, Kagran (?), fur surrounds 3-D celluloid Howdy faces, 3½" dia, rare, M, A...............$75.00

Howdy Doody's Embroidery Kit, Milton Bradley/Kagran, EX (EX box), A, $125.00.

Howdy Doody, figure, wood and composition, jointed, bright paint, original decal on stomach, 13", $150.00.

Howdy Doody, Electric Doodler, Wiry Dan version, contains 4 sheets w/various games, quizzes & mazes, M (EX+ box), A...$107.00

Howdy Doody, footstool, Wooden Ware, 1950s, features Howdy in graduation cap, It's Howdy Doody Time, scarce, NM, A $331.00

Howdy Doody, hat, NBC, red felt w/wht peak & wht braid, NM...$25.00

Howdy Doody, iron-on transfer, Howdy's face & name, 9x8", G (in pkg) $9.00

Howdy Doody, key chain, puzzle type, NM, J2 ....$20.00

Howdy Doody, lapel pin, Kagran, 1950s, plastic bust of Howdy on display card, ¾", NM+, A...........................$60.00

Howdy Doody, Magic Piano Xylo-Doodle instruction pamphlet, dtd 1948, w/songs, illus & directions, NM $22.00

Howdy Doody, night light, NBC, 1988, Howdy on pig, ceramic, 8½", MIB...$24.00

Howdy Doody, pen, Howdy figure w/moving mouth on top, MOC...$5.00

Howdy Doody, pin that talks, Chelsley Novelty, Howdy figure, plastic, 3½", M (G card)......................................$15.00

Howdy Doody, Put On Your Own Puppet Show Plastic Toys, Kagran, 1950s, figures w/movable mouths, 5", NMOC...$195.00

Howdy Doody, safe, bl plastic w/character portrait busts around dial w/Howdy portrait bust in center, 6", EX+, A....$226.00

Howdy Doody, shoes for Howdy Doody doll, wht w/bl trim, G $15.00

Howdy Doody, Slipperdoodle, box only for slippers, 3x7x10", EX+, A..$193.00

Howdy Doody, spoon, Kagran, 1950s, NM, C1 ....$45.00

Howdy Doody, squeeze toy, Clarabell, Peter Puppet Mfg, 7", NM (EX box) $250.00

Howdy Doody, squeeze toy, Dilly Dally, Peter Puppet Mfg, 7", NM (EX+ box) $250.00

Howdy Doody, towel, Clarabell, Cannon/Kagran, 1950s, Clarabell holds circus sign, 23", non-working squeaker, EX+, A..$182.00

Huckleberry Hound, bank, 1982, vinyl figure in sitting position, 5", NM, S2 ....$35.00

Huckleberry Hound, camera, 1960s, plastic, M (VG box), M5 ....$50.00

Huckleberry Hound, charm bracelet, 1959, sm metal Hanna-Barbera characters on bracelet, M (NM card) $40.00

Huckleberry Hound, club ring, 1961, metal, VG+, J2 ......$45.00

Huckleberry Hound, Friends Circus, Coleman, 1961, complete set of circus characters w/lion, pnt plastic, EX (EX box), A..$165.00

Huckleberry Hound, magic slate, 1961, features Huck, Jinx, Pixie & Dixie, NM, S2 ....$35.00

Huckleberry Hound, postcard, 1965, shows Huck snoozing, EX, J5 ....$10.00

Huckleberry Hound, TV tray, 1959, litho tin, shows Huck as William Tell shooting apple off Yogi's head, 16x21", NM, T2 ....$30.00

Huckleberry Hound & Cindy Lou, dolls, 1958, 15" & 17", NM, S9, pr $200.00

Huckleberry Hound & Yogi Bear, sand pail, Ohio Art, 1970s, NM, S2...$30.00

Huckleberry Hound & Yogi Bear, talking movie wheels, Movie Wheels Inc, 1960, complete w/record, MOC (sealed), T2 ....$24.00

Hunter, Police Accessory Set, Largo, 1984, dart gun & targets, MOC $25.00

Ignatz the Rat, figure, segmented wood w/pnt eyes & nose, wood ears, dowel legs, rope tail, 6", needs restrung, EX, A..$80.00

Impossibles, magic slate, Watkins, 1967, M $55.00

In Living Color, doll, Homey the Clown, 1992, stuffed cloth, 24", H4 ....$35.00

Incredible Hulk, bank, AJ Renzi, 1979, 8", NM, C1 ....$19.50

Incredible Hulk, Colorforms Set, MIB $36.00

Incredible Hulk, doll, Knickerbocker, 1978, stuffed, 16", NM, S2 ....$30.00

Incredible Hulk, figure, Applause, bendable, 6", MIP, K1 ..$6.00

Incredible Hulk, gumball machine, early 1980s, figural, 10½", MIP $20.00

Incredible Hulk, Hide-A-Way Playcase, Tara/Sears, 1978, M (sealed)...$35.00

Incredible Hulk, plate, 3 sections w/graphics around rim, Melmac, EX..$10.00

Incredible Hulk, playing cards, 1979, MIB (sealed) $5.00

Incredible Hulk, roller skates, Larami, 1970s, MIB..........$40.00

Incredible Hulk, Rub 'n Play Set, Colorforms, 1979, MIB.$12.00

Incredible Hulk & Spiderman, Shrinky Dinks Set, 1970s, MIB $35.00

Inspector Gadget, wastebasket, 1980s, NM, S2 ....$55.00

James Bond, Electric Drawing Set, Lakeside, 1966, NM (EX+ box)..$75.00

James Bond, figures, Gilbert, 1965, set of 10 movie characters, EX (EX box), J2 ....$170.00

James Bond, ID tags, Imperial, 1984, MOC, C1 ....$18.00

James Bond, Secret Agent 007 Action Toys Gun Case & M's Desk, Gilbert, 1965, M (EX bubble card) $50.00

Jeep (Popeye's dog), figure, King Features, ca 1935, standing upright w/decal on chest, pnt compo, 14", VG, A...$783.00

Jeep (Popeye's dog), figure, King Features, 1938, standing upright, jtd wood w/pnt features & name on chest, 4", NM, A...$500.00

Jetsons, candy box, Jetsons Candy Sprockets, features Elroy, George & Astro Dog, World Candies Inc, empty, 3", NM $80.00

Jetsons, Judy Jetson's Shoes, Gen Shoes/Hanna-Barbera, 1962, red w/image of Judy, rare, NM (EX shipping box), A $259.00

Jetsons, magic slate, Watkins Strathmore, 1960s, bl or yel background, EX, J5 ....$35.00

Jetsons, pencil sharpener, Colleen, crank operated, 5½", EX, A, $275.00.

Jetsons, puffy magnets, 1970s, set of 4 w/Mom, Dad, Elroy & Rosey, 4", M...$40.00

Joe Palooka, boxing gloves, B&M Sports, 1950s, 2 pr vinyl gloves w/laces & Joe's name, child-sz, EX (EX box), J5........$165.00

Joe Palooka, doll, daughter Joan, National, 1950s, cloth clothes w/vinyl head, hands & feet, 10", EX (damaged box) .$90.00

Joe Palooka, punching bag, Pioneer Rubber/c Ham Fisher, envelope shows Joe punching bag, NM, A $45.00

Johnny Appleseed, doll, Scerugo, 1954, The Apple Tree Planter, detailed rubber, 13", NM (VG box), T2 ....$198.00

Joker, see Batman

Kato, see Green Hornet

Kermit the Frog, see Muppets

King Kong, bank, Ricogen, 1977, shows King Kong standing on Empire State Building, pnt vinyl, 13", EX.................$60.00

King Kong, bank, 1978, plastic figure, 17", M..................$75.00

King Kong, figure, Monster-Nik, 1963, lg vinyl head on sm body, 4", M..$30.00

King Kong, jewelry box, Presents, 1990s, M $25.00

Knight Rider, clicker gun & holster set, MOC, S2 ....$20.00

Knight Rider, Colorforms, M (G box), S2 ....$20.00

Knight Rider, Impossible Stunt Set w/Motorized KITT Car, MIB, S2 ....$55.00

Knight Rider, intercom set, room-to-room phones w/30-ft cord, MIB, S2 ....$55.00

Knight Rider, KITT Dashboard, w/flashing lights & sound, MIB, S2 ....$55.00

Knight Rider, Knight Rider 2000 Turbo Boost & Launcher Set, 3¼" car & 7½" launcher, MOC, S2 ....$30.00

Knight Rider, Knight 2000 Crash Set, MIB, S2...............$45.00

Knight Rider, Knight 2000 Whip Shifter Vehicle, Kenner, 1984, w/T-pull strip, 7½", MIP, S2......................................$35.00

Knight Rider, rubber stamp set, 1982, MOC, S2 ....$15.00

Knight Rider, sleeping bag, w/tag, M, S2 ....$55.00

Knight Rider, slide-tile puzzle, Ja-Ru, 1982, MOC, S2 .....$25.00

Knight Rider, slot car race set, light-up, HO scale, MIB, S2 .$115.00

Knight Rider, sun visor & glasses, Laramie, 1982, MOC, C1.$14.00

Knight Rider, walkie-talkies, transistor set, MIB $45.00

Knight Rider, yo-yo, Larami, 1982, MOC, S2 ....$20.00

Krazy Kat, magic slate, Lowe, 1960s, Krazy Kat & friends graphics, EX, J5 ....$25.00

Krazy Kat, Toy Time Balloon counter display, 20 colorful 4" deflated balloons on display card, EX, J5..................$45.00

Krusty the Clown, see Simpsons

Land of the Giants, Cartoon Kit, Colorforms, 1968, MIB ..$90.00

Land of the Giants, movie viewer, Acme, 1968, plastic w/turning knob, w/2 boxes film, NMOC $65.00

Lariat Sam, magic slate, Lowe, 1962, lift-up erasable film on cb w/stylus, 8x12", VG+, T2 ....$15.00

Lassie, plate, Melmac, 1960s, 7", NM+ $20.00

Lassie, playset, Marx, 1992, MIB, D4 ....$60.00

Laugh-In, gumball machine display card, 1969, button & joke book offer, Rowan & Martin photo, 4x4", M, T2 ......$39.00

Laugh-In, helmet, German soldier type w/'Very Interesting,' NM, J2 ....$70.00

Laurel & Hardy, bank, Stan Laurel or Oliver Hardy figures, Play Pal, 1974, vinyl, 7½", EX, ea $45.00

Laverne & Shirley, Secretary Set, Harmony, 1977, MOC..$20.00

Li'l Abner, The Life & Times of the Shmoo, paperback, 1949, EX+, C1 ....$31.00

Linus, see Peanuts

Lion King, see Disney category

Little Audrey, tote bag, World Traveler, 1960, wht vinyl w/illus, 8x6x5", EX+, T2 ....$59.00

Little Bo-Peep, Phillip Segal Toys, England, 4 cast metal figures tied on card, Bo-Peep is 2", sheep are 1", EX (G box), A, $160.00.

Little Boy Blue, figure, Alan Toy, 1958, rubber, VG $18.00

Little Lulu, doll, cloth head, mask face w/pnt features, mitten hands, jtd shoulders & hips, orig outfit, early, 18", EX..............$295.00

Little Lulu, doll, early, 15", EX, J2 ....$300.00

Little Lulu, dolls, Little Lulu & Tubby, Georgine Novelties, orig tags, 15", scarce, EX, A, pr $1,378.00

Little Lulu, figures, Little Lulu & Tubby, Western Publishing, 1975, 3", EX+, A, pr $66.00

Little Orphan Annie, bank, Famous Artists Syndicate, 1936, 10¢ Register Bank, litho tin, 3", EX, A....................$330.00

Little Orphan Annie, clothespins, Transogram/Harold Gray, orig card contains 14 of 18 pins & 2 pulleys, 12", EX, A $70.00

Little Orphan Annie, doll, Famous Artists Syndicate, cloth & compo, 14½", G, A..................................$80.00

Little Orphan Annie, figures, Annie & Sandy, jtd wood, 5½", EX, I2 ....$149.00

Little Orphan Annie, paint and crayon box, Milton Bradley, 1934, complete with paints, crayons and cup, 14", EX+ (EX+ box), A, $105.00.

Little Orphan Annie, paint & crayon box, Milton Bradley, 1934, complete w/paints, crayons & cup, 14", EX+ (EX+ box), A....................................$105.00

Little Orphan Annie, pull toy, TrickyToy/FAS, 1930s, Sandy pulls Annie on wooden wheeled toy, EX, A............$150.00

Little Orphan Annie, see also Annie

Lost in Space, writing tablet, 1965, June Lockhart on cover, unused, NM $45.00

Lucy, see Peanuts

M*A*S*H, Doctor Set, 1981, MOC $20.00

Mammy & Pappy Yokum, nodders, Dogpatch USA, 1975, 8", EX, J2, pr..$100.00

Man From UNCLE, car, Carlos V/Spain, mk El Agente De CIPOL, wht w/yel decals, plastic, friction, 8½", NM (EX box)..$250.00

Man From UNCLE, flasher ring, flashes from Napoleon to Illya, M..$15.00

Man From UNCLE, Magic Tricks, MIB $150.00

Man From UNCLE, membership card, Ideal, 1960s, M....$15.00

Man From UNCLE, playing cards, Ed-U-Cards/MGM, 1965, 40 of 54 feature action photos w/Solo, NM (EX header card)..$40.00

Man From UNCLE, Secret Print Putty w/Spy Book, 1965, MOC, S2..$65.00

Martie the Martian, figure, c Donald Lee Cyr, 1950s, hard rubber, spring arms & legs w/suction cups, 6", NM (EX+ box), A..$254.00

Marvel Comics X-Men, figure, Cyclops, Just Toys, bendable, 6", MIP, K1..$5.00

Marvel Comics X-Men, figure, Wolverine, Just Toys, bendable, 6", MIP, K1..$5.00

Marvel Super Heroes, pennants, Capt America, Thor, Iron Man, Hulk or Sub-Mariner, RMS, 1966, set of 5, NM........$18.00

Marvel Super Heroes, stick-ons, Spiderman, Capt America & Thor, Our Way Studios, 1974, MIP, D9 ....$16.00

Mary Poppins, see Disney category

Masters of the Universe, bank, He-Man figure, NM (EX box), O1..$6.00

Masters of the Universe, bank, Skeletor, NM (EX pkg), O1..$6.00

Masters of the Universe, gumball bank, Castle Grayskull, NM (NM box), O1..$4.00

Masters of the Universe, puffy stickers & album set, NM (EX pkg), O1..$20.00

Masters of the Universe, record tote, for 45 rpms, VG, O1..$6.00

Masters of the Universe, talking toothbrush, He-Man, NM .$40.00

Masters of the Universe, tape player, He-Man & Skeletor figures on front, NM, S2..................................$45.00

Masters of the Universe, wall decoration, 3-D, NM (NM box), O1..$8.00

Maverick, see Western category

Max Headroom, candy container, figural bust, M, S2 ......$10.00

Max Headroom, mask, full head w/Velcro closure, rare, NM, S2..$155.00

Miami Vice, notebook folder, 1985, M $15.00

Mighty Mouse, bagatelle game, Imperial Toy, 1978, NM, T2..$8.00

Mighty Mouse, chalkboard set, Fleetwood, 1979, figure on corner, sm, MOC, S2..................................$25.00

Mighty Mouse, charm bracelet, 1950s, w/Terrytoon characters, EX (on damaged card), J5..$45.00

Mighty Mouse, doll, Viacom International, 1989, plush, 8", EX+, P3 ....$8.00

Mighty Mouse, figure, Jesco, bendable, 4½", MIP, K1 ....$5.00

Miss Piggy, see Muppets

Moon Mullins, Kayo, Uncle Willie and Emmy, figures, bisque, tallest figure is 3½", EX (original box), D10, $275.00.

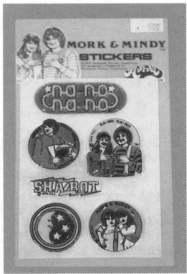

Mork and Mindy, stickers, Paramount Pictures Corp, 1979, MOC, $5.00.

Mortimer Snerd, Flexy doll, Ideal, 1940s, orig label, NM, A..$250.00

Mother Goose, doll, Mattel, 1962, talker, working, VG, J2 .$40.00

Mr Magoo, ring, w/2 of 4 different Magoo figures to put on ring, plastic, M (in bag w/colorful header card), H4 ....$12.00

Mr Magoo, tattoo wraper, Fleer, 1967, 1½x3½", M, T2 ...$15.00

Mr Peabody, figure, Jesco, 1991, bendable, 5", MIP, K1 .....$5.00

Mummy, doll, Remco, MIB $35.00

Mummy, figure, Novelty, 1979, bendable, NMOC, D9....$15.00

Munsters, Casting Set, Emenee/Castex, 1960s, complete w/molds & tools, NMIB $600.00

Munsters, figure, any character, Mini-Monster, Ideal, 1964, M, ea..$75.00

Muppet Babies, bank, Baby Kermit in pirate's outfit holding treasure chest, 1989, vinyl, 9", MIB, S2 ....$30.00

Muppet Babies, Shrinky Dinks, 1985, MIB, S2.................$15.00

Muppets, bank, Miss Piggy figure, Sigma, ceramic, 8", NM, S2 ....$65.00

Muppets, Christmas ornament, head of Kermit w/Santa hat & bells, Sigma, 1979, pnt papier-mache, NM, S2..........$35.00

Muppets, Christmas ornament, Sigma, 1979, features Miss Piggy's head, pnt papier-mache, NM, S2 ....$30.00

Muppets, figure, Miss Piggy, beanbag body w/vinyl head & rooted hair, VG, S2 ....$15.00

Muppets, floating soap dish, Kermit & Miss Piggy driving car, 1988, MIP $12.00

Mush Mouse, doll, Ideal, 1960s, solid-stuffed cloth body w/vinyl head, bendable arms & legs, 8", no vest o/w VG, H4 .$35.00

Nanny & the Professor, Colorforms, 1970, MIB...............$35.00

Natasha (Rocky & Bullwinkle), figure, Wham-O, 1972, MOC, S2..$20.00

Nexus, figure, Dark Horse Comics/China, 1993, Nexus crouched on lg rock in karate pose, hand-painted resin, MIB, H4 ....$65.00

Nightmare Before Christmas, see Disney category

Nightmare on Elm Street, Freddy Fright Squirter, 1989, detailed vinyl head squirts water, MIB, S2..........................$20.00

Nightmare on Elm Street, see also Friday the 13th

Olive Oyl, figure, Jesco, bendable, 3", MIP, K1.................$2.50

Olive Oyl, figure, Jesco, bendable, 6", MIP, K1.................$6.00

Olive Oyl, mirror, King Features, 1980, 6¾x5½", G...........$5.00

Olive Oyl, nodder, standing on rnd base, wood w/fabric collar & vinyl-like legs, 10", EX+, A.................................$205.00

Olive Oyl, tunic & mask w/Dick Tracy comic book & Motorola brochure, 1953, unused, NM (EX envelope), A $33.00

Olive Oyl & Wimpy, figures, Jaymar, articulated wood, 5" Olive Oyl & 4" Wimpy, NM, A, pr $125.00

Our Gang, clubhouse set, Hal Roach/MGM, 3-D cb clubhouse w/9 unpnt bsk figures, orig pnts & color-match card, MIB, A $732.00

Our Gang, Color Culture set w/theater, Gem Clay Forming Co/MGM, china, 9-pc, 2" to 5", NM (EX box), A..$364.00

Our Gang, see also Action Figures category

Pac-Man, belt, 1980, vinyl w/Pac-Man graphics, VG, S2.$25.00

Pac-Man, pocket game, Tomy, 1980s, Pac-Man tries to eat balls falling through maze, EX, S2 ....$20.00

Pac-Man, revolving color lamp, 1970s, S9......................$75.00

Partridge Family, dress-up set for David Cassidy, Colorforms, 1972, MIB $65.00

Peanuts, bank, Snoopy, pewter, VG, O1..........................$45.00

Peanuts, bank, Snoopy, 1973, standing wearing ball hat & mit, ceramic, NM, S2 ....$50.00

Peanuts, bank, Snoopy in bl jogging suit w/Woodstock, 1972, ceramic, 5½", EX, S2 ....$35.00

Peanuts, bank, Snoopy in Flying Ace airplane, ceramic, cracks & chips, G, S2 ....$15.00

Peanuts, bank, Snoopy on doghouse, ceramic, VG, S2/O1.$25.00

Peanuts, bank, Snoopy on soccer ball, ceramic, NM, S2 ..$45.00

Peanuts, bike horn, Snoopy, 1966, G, S2........................$10.00

Peanuts, Colorforms, 1969, Carry On Nurse Lucy, EX+ (EX box), T2 ....$20.00

Peanuts, Colorforms, 1969, Hold That Line Charlie Brown, EX+ (EX box), T2 ....$20.00

Peanuts, doll, Linus, Determined, 1970s, stuffed cloth, 14", EX, H4 ....$22.00

Peanuts, doll, Lucy, Determined, 1970s, stuffed cloth, 14", EX, H4 ....$22.00

Peanuts, doll, Peppermint Patty, Determined, 1970s, stuffed cloth, 14", EX, H4....................................$18.00

Peanuts, doll, Woodstock, 1972, VG, O1 ....$15.00

Peanuts, doll/cassette player, Snoopy, 24", G, O1............$35.00

Peanuts, figure, Belle, Determined, 1970s, Sleepy Time version from the Dress & Play series, vinyl, 9", EX, H4 ....$35.00

Peanuts, figure, Snoopy #376, w/red collar & molded ears, vinyl, 9", NM, S2 ....$45.00

Peanuts, figure, Snoopy as astronaut, Knickerbocker, 1965, 5", missing 2" Woodstock, H4 ....$50.00

Peanuts, figure, Snoopy as golfer, Determined, 1970s, vinyl, 9", H4 ....$35.00

Peanuts, figure, Snoopy as Red Baron, 1966, vinyl, 7", VG.$25.00

Peanuts, figures, Charlie Brown & Linus, jtd plastic w/cloth clothes, Linus w/chip on 1 heel, 7", H4, pr $40.00

Peanuts, figures, set of 5 w/Charlie Brown, Lucy, Snoopy, Schroeder & Linus, jtd vinyl w/cloth clothes, 7", EX, H4 ....$150.00

Peanuts, handlebar toy, Snoopy figure, 1971, MOC.........$10.00

Peanuts, jack-in-the-box, Snoopy, Mattel, NMIB............$75.00

Peanuts, magic slate, features Snoopy, Saalfield, 1967, activities on back, EX, T2 ....$20.00

Peanuts, magic slate, Saalfield, 1961, NM, T2 ....$49.00

Peanuts, nodder, Snoopy as Joe Cool, 5", EX, H4.............$35.00

Peanuts, pajama bag w/button, Snoopy figure, J5..............$42.00

Peanuts, paratrooper toy, Snoopy, 1980s, throw it up & it floats down, MOC, S2 ....$10.00

Peanuts, pull toy, Snoopy & Woodstock, VG, O1............$18.00

Peanuts, race car, features Lucy, diecast, MIP, S2.............$20.00

Peanuts, shampoo container, Snoopy on doghouse, Avon, 1970s, MIB $18.00

Peanuts, squeeze toy, Snoopy & Woodstock, G, O1 ....$7.00

Peanuts, squeeze toy, Snoopy as golfer, NM, O1 ....$3.50

Peanuts, toothbrush w/cup, Snoopy figure, battery-op, NMIB...$75.00

Peanuts, tote bag, Butterfly Originals, features Snoopy, canvas, NM, I2...$6.00

Peanuts, umbrella, Snoopy, 1965, S1 ....$26.00

Peanuts, vehicle, Snoopy on Station Wagon, diecast, MOC...$10.00

Pebbles, see Flintstones

Pee Wee's Playhouse, ball & dart set w/target, M (sealed), S2...$65.00

Pee Wee's Playhouse, Colorforms, lg, MIB, S2 ....$55.00

Pee Wee's Playhouse, Colorforms, sm set, MIB $25.00

Pee Wee's Playhouse, doll, Billy Baloney, 18", NMIB......$25.00

Pee Wee's Playhouse, doll, Chairry, 18", NRFB...............$35.00

Pee Wee's Playhouse, doll, Pterri, 18", NRFB..................$25.00

Pee Wee's Playhouse, doll, Vance, stuffed talker, lg, MIB, S2...$65.00

Pee Wee's Playhouse, figure, Randy & Globey, sm, MIP, S2, pr...$65.00

Pee Wee's Playhouse, see also Action Figures category

Pee Wee's Playhouse, Shrinky Dinks, rare, MIB, S2.........$45.00

Pee Wee's Playhouse, slumber bag, MIP, S2 ....$125.00

Pee Wee's Playhouse, yo-yo, 1980s, MOC $20.00

Penguin, see Batman

Pepe Le Peu & Fifi, figure, Applause, 1989, ceramic, rare, M, S2...$45.00

Peppermint Patty, see Peanuts

Phantom of the Opera, nodder, vinyl, 6", EX, J5 ....$45.00

Pink Panther, doll, 1989, 25th Anniversary, plush, 12", M, P3...$10.00

Pink Panther, figure, Jesco, bendable, 7", MIP, K1 ....$5.00

Pink Panther, figure, w/parachute, PVC, 4", EX, S2 ....$5.00

Pink Panther, figures, set of 6 in different outfits, PVC, 3", M, S2...$30.00

Pink Panther, Silly Putty, 1980, MOC, S2 ....$15.00

Pink Panther, wallet, 1961, child-sz, G, S2 ....$10.00

Planet of the Apes, Astronaut Virdon Mix 'n Mold, Catalog Shoppe, 1974, figure-casting set w/mold, powder & pnts, EX, D9...$32.00

Planet of the Apes, bank, Galen or Zaius vinyl figures, Play Pal, 1974, 11", EX, J5, ea $15.00

Planet of the Apes, kite, MIP, S2 ....$35.00

Pogo, figure, Alligator, Hound Dog, Owl or Turtle, Proctor & Gamble premium, 1969, vinyl, M, T1, ea $10.00

Pogo, figure, Howland Owl or Beauregard Hound, Proctor & Gamble, posable pnt vinyl, from set of 6, 4" or 5", M, T2, ea...$12.00

Pogo, figure, Pogo, Proctor & Gamble premium, 1969, striped shirt, M, T1...$12.00

Pokey, see Gumby

Police Academy, Shrinky Dinks, MIB, S2 ....$15.00

Popeye, balloon pump, 1957, cb cylinder w/metal top & bottom, EX, J5...$25.00

Popeye, bank, glazed ceramic w/pnt features & wooden corncob pipe, unmk, 7½", EX, A...$305.00

Popeye, Beach Set (sand toys), early, NMIP (sealed), J2..$85.00

Popeye, binoculars, Larami, 6¼", M (VG card) $20.00

Popeye, bubble set, King, 1936, 3-D Popeye soap head w/dish & 2 pipes, MIB, A...$80.00

Popeye, bubble set, Transogram, 2 pnt wood pipes & figural soap w/tin dish, soap used, rust on dish, VG (VG box), A...$15.00

Popeye, chalk, 6", most of contents, EX, M5 ....$25.00

Popeye, Colorforms, 1957, NM (VG+ box), C1..............$36.00

Popeye, corkscrew, figural w/corkscrew in base, marked Bulls on bottom, 6", EX pnt, A $175.00

Popeye, crib toy, prewar Japan, celluloid figure w/string & loop, 4", EX, A...$160.00

Popeye-Cheers Christmas Light Shades, Clemco Inc/King Features Syndicate, 1929, complete set of 8, each with paper decal, NM (NM box), A, $200.00.

Popeye, doll, Gund, 1960s, talker (squeeze chest), stuffed cloth w/vinyl head, 14", MIB, H4.................$120.00

Popeye, doll, Uneeda, 1974, 15", no clothing, VG, S2.....$30.00

Popeye, doll, Uneeda, 1979, 6", MIB, S2 ....$30.00

Popeye, figure, Jesco, bendable, 3", MIP, K1 ....$2.50

Popeye, figure, Jesco, bendable, 6", MIP, K1 ....$6.00

Popeye, flasher ring, S2...$30.00

Popeye, fly swatter, US Mfg Corp/KFS, 1936, Popeye illus on cb label, complete w/booklet, 26", scarce, EX, A $112.00

Popeye, Funny Face Maker, Jaymar/KFS, 1960s, turn 13" wheel & watch different faces appear, NM.......................$38.00

Popeye, hat, 1940s, bl cloth w/silkscreened details, wht plastic bill, quilted lining, old store stock, M, H4 ....$80.00

Popeye, lamp, 1940s, pnt slush-cast metal, 11½", VG, A.$173.00

Popeye, lantern, Linemar, King Features Syndicate, lithographed tin, 7½", NM+ (NM box), A, $900.00.

Popeye, motorcycle, Hubley, 1930s, pnt CI, mk Spinach, 5⅜", EX+, A $2,100.00

Popeye, motorcycle, Hubley, 1930s, pnt CI w/blk rubber tires, orig clicker, 8⅜", EX, A $5,000.00

Popeye, nodder, King Features Syndicate/Japan, stands on rnd base, pendulum-type lever, wood, 9", EX+, A $260.00

Popeye, paddle-ball paddle, 1960s, wood, ball missing, EX, J5...$10.00

Popeye, paint box, 1933, features Popeye, Olive Oyl & Sweet Pea, tin, EX, A...$25.00

Popeye, paper party cup, 1950s, Happy Birthday, 3", M, T2 .$8.00

Popeye, pencil box, Hassenfeld/KFS, 1950s, maroon w/paper label of Popeye on raft composed of pencils, EX+ $38.00

Popeye, pencil toppers, 1984, different characters, MOC, ea $10.00

Popeye, pipe, 1948, MOC, S1 ....$80.00

Popeye, pipe bubble blower & bubbles, MOC, S2 ....$20.00

Popeye, printing set, Stamperkraft, 1935 KFS, mk Popeye the Printer, unused, NM (EX box), A...........................$160.00

Popeye, Sparkle Paints, Kenner, 1966, w/glitter paints & brushes, w/5 action & 5 paint-by-number pictures, MIB, A..$90.00

Popeye, Super Race Car, w/launcher, NMOC, J2.............$20.00

Popeye, tattoos, Topps, 1958, 1st series, half-figure on bl ground, 1½x3½", NM, T2...$29.00

Popeye, Thimble Theatre Cutouts, Aldon/KFS, 1950s, theatre w/push-out figures & background on card, unused, NM ..$48.00

Popeye, Tube-a-Loones, 1980s, makes balloons, NM, S2 ...$5.00

Popeye, TV tray, King Features Syndicate, 1979, lithoed scene w/Popeye, Olive Oyl & Bluto, tin, 17", M, A............$35.00

Popeye, wallet, vinyl w/flasher on front, NM, J2 ....$55.00

Popeye & Olive Oyl, bank, ceramic spinach can, VG+, I2..$13.00

Porky Pig, bank, 1940s, compo figure, 6", trap missing, some wear, VG, J5...$45.00

Prince Valiant, coin, 1967, emb gold-tone, 1½" dia, EX, J5.$15.00

Prince Valiant, Dime Bank, KFS, 1954, litho tin, sq w/diagonal corners, 2½", EX+, A...$152.00

Prince Valiant, Jeweled Sword, Scabbard & Shield, Mattel, 1950s, tin, MIB, A...$295.00

Princess of Power, talking toothbrush, NM.....................$40.00

Punch & Judy, puppet theater, England, 1930s, complete w/8 movable characters, unassembled, NMIB, A $70.00

Quick Draw McGraw, drawing board, Whitman, 1959, graphics of Quick-Draw & friends, EX, J5...............................$25.00

Quick Draw McGraw, TV tray, 1960s, metal, unused, M, J2 .$45.00

Quick Draw McGraw, wiggle block, Kohner, 1960, hard plastic TV w/flasher images, 2x2x2", EX+, T2 ....$14.00

Raggedy Andy, doll, cloth, 12", NM, O1 ....$20.00

Raggedy Andy, shelf sitter, porcelain, G, O1....................$22.00

Raggedy Ann, bank, vinyl, 1972, 15", VG, S2.................$45.00

Raggedy Ann, beanbag chair, VG, O1 ....$38.00

Raggedy Ann, chalkboard, EX, O1.................................$28.00

Raggedy Ann, doll, cloth, handmade, 34", VG, O1 ....$55.00

Raggedy Ann, doll, cloth, 32", EX, O1 ....$75.00

Raggedy Ann, figure, w/playhouse, 1988, MOC, S2.........$15.00

Raggedy Ann, lamp/music box, Bobbs Merrill, 1976, VG, O1 ....$18.00

Raggedy Ann, popcorn tin, 24", VG, O1 ....$25.00

Raggedy Ann, stapler, 1975, figural, 5½", VG, S2 ....$25.00

Raggedy Ann, stove & refrigerator, 1970s, VG, O1 ....$55.00

Raggedy Ann, tea set, Banner, 1959, 25-pc set w/plastic cups, glasses & teapot, tin dishes w/silverware, unused, MIB, A...$180.00

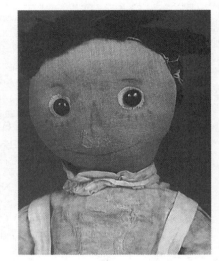

Raggedy Ann, doll, Volland, cloth with black shoe-button eyes, painted features, brown yarn hair, cardboard heart, red and white striped lower legs, brown feet for shoes, original print dress, white pinafore and bloomers, 16", G, A, $400.00.

Raggedy Ann & Andy, cradle, 1978, EX, O1 ....$45.00

Raggedy Ann & Andy, dolls, Georgene, 20", VG, O1, pr .$300.00

Raggedy Ann & Andy, dolls, Hallmark, 6", VG, O1, pr ..$22.00

Raggedy Ann & Andy, dolls, Knickerbocker/Hallmark, 4", VG, O1, pr..$25.00

Raggedy Ann & Andy, dolls, Mollye Goldman, 1920s, 18", some fading, 1 leg has split, A, pr $745.00

Raggedy Ann & Andy, lamp, porcelain, EX, O1 ....$45.00

Rambo, bank, figural, 1985, vinyl, 9", MIB.................$35.00

Rambo, bicycle toy, 1986, figural grenade squeeze horn & headband, MOC, S2...$20.00

Rambo, bike mirror, figural helicopter w/prop, guns & Rambo in window, MOC $25.00

Rambo, figure, Coleco, w/motorized battle action, 7", MOC, S2..$25.00

Rambo, Jungle Kit, 1985, w/makeup, bullets & headband, M (EX card), S2 ....$35.00

Rambo, M-24 assault rifle w/darts, grenades, etc, rare, MIB, S2 ....$135.00

Rambo, race set, Tyco, electric train & battle set, NM, S2.$95.00

Rambo, signal gun, 1985, MOC, S2 ....$20.00

Rat Finks, ring, Macman Enterprises, 1963, plastic 1¼" figure attaches & detaches, MIP, T2.......................$30.00

Rat Finks, ring, 1960s, w/1" figure, from gumball machine, NM, H4..$5.00

Ren & Stimpy, dolls, plush, dressed in Christmas outfits, 18", M, S2, pr..$50.00

Road Runner, rocket w/launcher & chute, Rayline, 1970s, MOC, S2..$40.00

Robin, see Batman

Robin Hood, hat w/feather, EX, J5 ....$15.00

Rocketeer, see Disney category

Rocky (movie), figure, Rocky, Ertl, 1981, 2", MOC, H4..$20.00

Rocky & Bullwinkle, clay set, Standard/Toykraft, 1960s, w/molds including Boris & cb cutouts of Rocky & Boris, EX, J5...$65.00

Rocky & Bullwinkle, Presto-Sparkle Painting Set, Kenner, 1962, M (EX box), J5...$65.00

Rocky Squirrel, figure, Jesco, bendable, MOC, T1 ....$10.00

Rocky Squirrel, figure, Wham-O, bendable, MOC, T1 ....$25.00

Rookies, Emergency Kit, Fleet, 1975, syringe & tweezers w/other items, MOC $25.00

Rookies, Target Practice Set, Fleetwood, 1975, w/dart pistol & 3 targets w/stands, MOC $35.00

Rootie Kazootie, club button, 1950s, color litho of Poison Zoomack, tin, 1", EX, J5 ....$15.00

Rootie Kazootie, handkerchief, 1950s, polka dots on cotton cloth w/gr trim, 9x9", EX, J5.....................................$25.00

Rootie Kazootie, Paint-A-Picture Set, Art Brown, 1950s, 1 of Rootie & 1 of Polka Dottie, no pnts, VG (VG box), J5..............$35.00

Scappy Doo, night light, 1980, reflects Scrappy Doo on wall, VG, S2 ....$35.00

Schroeder, see Peanuts

Scooby Doo, doll, 1970s, plush, 15", NM, S2 ....$25.00

Scooby Doo, figure, Bend-Em, 1992, 4", MOC, S2...........$15.00

Scooby Doo, figure, 1984, sitting, PVC, 2", NM, S2 ....$15.00

Scooby Doo, puffy magnets, set of 17 different featuring Scooby's Pals, M, S2..$10.00

Scooby Doo, rubber stamp, 1982, MOC, S2 ....$10.00

Scooby Doo, store display for puffy magnets, metal, M.....$70.00

Sesame Street, bank, Cookie Monster figure, bl vinyl, 1984, NM, S2...$35.00

Sesame Street, Christmas ornaments, 3" Grouch, 3¼" Elmo & 3½" Cookie Monster, set of 3, NM, S2 ....$45.00

Sesame Street, Cookie Monster roller, press head down & figure scoots away, 6½", EX, S2 ....$20.00

Sesame Street, figure, Big Bird, Applause, 1991, bendable, 6", MIP, K1..$6.00

Sesame Street, figure, Cookie Monster, Applause, 1991, bendable, 5½", MIP, K1...$6.00

Sesame Street, figure, Grover, Tara Toys, bendable, 3", MIP, K1 ....$6.00

Sherman (Rocky & Bullwinkle), figure, Wham-O, 1972, bendable, MOC, S2...$20.00

Shmoo, nesting dolls, celluloid, largest is 5½", NM, $85.00 for the set.

Simpsons, Bart Simpon Flip Face, Ja-Ru, 4x2¼", MOC, K1.$5.00

Simpsons, Bart Simpson Pinball, Ja-Ru, 9½x5½", MOC, K1 ....$3.00

Simpsons, Bart Simpson Rad Rollers, Spectra Star, 6 magnified marbles, MIP, K1 ....$5.00

Simpsons, chalk, Noteworthy, 1-sided sculptured colored chalk, 4", M, K1...$2.50

Simpsons, Crayon-By-Number, Rose Art, 6 pictures & crayons, MIB, K1...$6.00

Simpsons, doll, Bart, Dan Dee, stuffed body w/vinyl head, arms & legs, lt bl shirt & dk bl pants, 16", M, K1 ....$15.00

Simpsons, doll, Bart, Dan Dee, stuffed cloth in wht shirt w/red hearts, bl pants, No Kisses Please, 11", MOC, K1......$12.00

Simpsons, doll, Bart, Dan Dee, stuffed cloth w/suction cups on hands & feet, 8", M, K1...$10.00

Simpsons, doll, Bart, Dan Dee, stuffed w/vinyl head, arms & legs, lt bl shirt & dk bl pants, 10", M, K1....................$10.00

Simpsons, figure, Bart, Mattel, posable PVC w/5 interchangable quote balloons & accessories, MIP, K1 ....$10.00

Simpsons, figure, Homer, Marge or Bart, Presents, PVC, from 3½" to 4½", M, K1, ea...$3.50

Simpsons, figure, Homer, Mattel, posable PVC w/5 interchangable quote balloons & accessories, 5½", M, K1 ..$8.00

Simpsons, figures, all characters, Jesco, 1990, bendable, 2" to 7", MOC, K1, ea...$4.00

Simpsons, frisbee, Betra Plastics, Bart's head & Radical Dude on wht plastic, MIP, K1 ....$4.00

Simpsons, Fun Dough Model Maker, Rose Art, w/2 molds & 1 figure, 3 cans of dough & tools, MIB, K1 ....$12.00

Simpsons, Magic Paint Set, Rose Art, 1990, w/T-shirt, transfers, paints & brushes, MIB, S2 ....$25.00

Simpsons, paddle ball, Ja-Ru, wood paddle w/attached ball, 10", MIP, K1 ....$7.00

Simpsons, pencil sharpener, Noteworthy, 1" 3-D Bart inside snow dome, sharpener base, 2", MIP, K1.....................$5.00

Simpsons, poster, Western Graphics, Don't Have a Cow, Man!, 32x21", M, K1 ....$5.00

Simpsons, stamper kit, Rubber Stampede, 4 1x1" rubber stamps & ink pad, MOC, K1 ....$6.00

Simpsons, street sign, H&L Enterprises, Kid Zone w/family watching TV, 18x14", MIP, K1 ....$3.00

Simpsons, wallet, Imaginings 3, Bart Simpson Big Spender on purple vinyl, clear photo sleeves, MIP, K1 ....$5.00

Skeletor, see Masters of the Universe

Smokey & the Bandit, figure, Bandit, Ertl, 1982, MOC...$12.00

Smokey the Bear, see Advertising category

Smurfs, doll stroller, VG, S2 ....$25.00

Smurfs, figure, wearing wht hat & glasses carring book, ceramic, 3¾", NM, S2 ....$35.00

Smurfs, figure, wearing wht hat & laughing while opening gift, ceramic, 4", NM, S2 ....$35.00

Smurfs, figures, Bilken, 1988, set of 3, MIB, S2 ....$25.00

Smurfs, jack-in-the-box, 1982, plastic, VG, S2 ....$45.00

Smurfs, musical top, Ohio Art, 1982, litho tin, MIB, I2...$20.00

Smurfs, scooter, plastic, G, S2 ....$25.00

Snidley (Rocky & Bullwinkle), figure, Wham-O, 1972, bendable, MOC, S2 ....$75.00

Snoopy, see Peanuts

Snorky, see Banana Splits

Space Boy, squeak toy, figural, 1950s, 7", EX, J2.............$30.00

Space Kidettes, magic slate, Watkins, 1967, M $35.00

Space: 1999, Colorforms Adventure Set, 1976, unused, MIB $45.00

Spark Plug, wooden ride-on horse, 36x36x8", NM, D10, $650.00.

Spark Plug, floor toy, tin, w/rider, 9", EX, A................$1,650.00

Sparkle Plenty, see Dick Tracy

Spiderman, bank, Marvel Comics/Buddy L, 1986, figural head, MIB $20.00

Spiderman, belt buckle w/gumball dispenser, Superior, 1985, 3-D graphics, MOC...$30.00

Spiderman, Colorforms Set, 1974, EX (EX box), H4........$10.00

Spiderman, figure, Just Toys, bendable, 6", MIP, K1..........$5.00

Spiderman, figure, Mego, 1979, diecast metal, 5½", MIB, S2 ....$115.00

Spiderman, figure, Presents, vinyl, 13", M $40.00

Spiderman, Flip-It Flying Toy, 1977, balloon-like toy w/great graphics, MIP, S2...$35.00

Spiderman, gumball machine, figural, Hasbro, 1979, 11", incomplete, G, S2...$15.00

Spiderman, roller skates, 1979, red, blk & bl plastic, EX, I2 .$15.00

Spiderman, Shrinky Dinks, MIB, S2 ....$20.00

Spiderman, soap, 1979, figural, 6½", VG (rough box)......$15.00

Spiderman, squirt gun, Durham, 1970s, figural, EX $30.00

Spiderman, walkie-talkies, Marvel-Nasta/HK, red, bl & blk plastic, w/belt clip, battery-op, 5½", MIB, A $116.00

Spiderman, wall climber, PVC, w/suction cup, 3", M.......$25.00

Spiderman, wallet, 1987, flying through air graphics, VG, S2 ....$10.00

Spiderman, Web Maker Kit, Chemtoy, 1970s, M (G card) ..$25.00

Spiderman (Secret Wars), radio headset, 1984, w/figural ear pieces, MIB $40.00

Steve Canyon, Jet Helmet, Ideal, 1950s, w/sun visor & speaker mask, EX (EX box), A $50.00

Steve Canyon, membership card, 1959, M, T2 ....$5.00

Steve Canyon, Yankiboy outfit, 1959, jumpsuit and hat, features Steve Canyon Arrangers patch and others picturing spaceships, pin-on Lt Colonel emblems, identification card and instructions, MIB, A, $110.00.

Steve Scott, crayon & stencil set, Transogram, 1952, w/crayons, punch-out cards & color sheets, scarce, NM (EX box), A...$230.00

Super Circus, TV Color Show Drawing Kit, 1950s, litho cb box w/rotating coloring paper inside, MIB.......................$75.00

Super Heroes, Deformies, Japan, Spiderman, Wonder Woman, Batman & 3 other figures, pnt resin, set of 6, 1¾", H4 .$15.00

Superman, bank, Mego, w/closure, 8", VG, M5 ....$20.00

Superman, bank, Mego/National Pub, 1974, bust figure, plastic, 8", NM, A $60.00

Superman, candle holder set, 1979, MIB, S2 ....$10.00
Superman, Colorforms, 1978, NMIB..............................$20.00
Superman, figure, Bend-n-Flex, Mego, 6", EX, H4 ....$15.00
Superman, figure, Presents, w/stand, 15", M $30.00
Superman, movie viewer, National Prods, 1965, plastic viewer
    w/2 films, MOC, A $85.00
Superman, movie viewer & film, Acme, 1955, bl plastic viewer
    w/1 box of film, NMOC, A $105.00

Superman, record player, 1978, plastic and wood, multicolored graphics on all sides, with play-along record and book, scarce, EX+, A, $138.00.

Superman, Sparkle Paints, Kenner, 1966, complete w/pnt, glit-
    ter, brushes & pictures, scarce, MIB, A......................$90.00
Superman, squirt gun, Durham, 1960s-70s, figural, EX.....$40.00
Superman, stickpin, 1977, figural, M, S2 ....$10.00
Superman, swim fins, 1950s, gr, 10", no straps, VG, I2.....$15.00
Superman, Tim Store pamphlet, July 1946, features secret code
    story, ads & more, 16 pgs, EX, A................................$47.00
Superman, Tim Store pamphlet, June 1947, features comic sto-
    ries, ads & more, 35 pgs, EX, A $57.00
Superman, wallet, 1976, brn leather, EX, I2 ....$9.00
Superman, wastebasket (1st movie), EX $22.00
SWAT, Rescue Parachute, Fleet, MOC, C1....................$19.50
SWAT, rifle, Fleet, 1975, 20", MIP..................................$35.00
Sylvester, bank, 1970s, emb plastic, 9", NM, S2...............$25.00
Sylvester, figure, as St Louis Cardinal, Applause, 1991, bend-
    able, 3½", MIP, K1..$4.25
Tales of Wells Fargo, see Western category
Tarzan, Bop Bag, Multiple, 1968, NMIB, J2 ....$55.00
Tarzan, Cartoon Kit, Colorforms, 1966, EX (EX box), J2..$40.00
Tarzan, figure, Bend-n-Flex, Mego, wearing caveman-type outfit,
    6", NM, H4 ....$12.00
Tarzan, flasher ring, flashes from him standing to putting hands
    to mouth, S2 ....$45.00
Tarzan, magic slate, 1968, EX, J2 ....$28.00
Tarzan & Cheetah, figurine, 1930s, Cheetah between Tarzan's
    legs, pnt plaster, 4½", EX, A......................................$85.00
Tasmanian Devil, bank, Goad, 1990, ceramic figure w/Looney
    Tunes tag, 5½", EX+, A..$35.00

Tasmanian Devil, doll, Mighty Star, stuffed, 12", NM, S2..$30.00
Tasmanian Devil, figure, as New York Yankee, Applause, 1991,
    bendable, 3½", MIP, K1..$4.00
Tasmanian Devil, figure, Ertl, 1989, Taz on motorcycle, diecast,
    MOC, S2 ....$25.00
Tasmanian Devil, figure, vinyl, 6", M, S2 ....$25.00
Teenage Mutant Ninja Turtles, plate, bowl & mug, 1989,
    MIB $18.00
Teenage Mutant Ninja Turtles, wind sock, Raphael figure, Hang
    Arounds, MIB $10.00
Terminator 2, Color-By-Number Set, w/or w/out light-up, MIB,
    S2, ea..$25.00
Terminator 2, Cyberdyne Vinyl Kit, Tskuda, MIB, S2 .....$85.00
Terminator 2, temporary tattoos, MIP, S2 ....$25.00
Three Stooges, Colorforms Set, 1950s, gr box series, MIB...$175.00
Three Stooges, flasher rings, 1960s, silver-tone plastic, 3 differ-
    ent, M, ea $25.00
Thunderbirds, magic slate, Watkins, 1969, M $45.00
Thundercats, ring, 3-D secret compartment, MIP, S2 ......$15.00
TJ Hooker, ID, Wallet, Cuffs & Badge Set, 1982, MOC..$15.00
TJ Hooker LCPD, police car, Fleetwood, 1983, friction,
    MOC $20.00
Tom & Jerry, candy toppers, jtd acrobatic figures, M, S2,
    ea $10.00
Tom & Jerry, doll, Jerry, velvet w/orig Merry Thoughts tag, 6½",
    EX, A $90.00

Tom and Jerry, dolls, Georgene, 1949, stuffed cloth, original tag, 16" and 7", M, D10, $375.00 for the pair.

Tom & Jerry, jack-in-the-box, VG, J2 ....$50.00
Tom & Jerry, sand pail, Ohio Art, 1970s, VG, S2............$30.00
Tom & Jerry, stamp set, Ja-Ru, 1990, MOC, S2 ....$10.00
Tom & Jerry, toy shaving kit, Larami, 1989, w/cup, brush, razor
    & blades, MOC, S2 ....$20.00
Tom Corbett Space Cadet, book bag, 1950s, unusual, EX,
    J2...$175.00
Tom Corbett Space Cadet, field glasses, Herold Mfg, decaled
    gray metal w/red eyepcs, vinyl strap, 5", EX+ (VG+ box),
    A...$150.00
Tom Corbett Space Cadet, flasher ring, 1950s, shows Tom &
    gun, 1½", EX, J5..$15.00

Tom Corbett Space Cadet, hat, 1950s, silver w/bl trim, VG, J5 ....$15.00

Tom Corbett Space Cadet, Model Craft Molding Set, Kat Standley, 1950s, complete, VG, J5 ....$65.00

Tom Sawyer, Giant Crayons, Std Solophone, 1932, M (orig box) $30.00

Topo Gigio, bank, vinyl, unlicensed, in rare Santa suit w/beard, 1970s, NM, S2 ....$40.00

Topo Gigio, figure, celluloid w/outfit, pipe & 3-D glasses (eyes flicker), 6½", M, S2 ....$85.00

Topo Gigio, figure, plastic, 5", M, M5, $40.00.

Topo Gigio, figure, 11½", VG, S2 ....$95.00

Touche Turtle, doll, Ideal, 1962, stuffed cloth body w/vinyl head & felt hands (rpr), H4 ....$80.00

Tweety Bird, figure, France, Latex, 3¼", NM, S2 ....$25.00

Tweety Bird, night light, figural w/human-sz head, 18", NM, S2 ....$225.00

Ultraman, Deformies, Japan, w/6 Ultraman figures, pnt resin, 1¾", H4 ....$15.00

Uncle Sam, balancing bicycle, jtd flat figure pedals bicycle on wire w/balancing weight, wood base, 8¼", VG, A...$230.00

Underdog, bank, plastic figure, 11", minor pnt cracking o/w EX, A, from $40 to $60.00

Underdog, bank, 1960s, vinyl figure, 9½", EX, J5 ....$25.00

Underdog, bowl & cup, West Bend/US, illus action scenes surround hot/cold plastic 6" bowl & 4" cup, M, A $95.00

Underdog, figure, bendable, MOC, S2 ....$55.00

Underdog, harmonica, figural plastic, premium, NM, S2 .$95.00

V, bop bag, MIB..$75.00

V, figure, Enemy Visitor, LJN, 1984, MIB, S2 ....$50.00

Wally Walrus (Woody Woodpecker), figure, Walter Lantz, 1950s, pnt ceramic, NM, S2 ....$135.00

Wally Walrus (Woody Woodpecker), ring, wht w/gr emb figure, premium, NM, S2 ....$20.00

WCW Wrestlers, pencil hugger, Hulk Hogan, Applause, 2", MIP, K1 ....$2.25

Weird-Ohs, magic slate, Davy the Way-Out Cyclist, 1963, unused, MIP (sealed), T2 ....$59.00

Weird-Ohs, magic slate, Digger, 1963, lift-up erasable film sheet on cb w/pencil, unused, MIP (sealed), T2 ....$59.00

Where's Waldo, figure, Waldo or Wenda, Mattel, 1991, bendable, 5", MIP, K1, ea $6.00

Who Framed Roger Rabbit?, see Disney category

Wile E Coyote, doll, Mighty Star, 1971, hard-stuffed cloth, 16", EX, S2 ....$15.00

Wimpy, figure, 1940s, painted chalkware, You Bring the Ducks on base, 19", NM, D10, $450.00.

Wimpy, thermometer, King Features, 1981, plastic, 6½", VG $12.00

Winnie the Pooh, coat rack, honey tree w/Pooh & Tiger at top, 45½", I2 ....$35.00

Wizard of Oz, bank, Cowardly Lion, Arnart Imports, 1960s, 7", EX (orig box), S6 ....$100.00

Wizard of Oz, bank, Dorothy, Arnart Imports, 1960s, 7", NM+ (orig box), S6 ....$826.00

Wizard of Oz, bank, Scarecrow, Arnart Imports, 1960s, 7", NMIB, S6 ....$100.00

Wizard of Oz, bank, Tin Woodsman, Arnart Imports, 1960s, 7", MIB, S6 ....$135.00

Wizard of Oz, figure, bl monkey, Multi Toys, 1988, MIB, S2 ....$25.00

Wizard of Oz, foaming bath beads, Ansehi, 1976, complete set of 12, EX+ (window box), S6 ....$73.00

Wizard of Oz, magic set, EX, A...$15.00

Wizard of Oz, magic wand, Presents, 1989, MOC..............$5.00

Wizard of Oz, mobile, 6 punch-out cb sheets, instructions & 33⅓-rpm record w/Oz story, 1979, M (orig envelope) $25.00

Wizard of Oz, night light, Scarecrow, 1989, MIB $25.00

Wizard of Oz, Snack 'n Sip Pals, Cowardly Lion, NM (EX pkg), O1 ....$5.00

Wizard of Oz, trinket box, Presents, 1989, ruby slipper, MIB $15.00

Wizard of Oz, valentine, Am Colortype Co, 1940-41, Dorothy w/Toto & Scarecrow on yel brick road, 3x5", EX, S6 ..$120.00

Wizard of Oz, valentine, Am Colortype Co, 1940-41, Scarecrow & crabby crabapple tree, 3x5", NM, S6 ....$110.00

Wizard of Oz, valentine, Am Colortype Co, 1940-41, Scarecrow & Tin Woodman, 3x5", EX, S6 ....$114.00

Wizard of Oz, sand pail, Swift's Oz Peanut Butter, 1950s, red and yellow lithographed tin, 6½", EX, $125.00.

Wizard of Oz, wastebasket, Chienco, 1975, wraparound design of Oz map & characters, G, S6 .... $265.00
Wolfman, figure, Hamilton, vinyl, 14", M, S2 .... $35.00
Wolfman, lamp, mk Universal Studios, 1973, pnt plaster, EX, H4 .... $200.00
Wolfman, Magnet Disguise Set, 1987, MOC, S2 .... $20.00
Wolfman, pencil sharpener, UP Co, 1963, molded gr plastic bust on sharpener base, 3", unused, M, T2 .... $30.00
Wolfman, spoon, 1960s, figural, VG, S2 .... $25.00
Woodstock, see Peanuts
Woody Woodpecker, card set, 1950s, 2 decks featuring Woody in classic stance, w/carrying case, incomplete, VG, J5 .... $45.00
Woody Woodpecker, figure, 1980, playing baseball, 3½", some pnt loss, VG, S2 .... $20.00
Woody Woodpecker, jack-in-the-box, Mattel, head feather rpl, VG, S2 .... $85.00
Woody Woodpecker, lamp, plastic figure, S1 .... $25.00
Woody Woodpecker, ring, 1970s, wht plastic w/emb bl bust, NM, S2 .... $20.00
Woody Woodpecker, statuette, 1980, commemorating Woody's 40th birthday, pewter figure on rnd base, sgn Lantz, EX, A $158.00
Woody Woodpecker, 16mm film, Redwood Sap, EX (EX box), S2 .... $20.00
Yogi Bear, bank, Hanna-Barbera, 1961, figural plastic, 13", G, S2 .... $40.00
Yogi Bear, bean pinball game, 1970s, MOC, J5 .... $10.00
Yogi Bear, Colorforms Set, 1970s, EX (EX box), J2 .... $40.00
Yogi Bear, doll, 1989, plush, dressed as Santa, NM, S2 .... $10.00
Yogi Bear, lamp, 1960s, hard-plastic figure of Yogi on rnd base, 13", no shade, EX+, A $85.00
Yogi Bear, magic slate, 1960, lift-up erasable film on cb w/wood stylus, 8x12", NM, T2 .... $20.00
Yogi Bear, puffy sticker, 1977, MIP, S2 .... $10.00

Yogi Bear, xylophone, Green Monk/Hanna-Barbera, 1960s, litho tin, characters on keys, 9", NMIB, A, from $50 to **$75.00**

Chein

Though the company was founded shortly after the turn of the century, this New Jersey-based manufacturer is probably best known for the toys it made during the thirties and forties. Windup merry-go-rounds and Ferris wheels as well as many other carnival-type rides were made of beautifully lithographed tin even into the fifties, some in several variations. The company also made banks, a few of which were mechanical and some that were character-related. Mechanical, sea-worthy cabin cruisers, space guns, sand toys, and some Disney toys as well were made by this giant company; they continued in production until 1979.

Advisor: Scott Smiles (S10).

See also Banks; Disney.

WINDUPS, FRICTIONS AND OTHER MECHANICALS

Acrobatic Clown, 1950, NM, R7 .... $100.00
Alligator & Native, native jerks around as 'gator advances, opens & closes mouth, 15", NM (VG box), S10, from $275 to $325.00
Barnacle Bill, 1930s, sways side to side while moving about, 6", EX, S10, from $300 to $400.00

Bear, 1938, lithographed tin, EX, from $125.00 to $150.00.

Photo courtesy of Scott Smiles.

Boat, cruiser, 1940s, tin, 8½", EX $65.00
Broadway Trolley, ca 1935, 4-wheeled w/roof rod, 8", EX+, A $275.00
Cat w/Ball, 1950s, NM, S9 .... $135.00
Clown, ca 1930, tin clown in checked suit waddles around, 5½", EX, A $275.00
Disneyland Mechanical Ferris Wheel, c WDP, litho tin, 16", M (EX box), S10, from $750 to $850.00
Disneyland Roller Coaster, characters lithoed on side panels, 20", minor wear, missing cars o/w VG, A $200.00
Drum Major, 1930s, scarce, A $95.00

Drummer Boy, #109, 1930s, in red and blue uniform with red helmet, yellow drum, 9", EX, from $250.00 to $350.00.

Duck, 1930, 4", EX, R7 ....$35.00
Duck, 1930, 4", NM, R7 ....$50.00
Ferris Wheel, 16 gondolas w/carnival scene on base, litho tin, 16½", EX, A..$173.00
Hand-Standing Clown, balances on hands & moves back & forth, purple pants w/wht polka dots, 5", EX, S10, from $125 to $150.00
Hercules Ferris Wheel, mc litho tin, clockwork mechanism, 16½", EX, S10, from $225 to $275.00
Hercules Motor Express, 1930s, truck w/momentum action, 'Chein Balloon Cord' tin tires, 16", minor scratches o/w EX, A $450.00
Indian in Headdress, 1930s, EX, S10, from $150 to........$200.00
Merry-Go-Round, 1930, NM, R7 ....$450.00
Mister Rabbit, 1930s, red litho-dressed rabbit on wheels scoots along, 5½", EX, A..$125.00
Navy Frogman, tin diver moves plastic flippers, 11½", unused, M (EX card), from $175 to $225.00
Penguin, 1930, NM, R7 ....$60.00
Pig, 1938, EX, S10, from $125 to $150.00
Playland Merry-Go-Round, 5 carousel horses w/riders & 5 swans around perimeter, 10", EX+.................................$500.00
Playland Whip, 4 cars advance w/bell sounds, heads bob, carnival concession at center, EX (EX box), S10, from $750 to..$800.00
Popeye Floor Puncher, tin Popeye standing on rectangular platform punches celluloid punching bag, 7½", VG $900.00
Rabbit, advances on 3 red wheels, red, yel & blk litho tin, 5½", VG, S10 ....$150.00
Racer #3, ca 1925, yel litho tin, yel balloon tires, w/driver, 6½", VG, A $265.00
Red Checker Cab, 1924 model, litho tin, 8", scarce, EX, A.$475.00
Rocket Ride, 1935, 4 futuristic rockets w/2 figures in ea spin & fly out from tower w/bell noise, NM (EX+ box), A.$750.00
Roller Coaster, 1950, w/2 cars, EX+, from $225 to.........$250.00
Santa Claus Walker, litho tin, 5½", EX $600.00
Ski Boy, litho tin, 7", VG+, R7/S10..................................$150.00
Skin Diver, tin diver moves plastic flippers, 11½", M (EX window box), from $175 to $225.00

Touring Car, w/driver & passengers, VG+.....................$165.00
Toy-Town Helicopter, advances as props turn, tin w/lithoed pilot, 13", EX+ (G box), A..$80.00
Turtle w/Native on Back, 1950, NM, from $200 to........$225.00

US Army Sergeant, lithographed tin, 5½", EX, from $150.00 to $200.00.

US Army Sergeant, 5½", MOC, S10 ....$250.00
Walking Pelican, litho tin, 5", EX+, S10.......................$225.00
Walking Popeye, facing right, 6", non-working, VG, A.$310.00
Yellow Taxi, 1924, red & blk w/red tin tires, license mk NY 1924 #6415, Yellow Taxi Tel Main 6531 on doors, 8", EX+, A...$250.00

MISCELLANEOUS

Army Cannon Truck, ca 1935, spring-loaded cannon, army gr, 8", NM, A...$184.00
Army Truck, ca 1925, brn w/canvas bed topper, 8", NM, A...$295.00
Busy Mike, litho tin, sand toy, articulated monkey on red base, 7", G, A...$55.00
Cathedral, turn crank & music plays, 9½", EX+, S10, from $125 to...$150.00
Cathedral, turn crank & music plays, 9½", M (EX+ box), S10, from $175 to $200.00
Clown Roly Poly, rolls w/nodding head, litho tin, 6½", EX, from $250 to $300.00
Motor Express Stake Truck, gr, red & orange tin long-nosed truck w/long trailer, tin wheels, 15½", G, A...........$120.00
Music Maker, litho tin, crank-operated plinker w/frog graphics, scratches, 3½", VG, A $40.00
Open Roadster #221, early mk, orange & gr litho tin w/driver, features mounted rear tire, 8½", EX, A $250.00
Sedan, unmk, license plate dtd 1918, red w/gr trim, family & driver lithoed in windows, gold balloon tires, 6", VG, A...$90.00
Trolley, Broadway #270, litho tin floor toy, dirty, VG+, A...$70.00
Troop Carrier Truck, ca 1935, army gr, 8", EX+, A........$266.00

Chinese Tin Toys

China has produced toys for export since the 1920s, but most of their tin toys were made from the 1970s to the present. Collectors are buying them with an eye to the future, since right now, at least, they are relatively inexpensive.

Government-operated factories are located in various parts of China. They use various numbering systems to identify types of toys, for instance, ME (metal-electric — battery operated), MS (metal-spring — windup), MF (metal friction), and others. Most toys and boxes are marked, but some aren't; and since many of the toys are reproductions of earlier Japanese models, it is often difficult to tell the difference if no numbers can be found.

Prices vary greatly depending on age, condition, availability and dealer knowledge of origin. Toys currently in production may be discontinued at any time and may often be as hard to find as the earlier toys. Records are so scarce that it is difficult to pinpoint the start of production, but at least some manufacture began in the 1970s and 1980s. If you have additional information (toy name and number; description as to size, color variations, actions, type, etc.; and current market), please contact our advisor. In the listings below, values are for new-in-the-box items.

Advisor: Steve Fisch (F7).

#ME021, police car, current, 16½x5x5", F7, from $55 to...**$125.00**
#ME060, tank, remote control, 1970s, 7x4x4", F7, from $35 to...**$75.00**
#ME086, Shanghai bus, MIB, F7, from $85 to................**$150.00**
#ME087, Jetliner, 1980s, 19x18x3", from $55 to............**$125.00**
#ME089, Universe car, 1950s, MIB, F7, from $85 to......**$150.00**
#ME093, open-door trolley, current, 10x5x4", F7, from $25 to...**$35.00**
#ME100, robot, current, 12x4x6", F7, from $35 to.........**$125.00**
#ME102, spaceship, blows air, current, 13x5x4", F7, from $35 to...**$75.00**
#ME603, hen & chickens, MIB, F7, from $25 to..............**$50.00**
#ME610, hen laying eggs, current, 7x4x6", F7, from $25 to..**$50.00**
#ME611, News Car or World Cap Car, 5x16½x5", MIB, F7, from $55 to **$125.00**

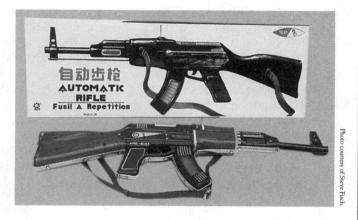

#ME614, automatic rifle, current, 23x2x8", from $25.00 to $35.00.

#ME677, Shanghai convertible, 1970s, 12x5x3", F7, from $60 to...**$100.00**
#ME679, dump truck, current, 13x4x3", F7, from $25 to .**$50.00**.
#ME699, fire chief car, 10x5x2", F7, from $25 to **$50.00**
#ME756, anti-aircraft armoured tank, MIB, F7, from $50 to.**$100.00**
#ME767, Universe boat, current, 10x5x6", F7, from $35 to..**$75.00**
#ME767, Universe boat, 1970s, 10x5x6", F7, from $75 to..**$150.00**
#ME770, Mr Duck, current, 9x7x5", from $25 to **$50.00**
#ME774, tank, remote control, 1970s, 9x4x3", F7, from $45 to...**$75.00**
#ME777, Universe Televiboat, current, 15x4x7", F7, from $35 to...**$75.00**
#ME777, Universe Televiboat, 1970s, 15x4x7", F7, from $75 to...**$150.00**
#ME801, Lunar explorer, 1970s, 12x6x4", F7, from $75 to.**$125.00**
#ME809, anti-aircraft armoured car, 1970s, 12x6x6", F7, from $75 to...**$100.00**
#ME821, giant cicada, 1970s, 10x4x4", F7, from $50 to.**$100.00**
#ME824, Patrol car, 1970s, 11x4x3½", from $35 to..........**$75.00**

#ME842, camel, discontinued, 10x4x7", from $35 to $50.00.

#ME884, Police car, VW bug style, current, 11½x4¾x5", F7, from $35 to...**$75.00**
#ME895, fire engine, 1970s, 10x4x4", F7, from $50 to **$85.00**
#MF032, Eastwind sedan, current, 6x2x2", F7, from $8 to .**$15.00**
#MF033, pickup truck, current, 6x2x2", F7, from $8 to....**$15.00**
#MF044, sedan, Nissan style, 1980s, 9x3½x3", F7, from $10 to..**$25.00**
#MF046, sparking carbine, current, 18x5x1", F7, from $20 to..**$35.00**
#MF083, sedan, current, 6x2x2", F7, from $8 to...............**$15.00**
#MF104, passenger plane, current, 9x10x3", F7, from $15 to ..**$25.00**
#MF111, ambulance, current, 8x3x3", F7, from $15 to **$20.00**
#MF132, ambulance, 1980s, 10x4x4", from $15 to.........**$35.00**
#MF134, tourist bus, current, 6x2x3", F7, from $15 to **$25.00**
#MF135, red flag convertible, MIB, F7, from $35 to.........**$75.00**
#MF136, double-decker train, current, 8x2x3", F7, from $15 to **$20.00**
#MF151, Shanghai pickup, 1970s, 12x4x4", F7, from $50 to...**$100.00**
#MF154, tractor, 1970s, 5x3x4", F7, from $25 to.............**$50.00**
#MF155, airplane, discontinued, 13x11x4", F7, from $15 to..**$35.00**
#MF163, fire truck, current, 6x2x3", F7, from $8 to **$15.00**
#MF164, construction truck, 1970s, 7x3x5", F7, from $35 to **$75.00**

#MF164, VW, current, 4x2x3", from $10 to $15.00
#MF170, train, current, 10x2x4", F7, from $15 to $25.00
#MF171, convertible, current, 5x2x2", F7, from $8 to......$15.00
#MF185, double-decker bus, current, 11x5x3", F7, from $15
    to $25.00
#MF193, soft-cover truck, 1970s, 11x3x4", F7, from $50 to..$75.00
#MF201, oil tanker, current, 14x4x4", F7, from $15 to $25.00
#MF202, jetliner, discontinued, 9x4x3", F7, from $15 to .$25.00
#MF206, panda truck, current, 6x3x2", F7, from $10 to...$20.00
#MF216, airplane, discontinued, 9x9x3", F7, from $15 to.$35.00
#MF239, tiger truck, current, 10x3x4", F7, from $15 to .$30.00
#MF249, flying boat, 1970s, 6x6x2", F7, from $35 to $75.00
#MF254, Mercedes sedan, current, 8x4x3", F7, from $15 to .$25.00
#MF274, tank, 1970s, 3x2x2", F7, from $8 to $15.00
#MF294, Mercedes sedan, litho, current, 7x3x2", F7, from $10
    to..$15.00
#MF304, race car, discontinued, 10x4x3", F7, from $15 to.$35.00
#MF310, Corvette, current, 3x2x3", F7, from $10 to $15.00
#MF316, Corvette, 1953, F7, from $20 to.........................$50.00
#MF317, Corvette convertible, current, 10x4x3", F7, from $20
    to $50.00
#MF320, Mercedes sedan, current, 7x3x2", F7, from $10 to .$20.00
#MF321, Buick convertible, current, 11x4x3", F7, from $20
    to...$50.00
#MF322, Buick sedan, current, 11x4x3", F7, from $20 to..$50.00
#MF326, Mercedes gull-wing sedan, 9x3x2", F7, from $15
    to..$25.00

#MF330, Cadillac sedan, current, 11x4x3", from $20.00 to $50.00.

#MF333, Thunderbird convertible, current, 11x4x3", F7, from
    $20 to $50.00
#MF340, Cadillac convertible, current, 11x4x3", F7, from $20
    to...$50.00
#MF712, locomotive, current, 7x2x3", F7, from $10 to....$15.00
#MF713, taxi, current, 5x2x2", F7, from $8 to.................$15.00
#MF714, fire chief car, current, 5x2x2", F7, from $8 to....$15.00
#MF716, ambulance, 1970s, 8x3x3", F7, from $15 to.......$30.00
#MF717, dump truck, discontinued, 10x3x3", F7, from $15
    to...$35.00
#MF718, ladder truck, current, 10x3x4", F7, from $15 to.$35.00
#MF721, light tank, current, 6x3x3", F7, from $15 to......$20.00
#MF722, jeep, current, 6x3x3", F7, from $15 to $20.00

#MF731, station wagon, current, 5x2x2", F7, from $8 to.$15.00
#MF732, ambulance, current, 5x2x2", F7, from $8 to $15.00
#MF735, rocket racer, current, 7x3x3", F7, from $15 to...$25.00
#MF742, flying boat, current, 13x4x4", F7, from $15 to...$35.00
#MF743, Karmann Ghia sedan, current, 10x3x4", F7, from $15
    to $45.00
#MF753, sports car, current, 8x3x2", F7, from $15 to.......$25.00
#MF782, circus truck, current, 9x3x4", F7, from $15 to ...$25.00
#MF787, Lucky open car, current, 8x3x2", F7, from $15 to.$25.00
#MF798, patrol car, current, 8x3x3", F7, from $15 to.......$25.00

#MF800, race car #5, discontinued, 6x2x2", from $10.00 to $25.00.

#MF804, locomotive, current, 16x3x5", F7, from $15 to..$25.00
#MF844, double-decker bus, current, 8x4x3", F7, from $15
    to..$20.00
#MF893, animal van, current, 6x2x3", F7, from $15 to....$20.00
#MF900, police car, current, 6x3x2", F7, from $8 to $15.00
#MF910, airport limo bus, current, 15x4x5", F7, from $20
    to $35.00
#MF923, torpedo boat, current, 8x3x3", F7, from $15 to .$25.00
#MF951, fighter jet, 1970s, 5x4x2", F7, from $15 to.........$25.00
#MF956, sparking tank, current, 8x4x3", F7, from $15 to .$20.00
#MF958, poultry truck, current, 6x2x2", F7, from $15 to.$20.00
#MF959, jeep, discontinued, 9x4x4", F7, from $15 to $20.00
#MF962, station wagon, 1970s, 9x3x3", F7, from $25 to..$45.00
#MF974, circus truck, current, 6x2x4", F7, from $15 to ...$20.00
#MF985, fowl transporter, current, 8x2x3", F7, from $15 to.$20.00
#MF989, noisy locomotive, 1970s, 12x3x4", F7, from $25
    to $50.00
#MF993, mini car, current, 5x2x2", F7, from $8 to...........$15.00
#MF998, sedan, current, 5x2x2", F7, from $8 to...............$15.00
#MS002, jumping frog, current, 2x2x2", F7, from $8 to ...$15.00
#MS006, pecking chick, 1970s, 2x1x1", F7, from $8 to....$15.00
#MS011, roll-over plane, current, 3x4x2", F7, from $10 to..$18.00
#MS014, single-bar exerciser, 1970s, 7x6x6", F7, from $25
    to $50.00
#MS042, swimming duck, current, 4x1x2", F7, from $8 to ..$15.00
#MS057, horse & rider, 1970s, 6x2x5", F7, from $18 to...$35.00
#MS058, old-fashion car, current, 3x3x4", F7, from $12 to..$20.00
#MS082, jumping frog, current, 2x2x2", F7, from $8 to ...$15.00
#MS083, jumping rabbit, current, 3x3x2", F7, from $8
    to $15.00
#MS085, xylophone girl, current, 7x3x9", F7, from $18 to..$35.00

#MS107, jumping Bambi, current, 5x1½x6", F7, from $12 to **$20.00**
#MS134, sparking jet, current, 5x5x3", F7, from $15 to ...**$30.00**
#MS166, crawling baby, vinyl head, current, 5x4x4¾", F7, from $12 to..**$20.00**
#MS203, train, current, 11x2x2", F7, from $8 to **$15.00**
#MS405, ice cream vendor, current, 4x3x4", F7, from $8 to..**$20.00**
#MS505, jumping zebra, current, 5x2x4", F7, from $8 to.**$20.00**
#MS565, drumming panda/wheel, current, 5x3x5", F7, from $8 to..**$20.00**
#MS568, sparrow, current, 5x2x2", F7, from $8 to **$15.00**
#MS569, oriole, current, 5x2x2", F7, from $8 to **$15.00**
#MS575, bear w/camera, current, 6x3x4", F7, from $15 to ..**$35.00**
#MS702, motorcycle, current, 7x4x5", F7, from $15 to....**$35.00**
#MS704, bird music cart, 1970s, 3x2x5", F7, from $15 to .**$25.00**
#MS709, motorcycle w/sidecar, current, 7x4x5", F7, from $15 to..**$35.00**
#MS710, tricycle, current, 5x3x5", F7, from $15 to..........**$20.00**
#MS713, washing machine, current, 3x3x5", F7, from $15 to.**$20.00**
#MS765, drummer, current, 5¼x3¼x6", F7, from $15 to.**$25.00**
#MS827, sedan, steering, 1970s, 9x3x3", F7, from $50 to .**$75.00**
#MS858, girl on goose, current, 5x3x5", F7, from $15 to .**$25.00**
#PMS102, rolling cart, current, 3x2x1", F7, from $15 to..**$20.00**
#PMS105, jumping dog, current, 3x2x6", F7, from $15 to.**$25.00**
#PMS106, jumping parrot, current, 3x2x6", F7, from $15 to...**$25.00**
#PMS108, duck family, current, 10x2x3", F7, from $15 to....**$25.00**
#PMS113, Fu dog, current, 4x2x3", F7, from $15 to.........**$25.00**
#PMS119, woodpecker, current, 3x2x6", F7, from $15 to .**$25.00**
#PMS210, clown riding bike, current, 4x2x5", F7, from $15 to **$25.00**
#PMS212, elephant on bike, current, 6x3x8", F7, from $15 to..**$35.00**
#PMS213, duck on bike, current, 6x3x8", F7, from $15 to ..**$35.00**
#PMS214, lady bug family, current, 13x3x1", F7, from $15 to..**$25.00**
#PMS215, crocodile, current, 9x3x1", F7, from $12 to.....**$20.00**
#PMS217, jumping rabbit, current, 3x2x6", F7, from $15 to..**$25.00**
#PMS218, penguin, current, 3x2x6", F7, from $15 to **$30.00**
#PS013, boy on tricycle, current, 2x4x4", F7, from $12 to .**$25.00**

Circus Toys

If you ever had the opportunity to go to one of the giant circuses as a child, no doubt you still have very vivid recollections of the huge elephants, the daring trapeze artists, the clowns and their trick dogs, and the booming voice of the ringmaster, even if that experience was a half century ago. Most of our circus toys are listed in other categories.

See also Battery-Operated Toys; Cast Iron, Circus; Chein, Windups; Marx, Windups; Windups, Friction and Other Mechanicals.

Circus Performers, Webber, 1912, jtd wood base w/center slots to fit cb clown w/drum & other figures, 14", VG+, A....**$145.00**
Clicker, circus elephant, mk Made in Japan, litho tin elephant balancing on a log, 2½", EX+, A.............................**$110.00**

Clever Clowns, Greycraft, Grey Iron Casting Company, 1930s, diecast figures, EX in box, D10, $750.00.

Elephant, Ringling Brothers, stuffed, 1987, S1 ....**$30.00**
Ringling's Performing Animals on Circus Wagon, wooden clown & bear balancing ball spin on tin wheels, EX+ (VG+ box), A..**$195.00**

Coloring, Activity and Paint Books

Coloring and activity books from the early years of the twentieth century are scarce indeed, and when found can be expensive if they are tied to another collectibles field such as Black Americana or advertising; but the ones most in demand are those that represent familiar movie and TV stars of the 1950s and 1960s. Condition plays a very important part in assessing worth, and though hard to find, unused examples are the ones that bring top dollar — in fact, as much as three to four times more than one even partially used.

Advisor: Diane Albert (T6).

See also Advertising

A-Team, activity book, Modern Promotions, 1983, M.......**$6.00**
Agent Zero, coloring book, EX, J2....................................**$20.00**
Alice in Wonderland, sticker book, Whitman, 1951, uncolored & most stickers unused, EX **$25.00**
Archie, coloring book, Whitman, NM, T2 ....**$8.00**
Attack! Fighting Men in Action, coloring book, Whitman, 1964, NM, T2 ....**$15.00**
Ballerina Barbie, coloring book, 1977, M, D2 ....**$8.00**
Bambi, cut-out book, features cb images of all characters, rare, NM, A **$110.00**
Barbie Trace & Color Book, 1984, M, D2............................**$3.00**
Barbie & Ken, coloring book, 1963, M, D2 ....**$50.00**
Barbie & Skipper, coloring book, 1973, features Barbie & Skipper dressed in Masquerade outfits, M, D2..................**$50.00**
Barbie Western, coloring book, 1982, M, D2......................**$3.00**
Bat Masterson, coloring book, VG, J2..............................**$20.00**
Batman, coloring book, various characters w/captions, NM, A...**$65.00**

Batman & Robin, coloring book, Whitman, 1966, M $35.00

Beatles, coloring book, 1964, 5 pgs neatly colored, VG, R2.$35.00

Bedknobs & Broomsticks, punch-out book, Whitman, 1971, M $35.00

Ben Casey, coloring book, Saalfield, 1963, EX, T2...........$18.00

Ben Hur, coloring book, Lowe, 1959, M $45.00

Betty Hutton & Her Girls, coloring book, Whitman, 1951, NM, T2 ....$29.00

Bewitched, activity book, Treasure Books, 1965, NM $15.00

Black Beards Ghost, coloring book, Whitman, 1968, few pgs colored o/w EX, P3 ....$15.00

Black Hole, activity book, Golden Books, 1979, NM, C1 .$18.00

Bonanza, coloring book, Saalfield, 1965, NM, C1 ....$45.00

Bozo the Clown, punch-out book, Whitman, 1966, M $25.00

Brave Eagle, coloring book, Whitman, 1955, EX+, C1 ....$15.00

Buffalo Bill Jr & Calamity Jane, coloring book, Whitman, 1957, EX, T2 ....$20.00

Bugs Bunny, Magic Coloring Book, Watkins-Strathmore, 1955, unused, EX $150.00

Bugs Bunny, sticker book, Whitman, 1953, unused, EX...$18.00

Bugs Bunny & Porky Pig, paint book, Whitman, 1946, 2 pgs colored, EX $18.00

Bullwinkle the Moose, coloring book, Whitman, 1960, EX..$45.00

Captain America, coloring book, Whitman, 1966, M $35.00

Captain Gallant, coloring book, Lowe, 1956, NM, C1.....$54.00

Captain Kangaroo, dot-to-dot book, Whitman, 1959, partially colored o/w EX..$15.00

Charmin' Chatty, coloring book, L6 ....$35.00

Chatty Baby, coloring book, L6...............................,.....$30.00

Ferdinand the Bull, cut-out & punch-out book, 1930s, minor wear to cover & spine o/w EX, J5 ....**$95.00**

Fighting Men in Action, coloring book, Whitman, 1963, NM, T2 ....**$18.00**

Fireball XL5, coloring book, Golden Books, 1963, M.......**$95.00**

Flash Gordon, coloring book, 1952, EX, J2 ....**$60.00**

Flintstones at the State Fair, sticker book, Whitman/Hanna-Barbera, 1966, NM **$25.00**

Flintstones Fishing Flop, coloring book, 1976, EX **$7.00**

Flipper, coloring & paint book, Whitman, 1967, EX+, T2 ..**$15.00**

Flipper, coloring book, Whitman, 1965, EX, T2 ....**$15.00**

Flipper, paint book, Whitman, 1984, partially used, G.......**$4.00**

Flipper, sticker book, Whitman, 1965, EX (NM folder), T2.**$18.00**

Garrison's Gorillas, coloring book, Whitman, 1967, M....**$35.00**

Gene Autry, coloring book, Whitman, 1951, EX, C1 ......**$54.00**

Gene Autry, paint book, 1940, EX, J2......................**$55.00**

Get Smart, coloring book, Artcraft, 1960s, some pgs colored, VG, J5 ....**$25.00**

Green Hornet, coloring book, Kato's revenge, Watkins, 1966, G..**$20.00**

Gumby & Pokey, coloring book, Western Publishing, 1966, several pgs colored o/w EX, H4................................**$8.00**

Hans & Fritz the Katzenjammer Kids, coloring book, Saalfield, 1917, scarce, VG, T2 ....**$39.00**

Happy Days, activity book, 1983, EX+, P3.......................**$5.00**

Hee Haw, coloring book, Artcraft, 1963, EX **$35.00**

Coronation Coloring Book, 1953, Queen Elizabeth on red cover, NM, $40.00.

Hopalong Cassidy, punch-out book, Whitman, 1951, makes Hoppy's Bar-20 Ranch, uncut and unpunched, NM, A, $250.00.

Dick Tracy, coloring book, Golden, w/collector cards on back cover, giant-sz, NM, P3....................................$4.00

Donald Duck, coloring book, Whitman, 1959, VG..........$15.00

Donny Osmond, activity book, Artcraft Keepsake, 1973, NM, C1..$15.00

Dr Dolittle, punch-out book, Whitman, 1967, M.............$30.00

Dr Kildare, coloring book, Lowe, 1963, NM, C1 ....$45.00

Dukes of Hazzard, coloring book, Hijacked, HC Rodeo, Stunt Show or Strike It Rich, EX, ea $10.00

Family Affair, coloring book, Whitman, 1968, EX $20.00

Hopalong Cassidy & the Abandoned Mine, coloring book, Lowe, 1950, 1 pg colored o/w EX $30.00

Hoppity Hopper, coloring book, Whitman, 1965, scarce, EX $45.00

Howdy Doody, coloring book set, Whitman, 1955, complete w/6 books featuring different characters, scarce, NM (NM box), A $395.00

Howdy Doody, follow-the-dots book, Whitman, 1955, few pgs colored, many puzzles neatly done, EX+ $28.00

Howdy Doody, Fun Book, Whitman, 1951, dot-to-dot, games, puzzles, etc, EX..$22.00

Huckleberry Hound, coloring book, Whitman, 1959, M..$25.00

Jetsons, coloring book, Rand McNally, 1986, NM.............$4.00

Jetsons, coloring book, Whitman, 1963, purple cover, VG..$15.00

Johnny Quest, coloring book, Whitman, 1965, scarce, NM, T2 ....$49.00

Knight Rider, activity book, NM.........................$7.00

Land of the Giants, coloring book, Whitman, 1960s, EX.$35.00

Lassie, coloring book, Whitman, 1974, M.........................$7.00

Lassie, coloring book, 1969, thick, M.........................$18.00

Laugh-In, punch-out & paste book, EX, J2 ....$10.00

Les Coloriages De Mickey, coloring book, Hachette, 1936, has been colored o/w EX, A........................$60.00

Lieutenant, coloring book, Saalfield, 1964, unused, scarce, NM..$50.00

Little Bo Peep, cut-out picture book, uncut, minor soiling & corners bent, A $30.00

Lone Ranger, coloring book, Whitman, 1957, NM, T2 ...$20.00

Lone Ranger, paint book, early, EX, J2 ....$55.00

Ludwig Von Drake, cut & color set, Hasbro, 1961, VG, J5 .$15.00

Magic Land of Alakazam, coloring book, Whitman, 1962, M..$125.00

Malibu Francie, coloring book, 1976, M, D2 ....$10.00

Man From UNCLE, coloring book, Watkins, 1965, M $40.00

Masters of the Universe, coloring book, M $5.00

Mickey & Minnie Mouse, coloring book, 1933, very rare, some pgs colored, VG, S2 ....$75.00

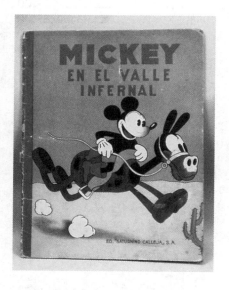

Mickey en el Valle Infernal, Spanish edition, 1930s, VG, from $50.00 to $100.00.

Moby Dick, coloring book, Whitman, 1968, 80 pgs, some pgs colored, VG $18.00

Moon Rockets, coloring book, 1930s, 13 pgs of early rockets & spaceships, M, A $80.00

Mr Magoo 1001 Arabian Nights, coloring book, Whitman, 1959, partially colored, VG, J5 ....$15.00

Munsters, sticker fun, Whitman, 1965, neatly used, J5.....$25.00

Nanny & the Professor, coloring book, Artcraft, 1969, VG.$20.00

National Velvet, coloring book, Whitman, 1961, EX+, T2.$14.00

Our Cowboy, coloring book, Merrill, 1950, EX, I2 ....$19.00

Partridge Family, coloring book, Artcraft, 1973, NM, C1 .$29.00

Peanuts, coloring book, Artcraft, 1970, features Peppermint Patty, crayon marks inside cover o/w VG, P3 ....$4.00

PJ & Her Friends, sticker book, 1975, NM, D2.................$20.00

Planet of the Apes, activity book, Saalfield #C3031, 1974, EX+ $8.00

Planet of the Apes, coloring book, Saalfield #C1531, 1974, EX..$8.00

Popeye, Color and Read Book, Whitman, 1972, 15¾x7½", NM, $10.00.

Popeye, coloring book, Whitman, 1968, NM, T2............$15.00

Popeye & Swee' Pea, coloring book, Whitman, 1970, VG+, T2..$10.00

Quick Draw McGraw, coloring book, Whitman, 1959, EX ..$55.00

Rango Texas Ranger, coloring book, EX $25.00

Reg'lar Fellers, paint book, Whitman, 1932, VG, T2 ....$39.00

Return of the Jedi, coloring book, Kenner, 1983, bar scene on front, NM, P9..$5.00

Return of the Jedi, coloring book, Kenner, 1983, Luke Skywalker on front, NM, P9..$5.00

Ricochet Rabbit, coloring book, Whitman, 1965, EX $30.00

Rocketeer, activity book, 5x7", M, H10 ....$5.00

Rocketeer, sticker book, M, H10 ....$3.00

Rocky Jones, coloring book, Whitman, 1951, lg-sz, some pgs colored, VG $15.00

Roger Rabbit, activity book, M $10.00

Roger Rabbit, paint-w/-water book, M $15.00

Round-Up Time, coloring book, Dell, 1954, several pgs colored o/w EX, T2..$8.00

Roy Rogers & Dale Evans, coloring book, Rodeo Days, Whitman, 1962, EX, T2..$15.00

Scooby Doo's All-Star Laff-a-Lympics, coloring book, Rand McNally, 1978, NM, C1..$21.00

Sergeant Bilko, coloring book, VG $20.00

Shazam, coloring book, Whitman, 1967, M.....................$30.00

Sigmond & the Sea Monsters, coloring book, Saalfield, 1974, EX+, C1 ....$21.00

Simpsons, color-by-number or paint-by-number books, EX, ea $8.00

Six Million Dollar Man, coloring books, Steve scuba diving, or Steve & girl, NM, ea $6.00

Six Million Dollar Man, dot-to-dot book, Steve sky diving on cover, M cover $6.00

Skipper, Scott & Beauty, sticker book, 1980, M, D2 ....$5.00

Snagglepuss & Yakky Doodle, coloring book, Whitman, 1962, EX..$45.00

Snow White & the Seven Dwarfs, cut-out book, Whitman, 1938, uncut, EX, A...$144.00

Star Trek, sticker book, Whitman, 1979, NM, C1 ....$14.00

Star Trek Rescue at Raylo, activity book, Whitman, 1978, M, S2 ....$20.00

Steve Canyon, coloring book, Seal, 1952, NM, C1 ....$54.00

Stingray, coloring book, Whitman, 1965, EX $35.00

Sun Valley Barbie & Ken, sticker book, 1975, M, D2 ....$8.00

Superboy, coloring book, Whitman, 1967, VG $25.00

Superman, color-by-number book, EX, J2 ....$23.00

Superman, coloring book, 1940, EX, A..........................$166.00

Superman, coloring book, 1979, some pgs colored o/w EX .$8.00

Superman, punch-out book, Saalfield, 1940, 62 punch-out figures, 6" Superman figure, rare, EX+, A $275.00

Superman, punch-out book, Whitman, 1966, M $65.00

Tales of Wells Fargo, coloring book, Watkins-Strathmore, 1957, NM...$25.00

Tammy's Vacation, coloring book, Watkins-Strathmore, 1963, some pgs colored, T2 ....$10.00

Tarzan, coloring book, Whitman, 1957, NM, C1 ....$49.00

Texas Ranger, coloring book, EX, J2 ....$25.00

That Girl, coloring book, Artcraft, 1966, EX....................$25.00

That Girl, coloring book, Saalfield, 1968, M $25.00

Three Stooges, activity book, Playmore, 1985, NM............$5.00

Time Tunnel, coloring book, Saalfield, 1966, EX+ $50.00

Tiny Chatty Baby, color-by-number book, L6 ....$50.00

Tiny Chatty Twins, coloring book, L6 ....$40.00

Tom & Jerry, coloring book, Whitman, 1959, EX $20.00

Tom Corbett Space Cadet, punch-out book, Saalfield, 1952, full-color heavy cb, unpunched, EX+ $75.00

Tonto, coloring book, Whitman, 1959, unused, NM $20.00

Top Cat, coloring book, Whitman, 1962, EX $35.00

Toxic Crusader, activity book, 1991, M, S2 ....$5.00

Tweety & Sylvester, coloring book, Whitman, 49¢ price on cover, VG, P3...$5.00

Underdog, coloring book, Whitman, 1972, some pgs colored, VG, I2 ....$4.00

Universal Studios, coloring book, Saalfield, 1964, illus w/studios sets & TV productions, EX+ $30.00

Wagon Train, coloring book, Whitman, 1959, unused, EX+..$30.00

Walter Lance Easy Way To Draw Book, Whitman, 1958, EX+, J2 ....$20.00

William Boyd & His Friend Danny, coloring book, 1951, EX+, C1..$27.00

Zedo Into Space, coloring book, 1950s, EX, J2 ....$20.00

Zorro (Walt Disney's), coloring & tracing book, Whitman, 1958, unused, EX $20.00

Comic Books

For more than a half a century, kids of America raced to the bookstand as soon as the new comics came in for the month and for 10¢ an issue kept up on the adventures of their favorite super heroes, cowboys, space explorers, and cartoon characters. By far most were eventually discarded — after they were traded one friend to another, stacked on closet shelves, and finally confiscated by Mom. Discount the survivors that were torn or otherwise damaged over the years and those about the mundane, and of those remaining, some could be quite valuable. In fact, first editions of high-grade comics books or those showcasing the first appearance of a major character often bring $500.00 and more. Rarity, age, and quality of the artwork are prime factors in determining value, and condition is critical. If you want to seriously collect comic books, you'll need to refer to a good comic book price guide such as Overstreet's. The examples we've listed here are worth from $5.00 and up; most of the higher end prices were realized at auction.

A Date With Judy, #3, 1948, VG, N2 ....$20.00

Absent-Minded Professor, Disney, 1961, EX, N2 ....$15.00

All Winners, #1, Blonde Phantom, VG+, A $259.00

All Winners, #18, VG, A...$165.00

All Winners, #2, glossy, EX, A..$484.00

Amazing Spiderman, Marvel #50, EX, A.......................$106.00

Uncle Wiggily and the Paper Boat, story and coloring book, American Crayon, 1943, 10 stories and 14 pictures to color, M, A, $80.00.

Amazing Fantasy, Marvel #15, introducing Spider Man, EX, $3,200.00.

Andy Panda, #345, 1951, EX-, N2 ....$10.00
Animal Comics, #9, 1944, Buy War Bonds, G-, N2 ....$15.00
Annette, #905, 1958, VG, N2 ....$15.00
Archie Pals & Gals, Giant Comic #26, EX+, C1 ....$16.00
Archie Pals & Gals, Giant Comics #29, Beatles satire, EX, C1 ....$21.00
Bat Masterson, #2, 1960, VG, N2 ....$10.00
Bat Masterson, #3, EX+, D8 ....$25.00
Bat Masterson, #4, C1 ....$27.00
Batman, DC #5, VG+, A $587.00
Batman, DC #13, G, A $130.00
Batman, DC #33, VG+, A $204.00
Batman, DC #39, EX, A $294.00
Batman, DC #43, EX, A $242.00
Batman/Superman Adventure, #279, EX+, C1 ....$19.00
Batman/Superman Adventure, #299, NM, C1 ....$17.00
Beany & Cecil, Dell #1, 1962, EX, C1 ....$48.00

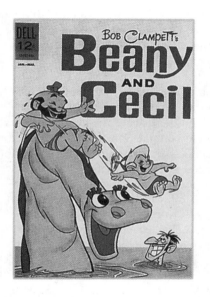

Beany and Cecil, Dell #3, NM, $60.00.

Beatles Complete Life Stories, Dell, 1964, VG, R2 ....$80.00
Beatles Story, Marvel, 1978, VG+, R2 ....$8.00
Big Land, Western Movie #812, Alan Ladd cover, EX+, D8 .$50.00
Bonanza, #1, EX $36.00
Bonanza, #10, EX-, C1 ....$25.00
Boris Karloff Thriller, #1, 1962, 80 pgs, EX, N2 ....$20.00
Buck Jones, #652, EX+, D8 ....$18.00
Buffalo Bill Jr, #7, EX+, D8 ....$18.00
Captain Action, #4, EX, D8 ....$18.00
Captain America, #9, VG+, A $275.00
Captain America, #16, G+, A $225.00
Captain America, #17, glossy, EX, A $468.00
Captain America, #20, EX, A $225.00
Captain America, Marvel #100, EX, A $97.00
Captain Marvel, Whiz #35, 1942, EX, C1 ....$69.00
Car 54 Where Are You?, Dell #12-108-311, EX $12.00
Casper the Friendly Ghost, #12, EX $6.00
Cheyenne, #6, EX+, D8 ....$30.00
Cheyenne, #9, NM, C1 ....$24.00
Cheyenne & Lost Gold of Lion Park, #6, G, D8 ....$10.00
Cisco Kid, #37, 1957, VG, N2 ....$20.00

Colt .45, #5, EX, D8 ....$20.00
Conan the Barbarian, #3, 1970, VG+, N2 ....$20.00
Darby O'Gill & Little People, Disney, 1959, EX-, N2 ......$25.00
Deputy Dawg Presents Dink & Hashimoto, #1, 1965, EX, N2 ....$30.00
Detective Comics, DC #44, G+, A $138.00
Detective Comics, DC #94, VG+, A $125.00
Detective Comics, DC #95, EX, A $160.00
Detective Comics, DC #97, VG+, A $100.00
Detective Comics, DC #105, EX, A $140.00

Detective Comics, DC #122, Batman and Robin Face the Catwoman, EX, $138.00.

Dick Tracy, #58, 1952, VG+, C1 ....$20.00
Doc Savage, #12, EX, C1 ....$92.00
Don't Give Up the Ship, Dell #1049, Jerry Lewis cover, VG+, T2 ....$10.00
Don Winslow, #61, 1948, EX+, C1 ....$26.00
Donald Duck Beach Party, #1, 1955, VG, N2 ....$10.00
Drumbeat, Western Movie #612, Alan Ladd cover, VG+, D8 ....$25.00
Dudley Do-Right, #5, 1971, VG, N2 ....$12.00
Fall of the Roman Empire, Gold Key, 1964, Stephen Boyd & Sophia Loren cover, VG+, T2 ....$7.00

Fantastic Four, Marvel #1, 1961, EX, very rare, A, $4,370.00.

Fantastic Four, Coming of Galactus, Marvel #48, 1st Silver Surfer, EX, A $178.00

Fantastic Four, Meet Doctor Doom, Marvel #5, 1st in series, VG, A $187.00

Fantastic Four, Skrulls From Outer Space, Marvel #12, G+, A...$214.00

Fantastic Voyages of Sinbad, #1, 1965, NM, N2 ....$15.00

Flash, Master of Mirrors, DC #105, G+, A..........$230.00

Flash Gordon, Dell #84, 1945, VG, A $135.00

Flash Gordon the Movie, #31, 1980, M, N2 ....$10.00

Flight Comics, #29, 1943, G, N2..$15.00

Flipper, #1, 1966, EX, N2 ....$20.00

Fox & the Crow, #18, 1954, VG, N2 ....$15.00

Frogmen, #3, 1962, VG, N2 ....$15.00

Incredible Hulk, Marvel #102, 1968, Big Premiere Issue, EX, $80.00.

Frontline Combat, EC Comics #1, 1951, EX, $125.00.

Garrison's Gorillas, #4, 1968, VG, N2 ....$10.00

Gene Autry, Dell #9, NM, C1..$79.00

Gene Autry, Dell #10, EX+, C1 ....$72.00

Gene Autry, Dell #12, 1944, VG, C1 ....$81.00

Gene Autry, Dell #13, EX, C1..$45.00

Gene Autry, Dell #20, EX+, C1 ....$54.00

Gene Autry, Dell #23, NM, C1 ....$45.00

Get Smart, #2..$35.00

Girl from UNCLE, #1, Goldberg, 1978, G.....................$15.00

Girl from UNCLE, #5, 1967, EX, N2 ....$15.00

Governor & JJ, #1, EX+, C1..$18.00

Green Hornet, #2, 1978, NM, C1 ....$90.00

Green Hornet, Dell #44, 1949, G+, C1 ....$31.00

Gunsmoke, #720, 1956, James Arness photo cover, VG, N2 ....$10.00

Hallelujah Trail, 1965, Burt Lancaster photo cover, VG, N2 ....$10.00

Have Gun Will Travel, #6, EX-, C1..................................$33.00

Hawkman, DC #1, VG+, A $55.00

Hopalong Cassidy, #27, EX+, D8 ....$45.00

Horsemasters, Disney, 1961, Annette photo cover, EX-, N2 ....$20.00

Human Torch, #3, EX, A $726.00

Human Torch, #23, EX, A $250.00

I Spy, #1, 1966, Cosby & Culp photo cover, EX-, N2 ......$30.00

I Spy, #2 or #3, C1, ea..$25.00

Incredible Hulk, #107, 1969, EX-, N2...............................$15.00

Jetsons, #14, EX, C1..$19.50

Jim Bowie, #993, VG, D8 ....$12.00

John Carter of Mars, #2, 1964, VG, N2 ....$10.00

John F Kennedy, Dell 12¢, 1964, 3rd printing, EX, I2 ......$16.00

Johnny Mac Brown, #645, D8 ....$30.00

Josie & the Pussycats, #66, 1972...$3.00

Kid Colt, #5, G, D8..$18.00

King of the Royal Mounted, #310, VG-, D8 ....$15.00

King Richard & the Crusaders, Dell #588, 1954, Rex Harrison cover, G-, T2...$10.00

Korg 70,000 BC, #1, 1975, VG+, N2 ....$10.00

Lancelot & Guinevere, 1963, G+, T2................................$10.00

Land of the Giants, #1, 1966-67, EX, S2..........................$35.00

Land of the Giants, #2, NM, C1..$36.00

Laramie, #1125, VG, D8 ....$18.00

Lawman, #11, EX, C1 ....$19.50

Left-Hand Gun, Western Movie #913, EX, D8 ....$40.00

Little Lulu, #49, EX, S2 ....$15.00

Little Lulu, #78, EX, S2 ....$20.00

Little Lulu, #111, G+, S2 ....$10.00

Little Lulu & Tubby, #17, EX, S2......................................$15.00

Lone Ranger, #2, 1952, EX-, N2..$15.00

Lone Ranger, #61, EX+, D8..$30.00

Lone Ranger, #73, EX+, D8..$30.00

Lone Ranger, #75, EX+, D8..$25.00

Lone Ranger, #83, EX+, D8..$25.00

Looney Tunes, #84, 1948, VG+, N2..................................$10.00

Lost in Space Family Robinson, #13, EX-, C1 ....$10.00

Man From UNCLE, #11, NM, C1......................................$28.00

Man From UNCLE, #5, EX+, C1/N2, from $17 to..........$20.00

Maverick, #1, 1958, VG, N2 ....$20.00

Maverick, #7, EX+, D8..$40.00

Maverick, #17, VG+, D8..$30.00

Maverick, #930, VG+, D8..$25.00

Maverick, #962, 1959, EX, C1..$31.00

Mission Impossible, #2, 1967, VG, N2 ....$12.00

Moby Dick, Dell #717, 1956, VG-, T2..............................$10.00

Mod Squad, #1, 1969, EX-, N2..$10.00

Munsters, #14, EX, C1..$18.00

My Favorite Martian, #1, 1963, EX, N2 ....$25.00
Nyoka the Jungle Girl, #39, 1950, VG, N2 ....$15.00
Outlaws of the West, Western Movie #33, VG+, D8 ....$8.00
Owl, #1, 1967, Birdman Bandits, VG, N2 ....$10.00
Pat Boone, DC #1, photo image on cover, scarce, EX, A .$34.00
Petticoat Junction, #3 ....$40.00
Popeye, #32, 1955, G, N2 ....$10.00
Punisher Bloodlines, #1, 1991, M, N2 ....$10.00
Quick-Draw McGraw, #14, 1964, VG, N2 ....$10.00
Range Riders, #15, EX+, D8 ....$15.00
Rat Patrol #3, Assignment Danger, EX, C1 ....$15.00
Real Fact Comics, DC Comics #11, Nov 1947, scarce, VG+, A $115.00
Real Fact Comics, How G-Men Are Trained, DC Comics #12, Jan 1948, scarce, EX+, A $115.00
Restless Gun, #934, EX+, D8 ....$35.00
Restless Gun, #986, VG+, D8 ....$18.00
Rex Allen, #8, EX+, D8 ....$35.00
Rex Allen, #13, EX+, D8 ....$28.00
Rex Allen, #16, D8 ....$28.00
Richie Rich Riches, #1, 1972, EX, N2 ....$10.00
Ricky Nelson, #998, 1959, VG+, C1 ....$46.50
Rifleman, #5, VG+, D8 ....$18.00
Rin-Tin-Tin, #6, 1954, VG, N2 ....$10.00
Rin-Tin-Tin, #7, 1955, EX, C1 ....$21.00
Rio Bravo, #1018, John Wayne, Ricky Nelson & Dean Martin color cover, EX, C1 ....$63.00
Rocketeer, Pacific Presents #1, H10 ....$8.00
Rocketeer, Pacific Presents On the Spot #2, H10 ....$8.00
Rocketeer, Starslayer #1, H10 ....$6.00
Rocky & Fiendish Friends in Hollywood, #2, 1962, EX-, N2 .$40.00
Rootie Kazootie, 3-D Dell #1, NM, C1 ....$230.00
Roy Rogers, #16, G+, D8 ....$20.00
Roy Rogers, #27, VG+, D8 ....$25.00
Roy Rogers, #38, G+, D8 ....$18.00
Roy Rogers, #75, EX+, D8 ....$30.00
Roy Rogers, #80, EX+, D8 ....$30.00
Roy Rogers, #82, EX+, D8 ....$24.00
Roy Rogers, #83, EX+, D8 ....$24.00
Roy Rogers, #88, EX+, D8 ....$24.00

Saint, Avon Periodicals #6, EX, $65.00.

Santiago, Western Movie #723, G+, D8 ....$20.00
Sea Hunt, #7, EX, C1 ....$29.00
Secret Agent, #2, EX+, C1 ....$15.00
Sensation Comics, DC #5, features Wonder Woman on cover, VG, A $93.00
Sergeant Preston, #22, EX+, D8 ....$18.00
Sergeant Preston, #30, G+, D8 ....$15.00
Shark Fighters, Dell, 1956, EX-, T2 ....$25.00
Sherlock Holmes, Dell #1169, 1960, EX-, N2 ....$40.00
Showcase Presents Aquaman & Aqualad, #30, 1961, VG-, N2 ....$60.00
Showcase Presents Challengers of the Unknown, DC #7, VG, A $125.00
Sir Walter Raleigh, Dell #644, 1955, VG-, T2 ....$10.00
Smokey Bear, True Story of Smokey Bear, 1969, EX, H4 ...$5.00
Son of Vulcan, #48, 1965, EX-, N2 ....$10.00
Space Mouse, Dell #1132, 1960, VG, N2 ....$10.00
Space War, #28, 1978, VG, N2 ....$10.00
Spin & Marty, Dell #767, Disney, VG, N2 ....$10.00

Sub-Mariner, Marvel #1, 2nd Series, 1968, NM, $120.00.

Sugarfoot, #1098, G+, D8 ....$18.00
Super Duck, #36, 1951, VG+, N2 ....$10.00
Superman, limited edition of extra-lg copy of 1938 1st edition, Golden Mint, 1974, EX, S2 ....$25.00
Tales of the Texas Rangers, #648, EX+, D8 ....$30.00
Tales of Wells Fargo, #876, EX, D8 ....$45.00
Tales of Wells Fargo, 4-Color Comic #127, EX+, C1 ....$23.00
Tex Taylor, #4, VG+, D8 ....$25.00
Texan, #1096, G+, D8 ....$18.00
Texas Rangers in Action, #8, VG+, D8 ....$25.00
Tom Corbett, #9, VG, C1 ....$15.00
Tom Thumb, Dell #972, 1958, VG, N2 ....$20.00
Top Cat, #5, 1963, VG, N2 ....$10.00
Treasure Island, Disney, 1955, EX-, N2 ....$10.00
Twilight Zone, #1, 1961, VG, N2 ....$10.00
Venus, #12, 1951, VG+, N2 ....$40.00
Venus, #17, EX, A $168.00
Voyage to the Bottom of the Sea, #7, 1967, EX, N2 ....$10.00
Wagon Train, #3, EX, D8 ....$18.00

Wagon Train, #5, VG+, D8 ....$16.00
Wanted by the FBI, 1948, Be on the Lookout for Ralph Roe, 52
 pgs, very rare, EX+, A..$90.00
War Comics, #48, 1957, VG, N2 ....$10.00
Wart & Wizard, #1, Disney, 1963, G+, N2......................$10.00
Western Marshal, #613, G+, D8 ....$12.00
Western Round-Up, #1, VG+, D8 ....$55.00
Western Round-Up, #20, EX, D8.......................................$38.00
Western Round-Up, #22, EX+, D8.....................................$40.00
Western Round-Up, #25, EX+, D8.....................................$50.00
Westward Ho the Wagons, 1956, Fess Parker cover, G, N2..$10.00
Wild Bill Elliott, #15, D8...$24.00
Wild Bill Elliott, #472, D8...$28.00
Wild Bill Elliott, #520, D8...$28.00
Wings of Eagles, Dell #790, 1957, John Wayne cover, VG+,
 T2..$30.00
World's Finest Comics, DC #11, features Batman & Robin in
 Victory Garden on cover, VG+, A $182.00
World's Finest Comics, DC #12, features Superman & Batman
 on cover, EX, A $264.00
Wyatt Earp, #4, EX, C1 ....$21.00
Wyatt Earp, #5, VG+, D8 ....$18.00
Wyatt Earp, #8, VG+, D8 ....$18.00
Wyatt Earp Frontier Marshall, #6, VG+, D8 ....$12.00

X-Men, Marvel #5, 1964, EX, $175.00.

Zane Gray's Stories of the West, #30, G+, D8 ....$9.00
Zane Grey's Nevada, #412, EX+, D8 ....$24.00
Zorro, Gold Key #5, EX...$6.00
Zulu, Gold Key, 1964, VG+, T2...$18.00
77 Sunset Strip, Dell #1159, VG, N2 ....$15.00

Corgi

Corgi vehicles are among the favorites of the diecast collectors; they've been made in Great Britain since 1956, and they're still in production today. They were well detailed and ruggedly built to last. Some of the most expensive Corgi's on today's collector market are the character-related vehicles, for instance, James Bond (there are several variations), Batman, and U.N.C.L.E.

Note: To avoid the idiosyncrasies of a numerical computer sort, we have inserted zeroes when necessary. For instance, #C50 was changed to #C050, otherwise it would have fallen between #C495 and #C804. Values are for mint-in-the-box examples.

Advisor: Irwin Stern (S3)

#C050, Massey-Ferguson 50B Tractor....................................$40.00
#C151, McLaren Yardley M19A $30.00
#C152, Ferrari 312 B2...$30.00
#C154, Lotus, John Player $35.00
#C154, Lotus, Texaco Special $35.00
#C155, Shadow F1 Racer..$35.00
#C156, Shadow F1, Graham Hill $30.00
#C158, Tyrrell-Ford Elf..$35.00
#C159, Indianapolis Racer $30.00
#C160, Hesketh Racer..$35.00
#C163, Santa Pod Dragster..$40.00
#C167, USA Racing Buggy $40.00
#C169, Starfighter Jet Dragster $40.00
#C170, John Woolfe's Dragster $40.00
#C268, Batman's Bat Bike..$50.00
#C275, Royal Wedding Mini Metro.......................................$20.00
#C276, Triumph Acclaim..$12.00
#C277, Triumph Driving School..$20.00
#C279, Rolls Royce Corniche...$40.00
#C280, Rolls Royce Silver Shadow $50.00
#C284, Citroen SM...$30.00
#C285, Mercedes Benz 240D..$15.00
#C286, Jaguar XJ12C...$40.00
#C287, Citroen Dyane..$20.00
#C288, Minissima...$20.00
#C289, VW Polo...$20.00
#C293, Renault 5TS...$20.00
#C294, Renault Alpine...$20.00
#C299, Ford Sierra 2.3 Ghia...$20.00
#C314, Supercat Jaguar...$25.00
#C315, Lotus Elite $25.00
#C327, Chevrolet Caprice Cab..$30.00
#C334, Ford Escort $15.00
#C338, Rover 3500 ....$25.00
#C345, Honda Prelude $20.00
#C346, Citroen 2 CV..$15.00
#C370, Ford Cobra Mustang $20.00
#C373, Peugeot 505...$20.00
#C374, Jaguar 4.2 Litre E Type..$70.00
#C374, Jaguar 5.3 Litre $70.00
#C378, Ferrari 308 GTS $20.00
#C382, Lotus Elite $20.00
#C393, Mercedes Benz 350SL, gr $100.00
#C393, Mercedes Benz 350SL, wht or bl..............................$50.00
#C400, VW Driving School, bl..$60.00
#C400, VW Driving School, red...$125.00
#C401, VW 1200..$50.00
#C405, Chevrolet Superior Ambulance.................................$25.00
#C405, Ford Milk Float $20.00

#C412, Mercedes Police Car, Police $50.00
#C412, Mercedes Police Car, Polizei................................$35.00
#C424, Security Van................................$20.00
#C425, London Taxi................................$25.00
#C426, Pinder Circus Booking Office $50.00
#C428, Renault Police Car $25.00
#C429, Jaguar Police Car $40.00
#C430, Porsche 924 Polizei $25.00
#C447, Renegade Jeep $15.00
#C448, Renegade Jeep $15.00
#C484, AMC Pacer, Rescue $25.00
#C484, AMC Pacer, Secours $50.00
#C489, VW Police Car $30.00
#C490, Caravan $25.00
#C490, VW Breakdown Truck $70.00
#C495, Opel Open Truck $15.00
#C804, Jaguar XK120 Rally $20.00
#C804, Jaguar XK120 Rally, w/spats $50.00
#C805, Mercedes Benz 300SC $20.00
#C810, Ford Thunderbird $20.00
#C900, German Tank $40.00
#C901, British Tank $40.00
#C902, American Tank $40.00
#C903, British Chieftain Tank $40.00
#C904, King Tiger Tank $40.00
#C905, SU-100 Tank Destroyer $40.00
#C906, Saladin Armoured Car $40.00
#C907, German Rocket Launcher $60.00
#C908, French Recovery Tank $60.00
#C909, Quad Gun Tractor, Trailer & Field Gun $60.00
#C920, Bell Helicopter $25.00
#C921, Hughes Helicopter $25.00
#C922, Sikorsky Helicopter $25.00
#C923, Sikorsky Helicopter, Military $25.00
#C924, Rescue Helicopter $25.00
#C925, Batcopter $50.00
#C926, Stromberg Helicopter $50.00
#C928, Spidercopter $90.00
#C929, Daily Planet Jetcopter $40.00
#C930, Drax Helicopter $40.00
#C1001, Corgitronics Firestreak $80.00
#C1002, Corgitronics Landtrain $50.00
#C1003, Ford Torino $30.00
#C1004, Corgitronics Beep-Beep Bus $40.00
#C1005, Police Land Rover $30.00
#C1006, Roadshow-Radio $50.00
#C1007, Land Rover, w/compressor $50.00
#C1008, Chevrolet Fire Chief $40.00
#C1009, Maestro MG 1600 ....$40.00
#C1011, Firestreak $40.00
#C1101, Hydraulic Crane $50.00
#C1105, Berliet Racehorse Transporter $60.00
#C1107, Berliet Container Truck $50.00
#C1118, Airport Emergency Tender $70.00
#C1143, American Le France Rescue Truck $120.00
#C1155, Skyscraper Tower Crane $60.00
#C1163, Circus Cannon Truck $65.00
#C1164, Dolphinarium $100.00

#D2022, Scanotron $60.00
#D2023, Rocketron $60.00
#D2024, Lasertron $60.00
#D2025, Magnetron $60.00
#0004S, Mercedes Benz 300 SL $90.00
#0010, Porsche 924 ....$20.00
#0050, Massey-Ferguson 65 Tractor $100.00
#0051, Massey-Ferguson Tipper Trailer $20.00
#0053, Massey-Ferguson Tractor Shovel $100.00
#0054, Fordson Half-Track Tractor $150.00
#0054, Massey-Ferguson Tractor Shovel $50.00
#0055, David Brown Tractor $50.00
#0055, Fordson Major Tractor $90.00
#0056, Plough $20.00
#0057, Massey-Ferguson Tractor & Fork $100.00
#0058, Beast Carrier $30.00
#0060, Fordson Power Major Tractor $90.00
#0061, Four-Furrow Plough $15.00
#0062, Ford Tipper Trailer $15.00
#0064, Conveyor on Jeep $70.00
#0066, Massey-Ferguson Tractor $80.00
#0067, Ford Super Major Tractor $90.00
#0069, Massey-Ferguson Tractor & Shovel $90.00
#0071, Fordson Disc Harrow $15.00
#0072, Ford 5000 Tractor & Trencher $100.00
#0073, Massey-Ferguson Tractor Saw $100.00
#0074, Ford 5000 Tractor & Scoop $90.00
#0100, Dropside Trailer $15.00

#0101, Platform Trailer......................................$15.00
#0102, Pony Trailer $15.00
#0104, Dolphin Cabin Cruiser $30.00
#0107, Batboat & Trailer $125.00
#0109, Penny Burn Trailer $50.00
#0112, Rice Horse Box $40.00
#0150, Surtees TS9 ....$35.00
#0150, Vanwall $65.00
#0150S, Vanwall $65.00
#0151, Lotus XI $75.00
#0152, BMR Racer..$80.00
#0153, Bluebird Record Car $125.00
#0153, Team Surtees...$30.00
#0154, Ferrari Formula 1 ....$50.00
#0155, Lotus Climax Racer $50.00
#0156, Cooper-Maserati $50.00
#0158, Lotus Climax...$50.00
#0159, Cooper-Maserati $45.00
#0161, Elf-Tyrrell Project 34 ....$50.00
#0161, Santa Pod Commuter...........................$35.00
#0162, Quartermaster Dragster $35.00
#0164, Wild Honey Dragster $40.00
#0165, Adams Bros Dragster............................$40.00
#0166, Ford Mustang $40.00
#0190, Lotus, John Player Special $65.00
#0191, Texaco McLaren-Marlboro...................$65.00
#0200M, Ford Consul $175.00

#0200, Ford Consul, $175.00.

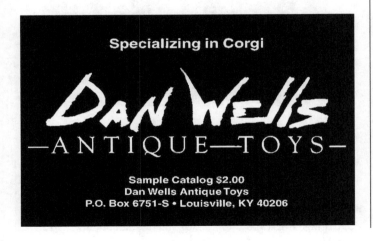
#0201, Austin Cambridge....................................$175.00
#0201, Saint's Volvo...$140.00
#0201M, Austin Cambridge..................................$200.00
#0202, Morris Cowley Saloon $175.00
#0202M, Morris Cowley $175.00
#0203, Mangusta de Tomaso $40.00
#0203, Vauxhall Velox $175.00
#0203M, Vauxhall Velox $250.00
#0204, Morris Mini-Minor $100.00
#0204, Rover 90 Saloon $175.00
#0204M, Rover 90 ....$200.00
#0205, Riley Pathfinder $130.00
#0205M, Riley Pathfinder $175.00
#0206, Hillman Husky Estate $130.00
#0206M, Hillman Husky Estate $150.00
#0207, Standard Vanguard $130.00
#0207M, Standard Vanguard $160.00
#0208, Jaguar 2.4 Saloon $150.00
#0208M, Jaguar 2.4 Saloon....................................$160.00
#0209, Riley Police Car $100.00
#0210, Citroen DS19 ....$90.00
#0210S, Citroen DS19..$90.00
#0211, Studebaker Golden Hawk $100.00
#0211M, Studebaker Golden Hawk........................$170.00
#0213, Jaguar Fire Chief $150.00
#0213S, Jaguar Fire Chief......................................$200.00
#0214, Ford Thunderbird..$95.00
#0214M, Ford Thunderbird....................................$300.00
#0214S, Ford Thunderbird.....................................$100.00
#0215, Ford Thunderbird Sport.............................$100.00
#0215S, Ford Thunderbird Sport $100.00
#0216, Austin A-40...$100.00
#0216M, Austin A-40 ....$300.00
#0217, Fiat 1800 ....$60.00
#0218, Aston Martin DB4.....................................$100.00
#0219, Plymouth Suburban $90.00
#0220, Chevrolet Impala $65.00
#0221, Chevrolet Impala Cab $90.00
#0222, Renault Floride $65.00
#0223, Chevrolet Police $65.00
#0224, Bentley Continental...................................$100.00
#0225, Austin 7, red $90.00
#0225, Austin 7, yel...$300.00
#0226, Morris Mini-Minor $100.00
#0227, Mini-Cooper Rally....................................$300.00
#0228, Volvo P-1800 ....$70.00
#0229, Chevrolet Corvair $50.00
#0230, Mercedes Benz 220......................................$75.00
#0231, Triumph Herald $100.00
#0232, Fiat 2100 ....$70.00
#0233, Heinkel Trojan $100.00
#0234, Ford Consul Classic $75.00
#0235, Oldsmobile Super 88....................................$75.00
#0236, Motor School, right-hand drive....................$70.00
#0237, Oldsmobile Sheriff's Car............................$100.00
#0238, Jaguar Mk 10, gr or silver..........................$200.00
#0238, Jaguar Mk 10, metallic gr, red or bl.............$100.00
#0239, VW Karmann Ghia $80.00

#0240, Fiat 500 Jolly	$150.00
#0241, Chrysler Ghia	$90.00
#0242, Fiat 600 Jolly	$175.00
#0245, Buick Riviera	$70.00
#0246, Chrysler Imperial, metallic turq	$250.00
#0246, Chrysler Imperial, red	$80.00
#0247, Mercedes Benz Pullman	$60.00
#0248, Chevrolet Impala	$60.00
#0249, Morris Mini-Cooper, wicker	$120.00
#0251, Hillman Imp	$75.00
#0252, Rover 2000, metallic bl	$65.00
#0252, Rover 2000, metallic maroon	$150.00
#0253, Mercedes Benz 220SE	$80.00
#0255, Motor School, left-hand drive	$200.00
#0256, VW 1200 East African Safari	$170.00
#0258, Saint's Volvo P1800	$150.00
#0259, Citroen Le Dandy, bl	$165.00
#0259, Citroen Le Dandy, maroon	$100.00
#0259, Penguin Mobile	$50.00
#0260, Renault R16	$40.00
#0260, Superman Police Car	$50.00
#0261, James Bond's Aston Martin DBS	$170.00
#0261, Spider Buggy	$60.00
#0262, Captain Marvel's Porsche	$50.00
#0262, Lincoln Continental Limo, bl	$165.00
#0262, Lincoln Continental Limo, gold	$80.00
#0263, Captain America's Jetmobile	$40.00
#0263, Rambler Marlin	$50.00
#0264, Incredible Hulk	$50.00
#0264, Oldsmobile Toronado	$60.00
#0265, Supermobile	$50.00

#0272, James Bond's Citroen 2CV	$50.00
#0273, Honda Driving School	$40.00
#0273, Rolls Royce Silver Shadow	$100.00
#0274, Bentley Mulliner	$75.00
#0275, Mini Metro, gold	$60.00
#0275, Mini Metro, other colors	$20.00
#0275, Rover 2000TC, gr	$60.00
#0275, Rover 2000TC, wht	$150.00
#0276, Oldsmobile Toronado	$70.00
#0277, Monkeemobile	$300.00
#0281, Metro Datapost	$15.00
#0281, Rover 2000TC	$140.00
#0282, Mini Cooper Rally Car	$90.00
#0283, DAF City Car	$40.00
#0284, Mercedes Benz 240D	$25.00
#0290, Kojak Buick, w/hat	$60.00
#0290, Kojak Buick, w/o hat	$100.00
#0291, AMC Pacer	$20.00
#0291, Mercedes Benz 240 Rally	$35.00
#0292, Starsky & Hutch's Ford Torino	$60.00
#0298, Magnum PI's Ferrari	$50.00
#0300, Austin Healey, bl	$300.00
#0300, Austin Healey, red or cream	$150.00
#0300, Chevrolet Corvette	$65.00
#0300, Ferrari Daytona	$20.00
#0301, Iso Grifo 7-Litre	$50.00
#0301, Lotus Elite	$20.00
#0301, Triumph TR2 Sports Car	$150.00
#0302, Hillman Hunter Rally, kangaroo	$130.00
#0302, MGA Sports Car	$140.00
#0302, VW Polo	$15.00
#0303, Mercedes Benz 300SL	$100.00
#0303, Porsche 924	$20.00
#0303, Roger Clark's Ford Capri	$75.00
#0304, Chevrolet SS350 Camaro	$60.00
#0304, Mercedes Benz 300SL	$100.00

#0266, Chitty-Chitty Bang-Bang, original, $350.00.

#0266, Chitty-Chitty Bang-Bang, replica	$100.00
#0266, Superbike	$40.00
#0267, Batmobile, red Bat hubs	$400.00
#0267, Batmobile, w/red whizzwheels	$500.00
#0267, Batmobile, w/whizzwheels	$100.00
#0270, James Bond's Aston Martin, w/tire slashers	$250.00
#0270, James Bond's Aston Martin, whizzwheels, 1/43 scale	$100.00
#0271, Ghia Mangusta de Tomaso	$50.00
#0271, James Bond's Aston Martin, 1/36 scale	$90.00

#0304S, Mercedes Benz 300 SL Hardtop, $90.00.

#0305, Mini Marcos GT 850	$50.00
#0305, Triumph TR3	$150.00
#0306, Fiat X1/9	$20.00
#0306, Morris Marina	$50.00
#0307, Jaguar E Type	$125.00

#0307, Renault..$15.00
#0308, BMW M1 Racer, gold plated.................$100.00
#0308, BMW M1 Racer, yel...............................$20.00
#0308, Monte Carlo Mini $100.00
#0309, Aston Martin DB4...................................$100.00
#0309, Aston Martin DB4, w/spoked hubs $170.00
#0309, VW Turbo...$20.00
#0310, Chevrolet Stingray, bronze.....................$160.00
#0310, Chevrolet Stingray, red or silver.............$65.00
#0310, Porsche 924..$20.00
#0311, Ford Capri, orange $120.00
#0311, Ford Capri, red.......................................$75.00
#0311, Ford Capri, w/gold hubs.......................$140.00
#0312, Ford Capri S...$25.00
#0312, Jaguar E Type..$100.00
#0312, Marcos Mantis...$40.00
#0313, Ford Cortina, bronze or bl......................$100.00
#0313, Ford Cortina, yel...................................$300.00
#0314, Ferrari Berlinetta Le Mans.......................$65.00
#0315, Simca Sports Car, metallic bl.................$170.00
#0315, Simca Sports Car, silver...........................$60.00
#0316, Ford GT 70..$40.00
#0316, NSU Sports Prinz.....................................$90.00
#0317, Monte Carlo Mini-Cooper.....................$175.00
#0318, Jaguar XJS...$20.00
#0318, Lotus Elan, copper.................................$300.00
#0318, Lotus Elan, metallic bl............................$80.00
#0318, Lotus Elan, wht.....................................$150.00
#0319, Jaguar XJS...$30.00
#0319, Lamborghini P400 GT Miura....................$30.00
#0319, Lotus Elan, gr & yel..............................$135.00
#0319, Lotus Elan, red or bl...............................$70.00
#0320, Saint's Jaguar XJS....................................$70.00
#0321, Porsche 924, metallic gr..........................$50.00
#0321, Porsche 924, red......................................$25.00
#0321, 1965 Monte Carlo Mini Cooper.............$300.00

#0321, 1966 Monte Carlo Mini Cooper with signatures, $600.00.

#0322, Rover Monte Carlo...................................$200.00
#0323, Ferrari Daytona 365 GTB4........................$25.00
#0324, Marcos Volvo 1800 GT.............................$70.00
#0325, Ford Mustang Competition $75.00
#0326, Chevrolet Police Car $30.00
#0327, MGB GT...$120.00
#0328, Hillman Imp Monte Carlo $110.00

#0329, Ford Mustang Rally..................................$40.00
#0329, Opel Senator, bl or bronze.......................$30.00
#0329, Opel Senator, silver.................................$50.00
#0330, Porsche Carrera 6, wht & bl.....................$110.00
#0330, Porsche Carrera 6, wht & red....................$50.00
#0331, Ford Capri Rally.......................................$80.00
#0332, Lancia Fulvia Sport, red or bl...................$50.00
#0332, Lancia Fulvia Sport, yel & bl...................$125.00
#0332, Opel, Doctor's Car...................................$40.00
#0333, Mini Cooper Sun/Rac.............................$400.00
#0334, Mini Magnifique......................................$70.00
#0335, Jaguar 4.2-Litre E Type..........................$100.00
#0336, James Bond's Toyota 2000GT..................$350.00
#0337, Chevrolet Stingray...................................$65.00
#0338, Chevrolet SS350 Camaro..........................$60.00
#0339, Rover 3500 Police Car.............................$25.00
#0339, 1967 Monte Carlo Mini Cooper..............$250.00
#0340, Rover Triplex..$20.00
#0340, 1967 Monte Carlo Sunbeam Imp.............$130.00
#0341, Chevrolet Caprice Racer..........................$20.00
#0341, Mini Marcos GT850..................................$50.00
#0342, Lamborghini P400 GT Miura.....................$50.00
#0342, Professionals' Ford Capri..........................$75.00
#0342, Professionals' Ford Capri, w/chrome bumpers.....$100.00
#0343, Pontiac Firebird.......................................$50.00
#0344, Ferrari 206 Dino Sport.............................$50.00
#0345, MGC GT, orange $300.00
#0345, MGC GT, yel...$100.00
#0347, Chevrolet Astro I.....................................$50.00
#0348, Pop Art, Mustang Stock Car....................$100.00
#0348, Vegas Ford Thunderbird............................$65.00
#0349, Pop Art, Morris Mini.............................$1,500.00
#0350, Thunderbird Guided Missile.....................$100.00
#0351, RAF Land Rover.......................................$70.00
#0352, Rover Vanguard Staff Car........................$100.00
#0353, Radar Scanner...$50.00
#0354, Commer Military Ambulance....................$100.00
#0355, Commer Military Police...........................$125.00
#0356, VW Personnel Carrier..............................$130.00

#0357, Land Rover Weapons Carrier, $170.00.

#0358, Oldsmobile Staff Car $100.00
#0359, Commer Army Field Kitchen....................$150.00
#0371, Porsche Carrera.......................................$40.00
#0373, VW 1200 Police Car..................................$75.00

#0376, Chevrolet Stingray Stock Car	$35.00
#0377, Marcos 3-Litre, wht & gray	$100.00
#0377, Marcos 3-Litre, yel or bl	$50.00
#0378, MGC GT	$140.00
#0380, Alfa Romeo P33	$40.00
#0380, Beach Buggy	$40.00
#0381, Renault Turbo	$15.00
#0382, Porsche Targa 911S	$45.00
#0383, VW 1200, red or orange	$60.00
#0383, VW 1200, Swiss PTT	$130.00
#0383, VW 1200, yel ADAC	$200.00
#0384, Adam Bros Probe 15	$30.00
#0384, Renault 11 GTL, cream	$15.00
#0384, Renault 11 GTL, maroon	$35.00
#0384, VW 1200 Rally	$70.00
#0385, Porsche 917	$40.00
#0386, Bertone Runabout	$35.00
#0387, Chevrolet Corvette Stingray	$100.00
#0388, Mercedes Benz C111	$40.00
#0389, Reliant Bond Bug 700 ES, gr	$100.00
#0389, Reliant Bond Bug 700 ES, orange	$60.00
#0391, James Bond's 007 Mustang	$250.00
#0392, Bertone Shake Buggy	$40.00
#0394, Datsun 240Z, East African Safari	$45.00
#0396, Datsun 240Z, US Rally	$40.00
#0397, Can Am Porsche Audi	$25.00
#0402, Ford Cortina, Polizei	$150.00
#0402, Ford Cortina, wht w/red stripe	$70.00
#0402, Ford Cortina GXL, Police, wht	$50.00
#0403, Bedford Daily Express	$170.00
#0403, Thwaites Dumper	$45.00
#0403M, Bedford KLG Plugs	$230.00
#0404, Bedford Dormobile, cream, maroon & turq	$100.00
#0404, Bedford Dormobile, yel, 2-tone bl	$200.00
#0404, Bedford Dormobile, yel w/bl roof	$125.00
#0404M, Bedford Dormobile	$170.00
#0404M, Bedford Utilicon Fire Tender	$200.00
#0405, Bedford Utilicon Fire Dept, red	$200.00
#0405, Bedford Utilicon Fire Tender, gr	$160.00

#0406, Land Rover, $75.00.

#0406, Mercedes Benz Ambulance	$25.00
#0406, Mercedes Benz Unimog	$50.00
#0407, Karrier Mobile Grocers	$150.00
#0408, Bedford AA Road Service	$150.00

#0409, Allis Chalmers Fork Lift	$30.00
#0409, Forward Control Jeep	$50.00
#0409, Mercedes Dumper	$50.00
#0411, Karrier Lucozade Van	$160.00
#0411, Mercedes 240D Taxi, blk or cream	$50.00
#0411, Mercedes 240D Taxi, orange	$75.00
#0411, Mercedes 240D Taxi, orange w/blk roof	$30.00
#0412, Bedford Ambulance, split windscreen	$120.00
#0412, Bedford Ambulance, 1-pc windscreen	$250.00
#0413, Karrier Bantam, w/suspension	$200.00
#0413, Karrier Bantam Butcher Shop	$160.00
#0413, Mazda Maintenance Truck	$50.00
#0414, Bedford Military Ambulance	$120.00
#0414, Coastguard Jaguar	$40.00
#0415, Mazda Camper	$40.00
#0416, Buick Police Car	$40.00
#0416, Radio Rescue Rover, bl	$100.00
#0416, Radio Rescue Rover, yel	$400.00
#0416S, Radio Rescue Rover, bl	$100.00
#0416S, Radio Rescue Rover, yel	$400.00
#0417, Land Rover Breakdown	$80.00
#0418, Austin Taxi	$40.00
#0419, Ford Zephyr Police Car, wht or cream	$100.00
#0419, Ford Zephyr, Politie	$300.00
#0419, Ford Zephyr, Rijks Politie	$350.00
#0419, Jeep	$30.00
#0420, Airborne Caravan	$100.00
#0421, Bedford Evening Standard	$200.00
#0422, Bedford Van, Corgi Toys, bl w/yel roof	$500.00
#0422, Bedford Van, Corgi Toys, yel w/bl roof	$200.00
#0422, Riot Police Wagon	$30.00
#0423, Rough Rider Van	$30.00
#0424, Ford Zephyr Estate	$85.00
#0426, Chipperfields Circus Booking Office	$300.00
#0428, Mister Softee Ice Cream Van	$175.00
#0430, Bermuda Taxi, metallic bl/red	$400.00
#0430, Bermuda Taxi, wht	$100.00
#0431, Vanatic Van	$30.00
#0431, VW Pickup, metallic gold	$300.00
#0431, VW Pickup, yel	$100.00
#0432, Vanatic Van	$30.00
#0433, VW Delivery Van	$100.00
#0434, VW Kombi	$100.00
#0435, Karrier Dairy Van	$125.00
#0435, Superman Van	$50.00
#0436, Citroen Safari	$100.00
#0436, Spidervan	$50.00
#0437, Cadillac Ambulance	$100.00
#0437, Coca-Cola Van	$40.00
#0438, Land Rover, gr	$60.00
#0438, Land Rover, Lepra	$375.00
#0439, Chevrolet Fire Chief	$100.00
#0440, Ford Cortina Estate, w/golfer & caddy	$160.00
#0440, Mazda Pickup	$25.00
#0441, Jeep	$25.00
#0441, VW Toblerone Van	$125.00
#0443, Plymouth US Mail	$100.00
#0445, Plymouth Suburban	$90.00

#0447, Walls Ice Cream Van $250.00
#0448, Police Mini Van, w/dog & handler $180.00
#0450, Austin Mini Van $100.00
#0450, Austin Mini Van, pnt grille $150.00
#0450, Peugeot Taxi $25.00
#0452, Commer Lorry..$125.00
#0453, Commer Walls Van $170.00
#0454, Commer Platform Lorry....................................$130.00
#0455, Karrier Bantam 2-Ton $100.00
#0456, ERF Dropside Lorry $100.00
#0457, ERF Platform Lorry $100.00
#0457, Talbot Matra Rancho, gr or red.........................$20.00
#0457, Talbot Matra Rancho, wht or orange $45.00
#0458, ERF Tipper Dumper..$70.00
#0459, ERF Moorhouse Van $375.00
#0459, Raygo Road Roller $15.00
#0460, ERF Cement Tipper..$90.00
#0461, Police Vigilant Range Rover, Police $35.00
#0461, Police Vigilant Range Rover, Politie...................$70.00
#0462, Commer Van, Co-op $125.00
#0462, Commer Van, Hammonds $150.00
#0463, Commer Ambulance $100.00
#0464, Commer Police Van, Police, bl $90.00
#0464, Commer Police Van, City Police $300.00
#0464, Commer Police Van, County Police, bl $90.00
#0464, Commer Police Van, Police, gr $700.00
#0464, Commer Police Van, Rijks Politie, bl $300.00
#0465, Commer Pickup Truck.......................................$60.00
#0466, Commer Milk Float, Co-op $160.00
#0466, Commer Milk Float, wht $60.00
#0467, London Routemaster Bus...................................$70.00
#0468, London Transport Routemaster Bus, Church's Shoes,
    red..$160.00
#0468, London Transport Routemaster Bus, Corgi Toys, brn, gr,
    cream $1,000.00
#0468, London Transport Routemaster Bus, Corgi Toys, red.$100.00
#0468, London Transport Routemaster Bus, Design Centre,
    red..$200.00
#0468, London Transport Routemaster Bus, Gamages, red...$200.00
#0468, London Transport Routemaster Bus, Madame Tussaud's,
    red..$200.00
#0468, London Transport Routemaster Bus, Outspan, red ..$60.00
#0470, Forward Control Jeep...$50.00
#0470, Greenline Bus $15.00
#0471, Karrier Snack Bar, Joe's Diner...........................$125.00
#0471, Karrier Snack Bar, Patates Frites $250.00
#0471, Silver Jubilee Bus $20.00
#0471, Woolworth's Silver Jubilee Bus $40.00
#0472, Public Address Land Rover $120.00
#0474, Ford Musical Walls Ice Cream Van $225.00
#0475, Citroen Ski Safari $150.00
#0477, Land Rover Breakdown $50.00
#0478, Forward Control Jeep, Tower Wagon..................$40.00
#0479, Mobile Camera Van $150.00
#0480, Chevrolet Impala Cab $75.00
#0481, Chevrolet Police Car $75.00
#0482, Chevrolet Fire Chief Car....................................$100.00
#0482, Range Rover Ambulance...................................$40.00

#0483, Dodge Tipper $55.00
#0483, Police Range Rover, Belgian $70.00
#0484, Livestock Transporter $60.00
#0485, Mini Countryman Surfer $200.00
#0485, Mini Countryman Surfer, unpnt grille $225.00
#0486, Chevrolet Kennel Service $100.00
#0487, Chipperfields Circus Parade $160.00
#0491, Ford Cortina Estate $100.00
#0492, VW Police Car, Politie.......................................$300.00
#0492, VW Police Car, Polizei $75.00
#0492, VW Police Car, wht w/gr mudguards $300.00
#0493, Mazda Pickup $25.00
#0494, Bedford Tipper, red & silver $160.00
#0494, Bedford Tipper, red & yel $70.00
#0497, Man From UNCLE, bl.......................................$250.00
#0497, Man From UNCLE, wht.....................................$600.00
#0499, Citroen, 1968 Olympics $160.00
#0500, US Army Rover...$400.00

#0503, Chipperfields Circus Giraffe Transporter, $100.00.

#0506, Sunbeam Imp Police $85.00
#0508, Holiday Minibus $100.00
#0509, Porsche Police Car, Polizei $80.00
#0509, Porsche Police Car, Rijks Politie.......................$125.00
#0510, Citroen Tour de France $100.00
#0511, Chipperfields Circus Poodle Pickup $600.00
#0513, Alpine Rescue Car..$350.00
#0647, Buck Rogers' Starfighter $65.00
#0648, Space Shuttle $40.00
#0649, James Bond's Space Shuttle $80.00
#0650, Boac Concorde, gold logo on tail $75.00
#0650, Boac Concorde, others......................................$20.00
#0651, Air France Concorde, gold tail design...............$140.00
#0651, Air France Concorde, others $20.00
#0652, Japan Air Line Concorde $400.00
#0653, Air Canada Concorde $300.00
#0700, Motorway Ambulance $20.00

#0701, Inter-City Minibus	$15.00
#0703, Breakdown Truck	$20.00
#0703, Hi-Speed Fire Engine	$20.00
#0801, Ford Thunderbird	$25.00
#0801, Noddy's Car	$400.00
#0801, Noddy's Car, w/blk-face golly	$1,000.00
#0802, Mercedes Benz 300SL	$20.00
#0802, Popeye's Paddle Wagon	$500.00
#0803, Beatle's Yellow Submarine	$500.00
#0803, Jaguar XK120	$20.00
#0804, Noddy's Car	$275.00

#0805, Hardy Boys Rolls Royce, $300.00.

#0806, Lunar Bug	$150.00
#0807, Dougal's Car	$250.00
#0808, Basil Brush's Car	$150.00
#0809, Dick Dasterdly's Racer	$150.00
#0811, James Bond's Moon Buggy	$500.00
#0831, Mercedes Benz 300SL	$20.00
#0851, Magic Roundabout Train	$350.00
#0852, Magic Roundabout Carousel	$700.00
#0853, Magic Roundabout Playground	$1,000.00
#0859, Mr McHenry's Trike	$200.00
#0927, Chopper Squad Helicopter	$50.00
#0931, Jet Police Helicopter	$40.00
#1100, Carrimore Low Loader, red cab	$140.00
#1100, Carrimore Low Loader, yel cab	$225.00
#1100, Mack Truck	$80.00
#1101, Carrimore Car Transporter, bl cab	$150.00
#1101, Carrimore Car Transporter, red cab	$75.00
#1102, Crane Fruehauf Dumper	$50.00
#1102, Euclid Tractor, gr	$150.00
#1102, Euclid Tractor, yel	$200.00
#1103, Airport Crash Truck	$75.00
#1103, Euclid Crawler Tractor	$125.00
#1104, Machinery Carrier	$125.00
#1104, Racehorse Transporter	$90.00
#1106, Decca Mobile Radar Van	$160.00
#1106, Mack Container Truck	$75.00
#1107, Euclid Tractor & Dozer, gr	$150.00
#1107, Euclid Tractor & Dozer, orange	$300.00
#1107, Euclid Tractor & Dozer, red	$375.00
#1108, Bristol Bloodhound & Launching Ramp	$125.00
#1108, Michelin Container Truck	$40.00
#1109, Bristol Bloodhound & Loading Trolley	$125.00
#1109, Michelin Truck	$40.00
#1110, JCB Crawler Loader	$60.00
#1110, Mobilgas Tanker	$250.00

#1110, Shell Tanker	$3,000.00
#1111, Massey-Ferguson Harvester	$150.00
#1112, Corporal Missile on Loading Ramp	$160.00
#1112, David Brown Combine	$100.00
#1113, Corporal Erector & Missile	$350.00
#1113, Hyster	$50.00
#1113, Hyster Sealink	$125.00
#1115, Bloodhound Missile	$100.00
#1116, Bloodhound Missile Platform	$80.00
#1116, Refuse Lorry	$30.00
#1117, Bloodhound Missile Trolley	$65.00
#1117, Faun Street Sweeper	$30.00
#1118, International Truck, Dutch Army	$300.00
#1118, International Truck, gr	$130.00
#1118, International Truck, US Army	$275.00
#1119, HDL Hovercraft	$80.00
#1120, Midland Coach	$250.00
#1121, Chipperfields Circus Crane	$200.00
#1121, Corgimatic Ford Tipper	$50.00
#1123, Chipperfields Circus Animal Cage	$100.00
#1124, Corporal Missile Launching Ramp	$70.00
#1126, Ecurie Ecosse Transporter	$200.00
#1126, Simon Snorkel Fire Engine	$50.00
#1127, Simon Snorkel Fire Engine	$100.00
#1128, Priestman Cub Shovel	$50.00
#1129, Mercedes Truck	$25.00
#1129, Milk Tanker	$250.00
#1130, Chipperfields Circus Horse Transporter	$250.00
#1130, Mercedes Tanker, Corgi	$25.00
#1131, Carrimore Machinery Carrier	$125.00
#1131, Mercedes Refrigerated Van	$20.00
#1132, Carrimore Low Loader	$250.00
#1132, Scania Truck	$20.00
#1133, Troop Transporter	$250.00
#1134, Army Fuel Tanker	$400.00
#1135, Heavy Equipment Transporter	$400.00
#1137, Ford Tilt Cab w/Trailer	$100.00
#1138, Carrimore Car Transporter, Corgi	$125.00

#1139, Chipperfields Circus Menangerie Truck, $500.00.

#1140, Bedford Mobilgas Tanker	$250.00
#1140, Ford Transit Wrecker	$25.00
#1141, Milk Tanker	$250.00
#1142, Holmes Wrecker	$150.00
#1144, Berliet Wrecker	$70.00
#1144, Chipperfields Circus Crane Truck	$600.00

#1145, Mercedes Unimog Dumper $50.00
#1146, Tri-Deck Transporter $160.00
#1147, Ferrymaster Truck $90.00
#1148, Carrimore Car Transporter...................$160.00
#1150, Mercedes Unimog Snowplough..............$60.00
#1151, Scammel Co-op Truck...........................$200.00
#1152, Mack Truck, Esso Tanker $75.00
#1152, Mack Truck, Exxon Tanker $140.00
#1153, Priestman Boom Crane $80.00
#1154, Priestman Crane $85.00
#1154, Tower Crane $75.00
#1156, Volvo Concrete Mixer $50.00
#1157, Ford Esso Tanker...................................$40.00
#1158, Ford Exxon Tanker $65.00
#1159, Ford Car Transporter $50.00
#1160, Ford Gulf Tanker $50.00
#1161, Ford Aral Tanker $70.00
#1169, Ford Guiness Tanker...............................$50.00
#1170, Ford Car Transporter $60.00

GIFT SETS CORGI

#01, Ford Sierra & Caravan................................$40.00
#01, Ford 500 Tractor & Beast Trailer...............$160.00

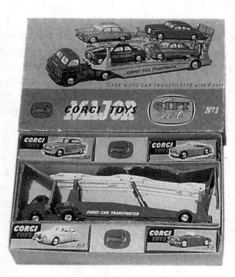

#1, Carrimore Transporter, $750.00.

#02, Land Rover & Horsebox $130.00
#02, Unimog Dumper.......................................$120.00
#03, Batmobile & Batboat, w/Bat hubs..........................$400.00
#03, Batmobile & Batboat, w/whizzwheels $200.00
#03, RAF Land Rover & Missile $200.00
#04, Country Farm Set......................................$75.00
#04, RAF Land Rover & Missile $500.00
#05, Agricultural Set $300.00
#05, Country Farm Set, w/no hay.....................$100.00
#05, Racing Car Set...$300.00
#06, Rocket Age Set......................................$1,000.00
#06, VW Transporter & Cooper Maserati $175.00
#07, Daktari Set...$150.00
#07, Tractor & Trailer Set $130.00
#08, Combine Harvester Set $400.00

#08, Lions of Longleat $200.00
#09, Corporal Missile & Launcher $600.00
#09, Tractor w/Shovel & Trailer.......................$200.00
#10, Centurion Tank & Transporter $120.00
#10, Rambler Marlin w/kayaks $200.00
#11, ERF Truck & Trailer $200.00
#11, London Set, no policeman $125.00
#11, London Set, w/policeman $50.00
#12, Circus Crane & Cage $300.00
#12, Glider Set...$75.00
#12, Grand Prix Set $400.00
#13, Fordson Tractor & Plough $150.00
#13, Peugeot Tour De France $90.00
#13, Renault Tour De France $150.00
#14, Giant Daktari Set $500.00
#14, Tower Wagon $100.00
#15, Land Rover & Horsebox...........................$100.00
#15, Silverstone Set......................................$1,500.00

#16, Ecurie Ecosse Transporter, $500.00.

#17, Land Rover & Ferrari $160.00
#17, Military Set $75.00
#18, Emergency Set..$75.00
#18, Fordson Tractor & Plough.......................$125.00
#19, Emergency Set..$75.00

#19, Chipperfields Land Rover with Elephant, $300.00.

#19, Flying Club Set $75.00
#20, Car Transporter Set...............................$1,000.00
#20, Emergency Set..$70.00
#20, Golden Guinea Set $300.00
#21, Chipperfields Circus Crane & Trailer $1,500.00
#21, ERF Milk Truck & Trailer.......................$350.00
#21, Superman Set...$225.00
#22, Farm Set...$1,000.00
#22, James Bond Set $250.00
#23, Chipperfields Circus Set, w/booking office..........$1,000.00
#23, Chipperfields Circus Set, w/Giraffe Truck $750.00
#23, Spiderman Set..$200.00

#24, Construction Set..$150.00
#24, Mercedes & Caravan $35.00
#25, Shell or BP Garage Set...........................$1,600.00
#25, VW Transporter & Cooper Maserati $160.00
#26, Beach Buggy Set..$50.00
#26, Matra Rancho & Racer..................................$75.00
#27, Priestman Shovel Set....................................$170.00
#28, Maxda & Dinghy $50.00
#28, Transporter Set..$800.00
#29, Ferrari Racing Set $70.00
#29, Tractor & Trailer..$120.00
#30, Grand Prix Set...$300.00
#30, Pinder Circus Rover & Trailer $100.00
#31, Buick Riviera & Boat $200.00
#31, Safari Set $70.00
#32, Tractor & Trailer..$160.00
#35, Chopper Squad $50.00
#35, London Set $170.00
#36, Tarzan Set $225.00
#36, Tornado Set $225.00
#37, Fiat & Boat..$50.00
#37, Lotus Racing Team $500.00
#38, Jaguar & Powerboat $60.00
#38, Mini Camping Set $60.00
#38, Monte Carlo Set..$1,000.00
#40, Avenger Set, gr Bentley................................$800.00
#40, Avenger Set, red Bentley..............................$600.00
#40, Batman Set $250.00
#41, Ford Transporter Set.....................................$800.00
#41, Silver Jubilee State Landau...........................$40.00
#42, Agricultural Set...$80.00
#43, Silo & Conveyor..$60.00
#44, Police Rover Set..$60.00
#45, All Winners Set...$750.00
#46, All Winners Set...$600.00
#46, Super Karts..$25.00
#47, Ford Tractor & Conveyor.............................$180.00
#47, Pony Club Set $50.00
#48, Ford Transporter Set.....................................$500.00
#48, Jean Richard's Circus Set $200.00
#48, Scammel Transporter Set $800.00
#49, Flying Club Set $50.00

HUSKIES

Huskies were marketed exclusively through the Woolworth stores from 1965 to 1969. In 1970, Corgi Juniors were introduced. Both lines were sold in blister packs. Models produced up to 1975 (as dated on the package) are valued from $15.00 to $30.00 (MIP), except for the character-related examples listed below.

Advisor: Irwin Stern (S3).

#1001A, James Bond Aston Martin, Husky on base.......$200.00
#1001B, James Bond Aston Martin, Junior on base, MIP.$175.00
#1002A, Batmobile, Husky on base, MIP $200.00
#1002B, Batmobile, Junior on base, MIP $175.00
#1003A, Bat Boat, Husky on base, MIP......................$125.00
#1003B, Bat Boat, Junior on base, MIP..........................$85.00

#1004A, Monkeemobile, Husky on base, MIP $200.00
#1004B, Monkeemobile, Junior on base, MIP $175.00
#1005A, UNCLE car, Husky on base, MIP $175.00
#1005B, UNCLE car, Junior on base, MIP.................$1,500.00
#1006A, Chitty-Chitty Bang-Bang, Husky on base, MIP.$200.00
#1006B, Chitty-Chitty Bang-Bang, Junior on base, MIP..$175.00
#1007, Ironsides Police Van, MIP.................................$125.00
#1008, Popeye Paddle Wagon, MIP $250.00
#1010 James Bond VW, MIP...$200.00
#1011, James Bond Bobsleigh, MIP................................$300.00
#1012, Spectre Bobsleigh, MIP $300.00
#1013, Tom's Go-Kart, MIP $75.00
#1014, Jerry's Banger, MIP $75.00
#1017, Ford Holmes Wrecker, MIP...............................$175.00

Dakins

Dakin has been an importer of stuffed toys as far back as 1955, but it wasn't until 1959 that the name of this San Francisco-based company actually appeared on the toy labels. They produced three distinct lines: Dream Pets (1960 – early 1970s), Dream Dolls (1965 – mid-1970s), and licensed characters and advertising figures, starting in 1968. Of them all, the latter series was the most popular and the one that holds most interest for collectors. Originally there were seven Warner Brothers characters. Each was made with a hard plastic body and a soft vinyl head, and all were under 10" tall. All in all, more than fifty cartoon characters were produced, some with several variations. Advertising figures were made as well. Some were extensions of the three already existing lines; others were completely original.

Goofy Grams was a series featuring many of their character figures mounted on a base lettered with a 'goofy' message. They also utilized some of their large stock characters as banks in a series called Cash Catchers. A second bank series consisted of Warner Brothers characters molded in a squatting position and therefore smaller. Other figures made by Dakin include squeeze toys, PVCs, and water squirters.

Advisor: Jim Rash (R3).

Alice in Wonderland, set of 3 w/Alice, Mad Hatter & the
     White Rabbit, artist Faith Wick, 18", EX+, H4 ......$550.00
Baby Puss, Hanna-Barbera, 1971, EX+, R3....................$100.00
Bambi, Disney, 1960s, MIP, R3 ....$35.00
Bamm-Bamm, complete w/bone & hat, 8", NM, S2.........$35.00
Bamm-Bamm, different outfit, no club or bone, NM, S2 .$20.00
Bamm-Bamm, Hanna-Barbera, w/club, 1970, MIP, R3 ....$50.00
Barney Rubble, Hanna-Barbera, 1970, EX, R3 ....$35.00
Bozo the Clown, Larry Harmon, 1974, EX, R3/H4/S2......$35.00
Bozo the Clown, MIP, H4 ....$50.00
Bugs Bunny, Great American Promo, 1976, stuffed, red, wht &
     bl, EX, S2 ....$20.00
Bugs Bunny, Warner Bros, 1971, MIP, R3 ....$30.00
Bugs Bunny, Warner Bros, 1976, MIB (cartoon theater box),
     R3 ....$40.00
Bugs Bunny, Warner Bros, 1978, MIP (fun farm bag), R3 .$20.00

Bugs Bunny, 1976, plush, lying on back, NM, S2 ....$20.00
Bullwinkle, Jay Ward, 1976, MIB (cartoon theater box), R3 ..$60.00
Bullwinkle, 1976, MIB, S2 ....$75.00
Cool Cat, Warner Bros, w/beret, 1970, EX+, R3 ....$40.00
Daffy Duck, Warner Bros, 1968, EX, R3 ....$30.00
Daffy Duck, Warner Bros, 1976, MIB (cartoon theater box), R3/S2 ....$40.00
Deputy Dawg, Terrytoons, 1977, EX, R3 ....$40.00
Dewey Duck, Disney, red shirt, straight or bent leg, EX, R3 .$30.00
Dino Dinosaur, Hanna-Barbera, 1970, EX, R3 ....$40.00
Donald Duck, Disney, 1960s, straight or bent leg, EX, R3.$20.00
Dudley Do-Right, Jay Ward, 1976, MIB (cartoon theater box), R3..$75.00
Dumbo, Disney, 1960s, cloth collar, MIB, R3...................$25.00
Elmer Fudd, Warner Bros, 1968, in hunting outfit w/rifle, EX, R3 ....$125.00
Elmer Fudd, Warner Bros, 1968, in tuxedo, EX, R3 ....$30.00
Elmer Fudd, Warner Bros, 1978, MIP (fun farm bag), R3..$35.00
Foghorn Leghorn, Warner Bros, 1970, EX+, R3 ....$75.00
Fred Flintstone, Hanna-Barbera, 1970, EX, R3................$35.00
Gigolo Giraffe, Dream Pet, stuffed, wearing top hat & tux collar w/tie, orig tag, NM, H4 ....$19.00
Glamour Kitty, 1977, wht cat w/gold crown, R3 ....$150.00
Goofy, Disney, 1960s, EX, R3...$20.00
Goofy Gram, Bloodhound, You Think You Feel Bad, EX, R3 ....$20.00
Goofy Gram, Dog, You're Top Dog, EX, R3 ....$20.00
Goofy Gram, Fox, Wanna See My Etching?, vinyl, 6", S2..$25.00
Goofy Gram, Kangaroo, w/hat & baby in pouch, NM, S2.$45.00
Goofy Gram, Lion, Sorry You're Feeling Beastly!, EX, R3.$20.00
Goofy Gram, Mouse, Merry Christmas, w/hat & scarf, EX, S2 ....$35.00
Goofy Gram, Scotty Dog, vinyl w/clothing, NM, S2........$35.00

Hokey Wolf, Hanna-Barbera, 1971, EX+, $250.00.

Hobo Joe, 1977, EX+, R3 ....$120.00
Hoppy Hopperoo, Hanna-Barbera, 1971, EX+, R3 ....$100.00
Huckleberry Hound, Hanna-Barbera, 1970, EX+, R3 ......$75.00
Huey Duck, Disney, gr shirt, straight or bent legs, EX, R3.$30.00
Jack-in-the-Box, bank, 1971, EX, R3 ....$25.00
Lion in a Cage, bank, 1971, EX, R3 ....$25.00

Louie Duck, Disney, bl shirt, straight or bent legs, EX, R3 ..$30.00
Merlin the Magic Mouse, Warner Bros, 1970, EX+, R3/S2..$25.00

Mighty Mouse, Terrytoons, 1978, EX, $100.00.

Mickey Mouse, Disney, 1960s, cloth clothes, EX, R3 ....$20.00
Miss Liberty Bell, 1975, w/hat, MIP, R3 ....$75.00
Monkey on a Barrel, bank, 1971, EX, R3 ....$25.00
Mouse on a Cheese Wedge, bank, 1971, EX, R3 ....$25.00
Olive Oyl, King Features, 1974, cloth clothes, MIP, R3...$50.00
Olive Oyl, King Features, 1976, MIB (cartoon theater box), R3...$50.00
Oliver & Co, doll, Francis, Sears Exclusive, 1988, plush, NM, S2 ....$25.00
Oliver & Co, doll, Oliver Dog, Sears Exclusive, 1988, plush, NM, S2..$25.00
Oliver Hardy, Larry Harmon, 1974, EX+, R3 ....$30.00
Oliver Hardy, w/tag, MIP, S2 ....$40.00
Pebbles Flintstone, Hanna-Barbera, 1970, EX, R3...........$35.00
Pepe Le Peu, Warner Bros, 1971, EX+, R3/H4 ....$75.00
Pink Panther, Mirisch-Freleng, 1971, EX+, R3 ....$50.00
Pink Panther, Mirisch-Freleng, 1976, MIB (cartoon theater box), R3 ....$50.00
Pinocchio, Disney, 1960s, cloth clothes, EX, R3 ....$20.00
Popeye, King Features, 1974, nodding head w/jtd arms, cloth clothes, spinach can in left hand, MIP, R3/S2...........$50.00
Popeye, King Features, 1976, MIB (cartoon theater box), R3 ....$50.00
Porky Pig, Warner Bros, 1968, EX+, R3...........................$30.00
Porky Pig, Warner Bros, 1976, MIB (cartoon theater box), R3..$40.00
Ren Hoek, Nickleodeon, 1993, water squirter, EX, R3.....$10.00
Road Runner, Warner Bros, 1968, EX+, R3 ....$30.00
Road Runner, Warner Bros, 1976, MIB (cartoon theater box), R3..$50.00
Rocky Squirrel, Jay Ward, 1976, MIB (cartoon theater box), R3..$60.00
Scooby Doo, Hanna-Barbera, 1980, EX, R3.....................$75.00
Scrappy Doo, Hanna-Barbera, 1982, EX+, R3 ....$75.00
Seal on a Box, bank, 1971, EX, R3...................................$25.00
Second Banana, Warner Bros, 1970, EX, R3/H4 ....$35.00
Smokey Bear, 1974, MIP, R3..$20.00

Smokey Bear, with shovel, vinyl with cloth pants, 8", NM, $40.00.

Snagglepuss, Hanna-Barbera, 1971, EX, $100.00.

Photo courtesy of Jim Rash.

Speedy Gonzalez, Warner Bros, 1968, EX+, R3 ....$25.00
Speedy Gonzalez, Warner Bros, 1976, MIB (cartoon theater box), R3 ....$50.00
Stan Laurel, Larry Harmon, 1974, EX+, R3 ....$30.00
Stimpy, Nickleodeon, 1993, water squirter, EX, R3..........$10.00
Swee' Pea, King Features, 1974, beanbag doll, VG, R3 ....$35.00
Sylvester, Warner Bros, 1968, EX+, R3 ....$20.00
Sylvester, Warner Bros, 1976, MIB (cartoon theater box), R3..$40.00
Sylvester, Warner Bros, 1976, 5¼", NM, S2 ....$20.00
Sylvester, Warner Bros, 1978, MIP (fun farm bag), R3 ....$20.00
Tasmanian Devil, Warner Bros, 1978, MIP (fun farm bag), R3 ....$400.00
Tiger in a Cage, bank, 1971, EX, R3 ....$25.00
Tweety Bird, Warner Bros, 1966, EX+, R3 ....$20.00
Tweety Bird, Warner Bros, 1976, MIB (cartoon theater box), R3..$40.00
Tweety Bird, Warner Bros, 1976, 3¾", NM, S2 ....$20.00
Tweety Bird, Warner Bros, 1978, MIP (fun farm bag), R3..$20.00
Uncle Bugs Bunny, Warner Bros, 1975, EX+, R3 ....$50.00
Underdog, Jay Ward, 1976, MIB (cartoon theater box), R3.$150.00
Wile E Coyote, Warner Bros, 1968, MIB, R3 ....$30.00
Wile E Coyote, Warner Bros, 1976, MIB (cartoon theater box), R3..$40.00
Wile E Coyote, Warner Bros, 1977, stuffed cloth, 11", M, C1 .$27.00
Yosemite Sam, missing pistols, H4 ....$16.00
Yosemite Sam, Warner Bros, 1968, MIB, R3 ....$30.00
Yosemite Sam, Warner Bros, 1976, MIP (fun farm bag), R3..$40.00

ADVERTISING

Bay View Eagle, 1976, bank, EX+, R3..............................$30.00
Bob's Big Boy, missing hamburger o/w VG, H4 ....$80.00
Bob's Big Boy, 1974, w/hamburger, EX+, R3 ....$190.00
Carnation's Mighty Dog, stuffed, orig tag, 1986, 10", M, S2 ..$45.00
Diaparene Baby, jtd vinyl, 1980, R3..................................$40.00
Freddie Fast, 1976, 7", R3 ....$95.00
Glamour Kitty, wht or blk, 1977, R3, ea............................$150.00
Hobo Joe, bank, 1977, missing trap, R3 ....$80.00
Hobo Joe, 1977, EX, R3..$120.00
Kernal Renk, American Seeds, 1970, rare, EX+, R3 ......$400.00
Li'l Miss Just Rite, 1965, EX+, R3 ....$75.00
Miss Liberty Belle, w/hat, 1975, M, R3 ....$75.00
Miss Liberty Belle, 1975, missing hat o/w EX, S2 ....$25.00
Quasar Robot, bank, 1975, M, R3......................................$175.00
RCA's Chipper Puppy Dog, NM..$15.00
RCA's Nipper Santa Dog, MIP $35.00
RCA's Nipper the Dog, 1980, plush, NM, S2 ....$25.00
Sambo Boy, 1974, plastic, EX+, R3 ....$75.00
Sambo's Tiger, in sitting position, 1977, stuffed, wearing T-shirt, 10", H4..$14.00
Sambo's Tiger, 1974, plastic, EX+, R3 ....$125.00
Woodsy Owl, 1974, EX, R3 ....$60.00
Woodsy Owl, 1974, MIP, R3 ....$85.00

Diecast

Diecast replicas of cars, trucks, planes, trains, etc., represent a huge corner of today's collector market, and their manufacturers see to it that there is no shortage. Back in the 1920s, Tootsietoy had the market virtually by themselves, but one by one other companies had a go at it, some with more success than others. Among them were the American companies of Barclay, Hubley, and Manoil, all of whom are much better known for other types of toys. After the war, Metal Masters, Smith-Miller and Doepke Ohlsson-Rice (among others) tried the market with varying degrees of success. Some companies were phased out over the years, while many more entered the market with fervor. Today it's those fondly remembered models from the fifties and sixties that many collectors yearn to own. Solido produced well-modeled, detailed little cars; some had dome lights that actually came on when the doors were opened. Politoy's were cleanly molded with good detailing and finishes. Mebetoys, an Italian company that has been bought out by Mattel, produced several; and some of the finest come from Brooklyn, whose Shelby (signed) GT-350H Mustang can easily cost you from $900.00 to $1,000.00 when you can find one.

In 1968 the Topper Toy Company introduced its line of low-friction, high-speed Johnny Lightning cars to be in direct competition with Mattel's Hot Wheels. To gain attention, Topper sponsored Al Unser's winning race car, the 'Johnny Lightning,' in the 1970 Indianapolis 500. Despite the popularity of their cars, the Topper Toy Company went out of business in 1971. Today the Johnny Lightnings are highly sought after and a new company, Playing Mantis, is reproducing many of the original designs as well as several models which never made it into regular production.

If you're interested in Majorette Toys, we recommend *Collecting Majorette Toys* by Dana Johnson; ordering information is given with Dana's listing under Diecast, in the section called Categories of Special Interest in the back of the book.

Advisor: Dan Wells (W1).

See also Corgi; Dinky; Diecast Collector Banks; Tootsietoy; Hot Wheels; Matchbox; Tekno.

ADJ, Citroen CX Station Wagon, Fire Chief, red, MIB, L1.$30.00
ADJ, Renault 12 Station Wagon, Fire Chief, red, MIB, L1.$30.00
Alezan, Alfa Romeo Evoluzione, dk red, MIB, L1 ....$65.00
All American, Hot Rod 3S-3305 California decal on rear plate, bl & wht, 9", VG, A $161.00
AMR, Abarth 1300, limited edition, red, MIB, L1........$375.00

AMR, Mercedes 500SL, cream, MIB, L1 ....$95.00
AMR, Morgan 2+2 Convertible, wht, MIB, L1 ....$65.00
AMR, Renault Alpine, limited edition, red, MIB, L1 ....$250.00
Autoreplica, Amilcar Italiana, bl, NMIB, L1 ....$45.00
Barclay, transport w/4 cars, hinged loading ramps, cars w/metal tires, truck w/blk rubber tires, 1950s, 5", MIP, A.....$100.00
Brooklyn, #6 Packard Light Eight Coupe, beige & brn, MIB, L1 ....$60.00
Brooklyn, #11 Lincoln Continental Mk II, metallic bl, MIB, L1 ....$65.00
Brooklyn, #12 Hudson Greater Murray Convertible, beige & brn, MIB, L1 ....$60.00
Brooklyn, #13 T-Bird, red, MIB, L1 ....$65.00
Brooklyn, #18 Packard Clipper, maroon, MIB, L1...........$62.00
Brooklyn, #26 Chevy Nomad Station Wagon, wht & turq, MIB, L1 ....$65.00
Brooklyn, #31 Pontiac Delivery Van, Modelex 92, metallic gr, MIB, L1 ....$175.00
Brumm, #r001 Morgan Cyclecar, gr, M, L1......................$22.00
Brumm, #r065 Fiat 1100 Sedan, dk bl, MIB, L1 ....$16.00
Brumm, #091 Alfa Romeo 1800, Police, blk, MIB, L1 .....$18.00
Bubby, #1032 Chevy Nova Sedan, red, M, L1 ....$58.00
Bubby, #1036 Fiat 128 Sedan, bl, M, L1 ....$38.00
Budgie, #56 Hertz Moving Van, gr, MBP, G3 ....$25.00
Budgie, #58 Modern Removals Van, tan, MBP, G3 ....$20.00
Can Am, Citroen SM Presidentielle Convertible, dk silver, MIB, L1 ....$135.00
CCC, Berliet PCK Fire, red, MIB, L1 ....$135.00
CCC, Delahaye Fourgon Mixte Fire, red, MIB, L1........$145.00
CCC, Delahaye T-40 Fire, red, MIB, L1 ....$145.00
Century, #8 Mercedes Benz 300CE, dk bl, MIB, L1 ....$92.00
Conquest, #1 Oldsmobile Starfire Convertible, bl & wht, MIB, L1 ....$185.00
Conquest, #3 Buick Special Sedan, fawn & bl, MIB, L1 .$185.00
Conrad, #1015 VW Santana, silver, M, L1 ....$38.00
Conrad, #1018 Graft & Stift Old Austrian Fire, red, NMIB, L1 ....$55.00
Conrad, #1034 Mercedes Race Car Carrier, bl, MIB, L1.$115.00
Conrad, #3053 Mercedes Tanker, Messer Griessheim, bl & yel, MIB, L1 ....$75.00
Cragstan, 1967 Corvair Coupe, gr, M, L1 ....$38.00
Cragstan, 1968 Chevy Impala Coupe, dk red, M, L1 ....$45.00
Crescent, BRM Formula 1, gr, MIB, L1 ....$115.00
Dinkum, Ford Falcon GT, red & blk, MIB, L1 ....$85.00
Dinkum, Holden FJ Panel Van, dk bl, MIB, L1 ....$75.00
Dinkum, Holden FJ Saloon, blk, MIB, L1 ....$75.00
Dinkum, Holden 214 Saloon, pale gr, MIB, L1 ....$85.00
Dubray, Peugeot 402, spare wheel, blk, M, L1 ....$60.00
Dubray, Peugeot 402 Fire Chief, Lyon, red, MIB, L1 ....$75.00
Dubray, Renault Viva Grand Sport Convertible, bl & blk, MIB, L1 ....$45.00
Dugu, 500A Topolino, dk gr, MIB, L1 ....$42.00
Edil Toys, ISO Grifo, metallic bl, NM, L1 ....$115.00
Eligor, #1010 Citroen 5CV Van, Nicholas, dk gr, MIB, L1.$16.00
Eligor, #1011 Citroen 5CV Van, Goodrich, orange, MIB, L1 ....$18.00
Eligor, #1013 Citroen 5CV Van, Lu-Lu, cream, MIB, L1.$16.00
Eligor, #1030 1930 Rolls Royce Limousine, silver, MIB, L1 .$18.00

Eligor, #1033 Citroen 11BL Fire Chief, red, MIB, L1 ....$25.00

Eligor, #1033 1938 Citroen 7CV, pewter, MIB, L1 ....$25.00

Eligor, #1040 Renault NN Torpedo (closed), fawn & bl, MIB, L1 ....$18.00

Eligor, #1041b Renault K Coupe de Ville, blk & red, MIB, L1 ....$22.00

Eligor, #1044 Mercedes Benz Hotel Kaysehof Limousine, brn, MIB, L1 ....$28.00

Eligor, #1048 Bentley T Saloon, navy, MIB, L1 ....$22.00

Eligor, #1049 Renault KZ Fire, red, MIB, L1 ....$25.00

Eligor, #1056 Citroen 5CV, First Alarm, red, MIB, L1 ....$28.00

Eligor, #1064 Opel 5CV Van, Ovomatine, dk bl, MIB, L1...$18.00

Eligor, #1080 Ford Pickup, blk, MIB, L1 ....$20.00

Eligor, #1083 Ford V8, San Francisco, red, MIB, L1 ....$25.00

Erie, Packard Roadster, aqua, wht rubber tires, 1936, rpt, A3 ....$50.00

Ertl, Ace Hardware, truck, 1/64 scale, MIB......................$35.00

Ertl, Campbell's Harvest of Good Foods, truck, 1/25 scale, MIB $25.00

Ertl, Dukes of Hazzard General Lee Car, 1/25 scale, 1981, MIB...$65.00

Ertl, grain truck, 1/25 scale, 1971-74, blue and red, EX, $100.00.

Ertl, John Deere Front End Loader, 1/64 scale, M $10.00

Ertl, John Deere Road Grater, 1/64 scale, M.....................$10.00

Ertl, Total Hardware Coast-to-Coast, truck, 1/25 scale, MIB.$40.00

Ertl, True Value, delivery truck, 1/25 scale, MIB, $30.00.

Ertl, Weyerhaeuser Log Truck, 1/25 scale, MIB...............$30.00

Esdo, Oldsmobile Omega, gold, MIB, L1 ....$45.00

Freewheels, Mercedes 190E, silver, MIB, L1 ....$10.00

FYP, Rolls Royce Silver Wraith, Gulbenkian, dk gr, MIB, L1...$425.00

Gad, Cadillac La Espada, yel, MIB, L1............................$165.00

Gama, #0894 BMW 733 Sedan, metallic gray, M, L1 ......$35.00

Gama, #0987 Mercedes Sportswagon SSK Convertible, wht & blk, NMIB, L1..$28.00

Govroski, GAZ Volga 24, metallic bl, MIB, L1 ....$28.00

Guisval, Cadillac V16, wht, M, L1 ....$8.00

Guisval, Renault Espace Police, dk bl, M, L1 ....$10.00

Heco, Rolls Royce Phantom III (Mini-Mini ltd edition), cream, MIB, L1..$115.00

Hubley, #457 Racer, red w/silver driver, 1950s, 7", MIB, A.$250.00

Hubley, American Eagle Carrier Plane, retractable wheels & folding wings, red & bl, 1971, NM (NM box), A......$97.00

Hubley, Bell Telephone Truck, hook & wench assembly w/accessories, army gr, 10", unused, M (VG box), A............$370.00

Hubley, Bulldozer, yel-gr w/blk rubber treads, movable treads, 9½", MIB, A $126.00

Hubley, Car Hauler, carries 3 sedans on trailer, red, 12½", NMIB, A...$450.00

Hubley, Convertible, gr w/NP windshield & steering wheel, blk rubber tires, 1940s, 7", M (G box), A $220.00

Hubley, Diesel Road Roller, orange & cream, clicker on rear wheels, 9¾", NM, A $190.00

Hubley, Fire Engine Set, 1950s, fire engine, station wagon, whistle & ladders, 5", M (Mighty-Metal Toys bubble card), A $125.00

Hubley, Motorcycle, red w/blk rubber tires, full-figure driver in blk, 8⅜", MIB, A...$700.00

Hubley, P-40 WWII Plane, 1950s, silver w/red wings, Flying Tiger decals, 7¾", M (Mighty-Metal Toys bubble card), A $160.00

Hubley, Stake Truck, 1946 Ford, orange cab w/CI stake bed, blk rubber tires, 9½", NM, A...................................$190.00

Hubley, Tiny Town, 1950s, blk car & bl race car on plastic trailer, 6", M (EX+ Mighty-Metal Toys bubble card), A $100.00

Hubley Kiddie Toys #45, 9" WWII fighter, 7" panel truck, 7" Jaguar convertible, 5½" tractor, ca 1950, NM (EX box), A $511.00

Idea, #3 Ferrari 250GT, silver & bl, M, L1 ....$35.00

Imperial, CHiPs Helicopter, 1980, M (NM card), C1 ......$21.00

Joal, #104 Renault 10 Sedan, wht, MIB, L1 ....$22.00

Joal, #110 Mercedes 300SL Convertible, blk, M, L1 ....$18.00

Joal, #114 Mercedes 230SL Convertible (closed), wht, M, L1 ....$18.00

Joal, #149a, Volvo Luxury Bus TWA, gray & wht, MIB, L1..$62.00

Johnny Lightning, AJ Foyt, purple, NM, W1 ....$55.00

Johnny Lightning, Al Unser Indy Special, Winner 1970, metallic bl, orig pipes & stickers, NM, W1 ....$39.00

Johnny Lightning, Baja, gold, VG-, W1............................$17.00

Johnny Lightning, Bonus White Wasp, repro, MBP, G3.$50.00

Johnny Lightning, Bug Bomb, metallic aqua, orig engines & pipes, NM, W1...$29.00

Johnny Lightning, Bug Bomb, purple, MBP, W1 ....$125.00

Johnny Lightning, Custom '32 Ford, metallic purple, missing radiator & pipes, EX+, W1 ....$7.50

Johnny Lightning, Custom Dragster, metallic purple, all pipes, missing canopy o/w NM, W1 ....$19.00

Johnny Lightning, Custom Eldorado, metallic brn, M, W1.$99.00

Johnny Lightning, Custom Eldorado, metallic purple, opening doors, EX-, W1 ....$39.00

Johnny Lightning, Custom Ferrari, metallic red w/wht interior, NM, W1 ....$29.00

Johnny Lightning, Custom GTO, red, P, W1 ....$20.00

Johnny Lightning, Custom Mako Shark, metallic bl, EX+, W1 ....$32.50

Johnny Lightning, Custom Spoiler, lime, MBP, W1 ....$95.00

Johnny Lightning, Custom Spoiler, metallic purple, orig canopy & wing, NM, W1......................$29.00

Johnny Lightning, Custom Turbine, metallic aqua, unpnt interior, orig top, EX, W1 ....$19.00

Johnny Lightning, Custom Turbine, orig top, metallic purple w/rare wht interior, NM, W1 ....$59.00

Johnny Lightning, Custom XKE, metallic purple, EX+, W1 ....$24.00

Johnny Lightning, Custom 32 Ford, aqua, MBP, W1 ....$75.00

Johnny Lightning, Double Trouble, metallic red, EX, W1..$39.00

Johnny Lightning, Flame Out, orig windshield & ladder, metallic purple, EX-, W1 ....$29.00

Johnny Lightning, Frantic Ferrari, metallic purple, orig engine, EX-, W1 ....$15.00

Johnny Lightning, Hairy Hauler, metallic purple, missing top & hook o/w EX+, W1 ....$17.00

Johnny Lightning, Nucleon, orig canopy & reactor, metallic purple, EX+, W1 ....$35.00

Johnny Lightning, Sand Stormer, purple, G, W1 ....$10.00

Johnny Lightning, Screamer, metallic purple, EX+, W1 ..$29.00

Johnny Lightning, Smuggler, orig whiskey barrel & engine, metallic purple, NM, W1 ....$29.00

Johnny Lightning, Triple Threat, orig pipes & engines, metallic purple, EX, W1 ....$32.50

Johnny Lightning, Vicious Vette, metallic red, EX+, W1 .$27.50

Johnny Lightning, Wild Winner, orange, MBP, W1......$275.00

K&R Replicas, Triumph TR6 Convertible, butterscotch, NMIB, L1 ....$65.00

KDN, #412-7 Skoda 110L, orange, MIB, L1 ....$12.00

KDN, #412-9 Tatra 613, pale bl, MIB, L1 ....$12.00

KDN, #494 Skoda 120LS, red, MIB, L1 ....$12.00

Kim Classics, 1960 Chrysler 300F, hardtop, claret, MIB, L1 ....$195.00

Lion Car, #12 Opel Rekord Coupe, petrol bl, rare, NM, L1..$145.00

Lion Car, #29 DAF 600 Variomatic, yel, rare, NM, L1 ..$115.00

Lion Car, DAF Eindhoven Truck, yel, M, L1 ....$45.00

Lion Car, DAF Zwanenberg Refrigerates Truck, wht, MIB, L1 ....$65.00

Lledo, #07PAT Ford Woody Wagon, Pat's Poodle Parlour, cream body, red chassis, M, C6......................$6.00

Lledo, #17PENN 1932 AEC Regal Single-Decker Bus, Pennine, M, C6......................$10.00

Lledo, #3STA Horse-Drawn Van, Staffordshire County Show, gr & cream, 1984, M, C6......................$6.00

Lledo, #54ROLLS 1929 Rolls Royce D Back, silver & bl, M, C6......................$8.00

Lledo, #6BM Model T Ford Van, British Meat, 1983, M, C6......................$6.00

Lledo, #6FAIRY Model T Van, Fairy Soap, M, C6.............$8.00

Lledo, #6MARA Model T Ford, Marcol Products, yel body, 1984, M, C6......................$10.00

Lledo, #8H2O Model T Tanker, Water Works, Rutland, M, C6......................$8.00

Lonestar, Cadillac Coupe De Ville, wht & bl, NM, L1 ....$95.00

Lonestar, Chevrolet Corvair, coral, M, L1 ....$65.00

Lonestar, Dodge Dart, Phoenix, metallic bl, M, L1 ....$95.00

Lonestar, Ford Sunliner Convertible, pale bl, MIB, L1 ..$115.00

Lusotoys, Citroen GS Pallas, Michelin, yel, NM, L1 ....$35.00

Macadam, Renault 1000Kg, Olibet, gray, MIB, L1 ....$45.00

Macadam, Renault 1000Kg, Valentine, dk gr, MIB, L1....$45.00

Madison, Chrysler 300C (hardtop), metallic red, MIB, L1.$165.00

Majorette, Scania Elf, wht, MIB, L1..................$35.00

McGregor, Lancia Di Lambda, brn, NM, L1 ....$5.00

McGregor/Politoys, Ford Taurus 20M Police, blk, NM, L1 .$16.00

Mebetoys, #A22 Corvette Pinin Farina, metallic bl, M, L1.$65.00

Mebetoys, #A43 Fiat 124 Roman Taxi, gr, NM, L1 ....$38.00

Mebetoys, #A48 Autobianchi A112, claret, NM, L1 ....$22.00

Mebetoys, #A50 Ferrari 365 GTC, chartreuse, NM, L1 ...$18.00

Mercury, #021-2 Ferves Ranger, orange, M, L1 ....$38.00

Mercury, #029 Rolls Royce Silver Cloud, dk gray, NM..$125.00

Mercury, #030 Bentley S Sedan, gray, NM......................$125.00

Mercury, #040-31-2 Maserati Racing, red, M, L1 ....$150.00

Mercury, #056 Mercedes W 194, silver, NM, L1 ....$95.00

Mercury, #069-1 Jack Demon's Dragster, yel, M, L1.........$38.00

Metal Masters Toy Set, complete w/Army Jeep, bus, truck & roadster, EX (VG box), A $201.00

Midgetoy, Army Ambulance, olive, blk rubber tires, VG-, W1 ....$9.00

Midgetoy, Army Truck, olive, blk rubber tires, EX+, W1...$9.00

Midgetoy, Convertible, bl, blk rubber tires, 1950s, EX+, W1 ....$13.50

Midgetoy, Convertible, red, blk rubber tires, 1950s, G-, W1 ....$9.00

Midgetoy, Corvette, gr, 1970s, VG, W1..................$1.00

Midgetoy, Corvette, yel, blk plastic tires, 1950s, VG, W1..$9.00

Midgetoy, El Camino, red, 1970s, VG, W1......................$2.00

Midgetoy, Indy Race Car, silver, blk rubber tires, 1950s, EX, W1 ....$13.50

Midgetoy, Jeep, military gr, crimped axles, 1950s, NM, W1 ....$3.50

Midgetoy, Jeep, red, blk plastic tires, 1960s, VG, W1 ....$2.50

Midgetoy, MG Sports Car, gr, 1960s, G+, W1 ....$2.00

Midgetoy, Pickup, Jeep cab-over, bl, blk rubber tires, 1950s, NM, W1 ....$13.00

Minialuxe, #04 Renault Paris Rome, brn, MIB, L1 ....$16.00

Minialuxe, #21 Renault Grande Remise, brn, MIB, L1 ....$16.00

Minialuxe, Hotchkiss Gregoire, dk gray, rare, NM, L1 .....$65.00

Minialuxe, Volvo 144 Sedan, butterscotch, M, L1 ....$35.00

Minimac, Scania Vabis, Transalfa, wht, M, L1 ....$48.00

Mira, Seat 128 Coupe, Michelin, wht, M, L1 ....$18.00

Mira, Seat 131 Coupe, Rallye, red, M, L1 ....$18.00

MOG, #5 Ferrari 400i Limousine, mint gr, wht roof & interior, limited edition of 200, MIB, L1 ....$215.00

Old Cars, Fiat Campagnola Fire Dept, Landes, red, MIB, L1 ....$45.00

Old Cars, Fiat Covered Van, Fire Dept, Mayenne, red, MIB, L1 ....$55.00

Old Cars, Fiat Van, Fire Dept, Eure & Loire, red, MIB, L1...$35.00

Patino, 1907 Peugeot Phaeton, pewter, MIB, L1 ....$45.00

Patino, 1938 Lagonda Raptide, pewter, MIB, L1 ....$45.00

Precision, 1954 Corvette Hardtop, pale bl, MIB, L1 ....$95.00

Progetta K, 1952 Ferrari Stradle, dk bl, MIB, L1 ....$38.00

Provence, Moulage K 081 Facel Vega Cabriolet, burgundy, MIB, L1 ....$95.00

Realistic Toy, Trailways Bus, red & wht, 9", EX, A........$280.00

Rextoys, 1938 #2 Cadillac 4-door Convertible (open), almond, MIB, L1 ....$35.00

Rextoys, 1938 #4 Cadillac, US Navy, bl, MIB, L1 ....$35.00

RW, 1927 BMW Cabriolet, bl, M, L1 ....$25.00

Safir, #12 Citroen B2 Ambulance, wht, M, L1 ....$65.00

Safir, #14 Fiat 8HP Victoria, red & gr, M, L1 ....$35.00

Schaback, #1018 VW Corrado Coupe, gray, MIB, L1 ......$25.00

Schaback, #1030 Audi 90 Quattro, gr, NM, L1 ....$15.00

Schaback, #1160 BMW ZI Spyder, red, MIB, L1 ....$25.00

Schuco, #611 Audi 80GL, orange, M, L1 ....$28.00

Schuco, #613 BMW Turbo Coupe, orange, M, L1 ....$28.00

Schuco, #619 VW Variant Station Wagon, champagne, MIB, L1 ....$35.00

Schuco, #622 Audi 50 Coupe, pumpkin, M, L1 ....$28.00

Schuco, #627 BMW 320 Coupe, dk orange, M, L1 ....$28.00

Schuco, #629 BMW 630 Coupe, chestnut, NM, L1 ....$15.00

Seriplastic, Chevrolet Truck, Coca-Cola, yel, M, L1........$12.00

Siku, #2519 Unimog Mercedes, w/trailer, gray, MIB, L1 ..$40.00

Siku, #2918 Ford Lemonade Truck, red, MIB, L1 ....$25.00

Siku, #2921 Mercedes Fire Truck, w/water cannon, red, MIB, L1 ....$25.00

Siku, #2922 Mercedes Cement Mixer, yel & red, MIB, L1..$32.00

Siku, #3732 Man Sarrasani Circus, w/animal cage, wht & gr, MIB, L1 ....$45.00

Siku, Unimog Mercedes, w/snowplow, orange, NM, L1 ...$15.00

SMTS, #RL4 Lotus Elite Rallye, 41 DAD, red, MIB, L1 .$135.00

Solido, #T12 Tank Transport Truck & Trailer, M, C6 ....$45.00

Solido, #132 1928 Mercedes SS Torpedo, MIB, C6 ....$25.00

Solido, #136 1930 Bugatti Royale, blk body, M, C6 ....$20.00

Solido, #140 1925 Panhard-Levassor, metallic gold, M, C6..$22.00

Solido, #144 1934 Voisin 17 CV Surbaissee, MIB, C6 .....$25.00

Solido, #145 1926 Hispano-Suiza, MIB, C6......................$25.00

Solido, #149 Renault 40 CV, burgundy, M, C6 ....$18.00

Solido, #154 1926 Renault 40 CV, MIB, C6 ....$25.00

Solido, #154BL 1929 Fiat 525 N, dk bl, MIB, C6.............$25.00

Solido, #156 1931 Duesenberg Type J, red/blk, M, C6 .....$25.00

Solido, #19 VW Gulf, gr, M, C6 ....$18.00

Solido, #198 Ford Fairlane Pickup (covered), gr, NM, L1 .$175.00

Solido, #203 Renault 4x4 Tous Terrains, M, C6 ....$50.00

Solido, #207 PT76 Amphibian Tank, M, C6......................$70.00

Solido, #21 Matra/Simca Bagheera, yel, M (EX box), C6..$15.00

Solido, #231 Sherman Tank, M (EX box), C6 ....$70.00

Solido, #32 Citroen 15 CV, blk, M, C6 ....$15.00

Solido, #321 Saviem Car Carrier, 2 trailers, bl cab, yel & silver trailers, M, C6 ....$65.00

Solido, #68 Porsche 934, wht, M, C6...............................$20.00

Spot On, #118 Isetta, gray, NMIB, L1 ....$135.00

Spot On, #119 Meadows Frisky Sports, aqua, NM, L1 ...$115.00

Spot On, #161 Land Rover, long wheel base, gray, NM, L1 .$85.00

Spot On, #215 Daimler Dart Convertible, pale bl, M, L1 ..$150.00

Spot On, #260 Rolls Royce Canberra III w/Queens, burgundy, NM, L1 ....$225.00

Starter, T-Bird, Coors, gold, MIB, L1...............................$35.00

Structo, Mack Log Carrier, yel, NM, L1 ....$45.00

Tin Wizard, #170 1963 Ford T-Bird Coupe, mauve, NMIB, L1 ....$165.00

Tomica, Corvette, yel, 1977, NM, A3................................$6.00

Tomica, Ford Model T/Mills Baking, wht, 1977, M, A3 ..$10.00

Tomica, Lamborghini Countach, blk, 1978, M, A3............$6.00

Tomica, Lotus Elite, ivory & gr, 1978, M, A3....................$6.00

Tomica, Mercedes 300SL, silver, 1978, M, A3 ....$8.00

Tomica, Morgan, red, 1977, M, A3....................................$6.00

Tomica, Packard, red, 1978, M, A3....................................$6.00

Tomica, Police Bus, blk & wht, M, G3..............................$20.00

Tomica, Porsche 911S, blk #7, 1978, M, A3......................$6.00

Tomica, Toyota LC Police, blk, 1978, EX, A3....................$8.00

Trax, #8002 Holden Pickup, gr, MIB, L1 ....$35.00

Trax, #8004 Holden Monaro Coupe, bl, MIB, L1 ....$35.00

Tri-ang Minic Ships, Neu Amsterdam Presentation, set of 10, EX (VG box), A..$250.00

Tri-ang Minic Ships, Neu Amsterdam Presentation, set of 10, NMIB, A..$400.00

Vitesse, #123.2 1938 BMW Cabriolet (closed), bl, MIB, L1 ....$35.00

Vitesse, #161 Mercedes 170 Porto Fire Dept, red, MIB, L1 ....$25.00

Vitesse, #210 Saurer Bailly Arola Truck, gr, MIB, L1.......$55.00

Vitesse, #290.2 Mercedes 170 Mercedes Service Van, bl, MIB, L1 ....$25.00

Vitesse, #390.4 1960 Impala Cabriolet, gr, MIB, L1 ....$25.00

Vitesse, #450.2 Buick Special Convertible, gold, MIB, L1..$25.00

Diecast Collector Banks

Thousands of banks have been produced since Ertl made its first model in 1981, the 1913 Model T Parcel Post Mail Service #9647. The Ertl company was founded by Fred Ertl, Sr., in

Dubuque, Iowa, back in the mid-1940s. Until they made their first diecast banks, most of what they made were farm tractors. Today they specialize in vehicles made to specification and carrying logos of companies as large as Texaco and as small as your hometown bank. The size of each 'run' is dictated by the client and can vary from a few hundred up to several thousand. Some clients will later add a serial number to the vehicle; Ertl does not. Other numbers that appear on the base of each bank are a 4-number dating code (the first three indicate the day of the year up to 365 and the fourth number is the last digit of the year, '5' for 1995, for instance.) The stock number is shown only on the box, never on the bank, so it is extremely important that you keep them in their original boxes.

Other producers of these banks are Scale Models, incorporated in 1991, First Gear Inc., and Spec-Cast, whose founders at one time all worked for the Ertl company.

In the listings that follow, unless another condition is given, all values are for banks mint and in their original boxes. (#d) indicates a bank that was numbered by the client, not Ertl.

Advisors: Art and Judy Turner (H8).

Key:
JLE — Joseph L. Ertl   NB — not a bank

ERTL

A&W Root Beer #2, 1905 Ford Delivery Van, #9827, H8 .**$35.00**
A&W Root Beer #3, 1918 Ford Runabout, #2972, T4/H8.**$30.00**
ABF Freight Comp, 1955 Chevy Cameo Pickup, #B123, H8.**$45.00**
Abilene TX Fire Fighters, 1926 Seagrave Fire Engine, #3729, H8 ....**$26.00**
AC Spark Plugs, 1950 Chevy Panel Truck, #2901, H8 ....**$34.00**
Ace Hardware #5, 1905 Ford Delivery Van, #9431, H8 ...**$25.00**
Agway #3, 1905 Ford Delivery Van, #9743, H8 ....**$45.00**
Agway Hellertown #1, 1932 Ford Panel Truck, #2184, T4 ..**$25.00**
Alan Kulwicki Racing, 1940 Ford, JLE, #6021, H8 ....**$60.00**
Alka Seltzer, 1932 Ford Panel Truck, #9737, H8 ....**$28.00**
Allen Organ Comp, 1931 Hawkeye, #9892, H8 ....**$45.00**
Alliance Racing, Dennis Setzer, Stearman Bi-Plane, #00386, H8 ....**$49.00**
Alliance Racing, R Pressley, 1948 Diamond T Tractor-Trailer, #9370, H8 ....**$49.00**
Allied Van Lines, 1950 Chevy Tractor-Trailer, #1354, H8 ..**$20.00**
Allis Chalmers, Vega Plane, #35023, H8 ....**$24.00**
Almond Joy, 1923 Chevy Van, #7653, H8/T4.................**$23.00**
Alta Vista, Iowa 100th Anniv, 1905 Ford Delivery Van, #B149, H8 ....**$29.00**
Alzheimers Assoc #1, 1913 Ford Model T, limited edition, #9680, P1 ....**$100.00**
American Red Cross #1, 1913 Ford Model T, #9294, H8.**$75.00**
American Store, 1913 Ford Model T, #9478, T4.............**$19.00**
Amoco, 1913 Ford Model T, #9150, H8........................**$125.00**
Amoco, 1929 Ford, #1530, H8 ....**$38.00**
Amoco, 1931 International Wrecker, #9000, T4 ....**$25.00**
Amoco, 1938 Dodge Airflow, JLE, #7000, H8.................**$35.00**
Amoco (Red Crown), 1923 Chevy Van, #1320, T4.........**$15.00**
Amoco #3, 1926 Mack Tanker, silver & blk, #9447, P1 .**$200.00**
Amoco Certicare, 1932 Ford Panel Truck, #7668, H8 .....**$49.00**

Amoco Convertible TK Dealer, 1948 Diamond T Tractor-Trailer, #8187, H8 ....**$22.00**
Amoco Motor Club, 1931 Hawkeye Wrecker, JLE, #9000, P1 ....**$25.00**
Amoco Oil #3, 1938 Dodge Airflow, JLE, #7008, H8.......**$34.00**
Amoco Red Crown, 1930 Diamond T Tanker, #9467, H8 ..**$22.00**
Amsouth, 1913 Ford Model T, #9454, H8 ....**$45.00**
Amstel Light Beer, 1931 Hawkeye, #9358, H8.................**$24.00**
Anheuser-Busch, 1926 Mack Crate Truck, #9047, T4 .....**$69.00**
Anheuser-Busch, 1931 Hawkeye, #7574, T4 ....**$19.00**
Anheuser-Busch #1 (silver spokes), 1918 Ford Barrel Truck, #9766, from $85 to **$125.00**
Anheuser-Busch #9, 1941 Ford Tractor-Trailer, #9553, H8.**$24.00**
Antique Power, 1923 Chevy Van, #9282, H8 ....**$29.00**
Arkansas Razorbacks, 1913 Ford Model T, #9353, H8 .....**$34.00**
Arm & Hammer, 1918 Ford Runabout, #B052, T4 ....**$39.00**
Arm & Hammer, 1923 Chevy Van, #2096, H8.................**$75.00**
Arm & Hammer, 1950 Chevy Panel Truck, #9859, H8.**$179.00**
Artwoods Town & Country, 1932 Ford Panel Truck, #9668, H8..**$45.00**
Ashland Oil Co, 1931 Hawkeye Tanker, #9757, H8 ....**$39.00**
Ashville Office Supply, 1931 Hawkeye, #9118, H8..........**$15.00**
Associated Grocers, 1913 Ford Model T, #9212, P1........**$50.00**
Atlanta Falcons, 1913 Ford, #1248, H8 ....**$35.00**
Atlantic City Show, 1931 Hawkeye Wrecker, #9634, H8.**$19.00**
Atlantic Oil, 1931 Hawkeye Wrecker, #7623, T4............**$27.00**
Atlas Van Lines, 1926 Mack, #9514, H8 ....**$95.00**

Baby Ruth, 1926 Mack, #9096, 1992, M, $40.00.

Baltimore Gas & Electric #1, 1932 Ford Panel Truck, #9153, P1 ....**$125.00**
Baltimore Gas & Electric #6, 1931 Hawkeye, #9848, T4 .**$25.00**
Banjo Matthews, 1932 Ford Panel Truck, #2191, P1........**$80.00**
Bardahl Oil, 1931 Hawkeye, #7672, H8..........................**$25.00**
Barq's Root Beer, 1913 Ford Model T, #9826, H8 ....**$49.00**
Barrett Jackson Car Auction, 1950 Chevy Panel Truck, #9361, H8..**$39.00**
Baseball II, California Angels, 1917 Ford, #B371, H8......**$18.00**
Beer Nuts, 1950 Chevy Panel Truck, #2118, from $15 to .**$25.00**
Bell Telephone, 1950 Chevy Panel Truck, #9203, H8.....**$39.00**
Bell Telephone Yellow Pages, 1926 Mack, #2142, H8 .....**$49.00**
Bethlehem Steel #2, Grumman Step Van, #3946, T4 ......**$29.00**
Big A, 1918 Ford Runabout, limited edition, #1324, P1...**$20.00**
Bit-O-Honey, 1923 Chevy Van, #1317, H8 ....**$23.00**

BJR Radiator Service, 1950 Chevy Panel Truck, #7614, H8 ....$95.00

Bobby Allison, 1940 Ford, JLE, #6014, H8 ....$65.00

Bobby Hillin (#d), 1940 Ford Barrel Truck, JLE, #6040, P1 ....$55.00

Boulder Beer, 1918 Ford, #9623, H8 ....$32.00

Brach's Candy, 1923 Chevy Van, #7675, from $25 to $35.00

Brendel's, 1917 Ford Model T, #9823, H8 ....$29.00

Brownies Muffler Wagon (#d), 1950 Chevy Panel Truck, #9894, P1 ....$25.00

Budweiser, 1913 Ford, #1315, H8 ....$195.00

Budweiser #1, 1913 Ford Model T, #1315, P1 ....$165.00

Burma Shave, 1929 International, JLE, #5016, H8 ....$38.00

Cal Tex, 1931 International Tanker, #4086, T4 ....$35.00

Cal Tex (sampler), 1931 International Tanker, #4087, T4 ....$45.00

Campbell's, Trolley, #B621, T4 ....$25.00

Campbell's, 1905 Ford Delivery, #9394, T4 ....$49.00

Campbell's, 1918 Ford Runabout, #9184, T4 ....$49.00

Campbell's, 1931 Hawkeye, #B623, T4 ....$19.00

Campbell's Baked Beans, 1918 Ford Runabout, #9184, H8 ...$65.00

Campbell's Soup #1, Vega Plane, #35005, H8 ....$34.00

Campbell's Tomato Juice, 1931 Hawkeye, #7537, H8 ......$35.00

Can-2 Motor Oil, 1931 International, JLE, #4103, H8 ....$29.00

Canada Dry, 1913 Ford Model T, #2133, H8 ....$125.00

Carl Budding, 1913 Ford Model T, #2106, H8/P1, from $45 to $55.00

Carlisle Prod Antiques, 1905 Ford Delivery Truck, #9315, H8 ....$25.00

Carlisle Prod Fall Car Show, 1931 Hawkeye Wrecker, #2195, H8 ....$21.00

Carlisle Thundering Herd, 1923 Chevy Van, #9051, H8 .$27.00

Carlisle Toy Show, 1950 Chevy Panel Truck, #2851, T4 ..$15.00

Carlos R Lefler #2, 1931 Hawkeye Tanker, #2945, T4 .....$25.00

Carlos R Lefler #3, 1925 Kenworth, #B212, T4 ....$27.00

Carnation, 1913 Ford Model T, #9178, H8 ....$34.00

Carnation, 1926 Mack, #9179, H8 ....$69.00

Carroll Manor Fire Comp, 1926 Seagrave Fire Engine, #7693, H8 ....$24.00

Case IH St Louis Trade Show, Vega Plane, #35047, H8 ..$39.00

Castrol Oil #2, 1926 Mack Tanker, #9464, H8/P1, from $49 to ....:......$55.00

Caterpillar, 1931 Hawkeye, #7714, H8 ....$27.00

Central Tractor, 1938 Chevy Van, #3836, T4 ....$20.00

Champion Spark Plug #1, 1918 Ford Runabout, #9067, H8 ..$39.00

Champlin Refining, 1931 International, JLE, #4088, H8 .$29.00

Check the Oil, 1931 Hawkeye Wrecker, #9599, T4 ....$15.00

Check the Oil, 1938 Chevy Van, #3226, T4 ....$27.00

Check the Oil #2, 1930 Diamond T Tanker, #9111, H8 ..$27.00

Chevron, 1931 Hawkeye Wrecker, #2962, T4 ....$25.00

Chicago Cubs, 1926 Mack, #7545, H8 ....$39.00

Chiquita Bananas, 1913 Ford Model T, #9662, H8 ....$65.00

Chiquita Bananas, 1931 Hawkeye Crate Truck, #9343, T4 .$19.00

Christmas '92, Horse & Wagon, #9780, T4 ....$17.00

Christmas #1, 1913 Ford Model T, #9584, H8 ....$85.00

Citgo, 1905 Ford Delivery Van, #9854, T4 ....$25.00

Citgo, 1918 Ford Barrel Truck, limited edition, #9456, P1 ...$75.00

Citgo, 1950 Chevy Panel, #7692, T4 ....$45.00

Citgo Lubricants, 1918 Ford Runabout, #9456, H8 ....$75.00

Classic Motorbooks, 1950 Chevy Panel Truck, #7567, T4 ...$19.00

Clearkote Protector, 1940 Ford, JLE, #6061, H8 ....$32.00

Clearly Canadian (#d), 1926 Mack, #9238, P1 ....$25.00

Clemson University, 1913 Ford Model T, #9775, H8 ....$49.00

Clyde Beatty Circus, 1937 Ford Tractor-Trailer, #9391, P1 ....$35.00

Co-op (The Farm Store), 1913 Ford Model T, #9245, H8 .$29.00

Coca-Cola, Air Express Plane, #B318, H8 ....$22.00

Coca-Cola, 1923 Chevy Van, #9432, T4 ....$25.00

Coca-Cola, 1925 Kenworth, #B398, H8 ....$18.00

Coca-Cola, 1929 International Tanker, JLE, #4075, H8 ..$34.00

Coca-Cola, 1931 International Tanker, #4075, T4 ....$49.00

Coca-Cola, 1955 Chevy Cameo Pickup, #B648, H8 ....$28.00

Coca-Cola Christmas, 1920 International, JLE, #3015, P1 ....$115.00

Collectors World, 1913 Ford Model T, #9137, H8 ....$34.00

Columbia Engine Co of NY, 1926 Seagrave Fire Engine, #9360, H8 ....$49.00

Conoco #7, 1925 Kenworth Stake Truck, #2778, P1 ....$25.00

Conoco Oil (sampler), 1929 International, JLE, #4004, H8 ..$45.00

Conoco Oil #1, 1926 Mack Tanker, #9750, P1 ....$200.00

Coors Brewing, 1925 Kenworth, #B201, T4 ....$25.00

Coors-Malted Milk, 1931 Hawkeye, #B233, H8 ....$18.00

Coors-Sussex Fair, 1931 International, JLE, #5002, H8 ...$27.00

Corona Beer, 1931 Hawkeye, #9255, H8 ....$39.00

Cossack Drill Team, 1938 Chevy Panel Van, #B077, H8 ..$59.00

Country Time Lemonade, 1913 Ford Model T, NB, #1640, H8 ....$28.00

Covington Savings & Loan, 1950 Chevy Panel Truck, #9216, H8 ....$95.00

Crown, 1931 Hawkeye Tanker, limited edition, #9652, P1 ....$20.00

Cub Foods, 1931 Hawkeye, #9042, H8 ....$29.00

Cumberland Valley, 1926 Mack, #9393, T4 ....$15.00

Cumberland Valley, 1955 Chevy Cameo Pickup, #9563, T4 .$19.00

Cumberland Valley, 1960 Ford 4x4 Pickup, #B288, T4 ...$19.00

Cumberland Valley Tractor Pull, 1926 Mack, #9393, H8 .$25.00

Custom Chrome, 1931 International Freight, #5006, T4 .$39.00

Dairy Queen, 1913 Ford Model T, #B306, T4 ....$27.00

Dallas Autorama, 1950 Chevy Panel Truck, #9349, H8 ...$44.00

Daytona Bike Week, 1938 Chevy Panel Van, #9354, H8 .$149.00

Dean Moon, 1950 Chevy Panel Truck, #9456, T4 ....$69.00

Decorah, 1913 Model T, #9134, T4 ....$10.00

Detroit News, 1913 Ford Model T, #1667, P1 ....$55.00

Diamond Motor Oil, 1931 International, JLE, #4079, H8 .$22.00

Diamond Salt, 1913 Ford Model T, #9414, H8/P1 ....$55.00

Dixie Brewing Co, 1937 Ford Tractor-Trailer, limited edition, #9278, H8 ....$125.00

Dobyns-Bennett High School, 1950 Chevy Panel Truck, #9516, H8 ....$69.00

Dominos Pizza, 1950 Chevy, #9460, H8 ....$45.00

Douglas County Republicans, 1913 Ford Model T, limited edition, #9369, P1 ....$145.00

Downtown M/C, Seattle WA, 1931 Hawkeye, #B103, H8 .$42.00

Dr Pepper, 1918 Ford, #7573, H8 ....$48.00

Dr Pepper (#d), 1913 Ford Model T, #9234, P1 ....$50.00

Dr Pepper #1, 1905 Ford Delivery Van, #9739, T4 ....$35.00

Drag Specialties #1, 1931 Hawkeye, #9084, H8 ....$195.00

Drag Specialties #2, 1931 Ford Panel Truck, #2525, T4...$59.00

Drake Hotel, 1913 Ford Model T, #2113, H8.................$125.00

Dubuque Fire Department, 1937 Ahrens-Fox Fire Engine, #9593, H8 ....$17.00

Dubuque Golf & Country Club, 1913 Ford Model T, #9726, H8 ....$75.00

Dyersville, IA Fire Dept #1, 1926 Seagrave Fire Engine, #9201, H8 ....$85.00

Eagles, 1931 Hawkeye, #B159, T4.................................$19.00

Eason (sampler), 1930 International, JLE, #4034, H8 ......$45.00

Eastman #4, 1913 Ford Model T, limited edition, #B118, P1 ....$50.00

Eastview Pharmacy, 1950 Chevy Panel Truck, #1317, H8..$125.00

Eastwood #1, 1950 Chevy Panel Truck, #9325, H8 ....$595.00

Eastwood #3, 1931 Hawkeye, #2985, T4..........................$49.00

Eastwood #4, 1937 Ford T/T, #7664, H8.......................$225.00

Eastwood #6, 1926 Seagrave Fire Engine, #1666, T4........$49.00

Eastwood #8, 1931 Hawkeye Wrecker, #9747, T4............$69.00

Edelbrock (sampler), 1931 International, #5055, H8 ....$29.00

Elizabeth College, 1913 Ford Model T, #2125, T4 ....$25.00

Enchanted Forest, 1923 Chevy Van, #9044, T4 ....$19.00

English Pub, 1920 International, JLE, #3003, P1 ....$15.00

Ertl Collectors Club Express, 1913 Ford Model T, #1668, P1 .$90.00

Ertl Replica, 1931 Hawkeye, #2088, T4............................$19.00

Ertl Safety, 1913 Ford Model T, #7554, P1 ....$80.00

Esso (sampler), 1939 Dodge Airflow, #B243, H8.............$79.00

Ethyl Gasoline, 1931 Hawkeye Tanker, JLE, #0880, P1 ...$30.00

Ethyl Gasoline, 1931 International, JLE, #4006, H8 ....$27.00

Ethyl Gasoline (sampler), 1932 Ford Panel Truck, #9898, H8 ....$45.00

Exxon, Vintage Plane, limited edition, #40015, H8.........$39.00

Farm Progress Show, 1930 International, JLE, #5008, H8.$20.00

Farmers Almanac, 1913 Ford Model T, #1359, H8...........$24.00

Field of Dreams, 1920 International, JLE, #3046, H8.......$28.00

Fina Oil, 1918 Ford Runabout, limited edition, #9502, T4 .$35.00

Fina Oil, 1926 Mack Tanker, #9186, T4...........................$39.00

Fina Oil, 1937 Ahrens-Fox Fire Engine, #2866, H8 ....$29.00

Firehouse Films, 1950 Chevy Panel Truck, #9369, H8...$125.00

First Tennessee Bank #1, 1917 Ford Model T, limited edition, #1318, P1 ....$160.00

Flav-O-Rich, 1913 Ford Model T, #9767, H8..................$19.00

Football-LA Rams, 1931 Hawkeye, #B162, H8 ....$17.00

Ford #2, 1913 Ford Model T, limited edition, #1322, P1..$90.00

Gilmore Oil (sampler), 1931 Hawkeye Tanker, #9891, P1.$110.00

Goodyear, 1917 Ford Model T, #9359, T4.......................$19.00

Goodyear (25th Anniversary), 1931 Hawkeye, #4957, T4.$25.00

Grapette Soda, 1940 Ford Delivery, JLE, #6002, P1 ....$30.00

Grapette Soda (sampler), 1940 Ford, JLE, #6001, H8 ......$45.00

Grauer's #3, 1955 Chevy Cameo Pickup, #2939, T4 ....$35.00

Gulf Oil, 1925 Kenworth Stake Truck, #9242, T4 ....$25.00

Gulf Oil, 1925 Kenworth Wrecker, #B107, H8 ....$45.00

Gulf Oil & Refining (#d), 1950 Chevy Panel Truck, #9156, P1 ....$145.00

Hamm's Beer, 1929 International, #1914, T4.....................$10.00

Hamm's Beer, 1931 Hawkeye, #7619, H8 ....$28.00

Hank Williams Jr, Vega Plane, #35045, H8......................$27.00

Happy Birthday, 1905 Ford Delivery Van, #9685, P1.......$14.00

Harley-Davidson, Motorcycle Sidecar, #1993, T4 ....$79.00

Harley-Davidson #1, 1918 Ford Runabout, #9784, H8 ..$595.00

Harley-Davidson #3, 1932 Ford Panel Truck, limited edition, #7525, P1 ....$275.00

Harley-Davidson #5, 1931 Hawkeye Tanker, #9164, limited edition, H8 ....$195.00

Harley-Davidson 90th Anniversary, 1934 Mack, JLE, #8008, H8 ....$69.00

Hawkeye Tech, 1913 Ford Model T, #9533, H8...............$25.00

Heartbeat of America, 1950 Chevy Panel Truck, #9561, H8 ....$25.00

Heartbeat of America (sm tires), 1950 Chevy, #9873, H8.$45.00

Heartland Popcorn, 1905 Ford Delivery Van, #9250, H8.$24.00

Heinekin Beer, 1931 Hawkeye, #9357, H8 ....$29.00

Heinekin Beer #1, 1918 Ford Barrel Truck, #9570, P1...$200.00

Hemp Bros, 1931 Hawkeye Wrecker, #2194, T4..............$35.00

Hershey's, Airplane, #B311, T4.......................................$22.00

Hershey's Almond, 1913 Ford Model T, gold, #2129, P1 .$85.00

Hershey's Auto Club, 1955 Chevy Cameo Pickup, #3815, T4 ....$39.00

Hershey's Transit, Trolley Car, #B310, P1 ....$20.00

Hills Dept Store, 1913 Ford Model T, #9768, H8.............$23.00

Hoffman LaRouche Set, 1905 Ford Delivery Van, #9974, T4 ....$199.00

Holley Performance Carburetors, 1955 Cameo Pickup, #7527, H8 ....$27.00

Hollycliff Farms, 1926 Mack, #977, H8...........................$45.00

Home Hardware #4, 1905 Ford Delivery Van, #9401, H8..$58.00

Homestead Collectibles, 1905 Ford Delivery Van, #9651, H8 ....$15.00

Hostess #1, 1913 Ford Model T, red spokes, #1661, P1 ....$70.00

House of Books, 1913 Ford Model T, #9256, H8 ....$40.00

Humble Oil, Stearman Plane, #37509, H8 ....$59.00

Humble Oil (sampler), 1951 GMC Panel Truck, #B546, T4 .$69.00

Hummelstown, 1955 Chevy Cameo Pickup, #9425, T4...$25.00

HWI Hardware, 1905 Ford Delivery Van, #9674, H8 ......$25.00

IGA, 1931 Hawkeye, #7696, H8/P1, from $20 to.............$24.00

Imperial Oil #1, 1931 Hawkeye Tanker, #9455, H8 ....$49.00

Indian Airplane, beige, #5010, T4 ....$29.00

Indian Motorcycle, Vega Plane, #35009, H8 ....$39.00

Indian Motorcycle Warrior (silver), 1940 Ford, JLE, #6023, H8 ....$49.00

Indianapolis 500, 1918 Ford Runabout, #9813, H8 ....$49.00

Iowa Gas, 1931 Hawkeye, #9589, H8...............................$49.00

Iowa Hawkeyes, 1926 Mack, #2135, H8 ....$65.00

IUE, 1950 Chevy Panel Truck, #7686, T4.......................$19.00

JC Penney, 1931 Hawkeye Wrecker, #9526, H8 ....$22.00

JC Penney #1, 1913 Model T, #1354, T4.........................$95.00

JC Whitney, 1923 Chevy Van, #B234, H8........................$32.00

JC Whitney, 1926 Seagrave Fire Engine, #B234, T4........$25.00

JF Good Co, 1913 Ford Model T, #9524, P1 ....$105.00

Jim Beam (District 5), 1918 Ford Barrel Truck, #2964, P1.$60.00

Jimmy's Autolite, 1938 Chevy Panel Truck, #9638, T4...$25.00

Jimmy's Fram Filters, 1950 Chevy Panel Truck, #2951, T4.$20.00

Jimmy's Goodyear, 1932 Ford Panel, #9387, T4 ....$25.00

JL Kraft, 1913 Ford Model T, limited edition, #2147, P1 .$70.00

Kendall Oil, 1931 Hawkeye Tanker, JLE, #4073, P1 ....$30.00

Key Aid Distributors, 1913 Ford Model T, #9175, H8......$65.00

Keystone Wood Products, 1950 Chevy Panel Truck, #9110, H8 ....$35.00

Kidde, 1913 Ford Model T, #9351, H8.....................$39.00

Kingsport Tennessee #1, 1918 Ford Runabout, limited edition, #9174, P1 ....$125.00

Kinsley Construction, 1932 Ford Panel Truck, #9824, H8.$25.00

Kodak, 1905 Ford Delivery Van, #9985, H8/P1................$75.00

Kraft Dairy Group, 1917 Ford Model T, #9675, H8..........$35.00

Kroger Foods, 1925 Kenworth, #3757, 1993, MIB, $25.00.

Kwik Shop, 1918 Ford Runabout, #B226, H8.................$21.00

Kyle Petty (sampler), 1950 Chevy Panel Truck, #2881, H8.$75.00

Lake Festival Toy & Card Show, 1920 International, JLE, #3004, P1 ....$20.00

Lake Speed, 1931 International, JLE, #5056, H8/P1 from $40 to...$45.00

Lancaster Anniversary, 1923 Chevy Van, #9387, T4.......$25.00

Lawry's Seasoning Salt, 1950 Chevy Panel Truck, #9159, H8.$28.00

Lea & Perrin, 1913 Ford Model T, limited edition, #9170, P1 ....$35.00

Lehman Hardware, 1926 Mack, #9477, H8 ....$25.00

Lepages Glue, 1913 Ford Model T, limited edition, #2120, P1 ....$30.00

Liberty, Model A Pumper, #2014, T4 ....$19.00

Lipton Tea #1, 1913 Ford Model T, limited edition, #7505, P1 ....$125.00

Madison Electric, 1913 Ford Model T, limited edition, #9589, P1 ....$80.00

Mailboxes Inc, 1932 Ford Panel Truck, #3645, T4...........$25.00

Marvel Mystery Oil, 1931 Hawkeye Tanker, #2157, T4...$19.00

Merit Oil, 1926 Mack Tanker, #9980, P1 ....$90.00

Mickey Thompson #5, 1938 Chevy Panel Van, #2090, T4.$39.00

Mike's Trainland #1, 1937 Ford Tractor-Trailer, #9850, H8.$59.00

Miller Beer, 1913 Ford Barrel Truck, #9277, H8 ....$45.00

Miller High Life (#d), 1913 Ford Model T, #9277, P1......$30.00

Mission Uniform, Grumman Step Van, #9119, H8..........$25.00

Mobil Oil, 1925 Kenworth Tanker, #9237, H8 ....$25.00

Mobil Oil, 1930 Diamond T Tanker, #9459, H8.............$32.00

Mobil Oil (new style), 1931 Hawkeye Tanker, #B278, T4.$25.00

Mobil Oil #6, 1931 Hawkeye Wrecker, #2127, T4.........$27.00

Mobilgas #6, 1931 Hawkeye Tanker, #9234, T4.............$25.00

Model T Ford Club, 1918 Ford Runabout, #9230, H8......$24.00

Montgomery Ward #2, 1917 Ford Model T, #9052, P1 ....$70.00

Montgomery Ward #3, 1926 Mack, #1363, T4.................$39.00

Mounds, 1923 Chevy Van, #7652, T4 ....$23.00

Mustang Club #1, 1932 Ford Panel Truck, #9732, P1 ......$65.00

Nintendo (#d), 1913 Ford Model T, limited edition, #2113, P1 ....$60.00

Oil Can Henry, 1931 Hawkeye Tanker, #9897, P1 ....$90.00

Oliver Tractors, Vintage Plane, #40008, H8.................$24.00

Otasco, 1918 Ford Runabout, #9777, H8....................$40.00

Otasco #1, 1913 Ford Model T, #1359, P1.................$90.00

Pennzoil, 1931 Hawkeye Wrecker, #2913, T4 ....$29.00

Pepsi, Santa #4, 1931 International, #5052, T4...............$25.00

Pepsi, 1931 International Tanker, #4113, T4 ....$25.00

Pepsi #6, Trolley Car, #B655, T4 ....$29.00

Phillips 66 (75th Anniversary), 1929 Tanker, JLE, #4030, P1 ....$120.00

Phillips 66 #5, 1925 Kenworth Tanker, #B707, T4 ....$25.00

Prairie Farms Milk, 1923 Chevy, #3558, 1993, M, $25.00.

Pumpkin World, 1950 Chevy Panel Truck, #1315, T4 ....$20.00

Quaker State (#d), 1926 Mack Tanker, #9196, P1 ....$65.00

Radio Flyer Wagons, 1931 Hawkeye Truck, #2128, P1 ....$55.00

Rain-X (#d), 1939 Dodge Air Flow, JLE, #7007, P1 ....$45.00

Red Crown Gasoline #1, 1931 Hawkeye Tanker, #7654, P1.$60.00

Richard Petty #1, 1913 Ford Model T, limited edition, #9573, P1 ....$175.00

Richard Petty #3, 1905 Ford Delivery Van, all bl, #9683, P1 .$300.00

Richard Petty/Petty Enterprises (bl & red), 1931 Tanker, JLE, #4101, P1 ....$30.00

Rogerstown Heritage Days #3, 1932 Ford Panel Truck, #2884, P1 ....$65.00

Ronald McDonald House, 1920 International, JLE, #3083, P1 ....$15.00

Scale Models, 1920 International, JLE, #3012, P1............$15.00

Scott Tissue, 1917 Ford Model T, gold spokes, #9652, P1.$65.00

Sea Coast #2, 1931 Hawkeye, #3736, T4 ....$39.00

Servistar, 1913 Ford Model T, #9036, T4 ....$17.00

Seven Eleven (#d), 1926 Mack Truck, #9155, P1 ....$30.00

Shell (new style), 1931 Hawkeye Tanker, #B276, T4 ......$25.00

Shell #2, 1931 Hawkeye Tanker, JLE, #4018, P1.............$45.00

Sico Independent Oil, 1930 Diamond T Tanker Truck, #9624, P1 ....$70.00

Sico Oil Co, 1925 Kenworth, #9224, T4 ....$25.00

Silver Springs Speedway, 1955 Chevy Cameo Pickup, #3789, T4 ....$29.00

Sinclair Oil, 1926 Mack Tanker, #2119, P1 ....$70.00

Smith Racing, 1938 Chevy Panel Van, #3826, T4 ....$29.00

Southern States #1, 1926 Mack Tanker, #9199, P1 ....$250.00

Soverign Bank, 1923 Chevy Van, #B637, T4 ....$19.00

Spec Cast #2, Roadster, #1527, T4 ....$29.00

Stanolind/Polarine #4, 1932 Ford Panel Truck, #7658, P1..$135.00

Steamtown USA, 1926 Mack Tanker, #9167, P1 ....$85.00

Storey Wrecker, 1931 Hawkeye Wrecker, #9006, T4.......$39.00

Sturgis, 1955 Chevy Cameo Pickup, #3612, T4 ....$69.00

Sturgis '93, 1931 International Freight, #5057, T4 ....$35.00

Sun Oils, 1930 International, JLE, #4037, P1 ....$35.00

Sun Records (#d), 1950 Chevy Panel Truck, #9169, P1 ..$60.00

Sunmaid Raisins, Grumman Step Van, #9576, T4 ....$35.00

Tennessee Homecoming '86, 1913 Ford Model T, #9420, P1 .$150.00

Texaco, 1929 Tanker, JLE, limited edition, #4028, P1...$105.00

Texaco #1, 1913 Ford Model T, #2128, P1 ....$850.00

Texaco #3, 1932 Ford Panel Truck, #9396, T4 ....$300.00

Texaco #5, 1918 Ford Runabout, #9740, T4 ....$90.00

Texaco #8, horse & wagon, #9390, T4 ....$25.00

Texas World Speedway, 1920 Ford, JLE, #3092, P1 ....$65.00

Thunderhills '93, 1905 Ford Delivery Van, #9433, P1 .....$70.00

Tisco, 1926 Mack Truck, #9948, P1 ....$80.00

Tower City, 1950 Chevy Panel Truck, #9012, T4 ....$25.00

True Value #6, 1905 Ford Delivery Van, #9301, T4........$29.00

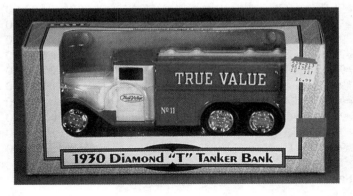

True Value #11, 1930 Diamond T Tanker, 1992, MIB, $20.00.

Trustworthy (sampler), 1918 Ford Runabout, #9302, T4 .$35.00

TRW, 1913 Ford Model T, #2887, P1 ....$95.00

Unique Gardens, 1926 Mack Tanker, #9122, P1 ....$60.00

University of Nebraska, 1913 Ford Model T, #1330, P1...$60.00

US Mail, 1938 Chevy Panel Van, #B447, T4 ....$27.00

USA Baseball, 1905 Ford Delivery Van, #9795, P1 ....$55.00

UTZ Chips #1, 1923 Chevy Van, #9398, T4 ....$19.00

Valvoline, 1932 Ford Panel Truck, #9259, T4 ....$20.00

Very Fine Apple Juice, 1923 Chevy Van, #3073, T4 ....$19.00

Western Auto, 1913 Ford Model T, #1328, P1 ....$90.00

Wheels of Time #3, 1923 Chevy Van, #B674, T4 ....$27.00

Wilwert #2, 1931 International Freight, #5024, T4..........$69.00

Wings of Texaco #1, Airplane, #3801, T4 ....$99.00

Winter Scene, 1920 International, JLE, #3014, P1...........$15.00

Wireless #2, 1950 Chevy Panel Truck, #2953, T4............$10.00

Wonder Bread #1, 1913 Ford Model T, #1660, P1 ....$65.00

FIRST GEAR

Adley, 1960 B-Mack, #19-1299, T4 ....$59.00

American Flyer, 1951 Ford Stake Truck, #19-0118, H8/T4 .$49.00

American Quarter Horses Assn, 1948 Diamond T Tractor-Trailer, #2780, H8 ....$28.00

Anheuser-Busch Eagle Snacks #1, 1951 Ford, #19-1121, H8 .$34.00

Anheuser-Busch Miss Budweiser, 1952 GMC Van, #10-1271, H8 ....$34.00

Arm & Hammer, 1952 GMC Stake, #19-1102, H8/T4....$32.00

Auto Parts, 1951 Ford DGV, #10-0102, T4 ....$29.00

Barq's Root Beer, 1951 Ford Bottle Truck, #19-1080, H8/T4.$32.00

Bitchin' Products, 1951 Ford DGV, #29-1252, T4...........$27.00

Boston Globe, 1951 Ford DGV, #29-1064, T4 ....$79.00

Burkhardt's Beer, 1952 GMC DGV, #19-1069, T4 ....$32.00

Campbell's Express, 1957 International DGV, #19-1217, T4..$33.00

Cape Cod Potato Chips, 1957 International Van, #19-1193, H8 ....$32.00

Central Tractor #1, 1951 Ford Grain Truck, #19-1011, T4.$39.00

Chicago Fire Dept, 1952 GMC, #19-1050, T4 ....$89.00

Citgo, 1957 International Tanker, #29-1248, H8............$59.00

Civil Defense, 1957 International, #19-1172, H8............$65.00

Custom Chrome, 1951 Ford DGV, #18-1161, T4 ....$39.00

Dad's Root Beer, 1951 Ford Bottle Truck, #19-1115, T4 .$33.00

Dean Moving, 1957 International Van, #19-0112, T4.....$45.00

Eagle Snack #2, 1952 GMC DGV, #19-1140, T4............$25.00

Eastwood, 1952 GMC Wrecker, #19-0109, H8/T4, from $60 to $80.00

Eastwood Museum, 1951 Ford DGV, #19-1010, T4 ....$75.00

Eastwood Museum, 1951 Ford Van, #19-0115, H8.........$125.00

Eastwood Museum, 1952 GMC Van, #19-0115, H8.........$49.00

Erector, 1957 International DGV, #19-0111, T4 ....$37.00

Eslinger Beer, 1952 GMC Stake, #19-1244, T4...............$32.00

Esso, 1957 International Tanker, Falstaff, 1952 GMC Van, #20-1245, T4 ....$35.00

First Gear Inc, 1951 Ford Stake Truck, #19-0120, H8......$40.00

GMC Sales & Service, 1952 GMC Wrecker, #10-1282, H8...$32.00

GMC Truck & Coach Division, 1952 GMC Stake Truck, #10-1253, H8 ....$29.00

Goodyear, 1937 Chevy, #15001, H8 ....$15.00

Great Northern, 1957 International DGV, #19-1175, T4.$32.00

Great Southern, 1960 B-Mack, #19-1225, T4 ....$59.00

Gulf, 1957 International, #19-1336, T4............................$35.00

Hershey's, Horse & Wagon, #39-0105, T4 ....$35.00

Hershey's Anniversary, 1960 B-Mack, #19-1288, T4 ....$59.00

Hershey's Antique Auto Club, 1951 Ford Bottle Truck, #19-1110, H8 ....$38.00

Hershey's Chocolate, 1951 Ford Van, #19-1002, H8........$29.00

Hershey's Milk Chocolate, 1957 International DGV, #19-1283, T4..$35.00

Hooker Headers, 1957 International, #10-1284, H8 ....$32.00

Hubbard Special, 1952 GMC, #19-1016, T4 ....$45.00

Indian Motorcycle, 1955 Chevy, #50021, H8..................$75.00

International Harvester, 1957 International F/T, #19-1289, T4 ....$35.00

Iola Car Show, 1940 Ford, #62504, H8 ....$25.00

JC Whitney #1, 1952 GMC DGV, #10-1147, T4............$35.00

Lakeside Dairy, 1952 GMC Van, #10-1216, T4 ....$31.00

Leffler Inc Carlos R #3, 1951 Ford, #28-1213, H8 ....$24.00

Leffler Oil, 1951 Ford Tanker, #28-1213, T4...................$25.00

Levy Moving Van, 1957 International Van, #18-1181, T4.$65.00

Lionel, 1960 B-Mack, #19-0116, T4 ....$175.00

Lionel #2, 1952 GMC DGV, #19-0108, T4....................$37.00

Mack (Eastwood), 1960 B-Mack, #19-0117, T4 ....$125.00

Marx Toys, 1957 International Fire Truck, #19-0113, T4 ..$37.00

Miss Budweiser, 1952 GMC DGV, #10-1271, T $32.00

Mobil Lube, 1952 GMC Tanker, #19-1230, T4................$32.00

Mobilgas, 1951 Ford Tanker, #29-1028, H8 ....$49.00

Model Railroad, 1951 Ford DGV, #19-0121, T4 ....$35.00

Mountain Dew, 1951 Ford Bottle Truck, #19-1075, T4 ...$29.00

Moxie, 1952 GMC Bottle Truck, #19-0119, T4...............$35.00

Nehi Cola, 1951 Ford Bottle Truck, #19-1099, T4...........$29.00

Nitro Cola, 1951 Ford Bottle Truck, #19-0114, T4 ....$35.00

Northern Pacific, 1957 International DGV, #19-1164, T4.$32.00

NY Central, 1957 International DGV, #10-1188, T4 ......$39.00

NY Central Pacemaker, 1960 B-Mack, #19-1095, T4 ......$55.00

NY Foam, 1957 International DGV, #19-1081, T4..........$32.00

Pabst Beer, 1952 GMC Van, #20-1226, T4 ....$35.00

Peach State, 1960 B-Mack, #19-1272, T4......................$65.00

Pepsi, 1951 Ford Bottle Truck, #19-0110, T4 ....$39.00

PIE #1, 1951 Ford DGV, #19-1006, T4 ....$135.00

Radio Flyer, 1960 B-Mack, #10-1346, T4 ....$89.00

RC Cola, 1951 Ford Bottle Truck, #19-1131, T4 ....$30.00

Rem Dove #2, 1951 Ford DGV, #10-1098, T4 ....$30.00

Rem Goose #5, 1952 GMC DGV, #10-1134, T4 ....$30.00

Roadway, 1960 B-Mack, #10-1211, T4 ....$55.00

Rock Island, 1957 International DGV, #19-1241, T4 ......$30.00

Rolling Thunder, 1951 Ford DGV, #28-1141, T4 ....$25.00

Smith & Wesson, 1957 International DGV, #18-1218, T4 .$37.00

Springfield Fire, 1957 International Wrecker, #10-1307, T4.$33.00

Stroh's Beer, 1952 GMC Van, #10-1353, T4...................$35.00

Texaco Pipeline, 1951 Ford State Truck, #19-1237, T4.$369.00

Tow Times #2, 1957 International Wrecker, #18-1297, T4.$49.00

US Mail, 1952 GMC Stake Truck, #19-1103, T4 ....$32.00

USA Bobsled, 1951 Ford DGV, #28-1151, T4 ....$25.00

Wayne Oil Comp, 1951 Ford Tanker, #19-1015, T4........$25.00

West Virginia, 1952 GMC Van, #19-1243, T4 ....$32.00

Winchester, 1957 International DGV, #18-1319, T4 ......$39.00

Winchester, 1960 B-Mack, #18-1320, T4.......................$69.00

Wolf's Head Oil, 1951 Ford DGV, #19-1132, T4 ....$35.00

Yellow Freight, 1960 B-Mack, #10-1293, T4 ....$55.00

Zephyr Gasoline, 1957 International DGV, #19-1166, T4..$32.00

1st Gear, 1951 Ford Half-Rack, #19-0120, T4 ....$37.00

Racing Champions

#0 Fisher/Dick McCabe, Grand Prix, new, #0494, P1 ......$25.00

#1 Goodyear Racing, Lumina, #0318, P1 ....$75.00

#1 Precision Production Racing, T-Bird, new, #2212, P1.$35.00

#2 Dupont/Ricky Craven, Lumina, new, #2258, P1 ....$25.00

#2 Ford Motorsports/Rusty Wallace, T-Bird, new, #2227, P1.$35.00

#3 Goodwrench/Dale Earnhardt, Lumina, new, #0465, P1/J1 ....$35.00

#3 Mom & Pops/Dale Earnhardt, Lumina, #0353, P1.......$35.00

#4 Kodak/Ernie Irvan, Lumina, #0344, P1 ....$35.00

#5 Tide/Ricky Rudd, Lumina, #0336, P1 ....$25.00

#6 Valvoline/Mark Martin, T-Bird, #0334, P1 ....$28.00

#7 Desert Storm/Alan Kulwicki, T-Bird, new, #00478, P1.$35.00

#7 Easter Seals/Jimmy Hensley, T-Bird, #0411, P1 ....$45.00

#7 Hooters/Alan Kulwicki, T-Bird, #00324, P1.............$150.00

#7 Manheim Auctions/Harry Gant, Lumina, new, #2270, P1..$60.00

#7 Morema/Harry Gant, Lumina, #0376, P1.................$45.00

#8 Raybestos/Sterling Marlin, T-Bird, #0337, P1 ....$35.00

#11 Budweiser/Bill Elliott, T-Bird, #0343, P1 ....$45.00

#12 Meinke/Jimmy Spencer, T-Bird, #0359, P1 ....$75.00

#15 Motorcraft/Geoff Bodine, T-Bird, #0338, P1 ....$30.00

#18 Interstate Batteries/Dale Jarrett, Lumina, #0345, P1 .$35.00

#19 Interstate Batteries/Dale Jarrett, Lumina, #2224, P1 .$25.00

#20 Fina/Joe Ruttman, T-Bird, #0330, P1 ....$55.00

#21 Citgo/Morgan Shepard, T-Bird, #0335, P1 ....$30.00

#24 Dupont/Jeff Gordon, Lumina, #0366, P1 ....$45.00

#26 Quaker State/Brett Bodine, T-Bird, #0339, P1 ....$20.00

#27 McDonald's/Hut Stricklin, T-Bird, #0323, P1 ....$35.00

#28 Texaco Box/Davy Allison, T-Bird, #0357, P1...........$75.00

#33 Leo Jackson/Harry Gant, Lumina, #2213, P1...........$35.00

#41 Mac Tools/Ernie Irvan, Lumina, #0452, P1 ....$35.00

#43 STP/Richard Petty, Pontiac, #0346, P1 ....$45.00

#44 STP/Rick Wilson, Grand Prix, #0360, P1 ....$35.00

#51 Racing Champion, Lumina, #0317, P1 ....$85.00

#55 US Air/Ted Musgrave, T-Bird, #0451, P1................$35.00

#93 AC Delco 500, Lumina, #0269, P1 ....$35.00

#93 Budweiser/Dover Downs, Pontiac, #0227, P1 ....$35.00

#93 CMS/Mello-Yellow, Lumina, #0439, P1 ....$30.00

#93 Hooters 500, T-Bird, #0440, P1...............................$35.00

#93 NASCAR Racing, Grand Prix, #0325, P1 ....$45.00

#93 Racing Collectible Collectors Club, Lumina, #0371, P1 .$75.00

#93 Thunder in the Glen, T-Bird, #0237, P1 ....$35.00

#94 Dallas Cowboys, Lumina, #0551, J1 ....$25.00

Spec-Cast

A&W Root Beer #5, 1932 Ford Panel Van, #1553, H8 ...$24.00

AC Delco (The Rock), Kenworth Tractor-Trailer, #0250, P1 ....$30.00

Alabama, 1955 Chevy, #50029, H8 ....$23.00

Allied Van Lines, Biplane, #37506, P1 ....$45.00

Allied Van Lines, 1929 Ford, #2551, H8 ....$20.00

Allis-Chalmers, 1929 Ford, #1015, H8............................$23.00

Allis-Chalmers, 1929 Roadster, #2000, P1......................$20.00

Amoco #2, Airplane, #35001, T4....................................$27.00

Amoco Diesel Fuel, 1929 Ford, #2015, H8 ....$32.00

Amoco Set Regular, 1937 Chevy Tanker, #17501, T4.....$59.00

Amoco/Standard Oil Co #2, Vega Plane, #35001, P1 ......$25.00

Atlanta Speedway's Hooters 500, 1929 Roadster, #0260, P1.$35.00

Bell System, 1931 Ford, #1004, H8 ....$24.00

Brett Bodine/Quakerstate, 1931 Panel, #0308, P1............$20.00

Brickyard 500, F-16 Falcon Jet, #00483, P1 ....$75.00

Buick Motorsports, 1929 Roadster, #1020, P1 ....$35.00

Butterfinger, 1929 Roadster, #1520, P1............................$20.00
California Highway Patrol, 1929 Ford, #2585, H8............$24.00
Campbell's A#3, Biplane, #37503, T4 ....$35.00
Campbell's Soup, 1937 Chevy, #10004, H8......................$22.00
Campbell's Soup, 1955 Chevy, #50013, P1......................$25.00
Charlotte Coca-Cola 600, Biplane, #00267, P1................$75.00
Charlotte Coca-Cola 600, 1955 Chevy Convertible, #0278, H8 ...$49.00
Charlotte Coca-Cola 600, Vega Plane, #00225, J1..........$65.00
Charlotte Coca-Cola 600, 1929 Roadster, #1013, P1.....$120.00
Charlotte/Hooters 500, Biplane, #0253, P1 ....$75.00
Chevrolet, KY, 1937 Chevy Pickup, #12506, H8 ....$19.00
Chevrolet Demo Car, 1937 Chevy, #10010, H8................$25.00
Chevrolet Expo A#1, Airplane, #35011, T4....................$29.00
Chevrolet Factory Service, 1937 Chevy Delivery, #15011, from
$19 to $25.00
Chevrolet Fire Dept, 1937 Chevy, #10006, H8 ....$19.00
Chevrolet Motor Co, 1955 Chevy, #50025, H8 ....$25.00
Chevrolet Parts & Service, 1955 Chevy Sedan, #50020, H8 .$22.00
Chevrolet-GM Parts #2, 1955 Chevy Cameo Pickup, #B071,
H8..$32.00
Chicago Auto Show, 1937 Roadster, #10017, P1 ....$25.00
Chicago 10th Anniv Bike Show, 1937 Chevy, #12504, H8.$34.00
Citgo, Airplane, #37502, T4 ....$29.00
Citgo, Vega Plane, #35012, from $25 to $45.00
Citgo, 1916 Studebaker, #27502, H8 ....$28.00
Citgo, 1929 Ford, #2514, H8 ....$19.00
Citgo/Wood Bros Racing, 1929 Ford, #0309, H8............$22.00
Clark Oil, 1929 Roadster, #1544, P1................................$20.00
Classic Auto, 1955 Chevy Convertible, #55002, H8........$22.00
Classic Auto Pickup, 1932 Ford, blk, #62503, H8 ....$25.00
Classic Auto Pickup, 1937 Chevy, red, #12516, H8.........$25.00
Classic Motorbooks, 1955 Chevy, #50032, H8 ....$28.00
Classic Street Rods, 1929 Ford, #2578, H8 ....$25.00
Coca-Cola 600, Kenworth Tractor-Trailer, #30001, H8 ..$44.00
Coca-Cola 600, 1929 Ford, #2711, H8..............................$75.00
Collectors Edition '92, 1929 Roadster, #1510, P1............$18.00
Conoco Oil, 1929 Ford, #2002, H8 ....$29.00
Dale Earnhardt, F-16 Falcon Jet, #00471, P1 ....$75.00
Darlington (w/flags), 1929 Panel, #2707, P1....................$45.00
Daytona Motorcycle, 1940 Ford, #6033, T4 ....$32.00
Daytona Speedway, 1931 Panel, #0209, P1......................$50.00
Daytona 500 STP, 1929 Roadster, #0231, P1 ....$45.00
Dead Stock/Mo's Mink Ranch, 1931 Panel, #25250, P1 ..$30.00
Dover Downs Bud 500, Kenworth Tractor-Trailer, #0230,
H8 ....$19.00
Drag Specialties #3, 1937 Chevy, #12510, H8..................$34.00
EAA #1 Winnie Mae, Vega Plane, #1161, H8 ....$29.00
EAA #2 Pioneer Airport, 1916 Studebaker Pickup, #1174,
H8 ....$32.00
Eastwood Auto Club, 1931 Ford Panel, #1735, P1 ....$65.00
Eastwood Auto Club #2, 1931 Ford Wrecker, #1303, H8..$19.00
Eastwood Auto Club #3, 1937 Chevy Panel Truck, #1162,
H8..$19.00
Eastwood Co #10, 1929 Ford, #1928, H8/T4, from $22 to.$25.00
Eastwood Co #14, 1937 Chevy, #1993, H8........................$34.00
Eastwood Co #2, Vega Plane, #35000, P1........................$30.00
Eastwood Co UK #1, 1929 Ford, #1992, H8......................$49.00
Eastwood Co UK #3, 1931 Ford, #1172, H8 ....$32.00

Exxon, Vega Plane, #40015, P1..$45.00
Fairway Foods, 1931 Panel, #2716, P1............................$18.00
Fina Oil, 1929 Ford Tanker, #2004, H8 ....$19.00
Ford, 1929 Ford, #1551, H8..$17.00
Ford Motorsports, Biplane, #00460, P1 ....$65.00
Ford Sales & Service, 1940 Ford, #67503, H8 ....$22.00
George Jones (The Possum), 1955 Chevy, #50023, P1.....$25.00
Gilmore, Airplane, #40022, T4..$29.00
Gulf #1, Vega Plane, #35006, from $27 to $35.00
Hamm's Beer, 1916 Studebaker, #27504, H8....................$22.00
Hamm's Beer, 1929 Ford Panel, #1014, J1........................$25.00
Harley-Davidson, 1929 Roadster, #1516, P1....................$85.00
Harley-Davidson, 1933 Motorcycle w/sidecar, #99199, H8.$85.00
Harley-Davidson #1, Vega Plane, #0820, H8 ....$295.00
Harry Gant #33, 1929 Ford, #0228, H8 ....$44.00
Heinz Pickle, 1929 Stake Truck, #1018, J1......................$20.00
Heinz 57, 1916 Studebaker, #22502, H8..........................$22.00
Hesston-Louisville Toy Show, 1929 Panel, #0161, P1......$20.00
Hooters Atlanta 500, 1929 Ford Panel, #2709, from $55 to.$75.00
Hooters/Richard Petty, Kenworth Tractor-Trailer, #0316,
P1 ....$80.00
House of Color, 1937 Chevy, #15013, H8 ....$29.00
Hurst Performance #6, 1931 Panel, #1164, P1..................$35.00
Indian A#2, Airplane, #40017, T4....................................$25.00
Indian Ace Motorcycle, 1929 Ford, #1059, H8 ....$35.00
Iowa Hawkeyes, 1929 Roadster, #1542, P1......................$25.00
Iowa State University, 1937 Roadster, #10012, P1..........$25.00
J&P Cycles #1, 1938 Chevy, #3834, H8............................$35.00
Jeff Gordon/Dupont, Airplane, #00377, T4......................$29.00
Jeff Gordon/Dupont, 1955 Chevy, #0027, J1....................$25.00
John Deere #4 '94, Biplane, #37516, J1............................$35.00
Kyle Petty #42, Biplane, #0448, J1....................................$55.00
Laconia Motorcycle Week, 1929 Ford Panel, #2553, H8 .$44.00
Liberty Classics Tanker, 1929 Kenworth, #2000, J1 ....$35.00
Louisville Slugger, 1929 Ford Panel, #1036, J1................$20.00
Magnolia Petroleum, 1935 Sterling, #4022, T4 ....$29.00
Massey Harris, 1929 Ford Panel, #1016, J1......................$20.00
Mello Yello, 1929 Ford Panel, #2710, J1..........................$45.00
Mid Atlantic Air Museum #2, Vintage Plane, #130500, H8 .$24.00
Minneapolis Moline Farm Equipment, Kenworth Tractor-
Trailer, #3006, J1..$20.00
Mobilgas A#1, Airplane, #35013, T4................................$27.00
Motorcraft, 1931 Panel, #00307, J1..................................$35.00
Nabisco, 1929 Ford Panel, #2508, J1................................$20.00
NASCAR Racing '93, Kenworth Tractor-Trailer, #00313,
J1..$30.00
NTPA, 1929 Roadster, #1524, J1......................................$25.00
Oliver, 1931 Panel, #2502, J1..$20.00
Olympia Beer, 1929 Ford, #3528, H8................................$19.00
Olympia Beer, Kenworth Tractor-Trailer, #30020, J1 ......$20.00
One Hot Night-Charlotte Speedway, 1931 Panel, #0224, J1.$40.00
Oreo Cookies, 1916 Studebaker, #25013, H8....................$21.00
Pabst Blue Ribbon, 1929 Roadster, #1512, J1 ....$25.00
Penzoil, Airplane, #35014, T4..$25.00
Pepsi, Lockheed Airplane, #46001, T4 ....$32.00
Pepsi, 1916 Studebaker Panel, #25015, T4......................$25.00
Pepsi, 1940 Ford, #67509, T4..$27.00
Pepsi, 1955 Chevy, #50012, J1..$25.00

Pepsi, 1955 Chevy Convertible, #55016, T4 ....$25.00
Piggly Wiggly Racing, Kenworth Tractor-Trailer, #00303, J1 ....$30.00
Police Dept #5, 1929 Ford Panel, #2507, J1 ....$25.00
Posies, 1931 Panel, #1993, J1 ....$25.00
Red Crown, Wrecker, #2036, J1 ....$25.00
Richard Petty #1, Airplane, #35003, T4 ....$69.00
Rockingham Speedway (The Rock), 1931 Panel, #0210, J1..$45.00
Route 66, 1929 Roadster, #1517, T4 ....$29.00
Royal Mail, 1931 Panel, #9002, J1 ....$25.00
Shell, Ford Model A Tanker, #02039, T4 ....$25.00
Shell (Gold), 1930 Kenworth, #2007, J1 ....$200.00
Shell A#2, Airplane, #35016, T4 ....$27.00
Sheriff, 1955 Chevy, #50019, J1 ....$25.00
Signal Gas, Airplane, #35018, T4 ....$19.00
Sonic Drive-In, 1931 Panel, #2582, J1 ....$25.00
Spec Cast, 1929 Panel, (2nd bank made), #1000, J1 ....$45.00
Stanavo Eagle, Airplane, #35050, T4 ....$29.00
Sunmaid Raisins, 1937 Chevy, #12505, J1 ....$20.00
Sunoco A#1, Airplane, T4 ....$27.00

Sunsweet, 1929 Ford, 75th Anniversary Edition, #1012, 1992, M, $35.00.

Sweet 'n Low, 1929 Roadster, #1554, J1 ....$25.00
Texaco, 1929 Ford, #2008, H8 ....$39.00
Total Performance, 1931 Panel, #1169, J1 ....$20.00
US Army Ambulance, 1937 Ambulance, #15018, J1 ....$25.00
Vic Edelbrock Sr, 1931 Roadster, #00236, J1 ....$35.00
Wix Filters, 1955 Chevy, #50001, J1 ....$35.00
Wood Brothers Racing, Kenworth Tractor-Trailer, #00311, J1 ....$35.00
Wood Brothers/Citgo, 1931 Roadster, #0309, J1 ....$25.00
Wrigley's Gum, Airplane, #40000, T4 ....$22.00

Dinky

Dinky diecasts were made by Meccano (Britain) as early as 1933, but high on the list of many of today's collectors are those from the decades of the fifties and sixties. They made commercial vehicles, firefighting equipment, farm toys, and heavy equipment as well as classic cars that were the epitome of high style, such as the #157 Jaguar XK120, produced from the mid-fifties

through the early sixties. Some Dinkys were made in France; since 1979 no toys have been produced in Great Britain. Values are for examples mint and in the original packaging unless noted otherwise.

Advisor: Irwin Stern (S3).
See also Soldiers.

#100, Lady Penelope's Fab 1, luminous pk $400.00
#100, Lady Penelope's Fab 1, pk $250.00
#101, Sunbeam Alpine $200.00
#101, Thunderbird II & IV, gr $225.00
#101, Thunderbird II & IV, metallic dk gr $350.00
#102, Joe's Car $170.00

#102, MG Midget, $300.00.

#103, Austin Healey 100 ....$250.00
#103, Spectrum Patrol Car $150.00
#104, Aston Martin DB3S $250.00
#104, Spectrum Pursuit Car $200.00
#105, Maximum Security Vehicle $150.00
#105, Triumph TR2 ....$250.00
#106, Austin Atlantic, bl or blk $200.00
#106, Austin Atlantic, pk $350.00
#106, Prisoner Mini Moke $300.00
#106, Thunderbird II & IV $150.00
#107, Stripey, The Magi Mini $400.00
#107, Sunbeam Alpine $150.00
#108, MG Midget $200.00
#108, Sam's Car, gold, red or bl $160.00
#108, Sam's Car, silver $120.00
#109, Austin Healey 100 ....$160.00
#109, Gabriel Model T Ford $150.00
#110, Aston Martin DB3S $150.00
#110, Aston Martin DB5 ....$125.00
#111, Cinderella's Coach $50.00
#111, Triumph TR2 ....$160.00
#112, Austin Healey Sprite $125.00
#112, Purdey's Triumph TR7 ....$60.00
#113, MGB $100.00
#114, Triumph Spitfire, gray, gold or red $125.00
#114, Triumph Spitfire, purple $170.00
#115, Plymouth Fury $125.00
#115, UB Taxi $70.00
#116, Volvo 1800S $85.00
#117, Four Berth Caravan $50.00

#118, Tow-Away Glider Set.............................$300.00
#120, Happy Cab $70.00
#120, Jaguar E-Type.....................................$100.00
#121, Goodwood Racing Gift Set $2,000.00
#122, Touring Gift Set.............................$2,000.00
#122, Volvo 265 Estate Car..........................$50.00
#123, Mayfair Gift Set.............................$3,000.00
#123, Princess 2200 HL.................................$50.00
#124, Holiday Gift Set.............................$1,000.00
#124, Rolls Royce Phantom V........................$90.00
#125, Fun A'Hoy Set....................................$300.00
#126, Motor Show Set $2,000.00
#127, Rolls Royce Silver Cloud III................$160.00
#128, Mercedes Benz 600..............................$80.00
#129, MG Midget..$500.00
#129, VW 1200 Sedan...................................$80.00
#130, Ford Consul Corsair...........................$100.00
#131, Jaguar E-Type 2+2..............................$160.00

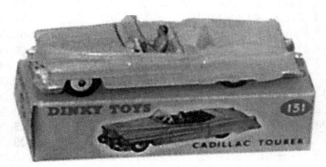

#131, Cadillac El Dorado, $200.00.

#132, Ford 40-RV $60.00
#132, Packard Convertible...........................$200.00
#133, Cunningham C-5R..............................$130.00
#133, Ford Cortina.......................................$80.00
#134, Triumph Vitesse.................................$100.00
#135, Triumph 2000.....................................$100.00
#136, Vauxhall Viva......................................$60.00
#137, Plymouth Fury....................................$150.00
#138, Hillman Imp..$65.00
#139, Ford Cortina.......................................$90.00
#139a, Ford Fordor Sedan, cream & red, or pk & bl.......$300.00
#139a, Ford Fordor Sedan, solid colors.........$160.00
#139am, US Army Staff Car $300.00
#139b, Hudson Commodore Sedan................$200.00
#140, Morris 1100...$60.00
#141, Vauxhall Victor....................................$60.00
#142, Jaguar Mark 10....................................$70.00
#143, Ford Capri...$100.00
#144, VW 1500...$60.00
#145, Singer Vogue.......................................$70.00
#146, Daimler V8...$100.00
#147, Cadillac 62..$100.00
#148, Ford Fairlane, gr.................................$120.00
#148, Ford Fairlane, metallic gr....................$220.00
#149, Citroen Dyane......................................$50.00
#149, Sports Cars Gift Set.........................$1,500.00

#150, Roll Royce Silver Wraith $100.00
#150, Royal Tank Corps Personnel................$300.00
#151, Royal Tank Corps Med Tank Set...........$600.00
#151, Vauxhall Victor 101 ....$100.00
#151a, Med Tank...$200.00
#151b, Six-Wheeled Covered Wagon..............$130.00
#151c, Cooker Trailer....................................$65.00
#151d, Water Tank Trailer..............................$75.00
#152, Rolls Royce Phantom V........................$90.00
#152, Royal Tank Corps Light Tank Set..........$600.00
#152a, Light Tank.......................................$160.00
#152b, Reconnaissance Car...........................$175.00
#152c, Austin 7 Car.....................................$200.00
#153, Aston Martin......................................$100.00
#153a, Jeep..$125.00
#154, Ford Taunus 17m..................................$50.00
#155, Ford Anglia..$150.00
#156, Mechanized Army Set.......................$7,000.00
#156, Rover 75, dual colors..........................$200.00
#156, Rover 75, solid colors.........................$150.00
#156, Saab 96..$80.00
#157, BMW 2000 Tilux..................................$100.00

#157, Jaguar XK120, red or yellow, $200.00.

#157, Jaguar XK120, wht or dual colors $350.00
#158, Riley...$160.00
#158, Rolls Royce Silver Shadow...................$100.00
#159, Ford Cortina MK II.............................$100.00
#159, Morris Oxford, dual colors...................$300.00
#159, Morris Oxford, solid colors..................$170.00
#160, Austin A30...$160.00
#160, Mercedes Benz 250 SE..........................$50.00
#160, Royal Artillery Personnel....................$300.00
#161, Austin Somerset, dual colors................$300.00
#161, Austin Somerset, solid colors...............$150.00
#161, Ford Mustang.......................................$70.00
#161, Mobile Antiaircraft Unit $1,000.00
#161a, Lorry w/Searchlight...........................$400.00
#161b, Antiaircraft Gun on Trailer $150.00
#162, Ford Zephyr.......................................$150.00
#162, Triumph 1300 ....$75.00
#162a, Light Dragon Tractor.........................$150.00
#162b, Trailer..$25.00
#162c, 18-Pounder Gun..................................$50.00
#163, Bristol 450 Coupe $80.00

#163, VW 1600 TL, metallic bl $150.00
#163, VW 1600 TL, red..$75.00
#164, Ford Zodiac MKIV, bronze $200.00
#164, Ford Zodiac MKIV, silver $100.00
#164, Vauxhall Cresta $150.00
#165, Ford Capri $100.00
#165, Humber Hawk $150.00
#166, Renault R16..$60.00
#166, Sunbeam Rapier $150.00
#167, AC Aceca, all cream $300.00
#167, AC Aceca, dual colors $160.00
#168, Ford Escort $80.00
#168, Singer Gazelle $160.00
#169, Ford Corsair..$80.00
#169, Studebaker Golden Hawk $170.00
#170, Ford Fordor, dual colors $300.00
#170, Lincoln Continental...$120.00
#170m, Ford Fordor US Army Staff Car $300.00
#171, Austin 1800...$90.00

#171, Hudson Commodore, dual colors, $350.00.

#172, Fiat 2300 Station Wagon..................................$80.00
#172, Studebaker Land Cruiser, dual colors...................$300.00
#172, Studebaker Land Cruiser, solid colors $160.00
#173, Nash Rambler $75.00
#173, Pontiac Parisienne $75.00
#174, Hudson Hornet $150.00
#174, Mercury Cougar $70.00
#175, Cadillac El Dorado $90.00
#175, Hillman Minx $160.00
#176, Austin A105, cream or gray $160.00
#176, Austin A105, cream w/bl roof, or gray w/red roof.$250.00
#176, NSU R80, metallic bl $180.00
#176, NSU R80, metallic red $65.00
#177, Opel Kapitan...$75.00
#178, Mini Clubman..$60.00
#178, Plymouth Plaza, bl w/wht roof $250.00
#178, Plymouth Plaza, pk, gr or 2-tone bl $170.00
#179, Opel Commodore...$70.00
#179, Studebaker President $160.00
#180, Packard Clipper $160.00
#180, Rover 3500 Sedan $25.00
#182, Porsche 356A Coupe, cream, red or bl..............$170.00
#182, Porsche 356A Coupe, dual colors.....................$300.00
#183, Fiat 600 ....$100.00

#183, Morris Mini Minor..$120.00
#184, Volvo 122S, red $100.00
#184, Volvo 122S, wht $375.00
#185, Alpha Romeo 1900..$125.00
#186, Mercedes Benz 220...$65.00
#187, De Tomaso Mangusta 5000 ....$65.00
#187, VW Karmann-Ghia Coupe $120.00
#188, Ford Berth Caravan $60.00
#188, Jensen FF..$75.00
#189, Lamborghini Marzal..$65.00
#189, Triumph Herald $125.00
#190, Caravan $60.00
#191, Dodge Royal Sedan, cream w/bl flash $260.00
#191, Dodge Royal Sedan, cream w/brn flash or gr w/blk flash $170.00
#192, Desoto Fireflite $160.00
#192, Range Rover..$50.00
#193, Rambler Station Wagon $75.00
#194, Bentley S Coupe $130.00
#195, Jaguar 3.4 Litre MKII $150.00
#195, Range Rover Fire Chief $60.00
#196, Holden Special Sedan $100.00
#197, Morris Mini Traveller, dk gr & brn.....................$400.00
#197, Morris Mini Traveller, lime gr...........................$300.00
#197, Morris Mini Traveller, wht & brn or med gr & brn.$100.00
#198, Austin Countryman, orange..............................$250.00
#198, Rolls Royce Phantom V $125.00
#199, Austin Countryman, bl......................................$100.00
#200, Matra 630..$50.00
#201, Plymouth Stock Car..$85.00
#201, Racing Car Set..$800.00
#202, Customized Land Rover....................................$50.00
#202, Fiat Abarth 2000...$50.00
#203, Customized Range Rover..................................$40.00
#204, Ferrari $40.00
#205, Lotus Cortina..$125.00
#205, Talbot Lago, in bubble pack $300.00
#206, Customized Corvette Stingray...........................$50.00
#206, Maserati, in bubble pack $360.00
#207, Alfa Romeo, in bubble pack $300.00
#207, Triumph TR7..$40.00
#208, Cooper-Bristol, in bubble pack.........................$300.00
#208, VW Porsche 914 ....$50.00
#209, Ferrari, in bubble pack $300.00
#210, Alfa Romeo 33...$50.00
#210, Vanwall, in bubble pack $200.00
#211, Triumph TR7 ....$60.00
#212, Ford Cortina Rally $135.00
#213, Ford Capri $75.00
#214, Hillman Imp Rally $90.00
#215, Ford GT Racing Car $70.00
#216, Ferrari Dino $50.00
#217, Alfa Romeo Scarabeo $40.00
#218, Lotus Europa $65.00
#219, Jaguar XJS Coupe $65.00
#220, Ferrari P5 ....$50.00
#221, Corvette Stingray..$40.00
#222, Hesketh Racing Car, dk bl................................$40.00

#222, Hesketh Racing Car, Olympus Camera $100.00
#223, McLaren M8A Can-Am......................................$40.00
#224, Mercedes Benz C111...$40.00
#225, Lotus Formula I Racer.......................................$40.00
#226, Ferrari 312/B2 ....$40.00
#227, Beach Buggy $40.00
#228, Super Sprinter $40.00
#236, Connaught Racer $125.00
#237, Mercedes Benz Racer $140.00
#238, Jaguar Type-D Racer..$125.00
#239, Vanwall Racer..$100.00
#240, Cooper Racer $50.00
#240, Dinky Way Gift Set $100.00
#241, Lotus Racer $45.00
#241, Silver Jubilee Taxi $50.00
#242, Ferrari Racer $50.00
#243, BRM Racer...$50.00
#243, Volvo Police Racer...$40.00
#244, Plymouth Police Racer.......................................$40.00
#245, Superfast Gift Set...$200.00
#246, International GT Gift Set $200.00
#249, Racing Car Gift Set..$1,500.00
#249, Racing Car Gift Set, bubble pack $2,000.00
#250, Mini Coopers Police Car $60.00
#251, USA Police Car, Pontiac....................................$75.00
#252, RCMP Car, Pontiac...$75.00
#254, Police Range Rover..$50.00
#255, Ford Zodiac Police Car $100.00
#255, Mersey Tunnel Police Van..................................$100.00
#255, Police Mini Clubman..$50.00
#256, Humber Hawk Police Car...................................$140.00
#257, Nash Rambler Canadian Fire Chief Car $100.00
#258, USA Police Car, Cadillac, De Soto, Dodge or Ford .$130.00
#259, Bedford Fire Engine $130.00
#260, Royal Mail Van..$150.00
#260, VW Deutsche Bundepost $170.00
#261, Ford Taunus Polizei $250.00
#261, Telephone Service Van $170.00
#262, VW Swiss Post PTT Car, casting #129 ....$100.00
#262, VW Swiss Post PTT Car, casting #181 ....$500.00
#263, Airport Fire Rescue Tender $70.00
#263, Superior Criterion Ambulance.............................$100.00
#264, RCMP Patrol Car, Cadillac................................$175.00
#264, RCMP Patrol Car, Fairlane $150.00
#265, Plymouth Taxi...$170.00
#266, ERF Fire Tender...$75.00
#266, ERF Fire Tender, Falck $100.00
#266, Plymouth Taxi, Metro Cab $200.00
#267, Paramedic Truck..$50.00
#267, Superior Cadillac Ambulance $100.00
#268, Range Rover Ambulance.....................................$40.00
#268, Renault Dauphine Mini Cab................................$150.00
#269, Jaguar Motorway Police Car $150.00
#269, Police Accident Unit...$50.00
#270, AA Motorcycle Patrol $100.00
#270, Ford Panda Police Car $70.00
#271, Ford Transit Fire, Appliance $100.00
#271, Ford Transit Fire, Falck $150.00

#271, TS Motorcycle Patrol $150.00
#272, ANNB Motorcycle Patrol $300.00
#272, Police Accident Unit...$60.00
#273, RAC Patrol Mini Van...$200.00
#274, AA Patrol Mini Van...$200.00
#274, Ford Transit Ambulance......................................$50.00
#274, Mini Van, Joseph Mason Paints $750.00
#275, Brink's Armoured Car, no bullion $75.00
#275, Brink's Armoured Car, w/gold bullion.................$200.00
#275, Brink's Armoured Car, w/Mexican bullion........$1,000.00
#276, Airport Fire Tender $85.00
#276, Ford Transit Ambulance......................................$70.00
#277, Police Land Rover..$40.00
#277, Superior Criterion Ambulance.............................$100.00
#278, Plymouth Yellow Cab $40.00
#278, Vauxhall Victor Ambulance $100.00
#279, Aveling Barford Diesel Roller..............................$60.00
#280, Midland Mobile Bank...$125.00
#281, Fiat 2300 Pathe News Camera Car $160.00
#281, Military Hovercraft $40.00
#282, Austin 1800 Taxi $85.00
#282, Land Rover Fire, Appliance.................................$50.00
#282, Land Rover Fire, Falck $80.00
#283, BOAC Coach $150.00
#283, Single-Decker Bus..$60.00
#284, London Austin Taxi $60.00
#285, Merryweather Fire Engine $75.00
#285, Merryweather Fire Engine, Falck.........................$150.00
#286, Ford Transit Fire, Appliance $80.00
#286, Ford Transit Fire, Appliance, Falck......................$160.00
#286, Police Accident Unit...$80.00
#288, Superior Cadillac Ambulance $80.00
#288, Superior Cadillac Ambulance, Falck....................$150.00

#289, Routemaster Bus, Esso, red, $50.00.

#289, Routemaster Bus, Esso, purple $750.00
#289, Routemaster Bus, Festival of London Stores $200.00
#289, Routemaster Bus, Madame Tussaud's...................$150.00
#289, Routemaster Bus, Silver Jubilee............................$40.00
#289, Routemaster Bus, Tern Shirts or Schweppes.........$150.00

#290, SRN-6 Hovercraft...$40.00
#291, Atlantean City Bus..$70.00
#293, Swiss Postal Bus $50.00
#294, Police Vehicle Gift Set...................................$200.00
#295, Atlantean Bus...$70.00
#296, Duple Luxury Coach.......................................$40.00
#297, Police Vehicles Gift Set $100.00
#297, Silver Jubilee Bus, National or Woolworth............$40.00
#298, Emergency Services Gift Set.....................$1,000.00
#299, Crash Squad Gift Set......................................$70.00
#299, Motorway Services Gift Set $1,600.00
#299, Post Office Services Gift Set $650.00
#300, London Scene Gift Set...................................$75.00
#302, Emergency Squad Gift Set..........................$100.00
#303, Commando Gift Set.......................................$120.00
#304, Fire Rescue Gift Set.......................................$120.00
#305, David Brown Tractor....................................$100.00
#308, Leyland 384 Tractor.....................................$100.00
#309, Star Trek Gift Set...$150.00
#319, Week's Tipping Farm Trailer..........................$40.00
#320, Halesowen Harvest Trailer $50.00
#320, Massey-Harris Manure Spreader...................$50.00
#322, Disc Harrow...$50.00
#323, Triple Gang Mower $50.00
#324, Hay Rake..$50.00
#325, David Brown Tractor & Harrow $150.00
#340, Land Rover $100.00
#341, Land Rover Trailer..$40.00
#342, Austin Mini Moke...$70.00
#342, Moto-Cart..$50.00
#344, Estate Car...$100.00
#344, Land Rover Pickup..$40.00
#350, Tony's Mini Moke..$130.00
#351, UFO Intersceptor...$75.00
#352, Ed Straker's Car, red $75.00
#352, Ed Straker's Car, yel or gold-plated.........$125.00
#353, Shado 2 Mobile...$80.00
#354, Pink Panther..$50.00
#355, Lunar Roving Vehicle......................................$55.00
#357, Klingon Battle Cruiser....................................$65.00
#358, USS Enterprise..$60.00
#359, Eagle Transporter..$65.00
#360, Eagle Freighter..$65.00
#361, Galactic War Chariot.......................................$55.00
#362, Trident Star Fighter...$55.00
#363, Cosmic Zygon Patroller, for Marks & Spencer........$60.00
#364, NASA Space Shuttle, w/booster..................$100.00
#366, NASA Space Shuttle, w/no booster...............$50.00
#367, Space Battle Cruiser..$80.00
#368, Zygon Marauder..$50.00
#370, Dragster Set...$70.00
#371, USS Enterprise, sm version $50.00
#372, Klingon Battle Cruiser, sm version...............$50.00
#380, Convoy Skip Truck..$20.00
#381, Convoy Farm Truck...$20.00
#382, Convoy Dumper...$20.00
#382, Wheelbarrow..$25.00
#383, Convoy NCL Truck...$30.00

#384, Convoy Fire Rescue Truck $25.00
#384, Grass Cutter..$25.00
#385, Convoy Royal Mail Truck...............................$30.00
#385, Sack Truck...$25.00
#386, Lawn Mower..$125.00
#390, Customized Transit Van..................................$50.00
#398, Farm Equipment Gift Set...........................$2,000.00
#399, Farm Tractor & Trailer Set..........................$200.00
#400, BEV Electric Truck..$50.00
#401, Coventry-Climax Fork Lift, orange $50.00
#401, Coventry-Climax Fork Lift, red......................$500.00
#402, Bedford Coca-Cola Lorry...............................$220.00
#404, Conveyancer Fork Lift.....................................$40.00
#405, Universal Jeep..$50.00
#406, Commer Articulated Truck............................$160.00
#407, Ford Transit, Kenwood or Hertz..................$120.00
#408, Big Bedford Lorry, bl & yel or bl & orange..........$400.00
#408, Big Bedford Lorry, maroon & fawn..............$160.00
#408, Big Bedford Lorry, pk & cream $2,000.00
#409, Bedford Articulated Lorry $130.00
#410, Bedford Van, Danish Post or Simpsons.............$100.00
#410, Bedford Van, MJ Hire, Marley or Collectors Gazette .$50.00
#410, Bedford Van, Royal Mail.................................$25.00
#411, Bedford Truck..$120.00
#412, Austin Wagon...$500.00
#412, Bedford Van AA...$40.00
#413, Austin Covered Wagon, dk bl & lt bl or red & tan .$650.00
#413, Austin Covered Wagon, maroon & cream or med bl & light bl $200.00
#413, Austin Covered Wagon, red & gray or bl & cream .$450.00
#414, Dodge Tipper, med bl or other colors.............$100.00
#414, Dodge Tipper, royal bl.....................................$200.00
#415, Mechanical Horse & Wagon..........................$200.00
#416, Ford Transit Van..$50.00
#416, Ford Transit Van, 1,000,000 Transits.............$200.00
#417, Ford Transit Van..$50.00
#417, Leyland Comet Lorry......................................$150.00
#418, Leyland Comet Lorry......................................$175.00
#419, Leyland Comet Cement Lorry........................$200.00
#420, Leyland Forward Control Lorry......................$100.00
#421, Hindle-Smart Electric Lorry...........................$100.00
#422, Thames Flat Truck, bright gr..........................$200.00
#422, Thames Flat Truck, dk gr or red.....................$100.00
#424, Commer Articulated Truck.............................$250.00

#425, Bedford TK Coal Lorry, $200.00.

#428, Trailer, lg	$40.00
#429, Trailer	$40.00
#430, Commer Breakdown Lorry	$1,000.00
#430, Johnson Dumper	$40.00
#431, Guy 4-Ton Lorry	$600.00
#432, Foden Tipper	$50.00
#432, Guy Warrior Flat Truck	$500.00
#433, Guy Flat Truck w/Tailboard	$350.00
#434, Bedford Crash Truck	$100.00
#435, Bedford TK Tipper, gray or yel cab	$100.00
#435, Bedford TK Tipper, wht/silver/bl	$250.00
#436, Atlas COPCO Compressor Lorry	$60.00
#437, Muir Hill Loader	$40.00
#438, Ford D 800 Tipper, opening doors	$50.00
#439, Ford D 800 Snow Plough & Tipper	$75.00
#440, Petrol Tanker, Mobilgas	$175.00
#441, Pertol Tanker, Castrol	$175.00
#442, Land Rover Breakdown Crane	$40.00
#442, Land Rover Breakdown Crane, Falck	$60.00
#442, Petrol Tanker, Esso	$175.00
#443, Petrol Tanker, National Benzole	$200.00
#448, Chevrolet El Camino w/Trailers	$350.00
#449, Chevrolet El Camino Pickup	$100.00
#449, Johnston Road Sweeper	$70.00
#450, Bedford TK Box Van, Castrol	$200.00
#450, Trojan Van, Esso	$175.00
#451, Johnston Road Sweeper, opening doors	$70.00
#451, Trojan Van, Dunlop	$175.00
#452, Trojan Van, Chivers	$175.00
#453, Trojan Van, Oxo	$300.00
#454, Trojan Van, Cydrax	$175.00
#455, Trojan Van, Brooke Bond Tea	$175.00
#465, Morris Van, Capstan	$300.00
#470, Austin Van, Shell-BP	$200.00
#471, Austin Van, Nestles	$200.00
#472, Austin Van, Raleigh Cycles	$200.00
#475, Ford Model T	$75.00
#476, Morris Oxford	$75.00
#477, Parsleys Car	$125.00
#480, Bedford Van, Kodak	$160.00
#481, Bedford Van, Ovaltine	$160.00
#482, Bedford Van, Dinky Toys	$160.00
#485, Ford Model T w/Santa Claus	$175.00
#486, Morris Oxford, Dinky Beats	$175.00
#490, Electric Dairy Van, Express Dairy	$100.00
#491, Electric Dairy Van, NCB or Job Dairies	$150.00
#492, Electric Mini Van	$325.00
#492, Loudspeaker Van	$100.00
#501, Foden Diesel 8 Wheel, 1st cab	$1,000.00
#501, Foden Diesel 8 Wheel, 2nd cab	$600.00
#502, Foden Flat Truck, 1st or 2nd cab	$1,000.00
#503, Foden Flat Truck, 1st cab	$1,200.00
#503, Foden Flat Truck, 2nd cab, bl & orange	$400.00
#503, Foden Flat Truck, 2nd cab, bl & yel	$1,000.00
#503, Foden Flat Truck, 2nd cab, 2-tone gr	$2,500.00
#504, Foden Tanker, red	$800.00
#504, Foden Tanker, 1st cab, 2-tone bl	$450.00
#504, Foden Tanker, 2nd cab, red	$600.00

#504, Foden Tanker, 2nd cab, 2-tone bl	$3,500.00
#505, Foden Flat Truck w/Chains, 1st cab	$2,000.00
#505, Foden Flat Truck w/Chains, 2nd cab	$400.00
#511, Guy 4-ton Lorry, 2-ton bl	$350.00
#511, Guy 4-ton Lorry, red, gr or brn	$900.00
#512, Guy Flat Truck, bl & red	$400.00
#512, Guy Flat Truck, other colors	$750.00
#513, Guy Flat Truck w/Tailboard	$400.00
#514, Guy Van, Lyons	$2,000.00
#514, Guy Van, Slumberland	$600.00
#514, Guy Van, Spratt's	$600.00
#514, Guy Van, Weetabix	$2,200.00
#521, Bedford Articulated Lorry	$200.00
#522, Big Bedford Lorry	$175.00

#531, Leyland Comet Lorry, blue and brown, $500.00.

#531, Leyland Comet Lorry, other colors	$300.00
#532, Bedford Comet Lorry w/Tailboard	$300.00
#533, Leyland Cement Wagon	$200.00
#551, Trailer	$60.00
#555, Fire Engine, w/extending ladder	$100.00
#561, Blaw-Knox Bulldozer	$100.00
#561, Blaw-Knox Bulldozer, plastic	$500.00
#562, Muir-Hill Dumper	$40.00
#564, Elevator Loader	$100.00
#571, Coles Mobile Crane	$75.00
#581, Horse Box, British Railway	$150.00
#581, Horse Box, Express Horse Van	$800.00
#582, Pullmore Car Transporter	$160.00
#591, AEC Tanker, Shell	$225.00
#601, Austin Para Moke	$60.00
#602, Armoured Command Car	$50.00
#604, Land Rover Bomb Disposal Unit	$65.00
#609, 105mm Howitzer & Gun Crew	$40.00
#612, Commando Jeep	$40.00
#615, US Jeep & 105mm Howitzer	$50.00
#616, AEC Articulated Transporter & Tank	$90.00
#617, VW KDF w/Anti-Tank Gun	$70.00
#618, AEC Articulated Transporter & Helicopter	$100.00
#619, Bren Gun Carrier & Anti-Tank Gun	$50.00
#620, Berliet Missile Launcher	$170.00
#621, 3-Ton Army Wagon	$100.00

#622, Bren Gun Carrier $40.00
#622, 10-Ton Army Truck $120.00
#623, Army Covered Wagon $60.00
#624, Daimler Military Ambulance $400.00
#625, Austin Covered Wagon $400.00
#625, 6-Pounder Anti-Tank Gun...................$40.00
#626, Military Ambulance............................$75.00
#640, Bedford Military Truck $400.00
#641, Army 1-Ton Cargo Truck....................$75.00
#642, RAF Pressure Refueler........................$150.00
#643, Army Water Carrier $75.00
#650, Light Tank $200.00
#651, Centurion Tank $70.00
#654, Mobile Gun $40.00
#656, 88mm Gun $40.00
#660, Tank Transporter................................$125.00
#661, Recovery Tractor $125.00
#662, Static 88mm Gun & Crew $40.00
#665, Honest John Missile Erector................$175.00

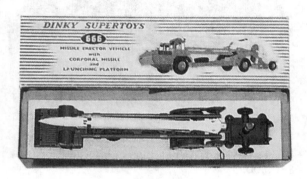

#666, Missile Erector Vehicle with Corporal Missile and Launching Platform, $300.00.

#667, Armored Patrol Car $40.00
#667, Missile Servicing Platform Vehicle $200.00
#668, Foden Army Truck...............................$50.00
#669, US Army Jeep.....................................$400.00
#670, Armoured Car $40.00
#671, MKI Corvette (boat) $25.00
#671, Reconnaissance Car.............................$180.00
#672, OSA Missile Boat $25.00
#672, US Army Jeep $100.00
#673, Scout Car $40.00
#674, Austin Champ, olive drab $50.00
#674, Austin Champ, wht, UN version $500.00
#674, Coast Guard Missile Launch.................$20.00
#675, Motor Patrol Boat $20.00
#675, US Army Staff Car $400.00
#676, Armoured Personnel Carrier $60.00
#676, Daimler Armoured Car, w/speedwheels ...$40.00
#677, Armoured Command Vehicle $100.00
#677, Task Force Set.....................................$70.00
#678, Air Sea Rescue $20.00
#680, Ferret Armoured Car $20.00
#681, DUKW $20.00
#682, Stalwart Load Carrier...........................$20.00

#683, Chieftain Tank $40.00
#686, 25-Pounder Field Gun $25.00
#687, Convoy Army Truck $20.00
#687, Trailer..$20.00
#688, Field Artillery Tractor $50.00
#689, Med Artillery Tractor $75.00
#690, Mobile Antiaircraft Gun $70.00
#690, Scorpion Tank $25.00
#691, Field Gun Unit $300.00
#691, Striker Anti-Tank Vehicle $45.00
#692, Leopard Tank $50.00
#692, 5.5 Med Gun $40.00
#693, 7.2 Howitzer $40.00
#694, Hanomag Tank Destroyer......................$50.00
#694, Howitzer & Tractor $300.00
#696, Leopard Antiaircraft Tank....................$50.00
#697, 25-Pounder Field Gun Set $150.00
#698, Tank Transporter & Tank $225.00
#699, Leopard Recovery Tank $50.00
#699, Military Gift Set $500.00
#700, Seaplane $150.00
#700, Spitfire MKII RAF Jubilee $150.00
#701, Shetland Flying Boat $600.00
#702, DH Comet Jet Airliner $200.00
#704, Avro York Airliner $160.00
#705, Viking Airliner $75.00
#706, Vickers Viscount Airliner, Air France $160.00
#708, Vickers Viscount Airliner, BEA $200.00
#710, Beechcraft S35 Bonanza $75.00
#712, US Army T-42A $75.00
#715, Beechcraft C-55 Baron $60.00
#715, Bristol 173 Helicopter..........................$75.00
#716, Westland Sikorsky Helicopter $60.00
#717, Boeing 737 ....$75.00
#718, Hawker Hurricane................................$70.00
#719, Spitfire MKII $70.00
#721, Junkers Stuka $70.00
#722, Hawker Harrier $100.00
#723, Hawker Executive Jet............................$60.00
#724, Sea King Helicopter $50.00
#725, Phanton II $100.00
#726, Messerschmitt, desert camouflage $100.00
#726, Messerschmitt, gray & gr $200.00
#727, US Air Force F-4 Phantom II.................$250.00
#728, RAF Dominie $60.00
#729, Multi-Role Combat Aircraft..................$60.00
#730, US Navy Phantom $70.00
#731, SEPECAT Jaguar $50.00
#731, Twin-Engine Fighter $50.00
#732, Bell Police Helicopter, M*A*S*H...........$100.00
#732, Bell Police Helicopter, wht & bl $50.00
#733, German Phantom II...............................$100.00
#733, Lockheed Shooting Star Jet Fighter $50.00
#734, P47 Thunderbolt..................................$80.00
#734, Submarine Swift...................................$50.00
#736, Bundesmarine Sea King $60.00
#736, Hawker Hunter $50.00
#737, P1B Lightning Fighter $75.00

#738, DH110 Sea Vixen Fighter $60.00
#739, Zero-Sen $75.00
#741, Spitfire MKII $65.00
#749, RAF Avro Vulcan Bomber $3,500.00
#750, Telephone Call Box $40.00
#751, Lawn Mower $100.00
#751, Police Box $40.00
#752, Goods Yard Crane $50.00
#753, Police Controlled Crossing $80.00
#755-6, Standard Lamp, single or dbl arm $25.00
#760, Pillar Box $25.00
#766, British Road Signs, Country set A $120.00
#767, British Road Signs, Country set B $120.00
#768m British Road Signs, Town set A $120.00
#769, British Road Signs, Town set B $120.00
#770, Road Signs, set of 12 ....$200.00
#771, International Road Signs, set of 12 ....$160.00
#772, British Road Signs, set of 24 ....$400.00
#773, Traffic Signal $25.00
#777, Belisha Beacon $15.00
#778, Road Repair Warning Boards $25.00
#781, Petrol Pumping Station, Esso $80.00
#782, Petrol Pumping Station, Shell $80.00
#784, Dinky Goods Train Set $50.00
#785, Service Station $240.00
#786, Tyre Rack $50.00
#787, Lighting Kit $35.00
#796, Healey Sports Boat $40.00
#798, Express Passenger Train $170.00
#801, Mini USS Enterprise $50.00
#802, Mini Klingon Cruiser $50.00
#815, Panhard Armoured Tank $150.00
#816, Berliet Missile Launcher $275.00
#817, AMX 13-Ton Tank $125.00
#822, M3 Half-Track $125.00
#884, Brockway Bridge Truck $300.00
#893, UNIC Boilot Car Transporter $175.00
#893, UNIC Pipe-Line Transporter $175.00
#900, Building Site Gift Set $1,500.00
#901, see #501
#902, see #502
#903, see #503
#905, see #505
#908, Mighty Antar w/Transformer $750.00
#911, see #511
#912, see #512
#913, see #513
#914, AEC Articulated Lorry $250.00
#917, Mercedes Benz Truck & Trailer $100.00
#917, Mercedes Benz Truck & Trailer, Munsterland $225.00
#917, see #514
#918, Guy Van, Ever Ready $350.00
#919, Guy Van, Golden Shred $1,200.00
#920, Guy Warrior Van, Heinz $2,500.00
#921, Bedford Articulated Lorry $135.00
#922, Big Bedford Lorry $400.00
#923, Big Bedford Van, Heinz Baked Beans can $450.00
#923, Big Bedford Van, Heinz Ketchup bottle $2,000.00

#924, Aveling-Barford Dumper $60.00
#925, Leyland Dump Truck $250.00
#930, Bedford Pallet-Jekta Van, Dinky Toys $400.00
#931, Bedford Comet Lorry, bl & brn $550.00
#931, Leyland Comet Lorry, other colors $200.00
#932, Leyland Comet Wagon w/Tailboard $200.00
#933, Leyland Cement Wagon $200.00
#934, Leyland Octopus Wagon, bl & yel $2,500.00
#934, Leyland Octopus Wagon, other colors $350.00
#935, Leyland Octopus Flat Truck w/Chains, bl cab ...$3,000.00
#935, Leyland Octopus Flat Truck w/Chains, gr & gray .$2,000.00
#936, Leyland 8-Wheel Test Chassis $140.00
#940, Mercedes Benz Truck $50.00
#941, Foden Tanker, Mobilgas $750.00
#942, Foden Tanker, Regent $600.00
#943, Leyland Octopus Tanker, Esso $500.00
#944, Shell-BP Fuel Tanker $300.00
#944, Shell-BP Fuel Tanker, red wheels $500.00
#945, AEC Fuel Tanker, Esso $100.00
#945, AEC Fuel Tanker, Lucas $150.00
#948, Tractor-Trailer, McLean $300.00
#949, Wayne School Bus $275.00
#950, Foden S20 Fuel Tanker, Burmah $75.00
#950, Foden S20 Fuel Tanker, Shell $100.00
#951, Trailer $40.00
#952, Vega Major Luxury Coach $125.00
#953, Continental Touring Coach $400.00
#954, Fire Station $300.00
#954, Vega Major Luxury Coach, no lights $100.00
#955, Fire Engine $100.00
#956, Turntable Fire Escape, Bedford $100.00
#956, Turntable Fire Escape, Berliet $300.00
#957, Fire Services Gift Set $500.00
#958, Snow Plough $300.00
#959, Foden Dumper, w/Bulldozer blade $100.00

#960, Lorry Mounted Concrete Mixer,
$100.00.

#961, see #561
#961, Vega Major Luxury Coach $250.00
#962, Muir-Hill Dumper $30.00

#963, Road Grader $40.00
#963, see #563
#964, Elevator Loader $80.00
#965, Euclid Rear Dump Truck $80.00
#965, Terex Dump Truck $250.00
#966, Marrel Multi-Bucket Unit $150.00
#967, Muir-Hill Loader & Trencher $40.00

#967, BBC TV Mobile Control Room, $200.00.

#968, BBC-TV Roving Eye Vehicle $225.00
#969, BBC-TV Extending Mast Vehicle $225.00
#970, Jones Cantilever Crane $100.00
#971, Coles Mobile Crane...............................$50.00
#972, Coles 20-ton Lorry, mounted crane, yel/blk $200.00
#972, Coles 20-ton Lorry, mounted crane, yel/orange....$100.00
#973, Eaton Yale Tractor Shovel $40.00
#973, Goods Yard Crane...................................$50.00
#974, AEC Hoyner Transporter.......................$100.00

#975, Ruston Bucyrus Excavator, $350.00.

#976, Michigan Tractor Dozer $40.00
#977, Servicing Platform Vehicle $250.00
#977, Shovel Dozer...$40.00
#978, Refuse Wagon $80.00
#979, Racehorse Transport...............................$400.00
#980, Coles Hydra Truck...................................$50.00
#980, Horse Box Express $650.00
#981, Horse Box, British Railways $200.00
#982, Pullman Car Transporter........................$120.00
#983, Car Carrier & Trailer $300.00
#984, Atlas Digger $55.00
#984, Car Carrier..$200.00
#985, Trailer for Car Carrier............................$80.00
#986, Mighty Antar Loader & Propeller..........$450.00
#987, ABC-TV Control Room $250.00
#988, ABC-TV Transmitter Van........................$300.00
#989, Car Carrier, Autotransporters $2,000.00
#990, Transporter Set..$2,000.00

#991, AEC Tanker, Shell Chemicals.............................$160.00
#992, Avro Vulcan Delta Wing Bomber $3,000.00
#994, Loading Ramp for #992.......................................$30.00
#997, Caravelle Air France $400.00
#998, Bristol Britannia Canadian Pacific.....................$350.00
#999, DH Comet Jet...$175.00

Disney

Through the magic of the silver screen, Walt Disney's characters have come to life, and it is virtually impossible to imagine a child growing up without the influence of his genius. As each classic film was introduced, toy manufacturers scurried to fill department store shelves with the dolls, games, battery-ops and windups that carried the likeness of every member of its cast. Though today it is the toys of the 1930s and 1940s that are bringing exorbitant prices, later toys are certainly collectible as well, as you'll see in our listings. Even characters as recently introduced as Roger Rabbit already have their own cult following.

For more information we recommend *Character Toys and Collectibles, First and Second Series*, and *Antique & Collectible Toys, 1870-1950*, by David Longest; *Stern's Guide to Disney Collectibles* by Michael Stern; *The Collector's Encyclopedia of Disneyana* by Michael Stern and David Longest; *Disneyana* by Cecil Munsey (Hawthorne Books, 1974); *Disneyana* by Robert Heide and John Gilman; *Walt Disney's Mickey Mouse Memorabilia* by Hillier and Shine (Abrams Inc, 1986); *Tomart's Disneyana Update Magazine* and *Elmer's Price Guide to Toys* by Elmer Duellman (L-W Books).

Advisors: Joel J. Cohen (C12); Don Hamm (H10) Rocketeer; Allen Day (D1), Roger Rabbit.

See also Battery-Operated; Books; Bubble Bath Containers; Character and Promotional Drinking Glasses; Character Clocks and Watches; Chein; Coloring, Activity and Paint Books; Dakins; Fisher-Price; Games; Lunch Boxes; Marx; Paper Dolls; Pez Dispensers; Plastic Figures; Pin-Back Buttons; Puppets; Puzzles; Records; Toothbrush Holders; View-Master; Western; Windups, Friction and Other Mechanicals.

Aladdin, pin, Aladdin figure, 1993, from Disney store, M, M8 ....$10.00
Alice in Wonderland, figure, March Hare, Gund/WDP, vinyl, 14", EX $25.00
Alice in Wonderland, painting on glass, tea party scene Alice, Mad Hatter & Hare, limited edition, fr, 8x10", EX, J5 ....$45.00
Babes in Toyland, Jumping Jack Soldier, Jaymar #1230/WDP, wood w/enamel, pull-string action, 10", rare, NM (VG+ box), A..$75.00
Baby Weems, child's knife, fork & spoon set, Bestmaid/WDP, beige plastic, rare, NMOC, A...................$40.00
Bambi, bank, Bambi figure, Leeds, china, EX, S1 ....$85.00
Bambi, bank, Flower figure, chalk, EX, S1 ....$50.00
Bambi, figure, Flower, Am Pottery, 1949, dk bl & wht glazed pottery, 5", scarce, M, A...............................$105.00

Bambi, figure, American Pottery Co., glazed ceramic with painted features, 8", EX, $175.00.

Bambi, friction toy, Flower, Linemar, 1950s, EX+ $45.00

Bambi, pencil sharpener, Bambi figure, 1940s, red Bakelite, rare, EX, M8 ....$50.00

Bambi, printing set, Multi Print/Italy, 7 stamps & ink pad, EX (orig box), M8 ....$45.00

Bambi, shoe polish, Baby Shoe White, EX (orig box), M5.$15.00

Bashful, see Snow White & the Seven Dwarfs

Beauty & the Beast, pin, Beast figure, 1990s, cloisonne & enamel, M, M8 ....$12.00

Bedknobs & Broomsticks, mobile, from video release, unpunched cb pcs, M...............................$15.00

Captain Hook, see Peter Pan

Chip & Dale, see Rescue Rangers

Cinderella, doll, Effanbee, 1985, MIB...............................$60.00

Cinderella, mold set, Model Craft, 1950s, complete, molds a bit dry, J5 ....$35.00

Cinderella, tea set, Japan, 1930s, china w/pnt scenes, 14 pcs, NM, A $295.00

Cinderella, Theatre de Marionettes, France, 1950s, complete w/theater, figures, scenery & booklet, unused, EX, A .$120.00

Cinderella, top, 1970s, figure pops up as musical top spins, VG (VG box), S2 ....$45.00

Daisy Duck, figure, Applause, bendable, 5½", MIP, K1 ......$6.00

Disney, calendar, Morrel's, 1942, 28x12", D10, M (original mailer), $320.00.

Disney, bubble gum wrapper, Gum Inc, 1930s, waxed, w/Mickey, Minnie, Pluto & Horace, 6x4½", NM, A $152.00

Disney, Casey Jr Character Train, wall decoration, fiberboard engine w/Donald, 5 cars lithoed w/Disney characters, NM, A $95.00

Disney, ceiling shade, 1950s, glass images of Mickey, Donald & Pluto holding balloons, 8" dia, EX+, A $60.00

Disney, Christmas lights, Disney Character Lites, Paramount/Japan, 1950s, 8 character-shaped pnt glass figures, MIB, A...$90.00

Disney, Christmas lights, Disneylights, Mazda/Thompson-Houston, 12 strung lamps w/decaled characters, EX+ (EX box), A $146.00

Disney, Christmas lights, Mickey Mouse Lights, Mazda/Thompson Houston, 12 strung lamps w/characters, NM (EX box), A $656.00

Disney, Christmas lights, NOMA, 1930s, set of 12 in different colors w/different decaled characters, EX+, A $80.00

Disney, drum set, 1980s, tin, paper and wood, 29", EX, $250.00.

Disney, Embroidery Set, Standard Toycroft, 1938, 5 cloth patterns & hoop, needle & thread, G (G box), A $17.00

Disney, Film Strip Projector, Johnsons/England, 1940s, w/11 filmstrips & 10 story sheets, EX (G box), A $176.00

Disney, Fun on Wheels Cars, Empire/WDP, set of 6 w/Donald, Mickey, Pluto, Goofy & Lady, plastic, 1½", MIB, A .$151.00

Disney, jewelry box, musical, wood w/Mickey, Donald, Nephews & Pluto on turntable on lid, 10", M, A...................$140.00

Disney, Krugs Bread cards, 1930, 19 borderless cards w/Disney photos on front, Mickey recipes on back, EX, J5 ....$95.00

Disney, lamp, Econlite/WDP, 1950s, merry-go-round w/plastic canopy & paper litho characters on tin base, A $305.00

Disney, lollipop jar, 1961, w/Mickey, Donald & Ludwig, MIB, A...$99.00

Disney, lunch pail, metal, lt gr w/many characters, pat #1737249, oval lid, 8½", lid wear, minor dent, A....$400.00

Disney, paint box, 1940s, litho tin w/images of Mickey, Donald & Pluto, EX, A $35.00

Disney, Plastic Palette Paint Set, Transogram, 1952, w/4 pictures, watercolors, etc, unused, VG+ (VG box), A ...$28.00

Disney, Playtime Plastics Nursery Tea Set, Gadeware, wht plastic, decals of various characters, 7-pc set, NM (VG+ box), A $125.00

Disney, rattle, NOMA, 1930s, yel hard plastic cylinder featuring Mickey, Minnie, Donald & Pluto, 4", EX, A $75.00

Disney, Rolykins, Marx, ca 1960, features Mickey & 5 other characters, ea w/ball bearing on bottom, M (NM card) .$75.00

Disney, rug, Alexander Smith, 1935, shows Mickey playing accordion while Minnie & Donald dance, wool, 38", EX, A...$180.00

Disney, sand pail, Chein, 1930s, features Mickey in Sky Hawk airplane & Minnie in boat, litho tin, 6", VG+, A ...$200.00

Disney, sand pail, Happynak, 1930s, 6", VG, M5 ....$100.00

Disney, sand pail, Happynak, 1940s, features Mickey, Minnie, Donald & Pluto, 4", EX+, A.....................$86.00

Disney, sand pail, Happynak, 1940s, features Mickey & Donald marching w/stars around them, 5", EX+, A................$81.00

Disney, sand pail, Happynak #7, 1930s, features Mickey leading band of Disney characters, 4½", G, A $39.00

Disney, sand pail & shovel, Ohio Art, 1938, features Mickey, Minnie, Donald, Pluto & Goofy, 12", EX, A $330.00

Disney, sand sifter, Ohio Art, ca 1930s, tin lithoed w/Disney characters, mesh bottom, 8" dia, EX, A $72.00

Disney, seed packets, 1970s, M, $10.00 each.

Disney, soap set, Kerk Guild, 1950s, set of 3 hand-painted figures of Mickey, Donald & Pluto, 4" ea, NM (EX box), A .$100.00

Disney, top, Chein, ca 1950, Mickey, Donald & Pluto playing musical instruments, tin, red wood knob, 7" dia, NM (M box), A $151.00

Disney, train set, pewter, NM (NM box), O1................$135.00

Disney, TV tray, early 1960s, Mickey & friends on bl background w/yel border, 19", NM+, M5 ....$12.00

Disney, viewer, England, 1948, w/12 vintage slides of Disney movies, NM (EX+ box), A......................................$82.00

Disney, World of Color pencil box, w/contents, 1950s, A.$15.00

Disney, yo-yo, 1970s Festival, features Mickey, Donald & Pluto, MIP, M3 ....$10.00

Disneyland, magic slate TV screen, EX+ $35.00

Disneyland, push plate, 1957, commemorates Disneyland opening, emb bronze, 10", M, A $221.00

Disneyland, tray, WDP/late 1950s, rectangular w/aerial view of Magic Kingdom as it appeared on opening day, 17", EX+, A..$66.00

Disneyland Alweg-Monorail, Schuco #6333, train runs by transformers on metal track, bl & gray plastic, EX+ (EX box), A $718.00

Disneyland Blocks, Halsam, 1960s, set of 20 wooden blocks w/letters, numbers & Disney characters, EX+ (EX+ box), A...$22.00

Disneyland Blocks, Halsam/WDE, 1939, 9 red & gr wooden blocks w/various characters, NM (EX 4" sq box), A..$182.00

Disneyland Gym, Plastic Playthings/WDP, 1950s, baby's play gym w/figures of Mickey, 10", NM (EX box), A $67.00

Disneyland Melody Player, Chein/WDP, tin lithoed w/Disney characters, 7" sq, NM+ (M box), A $285.00

Disneyland Tea Set, Chein, late 1950s, illus w/Mickey, Minnie & Pluto on metal, complete, EX (EX box), A $132.00

Disney's Wonderful World of Color, Paint-By-Number Set, Hasbro, 1960s, 6 pictures, 10 pencils & sharpener, NMIB (sealed)...$28.00

Doc, see Snow White & the Seven Dwarfs

Donald Duck, Art Stamp Picture Set, long-billed Donald on red background, EX (EX box), A $499.00

Donald Duck, balloon figure, WDP, 1940s, diecut cb face w/balloon for body, 11", NM...$50.00

Donald Duck, bank, ceramic, 1960s, S1 ....$30.00

Donald Duck, bank, Empire Toys, 1950s, hard plastic figure w/hands on belly, 10", EX......................................$125.00

Donald Duck, bank, figure as baby, 1983, S1 ....$10.00

Donald Duck, bank, late 1950s, TV shape w/picture of Donald & nephews on screen, ceramic, VG, S2 ....$65.00

Donald Duck, bank, Marx/WDP, litho tin register shape w/Disney characters in circus scenes, 4", EX, A...............$190.00

Donald Duck, bank, WDP/1939, mk Dime Register Bank, Donald guards money bags, sq litho tin w/diagonal corners, EX, A $429.00

Donald Duck, bank, 1930s, chalkware figure in bl shirt, silver tie & red cap, EX $215.00

Donald Duck, bank, 1930s, pnt cast-metal image of long-billed Donald, seated, 6", missing trap, G, A $575.00

Donald Duck, bank, 1970s, vinyl w/articulated arms that drop coins into pig, 9", NM, S2 ....$45.00

Donald Duck, doll, Deans Rag; 1930s, stuffed plush and felt, 24", EX, $350.00.

Donald Duck, bike toy, mk Japan, celluloid figure of Donald on coiled wire mount, 3½", NM, A $75.00

Donald Duck, bookends, Walt Disney USA, 1950, Donald standing w/books slung over shoulder, EX, A, pr...............$150.00

Donald Duck, camera, Herbert-George, ca 1950, blk plastic w/emb images of Donald & Nephews, unused, M (EX box), A $112.00

Donald Duck, camera, Herbert-George, ca 1950, blk plastic w/emb images of Donald & Nephews, EX, M8 ....$75.00

Donald Duck, cereal container/bank, Nabisco Caramel Wheat Puffs, 1966, pnt plastic, VG, H4 ....$15.00

Donald Duck, Colorforms, 1960, VG+ $24.00

Donald Duck, crib toy, celluloid, 4", EX, A $98.00

Donald Duck, doll, as sea captain (?), felt-covered w/glass eyes, dbl-breasted felt jacket & hat, 10", VG, A $75.00

Donald Duck, doll, Knickerbocker, 1936, stuffed, w/navy jacket & hat, VG, J5 ....$195.00

Donald Duck, doll, Lenci/Italian, 1940s-50s, 18", EX, $550.00.

Donald Duck, electric scissors, Linemar, scissors protruding from face, battery-op, 6", scarce, EX+ (VG box), A $435.00

Donald Duck, figure, Applause, bendable, 5", MIP, K1 ......$6.00

Donald Duck, figure, compo, partial Disney decal on foot, 1930, 6", VG+, M5...............$695.00

Donald Duck, figure, Disneykins, 1960s, EX, M8 ....$20.00

Donald Duck, figure, Hasbro, 1970s, in marching pose, squeeze hands to move feet, 15", VG, S2...............$35.00

Donald Duck, figure, Japan, 1930s, long-billed figure w/jtd arms & legs, 1 eye closed, celluloid, 5", EX, A $110.00

Donald Duck, figure, 1930s, long-billed Donald standing w/head turned sideways, chalkware, 7", chipping, G+, A $70.00

Donald Duck, figure, 1970s, carrying 2 purple shoes, ceramic, 5", NM, S2 ....$30.00

Donald Duck, ink blotter, Sunoco, M, C10 ....$12.00

Donald Duck, night light, 1960s, figural head, NM, S2....$35.00

Donald Duck, Pop Pal, Kohner, 1970s, push button & Donald pops from barrel, NM, S2 ....$25.00

Donald Duck, roly poly w/squeaker, mk Made in Japan, 1930s, press down on hat for squeaker, 6¾", scarce, EX, A ..$850.00

Donald Duck, squeeze toy, Donald leaning on red suitcase, 8", VG, S2 ....$20.00

Donald Duck, tea set, Japan, 1930s, lusterware teapot, sugar w/lid, 1 cup, featuring long-billed Donald, NM, A $181.00

Donald Duck, tea set, Japan, 1930s, pictures Donald tipping his hat, glazed ceramic teapot, creamer & sugar, EX+, A...........$256.00

Donald Duck, warming dish, ceramic w/metal pan, 3 compartments, 8", minor chips & crazing, A $40.00

Donald Duck, watering can, Ohio Art, 1930s, EX, D10, $275.00.

Donald Duck & Daisy, figures, prewar Japan, plastic, 3½", scarce (Daisy could be early Donna Duck), NM, A, pr $50.00

Donald Duck & Mickey Mouse, crayon tin, Transogram, VG+, A $25.00

Donald Duck & Mickey Mouse, paint box, Transogram, 1950, EX, A $25.00

Donald Duck and Pluto, car, Sun Rubber, 1940s, 7", EX, $160.00.

Dopey, see Snow White & the Seven Dwarfs

Duck Tales, backpack, bl, premium, MIP, S2 ....$15.00

Duck Tales, figure, Baggy Beagle, Just Toys, bendable, 6", MIP, K1 ....$5.00

Duck Tales, figure, Scrooge McDuck, Just Toys, bendable, 4½", MIP, K1 ....$5.00

Dumbo, figure, WD/Japan, 1960s, bl vinyl, NM, S2 ....$20.00

Dumbo, figure, 1950s, pnt plaster, 2½", EX, J5 ....$35.00

Fantasia, jack-in-the-box, EX (EX box), O1 ....$150.00

Ferdinand the Bull, figure, Brayton Laguna, blk, bl & pk glazed ceramic w/silver label, 9", rare, EX+, A $638.00

Ferdinand the Bull, figure, Ideal/W Dent, compo w/cloth flower in mouth, pnt bee on hip, 9½", EX, A $100.00

Ferdinand the Bull, figure, Seiberling, rubber, complete w/horns & tail, EX+, M8 ....$65.00

Ferdinand the Bull, pencil sharpener, 1930s, EX, J5 ....$25.00

Figaro, see Pinocchio

Flower, see Bambi

Geppetto, see Pinocchio

Goofy, diecast Goofy in sports car, Matchbox, MOC, S2.$40.00

Goofy, figure, Dakin-like w/removable clothes, NM, S2 ..$85.00

Goofy, figure, Gabriel, Goofy on trike, plastic w/wire legs, 5", EX+, M8 ....$20.00

Goofy, figure, 1970s, in pirate outfit, bendable, EX, S2 ....$20.00

Goofy, figure, 1970s, premium (?), pnt plastic, 2¼", M, S2 ....$20.00

Goofy, gumball dispenser, figural, 3", MOC, S2 ....$10.00

Goofy, yo-yo, Disney Festival, MOC, M3 ....$15.00

Grumpy, see Snow White & the Seven Dwarfs

Jamboree Bear, bank, WDP, 1960s, brn ceramic, 11", EX $48.00

Jiminy Cricket, see Pinocchio

Lady & the Tramp, figure, Lady, Hagen-Renaker, 1950, 1½", NM, M8 ....$35.00

Lady & the Tramp, figure, Lady, 1970s, ceramic, EX, M8 .$17.00

Lady & the Tramp, figure, Trusty, Hagen-Renaker, 1950s, 2", M, M8 ....$90.00

Lady & the Tramp, figures, General Mills premiums, 1955, 10 different, plastic, M, R3, ea $10.00

Lady & the Tramp, pull toy, Lady on gr plastic base, Eldon, 1955, EX+ $135.00

Lion King, pin, Simba figure, 1994, cloisonne & enamel, M, M8 ....$18.00

Little Mermaid, figure, Ariel, Just Toys, bendable, 6", MIP, K1 ....$4.00

Little Mermaid, figure, Flounder or Sebastian, Tyco, stuffed, MIB, S1, ea $18.00

Little Mermaid, figure, Sebastian, Just Toys, bendable, 3", MIP, K1 ....$4.00

Ludwig Von Drake, squeeze toy, Dell, 1950s-60s, 7½", VG, S2 ....$50.00

Mary Poppins, figure, ceramic, 1964, 8", NM+, M5 ....$65.00

Mary Poppins, needlepoint kit, 3 pictures w/foam fr, M ...$45.00

Mary Poppins, pop-up figures, Mary Poppins or Bert the Chimney Sweep, Nabisco premiums, 1965, M, R3, ea $5.00

Mickey Mouse, Art Set, Dixon/WDE, 1930s, box lid features Mickey in airplane waving goodbye to his pals, VG (VG+ box), A $149.00

Mickey Mouse, baby plate w/spoon & fork, Rogers Bros, 1930s, engraved silver plate, 9", EX, A $140.00

Mickey Mouse, baby rattle, prewar Japan, celluloid pie-eyed Mickey figure w/rubber loop handle, 6", NM, A $134.00

Mickey Mouse, balancing toy, Equilibrista, Estrella/Brazil, Mickey on bicycle balances on string, 9", EX (EX box), A $83.00

Mickey Mouse, balancing toy, WD/USA, 1930s, wooden pie-eyed Mickey does hand-controlled tricks on rod, 9", EX, A $128.00

Mickey Mouse, bank, early 1980s, standing vinyl figure, NM, S2 ....$20.00

Mickey Mouse, bank, Play-Pal, 1971, vinyl bust, 10¼", VG, S2 ....$45.00

Mickey Mouse, bank, Wolverine, ca 1960, put coins in Mickey & they automatically go to correct tubes, 12", EX, A $25.00

Mickey Mouse, beanie cap, unauthorized, 1930s, blk & yel w/image of Mickey waving, mk Yours Truly Mickey Mouse, EX+, A $55.00

Mickey Mouse, bottle stopper, prewar England, pnt metal rat-nosed Mickey w/hands on hips atop cork stopper, 5", VG, A $1,068.00

Mickey Mouse, bowl, Post Cereals, 1930s, red Beetleware w/emb letters & numbers around rim & Mickey, 5½", EX, A $11.00

Mickey Mouse, Bubble Buster, Kilgore/WDE, 1930s, CI grip & barrel w/paper litho covering, 8", NM, A $160.00

Mickey Mouse, camera, British ensign, 1930s, box-type w/raised image of Mickey, orig sticker, EX+ (VG box), A $220.00

Mickey Mouse, card holder, German (?), 1930s, blk & wht lead figure on base w/emb name, 2½", rare, EX, A..........$185.00

Mickey Mouse, cereal container/bank, Mickey figure, Nabisco Chocolate Wheat Puffs, 1966, pnt plastic, VG, H4...$15.00

Mickey Mouse, coloring sheets, WD/Big-Little Whitman, numerous (orig 320) sheets to 'Draw & Color,' VG (VG box), A $25.00

Mickey Mouse, crib toy, Occupied Japan, pnt plastic figure w/wire springs for arms & legs, 3", VG+ (NM box), A $91.00

Mickey Mouse, crib toy, 1930s, red & wht beaded wood figure of Mickey w/pie eyes, 6", EX+, A $230.00

Mickey Mouse, display card for lollipops, Brandle & Smith, 1930s, move Mickey's arm to change facial expression, EX, A $328.00

Mickey Mouse, doll, as Sorcerer, Applause, 1990, plush, 16", M $28.00

Mickey Mouse doll, Charlotte Clark, 1930s, 14", rare, M, $3,500.00.

Mickey Mouse, doll, Deans Rag; pre-1939, No 750611 under neck, velvet & cloth, 13", EX, A $242.00

Mickey Mouse, doll, Deans Rag; pre-1939, velvet & felt, all orig, 9", EX, A...$319.00

Mickey Mouse, doll, felt-covered w/bendable arms & legs, printed toothy grin, 12½", G, A...............................$100.00

Mickey Mouse, doll, Ideal, 1960s, inflatable, MIB, J5 ......$20.00

Mickey Mouse, doll, Knickerbocker, dressed in chaps & neckerchief, cloth & compo, pie-eyed, 12", G, A $140.00

Mickey Mouse, doll, Knickerbocker, stuffed, w/Mickey Mouse Club shirt, 14", EX, S1..$30.00

Mickey Mouse, doll, Knickerbocker, 1930s, stuffed, pie eyes & 4 fingers, red shorts & hard compo shoes, 12", G+, A.$149.00

Mickey Mouse, doll, Knickerbocker, 1930s, stuffed cloth w/red celluloid shoes, orig tag, 11½", EX+, A $750.00

Mickey Mouse, doll, Knickerbocker, 1940s, red & blk cloth w/yel hands & compo shoes, 11", EX, A.................$518.00

Mickey Mouse, doll, McCall, 1930s, stuffed cloth rat-nosed figure w/pie eyes, 15", NM+, A..................................$262.00

Mickey Mouse, doll, Playskool, 1980s, plush talker, NM (EX box), S2..$55.00

Mickey Mouse, doll, plush, Disney Channel promotion, EX, O1...$55.00

Mickey Mouse, doll, Steiff, early 1930s, original tag, 7½", M, D10, $2,500.00.

Mickey Mouse, doll, WDW/Horsman, 1972, talker, NM, S2..$195.00

Mickey Mouse, fan, barrel, MIB, S1 ....$20.00

Mickey Mouse, figure, Applause, bendable, 5", MIP, K1 ....$6.00

Mickey Mouse, figure, Borgfeldt, 1931, pnt wood w/disk-shaped hands & pnt chest label, 5", EX+, A.......................$575.00

Mickey Mouse, figure, ca 1933, hand-carved wood folk art image of Mickey as a Nazi, 4¾", NM, A..............................$567.00

Mickey Mouse, figure, Deans Rag image, pre-1939, china w/shades of bl & lavender, 2⅝", M, A $150.00

Mickey Mouse, figure, Dell, hitchhiking pose w/sack & pole over his shoulder, vinyl, 9", EX, A $14.00

Mickey Mouse, figure, Dolly Toy/WDE, 1930s, diecut cb w/movable arms & legs, pull-string action, 9½", EX (VG box), A $1,350.00

Mickey Mouse, figure, English china, Mickey in seated pose, gloss glaze, 1½", NM, A...$127.00

Mickey Mouse, figure, for Lionel circus train, compo, 5", scarce, EX+, A..$288.00

Mickey Mouse, figure, Fun-E-Flex, wood w/disk-shaped hands, red shorts, 9", NM (VG/EX box), A $2,650.00

Mickey Mouse, figure, Hasbro, 1970s, in marching pose, squeeze hands to move feet, 15", VG, S2 ....$35.00

Mickey Mouse, figure, Kay Kamen Inc, early 1930s, papier-mache, 44", P, A...$345.00

Mickey Mouse, figure, Mickey Mouse Corp/WD, 1940s, red & blk carved wood, yel hands & feet, 7", VG+, A $207.00

Mickey Mouse, figure, Nifty Fun-E-Flex/Borgfeldt, ca 1935, pnt jtd wood, 4-fingered pnt chest label, 7¼", EX+, A...........$650.00

Mickey Mouse figure, Nifty/Germany, jointed wood with lollipop hands, 1933, 7", EX, D10, $950.00.

Mickey Mouse, figure, prewar, boxing pose, compo, 9", very scarce, NM, A...$241.00

Mickey Mouse, figure, Seiberling, 1930s, blk hard rubber w/red & wht pnt, 3", EX, A...$50.00

Mickey Mouse, figure, Seiberling Latex/WD, 1930s, blk & red rubber w/wht pie eyes & buttons, 6", G+, A $22.00

Mickey Mouse, figure, 1930s, celluloid, Mickey w/hands on hips, 3¾", EX+, A $210.00

Mickey Mouse, figure, 1950s, cereal premium, red hard plastic, M, S2...$15.00

Mickey Mouse, figure, 1960s, pnt hollow plastic, 5½", G, S2 .$10.00

Mickey Mouse, figure, 1960s-70s, w/long face, plush & vinyl w/ground nut shells inside, VG, S2 ....$25.00

Mickey Mouse, fountain pen, Inkograph/WD, 1930s, blk w/Mickey decal, 5", EX, A...$65.00

Mickey Mouse, Fun Poncho, Ben Cooper, 1976, vinyl w/mask & hood, MIP, S2 ....$20.00

Mickey Mouse, Home Foundry, 1930s, figure casting set w/mold & most accessories, G, A...$358.00

Mickey Mouse, jack-in-the-box, Carnival, 1970s, VG, S2 .$35.00

Mickey Mouse, jack-in-the-box, Kohner, 1973, musical, piano shape, EX, I2 ....$35.00

Mickey Mouse, jam jar, glass emb w/Disney characters, Mickey's head on red lid w/slot, 6¼", VG, A $90.00

Mickey Mouse, lamp, plastic figure as base w/orig paper shade, S1 ....$35.00

Mickey Mouse, lamp, Soreng Manegold Co/WDE, 1930s, Mickey seated in chair w/book in left hand, some touchups o/w EX, A $800.00

Mickey Mouse, Magic Adder, 1960s, electric educational toy, VG (VG box), J5..$15.00

Mickey Mouse, night light, 1960s, figural head, NM, S2 .$35.00

Mickey Mouse, party favors, Paris France, ca 1933, paper litho envelope w/favors, unopened, 6", NM, A $50.00

Mickey Mouse, pencil box, Dixon, ca 1935, 2-sided cb figure w/pullout drawer, 8½", NM, A.....................................$245.00

Mickey Mouse, pencil sharpener, 'Chomps,' Hasbro, EX (EX box), O1...$45.00

Mickey Mouse, pencil sharpener, Plastic Novelties, 1935, hard plastic figure holding pencil, 1¾", EX, A...................$75.00

Mickey Mouse, pin, brass, hands on hips, standing in quarter turn, 6", EX, A...$250.00

Mickey Mouse, pin, Brier Mfg, 1930s, Mickey banging on drum, wood compo, 1½", M, M8 ....$85.00

Mickey Mouse, pin, 1930s, blk & wht enameled image of long-tailed Mickey, 1⅛", EX+, A $110.00

Mickey Mouse, planter, Leeds/WDP, Mickey dressed as Santa w/open sleigh, ceramic, 6½", M, A $105.00

Mickey Mouse, plaque, prewar, Mickey in uniform, tank & other pcs to pnt then pop out & mount, 14x10", MIP, A..$90.00

Mickey Mouse, plate, Bavarian, marked Made in Germany, 1932, 7", $275.00.

Mickey Mouse, plate, 50th birthday, NM (NM box), O1 ....$135.00

Mickey Mouse, phonograph, Vanity Fair, ca 1959, Mickey's head shape, plastic, battery-op, NM (M box), A...$125.00

Mickey Mouse, pull toy, jtd wood diecut Mickey pulls 2 lg tin wheels as head bobs up & down, Foreign mk, 12", EX+, A..$532.00

Mickey Mouse, purse, child's, 1960s-70s, plastic w/Mickey in inset, EX, S2...$40.00

Mickey Mouse, puzzle box, 1930s, European image of Mickey on narrow wooden box that makes coins disappear, 9", VG+, A..$70.00

Mickey Mouse, riding toy, tiny-tot sz, VG, S2 ....$20.00

Mickey Mouse, Roly Poly, England, Mickey figure atop wheel that rolls back & forth, NM (VG box), A..............$150.00

Mickey Mouse, Safety Blocks, American, 1930s, NM, D10, $225.00.

Mickey Mouse, sand pail, see Disney

Mickey Mouse, saxaphone, Czechoslovakian, litho tin w/image of Mickey, 16", EX+, A $290.00

Mickey Mouse, Schoolmaster Chalkboard, Falcon Toy, ca 1939, wood fr w/cb insert, 38x17", G, A...........................$109.00

Mickey Mouse, shoe polish, Scuffy, Mickey on box, full but contents dried out, EX+ (orig box), M5.........................$25.00

Mickey Mouse, Slugaroo, NM (EX box), O1 ....$45.00

Mickey Mouse, Sparkler, Nifty/Borgfeldt, early 1930s, 2-D head on stick, EX+ (rare VG box), A $1,430.00

Mickey Mouse, spoon, silver, pie-eyed Mickey, EX, O1 ...$38.00

Mickey Mouse, straws, 1960s-70s, 2 figural, MOC, S2 .....$20.00

Mickey Mouse, stroller, prewar Spain, metal 4-wheeled chair-type w/Mickey on backrest, 11", rare, EX, A $1,366.00

Mickey Mouse, tableware, Mickey & the Beanstalk, 7-pc, NM..$145.00

Mickey Mouse, Talkie Jecktor, 1934, with records and films, MIB, D10, $1,150.00.

Mickey Mouse, Talkie Jecktor records, Silly Symphony, Sieman/WD, 1930s, set of 3 in envelope, EX, A $201.00

Mickey Mouse, tea set, Japan, cream, blk & rust lustreware w/Mickey in hunting attire, 14-pc, EX+, A.............$1,401.00

Mickey Mouse, tea set, Japan, 1930s, 17-pc lusterware set featuring Mickey playing different musical instruments, NM (EX box), A $600.00

Mickey Mouse, tea set, Nifty/Germany, lustreware, EX (original box), $900.00.

Mickey Mouse, toilet soap, Cussons, figural, 5", NMIB, A.$45.00

Mickey Mouse, top, Lackawanna Mfg, 1930s, litho tin, 10", EX, A...$289.00

Mickey Mouse, tractor toy, Sun Rubber, 1930s, Mickey on red tractor w/wht wheels, M..................................$150.00

Mickey Mouse, watering can, Ohio Art, Mickey playing sax for Minnie, 6", EX+, A...$350.00

Mickey Mouse, watering can, Ohio Art, 1930s, cylinder-shaped w/long narrow spout, images of Mickey & chicken, 6", VG, A...$105.00

Mickey Mouse, wooden walker, American, 1930s, 12", EX, D10, $475.00.

Mickey Mouse, xylophone, WDE, 1930s, all wood w/classic pie-eyed Mickey figures stamped on ea key, w/sticks, 14", EX, A $100.00

Mickey Mouse & Donald Duck, bank, General Toy/Canada, 1940, red metal breadbox shape w/decal, VG+, A ..$110.00

Mickey Mouse & Donald Duck, bowls, Grape Nuts/WDE, Beetleware, 2 Mickeys & 4 larger Donalds in center, set of 6, NM, A $100.00

Mickey Mouse & Donald Duck, fire truck, Sun Rubber, pnt, VG+ $160.00

Mickey Mouse & Donald Duck, hangers, 1970s, plastic, MIP, S2 ....$20.00

Mickey Mouse & Donald Duck, Magic Slate Blackboard, 1950s, bold images of Mickey & Donald, orig stylus, EX, A .$80.00

Mickey Mouse & Minnie, biscuit tin, chased by lion, 10", VG/EX, A $500.00

Mickey Mouse & Minnie, card, WDE, 1935, Magic Movie Pallet, reversible, turn knob & Mickey & Minnie pose, EX, A $170.00

Mickey Mouse & Minnie, dolls, Applause, 1 pr of 2,000 made, plush, wood faces & feet, 15", ea MIB, S2, pr..........$250.00

Mickey Mouse & Minnie, figures, British, 1960s, china, Mickey & Minnie gardening, 2½", NM, A $55.00

Mickey Mouse & Minnie, hurdy-gurdy, England, 1950s, cast metal w/Minnie sitting atop & Mickey pulling, 3-pc, EX+, A $150.00

Mickey Mouse & Minnie, jewelry box, musical, wooden, VG, O1..$450.00

Mickey Mouse & Minnie, kaleidoscope, early 1950s, metal & paper w/graphics, EX, S2 ....$125.00

Mickey Mouse & Minnie, key chain, 1980s, flashes w/Mickey & Minnie kissing, NM, S2...$7.50

Mickey Mouse & Minnie, piano, Japan, 1930s, wood baby grand w/image of both playing piano, 11", VG+, A $374.00

Mickey Mouse & Minnie, pull toy, Nifty/Borgfeldt, 1935, compo ears, tin base, wood wheels, 11½", EX+, A $3,450.00

Mickey Mouse & Minnie, Scrap Book #640, WDE, pie-eyed Mickey & Minnie on cover, some pgs used, M8 ......$75.00

Mickey Mouse & Minnie, tambourine, tin & cloth w/image of Mickey juggling while Minnie swoons, 9", EX, A ...$299.00

Mickey Mouse & Minnie, umbrella, WDE, orange w/4 images, wood hdl, EX+, A...$115.00

Mickey Mouse & Minnie, washing machine, Ohio Art, pre-1939, lithoed images of Mickey & Minnie on wash day, 8", MIB, A $1,465.00

Mickey Mouse & Minnie & Pluto, figures, Fun-E-Flex, 1930s, EX 4" Mickey & Minnie, VG 3½" Pluto, A $295.00

Mickey Mouse & Pluto, sweater guard, 1940s, NM, O1 ...$97.50

Mickey Mouse Club, album, 1975, group picture on front, M (sealed), S2 ....$55.00

Mickey Mouse Club, bank, Mattel, 1957, tin & plastic, EX, I2 ....$100.00

Mickey Mouse Club, clubhouse playset, Romper Room/Hasbro, EX (EX box), S2 ....$95.00

Mickey Mouse Club, flasher ring, red plastic, rare, S2....$150.00

Mickey Mouse Club, harmonica, etched picture of Mickey, MOC, S2..$75.00

Mickey Mouse Club, Medical Kit, Hasbro, ca 1955, includes nursing items, NM (EX box), A $52.00

Mickey Mouse Club, Mousekaphone, Gong Bell/WDP, dial features Mickey's face, tin, 4", EX (EX box), A............$248.00

Mickey Mouse Club, phonograph needles on orig store card, Ectrovox/WDP, 1950s, Mickey atop record, NM (EX envelope), A..$287.00

Mickey Mouse Club, yo-yo, Duncan, clear w/inset photo, MIP, S2 ....$115.00

Mickey Mouse Club, Newsreel Projector, Mattel, 1950s, battery-operated tripod camera with film strips and record, MIB, $225.00.

Mickey Mouse Club, Western Wagon, 1950s, EX, D10, $250.00.

Minnie Mouse, bank, vinyl figure in pk outfit w/articulated arms that drop coins in basket, 11", EX, S2 ....$40.00

Minnie Mouse, bank, vinyl figure wearing red dress & bow w/yel shoes, 6", EX, S2 ....$25.00

Minnie Mouse, bank, 1970s, vinyl figure w/pk outfit & yel umbrella, NM, S2 ....$30.00

Minnie Mouse, doll, Knickerbocker, 1930s, polka-dot skirt, movable head, 14", EX, A $216.00

Minnie Mouse, figure, WDP, 1940s, pressed cotton w/pipe-stem limbs, yel fabric skirt, 3", NM, A....................................$80.00

Minnie Mouse, purse, 1970s, Pretty Minnie, MIP, S2 ......$15.00

Nightmare Before Christmas, doll, beanbag Santa, M, H9.$40.00

Nightmare Before Christmas, doll, Boogie, glow-in-the-dark mouth, makes noise, M, H9.......................................$45.00

Nightmare Before Christmas, figures, set of 5, pewter, M, H9 ....$100.00

Nightmare Before Christmas, jack-in-the-box, w/Jack figure, M, H9 ....$75.00

Nightmare Before Christmas, kaleidoscope, M, H9 ....$20.00

Nightmare Before Christmas, kite, H9 ....$8.00

Nightmare Before Christmas, pin, Jack as Santa, red enamel on pewter, M, H9..$30.00

Nightmare Before Christmas, pin, Jack as Santa, red rhinestones set in pewter, M, H9 ....$85.00

Nightmare Before Christmas, pin, Sally in the mirror, pewter, M, H9...$25.00

Nightmare Before Christmas, pin, Zero in the doghouse, pewter, M, H9...$25.00

Nightmare Before Christmas, sunglasses, features Jack's face across top, M, H9...$20.00

Oswald the Rabbit, doll, Ideal, 1930s, felt w/linen face & soft rubber hands, 21", VG, A...$55.00

Oswald the Rabbit, stroller, tin pram w/early image of Oswald, folding type, 5", EX, A...$110.00

Peter Pan, figure, Capt Hook, unlicensed, vinyl, 10", S2..$25.00

Peter Pan, figure, Peter Pan, unlicensed, vinyl, 10", MIB, S2 2 ....$25.00

Peter Pan, pincushion, 1950s, metal Tinkerbell figure on rnd red cloth top w/3-legged base, 3" dia, NM, A $32.00

Pinocchio, ball puzzle, Jiminy Cricket, 1960s, cereal premium, plastic w/colorful picture, 1", M, S2 ....$15.00

Pinocchio, bank, Play Pal, sitting on books, vinyl, 13", VG, S2 ....$40.00

Pinocchio, bank, Play Pal, vinyl figure, 7", VG, S2 ....$30.00

Pinocchio, bank, Play Pal, 1971, vinyl bust, EX, S2 ....$55.00

Pinocchio, doll, Jiminy Cricket, Gund, 1940s, rubber figure well-dressed in cloth clothes & hat, 14", EX, A....................$132.00

Pinocchio, doll, Jiminy Cricket, Gundikin label, stuffed body w/rubber head, NM, A..$40.00

Pinocchio, doll, Pinocchio, Crown (?)/WDP, ca 1940, compo w/jtd arms, 10", EX+, A...$350.00

Pinocchio, doll, Pinocchio, Gund/WDP, gold & red plush w/rubber head, w/tag, 13", NM, A............................$40.00

Pinocchio, doll, Pinocchio, Ideal, 1940, red & yel jtd wood w/compo head, pnt-on chest label, 10", VG, A $81.00

Pinocchio, doll, Pinocchio, Ideal, 1940, red & yel jtd wood w/compo head, pnt-on chest label, 10", EX+ (rare EX box), A $406.00

Pinocchio, doll, Pinocchio, pnt compo w/movable head & arms, cloth-clothed, 10½", G+, A $170.00

Pinocchio, figure, Jiminy Cricket, Ideal, 1939, jointed wood, 9", EX, $550.00.

Pinocchio, Eventyr Teater (theatre), European, 1939, complete w/stage, figures & scenery, unused, EX (EX box), A.**$120.00**

Pinocchio, figure, Gepetto, Multi Products/WDP, syrocco, EX+ **$150.00**

Pinocchio, figure, Jiminy Cricket, Ideal, jtd wood w/pnt eyes, open/closed mouth, wood hat w/felt brim, 8", EX, A .**$400.00**

Pinocchio, figure, Jiminy Cricket, Leisuramics, mail-in premium, unpnt ceramic, 12", MIB, S2 ....**$95.00**

Pinocchio, figure, Jiminy Cricket, Multi-Products, syroco, NM **$225.00**

Pinocchio, figure, Jiminy Cricket, 1960s, pk plastic, 5", EX, S2 ....**$20.00**

Pinocchio, figure, Pinocchio, Marx, w/stand, 3½", MIB, S2 ..**$55.00**

Pinocchio, figure, Pinocchio, Multi-Products, syrocco, NM.**$240.00**

Pinocchio, figure, Pinocchio, Rondect, 1960s, vinyl bust, 12", rare, EX, H4 ....**$45.00**

Pinocchio, mask, Figaro face, Gillette Blue Blade premium, 1939, folded, M8 ....**$8.00**

Pinocchio, mask, Geppetto face, Gillette Blue Blade premium, 1939, EX+, M8...**$15.00**

Pinocchio, music box, prewar France, rnd w/crank on top, lithoed graphics around side, 2½" dia, NM, A.........**$125.00**

Pinocchio, night light, Jiminy Cricket, hand-painted, EX (EX box), O1 ....**$22.00**

Pinocchio, pencil sharpener, Jiminy Cricket, wall mt, NM, I2 ....**$29.00**

Pinocchio, pencil sharpener, Jiminy Cricket figure, 1940s, Bakelite, EX, M8...**$35.00**

Pinocchio, rattle, sgn WD, image of Pinocchio & characters on both sides, celluloid w/red tubular hdl, 6", NM, A ..**$200.00**

Pinocchio, tea tray, WDP, 1939, Figaro watching Geppetto paint Pinocchio, litho tin, 10", EX, A...............**$75.00**

Pinocchio, wall plaque, Multi-Products, 1940s, Pinocchio characters in workshop, unpnt wood fiber, EX+, M8........**$65.00**

Pinocchio, wallet, Jiminy Cricket image, EX, O1 ....**$25.00**

Pinocchio, watch stand, 1940s, pnt ceramic figure, 3", NM, S2 ....**$85.00**

Pluto, bank, 1970s, vinyl figure w/articulated arm that drops coin into doghouse, 9", EX, S2 ....**$45.00**

Pluto, doll, Merry Thought/England, standing, plush w/oilcloth eyes, 12", VG, A **$15.00**

Pluto, figure, Walt Disney Prod, red-pnt wood Pluto on haunches w/head turned looking up, 11", scarce, EX+, A **$125.00**

Pluto, figure, 1960s-70s, bendable, 6", EX, S2....................**$20.00**

Pluto, lantern, Linemar, tin w/glass belly that lights, rubber ears, tail & tongue, 7", NM (EX box), A **$500.00**

Pluto, wagon pull toy with original Mickey Mouse silver-plate place setting (Wm Rogers), 1934, 10", rare, EX, D10, $900.00 to $1,200.00.

Pluto, pencil sharpener, sgn WDP, 1939, mustard-color Bakelite w/lt gr lithoed image of Pluto, EX+, A....................**$52.00**

Rescue Rangers, carryall bag, Chip & Dale images on red vinyl, premium, M **$20.00**

Rescue Rangers, figure, Chip or Dale, Just Toys, 4½", bendable, MIP, K1, ea...**$5.00**

Rescue Rangers, shoelace snappers, Chip & Dale, Hope Industries, MIP **$10.00**

Rescuers Down Under, figure, Bianca or Bernard, Applause, bendable, 2", MIP, K1, ea.................................**$2.50**

Rescuers Down Under, figure, Bianca or Bernard, Just Toys, bendable, 5", MIP, K1, ea................................**$5.00**

Robin Hood, water gun, 1973, figural, NMIB, A.............**$50.00**

Rocketeer, belt, turq or bl, child-sz, H10, ea....................**$30.00**

Rocketeer, display case for PVC figures, Applause, M, H10..**$8.00**

Rocketeer, doll, Applause, H10................................**$15.00**

Rocketeer, figure, bendable, M, H10........................**$6.00**

Rocketeer, figure, PVC, M, H10, ea **$2.00**

Rocketeer, Gee Bee plane, Spectra Star, $25.00; Gee Bee Plane, Spectra Star, $45.00.

Rocketeer, notebook, Mead, 4 different, H10, ea................**$4.00**

Rocketeer, pencil, helmet or flying figure, M, H10, ea **$2.00**

Rocketeer, poster, features the Disney Channel, M, H10.**$20.00**

Rocketeer, Rolalongs, set of 3 w/Rocketeer, plane & blimp, M, S2 ....**$30.00**

Rocketeer, slumber bag, H10................................**$45.00**

Scrooge McDuck, gum machine/bank, plastic figure, 13", MIB, S2 ....**$40.00**

Sleeping Beauty, Magic Bubble Wand, Gardner & Co, features Aurora, bubble solution has disintegrated, unopened, EX+, M8...**$25.00**

Sleeping Beauty, squeeze toy, Sleeping Beauty kneeling down w/forest animals, Dell, 1959, rubber, EX, M8.............**$45.00**

Sleepy, Smiley or Sneezy, see Snow White & the Seven Dwarfs

Snow White & the Seven Dwarfs, bank, WDE, 1938, mk Dime Register, litho tin w/diagonal corners, 2½", NM, A.............**$175.00**

Snow White & the Seven Dwarfs, bank, WDE, 1938, mk Dime Register, litho tin w/diagonal corners, 2½", EX, A......**$153.00**

Snow White & the Seven Dwarfs, bracelet, Flex-Let, enamel heart w/Snow White in center on expansion band, EX (EX box), A **$1,139.00**

Snow White & the Seven Dwarfs, candy containers, WDP/Germany, 8 pnt papier-mache figures w/glitter, ea 5", M **$425.00**

Snow White & the Seven Dwarfs, card album, pastel colors w/1937 graphics, w/100 affixed cards, EX, A $106.00

Snow White and the Seven Dwarfs, charm bracelet, marked Disney, $95.00.

Snow White & the Seven Dwarfs, Christmas lights, Noma, 6 shades, EX+ (EX+ box), M5 ....$160.00

Snow White & the Seven Dwarfs, doll, Grumpy, Gund, 1967, stuffed body & legs w/vinyl arms, 9", M (no bag or tag), H4 ....$12.00

Snow White & the Seven Dwarfs, doll, Happy, Gund, 1967, stuffed body & legs w/vinyl arms, 9", M (in bag), H4 .$18.00

Snow White & the Seven Dwarfs, doll, Sleepy, Gund, 1967, stuffed body & legs w/vinyl arms, 9", M (in bag w/tag), H4 ....$18.00

Snow White & the Seven Dwarfs, doll, Snow White, Applause, 13½", NM, I2 ....$15.00

Snow White doll, Krueger, musical, EX, D10, $750.00.

Snow White & the Seven Dwarfs, dolls, dwarfs, Knickerbocker, compo w/cloth clothing, set of 7, 9½", EX, A $825.00

Snow White & the Seven Dwarfs, dolls, dwarfs, Gund, solid-stuffed bodies & legs w/vinyl arms, set of 7, M (in orig bags), H4 ....$99.00

Snow White & the Seven Dwarfs, figure, Bashful, prewar England, pnt porcelain, 4", scarce, M, A......................$284.00

Snow White & the Seven Dwarfs, figure, Doc, prewar England, pnt procelain, 4", scarce, M, A.................................$265.00

Snow White and the Seven Dwarfs, figure, Dopey, Seiberling, 1940s, rubber, 5", EX, D10, $85.00.

Snow White & the Seven Dwarfs, figure, Grumpy, prewar England, pnt porcelain, 4", scarce, M, A........................$275.00

Snow White & the Seven Dwarfs, figure, Smiley, hollow vinyl, head turns, 4", EX, P3 ....$7.00

Snow White & the Seven Dwarfs, figure, Sneezy, prewar England, pnt porcelain, 4", scarce, M, A........................$275.00

Snow White & the Seven Dwarfs, figure, Snow White, chalk, EX, S1 ....$60.00

Snow White & the Seven Dwarfs, figure, Snow White, prewar English, pnt porcelain, 6", scarce, M, A...................$285.00

Snow White & the Seven Dwarfs, figure, Snow White, Wade England, NM+, M5 ....$135.00

Snow White & the Seven Dwarfs, figures, WDP, 1950s, complete set of dwarfs, soft rubber, 8", EX+, A $125.00

Snow White & the Seven Dwarfs, night light, WDE, 1938, tin w/litho cb Dopey figure on oval base, 4", VG, A.....$235.00

Snow White & the Seven Dwarfs, pin, Dopey figure, pressed wood, NM, J5..$25.00

Snow White & the Seven Dwarfs, pin, Snow White figure, 1930, pressed wood, NM, J5 ....$25.00

Snow White & the Seven Dwarfs, soap dish, floating, Snow White, S2...$25.00

Snow White & the Seven Dwarfs, stamp set, 1938, 8 colorful stamps on uncut sheet, EX, J5 ....$45.00

Snow White & the Seven Dwarfs, sweater guard, features Snow White & Doc, 1940s, NM, O1 ....$97.50

Sword in the Stone, placemat, 1963, EX............................$20.00

Three Little Pigs, bank, Chein, 1930s, lithoed pigs peer out window of tin house as wolf huffs & puffs, 3", EX+, A..$200.00

Three Little Pigs, bank, Mascon Toy, 1950s-60s, talking pig figure, 16", VG, S2 ....$125.00

Three Little Pigs, candy tin, Metal Box Co/England, prewar, rectangular w/diagonal corners, litho tin, NM+, A...$95.00

Three Little Pigs, soap, WDP, 1930s, set of 3 bars w/raised figures on ea, EX (EX box), A $75.00

Three Little Pigs, bank, Chein, 1930s, tin lithographed house, EX, D10, $175.00.

Three Little Pigs and Big Bad Wolf, candy pail, Mayfair, 3", VG/EX, D10, $110.00.

Tinkerbell, see Peter Pan

Uncle Scrooge, Gold Mobile Hand Car, Pride Lines, plated steel w/molded figures, O gauge, electric, 10", EX (EX box), A ..$160.00

Who Framed Roger Rabbit, bath set, 3-pc, M, S2 ....$65.00

Who Framed Roger Rabbit, doll, Roger Rabbit, Applause, stuffed, w/orig tag, 48", M, D1 ....$300.00

Who Framed Roger Rabbit, doll, Roger Rabbit, Playskool, stuffed, MIB, S2 ....$50.00

Who Framed Roger Rabbit, doll, Roger Rabbit, stuffed, 18", M, S2 ....$50.00

Who Framed Roger Rabbit, doll, Roger Rabbit, stuffed, 24", M, S2 ....$75.00

Who Framed Roger Rabbit, figure, Baby Herman, ceramic, Disney store item, M, S2...$45.00

Who Framed Roger Rabbit, figure, Benny the Cab, LJN, declared unsafe, produced but never marketed, MOC, D1, from $50 to..$75.00

Who Framed Roger Rabbit, figure, Benny the Cab, plush, MIB, S2 ....$50.00

Who Framed Roger Rabbit, figure, Eddie Valiant, LJN, bendable, 6", MOC, D1 ....$5.00

Who Framed Roger Rabbit, figure, Jessica, LJN, bendable, 6", MOC, D1 ....$30.00

Who Framed Roger Rabbit, figure, Jessica, ceramic, Disney store item, M, S2 ....$50.00

Who Framed Roger Rabbit, figure, Judge Doom, LJN, bendable, 6", MOC, D1...$5.00

Who Framed Roger Rabbit, figure, Roger Rabbit, Applause, PVC, M, D1 ....$5.00

Who Framed Roger Rabbit, figure, Roger Rabbit, ceramic, Disney store item, M, S2..$40.00

Who Framed Roger Rabbit, figure, Roger Rabbit on yel crate, Applause, PVC, M, O1..$10.00

Who Framed Roger Rabbit, figure, Smart Guy, LJN, bendable, 6", MOC, D1 ....$5.00

Who Framed Roger Rabbit, party bags for party favors, plastic, MIP, S2 ....$20.00

Who Framed Roger Rabbit, pins, Roger, Jessica, Doom, Weasle, Baby Herman & Benny, set of 6, cloisonne & enamel, M, M8 ....$40.00

Who Framed Roger Rabbit, plush stick-on, from Disneyland, MOC, S2..$25.00

Who Framed Roger Rabbit, tray, figural Jessica, M, S2..$70.00

Winnie the Pooh, baby rattle, figural, VG, S2.................$15.00

Winnie the Pooh, bank, ceramic Pooh Bear in sitting pose, 6¼", VG, S2 ....$30.00

Winnie the Pooh, bank, 1964, ceramic Pooh Bear w/honey pot, 5", light crack in back, VG, S2...................................$30.00

Winnie the Pooh, bulletin board, 17x24", EX, J2 ....$20.00

Winnie the Pooh, Christmas ornament, Eeyore figure, stuffed felt, EX, I2 ....$5.00

Winnie the Pooh, figure, Eeyore, Japan, 1970s, ceramic figure, S2 ....$45.00

Winnie the Pooh, Hunny Pumper Play Doh Set, Sears Exclusive, 1970s, NMIB, S2 ....$50.00

Winnie the Pooh, lamp, 1970s, Pooh & Eeyore figures, VG, S2 ....$35.00

Winnie the Pooh, plate, Melmac plastic, EX $15.00

Winnie the Pooh, Play-Doh Decorator Set, EX (EX box), J2, from $35 to...$45.00

Winnie the Pooh, squeeze toys, Sears/WDP, ca 1967, set of 6 rubber Pooh characters, from 3½" to 7½", EX, A $39.00

101 Dalmatians, figure, Perdita, Disneykins, 1960s, EX, M8..$65.00

101 Dalmatians, figure, Perdita or Pongo, Just Toys, bendable, 5", MIP, K1, ea..$5.00

101 Dalmatians, figure, 1960s, dog wearing fire hat & holding extinguisher, vinyl, 10", VG, S2................................$10.00

BISQUE FIGURES

Big Bad Wolf, prewar Japan, 3⅝", scarce sz, EX+, A.........$84.00

Donald Duck, prewar Japan, as admiral, 3¼", NM, A $90.00

Donald Duck, prewar Japan, long-billed Donald holding bugle, 3⅛", scarce, EX+, A..$50.00

Donald Duck, prewar Japan, long-billed Donald w/head turned, jtd arms, 5¾", NM, A $658.00

Donald Duck, prewar Japan, mk S1333, long-billed Donald holding flag w/head turned, 4", scarce, EX+, A $204.00

Donald Duck, prewar Japan, playing accordion, 5", EX+, A..$175.00

Donald Duck, prewar Japan, proud pose w/bill turned up, 3½", VG, A $58.00

Donald Duck, prewar Japan, proud pose w/bill turned up, 3½", NM, A...$121.00

Donald Duck, prewar Japan, seated on tricycle w/feet flat on ground, 3½", EX, A $123.00

Donald Duck, prewar Japan, long-billed Donald with head turned sideways, jointed arms, 5¾", M, $800.00.

Donald Duck, prewar Japan, standing, hands behind back, head turned, bill open, 3", EX+, A, from $85 to ..$120.00
Elmer Elephant, dtd 1936, 4¼", rare, NM, A $265.00
Goofy, prewar Japan, The Goof, 3⅝", scarce, NM, A $125.00
Horace Horsecollar, prewar Japan, 3⅝", scarce, EX+, A..$150.00
Mickey, Minnie & Pluto (Three Pals), Borgfeldt, 1930s, w/cane, w/umbrella, Pluto sitting, 3¾", NM+ (EX box), A.....$700.00
Mickey, Minnie & Pluto (Three Pals), Borgfeldt/WDE, prewar Japan, 4⅛", NM (EX box), A...................................$875.00
Mickey & Minnie Mouse, Japan, 1930, Mickey & Minnie arm in arm, 4½", NM+, A..$350.00
Mickey & Minnie Mouse, WDE/prewar Japan, Mickey w/hands on hips; Minnie in hat, hands on hips, 4", EX+, A, pr..$55.00
Mickey & Pluto, prewar Japan, Mickey riding Pluto, 3", EX, A $150.00

Mickey Mouse, movable arms, 5¼", EX, $600.00.

Mickey Mouse, prewar Germany, playing saxophone, 2½", rare, EX+, A...$187.00
Mickey Mouse, prewar Japan, as baseball catcher, 3¼", EX+, A...$350.00
Mickey Mouse, prewar Japan, holding song book while singing, 3½", EX, A..$72.00
Mickey Mouse, prewar Japan, in nightgown, 4", EX, A ..$90.00

Mickey Mouse, prewar Japan, movable arms, 9", NM (orig box), A...$1,050.00
Mickey Mouse, prewar Japan, playing accordion, 3¼", EX+, A...$300.00
Mickey Mouse, prewar Japan, playing banjo, 5½", NM, J2..$529.00
Mickey Mouse, prewar Japan, playing drum, 3½", EX+, A..$83.00
Mickey Mouse, prewar Japan, playing mandolin, cloth tail, 5¼", NM, A $280.00
Mickey Mouse, prewar Japan, playing various instruments, set of 4, 3½" ea, MIB, A $1,157.00

Mickey Mouse, with baseball bat, 3¼", EX, $250.00.

Mickey Mouse, prewar Japan, w/cane, 3¾", NM, A $100.00
Mickey Mouse, prewar Japan, w/cane, wearing felt hat, 4⅜", EX, A $60.00

Mickey Mouse in Canoe, prewar Japan, 2", VG, $1,200.00.

Mickey Mouse, prewar Japan, w/flag, 3¾", EX+, A...........$75.00
Mickey Mouse, prewar Japan, w/hands on hips, 2¾", NM, A $60.00
Mickey Mouse, prewar Japan, w/rifle, 3⅜", EX+, A..........$60.00
Mickey Mouse, prewar Japan, w/sword, 3¼", NM, A........$65.00
Minnie Mouse, prewar Japan, playing mandolin, 3⅝", NM, A $40.00
Minnie Mouse, prewar Japan, w/concertina, orig paper label, 3½", NM, A $95.00
Minnie Mouse, prewar Japan, w/folded umbrella, 3¾", EX+, A..$75.00
Minnie Mouse, prewar Japan, w/hands on hips, 2¾", NM, A $60.00

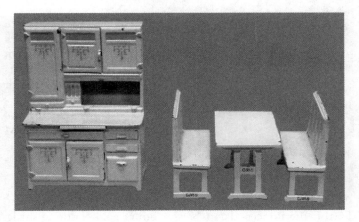

Minnie Mouse, movable arms, 5¼", D10, EX, $475.00.

Minnie Mouse, prewar Japan, w/umbrella & purse, 4⅜", EX, A $75.00
Pinocchio, prewar Japan, 3", EX, J2 ....$60.00
Snow White & the Seven Dwarfs, prewar Japan, Snow White w/3" dwarfs, set of 8, EX, A $224.00

Snow White and the Seven Dwarfs, boxed set, Snow White: 3¼", Dwarfs: 2½", MIB, $1,200.00.

Three Little Pigs, Borgfeldt/prewar Japan, holding trowel, playing flute & violin, 2½", M (EX box), A...................$535.00
Three Little Pigs, mk Foreign, 1933, farmer pig w/cloth clothing & jtd arms, 4", EX+, A $112.00
Three Little Pigs, prewar Japan, flute player, drummer & violinist, set of 3, 3½", VG (VG box), A $160.00
Three Little Pigs, prewar Japan, flute player (4¾"), drummer & violinist (3½") set of 3, EX, A $85.00

Dollhouse Furniture

Back in the forties and fifties, little girls often spent hour after hour with their dollhouses, keeping house for their imaginary families, cooking on tiny stoves (that often came with scaled-to-fit pots and pans), serving meals in lovely dining rooms, making beds, and rearranging furniture, most of which was plastic, much of which was made by Renwal, Ideal, Marx, Irwin, and Plasco. Jaydon made plastic furniture as well, but sadly never marked it. Tootsietoy produced metal items, many in boxed sets.

Of all of these manufacturers, Renwal and Ideal are considered the most collectible. Renwal's furniture was often detailed; some pieces had moving parts. Many were made in more than one color, often brightened with decals. Besides the furniture, they made accessory items as well as 'dollhouse' dolls of the whole family. Ideal's Petite Princess line was packaged in sets with wonderful detail, accessorized down to the perfume bottles on the top of the vanity. Ideal furniture and parts are numbered, always with an 'I' prexif. Most Renwal pieces are also numbered.

Advisor: Judith Mosholder (M7).

Acme, hammock, 2-tone colors, M7, ea............................$10.00
Acme, hammock, 2-tone colors, w/baby, M7, ea $12.00
Acme, rocker, yel & red, M7 ....$3.00
Acme, stroller, colors w/horse-head motif, M7, ea.............$8.00
Acme, stroller, pk w/bl top, M7...$8.00
Arcade, dining room set w/table & 6 chairs, hutch & sideboard, maroon-pnt CI, 3"-6", G+, A.....................................$300.00

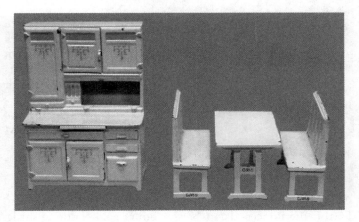

Arcade, kitchen set with Hoosier cabinet, table and 2 bench-style chairs, painted cast iron, NM, D10, $750.00.

Arcade, kitchen set w/Hoosier cabinet, ice box, sink, table & 2 chairs, pnt CI, 3"-8", G, A $110.00
Arcade, range, Hotpoint, footed electric type, drawers & doors open, tan-pnt CI w/gr trim, 6", VG, A $130.00
Arcade, range, Roper, gas type w/opening door, footed, red-pnt CI, 4½", VG, A...$70.00
Arcade, range, Roper, plated gas controls, footed, wht-pnt CI w/silver trim, VG, A...$100.00
Arcade, Standard sanitary tubs, dbl tubs on legs, yel-pnt CI, 3¼", G, A...$55.00
Best, bunk beds, bl, w/ladder, M7 ....$12.00
Best, chair, red, M7, ea...$2.00
Best, rocking horse, bl or pk, w/baby, M7.........................$12.00
Ideal, baby, w/pnt diaper, M7 ....$10.00
Ideal, buffet, drawer opens, ¾" scale, S13.......................$12.00
Ideal, chair, dining room; brn lyre-back w/bl seat, ¾" scale, S13...$7.00

Ideal, chair, folding; #I-1707, brn fr w/ivory seat, ¾" scale, S13 ....$20.00

Ideal, chair, lawn; #I-939, brn w/marbleized pk, ¾" scale, S13 ....$10.00

Ideal, chair, living room; marbleized gr, M7......................$12.00

Ideal, hamper, ivory, M7...$4.00

Ideal, highboy, brn, ¾" scale, S13..................................$12.00

Ideal, mangle, wht w/blk, M7 ....$12.00

Ideal, night stand, brn, ¾" scale, S13...............................$6.00

Ideal, radio, #I-999, brn, ¾" scale, S13.............................$6.00

Ideal, sewing machine, ¾" scale, S13.................................$8.00

Ideal, shopping cart, bl w/red wheels, wht basket, ¾" scale, S13 ....$10.00

Ideal, sofa, marbleized gr $20.00

Ideal, table, lawn; yel, rnd, ¾" scale, S13 ....$12.00

Ideal, toilet, ivory w/blk hdl, ¾" scale, S13 ....$10.00

Ideal, tub, ivory w/blk, M7..$6.00

Ideal, vanity, brn, w/mirror, no moving parts, ¾" scale, S13.$15.00

Ideal Petite Princess, coffee table, wht & gold, marbleized top, S13 ....$10.00

Ideal Petite Princess, dressing table, pk satin band, gold 3-way mirror, S13 ....$20.00

Ideal Petite Princess Heirloom Table Set, complete with table, bookends, books and lamp, M (EX box), $28.50.

Ideal Petite Princess, lamp, brass w/brn & gold plastic sq shade, S13 ....$8.00

Ideal Petite Princess, lyre table, wht & gold w/marbleized top, S13 ....$12.00

Ideal Petite Princess Royal Dressing Table, complete with vanity, chair and assorted bottles, M (EX box), $28.00.

Ideal Young Decorator, buffet, marbleized reddish brn, M7.$15.00

Ideal Young Decorator, dining room table & chairs, bright yel seat cushions, 7-pc, S13 ....$80.00

Irwin, broom, orange hdl, M7..$8.00

Irwin, mop, bl hdl, M7...$4.00

Jaydon, buffet, reddish brn, M7...$4.00

Jaydon, chair, reddish brn, M7..$1.00

Jaydon, cupboard, reddish brn, M7....................................$4.00

Jaydon, toilet, ivory w/red, M7..$5.00

JP Co, buffet, brn, M7...$4.00

JP Co, hutch, brn, M7..$4.00

Marx, accessory set, #1427, 1950s, complete w/20 figures, swimming pool, playground equipment, etc, MIB $150.00

Marx, bathtub, corner-type, ivory, ½" scale, M7................$2.00

Marx, bathtub, corner-type, pk w/fish decal, ¾" scale, S13 $12.00

Marx, bed, dbl-sleigh; bright yel w/rose decals, ¾" scale, chip on footboard, S13 ....$5.00

Marx, breakfront, mahogany, ¾" scale, S13.....................$10.00

Marx, buffet, dk maroon, hard plastic, ½" scale, M7...........$2.00

Marx, chair, barrel; red, back legs slightly chewed, ¾" scale, S13 ....$7.00

Marx, chair, captain's; yel, hard plastic, ½" scale, M7.........$2.00

Marx, chair, kitchen; wht, solid back, ¾" scale, S13...........$6.00

Marx, chair, living room; sq back, red, hard plastic, ½" scale, M7..$2.00

Marx, crib, bl, soft plastic, ½" scale, M7 ....$2.00

Marx, cupboard, china; dk brn, hard plastic, ½" scale, M7 .$2.00

Marx, hamper, pk, ¾" scale, S13.......................................$7.00

Marx, night stand, yel, hard plastic, ½" scale, M7..............$2.00

Marx, piano bench, yel, hard plastic, ½" scale, M7............$1.50

Marx, refrigerator, wht, ¾" scale, S13................................$5.00

Marx, sideboard, mahogany, ¾" scale, S13.......................$10.00

Marx, sink w/towel racks, pk, ¾" scale, S13 ....$10.00

Marx, sofa, gr or yel, hard plastic, ½" scale, M7 ....$2.00

Marx, sofa, mint gr, ¾" scale, S13 ....$10.00

Marx, sofa, 3-pc, pale bl, hard plastic, ½" scale, M7..........$5.00

Marx, table, dining; dk brn, hard plastic, ½" scale, M7.......$2.00

Marx, table, umbrella; yel, hard plastic, ½" scale, no umbrella, M7..$3.00

Marx, toilet, cream, ¾" scale, S13.....................................$6.00

Marx, TV/Hi-fi combination, bright gr, no moving parts, ¾" scale, S13...$5.00

Marx, vanity, bright yel w/silver-pnt mirror, ¾" scale, S13.$9.00

Marx, vanity, yel, hard plastic, ½" scale, M7......................$2.00

Mattel Littles, armoire, M7..$15.00

Mattel Littles, bathtub, M7 ....$10.00

Mattel Littles, chair, M7...$8.00

Mattel Littles, cradle, M7 ....$5.00

Mattel Littles, dresser, M7...$15.00

Mattel Littles, sink/icebox, M7..$15.00

Mattel Littles, sofa, M7..$12.00

Mattel Littles, stove, M7..$15.00

Mattel Littles, table, drop leaf; M7....................................$6.00

Mattel Littles, table, tilt top; M7..$8.00

Plasco, bathroom set w/sink, tub, toilet, hamper, vanity & bench, paper floor plan (orig box), M7 ....$90.00

Plasco, bathtub, wht, M7 ....$1.50

Plasco, buffet, brn or tan, M7, ea......................................$4.00

Plasco, chair, dining room; brn $3.00
Plasco, chair, kitchen; ivory, M7 ....$1.50
Plasco, chair, living room; gr or rose, ea $6.00
Plasco, chair, living room; yel, no base, S13 ....$3.00
Plasco, chair, patio; bl w/wht legs, S13 ....$7.00
Plasco, chaise lounge, red w/cream arms, S13 ....$12.00
Plasco, chest, ivory, 4-drawer, ftd, M7 ....$3.00
Plasco, coffee table, all colors, M7, ea $3.00
Plasco, grandfather clock, orig paper face, S13 ....$14.00
Plasco, highboy, ivory, M7 ....$15.00
Plasco, night stand, marbleized brn or tan, M7, ea $3.00
Plasco, sink, kitchen; mint gr, no base, S13 ....$5.00
Plasco, sofa, aqua, no base, S13 ....$5.00
Plasco, stove, wht, no base, S13 ....$4.00
Plasco, table, dining room; brn, M7 ....$8.00
Plasco, table, kitchen; all colors, ea $5.00
Plasco, table & 2 chairs, kitchen; wht $9.00
Plasco, toilet $5.00
Plasco, vanity, dk brn, straight sides w/rounded front, S13 .$8.00
Plasco, vanity, pk $5.00
Princess Patti, bathtub, no mirror or oil bottles, M7 ....$90.00
Princess Patti, kitchen sink, no accessories, M7 ....$90.00
Renwal, baby, #8, pnt or no pnt, M7, ea $8.00
Renwal, bathroom scale, #10, red, M7 ....$8.00
Renwal, bathtub, #95, pk w/bl spigots, S13 ....$6.00
Renwal, bathtub, #95, yel w/blk spigots, S13 ....$12.00
Renwal, bed, #81, brn w/ivory bedspread, S13 ....$10.00
Renwal, buffet, #D55, brn, drawer opens, M7 ....$8.00
Renwal, buffet, #D55, brn, no moving parts, M7 ....$6.00
Renwal, cabinet, china; #52, brn, S13 ....$6.00
Renwal, cabinet, china; #52, brn w/Cinderella decoration,
    S13 ....$6.00
Renwal, chair, #K63, all colors, M7, ea $3.00
Renwal, chair, barrel; #77, bl w/red base, S13 ....$10.00
Renwal, chair, club; #76, all plain colors, M7, ea $8.00
Renwal, chair, club; #76, colors w/stenciling, M7, ea $9.00
Renwal, chair, rocking; #65, blk w/stenciling, M7 ....$10.00
Renwal, chair, rocking; #65, red w/yel seat or yel w/red seat,
    M7, ea $6.00
Renwal, chair, teacher's; #35, brn, M7 ....$15.00
Renwal, china closet, #D52, brn, M7 ....$5.00
Renwal, clock, kitchen; ivory, M7 ....$20.00
Renwal, clock, mantel; #14, red or ivory, S13, ea $12.00
Renwal, desk, student's; #33, red, brn or yel, S13, ea $15.00
Renwal, doll, brother, #42, tan, metal rivets, pnt flakes on face
    & worn shoes, S13 ....$25.00
Renwal, doll, dad, #44, brn outfit, metal rivets, S13 ....$30.00
Renwal, doll, mom, #43, rose-pk outfit, metal rivets, S13 .$25.00
Renwal, doll, sister, #41, yel dress, M7 ....$20.00
Renwal, dustpan, #64, red, S13 ....$12.00
Renwal, end table, #L73, brn, rnd, M7 ....$5.00
Renwal, floor lamp, #70, red w/ivory shade, M7 ....$12.00
Renwal, hamper, #98, S13 ....$5.00
Renwal, highboy, #85, lt bl, no moving parts, S13 ....$10.00
Renwal, highboy, #85, woodtone, drawers open, S13 ....$10.00
Renwal, highchair, #30, pk, M7 ....$20.00
Renwal, ironing board, #32, bl, M7 ....$5.00
Renwal, Kiddie car, #27, red, bl & yel, S13 ....$40.00

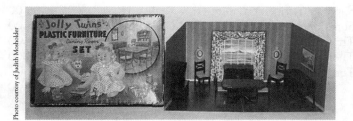

Renwal, Jolly Twins dining room set, complete, MIB, M7, from $100.00 to $125.00.

Renwal, Jolly Twins kitchen set, complete, MIB, M7, from $100.00 to $125.00.

Renwal, lamp, table; #71, brn w/ivory, M7 ....$8.00
Renwal, lamp, table; #71, red w/ivory shade, S13 ....$9.00
Renwal, night stand, #84, pk, S13 ....$3.00
Renwal, piano, #L74, M7 ....$20.00
Renwal, piano/vanity bench, #75, M7 ....$3.00
Renwal, playground seesaw, #21, bl, red & yel, melt mks on
    seats, S13 ....$15.00
Renwal, playpen, #118, pk w/bl base, mc beads, S13 ....$14.00
Renwal, potty chair, #36, pk, S13 ....$8.00
Renwal, radio, #16, brn, S13 ....$15.00
Renwal, radio, #18, console model w/slide-out record player, red,
    S13 ....$15.00
Renwal, refrigerator, #66, wht w/blk hdls, no moving parts,
    S13 ....$14.00
Renwal, server, #D54, all colors, opening drawer, M7, ea ...$8.00
Renwal, server, #54, brn, no moving parts, S13 ....$5.00
Renwal, sink, #68, wht w/blk hdls, no moving parts, S13 ...$7.00
Renwal, sink, #96, pk w/bl spigots, S13 ....$10.00
Renwal, smoking stand & ashtray, #13, red w/wht hdl, clear ash-
    tray, S13 ....$14.00
Renwal, sofa, #78, red w/mint gr cushions, S13 ....$11.00
Renwal, stool, #12, red w/ivory, M7 ....$10.00
Renwal, stove, #K69, all colors, M7, ea $10.00
Renwal, table, cocktail; #72, brn, M7 ....$5.00
Renwal, table, dining; #D51, orange, M7 ....$10.00
Renwal, table, kitchen; #67, ivory, M7 ....$5.00
Renwal, table, kitchen; #67, wht, M7 ....$6.00
Renwal, telephone, #28, yel w/red receiver, bl & wht cord,
    S13 ....$24.00
Renwal, toilet, #97, turq, S13 ....$12.00
Renwal, toilet, #97, wht w/blk hdl, S13 ....$10.00
Renwal, tricycle, #7, red & yel, S13 ....$22.00
Renwal, vacuum cleaner, red w/yel hdl & decal, M7 ....$25.00
Renwal, vanity, #82, filigree, cb back, no mirror, S13 ......$16.00
Renwal, washing machine, #31, bl, M7 ....$25.00

Superior, refrigerator, mint gr, ¾" scale, M7 ....$3.00
Superior, toilet, dk gr, ¾" scale, M7...................................$3.00
Thomas, cradle, pk & bl, unmk, M7....................................$4.00
Thomas, stroller, pk or bl, M7, ea..$5.00
Tootsietoy, bathroom, ivory-pnt cast metal, ivory & blk toilet,
    not orig set, 4-pc, VG/EX, G7 ....$80.00

Tootsietoy, bedroom set, pink-painted cast metal, 6 pieces, EX+ (VG red and green checked box with bright graphics), $120.00.

Tootsietoy, bedroom, various shades of bl-pnt cast metal, not
    orig set, 9-pc, VG/EX, G7 ....$120.00
Tootsietoy, bedroom, wht-pnt cast metal, pk chaise lounge, not
    orig set, 7-pc, VG/EX, G7 ....$125.00

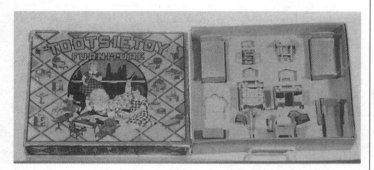

Tootsietoy, bedroom set, painted and flocked metal beds, dresser and 8 other pieces of pink furniture, minor paint chips, G (G box), A, $100.00.

Tootsietoy, dining room, brn-pnt cast metal, 1 pk chair, not orig
    set, 9-pc, VG/EX, G7..$90.00
Tootsietoy, kitchen, ivory-pnt cast metal, gr stove, not orig set,
    9-pc, VG/EX, G7...$105.00
Tootsietoy, living room, pnt cast metal, some marbleized pcs &
    some solid, not orig set, 17-pc, VG/EX, G7 ....$200.00
Tootsietoy, sitting room, brassy w/bl cushions, ivory-colored fire-
    place, not orig set, 11-pc, VG/EX, G7 ....$105.00

Dollhouses

Dollhouses were first made commercially in America in the late 1700s. A century later, Bliss and Schoenhut were making wonderful dollhouses that even yet occasionally turn up on the market, and many were being imported from Germany. During the forties and fifties, American toy makers made a variety of cottages; today they're all collectible.

Advisor: Bob and Marcie Tubbs (T5).

Bliss, Colonial-style mansion, 4 steps up to porch w/rnd columns
    & metal grillwork, 18x16x10", G-, A $275.00

Bliss, lithographed paper on wood, multicolor trim and window appointments, hinged front door, front wall opens for access to interior, porch repainted, 21¼", G, A, $300.00.

Bliss, litho paper on wood 2-story w/opening facade, wallpapered
    interior, 9", G+, A..$450.00
Bliss, stable, paper on wood w/opening loft doors, turned
    columns in front divide 3 stalls, 20", G+, A.........$1,700.00
Bliss type, dormer roof, 2-story, litho fretwork trim on porch w/4
    columns & spindle rails, 20x16", G, A $750.00
Converse, Horse Barn, emb & stenciled roof & gable ends, lift-
    off roof, w/2 pnt lead farm animals, 9½", G+...........$200.00
Converse, Red Robin Farm, lift-off roof, w/7 stenciled wood ani-
    mals, 12", VG $275.00
Dunham's, wood 4-story, printed brick, flat top, ea story is single
    room w/19th-century litho interior, 29", G, A.........$275.00
Marx, litho tin w/breezeway & doorbell, includes plastic furni-
    ture & accessories, unassembled, 21", NMIB, A......$100.00
Schoenhut, red tile roof, 2 turned wht porch posts, papered inte-
    rior, w/6 pcs of furniture, 13x17x13", EX, A $1,300.00
Schoenhut, 2-story w/4 rooms, yel w/wht trim, gr shutters, win-
    dow boxes w/flowers, roof folds, 18x19", VG, A.......$310.00
Unknown Maker, German, paper litho on wood, pnt roof, front
    door opens, electrified, 17", G-, A $400.00

Schoenhut, painted wood, fiberboard and cardboard, 2-story cottage with porch, 6 lithographed paper rooms and 2 hallways, chandelier, chimney, lift-off roof, ca 1920, 27½x23x23", VG+, A, $1,045.00.

Unknown Maker, German, 2-story w/fretwork, gr w/red roof, 1 side open, w/7 pcs of wood furniture, 14½", VG $800.00

SHOPS AND SINGLE ROOMS

Bake Shop, 3-sided pnt & papered wood w/counter, shelves & drawers, w/many bake-shop items, 26", EX+, A.........$650.00

Bathroom, German, early 1900s, pink and white tin, working plumbing and battery-operated light, 7x10x7", G-, A, $345.00.

Coffee Shop, 3-sided pnt & papered wood w/varnished counter & glass front doors, many coffee-related items, 21", VG, A $300.00
Corner Grocery, Wolverine, tin w/folding shelves, lithoed rear wall & counter, w/many grocery items, 15½", G, A..$110.00

Grocery Store, 3-sided pnt wood, back counter w/metal-labeled drawers in English, many store items, 20", EX, A....$500.00
Kitchen, pnt wood, w/accessories & shelves, table & chairs, 2 celluloid dolls 9" & 5", 34x17" base, G+, A $525.00
Modern Kitchen Set, Marx, litho tin diorama, rear wall lined w/cabinets, sink & appliances, w/accessories, 26", NMIB, A...$190.00
Newlyweds Bathroom #192, Marx, 1925, 3-sided litho tin room complete w/furniture, 3x5x3", NM (EX+ box), A...$400.00
Newlyweds Bedroom #191, Marx, 1925, 3-sided litho tin room complete w/furniture, cloth bedspread & pillows, 3x5x2", MIB...$305.00
Newlyweds Dining Room #194, Marx, 1925, 3-sided litho tin room complete w/furniture, 3x5x2", MIB...............$305.00
Newlyweds Kitchen #190, Marx, 1925, 3-sided litho tin room complete w/furniture, 3x5x3", M (G box), A..........$400.00
Newlyweds Library #105, Marx, 1925, 3-sided litho tin room complete w/furniture, 3x5x2", MIB........................$355.00
Newlyweds Parlor #193, Marx, 1925, 3-sided litho tin room complete w/furniture, 3x5x2", MIB........................$305.00
Store Counter, pnt wood w/cb labels in German, many store items, 10½", VG, A..$200.00
Tea Grocery Shop, lithoed paper on wood w/labels in German, wood, tin & cb tea containers, 14½", EX, A............$210.00
Toy Town Grocery Store, Parker Brothers, 3-sided w/lithoed paper over wood, many store items, 17", VG+, A ...$350.00
Tudor Stable, 3-sided pnt wood & stucco w/roof, 4 wood & compo animals, 14½", EX, A $160.00
Victorian Room, 3-sided wallpapered cb folding walls w/cloth curtains, upholstered & wood furniture, 21½", VG, A...$150.00
Wrapping Counter, pnt wood w/porcelain labels in German, lift-up desk, glass cabinet, w/holiday accessories, 21", EX, A .$575.00

Dolls and Accessories

Obviously the field of dolls cannot be covered in a price guide such as this, but we wanted to touch on some of the later plastic dolls from the fifties and sixties, since so much of the collector interest today is centered on those decades. For in-depth information on dolls of all types, we recommend the many lovely doll books written by authority Pat Smith; all are available from Collector Books.

See also Action Figures; Barbie and Friends; Celebrity Dolls; Character, TV and Movie Collectibles; GI Joe; and other specific categories.

BABY DOLLS

Aimee, Hasbro, 1972, plastic & vinyl, rooted hair, 18", EX $55.00
Baby Beans, Mattel, 1971, vinyl w/beanbag body, blond bangs, bl pnt eyes, sewn-on clothes, 11", EX.......................$20.00
Baby Belly Button, Ideal, 1970, plastic & vinyl, rooted blond hair, pnt eyes, redressed, 9", EX.................................$25.00
Baby Big Eyes, Ideal, 1954-59, soft vinyl, rooted curly hair, orig blanket & nightie, 20", EX....................................$50.00

Baby Crissy, Ideal, 1973-76, vinyl, rooted auburn hair grows w/arm movement, redressed, 24", EX $40.00

Baby First Step, Mattel, 1964, plastic & vinyl, blond hair, sleep eyes, battery-op, redressed, 18", EX $35.00

Baby Giggles, Ideal, 1967-69, vinyl, rooted blond hair, side-glancing eyes, pull hands together & she giggles, 18", EX...$120.00

Baby Huggams, Madame Alexander, 1963, soft stuffed body, redressed, 9", EX $20.00

Baby Laugh Alot, Remco, 1970, plastic & vinyl, all orig, 16", EX..$25.00

Baby Secret, Mattel, 1965, vinyl w/foam body, red hair, bl pnt eyes, pull-string talker, all orig, 18", EX $45.00

Baby Tweaks, Horsman, 1967, cloth & vinyl w/inset eyes, 20", EX..$30.00

Betsy Wetsy, Ideal, 1959, plastic & vinyl, molded hair, redressed, EX $55.00

Bizzie Lizzie, Ideal, 1971-72, vinyl, rooted blond hair, sleep eyes, irons, vacuums & dusts, battery-op, 18", EX $40.00

Bootsie, Horsman, 1969, plastic & vinyl, rooted blk hair, brn sleep eyes, all orig, 12", EX $15.00

Bucky Love Notes, Mattel, 1974, press body parts for tunes, all orig, 12", EX..$30.00

Carrie Cries, Sayco, 1963, plastic & vinyl, rooted hair, bl sleep eyes, all orig, battery-op, 19", EX $10.00

Cuddly Kissy, Ideal, 1964, vinyl & cloth, press stomach & she puckers up, all orig, 17", EX.................................$60.00

Dancerina, Mattel, 1968, complete w/pk outfit, shoes & crown, 24", VG+, I2 ....$39.00

Deluxe Kissy, Ideal, 1962, all orig, 22", M.........................$95.00

Floppy, Horsman, 1965, foam body & legs, rooted blond hair, bl sleep eyes, all orig, 18", EX $30.00

Gabbigale, Kenner, 1972, plastic & vinyl, blond hair, pnt eyes, all orig, battery-op, 18", EX $45.00

Kathy Tears, Madame Alexander, 1959-62, vinyl, closed mouth, 15", EX $70.00

Lazy Dazy, Ideal, 1971, vinyl & cloth, rooted blond hair, bl sleep eyes, all orig, 12", EX $20.00

Magic Meg, Uneeda, 1971, plastic & vinyl, rooted blond hair w/grow feature, bl sleep eyes, all orig, 16", EX $35.00

My Bottle Baby, Ideal, 1979-80, cloth & vinyl, rooted blond hair in pigtails, pull string for nursing sounds, 14", EX.....$25.00

Newborn Thumbelina, Ideal, 1968-72, vinyl & cloth, rooted blond hair, pull string & she squirms, 9", EX $30.00

Playpen Doll, Jolly Toys, 1967, nurser, plastic & vinyl, rooted hair, orig sleeper, 14", EX $12.00

Pretty Betty, Horsman, 1954, nurser, rooted brn hair, sleep eyes, redressed, 16", VG $25.00

Sister Small Talk, Mattel, 1967, plastic & vinyl, rooted blond hair, pnt eyes & teeth, all orig, 10", EX $25.00

Snuggles, Ideal, 1978-81, vinyl & cloth, rooted hair, pull string & she snuggles teddy bear or blanket, 12½", EX........$25.00

Sweet Cookie, Hasbro, 1972, vinyl w/rooted hair, all orig, EX .$35.00

Teensie Baby, Horsman, 1964, nurser, plastic & vinyl, pnt eyes, all orig, 12", EX $15.00

Tickletoes, Ideal, 1931-39, stuffed cloth w/rubber arms & legs, organdy dress, squeeze legs & she cries, 15", EX $100.00

Tiny Baby Tenderlove, Mattel, 1971, vinyl hair piece attached to vinyl head, 1-piece body and limbs, painted eyes, all original, M, $20.00.

Ginny Baby, Vogue, 1960s, vinyl and plastic, toddler body, M, $40.00.

Tippy Tumbles, Ideal, 1977, vinyl & plastic, rooted hair, stands on head & flips over, battery-op, 16½", EX $40.00

Tumbling Tomboy, Remco, 1969, plastic & vinyl, all orig, 16", EX...$25.00

Twinkle Eyes, Ideal, 1957-60, soft vinyl, rooted saran ponytail, orig pinafore & bonnet, 1957-60, 19", EX $55.00

Twistee, Jolly Toys, 1964, vinyl w/molded foam body, rooted brunette hair, blk sleep eyes, all orig, 16", EX............$25.00

BETSY MCCALL

The tiny 8" Betsy McCall doll was manufactured by the American Character Doll Co. from 1957 through 1963. She was made from high-quality hard plastic with a bisque-like finish and hand-painted features. Betsy came in four hair colors — tosca, red, blonde, and brunette. She had blue sleep eyes, molded lashes, a winsome smile, and a fully jointed body with bendable knees. On her back there is an identification circle which reads McCall Corp. The basic doll wore a sheer chemise, white taffeta panties, nylon socks, and Maryjane-style shoes and could be purchased for $2.25.

There were two different materials used for tiny Betsy's hair. The first was a soft mohair sewn into fine mesh. Later the rubber scullcap was rooted with saran which was more suitable for washing and combing.

Betsy McCall had an extensive wardrobe with nearly one hundred outfits, each of which could be purchased separately. They were made from wonderful fabrics such as velvet, taffeta, felt, and even real mink. Each ensemble came with the appropriate footwear and was priced under $3.00. Since none of Betsy's clothing was tagged, it is often difficult to identify other than by its square snap closures (although these were used by other companies as well).

Betsy McCall is a highly collectible doll today but is still fairly easy to find at doll shows. The prices remain reasonable for this beautiful clothes horse and her many accessories.

Advisor: Marci Van Ausdall (V2).

Doll, School Girl outfit, blue and white with red at waist, red shoes, 8", M, minimum value, $175.00.

Doll, both hair clips, G color, nude, EX, V2 ....$75.00
Doll, w/pk tissue & orig pamphlet, MIB, V2, from $150 to .$195.00
Doll, 1st year bridal outfit, complete, EX, V2 ....$150.00
Doll clothes pattern, McCall's, V2, from $5 to $7.50
Outfit, April Showers, EX, V2...$25.00
Outfit, depending on rarity, MIP, V2, minimum value $25.00
Outfit, Sunday Best, complete, EX, V2 ....$50.00
Pamphlet, orig, V2...$15.00

CHATTY CATHY

In their new book, *Chatty Cathy Dolls, An Identification & Value Guide*, authorities Kathy and Don Lewis (L6) tell us that Chatty Cathy (made by Mattel) has been the second most popular doll ever made. She was introduced in the 1960s and came as either a blond or a brunette. For five years, she sold very well. Much of her success can be attributed to the fact that Chatty Cathy talked. By pulling the string on her back, she could respond with eleven different phrases. During her five years of fame, Mattel added to the line with Chatty Baby, Tiny Chatty Baby and Tiny Chatty Brother (the twins), Charmin' Chatty, and finally Singin' Chatty. Charmin' Chatty had 16 interchangeable records. Her voice box was activated in the same manner as the above-mentioned dolls, by means of a pull string located at the base of her neck. The line was brought back in 1969, smaller and with a restyled face, but it was not well received.

Advisor: Kathy and Don Lewis (L6).

See Also Coloring, Activity and Paint Books; Paper Dolls; Puzzles.

Armoire, Chatty Cathy, L6 ....$125.00
Bedspread, Chatty Cathy, twin-sz, L6 ....$125.00
Carrying Case, Chatty Baby, pk or bl, L6.........................$20.00
Carrying Case, Tiny Chatty Baby, bl or pk, L6 ....$20.00
Cover & Pillow Set, Tiny Chatty Baby, L6 ....$55.00
Crib, Tiny Chatty Baby, MIB, L6 ....$175.00
Doll, Black Chatty Baby, M, L6 ....$325.00
Doll, Black Chatty Cathy, w/pigtails, M, L6....................$700.00
Doll, Black Chatty Cathy, 1962, pageboy style hair, M, L6.$450.00
Doll, Black Tiny Chatty Baby, M, L6 ....$275.00
Doll, Charmin' Chatty, auburn or blond hair, bl eyes, 1 record,
    M, L6...$95.00
Doll, Chatty Baby, open speaker, blond hair, bl eyes, M, L6 .$75.00
Doll, Chatty Baby, open speaker, brunette hair, bl eyes, M,
    L6..$80.00

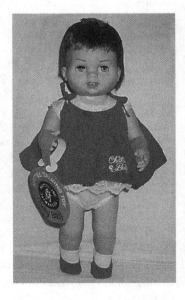

Doll, Chatty Baby, brunette, red pinafore over white romper, original tag, MIB, $120.00.

Doll, Chatty Baby, open speaker, brunette hair, brn eyes, M,
    L6..$90.00
Doll, Chatty Cathy, brunette hair, brn eyes, M, L6........$140.00
Doll, Chatty Cathy, later issue, open speaker grille, blond hair,
    bl eyes, M, L6..$130.00

Doll, Chatty Cathy, later issue, open speaker grille, brunette hair, bl eyes, M, L6 ....$135.00

Doll, Chatty Cathy, later issue, open speaker grille, brunette hair, brn eyes, M, L6 ....$145.00

Doll, Chatty Cathy, mid-year or transitional, brunette hair, brn eyes, M, L6 ....$135.00

Doll, Chatty Cathy, mid-year or transitional, brunette hair, bl eyes, M, L6 ....$125.00

Doll, Chatty Cathy, mid-year or transitional, open speaker, blond hair, bl eyes, M, L6 ....$120.00

Doll, Chatty Cathy, patent pending, brunette hair, bl eyes, M, L6 ....$130.00

Doll, Chatty Cathy, patent pending, cloth over speaker or ring around speaker, blond hair, bl eyes, M, L6 ....$125.00

Doll, Chatty Cathy, porcelain, 1980, MIB, L6 ....$700.00

Doll, Chatty Cathy, reissue, blond hair, bl eyes, M, L6 ....$55.00

Doll, Chatty Cathy, unmarked prototype, brunette hair, bl eyes, M, L6 ....$145.00

Doll, Chatty Cathy, unmarked prototype, brunette hair, brn eyes, M, L6 ....$155.00

Doll, Chatty Cathy, unmarked prototype, cloth over speaker, blond hair, bl eyes, M, L6 ....$135.00

Doll, early Chatty Baby, blond hair, bl eyes, ring around speaker, M, L6 ....$75.00

Doll, early Chatty Baby, brunette hair, bl eyes, M, L6 ......$85.00

Doll, early Chatty Baby, brunette hair, brn eyes, M, L6 ...$95.00

Doll, Singin' Chatty, blond hair, M, L6 ....$85.00

Doll, Singin' Chatty, brunette hair, M, L6 ....$90.00

Doll, Timey Tell, blond hair, bl eyes, M, L6 ....$55.00

Doll, Tiny Chatty Baby, blond hair, bl eyes, M, L6 ....$75.00

Doll, Tiny Chatty Baby, brunette, brn eyes, M, L6...........$90.00

Doll, Tiny Chatty Baby, brunette hair, bl eyes, M, L6......$80.00

Game, Charmin' Chatty, MIB, L6 ....$50.00

Jewelry Set, Chatty Cathy, MIP, L6................................$100.00

Nursery Set, Chatty Baby, NRFB, L6...............................$150.00

Outfit, Charmin' Chatty, Cinderella, MIP, L6 ....$75.00

Outfit, Charmin' Chatty, Let's Go Shopping, MIP, L6 ....$75.00

Outfit, Charmin' Chatty, Let's Play Birthday Party, MIP, L6 .$75.00

Outfit, Charmin' Chatty, Let's Play Nurse, MIP, L6 ....$80.00

Outfit, Charmin' Chatty, Let's Play Pajama Party, MIP, L6 .$75.00

Outfit, Charmin' Chatty, Let's Play Tea Party, MIP, L6 ..$90.00

Outfit, Charmin' Chatty, Let's Play Together, MIP, L6 ...$75.00

Outfit, Chatty Baby, Coverall Set, 2 colors, MIP, L6 ....$50.00

Outfit, Chatty Baby, Leotard Set, MIP, L6 ....$50.00

Outfit, Chatty Baby, Outdoors, MIP, L6 ....$60.00

Outfit, Chatty Baby, Party Pink, MIP, L6 ....$75.00

Outfit, Chatty Baby, Playtime, MIP, L6 ....$40.00

Outfit, Chatty Baby, Sleeper Set, MIP, L6 ....$50.00

Outfit, Chatty Cathy, Nursery School, MIP, L6 ....$85.00

Outfit, Chatty Cathy, Party Coat, MIP, L6 ....$90.00

Outfit, Chatty Cathy, Party Dress, bl gingham, MIP, L6.$100.00

Outfit, Chatty Cathy, Pink Peppermint Stick, MIP, L6 ...$85.00

Outfit, Chatty Cathy, Playtime, MIP, L6 ....$85.00

Outfit, Chatty Cathy, Sleepytime, MIP, L6 ....$80.00

Outfit, Chatty Cathy, Sunday Visit, MIP, L6 ....$100.00

Outfit, Chatty Cathy, Sunny Day, MIP, L6 ....$95.00

Outfit, Tiny Chatty Baby, Bye-Bye, MIP, L6 ....$60.00

Outfit, Tiny Chatty Baby, Dots-n-Dash, MIP, L6.............$80.00

Outfit, Tiny Chatty Baby, Fun Time, MIP, L6 ....$65.00

Outfit, Tiny Chatty Baby, Night-Night, MIP, L6.............$60.00

Outfit, Tiny Chatty Baby, Party Dress, bl gingham, MIP, L6 .$90.00

Outfit, Tiny Chatty Baby, Pink Frill, MIP, L6 ....$65.00

Pattern, Chatty Baby, uncut, L6.....................................$15.00

Pattern, Chatty Cathy, uncut, L6....................................$15.00

Pencil-Point Bed, Chatty Cathy, L6 ....$180.00

Play Hats, Charmin' Chatty, L6 ....$55.00

Play Table, Chatty Baby, L6 ....$95.00

Sticker Book, Tiny Chatty Baby, L6 ....$50.00

Stroll-a-Buggy, Chatty Baby, 9-way, complete, L6 ....$225.00

Stroller, Chatty Cathy, 5-way, complete, L6 ....$175.00

Stroller, Chatty Walk 'n Talk, L6 ....$150.00

Tea Cart, Chatty Cathy, 2 trays, L6 ....$90.00

Teeter-Totter, Tiny Chatty Baby Twins, L6...................$250.00

DAWN DOLLS BY TOPPER

Dawn and her friends were made by Deluxe Topper, ca 1970s. They're becoming highly collectible, especially when mint in the box. Dawn was a 6" fashion doll, part of a series sold as the Dawn Model Agency. They were issued in boxes already dressed in clothes of the highest style, or you could buy additional outfits, many complete with matching shoes and accessories.

Advisor: Dawn Parrish (P2).

Doll, Dawn, NRFB (2nd issue box), P2............................$20.00

Doll, Dinah, Dawn Model Agency, 1970-71, MIB, P2 .....$45.00

Outfit, Cupid's Beau, #8121, NRFB, P2 ....$20.00

Outfit, Fuchsia Flash, #0612, NRFB, P2..........................$30.00

Outfit, Gala Go-Go, #0621, NRFB, P2.............................$30.00

Outfit, Glamour Jams, #8124, NRFB, P2 ....$20.00

Outfit, Groovy Baby Groovy, #0620, NRFB, P2...............$30.00

Outfit, Pink Pussycat, #0616, NRFB, P2..........................$30.00

Outfit, Pink Slink, #8122, NRFB $15.00

Outfit, Twinkle Twirl, #8144, 1970, NRFB......................$12.00

Outfit, Up, Up & Away, #8394, missing shirt o/w complete, P2 ....$15.00

Outfit, Wedding Belle Dream, #0815, NRFB $18.00

FLATSYS BY IDEAL

Flatsy dolls were a product of the Ideal Novelty and Toy Company. They were produced from 1968 until 1970 in 2", 5" and 8" sizes. There was only one boy in the 5" line; all were dressed in seventies' fashions, and not only clothing but accessory items such as bicycles were made as well.

Advisor: Dawn Parrish (P2).

Bonnie Flatsy, sailing, NRFB (tear in cellophane), P2 .....$60.00

Candy Flatsy, Happy Birthday, NRFB, P2.........................$60.00

Carrie Flatsy, w/outfit, shoes & hair ribbon, P2 ....$12.00

Cory Fashion Flatsy, print mini-dress, NRFB, P2.............$60.00

Dale Fashion Flatsy, hot pk maxi, NRFB, P2 ....$60.00

Dale Fashion Flatsy, 2-pc wet-look outfit, NRFB, P2 ....$60.00

Fall Mini Flatsy Collection, NRFB, P2.............................$65.00

Gwen Fashion Flatsy, peach poncho, NRFB, P2................$60.00

Munch-Time Flatsy Clock, NRFB, P2 ....$75.00
Nancy Flatsy, nurse w/baby, NRFB, P2 ....$60.00
Sandy Flatsy, beach outfit, faded, NRFB, P2 ....$55.00
Summer Mini Flatsy Collection, NRFB, P2 ....$65.00

Flatsy in Locket/Frame, pink and red jacket and hat, red boots, MIP, from $50.00 to $60.00.

JEM DOLLS BY HASBRO

The glamorous life of Jem mesmerized little girls who watched her Saturday morning cartoons, and she was a natural as a fashion doll. Hasbro saw the potential in 1985 when they introduced the Jem line of 12" dolls representing her, the rock stars from Jem's musical group, the Holograms, and other members of the cast, including the only boy, Rio, Jem's road manager and Jerrica's boyfriend. Each doll was posable, jointed at the waist, head and wrists, so that they could be positioned at will with their musical instruments and other accessory items. Their clothing, their makeup, and their hairdos were wonderfully exotic, and their faces were beautifully modeled. The Jem line was discontinued in 1987 after being on the market for only two years. Our values are given for mint-in-box dolls. All loose dolls are valued at about $8.00 each.

Aja, bl hair, w/accessories, complete, MIB......................$40.00
Ashley, curly blond hair, w/stand, 11", MIB $20.00
Banee, waist-length straight blk hair, w/stand, MIB ...$20.00
Clash, straight purple hair, complete, MIB $40.00
Danse, pk & blond hair, invents dance routines, MIB $40.00

Jem Roadster, AM/FM radio in trunk (working), scarce, EX, $150.00.

Jem Soundstage, Starlight House #17, from $40 to...........$50.00
Jem/Jerrica, Glitter & Gold, w/accessories, MIB...............$50.00
Jetta, blk hair w/silver streaks, complete, MIB.................$40.00
Kimber, red hair, w/stand, cassette, instrument & poster, 12½",
    MIB $40.00
Krissie, dk skin w/dk brn curly hair, w/stand, 11", MIB $20.00

Pizzaz, chartreuse hair, one of 'The Misfits' (bad girls), complete, MIB, $40.00.

Raya, pk hair, complete, MIB...$40.00
Rio, Glitter & Gold, complete, 12½", MIB.......................$50.00
Roxy, blond hair, complete, MIB $40.00

Shana, purple hair, member of the Holograms Band, complete, from $30.00 to $40.00.

Stormer, curly bl hair, complete, MIB...............................$40.00
Video, band member who makes audio tapes, MIB $40.00

LIDDLE KIDDLES

From 1966 to 1971, Mattel produced Liddle Kiddle dolls and accessories, typical of the 'little kid next door.' They were made in sizes ranging from a tiny ¾" up to 4". They were all posable and had rooted hair that could be restyled. Eventually there were Animiddles and Zoolery Jewelry Kiddles, which were of course animals, and two other series that represented storybook and nursery-rhyme characters. There was a set of extraterrestrials, and lastly in 1979, Sweet Treets dolls were added to the assortment. Loose dolls, if complete and with all their original accessories, are worth about 25% less than the same mint in the box. Dressed, loose dolls with no accessories are worth 75% less. For more information, refer to *Little Kiddles, Identification and Value Guide*, by Paris Langford (Collector Books).

Advisor: Dawn Parrish (P2).

Anabelle Autodiddle, #3770, complete w/shoes & pusher, P2 ....$40.00
Apple Blossom Kologne, #3707, doll only w/5 flowers & pearls, P2 ....$10.00

Apple Blossom Kiddle Kologne, doll with green hair and blue painted eyes, 1966, complete, M, $25.00.

Babe Biddle, #3505, car only $15.00
Babe Biddle, #3505, complete $55.00
Bunson Burnie, #3501, MOC, P2 ....$125.00
Calamity Jiddle, #3506, complete, M, P2.........................$60.00
Case, bl, rnd w/zipper closure, EX, P2 ....$35.00
Case, purple, rnd w/zipper closure, EX, P2 ....$40.00
Case, turquoise, rectangular w/zipper closure, M..............$40.00
Cherry Blossom, #3790, w/outfit, headband, shoes & pusher, P2..$30.00
Cherry Delight Sweet Treat Cookies, #2818, MIP, P2 .....$20.00
Chitty-Chitty Bang-Bang Kiddle, #3597, MOC, P2 ......$250.00
Dainty Deer, #3637, missing pin, P2................................$30.00
Donald Duck Skediddler, #3628, MIB, P2 ....$75.00
Flower-Bracelet Jewelry Kiddle, #3747, charm only, P2 ...$10.00
Flower-Bracelet Jewelry Kiddle, #3747, MOC, P2............$25.00
Freezy Sliddle, #3516, missing boots, G, P2 ....$35.00
Frosty Mint Kone, #3653, doll only, P2 ....$13.00
Goofy Skediddle, #3627, MIB, P2 ....$75.00
Greta Grape, #3728, Canadian version, MIB $75.00
Greta Griddle, #3508, complete w/pk table, yel chairs & accessories, P2 ....$60.00
Harriet Helididdle, #3768, MIB, P2 ....$75.00
Harriet Helididdle, #3768, missing goggles, P2 ....$35.00

Henrietta Horseless Carriage, #3641, w/outfit & hat, pnt wear on feet, P2 ....$25.00
Honeysuckle Kologne, #3704, complete w/inner stand & tag, P2 ....$22.00
Howard Biff Boodle, #3502, complete w/wht shirt & red wagon, P2 ....$60.00

Kosmic Kiddle, Greenie Meenie, NM, O1, $125.00.

Kosmic Kiddle, yel w/gr spaceship, 1968, no base or antenna, H4..$65.00
Lady Crimson, #A3840, MOC, P2 ....$75.00
Lady Lace Tea Party Kiddle, #A3840, missing dome $35.00
Lady Lavender, #A3840, faded dress, P2 ....$20.00
Laverne Locket, #3718, 1976, MOC, P2..........................$25.00
Lickety Spliddle & Her Traveliddles, #3771, complete, P2 .$75.00
Liddle Diddle, #3503, checked pajamas, w/crib, EX, P2 ...$50.00

Liddle Kiddles Klub, case, EX, $20.00.

Liddle Middle Muffet, #3545, w/outfit, shoes & hair ribbons, P2 ....$30.00
Liddle Red Riding Hiddle, #3546, complete $40.00
Lola Liddle, #3504, complete, M, P2................................$60.00

Lolli-Mint, #3658, MOC $40.00
Lorelei Locket, #3717, doll w/hat only, 1976, P2 ....$9.00
Lorelei Locket, #3717, 1976, MOC, P2 ....$25.00
Loretta Locket, #3722, doll only, 1968, P2 ....$10.00
Loretta Locket, #3722, 1976, MOC, P2 ....$25.00
Louise Locket, #3721, locket only, missing door, P2............$3.00
Luana Locket, #3680, 1968, MOC, P2 ....$40.00
Lucky Lion, #3635, M (NM card), P2 ....$80.00
Mickey Mouse Skediddler, #3629, MIB, P2 ....$75.00
Millie Middle, #3509, missing shovel, outfit slightly faded, P2 ....$45.00
Miss Mouse, #3638, missing pin, P2 ....$35.00
Orange Ice Kone, #3654, doll only, P2 ....$13.00
Orange Olivia, #3730, Canadian version, MOC, P2 ....$75.00
Peter Paniddle, #3547, missing dagger, feather, book & wings, P2 ....$100.00
Plum Pretty Skediddle Play Clothes, #3585, MOC, P2 ....$25.00
Posies 'N Pink Skediddle Play Clothes, #3585, MOC, P2 .$25.00
Pretty Parlor, #3847, NMIB, P2 ....$55.00
Pretty Priddle, #3749, doll only $20.00
Rah Rah Skediddle, #3788, rpl shoes & pusher, P2 ....$30.00
Romeo & Juliet, #3782, NM, P2 ....$100.00
Rosemary Roadster, #3642, MOC, P2 ....$125.00
Sheila Skediddle, M, D2 ....$25.00
Shirley Skediddle, #3766, complete, P2 ....$25.00
Shirley Strawberry Kola, #3727, complete, P2 ....$40.00
Sizzly Friddle, #3513, complete, P2 ....$60.00
Slipsy Sliddle, #3754, complete, P2 ....$60.00
Snap-Happy Bedroom Furniture, #5172, missing bedspreads, P2 ....$15.00
Snap-Happy Patio Furniture, #5171, MIB, P2 ....$35.00

Storybook Kiddles Sweethearts, Rapunzel and the Prince, illustrated story inside, unopened, M, $125.00.

Suki Skediddle, #3767, MIB, P2 ....$50.00
Tracy Trikediddle, #3769, MIB, P2 ....$75.00
Tracy Trikediddle, #3769, wagon & trike only, M, D2 ....$30.00
Trikey Triddle, #3515, floral dress, MOC, P2 ....$100.00

Tutti-Frutti Kone, #3655, MOC, P2 ....$40.00
Vanilly Lilly Sweet Treat Cookies, #2819, MIP, P2 ....$20.00
Violet Kologne, #3703, doll only, P2 ....$4.00

Violet Kologne, #3706, 1966, complete, M, $25.00.

Windy Fliddle, #3514, missing maps, P2 ....$45.00
Windy Fliddle, #3514, M (EX card), P2 ....$100.00

STRAWBERRY SHORTCAKE

Strawberry Shortcake came on the market around 1980 with a bang. The line included everything to attract small girls. Swimsuits, bed linens, blankets, anklets, underclothing, coats, shoes, sleeping bags, dolls and accessories, games, and many other delightful items. Strawberry Shortcake and her friends were short lived, lasting only until the mid-1980s.

Advisor: Geneva Addy (A5).

Basinet, pink wicker on stand, 18x20", A5 ....$50.00
Book bag, A5 ....$8.00
Bunk Beds, wicker, 12x15", A5 ....$50.00
Carrying Case, strawberry form, hard plastic, 12", A5 ......$15.00
Doll, Raspberry Tart, Kenner, MIB $22.00

Doll, Strawberry Shortcake, Kenner, MIB, $22.00.

Figure, Purple Pie Man, poseable, 9", MIB, S2 ....$35.00
Figure, Purple Pieman w/Berry Bird, Kenner, MIB $25.00
Figure, Strawberry Shortcake or friends, miniature, ea $6.00
Gazebo, A5 ....$15.00
Night light, strawberry form, battery-op, A5 ....$12.00
Pony & Cart, A5 ....$8.00
Roller Skates, A5 ....$20.00
School Desk w/Seat, A5 ....$25.00

Strawberry-land Miniatures, Orange Blossom and Marmalade Painting a Picture, Kenner, MIB, $15.00.

TAMMY

In 1962 the Ideal Novelty and Toy Company introduced their teenage Tammy doll. Slightly pudgy and not quite as sophisticated-looking as some of the teen fashion dolls on the market at the time, Tammy's innocent charm captivated consumers. Her extensive wardrobe and numerous accessories added to her popularity with children. Tammy had a car, a house, and her own catamaran. In addition, a large number of companies obtained licenses to issue products using the 'Tammy' name. Everything from paper dolls to nurse's kits were made with Tammy's image on them. Her success was not confined to the United States, she was also successful in Canada and several other European countries.

Values quoted are for mint-in-box dolls. Loose dolls are generally about half mint-in-box value, as they are relatively common. Values for other items are for examples in mint condition but without their original packaging.

Advisor: Cindy Sabulis (S14).

Catamaran, M, S14 ....$150.00
Doll, Black Tammy, MIB, S14 ....$200.00
Doll, Bud, MIB, S14 ....$300.00
Doll, Dodi, MIB, S14 ....$65.00
Doll, Glamour Misty, MIB, S14 ....$90.00
Doll, Grown-Up Tammy, MIB, S14 ....$55.00
Doll, Patty (Montgomery Ward's Exclusive), MIB, S14.$125.00
Doll, Pepper, MIB, S14 ....$40.00
Doll, Pepper, orange hair, MIB, S14 ....$65.00
Doll, Pepper, 1965, slimmer body, MIB, S14 ....$50.00

Doll, Pos'n Dodi, MIB, S14 ....$75.00
Doll, Pos'n Pete, MIB, S14 ....$80.00
Doll, Pos'n Salty, MIB, S14 ....$80.00
Doll, Pos'n Tammy & Her Phone Booth, MIB, S14 ....$65.00
Doll, Tammy, straight legs, MIB, S14 ....$40.00
Doll, Tammy's Dad, MIB, S14 ....$45.00
Doll, Tammy's Mom, MIB, S14 ....$45.00
Doll, Ted, MIB, S14 ....$45.00
Tammy's Car, M, S14, minimum value $75.00
Tammy's Ideal House, M, S14, minimum value $100.00
Tea Set, M, S14 ....$150.00

TRESSY

American Character's Tressy doll was produced in this country from 1963 to 1967. The unique thing about this 11½" fashion doll was that her hair 'grew' by pushing a button on her stomach. Tressy also had a 9" little sister named Cricket. These two dolls had numerous fashions and accessories produced for them. Never-removed-from-box Tressy and Cricket items are rare, so unless indicated, values listed are for loose, mint items. A never-removed-from-box item's worth is at least double the item's loose value.

Advisor: Cindy Sabulis (S14).

Cricket, $20.00; Tressy, $15.00.

Photo courtesy of Cindy Sabulis.

Apartment, M, S14 ....$150.00
Beauty Salon, M, S14 ....$125.00
Carrying Case, features Cricket, M, S14 ....$25.00
Carrying Case, features Tressy, M, S14 ....$20.00
Doll, Cricket, M, S14 ....$20.00
Doll, Pre-Teen Tressy, M, S14 ....$50.00
Doll, Tressy, M, S14 ....$15.00
Doll, Tressy w/Magic Makeup Face, M, S14 ....$20.00
Doll Clothes Pattern, M, S14 ....$6.00
Gift Paks w/Doll & Clothing, NRFB, minimum value......$100.00

Hair Accessory Paks, NRFB, S14, ea................................$20.00
Hair Dryer, M, S14 ....$40.00
Hair or Cosmetic Accessory Kits, M, minimum value........$50.00
Millinery, M, S14..$150.00
Outfits, MOC, S14, ea...$20.00
Outfits, NRFB, S14, minimum value $40.00

Upsy Downsys by Mattel

The Upsy Downsy dolls were made by Mattel during the late 1960s. They were small, 2½" to 3½", made of vinyl and plastic, and some of the group were 'Upsies' that walked on their feet, while others were 'Downsies' that walked or rode fantasy animals while upsidedown.

Advisor: Dawn Parrish (P2).

Baby So-High, #3828, orange & gr windmill, 1 flap bent, P2 .**$12.00**
Miss Information, #3831, missing playland, P2 ....**$60.00**
Mother What Now, #3829, missing playland & curler, P2 .**$50.00**
Pocus Hocus, #3830, missing hat & dragon wagon, P2 .....**$50.00**
Tickle Pickle, #3825, missing playland & bridge, P2 ....**$55.00**

Farm Toys

It's entirely probable that more toy tractors have been sold than real ones. They've been made to represent all makes and models, of plastic, cast iron, diecast metal, and even wood. They've been made in at least 1/16th scale, 1/32nd, 1/43rd, and 1/64th. If you buy a 1/16th-scale replica, that small piece of equipment would have to be sixteen times larger to equal the size of the real item. Limited editions (meaning that a specific number will be made and no more) and commemorative editions (made for special events) are usually very popular with collectors. Many models on the market today are being made by the Ertl company; Arcade made cast-iron models in the '30s and '40s.

Advisor: John Rammacher (S5).

Agco Allison 6690 Tractor w/Duals, Ertl, 1/64 scale #1286,
    MIB, S5...**$3.45**
Agco R-52 Combine, Ertl, 1/64 scale, #1282, MIB, S5.......**$9.50**

Allis Chalmers Model G Tractor, shelf model, 1/16 scale, #402, MIB, from $25.00 to $30.00.

Allis Chalmers D-19, Ertl, Collector's Edition, 1/16, #2220,
    MIB, S5 ....**$40.00**
Allis Chalmers D-19, Ertl, shelf model, 1/16 scale, #2220,
    MIB, S5 ....**$21.00**
Allis Chalmers Disc, Am Precision, early 1950s, pnt coulters,
    6", VG, A...**$80.00**
Allis Chalmers Disc Harrow, Am Precision, early 1950s, orange,
    9", G, A...**$65.00**
Allis Chalmers Model C Tractor, Am Precision, orange,
    7½", EX, A..**$140.00**
Allis Chalmers Model C Tractor, Ertl, 1/43 scale, #2529, MIB,
    S5 ....**$5.25**
Allis Chalmers Model U Tractor w/Earth Hauler, Arcade,
    8", EX, A...**$180.00**
Allis Chalmers Model WC Tractor, Hubley, red w/bl driver,
    7", VG, A...**$160.00**
Allis Chalmers Tractor & Dump, Arcade, CI, red & gr w/rubber
    tires, 8", EX, A...**$110.00**
Allis Chalmers Tractor w/Scoop, Arcade, CI w/tin scoop, orange
    w/blk rubber tires, 7⅛", EX, A...........................**$525.00**
Avery Tractor, Hubley, blk, 4¼", VG, A.......................**$170.00**
Case Combine, Vindex, CI, red & silver, revolving cutter reel,
    imitation motor exhaust, 12¼", rare, NM, A **$5,700.00**
Case Hay Loader, Vindex, CI, red w/yel wheels, revolving
    chains & teeth, 9", EX, A **$5,200.00**
Case IH Fertilizer Truck, Ertl, 1/64 scale, #647, MIB, S5 ...**$6.00**
Case IH Forage Harvester, Ertl, 1/64 scale, #201, MIB, S5.**$2.50**
Case IH Grain Drill, Ertl, 1/16 scale, #269, MIB, S5........**$13.50**
Case IH Hay Rake, Ertl, 1/64 scale, #210, MIB, S5 ....**$2.75**
Case IH Maxxam 5120 Row Crop Tractor, Ertl, 1/16 scale,
    #634, MIB, S5 ....**$22.00**
Case IH Maxxum 5120 w/Duals, Ertl, 1/64 scale, #241, MIB, S5 ..**$3.85**
Case IH Maxxum 5140 w/Mechanical Front Assist, Ertl, 1/64
    scale, #240, MIB, S5 ....**$3.85**
Case IH Milk Truck, Ertl, 1/64 scale, #648, MIB, S5..........**$6.00**
Case IH Planter, Ertl, 1/64 scale, #478, MIB, S5 ....**$2.50**
Case IH Tractor w/Endloader, Ertl, 1/64 scale, #212, MIB,
    S5..**$5.00**
Case IH 1660 Combine, Ertl, 1/64 scale, #655, MIB, S5..**$10.50**
Case IH 1844 Cotton Picker, Ertl, 1/64 scale, #211, MIB,
    S5..**$5.90**
Case IH 2594 Tractor, Ertl, 1/64 scale, #227, MIB, S5 ....**$3.00**
Case IH 496 Wing Disk, Ertl, 1/64 scale, #694, MIB, S5....**$4.00**
Case IH 5130 Row Crop, 1991 Farm Show, Ertl, 1/64 scale,
    #229, MIB, S5...**$10.00**
Case IH 7120 w/Duals, Ertl, 1/64 scale, #626, MIB, S5 ......**$3.00**
Case IH 7130 Magnum Tractor, Ertl, 1/64 scale, #458, MIB,
    S5..**$3.00**
Case IH 7140 w/Mechanical Front Assist Tractor, Ertl, 1/64
    scale, #616, MIB, S5 ....**$2.90**
Case IH 7150 w/Front Wheel Assist, Farm Show 1992, Ertl, 1/64
    scale, #285, MIB, S5 ....**$10.00**
Case IH 7240 Magnum w/Mechanical Front Drive, Farm Show
    1994, Ertl, 1/16 scale, #2258, MIB, S5 ....**$37.00**
Case IH 7250 Magnum Mechanical Front Drive, Farm Show
    1994, Ertl, 1/64 scale, #4757, MIB, S5 ....**$8.00**
Case IH 9260 4-WD, 1993 Farm Show, Ertl, 1/64 scale, #231,
    MIB, S5..**$9.00**

Case L Tractor, Ertl, 1/43 scale, #2554, MIB, S5 ....$5.25

Case L Tractor, 150 Years Collector's Edition, 1/16 scale, #252, MIB, S5 ....$35.00

Case Uniloader, Ertl, 1/64 scale, #455, MIB, S5 ....$4.25

Case 3-Bottom Plow, Vindex, red w/lime gr spoke wheels, 10", very rare, EX, A..$1,200.00

Case 3-Bottom Tractor Plow, Vindex, CI, red & gr w/NP discs, 10¼", scarce, NM, A...$3,200.00

Case 500 Tractor, Ertl, 1/43 scale, #2510, MIB, S5 ....$5.25

Case 504 Turbo Tractor & Plow, Ertl, 1960s, MIB, S9 ..$165.00

Case 600 Tractor, Ertl, 1/16 scale, #289, MIB, S5 ....$20.00

Case 800 Tractor, Ertl, Collector's Edition, 1/16 scale, #695, S5 ....$40.00

Case 800 Tractor, Ertl, shelf model, 1/16 scale, #693, MIB, S5 ....$22.00

Case 5003 Deluxe Farm Set, Ertl, MIB, A, $175.00.

Caterpillar Diesel Tractor, Arcade, 1936, w/driver, pnt CI, yel w/metal tracks, exposed engine & radiator, 7", EX, A.$1,600.00

Caterpillar Tractor, Arcade, 1929, CI, bl w/red spoke wheels, NP driver & chain tracks, 5⅜", EX, A $1,600.00

Caterpillar Utility Truck, Ertl, 1/64 scale, #2411, MIB, S5 .$7.00

Caterpillar 2-Ton Tractor, Ertl, Collector's Edition, 1/16 scale, #2438, MIB, S5..$65.00

Caterpillar 2-Ton Tractor, Ertl, shelf model, 1/16 scale, #2438, MIB, S5..$19.00

Co-Op E3 Tractor, Advanced Products, orange, 7", G, A.$50.00

Cockshutt E3 Tractor, Advanced Products, tan, 8", M, A..$80.00

Cockshutt Wagon, Advanced Products, red, 9", rare, G, A $45.00

Cockshutt 30 Tractor, Lincoln Products, narrow front, 7¼", VG, A..$150.00

Cockshutt 30 Tractor, Lincoln Products, wide front, 7½", very rare, G, A..$400.00

Corn Binder, Arcade, 1-row, gr & yel, 3", VG, A..........$130.00

Corn Binder, Slik, 2-row, aluminum, 5", G, A $15.00

Deutz Allison Barge Wagon, Ertl, 1/64 scale, #2241, MIB, S5..$2.50

Deutz Allison R-50 Combine, Ertl, 1/64 scale, #1284, MIB, S5..$13.00

Deutz Allison Round Hay Processor, Ertl, 1/64 scale, #2216, MIB, S5..$2.50

Deutz Allison 6260 Tractor, Ertl, 1/64 scale, #1241, MIB, S5..$2.30

Deutz Allison 7085, 1990 Farm Show, Ertl, 1/64 scale, #1260, MIB, S5..$11.00

Deutz Allison 7085 Tractor w/Loader, Ertl, 1/64 scale, #2233, MIB, S5..$4.00

Deutz Allison 9150, Orlando Show Tractor, Ertl, 1/16 scale, #1280, MIB, S5..$190.00

Diesel Sd-3 Tractor, Shephard, 1950s, 7¾", rare, G, A ..$160.00

Diesel Tractor, Arcade, 1937, CI, red w/metal tracks, separate driver, 7⅝", VG, A...$1,400.00

Disk Harrow, Tru-Scale, yel decals, M (orig box), A........$80.00

Duetz Allison 6260 All Wheel Drive, Ertl, 1/64 scale, #2232, MIB, S5..$3.00

Farm Wagon, Arcade, CI w/NP wheels & wire hitch, 6¼", VG, A..$220.00

Farmall, Precision Series, Ertl, 1/16 scale, #284, MIB, S5.$95.00

Farmall Cub, Ertl, 1956-1958, 1/16 scale, #235, MIB, S5.$20.00

Farmall Cub, Ertl, 1959-1963, 1/16 scale, #652, MIB, S5.$18.00

Farmall F-20, Ertl, 1/16 scale, #260, MIB, S5...................$18.00

Farmall F-20 Precision Classic, Ertl, 1/16 scale, #294, MIB, S5..$92.00

Farmall Model M, Arcade, 7½", rpl tires, G, A $210.00

Farmall Model M Tractor, Arcade, gr w/wooden rear wheels, 5½", VG, A..$210.00

Farmall Model M Tractor, Tru-Scale, early 1950s, yel rim, 7½", G, A $40.00

Farmall Regular Tractor, Arcade, red, 6", VG, A...........$350.00

Farmall Regular Tractor, Arcade, 6", G, A $230.00

Farmall Super A Tractor, Ertl, 1/16 scale, #250, MIB, S5 ....$20.00

Farmall Super M-T-A Tractor, Ertl, 1/16 scale, #445, MIB, S5 ....$19.00

Farmall 350 Tractor, Ertl, 1/16 scale, #418, MIB, O1, $50.00.

Farmall 350 Tractor w/Wide Front End, Ertl, 1/43 scale, #2244, MIB, S5..$5.25

Ferguson TO 20 Tractor, Advanced Products, 3-point hookup, NM (orig box), A..$325.00

Flared Wagon, Tru-Scale, beige rims, 9½", EX, A $15.00

Ford F Tractor, Collector's Edition, Ertl, 1/16 scale, #872, MIB, S5..$45.00

Ford F Tractor, Ertl, 1/16 scale, #872, MIB, S5.................$22.00

Ford F-250 Pickup w/Livestock Trailer, Ertl, 1/64 scale, #311, MIB, S5..$5.00

Ford Model 9N Tractor, Arcade, 1939, CI, gray w/blk rubber tires, integral driver, 6⅜", EX, A $775.00

Ford Model 9N Tractor & Scoop Trailer, Arcade, CI, red w/blk rubber tires, silver hitch w/dump release, 15", EX, A $1,100.00

Ford New Holland Combine, Ertl, 1/64 scale, #815, MIB, S5...$10.50

Ford New Holland Hay Rake, 1/64 scale, #396, MIB, S5 ...$2.65

Ford Super Major Tractor, Ertl, 1/16 scale, #307, MIB, S5.$20.00

Ford Tractor w/Earth Hauler, Arcade, 14", VG, A.........$340.00

Ford TW35 Tractor, Ertl, 1/64 scale, #899, MIB, S5 ....$3.00

Ford 4000 Tractor, Hubley, bl & gray, 3-point hitch, 10½", G, A...$40.00

Ford 5640 w/Loader, Ertl, 1/64 scale, #334, MIB, S5 ....$4.25

Ford 6640 Row Crop Tractor, Ertl, 1/64 scale, #332, MIB, S5 ....$3.20

Ford 7740 Row Crop Tractor, Collector's Edition, 1/16 scale, #873, MIB, S5 ....$49.00

Ford 7740 w/Loader, Ertl, 1/64 scale, #387, MIB, S5 ....$4.55

Ford 7740 w/4WD, Ertl, 1/64 scale, #333, MIB, S5 ....$3.20

Ford 7840 w/Duals, Ertl, 1/64 scale, #335, MIB, S5 ....$3.00

Ford 8N Tractor, Ertl, 1/16 scale, #843, MIB, S5..............$17.00

Ford 8340 w/4WD, Collector's Edition, Ertl, 1/16 scale, #877, MIB, S5...$50.00

Ford 8730 Tractor, Ertl, 1/64 scale, #302, MIB, S5 ....$2.45

Ford 8730 Tractor w/Loader, 1/64 scale, #303, MIB, S5 .....$4.50

Ford 8830 Tractor w/Front Wheel Drive Assist, Ertl, 1/64 scale, #854, MIB, S5...$3.00

Ford 9N Tractor, Arcade, w/CI driver, gray, 7", VG, A .$270.00

Ford 961 Model Tractor w/Plow, Hubley, red & gray, 15", G, A...$75.00

Ford 961 Tractor, Ertl, 1/43 scale, #2508, MIB, S5 ....$5.25

Ford 961 Tractor, Hubley, red, w/3-point hitch, 10", G-, A..$15.00

Fordson Major Tractor, Chad Valley, w/3-point hookup, NM (orig box), A...$210.00

Fordson Model F Tractor, Ertl, 1/16 scale, #301, MIB, S5.$18.00

Fordson Tractor, Arcade, cast rims w/rubber tires, W&K mk on rear wheels, 6", G, A...$85.00

Fordson Tractor, Arcade, CI, gr w/red spoke wheels, NP integral driver, 5¾", VG, A...$375.00

Fordson Tractor, Arcade, cleated wheels, 5¼", G, A........$60.00

Fordson Tractor, Arcade, dk bl, spoke wheels, 4", VG, A .$80.00

Fordson Tractor, Arcade, gr w/red rims, 5¼", rpl driver, G, A, from $50 to $100.00

Fordson Tractor, Arcade, red w/gr spokes, 5½", G, A $160.00

Fordson Tractor, Arcade, spoked wheels, NP driver, 6", G, A...$120.00

Fordson Tractor, Arcade, wht tires, 5½", VG, A............$100.00

Fordson Tractor, Bing, litho tin w/up, 8", VG+, M5 ......$240.00

Fordson Tractor & Tripper Trailer, CI, dk gr & red, 8¼", EX, A...$225.00

Fordson Tractor w/Hay Rake, Arcade, CI, gr & red w/NP wheels on hay rake, 8½", EX, A...$475.00

Fordson Tractor w/Loader, Hubley, gr, 9", very rare, VG, A...$1,500.00

Fordson w/Pull Along, Arcade, CI, gray w/NP driver, gr attachment w/red wheels, 13½", VG, A.........................$145.00

Grain Drill, Tru-Scale, beige rims, 6½", EX, A................$40.00

Hay Baler, Tru-Scale, beige rims, 10", M, A...................$25.00

Hay Rake, Tru-Scale, 8", M, A...$5.00

Hesston Forage Harvester, Ertl, 1/64 scale, #2262, MIB, S5 .$2.50

Hesston 8400 Self-Propelled Windrower, Ertl, 1/64 scale, #2211, MIB, S5...$6.25

Heston SL-30 Skidsteer Loader, Ertl, 1/64 scale, #2267, MIB, S5...$4.25

Huber Roller w/Rake, Hubley, 8", EX, A.................................$400.00

Huber Steam Roller, Hubley, orange, 8", G, A...............$200.00

IH Anhydrous Ammonia Tank, Ertl, 1/64 scale, #1862, MIB, S5...$2.50

IH Corn Picker, Ertl, 1/16 scale, #666, MIB, S5 ....$15.00

IH Cub Tractor, Ertl, 1976-1979, 1/16 scale, #448, MIB, S5..$17.75

IH Farmall Diesel Tractor, National Farm Toy Show, Ertl, 1/43 scale, #4263, MIB, S5...$25.00

International 1066 5,000,000th Tractor, Ertl, 1/16th scale, MIB, $175.00.

IH 1566 Tractor w/Duals, Special Edition, Ertl, 1/16 scale, #4625, MIB, S5...$40.00

IH 1586 Tractor, Ertl, 1/16 scale, #463, MIB, S5..............$18.50

IH 1586 Tractor w/Loader, 1/16 scale, #416, MIB, S5......$22.00

International Track Tractor, Arcade, w/figure, CI, brass pattern, 8", EX, A $1,150.00

John Deere Barge Wagon, Ertl, 1/64 scale, #5529, MIB, S5..$2.30

John Deere Caterpillar, Ertl, 10½", M, $90.00.

John Deere Compact Utility Tractor, Ertl, 1/16 scale, #581, MIB, S5 ....$19.00

John Deere Cotton Picker, 1/80 scale, #1000, MIB, S5 ......$6.35

John Deere Farm Wagon, Vindex, CI, gr & red w/2 blk horses, running gear has working parts, 7½", scarce, EX, A...$1,700.00

John Deere Fertilizer Truck, Ertl, 1/64 scale, #5544, MIB, S54 ....$6.00

John Deere Flare Box Wagon, Ertl, 1/43 scale, #5637, MIB, S5 ....$5.25

John Deere Forage Wagon, Ertl, 1/64 scale, #567, MIB, S5 .$2.50

John Deere F145H 5 Bottom Plow, Precision Series, Ertl, 1/16 scale #5763, MIB, S5 ....$72.00

John Deere Gas Engine, Vindex, CI, gr w/yel logo, features working pulley & flywheels, EX, A $1,050.00

John Deere Grain Cart, Ertl, 1/64 scale, #5565, MIB, S5 ...$3.50

John Deere Grain Drill, Ertl, 1/64 scale, #5528, MIB, S5 ...$2.75

John Deere Hydra-Push Spreader, Ertl, 1/64 scale, #574, MIB, S5 ....$2.50

John Deere Manure Spreader, Vindex, CI, red w/yel wheels & logo, features operating spreader, 9¼", rare, NM, A $2,500.00

John Deere Manure Spreader, Vindex, red w/yel wheels, 14", very rare, VG, A $2,000.00

John Deere Model A Tractor, Arcade, NP driver, 7", EX, A .$425.00

John Deere Model A Tractor, Ertl, 1/16 scale, #539, MIB, S5 ....$16.00

John Deere Model A Tractor, Ertl, 1/43 scale, #5598, MIB, S5 ....$5.25

John Deere Model D Tractor, Vindex, gr w/yel wheels, orig decal, 6½", VG, A $1,100.00

John Deere Side Discharge Spreader w/PTO, Ertl, 1/32 scale, #5625, MIB, S5 ....$7.00

John Deere Skid Steer Loader, Ertl, 1/16 scale, #569, MIB, S5 ....$17.00

John Deere Sprayer, Ertl, 1/64 scale, #5553, MIB, S5 ....$2.75

John Deere Thresher, Vindex, CI, gr & silver w/yel wheels, removable straw stacker & grain pipe, 15", rare, NM, A $3,700.00

John Deere Thresher, Vindex, 12½", needs pick-up apron, very rare, VG, A $950.00

John Deere Utility Tractor, Ertl, 1/16 scale, #516, MIB, S5 ..$14.50

John Deere Utility Tractor w/Loader, 1/16 scale, #517, MIB, S5 ....$20.00

John Deere Van Brunt Drill, Vindex, CI, red & yel w/NP drill discs, 9¾", rare, NM, A $2,900.00

John Deere Waterloo Engine, Ertl, 1/16 scale, #5645, MIB, S5 ....$19.00

John Deere Waterloo Boy 2 HP Engine, Ertl, 1992, MIB, $20.00.

John Deere 12 A Combine, Collector's Edition, Ertl, 1/16 scale, #5601, MIB, S5 ....$44.00

John Deere 70 Tractor, Ertl, 1/16 scale, #5611, MIB, S5..$19.00

John Deere 338 Rectangular Baler, Ertl, 1/64 scale, #5646, MIB, S5 ....$3.10

John Deere 630 LP Tractor, Ertl, 1/16 scale, #5590, MIB, S5 ....$18.00

John Deere 630 LP Tractor, Ertl, 1/64 scale, #5600, MIB, S5 ..$2.85

John Deere 1949 Model AR Tractor, Ertl, 1/16 scale, #5680, MIB, S5 ....$22.00

John Deere 3010, Collector's Edition, Ertl, 1/16 scale, #5635, MIB, S5 ....$38.00

John Deere 4010 Diesel Tractor, Ertl, 1/16 scale, #5716, MIB, S5 ....$24.00

John Deere 4010 Gas Tractor, Collector's Edition, Ertl, 1/16 scale, #5716, MIB, S5 ....$40.00

John Deere 4020, Precision #3, Ertl, 1/16 scale, #5638, MIB, S5 ....$95.00

John Deere 4020 w/Wide Front End, Precision Classic, Ertl, 1/16 scale, #5549, MIB, S5 ....$95.00

John Deere 4455 w/Mechanical Front Drive Tractor, Ertl, 1/16 scale, #5584, MIB, S5 ....$25.00

John Deere 6400 Mechanical Front Wheel Drive, Ertl, 1/64 scale, #5729, MIB, S5 ....$3.10

John Deere 6400 Row Crop, Collector's Edition, Ertl, 1/16 scale, #5666, MIB, S5 ....$38.00

John Deere 6910 Self-Propelled Harvester, Ertl, 1/64 scale, #5658, MIB, S5 ....$8.95

John Deere 7800 Demonstrator Tractor, Ertl, 1/16 scale, #5719, MIB, S5 ....$85.00

John Deere 7800 Row Crop Tractor, Ertl, 1/64 scale, #5538, MIB, S5 ....$3.65

John Deere 7800 w/Duals, Ertl, 1/64 scale, #5649, MIB, S5.$3.75

John Deere 7800 w/Loader, Ertl, 1/64 scale, #5662, MIB, S5 ....$4.75

John Deere 8870 4WD Tractor, Ertl, 1/64 scale, #5791, MIB, S5 ....$4.75

Knudson 4360 4WD Tractor, Ertl, 1/64 scale, #4360, MIB, S5 ....$17.00

Knudson 4400 4WD Tractor, Ertl, 1/64 scale, #TF4400, 1 of 5,000 made, MIB, S5 ....$35.00

Massey-Fergeson Bale Processor, Ertl, 1/64 scale, #1093, MIB, S5 ....$2.45

Massey-Fergeson Challenger, Ertl, 1/16 scale, #1103, MIB, S5 ....$19.00

Massey-Fergeson 3070 Tractor, Ertl, 1/64 scale, #1177, MIB, S5 ....$3.00

Massey-Fergeson 3140 Front Wheel Drive, Ertl, 1/64 scale, #1107, MIB, S5 ....$3.50

Massey-Fergeson 44 Special Tractor, Ertl, 1/16 scale, #1115, MIB, S5 ....$18.00

Massey-Fergeson 699 Tractor w/Loader, Ertl, 1/64 scale, #1125, MIB, S5 ....$5.00

Massey-Harris Challenger Tractor, Ertl, 1/43 scale, #2511, MIB, S5 ....$5.25

Massey-Harris Combine, King, 10", VG, A $15.00

Massey-Harris Combine, Lincoln Products, self-propelled, 11½", VG, A $140.00

Massey-Harris Spreader, King Co, NM (orig box), A.......$30.00

Massey-Harris Wheel-Carried Disc, Zuehl, 5¼", G $80.00

Massey-Harris Wide Front Tractor, Ertl, 1/16 scale, #1292, MIB, S5...$19.00

Massey-Harris 44 Tractor, King, 7", G-, A........................$10.00

Massey-Harris 44 Tractor, Lincoln, 1950, sand cast, 8 slots in radiator grille, EX (original box), minimum value $100.00.

Massey-Harris 55, National Toy Show 1992, Ertl, 1/16 scale, #1292, MIB, S5...$60.00

McCormick, Cultivision Tractor, Arcade, 6¾", rare, VG+, A...$475.00

McCormick Corn Grinder, Arcade, 2-row, 6", G, A........$30.00

McCormick Dump Rake, Arcade, yel & red, 7", VG, A .$230.00

McCormick-Deering Cultivision Tractor, Arcade, w/driver, 6½" rpl tires, VG, A..$375.00

McCormick-Deering Dump Rake, Arcade, 5", G, A $75.00

McCormick-Deering Manure Spreader, Arcade, rubber tires, 14", VG, A...$110.00

McCormick-Deering Manure Spreader, pulled by 2 blk horses, CI w/NP wheels, 14", EX, A.....................................$650.00

McCormick-Deering Thresher, Arcade, CI, bl w/NP wheels, 9¼", VG, A..$900.00

McCormick-Deering Thresher, Arcade, CI, gr w/NP spoke wheels, 9½", rust on steel chute & pnt chips o/w VG, A........$600.00

McCormick-Deering Thresher, Arcade, 11", rpl straw shoot, VG, A $625.00

McCormick-Deering 10-20 Tractor, Arcade, CI w/cast rear rims, rubber tire band, 7½", EX, A.............................$190.00

McCormick-Deering 10-20 Tractor, Arcade, CI w/rubber tires & metal hubcaps, 7¼", EX, A..................................$550.00

McCormick-Deering 10-20 Tractor, Arcade, CI w/spoke wheels, 6½", G-, A...$50.00

McCormick-Deering 10-20 Tractor, Arcade, CI w/spoke wheels, 7¼", EX, A...$625.00

McCormick-Deering 2-Bottom Plow, Arcade, red w/yel spokes, 6½", G, A...$45.00

Minneapolis-Moline G-750, National Show 1994, Ertl, 1/43 scale, #2291, MIB, S5 ....$21.00

Monarch Tractor, Hubley, 1933, CI, gray & blk w/eccentric shaft to simulate up & down motion, 5¼", EX, A ...$675.00

Monarch Tractor, Hubley, 1933, CI, gray crawler, 3¼", EX, A $200.00

Monarch Tractor, Hubley, 1933, CI, olive-colored crawler, 4⅝", VG, A...$180.00

New Holland Hay Baler, Advanced Products, 1/16" scale, missing bale thrower, EX, A...$50.00

New Holland Mower Conditioner, Ertl, 1/64 scale, #322, MIB, S5..$2.55

New Holland Skid Loader, Ertl, 1/64 scale, #381, MIB, S5 .$4.25

Oh Boy Tractor, Kilgore, CI, orange & red w/NP wheels, 6", EX, A...$825.00

Oliver Corn Picker, Slik, 1948, from $95.00 to 265.00; Oliver Corn Picker, Slik, 1950, from $55.00 to $190.00; Oliver Grain Drill, Slik, 1950, from $65.00 to $190.00.

Oliver Disc, Slik, 1950, red, 8", from $10.00 to $35.00.

Oliver Hay Baler PTO, Slik, 10", rare, G, A..................$110.00

Oliver Hay Rake, Slik, 13", VG, A $85.00

Oliver Orchard Tractor, Hubley, dk gr, 5½", VG+, A ...$160.00

Oliver Orchard Tractor, Hubley, lt gr, 5", G, A $70.00

Oliver Plow, Arcade, red, 5½", VG, A $50.00

Oliver Single Gang Disc, Slik, 5¼", EX, A $10.00

Oliver Superior Grain Drill, NM (orig box), A $130.00

Oliver Superior Spreader, Arcade, yel, 9", G-, A...........$120.00

Oliver Superior Spreader, Arcade, yel, 9", VG+, A........$270.00

Oliver Tractor, Arcade, 1939, CI, red w/blk rubber tires, NP driver, 7¼", VG, A...$500.00

Oliver 1555 Diesel Tractor, Ertl, 1/16 scale, #2223, MIB, S5 ..$20.00

Oliver 2-Bottom Plow, Arcade, gr spokes, 5", EX, A......$150.00

Oliver 70 Tractor, Arcade, red, 7", VG, A $300.00

Oliver 77 Diesel Tractor, Slik, steerable, closed motor, 8", VG, A...$200.00

Oliver 77 Diesel Tractor, Slik, steerable open motor, 8½", G, A...$200.00

Oliver 77 Tractor, Slik, w/driver (non-drivable), 7½", VG, A...$120.00

Oliver 880 Tractor, Slik, gr, 8", G-, A $50.00

Portable Elevator, Tru-Scale, NM (orig box), A $10.00

Sickle Mower, Tru-Scale, 9", M, A $20.00

Thresher, Arcade, bl, 9½", G-, A $70.00

Thresher, Arcade, bl w/red trim, NP driver & chute, 10½", G+, A...$100.00

Thresher, Arcade, red, 9½", VG+, A $375.00
Thresher, Arcade, yel, 9½", EX, A $450.00
Tractor w/Loader, Slik, gr, 12", no driver, G-, A $10.00
Wagon, Arcade, red w/CI wheels, 6½", VG, A, from $65 to..$85.00
Wallis Tractor, Freidag, 1920s, CI, 4¾", rare, G-, A ...$2,400.00
Ward's Complete Toy Farm Set, Arcade, w/Oliver 70 tractor,
    mower, corn planter, plow & disc harrow, EX (orig box),
    A $700.00
White American 80 Front Wheel Drive, Ertl, 1/64 scale, #4285,
    MIB, S5 ....$2.75
Whitehead & Kales Wagon, Arcade, 8½", very rare, VG, A .$60.00
Whitewater Farm Wagon, Vindex, CI, gr & red w/2 blk horses,
    running gear has working parts, 7½", rare, EX, A..$3,400.00
Wil-Rich Chisel Plow, First Edition, Ertl, 1/64 scale, #9606,
    MIB, S5 ....$20.00
Wilkens Farm Wagon, w/blk horse & driver, CI & sheet metal,
    yel wagon, 13½", G, A $195.00
Wilkens Plow, w/blk horse & driver, CI, red w/yel chassis, 10",
    VG, A $2,100.00

Fast-Food Collectibles

Fast-food collectibles are attracting a lot of attention right
now — the hobby is fun and inexpensive (so far), and the little
toys, games, buttons and dolls originally meant for the kids are
now being snatched up by adults who are much more likely to
appreciate them. They were first included in kiddie meals in the
late 1970s. They're often issued in series of one to eight or ten
characters; the ones you'll want to watch for are Disney characters, popular kids' icons like Barbie dolls, Cabbage Patch Kids,
My Little Pony, Star Trek, etc. But it's not just the toys that are
collectible. So are the boxes, store signs and displays, and promotional items (like the Christmas ornaments you can buy for
99¢). Supply dictates price. For instance, a test market box
might be worth $20.00, a box from a regional promotion might
be $10.00, while one from a national promotion could be virtu-
ally worthless.

Toys don't have to be old to be collectible, but if you can
find them still in their original package, so much the better.
Though there are exceptions, a loose toy is worth one half to
two thirds the value of one mint in package. For more information we recommend *The Illustrated Collector's Guide to McDonald's*® *Happy Meal*® *Boxes, Premiums, and Promotions,*© by Joyce
and Terry Losonsky, and *Tomart's Price Guide to Kid's Meal Collectibles* by Ken Clee. Both are listed under Fast-Food Collectibles in the Categories of Special Interest section of this
book.

Advisors: Bill and Pat Poe (P10); Scott Smiles (S10), Foreign.

Arby's

Babar's Calendar Storybooks, set of 3, MIP, C3 ....$8.00
Babar's Puzzles, set of 4, MIP, C3 ....$15.00
Babar's Squirters, set of 3, MIP, C3 ....$10.00
Babar's Summer Slippers, 1991, set of 3, MIP, C3 ....$10.00
Babar's World Tour License Plates, 1990, P10, ea $3.00

Babar's World Tour Pull-Back Racers, 1992, MIP, P10, ea.$3.00
Babar's World Tour Squirters, 1992, set of 3, MIP, C3.....$10.00
Babar's World Tour Stampers, 1991, MIP, P10, ea $4.00
Babar's World Tour Vehicles, 1990, MIP, C3/P10, ea........$4.00
Babar's Wristpaks, set of 3, MIP, C3.................................$8.00
Kids' World Sticker Book, 1993, M, P10, ea $4.00
Little Miss, 1981, 9 different, P10, ea $4.00
Looney Toons Car Tunes, 1989, 6 different, P10, ea $3.00
Looney Toons Characters, 1987, 6 different, oval base, P10,
    ea $4.00
Looney Toons Fun Figures, 1989, Sylvester, Tasmanian Devil or
    Daffy Duck, P10, ea...$5.00
Looney Toons Holiday Figures, 1989, Bugs Bunny/Santa Claus,
    MIP, P10 ....$6.00
Looney Toons Pencil Toppers, 1988, 6 different, P10, ea...$5.00
Looney Toons Rings, Porky Pig, MIP, P10.......................$10.00
Mr Men, 1981, 10 different, P10, ea $4.00
Yogi & Friends Planters, set of 4, MIP, C3........................$12.00
Yogi & Friends Window Stickers, set of 4, MIP, C3.........$10.00
Yogi Bear Fun Squirters, 1994, MIP, C3/P10, ea.................$4.00

Big Boy

Action Figures, set of 4, MIP, C3 ....$20.00
Big Boy Racers, set of 3, MIP, C3 ....$15.00
Big Boy Stuffed Cloth Dolls, set of 3, MIP, C3 ....$75.00
Color...Own Window Clings, set of 4, MIP, C3 ....$24.00
Monster in My Pocket, MIP, C3, ea $3.00
Sports Figures, 1990, P10, ea $5.00
Time Capsule, Prehistoric Fun w/Pharaohs, MIP, C3 ....$5.00

Burger Chef

Action Figures, 1991, MIP, C3/P10, ea $3.00
Aladdin, 1992, MIP, P10, ea...$4.00
Aladdin Hidden Treasures, 1994, 5 different, MIP, P10, ea.$3.00
Alf, MIP, C3, ea $6.00
Archies, 1991, MIP, P10, ea $4.00
Barnyard Commandos, 1993, 4 different, all recalled, MIP, P10,
    ea $3.00
Beach Party, 1994, 5 different, MIP, P10, ea.....................$3.00
Beetlejuice, 1990, MIP, C3, ea $4.00
Bone Age, Smilodon, Dimetrodon or Tyrannosaurus Rex, P10,
    ea $5.00
Bonkers, 1993, Toots, Fall About Rabbit, Bonkers, Jitters or
    Detective Lucky Piquel, MIP, P10, ea $3.00
Capitol Critters, 1992, 4 different, MIP, P10, ea................$3.00
Captain Planet Flip-Over Star Cruisers, 1994, 4 different, MIP,
    P10, ea $3.00
Chipmunk Adventure, 1987, Alvin pencil topper, P10, ea .$4.00
Christmas Sing-A-Long Tapes, We Three Kings/O Holy Night,
    MIP, C3...$8.00
Cool Stuff, set of 5, MIP, C3 ....$15.00
Crayola Coloring Mystery Sets, 6 different, MIP, P10, ea...$4.00
Dino Crawlers, 1994, 5 different, MIP, P10, ea $3.00
Dino Meal, Wooly Mammoth, MIP, C3 ....$6.00
Glow-in-the-Dark Troll Patrol, 4 different, MIP, P10, ea...$3.00
Go-Go Gadget Gizmos, 1991, 4 different, MIP, P10, ea.....$4.00

Good Gobblin' Tricky Treaters, 1989, Zelda Zoombroom, Frankie Steen or Gourdy Goblin, P10, ea $3.00

Goof Troop Bowlers, 1992, Goofy, Max, Pete or PJ, MIP, P10, ea $3.00

It's Magic, 1992, 4 different, MIP, P10, ea $3.00

Kid Transporters, 1992, 6 different, P10, ea $3.00

Lickety Splits Rolling Racers, 1990, MIP, C3/P10, ea $3.00

Life Savers Freaky Fellas, 1992, w/Lifesavers, recalled, MIP, C3 ....$5.00

Life Savers Freaky Fellas, 1992, w/o Livesavers, P10, ea $3.00

Lion King, 1994, 7 different, MIP, P10, ea $4.00

Little Mermaid, 1993, 4 different, MIP, C3/P10, ea............$4.00

Matchbox Cars, MIP, C3, ea $7.00

McGruff Cars for You, 1991, set of 4 books w/tapes, MIP, C3/P10..$24.00

Mickey's Toontown w/Diarama, 1993, 4 different, MIP, P10, ea...$6.00

Mini Record Breakers, 1989, 6 different, P10, ea................$4.00

Mini Sports Games, 1993, set of 4, MIP, C3/P10 ....$12.00

Nerfuls, 1989, Bitsy Ball or Officer Bob, MIP, C3, ea.........$5.00

Phillies Photo Balls & Stand, set of 5, MIP, C3................$39.00

Pinocchio Summer Inflatables, 1992, MIP, P10, ea $4.00

Save the Animals, 1993, MIP, C3/P10, ea $4.00

Teenage Mutant Ninja Turtles, 1990, P10, ea $3.00

Water Mates, 1991, P10, ea $2.00

Z-Bots w/Pogs, 1994, MIP, P10, ea $4.00

BURGER KING

Action Figures, 1991, IQ Light Hair, Boomer Brown Glove, Jaws, Black Hair or Kid Vid, MIP, C11, ea $1.00

Archies, 1991, Archie or Veronica, MIP, C11, ea $2.00

Bulls Figures, set of 5, MIP, C11.....................................$20.00

Lion King, 1994, Rafiki, Scar, Simba, Mufasa or Ed the Hyena, MIP, C11, ea $3.50

Simpsons, Maggie with pacifier standing on turtle, Lisa playing saxophone with rabbit inside, M, $2.00 each.

Tricky Treaters, Zelda Zoombroom, Frankie Steen and Gourdy Goblin, M, $3.00 each.

DAIRY QUEEN

Alvin & the Chipmunks Music Makers, set of 4, MIP, C3.$19.00

Baby's Day Out Books, set of 4, MIP, C3 ....$15.00

Radio Flyer, 1991, M, P10, ea...$5.00

Rock-a-Doodle, 1992, MIP, P10, ea $7.00

Space Shuttle, set of 6, MIP, C3.......................................$19.00

DENNY'S

Adventure Seekers, 1993, MIP, C3/P10, ea $3.00

Dino-Makers, 1991, MIP, P10, ea..$3.00

Flintstone Dino-Racers, 1991, P10, ea................................$3.00

Flintstone Fun Squirters, 1991, MIP, P10, ea.....................$3.00

Flintstone Stone Age Cruisers, 1991, Barney, Wilma or Fred, M, $3.00 each.

Flintstone Glacier Gliders, 1990, C3/P10, ea $3.00

Flintstone Vehicles, 1990, P10, ea......................................$4.00

Jetsons Go Back to School, 1992, MIP, P10, ea $3.00

Jetsons Planets, 1992, MIP, P10, ea....................................$4.00

DOMINOS PIZZA

Avoid the Noid, 1988, Noid magician, MIP, P10 ....$5.00

Keep the Noid Out, 1987, He-Man Noid, MIP, P10 ....$5.00

Noid, bendable rubber, 1988, 7", NM, S2 ....$10.00

Noid Glider w/Power Prop, 1989, MIP, S2 ....$20.00

HARDEE'S

Beach Bunnies, 1989, P10, ea...$2.00

Dinosaur in My Pocket, 1993, MIP, C3/P10, ea..................$3.00

Eureka Castle Stampers, 1994, MIP, C3/P10, ea.................$3.00

Fender Benders, set of 5, MIP, C11 ....$8.00

Ghostbusters Blaster Toy, 3 different, recalled, MIP, S2 ..$20.00

Gremlin Adventures Read-Along Book & Record, 1984, M, P10, ea $6.00

Kazoo Crew Sailors, 1991, MIP, P10, ea.............................$3.00

Little Little Golden Books, 1987, M, P10, ea......................$6.00

Mickey's Christmas Carol, 1984, plush, M, P10, ea $6.00

Muppet Christmas Carol, finger puppet, 1993, MIP, P10, ea.$3.00

Smurfs Funmeal Pack, 1990, P10, ea $3.00

Tune-A-Fish, 1994, MIP, C3/P10, ea $3.00

Waldo & Friends Straw Buddies, 1990, P10, ea $3.00

Walt Disney Animated Film Classic, 1985, P10, ea............$6.00

JACK-IN-THE-BOX

Bendies, 1975, Jack, Shake Hans, Secret Sauce Agent or
  Clownie, G, P10, ea...$10.00
Garden Fun, set of 3, MIP, C3...................................$15.00
Jack Pack Puzzle Books, set of 3, MIP, C3 ....$14.00
Make-a-Scene, set of 3, MIP, C3...............................$12.00
Swiss Alps Character Figure, Imperial, rubber, NM, S2 ...$25.00

KENTUCKY FRIED CHICKEN

Rescuers Down Under, MIP, C3....................................$4.00
Sonic the Hedgehog, set of 5, MIP, C3 ....$15.00
Sports Ball, 1990, set of 4, MIP, C3 ....$10.00
Wild Friends Toy Books, set of 4, MIP, C3 ....$22.00

LONG JOHN SILVERS

Fish Car, plastic fish-shaped car, P10, ea..........................$3.00
Map Activities, 1991, MIP, P10, ea..................................$4.00
Once Upon a Forest, MIP, P10, ea $4.00
Sea Watchers, 1991, MIP, P10, ea..................................$5.00
Water Blasters, 1990, C3/P10, ea $4.00

MCDONALD'S

Airport, 1986, Fry Guy Flyer, Grimace Ace or Birdie Bent Wing
  Blazer, P10, ea...$3.00
Airport, 1986, under age 3, Fry Guy Flyer, orange, P10......$5.00
Airport, 1986, under age 3, Grimace Shuttler, bl, P10 ....$4.00
Alvin & the Chipmunks, 1991, Regional, set of 4, MIP,
  P10 ....$38.00
American Tale, 1986, Fievel's Boat Trip, Fievel's Friends or
  Tony & Fievel storybook, P10, ea $2.00
Animaniacs, 1994, 8 different, MIP, P10, ea......................$3.00
Astrosniks, 1983, Regional, any except Snikapotamus, P10,
  ea..$7.00
Astrosniks, 1983, Regional, Snikapotamus, P10.............$12.00
Back to the Future, 1992, Doc's Deloren (recalled), P10....$3.00
Back to the Future, 1992, Marty's Hoverboard, Einstein's Trav-
  eling Train or Vern's Junkmobile, P10, ea $2.00
Barbie/Hot Wheels, 1991, under age 3, any Barbie except Cos-
  tume Ball or Wedding Day Midge, MIP, P10, ea $4.00
Barbie/Hot Wheels, 1991, under age 3, Costume Ball or Wed-
  ding Day Midge, MIP, P10, ea....................................$7.00
Barbie/Hot Wheels, 1993, any Barbie except Rose Bride, MIP,
  P10, ea...$3.00
Barbie/Hot Wheels, 1993, any Hot Wheels except Hammer &
  Wrench, MIP, P10, ea $3.00
Barbie/Hot Wheels, 1993, under age 3, Hot Wheels Hammer &
  Wrench, MIP, P10, ea $4.00
Barbie/Hot Wheels, 1993, under age 3, Rose Bride, MIP, C10..$4.00
Barbie/Hot Wheels, 1994, 8 different Hot Wheels, MIP, P10,
  ea..$4.00
Barbie/Mini Streex (Hot Wheels), 1992, any Barbie, MIP, P10,
  ea..$3.00
Barbie/Mini Streex (Hot Wheels), 1992, any Mini Streex, MIP,
  P10, ea...$2.00

Barbie/Mini Streex (Hot Wheels), 1992, under age 3, Mini
  Streex Orange Arrow, MIP, P10 ....$4.00
Barbie/Mini Streex (Hot Wheels), 1992, under age 3, Sparkle
  Eyes, MIP, P10 ....$4.00
Barnyard (Old McDonald's Farm), 1986, 6 different, M, P10,
  ea..$8.00
Batman, 1992, Batman Press & Go, Batmobile, Cat Woman
  Coupe or Penguin, MIP, C11/P10, ea, from $2 to........$3.00
Batman Animated Series, 1993, Batman, Batgirl, Robin, Two-
  Face, Cat Woman, Poison Ivy, Riddler or Joker, MIP, P10,
  ea..$3.00
Batman Animated Series, 1993, under age 3, Batman, MIP, P10...$4.00
Beach Toy, 1989, Ronald Fun Flyer, MIP, C11 ....$1.50
Bedtime, 1989, foam wash mitt, bl, MIP, P10 ....$4.00
Behind the Scenes, 1992, 4 different, MIP, C11/P10, ea, from
  $1.25 to $2.00
Berenstain Bear Books, 1990, 7 different, M, P10, ea $2.00
Big Foot, 1988, purple pickup w/o Arch, MIP, C11 ....$8.00
Bobby's World, 1994, 4 different, MIP, C11/P10, ea, from $2
  to...$3.00
Cabbage Patch Kids/Tonka Trucks, 1992, any Cabbage Patch
  except under-age-3 Ribbons & Bows, MIP, C11/P10, ea,
  from $2 to...$3.00
Cabbage Patch Kids/Tonka Trucks, 1992, any Tonka except
  under-age-3 dump truck, MIP, P10, ea........................$3.00
Cabbage Patch Kids/Tonka Trucks, 1992, under age 3, Cabbage
  Patch Ribbons & Bows, MIP, P10................................$5.00
Cabbage Patch Kids/Tonka Trucks, 1992, under age 3, Tonka
  dump truck, MIP, P10..$4.00
Cabbage Patch Kids/Tonka Trucks, 1994, Mimi Kristina, Kimberly
  Katherine, Abigail or Michelle Elyse, MIP, P10, ea........$3.00
Cabbage Patch Kids/Tonka Trucks, 1994, Tonka loader, crane,
  grader or bulldozer, MIP, P10, ea...............................$3.00
Cabbage Patch Kids/Tonka Trucks, 1994, under age 3, Sarajane,
  MIP, P10 ....$5.00
Cabbage Patch Kids/Tonka Trucks, 1994, under age 3, Tonka
  dump truck, MIP, P10..$4.00
Camp McDonaldland, 1989, Utensils, MIP, C11 ....$2.50
Captain Hook Ball Puzzle, 1979, domed, EX, S2 ....$10.00
Carnival, set of 4, MIP...$20.00
Carnival, 1990, Regional, any except under-age-3 Grimace on
  rocker, MIP, P10, ea..$6.00
Carnival, 1990, Ronald, MIP, C11...................................$5.00
Carnival, 1990, under age 3, Grimace on rocker, P10 ....$7.00
Circus Parade, 1991, Regional, Ronald, Birdie, Fry Guy or Gri-
  mace, P10, ea $4.00
Connectibles, 1991, Regional/Fill-In, Birdie, Grimace, Hambur-
  glar or Ronald, MIP, P10, ea......................................$5.00
Crazy Creatures, 1991, 4 different, MIP, C11/P10, ea, from $3
  to...$4.00
Crazy Vehicles, 1991, Regional, Birdie, Grimace, Hamburglar or
  Ronald, MIP, P10, ea...$4.00
Design-O-Saurs, 1987, Hamburglar, Fry Guy, Grimace or
  Ronald, MIP, C11, ea $6.00
Dink the Little Dinosaur, 1990, Regional, 6 different, P10,
  ea..$5.00
Dino-Motion Dinosaurs, 1993, Baby Sinclair in eggshell, under-
  age-3 promo, MIP, P10 ....$4.00

Dino-Motion Dinosaurs, 1993, MIP, C11/P10, ea, from $1.50 to $2.00

Dinosaur Days, 1981, Ankylosaurus, Dimetrodon, Pteranodon, Stegosaurus, Triceratops or Tyrannosaurus Rex, M, P10, ea...$2.00

Dinosaur Talking Storybook w/Cassette, 1989, Creature in the Cave, MIP, C11 ....$7.00

Discover the Rain Forest, 1991, book, M, C11/P10, ea $2.00

Disney Favorites, 1987, Lady & the Tramp, Dumbo or Sword in the Stone, M, P10, ea $7.00

Duck Tales, I, 1987, U-3 Magic Motion Map & Decoder, MIP, P10 ....$6.00

Duck Tales I, 1987, 4 different, P10, ea............................$3.00

Duck Tales II, 1988, Launchpad, MIP, C11 ....$6.00

Duck Tales II, 1988, Scrooge McDuck, Webby, Launchpad or Donald's 3 nephews on jet ski, P10, ea.......................$4.00

Earth Days, 1994, tool carrier, bird feeder, globe terrarium or binoculars, MIP, P10, ea..................................$2.00

Feeling Good, 1985, Birdie the Early Bird/mirror, P10 ....$3.00

Feeling Good, 1985, Captain/red comb, P10......................$2.00

Field Trip, 1993, Explorer Bag, Nature Viewer, Leaf Printer or Kaleidoscope, MIP, C11/P10, ea, from $1.50 to...........$2.00

Fitness Fun/Michael Jordan, 1992, 8 different, MIP, P10, ea .$2.00

Flintstones, 1994, 5 different, MIP, C1/P10, ea, from $2.50 to...$3.00

Food Fun-Damentals, 1992, Milly, Otis, Slugger or Ruby, MIP, C11/P10, ea, from $1.50 ....$2.00

Friendly Skies, 1991, Grimace in wht plane, MIP, C11......$9.00

Friendly Skies, 1991, Ronald in wht plane, MIP, C11 ....$7.00

Friendly Skies, 1993, Ronald or Grimace in United gray, bl & red plane, MIP, P10, ea.....................................$10.00

Fry Benders, 1990, MIP, C11/P10, ea, from $4 to $5.00

Funny Fry Friends, 1989, set #1, Hoops, MIP, P10..............$5.00

Funny Fry Friends, 1989, set #7, Too Tall, gr, MIP, P10.....$4.00

Good Morning, 1991, clock, Ronald flying, MIP, C11/P10, from $1.50 to $3.00

Good Morning, 1991, toothbrush, Ronald in bed, MIP, P10 .$5.00

Gravedale High, set of 4, MIP $20.00

Grimace Watch, figural flip-top, M, S2.........................$10.00

Halloween Happy Meal, 1991, McBoo bag w/ghost in purple bow tie on purple ground, yel hdls, MIP, C11.............$1.00

Halloween McNuggets, 1993, MIP, C11/P10, ea, from $2.50 to...$3.00

Halloween McNuggets, 1993, under age 3, McBoo McNugget, P10...$4.00

Halloween Pails, 1990, M, P10, ea $2.00

Halloween Pails, 1992, w/cookie cutter on lid, M, P10, ea.$2.00

Halloween Pails, 1994, pumpkin, ghost, or witch, M, P10, ea...$3.00

Happy Birthday 15 Years, 1994, any except Barbie #2 (recalled) or under-age-3 Ronald McDonald, MIP, P10, ea.........$3.00

Happy Birthday 15 Years, 1994, under age 3, Ronald McDonald, MIP, P10 ....$5.00

Happy Pail, 1984, Olympic theme, w/lid, M, P10 ....$5.00

Happy Pail, 1986, w/lid, no shovel, M, P10, ea...................$5.00

Hook, 1991, Peter Pan, Mermaid, Hook or Rufio, MIP, C11/P10, from $2 to...$3.00

I Like Bikes, 1990, Birdie, Fry Guy or Grimace, P10, ea...$12.00

Jungle Book, 1989, any figure, MIP, C11/P10, ea, from $3 to $4.00

Jungle Book, 1990, Baloo, King Louie, Kaa or Shere Khan, MIP, P10, ea...$4.00

Lego Building Set, 1986, set B, MIP, C11/P4, from $4 to...$5.00

Lego Building Set, 1986, under age 3, Sailor, 5-pc, MIP, P10 ....$6.00

Lego Motion, 1989, Gyro Bird, Lightning Striker, Land Laser, Sea Eagle or Wind Whirler, MIP, P10, ea....................$5.00

Linkables, 1993, Birdie, Grimace or Ronald, MIP, C11, ea.$3.50

Little Engineer, 1987, Birdie, Fry Guy, Fry Girl or Grimace, w/partial decals, P10, ea...............................$2.00

Little Golden Book, 1982, 5 different, NM, P10, ea $3.00

Little Mermaid, 1989, Flounder, Ursula, Prince Eric w/Sebastian or Ariel, P10, ea...$2.00

Looney Tunes Quack Up Cars, 1993, MIP, P10, ea...........$3.00

M-Squad, 1992, Spycoder or Spy-Noculars, MIP, C11, ea .$2.00

M-Squad, 1993, 4 different, MIP, P10, ea $2.00

Mac Tonight, 1988, any in set, MIP, C11, ea $3.00

Mac Tonight, 1988, M, ea...$1.50

Magic School Bus, 1994, 4 different, MIP, P10, ea $3.00

Making Movies, 1994, 4 different, MIP, C11/P10, ea, from $1 to...$2.00

McCharacters on Bikes, 1991, Regional/Fill-In, Birdie on pk & bl bike or Ronald on red & yel bike, MIP, P10, ea $5.00

McDino Changeables, 1991, 8 different, MIP, C11, ea $1.50

McDonaldland Band, 1986, 6 different, M, ea $1.00

McDonaldland Dough, 1990, Fry Guy or Grimace, M, P10, ea...$5.00

McDonaldland Sailors, 1988, Hamburglar Pirate Ship, bl, M, P10...$6.00

McNugget Buddies, 1988, any except under-age-3 Daisy w/teddy bear $3.50

McNugget Buddies, 1988, Rocker, Snorkel, Boomerang or Sparky, MIP, C11, ea...$3.50

McNugget Buddies, 1988, under age 3, Daisy w/teddy bear, P10...$5.00

Mickey & Friends Epcot '94 Adventure, 1994, 8 different, MIP, C11/P10, ea, from $1.50 to $3.00

Mickey's Birthdayland, 1988, Donald or Minnie, MIP, P10, ea...$4.00

Mickey's Birthdayland, 1988, under age 3, Mickey or Donald, P10, ea...$6.00

Mighty Mini 4x4, 1991, Regional, Dune Buster, Li'l Classic, Cargo Climber or Pocket Pickup, MIP, C11/P10, ea, from $2 to...$3.00

Mighty Mini 4x4, 1991, Regional, under age 3, Pocket Pickup, MIP, P10 ....$5.00

Mix 'Em Up Monsters, 1988, Blibble, Thugger or Corkle, MIP, C11, ea...$4.00

Mix 'Em Up Monsters, 1989, Blibble, Corkle, Gropple or Thugger, P10, ea..$2.00

Moveables, 1988, Captain Crook or Fry Girl, P10, ea $5.00

Muppet Babies, 1990, Miss Piggy, Gonzo or Kermit, MIP, C11, ea...$5.00

Muppet Workshop, 1995, 4 different, MIP, P10, ea...........$3.00

Mystery of the Lost Arches, 1992, camera, micro-cassette, phone, or flashlight, MIP, C11/P10, ea, from $1.50 to.............$2.00

Mystery of the Lost Arches, 1992, under age 3, Magic Lens Camera, MIP, P10..$3.00

Nature's Helper, 1991, 5 different & under age 3, P10, ea, from $2 to...$3.00

New Archies, 1988, any in set, MIP, ea $6.00

Nickelodeon Game Gadgets, 1992, 4 different, MIP, C11/P10, ea, from $1 to $2.00

Oliver & Co, 1988, Francis, Georgette or Dodger, MIP, C11/P10, ea, from $2 to..$3.50

Out for Fun, 1993, 4 different, MIP, P10, ea $2.00

Peanuts, 1990, Snoopy's hay hauler, Charlie Brown's seed bag, Lucy's apple cart or Linuses' milk mover, MIP, C11/P10, ea $3.00

Peanuts, 1990, under age 3, Charlie Brown's egg basket or Snoopy's potato sack, MIP, P10, ea $5.00

Piggsburg Piggs, 1991, Regional, Porty w/Pig Head, Piggy w/Crackers or Rembrandt, P10, ea $4.00

Playmobile, 1982, Indian w/shield, spear & pipe, MIP, P10...$8.00

Polly Pocket/Attack Pack, 1995, 8 different, MIP, P10, ea.$3.00

Potato Heads, 1992, Regional, 7 different, MIP, ea $5.00

Raggedy Ann & Andy, 1989, Regional, set of 4, P10.......$25.00

Real Ghostbusters, 1987, wht ghost pencil sharpener, P10..$3.00

Rescuers Down Under, 1990, Cody or Wilbur, MIP, C11, ea $3.00

Ronald McDonald, figure, 1988, 3", M, $4.00.

Ronald McDonald Tree Ornament, mid-1980s, stuffed figure, 3", MIB..$5.00

Ronald McDonald Watch, figural flip-top, M, S2 ....$10.00

Runaway Robots, 1987, Beak, Bolt, Coil, Flame, Jab or Skull, P10, ea $3.00

Santa Claus the Movie, 1985, Elves at the Top of the World or Legend of Santa Claus storybook, P10, ea...................$3.00

Sea World of Texas, 1988, Regional, plush, 6", P10, ea......$6.00

Snow White & the Seven Dwarfs, 1992, MIP, ea..............$4.00

Snow White & the Seven Dwarfs, 1993, Dopey & Sneezy Spin, under age 3, MIP, P10..$4.00

Snow White & the Seven Dwarfs, 1993, Prince w/horse on gr base, MIP, P10 ....$5.00

Snow White & the Seven Dwarfs, 1993, Snow White w/wishing well, Prince w/horse (no base), Bashful or Doc, MIP, P10, ea $3.00

Snow White and the Seven Dwarfs, 1993, Snow White with wishing well, Witch, or Prince with horse, MIP, $3.00 each.

Sonic 3 the Hedgehog, 1994, any figure, MIP, C11/P10, ea, from $2 to...$3.00

Sports Ball, 1991, Basketball or Football, MIP, C11, ea $3.00

Stencils & Crayons, 1991, Fill-In, Grimace or Ronald, MIP, P10, ea $3.00

Super Looney Tunes, 1991, Bugs Bunny, Tasmanian Devil, Petunia Pig or Daffy Duck, MIP, C11/P10, ea..............$2.00

Super Looney Tunes, 1991, under age 3, Daffy Duck, MIP, P10 ....$4.00

Super Mario 3 Nintendo, 1990, Mario, Luigi, Goomba or Koopa, MIP, C11/P10, ea, from $2.50 ....$3.00

Super Mario 3 Nintendo, 1990, under age 3, standing Mario, MIP, P10 ....$4.00

Tail Spin, 1990, Kit, Molly or Wildcat, MIP, C11, ea........$2.00

Tinosaurs, set of 8, MIP...$40.00

Tinosaurs, 1986, Regional, 5 different, P10, ea $6.00

Tiny Toon Adventures/Flip Cars, 1990, 8 different, MIP, C11, ea $2.00

Tiny Toons, 1992, set of 8, MIP.......................................$24.00

Totally Toys, 1993, any except recalled Barbie dome, MIP, P10, ea $3.00

Turbo Macs, 1990, Birdie or Hamburglar, MIP, ea $3.00

Wild Friends, 1992, Regional, Elephant, Crocodile, Gorilla or Giant Panda, MIP, P10, ea $5.00

Winter Worlds, 1983, Hamburglar, MIP, C11 ....$3.00

Yo Yogi, 1992, Regional, Yogi, Huckleberry Hound, Cindy Bear or Boo Boo, MIP, P10, ea...$5.00

101 Dalmatians, MIP, $2.50.

Young Astronauts, 1992, Satellite Dish, Lunar Rover, Space Shuttle or Command Module, MIP, P10, ea...............$2.00
Young Astronauts, 1992, under age 3, Ronald in Lunar Rover, soft plastic, MIP, P10.....................$5.00
Zoo Face, 1988, 4 different, MIP, P10, ea...........................$4.00
101 Dalmatians, 1991, MIP, ea......................................$2.50

PIZZA HUT

Beauty and the Beast, hand puppets, set of 4, M, $5.00 each.

Drive to the Hoop, complete set of 4, MIP, C3 ....$10.00
Eureka's Castle Hand Puppets, 1990, rubber, 3 different, MIP, ea, P10.....................$5.00
Fievel Goes West, 1991, Fievel or Cat R Waul, M, P10, ea.$5.00
Garfield — Air Extremes, set of 5, MIP, C3 ....$22.00
Land Before Time Hand Puppets, 1988, any except Sharptooth, P10, ea..................$5.00
Marsupilami, set of 3, MIP, C3 ....$15.00
Young Indiana Jones, scope, C3 ....$6.00

ROY ROGERS

Be a Sport, magnets, set of 4, MIP, C3............................$22.00
Doodletop Jr, set of 4, MIP, C3 ....$19.00
Gater Tales, 1989, MIP, P10, ea.......................................$8.00
Ickky Stickky Bugs, set of 16, MIP, C3 ....$59.00
Swan Princess, set of 4, MIP, C3 ....$22.00

SONIC

Animal Squirters, set of 8, MIP, C3 ....$29.00
Brown Bag Juniors, 1989, MIP, P10, ea............................$5.00
Brown Bag Kids, 1993, on skis, snowboard or tube, MIP, ea $5.00
Dino Soakers, set of 4, MIP, C3 ....$16.00
Holiday Express, set of 4, MIP, C3 ....$22.00
Wacky Sacks, set of 24 w/6 styles in ea of 4 colors, MIP, C3..................$79.00
Wall Jacks, set of 4, MIP, C3...$16.00

SUBWAY

Cone Heads, set of 4, MIP, C3 ....$15.00
Explore Space, set of 4, MIP, C3 ....$15.00
Monkey Business, set of 5, MIP, C3 ....$15.00
Tom & Jerry, set of 4, MIP, C3 ....$15.00

TACO BELL

Busy World of Richard Scarry, Lowly Worm or Huckle Cat (recalled), MIP, C3, ea $8.00
Happy Talk Sprites, plush Spark, Twink or Romeo, P10, ea.$6.00
Hugga Bunch, 1984, plush Fluffer, Gigglet or Tuggins, P10, ea $8.00

TARGET MARKETS

Adventure Team Window Walkers, 1994, MIP, P10, ea....$4.00
Adventures in 3-D, Ramon Wins, MIP, C3 ....$5.00
Mutant Meal, 9 pogs w/card, set of 3 cards, MIP, C3........$18.00
Playful Pets, set of 3, MIP, C3 ....$19.00
Targeteers, 1992, MIP, P10, ea $5.00
Window Walkers, set of 4, MIP, C3.................................$15.00
X-Men, set of 3, MIP, C3..$11.00

WENDY'S

Alf Tales, 1990, P10, ea $3.00
Alien Mix-Ups, 1990, P10, ea $3.00
All Dogs Go to Heaven, 1989, P10, ea..............................$3.00
Cybercycles, 1994, gold, red or purple, MIP, ea $4.00
Definitely Dinosaurs, 1988 or 1989, P10, ea.....................$4.00
Dino Games, 1992, Egg Game or Dinosaur Puzzle, MIP, C11, ea $1.00
Endangered Animals, 1993, MIP, ea $2.00
Furskins Bears, 1986, plush, P10, ea $6.00
Gear Up, set of 5, MIP, C3 ....$15.00
Glo-Ahead, 1993, P10, ea...$2.00

Jetsons, George in spaceship, 1st series, 1989, MIP, $6.00.

Jetsons: The Movie, 1990, MIP, P10, ea............................$4.00
Kids 4 Parks, set of 5, MIP, C3 ....$18.00
Mighty Mouse, 1989, MIP, P10, ea...................................$4.00
Potato Head II, 1988, P10, ea $4.00
Speed Writers, 1991, MIP, P10, ea....................................$4.00
Wild Games, set of 6, MIP, C3...$15.00
World Wild Life, 1988, plush, M, P10, ea $5.00
Yogi Bear & Friends, 1990, MIP, P10, ea $4.00

White Castle

Bow Biters, 1989, MIP, P10, ea..$5.00
Camp White Castle, 1990, MIP, P10, ea........................$4.00
Castleburger Dudes, 1991, MIP, P10, ea.....................$5.00
Fat Albert & the Gang, set of 4, MIP, C3...........$28.00
Holiday Huggables, 1990, MIP, P10, ea $6.00
Silly Putty, set of 3, MIP, C3..$12.00
Super Balls, 1994, MIP, P10, ea......................................$5.00
Swat Kats, set of 3, MIP, C3..$10.00
Triassic Take-Aparts, set of 4, MIP, C3 ....$12.00
Water Balls, set of 4, MIP, C3 ....$15.00

Wienerschnitzel

Dinosaurs, Paddy Whacker, MIP, C3 ....$8.00
Dude Dex, set of 2, MIP, C3...$12.00
Frisbees & Balls, set of 4, MIP, C3.............................$19.00
Li'l Dude Classics Cassette Tapes, Night Before Christmas,
    C3 ....$5.00
Super Sucking Straws, set of 4, MIP, C3 ....$24.00
Superduper Balls, set of 4, MIP, C3 ....$20.00
Yo-Yos, set of 4, MIP, C3..$22.00

Foreign

Burger King, Cinderella, 1993, complete set, MIP, S10,
    from $40 to..$45.00
Burger King, Flinstones, complete set, MIP, C3/S10, from $35
    to...$45.00
Burger King, Snow White & the Seven Dwarfs, 1995, complete
    set, MIP, S10...$30.00
Burger King (England), Glow-in-the-Dark Trolls, set of 4, M,
    C3...$28.00
Burger King (England), Goof Troop, set of 4, MIP..........$20.00
Burger King (England), Peter Pan, set of 5, MIP $40.00
Burger King (England), Taz-Mania Crazies, set of 4, MIP,
    P10/S10, from $25 to...$30.00
McDonald's, Aladdin, 1994, complete set, MIP $25.00
McDonald's, Aladdin, 1994, complete set, MIP, w/4 Happy
    Meal boxes $30.00
McDonald's, Animated Batman, 1993, complete set, MIP,
    S10...$25.00
McDonald's, Aristocats, complete set, MIP, w/4 Happy
    Meal boxes $30.00
McDonald's, Astrix, 1994, complete set, MIP, w/4 Happy Meal
    boxes, P10...$28.00
McDonald's, Bambi, 1993, complete set, MIP, w/4 Happy Meal
    boxes, P10...$30.00
McDonald's, Barbie, complete set, MIP, S10, from $30 to .$35.00
McDonald's, Barbie/Attack Pack, set of 4 Attack Packs, MIP,
    w/4 Happy Meal boxes, P10 ....$30.00
McDonald's, Barbie/Attack Pack, 1993, Crystal Barbie, Holiday
    or Sea Holiday, MIP, P10, ea....................................$7.00
McDonald's, Bubble Games, set of 3, MIP, C3 ....$25.00
McDonald's, Connect-a-Car, 1991, set of 4, P10.............$18.00
McDonald's, Dinosaurs, complete set, MIP, S10, from $25
    to $30.00

McDonald's, Dragonettes, complete set, MIP, from $20 to..$25.00
McDonald's, Euro Disney, 1992, complete set, MIP $35.00
McDonald's, Flintstones, complete set, 1994, MIP, w/4 Happy
    Meal boxes, P10..$35.00
McDonald's, Garage/McVillage, Ronald, Grimace, Birdie or Fry
    Kids, MIP, P10, ea..$8.00
McDonald's, Jungle Book, complete set, S10, from $20 to..$25.00
McDonald's, Jungle Book, Mowgli in pot, Shere Kahn, King
    Louie or Kaa, MIP, P10, ea.......................................$6.00
McDonald's, Legos, complete set, MIP, P10 ....$28.00
McDonald's, Lion King, 1994, complete set, MIP, P10/S10,
    from $28 to..$35.00
McDonald's, McDonald's Band, complete set, MIP..........$25.00
McDonald's, McMusic, 1994, complete set, MIP, w/4 Happy
    Meal boxes, P10..$28.00
McDonald's, McRockin', 1992, 4 different, M, ea $5.00
McDonald's, Playdoh w/Dinosaur Mold, 1993, complete set,
    MIP, w/4 Happy Meal boxes, P10 ....$28.00
McDonald's, Rec-Ups, 1993, complete set, MIP, w/4 Happy
    Meal boxes $25.00
McDonald's, Rescuers Down Under, complete set, MIP, S10,
    from $25 to..$30.00
McDonald's, Rev-Ups, 1993, complete set, MIP, S10 ......$20.00
McDonald's, Space Launchers, complete set, MIP, S10, from
    $20 to...$25.00
McDonald's, Space Launchers, 1992, complete set, MIP, w/4
    Happy Meal boxes, P10 ....$28.00
McDonald's, Tail Spin, complete set, MIP, C11..............$25.00
McDonald's, Twisting Sports, complete set, MIP, S10, from $20
    to $25.00
McDonald's, Twisting Sports, 1993, complete set, MIP, w/4
    Happy Meal boxes $30.00
McDonald's, Water Pistols, 1993, 4 different, P10, ea......$10.00
McDonald's, Weather, 1993, complete set, MIP, w/1 bag,
    P10...$28.00
McDonald's, Winter Sports, 1994, complete set, MIP, S10,
    from $20 to..$25.00
McDonald's, Winter Sports, 1994, complete set, MIP, w/4
    Happy Meal boxes, P10 ....$35.00
McDonald's, World of Dinosaurs, 1994, complete set, lg, MIP,
    w/4 Happy Meal boxes, P10 ....$30.00
McDonald's (Australia), Aladdin Straw Grippers, 1994, set of 4,
    MIP, P10 ....$38.00
McDonald's (Australia), Flintstone Stationary Series, 1994, set
    of 4, P10...$38.00
McDonald's (Canadian), Cabbage Patch Kids, 1994, set of 5,
    MIB, P10...$25.00
McDonald's (Canadian), Farm Animals, set of 8, MIP, P3..$20.00
McDonald's (Canadian), Ice Pop Makers, set of 4, MIP, C3..$19.00
McDonald's (Canadian), Looney Tunes, set of 4, MIP, C3 .$23.00
McDonald's (Canadian), McDonald's Figurines, set of 4,
    MIP...$20.00
McDonald's (Canadian), Muppet Babies, set of 4, MIP, C3 .$29.00
McDonald's (Canadian), Peanuts, set of 4, MIP, C3 ....$30.00
McDonald's (France), Growing Figures, set of 3, MIP, C3 .$18.00
McDonald's (Germany), Akrobat, set of 3, MIP, C3........$15.00
McDonald's (Germany), Astromacs, set of 4, MIP, C3 ....$28.00
McDonald's (Germany), Garfield, set of 4, MIP, C3 ....$32.00

McDonald's (Holland), Ornajepakket, 1994, hat, referee whistle, sports face makeup & pin, MIP, P10..................$15.00
McDonald's (Japan), Musical Items, whistle or accordion, MIP, C3, ea $9.00
Pizza Hut, Gladiators, set of 6, MIP..................................$35.00

BOXES AND BAGS

Burger King, Bone Age, 1989, P10, ea.................................$7.00
Burger King, Critter Carton/Punch-Out Paper Masks, 1985, P10, ea...$18.00
Burger King, Dino-Meal, 1987, P10, ea.............................$6.00
Burger King, Fairy Tale Cassettes, 1989, P10, ea $6.00
Burger King, Trak-Pak, 1988, P10.....................................$8.00
Burger King, Tricky Treaters, Monster Manor, 1989, P10..$5.00
Denny's, Jetsons Fun Book & Menu, 1992, P10, ea $1.00
Hardee's, Cruisin' Back to School, 1994, P10 ....$2.00
Hardee's, Fender Benders 500 Racers, 1990, P10...............$3.00
Hardee's, Marvel Super Heroes, 1990, P10 ....$3.00
Hardee's, Muppet Christmas Carol, 1993, P10 ....$2.00

Hardee's, Old MacDonald Had a Farm, Little Golden Book series, 1 from series of 4, O1, $5.50 each.

McDonald's, Anamaniacs, C11, set of 4..............................$1.00
McDonald's, Back to the Future, 1992, P10, ea $2.00
McDonald's, Bambi, 1988, P10, ea.....................................$4.00
McDonald's, Barbie/Hot Wheels, 1991, P10, ea $2.00
McDonald's, Batman, 1992, P10, ea...................................$2.00
McDonald's, Batman, 1993, P10, ea...................................$1.00
McDonald's, Beach Toy, 1990, P10, ea...............................$3.00
McDonald's, Big Foot, 1987, M, C11, ea $10.00
McDonald's, Cabbage Patch Kids/Tonka, 1994, P10, ea $1.00
McDonald's, Carnival, 1990, P10, ea..................................$2.00
McDonald's, Changeables, 1987, P10, ea............................$3.00
McDonald's, Dink the Dinosaur, 1990, Dink, P10.............$4.00
McDonald's, Dino-Motion Dinosaurs, 1993, P10, ea.........$1.00
McDonald's, Duck Tales, set of 4, 1987, C11.....................$6.00
McDonald's, Feeling Good, 1985, set of 4, C11 ....$15.00
McDonald's, Garfield, 1989, set of 4, C11........................$8.00
McDonald's, Happy Birthday 15 Years, 1994, P10, ea $1.00
McDonald's, Hook, 1991, P10, ea $3.00
McDonald's, Jungle Book, 1989, set of 4, C11 ....$10.00

McDonald's, Mac Tonight, 1988, C11, ea $3.50
McDonald's, Nickelodeon, 1993, P10, ea............................$1.00
McDonald's, Real Ghost Busters, 1987, set of 4, C11.......$12.00
McDonald's, Rescuers Down Under, 1990, C11, ea...........$1.00
McDonald's, Snow White & the Seven Dwarfs, 1993, P10, ea..$2.00
McDonald's, Sports Ball, 1990, C11, ea $3.00
McDonald's, Super Looney Tunes, 1991, P10, ea $2.00
McDonald's, Super Mario, 1990, P10, ea $2.00
McDonald's, Tail Spin, 1990, C11, ea.................................$1.00
McDonald's, Turbo Mac, 1990, C11, ea..............................$3.00
McDonald's, Wild Friends, 1992, P10, ea............................$3.00
McDonald's, 101 Dalmatians, 1991, P10, ea $3.00
Wal-Mart, Lisa Frank, P10..$2.00
Wendy's, Fast Food Racers, 1990, P10................................$4.00
Wendy's, Weather Watch, 1991, P10 ....$2.00
Wendy's, Wendy & the Good Stuff Gang, 1989, P10 ....$3.00

MISCELLANEOUS

This section lists items other than those that are free with kids' meals, for instance, store displays and memorabilia such as Christmas ornaments and plush dolls that can be purchased at the counter.

Big Boy, sidewalk chalk, 4 colors, MIB, C3 ....$4.00
Burger King, bear, 1986, Crayola Christmas series, plush, P10, ea $5.00
Burger King, bucket, 1992, Aladdin, M, C3 ....$3.00
Burger King, calendar, 1992, 20 Years Magical, M, P10 .....$4.00
Burger King, cassette tape, Christmas Sing-a-Long, MIB, P10..$3.00
Burger King, coloring book, Keep Your World Beautiful, M, P10...$2.00
Burger King, doll, Magician, Knickerbocker, 1980, 18", MIB, S2..$65.00
Burger King, doll, Magician, 15", EX (orig box), J5 ....$45.00
Burger King, doll, Marvelous Magical Burger King, 13", P10.$8.00
Burger King, doll, older version w/human features, stuffed cloth, 13", H4...$8.00
Burger King, food playset, 1987, Whopper, fries & fixings, MIB, S2 ....$25.00
Burger King, puppet, The Many Faces of Alf, P10, ea $5.00
Chuck E Cheese, bank, figural, vinyl, EX $10.00
Chuck E Cheese, bank, Hillbillie Dog figure, vinyl, 6¼", VG...$8.00
Chuck E Cheese, doll, plush, 13", EX................................$15.00
Chuck E Cheese, wallet, w/picture of Chuck & Pizza Time Theater, tan, adult-sz, EX $5.00
Chuck E Cheese, watch, digital, premium, child-sz, VG ..$10.00
Chuck E Cheese, yo-yo, VG $3.00
Dominos Pizza, bookmark, 1989 ....$8.00
Dominos Pizza, doll, Noid, Rarity, 1988, plush, 19", MIP.$25.00
Dominos Pizza, pin-back button, Avoid the Noid Call Dominos Pizza, 2¼", M, P10...$2.00
Foreign, decals, McDonald character ruboffs, MIP, P10 .....$2.00
Foreign, display, Aladdin, S10, from $150 to..................$175.00
Foreign, display, Aristocats, S10, from $125 to...............$150.00
Foreign, display, Barbie/Hot Wheels, S10, from $175 to.$200.00

Foreign, display, Batman, S10, from $150 to $175.00

Foreign, display, Flintstones, S10, from $150 to $175.00

Foreign, display, Jungle Book, S10, from $125 to $150.00

Foreign, display, Lion King, S10, from $175 to..............$200.00

Foreign, pin, Grimace, Santa Claus, or Snowman, w/clip-on back, M, P10, ea..$5.00

Foreign, snow dome, Ronald ice skating, M, P10..............$5.00

Foreign, translite, Aladdin, S10, from $45 to....................$55.00

Foreign, translite, Barbie/Hot Wheels, S10, from $45 to..$55.00

Foreign, translite, Batman, S10, from $50 to....................$60.00

Foreign, translite, Beauty & the Beast, S10, from $50 to..$60.00

Foreign, translite, Euro Disney, S10, from $40 to.............$50.00

Foreign, translite, Flintstones, S10, from $40 to $50.00

Foreign, translite, Looney Tunes, S10, from $35 to..........$40.00

Foreign, translite, Tail Spin, S10, from $30 to..................$35.00

Hardee's, backpack, orange, MIP, P10..............................$3.00

Hardee's, car, Ertl, Hardee's #90, wht & orange, P10 ....$10.00

Hardee's, frisbee, yel letters on wht, 4¾", P10....................$2.00

Hardees, doll, Gilbert Giddy-Up, stuffed cloth, 15", EX, H4..$20.00

Jack-in-the Box, calendar, 1995, Star Trek, MIP, C3 ....$8.00

Jack-in-the Box, doll, Meatsa Meatsa Man, 1990, 5", P10..$3.00

Little Ceasers, doll, stuffed cloth, 6", H4..........................$10.00

McDonald's, band-aids, Curad Happy Strips, 1990, MIP, P10 ....$3.00

McDonald's, bank, plastic bottle form, 9", P10 ....$3.00

McDonald's, bank, 1975, Ronald's Singing Wastebasket, P10 ....$10.00

McDonald's, bank, 1985, Grimace, ceramic, 10", MIB.....$25.00

McDonald's, bank, 1993, Ronald's Happy Times, 7½", MIB, P10 ....$15.00

McDonald's, belt buckle, Hamburglar, bronze, M, C11....$15.00

McDonald's, book, 1988, Travel Fun, P10 ....$1.00

McDonald's, bop bag, Grimace, purple, 8", MIP, P10.........$4.00

McDonald's, calendar, 1991, Dino Fun Facts, M $1.00

McDonald's, cap, 1992, Season's Greeting, P10..................$3.00

McDonald's, car window cup holder, red, super sz, P10 ......$3.00

McDonald's, Christmas stocking, 1981, Ronald on thin vinyl, P10..$5.00

McDonald's, Christmas stocking, 1986, Fievel, P10, ea......$5.00

McDonald's, comb, 1980, figural Ronald McDonald, 6½", NM, ...$2.00

McDonald's, comic book, Brett Hull, MIP, C11, set of 3 ...$5.00

McDonald's, cookie cutter, 1978, Ronald or Grimace bust, red or yel plastic, P10, ea $3.00

McDonald's, cookie cutter, 1987, Fry Kid on unicycle, red or gr plastic, P10, ea $5.00

McDonald's, counter display, 1994, Barbie/Hot Wheels, P10 ....$100.00

McDonald's, counter display, 1994, Flintstones, P10........$60.00

McDonald's, counter display, 1994, Happy Birthday 15 Years, w/recalled Barbie, P10 ....$100.00

McDonald's, counter display, 1994, Magic School Bus, P10.$35.00

McDonald's, counter display, 1994, Mickey & Friends/Epcot '94 Adventure, P10...$75.00

McDonald's, display, Explore the Arts/Behind the Scenes, cb, M..$20.00

McDonald's, display, Natures Watch, cb, M.....................$20.00

McDonald's, display, 1989, stand-up cup display w/cup set, EX, S2...$85.00

McDonald's, display, 1990, Jungle Book, plexiglass, M, S2.$100.00

McDonald's, display, 1990, Super Mario 3, plexiglass, M .$100.00

McDonald's, display, 1990, Tail Spin, plexiglass, M.......$100.00

McDonald's, display, 1991, Michael Jordan Fitness Fun, cb, M..$25.00

McDonald's, display, 1991, Super Looney Tunes, plexiglass, M..$100.00

McDonald's, display, 1992, McSquad Secret Agent toys, cb, S2...$10.00

McDonald's, display, 1992, Tiny Toons, w/8 toys, cb, M .$10.00

McDonald's, doll, Baby Fozzie Bear, 1988, stuffed, M, C11.$3.00

McDonald's, doll, Fry Girl, 1987, cloth, 3½", M, C11 ....$5.00

McDonald's, doll, Hamburglar, 1972, 16", missing cape otherwise EX, $10.00.

McDonald's, doll, Hamburglar, w/cape, 16", VG, H4.......$12.00

McDonald's, doll, Ronald McDonald, cloth body w/vinyl head, hands & shoes, yarn hair, w/whistle, 20", EX, S2 ......$65.00

McDonald's, doll, Ronald McDonald, Hasbro, 1978, MIB, J2...$95.00

McDonald's, flasher ring, shows Ronald McDonald diving in water..$20.00

McDonald's, food tray, 3 sections, 6x9", 1987, P10 ....$4.00

McDonald's, football, 1993, Regional/Collegiate, Georgia Bulldogs or Georgia Tech Yellow Jackets, half-sz, P10, ea..$5.00

McDonald's, french fry container, Flintstones, set of 4, M, P10..$10.00

McDonald's, french fry container, Jurassic Park, set of 4, M, P10 ....$10.00

McDonald's, french fry container, Nothing But Net/Most Valuable Player, set of 6, M, P10 ....$15.00

McDonald's, game, 1993, Ronald Ring Toss, MIB, P10 ...$12.00

McDonald's, game cards, Dick Tracy/Crime Stoppers, MIP, C11, set of 12 ....$10.00

McDonald's, growth chart, Ronald McDonald, M, C11 .....$3.00

McDonald's, hand puppet, Ronald, 1990, plastic, P10........$1.00

McDonald's, lapel pin, Collector Ltd First Edition, P10.....$5.00

McDonald's, magic tablet, 1982, Tic-Tac-Teeth, M, P10 ..$1.00

McDonald's, magnet, Hamburglar in space, M, P10 ....$3.00

McDonald's, music box, plays Silent Night & Jingle Bells, 1990, 2¼x2½", MIB, P10 ....$25.00

McDonald's, ornament, 1982, Norman Rockwell holiday scene on brass, MIP, P10 ....$20.00

McDonald's, ornament, 1985, plush reindeer, P10 ....$5.00

McDonald's, ornament, 1988, plush Dodger, MIB, P10......$4.00

McDonald's, ornament, 1989, plush Flounder, MIB, P10...$4.00

McDonald's, ornament, 1990, Over One Million Holiday Wishes, MIB, P10 ....$25.00

McDonald's, ornament, 1990, plush Bernard or Miss Bianca, MIB, P10, ea $4.00

McDonald's, ornament, 1990-91, McHappy Holidays, MIB, P10 ....$25.00

McDonald's, ornament, 1993-93, Small Fry's First Christmas, MIB, P10 ....$20.00

McDonald's, pen, Holiday Greetings, red & gr, M, P10 .....$2.00

McDonald's, pin, Ken Griffey Jr Golden Moments, set of 3, MOC, P10 ....$10.00

McDonald's, pin-back button, I Support Ronald McDonald House, 3", P10 ....$3.00

McDonald's, pin-back button, Michael Jordan, C11 ....$1.00

McDonald's, plate, 1977, Four Season, M, P10, ea $6.00

McDonald's, plate, 1989, McNugget band, EX, I2 ....$5.00

McDonald's, plate, 1989, Ronald Rhyme, 9", M, P10........$5.00

McDonald's, playset, Playskool, 1974, rare, NMIB.........$100.00

McDonald's, pog, Ronald McDonald House, Hawaii, P10 .$2.00

McDonald's, popsicle mold, 1980, Ronald on hdl, P10 ......$4.00

McDonald's, postcard, 1970, Ronald McDonald, 3x5", unused, NM, T2 ....$12.00

McDonald's, puzzle, Springbok, 1992, 24x30", MIP, P10.$25.00

McDonald's, puzzle, 1991, limited edition for employees only, 1,000 pcs, MIB (sealed) $30.00

McDonald's, razor, 1986, Gillette Micro Track...................$2.00

McDonald's, record, 1970s, Ronald McDonald's Kids Radio Birthday Party, M (sealed), J5 ....$10.00

McDonald's, record, 1980, Share a Song From Your Heart, P10...$10.00

McDonald's, record, 1988, One Million Dollar Menu, cb, P10 ....$5.00

McDonald's, restaurant directory, 1989-1990, C11 ....$3.00

McDonald's, ring, Grimace 500 Smile Race or Spaceship Friendship, MOT, P10, ea...$5.00

McDonald's, ruler, 1981, Ronald, 6", P10 ....$2.00

McDonald's, shoelace ornament, 1986, Ronald, M, P10 ....$2.00

McDonald's, spoon, 1980, Ronald McDonald hdl, red plastic, NM..$2.00

McDonald's, stationery, 1980, w/McDonaldland letterhead, MIP, C11 ....$12.00

McDonald's, sunglasses, Ronald, Birdie or Hamburglar, MIP, C11/P10, ea, from $4 to $6.00

McDonald's, T-shirt, Batman Returns, issued to employees only, M $10.00

McDonald's, translite, 1988, Muppet Babies Stuffed Toys, C11 ....$10.00

McDonald's, translite, 1989, Lego Motion, 14x14" $10.00

McDonald's, translite, 1990, Frozen Yogurt $3.00

McDonald's, translite, 1990, Super Mario 3 Nintendo, C11.$10.00

McDonald's, translite, 1990, Tail Spin, 14x14", C11 ....$15.00

McDonald's, translite, 1991, Barbie/Hot Wheels, sm $10.00

McDonald's, translite, 1992, Cabbage Patch/Tonka.........$10.00

McDonald's, translite, 1992, Halloween Buckets, C11.......$8.00

McDonald's, translite, 1992, Tiny Toon Wacky Rollers, C11..$12.00

McDonald's, translite, 1992, Young Astronauts, C11.......$10.00

McDonald's, translite, 1993, Batman Returns 32-Oz Cups, 22x22", C11...$10.00

McDonald's, watch, quartz, Ronald on face, for employees only, MIB, S2..$55.00

McDonald's, whistle, 1985, McDonald's Tootler, gr, M, P10..$2.00

McDonald's (Australia), calendar, 1994 Colossal Calendar, P10...$5.00

McDonald's (Foreign), calendar, 1994, Super Action, P10 .$3.00

Pizza Hut, bank, 1969, Pizza Hut Pete figure, hard plastic, EX...$8.00

Pizza Hut, cookie cutter, plastic pizza, P10 ....$3.00

Pizza Hut, pin-back button, Book It, P10 ....$3.00

Pollo Loco, toy, rubber chicken w/stickers, MIP, C3 ....$5.00

Roy Rogers, Halloween bucket, glow-in-the-dark graphics, M, C3 ....$2.00

Sea Host Restaurant, push puppet, 1960s, plastic, 4", EX, J5..$25.00

Shoney's, bear, 1993, vinyl, M...$5.00

Fisher-Price

Fisher-Price toys are becoming one of the hottest new trends in the collector's marketplace today. In 1930 Herman Fisher, backed by Irving Price, Elbert Hubbard and Helen Schelle, formed one of the most successful toy companies ever to exist in East Aurora, NY. The company has seen many changes since then, the most notable being the changes in ownership. From 1930 to 1968, the company was owned by the individuals mentioned previously and a few stockholders. In 1969 the company was acquired by Quaker Oats, then in June of 1991 it became an independently owned company. But in November of 1993, one of the biggest undertakings in the toy industry took place: Fisher-Price became a subdivision of Mattel.

There are a few things to keep in mind when collecting Fisher-Price toys. You should count on a little edge wear as well as some paint fading or wear. The prices in the listings are for toys in that kind of condition. Pull toys found in mint condition are truly rare and command a higher value, especially if you find one with its original box. This also applies to playsets, but to command the higher prices, they must also be complete, with all pieces present. Another very important rule to remember is there are no set colors for pieces that came with a playset. Fisher-Price often substituted a piece of a different color when they ran short.

The company put much time and thought into designing their toys. They took care to operate by their 5-point creed: to make toys with (1) intrinsic play value; (2) ingenuity; (3) strong construction; (4) good value for the money; and (5) action. Some of the most sought-after pull toys are those bearing the Walt Disney logo.

The Toy Fest limited editions are a series of toys produced

in conjunction with Toy Fest, an annual weekend of festivities for the young and old alike held in East Aurora, NY. It is sponsored by the 'Toy Town USA Museum' and is held every year in August. Fisher-Price produces a limited-edition toy for this event. (For more information on Toy Fest and the museum, write to Toy Town Museum, P.O. Box 238, East Aurora, NY 14052.) For more information on Fisher-Price toys we recommend *Fisher-Price, A Historical Rarity Value Guide*, by John J. Murray and Bruce R. Fox, and *Modern Toys, American Toys, 1930-1980*, by Linda Baker.

Advisor: Brad Cassidy (C13). (Brad asks that he be allowed to thank his wife and three daughters, his brother Beau, Jeanne Kennedy and Deanna Korth, all of whom he feels have been very instrumental in his life and hold a special place in his heart.)

Note: Unless otherwise noted, prices are for examples that show only a little edge and paint wear and minimal fading (EX).
See also Clubs, Newsletters and Other Publications.

#0005 Bunny Cart, 1948, C13......$75.00
#0007 Doggy Racer, 1942, C13......$200.00
#0007 Doggy Racer, 1942, VG......$135.00
#0007 Looky Fire Truck, 1950, C13......$100.00
#0007 Looky Fire Truck, 1950, VG, J2......$60.00
#0008 Bouncy Racer, 1960, M......$35.00
#0010 Bunny Cart, 1940, C13......$75.00
#0012 Bunny Truck, 1941, C13......$75.00
#0015 Bunny Cart, 1946, C13......$75.00
#0020 Animal Cutouts, 1942, duck, elephant, pony or Scotty dog, C13, ea......$50.00
#0028 Bunny Egg Cart, 1950, C13......$75.00
#0050 Baby Chick Tandem Cart, 1953, no number on toy, C13......$100.00
#0052 Rabbit Cart, 1950, C13......$75.00
#0075 Baby Duck Tandem Cart, 1953, no number on toy, C13......$75.00
#0100 Dr Doodle, 1931, C13......$700.00
#0100 Musical Sweeper, 1950, plays Whistle While You Work, C13......$250.00
#0101 Granny Doodle, 1931, C13......$700.00
#0102 Drummer Bear, 1931, C13......$700.00
#0102 Drummer Bear, 1932, 2nd fatter & taller version, C13.$700.00
#0103 Barky Puppy, 1931, C13......$700.00
#0104 Looky Monk, 1931, C13......$700.00
#0105 Bunny Scoot, 1931, C13......$700.00
#0110 Chubby Chief, 1932, C13......$700.00
#0111 Play Family Merry-Go-Round, 1972, plays Skater's Waltz, w/4 figures, C13......$40.00
#0112 Picture Disk Camera, 1968, w/5 picture disks, C13..$30.00
#0114 Music Box TV, 1967, plays London Bridge & Row Row Row Your Boat as pictures pass screen, C13......$20.00
#0114 Sesame Street Music Box TV, 1984, plays The People In Your Neighborhood, C13......$10.00
#0120 Cackling Hen, 1958, wht, C13......$40.00
#0121 Happy Hopper, 1969, C13......$25.00
#0123 Cackling Hen, 1967, red litho, C13......$40.00
#0125 Music Box, 1967, C13......$40.00
#0125 Uncle Timmy Turtle, 1956, red, C13......$100.00

#0130 Wobbles, 1964, dog wobbles when pulled, C13......$50.00
#0131 Toy Wagon, 1951, C13......$250.00
#0132 Dr Doodle, 1958, C13......$100.00
#0132 Molly Moo Cow, 1972, C13......$35.00
#0135 Play Family Animal Circus, 1974, complete, C13.$50.00
#0136 Play Family Lacing Shoe, 1965, complete, C13......$40.00
#0137 Pony Chime, 1962, pk plastic wheels, C13......$50.00
#0138 Jack-in-the-Box Puppet, 1970, C13......$30.00
#0139 Tuggy Tooter, 1967, C13......$40.00
#0139 Tuggy Turtle, 1959, C13......$100.00
#0140 Coaster Boy, 1941, C13......$700.00
#0140 Katy Kackler, 1954, NMIB, A......$172.00
#0140 Katy Kackler, 1954, VG, R7......$80.00
#0145 Humpty Dumpty Truck, 1963, C13......$40.00
#0148, TV-Radio, 1959, Jack 'N Jill, C13......$40.00
#0149 Dog Cart Donald, 1936, C13......$700.00
#0150 Pop-Up-Pal Chime Phone, 1968, C13......$40.00
#0150 Teddy Tooter, 1940, C13......$400.00
#0150 Timmy Turtle, 1953, gr shell, C13......$100.00
#0151 Goldilocks & the Three Bears Play House, 1967, complete, C13......$50.00
#0152 Road Roller, 1934, C13......$700.00
#0155 TV-Radio, 1968 Jack & Jill, C13......$40.00
#0156 Circus Wagon, 1942, band leader in wagon, C13.$400.00
#0156 Juffy Dump Truck, 1971, C13......$40.00
#0156 TV-Radio, 1967, Baa-Baa Black Sheep, C13......$50.00
#0158 Katie Kangaroo, 1976, C13......$40.00
#0158 TV-Radio, 1967, Little Boy Blue, C13......$50.00
#0159 TV-Radio, 1961, Ten Little Indians, C13......$15.00
#0160 Donald & Donna Duck, 1937, C13......$70.00
#0161 Looky Chug-Chug, 1949, C13......$250.00
#0161 TV-Radio, 1968, Old Woman Who Lived in a Shoe, C13......$30.00
#0164 Mother Goose, 1964, C13......$40.00
#0166 Bucky Burro, 1955, C13......$250.00
#0166 TV-Radio, 1963, Farmer in the Dell, C13......$20.00
#0168 Magnetic Chug-Chug, 1964, C13......$50.00
#0168 Snorky Fire Engine, 1960, gr litho, 4 wooden firemen & dog, C13......$125.00
#0169 Snorky Fire Engine, 1961, red litho, 4 wooden firemen, C13......$100.00
#0170 Change-A-Tune Carousel, 1981, music box w/crank hdl, 3 molded records & 3 children figures, C13......$30.00
#0171 Toy Wagon, 1942, C13......$300.00
#0171 Toy Wagon, 1942, NMIB, J2......$750.00
#0172 Roly Raccoon, 1981, C13......$15.00
#0175 Gold Star Stagecoach, 1954, w/2 wood litho mail pouches, old store stock, M (EX box), A......$355.00
#0175 Gold Star Stagecoach, 1954, w/2 wood litho mail pouches, C13......$250.00
#0175 Kicking Donkey, 1937, C13......$450.00
#0177 Donald Duck Xylophone, 1946, 2nd version w/'Donald Duck' on the hat, C13......$300.00
#0177 Oscar the Grouch, 1977, squeeze bulb & Oscar peeks out of garbage can, C13......$40.00
#0185 Donald Duck Xylophone, 1938, mk WDE, C13..$800.00
#0190 Gabby Duck, 1939, C13......$350.00
#0191 Golden Gulch Express, 1961, C13......$100.00

#0192 Playland Express, 1962, C13.................................$100.00

#0195 Double-Screen TV Music Box, 1965, Mary Had a Little Lamb, C13 ....$20.00

#0195 Teddy Bear Parade, 1938, C13 ....$600.00

#0196 Double-Screen TV Music Box, 1964, Hey Diddle Diddle, C13 ....$30.00

#0200 Mary Doll, 1974, cloth body w/vinyl face & hands, removable apron & skirt, C13 ....$40.00

#0200 Winky Blinky Fire Truck, 1954, C13.................$100.00

#0201 Jenny Doll, 1974, cloth body w/vinyl head & arms, w/skirt, C13..$40.00

#0201 Woodsy-Wee Circus, 1931, complete, C13 ....$600.00

#0202 Natalie Doll, 1974, cloth body w/vinyl head & arms, w/skirt & bonnet, C13......................................$40.00

#0203 Audrey Doll, 1974, cloth body w/vinyl head & arms, w/jeans, C13..$40.00

#0204 Baby Ann Doll, 1974, cloth body w/vinyl head & arms, in nightgown & diaper, C13 ....$40.00

#0204 Black Elizabeth Doll, 1974, cloth body w/vinyl head & arms, in skirt, C13......................................$40.00

#0205 Woodsy-Wee Zoo, 1931, complete, C13 ....$600.00

#0206 Joey Boy Doll, 1975, cloth body w/vinyl head & arms, w/jacket & lace-&-tie sneakers, C13.......................$40.00

#0207 Woodsy-Wee Pets, 1931, complete, C13 ....$600.00

#0209 Woodsy-Wee Dog Show, 1932, complete, C13...$600.00

#0215 Fisher-Price Choo-Choo, 1955, engine w/4 cars, C13 .$85.00

#0234 Nifty Station Wagon, 1960, removable roof, 4 wooden family figures & dog, C13.....................................$250.00

#0250 Dollhouse, 1978, w/figures, furniture & accessories, C13 .$40.00

#0250 Performing Circus, 1932, w/figures, animals & accessories, C13 ....$950.00

#0251 Dinette, 1978, pedestal table w/4 chairs, C13, ea.....$2.00

#0252 Kitchen Appliances, 1978, oven range w/exhaust, refrigerator & sink, C13, ea...$2.00

#0253 Bathroom, 1978, sink, toilet & shower stall, C13, ea.$2.00

#0254 Chair & Fireplace, 1978, C13, ea $2.00

#0255 Bedroom Set, 1978, brass bed w/cover, dresser w/mirror & 3 drawers, C13, ea.....................................$2.00

#0256 Living Room Set, 1978, sofa w/cushion & coffee table, C13, ea..$2.00

#0257 Baby's Room, 1978, baby, crib, dresser & rocking horse, C13, ea...$2.00

#0258 Music Room, 1978, grand piano w/stool & stereo center, C13, ea..$2.00

#0259 Patio Set, 1978, redwood-type chair, chaise lounge, grill & collie dog, C13, ea...$2.00

#0260 Bed Set, 1978, bunkbeds w/mattress & female figure, C13, ea...$2.00

#0261, Desk Set, 1980, roll-top desk w/swivel chair & spinning globe, C13, ea..$2.00

#0262 Grandfather Clock & Rocker, 1980, C13, ea...........$2.00

#0263 Deluxe Decorator Set w/Lights, 1981, hutch w/2 compartments for AA batteries, 2 lamps, C13, ea....................$2.00

#0264 Dining Room Set, butterfly drop-leaf table w/wht bowl & 4 chairs, C13, ea..$2.00

#0265 Dollhouse Family, dad, mom & 2 daughters, C13, ea.$2.00

#0268 Wing Chair & Rug Set, chair w/footstool, lg potted plant & Oriental-like rug, C13, ea...............................$20.00

#0280 Dollhouse w/Lights, 1981, same as #250 but lighted, has battery compartment & 7 outlets, C13 ....$30.00

#0302 Chick Basket Cart, 1957, Easter only, C13 ....$40.00

#0303 Bunny Push Cart, 1957, Easter only, C13 ....$75.00

#0304 Running Bunny Cart, 1957, Easter only, C13.......$75.00

#0310 Mickey Mouse Puddle Jumper, 1961, C13 ....$125.00

#0310 Mickey Mouse Puddle Jumper, 1961, G, I2..........$50.00

#0325 Buzzy Bee, 1950, 1st version, C13 ....$40.00

#0333 Butch the Pup, 1951, C13.....................................$75.00

#0345 Penelope the Performing Penguin, 1935, w/up, C13 ....$700.00

#0350 Go 'N Back Mule, 1931, w/up, C13 ....$800.00

#0355 Go 'N Back Bruno, 1931, w/up, C13....................$800.00

#0358 Donald Duck Back-Up, 1936, w/up, C13............$800.00

#0360 Go 'N Back Jumbo, 1931, w/up, C13...................$800.00

#0365 Puppy Back-Up, 1932, w/up, C13 ....$800.00

#0400 Donald Duck Drum Major, 1946, C13.................$275.00

#0404 Bunny Egg Cart, 1949, C13..................................$50.00

#0404 Bunny Egg Cart, 1949, NM, S9.............................$135.00

#0404 Donald Duck Choo-Choo, 1940, 9½", C13..........$400.00

#0405 Lofty Lizzy, 1931, Giraffe Pop-Up Kritter, C13 ...$225.00

#0407 Chick Cart, 1950, Easter only, C13........................$50.00

#0407 Dizzy Dino, 1931, C13...$225.00

#0410 Stoopy Stork, 1931, C13.......................................$225.00

#0415 Lop-Ear Looie, 1934, C13.....................................$225.00

#0415 Super Jet, 1952, C13...$225.00

#0420 Sunny Fish, 1955, C13 ....$225.00

#0422 Jumbo Jitterbug, 1940, C13..................................$225.00

#0425 Donald Duck Pop-Up, 1938, C13 ....$400.00

#0432 Mickey Mouse Choo-Choo, 1938, C13 ....$600.00

#0432-532 Donald Duck Drum Major Cart, 1948, C13 .$300.00

#0432-532 Donald Duck Drum Major Cart, 1948, G, A.$127.00

#0433 Dizzy Donkey, 1939, C13 ....$100.00

#0434 Ferdinand the Bull, 1939, C13 ....$600.00

#0440 Goofy Gertie, 1935, C13.......................................$225.00

#0440 Pluto Pop-Up, 1936, mk WDE, w/oilcloth ears, C13 ....$225.00

#0444 Queen Buzzy Bee, 1959, red litho, C13 ....$40.00

#0445 Nosey Pup, 1956, C13...$75.00

#0448 Mini Copter, 1971, bl litho, C3.............................$25.00

#0450 Donald Duck Choo-Choo, 1941, 8½", C13.........$400.00

#0450 Donald Duck Choo-Choo, 1942, bl hat, C13......$200.00

#0454 Donald Duck Drummer, 1949, C13 ....$300.00

#0460 Dapper Donald Duck, 1936, C13 ....$600.00

#0463 or #463-550, Donald Duck Drum Major or Cart, 1939, mk WDE, C13, ea...$500.00

#0469 Donald Cart, 1940, C13 ....$400.00

#0474 Bunny Racer, 1942, C13.......................................$225.00

#0476 Cookie Pig, 1967, C13...$50.00

#0476 Mickey Mouse Drummer, 1941, C13 ....$300.00

#0477 Dr Doodle, 1940, C13...$225.00

#0478 Pudgy Pig, 1962, C13..$50.00

#0480 Leo the Drummer, 1952, C13................................$225.00

#0485 Mickey Mouse Choo-Choo, 1949, new litho version of #432, C13...$100.00

#0488 Popeye Spinach Eater, 1939, C13 ....$600.00

#0494 Pinocchio, 1939, C13..$600.00

#0499 Kitty Bell, 1950, C13..$100.00

#0500 Donald Duck Cart, 1937, Easter only, no number on toy, C13 ....$700.00

#0500 Donald Duck Cart, 1951, w/baton, gr litho background, C13 ....$350.00

#0500 Donald Duck Cart, 1953, new litho, VG+, J2 .....$220.00

#0500 Pick-Up & Peek Puzzles, 1972-1986, C13, ea $15.00

#0510 Strutter Donald Duck, 1941, C13 ....$300.00

#0530 Mickey Mouse Band, 1935, C13 ....$800.00

#0533 Thumper Bunny, 1942, C13 ....$500.00

#0544 Donald Duck, 1942, C13 ....$300.00

#0550 see #0463

#0557 Toy Lunch Kit, 1957, red, wht & gr plastic, C13...$40.00

#0604 Bunny Bell Cart, 1954, C13 ....$100.00

#0605 Donald Duck Cart, 1954, C13............................$300.00

#0605 Horse & Wagon, 1933, C13 ....$600.00

#0605 Woodsey Mayor Goodgrub Mole Book, 1981, 32 pgs, C13..$20.00

#0606 Woodsey Bramble Beaver Book, 1982, 32 pgs, C13.$20.00

#0607 Woodsey Very Blue Bird Book, 1981, 32 pgs, C13..$20.00

#0615 Tow Truck, 1960, C13 ....$75.00

#0616 Chuggy Pop-Up, 1955, C13 ....$100.00

#0616 Patch Pony, 1963, C13 ....$50.00

#0617 Prancing Pony, 1967, C13 ....$40.00

#0625 Playful Puppy, 1961, w/shoe, C13......................$50.00

#0626 Playful Puppy, 1963, w/shoe, C13......................$50.00

#0628 Tug-A-Bug, 1975, plastic, C13 ....$25.00

#0629 Fisher-Price Tractor, 1962, C13 ....$50.00

#0629 Fisher-Price Tractor, 1962, G............................$25.00

#0630 Fire Truck, 1959, C13..$50.00

#0634 Drummer Boy, 1967, wood w/plastic, C13 ....$50.00

#0641 Toot-Toot Engine, 1962, bl litho, C13 ....$75.00

#0642 Dinky Engine, 1959, blk litho, C13......................$75.00

#0642 Smokie Engine, 1960, blk litho, C13 ....$75.00

#0649 Stake Truck, 1960, C13 ....$50.00

#0653 Allie Gator, 1960, C13..$100.00

#0653 Allie Gator, 1960, VG+, I2 ....$75.00

#0654 Tawny Tiger, 1962, C13 ....$100.00

#0656 Bossy Bell, 1961, no bonnet, new litho design, C13 .$50.00

#0658 Lady Bug, 1961, C13..$50.00

#0659 Puzzle Puppy, 1976, 8-pc take-apart & put-together dog, C13..$15.00

#0662 Merry Mousewife, 1962, C13...............................$50.00

#0677 Picnic Basket, 1975, complete w/accessories, plastic, C13..$30.00

#0678 Kriss Krickey, 1955, C13 ....$100.00

#0684 Little Lamb, 1964, C13..$40.00

#0685 Car & Boat, 1969, w/trailer, mom & dad figures, C13 ....$40.00

#0686 Car & Camper, 1969, w/trailer, man & dog, C13..$50.00

#0686 Perky Pot, 1958, C13 ....$50.00

#0693 Little Snoopy, 1965, VG, P3 ....$10.00

#0695 Pinky Pig, 1956, missing wooden eyes, C13.........$100.00

#0695 Pinky Pig, 1958, litho eyes, C13.........................$100.00

#0698 Talky Parrot, 1963, C13 ....$100.00

#0700 Cowboy Chime, 1951, C13 ....$250.00

#0700 Popeye, 1935, hitting bell, C13 ....$700.00

#0700 Woofy Wowser, 1940, C13................................$400.00

#0703 Bunny Engine, 1954, C13...................................$100.00

#0703 Popeye the Sailor, 1936, C13 ....$700.00

#0705 Mini-Snowmobile, 1971, w/sled & 3 figures, C13 .$50.00

#0705 Popeye Cowboy, 1937, on horse, C13.................$700.00

#0711 Cry Baby Bear, 1967, C13 ....$40.00

#0711 Huckleberry Hound, 1961, for Sears only, C13 ...$300.00

#0711 Raggedy Ann & Andy, 1941, C13 ....$7.00

#0712 Fred Flintstone Xylophone, 1962, for Sears only, C13..$250.00

#0712 Teddy Tooter, 1957, C13 ....$250.00

#0714, Mickey Mouse Xylophone, 1963, $250.00.

#0715 Ducky Flip Flap, 1964, C13 ....$40.00

#0715 Peter Bunny Engine, 1941, C13 ....$225.00

#0717 Ducky Flip Flap, 1937, C13 ....$400.00

#0719 Cuddly Cub, 1973, C13 ....$20.00

#0719 Fisher-Price Choo-Choo Train, 1963, C13............$40.00

#0720 Fisher-Price Fire Engine, 1969, w/wooden-head driver & 2 fireman, C13 ....$20.00

#0720 Pinocchio, 1939, C13 ....$500.00

#0721 Peter Bunny Engine, 1949, C13 ....$200.00

#0724 Jolly Jalopy, 1965, C13 ....$15.00

#0725 Play Family Bath/Utility Room Set, 1972, w/4 wooden family figures & accessories, C13.........................$20.00

#0726 Play Family Patio Set, 1970, 4 family members w/dog & accessories, C13 ....$20.00

#0728 Buddy Bullfrog, 1959, yel body w/red litho coat, C13..$75.00

#0728 Buddy Bullfrog, 1961, gr coat w/red & wht pants, C13.$75.00

#0728 Play Family House Decorator Set, 1970, w/4 family figures & accessories, C13 ....$20.00

#0729 Play Family Kitchen Set, 1970, 4 family figures w/accessories, C13 ....$20.00

#0730 Racing Row Boat, 1952, C13 ....$350.00

#0732 Happy Hauler, 1968, wood farm tractor w/plastic cart, C13 ....$40.00

#0733 Mickey Mouse Safety Patrol, 1956, C13 ....$250.00

#0735 Juggling Jumbo, 1958, C13 ....$225.00

#0737 Galloping Horse & Wagon, 1948, C13................$250.00

#0738 Dumbo Circus Racer, 1941, w/rubber arms, C13 .$700.00

#0738 Shaggy Zilo, 1960, C13..$75.00

#0739 Poodle Zilo, 1962, C13 ....$75.00

#0741 Teddy Zilo, 1967, C13 ....$40.00

#0741 Trotting Donald Duck, 1937, Easter only, C13 ...$800.00

#0745 Elsie's Dairy Truck, 1948, w/2 bottles, C13 ....$400.00

#0746 Pocket Radio, 1977, It's a Small World, C13..........$20.00

#0750 Hot Wagon, 1938, C13 ....$400.00

#0750 Space Blazer, 1953, C13 ....$400.00

#0752 Teddy Xylophone, 1946, C13.............................$350.00

#0752 Teddy Xylophone, 1948, new litho version, C13 .$325.00

#0756, Pocket Radio, 1973, 12 Days of Christmas, C13 ...$20.00

#0757 Humpty Dumpty, 1957, C13 ....$225.00

#0758 Pocket Radio, 1970, Mulberry Bush, C13 ....$20.00

#0759 Pocket Radio, 1969, Do-Re-Me, C13 ....$20.00

#0760 Peek-A-Boo Block, 1970, C13............................$30.00

#0761 Play Family Nursery Set, 1973, family of 4 w/baby & accessories, C13 ....$8.00

#0762 Pocket Radio, 1972, Raindrops, C13....................$10.00

#0763 Farmer-In-Dell Music Box, 1962, yel or red litho, C13, ea $50.00

#0764 Pocket Radio, 1975, My Name Is Michael, C13 ....$15.00

#0765 Talking Donald Duck, 1955, C13 ....$125.00

#0765 Talking Donald Duck, 1955, EX+ (EX+ box), A .$278.00

#0766 Pocket Radio, 1968, Where Has My Little Dog Gone?, C13..$20.00

#0766 Pocket Radio, 1977, I'd Like To Teach the World To Sing, C13 ....$15.00

#0768 Pocket Radio, 1971, Happy Birthday, C13 ....$15.00

#0772 Pocket Radio, 1974, Jack & Jill, C13 ....$15.00

#0774 Pocket Radio, 1967, Twinkle Twinkle Little Star, C13 ....$20.00

#0775 Pocket Radio, 1967, Sing a Song of Pence, C13....$20.00

#0775 Pocket Radio, 1973, Pop Goes the Weasel, C13....$15.00

#0776 Gabbie Goofies, 1960, 13", EX+ (EX box), A........$95.00

#0777 Squeaky Clown, 1958, C13 ....$250.00

#0778 Ice Cream Wagon, 1940, C13 ....$350.00

#0778 Pocket Radio, 1967, Frere Jacques, C13 ....$15.00

#0779 Pocket Radio, 1976, Yankee Doodle, C13 ....$15.00

#0784 Mother Goose Music Cart, 1955, C13 ....$100.00

#0785 Blackie Drummer, 1939, C13 ....$450.00

#0786 Perky Penguin, 1973, C13 ....$30.00

#0793 Jolly Jumper, 1963, C13....................................$50.00

#0795, Mickey Mouse Drummer, 1941, G-, M5, $22.00.

#0795 Mickey Mouse Drummer, 1937, pie-eyed, rare, C13 .$700.00

#0795 Music Box Radio, 1981, When You Wish Upon a Star, C13 ....$10.00

#0795 Musical Duck, 1952, C13 ....$100.00

#0795 Tote-A-Tune Radio, 1984, Toyland, C13 ....$10.00

#0798 Chatter Monk, 1957, C13 ....$100.00

#0798 Chatter Monk, 1957, VG, I2 ....$78.00

#0798 Mickey Mouse Xylophone, 1938, w/hat, C13 ......$400.00

#0798 Mickey Mouse Xylophone, 1942, 2nd no-hat version, G..$248.00

#0799 Quacky Family, 1940, w/pamphlet featuring 15 toys, NM (G box), A...$238.00

#0800 Hot Diggety, 1934, w/up, C13 ....$700.00

#0810 Hot Mammy, 1934, w/up, C13 ....$700.00

#0870 Pull-a-Tune Zylophone, 1978, VG, O1 ....$6.00

#0909, Play Family Rooms, 1972, for Sears only, w/family of 4, dog & accessories, C13 ....$75.00

#0910 Change-A-Tune Piano, 1969, plays Pop Goes the Weasel, This Old Man & The Muffin Man, C13 ......$25.00

#0915 Play Family Farm, 1968, 1st version, C13 ....$40.00

#0916 Fisher-Price Zoo, 1984, family of 5 w/animals & accessories, C13...$35.00

#0919 Music Box Movie Camera, 1968, plays This Old Man, w/5 picture disks, C13 ....$25.00

#0926 Concrete Mixer, 1959, C13...............................$250.00

#0928 Play Family Fire Station, 1980, w/3 firemen, Dalmatian dog, truck w/2 horses, chief's car, ambulance, etc, C13 ....$75.00

#0929 Play Family Nursery School, 1978, 4-room playset w/figures, school bus & accessories, removable roof, C13 .$75.00

#0931 Play Family Hospital, 1976, w/figures, ambulance & accessories, C13..$100.00

#0932 Amusement Park, 1963, 6 wood figures w/vehicles & accessories, C13..$100.00

#0934 Play Family Western Town, 1982, w/4 figures, horses & accessories, C13..$75.00

#0937 Play Family Sesame Street Clubhouse, 1977, w/Sesame Street characters & accessories, C13..........................$75.00

#0938, Play Family Sesame Street, 1975, Sesame Street characters & accessories, C13...$75.00

#0940 Sesame Street Characters, 1977, C13, ea $3.00

#0942 Play Family Lift & Load Depot, 1977, 3 figures, vehicles & accessories, C13..$50.00

#0945 Offshore Cargo Base, 1979, 4 figures w/accessories, C1 ....$50.00

#0952 Play Family House, 1969, 1st version w/figures & accessories, C13..$50.00

#0960 Woodsey's Log House, 1979, w/figures & accessories, C13 ....$40.00

#0961 Woodsey's Store, 1980, w/figures, accessories & 32-pg book, C13 ....$40.00

#0962 Woodsey's Airport, 1980, w/figures, accessories & 32-pg book, C13 ....$40.00

#0969 Musical Ferris Wheel, 1967, 1st version w/4 wooden figures & accessories, plays In the Good Old Summer Time, C13..$40.00

#0972 Cash Register, 1960, w/3 wooden coins, C13.........$50.00

#0979 Dump Trucker Play Set, 1964, w/3 drivers & accessories, C13 ....$50.00

#0982 Hot-Rod Roadster, 1983, riding toy w/4-pc take-apart engine, C13..$50.00

#0983 Safety School Bus, 1959, w/6 figures, C13 ....$250.00

#0985 Play Family Houseboat, 1972, w/family, dog, boat & accessories, C13 ....$30.00

#0987 Creative Coaster, 1964, riding toy w/18 blocks & 6 wooden dowels, C13 ....$75.00

#0990 Play Family A-Frame, 1974, w/family, dog, vehicle & accessories, C13 ....$75.00

#0991 Circus Train, w/3 figures & 2 animals, NM $18.00

#0991, Musical Shoe, 1964, MIB, $110.00.

#0991 Play Family Circus Train, 1973, 1st version w/figures, animals & accessories, C13...$25.00

#0992 Play Family Car & Camper, 1980, w/family & accessories, C13 ....$30.00

#0993 Play Family Castle, 1974, 1st version w/figures & accessories, C13 ....$100.00

#0994 Play Family Camper, 1973, w/family, dog, boat & accessories, C13...$75.00

#0996 Play Family Airport, 1972, 1st version w/figures & accessories, C13...$75.00

#0997 Play Family Village, 1973, w/figures, vehicles & accessories, C13...$75.00

#0998 Music Box Teaching Clock, working, VG, O1 ......$25.00

#2500 Little People Main Street, 1986, w/figures, vehicles & accessories, C13...$25.00

#2525 Little People Playground, 1986, w/figures & accessories, C13...$15.00

#2526 Little People Pool, 1986, w/figures & accessories, C13 ....$15.00

#2551 Little People Neighborhood, 1989, w/figures, vehicles & accessories, C13 ....$40.00

#2552 McDonald's Restaurant, 1990, 1st version w/figures, vehicle & accessories, C13 ....$75.00

#2552 McDonald's Restaurant, 1991-92, 2nd version w/figures, vehicle & accessories, C13 ....$50.00

#5000 Dr Doodle, 1993-94, 1st Fisher-Price limited edition, 1 of 5,000, C13 ....$125.00

#6145 Jingle Elephant, 1993, Toy Fest limited edition, 1 of 5,000, C13 ....$75.00

#6550 Buzzy Bee, 1987, Toy Fest limited edition, 1 of 5,000, C13...$130.00

#6558 Snoopy Sniffer, 1988, Toy Fest limited edition, 1 of 300, C13 ....$625.00

#656 Bossy Bell, 1960, w/bonnet, C13 ....$60.00

#6575 Toot-Toot, 1989, Toy Fest limited edition, 1 of 5,000, C13 ....$135.00

#6590 Prancing Horses, 1990, Toy Fest limited edition, 1 of 5,000, C13 ....$60.00

#6592 Teddy Bear Parade, 1991, Toy Fest limited edition, 1 of 5,000, C13 ....$50.00

#6599 Molly Bell Cow, 1992, Toy Fest limited edition, 1 of 5,000, C13 ....$150.00

#8121 My Friend Karen Doll, 1990, was never produced, only 200 made, C13...$125.00

Furniture

Any item of furniture imaginable has been reduced to child size, and today these small-scale dressers, washstands, chairs, and tables are especially popular with doll collectors who use them to display a favorite doll. If you'd like to learn more, we recommend *Children's Glass Dishes, China, and Furniture, Vol I and II*, by Doris Anderson Lechler.

Key:
drw — drawer, drawers   fr — frame

Bed, walnut w/'spool' turnings, ornately shaped headboard, 23x18", EX, A $95.00

Carriage, wicker with unusual decoration on sides, Victorian era, 27x32", EX+, A, $350.00.

Chest, bird's-eye maple veneer on 3 drw & sides, glass knobs, ornate cut trim on bottom, 18x13", VG, A $120.00

Chest, Empire, 1 lg drw at top, 3 recessed drw below, dovetailed corners, metal pulls, 16x14", EX, A $180.00

Chest, walnut, Empire style, 2 sm top drw over 2 lg drw, dmn/circle design on sides, 13x14", EX, A $200.00

Chest, 3 drw w/knobs, 1 drw below w/out knobs, 2 handkerchief boxes, mirror, made from crates, 23x14", EX, A $135.00

Chest, 3-drw w/incised lines & pressed design, brass rosette pulls, mirror in back crest, 13x9", rpl mirror, EX, A............$50.00

Chest & dresser, maple, 4-drw chest w/fancy cut skirt, decorative top w/sm mirror, 11x9", 3-drw dresser w/mirror, EX, A........$125.00

Chest on chest, oak, 3 top drw, 2 bottom drw, wood knobs, incised lines, handkerchief box, mirror, 27x16", rfn, EX, A...$275.00

Clock, mk Plymires Cafe w/stars on metal pendulum, wood w/spindles & carved crown, Elgin pocket watch works, 20", EX, A $150.00

Cupboard, walnut, dbl doors on top w/stained glass windows, 2 doors w/raised panels on bottom, 24x16", EX, A.....$365.00

Cupboard, walnut, lg dbl doors w/raised panels, 3 shelves inside, lg bottom drw, early, 20x11", EX, A $525.00

Cupboard, walnut, step-back style, ornate jigsaw scrollwork panels in upper doors, 1920s, 35x20", EX, A.................$190.00

Cupboard, walnut, step-back style, 2-drw/panel-door base, 2 glass doors in top, fancy cornice, cut-out skirt, 29", EX, A $195.00

Desk, roll-top, alternate slats impressed w/design, 30x21", w/4-legged swivel oak chair, height adjusts, EX, A.........$350.00

Dresser, walnut, Victorian, mirror w/candle shelves & ornate scroll at top, 2 sm drw over 2 long drw, 20x11", EX, A........$350.00

Dresser, 2-drw, decorative keyholes & porcelain knobs, spoon cvg on top of swivel mirror & cut-out skirt, 32x22", EX, A $210.00

Dresser, 3-drw, tilt mirror w/spindle trim, 18x11", EX, A.$170.00

Dresser & Washstand, maple colored, dresser w/lg mirror, 1 drw, 2 doors, 14", washstand w/harp mirror fr, 13", EX, A....$150.00

Dressing Table, walnut w/marble top, sm swivel mirror, trn legs (may be rpl), 16x13x9", rpl mirror, EX, A $190.00

Dry Sink, made w/wood from crate, 1 lg door w/3 shelves, 22x20", EX, A..$85.00

Dry Sink, raised back, 2 drw w/porcelain knobs, 2 doors on bottom, 27x23", EX, A $210.00

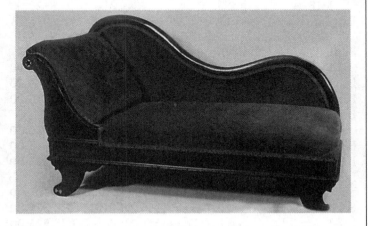

Fainting couch, Empire style with inlaid stars and bows, ornamental fretwork, red velvet upholstery, walnut frame, child size, 16½" at highest point, 32¾" long, EX/NM, from $800.00 to $1,000.00.

Pewter Cupboard, cherry stain, open top holds set of pewter dishes, spoon rack, porcelain knobs, 30x29", EX, A .$300.00

Rope Bed, maple, shaped legs w/decorative turnings, straw mattress, 4 pillows, 9x16", EX, A $100.00

Set, France, mahogany, 14" bed w/sliding doors, 11" chair w/hinged seat, table w/sliding top, 6" chest, EX, A .$425.00

Settee, Frederick Ducklow & Bros, Windsor style, contemporary, 24", A $110.00

Settee, Victorian, mauve velvet w/tufted back, ornately carved wooden fr, contemporary, 19x33", A $350.00

Settee, 2 armchairs, 4 side chairs, ornate carved pnt crests, upholstered, 9" tall, fragile but VG, A $895.00

Sideboard, oak, display shelf above mirror, 1 drw w/curved front, dbl lower doors w/pressed design, 25x18", rfn, EX, A .$130.00

Table, drop-leaf, walnut, oval top, 4 straight legs, 8x22", EX, A...$85.00

Table, tilt-top, walnut, 3-corner base w/pedestal, sq brad nails, early, 10" dia, VG, A...$235.00

Washstand, oak, short towel bar over 3 drw w/curved fronts & orig pulls, 30x22x9", rstr, A....................................$200.00

Games

Early games (those from 1850 to 1910) are very often appreciated more for their wonderful lithographed boxes than their 'playability,' and you'll find collectors displaying them as they would any fine artwork. Many boxes and boards were designed by commercial artists of the day. Games of the '20s and '30s are becoming more popular, especially ones with Art Deco or comic art. World War I and II games are also hot right now. Nostalgic TV games from the '50s and '60s have cooled off a bit in the last year or two.

When you buy a game, check to see that all pieces are there. Look on the instructions or in the box lid for a listing of contents. Value depends on rarity and condition of the box and playing pieces.

Advisor: Paul Fink (F3).

$1,000,000 Chance of a Lifetime, Cardinal, 1986, EX (EX box), M6 ....$22.00

$20,000 Pyramid, Milton Bradley, 1975, VG (VG box), M6 .$18.00

$64,000 Question, Lowell, 1955, G (VG box)..................$45.00

A-Team, Parker Bros, 1984, EX (EX box) $15.00

A-Team Water War Lawn Game, Lakeside, 1983, NM (shelf-worn box), S2 ....$50.00

Across the Continent, Parker Bros, 1952, EX (VG box)..$50.00

Addams Family, board game, Milton Bradley, 1973, EX (VG box), J5...$25.00

Addams Family, board game, Milton Bradley, 1973, M (NM box)...$35.00

Addams Family, card game, 1965, VG (VG box) $40.00

Addams Family Uncle Fester Mystery Trick, 1960s, light bulb lights up in mouth, EX (orig box), S2......................$195.00

ADT Messenger Boy, Milton Bradley, 1909, VG (VG box) .$175.00

Advance to Boardwalk, Parker Bros, 1985, VG (EX box), M6 ....$25.00

Adventures of Rin-Tin-Tin, Transogram, 1955, 17", unused, NMIB, A...$71.00

Adventures of R2-D2 (Star Wars), Kenner, 1977, VG (VG box), M6 ....$28.00

Adverteasing, Coleco, 1988, EX (EX box), M6 ....$25.00

Aeroplane Race, board game, Wolverine, litho tin w/game on both sides, minor scratches & rust.....................$65.00

Aggravation, CO-5, 1960s, EX (EX box), M6 ....$25.00

Air Force, Avalon Hill, 1980, EX (EX box), M6 ....$22.00

Airport, Dynamic, 1972, EX (EX box), M6 ....$35.00

Alfred Hitchcock Presents Why, 1958, NM (VG+ box), P3..$20.00

Alice in Wonderland, board game, 1923, EX (EX box) .$125.00

All About Cincinnati, All About Town, 1988, EX (EX box), M6...$25.00

All in the Family Game, Milton Bradley, 1972, NMIB, C1 .$27.00

All My Children, TSR, 1985, VG (M box), M6 ....$25.00

All the King's Men, Parker Bros, 1979, EX (EX box), M6 .$22.00

All Time Greats Baseball Game, Midwest Research, 1971, EX (EX box), M6...$32.00

Amazing Spider-Man Game, Milton Bradley, 1967, EX (EX box), M6 ....$25.00

Amusing Game of Innocence Abroad, Parker Bros, 1888, VG (G- box), M6..$210.00

Annie Oakley, board game, Milton Bradley, 1955, EX (VG box), M6 ....$45.00

Annie Oakley, board game, Milton Bradley, 1955, NM (NM box), C1 ....$75.00

Aquarius II, Gamescience, 1970, EX (EX box), M6 ....$55.00

Arnold Palmer's Inside Golf Game, 1961, old store stock, M (EX box)..$60.00

Around the World, Milton Bradley, 1962, VG (VG box), M6..$28.00

Around the World w/Nellie Bly, #4122, Milton Bradley, 1910s, VG (G box), M6...$165.00

As the World Turns, Parker Bros, 1966, EX (EX box) $35.00

Assembly Line, Selchow & Richter, 1960s, EX (EX box) ..$35.00

Assembly Line, Selchow & Righter, 1953, EX (VG box), M6..$70.00

Astro Launch, 3-D board game, Ohio Art, 1963, litho tin w/spring action, MIB, A $95.00

Astron, Parker Bros, 1955, EX (VG box).........................$60.00

Authors, Parker Bros, 1943, VG (VG box), M6 ....$25.00

Auto Game, Milton Bradley, ca 1906, G (G- box)...........$65.00

Aviation Game, card game, Milton Bradley, 1930s, complete with instructions, edge wear to box, A, $40.00.

Babes in Toyland, Whitman, 1961, M (EX box), M6 ......$70.00

Bang Box Game, Ideal, 1969, VG (G box), M6 ....$20.00

Barbar, 1968, NMIB, J2 ....$23.00

Barney Google & Spark Plug Game, Milton Bradley, VG (G box)..$125.00

Bas-ket, Cadaco-Ellis, 1956, EX (EX box) $35.00

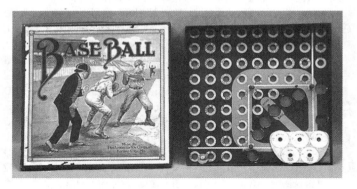

Base Ball, Pan American Toy Co., 1920s, NM, D10, $475.00.

Baseball, counter-top game, Akins, 1915, tin, 24", VG, A.$150.00

Baseball Bagatelle Game, Marx, 1960s, pinball action, litho tin & plastic, 10", NMIB, A...............................$65.00

Baseball Challenge, Tri-Valley Games, 1980, EX (EX box), M6...$38.00

Bat Masterson, board game, Lowell, 1958, w/3-D cb town, EX (EX box), H4 ....$50.00

Bataan: The Battle for the Phillipines, 1940s, G (EX box), M6...$65.00

Batman Shooting Range, target game, Marx, 1966, w/rare Bat-woman, EX (EX box), A $215.00

Batman Swoops Down, tiddly winks-type game w/plastic Batman figures, EX+ (EX box), A $105.00

Batman TV Game, Japan (not distributed in the US), cb, scarce, MIB, A..$120.00

Batman vs Joker, electronic arcade game, Blue Box, 1989, MIB, S2 ....$115.00

Battle Checkers: Beat the Axis; Penman, 1942, EX (G- box), M6..$42.00

Battle of Britain, Renwal, 1960s, MIB, M6 ....$45.00

Battleship, Milton Bradley, 1967, G (G box), M6...........$15.00

Beachhead Invasion Game, Warren-Bilt Rite, 1950s, EX (VG box), M6 ....$40.00

Beany & Cecil Jumpin' DJ, Mattel, NMIB, J2 ....$45.00

Beat the Clock, Milton Bradley, 1969, VG (VG box), M6.$25.00

Beatles Flip Your Wig Game, Milton Bradley, 1964, EX (VG box), M6 ....$105.00

Beetle Bailey, board game, Jaymar, 1956, NMIB $75.00

Ben Casey MD, board game, Transogram, 1960s, VG, J5.$25.00

Bermuda Triangle, Milton Bradley, 1975, EX (EX box), M6.$28.00

Bert Park's Break the Bank TV Quiz Game, Bettye-B, 1955, complete, EX+ (orig box) $45.00

Betsy Ross & the Flag, Transogram, 1961, VG (G box), M6.$28.00

Beverly Hillbillies, board game, 1963, EX $40.00

Beverly Hillbillies, card game, 1963, EX (EX box), C1/J2, from $18 to $25.00

Bible Characters, Nellie McGee, 1900s, EX (G box), M6.$28.00

Bible Picture Lotto, Warner Press, 1950s, EX (VG box), M6.$18.00

Big Board, Dadan Inc, 1958, EX (VG box), M6 ....$50.00

Big Board Stock Market Game, RJ McDonald, 1958, NM (EX box), T2 ....$59.00

Big Business, Transogram, 1948, VG (VG box) $20.00

Big Foot the Giant Snow Monster, Milton Bradley, 1977, MIB, H4 ....$10.00

Big League Baseball, 3M, 1967, EX (EX box) $30.00

Big Squeeze, Ideal, 1968, EX+ (EX+ box), J2 ....$35.00

Billionaire, Parker Bros, 1973, EX (EX box) $20.00

Bingo-Matic, Transogram, 1954, EX (VG box) $20.00

Bionic Woman, board game, Parker Bros, 1976, MIB (sealed), C1 ....$25.00

Bird Watcher Game, Parker Bros, 1958, EX (VG box), M6.$55.00

Birthday Game, Parker Bros, 1918, VG (G box), M6.......$65.00

Black Beauty Game, Transogram, 1958, M (EX box).....$125.00

Blackout, Milton Bradley, 1939, bl box, EX (VG box), M6.$65.00

Blarney Stones, Parker Bros, 1940, VG (VG box), M6 ....$45.00

Blondie Sunday Funnies, board game, Ideal, 1972, MIB, C1.$19.50

Blue Line Hockey, 3M, 1970, EX (VG box), M6 ....$48.00

Bobbsey Twins, Milton Bradley, 1957, EX (VG box).......$30.00

Booby Trap, Parker Bros, 1965, NMIB (10x18" box) $20.00

Boom or Bust, Parker Bros, 1951, EX (G box)................$125.00

Bowling Game, metal ball release attached to end of wood 'alley' w/10 wht pins & sm steel ball, 32", G, A $25.00

Bozo, Parker Bros, 1960s, VG (G box), M6 ....$26.00

Brady Bunch Hex-A-Game, Laramie, 1973, M (EX card), C1 ....$29.00

Branded, NMIB, J2 ....$60.00

Break the Bank, Bettye-B, 1955, EX (EX box), M6.........$48.00

Breakthru, 3M, 1965, EX (VG box), M6 ....$35.00

Brett Ball, Keltner, 1981, EX (EX box), M6 ....$45.00

Bridge Keno, Milton Bradley, 1930, EX (VG box), M6 ...$25.00

Broadside, Milton Bradley, 1962, EX (VG box) $45.00

Brownie Nine-Pins, Palmer Cox, 1883, G (G- box), A.$1,495.00

Buck Rogers Adventures in the 25th Century Game, Transogram, 1960s, M (NM box), C1 ....$55.00

Buck Rogers Combat, Built Rite, 1930s, features Rocket Ship Control Base, cb, 11", scarce, VG, A.....................$406.00

Buck Rogers Game of the 25th Century, board game, Lutz/Slesinger, 1934, EX (VG+ box), A, $526.00.

Buckaroo, Milton Bradley, 1940s, EX (EX box), M6........$45.00

Bullwinkle's Hide & Seek Game, Milton Bradley, 1961, EX (VG box) $50.00

Buster Brown Necktie Game, Buster's version of Pin the Tail on the Donkey, printed cloth ties, EX...........................$150.00

C&O/B&O, Avalon Hill, 1969, EX (EX box), M6........$105.00

Cabby!, Selchow & Righter, 1938, VG (VG box) $75.00

Call Me Lucky, Parker Bros, 1954, EX (G box), M6 ....$35.00

Calling All Cars, Parker Bros, 1940s, VG (VG box) $30.00

Calling Superman, Transogram, 1954, NM (EX+ box), A .$182.00

Calvin & the Colonel High Spirits Game, Milton Bradley, 1962, EX, T2 ....$39.00

Camp Granada, Milton Bradley, 1965, EX (VG box) $45.00

Campaign!, Saafield, Artcraft, 1961, EX (VG box), M6..$100.00

Candid Camera Game, Lowell, 1963, EX (EX box), M6..$50.00

Captain America, board game, Milton Bradley, 1977, MIB (sealed), C1...$15.00

Captain America, 1966, no comic, EX (EX box), J2 ....$35.00

Captain Kangaroo Kangadoodles Game, Hasbro, 1956, MIB (sealed), C1...$42.00

Captain Kangaroo Noah's Ark, card game, Fairchild, 1956, NMIB, T2 ....$20.00

Captain Video, board game w/spaceship, Milton Bradley, scarce, NMIB, A...$170.00

Car Travel Game, Milton Bradley, 1958, EX (VG box), M6..$26.00

Careers, Parker Bros, 1957, EX (EX box), M6 ....$32.00

Cargos (metal ships), Selchow & Righter, 1930s, EX (VG box) $50.00

Case of the Allusive Assassin, Ideal, 1967, EX (VG box), M6..$50.00

Casey Jones Game Box, Saafield, M (EX box), M6 ....$50.00

Casper the Friendly Ghost, Milton Bradley, 1959, EX (EX box) $15.00

Casper the Friendly Ghost Game, Cootie, 1974, NM (EX box), C1 ....$39.00

Casper the Friendly Ghost Light-Up Game, 1974, w/5" battery-op figure of Casper, NMIB..................................$40.00

Cat & Mouse, Parker Bros, 1964, EX (VG box), M6........$20.00

Catchword, Whitman, 1954, EX (G box), M6 ....$25.00

Cavalcade, Selchow & Righter, 1953, EX (VG box) $40.00

Champion Road Race, board game, M, D10, $165.00.

Championship Fight Game, Frankie Goodman, 1940s, M (VG box) $30.00

Charlie's Angels, board game, Milton Bradley, 1977, NM (EX box), C1 ....$19.00

Charlie's Angels (w/Farrah Faucett), Parker Bros, 1977, EX (EX box), from $19 to $28.00

Chick in the Coop, Gabriel, 1950s, EX (EX box).............$25.00

Children's Hour, Parker Bros, 1946, VG (VG box), M6..$45.00

Chinese Checkers & Telka, Parker Bros, 1938, EX (VG box), M6..$38.00

CHiPs, board game, Ideal, 1981, NM (EX box), C1.........$18.00

Chiromagica, McLoughlin Bros, early, hand inside window points to correct answer to question from question disk, 12", A..$130.00

Chit-Chat, Milton Bradley, 1963, MIB.............................$20.00

Chitty-Chitty Bang-Bang, board game, EX (EX box), J2 .$30.00

Chitty-Chitty Bang-Bang, board game, Milton Bradley, EX (VG box), J5..$25.00

Chug-a-Lug, Dynamic, 1969, M (VG box), M6 ....$25.00

Chutes Away, Gabriel, 1977, EX (orig box) $35.00

Clash of the Titans, board game, Whitman, 1981, EX, S2.$30.00

Classic MLB, board game, Game Time Ltd, 1987, EX (EX box), M6..$110.00

Cloak & Dagger, Ideal, 1984, EX (EX box), M6...............$45.00

Clown Toss, Wylder, EX+ (EX+ box)..............................$45.00

Clue, Parker Bros, 1950, VG (VG box), M6.....................$34.00

College Basketball, Cadaco-Ellis, 1954, M (VG box), M6.$45.00

Combat, board game, Ideal 1963, NM (EX+ box), C1 .....$72.00

Combat, Ideal, 1963, EX (VG box), M6 ....$45.00

Computer Vegas, Electric Data Control, 1971, EX (EX box), M6..$70.00

Connect, Galt & Co, 1969, EX (VG box), M6 ....$18.00

Constellation Station, Aristoplay, 1990, MIB (sealed), M6.$40.00

Contigo, 3M, 1971, MIB (sealed), M6 ....$45.00

Cootie, Schaper, 1949, EX (EX box)................................$25.00

Corporate Pursuit, Rachat Inc, 1986, EX (EX box), M6..$42.00

Countdown, Whitman, 1960s, VG (VG box), M6...........$17.00

Cowboy Roundup, Parker Bros, 1952, VG (G box), M6 ..$34.00

Crazy Clock, Ideal, 1960s, EX.......................................$50.00

Crosstown Game, Milton Bradley, 1956, EX (VG box) ...$35.00

D-Day, Avalon Hill, 1977, EX (VG box), M6..................$20.00

Daisy's Red Ryder Whirli-Crow Game, ca 1950, dbl row of crow targets, cork-shooting rifle, box dbls as target stand, MIB..$210.00

Dallas Card Game, Mego, 1980, MIB (sealed)................$12.00

Dark Tower, Milton Bradley, 1981, EX (VG box), M6 ....$70.00

Dastardly & Muttley Wacky Racers Game, VG, S2 ....$55.00

Davy Crockett Surprise Ball, Lester, 1953, compo figure of Davy w/30 games & surprise, 7", NM (in sealed plastic bag), A..$85.00

Dead Pan, Selchow & Righter, 1956, VG (G box) $20.00

Delta Force, Fun Designs, 1986, EX (EX box), M6...........$30.00

Deputy Dawg, Hecktor Heathcoat or Martin, puffy magnets, Terrytoons, 1979, 6", MIP, S2, ea $15.00

Derby Days, Parker Bros, 1930, w/hurdles, EX (G box), M6.$75.00

Detectives, board game, Transogram, 1961, NM (EX box).$50.00

Dick Tracy, card game, Whitman, 1937, complete set of 35, EX (EX box), A $45.00

Dick Tracy Crime Stopper, Ideal, 1963, w/plastic Crime Stopper control panel & decoder, MIB $110.00

Dick Tracy Super Detective Mystery Card Game, FAS, 1941, ea card depicts Tracy's friends & villains, NMIB, A $65.00

Dick Tracy Target Game, Marx, 1930s, 17½" dia board, EX, C1 ....$90.00

Dick Tracy: The Master Detective Game; Selchow & Righter, 1962, VG (G box), M6..$48.00

Dig, Parker Bros, 1959, EX (EX box) $15.00

Dirty Water, Urban Systems, 1971, EX (EX box), M6 .....$46.00

Disney, card game, 1950s, set of 3, NM (NM sealed box), O1..$15.00

Disneyland Express Card Games, Russell/WDP, 1950s, 6 games featuring 6 characters sealed in train box, 14", MIB, A......$75.00

Disneyland Game, Whitman, 1965, EX (VG box), M6 ...$50.00

District Messenger Boy, McLoughlin Bros, early, EX $350.00

Dobbin Derby, Cadaco-Ellis, 1950, VG (G- box), M6 .....$28.00

Doc Holiday Wild West, board game, Transogram, 1960, NMIB, T2..$49.00

Doc Holiday Wild West, board game, VG, T2 ....$15.00

Dog Race, Transogram, 1938, VG (VG box)....................$35.00

Dogfight, Milton Bradley, 1963, EX (VG box), M6 ....$46.00

Dollar a Second, Lowell, 1950s, EX (VG box), M6.........$38.00

Dominoes #4093, Halsom, MIB $22.00

Donald Duck Bean Bag Party Game, Parker Bros, 1939, EX (VG box), A..$95.00

Donald Duck's Party Game for Young Folks (Walt Disney's Own Game), Parker Bros, 1938, complete with playing pieces, spinner, tokens and instructions, EX+ (original box), A, $110.00; Walt Disney's Game Parade, set of 15 board games, 1938, complete with 65 playing pieces and instructions, EX (original box), A, $77.00.

Donald Duck Shooting Game, Chad Valley, 1930s, cb & paper, EX+, A..$253.00

Double Discoveries, Ravensburger, EX (EX box), M6......$35.00

Down You Go, Selchow & Righter, 1954, EX (VG box), M6..$35.00

Dracula Mystery Game, Hasbro, 1963, VG (VG box) ...$150.00

Dragnet Target Game, NMIB, W5.................................$45.00

Dragnet TV, board game, Transogram, 1957, NM (EX+ box), C1..$63.00

Dream House, Milton Bradley, 1968, EX (EX box) $30.00

Dubble-Up, Gabriel & Sons, 1930s, EX (VG box), M6 ...$35.00

Dunce, Schaper, 1955, EX (EX box), M6 ....$42.00

Dune, board game, Parker Bros, 1984, MIB (sealed), C1..$31.00

East Front, Control Box, 1976, EX, M6 ....$50.00

Easy Money, Milton Bradley, 1936, VG (VG box)...........$30.00

Edger Bergen's Charlie McCarthy Questions & Answers Game, 1938, M (slightly worn box), H4.............................$35.00

Emily Post Popularity Game, Selchow & Righter, 1970, M (EX box), M6..$45.00

Ernie Banks Ball 'n Strike Batting Game, 1970s, MIB $45.00

Escape From Death Star (Star Wars), Kenner, 1977, MIB, H4 ....$20.00

Escape From the Casbah, Selchow & Righter, 1975, EX (VG box) M6 ....$32.00

ESP, Dynamic, 1972, EX (EX box), M6....................$25.00

ET Speak & Spell Talking Game, Texas Instruments, MIB, S2 ....$95.00

Expanse, Milton Bradley, 1949, EX (VG box), M6 ....$55.00

Eye Guess, Milton Bradley, 1966, VG (VG box)..............$20.00

F-Troop, Ideal, 1965, EX (EX box), H4 ....$120.00

Facts in 5, 3M, 1967, EX (EX box)..................................$20.00

Fame & Fortune, Whitman, 1961, EX (EX box), M6.......$30.00

Family Game, Hasbro, 1967, VG (VG box), M6..............$38.00

Fang Face, Parker Bros, 1979, EX (EX box), M6..............$25.00

Fantastic Voyage, Milton Bradley, 1968, EX (EX box).....$15.00

Farming Game, Weekend Farmer, 1979, EX (VG box), M6 .$34.00

Fastest Gun, Milton Bradley, 1974, EX (EX box), M6 .....$40.00

Fat Albert, board game, Milton Bradley, 1973, VG (VG box) $20.00

Feed the Elephants, Cadaco-Ellis, 1952, EX (VG box), M6.$45.00

Felix the Cat, dexterity game, English, 1923, Felix tries to get mouse into cage, rnd metal fr, glass top, 2½", EX, A ..$150.00

Felix the Cat, Milton Bradley, 1960, VG (G box), M6 ....$35.00

Ferdinand's Chinese Checkers, Parker Bros, 1939, EX, D10, $150.00.

Finance, Parker Bros, 1962, EX (EX box), M6..................$30.00

Fireball Island, Milton Bradley, 1986, EX (VG box), M6.$24.00

Fishbait, Ideal, 1965, NMIB, J2 ....$55.00

Five Spot, Milton Bradley, 1931, VG (EX box), M6 ....$50.00

Flagship Airfreight, Milton Bradley, 1946, EX (G box), M6 .$70.00

Flintstones, card game, Ed-U-Cards, EX (EX box), H4 ......$6.00

Flintstones, Milton Bradley, 1971, EX (EX box), from $20 to..$25.00

Flipper Flips, board game, Mattel, 1965, M (EX box), J5 .$45.00

Flivver Game, Milton Bradley, 1920s, VG (G box), M6..$80.00

Floating Satellite, target game, unused, NMIB, J2..........$120.00

Flying Nun, board game, Milton Bradley, 1968, NM (EX+ box), C1..$72.00

Flying the Beam, Parker Bros, 1941, NMIB....................$100.00

Follow the Flag to Victory, Geo F Cram Co, 1942, VG (G box), M6 ....$55.00

Fonz, Milton Bradley, 1976, NM, J6............................$30.00

Fonzie's Real Cool Game, Parker Bros, VG (G box) $12.00

Football, Baseball & Checkers, Parker Bros, 1948, VG (G box), M6 ....$55.00

Fortune 500, Pressman, 1979, M (EX box), M6...............$50.00

Fox & Hounds, Parker Bros, 1948, VG (VG box) $35.00

Fox Hunt, ES Lowe, 1930s, EX (VG box).....................$30.00

Frontierland Game, Parker Bros, 1955, EX (VG box) $40.00

Fugitive, board game, Ideal, 1960s, EX...........................$100.00

Funny Face Disquise, Topper, 1967, MIB (sealed), T2.....$39.00

G-Man Carolyn Well's Fascinating Mystery Card Game, Milton Bradley, 1936, EX (orig box) $65.00

G-Men Clue Games, board games, Whitman, 1938, set of 3, scarce, NMIB..$165.00

Game of the States, Milton Bradley, 1960, EX (VG box), M6 ....$27.00

Gee-Wiz Racing Game, Wolverine, ball-bearing actuated, horses are propelled to finish line, 15", M (EX box), A.......$152.00

Generals, Ideal, 1980, EX (VG box), M6.........................$45.00

Geo-Graphy, Cadaco-Ellis, 1958, EX (VG box), M6 ....$26.00

George of the Jungle, Parker Bros, 1968, M (VG box), H4 .$79.00

GI Anvil of Victory, Avalon Hill, 1982, M (EX box), M6.$34.00

GI Joe Navy Frogman Game, Hasbro, 1967, EX (VG box), M6 ....$70.00

Ginasta, Kohner Bros, 1954, VG (VG box)......................$15.00

Global Pursuit, National Geography Society, 1987, EX (EX box), M6 ....$35.00

Globe-Trotters, Selchow & Righter, 1948, VG (G- box), M6 ....$30.00

Go, ES Lowe, 1951, EX (VG box), M6............................$40.00

Go Bang, Tivoli, Fox & Geese, McLoughlin, 1878, G (G box) $50.00

Godzilla Game, Mattel, 1978, M (EX box), M6 ....$90.00

Going to Jerusalem, Parker Bros, 1955, EX (EX box), M6..$45.00

Gold Star Marble Game, Lindstrom, 1933, NM (orig box).$90.00

Gomer Pyle Game, Transogram, 1960s, EX (EX box) $50.00

Good Neighbor Game, Whitman, 1942, EX (VG box), M6.$34.00

Great Charlie Chan Detective Mystery Game, Milton Bradley, 1937, VG (F box), M6..$58.00

Great Grape Ape, board game, Milton Bradley, 1975, EX (VG box), J5..$25.00

Green Hornet Switch Game, unpunched, unused, NMIB, H4 ....$175.00

Gremlins, card game, MIB, S2.....................................$30.00

Groucho Marx TV Quiz Game, Pressman, 1950s, unused, NM (EX+ box), A $100.00

Groucho Ring Toss, Spain, 1930s, bl & yel wood w/lithoed caricature of Groucho playing soccer, 16", EX, A $140.00

Hands Down, Ideal, 1964, EX (VG box), M6/T2.............$30.00

Hank Aaron Baseball Game, Ideal, 1973, VG, I2.............$48.00

Happiness, Milton Bradley, 1972, M (EX box)................$35.00

Happy Landing, Transogram, 1938, EX (EX box) $45.00

Hats Off, Transogram, 1941, EX..................................$30.00

Haunted Castle, pinball game, EX, J2 ....$25.00

Haunted Mansion Game, Walt Disney, 1975, 3-D plastic & cb, scarce, MIB, A $121.00

Have Gun Will Travel, board game, Parker Bros, 1959, NM (NM box)..$75.00

Hawaiian Punch Game, Mattel, 1978, VG (EX box), H4/M6..$28.00

Hector Heathcote's Silly Sidney the Absent-Minded Elephant Game, Transogram, 1963, EX+ (EX box), C1.........$110.00

Hex the Zig-Zag Game, Parker Bros, 1950, VG (G box), M6...$36.00

Hickety Pickety, Parker Bros, 1954, EX (VG box), M6....$35.00

Hippopotamus, puzzle game, Remco, 1961, electric, EX (EX box), from $30 to..$35.00

Hit the Beach, Milton Bradley, 1965, EX (EX box), M6..$55.00

Hollywood Stars, Whitman, 1955, VG (VG box), M6 ....$25.00

Honeymooners Game, Transogram, 1986, MIB (sealed), C1.$21.00

Hop-Off the New Airplane, board game, complete with playing pieces, and instructions, EX (original box), $300.00.

Hopalong Cassidy Dominoes, Milton Bradley, 1950, 30 punch-out cb dominoes (unpunched), NM+ (EX+ box), A .$333.00

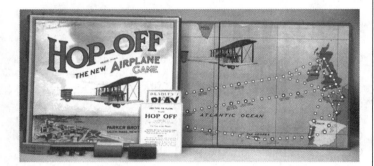

Hopalong Cassidy Game, board game, Milton Bradley, 1950, NM (EX lid with William Boyd illustration), $100.00.

Horse Racing Game, Milton Bradley, 1937, EX (VG box) .$40.00

How To Succeed, Hasbro, 1962, NM (EX+ box), T2 ....$118.00

Howdy Doody, card games, 1954, M, J5............................$15.00

Howdy Doody Bean Bag Game, toss beanbags into lassos, EX, A..$110.00

Howdy Doody Quiz, Multiple Products/Kagran, 1951, scarce, unused, EX+, A $205.00

Howdy Doody's Bowling Game, Parker Bros, 1949, 1 ball missing, EX+ (EX+ box), A $112.00

Howdy Doody's Own Game, Parker Bros, 1950s, roll ball to hit flip-over characters, 17", NM (EX box), A $85.00

Howdy Doody's Electric Carnival Game, Harett-Gilmar/Kagran, 1950s, NM unused (EX+ box), A, $118.00.

Howdy Doody's TV Game, Milton Bradley, 1950s, EX+ (VG box) $75.00

Howdy Doody's 3-Ring Circus, Wiry Dan Electric Game, Kagran, 1950s, rare, M (EX+ box), A $81.00

Huckleberry Hound Roll-A-Ball, Merit, NMIB, A...........$60.00

Huckleberry Hound Tiddly Winks, Chad Valley, 1960s, EX+, A...$35.00

Huckleberry Hound Western Board Game, Milton Bradley, 1959, EX (VG+ box), J5 ....$45.00

Hunch, Happy Hour Inc, 1956, EX (EX box), M6 ....$38.00

I Dream of Jeannie, Milton Bradley, 1960s, EX (VG box), J5...$45.00

I'm George Gobel & Here's the Game, Schaper, 1955, EX (VG box), M6 ....$45.00

I Spy, board game, Ideal, 1964, NM (NM box), C1 ....$75.00

Improved Game of Fish Pond, McLoughlin Bros, 1890, EX .$300.00

Incredible Hulk, smash-up action game, Ideal, 1979, VG (VG box), S2..$25.00

India, Milton Bradley, 1910s, VG (VG box) $30.00

Indian Raid, 3-D target game, fire gun at Indians, pnt wood & litho tin, scarce, MIB, A...$176.00

Indian Trail, 1930s, EX, D10, $250.00.

Indiana Jones Raiders of the Lost Ark, board game, Parker Bros, 1982, MIB (sealed), C1 ....$39.00

Input, Milton Bradley, 1984, EX (EX box), M6...............$25.00

Inspector Gadget Target Game, 1983, w/dart gun & action targets, MIB, S2...$85.00

Intrigue, Milton Bradley, 1950s, EX (EX box).................$35.00

Inventors, Parker Bros, 1974, EX (EX box), M6 ....$30.00

Ipcress File, Milton Bradley, 1966, EX (EX box) $25.00

Jack & the Beanstalk, Transogram, 1957, M (EX box) $25.00

Jacks, Grey Iron, 1930, MOC.......................................$30.00

Jackstraws #4093, Milton Bradley, EX (EX box)...............$20.00

James Bond, card game, orig box, EX, J2.........................$25.00

James Bond Secret Agent 007, Milton Bradley, EX (VG box)..$35.00

James Bond Secret Agent 007, Milton Bradley, 1964, NMIB, C1...$55.00

James Bond Thunderball, Milton Bradley, 1965, VG (VG box), D9...$33.00

James Bond 007: Goldfinger, Milton Bradley, 1966, M (EX box), M6...$60.00

Jeopardy (electric), Pressman, 1987, EX (EX box), M6....$35.00

Jet World, Milton Bradley, 1975, M (VG box), M6........$55.00

Jetsons Fun Pad Game, Milton Bradley, 1960s, EX..........$50.00

Jingo, Cadaco-Ellis, 1942, M (EX box), M6..................$45.00

Jumpin', 3M, 1964, EX (VG box), M6........................$85.00

Karate, Selchow & Righter, 1964, EX (VG box), M6......$40.00

Kentucky Derby, Whitman, 1969, EX (EX box)...............$30.00

Kentucky Jones, board game, T Cohn, 1965, contents sealed, M (NM box), C1...$36.00

Ker-Plunk Game, Ideal, 1967, EX (EX box) $20.00

King Kong, board game, 1976, NMIB, C1 ....$25.00

Kiss on Tour, board game, complete, J5 ....$65.00

Knapp Electric Questioner, Knapp Electric, EX (VG box).$25.00

Knight in Armor, target game, MT, litho tin, battery-op, NM (EX box), A...$204.00

Knight Rider Game, MIB (sealed), S2 ....$20.00

Knight Rider Pinball Game, 1982, table toy, 8", NM, S2.$10.00

Kopeefun, Embree Mfg, 1946, EX (EX box).......................$25.00

Kreskin, Milton Bradley, 1967, EX (EX box), S2.............$40.00

Kukla & Ollie, board game, Parker Bros, 1962, EX (orig box), T2...$40.00

Lai Shai, Karco Inc, 1943, VG (VG box), M6..................$40.00

Land of the Lost, Milton Bradley, 1975, EX (VG box).....$35.00

Laser Attack Game, Milton Bradley, 1978, EX (VG box), M6...$40.00

Laugh-In, Saafield, 1969, M (EX box), M6.....................$60.00

Laugh-In's Squeeze Your Bippie Game, Hasbro, 1968, EX (EX box) $45.00

Lay's Lunar Landing Game, Lay Packing Co, 1969, M (EX box), M6...$60.00

Leave It to Beaver, Hasbro, 1959, VG (G box) $35.00

Lese-Memory, Ravensburger, 1971, EX (EX box), M6 .....$18.00

Let's Play Tag, Milton Bradley, 1958, EX (VG box), M6.$24.00

Li'l Abner Board Game, Milton Bradley, 1946, EX+ (VG+ box), T2...$59.00

Li'l Abner Game, Parker Bros, 1969, VG (VG box), M6.$30.00

Little Chief, Whitman, 1959, EX (EX box) $20.00

Little League, board game, Milton Bradley, 1958, EX, J5 .$25.00

Little Orphan Annie Game, Milton Bradley, 1927, VG+ (G box), A...$94.00

Little Red Schoolhouse, Parker Bros, 1952, VG (G- box), M6...$28.00

Liz Taylor: Hollywood Starlet; Ideal, 1963, M (orig envelope), M6 ....$50.00

London Game, 7 Towns Ltd, 1972, EX (G box), M6 ....$45.00

Lone Ranger, board game, 1938, NMIB.........................$75.00

Lone Ranger & Tonto Board Game, Warren, 1978, EX, J5 .$15.00

Lone Ranger Game, Milton Bradley, 1966, EX (VG box), M6...$26.00

Lone Ranger Ring-Toss, Rosebud Art/Lone Ranger Inc, 1946, Lone Ranger on Silver attached to lever, rare, EX (VG box), A...$202.00

Lost in Space, card game, Japan, MIB (sealed), A.........$230.00

Lost in Space, Milton Bradley, 1965, EX+, M6/P3, from $95.00 to $110.00.

Lottery Game, Selchow & Righter, 1972, EX (VG box), M6...$40.00

Love Boat, board game, 1980, EX (VG box)....................$15.00

Lucky Star Gumball Game, Ideal, 1961, complete w/orig gumballs, M (NM box), T2...$49.00

Lucy's Tea Party Game, Milton Bradley, 1971, VG (G box)..$35.00

M*A*S*H, board game, Milton Bradley, 1981, EX, C1...$27.00

MacDonald's Farm Game, Selchow & Righter, 1948, EX (G box) $35.00

Mad Magazine, board game, Parker Bros, 1979, EX (EX box), from $15.00 to $25.00.

Magic Race, Lederer Co, 1930s, EX (VG box), M6..........$45.00

Magne-Rocket Launcher, target game, Toy Enterprises, 1950s, catch opponent's darts for points, VG, P4 ....$35.00

Mail Run, Quality Games, 1960, EX (G box), M6 ....$55.00

Major Bowes Amateur Hour Game, Warner Mfg, 1930s, VG (G box), M6 ....$55.00

Make-A-Million, Parker Bros, 1945, VG (VG box), M6 .$30.00

Mammoth Hunt, Cadaco, 1962, EX (EX box).................$25.00

Man From UNCLE, board game, Ideal, 1965, NMIB.......$55.00

Man From UNCLE, board game, Napoleon Solo, Ideal, 1965, VG+ (EX box), C1 ....$39.00

Man From UNCLE, card game, Milton Bradley, 1965, EX+ (EX box), O1/P3 ....$22.00

Man from UNCLE Shoot-Out Marble Game, plastic, G-, J5 .$10.00

Marble Bingo, Wolverine Supply, 1930s, EX (VG box), M6 .$70.00

Marlin Perkins Zoo Parade, Cadaco-Ellis, 1965, EX (EX box) $40.00

Mary Poppins, Whitman, 1964, EX (EX box), H4............$14.00

Masquerade Party, Bettye-B, 1955, VG (VG box), M6 ....$55.00

McHale's Navy, Transogram, 1962, EX (EX box) $50.00

Melvin the Moon Man, dice game, Remco, 1960s, EX, H4.$15.00

Mexican Pete, Parker Bros, 1940s, EX (VG box), M6......$45.00

Mickey Mouse & Donald Duck Speedway Game, EX (VG box), O1 ....$45.00

Mickey Mouse & Friends Dominoes, EX (EX box), O1 ...$10.00

Mickey Mouse Club Game, Whitman, 1955, EX (VG box) .$35.00

Mickey Mouse Library of Games, WDP, 1946, 6 boxed card games w/different characters in master case, scarce, MIB, A...$165.00

Mickey Mouse Party Game, Marx, pin the tail on Mickey, linen, uncut, EX+ (EX box), A $167.00

Mickey Mouse Scatter Ball, Marx, 1935, wooden spinner & 10 balls, EX, A..$275.00

Mickey Mouse Soldier Set, target game, British, 1935, 16 cb figures w/cork-shooting gun, lg-sz (rare), G (G box), A......$1,150.00

Mickey Mouse Space Quiz, math game, Unisonic, 1970s, figural Mickey in flying saucer, MIB, S2 ....$75.00

Mickey Mouse Spin 'n Win, NM (VG box), O1 ....$85.00

Middle Class Game, Klinemates, 1979, EX (EX box), M6 ..$30.00

Mighty Comics Super Heroes, board game, Transogram, 1960s, EX (VG box), J5 ....$45.00

Mighty Kong Big Mouth Target Game, Marx, battery-op, NM (EX box), A $305.00

Mind Over Matter, Ideal, 1967, EX (VG box), M6 ....$35.00

Model Shooting Gallery, Wyandotte, pnt & litho tin, 10¾", VG, A $35.00

Modern Battle Quadrigame, SPI, 1975, M (EX box), M6 ..$40.00

Monopoly, Parker Bros, 1954, Popular Edition, VG $25.00

Monopoly, Parker Bros, 1988, 50th Anniversary Edition, M (EX box) $35.00

Monster Game, Ideal, 1977, M (EX box), M6 ....$70.00

Monsters of Madness, board game, 1980s, MIB (sealed), S2 ..$35.00

Mork & Mindy, board game, Parker Bros, 1970s, VG, J5 .$20.00

Mother's Help for Rainy Days, Parker Bros, ca 1930, EX+ (orig box) $35.00

Mouse Trap, Ideal, 1963, EX (VG box) $45.00

Mr Brain's Electronic Kiddie Quiz, Jaymar, 1950s, battery-op, EX+ (EX+ box), A..$85.00

Mr Machine, Ideal, 1961, w/12" plastic Mr Machine figure, complete, NM (EX+ box), T2 ....$79.00

Mr Mad Game, Ideal, 1970, EX (EX box), M6 ....$75.00

Mr President, 3M, 1967, EX (EX box), M6.......................$35.00

Mr Ree, Selchow & Righter, 1946, EX (VG box) $45.00

Ms Pac-Man, table-top arcade game, Coleco, 1982, NM, S2 .$75.00

Munsters, card game, Milton Bradley, 1964, EX (EX box), H4 ....$25.00

Murder She Wrote, board game, 1985, MIB $15.00

Mystic Eye, Mr B Industries, 1953, EX (EX box), M6 ......$40.00

Name That Tune, Milton Bradley, 1957, VG (G box), M6 .$25.00

Nancy Drew Mystery, board game, Parker Bros, 1957, VG, T5 .$50.00

National Defense Shooting Game, Marx, G, A................$55.00

Neck & Neck, Yaquinto, 1981, MIB (sealed), M6 ....$25.00

Nemo, Lakeside, 1969, EX (VG box), M6 ....$34.00

New Bicycle Game, board game, Parker Bros, ca 1894, EX, A $650.00

New Game of Shuffle Board, Sam Gabriel & Sons, 1930s, EX (VG box) $50.00

Newlyweds Game, Hasbro, 1967, EX (VG box), M6.......$24.00

NFL Franchise, Rohrwood, 1982, M (EX box), M6.........$28.00

Nightmare on Elm Street The Game, Victory, 1987, MIB (sealed), S2 ....$45.00

No Time for Sergeants, Ideal, 1964, EX (EX box), M6 ....$55.00

Noah's Ark, Cadaco-Ellis, 1953, EX (VG box) $25.00

Number Game, Foxy Toys, numbers & math symbols locked in groove on rnd tin base w/groved bar across top, 13" dia, G, A $15.00

Odd Men, McLoughlin Bros, lg face in center of board, inner circle w/more faces, 17", EX, minimum value..........$600.00

Official Baseball Game, Milton Bradley, 1969, M (EX lg box), M6..$410.00

Official Baseball Game, Milton Bradley, 1970, EX (VG sm box) $135.00

Official Radio Football Game, Toy Creations, VG (G- box), M6 ....$40.00

Old Maid, Milton Bradley, 1936, EX (EX box), M6........$40.00

Operation, Milton Bradley, 1965, EX (EX box), M6.......$25.00

Organized Crime, Kowplow Games, 1974, EX (EX box), M6 ....$30.00

Outboard Motor Race, Milton Bradley, 1930s, EX (VG box), M6 ....$75.00

Outer Limits, board game, Milton Bradley, complete with insert, EX+ (EX+ box), A, $135.00.

Outwit, Parker Bros, 1978, EX (EX box), M6 ....$25.00

Over the Rainbow See-Saw Game, Milton Bradley, 1949, VG (VG box), M6...$34.00

Pac-Man, table-top mini arcade, G, S2 ....$50.00

Parcheesi, Selchow & Righter, 1938, EX (VG box) $15.00

Password, Milton Bradley, 1963, MIB $10.00

Pathfinder (David Jansen), board game, Milton Bradley, 1977, VG, J5 ....$15.00

Peter the Wolf (from the movie Make Mine Music), card game, complete w/booklet & rules, MIB, A $92.00

Petticoat Junction, board game, Standard Toykraft, 1960s, NM (EX+ box), P3, $95.00.

Petticoat Junction, board game, Standard Toykraft, 1960s, VG+ (VG box), J5 ....$35.00
Philip Marlow Game, Transogram, 1960, M (EX+ box) ..$60.00
Pink Panther, board game, Warren, 1970s, VG, J5/S2, from $30 to $35.00
Pinky Lee Who Am I Game, Ed-U-Cards, 1950s, EX+ (EX box), T2 ....$49.00
Pirate & the Traveler, Milton Bradley, 1953, MIB (sealed) .$25.00
Planet of the Apes, board game, Milton Bradley, 1974, M (EX+ box), C1 ....$54.00
Planet of the Apes, board game, Milton Bradley, 1974, VG (VG box), S2 ....$30.00
Popeye Ball Toss Game, 1960s, EX (VG box), J5 ....$45.00
Popeye Card Game, Parker Bros, 1983, MIB, C1 ....$18.00

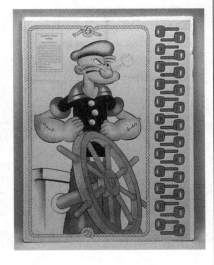

Popeye Party Game, uncut, 26½x19", NM (sealed package), D10, $75.00.

Popeye Pipe Toss Game, Rosebud/KFS, 1935, M (EX+ box), A $72.00
Popeye the Juggler, KFS, 1929, scarce, EX+, A $115.00
Prehistoric Pinball, Marx, NM (G+ box), A $168.00
Prince Valiant Crossbow Pistol Game, Parva, 1948, M (EX+ box), A $100.00
Pro Football (SI), Time Inc, 1970, EX (EX box), M6 ....$45.00
Probe, Parker Bros, 1964, EX (EX box) $15.00
Public Enemy No 1 Target Game, Marx, 1950s, 15", MIB, A .$121.00
Pull the Rug Out Game, Schaper, 1968, EX (EX box), M6 .$45.00
Punch & Judy, Parker Bros, G, A $175.00
Puss in Boots, McLoughlin Bros, 1887, VG, A $745.00

Pussy Cat Ten Pins, McLoughlin Bros, G, A $800.00
Put & Take, Schaper, 1956, EX (EX box) $15.00
Quarterback, Transogram, 1970, EX (VG box), M6 ....$50.00
Qubic, Parker Bros, 1965, EX (EX box), M6 ....$24.00
Quick Shoot, Ideal, 1970, EX (EX box), J2 ....$25.00
Quick Draw McGraw, card game, Ed-U-Cards, 1961, EX (VG box), S2 ....$20.00
Quick Draw McGraw Private Eye, board game, Milton Bradley, 1960, NMIB, C1 ....$81.00
Quiz Panel, Cadaco-Ellis, 1954, VG (G box), M6 ....$18.00
Rack-O, Milton Bradley, 1961, EX (EX box) $10.00
Radio Game, Milton Bradley, 1930s, VG (VG box) $85.00
Raggedy Ann, Milton Bradley, 1956, EX (VG box), M6 .$32.00
Rajah, ES Lowe, 1930s, EX (VG box), M6 ....$50.00
Rambo, hand-held electronic video game, 1988, MIB, S2 ...$25.00
Rambo P-38 Dart Gun Target Game, Arco, 1985, MOC, H4 ....$9.00
Ranger Commandos, Parker Bros, 1942, VG (VG box), M6..$70.00
Rat Patrol, Transogram, 1966, EX, H4 ....$30.00

Red Bird Base Ball Game, Measuregraph Co., 1930s, NM (lightly dented box with worn corners), D10, $475.00.

Red Herring, Cadaco-Ellis, 1945, VG (G box), M6 ....$30.00
Red Rover Game, Cadaco, 1963, EX (EX box), M6 ....$35.00
Red Star/White Star, SPI, 1972, EX (VG box), M6 ....$32.00
Regatta, Whitman, 1958, EX (EX box), M6 ....$35.00
Reminiscing, TDC Games, 1989, EX (EX box), M6 ....$20.00
Reward of Virtue, Ives, 1850, hand-colored folding board, complete, EX+, A $1,380.00
Rex Morgan MD, Sunday Funnies, board game, Ideal, 1972, MIB, C1 ....$21.00
Rich Uncle, Parker Bros, 1962, EX (VG box), M6 ....$35.00
Ricochet Rabbit & Droop-A-Long, board game, Ideal, 1964, EX, J5 ....$85.00
Ringmaster the Circus Game, Cadaco-Ellis, 1947, NMIB, A .$110.00
Risk, Parker Bros, 1968, wood pcs, EX (EX box), M6 ....$35.00
Road Runner Game, Milton Bradley, 1968, VG (EX box), M6 ....$38.00
Robb, McLoughlin Bros, Pat Dec 27 1892, plain non-litho box becomes table w/legs provided, 18x18", EX, A $105.00
Robocop, electronic table-top arcade, Remco, 1988, very rare, MIB, S2 ....$185.00
Rock 'Em Sock 'Em Robots, Marx, plunger activated, EX (EX box), A $213.00
Rock, Paper, Scissors Game, Ideal, 1967, EX (G- box), M6 .$20.00

Rocky, board game, 1985, MIB (sealed), J6 ....$18.00

Roman X, Selchow & Righter, 1964, EX (EX box), M6 ..$38.00

Rook, Parker Bros, Pat 1910, New Dixie-Boston edition, M (orig box) $10.00

Rough Rider Ten Pins, McLoughlin Bros, mixed set (orig rough box), A $500.00

Roulette Baseball, Bar-Zim Toy, 1930, G (G- box), M6 ..$40.00

Roy Rogers Horseshoe Set, Ohio Art, EX+ (EX box), A .$115.00

Roy Rogers Horseshoe Set, Ohio Art, NM (EX box), A ..$146.00

Roy Rogers Horseshoe Set, Ohio Art, VG+ (VG box), A .$87.00

Ruff & Ready Circus, board game, Transogram, 1962, NM (NM box) $60.00

Rumbo, Selchow & Righter, 1930s, VG (G box), M6 .....$30.00

Safari, Selchow & Righter, 1950, EX (VG box) $35.00

Saga, TSR, 1980, M, M6 ....$22.00

Satellite Target Game, USA, 1950s, plastic spring-action launcher & cb target, MIB, A $60.00

Say When!, Parker Bros, 1961, EX (EX box), M6 ....$32.00

Scarecrow Target Game, Ideal, 1965, VG (worn box), H4 ....$45.00

Scooby Doo & Scrappy Doo Game, Milton Bradley, 1983, EX (VG box), M6 ....$25.00

Scoop, Parker Bros, 1956, EX (G box), M6 ....$48.00

Score Four, Futuristic, 1967, EX (EX box), M6 ....$25.00

Scrabble, Selchow & Righter, 1953, EX (EX box), M6....$26.00

Scribbage, ES Lowe, 1963, EX (EX box), M6 ....$25.00

Scruples, Milton Bradley, 1988, EX (EX box) $15.00

Sea Battle, Kaywood Corp, 1940s, EX (EX box), M6 ....$48.00

Sea Raider, Parker Bros, 1940s, VG (VG box) $55.00

See New York ('Round the Town), Transogram, 1964, EX (EX box), M6 ....$38.00

Shakespeare, Avalon Hill, 1966, M (EX box), M6...........$32.00

Shenandoah, Battleline, 1975, M (EX box), M6 ....$85.00

Sherlock Holmes, board game, Parker Bros, 1904, NMIB, A $70.00

Sherlock Holmes, board game, Parker Bros, 1904, VG (VG box), M6 ....$45.00

Shifty Gear Game, Schaper, 1962, EX (VG box), M6 .....$38.00

Shooting Gallery, Wyandotte, 1930s, hit ducks w/dart pistol, wheel spins, EX (VG+ box), A $128.00

Shooting Gallery #151, Wolverine, gun on tin base shoots balls at 4 targets against wild animal backdrop, NM (EX box), A $176.00

Shotgun Slade, board game, Milton Bradley, 1960, EX (VG box), J5 ....$45.00

Sigmond & the Sea Monster, board game, Milton Bradley, 1975, M (NM box) $50.00

Simpsons, pinball game, Ja-Ru, 1989, all characters featured, 10", MOC, S2 ....$20.00

Sinbad, Cadaco, 1978, M (EX box), M6 ....$48.00

Six Million Dollar Man, board game, Parker Bros, 1975, MIB (sealed), M6 ....$28.00

Six Million Dollar Man Bionic Crisis, board game, Parker Bros, 1976, EX (VG box), P3 ....$5.00

Six Million Dollar Man Bionic Crisis, board game, Parker Bros, 1976, MIB (sealed), C1 ....$21.00

Skeet Shoot Game, Irwin Plastics, 1950s, MIB, S9 ....$225.00

Skill-Drive, Sidney Tarrson, 1950s, EX (VG box), M6....$35.00

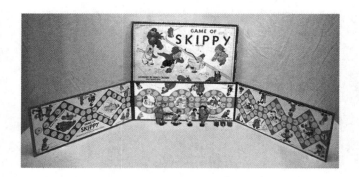

Skippy, board game, 1930s, M, D10, $225.00.

Skittle Score-Ball, board game, Aurora, 1971, EX (VG+ box), P3 ....$40.00

Skittles, Chad Valley, 1940s, features diecuts of Snow White & Dwarfs w/wooden bases & balls, EX+, A....................$90.00

Skudo, Parker Bros, 1949, EX (G box), M6 ....$45.00

Skunk, Schaper, 1953, EX (EX box) $25.00

Slalom Game, TN, 1960s, battery-op, scarce, NMIB, A ..$187.00

Smurf Ahoy Game, 1982, VG (VG box), S2 ....$20.00

Snagglepuss Fun at the Picnic, board game, Transogram, 1961, NM (EX+ box), C1 ....$72.00

Snake Eyes, Selchow & Righter, 1957, EX (G box), M6..$38.00

Snoopy & Red Baron Skill & Action Board Game, Milton Bradley, 1970s, M (EX box) $35.00

Snoopy Go Home, Milton Bradley, 1973, EX (EX box), M6 .$34.00

Snow White & the Seven Dwarfs (Walt Disney's Own Game), Parker Bros, 1938, EX+, A $330.00

Snuffy Smith Time's A-Wastin', board game, Milton Bradley, 1963, M (EX+ box), T2..$29.00

Solarquest, Western Publishing, 1986, EX (EX box), M6..$25.00

Sons of Hercules Game, Milton Bradley, 1966, EX (VG box), M6 ....$55.00

Sorry, Parker Bros, 1954, EX (VG box) $10.00

Soupy Sales Sez Go-Go-Go, Milton Bradley, 1960s, EX (VG box), H4 ....$35.00

Space Game, board game, Parker Bros, 1953, scarce, NMIB, A $176.00

Space Patrol Spinner Game, Japan, 1950s, NM, A $35.00

Space Pilot, Cadaco-Ellis, 1951, EX (VG box), M6 ....$65.00

Space Shooting Range, Automatic Toys USA, 1950s, players shoot cannon at revolving spaceships, tin, EX+ (VG+ box), A $400.00

Spartan, SPI, 1975, M (EX box), M6 ....$70.00

Special Agent, Parker Bros, 1966, G (VG box), M6 ....$20.00

Spelling Match, Cadaco-Ellis, 1954, EX (EX box), M6....$27.00

Spider-Man w/the Fantastic Four, board game, Milton Bradley, 1977, VG, S2 ....$20.00

Spiderman Chalk & Rechalk Game, Avalon, 1978, MIP (sealed), C1..$18.00

Spingo & Whirlette, Transogram, 1940, EX (VG box), M6 .$35.00

Spot Cash Game, Milton Bradley, 1959, VG (VG box), M6.$20.00

Spudsie Hot Potato Game, Ohio Art, 1960s, VG (VG box), S2 ....$50.00

Sputnick the Magnetic Satellite, space-race game, Maggie Magnetic/USA, 1950s, orbit rods attached to globe, MIB, A $100.00

Square Mile, Milton Bradley, 1962, EX (EX box), M6.....$65.00

Stage II, Milton Bradley, 1985, M (EX box), M6 ....$30.00

Starship Troopers, Avalon Hill, 1976, MIB (sealed), M6.....$30.00

Starsky & Hutch, Milton Bradley, 1977, EX (EX box), M6.$25.00

Steve Canyon Air Force Game, Lowell, 1959, EX (VG box), M6...$55.00

Stock Market Game, Whitman, 1968, EX (EX box), M6.$30.00

Straight Arrow, Selchow & Righter, 1950, EX (VG box)..$60.00

Stratego, Milton Bradley, 1961, VG (G box), M6............$25.00

Strategy: Game of Armies, Corey Games, EX (EX box), M6...$70.00

Streamline Express, 1936, VG (VG box), M6 ....$70.00

Stump, Milton Bradley, 1968, EX (EX box), M6.............$17.00

Sub Search, Milton Bradley, 1973, EX (EX box), M6 ......$45.00

Submarine Chaser, Milton Bradley, 1939, VG (VG box), M6...$80.00

Summit, Cameo-Milton Bradley, 1971, EX (VG box), M6.$65.00

Sunken Treasure, Parker Bros, 1948, EX (VG box)..........$35.00

Superman III Board Game, Parker Bros, 1982, M (EX+ box), C1...$24.00

Superman Junior Rubber Horseshoe Set, Super Swim Inc, 1950s, VG+ (VG+ box), A $51.00

Superstar Baseball, Time Inc, 1974, EX (VG box), M6....$40.00

Survive, Parker Bros, 1982, M (VG box), M6 ....$25.00

SWAT, board game, Milton Bradley, 1976, EX+ (EX box), C1...$21.00

Sweeps, All-Fair, 1940s, EX (VG box).............................$35.00

Swivel, Milton Bradley, 1972, EX (VG box), M6.............$20.00

Sword in the Stone Board Game, Parker Bros, 1968, EX, J5..$45.00

Tabloid Teasers, Pressman, 1991, MIB (sealed), M6 ....$25.00

Take 12, Phillips Publishing, 1959, EX (EX box), M6.....$25.00

Tangle, Selchow & Righter, 1964, EX (VG box), M6 .....$35.00

Tarzan, card game, Milton Bradley, 1983, MIB, S2 ....$10.00

Tarzan, card game (comic), Mattel, 1971, EX (on card), S2..$15.00

Tell It to the Judge, Parker Bros, 1959, VG (VG box), M6.$45.00

Terry & the Pirates Sunday Funnies, board game, Ideal, 1972, MIB, C1 ....$31.00

Thing Ding, Schaper, 1960s, VG (G box), M6 ....$95.00

Thinking Man's Football, 3M, 1969, EX (EX box), M6 ...$32.00

Three Little Pigs & the Big Bad Wolf, Freeman/WD, 1933, scarce, NM (EX+ box), A $232.00

Three Little Pigs & the Big Bad Wolf, Freeman/WD, 1933, scarce, EX (VG box), J2 ....$120.00

Three Men on a Horse, Milton Bradley, 1936, G (VG box) .$50.00

Three Stooges, video game, Pressman, 1986, M (sealed), S2.$40.00

Thunderbirds Game, Waddingtons, 1965, EX (EX box), M6...$70.00

Tic-Tac-Dough, Transogram, 1957, EX (EX box) $30.00

Tic-Tac-Dough, Transogram, 1957, VG (VG box), J5.....$15.00

Tickle Bee, Schaper, 1960s, VG (VG box), M6 ....$28.00

Tiddle-Tac-Toe, Schaper, 1955, EX (EX box), M6 ....$20.00

Tiddly Winks, 1963, w/Disney characters, S2....................$25.00

Tiger Island, Ideal, 1966, EX (VG box), M6.....................$30.00

Tip-It, Ideal, 1965, EX (VG box) $15.00

Toot! Toot!, Selchow & Righter, 1967, EX (VG box), M6.$27.50

Tootsie Roll Train Game, Hasbro 1969, MIB, H4............$39.00

Top-Ography, Cadaco-Ellis, 1951, EX (VG box), M6......$30.00

Toss Across, Ideal, 1970, EX (EX box), M6 ....$34.00

Toxic Crusaders Target Game, Troma, 1991, MIB, S2 ....$30.00

Toy Town Post Office, Milton Bradley, 1910, VG (G box).$100.00

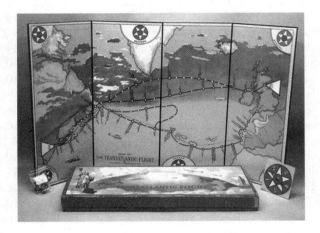

Transatlantic Flight, board game, 1930s, EX, $300.00.

Travel w/Woody Woodpecker, Cadaco-Ellis, 1956, EX (VG box), M6...$70.00

Treasure Hunt, Cadaco-Ellis, 1942, VG (VG box), M6...$45.00

Treasure Hunt, table-top pinball, Gotham #G-126, 17", A.$80.00

Triple Up, Ideal, 1977, VG (VG box), M6.......................$20.00

Troke, Selchow & Righter, 1967, VG (VG box), M6......$25.00

Tron, electronic, NMIB, J2 ....$85.00

Tru-Action Electric Football, Tudor, 1950s, VG (VG box), M6...$55.00

Truth or Consequences, Gabriel, 1955, EX (VG box), M6..$38.00

Turbo, Milton Bradley, 1981, EX (VG box), M6.............$25.00

Twelve O'Clock High, Ideal, 1965, EX (EX box)............$50.00

Twist, 3M, 1963, EX (VG box), M6 ....$25.00

Uncle Wiggily Game, board game, Milton Bradley, EX, $42.00.

Uncle Wiggily, Parker Bros, 1961, EX, S2 ....$10.00

Under-n-Over Marble Game, Marx, ca 1950, EX............$50.00

Undersea World of Jacques Costeau, Parker Bros, 1968, complete w/16-pg booklet, EX+, T2 ....$42.00

Universe, Parker Bros, 1967, EX (VG box), M6.............$34.00

Untouchables Target Game, Marx, w/up, 20", scarce, EX+ (EX box), A..$44.00

Upwords, Milton Bradley, 1983, MIB (sealed), M6.........$30.00

Vaquero, Wales Game System, 1952, M (VG box).........$40.00

Veda, The Magic Answer Man, Pressman, 1950s, VG (G-box), M6...$34.00

Video Village, Milton Bradley, 1960, EX (VG box), M6 .$30.00

Voyage to the Bottom of the Sea, Milton Bradley, 1964, M (EX box), M6 ....$50.00

Walt Disney's Casey Jr, EX (EX box), O1 ....$55.00

Walton's, Milton Bradley, 1974, EX (EX box), M6..........$28.00

We Play Store, Gabriel & Sons, 1930s, EX (VG box)......$50.00

Web of Gold, TSR, 1989, MIB (sealed), M6 ....$28.00

Weekend in Vegas, Research Games, 1974, EX (VG box), M6 ....$30.00

Welcome Back Kotter, board game, Ideal, EX (EX box) ..$25.00

Welfare, Jedco, 1978, VG (VG box), M6 ....$45.00

What's Up Doc?, Milton Bradley, 1978, EX (VG box), M6.$20.00

What Shall I Be? (boys), Selchow & Righter, 1968, EX (VG box), M6 ....$35.00

What Shall I Be? (girls), Selchow & Righter, 1976, EX (VG box), M6 ....$38.00

Wheeler Dealer, Ranco Games, 1977, EX (VG box), M6.$40.00

Whirling Words, Club Aluminum, 1942, EX (G box), M6..$32.00

Whodunit?, Selchow & Righter, 1972, EX (EX box), M6.$25.00

Why?, Milton Bradley, 1958, EX (VG box), M6 ....$30.00

Wide World, Parker Bros, 1957, EX (EX box).................$30.00

Wild Animal Picture Dominoes, Parker Bros, 1950s, EX (EX box), M6 ....$34.00

Win, Place & Show, Avalon Hill, 1966, EX (EX box), M6 .$38.00

Windigo, RW Associates, 1968, EX (VG box), M6 ....$35.00

Wings: The Air Mail Game, Parker Bros, 1928, EX (VG box), M6...$52.00

Wolfman, board game, Hasbro, 1963, EX (EX box), S2.$265.00

Wonderful Game of Oz, board game, Parker Bros, 1921, early version with pewter figures, wooden 'Wizard' cubes, dice cup, EX (EX box), $1,200.00.

Woody Woodpecker Flannel Game, 1973, VG (VG box), S2 ....$30.00

Woody Woodpecker Water Works Game, Whitman, 1972, EX (EX box), S2 ....$35.00

Word for Word (Merv Griffin), Mattel, EX (VG box), M6 .$35.00

Word Out, Milton Bradley, 1967, EX (VG box), M6.......$25.00

World War III, SPI, 1975, M (EX box), M6 ....$45.00

WOW Pillow Fight Game, Milton Bradley, 1969, VG (VG box), M6 ....$40.00

Wrestle Around Game, Ideal, 1969, EX (EX box), M6 ....$38.00

Yahtzee, ES Lowe, 1956, VG (VG box), M6 ....$20.00

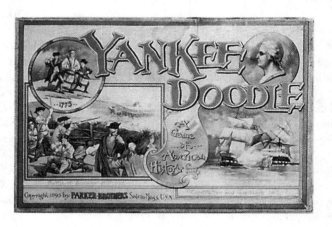

Yankee Doodle, Game of American History; Parker Bros, 1895, EX (EX box), $650.00.

Yertle, Dr Suess, NM $75.00

Yogi Bear, Pixie & Dixie Pile-On Game, Whitman, 1962, NM, C1..$31.00

You Don't Say, Milton Bradley, 1963, VG (VG box), M6.$25.00

Young People's Bible Game, Parker Bros, 1900s, EX (VG box), M6...$28.00

Zaxoon, Milton Bradley, 1983, EX (EX box), M6 ....$25.00

Zomax, Zomax Inc, 1989, M (EX sm box), M6................$50.00

Zoo-M-Roo, space pinball game, 1950s, EX+ (EX+ box), J2.$45.00

Zorro, board game, Parker Bros, 1966, NMIB, D9 ....$63.00

Zorro (Walt Disney's), Whitman, 1966, M (EX box), M6 ..$95.00

12 O'Clock High, Ideal, 1965, VG (VG box), J5/M6, from $45 to $50.00

1776, Avalon Hill, 1974, EX (M box), M6.....................$25.00

1863, Parker Bros, 1961, EX (EX box) $45.00

20,000 Leagues Under the Sea, 3-D board game, 1970s, M, S2..$35.00

300-Mile Race Game, Built-Rite, 1950s, EX+ EX box), T2 .$29.00

43 Sicily, International Team, M (shrink wrapped), M6..$65.00

77 Sunset Strip, Lowell, 1960, contents sealed, M (shelf-worn box) $50.00

Gasoline-Powered Toys

Two of the largest companies to manufacture gas-powered models are Cox and Wen Mac. Since the late fifties they have been making faithfully detailed models of airplanes as well as some automobiles and boats. Condition of used models will vary greatly because of the nature of the miniature gas engine and damage resulting from the fuel that has been used. Because of this, 'new in box' gas toys command a premium.

Advisor: Danny Bynum (B7).

Comet Model Hobby Craft Inc, Tiger Shark, ready-to-fly model plane, plastic, 13½", MIB, $175.00.

Cox, A-25 Dive Bomber, 1965-67, olive drab, EX, B7 .....$65.00

Cox, AA Fuel Dragster, 1968-70, bl & red, M, B7 ....$125.00

Cox, Acro Piper Cub, 1971-72, orange & wht, EX, B7 ....$35.00

Cox, AD-6 Skyraider, 1967-69, tan, wht & bl, M, B7 ......$75.00

Cox, Aerobat 150, E-Z Flyer Series, 1988-93, wht, EX, B7..$15.00

Cox, Airwolf, Wings Series, 1987-89, blk helicopter, M, B7 .$40.00

Cox, Army P-51B Mustang, 1963-70, olive drab, molded landing gear & razorback fuse, EX, B7......................................$35.00

Cox, Attack Cobra, Wings Series, 1993-95, blk helicopter, M, B7 ....$25.00

Cox, Avion Shinn, 1962, yel, EX, B7 ....$65.00

Cox, Baja Bug, 1968-73, yel & orange, M, B7 ....$65.00

Cox, Baron, Wings Series, 1980-81, blk, EX, B7 ....$15.00

Cox, Blue Angel, Wings Series, 1990-95, bl, M, B7 ....$30.00

Cox, Bushmaster, 1973-74, red & wht, pontoons & skis, EX, B7..$40.00

Cox, Cessna 150, Sure Flyer Series, 1976-78, wht, EX, B7.$20.00

Cox, Cessna 150, 1986-95, reissue, wht, M, B7 ....$30.00

Cox, Chopper, MIB, B7...$95.00

Cox, Commanche, Wings Series, 1987-92, reissue, wht, M, B7 ....$30.00

Cox, Commanche, 1960-64, tan & cream or maroon & chrome, .15 engine, M, B7 ....$125.00

Cox, Corsair II, 1970-72, chrome w/red & wht checkerboard on wing, EX, B7, ea..$45.00

Cox, Corvette, blk plastic body, metal fr, 9", VG, A......$175.00

Cox, Corvette, 1966, red plastic body w/metal fr, VG, B7 .$100.00

Cox, Cosmic Wind, Wings Series, 1986-89, red, EX, B7 .$20.00

Cox, Crusader, 1976-79, wht & bl, EX, B7 ....$40.00

Cox, Curtiss Pusher, 1960-62, Wright Bros biplane, blk & orange, EX, B7 ....$70.00

Cox, Dan Gurney Indy Car, bl or red, EX, B7, ea.............$75.00

Cox, Delta F-15, Wings Series, 1981-86, gray, M, B7.......$25.00

Cox, Desert Defender, Wings Series, 1991-93, M, B7 ......$25.00

Cox, Dune Buggy, M, B7...$65.00

Cox, F-1 Sport Trainer, 1971-83, pk w/bl canopy, M, B7.$45.00

Cox, F-18 Eagle, Wings Series, 1977-79, blk, EX, B7 ....$15.00

Cox, FA-18 Hornet, Wings Series, 1991-95, lt gray, M, B7 .$30.00

Cox, Falcon, Wings Series, 1977-79, wht, M, B7 ....$25.00

Cox, Firebird, E-Z Flyer Series, 1993-95, red w/muffler, M, B7 ....$25.00

Cox, Flight Trainer, V: TD-4, 1956-59, red & bl or bl & yel, EX, B7 ....$45.00

Cox, Flying Circus, V:TD-3, 1958-61, wht w/red checkerboard wing, engine w/metal tank, M, B7..............................$95.00

Cox, Fokker D-7, Wings Series, 1990-91, bl-gray & lt gray, reissue, M, B7 ....$30.00

Cox, Fokker D-7, 1972-74, red & bl, M, B7.....................$50.00

Cox, Fokker Tri-plane, Wings Series, 1990-91, reissue, red, M, B7 ....$35.00

Cox, Fokker Tri-plane, 1973-74, red, EX, B7...................$35.00

Cox, Golden Bee, .049 engine, M, B7...............................$20.00

Cox, Invader, Wings Series, 1980 only, Buck Rogers Series flying saucer, blk, M, B7 ....$45.00

Cox, Kitty Hawk Spitfire, gr w/yel tail & lettering, EX, B7 .$60.00

Cox, L-4 Grasshopper, 1963-70, Army Piper Cub, olive drab, M, B7 ....$75.00

Cox, Li'l Stinker, 1958-64, biplane w/.020 engine, red & wht, EX, B7 ....$70.00

Cox, Mantis, Wings Series, 1977-79, yel, EX, B7 ....$15.00

Cox, Marine Corsair, Wings Series, 1994-95, bl, M, B7...$25.00

Cox, ME-109 Stunt Flyer, Wings Series, 1994-95, blk & wht, styrofoam wing, M, B7 ....$25.00

Cox, Mercedes Benz W196 Race Car, 1963-65, red, EX, B7 .$85.00

Cox, Mini Stunt, 1969-70, biplane w/.020 engine, lime gr, EX, B7 ....$45.00

Cox, Miss America, Wings Series, 1990-91, reissue, red, wht & bl, wire landing gear, M, B7 ....$35.00

Cox, Miss America P-51, 1971-72, red, wht & bl, molded landing gear, EX, B7 ....$45.00

Cox, Navy Corsair, 1968-72, bl, EX, B7............................$45.00

Cox, Navy Helldiver, 1963-66, lt bl & dk bl, EX, B7 ....$65.00

Cox, P-19, Wings Series, 1981-84, red & wht, M, B7 ......$40.00

Cox, P-39 Air Cobra, Sure Flyer Series, 1976-79, bl, EX, B7 ....$20.00

Cox, P-39 Air Cobra, Wings Series, 1986-94, reissue, tan, M, B7 ....$30.00

Cox, P-40, 1969-70, tan w/gr or blk camo, EX, B7 ....$40.00

Cox, P-40, 1978-91, gr w/camo, plastic tank in fuselage, M, B7 ....$45.00

Cox, P-40 Flying Tiger, 1959-60, tan, mk Flying Tiger on fuselage, inverted engine, VG, B7 ....$35.00

Cox, P-40 Warhawk, 1961-68, tan w/inverted engine & pnt pilot, EX, B7...$45.00

Cox, P-51 Bendix Racer, 1963-64, red & yel, molded landing gear, EX, B7 ....$65.00

Cox, P-51 Mustang, Wings Series, 1979-80, olive drab, sidemount engine, EX, B7...$30.00

Cox, P-51 Mustang, Wings Series, 1981 only, Red Baron, M, B7 ....$55.00

Cox, P-51 Mustang, Wings Series, 1981-90, gray, upright engine, EX, B7 ....$20.00

Cox, P-51 Mustang, 1975-77, gray w/WWII Invasion stripes & side-mounted engine, M, B7................................$40.00

Cox, P-51D Mustang, 1971-78, olive drab, bubble canopy & bolted-on landing gear, EX, B7 ....$35.00

Cox, Phantom 5, Wings Series, 1982-86, gr, M, B7 ....$25.00

Cox, Pinto/Vega, M, B7..$75.00

Cox, Piper Commanche, Sure Flyer Series, 1976-77, wht, EX, B7..$20.00

Cox, Pitts Special, 1968 only, .020 powered biplane, wht, EX, B7..$45.00

Cox, Pontiac GTO, 1968, lt bl, EX, B7............................$75.00

Cox, PT-19 Flight Trainer, yellow and blue, EX, B7, $35.00.

Photo courtesy of Danny Bynum.

Cox, PT-19, 1960-65, bl & yel, open front nose, EX, B7 .$35.00

Cox, QZ PT-19, 1966-69, red & wht, Quiet Zone, M, B7..$60.00

Cox, RAF Spitfire, 1964-65, lt gr w/camo, EX, B7 ....$55.00

Cox, Red Devil, Wings Series, 1980 only, red, M, B7 ......$25.00

Cox, Red Knight, 1970-72, biplane w/.020 engine, dk red, M, B7 ....$60.00

Cox, Rivets Racer, 1971-73, red & yel, pilot figure, EX, B7 .$40.00

Cox, Ryan PT-20, 1969-70, .020 engine, olive drab & yel, EX, B7..$45.00

Cox, Ryan ST-3, 1969-70, .020 engine, wht & bl, 2 pilots, B7 ..$45.00

Cox, Sandblaster, 1968-72, br & tan, M, B7.....................$65.00

Cox, Shrike, 1968, yel, M, B7 ....$65.00

Cox, Shrike, 1972, gr, B7..$55.00

Cox, Shrike, 1974, red, B7...$50.00

Cox, Sky Commando, Wings Series, 1983 only, gr man, red rotors, EX, B7...$25.00

Cox, Sky-Copter, 1975-76, yel & orange, metal-tanked engine, M, B7..$45.00

Cox, Sky-Copter, 1976-79, yel & orange, plastic gas tank, EX, B7..$40.00

Cox, Sky-Jumper, Wings Series, 1989-95, helicopter, olive drab, M, B7 ....$35.00

Cox, Sky-Ranger, Wings Series, 1980-89, helicopter, wht, EX, B7..$25.00

Cox, Skymaster, Sure Flyer Series, 1976-79, orange, M, B7 .$35.00

Cox, Snowmobile, 1968, silver, M, B7 ....$95.00

Cox, Sopwith Camel, Wings Series, 1981 only, tan & bl, EX, B7..$25.00

Cox, Sopwith Camel, Wings Series, 1990-91, olive gr & cream, reissue, EX, B7 ....$20.00

Cox, Sopwith Camel, 1972-74, yel & bl, EX, B7.............$30.00

Cox, Spitfire, Wings Series, 1979-80, reissue, lt bl, EX, B7 .$30.00

Cox, Spook, 1964, wht flying wing kit w/engine, M, B7 ..$85.00

Cox, Star Cruiser, Wings Series, 1978-79, EX, B7............$25.00

Cox, Starfighter, Wings Series, 1980 only, Buck Rogers series, wht, M, B7 ....$50.00

Cox, Stealth Bomber, Wings Series, 1987-89, blk, EX, B7.$25.00

Cox, Stuka, 1962-65, gr, w/molded landing gear, EX, B7 .$60.00

Cox, Stuka, 1965-81, blk w/landing gear molded into wing, EX, B7..$45.00

Cox, Stuka, 1981-87, blk w/landing gear bolted onto wing, M, B7..$70.00

Cox, Stuka, 1987-89, blk w/landing gear bolted onto the wing, upright engine, M, B7 ....$60.00

Cox, Super Chipmunk, Wings Series, 1988-93, reissue, wht & red, M, B7 ....$30.00

Cox, Super Chipmunk, 1975-82, red, wht & bl, M, B7....$40.00

Cox, Super Cub 105, 1959-61, Civil Air Patrol version, yel & bl, M, B7 ....$90.00

Cox, Super Cub 150, red & cream, plastic wheel pants, M, B7..$55.00

Cox, Super Cub 150, 1961-62, red & cream, upright engine w/metal tank, EX, B7...$45.00

Cox, Super Cub 150, 1963-65, red & cream, plastic tank in fuselage, M, B7 ....$60.00

Cox, Super Sabre F-100, 1958-63, .020 engine, wht or gray, M, B7..$95.00

Cox, Super Sport II, Wings Series, 1982-90, yel, EX, B7..$20.00

Cox, Super Stunter, 1974-79, blk & bl, EX, B7 ....$30.00

Cox, T-28 Trainer, 1966-67, yel, EX, B7 ....$45.00

Cox, Thimble Drome Champion Racer, red & bl, no engine, 10", EX..$125.00

Cox, Thimble Drome Champion Racer, red & bl, w/engine, 10", EX, J2 ....$325.00

Cox, Thimble Drome Prop Rod, bl plastic body w/metal chassis, EX, B7 ....$80.00

Cox, Thimble Drome Prop Rod, red plastic body w/metal chassis, EX, B7 ....$75.00

Cox, Thimble Drome Prop Rod, red plastic body w/metal chassis, M, B7 ....$75.00

Cox, Thimble Drome Prop Rod, yel plastic body w/metal chassis, EX, B7 ....$85.00

Cox, Thunderbolt, E-Z Flyer Series, 1993-95, blk w/muffler, M, B7..$25.00

Cox, Top Gun, Wings Series, 1988-90, gray, M, B7.........$30.00

Cox, UFO Flying Saucer, Wings Series, 1990-91, wht, M, B7..$25.00

Testors, Cosmic Wind Racer, blk or orange, M, B7..........$20.00

Testors, Fly 'em, Red Albatross, NM, B7 ....$25.00

Testors, Fly 'em, Sopwith Camel, EX+, B7 ....$20.00

Testors, Fly 'em, Zero, M, J2 ....$30.00

Testors, OD P-40, NM, B7 ....$15.00

Testors, OD P-51 Mustang, VG, J2 ....$20.00

Testors, Sopwith Camel, VG, B7 ....$20.00

Testors, Sprite Indy Car, 1966-68, wht, M, B7 ....$75.00

Wen-Mac, A-24 Army Attack Bomber, 1962-64, olive drab, EX, B7 ....$45.00

Wen-Mac, Aeromite, 1950-53, blk, Baby Spitfire engine, EX, B7 ....$55.00

Wen-Mac, Aeromite, 1956-64, red, bl, yel, blk & chrome, VG, B7 ....$25.00

Wen-Mac, Albatross, Flying Wings, red, wht & bl, EX, B7 .$40.00

Wen-Mac, AT-6, 1963-64, olive drab, M, B7 ....$75.00

Wen-Mac, B-33 Debonair, 1962-64, gr, yel & chrome, EX, B7 ....$45.00

Wen-Mac, Basic Trainer, 1962-64, red, bl, yel, blk & chrome, VG, B7 ....$35.00

Wen-Mac, Beechcraft M-35, 1958-64, bl, gr, yel & wht, EX, B7 ....$40.00

Wen-Mac, Cessna 175 Trainer, Vacuum Formed, 1962-64, red & wht, EX, B7 ....$40.00

Wen-Mac, Cutlass, 1958-60, bl, blk & yel, EX, B7 ....$45.00

Wen-Mac, Eagle, Flying Wings, 1963-64, red, wht & bl, EX, B7 ....$40.00

Wen-Mac, Earth Satellite, 1960-64, red flying saucer, VG, B7 ..$25.00

Wen-Mac, Falcon, Flying Wings, 1963-64, red, wht & bl, EX, B7 ....$40.00

Wen-Mac, Fan/Jet XL600, 1958-60, red Delta wing, rear engine, EX, B7 ....$45.00

Wen-Mac, Flying Platform, 1956-58, olive drab, USN emblems, EX, B7 ....$65.00

Wen-Mac, F4U Marine Fighter Corsair, 1959-62, chrome, EX, B7 ....$40.00

Wen-Mac, Giant P-40 Flying Tiger, Vacuum Formed, 1959-69, wht, EX, B7 ....$40.00

Wen-Mac, Giant P-51 Mustang, Vacuum Formed, 1959-60, wht, EX, B7 ....$40.00

Wen-Mac, Hawk, Flying Wings, 1963-64, yel & wht, VG, B7 ....$20.00

Wen-Mac, Indy Special Race Car, 1964-66, yel, EX, B7 ..$65.00

Wen-Mac, Marine Corsair, 1958-64, red, EX, B7 ....$40.00

Wen-Mac, Mustang Coupe, 1965, orange, NMIB, W5 ..$300.00

Wen-Mac, Mustang Fast-Back, 1968, bl, EX, W5 ....$120.00

Wen-Mac, Navy Corsair, 1958-64, bl, VG, B7 ....$25.00

Wen-Mac, Navy SNJ-3, 1963-64, lt bl, M, B7 ....$75.00

Wen-Mac, Night Fighter, 1952-55, bl, Wen-Mac engine, EX, B7 ....$75.00

Wen-Mac, P-26 Pursuit, 1958-62, bl & yel, EX, B7 ....$65.00

Wen-Mac, P-38 Lightning, 1959-64, red, gray, tan & chrome, 2 engines, EX, B7 ....$75.00

Wen-Mac, P-39 Air Cobra, 1962-64, olive drab, M, B7 ...$70.00

Wen-Mac, P-63 King Cobra, 1962-64, chrome, EX, B7 ...$45.00

Wen-Mac, RACF Banshee Raider, 1963-64, blk, EX, B7 .$45.00

Wen-Mac, RAF Day Fighter, 1963-64, wht, EX, B7 ....$45.00

Wen-Mac, SBD-5 Navy Dive Bomber, 1962-64, dk bl, VG, B7 ....$25.00

Wen-Mac, Thunderbird, Fling Wings, 1963-64, lt bl & wht, EX, B7 ....$40.00

Wen-Mac, Turbo-Jet, 1958-64, red & cream or red & chrome, EX, B7 ....$40.00

Wen-Mac, US Army Hovercraft, 1960-64, olive drab, EX, B7 ....$40.00

Wen-Mac, Yellow Jacket Corsair, 1959-64, yel, EX, B7 ...$40.00

GI Joe

GI Joe, the most famous action figure of them all, has been made in hundreds of variations since Hasbro introduced him in 1964. The first of these jointed figures was 12" tall; these can be identified today by the mark each carried on his back: GI Joe T.M. (trademark), Copyright 1964. They came with four different hair colors: blond, auburn, black, and brown, and each had a scar on his right cheek. They were sold in four basic packages: Action Soldier, Action Sailor, Action Marine, and Action Pilot. A Black figure was included in the line, and there were representatives of many nations as well — France, Germany, Japan, Britain, Canada, Russia, and Australia. Talking GI Joes were issued in 1967 when the only female (the nurse) was introduced. Besides the figures, uniforms, vehicles, guns, and accessories of many varieties were produced. The Adventure Team series, made from 1970 to 1976, included Black Adventurer, Air Adventurer, Talking Astronaut, Sea Adventurer, Talking Team Commander, Land Adventurer, and several variations. Joe's hard plastic hands were replaced with kung fu grips, so that he could better grasp his weapons. Assorted playsets allowed young imaginations to run wild, and besides the doll-size items, there were wristwatches, foot lockers, toys, and walkie-talkies made for the kids themselves. Due to increased production costs, the large GI Joe was discontinued in 1976.

In 1982 Hasbro brought out the 'little' 3¾" GI Joe figures, each with its own descriptive name. Of the first series, some characters were produced with either a swivel or straight arm. Vehicles, weapons, and playsets were available, and some characters could only be had by redeeming flag points from the backs of packages. This small version proved to be the most successful action figure line ever made. Loose items are common; collectors value those still mint in the original packages at two to four times higher.

In 1993 Hasbro reintroduced the 12" line while retaining the 3¾" size. The highlights of the comeback are the 30th anniversary collection of six figures which are already selling in the collector's market at well above retail ($29.00): Soldier, $80.00; Sailor, $80.00; Marine, $50.00; Pilot, $80.00; Black Soldier, $180.00; and Green Beret, $285.00.

Production of the 3¾" figures came to an end in December 1994, but we may see GI Joe again in 1996. For more information we recommend *Collectible Action Figures* by Paris and Susan Manos (Collector Books); *Encyclopedia to GI Joe* and *The 30th Anniversary Salute to GI Joe*, both by Vincent San Telmo; *Official Guide to Collecting and Completing 3¾" Series and Hall of Fame: Vol I*, *Official Guide To Collecting and Completing 3¾" Series and Hall of Fame: Vol II*, and *Official Guide To GI Joe: '64-'78*, all by James DeSimone. There is also a section on GI Joe in *Dolls in Uniform*, a new publication by Joseph Bourgeois (Collector Books). Note: all items are American issue unless indicated otherwise.

Advisor: Cotswold Collectibles (C6).

See also Games; Lunch Boxes.

12" GI JOE FIGURES

Action Pilot, complete w/accessories, EX, C6 ....$129.00

Action Soldier, complete w/accessories, EX, C6.............$215.00

Action Soldier, complete w/accessories, MIB, C6 ....$325.00

Air Adventurer, blond, bearded, hard hands, orange flight suit w/insignia, boots, holster & pistol, EX, C6 ....$89.00

Air Force Cadet, complete w/accessories, EX, C6 ....$345.00

Air Police, complete w/accessories, EX, C6 ....$265.00

Atomic Man (no copter), camo shirt, brn shorts, EX, C6 ..$45.00

Australian Jungle Fighter, complete w/accessories & outfit, NM, C6 ....$269.00

Black Action Soldier, complete w/accessories, NM, C6.$649.00

Black Adventurer, tan shirt & pants, decal, boots, holster & pistol, EX, C6 ....$125.00

British Commando, complete w/accessories, EX, C6......$299.00

Combat Construction, complete w/accessories, EX, C6 .$325.00

Combat Marine, complete w/many accessories, EX, C6 .$245.00

Copter Rescue, w/bl flight suit, boots & camera, EX, C6 .$75.00

Danger Ray Detection, w/gray suit, bl pants, magnetic ray detector, solar communicator, EX, C6 ....$85.00

Deep Sea Diver, complete w/accessories, EX, C6 ....$185.00

Fight for Survival, w/brn shirt & pants, Australian bush hat, machete, EX, C6 ....$95.00

French Resistance Fighter, complete w/accessories, NM, C6 .$259.00

German Stormtrooper, complete w/accessories, EX, C6.$325.00

Green Beret, w/scarf (hand-painted silk), EX, C6 ....$225.00

Heavy Weapons, complete w/accessories, NM, C6 ....$329.00

High Voltage Escape, w/silver net jumpsuit, boots, face shield, sign, wire cutters & belt, EX, C6 ....$89.00

Intruder Commander, #8050, M (EX card), C6..............$150.00

Japanese Imperial Soldier, complete w/accessories, EX, C6.$600.00

Man of Action, #7284, Kung Fu grip, shirt, pants, boots & rifle, VG+ (VG+ box), C6 ....$149.00

Marine Flame Thrower, complete w/accessories, EX, C6 .$185.00

Military Police, complete w/accessories, NM, C6...........$245.00

Navy Attack, complete w/accessories, EX, C6................$225.00

Navy Machine Gunner, complete, EX, C6 ....$195.00

Race Car Driver, EX, C6 ....$129.00

Russian Infantry Man, red hair, rare, NM (EX box), $2,800.00; British/Canadian Commando, blond hair, rare variation, professional repair, NM (EX box), $1,800.00.

Scuba Diver, complete w/accessories, VG+, C6 ....$175.00

Shore Patrol, w/helmet, complete w/accessories, EX, C6.$265.00

Shore Patrol, w/sailor hat, complete w/accessories, EX, C6.$195.00

State Trooper, EX, C6 ....$349.00

Talking Action Soldier, complete w/accessories, EX, C6.$149.00

Talking Astronaut, blond hair, with instructions and insert, EX (VG+ box), A, $300.00.

Talking Team Commander, brn beard, dog tags, voice, EX, C6..$125.00

Tank Commander, radio w/incomplete decals & no tripod o/w EX, C6 ....$295.00

US Marine Dress Blues, complete w/accessories, EX, C6 .$169.00

West Point Cadet, wht rifle, complete w/accessories, EX, C6..$265.00

ACCESSORIES FOR 12" GI JOE

Action Pilot Scramble Helmet, #7810, MOC, C6 ....$225.00

Adventure Foot Locker, EX, C6......................................$49.00

Adventure of the Secret Mission to Spy Island, #7922, 1969, M (NM sealed box), C6...$565.00

Adventure of the 8 Ropes of Danger, #7950, 1969, M (NM sealed box), C6 ....$525.00

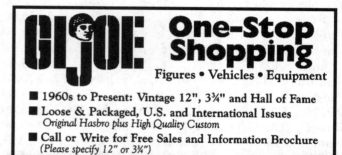

Air Force Academy Dress Cap, EX, C6 ....$5.00
Air Force Academy Epaulette, EX, C6............................$20.00
Air Force Academy M1 Rifle, wht, Action Man, EX, C6...$8.00
Air Force Academy M1 Rifle, wht, EX, C6......................$20.00
Air Force Academy Sash, EX, C6....................................$65.00
Air Force Academy Shoes, EX, C6, pr..............................$8.00
Air Force Academy Shoulder Belt, EX, C6.....................$65.00
Air Force Academy Sword & Scabbard, EX, C6.............$25.00
Air Force Academy Trousers, Action Man, EX, C6 ....$20.00
Air Force Academy Trousers, EX, C6.............................$45.00
Air Force Academy Tunic, EX, C6 ....$75.00
Air Force Dress Cap, EX, C6 ....$20.00
Air Force Dress Cap (hard), EX, C6................................$5.00
Air Force Dress Shoes, EX, C6, pr...................................$8.00
Air Force Dress Trousers, EX, C6...................................$15.00
Air Force Dress Tunic, no bars or wings, EX, C6............$25.00
Air Force Dress Tunic, w/bars & wings, EX, C6.............$45.00
Air Force Shirt, EX, C6...$15.00
Air Force Tie, EX, C6..$18.00
Air Police Helmet, EX, C6 ....$45.00
Air Vest, orange plastic, EX, C6.....................................$11.00
Ammo Box, gr, Action Man, EX, C6 ....$5.00
Ammo Box, gr, GI Joe logo, EX, C6.................................$8.00
Ammo Box, Russian, EX, C6...$25.00
Ammo Box, US Navy, bl, EX, C6....................................$20.00
Ammo Pouch, German, EX, C6..$8.00
Ammo Pouch, Japanese, EX, C6.....................................$10.00
Ammo Pouch, US, EX, C6 ....$3.00
Annapolis Cadet's Belt, EX, C6 ....$70.00
Annapolis Cadet's Cap, EX, C6......................................$15.00
Annapolis Cadet's M1 Rifle, wht, Action Man, EX, C6.....$8.00
Annapolis Cadet's M1 Rifle, wht, EX, C6 ....$20.00
Annapolis Cadet's Sword & Scabbard w/Slings, EX, C6..$80.00
Annapolis Cadet's Trousers, Action Man, EX, C6 ....$20.00
Annapolis Cadet's Trousers, EX, C6 ....$45.00
Annapolis Cadet's Tunic, EX, C6....................................$95.00
Aqua Foot Locker, EX, C6...$49.00
Argyle & Sutherland Highlanders' Puttee, Action Man, EX,
   C6..$15.00
Argyle & Sutherland Highlanders' Tunic, Action Man, VG,
   C6 ....$45.00
Argyle's Kilt, Action Man, EX, C6 ....$40.00
Army Sweater, gr, Action Man, EX, C6............................$5.00
Astronaut Boots, plastic, EX, C6, pr...............................$12.00
Astronaut Chest Pack, Propellant Gun & Tether Cord, EX,
   C6..$23.00
Astronaut Flight Suit, wht, EX+, C6..............................$49.00
Astronaut Flight Suit, wht, no flap, VG+, C6 ....$28.00
Astronaut Gloves, EX, C6, pr..$12.00
Astronaut Helmet, no mike, EX, C6 ....$10.00
Astronaut Helmet, w/mike, EX, C6 ....$30.00
Astronaut Pack, EX, C6...$12.00
Astronaut Propellant Gun & Wand, EX, C6...................$10.00
Astronaut Soft Booties, EX, C6, pr $12.00
Astronaut Suit, 1 zipper, EX, C6 ....$20.00
Astronaut Suit, 2 zippers, EX, C6 ....$25.00
Astronaut Suit, 3 zippers, EX, C6 ....$30.00
Astronaut Tether Hose, EX, C6 ....$7.00

Australian Belt, EX, C6...$15.00
Australian Entrenching Tool, EX, C6...............................$5.00
Australian Hat, EX, C6..$30.00
Australian Jacket, no chevrons, EX, C6..........................$25.00
Australian Jacket, w/chevrons, EX, C6 ....$45.00
Australian Jungle Fighter Equipment, #8305, MOC, C6 .$325.00
Australian Medal, Victoria Cross, EX, C6......................$15.00
Australian Shorts, EX, C6...$22.00
Australian Sock, EX, C6, ea..$15.00
Bag w/Ammo Strip, Action Man, EX, C6.........................$4.00
Bandolier, Action Man, EX, C6..$4.00
Battle of Britain Flying Helmet, no O2 mask, Action Man, EX,
   C6..$30.00
Battle of Britain Jacket, Action Man, EX, C6.................$20.00
Battle of Britain Life Vest, Action Man, EX, C6 ....$30.00
Battle of Britain Trousers, Action Man, EX, C6 ....$8.00
Bayonet, Japanese, Hasbro orig, EX, C6.........................$65.00
Bayonet, US, Hasbro orig, EX, C6..................................$25.00
Bazooka, EX, C6..$20.00
Bazooka, gr, Action Man, EX, C6 ....$18.00
Bazooka Shell, EX, C6..$4.00
Beachhead Assault Field Pack, #7713B, MOC (no sticker),
   C6..$69.00
Belt, brn web, Action Man, EX, C6 ....$3.00
Belt, gr web, Action Man, EX, C6....................................$6.00
Belt, gr web, EX, C6..$10.00
Belt, gr web, w/ammo pouches, EX, C6...........................$15.00
Belt, tan web, EX+, C6..$12.00
Belt, w/ammo pouch, US, Action Man, EX, C6 ....$4.00
Belt, w/ammo pouch, wht, G+, C6..................................$12.00
Belt, web, w/canteen & cover, EX, C6.............................$22.00
Belt, web, w/first-aid pouch, EX, C6...............................$16.00
Belt, web, w/45 holster, Action Man, EX, C6..................$10.00
Billy Club, EX, C6...$5.00
Binoculars, red or blk, EX, C6, from $6 to.......................$7.00
Bivouac Machine Gun, #7514, MOC, C6 ....$60.00
Bivouac Sleeping Bag, #7515, MOC, C6 ....$52.00
Bivouac Tent Set, #7516, complete w/accessories, M (VG box),
   C6...$1,050.00
Boots, blk, short, EX, C6, pr...$7.00
Boots, blk, tall, Action Man, EX, C6, pr...........................$7.00
Boots, blk, tall, EX, C6, pr..$12.00
Boots, brn, short, EX, C6, pr...$30.00
Boots, German/Russian, EX, C6, pr................................$35.00
Bouy, Breeches; EX, C6...$55.00
British Belt, EX, C6 ....$15.00
British Canteen, EX, C6...$20.00
British Canteen Cover, EX, C6..$18.00
British Gas Mask, EX, C6..$30.00
British Gas Mask Satchel, Action Man, EX, C6 ....$5.00
British Gas Mask Satchel, EX, C6...................................$30.00
British Helmet, EX, C6..$20.00
British Jacket, EX, C6..$39.00
British Medal, Action Man, EX, C6..................................$8.00
British Medal, Victoria Cross, EX, C6.............................$15.00
British Military Police Armband, EX, C6..........................$5.00
British Military Police Cap, EX, C6 ....$8.00
British Officer's Cap, w/badge, EX, C6.............................$7.00

British Sten Gun, Action Man, no clip, EX, C6 ....$5.00
British Sten Gun, no clip, EX, C6 ....$25.00
British Trousers, EX, C6 ....$28.00
Bunk Bed, Action Man, EX, C6 ....$25.00
Bunk Bed, EX, C6 ....$39.00
Camera, box style, EX, C6 ....$4.00
Camera, movie, EX, C6 ....$5.00
Canteen, Action Man, EX, C6 ....$2.00
Canteen, EX, C6 ....$5.00
Canteen & Cover, Hasbro, EX, C6 ....$16.00
Canteen & Cover, plastic, Action Man, EX, C6 ....$6.00
Cap, gr fatigue, EX, C6 ....$5.00
Capture of the Pygmy Gorilla, #7437, M (EX+ box), C6.$249.00
Carbine, Action Man, EX, C6 ....$10.00
Carbine, w/orig sling, EX+, C6 ....$22.00
Carbine, w/rpl sling, Hasbro, EX, C6 ....$16.00
Chest, blk, EX, C6 ....$3.00
Chest, Trans-Polar, Action Man, EX, C6 ....$5.00
Clipboard, no pencil, EX, C6 ....$20.00
Clipboard Pencil, EX, C6 ....$5.00
Combat Camouflage Netting Set, #7511, MOC, C6........$21.00
Combat Field Jacket Set, #7502, complete w/accessories, M
    (NM box), C6..$250.00
Combat Knuckle Knife, EX, C6....................................$5.00
Combat Mess Kit, #7509, MOC, C6 ....$50.00
Combat Sandbags Set, #7508, MOC, C6......................$28.00
Command Post Poncho, #7519, MOC, C6 ....$55.00
Command Post Poncho Set, #7516, complete w/accessories, M
    (NM box), C6..$169.00
Communications Field Set, #7703, MOC, C6 ....$85.00
Compass, Action Man, EX, C6......................................$2.00
Crash Crew Boots, silver, EX, C6, pr............................$12.00
Crash Crew Gloves, EX, C6, pr $20.00
Crash Crew Hood, EX, C6..$8.00
Crash Crew Set, #7820, MIP, C6 ....$300.00
Crash Crew Trousers, silver, EX, C6 ....$20.00
Crash Crew Tunic, silver, EX, C6 ....$30.00
Crash Crew Utility Belt, w/3 tools, EX, C6..................$24.00
Dangerous Climb, #7309E, 1973, M (EX box), C6..........$30.00
Deep Freeze Boots, wht, EX, C6, pr............................$10.00
Deep Freeze Parka, EX, C6 ....$45.00
Deep Freeze Supply Sled, EX, C6 ....$12.00
Deep Freeze Trousers, EX, C6 ....$24.00
Demolition, #7370, M (NM box), C6..........................$85.00
Desert Patrol Driver's Jacket, EX, C6..........................$125.00
Desert Survival, Action Outfit, M (EX card), C6............$30.00
Detonator, EX, C6 ....$7.00
Devil of the Deep, #7439, MIB (sealed), C6..................$195.00
Diver's Air Hose & Gauge, EX, C6 ....$10.00
Diver's Belt, covered weights, EX, C6 ....$17.00
Diver's Belt, exposed weights, EX, C6..........................$22.00
Diver's Bouy, EX, C6..$4.00
Diver's Gloves, EX, C6, pr $5.00
Diver's Helmet & Collar, GI Jo logo, EX, C6 ....$20.00
Diver's Helmet & Collar, no logo, EX, C6....................$14.00
Diver's Suit, G-, C6..$5.00
Diver's Weighted Shoes, EX, C6, pr............................$10.00
Dog Tag, metal, Action Man, EX, C6............................$15.00

Dog Tag, metal, EX, C6..$20.00
Dog Tag, plastic, Adventure Team, EX, C6....................$14.00
Dog Tag, plastic, child's, GI Joe, EX, C6......................$35.00
Duffle Bag, Action Man, EX, C6 ....$6.00
Duffle Bag, VG, C6 ....$7.00
Dynamite, EX, C6, per stick..$.50

Emergency Rescue, GI Joe Adventure Team, 1972-75, MIB, $70.00.

Engineer's Transit & Tripod, EX, C6 ....$80.00
Entrenching Tool & Cover, Hasbro, EX, C6 ....$25.00
Fangs of the Cobra, #8028, M (EX card), C6................$125.00
Fatigues, camo, EX+, C6..$20.00
Fatigues, gr drab, Action Man, EX+, C6 ....$10.00
Fatigues, olive drab, VG, C6..$15.00
Field Jacket, EX, C6 ....$25.00
Field Telephone, brn, EX, C6 ....$9.00
Field Telephone, brn camo, EX, C6 ....$15.00
Field Telephone, gr camo, EX, C6 ....$100.00
Field Telephone, gray, EX, C6......................................$37.00
Fight for Survival, Action Outfit, complete w/accessories, 1975,
    M (NM card), C6 ....$30.00
Fighter Pilot's Helmet, gold, EX, C6 ....$95.00
Fire Axe, gr, EX, C6 ....$5.00
Fire Axe, red, EX, C6 ....$9.00
Fire Extinguisher, chemical, EX, C6............................$20.00
Fire Extinguisher, sm, EX, C6......................................$12.00
Firefighting Backpack, water container w/hose & nozzle, EX,
    C6 ....$18.00
Fireman's Helmet, Action Man, EX, C6........................$12.00
First-Aid Box, EX, C6..$12.00
First-Aid Case, Action Man, EX, C6..............................$3.00
First-Aid Pouch, gr, EX, C6 ....$7.00
Flag, Army, Marines, Air Force, Navy or Stars & Stripes, Hasbro
    orig, EX, C6 ....$35.00
Flame Thrower, camo, EX, C6 ....$17.00
Flashlight, red, EX, C6 ....$9.00
Footlocker, wood, w/tray & illus, EX, C6 ....$39.00
French Beret, EX, C6..$35.00
French Jeans, EX, C6 ....$18.00
French Machine Gun, EX, C6 ....$12.00
French Medal, EX, C6 ....$15.00
Gas Mask Shoulder Bag, Action Man, EX, C6 ....$5.00
German Belt, w/ammo pouch, EX, C6 ....$20.00
German Grenade, EX, C6 ....$8.00

German Holster, Action Man, EX, C6.........................$5.00
German Holster, EX, C6...$10.00
German Jacket, EX, C6..$37.00
German Luger, Action Man, EX, C6..........................$5.00
German Medal, Action Man, EX, C6.........................$10.00
German Medal, EX, C6...$20.00
German Officer's Cap, Action Man, EX, C6..............$10.00
German Officer's Cavalry Trousers, Action Man, EX, C6 .$10.00
German Officer's Jacket, Action Man, EX, C6 ....$8.00
German Pack, Action Man, EX, C6...........................$5.00
German Pack, EX, C6...$19.00
German Schmeisser, Action Man, EX, C6 ....$20.00
German Schmeisser, EX, C6....................................$45.00
German Stormtrooper's Equipment, #8300, MOC, C6..$285.00
German Stormtrooper's Jacket, Action Man, EX, C6 ......$10.00
German Trousers, EX, C6.......................................$28.00
Goggles, Action Man, gr, EX, C6...............................$6.00
Goggles, gr, wht trim, EX, C6...................................$8.00
Grease Gun MP45, Action Man, EX, C6.....................$5.00
Green Beret Hat, blk, w/badge, EX, C6.....................$22.00
Green Beret Hat, dk bl, EX, C6................................$18.00
Green Beret Scarf, EX, C6......................................$65.00
Green Beret Shirt, EX+, C6 ....$36.00
Green Beret Trousers, EX+, C6................................$25.00
Green Beret Weapons, complete, 1993, M $6.50
Grenade, US, EX, C6...$.50
Grenade Launcher, no sling, Action Man, EX, C6..........$10.00
Grenade Launcher, w/rpl sling, EX, C6.....................$20.00
Grenadier Guard's Bayonet & Scabbard, wht, Action Man, EX,
   C6...$8.00
Grenadier Guard's Jacket, Action Man, EX, C6.............$13.00
Harpoon, EX, C6...$5.00
Heavy Weapons Flak Vest, EX, C6 ....$69.00
Helicopter Pilot's Coveralls, Action Man, EX, C6 ....$8.00
Helmet, camo, EX, C6...$32.00
Helmet, gr, EX, C6..$25.00
Hunting Rifle, Action Man, EX, C6 ....$2.00
Hurricane Spotter, #7343, 1975, M (rare VG 11x13x½" box),
   C6..$49.00
Ike Jacket, Military Police, brn, EX, C6 ....$25.00
Japanese Bayonet, EX, C6......................................$65.00
Japanese Belt, w/2 ammo pouches, EX, C6 ....$39.00
Japanese Helmet, EX, C6..$20.00
Japanese Holster, EX, C6..$35.00
Japanese Medal, EX, C6..$70.00
Japanese Nambu Pistol, EX, C6...............................$49.00
Japanese Pack, EX, C6..$30.00
Japanese Shirt, EX, C6..$10.00
Jettison to Safety, #7332, Canadian, M (EX- box), C6 ..$119.00
Jungle Ordeal, Action Outfit, MOC, C6 ....$30.00
Karate, #7372, M (EX box), C6...................................$95.00
Landing Signal Officer, #7621, MIP, C6.....................$575.00
Landing Signal Officer, #7626B, MOC (no sticker), C6..$112.00
Landing Signal Officer's Coveralls, EX+, C6 ....$55.00
Landing Signal Officer's Headgear, complete, EX, C6......$60.00
Landing Signal Officer's Paddle, EX, C6, ea $18.00
Lewis Gun & Tripod, Action Man, EX, C6.....................$10.00
Life Raft, blk w/anchor, EX, C6................................$20.00

Life Ring, #7627, MOC, C6 ....$45.00
Life Ring, EX, C6...$25.00
Life Vest, orange, padded, EX, C6 ....$18.00
Life Vest, yel, padded, EX+, C6...............................$40.00
Lifeguard's Cuirass, back & front, Action Man, EX, C6...$50.00
Lifeguard's Helmet, Action Man, EX+, C6.................$45.00
Lifeguard's Jacket, Action Man, EX, C6 ....$15.00
Lifeguard's Shoulder Pouch, Action Man, EX, C6..........$45.00
Machete & Scabbard, EX, C6....................................$9.00
Machine Gun, M30, w/tripod, EX, C6.......................$18.00
Machine Gun, M60, w/bipod, EX, C6........................$60.00
Map & Case, orange, EX, C6....................................$14.00
Marine Dress Parade Set: Photo Box, #7710, wht belt & rifle,
   VG (VG box), C6...$775.00
Marine Flame Thrower Set, #7718B, MOC, C6...............$80.00
Marine Parachute Pack, #7709B, no helmet sticker, MOC,
   C6..$72.00
Marine Paratrooper Helmet Set, #7707, MOC, C6.........$55.00
Marine Small Medic Set, #7720, MOC, C6...................$80.00
Medic Bag, EX, C6..$15.00
Medic Bandage, EX, C6..$1.00
Medic Crutch, EX, C6..$8.00
Medic Plasma Bottle, EX, C6...................................$12.00
Medic Red Cross Armband, EX, C6...........................$12.00
Medic Red Cross Helmet, EX, C6.............................$45.00
Medic Splint, EX, C6..$1.00
Medic Stethoscope, EX, C6.....................................$12.00
Medic Stretcher, EX, C6..$25.00
Mess Kit, EX, C6..$10.00
Military Police Armband, EX, C6..............................$22.00
Military Police Billy Club, EX, C6 ....$5.00
Military Police Helmet, EX+, C6...............................$40.00
Military Police Helmet & Small Arms, #7526, MOC, C6 ..$80.00
Military Police Scarf, EX, C6....................................$30.00

Military Police
Set, #7521, MIB,
from $1,000.00
to $1,200.00.

Military Police Set, #7521, complete w/accessories, M (EX box),
   C6...$1,000.00
Military Police Trousers, #7525, brn, MOC, C6...............$70.00
Military Police Trousers, EX, C6...............................$20.00

Mine, EX, C6 ....$4.00

Mine Detector & Harness, EX, C6 ....$35.00

Mine Shaft Breakout, #7331, Canadian, M (EX- box), C6 .$119.00

Mortar, Action Man, EX, C6 ....$39.00

Mortar, complete (no shells), EX, C6 ....$49.00

Mortar, no chain, EX, C6 ....$45.00

Mortar Shell, EX, C6 ....$5.00

Motorcyclist's Boots, Action Man, EX, C6 ....$10.00

Mountain Troops, #7530, MIP, C6 ....$185.00

MP Duffle Bag, #7523, MOC, C6 ....$40.00

Mystery of the Boiling Lagoon, #7431-16, VG+ (VG+ box),
    C6 ....$165.00

Navy Attack, #7607, MIP, C6 ....$189.00

Navy Frogman, #7602, M (EX sealed photo box), C6 ....$850.00

Navy Frogman, #7602A, M (EX- sealed window box), C6 .$825.00

Navy Frogman Accessories, #7605A, MOC, C6 ....$50.00

Navy Frogman Scuba Tanks, #7606, MOC, C6 ....$45.00

Nurse's Dress, EX, C6 ....$225.00

Pack, gr or winter wht, EX+, C6, ea $23.00

Paddle, blk, EX, C6 ....$6.00

Parachute, orange, Action Man, EX, C6 ....$8.00

Parachute, red & wht, EX, C6 ....$20.00

Parachute, reserve, Action Man, EX, C6 ....$4.00

Parachute Pack, gr, cloth, EX+, C6 ....$29.00

Parachute Pack, w/chute, bl, plastic, EX, C6 ....$35.00

Parachute Pack, w/chute, gr, plastic, EX, C6 ....$65.00

Parka, red, Action Man, EX, C6 ....$5.00

Parka, red, US Flag, EX, C6 ....$20.00

Peril of the Raging Inferno, #7416, MIB, C6 ....$325.00

Photo Recon, Action Outfit, 1975, MOC, C6 ....$30.00

Pick, EX, C6 ....$5.00

Pilot's Cap, bl, EX, C6 ....$14.00

Pilot's Flight Suit, gray, EX+, C6 ....$37.00

Pilot's Flight Suit, orange, w/waist tabs, EX, C6 ....$32.00

Pilot's G-Pants, EX, C6 ....$150.00

Pilot's Helmet, blk, SAS, Action Man, EX, C6 ....$20.00

Pilot's Helmet, gold, w/visor, no O2 mask, EX, C6 ......$35.00

Pilot's O2 Mask & Hose, attachments broken, EX, C6 ....$5.00

Pilot Survival Set, #7801, MIP, C6 ....$950.00

Pistol, Lebel revolver, Action Man, EX, C6 ....$3.00

Pith Helmet, EX, C6 ....$8.00

Poncho, gr or camo, EX+, C6, ea $25.00

Projectile, 106mm, EX, C6 ....$8.00

Pup Tent, EX, C6 ....$6.00

Race-Car Driver's Coveralls, EX, C6 ....$19.00

Race-Car Driver's Helmet, EX, C6 ....$35.00

Radiation Detection, #7341, MIB, C6 ....$75.00

Radio, backpack; bl, EX, C6 ....$50.00

Radio, backpack; gr or camo, EX, C6, ea $25.00

Rescue Ring, EX, C6 ....$25.00

Rifle, Action Man, M1, EX, C6 ....$8.00

Rifle, M1, Hasbro orig, EX, C6 ....$20.00

Rifle, M16, Action Man, EX, C6 ....$12.00

Rifle, M16, Hasbro orig, EX, C6 ....$20.00

Rifle, NATO FLN, Action Man, EX, C6 ....$4.00

Rifle Rack, EX, C6 ....$12.00

Royal Canadian Mounted Police Sam Browne Belt, EX, C6 .$45.00

Royal Canadian Mounted Police Stetson, EX, C6 ....$30.00

Russian Ammo Box, EX, C6 ....$15.00

Russian Ammo Clip, EX, C6 ....$10.00

Russian Anti-Tank Grenade, EX, C6 ....$15.00

Russian Belt, EX, C6 ....$20.00

Russian Binoculars, w/brn case, EX, C6 ....$45.00

Russian Fur Hat, EX, C6 ....$65.00

Russian Infantry Equipment, #8302, MOC, C6 ....$250.00

Russian Machine Gun Bipod, EX, C6 ....$30.00

Russian Medal, EX, C6 ....$20.00

Russian Trousers, EX, C6 ....$29.00

Russian Tunic, EX, C6 ....$38.00

Sabotage Set, #7516A, complete w/accessories, M (NM box),
    C6 ....$1,075.00

Sailor's Cap, EX, C6 ....$10.00

Sailor's Cap, Hong Kong mk, EX, C6 ....$5.00

Sailor's Dress Parade Set, #7619A, MOC, C6 ....$73.00

Sailor's Dress Tunic, w/tie, full underarm zipper, EX, C6 .$37.00

Sailor's Dungarees, EX+, C6 ....$15.00

Sailor's Shirt, EX+, C6 ....$20.00

Sandbag, lg, EX, C6 ....$4.00

Sandbag, sm, EX, C6 ....$2.00

Scramble Pilot's Air Vest & Accessories, #7809, MOC, C6 ...$90.00

Scramble Pilot's Helmet, wht, EX, C6 ....$95.00

Scramble Pilot's Parachute Pack, #7811, MOC, C6 ....$70.00

Scuba Bottoms, #7604, MOC, C6 ....$59.00

Scuba Bottoms, blk, EX, C6 ....$34.00

Scuba Fins, EX, C6, pr $3.00

Scuba Headpiece, blk, VG-, C6 ....$18.00

Scuba Mask, blk, rpl strap, EX, C6 ....$6.00

Scuba Tanks, silver, EX, C6 ....$15.00

Scuba Tanks, wht, Action Man, EX, C6 ....$5.00

Scuba Top, blk, EX, C6 ....$34.00

Sea Bag, EX+, C6 ....$22.00

Sea Hammer, EX, C6 ....$12.00

Sea Rescue Set, #7601, MIP, C6 ....$950.00

Search for the Abominable Snowman, #7430, MIB (sealed),
    C6 ....$295.00

Secret Agent, Action Outfit, 1975, MOC, C6 ....$30.00

Shoes, dress, EX, C6, pr $10.00

Shore Patrol Armband, EX, C6 ....$25.00

Shore Patrol Dress Pants, #7614, MOC, C6 ....$75.00

Shore Patrol Helmet, EX+, C6 ....$45.00

Shore Patrol Helmet Set, #7616B, MOC (no sticker), C6 .$85.00

Shore Patrol Sea Bag, #7615, MOC, C6 ....$40.00

Shore Patrol Set, #7612A, rare version w/shoes, M (VG box),
    C6 ....$900.00

Shoulder Holster (blk) & Revolver, EX, C6 ....$25.00

Shovel, EX, C6 ....$6.00

Signal Lamp, plastic lens, EX, C6 ....$10.00

Signal Pistol, Action Man, EX, C6 ....$2.00

Signal Pistol, EX, C6 ....$4.00

Ski Poles, EX, C6, pr $20.00

Skis, EX, C6, pr $35.00

Sleeping Bag, EX+, C6 ....$16.00

Slicker Bottom, Breeches Bouy, EX, C6 ....$30.00

Sniper Patrol, Defender's Outfit, #9028B, rifle missing, EX card,
    C6 ....$9.00

Snow Troop Bear Parka, EX, C6 ....$25.00

Snow Troop Boots, blk, EX, C6, pr $10.00
Snow Troop Trousers, EX, C6 ....$12.00
Snowshoes, red, EX, C6, pr $25.00
Snowshoes, wht, EX, C6, pr $15.00
Sock, dk brn, EX, C6, ea $8.00
Sonic Rock Blaster, #7312, MOC, C6 ....$28.00
Space Boots, Action Man, EX, C6, pr $5.00
Space Capsule w/Flotation Collar, #5979A, Sears edition, complete w/accessories, NM (NM box), C6 ....$565.00
Spare Tire, Desert Tan, EX, C6 ....$7.00
Spare Tire, gr, EX, C6 ....$5.00
Sten Gun, no clip, Action Man, EX, C6 ....$5.00
Sterling Submachine Gun, no clip or sling, Action Man, EX, C6 ....$3.00
Stocking Cap, plastic, EX, C6 ....$8.00
Supply Sled, G-, C6 ....$8.00
Sweater, blk, EX, C6 ....$9.00
Swimming Trunks, Navy bl, EX, C6 ....$9.00
Tank Commander's Beret, Action Man, EX, C6 ....$5.00
Tank Commander's Helmet, Action Man, EX, C6 ....$20.00
Tank Commander's Helmet, EX, C6 ....$100.00
Tank Commander's Leather Jacket, EX, C6 ....$60.00
Tank Commander's Radio & Tripod, EX, C6 ....$100.00
Tent, gr or camo, no stakes or poles, EX, C6, ea $12.00
Tent Stakes & Poles, EX, C6 ....$7.00
Trousers, bl, Action Man, EX, C6 ....$2.00
Trousers, jeans, Action Man, EX, C6 ....$3.00
Underwater Knife & Scabbard, EX, C6 ....$10.00
United Nations Beret, Action Man, EX, C6, ea $12.00
US Air Force Dress Uniform Set, #7803, MIP, C6 .....$1,900.00
US Marine Dress Blues, complete w/accessories, EX, C6 .$169.00
USMC Dress Cap, EX, C6 ....$7.00
USMC Trousers, EX+, C6 ....$23.00
Volcano Jumper, #7344, M (EX+ box), C6 ....$75.00
Walkie-Talkie, EX, C6 ....$6.00
West Point Cadet's Trousers, Action Man, EX, C6 ....$20.00
West Point Cadet's Trousers, EX, C6 ....$45.00
West Point Cadet's Tunic, EX, C6 ....$70.00
West Point Shako & Plume, EX, C6 ....$10.00
West Point Shoulder Belt, Action Man, EX, C6 ....$32.00
West Point Sword & Scabbard, EX, C6 ....$25.00
Wire Roll, copper, EX, C6 ....$6.00
Wire Roll, gray, EX, C6 ....$3.00
Wrist Depth Gauge, EX, C6 ....$8.00
Wristwatch, EX, C6 ....$5.00

1964-1969 Paperwork

Air Force Manual, lg, EX $6.00
Air Force Manual, sm, EX $6.00
Army Manual, came w/boxed dolls, sm, EX $6.00
Army Manual, lg, EX $3.00
Counter Intelligence Manual, sm, EX $25.00
Fold-Out Equipment List for Army, Marine, Pilot or Sailor, EX, ea $3.00
Marine Manual, came w/boxed dolls, sm, EX $6.00
Marine Manual, lg, EX $4.00

Navy Manual, lg, EX $4.00
Navy Manual, sm, EX $6.00
Official Gear & Equipment Manual, all color pictures, EX..$5.00

Vehicles for 12" GI Joe

Badger Attack Jeep, Hall of Fame, 1991, MIP $12.00
Chest Winch, #7313, M (NM card), C6 ....$28.00

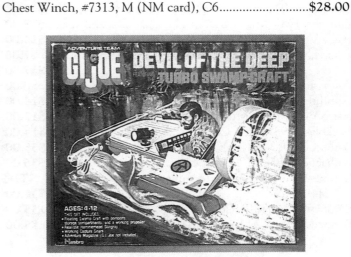

Devil of the Deep Set with Turbo Swamp Craft, 1974-75, MIB, $195.00.

Drag Bike, Action Pack, #7364, red & chrome, Canadian, M (EX box), C6 ....$95.00
Frogman & Sea Sled, #8050, complete w/accessories, NM (NM box), C6 ....$449.00
German Staff Car, #5652, complete w/accessories, Irwin produced, EX (NM brn shipping carton), C6 ....$695.00
Helicopter, #7380, M (NM sealed box), C6 ....$225.00
Ice Sabre Arctic Assault Vehicle, Hall of Fame, 1991, MIP.$15.00
Rescue Raft, gr hard plastic pack w/compass, 2-pc paddle, orange raft, EX, C6 ....$35.00

Space Capsule, with authentic space suit, with record and instructions, M (VG+ box), A, $225.00.

Underwater Explorer, Action Pack, #7354, 1-man underwater sled, Canadian, M (EX+ box), C6 ....$75.00
Windboat, #7353, bl, plastic, Canadian, M (EX box), C6..$75.00
5-Star Jeep & Trailer, #7000, complete w/accessories, EX (G box), C6 ....$385.00

3¾" GI JOE FIGURES

Ace, w/accessories, 1983, C6 ....$16.00
Ace, w/ID card, 1983, M (in factory bag), H4 ....$27.00
Airborne, no ID card o/w complete w/accessories, 1983, VG+,
   H4 ....$16.00
Airborne, 1983, MIP, C6...$47.00
Airtight, no ID card o/w complete w/accessories, 1984, VG+ .$10.00
Airtight, 1985, MIP, C6 ....$38.00
Alley Viper, 1989, M (pkg faults), C6.................................$14.00
Alpine, w/backpack & pick only, 1984, VG+ $7.00
Alpine, 1985, MIP, C6 ....$37.00
Ambush, 1990, M (pkg faults), C6 ....$8.00
Annihilator, 1989, MIP, C6 ....$14.00
Astro Viper, 1988, MIP, C6 ....$12.00
Backblast, 1989, MIP, C6 ....$14.00
Barbecue, 1983-85, MOC, from $25 to $35.00
Barbecue, 1985, MIP, C6...$36.00
Baroness, no ID card o/w complete w/accessories, 1984, VG+,
   H4 ....$30.00
Baroness, 1984, MIP, C6 ....$135.00
Barracuda, 1985, M (pkg faults), C6...................................$5.00

BATS, 1986, missing 3 aim attachments, $8.00.

BATS, w/accessories, 1986, C6 ....$12.00
Battle Corp Bazooka, 1993, M (pkg faults), C6 ....$4.00
Battle Corp Beach-Head, 1993, M (pkg faults), C6............$4.00
Battle Corp Cross-Country, 1993, MIP, C6 ....$5.00
Bazooka, Tiger Force, 1988, MIP, from $18 to.................$25.00
Bazooka, 1983-85, MOC, H4 ....$25.00
Bazooka, 1985, MIP, C6 ....$35.00
Beachhead, 1983-85, MOC, H4...$22.00
Beachhead, 1986, MIP, C6..$33.00
Big Boa, 1987, MIP, C6 ....$25.00
Black Major, Action Force, MIP, C6 ....$7.50
Blades, 1983, MIP, C6 ....$10.00
Blaster, English, MIP, C6 ....$20.00
Blizzard, w/accessories, 1988, C6..$8.00
Blocker, English, 1987, MIP, C6 ....$20.00
Blowtorch, 1984, M (pkg faults), C6....................................$33.00

Breaker, Japanese, 1983, MIP, C6 ....$22.00
Breaker, 1983, MIP, C6 ....$58.00
Budo, complete w/accessories, 1988, VG+, H4...............$6.00
Budo, 1988, M (pkg faults), C6 ....$16.00
Bullhorn, 1990, MIP, C6 ....$14.00
Buzzer, 1985, M (pkg faults), C6 ....$28.00
Captain Grind-Iron, 1990, MIP, C6......................................$11.00
Charbroil, red or blk eyes, MIP, C6, ea $18.00
Chuckles, w/accessories, 1987, EX, C6 ....$7.00
Chuckles, 1987, MIP, C6...$23.00
Clutch, w/accessories, 1982, EX, C6 ....$20.00
Cobra Commander, Action Force, 1983, EX $35.00
Cobra Commander, w/battle armor, 1987, MIP, C6........$29.00
Cobra Commander/Hood, mail-order, no ID card o/w complete
   w/accessories, 1983, VG+, H4 ....$18.00
Cobra FANG, w/accessories, 1983, C6 ....$10.00
Cobra Hiss Driver, w/ID card, 1982, M (in factory bag), H4 .$15.00
Cobra Officer, no ID card o/w complete w/accessories, 1982,
   VG+, H4 ....$10.00
Cobra Officer, 1983, M (pkg faults) $62.00
Cobra Soldier, w/accessories, 1982, C6 ....$18.00
Cobra Soldier, 1983, MIP, C6 ....$72.00
Cobra Stinger Driver, w/ID card, 1982, M (in factory bag),
   H4..$15.00
Copperhead, w/ID card, 1984, MIP, H4..............................$10.00
Countdown, 1989, M (pkg faults), C6 ....$14.00
Crankcase, w/accessories, 1985, EX, C6 ....$14.00
Crankcase, w/ID card, 1985, M (in factory bag) $24.00
Crazylegs, no ID card o/w complete w/accessories, 1987, VG+,
   H4..$4.00
Crazylegs, no weapons or accessories, 1987, G, C6 ....$5.00
Crazylegs, 1986, MOC, H4...$12.00
Crimson Guard, 1985, MIP, C6..$42.00
Croc Master, 1987, M (pkg faults), C6................................$22.00
Cross-Country, w/accessories, 1986, C6 ....$8.00
Crystal Ball, complete w/accessories, 1986, VG+, H4 ....$7.00
Crystal Ball, 1987, MIP, C6..$15.00
Dee-Jay, complete w/accessories, 1988, VG+, H4...............$6.00
Dee-Jay, 1989, M (pkg faults), C6 ....$10.00
Deep Six, 1989, M (pkg faults), C6 ....$11.00

Dial-Tone, 1983, MIP, $30.00.

Dial-Tone, no weapons or accessories, 1986, G, C6 ....$6.00
Doc, 1983, M (pkg faults) $38.00
Dojo, 1992, MIP, C6 ....$12.00
Duke, Tiger Force, no ID card o/w complete w/accessories, 1988, VG+, H4 ....$4.00
Duke, 1984, MIP, C6 ....$105.00
Duke, 1992, MIP, C6 ....$10.00
Duke First Sergeant, mail-order figure, no ID card o/w complete w/accessories, 1983, VG+, H4 ....$16.00
Dusty, no ID card or bipod, o/w complete w/accessories, 1984, VG+, H4 ....$5.00
Dusty, 1985, M (pkg faults), C6 ....$30.00
Eels, 1985, M (pkg faults), C6 ....$45.00
Falcon, 1987, MIP, C6 ....$25.00
Fast Draw, 1987, M (pkg faults), C6 ....$21.00
Ferret, w/accessories, 1988, EX, C6 ....$8.00
Firefly, 1984, MIP, C6 ....$110.00
Flak-Viper, 1992, M (pkg faults), C6 ....$7.00
Flash, no ID card o/w complete w/accessories, 1982, VG+, H4 ....$20.00
Flash, 1982, EX (orig pkg) $65.00
Flint, 1985, M (pkg faults), C6 ....$45.00
Footloose, no ID card o/w complete w/accessories, 1984, VG+, H4 ....$7.00
Footloose, Slaughter's Marauders, 1989, MIP, C6 ....$20.00
Footloose, 1985, MIP, C6 ....$36.00
Frag-Viper, 1989, MIP, C6 ....$14.00
Frostbite, w/ID card, 1985, M (in factory bag), H4 ....$10.00
General Flagg, 1992, MIP, C6 ....$6.00
General Hawk, w/sonic jet pack & file card, 1994 Convention, MIP, C6 ....$10.00
Glider, w/Spirit, 1992, MIP, C6 ....$15.00
Gnawgahyde, 1989, M (pkg faults), C6 ....$14.00
Golobulus, no ID card o/w complete w/accessories, 1987, VG+ $10.00
Grunt, no ID card o/w complete w/accessories, 1982, VG+, H4 ....$20.00
Grunt, no ID card o/w complete w/accessories, 1983, VG+, H4 ....$16.00
Grunt, 1983, M (pkg faults), C6 ....$42.00
Gung-Ho, 1986, MOC $18.00
Gyro-Viper, w/accessories, 1987, C6 ....$8.00
Hardball, 1988, M (pkg faults), C6 ....$14.00
Hawk, 1986, MIP, C6 ....$46.00
Headhunters, w/rocket launcher, 1992, MIP, C6 ....$6.00
Heavy Duty, 1991, MIP, C6 ....$10.00
Heavy Metal, complete w/accessories, 1985, VG+ $22.00
HISS Driver, w/accessories, 1983, C6 ....$13.00
Hit & Run, 1988, MIP, C6 ....$22.00
Hydro-Viper, w/accessories, 1988, C6 ....$7.00
Ice Sabre, 1991, MIP, C6 ....$12.00
Iceberg, w/ID card, 1986, M (in factory bag), H4 ....$10.00
Iceberg, 1983-85, MOC $32.00
Iceberg, 1986, M (pkg faults), C6 ....$22.00
Iron-Grenadiers, 1988, G (no weapons or accessories), C6 ....$4.00
Jinx, w/ID card, 1987, M (in factory bag), H4 ....$10.00
Jinx, 1987, M (pkg faults), C6 ....$22.00

Keel-Haul, Admiral USS Flagg, complete w/accessories, 1985, VG+ $34.00
Keel-Haul, w/ID card, 1989 mail-order figure, M (in factory bag), H4 ....$10.00
Knockdown, English, 1989, MIP, C6 ....$22.00
Lady Jaye, India, 1985, M (pkg faults), C6 ....$15.00
Lady Jaye, 1985, M (pkg faults), C6 ....$70.00

Lady Jaye, 1985, missing camera, $25.00.

Lampreys, complete w/accessories, 1985, VG+, H4 ....$8.00
Lampreys, w/ID card, 1985, M (in factory bag), H4 ....$10.00
Laser-Viper, 1990, MIP, C6 ....$12.00
Law & Order, no ID card or dog, o/w complete w/accessories, 1987, VG+ $5.00
Leatherneck, 1983-85, MOC, H4 ....$25.00
Leatherneck, 1986, M (pkg faults), C6 ....$22.00
Lifeline, no ID card o/w complete w/accessories, 1985, VG+, H4 ....$7.00
Lifeline, Tiger Force, 1988, MIP, C6 ....$18.00
Lifeline, 1986, MIP, C6 ....$35.00
Lift Ticket, 1986, M (pkg faults), C6 ....$25.00
Lightfoot, 1988, MIP, C6 ....$18.00
Low-Light, Slaughter's Marauders, 1989, M (pkg faults), C6..$13.00
Low-Light, 1983-85, MOC, H4 ....$22.00
Low-Light, 1986, MIP, C6 ....$32.00
Mainframe, 1986, M (pkg faults), C6 ....$22.00
Major Bludd, w/accessories, 1983, EX, C6 ....$16.00
Mercer, figure only, 1987, VG $5.00
Mercer, 1990, MOC, H4 ....$12.00
Monkey Wrench, w/accessories, 1986, EX, C6 ....$7.00
Monkey Wrench, 1983-85, MOC, H4 ....$20.00
Motorviper, w/ID card, 1986, M (in factory bag), H4 ....$10.00
Motorviper, 1986, M (pkg faults), C6 ....$17.00
Muskrat, figure only, 1988, VG, H4 ....$2.00
Muskrat, 1988, MIP, C6 ....$18.00
Muton, Action Force, MIP, C6 ....$5.00
Mutt & Junkyard, Slaughter's Marauders, 1989, MIP, C6..$20.00
Mutt & Junkyard, 1984, M (orig pkg), C6 ....$30.00
Night Creeper, 1990, M (orig pkg), C6 ....$10.00
Outback, w/accessories, 1987, EX, C6 ....$7.00

Overlord, w/accessories, 1990, C6 ....$6.00
Pathfinder, 1990, MIP, C6.......................................$11.00
Polar Battle Bear, 1983, EX (orig pkg), C6 ....$25.00
Psyche-Out, complete w/accessories, 1987, VG+, H4........$6.00
Psyche-Out, 1987, MOC $22.00
Python Patrol Trooper, 1989, MIP, C6 ....$13.00
Q Force Aqua Trooper, Action Force, MIP, C6 ....$7.50
Q Force Deep Sea Defender, Action Force, MIP, C6 ....$7.50
Quick Kick, w/accessories, 1985, EX, C6 ....$10.00
Range-Vipers, 1990, MIP..$11.00
Raptor, 1986, MOC $20.00
Recoil, no weapons or accessories, 1989, G, C6.................$4.00
Recoil, 1989, MIP, C6 ....$15.00
Recondo, no weapons or accessories, 1984, EX, C6..........$10.00
Recondo, 1983-85, MOC, H4 ....$25.00
Red Star, 1991, MIP, C6..$8.00
Repeater, 1988, MIP, C6 ....$21.00
Rip Cord, no weapons or accessories, 1984, G, C6 ....$10.00
Ripper, no ID card o/w complete w/accessories, 1984, VG+,
 H4 ....$7.00
Ripper, 1985, MIP, C6...$36.00
Road Pig, 1988, M (pkg faults), C6 ....$17.00
Roadblock, Tiger Force, 1988, M (pkg faults), C6............$18.00
Roadblock, w/accessories, 1984, EX, C6 ....$16.00
Roadblock, w/machine gun & tripod only, 1986, VG+, H4 .$7.00
Roadblock, 1984, MIP, C6 ....$48.00
Roadblock, 1986, MIP, C6 ....$36.00
Rock-Viper, 1990, MIP, C6.......................................$15.00
Rolling Thunder, English, 1988, MIP, C6 ....$29.00
Royal Guard, figure only, 1987, VG $7.00
Rumbler, no weapons or accessories, 1987, G, C6 ....$9.00
Salvo, 1990, M (pkg faults), C6.....................................$8.00
SAW Viper, complete w/accessories, 1989, VG+, H4........$5.00
SAW Viper, figure only, 1990, VG, H4 ....$2.00
SAW Viper, 1990, MIP, C6 ....$12.00
Sci-Fi, missing ID card & hose o/w complete w/accessories,
 1986, VG+, H4 ....$5.00
Sci-Fi, 1986, MIP, C6 ....$32.00
Scoop, w/accessories, 1989, C6 ....$6.00

Scrap Iron, 1984, missing several accessories, $10.00.

Scrap Iron, 1984, MIP, C6.......................................$42.00
Sea Slug (Sea Ray Driver), complete w/accessories, 1987,
 VG+ $10.00
Sgt Slaughter, mail-order figure, complete w/accessories, 1985,
 VG+, H4 ....$20.00
Sgt Slaughter, Slaughter's Marauders, 1989, MIP, C6 ......$18.00
Shipwreck (w/parrot), 1985, MIP, C6 ....$60.00
Shockwave, English, 1988, MIP, C6 ....$15.00
Short Fuse, mail-order figure, 1983, MIP, H4 ....$28.00
Short Fuse, no ID card o/w complete w/accessories, 1982, VG+,
 H4 ....$20.00
Sky Hawk, 1984, M (pkg faults), C6 ....$18.00
Sky Sharc, 1990, MIP, C6 ....$20.00
Slice, 1992, MIP, C6..$15.00
Slip Stream, w/accessories, 1986, EX, C6......................$10.00
Snake Armor, w/accessories, bl, 1984, EX, C6................$25.00
Snake Eyes, no ID card o/w complete w/accessories, 1985, VG+,
 H4 ....$25.00
Snake Eyes, w/accessories, 1982, VG+, H4 ....$45.00
Snake Eyes, w/accessories, 1985, EX, C6......................$20.00
Snake Eyes, 1985, MIP, C6 ....$110.00
Sneak Peak, Night Force, no ID card o/w complete w/acces-
 sories, 1987, VG+ $12.00
Sneak Peak, 1987, M (pkg faults), C6...........................$17.00
Snow Job, no accessories, 1983, VG $9.00
Snow Job, 1983, MIP, C6 ....$45.00
Snow Serpent, 1983-85, MIP, C6/H4, from $46 to $58.00
Space Engineer, Action Force, MIP, C6 ....$7.50
Space Security Trooper, Action Force, MIP, C6 ....$7.50
Spearhead & Max, 1988, MIP, C6 ....$18.00
Special Mission Brazil Leatherneck, no weapons or accessories,
 C6..$18.00
Spirit, 1984, MIP, C6...$45.00
Stalker, w/accessories, 1982, C6 ....$20.00
Steel Brigade, mail-order figure, no ID card o/w complete w/
 accessories, 1984, rare, VG+, H4 ....$25.00
Steeler, 1983, MIP, C6...$38.00
Storm Eagle, 1992, MIP, C6 ....$12.00
Storm Shadow, no ID card o/w complete w/accessories, 1988,
 VG+, H4 ....$7.00
Strato Viper, w/accessories, 1986, EX, C6.....................$10.00
Stretcher, 1990, M (pkg faults), C6..............................$12.00
Sub-Zero, 1990, MIP, C6..$12.00
Swampmasher, 1988, MIP, C6 ....$14.00
T'Jbang, 1992, M (pkg faults), C6 ....$8.00
Talking Battle Commander General Hawk, w/Sonic Voice Back
 Pack, gold, 1991, MIP, C6 ....$12.00
Techno-Viper, 1987, MIP, C6.....................................$23.00
Tele-Vipers, w/accessories, 1985, EX, C6.......................$9.00
Thrasher, no weapons or accessories, 1986, EX, C6...........$6.00
Tiger Shark, Tiger Force, 1988, MIP, C6 ....$18.00
Topside, 1990, M (pkg faults), C6................................$10.00
Torch, 1985, MIP, C6..$37.00
Torpedo, w/flipper & oxygen tank only, 1983, VG+ $11.00
Torpedo, 1983, EX (orig pkg)....................................$47.00
Toxo-Viper, 1988, M (pkg faults), C6...........................$14.00
Tripwire, no ID card o/w complete w/accessories, 1983, VG+,
 H4 ....$10.00

Tripwire, Tiger Force, 1988, M (pkg faults), C6 ....$14.00
Tripwire, 1983, M (pkg faults), C6..............................$38.00
Tunnel Rat, 1987, M (pkg faults), C6.............................$22.00
Undertow, w/accessories, 1990, C6 ....$5.00
Voltar, Action Force, Great Britain, 1989, MOC, H4 .....$20.00
Wetsuit, complete w/accessories, 1986, VG+ $13.00
Wild Bill, w/accessories, 1983, EX, C6............................$14.00
Wild Weasel, w/accessories, 1984, EX, C6........................$18.00
Windchill, no weapons or accessories, 1989, G, C6............$5.00

Zandar, 1986, no accessories, $4.00.

Zandar, 1986, MIP, C6 ....$18.00
Zanzibar, complete w/accessories, 1985, VG+, H4..............$8.00
Zap, 1983, MIP, C6..$58.00
Zarana, no ID card o/w complete w/earrings & accessories, 1986, VG+ $15.00
Zarana, no ID card or earrings o/w complete w/accessories, 1984, VG+ $6.00

ACCESSORIES FOR 3¾" GI JOE

Air Defense Battle Station, 1985, EX (orig pkg), C6 ....$12.00
Air Defense Pack, 1985, MIP $15.00
Ammo Dump Unit, 1985, EX (orig pkg), C6....................$10.00
Battle Gear Accessory Pack #1, 1983, MIP.......................$16.00
Bivoac Battle Station, w/accessories, 1983, EX..................$7.00
Bomb Disposal Unit, 1985, MIP...$8.00
Enemy Battle Gear, Action Force, MIP, C6 ....$3.00
Forward Observer Unit, w/accessories, 1985, EX, C6 ....$8.00
Missile Defense Unit, 1984, MIP $20.00
Mountain Howitzer, w/accessories, 1984, EX.....................$8.00
Q Force Battle Gear, Action Force, MIP, C6.......................$3.00
SAS Parachutist Attack, Action Force, MIP.......................$25.00
Sky Patrol Airwave, w/parachute pack, 1990, MIP, C6....$18.00
Sky Patrol Drop Zone, w/parachute pack, brn, 1990, MIP, C6.$18.00
Space Force Battle Gear, Action Force, MIP, C6 ....$3.00
Transportable Tactical Battle Platform, w/accessories, 1985, EX, C6 ....$22.00

VEHICLES FOR 3¾" GI JOE

Air Commando Glider, w/Cloudburst, 1990, MIP, C6.....$12.00

Aircraft Carrier USS Flagg, w/Admiral Keel-Haul, 1984, MIP $250.00
Amphibious Personnel Carrier, 1983, M (pkg faults), C6 ..$46.00
Arctic Blast, w/Windchill, 1989, EX (orig pkg), C6 ....$15.00
Battle Copter, w/Ace, bl, 1992, MIP, C6.............................$10.00
Chameleon Swamp Skier, w/Zartan, w/accessories, 1984, M (M box)..$95.00
Cobra Battle Copter, w/Heli-Viper, pk, 1992, MIP, C6 .....$9.00
Cobra Feret ATV, 1985, MIP...$8.00
Cobra Jet Skystriker (XP-14F), w/Ace & accessories, 1983, EX, C6 ....$32.00
Cobra Stellar Stiletto, w/Star-Viper, 1988, EX (orig pkg), C6.$21.00
Cobra Stun Vehicle, w/Motorviper, 1986, MIP..............$41.00
Cobra Water Moccasin, w/Copperhead, 1984, MIP $50.00
Darklon's Evader, w/Darklon, 1989, MIP, C6..................$26.00
Desert Fox 6WD Jeep, w/Skidmark, Night Force, Toys 'R Us, 1988, MIP..$33.00
Devilfish Attack Boat, 1986, MIP.....................................$15.00
Dragonfly Assault Helicopter, w/Wild Bill, 1983, EX (orig pkg) $80.00
Dragonfly Assault Helicopter, w/Wild Bill, 1983, MIP ..$100.00
Dreadnok Cycle, 1987, MIP $17.00
Eliminator 4WD Vehicle, Battle Force 2000, 1987, MIP .$25.00
FLAK Attack Cannon, 1982, MIP.....................................$25.00
LCV Recon Sled, 1986, EX (orig pkg), C6 ....$12.00
Mauler Tank MBT (no driver), w/accessories, 1985, C6 ..$15.00
Motorized Battle Wagon, 1991, MIP, C6...........................$32.00
Mudbuster, 1993, EX (orig pkg), C6..................................$8.00
Night Boomer, Attack Jet, 1989, MIP................................$55.00
RAM Motorcycle, 1982, MIP...$45.00
Roboskull, w/Air Wolf, Action Force, M (pkg faults), C6 .$24.00
Silent Attack Kayak, Action Force, M (pkg faults), C6 ...$25.00
Sky Hawk, VTOL Copter, 1984, MIP................................$18.00
Slugger (no driver), w/accessories, 1984, C6....................$12.00
Snow Cat Artic Vehicle, w/Frostbite, 1985, MIP $40.00
Space Capsule, w/outfit, accessories & soundtrack of Mercury flight, complete, EX+ (orig box), T2..........................$98.00
Tiger Cat, w/Frostbite, Tiger Force, 1988, MIP $25.00
Vamp Mark II, Convention '93, MIP, C6..........................$14.00
Vector Jet, Battle Force 2000, 1987, MIP $25.00
Whale Hovercraft w/Cutter, 1984, MIP.............................$70.00
Whirlwind Twin Battle Gun, 1983, MIP............................$32.00
Wolverine Armored Missile Vehicle, w/Cover Girl, w/accessories, 1983, MIP $75.00

MISCELLANEOUS

Gun and Holster Set, Halco, 1950s, 6½" Hubley .45 cap gun in leather holster, M (EX box), A, $200.00.

Signal Flasher, battery-operated, MIB, O1, $45.00.

Volcano Jumper, MIB, $85.00.

Guns

Until WWI, most cap guns were made of cast iron. Some from the 1930s were nickel-plated, had fancy plastic grips and were designed with realistic details like revolving cylinders. After the war, a trend developed toward using cast metal, a less expensive material. These diecast guns were made for two decades, during which time the TV western was born. Kids were offered a dazzling array of weapons, endorsed by stars like the Lone Ranger, Gene, Roy and Hoppy. Sales of space guns, made popular by Flash Gordon and Tom Corbett, kept pace with the robots coming in from Japan. Some of these early tin lithographed guns were fantastic futuristic styles that spat out rays of sparks when you pulled the trigger. But gradually the space race lost its fervor, westerns were phased out, and guns

began to be looked upon with disfavor by the public in general and parents in particular. Since guns were meant to see lots of action, most will show wear. Learn to be realistic when you assess condition; it's critical when evaluating the value of a gun.

Advisor: Bill Hamburg (H1); Jim Buskirk (B6), BB Guns.

MISCELLANEOUS

Hubley Automatic Tommy Gun, 10", EX, $25.00.

Aids Atomic Airblaster Space Gun, w/target, EX, J2 ....$60.00
BCM Space-Outlaw Atomic Pistol, 1960s, diecast w/bright silver finish, movable front sight, 10", MIB.................$200.00
BCM Space-Outlaw Atomic Pistol, 1960s, diecast w/bright silver finish, movable front sight, 10", VG $125.00
Boyville Texan Jr Cap Gun & Holster, NP w/ivory plastic grip, tooled leather holster, NM (G box)........................$125.00
Chinese Space Gun, 1980s, litho tin w/flint action, red dome on top mk MF 227, 6½", MIB, P4 ....$25.00
Cordeice Industries Tripod Machine Gun, 1950s, plastic & diecast w/aluminum barrel, fires roll caps, 31", M ...$100.00
Daisy #72 Squirt-O-Matic, early, EX, J2 ....$50.00
Diamond Pellet Gun, shoots 50 reloadable pellets, brn & blk plastic, 4", MOC, A...$30.00
Esquire Action Miniatures No 10 Authentic Derringer, 1960s, cap pistol, diecast w/bronze finish, 2", MOC, P4.......$15.00
Esquire Action Miniatures No 11 Official Snub Nose 38, 1960s, cap pistol w/spinning chamber, diecast, 2", MOC, P4..$15.00
Esquire Pony Boy Cowboy Outfit, dbl leather holster w/2 cap guns, NM (EX+ box), A..$250.00
Futuristic Products Strato Repeater Cap Gun, ca 1950, heavy metal space gun, 9", unused, M (EX box) $400.00
Futuristic Products Strato Repeater Cap Gun, ca 1950, heavy metal space gun, 9", NM (G box) $275.00
Haji Atomic Gun, 1969, red, gray & yel litho tin w/plastic muzzle, sparking action, 9", M, P4 ....$55.00
Haji Over & Under Reciprocating Ray Gun, 1960s, litho tin & plastic, 8½", flint not working o/w VG, P4 ....$40.00
Halco Texan Holster Set w/Cap Guns, 2 8" cap guns w/leather grips, emb leather dbl holster, M (M window box) .$100.00
Hamilton Smoking Cheyenne Shooter Cap Gun, metal w/simulated pearl grips, 9½", unused, NM+ (VG+ box).......$75.00
Hiller Atom Ray Gun, 1930s, cast-metal water gun w/Atom Ray Gun emb on water tank, 6", EX $300.00
Hubley Army .45 Cap Gun, blk metal w/wht plastic inset grips, 6½", unused, M (G box)..$125.00
Hubley Atomic Disintegrator Cap Gun, 1930, EX, R7 ..$350.00

Hubley Authentic Colt Gun Replicas, Colt 45 '1860' w/6 cap-loading cartridges, Colt Detective Special, M (EX+ box)..**$375.00**

Hubley Automatic Cap Pistol No 290, diecast w/NP finish, brn checked grips, 6½", VG **$75.00**

Hubley Cap Pistol, plastic horsehead grip, 7", EX, $55.00.

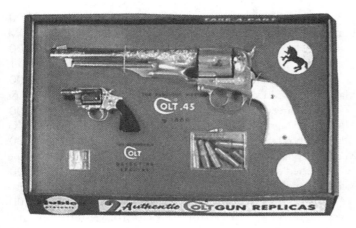

Hubley Colt Replicas, Western Colt .45 of 1860, gold-tinted chamber, with 6 cartridges, 14", and Detective Special with 6 bullets, 4", both metal with plastic grips, M (EX+ box), $375.00.

Hubley Colt .45 Cap Pistol, 1959, diecast, ivory grips, revolving cylinder w/open chamber ends, 13", NMIB **$250.00**

Hubley Cowboy Gold-Plated Classic Pistol, longhorns on blk plastic grips, 11½", unused, M (scarce EX+ box).....**$200.00**

Hubley Cowboy Jr Cap Gun, 1950s, diecast w/wht plastic steer grips, 9", EX **$75.00**

Hubley Cowboy Repeating Cap Pistol, NP w/longhorns on ivory plastic inset grips, 12", MIB....................**$175.00**

Hubley Dagger Derringer, over & under w/slide-out dagger in barrel, barrel flips to load cartridges, 6¾", NM **$75.00**

Hubley FBI Jr Holster Set, 1950s, 6½" Trooper cap gun in leather holster mk FBI Jr w/Sgt Eddy signature, MIB **$100.00**

Hubley Flintlock Pistol No 280, 1954, NP finish, brn swirl plastic stock, single action 2-shot, dbl barrel, 9", M **$50.00**

Hubley Patrol Cap Pistol, NP CI w/brn grips, 6", G, A **$30.00**

Hubley Pirate Cap Pistol, 1950, side-by-side flintlock style w/diecast fr & plastic grips, dbl hammers & trigger, VG, P4...........**$65.00**

Hubley Ric-o-Shay Cap Gun, heavy metal w/flip-out cylinder, blk plastic grip, makes ricochet noise, 12", M (EX+ box) .**$225.00**

Hubley Rifleman Flip Special, 1959, NP, brn plastic stocks, ring-lever action fires single or rapid fire, 32", VG, P4 ...**$165.00**

Hubley Rodeo Cap Gun, metal w/ivory plastic grips, 7", unused, MIB **$75.00**

Hubley Scout Rifle, 1959, diecast w/brn plastic stocks, western scenes on both sides of fr, lever action, 36", VG, P4 .**$75.00**

Hubley Smoking Texan Jr Cap Pistol, NP CI w/emb steer on plastic pearly inset grips, 9", NM (VG+ box), A.....**$100.00**

Hubley Smoking Texan Jr Cap Pistol, NP CI w/emb steer on plastic pearly inset grips, 9", unused, M (EX+ box).**$150.00**

Hubley Texan Pistol, gold-plated metal cap gun with longhorn relief on black plastic grip, 9", M (EX+ box), $200.00.

Hubley Texan Cap Pistol, diecast w/NP finish, blk plastic steer head grips, revolving cylinder, 9½", VG, P4 ....**$85.00**

Hubley Victory Army .45 Play Cap Gun, Army .45 emb on blk metal barrel, ivory grips, 6½", unused, NM (EX box), A **$80.00**

Ives Clown on Powder Keg Cap Pistol, 1892, cast iron, hinged clown figure falls toward grip, ornate molded patterns, 3¾", VG, $450.00.

J&E Stevens Automatic Repeating Cap Pistol, NP CI, 4⅜", NMIB, A..**$110.00**

Kadet Civil War Pistol Musket, Savannah Tenn, wood & metal, w/ramrod, cork, balls, target & stand, 13½", MIB, A..**$100.00**

Kenton Bull's-Eye Cap Gun, 1940, blk w/hat & spurs on ivory plastic grips, 6½", M (EX box w/orig price tag) **$175.00**

Kenton Law Maker Cap Pistol, 1930s, cast iron with plastic inset grips, rare, 8½", M (EX+ box), $175.00.

Kenton Lightning Express Animated Cap Pistol, cast iron, working, 4¾", VG, $175.00; Ives Butting Heads Animated Cap Pistol, black monochrome on cast iron, working, 4¾", VG, $450.00.

Kenton Magic 22 Caliber Blank Pistol, NP & japanned CI, 6¼", VG, A **$40.00**

Keystone Bros Lasso 'Em Bill Holster Set, 2 gold-tone cap guns w/blk grips in dbl lt tan leather holsters, 11", MIB ..**$400.00**

Kilgore American Cap Gun, 1930s, CI w/emb eagles on plastic ivory grips, spinning cylinder, 9½", rare, EX............**$400.00**

Kilgore Buck Cap Pistol, scrolled metal w/antlered deer on grips, 7", unused, MIB **$75.00**

Kilgore Champion Fast Draw Pistol, 1950s, cap gun w/timer in grip which records your draw time, M (EX+ box) ...**$150.00**

Kilgore Eagle 6-Shooter Cap Gun, scrolled metal w/flying eagle emb on grips, 8", unused, MIB......................**$75.00**

Kilgore Invincible Cap Gun, NP CI, buffed finish, 6½", G .**$40.00**

Kilgore Long Tom Disk Cap Pistol & Holster, 1930s, NP CI w/ivory plastic grips, studded holster, 10½" rare, EX, A **$425.00**

Kilgore Longboy Cap Gun, NP CI, working, 11", EX, A..**$110.00**

Kilgore Machine Gun, 1930s, NP CI, orig lever, 5½", NM, A **$165.00**

Kilgore Mascot Automatic 50-Shot Repeater Cap Pistol, 1936, NP CI, 3⅞", unfired, MIB, P4 ....**$110.00**

Kilgore Ranger Cap Pistol, metal, plastic inset grip w/emb cowboy, 9", unused, MIB.................................**$75.00**

Kilgore Rawhide Cap Whip, ca 1960, plastic tube w/cap insert fires when rawhide whip is cracked, 15", MIP, P4 .....**$45.00**

Kilgore Western Squirt Pistol, red plastic, 8", unused, NMIB, J2..**$65.00**

KO Mars Rifle, litho tin w/red plastic barrels, fires w/sparking action & sound, friction, VG (worn box), A.............**$65.00**

KO Space Pilot X-Ray Gun, shoots sparks w/gun noise, plastic, 8½", M (EX box), A......................................**$150.00**

KO Space Super Jet Gun, 1957, litho tin & plastic, sparking action, reciprocating bullet in barrel, 9½", MIB, P4..**$125.00**

Kusan Astro Zapper No 64B, late 1970s(?), blk plastic guns fires red plastic balls, 12", MIB (sealed), P4......................**$35.00**

Langson Super-Numatic Paper Popper, 1950s, diecast w/gray metal finish, fires roll paper, 6½", VG.......................**$45.00**

Leslie-Henry Texas Ranger Star Gun & Holster Set, 1950s, gold finish w/blk plastic grips, brn plastic holster, NMIB, P4 ...**$135.00**

Lone Star Miniature Tommy Gun, 1960s, diecast, fires single shot caps & plastic bullets, 6½", NMOC, P4.............**$15.00**

Lone Star Scout Cap Pistol, diecast w/red plastic grips, 7", NM (EX+ box), A...**$100.00**

Marklin Coastal Defense Gun, olive gr pnt metal w/brass barrel, intricate breech to fire sm charge, 10", VG **$400.00**

Marklin Coastal Defense Gun, olive gr pnt metal w/brass barrel & plated direction & elevating adjustments, 6", G+, A.**$160.00**

Marushin Magnum Force 44 Magnum Cap Gun, chrome, VG (orig box), S2 ....**$175.00**

Marx Airplane Cap Pistol, 1950s, blk hard plastic jet shape attached to gun hdl, 9½", rare, NM (EX box), A **$150.00**

Marx Army Pistol #45, ca 1940, blk tin w/blk & red plastic spinning cylinder, yel & red hdl, 9", EX (EX box) **$125.00**

Marx Blaze Away Dart Pistol, ca 1950, tin western-type gun shoots suction darts, 9", unused, M (EX box), A **$130.00**

Marx Blue & Gray Shell Shooting Civil War Cavalry Pistol, 1960, plastic w/diecast works, 10", MOC.................**$125.00**

Marx Commando Cap Gun, features simulated lever to switch from semiautomatic to fully automatic, 13", EX+ (EX box) **$75.00**

Marx Famous Firearms Deluxe Edition, 1959, set of 9 miniature historic guns w/4 holsters, M (EX box) **$100.00**

Marx Miniature Sharps Carbine, Famous Firearms Series, 1960s, diecast w/blk finish, brn plastic stock, 7¼", MOC, P4.**$15.00**

Marx Patrol Leader Infantry Carbine, plastic, fires wooden bullets, 21½", MOC, P4....................................**$75.00**

Marx Rex Mars Planet Patrol Flashlight Gun, plastic, clicks while shooting beam of light, battery-op, NM (EX box) **$175.00**

Marx Rex Mars Planet Patrol Space Rifle, 22", EX **$200.00**

Marx Thundergun Rifle, 1960s, brn & blk plastic w/diecast works, 36", NMIB, P4.......................................**$125.00**

Marx Thundergun Western Revolver Cap Gun, smokes w/super sound, emb ivory plastic grips, 12", MIB.................**$275.00**

Marx Wild West Cap Rifle, ca 1959, w/telescope sight, 27", M (VG box) **$100.00**

Marx Wild West Cap Rifle, w/sight, 30", NM, J2...........**$100.00**

Marx WWSA-05 Special Mission Tommy Gun, 1960s, bl & brn plastic, folding stock, friction, 20", MOC, P4 ....**$75.00**

Mattel Agent Zero-M Movie Shot, 1965, plastic w/diecast works, barrel extends & fires, w/up, 8", VG, P4.........$65.00

Mattel Agent Zero-M Snap-Shot Camera Pistol, 1964, plastic w/diecast works, M (NM box), M5 ....$80.00

Mattel Agent Zero-W Rapid Fire Special Rifle, 1965, blk plastic w/brn stocks, crack noise when fired, 26", NM, P4....$75.00

Mattel Fanner-50 Cap Pistol, 1957, later cartridge-loading version, complete with unopened 'Bullet Pak' of 8 cartridges, M (EX+ box), $250.00.

Mattel Fanner-50 Cap Pistol w/Swivelshot Trick Holster, 1950s, 6 cartridge-loading bullets, 10½", NM (EX box)..........$200.00

Mattel Fanner-50 Deputy Holster & Pistol, smoking action, 11", NM (NM box)...$225.00

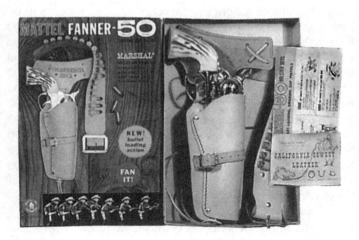

Mattel Fanner-50 Marshal Holster and Pistol Set, 11" pistol with revolving cylinder, with 18 bullets, complete and unused, NM (NM box), $275.00.

Mattel Official Detective Snub-Nose .38 Shootin' Shell Cap Pistol, 1960, diecast, EX, J2 ....$50.00

Mattel Official Detective Snub-Nose .38 Shootin' Shell Cap Pistol, 1960, diecast, blk vinyl shoulder holster, NMIB, P4 ....$165.00

Mattel Shootin' Shell .45 cap pistol, 1960, diecast w/plastic stag grips, 11", VG, P4...$165.00

Mattel Shootin' Shell Buckle Gun Western Belt Set, 1958, gun pops out of belt buckle, MIB $65.00

Mattel Shootin' Shell Fanner Cap Pistol, 1950s, w/spring-loaded bullets in pouch, 9", NM (M box), A $225.00

MT Friction Ray Gun, 1970s, gold plastic w/red & gr windows, 11½", VG, P4...$25.00

Nichols Buccaneer Shell-Firing Flintlock Pistol, 1958, diecast, shoots red plastic bullets, 3½", MOC $50.00

Nichols Dyna-Mite Derringer diecast with nickel finish, white grips, $35.00.

Nichols F-500 Fury Machine Gun, ca 1959, shoots up to 500 caps w/loud machine-gun noise, 28", NM (EX box) $200.00

Nichols Mustang 500 Cap Gun, scrolled barrel & body w/gold-tinted hammer & lever, plastic grip, 12½", M (EX box), A $275.00

Nichols Paint Cap Pistol, 1950s, diecast, flip-out cylinder, 3½", MOC, P4..$35.00

Nichols Stallion .38 Six-Shooter Cap Gun, cartridge loading, w/cartridges, 9½", unused, M (EX+ box), A $157.00

Nichols Stallion .45 Mark II, cartridge-loading gun w/interchangeable blk & pearly grips, w/cartridges, M (EX box), A...$272.00

Nichols Stallion .45 Six-Shooter Cap Pistol, 1950s, diecast, wht plastic stallion grips w/red jewels, 12", NMIB, P4 ...$285.00

Nichols Stallion 41-40 Six-Shooter Cap Gun, NP w/ivory plastic grips, cartridge loading, 10¼", NM (G box), A..$252.00

Nu-Age Smoke-Ring Space Gun, 1950s, plastic & metal, complete w/3 packs of smoke pellets, 9½", EX+ (EX box) $100.00

Ohio Art AstroRay Flashlight Target Gun, 1950s, M (EX box), A $50.00

Ohio Art Sheriff's Derringer Pocket Pistol, red & silver cast metal, pocket-sz w/cap-loading bullet, MOC............$50.00

Palmer Plastics Cap Firing Space Gun, 1950s, blk plastic w/diecast mechanism, lift-up magazine door, 6", M, P4...............$30.00

Palmer Plastics Ray Gun Water Pistol, 1950s, translucent orange plastic, 5½", M, P4...$20.00

Ranger Cosmic Ray Gun, ca 1950, tin & plastic gun shoots sparks, 9", needs flint, NM (EX box) $150.00

Remco Monkey Division 3-in-1 Monkey Gun, 1964, plastic, fires grenades from spring launcher, battery-op, VG, P4 ....$55.00

Schmidt Patrol Cap Pistol, 1950s, diecast w/copper cross-hatched grips, scrollwork on fr, 10", VG, P4.............$85.00

Stevens Bang-O Cap Pistol, 1938, NP CI, wht plastic grips w/horse head & cowboy, 7", NM, P4.........................$90.00

Stevens Cowboy Cap Pistol & Holster, unfinished CI w/blk holster, 3½", EX, A..$65.00

Stevens Jet Jr Space Cap Gun, 1949, diecast w/silver-coated finish, 6⅜", VG...$175.00

Stevens Peacemaker, NP CI w/emb tenite inset grips, 8½", M (G box)...$175.00

Stevens Rapid Load Cap Pistol, CI snub nose w/diamond-emb hdl, spring mechanism, working, 6¼", G, A.............$65.00

Stevens Scout Cap Gun, CI, buffed finish, 7", G, A.........$20.00

Stevens Spitfire Gun, NP CI w/3 Spitfire planes emb on ivory-colored grips, 5", scarce, MIB, A..............................$160.00

Stevens 49-ER, copper-tone metal w/emb Conestoga wagon & cowboy, jeweled plastic grips, M (EX+ box)............$400.00

TN Atomic Ray Gun, 1950s, gold & silver litho tin, flashing lights & sound, battery-op, 18", scarce, MIB..........$225.00

TN Double Barrel Machine Gun, litho tin, magazine revolves, sparks & sounds, friction, 12½", MIB, A.................$100.00

TN Double Barrel Pirate Pistol, mk Flintlock, brn, silver & gold litho tin w/multiple gun sounds, 12", MIB...............$100.00

TN Sparkling Space Control Ray Gun, 1950s, barrel sparks, litho tin, friction, scarce, NMIB...............................$100.00

Topper/Deluxe Reading Cane Shooter, 1966, blk plastic cane w/gold lion head shoots bullets & grenade, 31", MOC, P4..$55.00

Topper/Deluxe Reading Multi-Pistol 09, 1965, plastic, fires bullets or grenades, NMIB...$75.00

Twentieth Century Products Super Site Magic Bullet Gun, 1950s, plastic, clicker action, 9", VG, P4....................$20.00

USA Jr Sheriff & Ranger Accessories, 1950s, complete w/gun, holster, mask & accessories, NMIB...........................$75.00

USA Ruff & Ready Holster Set, NP gun w/tan longhorn grips w/jeweled holster, 8½", EX+ (EX box), A...............$112.00

Wyandotte Dart Pistol, 1950s, NMIB, J2.........................$75.00

BB Guns

Daisy (Early), break action, wire stock, B6.....................$350.00

Daisy (Early), top lever, wire stock, B6..........................$450.00

Daisy #011, lever action, wood stock, B6..........................$50.00

Daisy #012, break action, wood stock, B6.........................$35.00

Daisy #025, pump action, pistol-grip wood stock, B6.......$35.00

Daisy #025, pump action, straight wood stock, B6............$50.00

Daisy #030, lever action, wood stock, B6..........................$40.00

Daisy #040, military, lever action, wood stock, B6...........$85.00

Daisy #040, military w/bayonet, lever action, wood stock, B6 .$185.00

Daisy #050, copper-plated, lever action, blk wood stock, B6 .$65.00

Daisy #104, dbl barrel, wood stock, B6...........................$300.00

Daisy #106, break action, wood stock, B6.........................$15.00

Daisy #106, pump action, wood stock, B6.......................$100.00

Daisy #107, Buck Jones, pump action, wood stock, B6.....$80.00

Daisy #107, pump action, plastic stock, B6.......................$20.00

Daisy #140, Defender, lever action, wood stock, B6.........$90.00

Daisy #195, Buzz Barton, lever action, wood stock, B6.....$65.00

Daisy Model A, break action, wood stock, B6.................$125.00

Daisy Model B, lever action, wood stock, B6....................$65.00

Daisy Model C, break action, wood stock, B6.................$100.00

Daisy Model H, lever action, wood stock, B6....................$75.00

Daisy Model 102 #36, lever action, wood stock, B6.........$25.00

Daisy Model 1938B, Christmas Story Special Model, B6 .$35.00

Daisy Model 21, 1968, dbl barrel, plastic stock, B6........$175.00

Daisy Model 33 #101, lever action, wood stock, B6.........$25.00

Daisy Model 33 #103, Buzz Barton, B6.............................$95.00

Daisy Model 33 #103, lever action, wood stock, B6.........$75.00

Daisy Model 36 #101, lever action, wood stock, B6.........$25.00

Daisy Model 36 #195, Buzz Barton, lever action, wood stock, B6..$70.00

Daisy Model 38 #100, break action, wood stock, B6........$25.00

Daisy Model 39 #108, lever action, wood stock, B6.........$45.00

Daisy Model 40 #111, Red Ryder, aluminum lever, B6 ....$40.00

Daisy Model 40 #111, Red Ryder, iron lever, B6 ....$50.00

Daisy Model 40 #111, Red Ryder, plastic stock, B6.........$30.00

Daisy Model 94, Red Ryder, 1955, plastic stock, B6........$35.00

Daisy 1000 Shot, lever action, wood stock, B6...............$150.00

Daisy 500 Shot, lever action, wood stock, B6.................$125.00

King (New), break action, wood stock, B6.........................$75.00

King (New), repeater, break action, wood stock, B6 ....$80.00

King #0001, break action, all wood, B6.............................$45.00

King #0002, break action, wood stock, B6.........................$45.00

King #0004, lever action, wood stock, B6..........................$80.00

King #0005, lever action, wood stock, B6..........................$80.00

King #0005, pump action, wood stock, B6.........................$65.00

King #0010, break action, wood stock, B6.........................$30.00

King #0017, break action, wood stock, B6.........................$65.00

King #0021, lever action, wood stock, B6..........................$55.00

King #0022, lever action, wood stock, B6..........................$55.00

King #0024, lever action, wood stock, B6..........................$65.00

King #0055, lever action, wood stock, B6..........................$35.00

King #2136, lever action, wood stock, B6..........................$20.00

King #2236, lever action, wood stock, B6..........................$20.00

King #5533, lever action, wood stock, B6..........................$35.00

King #5536, lever action, wood stock, B6..........................$40.00

King Chicago, break action, all wood, B6........................$100.00

Character

Al Capone Miniature Machine Gun, Victory/Carib, Florida souvenir, diecast, 6", MIB, P4..$18.00

Bat Masterson Gun & Holster Set, Carnell, 1960, w/cane & vest, MIB, J2...$350.00

Batman Escape Gun, Lincoln, 1966, dual-action gun launcher fires bat darts & gyros, plastic & rubber, MOC, A.....$55.00

Billy the Kid Cap Gun, Stevens, NP CI, red star on ivory plastic grips, 6¾", NM...$125.00

Buck Rogers Sonic Ray Flashlight Gun, Norton-Honer, 1952, gr, red & yel plastic, battery-op, 7½", M (EX box), A ..$200.00

Buck Rogers Sonic Ray Gun, Commonwealth, buzzes & flashes, battery-op, complete w/secret code book, 7", scarce, MIB, A $165.00

Buck Rogers XZ-35 Pop Pistol (Wilma's gun), Daisy, 1935, pressed steel w/bl metal finish, 8", VG....................$200.00

Buck Rogers XZ-38 Disintegrator Pistol, Daisy, 1936, pressed steel w/copper finish, G, P4..................................$150.00

Buck Rogers U-238 Atomic Pistol Holster Set, Daisy, 1930s, spark action, 10", no holster otherwise EX (G- box), $450.00; Buck Rogers U-235 Atomic Pistol, metal pop gun, minor paint chips, no sparking action, VG (G box), $375.00.

Buck Rogers XZ-38 Disintegrator Pistol, Daisy, 1936, pressed steel w/copper finish, VG+.....................................$200.00

Buffalo Bill Cap Pistol, Kenton, CI w/long barrel, emb hdl, 13½", VG, A...$120.00

Buffalo Bill Cap Pistol, Stevens, cast iron with tenite grips, unused store stock, 8", M (EX box), $175.00.

Davy Crockett Flintlock Jr Cap Gun w/Dell Comic #631, Halco, 1955, includes fringed leather holster, EX+ (EX box), A..$175.00

Davy Crockett Indian Scout Set, Kilgore, w/Hawkeye cap gun & Indian belt, MOC...$75.00

Dick Tracy Cap Pistol, Hubley, NP CI, 4¼", EX (sealed in orig bubble-pack), A...$55.00

Dick Tracy Jr Pistol, Marx, 1936, blk tin w/decal, 4", M (G box) $150.00

Dick Tracy Shoulder Holster Set, John Henry, plastic & litho tin, MOC, A $70.00

Dragnet Police Outfit, Hubley, 6½" Trooper gun in leather shoulder holster mk Dragnet, w/accessories, MIB, A $150.00

Dragnet Snub Nose Cap Pistol, Knickerbocker, 1960s, plastic & diecast, gold Dragnet & 714 badge on grip, 7", M, P4.$55.00

Flash Gordon Click Ray Pistol, Marx, 1930s, MIB, $275.00.

G-Man Automatic Pistol, Marx, 1930s, blk automatic wind rapid-fire sparking gun, w/label, 4", VG+, A $273.00

G-Man Cap Gun, Kilgore, 1930s, NP CI w/emb G-Man, scarce, EX+, A...$190.00

G-Man Machine Gun, Linemar, moving bullet creates muzzle flash, litho tin, battery-op, 19", MIB.......................$200.00

G-Man Machine Gun, Marx, 1930, sparks w/machine gun noise, tin & wood stock, 24", NM (EX box) $250.00

Gene Autry Cap Pistol, Kenton, NP CI, wht grips w/emb horse & rider, 8¼", never fired, EX, A $200.00

Gene Autry Cap Pistol, Leslie-Henry, 1950s, diecast w/NP finish, wht plastic horse-head grips, 11", NM, P4 ....$200.00

Gene Autry Golden Pistol No 103, Leslie-Henry, 1950s, diecast w/wht plastic grips, lever release, 7½", NMIB, P4 ...$285.00

Gene Autry's Repeating Cap Pistol, Kenton, cast iron with facsimile signature, plastic grips, 8½", EX+ (EX+ box), $250.00.

GI Joe Gun & Holster Set, Halco, 1950s, 6½" Hubley cap gun in tan leather holster mk GI Joe, NM (EX+ box), A...$200.00

Gunsmoke Double Holster Gun Set, Leslie-Henry, copper-clad grips, EX...$25.00

I Spy Official Shoulder Holster Set, Rayline, from 1966 movie, pellet gun & holster, NM (EX card), A $55.00

Hopalong Cassidy Pistol and Spurs, Wyandotte, 1950, cast metal with plastic inset grips, 8½", and metal spurs with longhorn decoration and leather straps, unused, M (EX box), $850.00.

James Bond Goldfinger 100-Shot Repeater Cap Pistol, Lone Star, 1960s, w/silencer, NMIB $150.00

James Bond 007 Cap Gun, Glidrose, 1960s, blk metal w/plastic grips & silencer, 6", NM (EX+ box), A $130.00

James Bond 007 Moonraker Cap Gun, Lone Star, 17", M (NM box), M5 ....$70.00

Johnny Ringo Gun & Holster, Marx, 1960, blk metal, ivory plastic grip, rubber-type holster, 10", NM (EX display card) .$125.00

Johnny West Ranch Rifle, Marx, 1960, repeater w/built-in noisemaker & speaker, 26" $75.00

Kansas Kid Pistol, Cresent Toy, 1970(?), diecast w/blk pnt finish, wht plastic grips, 10½", MIB, P4 ....$55.00

Kit Carson Cap Gun, Kilgore, gold-tone, 10", VG+........$65.00

Kit Carson Cowboy Cap Guns, Pal Tom, 1946, diecast, w/holster, bullets & 2 guns, NM (EX+ box) $150.00

Lone Ranger Cap Gun, Kilgore, 1939, nickel-plated cast iron, early style with Lone Ranger on grips, 8½", EX (G box), $450.00.

Lone Ranger Cap Gun, Steve Larabee, England, ca 1950, metal, inscribed Steve Larabee, 7½", M (EX box), A...........$85.00

Lone Ranger Carbine Cap Rifle, Marx, plastic w/Lone Ranger in script on stock, 26", EX+ (G box), A $150.00

Lone Ranger Rifle, Hubley, 1973, 29", EX, J2..................$90.00

Man From UNCLE Napoleon Solo Cap Pistol, Ideal, 1965, assembles into 27" rifle w/silencer, scope & stock, 7", VG, P4...$135.00

Matt Dillon Marshall Gun & Holster Set, John Henry, w/jail keys, handcuffs & badge, MOC (sealed), J2 ....$145.00

Mickey Mouse Pop Shot Rifle, Durham, 1977, automation pump action w/balls, 1977, MIB, C1....................................$30.00

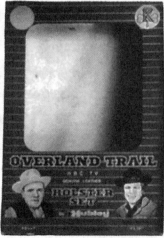

Overland Trail Holster Set, Hubley, 1960, 2 'Flip' cap guns with black simulated leather grips, double leather holster with stagecoach silkscreen, MIB, $400.00.

Popeye Pirate Pistol, Marx, 1935, litho tin w/Popeye as pirate on grip, 10", EX+ (VG box) $450.00

Rambo Motorized M-16 Water Gun, LJN, 1985, MIB, S2.$125.00

Red Ranger Engraved-Gold Repeating, Wyandotte, gold-plated w/lavender-tone grips, NM (EX box).......................$300.00

Rookies Dart Pistol & Scope, Fleetwood, 1975, MOC, H4 ..$8.00

Rookies Official Cap Pistol, Fleetwood, 1975, MOC, H4...$6.00

Roy Rogers' Riders Official Signal Gun, Langson, diecast w/Morse code on grips, 5", rare, non-working o/w EX (VG box), A..$150.00

Roy Rogers Cap Gun, Kilgore, 9", VG, J2......................$125.00

Roy Rogers Cap Pistol, Schmidt, 1950s, diecast w/NP finish, copper grips, 10", G, P4 ....$75.00

Roy Rogers Carbine Cap Rifle, Marx, plastic w/Roy Rogers in script on stock, 26", NM (G box), A $220.00

Roy Rogers Combination Set, Classy Products/Roy Rogers, 1958, complete with pair of 10" cap pistols, double holster, metal spurs and set of metal bullets along with western tie, EX (EX- box), $850.00.

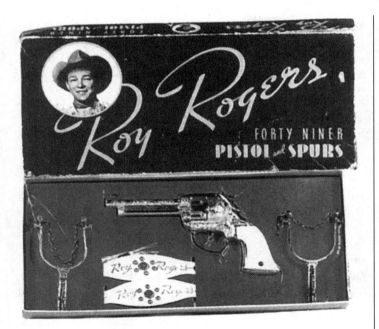

Roy Rogers Forty Niner Pistol and Spurs Set, Leslie-Henry, 9" golden cap pistol with plastic grips, 2 golden spurs with metal chains and wristlets with center simulated jewel, NM (VG+ box), $800.00.

Roy Rogers Shootin' Iron, Kilgore, diecast pistol w/horse heads on simulated pearl grips, 10", NM (EX+ box), A $40.00
Roy Rogers Shootin' Iron, Kilgore, diecast pistol w/Roy & raised image of Trigger on grips, 9", EX (EX box)..............$250.00
Superman Krypto Ray Gun w/Film, Daisy, 1939, pressed steel, Superman emb on barrel, battery-op, 7", NM (EX box).........$650.00
Superman Krypto Ray Gun w/Film, Daisy, 1939, pressed steel, Superman emb on barrel, battery-op, 7", VG $300.00

Superman Krypto Ray Gun, Daisy, 1939, Superman embossed on barrel, battery-operated, 7", NM (EX box), $650.00.

Tom Corbett Atomic Rifle, Marx, futuristic plastic w/telescopic sight, 23", EX+ (VG+ box) $300.00
V (TV Show) .45ER Pistol & Holster, Arco, 1984, w/ricochet sound, MOC, S2 ....$75.00
V (TV Show) Gundam Beam Rifle, Bandai, w/light & sound, S2 ....$75.00
V (TV Show) P.38 pistol dart gun, Arco, 1975, MOC, S2..$75.00
Wagon Train .44 Western Six-Gun, Leslie-Henry, scrolled gold-tone barrel w/plastic grips, chamber spins, NM (EX box), A $275.00

Wagon Train Gun and Holster Set, Leslie-Henry, 1958, diecast pistol marked Wagon Train with horse head on plastic grips, complete with leather belt, buckle, 3 bullets and ornate holster with jewel design, NM (EX box with Ward Bond and Robert Horton on lid), $250.00.

Wild Bill Hickok Cap Pistol, Leslie-Henry, 1950s, diecast w/NP finish, wht plastic horse-head grips, 9", VG, P4.........$90.00
Wild Bill Hickok Gun & Holster, Leslie-Henry, single, VG+.$150.00
Wild Bill Hickok Marshall Double Gun Set, Halco/Leslie-Henry, 1960s, diecast w/bronze steer-head grips, 9½", NM..$325.00

Wyatt Earp Buntline Special Cap Gun, Lonestar, silvered diecast metal, 100-shot repeater, 7", with EX holster, VG+ (VG+ box), A, $120.00.

Wyatt Earp Frontier Marshall Set, Service Mfg, dbl holster w/2 guns, mk Wyatt Earp, 8½", M (EX+ box)................$350.00

RELATED ITEMS AND ACCESSORIES

Box, Cowboy Repeating Cap Pistol, Hubley, 5x11", VG, J2 .$45.00

Box, Hopalong Cassidy Gold-Plated Repeating Cap Pistol, All Metal Prod, cb, features Hoppy & Topper, 9½x4", VG+ $100.00

Box, Lone Ranger Pistol, Marx, 1938, yel cb w/close-up of Lone Ranger & Silver, Hi-Yo Silver!, EX+, A....................$55.00

Caps, box of 104 Kilgore #514 rnd caps for single-shot guns, MIB, A $5.00

Caps, Greenie Stik-'Em, Mattel, 1958, would stick to end of bullets, 100 per box, MIB, T2 ....$5.00

Caps, 5 rolls Kilgore #150 perforated 250-shot roll caps, MIB..$5.00

Display Box, Nichols Fury 500 Shot Roll Caps, w/6 pkgs of shot caps, 12", M, A $70.00

Display Box, Nichols Tophand 250 Shot Roll Caps, w/12 boxes of cap rolls, M (sealed), A $75.00

Holster, Buck Rogers XZ-35, Daisy, 1935, 9½", VG, P4.$145.00

Holster, Gunsmoke Matt Dillon, dbl holster, VG+, J2.....$60.00

Holster, Keystone Bros, marked Top Grain Cowhide, 'jewel' decoration, EX, $65.00.

Holster, Roy Rogers Double R Bar, Classy, 1950s, tan & brn w/logo & signature, bullets & store bag, NM, A $250.00

Holster, Sheriff's, USA, blk leather & tin embellished w/bl jewels & metal studs, MIB, A $150.00

Holster, Western Ranger 2 Gun BYK-Olster (sic), studded leather designed to be hung on post of bike, scarce, MIB......$100.00

Halloween

Halloween is a uniquely American holiday melded from the traditions of superstitions brought to the new world from Germany and Scotland. St. Matrimony was reportedly the patron saint of this holiday, as it was at this time of the year when the harvest was safely in that betrothals and weddings took place.

Most activity for the holiday focused on getting young eligible people married. Trick or Treat was a way of getting rid of bothersome younger siblings. Robert Burns, the poet of Scotland, was a major influence on the folklore of the holiday. In this country today, Halloween is a holiday with little or no association with earlier religious rites of any group. It's an evening of fun, frolic, and fantasy filled with lots of sugar and calories!

Advisor: Pamela E. Apkarian-Russell, The Halloween Queen (H9).

See also Halloween Costumes.

Banjo, orange w/blk bat & owl, tin, 9", NM, A $190.00

Basket, pumpkin face on side, appears carved from pumpkin, pnt cb on wood base, 8", EX, A $200.00

Bucket, Incredible Hulk figure, 1979, EX, S2 ....$10.00

Bucket, Spiderman figure, 1979, EX...............................$10.00

Bucket, Wendy from Casper the Friendly Ghost, NM, S2 ....$20.00

Candle, jack-o'-lantern, orange w/gr stem, paper base, Gurley, 4", A..$25.00

Candle, jack-o'-lantern, orange w/incised wht eyes, gr stem, Gurley, 5", A...$30.00

Candle, seated witch stirring bubbling cauldron in cave-like setting, yel, bl, gr & orange, 7½" $50.00

Candle, skull shape, blk, yel & red, Gurley, 4½" $20.00

Candy Box, cat pulling cart, stenciled plywood w/wheels, 9", EX, A..$140.00

Candy Container, blk cat, fur-covered papier-mache figure w/glass eyes, 7½", EX $450.00

Candy Container, cabbage-head vegetable man, papier-mache, 6½", VG..$700.00

Candy Container, goblin astride pumpkin w/cat, papier-mache, base opening, mk Germany, 6", EX, A....................$300.00

Candy Container, jack-o'-lantern, cb w/whimsical features, Ann-Dee, 4", EX-, A $60.00

Candy Container, melon head on spring legs, pressed cb, mk Germany, 6", VG, A..$220.00

Candy Container, witch, Germany, 1940s, cardboard, 8½", EX/NM, $185.00.

Candy Container, pear-head vegetable man, papier-mache, 6½", VG $700.00

Candy Container, pumpkin-head baby, pressed cb & papier-mache w/melon legs & feet, 3", VG, A....................$185.00

Candy Container, pumpkin-head lady, papier-mache, mk Germany, 5½", EX...$300.00

Diecut, blk cat in orange costume w/moon & stars, German, 1920s, 20", EX..$95.00

Diecut, devil w/pitchfork held across chest, witch w/broom over shoulder, emb cb, German, 15½", VG+, A $70.00

Diecut, embossed cat with saxophone, Germany, 12", NM, D10, $95.00.

Diecut, pumpkin man in orange & blk harlequin design playing horn, German, 1920s, 15", EX.................................$95.00

Fan, 5 orange paper teardrop-shaped sections w/blk cat features wooden sticks, German, 12", EX $45.00

Garland, orange & blk crepe-paper cut-out jack-o'-lanterns & witches, 1920s, 72", unused, A $40.00

Horn, carrot face, hand-painted cb & wood, 7", EX.......$150.00

Jack-in-the-Box, devil, compo head, crepe-paper robe, box decorated in Halloween colors, 3½", EX, A $250.00

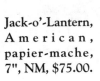

Jack-o'-Lantern, American, papier-mache, 7", NM, $75.00.

Jack-o'-Lantern, molded tin w/cut-out features, Jack O Lantern Co, Toledo O, 7", VG, A $495.00

Jack-o'-Lantern, paper accordion type, dbl-sided, German, 1910, 24" dia, sm tears, A $80.00

Jack-o'-Lantern, pulp, American, 1940s, 8", NM $125.00

Jack-o'-Lantern w/Hat, papier-mache w/mc paper insert, 6", VG, A $140.00

Jumping Jack, pumpkin head & body, papier-mache & wood w/moving eyes, legs & arms move, 11", EX-, A $350.00

Lantern, black cat, Germany, 1930s, cardboard, 4", M, $250.00.

Lantern, cat, 1910, red compo w/yel eyes, 5", very rare, EX.$600.00

Lantern, cat on fence, papier-mache w/mc paper inserts, 7½", EX, A $100.00

Lantern, cat's head, pressed cb w/paper inserts, long ears, gr eyes, pnt face, 3¼", EX......................................$250.00

Lantern, cat's head, 1930s, orange papier-mache, fierce-looking w/paper eyes & mouth insert intact, 3", NM $200.00

Lantern, cat's head w/open mouth, papier-mache w/paper insert, 3", VG, A...$220.00

Lantern, dbl-sided owl's face, cb, American, 1930s, 8x11", EX, A $200.00

Lantern, vegetable person, Germany, 1920s, 6½", EX/NM, $165.00.

Lantern, devil's head, orange papier-mache, wire hdl, mk Germany, 1930s, 5½", NM................$150.00

Lantern, devil's head, papier-mache w/paper insert, 4", EX.$400.00

Lantern, devil-faced witch's head, heavy papier-mache w/paper insert, 4", VG+, A................$525.00

Lantern, pumpkin man, plaster & papier-mache w/paper insert, very lg head, 6", EX, A................$550.00

Lantern, skull, papier-mache, 3", VG, A................$165.00

Lantern, skull, pulp, yel w/red eyes & mouth insert, 4½", rare, EX, A................$325.00

Lantern, watermelon face, pressed cb w/paper insert & glass nose, 4", EX, A................$550.00

Lantern, watermelon, Germany, 1910-20, cardboard with paper features, 3¼", EX, $350.00.

Lantern, witch, Germany, 1920s, 4½", VG+, D10, $800.00 to $1,200.00.

Match holder, devil's head, high glaze china, striker on back, German, 2½", EX, A................$60.00

Nodder, pumpkin head, papier-mache w/metal nodding bar, 5¼", EX-, A................$185.00

Nodder, pumpkin-head cowboy, papier-mache on masonite base, 8½", NM, A................$300.00

Nodder, pumpkin-head lady, papier-mache w/high-gloss pnt, cb base, mk Germany, 9", EX, A................$400.00

Nodder, skeleton, papier-mache, dressed in knee-length wht robe, mk Germany, 8", EX................$200.00

Nodder, witch, Germany, papier-mache, 8", EX, D10, $480.00.

Noisemaker, children discover the great pumpkin, tin, Chein, NM................$50.00

Noisemaker, compo blk cat on wood rachet, German, 8", EX................$150.00

Noisemaker, compo devil's head on wood rachet, German, 1920s, 7x5", EX................$175.00

Noisemaker, pumpkin-head ball on rachet mechanism, cb & wood, 8", EX................$125.00

Noisemakers, T Cohn, tin rattle type, $15.00 each.

Pipe, orange paper litho w/blk pumpkins & witches, German, 6", EX................$100.00

Postcard, girl & boy pop popcorn while gazing into fire, HB Griggs, M, H9................$14.00

Postcard, girl in witch's outfit w/cat in jack-o'-lantern, Whitney, M, H9................$14.00

Postcard, girl on jack-o'-lantern plays w/blk kitty, Winch, 1914, M, H9..$65.00

Postcard, jack-o'-lantern man & devil pull cracker apart, Tuck, M, H9...$14.00

Postcard, 3 girls bobbing for apples, red border, Tuck, art by Brundage, M, H9 ....$16.00

Tea set, teapot, creamer & sugar bowl, all modeled as pumpkin faces, German, EX $250.00

Toy, pumpkin man playing accordion, plastic, 1950s, 5", M $35.00

Toy, scarecrow on wheels, plastic, 1950s, 5", M, A $35.00

Halloween Costumes

During the fifties and sixties Ben Cooper and Collegeville made Halloween costumes representing the popular TV and movie characters of the day. If you can find one in excellent to mint condition and still in its original box, some of the better ones can go for over $100.00. MAD's Alfred E. Neuman (Collegeville, 1959-60) usually carries an asking price of $150.00 to $175.00, and The Green Hornet (Ben Cooper, 1966), $200.00. Earlier handmade costumes are especially valuable if they are 'Dennison-Made.'

Advisor: Pamela E. Apkarian-Russell, The Halloween Queen (H9).

Addams Family, Lurch, Ben Cooper, NMIB....................$45.00
Addams Family, Morticia, Ben Cooper, 1965, MIB..........$75.00
Alf, plush w/full head, MIB $25.00
Andromeda Lady Space Fighter, EX (EX box)................$30.00
Astro Boy, mask only, bl hair, 1960s, EX $10.00
Atom Ant, Ben Cooper, 1965, G.....................................$15.00
Banana Splits, Bingo, Ben Cooper, 1968, NM................$20.00
Barbie, Collegeville, 1975, MIP......................................$65.00
Barbie Super Star Bride, Collegeville, 1975, MIP, D2 ......$75.00
Batman, mask only, Ben Cooper, 1976, EX.......................$5.00
Beatles, Ringo Starr, mask only, G, R2 ....$40.00
Beatles, set of 4 rubberized plastic masks on orig header card mk Strange Mask, EX $150.00
Bret Maverick, Collegeville, 1959, MIB...........................$55.00
Bride of Frankenstein, 1980, MIB, J2 ....$45.00
Buck Rogers, Ben Cooper, 1978, MIB, C1 ....$27.00
Bugs Bunny, MIB, S1..$25.00
Bunny (Bunny & Clyde), Collegeville, 1960s, EX (EX box), J5 ....$25.00
Casper the Friendly Ghost, pajama costume, NMIB.........$20.00
CHiPs, motorcycle cop costume, 1978, M (G box) $25.00
Cinderella, Ben Cooper, 1960s, EX (EX box), J5..............$20.00
Colonel Sanders, mask only, EX....................................$15.00
Daniel Boone, Ben Cooper, 1960s, EX w/VG mask (worn box), J5 ....$25.00
Devil, Kusan, 1974, G (G box) $20.00
Dick Dastardly, Ben Cooper, 1969, MIB..........................$35.00
Donald Duck, long-billed mask w/sailor cap, wht pants w/feather tail, yel cloth-webbed gloves, 1930s, EX (EX box), A $1,047.00

Donald Duck, Collegeville, NMIB, $35.00.

Frankenstein, 1980, MIB $20.00
Gremlins, Gizmo, Ben Cooper, 1982, MIB $20.00

Gumby, Collegeville, EX (G box), $35.00.

Hopalong Cassidy, mask only, Latex, 1950, MIB..............$95.00
Howdy Doody, mask only, cloth, early, VG $35.00
Incredible Hulk, Ben Cooper, 1977, M (NM box), C1 ....$20.00
Jolly Green Giant, Halco, 1960s, EX (orig box), J5..........$35.00
Jolly Green Giant, Kusan, 1960s, MIB, H4 ....$35.00
King Kong, Ben Cooper, 1976, MIB, H4 ....$20.00
Lilly Munster, Ben Cooper, 1965, M (NM box).............$200.00
Mickey Mouse Fun Poncho, Ben Cooper, 1976, MIP.......$25.00
Mummy, Ben Cooper, 1963, MIP...................................$50.00
Planet of the Apes, Warrior, Ben Cooper, 1970s, EX (VG box), J5 ....$20.00
Psychedelic, Peter Max type, Halco, 1960s, EX (orig box), J5 ....$25.00
Quick Draw McGraw, Ben Cooper, 1959, M (VG box)...$45.00
Raggedy Ann, EX (G box), O1..$8.00

Rocketeer, Ben Cooper, MIB, H10 ....$150.00
Roger Rabbit, Ben Cooper, 1980s, MIB $35.00
Samantha (Bewitched), EX, J2.....................................$40.00
Secret Squirrel, Ben Cooper, 1967, NM $25.00
Smokey the Bear, 1960s, NM $35.00
Spiderman, 1979, NMIB, S2 ....$20.00
Star Wars, Ewok, NM (Darth Vader box), S2 ....$15.00
Star Wars, Storm Trooper, Ben Cooper, 1980, VG+ (orig card),
    I2 ....$10.00
Star Wars, Yoda, EX (G box) $20.00
Star Wars Fun Poncho, Darth Vader, Ben Cooper, 1977, MIP
    (sealed)...$20.00
Superman, Ben Cooper, 1970, cloth, M..........................$40.00
Superman, Ben Cooper, 1970, cloth, VG (worn box), J5.$20.00
Tasmanian Devil, 1987, MIB, S2 ....$15.00

Alkali Ike, w/horse, 8", EX+ $65.00
Babe Ruth, slightly discolored o/w EX+ $245.00
Bat Masterson, 9½", MIB $250.00
Brave Eagle, on wht walking horse, w/bow & arrow, knife, etc,
    EX, I2 ....$135.00
Bret Maverick, w/horse & saddle, hat & guns, NM, from $235
    to $300.00
Buffalo Bill, w/horse & accessories, 9½", M, from $250 to .$275.00
Bullet, #700, EX+..$55.00
Cactus Pete, w/horse, 8", M $80.00
Cheyenne, bagged accessories, NM (EX+ box), I2 ....$375.00
Cheyenne, w/horse, 5½", MOC, from $50 to...................$85.00
Chief Thunderbird, w/horse, VG+..................................$55.00
Chief Thunderbird, w/horse & accessories, NM, from $115
    to $150.00

Teenage Mutant Ninja Turtle, mask only, copyright Premo & Remco Toys, made in China, NM, $3.00.

Cochise of Broken Arrow, 8" figure on 8" horse (not original) with saddle, EX, $70.00.

Touche Turtle, Ben Cooper, 1965, MIB $75.00
Wizard of Oz, Straw Man, Ben Cooper, 1960s, MIB $75.00
Wolf, Kusan, 1974, G $10.00
Wolfman, mask only, early 1960s, EX $15.00
Yogi Bear, 1963, flannel front, EX, S2 ....$25.00
Zorro, Ben Cooper, 1960s, EX (EX box), S2 ....$65.00

Hartland Plastics, Inc.

Hartland Plastics, Inc., was formed in Hartland, Wisconsin, in the 1940s. The durable material used to make the figures was cellulose acetate. Figures were hand painted with an eye for detail. The Western and Historic Horsemen, Miniature Western Series, Authentic Scale Model Horses, Famous Gunfighter Series, and the Hartland Sports Series of Famous Baseball Stars were a symbol of the fine workmanship of the '40s, '50s and '60s. (There were also football, bowling and religious statues.) For more information we recommend *Hartland Horses and Riders* by Gail Fitch.

See Also Clubs, Newsletters and Other Publications.

Dale Evans & Buttermilk, 1950s, complete w/tag, 9½", A.$219.00
Dick Groat, M...$900.00
Ernie Banks, slightly discolored o/w EX+ $275.00
Ernie Banks, w/bat, sm, M, from $425 to $475.00
General Custer, w/horse & accessories, 9½", NMIB.......$180.00

George Washington on horse (not original), missing hat and sabre, otherwise NM, $120.00.

General George Washington, w/horse & accessories, 9½", MIB $250.00
Hank Aaron, slightly discolored, rpl bat o/w EX $170.00
Hank Aaron, w/bat, lg, M, from $325 to......................$350.00

Horse, reddish-brown with white feet, 8", NM, $18.50.

Jim Bowie, w/horse & accessories, NM $200.00
Jim Hardie, w/horse, 9½", EX..$85.00
Josh Randall, w/horse & accessories, 9½", M, from $500 to ..$525.00
Little Leaguer, 4", M...$265.00
Lone Ranger, w/Silver, 9½", complete, VG $65.00
Matt Dillon, complete except gun, EX+ (orig box), I2 ..$275.00
Matt Dillon, w/horse, 5½", MOC, from $50 to.................$85.00
Mickey Mantle, EX...$250.00
Mickey Mantle, w/bat, 1 of 150,000, med, M, from $400 to..$425.00
Minor Leaguer, 4", M, from $160 to................................$185.00
Rocky Colavito, w/bat, 1 of 10,000, med, M, from $1,000 to...$1,300.00
Roger Maris, w/bat, slightly discolored o/w EX..............$290.00
Roy Rogers & Trigger, #806, 1950s, complete, 9½", EX+, A $219.00

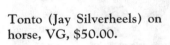
Tonto (Jay Silverheels) on horse, VG, $50.00.

Roy Rogers & Trigger, #806, 1950s, complete, 9½", EX+ (EX box), A...$303.00
Sgt Lance O'Rourke, w/horse, 9½", EX......................$125.00
Sgt Preston, w/horse & accessories, NM $225.00
Stan Musial, slightly discolored o/w EX+.......................$220.00
Tonto, w/Scout, complete, 9½", VG+.............................$65.00
Vint Bonner, 9½", VG+ $80.00
Willie Mays, w/orange glove, NM................................$375.00
Wyatt Earp, w/horse, 5½", MOC, from $50 to...............$85.00
Wyatt Earp, w/horse & accessories, 9½", NM..............$175.00
Yogi Berra, w/mask, NM..$325.00

Horses

Horse riding being the order of the day, many children of the 19th century had their own horses to ride indoors; some were wooden while others were stuffed, and many had glass eyes and real horsehair tails. There were several ways to construct these horses so as to achieve a galloping action. The most common types had rocker bases or were mounted with a spring on each leg.

Gliding Horse, early 1900s, pnt wood, dapple gray on red base, leatherette saddle, inset eyes, 36", ears missing, G, A .$345.00

Riding horse, stuffed cloth with fur mane, string tail, glass eyes, remounted on wooden platform with hard rubber wheels, worn, 28" long, G, A, $130.00.

Rocking Horse, brn-stained wood w/blk hooves on wood base, curved metal rockers, orig blk saddle, 38", VG, A...$400.00
Rocking Horse, carved & pnt 1-pc wood body w/applied legs on 48" red wood runners, leather saddle, 32", crazing, G, A...$375.00
Rocking Horse, Gibbs, paper litho on wood w/tin legs & wood rockers, 9", some scratches on litho, split on chest, VG, A...$240.00
Rocking Horse, wood horse w/leather seat on wood rockers w/4 sm CI wheels, 31" long, G, A $60.00
Rocking Horse, 1890s, carved wood, dapple gray w/pnt eyes, w/hair mane & tail, red rockers, 51", some wear, A ..$500.00

Rocking horse, painted wood, leather saddle, missing ears and tail, 51", G, A, $1,200.00.

Hot Wheels

When they were introduced in 1968, Hot Wheels were an instant success. Sure, their racy style and flashy custom paint jobs were instant attention-getters, but what the kids loved most was the fact that they were fast! The fastest on the market! It's estimated that more than two billion Hot Wheels have been sold to date — every model with a little variation, keeping up with new trends in the big car industry. The line has included futuristic vehicles, muscle cars, trucks, hot rods, racers, and some military vehicles. Lots of these can still be found for very little, but if you want to buy the older models (collectors call them 'Red Lines' because of their red sidewall tires), it's going to cost you a little more, though many can still be found for under $25.00. By 1971, earlier on some models, black-wall tires had become the standard. A line of cars with Goodyear tires called Real Riders were made from 1983 until about 1987. Though recent re-releases have dampened the collector market somewhat, cars mint and in the original packages are holding their values and are still moving well. Near-mint examples (no package) are worth about 40% to 50% (of MIP), excellent condition only about 25% to 35%. Collector pin-back buttons included in some of the packaging are worth from $3.00 to $5.00.

Advisor: Aquarius Antiques (A3); all photos courtesy Mike's General Store (M5).

'31 Classic Woody, red line tires, metallic bl w/smooth blk roof, NM+, W1 ....$24.00
'31 Classic Woody, red line tires, rose, M $40.00
'32 Classic Vicky, red line tires, metallic gr w/smooth blk roof, NM+, W1 ....$37.50
'34 Ford 3-Window Coupe, blk walls, purple, 1988, MIP, A3 ....$10.00
'36 Classic Coupe, red line tires, metallic purple w/blk roof, NM, W1 ....$28.00
'37 Bugatti, wht-walls, red & blk, 1981, MIP, A3 ....$8.00
'55 Chevy, blk walls, red & wht, MBP, W1 ....$22.50
'57 Chevy, blk walls, yel w/flames, MBP, J1 ....$4.00
'57 Chevy, Power Commando Racer, blk walls, gr, India, M (EX bubble pack), C6 ....$8.00
'57 Classic Bird, red line tires, metallic bl, NM, W1 ....$24.00

'57 Classic T-Bird, red line tires, purple, w/button, MBP $120.00
'57 T-Bird, blk walls, gold, Gleem Team, MBP, J1 ....$2.00
'63 Split Window Corvette, blk walls, blk, plastic base, MBP, W1 ....$10.00
'65 Mustang Convertible, wht-walls, red, 1983, MIP, A3 $10.00
Alive '55, red line tires, yel, NM+, W1 ....$45.00
AMX/2, red line tires, metallic red, NM, W1 ....$27.50
AMX/2, red line tires, purple, w/button, MBP $95.00
Auburn 852, blk walls, gr, M, J1 ....$4.00
Auburn 852, blk walls, metallic gold, 1983, MIP, A3 ....$8.00
Auburn 852, blk walls, red w/blk fenders, MBP, J1 ....$8.00
Backwoods Bomb, red line tires, gr, 1975, EX, A3 ....$10.00
Baja Breaker, blk walls, orange & bl, 1983, MIP, A3 ....$10.00
Beach Bomb, red line tires, aqua, w/button, MBP $150.00
Beach Bomb, red line tires, orig boards, metallic bl, NM+, W1 ....$59.00
Beatnik Bandit, red line tires, metallic bl, NM+, W1 ....$15.00
Big Bertha Tank, blk walls, lt tan & camo, MBP, J1 ....$2.00
Blazer 4x4, blk walls, silver & bl or metallic bl, MBP, J1 ....$5.00
Blown Camaro Z-28, blk walls, aqua, gold hubs, MBP, J1 ..$4.00
Blown Camaro Z-28, blk walls, blk, rare, M, J1 ....$6.50
Boss Hoss, red line tires, chrome, M $50.00
Brabham Repco F1, red line tires, orig decal, metallic aqua, NM+, W1 ....$13.50
Bronco 4x4, blk walls, wht, smooth tires, MBP, J1 ....$4.00
Bugeye, red line tires, metallic red, NM, W1 ....$35.00
Buzz-Off, blk walls, gold, NM, W1 ....$7.00
Cadillac Seville, blk walls, metallic gold, 1982, MIP $8.00
Carabo, red line tires, metallic red, NM, W1 ....$29.00
Cat Bulldozer, blk walls, yel & wht, MBP, W1 ....$6.00
Chaparral 2G, red line tires, wht, NM+, W1 ....$20.00
Chevy Monza 2+2, India, blk walls, red, M (EX bubble pack), C6 ....$8.00
Chevy Stocker, blk walls, blk, #3, MBP, J1 ....$4.00
Classic '57 T-Bird, red line tires, red, w/button, MBP, G3 .$85.00
Classic Cobra, blk walls, red, MBP $4.00
Classic Cobra, blk walls, wht, older issue, M, W1 ....$7.50
Classic Cord, red line tires, metallic lt gr, orig top, NM+, W1 ....$169.00
Classic Nomad, red line tires, bl, w/button, MBP $150.00
Classic Nomad, red line tires, metallic lime, NM+, W1 ...$44.00
Classic Nomad, red line tires, 1970, VG, A3 ....$15.00

Cockney Cab, red line tires, metallic bl, NM+, W1 ....$54.00

Command Tank, blk walls, tan & camo, MBP, J1 ....$4.00

Corvette Stingray, red line tires, red, G+ $9.00

Custom AMX, red line tires, metallic yel, NM $50.00

Custom AMX, red line tires, orange (unusual), M $75.00

Custom Barracuda, red line tires, metallic brn, NM+, W1.$49.00

Custom Camaro, red line tires, metallic red, NM-, W1....$69.00

Custom Charger, red line tires, bl, NM $80.00

Custom Continental Mk III, red line tires, gold, w/button, MBP,
  G3 ....$125.00

Custom Continental Mk III, red line tires, metallic bl, NM,
  W1 ....$26.00

Custom Continental Mk III, red line tires, lime, 1969, NM,
  A3...$10.00

Custom Continental Mk III, red line tires, purple, M $55.00

Custom Corvette, India, blk walls, red, M (open pkg), C6.$5.00

Custom Corvette, red line tires, antifreeze, M $135.00

Custom Corvette, red line tires, aqua, w/button, MBP...$175.00

Custom Corvette, red line tires, metallic bl, NM, W1 .....$54.50

Custom Cougar, red line tires, bl, M $95.00

Custom Cougar, red line tires, gold w/blk roof, NM, W1 .$44.00

Custom Cuda, red line tires, purple, M $75.00

Custom Dodge Charger, red line tires, metallic lime, NM+,
  W1 ....$89.00

Custom Eldorado, red line tires, aqua, w/button, MBP...$140.00

Custom Eldorado, red line tires, brn, M, from $40 to $50.00

Custom Eldorado, red line tires, metallic orange w/blk roof, NM,
  W1 ....$39.00

Custom Firebird, red line tires, metallic olive, NM+, W1 .$30.00

Custom Fleetside, red line tires, metallic orange, NM, W1.$35.00

Custom Fleetside, red line tires, purple, M.......................$35.00

Custom Mustang, red line tires, metallic brn, NM, W1 ...$49.00

Custom Mustang, red line tires, red, NM $60.00

Custom Police Cruiser (Plymouth), red line tires, wht w/clear
  dome, MBP, W1 ....$179.00

Custom VW, red line tires, brn, M $19.00

Custom VW, red line tires, metallic red, NM+, W1.........$19.00

Datsun 200SX, blk walls, metal-flake gold, 1983, MIP, A3 .$10.00

Demon, red line tires, metallic bl w/smooth blk roof, NM,
  W1 ....$9.00

Demon, red line tires, metallic orange, 1969, EX, A3.........$5.00

Deora, red line tires, metallic orange, orig boards, NM+, W1..$49.00

Dixie Challenger, blk walls, orange, 1979, M, A3 ....$5.00

Dodge Viper, blk walls, red, MBP, J1.................................$2.00

Double Vision, red line tires, dk bl, NM+ $75.00

Dream Van, India, blk walls, bl w/blk & yel stripes, M (open
  pkg), C6 ....$5.00

Driven to the Max Dragster, blk walls, orange, MBP, J1 ....$4.00

Dune Daddy, red line tires, red w/brn interior, NM+, W1.$89.00

Evil Weevil, red line tires, metallic bl, orig stickers, NM,
  W1..$39.00

Fangster, blk walls, gr, MBP, W1 ....$9.00

Ferrari Testarosa, blk walls, wht w/blk interior, MBP, W1 ..$10.00

Ferrari 312P, red line tires, yel, orig stickers, NM+ $100.00

Ferrari 348, blk walls, metallic lt gray, silver hubs, MBP, J1..$3.00

Fire Chief Cruiser (Plymouth Fury), red line tires, red, MBP,
  W1 ....$40.00

Flame Runner, blk walls, metallic gold, NM+, W1.............$5.00

Flat Out 442, blk walls, yel, gold hubs, MBP, J1 ....$7.00

Ford Aerostar Van, blk walls, blk, Rollerblade, MBP, J1 ....$3.00

Ford Aerostar Van, blk walls, wht, Speedie Pizza, MBP, J1...$4.00

Ford J-Car, red line tires, wht enamel, orig stickers, EX+,
  W1 ....$12.00

Ford Mk IV, red line tires, metallic brn, NM, W1 ....$12.50

Funny Money, red line tires, plum, NM, W1 ....$29.00

Grass Hopper, red line tires, metallic bl, orig top, NM, W1 .$34.50

Grass Hopper, red line tires, purple, 1975, EX, A3 ....$10.00

Grass Hopper, red line tires, salmon pk, w/button, MBP, G3 .$150.00

Gremlin Grinder, red line tires, chrome, VG, W1 ....$8.00

Hairy Hauler, red line tires, metallic gr, NM+, W1 ....$26.00

Heavy Chevy, red line tires, metallic orange, orig stickers, NM+,
  W1 ....$39.00

Heavy Chevy, red line tires, red, M..................................$55.00

Heavy Chevy, red line tires, red, w/button, MBP $125.00

Heavyweights, Ambulance, red line tires, metallic brn, NM,
  W1 ....$29.00

Heavyweights, Cement Truck, red line tires, metallic bl, NM,
  W1 ....$22.00

Heavyweights, Fire Engine, red line tires, metallic red w/blk
  interior, MBP...$125.00

Heavyweights, Fire Engine, red line tires, red, w/button,
  MBP $125.00

Heavyweights, Moving Van, red line tires, metallic gr w/wht
  trailer, MBP, W1 ....$59.00

Heavyweights, Racer Rig, red line tires, metallic red, NM+,
  W1 ....$89.00

Heavyweights, Snorkel, red line tires, metallic gr, VG+,
  W1 ....$29.50

Heavyweights, Tow Truck, red line tires, metallic gr, NM,
  W1 ....$21.00

Heavyweights, Waste Wagon, red line tires, metallic gr, NM+,
  W1 ....$69.00

Hiway Hauler, blk walls, aqua & wht, MBP, J1................$4.00

Hiway Hauler, blk walls, red & wht, Pepsi, MBP, J1...........$6.00

Hiway Hauler, Ocean Pacific Delivery, India, blk walls, MBP,
  G3 ....$20.00

Hiway Robber, red line tires, red, NM, W1 ....$99.00

Hood, red line tires, metallic gr, NM+, W1 ....$29.00

Hot Bird, blk walls, metal-flake blk, MBP, J1....................$2.00

Hot Bird, blk walls, metal-flake bl w/tan interior, MBP, W1 .$4.50

Hot Heap, red, M, (NM card), M5, $125.00; Sidekick,
aqua, M (NM card), M5, $50.00.

Hot Heap, red line tires, metallic pk, scarce color, NM+ .$60.00

Hummer, blk walls, dk tan w/dk brn & orange camo, MBP, J1 ....$3.00

Indy cars, larger scale, each 8", MIB, M5, $35.00 each.

Indy Eagle, red line tires, gold chrome (scarce), NM, W11 .$99.00

Indy Eagle, red line tires, metallic red, NM+, W1 ....$13.00

Jack Rabbit Special, red line tires, wht w/blk interior, flower decal, NM, W1 ....$14.00

Jaguar XJS, blk walls, metal-flake brn, NM+, W1 ....$27.00

Jet Threat, red line tires, metallic gr, NM+, W1 ....$34.00

Kenworth Big Rig, blk walls, blk, MBP, J1 ....$2.00

King Kuda, red line tires, chrome, M $60.00

King Kuda, red line tires, metallic gr, orig stripes & numbers, NM+, W1 ....$39.00

Lamborghini Countach, blk walls, wht, MBP, W1 ....$5.00

Landlord, blk walls, orange, 1982, MIP, A3 ....$10.00

Large Charge, blk walls, chrome, NM, W1 ....$9.00

Large Charge, red line tires, gr, NM, W1 ....$29.00

Letter Getter Van, blk walls, wht & bl, US Mail, MBP, J1 ..$7.00

Light My Firebird, red line tires, aqua, M $30.00

Light My Firebird, red line tires, metallic gr, orig stickers, NM+, W1 ....$34.50

Lincoln Continental, lime gold, M (wavy card), M5, $60.00; Snake Funny Car, M (EX card), M5, $275.00; Mongoose Funny Car, blue, M (EX+ card), M5, $200.00; Python, blue, M (NM card), M5, $50.00.

Lola GT-70, red line tires, dk gr, orig stickers, NM+, W1 ..$10.00

Lotus Turbine, red line tires, metallic purple, orig decal, NM+, W1 ....$13.50

Lowdown, red line tires, gold, 1977, EX, A3 ....$10.00

Mantis, red line tires, metallic olive, w/button, Canadian, MBP, W1 ....$40.00

Maserati Mistral, red line tires, metallic purple, NM, W1 ..$52.50

Mazda MX-5 Miata, blk walls, convertible, red, European, MIB, C6 ....$1.50

Mazda MX-5 Miata, blk walls, yel w/lime hubs, MBP, J1 ....$3.00

Mercedes Benz 280SL, red line tires, dk bl, 1973, NM, W1 ....$149.00

Mercedes 380 SEl, blk walls, wht, MBP, J1 ....$4.00

Mercedes 540K, blk walls, metal-flake purple, MBP, J1 ......$2.00

Mighty Maverick, red line tires, magenta, w/button, MBP .$125.00

Mighty Maverick, red line tires, metallic olive, missing side stickers, NM, W1 ....$30.00

Mini Truck, blk walls, orange w/bl interior, MBP, J1 ....$2.00

Minitrek, blk walls, wht, 1983, MIP, A3 ....$10.00

Mirada Stocker, blk walls, metal-flake gold, 1983, MIP, A3 ..$10.00

Mod Quad, red line tires, metallic lt gr, M, W1 ....$28.00

Mongoose Funny Car, red line tires, no decals, 1969, VG ..$20.00

Mongoose Funny Car, red line tires, red, M $85.00

Mongoose Funny Car, red line tires, red, w/sticker sheet, M .$125.00

Mongoose II Funny Car, red line tires, metallic bl, missing stickers, NM, W1 ....$69.00

Mongoose Rail Dragster, red line tires, metallic bl, NM+, W1 ....$59.00

Monster Vette, blk walls, yel w/flames, European, MIB, C6 ..$1.50

Monte Carlo Stocker, blk walls, dk bl w/gr, yel & wht tampo, M $25.00

Monte Carlo Stocker, red line tires, yel, NM, W1 ....$26.50

Mustang, red line tires, w/louvered window, bl, NM $395.00

Mustang Boss Hoss, red line tires, chrome, club car, NM+, W1 ....$49.00

Mustang Boss Hoss, red line tires, chrome, M $55.00

Mustang Boss Hoss, red line tires, emerald gr, w/button, MBP $350.00

Mustang Stocker, red line tires, yel, MBP $240.00

Mutt Mobile, red line tires, metallic aqua, rare MBP, W1 .$139.00

Neet Streeter, blk walls, maroon, 1975, NM, A3 ....$10.00

Neet Streeter, blk walls, red, 1983, MIP, A3 ....$15.00

Nissan 300ZX, blk walls, metal-flake red, MBP, W1 ....$7.00

Nitty Gritty Kitty, red line tires, gr, #3, w/button, MBP ..$125.00

Nitty Gritty Kitty, red line tires, orange, M $35.00

Nomad, Seattle Toy Show, blk & wht, w/button, MBP, G3 .$12.00

Noodle Head, red line tires, metallic med bl, NM+, W1 ..$59.00

Noodle Head, red line tires, olive, M $85.00

Open Fire, red line tires, gold, M $95.00

Open Fire, red line tires, metallic magenta, MBP, W1 ...$299.00

Oscar Meyer Wienermobile, blk walls, tan & red, MBP, J1 ..$3.00

Osh Kosh Snowplow, blk walls, metal cab, orange hopper, MBP, J1 ....$3.00

P-911 Turbo, blk walls, blk, gold hubs, M, J1 ....$5.00

Paddy Wagon, red line tires, bl, gold letters, NM+, W1 ...$10.00

Paddy Wagon, red line tires, bl, 1969, NM, A3 ....$5.00

Peeping Bomb, red line tires, metallic pk (rare), EX $30.00

Peterbilt Dump Truck, blk walls, metal-flake bl, MBP, W1 .$6.00

Peterbilt Tanker, blk walls, red cab, MBP, J1 ....$4.00

Peterbilt Tanker, California Construction, blk walls, orange, MBP, J1 ....$6.00

Pipe Jammer, blk walls, yel, chrome driver, MBP, J1 ....$2.00

Pit Crew Car, red line tires, wht, rare MBP, W1 ....$299.00

Poison Pinto, red line tires, gr, 1976, NM+, A3 ....$10.00

Poison Pinto, red line tires, lt gr, VG+, W1 ....$8.50

Pontiac Fiero, blk walls, metal-flake gr, silver hubs, MBP, J1 ....$3.00

Porsche 917, red line tires, metallic gr, orig stickers, NM, W1 ....$15.00

Porsche 959, blk walls, bl, MBP, W1 ....$10.00

Porsche 959, blk walls, red, MBP, J1 ....$2.00

Power Pad, red line tires, hot pk, w/button, MBP $200.00

Power Pad, red line tires, metallic gr, orig top, M, W1 .....$49.00

Power Plower, blk walls, purple w/yel blade, MBP, J1 ....$2.50
Predator, blk walls, metallic purple, unlisted color, M, W1 ..$6.00
Proper Chopper, blk walls, wht & bl, MBP, J1 ....$4.00
Prowler, red line tires, dk bl, NM $90.00
Prowler, red line tires, gr, M $110.00
Python, red line tires, gold, M $25.00
Python, red line tires, metallic purple, NM, W1 ....$19.00
Race Bait 308, blk walls, metal-flake, gray, M, J1 ....$5.00
Ramblin' Wrecker, red line tires, wht w/phone & bl windshield,
    NM, W1 ....$19.00
Range Rover, blk walls, wht, MIB, C6 ....$1.50
Red Alert, Hot Shots, red line tires, MBP, G3 ....$75.00
Red Baron, red line tires, red, sharp point, no sticker version,
    NM+, W1 ....$29.00
Red Baron, red line tires, red, 1969, NM, A3 ....$10.00
Rescue Ranger, blk walls, Real Rider, gr, M, W1 ....$10.00
Rescue Ranger, India, Emergency Unit, blk walls, red, M (EX
    bubble pack), C6 ....$8.00
Road King, red line tires, yel, missing sm lever o/w complete,
    VG, W1 ....$399.00
Rock Buster, blk walls, gr, 1975, M, A3 ....$10.00
Rock Buster, red line tires, Super Chrome, NM-, W1 ....$15.00
Rock Buster, red line tires, yel, 1975, NM, A3 ....$10.00
Rocket Bye Baby, red line tires, metallic bl, NM+, W1 ......$59.00
Rodzilla, blk walls, purple, MBP, J1 ....$2.00
Roll Patrol, blk walls, lt tan w/camo on hood, MBP, J1 ......$3.00
Rolls Royce, blk walls, bl, 1983, MIP, A3 ....$8.00
Rolls Royce Silver Shadow, red line tires, metallic gr, NM+,
    W1 ....$49.00
Royal Flash, blk walls, orange, 1982, MIP, A3 ....$10.00
Ruby Red Passion, wht-walls, red, 1992, MIP $25.00
Ruby Red Passion, wht-walls, metal-flake red, MBP $25.00
S'Cool Bus, red line tires, yel, orig blower, prop, seats & sticker,
    NM, from $129 to $175.00
Sand Crab, red line tires, metallic gr, NM+, W1 ....$19.00
Sand Crab, red line tires, metallic pk, 1969, VG+, A3 ....$8.00
Sand Drifter, red line tires, yel, NM, W1 ....$29.00
Seasider, red line tires, gr, M $85.00
Seasider, red line tires, lime gr, w/button, MBP $175.00
Seasider, red line tires, metallic gr, NM, W1 ....$56.00
Shelby Turbine, red line tires, metallic red, MBP, W1 ....$39.00
Sheriff Patrol, blk walls, blk & wht, 1982, MIP, A3 ....$10.00
Short Order, red line tires, metallic gr, MBP, W1 ....$189.00
Show Off, red line tires, lt gr, NM $90.00
Silhouette, red line tires, metallic brn, NM, W1 ....$19.00
Six Shooter, red line tires, metallic magenta, M, W1 ....$99.00
Snake Funny Car, red line tires, no decals, 1969, VG $15.00
Snake Funny Car, red line tires, yel, 1969, NM $35.00
Snake II Funny Car, red line tires, wht, NM, W1 ....$39.00
Snake Rail Dragster, red line tires, wht, NM+, W1 ....$59.00
Sol-Aire CX4, blk walls, blk, #33, older issue, MBP, J1 .....$3.00
Special Delivery, red line tires, metallic bl, NM+, W1 .....$39.00
Special Delivery, red line tires, metallic bl, rare MBP,
    W1 ....$169.00
Splittin' Image, red line tires, metallic red, NM, W1 ....$10.00
Spoiler Sport, blk walls, gr, MBP, W1 ....$13.50
Spoiler Sport, blk walls, wht, 1982, MIP, A3 ....$10.00
Staff Car, red line tires, olive, very rare, M $600.00

Staff car, rare, came only in gift set, EX, M5, $300.00.

Steam Roller, red line tires, wht, NM, W1 ....$29.00
Street Snorter, red line tires, red, NM-, W1 ....$149.00
Strip Teaser, red line tires, metallic aqua, NM, W1 ....$49.00
Sugar Caddy, red line tires, metallic purple, NM, W1 ....$34.00
Sugar Caddy, red line tires, red, 1971, VG+, A3 ....$10.00
Superfine Turbine, red line tires, lt bl, NM+, W1 ....$299.00
Supervan, blk walls, wht w/flames, NM, W1 ....$19.00
Supervan, red line tires, plum, NM, W1 ....$79.00
Sweet 16, red line tires, bl, NM $125.00
T-Bucket, blk walls, blk, MBP, W1 ....$9.00
T-Totaler, blk walls, blk, 1976, NM+, A3 ....$10.00
T-4-2, red line tires, metallic lime, NM, W1 ....$29.00
Tall Ryder, blk walls, metallic silver, MBP, J1 ....$4.00
Thing, blk walls, bl, MBP, W1 ....$21.50
Thrill Driver's Torino, blk walls, red or wht, NM, ea $85.00
Thunderstreak, blk walls, bl & gr, Hot Wheels #1, MBP, J1 ...$5.00
Thunderstreak, blk walls, Park n' Plates, dk bl, MBP, W1 ...$21.50
TNT Bird, red line tires, metallic gr, NM+, W1 ....$27.00
Torino Stocker, red line tires, red, NM, W1 ....$39.00
Tow Truck, red line tires, purple, M $55.00
Tri-Baby, red line tires, metallic gr, MBP, W1 ....$55.00
Tricar X8, blk walls, red, 1983, MIP, A3 ....$8.00
Truckin' A, blk walls, yel, 1977, NM, A3 ....$10.00

Turbofire, aqua, M (NM card), M5, $45.00; TNT Bird, green, M (NM card), M5, $90.00; What 4, green, M, (EX card), M5, $180.00.

Turbofire, red line tires, metallic purple, NM, W1 ....$19.00
Twinmill, red line tires, lt bl, Shell promo, EX, W1 ....$16.50
Vampyra, blk walls, blk, MBP, J1 ....$2.00
VW Bug, blk walls, purple, MBP, J1 ....$2.00
VW Bug, blk walls, red, MBP, J1 ....$4.00
Warmouth, red line tires, wht, metal base, EX, W1 ....$12.00
Warpath, red line tires, red, 1973, NM+, A3 ....$10.00
What 4, red line tires, metallic purple, NM+, W1 ....$79.00
Xploder, red line tires, bl, NM $100.00

Xploder, red line tires, yel, EX-, W1..................$44.50

Snake Rear Engine Dragster, M (NM card), $150.00;
Mongoose Rear Engine Dragster, M (NM card), $150.00.

RUMBLERS HOT WHEELS

Choppin' Chariot, no driver, NM+, W1...............$39.00
Devil's Deuce, yel w/orange driver, EX, M5............$50.00
High Tailer, bl & wht driver, NM, W1.................$32.00
Praying Mantis, lime, M...............................$85.00
Road Hog, bl, NM+, W1................................$39.00
Snorter, yel w/brn driver, EX+ (crease in middle of card),
    M5..$50.00
Torque Chopper, red, missing training wheels, NM+, W1.$39.00
3 Squealer, orange w/bl driver, EX+ (crease in middle of card),
    M5..$25.00

SIZZLERS

Back Fire, lt metallic gr, NM, W1.....................$19.00

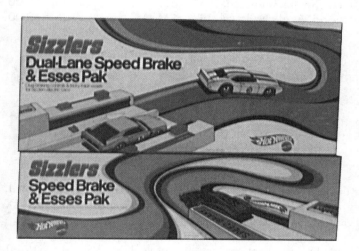

Dual-Lane Speed Brake & Esses Pak, MIB, M5, $30.00;
Speed Brake & Esses Pak, MIB, M5, $15.00.

Hot Head, metallic gr, EX+, W1........................$14.50
Indy Eagle, metallic bl, NM, W1.......................$19.00
Law Mill, Fat Daddy, police car hot rod, wht, NM, W1...$79.00
Live Wire, metallic orange, NM+, W1...................$19.00
Mustang, metallic orange, orig wing, NM, W1...........$29.00

Revvin' Heaven, metallic magenta, NM-, W1............$17.50
Spoil Sport, metallic bl, orig wing, NM-, W1..........$17.50
Spoil Sport, metallic magenta, orig wing, NM, W1......$19.00
Van, chrome, NM, G3..................................$20.00

ACCESSORIES

Belt Buckle, 1984, red & bl belt, Lee Comp, EX, W1....$16.00
Button, metal, Brabham Repco F1, NM+, W1.............$2.50
Button, metal, Chaparral 2G, NM, W1..................$2.00
Button, metal, Classic Nomad, NM+, W1................$5.00
Button, metal, Custom Camaro, NM+, W1................$4.00
Button, metal, Custom Corvette, NM, W1...............$3.50
Button, metal, Custom Firebird, NM, W1...............$3.50
Button, metal, Eevil Weevil, NM-, W1.................$5.00
Button, metal, Ford J-Car, NM, W1....................$2.00
Button, metal, Hot Heap, NM, W1......................$3.00
Button, metal, Indy Eagle, NM, W1....................$2.50
Button, metal, Jack Rabbit Special, NM+, W1..........$3.50
Button, metal, King Kuda, EX, W1.....................$2.00
Button, metal, Lotus Turbine, NM, W1.................$2.50
Button, metal, Mercedes Benz 280SL, NM+, W1..........$3.50
Button, plastic, Bye Focal, M, W1....................$7.50
Button, plastic, Grasshopper, M, W1..................$5.00
Button, plastic, Heavyweights, Racer Rig, M, W1......$9.50
Button, plastic, Ice T, M, W1........................$7.50
Button, plastic, Jet Threat, M, W1...................$7.50
Button, plastic, Mod Quad, M, W1.....................$7.00
Button, plastic, Mongoose II, M, W1..................$15.00
Button, plastic, Snake II, M, W1.....................$15.00
Button, plastic, T-4-2, M, W1........................$7.50
Car Carrier Showcase Plaque, M (EX card), W1.........$35.00
Case, Collectors Case, 1968, 24-car, wht & purple cars on front,
    NM, W1..$26.00
Case, Collectors Case, 1970, 24-car, Mustang & Camaro on
    front, NM, W1...$29.00
Case, Collectors Case, 1981, missing hdl, VG, W1.....$4.00
Case, Collectors Race Case, 1970, 48-car, Porsche & Ferrari on
    front, EX, W1...$27.50
Case, Collectors Race Case, 1970, 72-car, Snake & Mongoose
    on front, EX, W1......................................$49.00
Case, Mattel Miniature Car Collectors Case, 1966, 48-car, pre
    Hot Wheel, EX, W1....................................$17.50

Flyin' Circus, copyright 1971, complete, M (EX box), M5,
$450.00.

Case, Rally Case, 1968, 12-car, VG+, W1 ....$12.50
Case, Super Rally Case, 24-car, plastic wheel insert, EX,
  W1 ....$17.50
Custom Shop Showcase Plaque, 1969, red, M (EX card),
  W1 ....$17.00
Dual-Lane Speedometer, MIB, M5 ....$24.00
Hot Ones Stamper 3 Pack, 1985, Camaro Z28, P911, '80s Fire-
  bird, MBP, W1..$26.00
Lap Counter, 1970, M (water damage o/w VG box), W1..$11.50
Pop-Up Speed Shop, 1968, purple Custom Fleetside, w/button,
  MIP, W1 ....$224.00
Real Riders Stamper 3 Pack, 1985, Baja Bug, Bywayman, Dream
  Van XGW (wht hub), MBP, W1 ....$59.00

Sky Show Deora, aqua, Canada, NM decals (EX rare box), M5, $180.00.

Sky Show Set, MIB...$650.00
Starting Gate, 2-car, 1967, NM $5.00

Super-Charger, MIB, M5, $35.00; Dual-Lane Speedometer, MIB, M5, $24.00; 2-Way Supercharger, MIB, M5, $32.00.

15th Anniversary Belt Buckle 3 Car Set, 1983, '67 Camaro,
  P928 & Longshot, MBP, W1 ....$49.00
20th Anniversary Pack, 1988, Ferrari Testarosa (chrome),
  Sharkruiser, Jeep CJ7, MBP, W1.........................$14.50

Housewares

Back in the dark ages before women's lib and career-minded mothers, little girls emulated mommy's lifestyle, not realizing that by the time they grew up, total evolution would have taken place before their very eyes. They'd sew and bake, sweep, do laundry and iron (gasp!), and imagine what fun it would be when *they* were big like mommy. Those little gadgets they played with are precious collectibles today, and any child-size house-

ware item is treasured, especially those from the forties and fifties. Values are suggested for items in excellent condition unless noted otherwise.

CLEANING AND LAUNDRY

Child's Lawnmower, Arcade, salesman's sample, steel parts, wooden handle and roller, yellow with red tread, 26½", M, A, $325.00; Broom, Arcade, salesman's sample, red handle, straw bristles, 27", M, A, $130.00; Garden Set (rake, hoe and spade), Arcade, salesman's sample, metal parts, 36" to 38" long, M, A, $525.00.

Broom, Arcade, saleman's sample, straw bristles w/red hdl, 27",
  M, A...$130.00
Susy Goose Sweeper, Kiddie Toys, litho tin & wood push type,
  M...$35.00

Maytag Washing Machine, Hubley, late 1920s, 8,000 made in red or blue, 7½", VG, $750.00.

Photo courtesy of Nate Stoller.

Washer, Wee Washer stenciled in wht on bl pnt, wood & galvanized tin, 18½", EX, A...$210.00
Washing Machine, Wolverine, glass & tin, 9¾", A..........$55.00

COOKING

Canisters, metal w/Coffee, Tea, Sugar, Flour, Cake & Bread in script, set of 6, EX...$130.00
Colander, metal w/bl & wht marble design, 2-hdl, 4½" dia, EX..$150.00
Cooking Set, Revere Ware, metal w/blk hdls, 7-pc set w/pot, bowl, teakettle, skillet, saucepan & toast rack, EX ..$130.00
Potato Masher, Steffen, wire w/bl & wht hdl, EX.............$12.00
Rolling Pin, wood w/bl & wht wood hdls, EX...................$12.00
Slotted Spoon, Steffen, 3-slotted metal w/bl & wht wood hdl, EX...$10.50
Stove, Baby, name emb on oven door, EX......................$350.00
Stove, Bing, footed bl steel 4-burner w/polished trim, alcohol fired, w/4 pcs bl & wht enamelware, 16", VG, A $600.00
Stove, Buck's Jr Range, St Louis MO, new body & pnt, recast parts, 26"...$850.00
Stove, Cresent, plated CI & steel 4-burner w/ornate front, stovepipe & shelf, 4-footed, w/4 pcs CI cookware, 12", EX, A...$230.00
Stove, Dainty, Reading Stove Works, PA, 7x13x8", VG.$150.00
Stove, Eagle, plated CI & steel 6-burner w/ornate front, stovepipe w/shelf, 11", G, A $110.00
Stove, Eagle, sm, EX $200.00
Stove, Eclipse, EX..$175.00
Stove, footed ornate CI w/stovepipe shelf, 16", G-, A......$85.00

Stove, Kenton/Royal, polished CI & steel footed 4-burner w/ornate pipe shield, 10", no stovepipe, VG, A $100.00
Stove, Little Fanny, EX $300.00
Stove, Little Giant, unmk/unidentified, 7½x8½x11", EX orig $675.00
Stove, Little Willie, EX $75.00
Stove, Queen, 15" long, no shelves, EX....................$1,000.00
Stove, Queen, 9"long, no shelves, EX...........................$500.00
Stove, Rival, top warmers & oven, several accessories, 14", NM...$1,350.00
Stove, Rival, 12" long, no shelves, EX $900.00
Stove, Royal, sm, EX $200.00
Stove, The Pet, Young Bros, Albany NY, 10½x6x8½"...$165.00
Teakettle, porcelain, rnd w/flat bottom, S-shaped spout, bail hdl, EX $175.00

NURSERY

Baby Buggy, 1890, Joel Ellis type, wood w/red & wht pnt, fancy metal canopy supports, 3 wheels, 27x24", G, A.......$375.00
Carriage, ca 1870, blk & red wood w/spoke wheels, cloth convertible top w/fringe, 35", G-, A $200.00
Carriage, early, wht w/bl 4-wheeled wood fr w/dk bl tufted cloth seat & canopy, gold trim, 48", G, A........................$450.00
Carriage, early, 3-wheeled pnt wood w/canvas canopy & iron fittings, tufted leather seat & footrest, 21", VG+, A...$165.00
Carriage, early 1900s, wicker, cloth-covered parasol, brocade upholstery, 32", some damage, A $345.00
Carriage, mid-19th century, pnt wood & metal w/leatherette upholstry, convertible canopy, 29¾", G, A $489.00

Stove, Karr Range Co, painted sheet metal with blue and white finish, nickel-plated trim and iron accessories, removable grill, 21", NM, A, $3,000.00.

Carriage, wicker and wood, mounted on metal springs and wheels, replaced lining, 29", G+, A, $300.00.

Stove, Karr, Qualified, Belleville, IL, bl porcelain w/nickel, 1925, EX (repro in 1960s, same value for repro as orig) ..$2,500.00
Stove, Kenton/Royal, blk CI & steel 4-burner w/ornate front & working grates, 10", rpt, no stovepipe, G, A $45.00

Carriage, wicker, ornate spirals, footrest moves w/back to sit up or lie down, parasol, metal wheels, 36", EX, A.....$1,075.00
Carriage, wicker, wood floor, fr & wheels, 24", EX, A....$135.00
Carriage, wood, brn w/mc stencil, wood wheels w/metal rims, wood canopy w/oilcloth cover & fringe, 31x30", VG, A.....$575.00

Carriage, wood, pnt blk w/gold stencil, wood canopy covered w/oilcloth, wood rim wheels, 27", orig, EX, A $450.00

Carriage, wood, shaped sides, red w/blk stencil & bl stencil, pnt wood canopy, 4 lg wheels, 27", EX, A.....................$375.00

Carriage, wood & wicker w/wooden balls, curved hdl, metal fr & wheels, upholstered seat, parasol, 24x37", VG, A ...$300.00

Carriage, 1880s, pnt wood w/iron canopy fr, orig bl cloth canopy, blk & gold pnt wood spoke wheels, 27x34", EX, A $259.00

Carriage, 1880s, wood w/spindle & ball design, 4 wood wheels, hdl & handrest, 24x31", EX, A $200.00

Carriage, 1890s, wicker, front folds to be carriage or buggy, wire wheels, 29x20", orig finish, EX, A............................$259.00

Stroller, ornate wicker sides, footrest & back, wood fr, velvet upholstery w/matching ruffled pillow, 29", EX, A ...$440.00

Stroller, wood & wicker body w/wood knob trim, gr metal fr & wheels, parasol, 27", EX, A.......................................$475.00

Stroller, wood dowel-built w/a few lg balls as trim, metal wheels, pnt red w/gold accents, 25", EX, A $125.00

SERVING

Breakfast Set, Japan, wht w/pnt intersecting bl lines, biscuit jar, 2 teapots, cheese/butter dish & 8 more pcs, EX, A..$350.00

Castor Set, 2 cruets w/stoppers & 2 w/metal lids for shakers, sm 3-D girl on rim of hdl, 6½", EX, A $140.00

Castor Set, 4 glass condiment bottles w/stoppers in metal stand, rare sz, 2½", 1 bottle damaged, A $75.00

Dinner Set, Ridgways, Maiden Hair Fern lettered in banner, wht w/brn ferns, 27 pcs, VG, A $45.00

Dish, Czechoslovakia, 2 Kewpies in center, bird & frog on rim, Baby lettered above Kewpies, 5½", EX, A $175.00

Plate, Union Pacific Tea Co, 1907, litho tin w/children & bears in snow battle, 8⅛", EX, A...$115.00

Tea Set, Allerton's England, pk flowers w/mauve designs & gr leaves, mauve lustre trim, pot, 4 cups & 7 saucers, G, A...........$160.00

Tea Set, Bennett S-V Baltimore, Kewpie on ea pc, wht w/bl & rust color, 4 cups & saucers, EX, A $200.00

Tea Set, English, bluish w/flow-bl like flowers & vines, w/3 cups, 5 saucers, 4 plates & waste bowl, G, A $225.00

Tea Set, English Staffordshire, M mk, 1890s, flowers & vines blk transfer, 5 cups & 4 saucers, G, A $200.00

Tea Set, German, c Rose O'Neill Wilson Kewpie, wht w/pk touches, daisies & Kewpies, w/6 cups, saucers & plates, EX, A $1,300.00

Tea Set, German, Indian decal & gold trim on ornate shapes, w/4 cups & saucers, VG, A......................................$150.00

Tea Set, German, 1915, wht w/cobalt bands & sm bl flowers, 6 cups & saucers, EX (box bottom only), A $225.00

Tea Set, ironstone, w/6 cups, saucers, & plates, EX (VG box illus w/child & dog), A $105.00

Tea Set, Kate Greenaway, w/6 cups, saucers & plates, EX, A..$240.00

Tea Set, Little Miss Homemaker, Plastic Art, 15 pcs, MIB .$25.00

Tea Set, Minton Gaudy type, #664 in scroll on bottom, orange, dk bl & gold on wht, 15 pcs, EX, A $210.00

Tea Set, mk Basket #204, early English shapes, w/6 cups, saucers, 2 plates & waste bowl, rare, EX, A...........................$525.00

Tea Set, Noritake, wht w/plain gold bands, w/4 cups, saucers, plates, knives, forks & spoons, unused, (EX box), A .$85.00

SEWING

Little Red Spinning Wheel, Remco, 1961, EX (orig box), S1 ....$75.00

Sewing Machine, Casige, Germany/British Zone, works perfectly, EX, P3 ....$50.00

Sewing Machine, Singer, ca 1930s, EX (orig box).........$110.00

Sewing machine, Singer Model K-20, ca 1920s, EX, working, $135.00.

MISCELLANEOUS

Adding Machine, Wolverine, litho tin, M.......................$22.00

Bathtub, canvas in oval oak fr w/turned legs, folding, 8x11", EX, A $275.00

Garden Set, Arcade, salesman's sample, rake w/red hdl, hoe w/gr hdl & spade w/bl hdl, 36"-38", M, A.......................$525.00

Lawnmower, Arcade, salesman's sample, early push mower w/metal blades, yel & red w/wood hdl, 26½", M, A ..$325.00

Tea Set, German G (crown) H mark, pink lustre with pictures of children, serves three, VG, A, $275.00.

Scales, Toledo, orange CI, 6x5½", EX $219.00

Tub & Shower, German, pnt tin w/early wht tub & pump shower on emb wall, beveled base, 7", VG, A $275.00

Keystone

Though this Massachusetts company produced a variety of toys during their years of operation (ca 1920-late '50s), their pressed-steel vehicles are the most collectible, and that's what we've listed here. As a rule they were very large, with some of the riders more than 30" in length.

Army Truck, pnt khaki w/canvas cover, pnt flaking, 26½", VG, A $375.00

Coal Car, blk 4-wheeled type w/steering wheel, 19", rstr, EX, A $50.00

Dump Truck, Packard type w/lever-operated dump bed, 26", G, A $180.00

Dump Truck, pnt, gr cab w/orange dump, metal wheels, 23½", G, A $210.00

Dump Truck, red w/open cab, scissor dump mechanism, spoked wheels, 26", G-, A $150.00

Fire Department Ladder Truck, Packard type w/2 ladders, 8", scratches, G $300.00

Keystone Fleet, 1940s, sailboat, speedboat & canoe w/sail, wood & paper, set of 3, NM (EX+ box), A $110.00

Locomotive, rider, blk & red 6-wheel style w/lever whistle, 25", G-, A $60.00

Locomotive, rider, pnt steam type w/added electric lights, 26½", G, A $210.00

Locomotive, rider, red & blk 4-wheel type w/brass trim, sm steering wheel, 26", G-, A $90.00

Locomotive, rider, 2-tone w/NP trim, mk Keystone RR 6400, 25½", rstr, EX, A $150.00

Locomotive, rider, 2-tone 4-wheel type w/brass trim, mk Keystone RR 6400, 26", rstr, EX, A $110.00

Pullman Car, has hinged roof to operate steering, 25", rstr, EX, A $145.00

Pullman Car, pnt, orange & blk w/hinged opening top, 25", G, A $220.00

Railroad Engine, rider, red and black, EX, A, $275.00.

Railroad Wrecking Car, rider, blk & yel w/steering & operating crane, 19", rstr, EX, A $100.00

Railway Express Truck, pnt, screen-side truck, 2-pc wheels, 26", rpt, G, A $500.00

Sand Loader, yel & blk w/crank & chain operation, 17½", G, A $50.00

Steam Shovel, rider, red and black with metal wheels, 20¾", VG, $150.00.

Steam Shovel, rider, red & gray w/extended shovel boom, steering hdls, 20", G, A $35.00

US Army Troop Carrier, open cab with green canvas top over bed, 26", restored, VG, A, $200.00.

US Mail Truck, 1927, rstr, NM, R7............................$2,000.00

Water Tower Fire Truck, red w/decal reading Keystone Water Tower With Real Pump on water tank, 32", rstr, EX, A $450.00

Lehmann

Lehmann toys were made in Germany as early as 1881. Their early toys were sometimes animated by means of an inertia-generated flywheel; later, clockwork mechanisms were used. Some of their best-known turn-of-the-century toys were actually very racist and unflattering to certain ethnic groups. But the wonderful antics they perform and the imagination that went into their conception have made them and all the other Lehmann toys favorites with collectors today. Though the company faltered with the onset of WWI, they were quick to recover and during the war years produced some of their best toys, several of which were copied by their competitors. Business declined after WWI. Lehmann died in 1934, but the company continued for awhile under the direction of Lehmann's partner and cousin, Johannes Richter.

Advisor: Scott Smiles (S10).

WINDUPS, FRICTIONS AND OTHER MECHANICALS

Adam the Porter, #689, 8", G, from $500 to...................$550.00
AHA Delivery Van, driver in early van w/open cab, litho tin, 5", EX, A...$700.00
Alabama Coon Jigger, #695, NM (G- box), M5............$810.00
Alabama Coon Jigger, blk-skinned jigger in blk jacket & red pants atop red, blk & wht mk base, 10", EX, A.......$650.00

Alabama Coon Jigger, box only, EX, from $300.00 to $450.00.

ALSO Automobile, driver in early open car, gr w/bl trim, wht balloon tires w/red spokes, 3¾", M, A......................$475.00
Anxious Bride Nanni, lady w/head bowed in 2-wheeled carriage pulled by driver on 3-wheeler, 8¼", VG, S10.......$2,000.00
Auto Post, driver in early van w/open cab, yel litho tin w/wht spoked tires, clockwork, 5" long, EX, A................$1,350.00
Autobus, red w/yel striping & wht top, 8", EX, S10....$2,250.00
Autobus, red w/yel striping & wht top, 8", front wheel separated, VG, M5...$675.00
Baker & Sweep, baker on front of 3-wheeled cart w/sweep on back, hand-painted & litho tin, 5½", M (orig box), A...$5,200.00
Balky Mule, clown drives mule cart as he bounces up & down, 7½", EX (VG+ box w/instructions), M5.................$600.00
Balky Mule, clown drives mule cart as he bounces up & down, 7½", EX+ (EX box), S10, from $700 to $750.00
Bucking Bronco, see Wild West Bucking Bronco
Climbing Monkey, Pat 1892, monkey climbs up string when finger loops are pulled, 8", VG+, S10..........................$175.00

Climbing Monkey, Pat 1892, monkey climbs up string when finger loops are pulled, 8", EX (G box), S10 ....$300.00
Dancing Sailor, #535, 8", EX+ (EX box), M5.................$935.00
Dancing Sailor, tin figure in cloth sailor suit, mk SMS Bradenburg, 8", EX, S10, from $650 to................................$750.00

Dare Devil, lithographed tin figure in cart pulled by zebra, 7", scratches and dark finish otherwise VG, from $425.00 to $475.00.

DUO Rooster & Rabbit, rabbit atop 2-wheeled egg pulled by rooster, litho tin, clockwork, 6½", M, A..................$925.00
Echo Motorcycle #725, pnt & litho tin, 8¼", EX, A...$1,600.00
EPL-11 Zeppelin, litho tin w/celluloid props, 9½", missing props o/w EX, A $225.00
Express, man pulling 2-wheeled enclosed cart, 6", VG+, A...$350.00
Flying Bird, pnt tin w/pasteboard wings, 10" wingspan, M, A...$325.00
Gustav the Miller, pull-string action w/figure moving up & down on windmill pole, bag drops on head at top, 18", MIB, A...$300.00
Hansom Cab, driver atop pk cab w/gold trim carrying 2 passengers, wht spoked wheels, 5½", EX, from $2,000 to $2,200.00

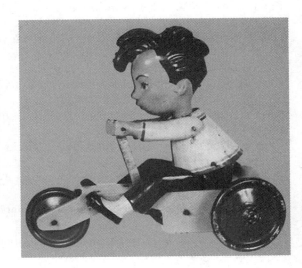

Heini, boy on scooter with back-and-forth action, 5x6", EX, A, $700.00.

ITO Sedan, driver in red & blk litho tin car w/gold trim, red spoked wheels, 6½", M, A $800.00

Kadi, litho tin, 6½", EX, A...$1,050.00

Lana Sedan, yel & blk litho tin, clockwork, 7" long, EX, A $2,500.00

Masayama (Rickshaw), 1927, w/driver & passenger, litho tin, clockwork, 6¾", EX, (G- box), A $2,000.00

Masayama (Rickshaw), 1927, w/driver & passenger, litho tin, clockwork, 6¾", MIB, A $3,400.00

Motorcoach, w/driver, pnt & litho tin, 5", G, S10, from $600 to...$650.00

NA-OB, 1907, donkey cart w/driver advances as offset wheels cause wagon to move erratically, tin, 6", EX, A.......$485.00

New Century Cycle, Black man holds umbrella over man on 3-wheeled vehicle, 5", G, from $425 to.....................$475.00

New Century Cycle, Black man holds umbrella over man on 3-wheeled vehicle, 5", EX+, A $1,550.00

OHO Automobile, man driving early open auto, 3¾", EX+, M5..$390.00

OHO Automobile, man driving early open auto, 3¾", M, A...$475.00

Paddy Pig, man riding pig, pig goes in circles, man goes sideways, 5¾", EX+, S10, from $1,200 to $1,250.00

Paddy Pig, man riding pig, pig goes in circles, man goes sideways, 5¾", G, S10, from $675 to......................................$725.00

PANNE Touring Car, driver in gray & red open car, wht tires w/red spokes, 6½", EX, A $1,000.00

Quack-Quack Duck Cart, mother duck pulling 3 ducklings in cart, litho tin, 7", MIB, A..$775.00

Racer w/Garage, yel Galop racer, litho tin 6¼" garage, EX, A...$1,300.00

Rigi 900 Cable Car, 1950, w/figures, MIB, R7 ....$325.00

Rigi 900 Cable Car, 1950, w/figures, NM, R7................$225.00

Royal Mail Truck EPL No 585, ca 1927, red & beige litho tin, 6½", EX, A $2,300.00

Sedan w/Garage, gr early auto, in litho tin 6¼" garage, EX, A...$700.00

Stubborn Donkey, clown drives mule cart w/tumbling clowns lithoed on wheels, 7½", NM (G box), from $600 to $650.00

Tap-Tap Man w/Wheelbarrow, litho tin, 6", EX, A.......$350.00

Tap-Tap Man w/Wheelbarrow, wht hat & pants, bl coat & blk boots, litho tin, 6½", NM (EX box), $600 to...........$650.00

Toy Balloon Jupiter, figure waving American flag in hot-air balloon, tin, hand-manipulated, 5¼", EX (orig box), A $5,600.00

Tut-Tut, man in open car blowing horn, pnt & litho tin, 7", NM, from $1,500 to $2,000.00

Tut-Tut, man in open car blowing horn, pnt & litho tin, 7", VG, S10...$1,000.00

Tyrus Walking Dog, brn & wht litho tin dog, clockwork, 6", EX, A...$625.00

UHU Amphibious Car, pnt tin driver in pnt tin car w/lithoed windshield, 9", EX, A $2,000.00

Walking Sailor, cloth-dressed tin figure in Columbia hat, 7½", G, from $500 to $550.00

Wild West Bucking Bronco, pnt tin cowboy & horse on platform, EX+ (NM box), S10, from $1,000 to $1,200.00

Photo courtesy of Scott Smiles.

Wild West Bucking Bronco, painted tin cowboy and horse on platform, VG+, $750.00.

Zig-Zag, 2 men at steering wheels facing each other between 2 lg wheels, litho tin, clockwork, 4¼", flaking, G, A **$825.00**

Zig-Zag, two men at steering wheels facing each other between two large wheels, lithographed tin, clockwork, 4¼", NM, from $2,000.00 to $2,200.00.

Zulu Ostrich Mail #721, Black driver on ostrich-driven 2-wheeled cart, yellow with red trim, clockwork, 6", EX, $400.00.

Zulu Ostrich Mail #721, Black driver on ostrich-driven 2-wheeled cart, yel litho tin w/red trim, 6", M, from $625 to...$675.00

Lunch Boxes

When the lunch box craze began in the mid-1980s, it was only the metal boxes that so quickly soared to sometimes astronomical prices. But today, even the plastic and vinyl ones are collectible. Though most lunch box dealers agree that prices have become much more reasonable than they were at first, they're still holding their own and values seem to be stabilizing. So pick a genre and have fun. There are literally hundreds to choose from, and just as is true in other areas of character-related collectibles, the more desirable lunch boxes are those with easily recognized, well-known subjects — western heroes, TV, Disney and other cartoon characters, and famous entertainers. Thermoses are collectible as well. In our listings, values are just for the box unless a thermos is mentioned in the description. If you'd like to learn more about them, we recommend *A Pictorial Price Guide to Metal Lunch Boxes and Thermoses* and a companion book *A Pictorial Price Guide to Vinyl and Plastic Lunch Boxes* by Larry Aikins. For more pricing information, Philip R. Norman (Norman's Olde Store) has prepared a listing of hundreds of boxes, thermoses, and their variations. He is listed in the Categories of Special Interest under Lunch Boxes.

Advisor: Terri Ivers (I2).

METAL

Bonanza, 1965, brown rim, with thermos, NM, M5, $110.00.

A-Team, 1985, w/plastic thermos, M, N2..........................$25.00
Adam-12, 1972, VG, I2...$20.00
America on Parade, w/thermos, EX, I2 ....$25.00
Animal Friends, 1975, blk letters, EX-, N2 ....$30.00
Annie, 1981, w/plastic thermos, EX, N2...........................$20.00
Annie Oakley & Tagg, Aladdin, 1956, w/thermos, EX, A..$205.00
Archies, 1969, w/plastic thermos, VG, I2 ....$69.00
Astronaut, 1960, dome top, EX-...................................$125.00
Barn, doors open, dome top, EX+, M5.............................$55.00
Battlestar Galactica, 1978, w/thermos, EX, I2 ....$35.00
Beatles, Aladdin, 1965, EX, C1..................................$450.00

Beatles, Aladdin, 1965, VG, I2 ....$275.00
Bedknobs & Broomsticks, 1972, VG+, I2......................$23.00
Bee Gees, 1978, features Barry, EX, I2 ....$32.00
Berenstain Bears, 1983, EX, I2 ....$26.00
Beverly Hillbillies, 1963, w/thermos, G+, I2.................$88.00
Bingo, 2 hdls, M, N2...$28.00
Bionic Woman, 1977, EX, I2...$25.00
Black Hole, 1979, EX, I2 ....$35.00
Bobby Sherman, 1972, EX+, C1....................................$69.00
Bobby Sherman, 1972, w/thermos, G, I2 ....$52.00
Bond XX, VG, M5..$90.00

Brave Eagle, VG+, M5, $75.00.

Buccaneer, 1957, dome top, VG+, N2............................$150.00
Buck Rogers, 1979, G+, I2...$18.00
Bugaloos, 1971, VG, from $40 to $65.00
Campus Queen, 1967, VG+, I2......................................$18.00
Canadian Birds, EX, M5...$200.00
Canadian Train, NM, M5...$60.00
Captain Kangaroo, 1964, w/thermos (no cup), VG+, I2 ..$199.00
Care Bear Cousins, 1985, w/thermos, VG, I2 ....$12.50
Care Bears, 1983, w/thermos, VG+, I2...........................$10.00
Chan Clan, 1973, w/thermos, NM, I2.............................$65.00
Charlie's Angels, 1978, w/thermos, VG, I2.....................$26.00
Clash of the Titans, 1981, EX, I2 ....$30.00
Corsage, 1964, EX, N2..$30.00
Corsage, 1964, VG+, I2...$23.00
Curiosity Shop, 1972, EX, N2 ....$50.00
Cyclist, 1979, EX $45.00
Davy Crockett, Holtemp, 1955, w/thermos, VG+, I2 ....$119.00

Davy Crockett, VG+, M5, $80.00.

Dick Tracy, Aladdin, 1967, G/M, from $100.00 to $200.00.

Disney Express, 1979, w/thermos, VG+, I2 ....$10.00
Disney Fire Fighters, 1969, dome top, EX+, I2 ....$70.00
Disney School Bus, orange, dome top, w/thermos, EX, I2 ..$29.00
Disneyland Castle, 1957, VG, N2 ....$59.00
Dr Doolittle, 1967, Canadian, EX, M5 ....$100.00
Dragon's Lair, 1983, w/plastic thermos, VG+, N2 ....$25.00
Dudley Do Right, w/generic thermos, NM, A $1,170.00
Dukes of Hazzard, 1980, VG, N2 ....$9.00
Dukes of Hazzard, 1980, w/thermos, EX, I2 ....$18.00
Dynomutt, 1976, EX, I2 ....$35.00
Emergency, 1977, dome top, VG+, I2 ....$69.00

**Empire Strikes Back, 1980, Swamp,
with thermos, EX, $40.00.**

Empire Strikes Back, 1980, Spaceship, VG+, N2 ....$16.00
Evel Knievel, Aladdin, 1974, VG+ $38.00
Evel Knievel, Aladdin, 1974, w/thermos, EX, I2 ....$42.00
Fall Guy, Aladdin, 1981, w/plastic thermos, EX, I2 ....$20.00
Fall Guy, Aladdin, 1981, w/plastic thermos, M $37.00
Family Affair, 1969, metal, w/thermos, EX, I2 ....$90.00
Fat Albert & the Cosby Kids, 1973, w/thermos, EX, I2 ....$40.00
Flintstones, Aladdin, 1962, red trim, w/thermos (no stopper),
 EX, A $160.00
Flipper, Thermos, 1967, w/thermos, EX, N2 ....$100.00
Flipper, Thermos, 1967, w/thermos, NM, A $180.00

Fox & the Hound, Aladdin, 1981, w/thermos, EX+ $30.00
Fox & the Hound, Aladdin, 1981, w/thermos, VG $18.00
Fraggle Rock, 1984, NM, I2...$16.00
Fruit Basket, 1975, EX, N2 ....$35.00
Funtastic World of Hanna-Barbera, Flintstones on front, Yogi &
 friends on back, G, I2 ....$32.00
Gene Autry Melody Ranch, Universal, 1954-55, w/thermos,
 NM, from $400 to..$500.00
Gene Autry Melody Ranch, Universal, 1954-55, w/thermos,
 VG, I2 ....$200.00
Gentle Ben, 1968, VG, P9...$40.00
Gentle Ben, 1968, w/thermos, EX, I2 ....$79.00
Ghostland, 1977, EX, N2 ....$35.00
GI Joe, 1967, EX-, I2...$78.00
GI Joe, 1967, G, N2..$26.00
Green Hornet, Thermos, w/thermos, EX+, A $276.00
Gremlins, 1984, w/plastic thermos, VG+, I2......................$8.00
Grizzly Adams, Aladdin, 1977, dome top, NM, A $65.00
Gunsmoke, 1959, EX, I2 ....$70.00
Gunsmoke, 1973, NM, I2 ....$89.00

**Gunsmoke, double LL version, crack on lid other-
wise NM, EX+ thermos, M5, $350.00.**

Hair Bear Bunch, 1971, VG, I2 ....$29.00
Hair Bear Bunch, 1971, w/plastic thermos, EX $55.00
Hansel & Gretel, 1977, EX- $35.00
Happy Days, 1976, EX-, N2 ....$25.00
Happy Days, 1976, G+, I2 ....$16.00
Hardy Boys Mysteries, 1977, EX, I2/N2 ....$22.00
Harlem Globetrotters, 1971, VG+ $29.00
He-Man & Masters of the Universe, 1984, EX $13.00
Heathcliff, 1982, w/thermos, EX, I2 ....$19.00
Hector Heathcote, 1964, EX, I2 ....$109.00
Hee Haw, Thermos, 1970, NM $38.00
Holly Hobbie, 1972, bl rim, EX, I2 ....$12.00
Holly Hobbie, 1973, park bench scene, EX, N2................$17.00
Holly Hobbie, 1975, profile w/flowers, EX, I2 ....$13.00
Hong Kong Phooey, 1975, VG, N2 ....$25.00
Hopalong Cassidy, Aladdin, bl, EX+, M5 ....$160.00
Hopalong Cassidy, Aladdin, ca 1950, red, EX, A $130.00
Hopalong Cassidy, Aladdin, ca 1950, red, w/thermos, NM,
 A $175.00

Hot Wheels, 1969, VG+, I2 ....$59.00

How the West Was Won, 1978, EX, I2/N2 ....$35.00

Huckleberry Hound & His Friends, 1961, VG+, M5........$85.00

Indiana Jones & the Temple of Doom, 1984, sword scene, VG+, I2 ....$15.00

It's About Time, Aladdin, VG, A $86.00

Jet Patrol, 1957, EX, M5..............................$250.00

Jetsons, Aladdin, 1963, dome top, EX-, I2 ....$515.00

Jetsons, Aladdin, 1963, dome top, yel trim, G, A..........$185.00

Joe Palooka, Continental Can, 1948, EX+, A $80.00

Julia, w/thermos, EX+, P9 ....$65.00

Junior Miss, 1966, girl w/bird, EX- $37.00

King Kong, 1977, w/thermos, VG, I2 ....$20.00

Kiss, 1977, EX+, I2 ....$100.00

Knight Rider, 1982, w/thermos (no cup), EX, I2 ....$13.00

Korg, Thermos, 1975, NM+, C1 ....$59.00

Krofft Supershow, 1976, w/thermos, VG, I2 ....$35.00

Kung Fu, King Seeley, 1974, w/thermos, M (NM box).....$55.00

Kung Fu, King Seely, 1974, VG+, I2 ....$18.00

Land of the Giants, Aladdin, 1968, gr trim, w/thermos, EX+, A $110.00

Laugh-In, 1968, helmet scene on bk, G, I2 ....$25.00

Lawman, Thermos, 1961, EX, A $75.00

Legend of the Lone Ranger, 1980, EX-, N2 ....$25.00

Life & Times of Grizzly Adams, 1977, VG, I2 ....$41.00

Little House on the Prairie, 1978, w/thermos (no cup), VG+, I2 ....$42.00

Muppet Show, 1978, EX, I2..............................$14.00

Muppets, 1979, Kermit on back, VG+, I2 ....$10.00

NFL, 1978, helmets on band, EX-, N2 ....$19.00

Osmonds, 1973, EX, I2 ....$33.00

Pac-Man, VG $9.00

Pac-man, Aladdin, 1980, yel trim, w/thermos & tag, NM, A $20.00

Partridge Family, 1971, EX, I2 ....$45.00

Peanuts, 1966, tan rim, w/metal thermos, EX-, N2...........$40.00

Pebbles & Bamm-Bamm, 1971, EX, I2 ....$65.00

Pete's Dragon, 1978, EX, I2/N2 ....$27.50

Pigs in Space, 1979, VG+, I2 ....$21.00

Pink Gingham, 1976, EX $25.00

Pink Panther & Sons, 1984, EX-, N2 ....$20.00

Pinocchio, 1971, EX, I2 ....$45.00

Plaid, Aladdin, red & blk, w/thermos (no cup), EX+, A ..$15.00

Plaid Scotch, Ohio Art, 1964, yel hdl, EX, I2 ....$8.00

Planet of the Apes, Aladdin, 1974, EX, C1 ....$69.00

Planet of the Apes, Aladdin, 1974, w/thermos, EX+, P9 ..$80.00

Popeye, Aladdin, 1980, EX $26.00

Popeye, Thermos, 1964, blk trim, w/thermos, EX, A......$105.00

Popples, 1986, w/worn thermos, EX, I2 ....$6.00

Porky's Lunch Wagon, dome top, EX+, P9 ....$250.00

Pro Sports, 1962, EX $55.00

Raggedy Ann & Andy, VG+, I2 ....$13.00

Rambo, 1985, VG, I2 ....$7.00

Lone Ranger, EX+, M5, $38.00; Monroes, EX+, M5, $100.00.

Lone Ranger, 1954, red band, EX+, P9 ....$325.00

Looney Toons TV Set, 1959, G+, M5 ....$70.00

Looney Toons TV Set, 1959, VG, I2 ....$120.00

Lost in Space, dome top, EX+, A $400.00

Magic Kingdom, Aladdin, 1979, w/thermos & tag, bl trim, M, A $35.00

Magic of Lassie, 1978, EX, N2 ....$26.00

Mickey & Donald, 1954, VG+, I2 ....$190.00

Mickey Mouse Club, 1977, w/thermos, EX, I2 ....$23.00

Mod Tulips, 1962, dome top, EX, N2 ....$225.00

Monroes, 1967, VG, N2 ....$79.00

Mork & Mindy, Thermos, 1978, VG, N2 ....$20.00

Mork & Mindy, Thermos, 1978, w/plastic thermos, EX ...$38.00

Mr Merlin, w/plastic thermos, EX, I2 ....$23.00

Munsters, Thermos, 1965, blk trim, w/thermos, NM, A ..$250.00

Rat Patrol, EX, $70.00.

Red Barn, 1957, dome top, open doors, VG, N2 ....$39.00

Red Barn, 1971, dome top, metal thermos, EX+ $110.00

Return of the Jedi, 1983, w/plastic thermos, VG+, I2.......$25.00

Road Runner, 1970, G+, N2 ....$17.00

Ronald McDonald Sheriff of Cactus Canyon, 1982, w/thermos, VG, I2 ....$18.00

Rose Petal Place, 1983, EX $25.00

Rough Rider, 1972, EX+, N2 ....$50.00

Roy Rogers & Dale Evans, Thermos, 1953, Roy on Trigger, wood-grain trim, w/thermos (no stopper), EX $95.00

Roy Rogers & Dale Evans, Thermos, 1958, EX, A $110.00

Roy Rogers & Dale Evans Double R Bar Ranch, 1954, bl bands, EX, I2 ....$105.00

Roy Rogers' Chow Wagon, dome top, with thermos, NM, $250.00.

Satellite, Thermos, 1958, VG, I2 ....$35.00
School Days, 1960, VG+ $45.00
Scooby Doo, 1973, yel rim, VG, N2.................................$18.00
Scooby Doo, 1973, yel rim, w/thermos, NM, P9 ....$70.00
Secret Wars, 1984, EX, I2 ....$19.00
See America, Ohio Art, EX, P9..$45.00
Sesame Street, 1979, w/thermos (no cup), NM, I2 ....$19.00
Six Million Dollar Man, 1974, VG+, N2 ....$17.00
Six Million Dollar Man, 1974, w/thermos, G, I2 ....$12.00
Snow White (Disney), 1975, EX-......................................$40.00
Space 1999, 1975, w/plastic thermos, EX-........................$40.00
Speed Buggy, Thermos, 1974, w/plastic thermos, unused, NM+, C1..$60.00
Sport Goofy, Aladdin, 1983, EX, I2 ....$10.00
Sport Goofy, Aladdin, 1983, yel trim, w/thermos, NM, A .$25.00
Sport Goofy, 1984, EX-..$20.00
Sport Skwirts, 1982, EX, I2..$22.00
Star Trek the Motion Picture, 1979, EX, I2......................$39.00
Star Trek the Motion Picture, 1979, w/thermos, M, A ..$125.00
Star Wars, 1977, characters on band, w/thermos, EX+ $36.00
Steve Canyon, 1959, EX, I2 ....$180.00
Strawberry Shortcake, 1980, w/thermos, EX, I2 ....$8.00
Submarine, 1960, rope hdl, G, I2 ....$29.00
Super Friends, 1976, G, I2 ....$16.00

Super Heroes, Aladdin, 1976, black trim, NM+, $40.00.

Super Powers, 1983, EX, I2..$26.00
Superman, c Nat'l Comics Pub Inc, 1954, Superman fighting lg robot, EX, A...$750.00
Superman, 1978, w/plastic thermos, EX, I2.....................$20.00
Superman, 1978, w/plastic thermos, NM, C1 ....$39.00

Superman, 1954, inside painted white, some spilled onto sides, sides slightly wavy, M5, $405.00.

Tarzan, Aladdin, 1967, gr trim, EX, A $65.00
Teen School Days, Thermos, 1960, dome top, EX, A $65.00
Teen School Days, Thermos, 1960, rectangular, EX........$30.00
Teenager, 1957, dome top, NM, I2 ....$75.00
Three Little Pigs, 1982, EX...$45.00

Tom Corbett Space Cadet, EX+, M5, $330.00.

Transformers, 1986, EX, N2 ....$10.00
Transformers, 1986, w/plastic thermos, EX, I2.................$16.00
Traveler, 1962, red trim, EX...$60.00
Traveler, 1964, brn, EX, N2 ....$60.00
UFO, 1973, VG+, I2..$38.00
Underdog, w/thermos, scarce, NM, A $1,235.00
Universal Monsters, 1979, G, I2.......................................$18.00
US Mail, 1969, dome top, w/plastic thermos, EX $50.00
V, 1985, EX-, N2 ....$98.00
Voyage to the Bottom of the Sea, 1967, w/thermos, VG, I2...$125.00

Wagon Train, 1964, VG, I2 ....$72.00
Walt Disney World, 1972, VG, I2.................................$14.00
Washington Redskins, 1970, VG, N2 ....$145.00
Welcome Back Kotter, 1976, w/plastic thermos, EX-, N2 ..$45.00
Welcome Back Kotter, 1977, EX, N2............................$35.00
Welcome Back Kotter, 1977, w/thermos, VG, I2 ....$23.00
Wild Bill Hickok & Jingles, 1955, EX, I2 ....$62.00
Wild Frontier, 1977, EX+, N2......................................$52.00
Wild Frontier, 1977, VG, N2..$25.00
Woody Woodpecker, 1972, VG, I2 ....$48.00
Yankee Doodle, 1975, w/plastic thermos, EX, N2 ....$40.00
Yogi Bear & Friends, 1963, EX+, M5.............................$80.00
Zorro, 1958, blk rim, EX+, I2 ....$80.00
18 Wheeler, 1978, EX, N2...$57.00

PLASTIC

A-Team, 1983, red, EX, I2 ....$6.00
A-Team, 1985, red, w/thermos, EX, I2............................$10.00

A-Team, Thermos, 1985, NM, $5.00.

Alf, Thermos, 1987, red, w/thermos, VG+, I2 ....$5.00
Batman, 1982, Joker, bl, w/thermos, EX, I2 ....$8.00
Batman, 1991, Batman throwing rope on rooftop, bl, w/thermos, EX, I2 ....$5.00
Beauty & the Beast, Aladdin, purple, w/thermos, EX, I2....$7.00
Benji, 1974, bl, EX, I2...$12.00
Betsy Clark, 1976, yel, w/thermos, old store stock, M, I2 .$40.00
Beverly Hills 90210, purple, w/thermos, VG, I2 ....$5.00
Bozostuffs, 1988, red, w/thermos, EX, I2 ....$15.00
Cabbage Patch Kids, 1983, yel, w/thermos, EX, I2.............$6.00
California Raisins, 1988, NM, N2.....................................$15.00
Chicklets, 1987, w/thermos, M, N2 ....$50.00
Dark Crystal, 1982, w/thermos, VG+, I2...........................$8.00
Deka 4/4, 1988, w/thermos, M, N2 ....$35.00
Garfield, 1978, red, Odie kissing Garfield, w/thermos, EX+, I2 .$6.00

Hot Wheels, Thermos, 1984, red, EX, I2 ....$10.00
Howdy Doody, 1977, EX, N2 ....$30.00
Inspector Gadget, 1983, bl, EX, I2....................................$4.00

Jem, Aladdin, bright yellow background, with thermos, NM, $10.00.

Jetsons, 1987, 3-D, purple, w/thermos, M $60.00
Little Mermaid, purple, w/thermos, EX, I2 ....$7.00
Mighty Mouse, 1979, EX, N2 ....$20.00
Minnie Mouse, 1992, figural head, w/thermos, EX, I2 ......$19.50
Miss Piggy, 1980, yel, Miss Piggy riding motorcycle, EX, I2 ..$12.00
Moon Dreamers, Aladdin, 1987, bl, w/thermos, VG+, I2....$5.00
My Little Pony, Aladdin, 1989, bl w/merry-go-round scene, w/thermos, minor scuffs on rim o/w EX, I2..................$6.00
New Kids on the Block, 1990, orange, w/thermos, NM, I2.$8.00
Pee Wee Herman, 1987, w/thermos, EX, N2 ....$15.00
Popeye, 1979, dome top, EX, N2 ....$40.00

Pink Panther and Sons, 1984, with thermos, EX, $12.00.

Punky Brewster, 1984, w/thermos, M $30.00
Punky Brewster, 1984, w/thermos, VG+, I2 ....$14.00
Rainbow Brite, 1984, yel, w/thermos, EX, I2 ....$5.00
Return of the Jedi, 1983, Wicket & R2-D2, red, w/thermos, EX, I2 ....$13.00
Smurf, 1984, bl w/fishing scene, toadstool thermos, VG+, I2 ....$5.00
Smurfette, pk w/flowers & butterflies, VG, I2 ....$6.00
Snoopy, 1978, bl, dome top, EX, I2 ....$5.00
Snoopy & Woodstock, 1971, dome top, w/thermos, EX, N2 .$25.00
Sport Billy, 1982, w/thermos, EX, N2 ....$35.00
Star Trek the Next Generation, 1988, purple, EX, I2 ....$10.00
Tang Trio, 1988, orange, w/thermos, M, N2 ....$40.00
Teenage Mutant Ninja Turtles, 1990, bl, w/decaled thermos, EX, I2 ....$5.00
Tiny Toon Adventures, 1990, purple, EX+, I2 ....$4.00

Toronto Blue Jays, with thermos, NM, $50.00.

Treasure Trolls, 1992, purple, w/thermos, NM, I2 ....$7.00
Washington Redskins, dome top, EX, N2 ....$25.00
Who Framed Roger Rabbit?, red, EX, I2 ....$6.00
Wizard of Oz, Aladdin, 1989, bl, w/thermos, VG, I2 ....$25.00
Wuzzles, 1985, dome top, w/thermos, VG, N2 ....$20.00
WWF w/Hulk Hogan, 1987, bl, w/thermos, EX, I2 ....$12.00
Yogi's Treasure Hunt, 1987, 3-D, gr, w/thermos, M, N2 ..$65.00
101 Dalmatians, red, w/thermos, EX, I2 ....$5.00

VINYL

Barbie and Midge, black, with thermos, EX, $125.00; World of Barbie, blue, with thermos, NM, $40.00.

All Dressed Up, bl, w/styrofoam thermos, NM, I2 ....$75.00
Alvin & the Chipmunks, 1963, gr, NM, I2 ....$285.00
Annie, 1981, w/plastic thermos (no cup or cap), VG, I2..$25.00
Barbie & Midge, 1963, w/metal thermos, EX, N2 ....$125.00
Barbie & Midge, 1965, blk, EX....................................$75.00
Beatles, Airflite, red, G, I2 ....$450.00
Betsy Clark, w/thermos, store stock, M, I2 ....$75.00
Boston Red Sox, wht, w/styrofoam thermos, NM, I2 ....$70.00
Buck Rogers in the 25th Century, 1979, w/plastic thermos, G, I2 ....$20.00
Captain Kangaroo, 1964, red, VG, I2 ....$185.00
Charlie's Angels, 1977, brunch bag, w/thermos, NM, I2 ..$90.00
Dawn, 1970, wht, w/thermos, EX, I2 ....$99.00
Deputy Dawg, Thermos, 1962, rare, EX, A....................$350.00
Donny & Marie, Aladdin, 1976, wht, EX, C1 ....$42.00
Engine Co #1, 1974, dome top, EX, N2 ....$90.00
Flying Nun, 1968, EX-, N2...$175.00
Kewtie Pie, 1964, w/metal thermos, EX $190.00
Ladybug, 1978, w/drawstring closure, EX, N2 ....$39.00
Mardi Gras, 1971, w/thermos, EX, N2 ....$75.00
Monkees, King Seeley/Raybert, 1967, w/thermos, EX $250.00
Peanuts, 1969, Peanuts playing baseball, red, EX, N2.......$60.00
Peanuts, 1977, brunch bag w/plastic thermos, EX, N2......$75.00
Pink Panther, 1980, vinyl, EX, N2 ....$75.00
Planters Peanuts, brunch bag, EX+, P9 ....$40.00
Shari Lewis, 1963, blk, NM, C1 ....$360.00

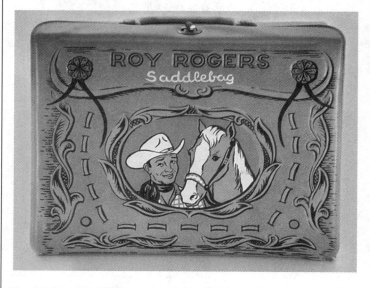

Roy Rogers Saddlebag, American Thermos, 1960, tan background, NM, $195.00.

Speedy Turtle, 1978, w/drawstring closure, EX, N2 ....$39.00
Strawberry Shortcake, 1980, w/plastic thermos, EX, N2 ....$40.00
Tic Tac Toe, 1977, red, EX, N2 ....$50.00
Tinkerbell, 1969, EX, N2 ....$200.00
Tropical Swim Club, red, EX, N2....................................$55.00
US Space Shuttle Challenger, 1986, puffy, M, N2 ....$250.00
Wonder Woman, 1978, EX, N2 ....$175.00
Ziggy, 1979, EX, N2 ....$60.00

THERMOSES

Beverly Hillbillies, Thermos, metal with plastic cup, EX+, $60.00.

ABC Sports, 1976, metal, G, N2.......................................$12.00
Addams Family, 1974, plastic, no cup, EX, I2....................$12.00
Aladdin, litho plastic, EX, I2..$3.00
Annie Oakley, Canadian, EX-, M5....................................$70.00
Archies, 1969, plastic w/glass liner, EX, N2......................$30.00
Babar, 1988, plastic, M, I2..$2.00
Banana Splits, 1969, metal, red cup, EX, I2......................$55.00
Barbie, 1962, blk w/tan cup, EX, I2.................................$33.00
Baseball, red cap, yel background, EX+, M5.....................$39.00
Bionic Woman, 1977, plastic, EX, N2...............................$12.00
Buccaneer, yel background, EX+, M5................................$35.00
Campbell's Soup Fuel For Fitness, 1984, plastic, Official Soup
     Winter Olympics Sarajevo emblem, M, I2.................$16.00

Casper the Ghost, Thermos, metal with plastic cup, EX+, $80.00.

Chan-Clan, Thermos, 1973, NM, C1 ....$18.00

Chitty-Chitty Bang-Bang, 1968, metal, EX, I2 ....$22.00
Chuck Conners, Cowboy in Africa, 1958, EX+, C1 ....$49.00
Cracker Jack, 1979, plastic, EX, N2 ....$20.00
Davy Crockett, Holtemp, steel & glass, 1950s, NM, C1 ..$54.00
Dawn, Topper Aladdin, 1970, plastic, yel & wht, EX+, I2 ..$29.00
Disneyland Castle, 1957, metal, EX, I2 ....$38.00
Donny & Marie, 1976, long-hair version, plastic, yel, no stopper,
     NM, I2 ....$12.00
Duchess, 1960, metal, EX, N2 ....$25.00
Dunkin' Donuts, metal, G-, N2 ....$7.00
Dunkin' Donuts, plastic w/glass liner, EX, N2 ....$20.00
Evel Knievel, 1974, plastic, EX, N2 ....$12.00
Flintstones, 1962, metal, EX+, N2 ....$70.00
Flintstones, 1964, metal, yel w/picnic scene, VG, I2 ....$33.00
Flying Nun, 1968, metal, no cup or stopper, VG, I2 ....$25.00
Game Birds & Fish, 1973, EX, I2 ....$12.00
GI Joe, 1967, metal, EX, N2 ....$35.00
Gigi, 1962, metal, red cup & cap, EX, I2 ....$18.00
Green Hornet, 1967, metal, red cup, EX+, I2 ....$83.00
Holly Hobbie, 1979, plastic, EX, I2 ....$4.00
Howdy Doody, 1977, plastic, dk red cup, EX, I2 ....$12.00
Huckleberry Hound & Friends, 1961, metal, blk cup & red stop-
     per, NM, I2 ....$50.00
It's a Small World, metal, wht cup, EX+, I2 ....$35.00
James Bond, EX, M5 ....$50.00
Junior Nurse, 1963, metal, EX, I2 ....$45.00
Land of the Giants, 1968, plastic, EX+, I2 ....$25.00
Land of the Lost, 1975, plastic, VG, N2 ....$15.00
Looney Tunes, 1959, EX+, C1 ....$60.00
Love, 1972, plastic w/glass liner, EX, N2 ....$25.00
Magic of Lassie, 1978, plastic, EX, I2 ....$18.00
Mary Poppins, 1964, metal, VG+, I2 ....$24.00
Mighty Mouse, 1979, plastic, EX, I2 ....$13.00
Outdoor Sports, 1960, metal, EX, N2 ....$50.00
Partridge Family, 1971, metal, EX, N2 ....$35.00
Peanuts, 1966, metal, no cup, VG+, I2 ....$10.00
Planet of the Apes, 1974, plastic, no cup, G, I2 ....$7.00
Pussycats, 1968, metal, no cup, VG, I2 ....$12.00
Pyschedelic Blue, 1970, metal, VG, N2 ....$12.00
Robin Hood, 1956, gr cap, EX+, M5 ....$50.00
Robin Hood, 1956, metal, no cap or cup, G, I2 ....$24.00
Rough Rider, 1972, plastic, EX, N2 ....$20.00
Shari Lewis, 1963, EX, I2 ....$36.00
Space 1999, 1975, plastic, EX, N2 ....$12.00

Superman, Canadian, lg Superman, red cap, bl band at bottom, rare, EX+, M5 ....\$50.00
Superman, 1967, metal, EX, N2 ....\$45.00
Tarzan, Canadian, swinging on vine, EX+, M5 ....\$43.00
Tarzan, 1966, metal, no cup, VG+, I2..............\$25.00
Tom Corbett Space Cadet, Aladdin, 1952, metal, no cup, G+, I2 ....\$45.00
Tom Corbett Space Cadet, Aladdin, 1952, metal w/plastic lid, 7", NM........................\$75.00
Treasure Chest, 1961, metal, EX, N2 ....\$89.00
Wags & Whiskers, 1978, plastic, yel cup, EX, I2 ....\$5.00
Winnie the Pooh, 1976, plastic, EX, N2 ....\$20.00
Winston Cigarettes, plastic w/glass liner, EX, N2.............\$35.00
Wonder Woman, 1977, plastic, EX, I2.............\$15.00
Woody Woodpecker, 1972, plastic w/glass liner, EX, N2.........\$40.00

Buccaneer, EX+, \$35.00; Hopalong Cassidy, EX+, \$80.00; Robin Hood, red cap, EX+, \$30.00; Ovaltine, 1976 Olympics, NM, \$15.00; Monkees, EX+, \$75.00; Popeye, EX, \$38.00; Roy Rogers, EX+, \$58.00.

Marbles

Antique marbles are divided into several classifications: 1) Transparent Swirl (Solid Core, Latticinio Core, Divided Core, Ribbon Core, Lobed Core, and Coreless); 2) Lutz or Lutz-type (with bands having copper flecks which alternate with colored or clear bands; 3) Peppermint Swirl (made of red, white, and blue opaque glass); 4) Indian Swirl (black with multicolored surface swirls); Banded Swirl (wide swirling bands on opaque or transparent glass); 6) Onionskin (having an overall mottled appearance due to its spotted, swirling lines or lobes: 7) End of Day (single pontil, allover spots, either 2-colored or multicolored); 8) Clambroth (evenly spaced, swirled lines on opaque glass); 9) Mica (transparent color with mica flakes added); 10) Sulphide (nearly always clear, colored examples are rare, containing figures). Besides glass marbles, some were made of clay, pottery, china, steel, and even semiprecious stones.

Most machine-made marbles are still very reasonable, but some of the better examples may sell for \$50.00 and up, depending on the colors that were used and how they are defined. Guineas (Christensen agates with small multicolored specks instead of swirls) sometime go for as much as \$200.00. Mt. Peltier comic character marbles often bring prices of \$100.00 and more with Betty Boop and Kayo being the rarest and most valuable.

From the nature of their use, mint-condition marbles are extremely rare and may be worth as much as three to five times more than one that is near-mint, while chipped and cracked marbles may be worth half or less. The same is true of one that has been polished, regardless of how successful the polishing was. If you'd like to learn more, Everett Grist has written three books on the subject that you will find helpful: *Antique and Collectible Marbles*, *Machine Made and Contemporary Marbles*, and *Everett Grist's Big Book of Marbles*.

Artist-Made, crown filigree & peppermints, contemporary, by Bill Burchfield, 1", M.................\$35.00
Artist-Made, onionskin lutz, wht, bl & cranberry, sgn Harry Boyer, 1½", M, A \$85.00
Banded Lutz, handmade, peewee, clear base w/4 lt bl bands, lutz bands edged in wht, ½", NM, A \$80.00
Banded Opaque, handmade, semitranslucent milky wht w/slight opalescent glow, semitranslucent pk center band, ¾", NM, A \$105.00
Banded Opaque Lutz, handmade, semiopaque amethyst w/2 lutz bands edged in wht, 4 olive gr strands, ¾", EX+, A.\$140.00
Banded Swirl, bubble-filled transparent core, 4 wide alternating outer bands of translucent colors, 1⅝", rare, NM, A ..\$130.00
Banded Swirl, handmade, transparent amber w/1 subsurface wht band, ⅝", EX+, A.....................\$40.00
China, 2-color design, glazed, ⅝", M................\$25.00

Chinko-Checko-Marblo, Berry Pink Inc, solid colors in red, yellow, blue, green, black and white, \$50.00.

Clambroth, handmade, cranberry w/gray stripes, ⅝", several tiny flakes on surface o/w NM, A \$140.00

Clambroth, handmade, opaque blk w/wht stripes, ⅝", NM, A $210.00

Clambroth, handmade, opaque wht w/lime gr stripes, ⅝", several sm surface chips/overall roughness, G+, A.................$80.00

Clambroth, handmade, semiopaque wht base w/18 alternating bl & pk stripes, ⅝", EX+, A $80.00

Clambroth, semiopaque wht base w/lime gr & pale bl stripes, ⅝", several mars/some glass missing, G+, A......................$60.00

Comic Strip, Annie, blk transfer on wht w/lt red patch, Peltier, ⅝", NM, A $110.00

Comic Strip, Bimbo, blk transfer on mustard w/lt red patch, Peltier, ⅝", NM, A $140.00

Custard Swirl, handmade, semiopaque w/red outer bands & 1 opaque wht band, ⅝", NM, A $75.00

Divided Core Swirl, yel & red inner bands, wht & yel inner threads, 3-color outer bands, ⅝", M $25.00

Divided Core Swirl, 3 wide 3-color inner bands, 5 sets of alternating wht & yel threads, 1¾", M..........................$100.00

End of Day, cloud type w/mica, yel core w/transparent red & opaque gr splotches, single pontil, 2", rare, EX+, A ..$485.00

End of Day, handmade, onionskin lutz, dk gr bands w/lutz covering entire core surface, ⅝", M, A $210.00

End of Day, handmade, onionskin lutz, opaque yel onionskin core coated w/fine layer & heavy bands of lutz, ⅝", M, A ..$175.00

End of Day, handmade, onionskin lutz, semiopaque wht & bright yel w/4 bands of lutz, ½", EX+, A $160.00

End of Day, handmade, onionskin lutz, semiopaque wht & gr bands, 40% of surface is lutz bands, ½", NM, A.......$160.00

End of Day, handmade, onionskin lutz, translucent wht & lt bl & wht bands covered w/finely ground lutz, ½", M, A...$160.00

End of Day, onionskin, opaque wht & transparent pk w/sm splotches of bl & yel, 1¾", NM, A.............................$215.00

End of Day, onionskin w/mica, yel core covered w/transparent red splotches, 1⅝", minor scratches o/w NM, A......$360.00

End of Day, 4-panel onionskin, opaque wht & bl alternating w/opaque yel & translucent red, 1½", M, A $295.00

End of Day, 4-panel onionskin w/bl on mustard & red on mustard, 2¼" (unusual sz), needs polished, G, A $235.00

Gooseberry, clear gr w/wht swirl at surface, ⅝", M $250.00

Indian, slag-type, opaque blk w/dk red bands, ¾", NM.....$40.00

Indian Lutz, handmade, opaque blk base w/slag-type stripes & lutz bands cased in clear glass, ⅝", NM, A...............$460.00

Indian Lutz, handmade, opaque blk w/lutz stripe edged in wht & yel, ⅝", rare, M, A $405.00

Indian Swirl, blk w/earth-tone swirls at surface, ⅝", M $85.00

Indian Swirl, handmade, opaque blk base w/clear overglaze, gr & wht outer bands w/1 set of pk & wht, ½", NM, A $85.00

Indian Swirl, handmade, opaque blk w/2 sets of lt bl outer bands edged in wht, ¾", minor rough spots o/w NM, A $85.00

Indian Swirl, handmade, semitranslucent amethyst w/4 olive gr outer bands edged in various colors, ⅝", EX+, A $80.00

Joseph Swirl, bl-tinted glass, mc swirl, ⅝", M.....................$85.00

Latticinio Swirl, alternating yel & wht core, 3 translucent red & gr outer bands alternating w/red & bl, 1⅝", NM, A ..$40.00

Latticinio Swirl, dk orange core in clear glass, 3 translucent bl & 3 opaque wht outer bands, ¾", NM, A......................$50.00

Latticinio Swirl, wht & yel core w/2 red, wht & bl outer ribbon swirls, 1⅝", rare, NM, A $110.00

Latticinio Swirl, wht core in clear glass w/8 mc outer bands, 2⅛", bands not formed correctly & few chips, G, A...........$95.00

Latticinio Swirl, yel core, blk & red outer bands, 1¾", M ..$85.00

Line Crockery, zigzag bl lines in clay, ⅝", M.....................$10.00

Lutz, aqua w/wht & wht-bordered gold swirl at surface, ⅝", M...$165.00

Lutz, clear w/bl, wht & gold surface swirls, ⅝", M $100.00

Lutz, opaque bl w/wht & wht-bordered gold swirl at surface, ⅝", M...$200.00

Machine-Made, bl guinea, single-seam diaper-fold design w/gr, bl & orange flecks, Christensen Agate, ⅝", M, A ...$395.00

Machine-Made, bl oxblood corkscrew, Akro Agate, ⅝", rare, M, A $65.00

Machine-Made, brick-type, oxblood base w/blk lines & sm bl & wht splotches, MF Christensen & Son, ⅝", M, A $70.00

Machine-Made, brick-type, oxblood w/several wht patches & blk lines, MF Christensen & Son, ⅝", NM, A...........$50.00

Machine-Made, carnelian oxblood w/few swirls of milky wht & 1 oxblood corkscrew, rare, ⅝", NM, A $50.00

Machine-Made, egg yolk oxblood, semitranslucent milky wht & semiopaque yellow, Akro Agate, ⅝", NM, A.............$45.00

Machine-Made, lemonade & oxblood, Akro Agate, ½" to ¾", M, ea $75.00

Machine-Made, opaque blk w/gray snowflakes, 2", M, A .$25.00

Machine-Made, oxblood swirl, Akro Agate, ½" to ¾", M, ea ..$20.00

Machine-Made, purple slag, melted pontil, ⅞", NM.........$40.00

Machine-Made, swirl oxblood corkscrew, transparent base, Akro Agate, ⅝", rare, M, A $85.00

Machine-Made, translucent milky wht & semiopaque electric red swirl, Am Agate/Christensen Agate, ¾", M, A ...$20.00

Machine-Made, transparent amber w/aventurine, ⅞", M, A..$30.00

Machine-Made, 3-color Rainbo, 'Ketchup & Mustard,' wht base w/red & yel ribbon swirls, Peltier, ⅝", NM, A $35.00

Machine-Made, 3-color Rainbo, 'Patriot or Liberty,' wht base w/red & slate bl ribbon swirls, Peltier, ⅝", NM, A $45.00

Machine-Made, 3-color Rainbo, 'Superman,' lt bl base w/red & yel ribbon swirls, Peltier, ⅝", NM, A $65.00

Machine-Made, 3-color Rainbo, opaque wht base w/4 bands of translucent red & 2 opaque blk, Peltier, ⅝", M, A $35.00

Machine-Made, 3-color Rainbo w/aventurine, wht, red & blk, Peltier, ⅝", NM, A..$65.00

Machine-Made, 4-color Popeye, opaque purple, yel, wht & clear, Akro Agate, ⅝", NM, A $50.00

Mica, transparent gr w/flecks, ⅝", M $20.00

Opaque Glass Swirl, sky blue and aqua with gold lutz-type band in center, ⅝", $200.00; 1¾", $1,250.00.

Onionskin, red, gr & wht, cloud type w/mica, 1¾", M ...$450.00

Onionskin, red, yel, bl & yel ribbons w/lt swirl, mica flecks over-all, 1¾", M $500.00

Onionskin, red & wht ribbons w/lt swirl, mica flecks, 1¾", M.$450.00

Onionskin, 4-lobed in red & wht w/sm bl flecks, pk blends between red & wht, 1¾", M $400.00

Onionskin, 4-lobed w/1 yel swirl & red flecks, 1 wht swirl w/gr flecks, mica & blk flecks, 1¾", M............................$200.00

Peppermint Swirl, handmade, beach-ball style, 4 red & bl bands alternating w/wht, ⅝", NM, A $85.00

Peppermint Swirl, handmade, clear core w/opaque red, wht & bl outer bands, ⅝", EX+, A................................$95.00

Peppermint Swirl, handmade, opaque bl & wht bands w/3 semi-translucent red bands on ea wht, ¾", NM, A $120.00

Peppermint Swirl, opaque, red, wht & bl, ⅝", M............$100.00

Ribbon Core Lutz, blood red w/wht-bordered gold swirl, ⅝", M..$275.00

Ribbon Core Swirl, alternating stripes of opaque red, wht & yel, 1¼", several dings o/w VG, A...............................$90.00

Ribbon Core Swirl, handmade, blk & wht core w/2 sets of blk & cranberry outer bands, 2⅛", M, A $45.00

Ribbon Core Swirl, mc core edged w/2 colorful bands, ¾", edging bands slightly separated o/w NM, A....................$70.00

Ribbon Core Swirl, opaque wht w/pk on 1 side & bl on the other, no outer bands, ⅝", EX+, A...........................$50.00

Ribbon Core Swirl, peppermint twist at center in clear glass, ⅝", M..$50.00

Ribbon Core Swirl, 8 red stripes alternating w/wht & edged in bl at center, 2 yel 9-thread outer swirls, ⅝", M $35.00

Ribbon Lutz, handmade, clear base w/translucent yel & lt gr ribbon edged w/lutz bands, ⅝", NM, A...................$160.00

Ribbon Lutz, handmade, opaque lt bl & transparent vaseline, lutz edges w/opaque wht stripes, ⅝", EX+, A...........$140.00

Ribbon Lutz, handmade, wht core edged in lutz & transparent cranberry, ⅝", EX+, A...$175.00

Slag w/Mica, handmade, pk, bl & wht core w/lg flakes of mica encased in clear glass, 2", M, A $45.00

Solid Core Swirl, handmade, opaque wht core w/dk bl strands, alternating purple & yel outer bands, 2⅛", M, A.......$60.00

Solid Core Swirl, red & wht core edged in yel threads, dk bl & wht outer threads, 1¾", M......................................$125.00

Solid Core Swirl, translucent yel core w/4 outer bands of opaque red, wht & gr, ½", rare, M, A $80.00

Solid Opaque, 2 pontils, ⅝", M $350.00

Sulfide, baboon on all fours, 1¾", minor chips o/w NM, A..$145.00

Sulfide, bird (probably a grouse), 1½", air bubble around figure & tiny subsurface moons o/w NM, A $70.00

Sulfide, child w/hammer, 1¾", M....................................$600.00

Sulfide, cow, 1¾", M...$150.00

Sulfide, eagle, 1¾", M...$400.00

Sulfide, horse, 1¾", M...$150.00

Sulfide, lg #7, 1⅝", few chips/subsurface moons, G, A $215.00

Sulfide, little boy blowing a horn seated on hobby horse, 1⅞", NM, A $225.00

Sulfide, peasant boy seated on stump w/legs crossed, 1¾", NM, A..$270.00

Sulfide, rabbit, 1¾", M...$150.00

Sulfide, rearing horse in tinted amber glass, 2⅛", M, A....$120.00

Sulfide, standing male lion, 1⅞", heat fracture to figure & minor cloudiness to marble surface o/w NM, A....................$80.00

Transitional, transparent lt gr w/opaque wht loops, melted pontil, ⅝", NM, A..$55.00

Marx

Louis Marx founded his company in New York in the 1920s. He was a genius not only at designing toys but also marketing them. His business grew until it became one the largest toy companies ever to exist, eventually expanding to include several factories in the United States as well as other countries. Marx sold his company in the early 1970s; he died in 1982. Though toys of every description were produced, collectors today admire his mechanical toys above all others.

Advisor: Scott Smiles (S10), windups; Tom Lastrapes (L4), battery-ops.

See also Advertising; Banks; Character, TV and Movie Collectibles; Dollhouse Furniture; Games; Guns; Plastic Figures; Playsets; and other categories. For toys made by Linemar (Marx's subsidiary in Japan), see Battery-Operated Toys; Windups, Friction and Other Mechanicals.

BATTERY-OPERATED

Electric Marx Mobile, painted and lithographed tin, push-button controls, 30", G+, A, $95.00.

Aircraft Carrier, 21", missing 2 missiles & airplane, EX, M5 ....$265.00

Atomic Submarine, lights & fires missiles, litho tin & plastic, remote control, 13", non-working, VG (orig box), A $160.00

Brewster the Rooster, plush rooster travels around, lifts head, opens beak & crows, 10", M (EX box)....................$145.00

Brightlite Filling Station, litho tin, 9½", NM, A............$525.00

Bristol 188 Jet, tin jet w/plastic belly advances as engines flash, 15", NM (EX box), A..$205.00

Buttons the Puppy w/a Brain, plush w/litho tin eyes & base, 8 buttons control actions, MIB $395.00

Catfish Tug Boat, Hong Kong, ca 1960, shakes w/bump-&-go action, rat-a-tat & horn noise, lights, 15", NM (EX box), A **$154.00**

Clang-Clang Locomotive, early 1960s, advances w/lights & sound, 13", MIB **$78.00**

Colonel Hap Hazard, walks while arms move & antenna spins, mostly tin, 11½", NM+ (EX+ box), A **$1,450.00**

Electric Lighted Filling Station, 1930, station mk Sunny Side, gas pumps, car & lift, non-working, EX (EX box), A......**$526.00**

Electric Robot, side-to-side motion w/light-up eyes & buzzing sound, red & blk plastic, 15", EX+ (NM box), A **$394.00**

Electric Robot & Son, advances & lifts child up & down, light-up eyes & buzzer, plastic, 15", rare color, NM (NM box), A **$595.00**

Flashy Flickers Picture Gun, ray gun projector shows color films of various characters, tin & plastic, EX (EX box), A.**$95.00**

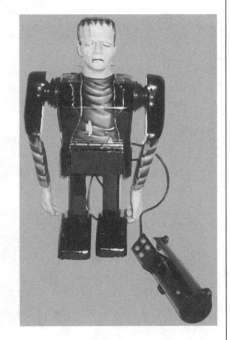

Frankenstein, 1950s, lithographed tin, remote control, EX, $875.00.

Fred Flintstone on Dino, purple & blk plush w/litho tin & plastic, 19", EX (VG box) **$750.00**

Hootin' Hollow Haunted House, push-button actions, 10", EX+, A **$800.00**

Marx-a-Copter, 1958, circles pylon, bombs sub & rescues men, plastic, missing tower o/w NMIB **$125.00**

Mickey Mouse on Big-Wheel, advances w/sound, NMIB, W5 ....**$275.00**

Mighty Kong, walks, stops, beats chest & growls, plush over tin, 11½", MIB **$650.00**

Mr Mercury, man behind face visor walks, bends over & grasps objects, tin w/plastic, remote control, 13", NM, A..**$600.00**

Mr Mercury, man behind face visor walks, bends over & grasps objects, tin w/plastic, remote control, 13", VG, A ..**$250.00**

Nutty Mad Car, vinyl head flips around in litho tin car w/crazy actions & engine noise, 9", MIB **$675.00**

Nutty Mad Indian, Indian rocks while beating drum, tongue moves as war hoops are made, tin & vinyl, 12", M (G box), A **$175.00**

Walking Plenty, figure holding baby & gift wobbles while hat moves, 8¼", VG, A **$190.00**

Willy's Jeep, 1950, w/lights & horn, VG+, R7.................**$45.00**

Whistling Spooky Kooky Tree (Summer version), bump-and-go action, 13", EX (VG box), A, $1,900.00.

Yeti the Abominable Snowman, advances with shrieks and grunting noise, plush over tin, 11", NM (NM box), A, $860.00.

PRESSED STEEL

Army Transport Truck, marked USA 41573147, original canvas top, 13½", NM, A, $250.00.

Army Truck, olive drab w/NP grille, 10", VG, A..............$90.00

Army Truck, 1950, canvas top, 18", G, R7.....................$125.00

Army Truck, 1950, canvas top, 18", NM, R7 ....$200.00

Car Carrier, gray, bl & red w/NP grille, carries 2 plastic cars, wood wheels, 13¾", EX $80.00

Coal Truck, red & bl w/blk tires & red hubcaps, Lumar Coal stamped on sides, 11¼", G..$40.00

Combat Aircraft, 4-prop w/tin nose cone, litho tin side plates picture uniformed gunner & airman, 10", EX, A.....$450.00

Deluxe Pickup Truck, bl & yel w/NP grille, decals on doors, electric headlights, 14½", NMIB..............................$500.00

Dump Truck, bl w/red bed, NP grille, electric lights, 10½", G+, A $60.00

Dump Truck, silver w/blk grille & bumper, Dept Street Cleaning stamped on side, blk wood wheels, 11", VG $150.00

Fire Engine, 1935, red & yel w/blk rubber tires, 14½", EX, A $900.00

Fire Truck, red w/ride-on seat, siren & bell, 30½", G-, A.$110.00

Garbage Truck, wht w/blk & red letters on van, rear door slides open, litho tin wheels, 13⅜", VG+ $220.00

Gold Star Hauler w/Van & Trailer, 1950s, red & wht w/plastic tires, rear doors open, 21", NM (EX box), A $330.00

Ice Truck, red and yellow with Polar Ice Co decal, tin balloon tires, complete with glass ice cubes and tin tongs in original truck bed insert, 12", M (original box), A, $545.00.

Joy Gasoline Trailer Truck, red & yel w/NP grille, wood wheels, clockwork mechanism, 14½", VG+ $110.00

Pathe News Car, NP grille, litho tin newsreel camera mounted on top, 10", VG...$1,100.00

Race Car, red w/rubber wheels, electric lights, 8½", VG+, A.$150.00

Stake Body Trailer, gray, gr & blk w/Tri-City Freight decal, plastic wheels, 19", NMIB $225.00

Steam Roller, ca 1940, chrome-plated, 11⅜", EX $60.00

Super Styled Streamline w/Garage, 1930s, silver car w/red & gr garage, EX+ (scarce EX box), A $260.00

US Army Jeep w/Searchlight Trailer, mk Lumar on blk rubber tires, 22", NM (NM box), A $275.00

US Army Truck w/Searchlight Trailer, 1956, army gr w/tan canvas bed cover, battery-op light, 27", MIB, A $380.00

US Navy Jeep w/Searchlight Trailer, 1950s, trailer w/plastic engine & battery-op searchlight, 21", MIB, A.........$586.00

Railway Express Truck, green with multicolored decals, black rubber tires marked Wyandotte, complete, 20", EX (EX box), A, $675.00.

WINDUPS, FRICTIONS AND OTHER MECHANICALS

Airplane & Hanger, red litho tin plane w/red & yel hanger, 6" plane, EX $225.00

Amos 'N Andy Fresh Air Taxi, 1930s, Amos 'N Andy with dog in open car, 7½", EX, $900.00.

Amos Walker, litho tin figure wearing 'Taxi' hat, eyes move, 10½", EX, A...$450.00

Army Bomber #6, olive gr, twin-engine w/tin wheels & metal props, 14" wingspan, VG+, A $275.00

Auto Mac Truck Driver, 1950s, advances & stops, Mac turns head as bed dumps, red & gr plastic, NM (EX box), A $125.00

Automatic Brake Car, 1950s, set distance in feet, push lever & car travels distance, yel plastic, 9", NM (EX box), A $125.00

Automatic Car Wash, car w/family lithoed in windows enters & exits 9x6" car wash, 6½" car, NM (EX+ box), A.....$500.00

Balky Mule, 1950s, farmer drives 2-wheeled mule cart, 8", MIB, from $250.00 to $350.00.

Balky Mule, 1950, NM, R7 ....$125.00

Ballerina, 1930s, insert toothed gear rod & ballerina dances around, 6", NM...$175.00

Barrel Wagon, 2 donkeys pull wagon w/farmer driver, wagon lithoed w/barrels, 10", EX............................$150.00

Be Bop Jigger, yel plastic figure on mc litho tin drum base, clockwork mechanism, 10", EX (orig box), S10 ......$275.00

Bear Cyclist, 1925, push down lever & bear pedals tricycle, litho tin, 6", EX, A..$225.00

Beat It the Komikal Cop Car, travels in circular motion, front end lifts, 7", EX, S10, from $475 to..........................$550.00

Betty Rubble Car, 1962, litho tin car w/vinyl-headed Betty, 4", EX $200.00

Big Parade, 1926, soldiers, cannon & ambulance move along track, 24", VG (orig box), S10..............................$600.00

Big-3 Aerial Acrobats, 1930, litho tin, 11", VG (EX box), A $225.00

Blondie's Jalopy, forward & reverse action, litho tin, 16¾", EX, A..$2,600.00

Buck Rogers 25th Century Rocket Ship, 1930s, advances with noise and sparks, tin with celluloid shield, 13", EX (EX box), $1,250.00.

Buck Rogers Rocket Police Patrol, advances w/noise & sparks, litho tin, 11½", VG, A $425.00

Bulldozer, early dozer w/stand-up driver travels forward & backward, red litho tin w/blk & yel accents, 8", EX+, A ..$220.00

Busy Bridge, 1930s, autos go in & out of terminals across bridge, traffic cop in center, tin, 24", NM, from $575 to.....$660.00

Busy Bridge, 1930s, autos go in & out of terminals across bridge, traffic cop in center, litho tin, 24", G, A $350.00

Busy Miners, coal cart w/2 men travels from station to mine entrance, litho tin, 16", EX (NM box) $350.00

Butter & Egg Man, walks w/suitcase mk Fresh Country Butter & mallard w/sign mk Eggs Lain in Order, 8", M, S10 ..$1,200.00

Butter & Egg Man, walks w/suitcase mk Fresh Country Butter & mallard w/sign mk Eggs Lain in Order, 8", VG, S10 ..$650.00

Butterfly, moves forward & tumbles, 8", EX, A.................$25.00

Campus Car, 4 college men in yel crazy car lettered w/puns, 5½", EX, from $250 to $335.00

Captain America, Marvel Comics, 1968, 5½", MIB, S2...$95.00

Car Carrier #7, red truck carries 3 cars on trailer, litho tin, 23", EX, A..$2,000.00

Careful Johnnie, 1950s, Johnnie drives car w/non-fall action, plastic & tin, 7", NMIB, S10................................$750.00

Carousel Truck, litho tin carousel w/plastic horses spins around on bl truck, friction, 7½", NM (EX box), A $135.00

Charleston Trio, 1921, jigger dances, little boy plays violin and dog with cane jumps, lithoed audience watches, EX, $850.00.

Charlie McCarthy & Mortimer Snerd Coupe, 1930s, travels w/actuated bumpers as heads turn, tin, 16½", EX, A...........$1,800.00

Charlie McCarthy in His Benzine Buggy, 1938, Charlie's head spins as crazy action car advances, 7", MIB, A $1,540.00

Charlie McCarthy Walker, 8", VG, A $225.00

Chrysler Coupe, ca 1925, blk, yel & red litho tin w/driver, rear spare, Chrysler emb on front, 8¾", EX+, A $364.00

City Coal Truck, litho tin silver Mack w/red interior bed, 13", G, A $95.00

Climbing Fireman, red, yel & bl, litho tin, clockwork mechanism, 12½", EX, S10, from $375 to $425.00

Climbing Fireman, red, yel & bl, litho tin, clockwork mechanism, 12½", VG, S10, from $300 to $350.00

Climbing Sailor, pull cords for climbing action, litho tin, 7", G, A $25.00

Coo Coo Car, 1931, advances in circular motion with full-figure driver moving up and down, 8", EX+ (VG+ box), $750.00.

Cowboy Rider, ca 1939, rearing horse vibrates as cowboy spins lasso & arms swing holding gun, tin, 8", NM (VG box), A $300.00

Dagwood Aeroplane, travels w/crazy action as Dagwood's head bobs, litho tin, 9", NM (VG box).........................$1,700.00

Dagwood the Driver, litho tin, eccentric clockwork, 8", VG, S10..$750.00

Dan Dipsy Car, ca 1950, head bobs as crazy-action car advances, tin w/plastic figure, 6", EX (orig box) $300.00

Dapper Dan Coon Jigger, tin Black man dances on yel stage lithoed w/Black figures, 11", NM (EX box), from $900 to $1,000.00

Desoto Taxi 3601 X, rare prototype, plunger-activated horn on roof, gr & yel, 10", VG, A $200.00

Dick Tracy Siren Squad Car, metallic gr w/various characters lithoed on windows, battery-op light, 11", NMIB, A .$400.00

Dick Tracy Sparkling Riot Car, various characters lithoed on windows, friction, 6", NM (EX box), A $366.00

Disney Parade Roadster, Walt Disney Productions, lithographed tin with plastic figures, 11", NM (EX box), A, $650.00.

Disneyland Express, 1950s, plastic engine & 3 litho tin cars navigate track w/2 tunnels, 21", EX (VG box), A.........$439.00

Donald Double (prototype), mk Erie- x1073 -9/17/47 on bottom, tin w/hand-painted figures on seesaw, 12", VG, A ...$810.00

Donald Duck, see also Twirling Tail Donald

Donald Duck Duet, 1946, Donald & Goofy standing on drums, litho tin, 10", EX (VG box), S10.........................$1,200.00

Donald Duck Duet, 1946, Donald & Goofy standing on drums, litho tin, 10", EX, S10...$1,000.00

Donald Duck Racing Kart, WDP, 1960s, full-figure Donald holding steering wheel, plastic, friction, 6", NM (EX box), A $176.00

Donald the Driver, WDP, advances as Donald waves & nods head, litho tin, 6½", EX+ (EX box), A $660.00

Donald the Skier, wht plastic w/litho tin skis, clockwork mechanism, 10½", EX (orig box)..$400.00

Donkey Cart, 1950, tin cart lithoed w/barrels advances as donkeys move up & down, 10¼", NM (EX+ box).........$250.00

Dottie the Driver, ca 1950, Dottie's head bobs up & down while car travels w/non-fall action, 6½", NM (EX box), A.$265.00

Doughboy Tank, 1930, soldier w/gun pops out of litho tin tank w/2 side turrets, 9¼", EX+ (G box), A...................$475.00

Doughboy Tank, 1930, soldier w/gun pops out of litho tin tank w/2 side turrets, 9¼", NM, A................................$375.00

Doughboy Tank, 1930s, soldier w/gun pops out of litho tin tank w/2 side turrets, 9¼", VG, S10 ....$250.00

Drive-Ur-Self Car, advances and turns any direction with pull string, 14", NM (scarce box), $850.00.

Dumbo the Acrobatic Elephant, Walt Disney Productions, 1941, performs flips, lithographed tin, 4", NM (EX box), from $750.00 to $850.00.

Drummer Boy, ca 1935, advances while playing wheeled drum, litho tin, 8", NMIB, A $1,200.00

Drumming Soldier, marching drummer in red & yel uniform, 9", few scratches o/w EX, A $110.00

Ferdinand & Matador, Walt Disney Productions, 1938, advances as bull and matador move toward each other, 7", scarce, NM (EX+ box), from $1,100.00 to $1,200.00.

Ferdinand the Bull, standing w/flower & butterfly, litho tin, 5¾", EX (EX box), A...$230.00

Fire Chief Car, 1950s, friction with battery-operated lights and siren sound, MIB, from $300.00 to 350.00.

Flintstones, see Betty Rubble Car, Fred Flintstone Car, Hopping Fred Flintstone & Hopping Dino

Flippo the Jumping Dog, 1930s, litho tin dog leans over, jumps & performs flips, 4", EX+ (NM box), S10 ....$300.00

Frankenstein, Universal Pictures/HK, tin & plastic figure walks w/step-over action as arms move, VG, A.................$180.00

Fred Flintstone Car, Hanna-Barbera, 1962, litho tin w/vinyl-headed figure, friction, 4", NM (EX+ box) $500.00

Funny Flivver, 1926, eccentric car w/comical driver advances in erratic motion, 7½", EX+ (EX+ box)......................$900.00

George Jetson, see Hopping George Jetson, Jetson Express

George the Drummer Boy, moving-eye version, 1930s, beats drum and plays cymbals, 9", EX, from $275.00 to $350.00.

Photo courtesy of Scott Smiles.

George the Drummer Boy, moving-eye version, beats drum & plays cymbals, 9", NM, S10, from $350 to $400.00

George the Drummer Boy, stationary-eye version, beats drum & plays cymbals, 9", EX+ (EX box), S10, from $250 to .$300.00

Go-Kart Racer, 1960s, plastic w/full-figure driver, friction, 5½", EX+ (VG box) $75.00

Gobbling Goose, goose pecks at ground while laying wooden golden eggs, 9", NMIB..$200.00

Goofy the Gardener, Goofy pushes wheelbarrow, litho tin, VG+ $500.00

Greyhound Coast-to-Coast Bus, 1930s, litho tin w/logo & Atlantic Greyhound Line Seats 29, 10", VG, A......$300.00

Harold Lloyd Funny Face Walker, 1930s, face changes expressions as he advances, 11", VG (G box), $525.00.

Hee-Haw, 1925, farmer drives mule cart w/5 milk cans in back, 10½", NM (EX box), S10..$525.00

Hey-Hey Chicken Snatcher, 1925, Black man being bitten by dog while trying to snatch chicken, EX, S10, from $1,100 to...$1,200.00

Honeymoon Express, 1930, locomotive & cars circle base w/3 tunnels & station house, litho tin, EX (NM box), S10...$300.00

Hopping Astro, hops on 2 lg hind feet, gray litho tin w/orig ears & tail, 4½", NM+, A...$400.00

Hopping Astro, 4½", EX+, M5.....................................$265.00

Hopping Barnaby Banana, 1950s, litho tin, MIB, D10...$100.00

Hopping Corkie Corn, 1950s, litho tin, MIB, D10.........$100.00

Hopping Dino, 4", G, M5...$95.00

Hopping Fred Flintstone, 3½", EX+, M5 ....$295.00

Hopping George Jetson, 1963, mc litho tin, clockwork mechanism, 3½", NM (G- box).......................................$875.00

Hopping Little Pig, plays flute, litho tin, 4", VG (orig box)..$175.00

Hopping Munchie Melon, 1950s, litho tin, MIB, D10...$100.00

Hoppo the Waltzing Monkey, hops & plays cymbals, red & yel outfit, VG (orig box), A...$200.00

Huckleberry Hound, litho tin w/vinyl head, friction, 4", EX (EX box)...$250.00

Indian Motorcycle w/Sidecar, tin, 6½", non-working, G, A...$225.00

Insect Robot, 1968, tin bug-eyed insect w/rubber antennas, 6", NM..$100.00

International Agent Car, vinyl-headed driver in litho tin car, friction, 4", NM (M box), A $150.00

Jetson Express, tin train w/George & family lithoed in windows of engine & cars, 13", NM, A $400.00

Joe Penner & His Duck, 1934, advances w/shuffling feet as his hat tips, litho tin, 8", EX, S10.................................$650.00

Joy Rider, 1928, tractor-type vehicle w/driver & rear trunk advances in erratic motion, litho tin, 8", EX, A......$300.00

Jumpin' Jeep, four soldiers travel in jeep with crazy-car action, 5½", EX+, S10, $225.00.

Jumpin' Jeep, 4 soldiers travel in jeep w/crazy-car action, 5½", MIB, S10..$350.00

King Kong, see Mechanical Gorilla

King Racer, 1920s, w/driver, tin, 9", NM, S9..................$750.00

King Roadster, yel w/gr wheels, bl top, blk trim, driver, 9", G, A...$485.00

Knock-Out Champs, 7", EX (G- box), A.......................$350.00

Limping Lizzy, 1925, advances & rocks, blk tin lettered w/various sayings, EX (VG box), A $700.00

Little Orphan Annie & Sandy, 1930s, Annie jumps wire rope, Sandy carries satchel, D10, $750.00 for the pair.

Lone Ranger, see Range Rider

Looping Plane, 1930s, acrobatic plane w/pilot advances, flips over, rights itself & advances, 7½", EX+ (VG box) ..$450.00

Mack Truck, ca 1930, dump truck, driver at wheel, 9", VG, A...$350.00

Magic Garage, 1950s, litho tin car hits garage door, door opens & car enters, 10x8" garage, EX+ (NM box) $300.00

Main Street, trolleys & trucks move along track between buildings, traffic cop in center, 24", VG, S10 ....$375.00

Mammy's Boy, ca 1925, Black man w/cane sways as eyes shift, litho tin, EX+ (G box), A.....................................$1,400.00

Marvel Super Hero Tricycle (Spiderman), 1968, red & bl plastic Spiderman on tin bike, 4", M (EX box), A..............$352.00

Mechanical Gorilla (King Kong), walks & beats his chest, opens mouth & growls, tin, plush & plastic, 8", EX, S10 ..$350.00

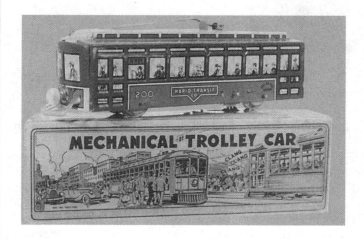

Mechanical Trolley Car (Rapid Transit), red, green and cream with passengers lithoed in windows, battery-operated headlight, 9", EX (EX box), from $500.00 to $550.00.

Merchant's Transfer Truck, red & yel litho tin Mack stake truck, 11", G, A...$100.00

Merry Makers, litho tin version w/no backdrop & band leader sitting on piano, 9¼", NM, S10.........................$1,000.00

Mickey Mouse Dipsy Car, 1950s, head bobs while crazy car travels, plastic figure, tin car, 6", NM, from $500.00 to $600.00.

Mickey Mouse Dipsy Car, 1949, head bobs while crazy car travels, plastic figure, tin car, 6", NM (VG box), from $750 to...$850.00

Mickey Mouse Express, Mickey in airplane flies above train track w/Disneyville station in center, 9" dia, NM (VG box), A...$875.00

Mickey Mouse Racing Kart, WDP, 1960s, full-figure Mickey holding steering wheel, plastic, friction, 6", NM (EX box), A...$125.00

Mickey Mouse w/Whirling Tail, WDP, 1950s, Mickey vibrates around as tail spins, plastic, 7", NM, A....................$125.00

Mickey the Musician, 1950s, plastic Mickey leans over & plays tin xylophone on sq tin base, 12", MIB, A..............$700.00

Midget Racer #11, 1950, dk bl racer w/driver, blk rubber tires, NM (EX box), A.......................................$175.00

Midget Racer #3, 1930, EX+, R7.................................$145.00

Midget Racer #5, 1930, VG+, R7.................................$125.00

Midget Racer #7, 1930, EX+, R7.................................$145.00

Milton Berle Car, ca 1950, Milty's head spins while driving crazy car, litho tin w/plastic hat, 6", VG, A....................$275.00

Milton Berle Car, ca 1950, Milty's head spins while driving crazy car, litho tin w/plastic hat, 6", NM+ (EX+ box), A..$675.00

Monkey Cyclist, litho tin monkey w/cb arms on bl cycle, 6", EX (EX box)...$225.00

Moon Mullins & Kayo Handcar, 1930s, flat litho tin figures on car, 6", EX (EX box), A.......................................$990.00

Mortimer Snerd's Hometown Band, advances & beats drum, litho tin, 8½", VG, S10, from $850 to.....................$950.00

Mysterious Pluto, WDP, press down on his tail & Pluto scoots along, yel tin w/orig rubber ears, 9", EX (EX box), A...$480.00

Munchie Melon and Corkie Corn, tin, friction, MIP, D10, $100.00 each.

Mystery Car, red sheet metal w/wooden wheels, self-winding motor, 9¾", EX, A...$350.00

Mystery Tunnel, 2 cars travel track through tunnel lithoed w/gas station & Community Shopping Center, MIB, A...$675.00

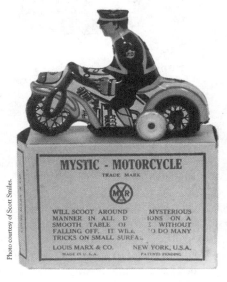

Mystic Motorcycle, 1936, cop on cycle advances with non-fall action, 4¼", MIB, from $250.00 to $300.00.

Photo courtesy of Scott Smiles.

Old Jalopy, blk, red & yel, clockwork mechanism, litho tin, 6¾", EX, S10...$200.00

PD Police Cycle, 1930s, litho tin w/policeman & sidecar, wood wheels, 3½", NM, A...$375.00

Pinched, 1930, truck goes in circle under 2 bridges, tunnel & station, includes cops & restaurant, 10", EX, S10....$600.00

Pinocchio, 1939, waddles from side to side as eyes move, litho tin, 8", EX (G box)...$650.00

Pinocchio the Acrobat, WDE, 1939, sways on rocker base w/bright graphics, 16", NM, A.................................$500.00

Pinocchio the Acrobat, WDE, 1939, sways on rocker base w/bright graphics, 16", G, A.....................................$250.00

Pluto, see Mysterious Pluto, Rollover Pluto, Twirling Tail Pluto & Wise Pluto

Police Motorcycle w/Sidecar, 1930s, red cycle w/driver in bl, wood tires, 3½", NM, S10 ....$275.00

Popeye, see also Walking Popeye

Popeye & Olive Oyl Jiggers, 1934, Olive Oyl plays accordion & sways while Popeye dances on roof, 9", EX (EX box), A...$1,700.00

Popeye & Olive Oyl Jiggers, 1934, Olive Oyl plays accordion & sways while Popeye dances on roof, 9", VG, A........$750.00

Popeye Dipper Dumper, 1930s, pnt celluloid Popeye figure in litho tin open truck w/dumping action, 9½", EX.....$550.00

Popeye Express, King Features Syndicate, 1930s, lithographed tin, 9" dia, MIB, from $1,750.00 to $1,850.00.

Popeye Express w/Parrot, parrot sits atop crate in wheelbarrow pushed by Popeye, 8½", G, A...................................$375.00

Popeye Express w/Parrot, 1932, parrot pops out of trunk in wheelbarrow pushed by Popeye, 8½", scarce, NM (G box), A...$2,250.00

Popeye Jigger, box only, litho cb featuring Popeye dancing atop boxcar, vertical, EX, A..$200.00

Popeye the Champ, Popeye & Bluto on revolving platform, celluloid & litho tin, clockwork mechanism, VG (orig box) $1,650.00

Popeye the Pilot Airplane, early version w/erratic action, red, yel & bl litho tin, 8½", VG, A.......................................$700.00

Porky Pig, 1939, vibrates as he twirls umbrella, litho tin, 8", EX (VG+ box), from $450 to......................................$500.00

Porky Pig, 1939, vibrates as he twirls umbrella, litho tin, 8", NM (EX box), A...$950.00

Racer, 1930s, driver in red, yel & blk boat racer w/red hubs on blk tin tires, 13", EX, A...$230.00

Racer, 1950, litho tin w/plastic driver, 16½", EX+, R7 ..$350.00

Racer #4, 1930s, red, orange, yel & blk litho tin w/balloon tires, 5", EX...$225.00

Range Rider, 1938, Lone Ranger on Silver swings his lasso, rocker base, litho tin, NMIB, S10 ....$650.00

Range Rider, 1938, Lone Ranger on Silver swings his lasso, rocker base, litho tin, EX, S10................................$350.00

Red Cap Porter, 1930, litho tin Black porter w/toothy grin & fast-moving legs carrying 2 bags, 8¼", scarce, EX, A $750.00

Red the Iceman, walks carrying block of ice, litho tin, 9", rare, NMIB $2,000.00

Reversible 1930s Coupe, red litho tin w/front & back bumpers, 16¾", EX, A...$475.00

Rex Mars Planet Patrol, 1950s, advances as astronaut pops up, gun sounds & sparks, litho tin, 10", MIB, from $500 to...$550.00

Ride 'Em Cowboy, ca 1925, celluloid cowboy spins lasso as tin horse advances, 6", rare, EX (EX box), A $275.00

Photo courtesy of Scott Smiles.

Ring-A-Ling Circus, 1925, animals and figures on lithoed base, EX, from $1,400.00 to $1,500.00.

Roadside Rest Service Station, coupe w/battery-op lights & clockwork motor, litho tin, 13½", non-working, VG, A $675.00

Rocket Racer, 1930s, litho tin, VG+, R7.......................$350.00

Rollover Plane, pilot in litho tin plane, 6" wingspan, M, A...$325.00

Rollover Pluto, WDP, 1939, Pluto advances & rolls over, tail spins, w/instructions, 8", EX (EX box), A...............$525.00

Rookie Cop, cycle advances, falls over & gets back up, w/siren sound, litho tin, 8½", EX (EX box), A.....................$525.00

Rookie Pilot, 1940, advances in erratic motion, pilot in cockpit, red & yel litho tin, EX, S10, from $550 to...............$650.00

Rookie Pilot, 1940, advances in erratic motion, pilot in cockpit, yel & red litho tin, EX (VG+ box), S10, from $650 to...$750.00

Roy Rogers Stagecoach Wagon Train, ca 1950, 2-horse plastic stage pulls 3 tin wagons, 14¼", NM (EX box) $300.00

Royal Coupe, 1930, litho tin w/tin driver, lift-up rumble seat, NM (EX+ box), A..$1,650.00

Sabre Car, gr plastic roadster w/sparkling exhaust & siren, needs flint o/w NM (EX box) $150.00

Sam the Gardener, 1940, plastic and tin, complete with tools, NM (EX box), A, $450.00.

Photo courtesy of Continental Hobby House.

Sam the Gardener, 1940, plastic & tin, NM, R7 ....$250.00

Sandy's Dog House (Orphan Annie), 1938, push down on tail & dog scoots w/ball, tin w/rubber ears, 8", NM (EX box), A $1,125.00

Scottie the Guid-A-Dog, 1930s, guide along w/attached leash, blk w/red saddle, 12", NM (EX box), from $475 to .$525.00

Sedan, red stylized auto w/long-nosed hood, bump-&-go action, 15", non-working, G, A...$170.00

Silver Streak Racer, 1950s, Indy-style plastic racer w/driver, chrome-like finish, blk rubber tires, 6", NM (EX box), A $250.00

Skybird Flyer, ca 1935, 2 planes circle control tower, gaining altitude as they spin, litho tin, EX+ (EX box), A $700.00

Skyview Yellow Cab, 1950s, w/driver & women passengers at windows, litho tin w/wood wheels, 7", EX $250.00

Sleek Coupe w/Trailer, trailer mk Lonesome Pine, litho tin, 22½", EX, A...$850.00

Smokey Joe the Climbing Fireman, 1930s, fireman climbs ladder attached to base, litho tin, NM (EX box), from $500 to...$550.00

Somstepa Jigger, 1925, Black jigger dances on stage lithoed w/depictions of children, 8", scarce, EX $750.00

Space Creature, advances w/sound, yel cone-shaped body w/blk antennae & rubber ears, 5½", EX $75.00

Space Mobile, Japan, litho tin vehicle & track, EX (VG box) $150.00

Sparkling Airplane, mk US Army 712, advances & sparks, litho tin w/balloon tires, 8", NM (EX box), A $475.00

Sparkling Luxury Liner, litho tin, friction, 15", NM (VG box), A $232.00

Sparkling Mountain Climber, engine & car travel suspended tracks, 8", needs flint, NM (VG box) $150.00

Sparkling Rocket Fighter Ship, 1930s, advances w/noise & sparking action, pilot in open cockpit, 12", NM (EX box), A...$1,000.00

Sparkling Siren Police Squad Motorcycle, 1940, includes sidecar, travels w/siren noise, needs flint, NM (EX+ box), A..$875.00

Sparkling Soldier, ca 1930, WWI litho tin soldier crawls on belly, NM (EX box), A...$400.00

Sparkling Tank, 1930s, litho tin, 4", needs new flint o/w NM (EX+ box), A...$200.00

Sparkling Warship, USS Washington w/deck planes & depth charges, litho tin, 14", NM (G box) $250.00

Speed Boy Delivery Cycle, 1930s, litho tin, 10", M, S10...$550.00

Speed Boy Delivery Cycle, 1930s, litho tin, 10", VG+, S10 ..$350.00

Speed King Racer, driver in cream & red litho tin racer w/fins, 16", non-working, some underside scratches, G, A .$125.00

Speed Racer, ca 1950, Indy-type tin racer w/plastic driver, blk tin tires, 12", NM (EX+ box), A $400.00

Speed Racer #3, open racer w/driver, litho tin w/balloon tires, 6¼", NM (EX+ box)...$350.00

Speed-Way Coupe, 1930, red & blk litho tin w/wht spoked balloon tires, battery-op lights, 8", NM, from $500 to .$550.00

Speed-Way Coupe, 1930, red & blk litho tin w/wht spoked balloon tires, battery-op lights, 8", NM (EX box), A ...$775.00

Smokey Joe the Climbing Fireman, 1930s, fireman climbs ladder attached to base, EX, from $350.00 to $450.00.

Photo courtesy of Scott Smiles.

Spic and Span, 1924, two Black minstrels on stage marked The Hams What Am, 10½", VG, A, $1,150.00.

Spiderman, see Marvel Super Hero Tricycle

Streamline Coupe Racer, yel, red & gr litho tin w/driver, rear spare, 9", VG, A $325.00

Streamline Speedway, 2 cars travel sectioned track w/graphics of US cities, VG (VG box), A $150.00

Streamline Train, 1930s, litho tin, 36" track, rare, NM (G box), A...$200.00

Subway Express, 1950, train travels in plastic tunnel on base lithoed with city and dock scenes, 9" dia, NM, $250.00.

Subway Express, 1950, train travels in plastic tunnel on rnd base lithoed w/city & dock scenes, 9" dia, M (EX+ box), A.$350.00

Thor Car, Marvel Comics, 1968, vinyl-headed figure in tin car lithoed w/Marvel characters, friction, 4", NM, A....$100.00

Tick & Tack the Tumbling Two, litho tin, 18", VG (orig box) $210.00

Tidy Tim, figure pushes barrel w/broom & shovel, litho tin, 9", NMIB, from $850 to..$900.00

Tom & Jerry Go Kart, MGM, 1973, Tom driving while Jerry points gun at his head, plastic, friction, 6", NM (NM box), A $150.00

Tom Corbett Rocket Ship, 11½", EX, A $350.00

Tom Tom Jungle Boy, native rocks back & forth while beating drum, litho tin, 7", NM (G box), A.........................$300.00

Toyland Milk Wagon, brn horse pulls wagon w/red roof, 10", EX (orig box), S10...$375.00

Tractor-Trailer Set, farmer on tractor w/plow pulling wagon w/balloon tires, litho tin, 8", NM (EX box), A........$335.00

Tricky Fire Chief — Where's the Fire?, ca 1925, car travels w/non-fall action around lithoed base, EX+ (G box) $450.00

Tricky Motorcycle, police motorcyclist advances & turns, litho tin, 4½", EX (NM box), S10 ....$325.00

Tricky Taxi on Busy Street, taxi moves in all directions on base, litho tin, 10" base, EX, A $400.00

Turnover Tank, 1940-44, advances & rolls over, litho tin, EX, S10 from $125 to $150.00

Twirling Tail Donald, WDP, Donald vibrates around as tail spins, plastic, 6½", EX, A $85.00

Twirling Tail Pluto, WDP/Hong Kong, 1960, Pluto vibrates around as tail spins, plastic, 5", M (EX box), A.......$195.00

Tumbling Monkey, 1942, spins head over heels between two chairs, lithographed tin, 5", EX, from $175.00 to $225.00.

Uncle Wiggily Car, 1935, travels w/crazy action as Uncle Wiggily's head turns, Easter motif on car, 8", NM (VG box), A..$1,500.00

US Army Truck #F63, litho tin w/canvas top, 5", EX+, A $250.00

Walking Popeye, King Features, 1930s, carries 2 cages w/lithoed parrots, 8¼", NM (EX box), from $750 to $850.00

Walking Tiger, walks upright w/swinging arms, turns head & roars, holds flower in right hand, plush & celluloid, 8", MIB...$147.00

Walt Disney's Television Car, WDP, ca 1949, Disney characters lithoed on tin car w/TV screen on roof, 8", NM (VG box) $1,000.00

Wee Scottie, 1930s, advances as front legs move, litho tin, 5", EX, S10, from $200 to $250.00

Whee-Whiz Auto Racer, 1925, cars race around dish-shaped track that rocks up & down, 13" dia track, G+, S10..........$350.00

Whoopee Car, eccentric clockwork, mc litho tin, 8", G, S10...$250.00

Whoopee Cowboy, 1932, cowboy moves up & down as crazy car travels, happy cow faces on wheels, 8", G, S10, from $250 to $300.00

Whoopee Cowboy, 1932, cowboy moves up & down as crazy car travels, happy cow faces on wheels, 8", NM $450.00

Wise Pluto, 1939, advances to edge of table and stops automatically, 8", MIB, from $375.00 to $475.00.

Wonder Cyclist, boy rides trike & moves handlebars to change direction, bell rings, 8", NM (EX+ box), S10 ....$600.00

Wonder Cyclist, boy rides trike & moves handlebars to change direction, bell rings, 8", VG, S10 ....$375.00

World War I Tank, ca 1925, advances & runs upsidedown on rubber treads, EX+, A..$275.00

Yellow Cab, 1940s, yellow with red lettering, passengers lithoed in windows, D10, $250.00.

Yogi Bear Car, Hanna-Barbera, 1962, vinyl-headed Yogi in red tin car, friction, 4", EX, A $153.00

Zippo the Climbing Monkey, hat marked Zippo, complete with string and hooks, 9½", EX (EX box), from $350.00 to $400.00.

Zulu Playing Drums, tin, 6½", EX, A $55.00

MISCELLANEOUS

Fix All Tractor, orange plastic, take apart & reassemble w/tools, 9¼", VG (VG box), A...$65.00

Glendale Station, litho tin, bi-level base, scratches, 10x20½", VG, A $70.00

Grand Central Station, litho tin, streamlined, gold finish, 2-wheel trailer, front canopy & opening doors, 11x17", VG, A $140.00

Happi-Time Service Station, 1950s, appears unused, NM+ (EX+ box), A...$350.00

Hometown Movie Theatre #170, 1925, turn knobs to view paper roll movie on litho tin theater, 5", MIB, A..............$415.00

Irrigated Garden #6021, MIB (sealed), from $40 to..........$50.00

Junior Dual Typewriter, 1950, NM, R7.............................$65.00

Little Orphan Annie Stove, 1930s, electric, Annie & Sandy graphics, 3 oven doors, 8x9½x5", working, NM, C1 ..$225.00

Minit Car Wash, litho tin, spring-hinged doors at ends, 9", G+, A $35.00

Pet Shop Delivery Truck, sides flip up to show 6 cubicles holding 6 different dogs, plastic, 11" long, EX (EX box)........$210.00

Press Lever Top Set, complete w/2 litho tin globes, EX+ (VG box), A...$175.00

Press Lever Top Set, complete w/2 tin globes, MIB, A...$232.00

Service Gas Station, 1920s, lithoed gas station w/pump island out front, lettered marquee on roof, NM (EX box), A..$880.00

Service Station w/Take-A-Part Car, ca 1950, dbl-bay station complete w/many accessories, scarce, NM (EX box), A..$352.00

Store Display, Miniature Masterpieces, 69¢ Per Set, 1960s, 18 scenes w/plastic figures in cb display, NM (EX card), A $160.00

Matchbox

The Matchbox series of English and American-made autos, trucks, taxis, Pepsi-Cola trucks, steamrollers, Greyhound buses, etc., was very extensive. By the late 1970s, the company was cranking out more than 5 million cars every week, and while those days may be over, Matchbox still produces about 75 million vehicles on a yearly basis.

Introduced in 1953, the Matchbox Miniatures series has always been the mainstay of the company. There were 75 models in all but with enough variations to make collecting them a real challenge. Larger, more detailed models were introduced in 1957; this series, called Major Pack, was replaced a few years later by a similar line called King Size. To compete with Hot Wheels, Matchbox converted most models over to a line called SuperFast that sported thinner, low-friction axles and wheels. (These are much more readily available than the original 'regular wheels,' the last of which were made in 1969.) At about the same time, the King Size series became known as Speed Kings; in 1977 the line was reintroduced under the name Super Kings.

In the early '70s, Lesney started to put dates on the baseplates of their toy cars. The name 'Lesney' was coined from the first names of the company's founders. The last Matchboxes that carried the Lesney mark were made in 1982. Today many models can be bought for less than $10.00, though a few are priced much higher.

In 1988, to celebrate the company's 40th anniversary, Matchbox issued a limited set of five models that except for minor variations were exact replicas of the originals. These five were repackaged in 1991 and sold under the name Matchbox Originals. In 1993 a second series expanded the line of reproductions.

Another line that's become very popular is their Models of Yesteryear. These are slightly larger replicas of antique and vintage vehicles. Values of $20.00 to $60.00 for mint-in-box examples are average, though a few sell for even more.

Sky Busters are small-scale aircraft measuring an average of 3½" in length. They were introduced in 1973. Models currently being produced sell for about $4.00 each.

To learn more, we recommend *Matchbox Toys, 1948 to 1993*, by Dana Johnson, and a series of books by Charlie Mack: *Lesney's Matchbox Toys* (there are two: *Regular Wheel Years* and *Super Fast Years)* and *Universal Years*.

To determine values of examples in conditions other than given in our listings, based on MIB or MOC prices, deduct a minimum of 10% if the original container is missing, 30% if the condition is excellent, and as much as 70% for a toy graded only very good. In the following listings, we have added zeroes ahead of the numbers to avoid the idiosyncrasies of computer sorting.

Advisors: Mark Giles (G2) 1-75 Series; Dan Wells (W1) King Size, Speed Kings and Super Kings; Matchbox Originals; Models of Yesteryear; Skybusters.

Key:
LW — Laser Wheels (introduced in 1987)
reg — regular wheels (Matchbox Miniatures)
SF — SuperFast

I-75 SERIES

01-A, Diesel Road Roller, reg, lt gr, VG+ $32.50
01-B, Road Roller, reg, lt gr, G, W1 ....$19.00
01-D, Aveling Barford Road Roller, reg, NM, W1 ....$12.00
01-E, Mercedes Truck, reg, orange canopy, MIB, W1 ......$15.00
01-F, Mercedes Benz Lorry, SF, gold w/yel canopy, EX.....$11.00
01-F, Mercedes Benz Lorry, 1970, SF, red w/yel canopy, M ..$5.00
01-G, Mod Rod, SF, w/label, VG, G2 ....$6.00
01-G, Mod Rod, SF, yel, red wheels, bear label, EX, W1 ....$7.50
01-G, Mod Rod, 1971, SF, yel, spotted cat emblem, MBP ..$10.00
01-H, Dodge Challenger, SF, red w/wht interior, NM, W1.$4.00
01-H, Dodge Challenger, 1976, SF, red, wht roof, chrome interior, MIB, J1 ....$6.50
01-I, Revin' Rebel Dodge Challenger, 1982, SF, orange, wht roof, MIB, J1...$7.00
01-J, Toyman Dodge Challenger, 1983, SF, yel, blk top, MBP $4.00
01-N, Dodge Challenger Hemi, 1993, SF, metallic bl, wht roof, MBP, J1 ....$2.00
02-B, Dumper, reg, #2 cast, orig driver, NM, W1 ....$39.00
02-C, Muir Hill Dumper (Laing), reg, red w/gr dumper, M, J1 .$20.00
02-D, Mercedes Trailer, reg, orange canopy, MIB, W1 ....$11.00
02-G, Hovercraft, SF, avocado, blk hull, silver scoop, Rescue labels, MIB, W1 ....$10.00
02-H, S-2 Jet, 1981, SF, blk, yel wings, MIB, J1..................$6.00
02-I, Pontiac Fiero, 1985, SF, wht, bl lettering, MIB..........$4.00
02-K, Corvette Grand Sport, 1990, SF, bl, MIB, J1 ....$2.00
03-A, Cement Mixer, reg, EX, W1.......................................$26.00
03-B, Bedford Tipper, reg, maroon dumper, EX-...............$11.00
03-C, Mercedes Benz Ambulance, reg, MIB $15.00
03-E, Monteverdi Hai, 1973, SF, orange, MBP..............$8.00

03-F, Porsche Turbo, SF, brn w/cream interior, blk base, M (EX box), W1 ....$9.00
04-C, Triumph Motorcycle & Sidecar, reg, M..................$48.00
04-D, Dodge Stake Truck, reg, gr stakes, MIB, W1 ....$13.00
04-G, Pontiac Firebird, SF, lt bl, dot-dash wheels, NM+, W1..$5.00
04-H, '57 Chevy, SF, lt purple, M (cracked blister, wrinkled card), W1 ....$7.50
05-D, London Bus, reg, decals, NM+ $21.00
05-E, Lotus Europa, SF, pk, unpnt base, no labels, NM $11.50
05-G, US Mail Jeep, 1978, SF, bl & wht, MIB, J1 ....$8.00
05-H, Golden Eagle Jeep, 1982, SF, red, MBP $3.50
06-C, Euclid Quarry Truck, reg, G $4.00
06-C, Euclid Quarry Truck, reg, solid tires, MIB $37.00
06-D, Ford Pickup Truck, reg, silver grille, MIB $12.00
06-F, Mercedes 350SL, SF, orange, M (NM box), W1 ....$9.00
06-G, IMSA Mazda, 1983, SF, bl, MIB, J1.........................$3.00
06-L, Excavator, 1992, SF, yel, blk stripes & shovel, MBP, J1.$2.00
07-A, Milk Float, reg, wht, NM+, W1 ....$82.50
07-B, Ford Anglia, reg, blk wheels, EX+ $26.00
07-B, Ford Anglia, reg, silver wheels, VG+, W1..............$13.50
07-C, Ford Refuse Truck, reg, scalloped side plates, MIB, W1 ....$16.00
07-F, VW Gulf, 1976, SF, metallic gr, MIB, J1/C6 ....$5.00
07-J, Porsche 959, 1987, SF, dk gray, MBP, J1 ....$3.00
07-L, T-Bird Stock Car, 1993, SF, wht graphics, MBP, J1..$2.00
08-C, CAT Tractor, reg, yel w/blk plastic rollers, orig treads, MIB $48.00
08-E, Ford Mustang, reg, wht, NM $15.50
08-F, Ford Mustang, SF, wht w/red interior, NM-, W1 ....$29.00
08-H, Pantera, 1975, SF, wht, MIB, J1 ....$5.50
08-J, Greased Lightning Pantera, 1983, SF, red, MIB, J1....$4.00
08-K, Scania T-142, 1986, SF, wht, MIB $4.00
08-M, Mack CH-600, 1990, SF, wht, MIB, J1 ....$3.00
08-N, Airport Fire Tender, 1992, bright orange, MIB, J1 ...$2.50
09-A, Dennis Fire Escape, reg, no # cast, gold trim, NM..$60.00
09-C, Merryweather Marquis Fire Engine, reg, gold ladder, MIB...$23.50
09-D, Boat & Trailer, reg, M $14.00
09-E, AMX Javelin, 1971, SF, lime gr, MIB, J1...................$9.00
09-F, Ford Escort RS 2000, SF, wht w/tan interior, charcoal base, clear windows, Dunlop labels, MIB $7.00
09-G, Fiat Abarth, 1982, SF, wht, MIB, J1 ....$4.00
10-B, Mechanical Horse & Trailer, reg, VG....................$45.00

10-C, Sugar Container Truck, reg, no-crown decal, M (NM box), W1 ....$59.00

10-D, Pipe Truck, reg, silver grille, 7 pipes, NM+, W1.....$12.00

10-G, Plymouth Grand Fury Police, 1979, SF, blk & wht or wht & bl, MBP, J1, ea $4.00

10-H, Buick LeSabre Stock Car, 1987, SF, blk & wht, MBP, J1 ....$3.00

11-B, Road Tanker, reg, gray wheels, red w/silver trim, Esso decal, NM $38.00

11-C, Jumbo Crane, reg, red weight box, MIB.................$16.00

11-D, Scaffolding Truck, reg, MIB, W1 ....$20.00

11-F, Flying Bug, SF, metallic red, heart label, NM+, W1 .$14.00

11-G, Bedford Car Transporter, 1976, SF, orange cab, M, J1..$4.00

11-G, Bedford Car Transporter, 1976, SF, red cab, MBP, J1..$6.00

11-I, IMSA Mustang Mack I, 1983, SF, blk, MBP $3.00

12-A, Jeep, reg, EX, W1...$29.00

12-C, Safari Land Rover, reg, bl, tan luggage, MIB, W1 ..$15.00

12-E, Setra Coach, SF, burgundy w/wht roof, gr window, MBP $11.00

12-F, Big Bull Bulldozer, 1975, SF, orange & gr, M, J1 ....$6.00

12-G, Citroen Station Wagon, 1979, SF, metallic bl, MIB, J1 ....$6.00

13-A, Bedford Wrecker, metal wheels, VG+ $30.00

13-C, Thames Wrecker, reg, gray plastic hook, EX, W1 ..$19.00

13-D, Dodge Wrecker, yel cab, gr bed, red hook, MIB $18.00

13-F, Baja Dune Buggy, 1971, SF, metallic gr, flower emblem, MIB $10.00

13-G, Snorkel Fire Engine, 1977, SF, red, yel boom, MIB..$6.00

13-H, 4x4 Dunes Racer, 1982, SF, lt orange, MIB, J1.........$4.00

14-B, Daimler Ambulance, reg, cream, no decals, VG-, W1 .$10.00

14-C, Bedford Ambulance, reg, MIB, W1......................$34.00

14-D, ISO Grifo, reg, NM+, W1 ....$13.00

14-E, ISO Grifo, SF, bl w/wht interior, unpnt base, 5-spoke wheels, MIB $12.00

14-F, Rallye Royale, SF, silver, blk base, MIB, W1 ....$10.00

15-A, Prime Mover, reg, orange w/silver trim, metal wheels, NM+, W1 ....$31.50

15-C, Tippax Refuse Truck, reg, peep hole, MIB, W1 .....$24.00

15-D, VW 1500 Saloon, reg, labels, M (EX+ box) $14.00

15-F, Hi-Ho Silver VW, 1971, SF, silver & blk, MIB, J1 ...$6.50

15-G, Ford Forklift, 1972, SF, red, gray forks, MBP, J1.......$5.00

15-N, Sunburner (Dodge Viper), 1992, SF, bright gr & yel, MBP, J1 ....$2.00

16-A, Atlantic Trailer, reg, VG-, W1 ....$14.50

16-C, Scammell Mountaineer Snowplow, reg, rare gray wheels, red & wht decals, M (NM+ box) $75.00

16-D, Case Bulldozer, reg, MIB.................................$36.00

16-E, Badger Exploration Truck, SF, lt bronze, cream antenna, NM $11.00

16-E, Badger Exploration Truck, SF, metallic orange, blk antenna, MBP $12.00

16-F, Pontiac Firebird Trans Am, 1979, SF, gold, MBP, J1 ..$5.00

16-H, Formula Racer, 1984, SF, red, MIB $4.00

16-J, Ford LTD Police, 1990, SF, wht, MIB, J1 ....$2.50

17-A, Bedford Removals Van, reg, metal wheels, gr, solid letters, NM, W1 ....$49.00

17-B, Austin Taxi, reg, scarce silver wheels, EX, W1 ....$49.00

17-C, Hoveringham Tipper, reg, red base, M (NM box) ..$20.00

17-E, Horse Box, SF, red, no horses, MIB $16.00

17-H, AMX Pro Stocker, 1983, SF, gray, MIB..................$6.00

18-D, CAT D8 Bulldozer, reg, orig tread, blk plastic rollers, NM $25.00

18-E, Field Car, reg, unpnt base, red wheels, orig top, M .$15.00

18-H, Extending Ladder Fire Engine, SF, bright orange, MIB $3.00

19-A, MG Sports Car, reg, VG+ $30.00

19-D, Lotus Racing Car, reg, gr, labels, NM+ $19.00

19-F, Road Dragster, 1970, SF, red, M, J1 ....$6.00

19-H, Peterbilt Cement Truck, 1982, SF, gr & orange, MBP, J1 ....$4.00

20-A, Stake Truck, reg, metal wheels, silver grille & tanks, VG+ $28.00

20-C, Chevy Impala Taxi, reg, orange w/ivory interior, unpnt base, MIB $19.00

20-D, Lamborghini Marzal, SF, red, no labels, M (NM box), W1 ....$15.00

20-E, Police Patrol Range Rover, 1975, SF, wht, MBP, J1 ..$5.00

21-A, Long Distance Coach, reg, metal wheels, VG-, W1 .$14.50

15-J Peugeot 205 Turbo 16, 1985, MIB, $6.00.

21-C Commer Milk Truck, 1961, MIB, $35.00.

15-K, Saab 9000 Turbo, 1988, SF, metallic red, MIB $4.00

15-M, Alfa Romeo SZ Coupe, 1991, SF, red w/blk roof, MIB $2.00

21-D, Foden Concrete Truck, reg, M (NM-, box), W1 ....$13.50

21-F, Road Roller, 1973, SF, yel, blk rollers, MIB, from $6 to $8.00

21-G, Renault 5TL, 1978, SF, yel, tan interior, MIB, J1.....$5.00

21-I, Breakdown Van, 1986, SF, Action Pack, orange, MBP, J1 ....$4.00

22-A, Vauxhall Cresta, reg, metal wheels, M (G- box) $40.00

22-C, Pontiac Grand Sports Coupe, reg, MIB $15.50

22-E, Freeman Intercity Commuter, SF, purple, VG+, W1 ....$4.00

22-F, Blaze Buster Fire Engine, 1975, SF, red, chrome interior, MIB, from $5 to $6.50

23-B, Berkely Cavalier Trailer, reg, lime gr, NM $38.00

23-D, House Trailer Caravan, reg, pk, M, W1 ....$15.00

23-E, Atlas Truck, 1975, SF, bl, orange dumper, chrome interior, MIB $10.00

24-B, Weatherhill Hydraulic Excavator, reg, M, W1 ....$27.50

24-C, Rolls Royce Silver Shadow, reg, MIB, W1 ....$15.00

24-F, Diesel Shunter, 1975, SF, yel, MIB $7.00

24-G, Datsun 280ZX, 1982, SF, blk & gold, M, J1 ....$3.00

24-J, Ferrari F40, 1989, SF, red, MBP, J1 ....$2.00

25-A, Dunlop Van, reg, NM+, W1 ....$42.00

25-B, VW 1200 Sedan, reg, silver-gray wheels, gr window, NM+ $46.50

25-C, BP Petrol Tanker, reg, gr, NM+, W1 ....$16.00

25-D, Ford Cortina, reg, NM $12.50

25-E, Ford Cortina, SF, bl, VG, G2 ....$10.00

25-F, Mod Tractor, 1972, SF, purple, M................$11.00

25-G, Flatcar w/Container, 1978, SF, blk, M $6.00

25-H, Toyota Celica, SF, bl, M (EX box), W1 ....$7.50

26-B, Foden Concrete Truck, reg, orange barrel, M, W1 .$18.00

26-C, GMC Tipper Truck, reg, NM, W1 ....$8.00

26-F, Site Dumper, 1976, SF, yel w/red dumper, MBP or MIB, C6/J1 ....$5.00

26-G, Cosmic Blues, 1980, SF, wht, MIB................$10.00

27-C, Cadillac Sixty Special, reg, lilac & pk w/red base, gr windows, M (NM box) $49.00

27-D, Mercedes Benz 230SL, reg, NM+, W1 ....$12.50

27-F, Lamborghini Countach, SF, MIB, C6 ....$8.00

27-G, Swing Wing Jet, SF, red & wht, Jet Set on wings, MBP, J1 ....$4.50

27-H, Jeep Cherokee, 1987, SF, wht, Quadtrack, MIB, J1..$3.50

28-A, Bedford Compressor Truck, reg, orange, M (NM box) $45.00

28-B, Thames Compressor Truck, reg, VG $11.00

28-C, Jaguar Mk 10, reg, metallic lt brn, M $18.00

28-C, Jaguar MK 10, reg, scarce pnt motor version, NM..$16.00

28-C, Jaguar MK 10, reg, unpnt motor, broken tow hook, NM, W1................$5.00

28-D, Mack Truck, reg, red hubs, M $16.00

28-E, Mack Dump Truck, SF, pea gr, unpnt base, M (EX+ box)................$17.00

28-I, Dodge Daytona Turbo Z, 1984, SF, maroon, MIB......$2.00

28-M, Fork Lift Truck, 1991, SF, med gr, MBP, J1 ....$2.00

29-B, Austin A55 Cambridge Sedan, reg, NM, W1 ....$24.00

29-C, Fire Pumper Truck, reg, red, M, from $11 to..........$14.00

29-E, Racing Mini, 1970, SF, orange, MIB, J1 ....$8.00

29-F, Shovel Nose Tractor, 1976, SF, yel w/red shovel or orange w/blk shovel, MBP, J1 ....$5.00

30-C, 8-Wheel Crane, reg, yel hook, M (NM box), W1 ..$16.00

30-F, Swamp Rat, 1976, SF, Army gr, MIB, J1/W1 ....$5.00

30-H, Peterbilt Quarry Truck, 1982, SF, yel w/gray dumper, MBP $5.00

31-A, Ford Station Wagon, reg, VG, W1 ....$16.00

31-B, Ford Fairlane Station Wagon, reg, gr & pk, gr window, red base, NM, W1 ....$49.00

31-F, Caravan Travel Trailer, 1977, SF, wht w/orange trim, M, J1 ....$4.50

31-J, Rover Sterling, 1988, SF, metallic red, MIB................$3.00

31-L, Nissan Prairie Van, 1991, SF, bl over silver, MBP, J1..$2.50

31-M, Jaguar XJ220, 1993, SF, med bl, MBP, J1 ....$2.00

32-A, Jaguar XK140, reg, cream, EX, W1 ....$34.00

32-B, Jaguar XKE, reg, clear windows, wire wheels, NM+, W1 ....$29.00

32-C, Leyland Petrol Tanker, reg, gr w/silver grille, NM-, W1 ....$8.00

32-D, Leyland Petrol Tanker, SF, gr w/wht tank, silver base, NM $10.00

32-F, Field Gun, SF, olive, olive guard, tan base, blk wheels, M $4.50

33-A, Ford Zodiac MKII Sedan, reg, dk gr, no windows, M (NM box) $50.00

33-B, Ford Zephyr 6 MKIII, 1963, reg, teal gr, M $24.00

34-A, VW Microvan, reg, metal wheels, M $48.00

34-B, VW Camper, reg, lt gr, knobby tires, M (NM box)...$50.00

34-C Volkswagen Camper, 1967, raised roof with windows, silver, MIB, $50.00.

34-E, Formula One Racer, 1971, SF, yel, MIB, J1 ....$6.00

34-F, Vantastic, 1975, SF, orange w/chrome engine, MBP.$9.00

34-G, Chevy Pro Stocker, 1981, SF, wht, MBP $5.50

34-J, Ford RS 200, 1987, SF, bl, MBP $4.00

35-B, Snowtrac Tractor, reg, cast letters, orig treads, NM..$29.00

35-C, Merryweather Fire Engine, SF, red w/gray base, 2 clips, 5-spoke wheels, MBP, W1 ....$15.00

35-F, Trans Am w/T-Roof, 1982, SF, blk w/red interior, MIB, J1 ....$4.00

35-I, Land Rover 90, 1990, SF, bl, MBP................$2.00

36-A, Austin A50, reg, NM+ $40.00

36-B, Fandango, SF, red w/ivory interior, unpnt base, clear windows, bl prop, label, NM................$10.00

36-B, Lambretta Scooter & Sidecar, reg, NM, W1 ....$39.50

36-C, Opel Diplomat, reg, gold w/silver motor, MIB.......$11.00

36-E, Draguar, SF, MIB, C6................$15.00

36-G, Refuse Truck, 1980, SF, red w/yel dumper, MIB, J1 .$5.00

37-A, Coca-Cola Truck, reg, uneven load, sm letters, M .$83.00

37-C, Dodge Cattle Truck, reg, M......$18.00

37-F, Soopa Coopa, SF, MIB $14.00

37-G, Skip Truck, 1976, SF, red & yel buckets, chrome interior, MIB $5.00

37-H, Maserati Bora Sunburner, 1982, SF, blk, MBP, J1 ....$4.50

38-A, Karrier Refuse Collector, reg, gray, gray wheels, M ..$38.00

38-C, Honda Motorcycle & Trailer, reg, yel trailer, labels, NM+ $20.00

38-G, Camper Pickup Truck, 1980, SF, red & tan, MIB ..$10.00

38-H, Model A Truck, 1982, SF, bl w/blk lettering, MBP ..$7.00

39-B, Pontiac Convertible, reg, yel, ivory steering wheel, blk base, NM+, W1 ......$36.00

39-C, Ford Tractor, reg, bl & yel, M (NM box)......$15.00

39-D, Clipper, 1973, SF, metallic purple, gr base, MIB $10.00

39-E, Rolls Royce Silver Shadow II, 1979, SF, metallic red, MBP $6.50

40-A, Bedford Tipper Truck, reg, M (EX- box) $38.00

40-B, Leyland Royal Tiger Coach, reg, M......$22.00

40-C, Hay Trailer, reg, orig bales, M (NM box), W1 ......$13.50

40-E, Bedford Horse Box w/2 Horses, 1977, SF, orange cab, ivory box, brn door, M $8.00

40-F, Corvette T-Roof, 1982, SF, bl w/gray side pipes, MIB ..$4.50

41-C, Ford GT Race Car, reg, wht, yel hubs, decal, NM+..$16.00

41-D, Ford GT Race Car, SF, wht w/blk base, label, 5-spoke wheels, M (NM box) $12.50

41-G, Kenworth Conventional Aerodyne, 1982, SF, red, MIB, J1 ......$4.00

42-A, Bedford Evening News, reg, NM, W1......$44.00

42-B, Studebaker Lark Wagonaire, reg, orig hunter & dog still on tree, MIB......$22.00

42-C, Iron Fairy Crane, reg, MIB $19.50

42-E, Tyre Fryer, SF, bl, EX $6.50

42-F, Mercedes Container Truck, 1977, SF, red, MIB, J1 ...$6.00

43-A, Hillman Minx, reg, bl/gray, NM+ $30.00

43-B, Averling Bedford Tractor Shovel, reg, yel, red driver & base, M, W1 ......$29.00

43-C, Pony Trailer w/2 horses, 1968, reg, yel & gr base, MIB, J1 ......$15.00

43-E, VW Bug Dragon Wheels, SF, gr, blk base, 5-spoke wheels, M $12.00

43-F, 0-4-0 Steam Locomotive, 1978, SF, red & blk, #4345, MBP, J1 ......$5.00

43-K, Lincoln Town Car, 1989, wht, MBP $2.00

44-A, Rolls Royce Silver Cloud, reg, silver wheels, M $37.00

44-B, Rolls Royce Phantom V, reg, M $33.00

44-C, GMC Refrigerator Truck, reg, MIB......$18.00

44-F, Passenger Coach Train Car, SF, red, NM+ $6.00

45-A, Vauxhall Victor, reg, no-window version, NM $31.00

45-B, Ford Corsair, reg, all orig, MIB $19.50

45-C, Ford Group 6, 1970, SF, metallic red, MIB......$15.00

45-D, BMW 3.0 CSL, 1976, SF, orange, MIB......$7.00

46-A, Mercedes 300SE, SF, gold, closed doors, NM+......$6.50

46-A, Morris Minor, reg, metal wheels, dk gr, NM+ $50.00

46-B, Pickford's Removal Van, reg, 3-line decal, NM+, W1 ......$39.00

46-C, Mercedes 300SE, 1968, reg, gr, M, J1 ......$15.00

46-E, Stretcha Fetcha, SF, wht w/lt yel interior, red base, bl window, 5-spoke wheels, Ambulance label, M $10.00

46-F, Ford Tractor, 1978, SF, bl w/yel harrow, MIB, from $4 to $6.00

46-G, Hot Chocolate VW Beetle, 1982, SF, blk & bronze, MIB $8.00

47-A, One-Ton Trojan Van, M $34.00

47-B, Commer Ice Cream Canteen, bl, oval roof decal, plain side decal, M (VG- box)......$26.00

47-C, DAF Tipper Truck, reg, silver & yel, gray top, NM+ $16.00

47-E, Beach Hopper, 1974, SF, bl w/pk spots, orange interior, MIB, J1 ......$6.00

47-F, Panier Locomotive, 1979, gr, MIB, J1 ......$5.00

47-G, Jaguar SS, SF, red hood & body, tan interior, blk base, MIB $3.00

48-B, Sports Boat & Trailer, reg, red deck, wht hull, dk bl trailer, NM+......$28.50

48-C, Dodge Dump Truck, reg, full-length base, MIB, W1 .$16.00

48-F, Sambron Jacklift, 1977, SF, yel, MIB $6.00

48-G, Red Rider, 1982, SF, red, MIB, J1 ......$2.50

48-J, Pontiac Firebird Racer, 1993, blk w/pk chassis, MBP, J1..$2.00

49-A, M3 Personnel Carrier, reg, blk plastic rollers, NM+, W1 ......$29.00

49-B, Unimog, reg, tan & aqua, M, W1 ......$15.00

49-E, Crane Truck, 1976, SF, yel w/yel boom, MIB, J1 ......$5.00

49-H, Peugeot Quasar, 1987, SF, maroon, MIB, J1 ......$2.50

50-A, Commer Pickup Truck, reg, gray wheels, tan, EX, W1 .$27.50

50-B, John Deere Tractor, reg, gray wheels, MIB......$24.00

50-C, Kennel Truck, reg, wht grille, smooth bed, 4 orig dogs, NM+, W1 ......$19.00

50-E, Articulated Truck, 1973, SF, yel cab, bl dumper, MBP, J1/C6 ......$5.50

50-H, Chevy Blazer, 1985, SF, wht, MBP $3.00

51-B, John Deere Tractor, reg, gray wheels, orig barrels, NM $12.00

51-C, 8 Wheel Tipper Truck, reg, yel, Douglas labels, orange truck, MIB......$15.00

51-E, Citroen SM, SF, bl, M (EX box)......$10.50

51-F, Combine Harvester, SF, MIB $7.50

51-G, Midnight Magic, 1982, SF, blk, MIB $5.50

51-J, Camaro IROC-Z, 1985, SF, yel, MIB......$2.00

52-A, Maserati 4 CLT Racer, reg, red decals, orig driver, VG $13.00

52-B, BRM Racing Car, reg, bl, decals, NM $13.00

52-C, Dodge Charger, SF, metallic lime, red base, no labels, M (NM box) $13.50

52-D, Police Launch, SF, MIB, C6 ......$5.00

53-B, Mercedes Benz 220 SE, reg, red, NM+, W1 ......$29.00

53-C, Ford Zodiac MK IV Sedan, reg, silver/bl, NM $14.00

53-D, Ford Zodiac, SF, lt gr, M (NM box) $15.00

53-E, Tanzara, 1972, SF, wht, M, J1 ......$5.00

53-F, CJ-6 Jeep, 1977, SF, red w/tan roof, MBP, J1......$4.50

54-A, Saracen Personnel, reg, MIB $25.00

54-B, S&S Cadillac Ambulance, reg, decals, NM $17.00

54-E, Personnel Carrier, 1976, SF, Army gr, MIB......$6.00

54-G, NASA Tracking Vehicle, 1982, SF, wht, MIB, J1 ...$5.00

54-I, Chevrolet Lumina Stocker, 1990, SF, bl, MBP, J1.....$3.00

55-B, Ford Fairlane Police Car, reg, metallic bl, MIB.......$34.00

55-C, Ford Galaxie Police Car, reg, decals, red dome, NM+, W1 ....$23.00

55-D, Mercury Police Car, reg, bl dome, MIB.................$17.00

55-E, Mercury Police Car, SF, wht w/bl dome light, MIB...$17.00

55-G, Hellraiser, 1975, SF, wht, red interior, chrome engine, M $9.00

55-H, Ford Cortina 1600GL, SF, MIB, C6/J1 ....$5.00

56-A, London Trolley Bus, reg, red trolley poles, NM-, W1 ....$54.00

56-B, Fiat 1500 Sedan, reg, aqua, tan luggage, MIB.........$19.00

56-E, Mercedes 450SEL, 1979, SF, bl, MIB.....................$6.50

57-A, Wolseley 1500, reg, lt gr, gray wheels, MIB...........$42.50

57-B, Chevy Impala, reg, blk base, MIB..........................$34.50

57-C, Land Rover Fire Truck, reg, decals, orig ladder, MIB, W1 ....$21.00

57-D, Land Rover Fire Truck, SF, labels, MIB.................$29.00

57-F, Wild Life Truck, 1973, SF, yel, MIB $8.50

58-B, Drott Excavator, reg, orange body, silver motor & base, blk plastic rollers, orig tread, NM+ $31.00

58-E, Woosh n' Push, 1972, SF, yel, MIB $11.00

58-F, Faun Dump Truck, 1976, SF, yel, MIB, J1/W1 ....$5.00

58-G, Ruff Trek Racing Pickup, 1983, SF, gold, MIB.........$8.00

59-A, Ford Thames Singer Van, reg, lt gr, NM-, W1 ....$34.50

59-C, Ford Galaxie Fire Chief Car, reg, hood & side decals, NM+ $14.00

59-F, Planet Scout, SF, MIB, C6 ....$10.00

59-G, Porsche 928, 1980, SF, goldfish tan, MIB, J1 ....$5.50

60-A, Morris J-2 Pickup, reg, gray wheels, red & blk decals, w/window, M $47.50

60-B, Leyland Site Office Truck, 1966, reg, gr & yel, M, J1 ..$13.00

60-B, Site Hut Truck, reg, M.......................................$13.00

60-Ea, Mustang Piston Popper, 1982, SF, yel, M, J1 ....$4.00

60-F, Pontiac Firebird Racer, 1984, SF, wht, MBP, J1 ....$3.00

61-A, Ferret Scout Car, 1959, reg, Army gr, M $30.00

61-B, Alvis Stalwart, reg, gr hubs, decals, NM.................$19.00

61-C, Blue Shark, SF, dk bl, clear window, silver gray base, label, M (EX box) $11.00

61-E, Peterbilt Wrecker, 1982, wht & orange, MIB, J1 ......$4.00

62-A, General Service Lorry, reg, VG.............................$17.00

62-B, TV Service Van, reg, all orig, MIB........................$30.00

62-C, Mercury Cougar, reg, NM+, W1 ....$12.50

62-D, Mercury Cougar, SF, metallic gr, M (EX box) $12.00

62-F, Renault 17TL, SF, red, label, M (EX box), W1 ....$7.50

62-I, Rolls Royce Silver Cloud, 1985, SF, cloud cream, MBP.$2.00

63-B, Foamite Airport Crash Tender, reg, gold nozzle, MIB.$28.00

63-D, Dodge Crane Truck, SF, yel, blk axle covers, M (NM box) $19.00

63-E, Freeway Tanker, 1973, SF, red & wht, MIB, J1 ....$6.50

64-A, Scammel Breakdown Truck, reg, gray plastic hook, NM+ $35.00

64-B, MG 1100 Sedan, reg, NM+ $17.00

64-B, MG 1100 Sedan, 1964, SF, gr, M $17.00

64-E, Fire Chief Car, SF, red, outlined shield labels, M......$8.00

64-F, CAT Bulldozer, 1979, SF, yel & tan cab, orange rollers, MBP, J1 ....$5.00

65-A, Jaguar 3.4 Litre Saloon, reg, bl, M........................$35.50

65-C, Claas Combine Harvester, reg, NM+.....................$11.00

65-Ea, Airport Coach, 1977, SF, bl & wht, American Airlines, MBP $6.00

66-A, Citroen DS19, reg, NM+ $48.50

66-B, Harley-Davidson Motorcycle & Sidecar, reg, NM+..$58.50

66-C, Greyhound Bus, reg, silver, gray lettering, M..........$20.00

66-Cb, Greyhound Bus, reg, amber windows, decals, VG...$6.50

66-E, Mazda RX 500, SF, dk gr, tampo, M (EX box), W1 ..$10.00

66-F, Ford Transit, SF, MIB, C6/J1, from $5 to..................$6.50

66-G, Tyrone Malone Super Boss, 1982, SF, wht, MIB, J1.$4.50

67-B Volkswagen 1600TL, 1967, MIB, $25.00.

67-B, VW 1600TL Fastback, reg, NM.............................$16.00

67-C, VW 1600TL Fastback, SF, purple, NM+ $19.00

67-D, Hot Rocket Ford Capri, SF, orange, M (VG box), W1.$10.00

67-F, Datsun 260Z, 1978, SF, metallic wine red, M, J1.......$4.50

68-B, Mercedes Coach, reg, orange, NM+ $16.00

68-C, Porsche 910, 1970, SF, metallic red, MBP $10.00

68-E, Chevy Van, SF, MIB, C6 ....$5.00

68-F, Dodge Caravan, 1984, SF, blk w/gold stripes, MIB....$2.00

69-D, Turbo Fury, SF, NM, W1......................................$5.00

69-E, Armored Truck, 1978, SF, red, MBP $8.00

70-B, Ford Grit Spreader, reg, gray pull, NM+.................$16.00

70-F, Ferrari 308 GTB, 1981, SF, red-orange, M, J1 ....$4.50

71-B, Jeep Gladiator Pickup, reg, wht interior, NM $22.50

71-C Ford Wrecker, Esso, 1968, MIB, $20.00.

71-F, Dodge Cattle Truck, 1976, SF, bronze cab, blk cattle, MIB, J1 ....$5.00

72-B, Jeep, reg, NM $14.50

72-D, Hovercraft SRN6, SF, MIB $10.00

72-E, Maxi Taxi, 1973, SF, yel, MBP $7.00

72-F, Bomag Road Roller, 1979, SF, yel w/blk rollers, MIB, J1 ....$5.00

73-B, Ferrari F1 Racer, reg, wht driver, M (EX+ box) $31.50

73-F, Weasel Armored Vehicle, 1974, SF, metallic gr, MIB, J1 ....$6.00

73-G, Ford Model A, SF, gr w/dk gr fenders, EX+ $6.50

74-A, Mobile Refreshment Canteen, reg, silver, lt bl base, NM $46.50

74-B, Daimler London Bus, 1966, reg, gr, M....................$23.00

74-D, Toe Joe Wrecker, 1972, SF, metallic gr, MBP $8.00

74-F, Dodge Charger Orange Peel, 1982, SF, wht & orange, M $4.50

75-B, Ferrari Berlinetta, reg, gr w/wht wheels, NM $29.00

75-C, Ferrari Berlinetta, SF, red, plain grille, M (NM box) .$20.50

75-D, Alfa Carabo, SF, MIB, C6 ....$12.00

75-G, Ferrari Testarosa, 1987, SF, red, MBP, J1 ....$2.50

KING SIZE, SPEED KINGS AND SUPER KINGS

K01B, Hoveringham Tipper Truck, 1964, M (G box), W1.$42.00

K02B, KW Dump Truck, 1964, MIB, $25.00.

K02B, Kenworth Dump Truck, 1964, NM-, W1 ....$12.50

K03B, Hatra Tractor Shovel, 1965, NM-, W1...............$15.50

K05B, Racing Car Transporter, 1967, EX, W1 ....$14.00

K05C, Muir Tractor & Trailer, 1972, yel w/red hubs, MIB, J1 ..$20.00

K06B, Mercedes Ambulance, 1967, EX, W1......................$7.50

K07A, Curtis Wright Rear Dumper, 1961, VG, W1 ....$12.00

K07B, Refuse Truck, 1967, blk walls, EX+, W1 ....$9.00

K08B, Guy Warrior Car Transporter, 1975, aqua w/orange trailer, EX+, W1 ....$32.00

K09A, Diesel Road Roller, 1962, M- (G box), W1 ....$34.00

K09B, Claas Combine Harvester, 1967, gr, NM-, W1......$17.00

K10A, Aveling Barford Tractor Shovel, 1963, bl-gr, red hubs, VG, W1 ....$17.00

K10B, Pipe Truck, 1967, EX+, W1 ....$11.00

K10D, Bedford Car Transporter, 1981, bl & wht, MIB, J1 ..$20.00

K13A, Ready Mix Concrete Truck, red hubs, decals, NM, W1 ....$19.00

K14A, Taylor Jumbo Crane, 1964, yel weight box, NM, W1 ....$14.00

K15A, Merryweather Fire Engine, 1964, M (NM box), W1..$42.00

K15B, London Bus, 1973, Berlin Anniversary Issue, tan, MIB, J1 ....$15.00

K16G, Articulated Petrol Truck, 1974, red & wht, Texaco, MIB, J1 ....$18.00

K17B, Container Truck, 1974, wht & gr, 7-Up, MIB, J1 .$20.00

K19A, Scammell Tipper Truck, 1967, NM, W1..............$19.00

K20B, Cargo Hauler & Pallet Loader, 1973, gr, MIB, J1 ..$20.00

K20C, Peterbilt Wrecker, SF, 1979, dk gr, red dome lights, unpnt base, EX, W1 ....$14.00

K21A, Mercury Cougar, 1968, gold w/red interior, NM-, W1 ....$13.00

K21C, Tractor Transporter & 2 Mod Tractors, 1974, purple, MIB, J1 ....$20.00

K21D, Ford Transcontinental, 1978, gr & wht, MIB, J1 ..$25.00

K24B, Scammell Container Truck, 1977, red & wht, M, J1 ....$10.00

K31B, Peterbilt Refrigerator Truck, 1979, bl, MIB, J1......$20.00

K36B, Transporter w/Shovel Nose & Site Dumper, 1978, yel, MIB, J1 ....$20.00

K39B, Simon Snorkel Fire Engine, 1980, red w/wht boom, MIB, J1 ....$15.00

K48A, Mercedes 350 SL, 1973, orange, M, L1 ....$20.00

K49A, Leyland Ambulance, 1973, wht, M, L1 ....$15.00

K56A, Maserati Bora, 1976, silver, M, L1 ....$15.00

K59A, Capri II, 1976, wht w/blk roof, MIB, J1 ....$13.00

K60, Ford Mustang Cobra, red, M, L1 ....$24.00

K62A, Citroen SM, 1977, Emergency Doctor, wht, M, L1...$28.00

K86A, VW Golf (w/gas pump), 1981, wht, MIB, J1 ....$12.00

K98B, Porsche 944, 1983, gold, MIB, J1...........................$8.00

K133A, Iveco Refuse Truck, 1986, $10.00.

K139A, Iveco Tipper Truck, Department of Highways, 1987, $10.00.

MATCHBOX ORIGINALS

01-Lb, Averling Barford Road Roller, 1991, bl, dbl roof posts, MBP, J1 ....$4.00

04-Jb, Massey-Harris Tractor, 1991, gr, press-fit axles, MBP, J1 ....$3.00

05-Jb, London Bus, 1991, red, MBP, J1 ....$3.00

06-K, Euclid Dump Truck, 1993, bl w/gray dumper, MBP, J1 ....$3.00

09-Jb, Dennis Fire Engine, 1991, red, MBP, J1 ....$4.00

13-J, Bedford Wreck Truck, 1993, red w/yel boom, MBP, J1 ..$3.00

19-I, MGA Roadster, 1993, dk gr, cream driver, MBP, J1 ..$3.00

26-K, Foden Ready Mix Concrete Truck, 1993, MBP, J1...$3.00

32-I, Jaguar XK 140 Coupe, 1993, blk, MBP, J1 ....$3.00

MODELS OF YESTERYEAR

Y-01A, 1925 Allchin Traction Engine, 1956, blk flywheel, partial gold drum, riveted axle, NM+, W1.....................$79.00

Y-01B, 1911 Ford Model T, 1964, red, blk top, grille & seats, single brake lever, brass wheels, M (NM box), W1 ...$31.00

Y-01B, 1911 Ford Model T, 1968, cream w/maroon top, MIB, J1 ....$18.00

Y-01C, 1936 Jaguar SS/100, wht, M.................................$10.00

Y-01C, 1936 Jaguar SS/100, yel body, diorama, MIB, C6.$15.00

Y-01C, 1936 Jaguar SS/100, 1977, MIB, $15.00.

Y-02A, 1911 B-Type London Bus, 1956, NM (EX box)...$90.00

Y-02B, 1911 Renault 2-Seater, 1963, 4-prong spare holder, M (EX box), W1 ....$29.00

Y-02C, 1914 Prince Henry Vauxhall, 1970, red body, M, C6 ....$18.00

Y-03B, 1910 Mercedes Benz Limo, 1966, cream w/gr roof & seats, gr radiator, NM, W1 ....$19.00

Y-03C, 1934 Riley MPH, 1974, bl w/wht interior, MIB, J1 .$18.00

Y-03C, 1934 Riley MPH, 1974, purple, M, C6 ....$22.00

Y-03C, 1934 Riley MPH, 1974, red, M, C6 ....$16.00

Y-03D, Ford Model T Tanker, 1981, gr w/wht roof, MIB, J1 ..$12.00

Y-04A, 1928 Sentinel Steam Wagon, 1956, bl w/gold tool box, crimped axles, NM, W1 ....$80.00

Y-04B, Shand-Mason Horse-Drawn Fire Engine, 1960, EX+ (EX box), C6..$125.00

Y-04B, 1909 Opel Coupe, 1967, wht, M, L1 ....$16.00

Y-04B, 1909 Opel Coupe, 1967, wht w/smooth tan roof, red seats & radiator, M (EX box), W1 ....$24.00

Y-04D, 1930 Deusenberg Model J Town Car, 1976, gr, M, L1.$16.00

Y-04D, 1930 Deusenberg Model J, 1976, red, M, C6........$16.00

Y-05B, 1929 4½ Litre Bentley, 1962, gr w/silver radiator, decal, C-type base, M, W1..$35.00

Y-05C, 1907 Peugeot, 1969, MIB, $25.00.

Y-05D, 1927 Talbot Van, 1978, Chocolate Menier, M, C6 .$18.00

Y-05D, 1927 Talbot Van, 1978, Dunlop, M $15.00

Y-05D, 1927 Talbot Van, 1978, Everready, M.................$15.00

Y-05D, 1927 Talbot Van, 1978, yel, VG+, W1 ....$6.50

Y-05D, 1927 Talbot Van, 1978, MIB, $20.00.

Y-05E, Titan Bus, 1989, gr, Robin Starch, MIB...............$15.00

Y-06A, 1916 AEC Type Lorry, 1957, gray w/silver radiator, gray driver, unpnt wheels, riveted axles, rare version, NM, W1 ....$89.00

Y-06C, 1913 Cadillac, 1967, gold w/smooth dk red roof, seats & radiator, brass wheels, M, W1 ....$20.00

Y-07A, 4-Ton Leyland Van, 1957, NM (VG box) $90.00

Y-07C, 1912 Rolls Royce, 1968, gold w/ribbed dk red roof, blk seats & radiator, NMIB, W1 ....$11.00

Y-08A, 1926 Morris Cowley Bullnose, tan w/gold trim, unplated wheels, NM, W1 ....$80.00

Y-08B, 1914 Sunbeam Motorcycle & Sidecar, silver, dk gr sidecar seat, NM, W1...$33.00

Y-08C, 1914 Stutz Roadster, dk metallic red, tan roof, copper gas tank, NM, W1 ....$19.00

Y-08D, 1945 MG/TC, 1978, MIB, $25.00.

Y-08D, 1945 MG TC, 1978, bl w/tan roof, M, J1 ....$12.00

Y-08E, 1917 Yorkshire Steam Wagon, 1987, maroon Johnny Walker logo, M..$15.00

Y-08E, 1917 Yorkshire Steam Wagon, 1987, William Prichard, M...$15.00

Y-09A, 1924 Fowler Big Lion Showman's Engine, 1958, gold boiler door & roof supports, maroon base, VG+, W1..$29.00

Y-09A, 1924 Fowler Big Lion Showman's Engine, 1958, NM (EX+ box)...$80.00

Y-09B, 1912 Simplex, 1968, gr w/smooth tan roof, red seats, dk red grille, brass wheels, NM, W1..........................$15.00

Y-09B, 1912 Simplex, 1968, NM (EX+ box).....................$20.00

Y-10A, 1908 Grand Prix Mercedes, 1958, cream w/gr seats, plated parts & wheels, gold trim, M, W1 ....$62.00

Y-10B, 1928 Mercedes Benz 36/220, 1963, wht w/red seats, tan dash & floor, NM, W1 ....$17.00

Y-10C, 1906 Rolls Royce Silver Ghost, 1969, silver, MIB, J1...$18.00

Y-11A, 1920 Averling Porter Steam Roller, 1958, gr w/blk fly-wheel, partial gold trim, M, W1 ....$109.00

Y-11B, 1912 Packard Landaulet, 1964, dk red w/blk seats, brass trim, 3-prong spare holder, NM+, W1 ....$23.00

Y-11C, 1938 Lagonda Drophead Coupe, 1972, MIB, $25.00.

Y-11C, 1938 Lagonda Drophead Coupe, 1972, cream w/blk cha-sis, solid chrome wheels, NM (EX- box), W1 ....$16.00

Y-12A, 1899 London Horse-Drawn Bus, 1959, NM (NM box), C6..$99.00

Y-12A, 1899 London Horse-Drawn Bus, 1959, red w/beige seats, gold collars on lt brn horses, unpnt underside, NM+, W1 ....$89.00

Y-12B, 1909 Thomas Flyabout, 1967, bl w/smooth tan roof, roof pins in red seats, type-C base, MIB, W1....................$30.00

Y-12C, 1912 Ford Model T Truck, 1978, Baxter's, M, C6..$12.00

Y-12C, 1912 Ford Model T Truck, 1978, Captain Morgan, M...$18.00

Y-12C, 1912 Ford Model T Truck, 1978, Harrod's, M, C6..$15.00

Y-13A, 1862 American General Class Sante Fe Locomotive, 1959, dk gr w/red base rivets, gold condenser/stack rim, M-, W1 ....$98.00

Y-13B, 1911 Damler, 1966, yel w/blk seats, brass wheels, type-A base, 1st version of this model, M, W1 ....$32.00

Y-13C, 1918 Crossley RAF Tender, 1974, bl w/tan roof, wht seats & olive radiator, type-B base, M (EX box), W1 ....$62.00

Y-13C, 1918 Crossley RAF Tender, 1974, Carlsberg, M, C6.$15.00

Y-13C, 1918 Crossley RAF Tender, 1974, Warings, M, C6..$20.00

Y-14B, 1911 Maxwell Roadster, 1965, turq w/smooth blk roof, dk red seats, blk radiator & copper tank, M, W1 ....$17.00

Y-14C, Stutz Bearcat, 1974, cream w/gr fenders, MIB......$15.00

Y-14D, 1935 ERA Race Car, 1986, bl & yel, #4, MIB......$12.00

Y-15A, 1907 Rolls Royce Silver Ghost, 1960, lt metallic gr w/blk seats, brass A wheels, B spare, MIB, W1 ....$34.00

Y-15B, 1930 Packard Victoria, 1969, cream w/brn fenders, MIB, J1...$12.00

Y-15B, 1930 Packard Victoria, 1969, metallic lime gold w/red seats & radiator, bl top & trunk, M (EX- box), W1 ..$19.00

Y-15C, 1920 London Tram, 1987, M.............................$15.00

Y-16A, 1904 Spyder, 1961, pale yel radiator shell, A base, type-2 chasis panel, NM, W1 ....$17.50

Y-16B, 1928 Mercedes Benz SS Coupe, 1972, bl w/gray side pan-els, MIB..$20.00

Y-16B, 1928 Mercedes Benz SS Coupe, 1972, red body, M.$15.00

Y-17A, 1938 Hispano Suiza, 1975, 2-tone gr, blk roof, M..$18.00

Y-18A, 1937 Cord 812, 1979, red, M...........................$15.00

Y-19A, 1935 Auburn 851 Boattail Speedster, 1980, M....$15.00

Y-20A, 1937 Mercedes Benz 540K, 1981, MIB, $20.00.

Y-20A, 1937 Mercedes Benz 540K, 1981, silver, M, L1....$15.00

Y-22A, 1930 Ford Model A Van, 1982, Maggi, M, C6.....$12.00

Y-22A, 1930 Ford Model A Van, 1982, Oxo, M, C6 ....$10.00

Y-22A, 1930 Ford Model A Van, 1982, Palm Toffee, M..$15.00

Y-23A, 1922 AEC S Type Omnibus, 1982, M..................$15.00

Y-23B, 1930 Mack Tanker, 1989, M (NM box), C6 ....$14.00

Y-24A, 1927 Bugatti T44, 1983, M, C6..........................$12.00

Y-25A, 1910 Renault Type AG, 1983, M........................$15.00

Y-26A, 1918 Crossley Beer Lorry, 1983, M, C6...............$10.00

Y-29A, 1919 Walker Electric, 1985, gr, M (special box), J1..$8.00

Y-30A, 1920 Mack Truck, 1985, bl w/gray mudguards & cab steps, M, C6 ....$25.00

Y-40A, 1931 Mercedes Benz Type 770, 1991, gray w/bl roof, M, C6...$10.00

SKYBUSTERS

SB01, Learjet, wht, US Air Force, MBP, J1 ....$4.00
SB02, A-7D Corsair, tan, gr camo, USAF, MBP, J1 ....$4.00
SB04, Mirage F-1, orange, MIB, J1....................................$6.00
SB12C, Mission Chopper, gr & tan, MBP, J1 ....$3.00
SB16, F4U-4 Corsair, bl, Navy, MIB, J1 ....$10.00
SB20, Helicopter, Army gr, MBP, J1................................$10.00
SB21, Lightning, olive gr, MBP, J1 ....$10.00
SB31, Boeing 747-400, gray & bl, MBP, J1 ....$3.00
SB32, Fairchild A-10, gray & gr camo, MBP, J1 ....$4.00
SB34, Lockheed C-130 Hercules, wht & silver, USCG, MIB, J1..$4.00
SB36, F-117 Stealth Fighter, blk, MBP, J1 ....$4.00
SB38, BAE 146, wht, MIB, J1...$4.00

ACCESSORIES

Case, Collectors Case, 1965, 40-car, #53 & #6 on sides, orig store tag, EX+, W1...$23.00
Case, Collectors Case, 1968, 48-car, #41 on front, plastic trays, NM, W1..$21.00
Case, Collectors Case, 1968, 72-car, #75 Ferrari on front, plastic trays, NM, W1 ....$29.00
Case, Collectors Mini-Case, 1967, 18-car, Ford Mustang on front, NM, W1...$26.00

Model Kits

Figure-type model kits have drastically increased in value over the past five to eight years, especially those made by Aurora during the 1960s. Though model kits were popular with kids of the fifties who enjoyed the challenge of assembling a classic car or two or a Musketeer figure now and then, when the monster series hit in the early 1960s, sales shot through the ceiling. Made popular by all the monster movies of that decade, ghouls like Vampirella, Frankenstein and the Wolfman were eagerly built up by kids everywhere. They could (if their parents allowed them to) even construct an actual working guillotine. Aurora had other successful series of figure kits, too, based on characters from comic strips and TV shows as well as a line of sports stars.

But the vast majority of model kits were vehicles. They varied in complexity, some requiring much more dexterity on the part of the model builder than others, and they came in several scales, from 1/8 (which might be as large as 20" to 24") down to 1/43 (generally about 3" to 4"), but the most popular scale was 1/25 (usually between 6" to 8"). Some of the largest producers of vehicle kits were AMT, MPC, and IMC. Though production obviously waned during the late 1970s and early '80s, with the intensity of today's collector market, companies like Ertl (who now is producing 1/25 scale vehicles using some of the old AMT dies) are proving that model kits still sell very well.

As a rule of thumb, assembled kits (built-ups) are priced at about 25% to 50% of the price range for a boxed kit, but this is not always true on the higher-priced kits. One mint in the box with the factory seal intact will often sell for up to 15% more than if the seal were broken. Condition of the box is crucial. For more information, we recommend *Aurora History and Price Guide* by Bill Bruegman.

Advisors: Mike and Kurt Fredericks (F4); John and Sheri Pavone (P3)

Adams, Thor Rocket — White Sands #162, 1958, 1/87, MIB, G5 ....$109.00
Adams, Vanguard #161, 1958, 1/80, MIB, G5..............$169.00
Addar, Blue Jays #250, 1975, MIB, G5 ....$20.00
Addar, Jaws Diorama #231, MIB, G5................................$34.00
Addar, Planet of the Apes, Cearer, no instructions, EX (EX box), J2...$45.00
Addar, Planet of the Apes, Cornelius, 1973, MIB (sealed), D9 ....$34.00
Addar, Planet of the Apes, Dr Zaius, 1973, EX (EX box), D9.$35.00
Addar, Planet of the Apes, Dr Zauis, 1973, NM (in long box), S2...$50.00
Addar, Planet of the Apes, General Aldo, EX (EX box) ..$38.00
Addar, Planet of the Apes, Scenes in a Bottle, Cornfield Roundup, 1975, 1/32, M (orig box), G5/J2, from $35 to...$45.00
Addar, Planet of the Apes, Stallion & Soldier, MIB (sealed) .$200.00
Addar, Spirit in a Bottle (phantom-like monster in a cemetery), 1975, MIB (sealed), H4 ....$29.00

Addar Super Scenes, Planet of the Apes, Treehouse, 1975, MIB (sealed), $35.00; Addar Super Scenes, Planet of the Apes, Jail Wagon, 1975, missing printed background scene otherwise MIB, $25.00.

AEF Designs, Aliens Frost #AM-3, 1/35, MIB, G5..........$34.00
AEF Designs, Aliens Ripley #AC-1, 1/35, MIB, G5........$34.00

AEF Designs, Aliens Warrior Alien A #AX-1, 1/35, MIB, G5 ....$49.00

AEF Designs, Aliens Wierzbowski #AM-8, 1/35, MIB, G5 .$39.00

Airfix, Apollo Saturn V #911, 1968, 1/144, MIB, G5 ......$59.00

Airfix, Astronauts #41, 1978, 1/75, MIB, G5..................$26.00

Airfix, Bristol Bloodhound #2309, 1977, 1/76, MIB, G5..$19.00

Airfix, High Chaparral Set #38, 1/75, MIB, G5..............$14.00

Airfix, Lunar Module #3013, 1975, 1/72, MIB, G5 ....$18.00

Airfix, Monkeemobile #831, 1967, 1/24, MIB, G5.........$154.00

Airfix, Queen Elizabeth I #3543, Famous Women in History, 1974, 1/12, MIB, G5 ....$24.00

Airfix, Russian Vostok #05172, 1991, 1/144, MIB, G5 ....$21.00

Airfix, Space: 1999, Eagle Transporter #6174, 1976, 1/72, MIG, G5 ....$109.00

Airfix, 2001: A Space Odyssey, Orion #05175, 1980, 1/144, MIB, G5 ....$49.00

Alabe, Neanderthal Man #2963, 1976, 1/8, MIB, G5 ......$64.00

ALT, Robocop, 1/6, MIB, G5..$59.00

AMF, Cargo Ship (Dolphin), 1963, battery-op, assembles & disassembles, turn switch & prop spins, NM+ (EX box), A $175.00

AMT, Apollo Spacecraft #S955, 1970, 1/200, MIB, G5 ..$11.00

AMT, BJ & the Bear Big Rig, 1980, MIB (sealed), C1.....$36.00

AMT, Family Sedan, MIB (sealed) $145.00

AMT, Farrah's Foxy Vette, MIB (sealed), J2 ....$30.00

AMT, Ford Pickup, 1977, MIB, J2 ....$55.00

AMT, Get Smart Car, 1967, NMIB, J2............................$165.00

AMT, Graveyard Ghoul Duo, MIB, J2 ....$200.00

AMT, Hero (Chrysler Imperial from TV show), 1966, EX (EX box), D9 ....$55.00

AMT, Kiss Custom Chevy Van #250, 1977, MIB $80.00

AMT, Kiss Custom Chevy Van #250, 1977, MIB (sealed).$95.00

AMT, Man From UNCLE Car #912, 1967, 1/25, MIB, G5.$249.00

AMT, Munster Ghoul Duo #309, 1/25, MIB, G5 ....$144.00

AMT, Munster Koach, 1964, orig issue, 1/25, NMIB, J2.$300.00

AMT, Munster Koach, 1965, 1/25, EX+ $175.00

AMT, Munsters, Grandpa's Dragula #905, 1964, 1/25, MIB, G5 ....$269.00

AMT, My Mother the Car (TV Show), NMIB $49.00

AMT, Star Trek, K-7 Space Station #K955, 1976, 1/7600, MIB, G5 ....$74.00

AMT, Star Trek, Space Ship Set, 1976, MIB (sealed) $45.00

AMT, Star Trek, Spock w/Snakes, 1973, assembled, EX+, C1 ....$72.00

AMT, Star Trek, Spock w/Snakes, 1973, assembled & pnt, needs rpr, D9..$43.00

AMT, Star Trek, USS Enterprise, 1975, MIB (sealed), C1/D9, from $35 to..$57.00

AMT, Star Trek, USS Enterprise Command Bridge, 1975, MIB (sealed), C1..$77.00

AMT, Star Trek, USS Enterprise Exploration Set, 1974, MIB (sealed), D9..$38.00

AMT, Star Trek the Motion Picture, USS Enterprise #970, 1979, 1/500, MIB, G5..$79.00

AMT, Star Trek the Motion Picture, Vulcan Shuttle #972, 1979, 1/50, MIB, G5..$59.00

AMT, Vega/Astre Funny Car Kit, MIB (sealed), J2 ....$35.00

AMT, 1949 Mercury, assembled, NM (NM box), J2........$25.00

AMT, 1957 Ford Fairlane 500, VG+, J2 ....$25.00

AMT, 1958 Chevrolet Impala, Trophy series, M (EX box), $110.00.

AMT, 1966 Ford Falcon, NMIB, from $75 to..................$90.00

AMT, 1966 Ford Galaxy 500XL Convertible, NMIB, J2 .$90.00

AMT, 1968 Corvair #5728, w/Yenko Stinger Customizing Kit, unassembled, complete, A3 ....$50.00

AMT/Ertl, Airwolf Helicopter, 1984, 1/48 scale, MIB (sealed) $30.00

AMT/Ertl, Batman Batwing #6970, 1990, 1/25, MIB, G5..$39.00

AMT/Ertl, Dick Tracy Coup #6107, 1990, 1/25, MIB, G5 .$9.00

AMT/Ertl, Ghostbusters II ECTO 1-A #6017, 1989, 1/25, MIB, D9/G5, from $12 to **$19.00**

AMT/Ertl, Monkees Monkeemobile #6058, 1990, 1/24, MIB, G5 ....**$54.00**

AMT/Ertl, Munster Koach & Dragula Car #8059, 1991, 1/25, MIB, G5 ....**$59.00**

AMT/Ertl, Robo 1 Police Car, 1990, MIB (sealed), D9......**$9.00**

AMT/Ertl, Star Trek, Galileo II Shuttlecraft #6006, 1991, 1/35, MIB, G5 ....**$7.00**

AMT/Ertl, Star Trek, USS Enterprise, 1983, MIB (sealed), D9 ....**$15.00**

AMT/Ertl, Star Trek: Deep Space Nine, Runabout Rio Grande #8741, 1993, 1/72, MIB, G5 ....**$16.00**

Anubis Productions, Cool World Holly Wood #9301, 1993, MIB, G5 ....**$89.00**

Anubis Productions, Five Million Years to Earth Martian #9101, 1991, MIB, G5 ....**$44.00**

Anubis Productions, Star Trek, Doomsday Machine #9211, 1992, MIB, G5 ....**$39.00**

Anubis Productions, Star Trek III, Federation Spacedock #9207, 1992, MIB, G5 ....**$109.00**

Anubis Productions, Star Wars, Death Star #9203, 1992, MIB, G5 ....**$49.00**

Anubis Productions, Wizards Peace #9212, 1992, MIB, G5.**$199.00**

Aoshima, Back to the Future II, Delorian #1500, 1989,1/24, MIB, G5 ....**$29.00**

Aoshima, Batmobile, 1989, can be motorized, 1/32 scale, MIB, S2 ....**$55.00**

Aoshima, Eagle 5-Apollo LEM #SS01, 1975, 1/40, MIB, G5 ....**$49.00**

Aoshima, Ideon: Space Runaway Clawed Walker #AM03, 1/760, MIB, G5 ....**$14.00**

ATL, Blade Runner, Spinner, MIB, G5 ....**$64.00**

ATL, Star Trek, Dreadnought, 1/2000, MIB, G5 ....**$54.00**

Atlantic, Actarus Figure Set #GK1, 1978, MIB, G5.........**$19.00**

Atlantic, Geronimo & the Apaches #4002, 1/75, MIB, G5 ....**$16.00**

Aurora, Addams Family Haunted House, 1964-65, 1/64, assembled & pnt, G- pnt, H4 ....**$180.00**

Aurora, Addams Family Haunted House, 1964-65, 1/64, MIB **$995.00**

Aurora, Alfred E Neuman #802, 1965, MIB (sealed), P3..**$400.00**

Aurora, Allosaurus #736, Prehistoric Scenes, 1971, incomplete (EX box), D9..**$69.00**

Aurora, American Astronaut #409, 1967, 1/12, MIB, G5..**$114.00**

Aurora, Anzio Beach #339, 1968, assembled, EX (EX box), J2 ....**$75.00**

Aurora, Apache Warrior on Horse #401, 1960, 1/8, MIB .**$400.00**

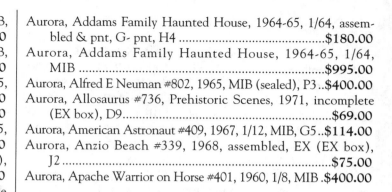

Aurora, Avro Arrow CF-105, MIB, $400.00.

Aurora, Batcycle, photocopy instruction & decal sheet, NMIB (EX box) **$450.00**

Aurora, Batman #467, orig issue, 1964, 1/8, M (EX box), from $250 to **$300.00**

Aurora, Batplane, unassembled, M (EX+ box), H4.......**$250.00**

Aurora, Big Frankie #470, see Gigantic Frankenstein #470

Aurora, Black Fury #400, King of the Wild Horses, reissue, 1969-75, MIB (sealed) **$45.00**

Aurora, Black Knight of Nurnberg #K-3, orig issue, 1956-62, MIB (box w/knight in wide stance & hand at hip) ...**$50.00**

Aurora, Blue Knight of Milan #472, reissue, 1963-68, 1/8, MIB **$35.00**

Aurora, Boeing F4B4, 1959, NMIB, J2..........................**$45.00**

Aurora, Addams Family Haunted House, 1964-1965, 1/64, assembled, missing ghosts, $275.00.

Aurora, Captain Action #480, 1966-1967, original issue, MIB (sealed), $355.00.

Aurora, Captain America #476, 1966, original issue, MIB, $300.00.

Aurora, Captain Kidd #464, 1965, 1/11, MIB....................$85.00

Aurora, Cave, Prehistoric Scenes, 1971, M (EX+ sealed 2nd issue box), M5...$32.00

Aurora, Chevy Custom Pickup, 1963, MIB (sealed), D9 .$23.00

Aurora, Chinese Girl #416, Guys & Gals Series, 1955, 1/8, MIB, G5...$70.00

Aurora, Creature #426, orig issue, 1963-68, metallic gr, MIB, minimum value...$500.00

Aurora, Creature From the Black Lagoon #653, Monsters of the Movies, Glow-in-the-Dark, 1975, assembled, EX+, J2..$80.00

Aurora, Creature From the Black Lagoon #653, Monsters of the Movies, Glow-in-the-Dark, 1975, M (orig box), M5 .$259.00

Aurora, Cro-Magnon #730, Prehistoric Scenes, 1971, MIB (sealed), D9..$35.00

Aurora, Crusader #K-7, orig issue, 1959-62, MIB...........$225.00

Aurora, Cunningham Phantom Sports Car, EX (EX box), J2..$25.00

Aurora, D'Artagnan the Musketeer #410, 1965, 1/8, MIB, G5...$214.00

Aurora, Douglas M2 Mail Plane, 1957, MIB, J2 ....$55.00

Aurora, Dr Doolittle & the Pushmi Pullyu #814, 1968, MIB...$95.00

Aurora, Dr Jekyll & Mr Hyde #462, Monster Scenes, 1971, MIB (sealed) $150.00

Aurora, Dr Jekyll & Mr Hyde #482, Glow-in-the-Dark, 1969, 1/8, MIB, G5...$169.00

Aurora, Dr Jekyll & Mr Hyde #654-655, Monsters of the Movies, Glow-in-the-Dark, 1975, assembled, NM, J2, pr...$70.00

Aurora, Dracula #424, orig issue, 1962, assembled, EX pnt, H4..$35.00

Aurora, Dracula #454, Frightening Lightning, Glow-in-the-Dark, 1969, assembled, VG (VG box), H4..............$180.00

Aurora, Dracula #656, Monsters of the Movies, 1975, MIB (sealed), J2...$275.00

Aurora, Dracula's Dragster #466, 1964, assembled, complete $200.00

Aurora, Dracula's Dragster #466, 1964, box only, w/instructions, NM, P3 ....$225.00

Aurora, Dutch Boy #413, Guys & Gals Series, 1955, 1/8, MIB, G5...$46.00

Aurora, Flying Saucer, see Invaders Flying Saucer

Aurora, Forged Foil Buffalo, 1969, gold, MIB (sealed), I2 ..$65.00

Aurora, Forged Foil Stallion, 1969, MIB, I2 ....$59.00

Aurora, Forgotten Prisoner of Castle-Mare, 1992, MIB, H4.$29.00

Aurora, Forgotten Prisoner of Castle-Mare #422, Famous Monsters, 1966, assembled & pnt, D9 ....$65.00

Aurora, Forgotten Prisoner of Castle-Mare #422, Famous Monsters, 1966, assembled & pnt, EX (EX box) $100.00

Aurora, Forgotten Prisoner of Castle-Mare #453, Glow-in-the-Dark, partially assembled (orig box), G5 ....$139.00

Aurora, Frankenstein, see also Gigantic Frankenstein

Aurora, Frankenstein #423, 1961, MIB, $300.00.

Aurora, Frankenstein #423, 1961, assembled, G- pnt, H4..$25.00

Aurora, Frankenstein #449, Glow-in-the-Dark, 1972, partially assembled, w/instructions, EX (EX box), H4 ....$85.00

Aurora, Frankenstein #633, Monster Scenes, 1971, 1/13, MIB, from $150 to $175.00

Aurora, Frankenstein #651, Glow-in-the-Dark, 1975-77, assembled, EX...$25.00

Aurora, Frankenstein's Fliver #465, 1964, assembled, incomplete, D9...$27.00

Aurora, Ghidrah #658, Monsters of the Movies, 1975, orig instructions, partially assembled, EX (orig box) $275.00

Aurora, Gigantic Frankenstein #470, 1964-65, assembled (orig box), G5...$599.00

Aurora, Gigantic Frankenstein #470, 1964-65, partially assembled (orig box), from $700 to $800.00

Aurora, Gladiator, see Roman Gladiator

Aurora, Godzilla #466, Glow-in-the-Dark, 1969, MIB, G5...$219.00

Aurora, Godzilla #468, Glow-in-the-Dark, 1972, assembled, NM, J2 ....$60.00

Aurora, Godzilla #468, Glow-in-the-Dark, 1972, M (EX box) $175.00

Aurora, Godzilla #469, orig issue, 1964, bright fuchsia, assembled, incomplete, D9 ....$39.00

Aurora, Green Beret #413, US Army Special Forces, 1966-67, 1/12, MIB, from $150 to...$200.00

Aurora, Gruesome Goodies #634, Monster Scenes, 1971, MIB (sealed), J2 ....$85.00

Aurora, Guillotine #800, Canadian issue, M (worn box), J2 ..$575.00

Aurora, Guillotine #800, Chamber of Horrors, 1964, Block A base, complete, D9...$169.00

Aurora, Guillotine #800, Madame Tussaud's Chamber of Horrors, 1964, orig issue, partly assembled, NMIB.........$475.00

Aurora, Hulk #184, Comic Scenes, 1974-75, MIB $85.00

Aurora, Hulk #421, 1966, orig issue, 1/12, MIB $300.00

Aurora, Hunchback of Notre Dame #460, orig issue, 1964, NMIB (Anthony Quinn likeness on box), J2..........$270.00

Aurora, Hunchback of Notre Dame #481, Glow-in-the-Dark, 1969-75, NMIB, J2 ....$100.00

Aurora, Invaders Flying Saucer #256, reissue, 1975, 1/72, assembled, missing base & instruction sheet (EX box), D9 ..$39.00

Aurora, Invaders Flying Saucer #256, reissue, 1975, 1/72, MIB, G5 ....$99.00

Aurora, Invadors UFO #813, 1968, w/7 figures, assembled & partial pnt, incomplete, D9 ....$35.00

Aurora, James Bond 007 #414, 1966, 1/8, MIB, G5 ....$599.00

Aurora, Jesse James, see US Marshal (reissue)

Aurora, John F Kennedy #851, Great American Presidents, 1965, 1/8, EX (EX box), D9....................................$89.00

Aurora, John F Kennedy #851, Great American Presidents, 1965, 1/8, assembled & pnt, incomplete, D9 ....$32.00

Aurora, John F Kennedy #851, Great American Presidents, 1965, 1/8, NMIB, J2 ....$125.00

Aurora, Jungle Swamp #740, Prehistoric Scenes, 1972, 1/13, M (orig box), G5...$159.00

Aurora, King Kong #468, Glow-in-the-Dark, 1972, M (NM box)...$225.00

Aurora, King Kong #468, orig issue, 1964, M (EX+ box).$695.00

Aurora, Land of the Giants Rocket Transport Spindrift #255, reissue, 1975, 1/64, MIB, G5 ....$109.00

Aurora, Land of the Giants Snake Scene #816, 1968, assembled & partially pnt, complete, D9 ....$169.00

Aurora, Land of the Giants Snake Scene #816, 1968, rare, NM (EX+ box), P3...$475.00

Aurora, Lone Ranger #808, orig issue, 1967, MIB, J2.....$200.00

Aurora, Lost in Space Cyclops Diorama #419, 1967, 1/32, sm-sz, M (orig box), G5..$389.00

Aurora, Lost in Space Diorama #816, 1968, 1/48, M (orig box), G5..$500.00

Aurora, Lost in Space Robot #418, 1968, assembled, incomplete, D9...$39.00

Aurora, Man From UNCLE, Ilya Kuryakin #412, 1966, MIB...$225.00

Aurora, Man From UNCLE, Napoleon Solo #411, 1966, EX (EX box), H4...$150.00

Aurora, Maseratti 3500 GT, 1964, MIB (sealed), J2 ....$50.00

Aurora, Monster Customizing Kit #1, NMIB, J2 ....$200.00

Aurora, Mummy #427, orig issue, 1963, assembled & partially pnt, complete, D9 ....$23.00

Aurora, Mummy #452, Glow-in-the-Dark, 1972, 1/8, MIB, G5 ....$84.00

Aurora, Mummy's Chariot #459, 1965, MIB, G5 ....$699.00

Aurora, Mummy #427, 1963, MIB, $200.00.

Aurora, Munsters' Living Room #804, 1964-65, 1/16, MIB $1,295.00

Aurora, NFL Miniatures #824, 1967, 1/32, MIB, G5........$94.00

Aurora, Odd Job #415, 1966, M (EX box).....................$325.00

Aurora, Pain Parlor #635, Monster Scenes, 1971, MIB (sealed), J2..$100.00

Aurora, Pan Am Space Clipper: 2001 #148, orig issue, 1964, 1/144, MIB, G5...$209.00

Aurora, Phantom of the Opera #428, orig issue, 1966, assembled, EX+, J2...$45.00

Aurora, Phantom of the Opera #428, orig issue, 1966, partially assembled, 2 pcs missing (G box), H4.....................$80.00

Aurora, Phantom of the Opera #451, Glow-in-the-Dark, 1972, M (EX box)..$85.00

Aurora, Ragnarok Orbital Interceptor #251, 1975, 1/200, MIB, G5 ....$74.00

Aurora, Red Knight of Vienna #474, 1963, 1/8, MIB, G5..$54.00

Aurora, Robin the Wonder Boy #488, orig issue, 1966, 1/12, MIB (sealed) $95.00

Aurora, Rodan #657, Monsters of the Movies, 1975, assembled, complete $175.00

Aurora, Roman Gladiator w/Trident #406, orig issue, 1959, 1/8, MIB...$195.00

Aurora, SE-5 Scout, 1956, EX (VG+ box), D9................$25.00

Aurora, Seaview Nuclear Submarine #253, Voyage to the Bottom of the Sea, reissue, 1975, MIB, H4 ....$125.00

Aurora, Seaview Submarine #707, Voyage to the Bottom of the Sea, orig issue, 1966, M (EX orig 16" long box) $275.00

Aurora, Spartacus #405, 1965, assembled, no left arm o/w EX, J2..$65.00

Aurora, Spartacus #405, 1965, M (NM box)..................$225.00

Aurora, Spiderman #477, orig issue, 1966, assembled, spider web missing o/w complete, D9....................................$54.00

Aurora, Spindrift Spaceship, see Land of the Giants

Aurora, Stanley Steamer, NMIB, J2................................$35.00

Aurora, Star Trek, Klingon Battle Cruiser #923, 1969, 1/635, MIB, G5...$69.00

Aurora, Superboy #186, Comic Scenes, 1974, MIB (sealed), D9 ....$69.00

Aurora, Tar Pit #735, Prehistoric Scenes, 1971, M (EX+ box), P3 ....$125.00

Aurora, Tarzan #181, Comic Scenes, 1974, MIB (sealed), H4 ....$60.00

Aurora, Tarzan #820, 1967, assembled, needs rpr, D9 ......$23.00

Aurora, Tarzan #820, 1967, orig issue, M (NM sealed box), J2 ....$150.00

Aurora, Tonto #183, Comic Scenes, 1974, MIB (sealed).$45.00

Aurora, Tonto #809, orig issue, 1967, assembled & pnt, eagle's foot needs rpr, D9 ....$23.00

Aurora, Totem Craft (Alaskan) #452, 1959, 1/8, MIB.....$85.00

Aurora, Totem Craft (Indian) #451, 1959, 1/8, MIB $85.00

Aurora, UFO, see Invaders UFO

Aurora, US Marines #412, 1959, assembled & pnt, incomplete, D9 ....$19.00

Aurora, US Marshal (Jesse James) #408, reissue, 1966, 1/8, MIB $75.00

Aurora, US Marshal #408, 1958, 1/8, MIB....................$125.00

Aurora, US Sailor #410, 1957, 1/8, MIB, G5/J2, from $59 to $65.00

Aurora, Vampirella #638, Monster Scenes, 1971, MIB, G5 ....$144.00

Aurora, Victim #632, Monster Scenes, 1971, orig issue, M (NM sealed box) $65.00

Aurora, Viking #K-6, 1959, 1/8, MIB, from $185 to $225.00

Aurora, Witch #470, Glow-in-the-Dark, 1972, EX (EX box), J2 ....$135.00

Aurora, Witch #470, Glow-in-the-Dark, 1972, MIB (sealed) $250.00

Aurora, Witch #483, orig issue, 1965, assembled, incomplete, D9 ....$32.00

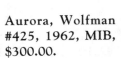

Aurora, Wolfman #425, 1962, MIB, $300.00.

Aurora, Wolfman #425, orig issue, 1962, assembled, G- pnt, H4 ....$25.00

Aurora, Wolfman #450, Glow-in-the-Dark, 1972, 1/8, MIB, G5 ....$74.00

Aurora, Wolfman #652, Monsters of the Movies, 1975, MIB (sealed), J2 ....$255.00

Aurora, Wolfman's Wagon #458, 1965, partially assembled (EX box), from $300 to...$350.00

Aurora, Wooly Mammoth #743, Prehistoric Scenes, 1971, 1/13, MIB, G5 ....$89.00

Aurora, WWI Breguet 14 Aircraft, 1963, NMIB, J2.........$45.00

Aurora, WWI Sopwith Camel Aircraft, 1956, MIB, J2 ....$50.00

Bachmann, Animals of the World, Deer #7105, MIB, G5 .$46.00

Bachmann, Animals of the World, Tiger #7100, 1/12, MIB, G5 ....$54.00

Bachmann, Birds of the World, Baltimore Oriole #9000, 1/1, MIB, G5 ....$34.00

Bachmann, Birds of the World, Canary, NM (EX box), $25.00.

Bachmann, Birds of the World, Meadowlark #9202, 1/1, MIB, G5 ....$54.00

Bachmann, Dogs of the World, Dalmatian #8008, 1/6, MIB, G5 ....$39.00

Bachmann, Dogs of the World, Poodle #8007, 1/6, MIB, G5 ....$26.00

Bandai, Baltanselzin #0503524, 1984, 1/350, MIB, G5 ....$16.00

Bandai, Galaxy Express Space Train 999 #36005, MIB, G5 ..$29.00

Bandai, Gundam Frau Baw #36228, 1/20, MIB, G5............$9.00

Bandai, Gundam Kal Shiden #36227, 1/20, MIB, G5 ......$11.00

Bandai, Macross VF-1A Valkyrie #0030496, 1990, 1/72, MIB, G5 ....$33.00

Bandai, Space Shuttle #37020, 1981, 1/144, MIB, G5 .....$14.00

Bandai, Star-Blazers Space Cruiser Yamato #36033, 1/500, MIB, G5 ....$69.00

Bandai, Xabungie Walker Machine Iron Gear #36419, 1/1000, MIB, G5 ....$9.00

Bandai, Z-Ton #3564, 1990, 1/350, MIB, G5.....................$9.00

Billiken, Creature From the Black Lagoon, MIB, H4 .....$120.00

Billiken, Frankenstein, MIB, H4 ....$110.00

Billiken, Joker, 1989, 1/6, MIB, G5............................$174.00

Billiken, Predator, vinyl, MIB, G5 ....$94.00

Billiken, Saucer Man, MIB, H4....................................$80.00

Billiken, Seventh Voyage of Sinbad Cyclops, MIB, G5 .$254.00

Billiken, The Beast From 20,000 Fathoms Rhedosaurus, MIB, G5 ....$309.00

Billiken, Thing, MIB, G5 ....$270.00

Billiken, Ultraman, 1987, vinyl, 10½", assembled, VG, D9 ....$27.00

Bryan, Dracula Renfield, 1991, 1/6, MIB, G5 ....$69.00

Bryan, Silence of the Lambs, Dr Lecter, MIB, G5 ....$84.00

Cashulette Engineering, Titan/Gemini Rocket, 1/95, G5 .$149.00

Classic Plastic, Terminator 2, Sarah Conner #1007, 1992, MIB, G5 ....$121.00

Collect-Aire, 2001: A Space Odyssey, Orion Shuttle, MIB, G5 ....$29.00

Comet Miniatures, Blakes 7-Terry Nation's DSV 1 the Liberator #006, MIB, G5 ....$29.00

Comet Miniatures, Forbidden Planet Robby #008, 1990, 1/8, MIB, G5 ....$94.00

Comet Miniatures, Thunderbird 1 #04, MIB, G5 ....$49.00

Constructo, US Eagle Ship, wood & cloth, 300-pc, MIB, A .$125.00

Dark Horse, Frankenstein #22, 1991, 1/8, cold cast, MIB, G5 ....$99.00

Dark Horse, King Kong #1092, 1992, MIB, G5 ....$99.00

Deluxe Vacumform, Proteus Fantastic Voyage, MIB, G5 .$34.00

Eldon, Invador Show Car, EX (EX box), J2 ....$30.00

Entex, Battle of the Planets G-1SP Spaceship #8402, 1978, MIB, G5 ....$29.00

Entex, Battle of the Planets Space Station #8411, 1978, MIB, G5 ....$54.00

Entex, Message From Space Star Cruiser Llabe #8427, 1978, MIB, G5 ....$29.00

Ertl, A-Team Van, 1983, MIB, S2 ....$20.00

Ertl, Batmobile, 1989, MIB (sealed), S2 ....$20.00

Ertl, Batmobile Powerracer, 1990, motorized, MIB, S2 ....$35.00

Ertl, Dick Tracy's Getaway Car, 1990, MIB (sealed), S2 ..$20.00

Esci, Flag Raising on Iwo Jima #8062, 1/72, MIB, G5 ....$9.00

Fun Dimensions, Six Million Dollar Man, Bionic Bustout, 1974, unassembled, complete (EX box), D9 ....$13.00

Furuta, Thunderbird 1, MIB, G5 ....$7.00

General Products, Captain Scarlet Gerry Anderson SPV, 1/35, MIB, G5 ....$95.00

General Products, War of the Worlds, Martian War Machine #005, 1/72, MIB, G5 ....$74.00

Geometric Designs, Star Trek: The Next Generation Captain Jean Luc Picard, 1992, 1/6, MIB, G5 ....$59.00

Glencoe, Retriever Rocket #05002, 1/72, MIB, G5 ....$19.00

Glencoe, US Paratrooper #05902, 1991, 1/10, MIB, G5 ....$8.00

Globe, 50-ton steel boxcar, 1948-early '50s, NP brass, assembled, NM, A3 ....$45.00

Gunze Sangyo, Dorvack Variable Gun Calibur #826, 1984, 1/72, MIB, G5 ....$9.00

Gunze Sangyo, Dorvack Variable Machine Bonaparte #805, 1983, 1/100, MIB, G5 ....$9.00

Halcyon, Alien, Armored Personnel Carrier #01, 1987, 1/35, MIB, G5 ....$36.00

Halcyon, Alien, Face Hugger #V02, 1991, 1/1, MIB, G5 ..$112.00

Halcyon, Alien, Power Loader w/Ripley #03, 1991, 1/12, MIB, G5 ....$58.00

Halcyon, Alien, Warrior, 1991, 1/5, MIB, G5 ....$69.00

Halcyon, Alien, 3-Face Hugger & Queen Fetus #06, 1992, 1/1, MIB, G5 ....$106.00

Hasegawa Minicraft, Space Shuttle w/Boosters #001, 1985, 1/200, MIB, G5 ....$29.00

Hawk, Explorer 18 Earth Satellite, NMIB, J2 ....$60.00

Hawk, Frantics Steel Pluckers, box only, EX, J2 ....$35.00

Hawk, Indian Totem Poles Grave of Ske-Dans Totem #556, 1966, MIB, G5 ....$29.00

Hawk, Killer McBash, 1964, assembled & pnt, EX, D9 ....$75.00

Hawk, Silly Surfers, Hodad, MIB (sealed), P3 ....$125.00

Hawk, Silly Surfers, Hodad Makin' the Scene #543, 1964, MIB $110.00

Hawk, Silly Surfers, Hot Dogger, MIB (sealed), P3 ....$125.00

Hawk, Silly Surfers, Hot Dogger & Surf Bunny Riding Tandem, 1965, MIB (torn seal) $100.00

Hawk, Silly Surfers, Woodle on Surfari #540, 1964, MIB, G5 ..$124.00

Hawk, Vanguard Satellite #515, 1958, 1/5, MIB, G5 ....$69.00

Hawk, Weird-Ohs, Daddy, M (EX box), P3 ....$90.00

Hawk, Weird-Ohs, Daddy the Suburbanite #532, 1963, MIB, G5 ....$124.00

Hawk, Weird-Ohs, Davy the Way-Out Cyclist, 1963, EX (EX box) $65.00

Hawk, Weird-Ohs, Drag Bag, box only, NM $40.00

Hawk, Weird-Ohs, Endsville Eddie #537, 1963, MIB, G5/P3, from $89 to $100.00

Hawk, Weird-Ohs, Sling Rave Curvette, 1964, M (EX box), H4 ....$35.00

Horizon, Batman Returns, Cat Woman #032, 1992, 1/6, MIB, G5 ....$54.00

Horizon, Bride of Frankenstein #003, 1988, MIB, G5 ......$49.00

Horizon, Carnage #051, 1993, 1/6, MIB, G5 ....$54.00

Horizon, Freddy Krueger, assembled, 18", NM, S2 ....$85.00

Horizon, Ghost Rider #024, 1993, 1/6, MIB, G5 ....$54.00

Horizon, Indiana Jones #34, 1993, 1/6, MIB, G5 ....$48.00

Horizon, Invisible Man #005, 1988, MIB, G5 ....$29.00

Horizon, Jurassic Park, Brachlosaur Brontosaurus #064, 1993, 1/19, MIB, G5 ....$127.00

Horizon, Jurassic Park, Velocripator #061, 1993, 1/5, MIB, G5 ....$48.00

Horizon, Mole Man #002, 1988, MIB, G5 ....$29.00

Horizon, Punisher #007, 1988, MIB, G5 ....$19.00

Horizon, Spiderman #006, 1988, MIB, G5 ....$29.00

Horizon, Terminator 2, Aerial Hunter Killer #047, 1993, 1/35, MIB, G5 ....$79.00

Horizon, Terminator 2, T-800 Terminator #020, 1991, 1/5, MIB, G5 ....$54.00

Horizon, Tyrannosaurus Rex #027, 1992, 1/30, MIB, G5 .$16.00

Horizon, Wolfman #038, 1993, 1/6, MIB, G5 ....$59.00

Horizon, Wolverine #015, 1990, 1/6, MIB, G5 ....$39.00

Hubley, Duesenberg SJ Town Car, metal kit, EX (EX box) ..$75.00

Hubley, 1930 Packard Roadster, metal kit, NMIB, J2 ......$35.00

Huia, Robocop, ED-209 Robot, 1987, 1/16, MIB, G5 ......$79.00

Huia, Robocop, 1987, vinyl, assembled & pnt, 1/16, worn pnt, D9 ....$27.00

Huia, Robocop, 1987, vinyl, 1/16, MIB, G5 ....$117.00

Ideal, Jaguar, NMIB, J2 ....$25.00

Imai, Armored Knights, Kurfurst Friedrich I #1392, 1984, 1/12, MIB, G5 ....$24.00

Imai, Batmobile #1397, 1984, 1/32, MIB, G5 ....$24.00

Imai, BB 1 Missile #524, 1/24, MIB, G5 ....$200.00

Imai, Captain Scarlet, Patrol Car #1204, 1982, MIB, G5 .$15.00

Imai, Gignator #1782, 1989, MIB, G5 ....$64.00

Imai, Macross, Destroid Phalanx #1227, 1/100, MIB, G5.**$16.00**

Imai, Orguss Gerwalk #1338, 1/72, MIB, G5 ....**$11.00**

Imai, Thunderbirds, Zero X #060, MIB, G5 ....**$21.00**

Imai, UFO Sky I #1241, 1983, MIB, G5 ....**$34.00**

Irwin Plastics, Build a Car Kit w/2 Fords, 1950s, NMIB, S9 ....**$400.00**

Italeri, Lockheed TR1A/B Sky Patrol #822, 1/48, MIB, G5 ..**$4.00**

ITC, Explorer Satellite I #3673, 1959, 1/6, MIB, G5 .....**$274.00**

ITC, Soviet Amphibious Launcher w/BB-1 Missile #3812, 1960, 1/32, MIB, G5 ....**$144.00**

ITC, Soviet Amphibious Carrier #3811, 1/32, MIB, G5 ..**$49.00**

ITC Model Craft, Marvel Metal Giraffe, 1960, EX (EX box), D9 ....**$45.00**

JAM, Robocop ED-209 Robot #2, 1987, MIB, G5 ....**$19.00**

JRC, Alien, Face Hugger, #ORGSB, 1984, MIB, G5 ....**$60.00**

K&B, De Havilland DH-10A WWI Aircraft, MIB, J2 .....**$30.00**

Kaiyodo, Alien, Warrior #1, 1986, 1/9, MIB, G5 ....**$114.00**

Kaiyodo, Gremlins II, Mogwai Mohawk, 1990, soft vinyl, unassembled, complete, D9 ....**$23.00**

Lark, UFO Lunar Carrier #3, 1/144, MIB, G5 ....**$144.00**

Lark, UFO Lunar Module #P2, 1/144, MIB (plain box), G5 ..**$69.00**

Lifelike, Dimetrodon #278, 1/12, MIB, G5 ....**$18.00**

Lifelike, Hawk Missile Battery #661, 1974, 1/40, MIB, G5...**$54.00**

Lindberg, Black Bat, 1966, MIB, H4 ....**$125.00**

Lindberg, Dune Tiger, 1969, motorized, MIB, J2 ....**$40.00**

Lindberg, FBU Crusader Jet #548, 1/48, MIB, G5 ....**$8.00**

Lindberg, Flying Saucer, assembled, EX, J2 ....**$55.00**

Lindberg, Goofy Klock, MIB, J2 ....**$200.00**

Lindberg, Human Brain, 1972, life-sz, NMIB, S2 ....**$20.00**

Lindberg, Northrop Shark Missile #687, 1988, 1/48, MIB, G5 ....**$16.00**

Lindberg, Republic XF-91 Thunderceptor Jet, MIB..........**$30.00**

Lindberg, Satellite w/3-Stage Launching Rocket, 1950s, MIB, J2...**$225.00**

Lindberg, UFO #1152, 1976, 1/48, MIB, G5 ....**$34.00**

Lunar Models, Forbidden Planet C57-D #SF013, 1987, MIB, G5 ....**$69.00**

Lunar Models, Jupiter II #SF007, 1986, 1/35, MIB, G5 ....**$79.00**

Macros Miniatures, US Astronaut on the Moon #508, 1992, 1/12, MIB, G5 ....**$35.00**

Mantua, West Fruit reefer, 1948-early 50s, HO scale, NM, A3 ....**$25.00**

Mantua, 8-wheeled caboose, 1948-early 50s, assembled & pnt, HO scale, NM, A3..**$30.00**

Marx, Creature From the Black Lagoon, 1/12, MIB, G5 ..**$16.00**

MCP, Six Million Dollar Bionic Bustout, MIB (sealed) ...**$40.00**

Mego, Killer Kane #85001, Buck Rogers TV show, 1979, MIB, G5 ....**$26.00**

Mego, King Kong's Last Stand, 1976, MIB, S2 ....**$50.00**

Monogram, Apollo-Saturn, 1968, missing decal sheet o/w complete (EX box), D9...**$53.00**

Monogram, Bathtub Buggy, NMIB, J2 ....**$45.00**

Monogram, Battlestar Galactica #6028, 1979, MIB, G5 ..**$249.00**

Monogram, Battlestar Galactica Cylon Base Star #6029, 1979, EX (G box), D9..**$48.00**

Monogram, Battlestar Galactica Cylon Base Star #6029, 1979, MIB...**$95.00**

Monogram, Battlestar Galactica Cylon Raider #6026, 1979, 1/48, MIB, G5 ....**$89.00**

Monogram, Beer Wagon, 1967, NMIB, J2 ....**$30.00**

Monogram, Boot Hill Express, 1967, EX (EX box), D9 ...**$50.00**

Monogram, Buck Rogers Starfighter #6030, 1979, 1/48, MIB, G5 ....**$44.00**

Monogram, Daytona Spider #2737, 1986, 1/24, MIB, G5 .**$13.00**

Monogram, Elvira's Macabre Mobile (1958 Ford T-Bird), 1988, MIB (sealed), J2...**$20.00**

Monogram, F-104G Starfighter #5447, 1986, 1/48, MIB, G5 .**$6.00**

Monogram, First Lunar Landing #5503, 1979, 1/48, MIB, G5 ....**$34.00**

Monogram, Frankenstein #6007, 1983, 1/8, MIB, G5 ......**$69.00**

Monogram, Futurista, NMIB, J2.....................................**$190.00**

Monogram, Go-Bots, Cy-Kill, 1984, MIB (sealed), D9 ....**$25.00**

Monogram, Go-Bots, Leader-1, 1984, MIB (sealed), D9 ..**$25.00**

Monogram, Hellcat F65-5 WWI Aircraft, 1963, NMIB, J2.**$35.00**

Monogram, Li'l Coffin, 1966, EX (EX box), D9 ....**$63.00**

Monogram, Masters of the Universe, Attack Trak, 1983, MIB (sealed), D9...**$25.00**

Monogram, Masters of the Universe, Roton Assault Vehicle #6016, 1984, MIB (sealed), D9 ....**$25.00**

Monogram, Masters of the Universe, Talon Fighter, 1983, MIB (torn seal), D9...**$25.00**

Monogram, Miami Vice, Daytona Spider, 1986, NMIB, S2 .**$25.00**

Monogram, Mustang GT Convertible #2771, 1987, 1/24, MIB, G5 ....**$13.00**

Monogram, New Monkees Mustang GT Convertible #2771, 1987, 1/24, MIB, G5...**$13.00**

Monogram, Phantom of the Opera #1624, 1992, 1/8, MIB, G5 ....**$16.00**

Monogram, Rascal Missile #42, 1958, 1/48, MIB, G5 ....**$314.00**

Monogram, Red Baron, Tom Daniels, 1968, NMIB, J2 ....**$35.00**

Monogram, Sand Crab, Tom Daniels, 1969, NMIB, J2 ....**$55.00**

Monogram, Space Buggy #194, 1969, 1/48, MIB, G5 ....**$89.00**

Monogram, Space Shuttle Challenger #5702, 1979, 1/72, MIB, G5 ....**$12.00**

Monogram, Superman, 1974, assembled & pnt, needs rpr, D9 ....**$18.00**

Monogram, Terry Labonte's Piedmont 1984 Monte Carlo SS, #2299, complete, VG, A3..**$25.00**

Monogram, TV Orbitor #44, 1959, 1/96, MIB, G5 ....**$149.00**

Monogram, Tyrannosaurus Rex #6077, 1987, 1/13, MIB, G5 ....**$19.00**

Monogram, US Navy Frogman Demolition Team & LCP (R) Boat, 1959, NMIB, J2..**$210.00**

Monogram, Wooly Mammoth #6041, 1979, 1/13, MIB, G5 ..**$21.00**

Monogram, 2½-ton truck, Amor series, 1972, MIB (sealed), J2...**$30.00**

Monogram/Bandai, Battlestar Galactica, Cylon Base Star, #37024, 1981, MIB, G5 ....**$90.00**

MPC, Advanced Dungeons & Dragons Orc War #2101, 1982, MIB, G5 ....**$26.00**

MPC, Alien, box only, 1979, EX, H4................................**$20.00**

MPC, Alien #O1961, orig movie, 1979, 1/10, MIB, G5...**$64.00**

MPC, Andy Granatelli's Indy Turbine Car #40, assembled, EX (EX box), J2..**$38.00**

MPC, Bionic Woman Repair Lab, 1970s, MIB (sealed), C1 ....**$36.00**

MPC, Black Belt Firebird Funny Car, 1981, MIB...........**$30.00**

MPC, Black Hole, Maximillian Robot #1982, 1979, 1/12, MIB, G5 ....$26.00

MPC, Black Hole, Maximillian Robot #1982, 1979, 1/12, MIB (sealed), D9..$35.00

MPC, Black Hole, Vincent Robot #1981, 1979, 1/12, MIB (sealed, D9 ....$34.00

MPC, Columbia Space Shuttle, 1982, incomplete (EX box), D9 ....$10.00

MPC, Dark Shadows, Barnabas Collins #A550, 1969, 1/8, MIB, G5 ....$119.00

MPC, Don Garlits' Rear-Engine Dragster, MIB (sealed), $60.00.

MPC, Don Garlits & His 426 Heni, few pcs assembled, MIB, H4 ....$30.00

MPC, Dukes of Hazzard, Daisy's Jeep CJ #0662, 1980, 1/25, MIB, G5 ....$29.00

MPC, Elegant Farmer Wild Wheelbarrow Show Rod, NMIB $55.00

MPC, George Barris Mail Truck, 1968, M (EX+ box), P3 .$75.00

MPC, Happy Days, Fonz & Bike #0634, 1976, 1/12, MIB, G5 ....$52.00

MPC, Hogan's Heros, Jeep #402, 1968, 1/25, MIB, G5 ....$69.00

MPC, Hot Curl, Surfer's Idol, 1960s, NMIB (sealed), D9 ..$54.00

MPC, Hot Rodder Tall T, NMIB (sealed) $300.00

MPC, Hotshot & Hot Dog #103B, MIB, G5 ....$50.00

MPC, Incredible Hulk, 1978, MIB (sealed), C1 ....$45.00

MPC, Killer Cuda Street Rod, 1978, MIB $45.00

MPC, Monkeemobile, assembled, EX (EX box), H4 ....$55.00

MPC, Pilgrim Observer Space Station #9001, 1970, 1/100, MIB (sealed), D9..$39.00

MPC, Pilgrim Observer Space Station #9001, 1970, 1/100, MIB...$30.00

MPC, Pirates of the Caribbean, Dead Man's Raft #5005, Disney, 1972, MIB, G5 ....$164.00

MPC, Pirates of the Caribbean, Dead Men Tell No Tales #5001, Disney, 1972, 1/12, MIB, G5...............................$149.00

MPC, Pirates of the Caribbean, Freed in the Nick of Time, NMIB, J2...$85.00

MPC, Pirates of the Carribean, Freed in the Nick of Time, MIB (sealed), P3 ....$110.00

MPC, Schwinn 5-Speed Sting-Ray, EX (EX box), J2 ....$90.00

MPC, Six Million Dollar Man Evil Rider, MIB (sealed) ..$40.00

MPC, Space: 1999, Eagle I Transporter #S1901, 1975, 1/72, MIB, G5 ....$109.00

MPC, Spiderman #1931, 1978, 1/8, MIB, G5 ....$54.00

MPC, Star Wars, A-Wing Fighter, 1983, MIB (sealed), D9 .$8.00

MPC, Star Wars, B-Wing Fighter, 1983, MIB (sealed), D9..$8.00

MPC, Star Wars, Battle on Ice Planet Hoth #1922, 1981, 1/75, MIB, G5 ....$49.00

MPC, Star Wars, Boba Fett's Slave I #1919, 1982, 1/72, MIB, G5 ....$85.00

MPC, Star Wars, C-3PO #1901, 1984, MIB, G5 ....$16.00

MPC, Star Wars, C-3PO #1901, 1984, MIB (sealed), D9 ..$23.00

MPC, Star Wars, C-3PO #1913, 1977, MIB (sealed), D9 ..$25.00

MPC, Star Wars, Darth Vader #1916, 1979, 1/8, MIB, G5 ..$14.00

MPC, Star Wars, Darth Vader #1916, 1979, 1/8, MIB (sealed), D9..$32.00

MPC, Star Wars, Darth Vader's TIE Fighter #1915, 1978, 1/48, NM (G- box), D9 ....$14.00

MPC, Star Wars, Darth Vader's TIE Fighter #1915, 1978, 1/48, MIB (sealed), D9 ....$35.00

MPC, Star Wars, Millennium Falcon #1925, 1979, illuminated version, 1/72, M (EX+ box), C1 ....$120.00

MPC, Star Wars, R2-D2 #1912, 1977, MIB (sealed), G5 .$59.00

MPC, Star Wars, R2-D2 #1912, 1977, M (EX box), D9 .$23.00

MPC, Star Wars, Snow Speeder #1917, 1980, 1/35, MIB, G5 ..$8.00

MPC, Star Wars, X-Wing Fighter, 1977, M (VG box), D9.$28.00

MPC, Star Wars, X-Wing Fighter #1971, 1983, MIB (sealed), D9..$17.00

MPC, Star Wars (ESB), Encounter w/Yoda on Dagobah, 1981, MIB (sealed), C1/D9, from $25 to $39.00

MPC, Star Wars TIE Interceptor #1972, 1983, MIB (sealed), D9/G5/P9, from $10 to $15.00

MPC, Star Wars TIE Interceptor #1972, 1983, 1/48, MIB, G5 ....$14.00

MPC, Super Powers #1701, Superman, 1984, 1/8, assembled & pnt, need rpr, D9.......................................$13.00

MPC, Super Powers #1701, Superman, 1984, 1/8, EX (EX box), D9..$20.00

MPC, Super Powers #1701, Superman, 1984, 1/8, MIB, G5.$40.00

MPC, Super Powers #1702, Batman, 1984, EX (VG box), H4 ....$28.00

MPC, Super Powers #1702, Batman, 1984, 1/8, MIB, G5 ..$44.00

MPC, Tall T w/Stoker McGurk #102, 1964, MIB, G5 ...$100.00

MPC, Titan IIIC #1902, 1/100, MIB, G5 ....$194.00

MPC, Welcome Back Kotter, Sweat Hog's Car #641, 1976, 1/25, MIB, G5 ....$26.00

MPC, Zinger Super-Drag, NMIB (sealed), J2 ....$50.00

MPC/Ertl, Star Wars, Darth Vader #8154, 1992, 1/8, MIB, G5 ....$9.00

Multiple, Disappearing Lady #1257, World's Greatest Stage Illusions series, 1966, MIB, G5 ....$134.00

Multiple, Lady Floating on Air #1256, World's Greatest Stage Illusions series, 1966, MIB, G5...............................$163.00

Multiple, Rube Goldberg's Automatic Baby Feeder, MIB (sealed), P3 ....$125.00

Multiple, Rube Goldberg's Back Scrubber & Hat Remover, M, P3...$100.00

Multiple, Rube Goldberg's Painless False Tooth Extractor, M, P3...$100.00

Multiple, Rube Goldberg's Signal Device for Shipwrecked Sailors, MIB (sealed), P3 ....$125.00
Nemotechnik, Invaders Killer Disk #02, 1/1, MIB, G5 ....$16.00
Nemotechnik, Star Trek III, Communicator #05, 1/1, MIB, G5 ....$34.00
New Future, Star Trek III, Klingon Communicator #04, 1990, 1/1, MIB, G5 ....$43.00
Nikken, Eagle Apollo Lunar Module #001, 1969, 1/80, MIB, G5 ....$21.00
Nitto, Gyeronia #23067, 1/480, MIB, G5 ....$19.00
Nitto, US Armored Half-Track #74, 1/35, MIB, G5 ....$16.00
Ogonyek (USSR), Solyuz I #32, 1/30, MIB, G5 ....$84.00
Otaki, Atragon Sub #12, 1/800, MIB, G5 ....$16.00

Palmer Plastics, Atlantic Sailfish, Animals of the World series, 1950s, rare, unassembled and complete (EX box); Palmer Plastics, Shoveler Duck, Animals of the World series, 1950s, rare, unassembled and complete (VG box), from $25.00 to $50.00 each.

Palmer Plastics, Atlantic Sailfish #23, Scout Award Trophies, MIB, G5 ....$36.00
Palmer Plastics, Kodiak Bear, Animals of the World series, 1950s, assembled, complete (EX box) $35.00
Palmer Plastics, Spanish Conquistador #32, 1/5, MIB, G5 ..$76.00
Palmer Plastics, Visible Dissecting Frog, 1950s, unassembled, complete (EX box), D9...$43.00
Palmer Plastics, White-tail Deer, Animals of the World Series, 1950s, unassembled, complete (EX box), D9.............$24.00
Parks, Born Losers series, Napoleon, 1965, assembled & pnt, incomplete, D9 ....$27.00
Plasticart #5024, 1977, 1/25, MIB, G5 ....$22.00
Precision, Fighting Blue Marlin #101, 1958, MIB, G5 .....$39.00

Premiere, Star Trek Phaser II, 1993, 1/1, MIB, G5 ....$19.00
Pyro, Corythosaurus #280, 1968, 1/50, MIB (partially sealed), D9...$20.00

Pyro, Ghost Rider, 1970, MIB (seal torn), $25.00.

Pyro, Protoceratops #279, 1968, 1/8, MIB, G5...............$34.00
Pyro, Ring-Necked Pheasant, Mark Trail series, 1958, unassembled, complete (EX box), D9....................................$34.00
Pyro, Volkswagen Beetle, plastic, battery-op, EX (orig box), A $30.00
Pyro, Western series, Cowboy, 1950s, paint-by-number, MIB, H4 ....$39.00
Remco, Flintstones Motorized Sports Car & Trailer, 1961, missing 1 pc & Barney figure o/w EX (VG box), H4........$99.00
Remco, Showboat, 1950s, EX (EX box), S9.....................$85.00
Renwal, Andrew Jackson Polaris Nuclear Submarine, EX (EX box), J2...$45.00
Renwal, Hawk Guided Missiles #558, 1974, 1/32, MIB, G5 ....$46.00
Renwal, Human Skeleton, 1950s-early '60s, unassembled, complete (EX+ box), D9 ....$35.00
Renwal, Visible Man #800, 1/5, MIB, G5 ....$24.00
Revell, Alien Invader #8001, 1979, 1/144, MIB, G5 ....$20.00
Revell, American Airlines DC-7 Flagship, 1955, MIB, J2..$60.00
Revell, Apollo Lunar Module #1861, 1975, 1/48, MIB, G5.$53.00

Revell, Brother Rat Fink...on a Bike! Custom Monster series, MIB, O1, $80.00.

Revell, Astronaut in Space #1841, 1968, 1/12, MIB, G5 .$86.00

Revell, Beatles, Ringo Starr #1351, 1964, partially assembled, (VG box), R2 ....$175.00

Revell, Beatles, Ringo Starr #1351, 1964, 1/8, MIB, G5......$299.00

Revell, Billy Carter's Redneck Power, 1978, MIB (torn seal), D9 ....$16.00

Revell, Black Panther, Endangered Species series, 1974, MIB (sealed), D9..$32.00

Revell, Boeing IM-99 Bomarc Guided Missile, 1957, MIB, J2 ....$100.00

Revell, Bounty, 1960s, NMIB, S2 ....$35.00

Revell, Challenger & Boosters #4528, 1982, 1/288, MIB, G5..$6.00

Revell, Chance Vought Cutlass F7U-3 Jet Fighter, 1950s, MIB, J2 ....$60.00

Revell, Chance Vought Regulus II #8633, 1983, 1/68, MIB, G5 ....$31.00

Revell, Charlie's Angels, Van #1397, 1977, 1/25, MIB, G5 .$26.00

Revell, Chicken Little, Miracle of Life in an Eggshell, 1976, M (EX box), D9...$58.00

Revell, CHiPs, Kawasaki, NM (G box), O1 ....$18.00

Revell, Chopped Hog, 1969, 1/8 scale, EX (EX box), J2 ..$50.00

Revell, Columbia & Eagle-Apollo 11, 1969, MIB (sealed), D9 ....$38.00

Revell, Condor #702, Endangered Species series, 1974, MIB, G5 ....$35.00

Revell, Corvette (1966), Model Builders Club kit, M (sealed mailing box), A3..$25.00

Revell, DC-7 Mainliner United Flight 707 Airport Scene, 'S' Kit, 1955, NMIB, J2 ....$250.00

Revell, Deal's Wheels Baron & Fundecker Fokker #190, 1971, MIB, G5 ....$49.00

Revell, Disney Peter Pan Pirate Ship #364, 1969, partially assembled (orig box), G5..$59.00

Revell, Dr Seuss, Gowdy the Dowdy Crackle, MIB, H4.$150.00

Revell, Dr Seuss, Tingo the Noodle Top Strudel, 1960s, MIB, H4 ....$175.00

Revell, Dune Sand Worm #1778, 1985, 1/300, MIB, G5 .$39.00

Revell, Enterprise & Space Lab, 1978, MIB (sealed), D9.$28.00

Revell, Famous Racer #13, Don 'Big Daddy' Garlits Rear Engine Dragster, #H-1460, 1974, unassembled, no slicks on rim, A3 ....$50.00

Revell, Famous Racers #16, Keeling's & Clayton's California Charger, #H-1461, 1974, unassembled, complete, A3 ..$50.00

Revell, Gemini Astronaut, 1967, MIB, D9 ....$69.00

Revell, Gemini Capsule #1836, 1965, 1/24, MIB, G5 .....$99.00

Revell, Great Waldo Pepper Sopwith Camel, 1975, partially assembled, (Robert Redford photo on EX box), D9.....$9.00

Revell, History Makers German V-2 Missile #8601, 1982, 1/54, MIB, G5 ....$29.00

Revell, LaCrosse Missile w/Mobile Launcher, MIB, J2.....$45.00

Revell, Magnum PI 308 GTS Ferrari, 1982, MIB (sealed), C1 ....$27.00

Revell, McDonald's Funny Car, 1993, MIB, P10.............$10.00

Revell, McDonald's Rail Dragster, 1993, MIB, P10.........$10.00

Revell, Mickey Thompson's Challenger I Landspeed Car, VG+ (VG+ box), J2..$45.00

Revell, Midnight Cowboy Custom Chevy Wrecker Truck, 1978, MIB, H4 ....$65.00

Revell, Mr Gasser, 1st in series of Custom Monster kits by Ed Roth, MIB, H4..$50.00

Revell, North American X-15 #164, 1/65, MIB, G5 ....$29.00

Revell, Northern White Rhino #700, Endangered Species 1974, MIB, G5 ....$16.00

Revell, Northrup Shark Missle #1801, 1957, 1/96, MIB, J2..$85.00

Revell, Pappy Boyington's Corsair #580, 1976, 1/32, MIB, G5 ....$29.00

Revell, Polar Bear, Endangered series, 1974, MIB (sealed), D9 ....$30.00

Revell, Polaris Nuclear Submarine #437, 1975, 1/261, MIB, G5 ....$14.00

Revell, Regulus II Missile #1815, 1958, 1/68, MIB...........$80.00

Revell, Sleazy Rider, #H-903, Freaky Riders series, assembled (VG box), O1, $60.00.

Revell, Space Explorer Solaris #1851, 1969, 1/60, MIB, G5 ..$194.00

Revell, Space Shuttle Challenger, 1986, pulled from market, MIB (sealed), S2 ....$95.00

Revell, Space Shuttle Enterprise #200, 1978, 1/144, MIB, G5 ....$19.00

Revell, Talos Anti-Aircraft Missile, 1957, MIB, J2 ....$75.00

Revell, Tranquility Base #8604, 1982, 1/48, MIB, G5......$20.00

Revell, US Army Nike Hercules #1804, 1958, 1/40, MIB, from $120 to..$150.00

Revell, US Army Tactical Missile Set, 1958, MIB, J2......$65.00

Revell, US Navy Hospital Ship 'Haven,' 1955, MIB, J2 ..$165.00

Revell, USS Alabama Battleship, 1969, MIB (sealed), J2 ..$45.00

Revell, USS John Paul Jones Navy Destroyer, 1971, MIB (sealed), J2 ....$45.00

Revell, USS Missouri Battleship #301, 1973, 1/535, MIB, G5 ....$16.00

Revell, WWI Dog Fighters Gift Set, 1967, set includes 4 planes, NMIB, J2 ....$130.00

Revell, X-17 Lockheed Re-entry Research Missile, 1957, MIB, J2 ....$75.00

Richman, Batmobile, Build Your Own, remote control, 21", M, S2 ....$250.00

Screamin', Rocketeer, MIB, H10................$60.00
Stombecker, Walt Disney Satellite Launcher, 1950s, MIB, J2................$190.00
Superior Plastics, Deep Sea Lobster, 1962, M (G box), D9 ..$39.00
Tskuda, Gremlins, Mohawk figure, life-sz, MIB, S2 ....$600.00
Ulrich, Rock Island Hopper, 1948-early '50s, HO scale, M, A3................$20.00
US Navy F-4J #5805, 1981, 1/48, MIB................$9.00

Movie Posters and Lobby Cards

This field is a natural extension of the interest in character collectibles, and one where there is a great deal of activity. There are tradepapers that deal exclusively with movie memorabilia, and some of the larger auction galleries hold cataloged sales on a regular basis. The hottest genre right now is the monster movies, but westerns and Disney films are close behind.

Advisors: John and Sheri Pavone (P3)

Asylum, 1972, lobby card set, NM, P3 ....$45.00
Beast From the Haunted Cave, 1959, lobby card scene #2, NM, P3 ....$15.00
Beast of the Yellow Night/Creature With the Blue Hand, 1971, 1-sheet, 27x41", EX, P3 ....$45.00
Ben, 1972, 1-sheet, 27x41", EX, P3................$40.00
Beyond the Door, 1974, 1-sheet, 27x41", EX, P3 ....$20.00

Charlie Chaplin Cavalcade, 1920s, features Chaplin's best films, red and black lettering, 41x27", minor soiling, $160.00.

Chambers of Horrors, 1966, lobby card set, NM, P3 ....$50.00
Diary of a Madman, 1963, 1-sheet, 27x41", EX+, P3........$65.00

Die Monster Die, 1965, lobby card set, NM, P3 ....$65.00

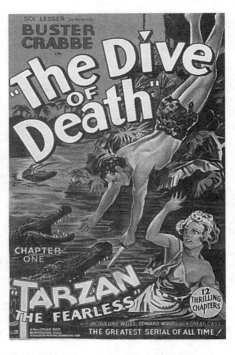

Dive of Death, Tarzan the Fearless, 1933, 1-sheet, linen backed, 41x27", EX, $800.00.

Dracula, the Vampire Thriller, lobby card, Universal, 1931, 11x14", NM, A, $10,925.00.

Dr Phibes Rises Again, 1972, 1-sheet, 27x41", EX, P3 .....$50.00
Frankenstein & the Monster From Hell, 1973, 1-sheet, 27x41", EX+, P3................$60.00
Frankenstein Created Woman/Curse of the Mummy's Shroud, 1967, 1-sheet, 27x41", EX+, P3................$55.00
Frankenstein Meets the Space Monster/Curse of the Voodoo Woman, 1965, 1-sheet, 27x41", EX+, P3 ....$600.00
Frankenstein Must Be Destroyed, 1970, 1-sheet, 27x41", NM, P3 ....$75.00
Frogs, 1972, lobby card set, NM, P3 ....$45.00
Frogs, 1972, 1-sheet, 27x41", NM, P3 ....$70.00
From Beyond the Grave, 1974, 1-sheet, 27x41", NM, P3.$75.00
Halloween II, 1981, lobby card set, NM, P3 ....$40.00
Halloween II, 1981, 1-sheet, 27x41", NM, P3 ....$65.00

Heroes of Telemark, lobby card set, EX, P3 ....$50.00
Hound of the Baskervilles, 1959, scene card, NM, P3 ......$25.00
Hunchback of Notre Dame, 1957, scene card, EX, P3......$25.00
Island of Terror/The Projected Man, 1966, 1-sheet, 27x41", EX, P3 ....$50.00
Kelley's Heroes, 1971, 1-sheet, 27x41", VG, P3 ....$45.00

Magic World of Topo Gigio, 1965, lobby card, NM, $45.00.

Mrs Brown You Have a Lovely Daughter (Herman's Hermits), 1968, 1-sheet, 27x41", EX, P3 ....$50.00
Murders in the Rue Morgue, 1971, lobby card, NM, P3 ...$35.00
Night of the Lepus, 1972, 1-sheet, 27x41", VG, P3..........$30.00
Return of Count Yorga, 1971, lobby card set, NM, P3 .....$45.00
Return of Count Yorga, 1971, 1-sheet, 27x41", NM, P3 ..$85.00
Scream & Scream Again, 1970, 1-sheet, 27x41", NM, P3 ..$95.00

Son of Dracula, Universal, 1943, 1-sheet, linen backed, 41x27", M, $25,000.00.

Tales from the Crypt, 1972, 1-sheet, 27x41", EX, P3 ....$75.00
Taste the Blood of Dracula, 1-sheet, 27x41", NM, P3....$125.00
Ten Little Indians, 1966, 1-sheet, 27x41", NM, P3 ....$65.00
Terror in the Wax Museum, 1973, 1-sheet, 27x41", EX, P3 .$60.00
Terror in the Wax Museum, 1973, lobby card set, NM, P3 ..$40.00
Three Stooges Meet Snow White, insert card, 14x36", VG+, P3 ....$65.00
Three Stooges/Around the World in a Daze, 1963, insert card, 14x36", EX, P3...$75.00
Three Stooges/Hercules, 1962, 1-sheet, 27x41", EX, P3...$95.00
Twice Told Tales, 1963, ½-sheet, 22x28", VG, P3...........$55.00
Two on a Guillotine, 1965, 1-sheet, 27x41", NM, P3 ......$60.00
Who Framed Roger Rabbit?, Disney, 1-sheet, 27x41", M, D1 ..$35.00

Musical Toys

Whether meant to soothe, entertain or inspire, musical toys were part of our growing-up years. Some were as simple as a windup music box, others as elaborate as a lacquered French baby grand piano.

See also Disney; Character, TV and Movie Collectibles.

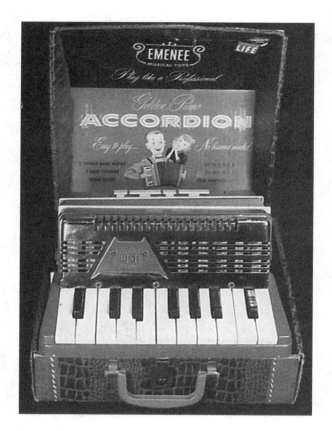

Accordion, Emenee, 1957, plastic body with eighteen keys and fifty-two tuned reeds, cardboard case with song book and harness strap, extends to 24", EX+, $45.00.

Accordion, Everest, 1940s, 5x6", works, NM (orig box) ..$35.00
Accordion, Hohner/prewar, works, EX $165.00

Blow-a-Tune, Kenner, 1949, crank hdl & blow to turn Happy Birthday disk, M (EX box), D9....................$23.00
Guitar, Mattel, w/Mother Goose graphics, NM, S2..........$55.00
24-Key Portable Organ, SUN, 1960, MIB, R7................$100.00

Noah's Ark

What Bible story is more delightful to children than Noah's? In the late 1800s, Bliss produced arks of various sizes along with animal pairs made of wood with applied paper lithographed details. Others imported from Germany had hand-carved or composition animals, some rather primitive, others wonderfully detailed. They're seldom found today at all, and when they are, the set is seldom complete.

Converse, emb & stenciled wood, hinged roof & side storage compartment, no animals, 18½", EX $200.00
Germany, paper litho on wood, w/9 sm carved animals, 11", EX $195.00

Lithographed wood ark with hinged roof, includes 47 painted wood animals and 2 figures, 12", VG, A, $675.00.

Paper litho on wood, lift-off roof & side, 65 pnt wood animals, late 19th century, 45", VG, A $2,530.00
Wood, ca 1900, pnt, 15 prs of carved & pnt animals w/Noah & wife, 17¾", few legs missing o/w G, A $460.00

Nodders

Nodders representing comic characters of the day were made in Germany in the 1930s. These were small doll-like figures approximately 3" to 4" tall, and the popular ones often came in boxed sets. But the lesser-known characters were sold separately, making them rarer and harder to find today. While the more common nodders go for $125.00 and under, Ambrose Potts, The Old Timer, Widow Zander and Ma and Pa Winkle often bring about $350.00 — Happy Hooligan even more, about $600.00. (We've listed the more valuable ones here; any German bisque nodder not listed is worth $125.00 or under.)
    Advisor: Doug Dezso (D6).
See also Sports Collectibles.

Ambrose Potts, German, pnt bsk, NM..........................$350.00
Auntie Blossom, German, pnt bsk, NM.........................$150.00

Buttercup, German, pnt bsk, NM..................................$250.00
Chubby Chaney, German, pnt bsk, NM.........................$250.00
Corky, German, pnt bsk, NM..$475.00
Fanny Nebbs, German, pnt bsk, NM $250.00
Ferina, German, pnt bsk, NM $350.00
Grandpa Teen, German, pnt bsk, NM $350.00
Happy Hooligan, German, pnt bsk, NM.........................$600.00
Harold Teen, German, pnt bsk, NM..............................$150.00
Junior Nebbs, German, pnt bsk, NM $500.00
Lillums, German, pnt bsk, NM......................................$150.00
Little Annie Rooney, German, pnt bsk, arms move, NM $250.00
Little Egypt, German, pnt bsk, NM................................$350.00
Lord Plushbottom, German, pnt bsk, NM $150.00
Ma or Pa Winkle, German, pnt bsk, ea..........................$350.00
Mary Ann Jackson, German, pnt bsk, NM $250.00
Min Gump, German, pnt bsk, NM $150.00
Mr Bailey, German, pnt bsk, NM..................................$150.00
Mr Bibb, German, pnt bsk, NM $400.00
Mr Wicker, German, pnt bsk, NM.................................$250.00
Mushmouth, German, pnt bsk, NM...............................$350.00
Mutt or Jeff, German, pnt bsk, NM, ea $250.00
Nicodemus, German, pnt bsk, NM $350.00
Old Timer, German, pnt bsk, NM $350.00
Our Gang Set, pnt bsk, 6-pc, MIB $1,200.00
Pat Finnegan, German, pnt bsk, NM $400.00
Pete the Dog, German, pnt bsk, NM $150.00
Rudy, German, pnt bsk, NM...$250.00
Scraps, German, pnt bsk, NM.......................................$250.00
Uncle Willie, German, pnt bsk, NM $350.00
Widow Zander, German, pnt bsk, NM...........................$400.00
Winnie Winkle, German, pnt bsk, NM..........................$150.00

Optical Toys

Compared to the bulky viewers of years ago, contrary to the usual course of advancement, optical toys of more recent years have tended to become more simplified in concept.
See also View-Master and Tru-View.

Irwin Projector, 1930s, metal, red and gray, Popeye film included, minor wear to film (worn box), $150.00.

Give-A-Show Projector, projects 5-ft sq image of Popeye, Three Stooges, Pinocchio & others, plastic, battery-op, VG+, A..................$95.00

Give-A-Show Projector Slide Set, Kenner, 1970, 35 slides featuring Popeye, Lassie, Superman & others, NM (EX box), S2 ....$25.00

Irwin Film Projector, 1920s, w/Betty Boop, Koko, Felix, Minnie & more on labels, battery-op, 5", rare, VG+ (VG box), A $479.00

Kaleidoscope, cb w/Disney graphics, older style, EX.........$65.00

Kaleidoscope, Stevens, 1950s, w/3 snap-in heads, very rare, NMIB, S2.............................$110.00

Magic Lantern, Bing, electric, w/some slides, 11", EX+, M5.$100.00

Magic Lantern, Ernst Planck, Germany, pnt tin w/oil burner, 10 slides, wood case w/labels, 8", VG...........................$325.00

Magic Lantern, Germany, pnt & emb tin & brass, figure supports lens, w/3 disks & 7 slides, orig case, 14½", VG.........$425.00

Marvel Super Heroes See-a-Show Viewer, Kenner, 1966, EX $150.00

See-A-Show Stereo Viewer Set, Kenner, 1969, unused, NMOC, J2 ....$40.00

Zeotrope, Milton Bradley, patent 1867, 18 paper strips, orig label under drum, 12½x12" dia, EX, A.........................$1,035.00

Paper Dolls

Turn-of-the-century paper dolls are seldom found today and when they are, they're very expensive. Advertising companies used them to promote their products, and some were printed on the pages of leading ladies' magazines. By the 1920s most paper dolls were being made in book form — the doll on the cover, the clothes on the inside pages. Because they were so inexpensive, paper dolls survived the Depression and went on to peak in the 1940s. Though the advent of television caused sales to decline, paper doll companies were able to hang on by making paper dolls representing Hollywood celebrities and TV stars. These are some of the most collectible today. Even celebrity dolls from more recent years like the Brady Bunch or the Waltons are popular. Remember, condition is very important; if they've been cut out, even when they're still in fine condition and have all their original accessories, they're worth only about half as much as an uncut doll.

For more information, refer to *Collecting Toys*, by Richard O'Brien and *Toys, Antique and Collectible*, by David Longest.

Annie Oakley, Whitman #2056, 1955, w/Annie, Tagg & Lofty, cut, complete, NM......................$45.00

Archies, Whitman, 1969, complete w/5 dolls, EX, D9 .....$20.00

Baby Doll, Lowe #9119, 1964, MIB..................................$20.00

Baby Sister & Baby Brother, Merrill #2571, M (orig folder).$25.00

Barbie, Skipper & Skooter, 1966, EX, D2 ....$20.00

Barbie, Western Publishing #1690, 1990, M......................$2.50

Barbie & Francie Magic Stay-on Fashions, 1966, cut, NM, D2 ....$30.00

Barbie Ballerina, 1977, uncut, D2 ....$15.00

Barbie Christmas Time, 1984, M, D2 ....$6.00

Barbie Country Camper, 1973, uncut, D2................$10.00

Barbie Goin' Campin', 1974, uncut, D2.................$15.00

Barbie Sweet 16, 1974, uncut, D2 ....$12.00

Beverly Hillbillies, Whitman, 1964, uncut, M (NM folder), C1.................................$70.00

Blondie, Whitman #981, 1944, cut, complete, NM..........$35.00

Brady Bunch Paper Doll Book, Whitman, 1973, uncut, M (NM folder), C1.................................$80.00

Bride & Groom, Western Publishing, #1501, 1988, NM....$3.00

Buffy & Mrs Beasley, see Family Affair

Candy & Her Cousins, 1961, cut, complete, NM (orig folder).$18.00

Cathy Quick-Curl, Whitman #1977, 1975, M..................$10.00

Charmin' Chatty, uncut, L6 ....$50.00

Chatty Baby, uncut, L6...$50.00

Chatty Cathy, uncut, w/carry-all, L6....................$50.00

Chatty Twins, uncut, L6.......................................$45.00

Children in the Shoe, Merrill #1562, 1949, NM (orig folder).$40.00

Dawn & Her Friends, 1972, M, D2...........................$25.00

Debbie Reynolds, Whitman #1956, 1960, cut, complete, NM...............................$25.00

Diana Lynn, Saalfield #2611, 1953, M.....................$55.00

Fairy Princess, Merrill #1548, 1950s, M $45.00

Family Affair, Whitman, 1968, Buffy & Mrs Beasley dolls w/5 pgs of outfits, uncut, M, D2 ....$35.00

First Ladies of the White House, Whitman #2164, 1937, M.$30.00

Flower Girl, Saalfield #4473, 1966, M.....................$12.50

Flying Nun, 1969, uncut, NM, J2 ....$45.00

Francie w/Growin' Pretty Hair, 1973, M, D2 ....$50.00

George Bush & Family, M, S1 ....$10.00

George Washington, Milton Bradley, 1923, uncut, NMIB.$50.00

Ginghams Visit Grandma, Whitman #1987, 1981, M......$12.00

Great Shape Barbie, Ken & Skipper, 1985, uncut, D2 ....$6.00

Green Acres, Whitman, 1967, Oliver & Lisa dolls w/6 pgs of outfits, uncut, M $32.00

Groovin' World of Barbie & Her Friends, 1971, uncut, D2..$15.00

Hayley Mills, Whitman, 1960s, cut, EX, J5......................$15.00

Hi Dottie, Whitman #1997, 1972, M.............................$12.00

It's a Small World, Disney/Whitman, 1966, EX (orig folder) .$22.00

Jane Powell Cut-Out Dolls, Whitman, 1952, EX, $60.00

Janet Leigh, Cutouts and Coloring, 2 books in 1, 1953, M, $75.00.

Jewel Secrets Barbie, Ken, Whitney & Skipper, 1987, M, D2 ....$5.00
Julia, 1968, uncut, M, D2..$50.00
Kewpies, 1960s, uncut, M, J5.......................................$25.00
Laugh-In, Saalfield, 1969, unused, M (NM folder), C1 ....$55.00
Lennon Sisters, Whitman #1995, cut, complete, NM $15.00
Liddle Kiddles, 1966, M, D2 ....$75.00
Linda (Mouseketeer), uncut, NM, J5 ....$45.00
Little Lulu, Whitman, 1972, EX (EX box), J2 ....$30.00
Lollipop Crowd, 1940s, cut, complete, NM $14.00
Lost Horizon, 7 celebrity dolls from musical, M...............$25.00
Malibu Francie, 1973, uncut, D2 ....$15.00
Marie Osmond, 1970s, uncut, EX, J5 ....$35.00
Mary Poppins, 1960s, uncut, NM, J5.............................$25.00
Moonspinners, Haley Mills, Whitman, 1964, NM (NM folder), A $75.00
Nanny & the Professor, Saalfield, 1971, NM, J5 ....$35.00
Paper Dolls Around the World, Saalfield #4281, 1971, M .$5.00
Partridge Family, Artcraft, 1972, cb stand-ups of entire group, NM...$45.00
Peggy & Peter, Lowe, 1962, M (NM folder) $55.00
Perfume Pretty Barbie, Ken & Whitney, 1988, M, D2 ....$5.00
Petticoat Junction, 1 pg cut, EX, J5 ....$35.00
Princess of Power, 1985, M, D2 ....$25.00
Quick Curl Barbie, Francie, Kelly & Skipper, 1973, M, D2....$20.00
Raggedy Ann & Andy, Whitman, 1970, EX, J5 ....$15.00
Raggedy Ann & Andy, 1960s, uncut, NM, J5 ....$25.00
Ricky Nelson, Whitman, 1959, NM $50.00
Rock Hudson, Whitman #2087, 1957, uncut, NM...........$60.00
Ronald Reagan & Family, 1980, uncut, M.......................$20.00
Roy Rogers & Dale Evans, Whitman, 1950, complete & uncut, NM, A $125.00
Storybook Paper Dolls, Saalfield, 1960s, M (NM folder)....$8.00
Sugar & Spice, Saalfield #3961, 1969, M $8.00
Sunsational Malibu Barbie, 1983, uncut, D2......................$5.00
Superstar Barbie, Whitman #1983, 1977, M.....................$12.00
Superstar Barbie, 1989, M, D2 ....$5.00
Tiny Thumbelina, Whitman, 1963, M, C1...........................$35.00
Tricia Nixon, Saalfield #1248, 1970, M............................$18.00

Tropical Barbie, Ken, Miko & Skipper, 1986, M, D2 ....$5.00
Tuesday Weld, Saalfield #5112, 1960, cut, complete, NMIB .$28.00
Twirly Curls Barbie, 1983, uncut, D2..............................$7.00
Walt Disney's Mouseketeers, Whitman #1974, cut, complete, NM..$15.00
Waltons, Whitman, 1974, incomplete, G (orig box), S2........$10.00
Welcome Back Kotter, Toy Factory, 1976, MIB (sealed), I2 .$25.00

Shirley Temple Standing Doll, Saalfield #1727, 1935, boxed set, minimum value $60.00.

MAGAZINE PAPER DOLLS

Adventures of Polly and Peter Perkin, Pictorial Review, July 1933, $14.00.

Barbara, Jack & Jill, March 1941 ....$8.00

Beauty & the Beast, National Doll World, September-October 1982...$4.00

Becky Thatcher, National Doll World, November-December 1983...$3.00

Betsy McCall & the Westminster Dog Show, McCall's, February 1961...$3.00

Betsy McCall Becomes a Sister, McCall's, February 1966...$3.00

Betsy McCall Christmas Morning, McCall's, December 1963 ....$3.00

Betsy McCall Clown for a Day, McCall's, April 1971 ....$2.00

Betsy McCall Goes Dog Walking, McCall's, August 1964 .$3.50

Betsy McCall Goes to School, McCall's, September 1958 .$4.00

Betsy McCall in Colonial Williamsburg, McCall's, February 1960...$4.00

Betsy McCall Learns To Skate, McCall's, April 1980 ....$2.00

Betsy McCall Meets a Witch, McCall's, October 1952 .....$4.00

Betsy McCall's Big Surprise, McCall's, February 1965........$2.50

Betsy McCall's Trip to New York, McCall's, February 1963 ....$4.00

Betsy McCall Takes a Trip Down the Mississippi, McCall's, April, 1960...$3.50

Betsy McCall Turns Magician, McCall's, March 1978 ....$2.00

Betsy McCall Visits Roy Rogers' Ranch, McCall's November, 1959...$2.50

Betsy McCall Visits the Plaza, McCall's, April 1972 ....$2.00

Betty Bonnet, Ladies' Home Journal, March 1915 ....$16.00

Christopher, Jack & Jill, April 1948.............................$4.00

Cinderella, Ladies' Home Journal, June 1913.............$14.00

Dolly Dingle as Cinderella, Pictorial Review, March 1927 .$15.00

Dolly Dingle's Little Cousin Peter, Pictorial Review, September 1920 ....$20.00

Dolly Dingle's Little Cousin Robin, Pictorial Review, March 1924 ....$17.00

Dolly Dingle's Playmates, Pictorial Review, May 1929 ....$14.00

Dolly Dingle's World Flight: Italy, Pictorial Review, December 1932 ....$14.00

Dolly Dingle Takes Up Grand Opera, Pictorial Review, August 1921 ....$15.00

Goosey, Goosey, Gander, Woman's Home Companion, April 1921 ....$10.00

Heeza Fraid, the Trick Elephant, Child Life, August 1922 .$8.00

Heidi & Her Father, Jack & Jill, 1952 ....$7.00

Jack & Jill, McCall's, January 1921 ....$14.00

Jack & Peggy at the Zoo, McCall's, January 1918 ....$8.00

Jack & the Beanstalk, Ladies' Home Journal, June 1913 ..$18.00

Jackie Coogan, Woman's Home Companion, May 1925 .$22.00

Jean, Wee Wisdom, May 1953...$3.00

June's Spring Clothes, Canadian Home Journal, April 1937, minimum value $12.00.

Katje & Pieter of Holland, Children's Activities, March 1937 ....$6.00

Katrinka, Good Housekeeping, 1923 ....$10.00

Kewpie, National Doll World, November-December 1979 ..$3.00

Kristin of Norway & Siglinda of Sweden, Children's Play Mate, 1952...$8.00

Lettie's Brother, Ladies' Home Journal, June 1909 ....$18.00

Lettie's Twin Brother & Sister, Ladies' Home Journal, November 1908 ....$10.00

Little Boy Blue & Little Bo Peep, Children's Play Mate, October 1941 ....$8.00

Little Tommy Tucker, Woman's Home Companion, May 1920 ....$12.00

Margaret Butterick's Little Sister Betty, Delineator, October 1913 ....$22.00

Marilyn Maxwell, Life, February 23, 1948........................$10.00

Miss Muffet, Woman's Home Companion, July 1920.......$12.00

Nipper Takes His Camera to the Circus, McCall's, May 1925..$8.00

Peggy Perkins' Brother Bobby, Ladies' Home Journal, January 1919 ....$10.00

Dolly Dingle, Pictorial Review, April 1933, $14.00.

Peter Pan, Woman's Home Companion, August 1925.....$20.00
Polly, Good Housekeeping, April 1919............................$10.00
Polly & Peter Perkins & Peter Pumpkin-Eater, Pictorial Review,
    October 1934 ....$9.00
Pollykins Pudge, McCall's, July 1919 ....$14.00
Robin Hood, McCall's, April 1923....................................$5.00
Santa's Trans-Atlantic Flight, Delineator, December 1919..$12.00
Shirley Mason, Ladies' World, January 1917.....................$8.00
This Is Deborah, Wee Wisdom, March 1955 ....$4.00
Three Little Nixons, Life, May 8, 1970............................$10.00
Wendy, Wee Wisdom, July 1954..$3.00

Pedal Cars and Other Wheeled Goods

Just like Daddy, all little boys (and girls as well) are thrilled and happy to drive a brand new shiny car. Today both generations search through flea markets and auto swap meets for cars, boats, fire engines, tractors and trains that ran not on gas but pedal power. Some of the largest manufacturers of wheeled goods were AMF (American Machine and Foundry Company), Murray, and Garton. Values depend to a very large extent on condition, and those that have been restored may sell for upwards of $500.00, depending on year and model.

Advisor: Nate Stoller (S7).

Car, Gendron, yellow with red stripes, black fenders and trim, folding windshield, restored, 38", VG+, $1,500.00.

Apperson Roadster, Am National, 1925, yel w/blk & red, rear spare,
    2-pc windshield w/wind wings, 55", some rstr, A $3,600.00
Atomic Missile, Murray, 1950s, bl & gray pressed steel, US Navy
    Blue Angels, chain drive, 48", rpt, NM $1,500.00
Auburn Roadster, Am National, ca 1927, orig 2-tone gr pnt
    w/yel pinstripe, spoke wheels, metal seat, 50", some wear,
    A..$4,300.00
BMC Station Wagon, Jetliner, 1950s, gr pressed steel, chain
    drive, hard rubber wheels, silver hubs, 40", rpt, EX+.$950.00

Buick Roadster, Am National, 1927, gray-gr w/red trim, rumble seat
    & opening door, w/picnic jug & basket, 68", rstr, A.$5,200.00
Buick Roadster, Toledo, 1933, red & gr w/yel pinstripe, red wheels,
    flared fenders, orig pnt, 48", some wear, A $3,100.00
Buick 5-Wheel Roadster, Steelcraft, 1928, tan & bl w/red pinstripe,
    windshield w/wind wings, chrome grille, 53", rstr....$4,500.00
Cadillac, Am National, 1920, orig red pnt, hood opens to motor,
    rear spring suspension, spoke wheels, 48", rare, EX.$7,500.00
Cadillac, Steelcraft, ca 1924, orig red pnt w/yel & blk trim, cowl &
    headlights, windshield w/wind wing, 47", worn, A.$3,200.00
Cadillac Roadster, Am National, 1928, red, tan & blk w/pinstripe
    trim, red wheels, rear-mounted spare, 52", rstr, A...$4,300.00
Car, Keystone, ca 1915, orig red & blk pnt w/yel trim, butterfly
    fenders over wide-spoked wheels, 43", EX $550.00
Chrysler Airflow, Am National, 1935, orig red & cream pnt, metal
    fold-down top, working lights & horn, 51", worn ...$9,500.00
Chrysler, Steelcraft, ca 1933, yel & blk open convertible w/chrome
    wheels, side spare & trim, cowl lights, 50", EX........$3,000.00
Chrysler, Toledo Wheel Co, ca 1930, beige w/red trim, yel fend-
    ers, red hubs & brn seat, rear spare, 49", rstr, A ...$3,000.00
Cord Roadster, Gendron, 1931, dk bl w/lt bl & red pinstripe,
    wht balloon tires w/red spokes, 58", rstr, A $4,500.00
Custer Electric Car, ca 1924, tan & blk battery-op sidewalk car
    w/simple styling, front headlights, red wheels, 60", A.$750.00
Dan Patch Car, ca 1920, orig red pnt w/blk trim, brass headlights
    & horn, rear gas tank, gear drive, 66" $1,250.00
Delahaye, Eureka, sleek styling w/lt bl rpt over rough body,
    pneumatic blk-wall tires w/chrome hubs, 67", A $750.00
Dodge Roadster, Am National, 1926, tan & blk w/red trim,
    spoke wheels, red pleated seat, horn, 52", rstr $4,500.00
Fast Mail Locomotive, Toledo Wheel Goods, orig red pnt w/blk
    trim, wht stenciled lettering, 42½", EX, A $1,700.00
Federal Dump Truck, Toledo, 1925, red & blk w/chrome grille,
    wht-wall tires, cowl lights, front crank, 60", rstr, A.$1,700.00
Fire Chief's Car, Gendron, ca 1927, blk & red w/rear rnd open-
    ing tool box, red wheels, 50", rstr, A $2,000.00
Fire Pumper #6, Toledo, ca 1924, red w/yel & bl trim, NP radia-
    tor band & boiler tank, red wheels, 63", rstr, A ...$2,500.00
Fire Truck, Am National, 1930, water tower truck w/orig red pnt,
    electric horn & lights, pneumatic tires, 86", rstr, A.$7,500.00
Fire Truck, Am National, 1935, red 2-passenger mk AFD, pneumatic
    spoked tires, w/boots & helmet, hose reel, 70", rstr....$6,500.00
Fire Truck #2, Am National, red ladder type w/yel trim, rear spring
    suspension, wht tires w/red spokes, 72", rstr, A.......$1,700.00
Hi-Speed Gas Dump Truck, Steelcraft, ca 1929, red & blk open truck
    w/wht lettering, red wheels, 62", rstr fenders, EX, A ..$2,900.00
Jordan Roadster, Am National, bl w/yel pinstripe, blk fenders &
    headlights, wood running boards, bl wheels, 40", rstr.$3,750.00
Jordan Roadster, Gendron, ca 1927, gr w/red trim & hubs, wind-
    shield w/wind wings, rear spare, 53", rstr, A $3,700.00
Kidillac, Garton, pnt salmon & silver pressed-steel Cadillac w/
    plush upholstery, covered rear spare, 43", rstr, EX ...$1,500.00
Lincoln, Grendron, 1928, wht & blk w/red & blk pinstripe, red
    hubs, hand brake, wind screen, 46", rstr suspension..$2,500.00
Lincoln Tandem, Am National, ca 1935, red w/blk fenders, wire
    wheels w/pneumatic tires, rstr, 66" $7,500.00
Lincoln Zephyr, Garton, ca 1937, cream w/orange trim & red pin-
    stripe, cream wheels w/chrome hubs, 45", rstr, A...$3,900.00

Lincoln, ca 1935, lime green with forest green fenders and running boards, split windshield with side panes, electric lights, restored, 45", $8,000.00.

Little Joe, Steelcraft, 1950s, red & gray pressed steel, metal rods, hard rubber tires, Peugeot crest, 37", EX, rpt $750.00

Mack Dump Truck, Steelcraft, red flat-bed type w/yel pinstripe, red wheels, blk steering & fr, 44", rstr....................$1,250.00

Mack 2½-Ton Dump Truck, Steelcraft, ca 1930, dk red w/yel pinstripe, pneumatic tires w/red wheels, 50", A ...$1,800.00

Murray Skipper Motor Boat, Murray, 1960s, wht & bl steel, front lights, rear recast Mercury engine, 46", NM, rpt ...$1,500.00

National Pedal Car, Am National, ca 1928, bl & blk w/yel trim, red wood spoke wheels, 48", rstr, 47" $2,500.00

Packard, Am National, 1928, yel & blk w/red wheels & folded convertible top, fully sprung chassis, 50", rstr.......$5,500.00

Packard Electric Car, Am National, 1927, red w/yel interior, fat-man steering wheel, rare, 71", rough & incomplete, A.......$2,300.00

Packard Roadster, Gendron, 1928, bl w/blk & wht trim, w/rumble seat, 2-pc windshield & side spare, 68", rare, rstr, A.$5,700.00

Packard Roadster, Steelcraft, 1924, red & blk w/red wheels, rear spare, hand brake, 54", rstr suspension, A $3,900.00

Paige Roadster, Am National, 1925, brn w/orange trim, V-shaped radiator hood, 53", orig condition w/rpt fenders, A...$4,200.00

Pierce Arrow, Am National, gr & tan w/wht trim & pinstripe, tan wheels w/chrome hubs, pneumatic tires, 45", rstr, A .$4,300.00

Pierce Arrow, Steelcraft, ca 1935, blk & gr w/yel & gray trim, gr spoke wheels w/chrome hubs, 43", rstr, A $3,300.00

Pioneer Air Express Plane, Marx, 1920s, litho tin w/Indian, 25½" wingspan, 24", G, A $230.00

R&S Special Race Car, Triang, 1950s, #6 on red pressed steel, metal rods, hand brake, 50", EX+, rpt, A.................$575.00

Race Car #6, Gendron, ca 1924, orig red pnt w/yel pinstripe, 53", some wear, A...$3,600.00

Racer, contemporary aluminum body w/side exhaust, spoked bicycle-type tires, 61", A.......................................$1,500.00

Red Bird Roadster, Am National, 1924, red w/yel pinstripe & blk trim, tool-box trunk, orig pnt, 50", some wear, A .$2,700.00

Red Wing Airplane, Am National, 1930s, 30" wingspan, 50", lt old rpt, lt rust o/w G, A.......................................$1,955.00

Roadster, Steelcraft, 1932, smoke gray w/red fenders, rear spare, 53", rstr, A...$3,500.00

Roadster, Torck, orig 2-tone gr & cream pnt w/chrome front & rear bumpers, red wheels, lg chrome hubs, 45", some wear, A $275.00

Roamer, Am National, 1927, gr w/yel & blk trim, red hubs, open convertible top, Alemite lubrication, 49", rstr $3,750.00

Roamer Shaft-Drive, Am National, ca 1927, gr & cream, windshield w/wind wings, open convertible top, 51", rstr, A $4,700.00

Shaft Drive Car, Am National, ca 1928, bl w/blk & red trim, rear spare, rare drive mechanism, 48", rstr, A.......$3,600.00

Skippy Chrysler Airflow, Am National, ca 1935, orig cream & tan pnt, emb hubs, working high-low beam headlights, G, A....$4,200.00

Skippy Chrysler Airflow, Gendron, ca 1935, cream & tan w/red wheels & chrome hubs, pneumatic tires, 45", rstr, A.$2,800.00

Skippy Fire Truck, Gendron, ca 1940, red w/pneumatic tires w/red spoked wheels, hose reel & side ladders, 56", rstr, A.$4,000.00

Skippy Pontiac, Gendron, ca 1935, orig red pnt w/wht Pontiac logo, red spoke wheels, electric lights, 45", G, A .$3,400.00

Skippy Roadster, Gendron, ca 1939, cream w/red hood & trim, red cut-out wheels w/chrome hubs, 39", rstr, A....$1,800.00

Skippy Shark-Nose Graham, Am National, ca 1938, bl w/cream fenders & wheels, chrome hubs, 48", rstr, A $4,000.00

Skippy Speedster, Gendron, ca 1935, orig red pnt w/wht trim, red-striped wht wheels, fender lights, squeeze horn, 45", A.$2,600.00

Skylark Airplane, Am National (?), ca 1928, orig red & gr pnt, 23" wingspan, some wear, A $2,700.00

Speed Racer, 1950s, metal w/single seat, center hdl pushes to power, 41", NM, rpt, A...$345.00

Spirit of America Airplane, Steelcraft, ca 1926, orig finish w/rare chain-drive mechanism, 50", G-, A...........$3,200.00

Spirit of St Louis Plane, painted sheet metal, silver with red and blue lettering and stripes, wood steering wheel, 59" long, replaced stabilizers and fin, G, $2,700.00.

Spirit of St Louis, Am National, 1932, gray & red w/bl & yel trim, pneumatic tires w/red spokes, 36" wingspan, rstr, A .$4,500.00

Studebaker Roadster, Steelcraft, 1935, bl & blk w/wht trim, bl wheels w/chrome hubs, simulated wht-walls, 46", rstr, A.......$2,900.00

Stutz Roadster, Garton, ca 1924, orig brn & blk pnt w/pinstripe, rare tool box, 47", much wear, A.........................$3,100.00

Stutz Roadster, Steelcraft, 1929, lt gr w/red pinstripe & blk trim, cowl lights, spoked wht-walls, 52", rstr, A............$4,000.00

Sunbeam Racer #8, Gendron, ca 1932, red & blk, wht pinstripe, yel wheels, wht balloon tires, side exhaust, 70", rstr, A ...$3,600.00

Super Charger Deluxe, Steelcraft, 1941, blk w/wht pinstripe, pneumatic wht-walls, red wheels, chrome hubs, 53", rstr, A $4,000.00

Super Charger Deluxe, Steelcraft, 1941, red rpt w/red wheels, pneumatic blk-walls, red wheels, chrome hubs, EX body, A $2,900.00

T-Bird, Murray, 1960s, dusty rose pressed steel w/steel rods for action, hard rubber wheels & hub, 32", NM, rpt, A $1,610.00

Torpedo, Murray, 1950s, yel pressed steel, metal rods, hard rubber wheels, silver hubs, 40", NM, rpt....................$3,750.00

Tractor Junior, BMC Mfg, red sheet metal w/blk rubber tires, wht lettering, 34", M, A $650.00

Triang Car, English, ca 1928, orig red & blk pnt, red wheels, opening door, side-mounted lights, 32", worn, A $950.00

Velie Roadster, Am National, gr w/yel pinstripe & red wheels, windshield, lights & steering wheel in blk, 35", rstr $3,500.00

White Dump Truck, Am National, ca 1924, gr & blk w/yel pinstripe, chrome grille, gr wheels, 58", amateur rstr, A $1,800.00

White Trucking Dump Truck, Am National, ca 1935, bl & orange, tires w/silver sidewalls, orange wheels, 54½", rstr.....$3,200.00

Wills Sainte Clare, American National, painted sheet metal on wood chassis, blue with yellow trim, red wheels, includes front license plate, spotlight, working horn and hand brake, restored, 46", G, $3,500.00.

Zephyr Deluxe, Steelcraft, ca 1941, blk & wht w/wht pinstripe, blk wheels w/chrome hubs, pneumatic wht-walls, 42", A $2,600.00

Scooters

Coaster Craft, orig red pnt w/rear flared fender, red wheels w/yel stripe, rear wheel kickstand, unused, M, A $190.00

Gendron Skippy, ca 1940, red streamlined style w/wht pinstripe, front & rear fenders, wht tires, 43", rstr................$2,750.00

Scooter, orig gr pnt w/wood footrest, 12x2¾" pneumatic tires, G, A $150.00

Wagons

Georgie, gray pnt wood w/pnt landscapes on ends, Georgie on on sides w/gold trim, wood spoke wheels, 28" bed, VG+, A $650.00

Peerless Wagon, stenciled and painted wood, red and black lettering on yellow and red, metal wheels with hard rubber tires, 43", VG, $290.00.

Sherwood Spring Coasters, pnt wood w/stenciled lettering, sm steel spoke wheels, spring loaded, 41", G+, A $400.00

Skippy Deluxe, ca 1935, streamlined w/wht trim, front headlights & hdl, red & wht wheels w/chrome hubs, 40", rstr ..$2,500.00

Penny Toys

Penny toys were around as early as the late 1800s and as late as the 1920s. Many were made in Germany, but some were made in France as well. With few exceptions, they ranged in size from 5" on down; some had moving parts, and a few had clockwork mechanisms. Though many were unmarked, you'll sometimes find them signed Kellermann, Meier, Fischer, or Distler, or carrying an embossed company logo such as the dog and cart emblem. They were made of lithographed tin with exquisite detailing — imagine an entire carousel less than 2½" tall. Because of a recent surge in collector interest, many have been crossing the auction block of some of the country's large galleries. Our values are prices realized at several of these auctions.

Advisor: Jane Anderson (A2).

Baby Carriage, Meier, green with maroon trim, red wheels, lithographed tin, 3⅜", EX, A, $425.00.

Airplane, Germany, ca 1915, yel wings, 3½" wingspan, EX, A..**$431.00**

Airplane, Germany, litho tin w/open cockpit & pilot, 4", EX, A...**$120.00**

Airplane & Hangar, G Levy/Germany, hangar lithoed w/people watching planes, monoplane w/pilot, EX+, A.........**$556.00**

Auto Coach w/Driver, Meier, litho tin, 2 passengers appear in window, 3½", VG, A...**$110.00**

Beetle, Germany, on wheels, legs move, 3", EX, A...........**$79.00**

Biplane, Meier, ca 1910, with pilot, tin, EX+, A, $970.00; Biplane, Distler, ca 1910, with pilot, tin, EX+, A, $825.00.

Boat, Germany, ca 1915, man seated in boat w/yel deck & red sides, 2 wheels, 4¾", VG, A.....................................**$250.00**

Boat Swing, Meier/Germany, early 20th century, litho tin w/2 figures, 3¼", G, A...**$633.00**

Boat Tail Racer, Germany, red w/goggled driver, 3", EX+, A..**$260.00**

Boat Tail Racer, Kellermann/Germany, yel litho tin w/driver, 3½", NM, A...**$222.00**

Boat-Tail Racer w/Driver, Germany, bl racer w/blk & yel trim, brn driver, 4¾", G+, A...**$200.00**

Boy in Highchair, Germany, bottom swings out to become table, tin, 3", VG, A..**$182.00**

Boy on Cart, Meier, yellow with red wheels, boy in blue and white, rocks when pushed, tin, 3⅛", VG, A, $650.00.

Boy on Sled, Germany, boy in boots & scarf, litho tin, 2½", EX+, from $300 to...**$400.00**

Buster Brown Roly Poly, Germany, ca 1910, winking figure on wheels, celluloid, 2¼", scarce, EX, A.......................**$182.00**

Butterfly, Einfalt, mk Souvenir From Universal Theatres Concession..., advances w/flapping wings, tin, 2", NM, A...**$144.00**

Cannon, Germany, spring-loaded tab shoots cannon, 2¼", EX, A...**$40.00**

Car, Meier/Germany, sticker reads Automobile Show 1903, may be promotional, 3", EX+, A.....................................**$225.00**

Car w/Driver, Meier/Germany, mk 948 on ea side, cream w/red & gr highlights, 3½", EX, A.....................................**$460.00**

Carousel, Meier/Germany, early 20th century, litho tin, 2½", G, A...**$230.00**

Chinese Man w/Parasol, Distler, 1920s, full-figure man on wheeled toy, litho tin, 3½", EX+, from $250 to.......**$500.00**

Convertible Highchair, Meier/Germany, litho tin, 3", G, A.**$144.00**

Court Jester, embossed tin figure in bloomer-type knee pants and tights on 4-wheeled base, 4", rare, G, A, $650.00.

Dancing Man, marked Germany, lithographed tin figure on rectangular footed box, 3¾", EX, $495.00.

Elephant & Cart, nodder, NM $350.00

Elk, Germany, on wheeled platform, 5", EX+, A............$250.00

Fire Engine, Germany, driver w/4 full-figure fireman seated at rear, adjustable ladder, 4", EX, A $165.00

Fire Engine, Meier/Germany, 2 figures seated back to back in open red truck w/yel ladder above, VG, A..............$226.00

Fire Engine Set, Fischer/Germany, pumper truck, ladder truck, hose truck, 3", M (NM box), A $1,000.00

Fire Engine w/ladder, Germany, nickel w/full-figure litho driver, red, yel & gr, 4¾", VG+, A.....................$185.00

General Omnibus, Fischer/Germany, litho tin w/driver, VG, A...$366.00

Horse & Coach w/Driver, Germany, mc litho tin, 5", EX+, A...$244.00

Horse and Jockey, on 4-wheeled rectangular base, 5", EX, $495.00.

Horse-Drawn Ambulance, Meier, ca 1910, 4", EX, S9 ....$750.00

Horseless Carriage, Meier, litho tin, stained tin wheels, inertia drive, w/driver, rare, 3¾", EX, A.................$2,000.00

Jockey on Rocking Horse, rockers w/racing graphics, 4", G, A...$200.00

Leopard, Germany, spotted leopard on wheeled base, 3¼", NM, A...$225.00

Limousine, Fischer/Germany, butler driver, yel w/red roof & running boards, gr trim, wht balloon tires, 4", EX+, A...$330.00

Limousine, Fischer/Germany, w/driver, brn, 4", VG+....$185.00

Limousine, Germany, center door & driver, brn w/yel & blk striping, 4", G, A.....................................$100.00

Limousine, Germany, door opens to butler driver & passengers, wht w/gold trim & bl running board, 3", NM, A.....$333.00

Limousine, Germany, w/driver, bl & cream w/lt brn trim, silver roof, 4¾", EX, A.....................................$165.00

Limousine, Germany, w/driver, yel w/blk roof & trim, w/up, 4", A...$250.00

Man w/Wheelbarrow, litho tin, pipe in mouth, striding, 3", EX, A...$120.00

Ocean Liner, Meier/Germany, yel w/red & gr trim, red twin stacks, flags fore & aft, 4½", VG, A $185.00

Panel Truck, Fischer/Germany, wood-grained w/dbl oval rear windows, uniformed driver, 4", VG, A $175.00

Panel Truck, Fischer/Germany, wood-grained w/dbl oval rear windows, uniformed driver, 4", EX+, A $270.00

Parrot in Cage, Meier/Germany, gr parrot slides on perch in gold-tone cage w/red base, tin, 4", EX+, A $430.00

Phonograph, Meier/Germany, early megaphone type, turn crank for plink-plink noise, 3½", EX, A...................$147.00

Pool Player, Germany, man at red pool table, complete w/ball & spring-loaded pool stick, 4", NM, A.................$125.00

Sand Pail, unmk, litho tin w/children at play, bail hdl, 2½", EX, A...$72.00

Sewing Machine, Meier/Germany, turn crank to activate machine, tin, 3", EX, A.................................$125.00

Spinning Boy & Girl, Meier/Germany, early 20th century, litho tin, 2½", G, A...$978.00

Squirrel Cage Whistle, Germany, litho tin, blowing whistle causes cage to spin, 4½", EX, A........................$165.00

Stake Truck, Germany, orange open cab w/driver, brn fr & spoke wheels, 4", G, A.................................$60.00

Sword Fighters, Kellermann/Germany, early 20th century, litho tin, squeeze for action, w/clicker, 3", EX, A.............$288.00

Taxi Cab, Distler, litho tin, driver in open car, inertia mechanism, 3¼", VG+, A.....................................$275.00

Touring Car, Distler, litho tin, driver in open car, 3½", EX+, A...$120.00

Touring Car, Distler, litho tin, highly detailed w/driver & opening door, 3¾", EX, A.................................$385.00

Touring Car, G Levy/Germany, driver in open lt gr car w/purple trim & wht balloon tires, w/up, 5", EX+, A.............$341.00

Touring Car, Germany, driver in open dk bl car w/red trim, 4½", NM, A...$213.00

Touring Car, Germany, litho tin, w/driver, w/up, 4", EX, A...$150.00

Touring Car, litho tin, driver in open front seat under extended roof, 4¾", EX, from $350 to..........................$375.00

Touring Car w/Roof Rack, litho tin, w/driver, w/up, 4½", EX, A...$220.00

Train, engine & 2 cars, 6", EX+, M5............................$110.00

Train, Germany, engine w/coal tender & 6 cars, 4", NM, A...$285.00

Train, unmk, early engine w/coal & passenger cars, 8", EX+, A $366.00

Trolley Car, Kellermann, tin, passengers lithoed in windows, w/roof wire, 3", EX+ $500.00

Truck, litho tin, w/driver, open bed, 4½", EX, A............$495.00

Vis-A-Vis, Meier, litho tin driver in red car w/inertia mechanism, 3", EX-, A...$365.00

Watering Can, Germany, w/spring-loaded lid, 3", EX, A...$94.00

Whistle, Germany, blow whistle & dog spins on top of stage, 4", EX+, A...$100.00

Pez Dispensers

Every few years a collecting phenomenon occurs, and none has been quite as intense in recent memory as the Pez craze. Pez was originally designed as a breath mint for smokers, but by the fifties kids were the target market, and the candies were packaged in the dispensers that we all know and love today. There is already more than three hundred variations to collect, and more arrive on the supermarket shelves every day. Though early on collectors seemed to prefer the dispensers without feet, that attitude has changed, and now it's the character head they concentrate on. Feet were added in 1987, so if you were to limit yourself to only feetless dispensers, your collection would be far from complete. Some dispensers have variations in color and design that can influence their values. Don't buy any that are damaged, incomplete, or that have been tampered with in any way; those are nearly worthless. For more information refer to *A Pictorial Guide to Plastic Candy Dispensers Featuring Pez* by David Welch and *Collecting Toys #6* by Richard O'Brien. Values are for mint-condition dispensers unless noted otherwise.

Advisor: Richard Belyski (B1).

Angel, no feet, 1970s, B1	$25.00
Annie, no feet, B1	$55.00
Arlene, w/feet, pk girl, from $1 to	$3.00
Barney Bear, no feet, H4	$35.00
Barney Bear, w/feet, B1	$25.00
Barney Rubble, w/feet, gr, P10	$3.00
Baseball Glove, no feet	$150.00
Batgirl, no feet, soft head, EX, from $50 to	$65.00
Batman, no feet, H4	$12.00
Batman, no feet, w/cape, B9	$120.00
Batman, w/feet, bl or blk, ea, from $1 to	$3.00
Betsy Ross, no feet, B9	$60.00
Bouncer Beagle, w/feet, M, B1	$6.00
Boy, w/feet, brn hair, from $3 to	$8.00
Bozo, no feet, diecut, B9	$125.00
Bugs Bunny, no feet, old, from $10 to	$15.00
Bugs Bunny, w/feet, from $1 to	$3.00
Candy Shooter, no feet, red, B9	$45.00
Captain America, no feet, S2	$45.00
Casper, no feet	$70.00
Charlie Brown, w/feet, from $1 to	$3.00
Charlie Brown, w/feet, frown, eyes closed, B1	$25.00
Charlie Brown, w/feet, frown, B1	$6.00
Chick, w/feet, from $1 to	$3.00
Chick (no hat), B9	$50.00
Chick in Egg, no feet, H4	$12.00
Chick in Egg, no feet, w/hair	$50.00
Chick in Egg, w/feet, H4	$1.00
Clown, no feet, no feet, B9	$65.00
Clown, w/feet, whistle head, B1	$6.00
Cockatoo, no feet, bl face, red beak	$30.00
Cool Cat, w/feet	$30.00
Cow (A), no feet, bl, B9	$40.00
Cow (B), no feet, bl & flesh-colored, B9	$45.00

Creature From the Black Lagoon, no feet, B1	$185.00
Crocodile, no feet, B9	$55.00
Daffy Duck, no feet, H4	$15.00

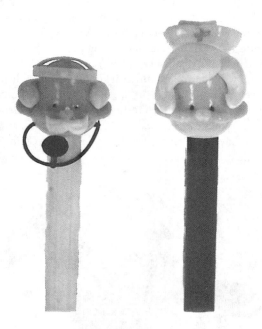

Doctor, M, $70.00; Nurse, blond hair, M, $80.00.

Daffy Duck, w/feet, from $1 to	$3.00
Dalmatian Pup, w/feet, B1	$25.00
Daniel Boone, no feet, B1	$110.00
Dino, w/feet, purple, from $1 to	$3.00
Dinosaur, w/feet, from $1 to	$5.00
Donald Duck, no feet, diecut, B9	$115.00
Donald Duck, no feet	$15.00
Donald Duck, w/feet, bl w/yel bill, from $1 to	$3.00
Donald Duck's Nephew, no feet	$20.00
Donald Duck's Nephew, w/feet, gr or bl hat, ea, B1	$6.00
Donald Duck's Nephew, w/feet, red hat, B1	$10.00
Donkey, w/feet, whistle head, B1	$6.00
Droopy Dog, no feet, plastic swivel ears, MIP, B1	$15.00
Droopy Dog, w/feet, B9	$8.00
Droopy Dog, w/feet, pnt ears, B1	$6.00
Dumbo, w/feet, bl head, B1	$25.00

Elephant, orange and blue, with flat hat, M, $50.00; Tom, M, $45.00.

Erie Specters, no feet, 6 different, B1, ea, from $75 to	$95.00
Fat-Ears Rabbit, no feet, pk head	$15.00
Fat-Ears Rabbit, no feet, yel head	$10.00
Fireman, no feet	$30.00
Fishman, no feet, gr, B1	$185.00
Foghorn Leghorn, w/feet, B1	$35.00
Football Player, no feet, red w/wht helmet	$95.00
Fozzie Bear, w/feet, from $1 to	$3.00
Fred Flintstone, w/feet, B1, from $1 to	$3.00
Frog, w/feet, whistle head, B1	$30.00
Garfield, w/feet, teeth, B1, from $1 to	$10.00
Garfield, w/feet, w/visor, from $1 to	$3.00
Girl, w/feet, blond hair, B1	$15.00
Girl, w/feet, yel hair, B1	$6.00
Gonzo, w/feet, from $1 to	$3.00
Goofy, no feet, old, B1	$25.00
Goofy, w/feet, from $1 to	$3.00
Gorilla, no feet, blk head	$45.00
Green Hornet, 1960s, from $150 to	$250.00

Gyro Gearloose, w/feet, B1	$6.00
Henry Hawk, no feet, B1	$55.00
Hulk, no feet, dk gr, MIP	$20.00
Hulk, no feet, lt gr, B9	$10.00
Hulk, w/feet, lt gr, remake, B1	$5.00
Icee Bear, w/feet, foreign card, B1	$15.00
Icee Bear, w/feet, special winter card, B9	$25.00
Indian, w/feet, whistle head, B1	$6.00
Indian Brave, no feet, reddish, B9	$140.00
Indian Chief, no feet, marbleized, B9	$45.00
Indian Chief, no feet, yel headdress, B1	$55.00
Indian Squaw, no feet, w/headband, B1	$65.00
Jerry Mouse, see also Muscle Mouse	
Jerry Mouse, w/feet, plastic face, B1	$15.00
Jerry Mouse, w/feet, pnt face, B1	$8.00
Joker (Batman), no feet, soft head	$70.00
King Louie, no feet, B1	$35.00
Knight, no feet, B1	$125.00
Koala, w/feet, whistle head, B1	$30.00
Lamb, no feet, B1	$15.00
Lamb, w/feet, from $1 to	$3.00
Lamb, w/feet, whistle head, from $15 to	$25.00
Li'l Bad Wolf, w/feet, B1	$25.00
Lion's Club Lion, A	$950.00
Lion w/Crown, no feet	$55.00
Lion w/Crown, no feet, costume, B9	$85.00
Lucy, w/feet, from $1 to	$3.00
Lucy, w/feet, wht eyes	$45.00
Maharajah, no feet, from $45 to	$50.00
Make-A-Face, works like Mr Potato Head, B1, from $15 to	$27.00
Mary Poppins, no feet, B1, minimum value	$500.00
Merlin Mouse, w/feet, B1	$10.00
Mexican, no feet, B9	$65.00
Mickey Mouse, no feet, removable nose or cast nose, ea, from $10 to	$15.00
Mickey Mouse, w/feet, from $1 to	$3.00
Mimic Monkey (monkey w/ball cap), no feet, several colors, ea, from $25 to	$35.00
Miss Piggy, w/feet, eyelashes, B1	$10.00
Miss Piggy, w/feet, MIP, from $1 to	$3.00
Monkey Sailor, no feet, from $25 to	$35.00
Mowgli, w/feet, B1	$30.00
Mr Ugly, no feet, from $25 to	$39.00
Muscle Mouse (gray Jerry), w/feet, plastic nose or pnt face, B1, ea	$10.00
Nermal, w/feet, gray, from $1 to	$3.00
Nurse, no feet, brn hair, B1	$75.00
Octopus, no feet, blk, B9	$40.00
Olive Oyl, no feet, B1, minimum value	$125.00
Olympic Wolf, A	$600.00
Orange, no feet, B9	$75.00
Panda, no feet, diecut eyes, B1	$25.00
Panda, w/feet, remake, B1, from $1 to	$3.00
Panda, w/feet, whistle head	$6.00
Papa Smurf, w/feet, B1	$10.00
Parrot, w/feet, whistle head, B1	$6.00
Pebbles Flintstone, w/feet, B1, from $1 to	$3.00
Penguin (Batman), no feet, soft head	$70.00

Peter Pez, w/feet, remake, B1 ....$5.00
Peter Pez (A), no feet $65.00

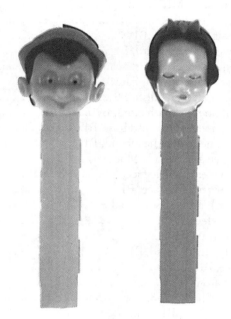

Pinocchio, M, $90.00; Snow White, M, $65.00.

Pirate, no feet, from $25 to $40.00
Pluto, no feet, red..$25.00
Pluto, w/feet, red, from $1 to $3.00
Police Style Whistle, w/feet, B1, $1 to $3.00
Policeman, no feet, B1 ....$30.00
Popeye (B), no feet $40.00
Popeye (C), no feet, w/removable pipe $45.00
Practical Pig (B), no feet, B9 ....$30.00
Psychedelic Eye, no feet, from $350 to............................$450.00
Psychedelic Flower, no feet, B1, from $375 to $400.00
Pumpkin (A), no feet, from $10 to....................................$15.00
Pumpkin (B), w/feet, new, foreign card, B1, from $1 to......$3.00
Raven, no feet, yel beak $30.00
Regular (looks like Bic lighter), many variations, no feet, ea,
     minimum value..$100.00
Rhino, w/feet, whistle head, B1 ....$6.00
Ringmaster, no feet...$125.00
Road Runner, w/feet, B1 ....$6.00
Rooster, w/feet, whistle head, B1.....................................$25.00
Rooster, w/feet, wht or yel head, ea..................................$25.00
Rudolph, no feet $25.00
Santa Claus, no feet, full body..$125.00
Santa Claus (A), no feet, steel pin, from $95 to $125.00
Santa Claus (B), no feet, B1 ....$85.00
Santa Claus (C), no feet, from $5 to $15.00
Santa Claus (C), w/feet, B1, from $1 to $3.00
Scrooge McDuck (A), no feet, B1 ....$20.00
Scrooge McDuck (B), w/feet, B1 ....$6.00
Sheik, no feet $40.00
Skull (A), no feet, from $5 to..$10.00
Skull (B), w/feet, from $1 to $3.00
Smurf, w/feet, B1 ....$6.00

Smurfette, w/feet, I2...$8.00
Snoopy, w/feet, from $1 to $5.00
Snowman (A), no feet, from $5 to $10.00
Snowman (B), w/feet, B1, from $1 ....$5.00

Space Gun, MIP, from $125.00 to $150.00.

Space Trooper Robot, no feet, full body, from $250 to...$325.00
Spaceman, no feet, DBP stem, B9 ....$95.00
Speedy Gonzales, w/feet, B1 ....$6.00
Speedy Gonzoles, no feet, H4 ....$15.00
Spiderman, no feet..$15.00
Spiderman, w/feet, from $1 to...$3.00
Spike, w/feet, B1..$6.00
Sylvester, w/feet, cream whiskers, B1 ....$5.00
Sylvester, w/feet, wht whiskers, B1 ....$2.00
Teenage Mutant Ninja Turtles, w/feet, 8 variations, B1, ea...$1.50
Thor, no feet, B1..$150.00
Thumper, w/feet, no copyright $30.00
Tiger, w/feet, whistle head, B1 ....$6.00
Tinkerbell, no feet, B9...$100.00
Truck, many variations, ea, from $1 to $100.00
Tweety Bird, no feet...$15.00
Tweety Bird, w/feet, from $1 to $3.00
Tyke, w/feet, B1 ....$6.00
Uncle Sam, no feet, B9 ....$70.00
Wile E Coyote, w/feet, B1 ....$25.00
Winnie the Pooh, w/feet, B1 ....$25.00
Witch, 3-pc; w/feet, from $1 to..$3.00
Witch (A), 3-pc; no feet, B9 ....$10.00
Wonder Woman, no feet, soft head, from $60 to.............$75.00
Wonder Woman, w/feet, from $1 to...................................$3.00
Woodstock, w/feet, from $1 to $3.00

Woodstock, w/feet, pnt feathers, B1 .... $12.00
Yappy Dog, no feet, gr, B9 .... $35.00
Zorro, no feet, w/Zorro logo, B1 .... $75.00

MISCELLANEOUS

Coloring Book, Saftey #2, non-English, B1 .... $15.00
Flintstone's Dice Game (like Candyland), German, B1 ... $15.00
Greeting Card, same picture as Hallmark puzzle, B1 .... $8.00
Lapel Pins, older style, 10 different, B9, ea $10.00
Muppets Gift Set, B9 .... $25.00
Paper Cap, B9 .... $10.00
Peter Pez Bag, hot pk, lg, B9 .... $10.00
Peter Pez Counter Display, 2 Lucite bowls & header card, B9 .. $25.00
Puzzle, Ceaco, 1991, out of production, 125 pcs, B1 .... $20.00
Puzzle, Springbrook/Hallmark, 500 pcs, B1 .... $10.00
Stand, plastic w/fuzz, holds 6 non-footed dispensers, B1 ..... $9.00

Pin-Back Buttons

Pin-back buttons produced up to the early 1920s were made with a celluloid covering. After that time, a large number of buttons were lithographed on tin; these are referred to as tin lithos.

Character and toy-related buttons represent a popular collecting field. There are countless categories to base a collection on. Buttons were given out at stores and theatres, offered as premiums, attached to dolls or received with a club membership.

In the late forties and into the fifties, some cereal companies packed one in boxes of their product. Quaker Puffed Oats offered a series of movie star pin-backs, but probably the best known are Kellogg's Pep Pins. There were eighty-six in all, so theoretically if you wanted the whole series as Kellogg hoped you would, you'd have to buy at least that many boxes of their cereal. Pep pins came in five sets, the first in 1945, three more in 1946, and the last in 1947. They were printed with full-color lithographs of comic characters licensed by King Features and Famous Artists — Maggie and Jiggs, the Winkles, and Dagwood and Blondie, for instance. Superman, the only D.C. Comics character, was included in each set. Most Pep pins range in value from $10.00 to $15.00 in NM/M condition; any not mentioned in our listings fall into this range. There are exceptions, and we've made sure they're evaluated below.

Nearly all pin-backs are collectible today with these possible exceptions: common buttons picturing flags of various nations, general labor union buttons denoting the payment of dues, and common buttons with clever sayings. Be sure that you buy only buttons with well-centered designs, well-alligned colors, no fading or yellowing, no spots or stains, and no cracks, splits, or dents. In the listings that follow, sizes are approximate.

Advisor: Doug Dezso (D6), Kellogg's Pep Pins.

Archie, features Betty & Let's Go Slurpin', litho tin, 1978, 1",
     VG, J5 .... $10.00
Archie, features Reggie & Keep on Grovin', litho tin, 1978, 1",
     VG, J5 .... $10.00

Al Kaline Day, Tiger Stadium, Aug 2, 1970, color photo, 2¼", M, $35.00.

Archie Fan Club, Official Member, blk, wht, bl & orange, 1½",
     EX $15.00
Babe Ruth, Baseball Club Member, blk & wht, ⅞", EX $40.00
Batman, Pow, red, wht, bl & blk litho, 1966, 1", EX $25.00
Big Boy, National Club Member, red, gr, brn & wht litho, 1⅛",
     EX $40.00
Cat in the Hat, Happy 30th Birthday, blk, wht & orange 1987,
     2½", EX $25.00
Cisco Kid, Triple S Club, red, wht & yel litho, 1⅜", EX .. $65.00
Cracker Jack, lady's head, mc, 1910, 1¼" $50.00
Daisy Air Rifles, boy w/rifle, mc, ⅞", EX $110.00
Duncan Yo-Yo Tourney, yo-yo head figure, red & wht litho, ¾",
     EX $25.00
Effanbee Dolls, Finest & Best, w/bluebird, red & bl on gold, ¾",
     EX $30.00
Elvis, Love Me Tender, blk & wht litho on gold record, 1956,
     ⅞", EX $50.00
Elvis, Love Me Tender, flasher, blk & wht on bl, 1956, 2½",
     EX $35.00
Fonzie, Sit on It, color photo on red & yel, 1976, 3½", EX .. $10.00
Gene Autry, Official Club Badge, blk & wht w/orange rim, 1¼",
     EX $30.00
Gene Autry & Champion, blk & wht on silver star, 1¾", EX . $50.00
Goofy/I'm Goofy About Disneyland, flasher, mc, 2½", EX . $25.00

Herman's Hermits, I Love Herman's Hermits, red and white with black and white photos, 3½", M, $25.00.

Hopalong Cassidy, Ask Me About the Savings Club, tin, 1950, 3", EX, J5/01 from $40 ....$45.00

Hopalong Cassidy's Saving Rodeo: Wrangler, 1950s, light blue background; Trail Boss, 1950s, light green background; Tenderfoot, 1950s, yellow background; all M condition, $25.00 each.

Howdy Doody, It's Howdy Doody Time, 1980s, 2¼", M $5.00

Howdy Doody, It's Howdy Doody Time w/full-figure Howdy & head shots of friends, 1980s, 6", NM $18.00

Howdy Doody, It's Howdy Doody Time!, blk on orange, 1¾", EX $15.00

Ideal, Fun & Games Day, gr, bl, red & wht, 4", EX $25.00

Jimmy Durante, Gimme the Candidate, red, wht, bl & blk litho, 1⅛", EX $15.00

Jimmy Durante & Umbriago (puppet), blk & wht on orange, 1940s, 1⅛", EX...$25.00

Jimmy Durante for President, mc, 1¼", M11 ....$20.00

Joe DiMaggio, NY Yankees, blk & wht photo, 1¾", EX ...$35.00

Kiss, Madison Square Garden, WPLJ Radio, NYC, Dec 1977, M...$18.00

Led Zeppelin Summer Fest, Buffalo, New York, 1977, 3", NM.$10.00

Li'l Abner, blk & wht on bl ground, 1940s, 1¼", EX........$65.00

Little King, blk, red & flesh on yel litho, 1950s, ⅞", EX ..$15.00

Little King, litho tin, 1960s, 1", EX, J5 ....$10.00

Lone Ranger, Sunday Herald Examiner, blk, wht & orange litho, 1", EX...$35.00

Lone Ranger on Silver, mc, 1949, 1¼", EX.......................$30.00

Marble Champion, wht lettering on dk bl, 1¼", EX.......$100.00

Matchbox Collector, box pictures car, red, wht, bl & yel litho, 1⅜", EX...$20.00

Mickey Mantle, Lee Jeans, 1960s, 3", NM $15.00

Mickey Mantle, 1969, ⅞", EX...$6.00

Mod Mickey, Benay-Albee, late 1960s, 3½" $20.00.

Mickey Mouse Club, mc w/red rim, 1960s, 3", EX $10.00

Mickey Mouse/I Like Disneyland, flasher, 1970s, 2½", M, S2 .$25.00

Mr Peanut, Vote the People's Choice, red, blk & wht, 1¼", EX...$25.00

Mummy, Universal Pictures, bl, red & wht, 1960s, 3½", EX .$25.00

Mummy, Universal Pictures, blk & wht on red, 1966, ⅞", EX.$12.50

Mutt & Jeff, portraits on gr ground, 1940s, 1¼", EX.........$65.00

My Pal Roy Rogers, 1950s, 2¼", NM $10.00

Peter Pan, Benay-Albee, multicolored, 3½", $18.00.

Popeye the Sailor, 1980s, 1¼", M.....................................$4.00

Popeye the Sailor Man, red, bl, blk & wht, 3½", EX $30.00

Psycho Comics Fan Addict Member, celluloid, 2", EX, J5 ..$10.00

Red Ryder, I Have Entered the Pony Contest, blk on yel litho, 1", EX...$25.00

Rin-Tin-Tin, Every Kid Needs a Super Dog, blk & wht, 2¼", EX...$5.00

Roberto Clemente, photo, 1969, ⅞", M $6.00

Roberto Clemente, Pittsburgh Pirates, blk, wht, red & bl, 1969, 3½", EX $25.00

Rocketeer, flasher, only 100 made, M, H10 ....$100.00

Rootie Kazootie Club, featuring Squeako Mouse, Mr Deetle Dootle or Poison Zoomack, litho tin, 1950s, EX, J5, ea.....$25.00

Rootie Kazootie Club, pictures Rootie, blk, wht & orange, 1⅛", EX...$25.00

Roy Rogers, My Pal, blk & wht w/red rim, 1950s, 1¾", EX .$150.00

Santa, Merry Christmas/Fun Book, red & gr on wht, 2⅛", EX.$18.00

Santa, Merry Christmas/Happy New Year, mc, 1950s, 1¼", M11...$10.00

Shirley Temple Doll, The World's Darling, brn & pk photo, 1¼", EX...$450.00

Snoopy as Red Baron, Millbrook Bread 1970, 1½", H4 ......$2.00

Snoopy Wearing Crown, Millbrook Bread, 1970, 4", H4 ...$2.00

Snow White, Jingle Club Member, red, wht & bl, 1938, 1¼", M, M8..$45.00

Star Trek, Captain Kirk, mc, 1969, 1¼", EX....................$15.00

Sunset Carson, blk & wht, 1¾", EX $50.00

Superman, Action Comics Magazine, orange & dk bl on cream, ⅞", EX...$75.00

Superman, figural, 1940s, lg, EX, C10 ....$85.00

Tarzan, w/apes on yel ground, cello, art by Foster, 1973, 3", NM, C1...$18.00

Tarzan, w/lion on bl ground, cello, art by Frazetta, 1973, 3", NM, C1 ....$24.00
Ted Williams, Boston Red Sox, blk & wht, 1¼", EX $10.00
Tom & Jerry, Stroehmann's Bread, red, wht & blk litho, 1⅛", EX $18.00
Tom & Jerry, Sunbeam Bread, 1960s, 1¼", M $6.00
Winnie the Pooh, 1960s, 3½", EX, J5 ....$10.00
Yellow Kid, Hogan's Alley advertising on shirt, yel & wht on gr, ⅞", EX $85.00
Yogi Bear for President, red, wht & bl, 1964, ⅞", EX $10.00
Zorro/7-Up, Disney, blk, wht & orange, 1957, 1⅜", NM .$12.00

KELLOGG'S PEP PINS

BO Plenty, NM...$30.00
Corky, NM..$16.00
Dagwood, NM...$30.00
Dick Tracy, NM..$30.00
Early Bird, NM...$6.00
Fat Stuff, NM...$15.00

Felix the Cat, NM, $75.00.

Flash Gordon, NM...$30.00
Goofy, NM..$10.00
Gravel Gertie, NM $15.00
Harold Teen, NM $15.00
Inspector, NM...$12.50
Jiggs, NM...$25.00
Judy, NM...$10.00
Kayo, NM...$20.00
Little King, NM $15.00
Little Moose, NM $15.00
Maggie, NM..$25.00
Mama De Stross, NM $30.00
Mama Katzenjammer, NM $25.00
Mamie, NM...$15.00
Navy Patrol, NM...$6.00
Olive Oyl, NM...$30.00
Orphan Annie, NM..$25.00
Pat Patton, NM...$10.00
Perry Winkle, NM $15.00
Pop Jenks, NM..$15.00
Popeye, NM..$30.00
Rip Winkle..$20.00

The Phantom, NM, $75.00

Skeezix, NM..$15.00
Superman, NM..$35.00
Toots, NM...$15.00
Uncle Walt, NM..$20.00
Uncle Willie, NM...$12.50
Winkles Twins, NM..$75.00
Winnie Winkle, NM...$15.00

Pipsqueaks

Pipsqueak toys were popular among the Pennsylvania Germans. Many featured animals made of painted papier-mache, some were on spring legs. All had bellows that produced a squeaking sound, hence the name. Early toys had bellows made from sheepskin. Cloth bellows followed, and on later examples, the bellows were made of paper.

Cat w/Two Kittens, striped flocking, animated mouth, 7", VG $450.00

Chicken in Coop, painted plaster chicken pops out of wooden coop with paper lithographed roof, 4¾", paper loss on roof otherwise VG, A, $30.00; Rabbit and Eggs on Bellows Base, painted composition, not working, G, A, $65.00.

Goose, papier-mache, mc pnt, spring legs, squeaks, 6", rprs..$150.00
Horse in Cage, dapple gray flannel coat, glass eyes, 9", EX $475.00
Parrot on Stump, papier-mache, squeaks, EX color, 4"...$145.00

Rooster in House, paper on wood, cloth & feather bird, door opens, bird chirps & swings out, 6½", VG, A $200.00

Sheep in Cage, wood & paper, silent, 5¾" $150.00

Plastic Figures

Plastic figures were made by many toy companies. They were first boxed with playsets, but in the early fifties, some became available individually. Marx was the first company to offer single figures (at 10¢ each) and even some cereal companies included one in boxes of their product. (Kellogg offered a series of 16 54mm Historic Warriors and Nabisco had a line of ten dinosaurs in marbleized, primary colors.) Virtually every type of man and beast has been modeled in plastic, today some have become very collectible and expensive. There are lots of factors you'll need to be aware of to be a wise buyer. For instance, Marx made cowboys during the mid-sixties in a flat finish, and these are much harder to find and more valuable than the later figures with a waxy finish. Marvel Super Heroes in the fluorescent hues are worth about half as much as the earlier, light gray issue. Because of limited space, it isn't possible to evaluate more than a representative few of these plastic figures in a general price guide, so if you'd like to learn more about them, we recommend *Geppert's Guide* by Tim Geppert. See the Clubs and Newsletters section for information on how to order the *Plastic Figure & Playset Collector* magazine.

Advisors: Mike and Kurt Fredericks (F4).

See also Playsets.

ACTION AND ADVENTURE

Ajax, Spacemen, glow-in-the-dark, M, ea..........................$10.00

Ajax, Spacemen, M, ea $7.00

Ajax, Spacemen, w/helmet, MIB......................................$15.00

Archer, Spacemen, M, ea, from $5 to $10.00

Archer, Spacemen, robot, hard plastic, M, from $15.......$25.00

Archer, Spacemen, space GI, metallic gr, M.....................$7.00

Archer, Spacemen, woman w/helmet, EX.........................$5.00

Best, Spacemen, w/gun, red hard plastic, VG $40.00

Crescent, Robin Hood, 5-pc set, NM (G box)................$60.00

Giant, Spacemen, HO scale, M, ea....................................$2.00

Ideal, Arctic, penguin, wht, M..$4.00

Ideal, Underwater Adventure, diver, red, M $5.00

Ideal, Untouchables, gangster w/tommy gun or satchel, red, M, ea $6.00

Lido, Captain Video, 4", VG+..$15.00

Lido, Spacemen, M, ea..$7.50

Marx, Aliens, 35mm, M, ea $6.00

Marx, Astronauts, 35mm, w/1" ring on head, M, ea $5.00

Marx, Ben Hur, chariot w/4 horses & driver, M $62.00

Marx, Cape Canaveral, 54mm, astronaut, lt bl, M $10.00

Marx, Cape Canaveral, 54mm, ground crewman, metallic bl, M $4.00

Marx, Caveman, 6", w/rock, NM......................................$8.00

Marx, Cavemen, 6", lt orange, 1962, set of 6, NM $45.00

Marx, Eskimos, dog sled w/harness & pack, M, from $18 to ..$25.00

Marx, Eskimos, igloo, M $14.00

Marx, Eskimos, w/paddle, M...$20.00

Marx, Jungle Jim or Daktari, chief w/top hat & cigar, M..$20.00

Marx, Jungle Jim or Daktari, climbing monkey, M $5.00

Marx, Jungle Jim or Daktari, dead tiger & pole, M, from $15 to $20.00

Marx, Jungle Jim or Daktari, hunter, cream soft plastic, no name on base, M..$20.00

Marx, Jungle Jim or Daktari, hunter w/rifle, M $10.00

Marx, Jungle Jim or Daktari, jeep driver, M $8.00

Marx, Jungle Jim or Daktari, lost hunter, M $20.00

Marx, Jungle Jim or Daktari, missionary, M $35.00

Marx, Jungle Jim or Daktari, native, lt brn, M $6.00

Marx, Jungle Jim or Daktari, native policeman, brn, M ...$20.00

Marx, Jungle Jim or Daktari, ostrich or lion, M, ea............$8.00

Marx, Jungle Jim or Daktari, Paula, M $35.00

Marx, Jungle Jim or Daktari, Tamba or Judy the Chimp, M, ea from $15 to..$25.00

Marx, Jungle Jim or Daktari, tiger or giraffe, M, ea $5.00

Marx, Jungle Jim or Daktari, witch doctor, M..................$10.00

Marx, Lassie, 60mm, cream, M...$12.00

Marx, Lost in Space, Will Robinson, M..........................$45.00

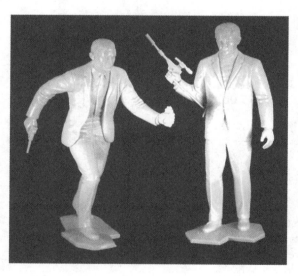

Marx, Man From UNCLE, Napoleon Solo, 6", M; Marx, Man From UNCLE, Illya Kuryakin, 6", M, from $20.00 to $25.00 each.

Marx, Man From UNCLE, THRUSH officer, 6", $18.00.

Marx, Monsters, 6", Frankenstein, bl, 1960s, NM $10.00

Marx, Monsters, 6", Frankenstein, lt orange, 1960s, M $25.00

Marx, Phantom of the Opera, orange, NM $20.00

Marx, Pirates, 60mm, bl, M, ea.................................$12.00

Marx, Pirates, 60mm, cream, M, ea $20.00

Marx, Robin Hood, 54mm, Friar Tuck or Little John, cream, M, ea...$12.00

Marx, Robin Hood, 54mm, minstrel, red or yel, M, ea $4.00

Marx, Robin Hood, 54mm, Sheriff of Nottingham, red, M $5.00

Marx, Robin Hood, 60mm, Little John, M $15.00

Marx, Robin Hood, 60mm, Maid Marian, M...................$10.00

Marx, Robin Hood, 60mm, Richard Green, gr, NM.........$65.00

Marx, Robin Hood, 60mm, Sir Gawain, M......................$15.00

Marx, Robin Hood, 60mm, 22-pc set, MIP.....................$150.00

Marx, Secret Agent, 6", w/pistol, bl, EX $14.00

Marx, Sky King, Penny, red..$12.00

Marx, Sky King, sheriff, red, M.......................................$18.00

Marx, Super Heroes, 6", Captain America, gr, NM $14.00

Marx, Tom Corbett Space Cadet, 45mm, alien, bl or orange, M, ea...$12.00

Marx, Tom Corbett Space Cadet, 45mm, alien crawling, M...$12.00

Marx, Tom Corbett Space Cadet, 45mm, cadet, dk bl, M ..$10.00

Marx, Tom Corbett Space Cadet, 45mm, cadet, gray, M, from $3 to $6.00

Marx, Tom Corbett Space Cadet, 45mm, female cadet, gray, M $9.00

Marx, Tom Corbett Space Cadet, 45mm, space car, complete, M...$65.00

Marx, Tom Corbett Space Cadet, 45mm, spaceman, bl, M..$7.00

Marx, Tom Corbett Space Cadet, 45mm, spaceman, metallic bl or orange, M, ea $9.00

Marx, Underwater Adventures, fish, 8-pc set, M $25.00

Marx, Underwater Adventures, skin diver, M....................$8.00

Marx, Untouchables, Al Capone, M $7.00

Marx, Untouchables, Elliott Ness, NM...........................$13.00

Marx, Untouchables, flapper lady, M $12.00

Marx, Untouchables, Rolls Royce, NM...........................$65.00

Mattel, Big Jim, gorilla, MIB $50.00

Mattel, Lost in Space, Will Robinson, M.........................$45.00

Miller, Jungle Natives, w/pack on head, M $18.00

Miller, Jungle Natives, w/spear & shield, M....................$18.00

MPC, Monsters, Grim Reaper, M.....................................$8.00

MPC, Monsters, Hangman, M...$8.00

Pal, Alaskan Eskimo Life, soft plastic, 12-pc set, MIP $50.00

Palmer, Monsters, Frankenstein, M.................................$22.00

Palmer, Monsters, Wolfman, M.......................................$22.00

Pecos, Pirates, Blackbeard, red w/blk accessories, M.........$72.00

Plasticraft, Pirates, pnt, M, ea..$10.00

Premier, Spacemen, M, ea $10.00

Superior, Captain Video, GIs, M, ea $5.00

Superior, Captain Video, spaceman, M............................$15.00

Tim-Mee, Pirates, M, ea..$8.00

Timpo, Frozen North, Eskimos; 5-pc w/dog sled & 4 dogs, MIB $95.00

Timpo, Romans, mounted, M, ea $35.00

Timpo, Romans, on foot, M, ea..$15.00

CAMPUS CUTIES AND AMERICAN BEAUTIES

Marx, American Beauties, ballerina, ca 1955, NM..........$17.00

Marx, American Beauties, hula dancer, hard plastic, peach, NM...$16.00

Marx, American Beauties, reclining nude, M $40.00

Marx, Campus Cuties, 6", Dinner for Two, M, from $8 to .$10.00

Marx, Campus Cuties, 6", Lodge Party, M, from $8 to $10.00

Marx, Campus Cuties, 6", Nighty Night, M, from $8 to...$10.00

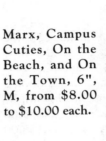
Marx, Campus Cuties, On the Beach, and On the Town, 6", M, from $8.00 to $10.00 each.

Marx, Campus Cuties, 6", Shopping Anyone, M $7.50

Marx, Campus Cuties, 6", Stormy Weather, M, from $8 to..$10.00

CIRCUS AND ANIMALS

Airfix, Animal Farm Stock, HO scale, 1st series, MIB $15.00

Ajax, Prehistoric Animals, Tyrannosaurus Rex or Plateosaurus, M, ea...$5.00

Auburn, Farm Animals, M, ea $2.00

Auburn, Wild Jungle Animals, M, ea...............................$5.00

Chitech, 3-headed dragon, gr, 1984, 11", D9 ....$7.00

Marx, Birds, 60mm, M, ea...$2.00

Marx, Blue Ribbon Dogs, pnt plastic, 1960s, 10 in set, NM (NM boxes), ea $8.00

Marx, Fish, 60mm, deep sea species, M, ea $10.00

Marx, Prehistoric Animals, Kronosaurus, lt gr soft plastic, M .$10.00

Marx, Prehistoric Animals, Tyrannosaurus Rex, potbellied, marbled soft plastic, M..$15.00

Marx, Super Circus, balloon vendor w/mc balloons, M $8.00

Marx, Super Circus, Cliffy the Clown, M $10.00

Marx, Super Circus, gorilla w/raised arms, M $3.50

Marx, Super Circus, Mary Hartline, M $10.00

Marx, Super Circus, seal w/ball, gray, M $5.00

Marx, Super Circus, seated lion, M $3.50

Marx, Super Circus, waving clown, vinyl, M $20.00

Miller, Jungle Animals, elephant, M, minimum value $50.00

Miller, Jungle Animals, hippo, M, minimum value $50.00

Miller, Prehistoric Animals, Stegosaurus, minimum value..$50.00

MPC, Animal Land, 10-pc set, MIB $40.00

MPC, Farm Animals, complete set, MIP.........................$16.00

MPC, Fish, barracuda, M $5.00

MPC, Jungle Animals, gorilla, M $6.00

Ohio Art, Farm Animals, vinyl, M, ea $2.00

Palmer, Circus, clown, M $7.00

Palmer, Circus, midget, M $5.00

Palmer, Circus, ringmaster, M $5.00

Palmer, Circus, strongman, M $7.00

Palmer, Circus, sword swallower, M $9.00

COMIC, DISNEY AND NURSERY CHARACTERS

Ideal, Comic Strip, Batman, w/accessories, M $35.00

Ideal, Comic Strip, Brainstorm, M $40.00

Ideal, Comic Strip, Joker, NM.......................................$35.00

Lido, Disney, Zorro; 54mm, Zorro, MIP $18.00

Lido, Foreign Legion & Arabs, 20 French, 14 Arabs, 4 horses &
5 camels, MIB $60.00

Marx, Comic Strip, 54mm, Prince Valiant or Sir Gawain, M,
ea...$25.00

Marx, Comic Strip, 60mm, BO Plenty, M.........................$8.00

Marx, Comic Strip, 60mm, Cookie, M $6.00

Marx, Comic Strip, 60mm, Dagwood, pnt soft plastic, M...$25.00

Marx, Comic Strip, 60mm, Daisy Mae, pnt soft plastic, M...$25.00

Marx, Comic Strip, 60mm, Hook, short sword, M $4.00

Marx, Comic Strip, 60mm, Huey, M $6.00

Marx, Comic Strip, 60mm, Jiggs, gr, M $10.00

Marx, Comic Strip, 60mm, Jiggs, M $7.00

Marx, Comic Strip, 60mm, Jughead, M $8.00

Marx, Comic Strip, 60mm, Li'l Abner, M.........................$7.00

Marx, Comic Strip, 60mm, Loweezy, M $8.00

Marx, Comic Strip, 60mm, Sarge (Beetle Bailey), M $15.00

Marx, Comic Strip, 60mm, Snuffy Smith, M $9.00

Marx, Comic Strip, 60mm, Sut Tattersal, M......................$9.00

Marx, Disney, Babes in Toyland; 60mm, any figure, M, ea..$25.00

Marx, Disney, Bambi; 6", Bambi, M $12.00

Marx, Disney, Peter Pan; 6", Peter Pan, M, from $12 to...$15.00

Marx, Disney, Peter Pan; 6", Tinker Bell, M....................$15.00

Marx, Disney, Peter Pan; 60mm, Peter Pan, Captain Hook or
Wendy, M, ea...$5.00

Marx, Disney, Pinocchio; 6", Jiminy Cricket, M................$8.00

Marx, Disney, Snow White & the Seven Dwarfs; 6", Snow
White, M $12.00

Marx, Disney, Zorro; 54mm, Don Alejandro, gray, M $18.00

Marx, Disney, Zorro; 54mm, Don Diego or Don Alejandro,
cream, M, ea...$30.00

Marx, Disney, Zorro; 54mm, Zorro, w/blk horse, M..........$28.00

Marx, Disney, 6", Donald Duck, M $12.00

Marx, Disney, 6", Goofy, red, M $10.00

Marx, Disney, 6", Mickey Mouse, M, from $8 to $12.00

Marx, Disneykins, Ludwig Von Drake, M $25.00

Marx, Disneykins, Mowgli, M $35.00

Marx, Disneykins, 34-pc set, 1960, 1½" ea, NM+ (EX compart-
mented 12" sq box), A, from $250 to.....................$295.00

Marx, Disneykins, 60mm, Blue Fairy, MIB $35.00

Marx, Disneykins, 60mm, Captain Hook, MIB $35.00

Marx, Dollhouse, Disney, 60mm, set of 6, movable limbs,
MIB $50.00

Marx, Fairykins, Humpty Dumpty, M $15.00

Marx, Hanna-Barbera, Flintstones; 54mm, Barney Rubble, bl,
M $10.00

Marx, Hanna-Barbera, Flintstones; 54mm, Betty Rubble, cream,
M $6.00

Marx, Hanna-Barbera, Flintstones; 54mm, Fred Flintstone, bl,
M $10.00

Marx, Hanna-Barbera, Flintstones; 54mm, Fred's house, gray,
M $8.00

Marx, Hanna-Barbera, Flintstones; 60mm, any other than main
character, M, ea $5.00

Marx, Hanna-Barbera, TV Tinykins; Hokey Wolf & Ding-a-
ling, M, pr $50.00

Marx, Hanna-Barbera, TV Tinykins; Quick Draw McGraw, 2",
NM, T2 ....$15.00

Marx, Hanna-Barbera, TV Tinykins; Super Snooper, M..$25.00

Marx, Hanna-Barbera, TV Tinykins; Yogi Bear & Cindy Bear,
M, pr...$40.00

Marx, Howdy Doody, 60mm, Clarabell, wht hard plastic, M...$35.00

Marx, Nursery Rhymes, Jack climbing beanstalk, M..........$8.00

Marx, Nursery Rhymes, Jack w/pail, M $8.00

Marx, Nursery Rhymes, Little Red Riding Hood $8.00

Marx, Nursery Rhymes, Mama Bear, M $5.00

Marx, Nursery Rhymes, Old Mother Hubbard, M $8.00

Marx, Nursery Rhymes, Simple Simon, M $5.00

Marx, Tom & Jerry, 6" & 4", 1963, NM, C1, pr $54.00

Marx, TV Fairykins, Goldilocks & 3 Bears, M.................$75.00

Marx, 101 Dalmatians, unpnt wht, 1960s, 8-pc set, NM, M8..$35.00

MPC, Comic Strip, Beetle Bailey, M $35.00

FAMOUS PEOPLE AND CIVILIANS

Auburn, Civilians & Workmen, police motorcycle, from $25
to..$35.00

Marx, American Beauties, 60mm, flesh, 8-pc set, MIP...$100.00

Marx, Civilians & Workmen, 3", construction worker, M .$5.00

Marx, Civilians & Workmen, 3", fireman w/extinguisher, cream,
M $6.00

Marx, Civilians & Workmen, 35mm, airport attendant, M..$1.50

Marx, Civilians & Workmen, 35mm, motorcycle cop, M ..$6.00

Marx, Civilians & Workmen, 45mm, construction worker,
M $3.00

Marx, Civilians & Workmen, 45mm, train conductor, M..$4.00

Marx, Civilians & Workmen, 6", construction vehicle driver,
M $25.00

Marx, Civilians & Workmen, 60mm, Boy Scout, M $10.00

Marx, Civilians & Workmen, 60mm, Boy Scout w/basketball,
bl, M $10.00

Marx, Civilians & Workmen, 60mm, skyscraper civilians, 16-pc
set, cream, MIP..$130.00

Marx, Civilians & Workmen, 60mm, woman w/child, cream,
M $7.00

Marx, Football, 54mm, complete set w/Tom Landry, red, M..$60.00

Marx, Football, 54mm, 32-pc, red soft plastic, MIP.........$80.00

Marx, Presidents & Politicals, 60mm, Dwight D Eisenhower, raised arms, soft plastic, no date, M..............$20.00

Marx, Presidents & Politicals, 60mm, Nelson Rockefeller, pnt version, M..............$25.00

Marx, Presidents & Politicals, 60mm, President Eisenhower, M..............$20.00

Marx, Presidents & Politicals, 60mm, President Johnson, M..$20.00

Marx, Presidents & Politicals, 60mm, President Kennedy, pnt, M..............$50.00

Marx, Presidents & Politicals, 60mm, Winston Churchill, hard plastic, M..............$20.00

Marx, Queen Elizabeth II Coronation, 60mm, Duke of Edinburgh, wht hard plastic, M..............$20.00

Marx, Queen Elizabeth II Coronation, 60mm, Duke of Windsor, wht hard plastic, M..............$15.00

Marx, Queen Elizabeth II Coronation, 60mm, Princess Margaret, wht hard plastic, M..............$18.00

Marx, Religious, 60mm, Andrew, hard plastic, M..............$5.00

Marx, Religious, 60mm, Jesus Christ, 1st version, w/left hand raised, M..............$15.00

Marx, Religious, 60mm, Pope Pius XII, M..............$12.00

MPC, Fire Rescue, 3 figures w/accessories, MIB..............$12.00

MILITARY AND WARRIORS

Airfix, Washington's Army, HO scale, MIB..............$25.00

Airfix, Waterloo, HO scale, French Artillery, MIB..........$15.00

Airfix, WWI, HO scale, British Infantry, 1st series, MIB.$20.00

Auburn, WWII, 60mm, GIs, M, ea..............$2.00

Auburn, WWII, 60mm, GIs, vinyl, 5-pc set, MIP..............$15.00

Britain, Revolutionary War, advancing colonial scout, pnt, M..............$9.00

Britains, Foreign Legion & Arabs, Arab standing, M.......$10.00

Britains, Foreign Legion & Arabs, Legionnaire standing, M..$8.00

Britains, War of the Roses, British foot archer, M............$15.00

Britains, War of the Roses, British mounted & attacking w/lance or sword, M, ea..............$35.00

Britains, Waterloo, British infantry detail, 7-pc set, MIB.$75.00

Comansi, Knights, 28mm, soft plastic, M..............$2.50

Crescent, WWII, British Red Devil, M..............$7.00

Elastolin, American Revolution, 70mm, Colonial drummer, M..............$10.00

Elastolin, Knights, 70mm, Sir Gawain w/helmet, M.........$12.00

Giant, Vikings, M, ea..............$3.00

Goldmarx, Egyptian w/spear at chest, M..............$23.00

Goldmarx, Viking w/shield & axe, M..............$20.00

Goldmarx, WWII, English soldier running w/rifle, M......$25.00

Ideal, Battle Action, GI firing rifle, gray, M..............$6.00

Ideal, Knights, mounted, M, ea..............$10.00

Ideal, Knights, yel soft plastic, 12-pc set, M..............$80.00

Ideal, Knights on foot, red or yel, ea..............$6.00

Ideal, Mitchell Bomber, 1/72 scale, silver, M..............$25.00

Ideal, PT Boat #19, 60mm, silver & red, M..............$25.00

Ideal, War of 1812, soldier, M, ea..............$5.00

Ideal, WWII, 54mm, GIs, M, ea..............$5.00

Ideal, WWII, 60mm, GIs, vinyl, M, ea..............$5.00

Ideal, WWII, 60mm, Sailors, vinyl, M, ea..............$10.00

Kinderegg, Samurai, 54mm, warrior, M..............$15.00

Lido, Annapolis Cadets, 22-pc set, MOC..............$80.00

Lido, Foreign Legion & Arabs, camel, M..............$4.00

Lido, Foreign Legion & Arabs, M, ea..............$2.00

Lido, Knights, mounted, M, ea..............$5.00

Lido, Spirit of '76, 11-pc, MOC..............$40.00

Lido, West Point Academy, 22-pc set, MOC..............$80.00

Lido, WWII, Germans, M, ea..............$1.00

Lido, WWII, GIs, olive drab, M, ea..............$1.25

Lone Star, WWII, British Red Devil, M..............$12.00

Lone Star, WWII, German w/grenade, gray, M..............$3.50

Marx, Air Force, 35mm, M, ea..............$1.00

Marx, Air Force, 45mm, metallic, M, ea..............$1.00

Marx, American Revolution, HO scale, Paul Revere w/horse, M..............$15.00

Marx, American Revolution, 60mm, General George Washington, pnt, NM..............$10.00

Marx, Army, 45mm, GIs, M, ea..............$.50

Marx, Captain Gallant of the Foreign Legion, 22-pc set, MIP..............$175.00

Marx, Civil War, Confederate; 54mm, flagbearer, M.......$22.00

Marx, Civil War, Confederate; 54mm, foot soldier, M, ea .$1.50

Marx, Civil War, Confederate; 54mm, sentinel, M..............$5.00

Marx, Civil War, Confederate; 54mm, soldier firing, M.....$4.00

Marx, Civil War, Confederate; 60mm, soldier firing, M...$25.00

Marx, Civil War, Union; 54mm, flagbearer, M..............$6.00

Marx, Civil War, Union; 54mm, mounted soldier, M......$10.00

Marx, Civil War, Union; 54mm, soldier firing, M..............$4.00

Marx, Civil War Leaders, 54mm, Abraham Lincoln, General Grant or General Lee, cream, M, ea..............$9.00

Marx, Civil War Leaders, 54mm, General Grant, soft plastic, sq base, M..............$24.00

Marx, Civil War Leaders, 54mm, Jefferson Davis, M..........$8.00

Marx, Foreign Legion & Arabs, 60mm, Legionnaire, bl, M, ea..$9.00

Marx, Foreign Legion & Arabs, 60mm, Legionnaire, silver, M, ea..............$5.00

Marx, Gallant Men, 54mm, Captain Benedict, dk gr, M..$25.00

Marx, Gallant Men, 54mm, Captain Benedict, lt drab olive, M..............$20.00

Marx, Gallant Men, 54mm, Lt Kimbro, lt olive drab, M..$20.00

Marx, Gallant Men, 54mm, Private D'Angelo, dk gr, M..$25.00

Marx, Gallant Men, 54mm, Sergeant McKenna, dk gr, M.$25.00

Marx, Knights, 54mm, horse, M..............$2.00

Marx, Knights, 6", w/shield, EX, J5..............$15.00

Marx, Knights, 60mm, horse, M..............$20.00

Marx, Knights, 60mm, mounted, w/separate lance, silver, M .$20.00

Marx, Knights, 60mm, mounted on running horse, cream, M..$18.00

Marx, Mexican War, 60mm, advancing w/rifle, metallic bl, M..............$20.00

Marx, Mexican War, 60mm, standing & shooting rifle, metallic bl, M..............$15.00

Marx, Revolutionary War, Colonial, M..............$3.00

Marx, Revolutionary War, rose, 17-pc set, MIB..............$75.00

Marx, Robin Hood, 60mm, Merryman, M..............$6.00

Marx, Romans, 6", Marius, MIB..............$10.00

Marx, Vikings, 6", Ericson, MIB..............$10.00

Marx, Vikings, 6", Gustaf, MIB..............$10.00

Marx, Vikings, 6", Olaf, MIB..............$10.00

Marx, Warriors of the World, 60mm, Bjorni, M..............$10.00

Marx, Warriors of the World, 60mm, Egyptian archer, pnt hard plastic, M $150.00

Marx, Warriors of the World, 60mm, Laelius, M $9.00

Marx, Warriors of the World, 60mm, Peter Mayers, M $6.00

Marx, Warriors of the World, 60mm, Revolutionary War Colonist, M $6.00

Marx, Warriors of the World, 60mm, Romans, M, ea $13.00

Marx, Warriors of the World, 60mm, Romans, soft plastic, M, ea...$50.00

Marx, Warriors of the World, 60mm, Tiberius, M $9.00

Marx, Warriors of the World, 60mm, US Combat Soldiers, Charley Hamilton or Hank Myers, MIB, ea...............$12.00

Marx, Warriors of the World, 60mm, Vikings, w/spear down, silver soft plastic, M...$75.00

Marx, Warriors of the World, 60mm, Vikings, 8-pc set, MIB..$36.00

Marx, Warriors of the World, 60mm, Yank, hard plastic, M, ea...$6.00

Marx, West Point Cadets, 54mm, guard, rifle on ground, wht, M $9.00

Marx, West Point Cadets, 54mm, marching, dress uniform, wht, M $8.00

Marx, West Point Cadets, 54mm, marching in overcoat, wht, M $8.00

Marx, West Point Cadets, 60mm, cadet parade rest, gray, M...$15.00

Marx, West Point Cadets, 60mm, marching in overcoat, gray, M...$12.00

Marx, West Point Cadets, 60mm, officer w/sword, gray, M ...$15.00

Marx, WWI, 60mm, US marching doughboy, M $15.00

Marx, WWII, Army Air Corp; 54mm, 11-pc set w/2 jets, gray, MIP $30.00

Marx, WWII, British; 6", soldier w/grenade & rifle, pnt, 1963, NM...$20.00

Marx, WWII, British; 6", soldier w/mine detector, NM ...$25.00

Marx, WWII, British; 6", soldier w/rifle, NM $25.00

Marx, WWII, French; 54mm, foot soldier, M $8.00

Marx, WWII, Gallant Men; 54mm, Lt Kimbro, olive drab, M...$25.00

Marx, WWII, German; 6", infantryman w/raised rifle, pnt, NM...$10.00

Marx, WWII, Germans; 54mm, 16-pc set, dk gray, MIP ..$22.00

Marx, WWII, GIs; 54mm, 2nd series, dk olive drab, 22-pc set, M...$65.00

Marx, WWII, GIs; 54mm, 2nd series poses, 12 poses w/stretcher, dk olive drab, 16-pc set, M $50.00

Marx, WWII, GIs; 6", seated MP, wht, M.......................$10.00

Marx, WWII, GIs; 60mm, band members w/clarinet, cymbals or tuba, vinyl, M, ea...$15.00

Marx, WWII, GIs; 60mm, chaplin w/Bible, M..................$9.00

Marx, WWII, GIs; 60mm, nurse w/plasma bottle, M.........$9.00

Marx, WWII, GIs; 60mm, soldier w/wounded man on shoulder, M...$8.00

Marx, WWII, GIs; 60mm, w/mine detector, M $10.00

Marx, WWII, Japanese; 54mm, khaki, M..........................$2.00

Marx, WWII, Japanese; 54mm, khaki, 12-pc set, MIP $40.00

Marx, WWII, Japanese; 54mm, officer w/sword, pnt, NM..$15.00

Marx, WWII, Japanese; 6", lt orange, 1963, 6-pc set, NM...$38.00

Marx, WWII, Marines; 54mm, dk gr, M, ea $3.00

Marx, WWII, Russians; 6", lt olive, 6-pc set, M.............$55.00

Marx, WWII Leaders, 60mm, General MacArthur, ivory, M..$12.00

Marx, WWII Leaders, 60mm, General Patton, ivory, M $9.00

Marx, WWII Leaders, 60mm, General Patton, soft plastic, sq base, M $12.00

Marx, WWII Leaders, 60mm, General Snyder, wht hard plastic, M $12.00

MPC, Cowboys & Indians, MPC, MIP, ea......................$15.00

MPC, Soldiers of the World, 54mm, Germans, complete set, MIP $95.00

MPC, Wild West Target Shoot, M (NM box)................$27.00

MPC, WWII, 54mm, Russians, 8-pc set, MIP.................$12.00

Plasticraft, WWII, GIs; 60mm, M, ea............................$3.00

Plasticraft, WWII, GIs; 60mm, 7-pc set, MIP $10.00

Preiser, Roman, 70mm, pnt, MIB.................................$10.00

Premier, WWII, GIs, 12-pc set, MIB.............................$12.00

Pyro, Army Attack Launch, olive drab, M.....................$12.00

Remco, WWI, British officer, M....................................$7.00

Starlux, Napoleonic, French; 65mm, foot soldier, M........$15.00

Starlux, Napoleonic, Prussian; 65mm, foot soldier, M......$15.00

Starlux, Napoleonic, Russian; 65mm, soldier, mounted, M..$20.00

Thomas, Army Tow Truck, drab olive, M $10.00

Tim-Mee, Civil War, Union officer, M...........................$15.00

Tim-Mee, kneeling soldier with large weapon, 4½", M, $4.00.

Tim-Mee, Knights, mounted, w/lance, M $12.00

Tim-Mee, WWII, armored car, swivel turret & blk rubber tires, 1950s, M...$28.00

Tim-Mee, WWII, GIs; 60mm, 12-pc set, MIP $8.00

Tim-Mee, WWII, troop truck w/removable cover, M.........$8.00

Timpo, Arabs, camel, M $30.00

Timpo, Arabs, horse, M...$20.00

Timpo, Arabs, mounted, M, ea....................................$25.00

Timpo, Arabs, on foot, M, ea $15.00

Timpo, Knights, mounted w/shield, mc, M, ea $20.00

Timpo, Knights, on foot, M, ea $10.00

Werner, WWII, GIs; 60mm, throwing grenade, M............$4.00

NUTTY MADS

Marx, All-Heart Hogan, pk, 1960s, EX, D9 ....$18.00
Marx, Bullpen Boo-Boo, red, M, from $15 to...................$18.00
Marx, Chief Lost Tee-Pee, pk, 1960s, 50% pnt, EX, D9...$15.00

Marx, Chief Lost Tee-Pee, 1963, green, 6", M, $20.00.

Marx, Dippy the Deep Diver, lt gr or purple, 1960s, EX, D9, ea, from $8 to $12.00
Marx, Donald the Demon, dk gr, EX, O1 ....$25.00
Marx, Donald the Demon, dk red, EX, O1 ....$20.00
Marx, End Zone Eddy, bright florescent orange, 1960s, EX, from $15 to $20.00
Marx, End Zone Eddy, red, T1, from $25 to.....................$35.00
Marx, Gutterball Annie, gr, NM, from $25 to $35.00
Marx, Manny the Reckless Mariner, J2/T1, from $20 to ..$23.00
Marx, Rocko the Champ, NM, J2 ....$23.00

Marx, Roddy the Hotrod, green, M, $30.00.

Marx, Suburban Sidney, NM, J2 ....$23.00
Marx, The Thinker, pk, NM $14.00
Marx, Waldo the Weightlifter, NM, J2/T1, from $20 to ..$23.00

WESTERN AND FRONTIER HEROES

Airfix, US Cavalry, HO scale, 1st series, MIB $20.00
Airfix, Wagon Train, HO scale, 1st series, MIB $30.00
Ajax, Indians, combat pose, MOC, ea $13.00
Auburn, Indians, mounted, rubber, M, ea $7.00
Auburn, Pioneers, M, ea $4.00
Britains, Cowboys & Indians, Apache, standing, M $6.00
Britains, Cowboys & Indians, cowboy, standing, M...........$2.00
Elastolin, Cowboys, 70mm, running w/rifle, M $10.00
Elastolin, stagecoach, M $45.00
Ideal, Famous Frontier Americans, 5", Pat Brady, M $10.00
Ideal, Famous Frontier Americans, 5", Roy Rogers, M $10.00
Ideal, Pioneers, ea..$7.00
Lido, Western Frontier, complete set, MIP $35.00
Marx, Cavalry, 45mm, flagbearer, M................................$10.00
Marx, Cavalry, 45mm, horse, M $7.00
Marx, Cavalry, 54mm, firing, riding or wounded, turq, M, ea..$3.00
Marx, Cavalry, 54mm, wagon driver, cream, M.................$12.00
Marx, Cowboys, 3", drawing pistol, tan, M $7.00
Marx, Cowboys, 60mm, M, ea $5.00
Marx, Famous Frontier Americans, 35mm, Matt Dillon, cream, M...$10.00
Marx, Famous Frontier Americans, 45mm, Davy Crockett, cream soft plastic, no name on base, M.....................$25.00
Marx, Famous Frontier Americans, 5", Dale Evans, seated, cream, M $10.00
Marx, Famous Frontier Americans, 5", Roy Rogers & Trigger, w/pistol, brn, M $10.00
Marx, Famous Frontier Americans, 54mm, Bullet, cream, M..$15.00
Marx, Famous Frontier Americans, 54mm, Cilla, hard plastic, M...$22.00
Marx, Famous Frontier Americans, 54mm, Dale Evans, cream, M...$15.00
Marx, Famous Frontier Americans, 54mm, Flint McCullough (Wagon Train), cream soft plastic, M........................$75.00
Marx, Famous Frontier Americans, 54mm, James Otis, cream, M...$25.00
Marx, Famous Frontier Americans, 54mm, Lone Ranger, mounted w/pistol, cream, M $20.00
Marx, Famous Frontier Americans, 54mm, Mark McCain, cream, M $40.00
Marx, Famous Frontier Americans, 54mm, Pat Brady, cream, M $15.00
Marx, Famous Frontier Americans, 54mm, Roy Rogers, mounted w/pistol, cream, M $18.00
Marx, Famous Frontier Americans, 54mm, Seth Adams (Wagon Train), cream soft plastic, M $75.00
Marx, Famous Frontier Americans, 54mm, Tonto, cream, M..$20.00
Marx, Famous Frontier Americans, 54mm, Wyatt Earp, cream, M...$35.00
Marx, Famous Frontier Americans, 60mm, Bullet, M.......$10.00
Marx, Famous Frontier Americans, 60mm, Dale Evans, cream, M...$12.00

Marx, Famous Frontier Americans, 60mm, General Custer, M..$25.00

Marx, Famous Frontier Americans, 60mm, Lone Ranger, mounted w/pistol, cream, M $24.00

Marx, Famous Frontier Americans, 60mm, Pat Brady, cream, M $12.00

Marx, Famous Frontier Americans, 60mm, Roy Rogers, standing or mounted, cream, M, ea..........................$20.00

Marx, Famous Frontier Americans, 60mm, Sitting Bull, M ..$6.00

Marx, Famous Frontier Americans, 60mm, Tonto, standing, cream, M $20.00

Marx, Frontiersmen, 6", swinging musket, red or tan, M, ea..$8.00

Marx, Indians, 45mm, horse, M..$4.00

Marx, Indians, 60mm, M, ea..$5.00

Marx, Pioneers, 45mm, silver or tan, M, ea.......................$4.50

Marx, Pioneers, 45mm, wounded, M................................$10.00

Marx, Pioneers, 54mm, silver or lt bl, M, ea.....................$3.00

Marx, Pioneers, 60mm, standing & shooting rifle, cream, M..$8.00

Marx, Pioneers, 60mm, woman loading rifle, cream, M ...$10.00

Marx, Ranch Kid, 60mm, M..$25.00

MPC, Cowboys, MIP, ea..$28.00

Plasticraft, Pioneers, M, ea..$6.00

Rel, Indians, mounted, M, ea...$4.00

Rel, Pioneers, mounted, M, ea..$4.00

Stuart, Famous Frontier Americans, Pat Brady, squatting position, M $3.00

Stuart, Indians, mounted, M, ea $3.00

Tim-Mee, Pioneers, mounted, M, ea $5.00

Timpo, Wild West City, Golden Nugget Saloon, MOC ..$38.00

Werner, Cowboys, standing & firing rifle, M $4.00

Plasticville

From the 1940s through the 1960s, Bachmann Brothers produced plastic accessories for train layouts such as buildings, fences, trees, and animals. Buildings often included several smaller pieces — for instance, ladders, railings, windsocks, etc. — everything you could ever need to play out just about any scenario. Beware of reissues.

Advisor: Gary Mosholder, Gary's Trains (G1).

#AD-4 Airport Administration Building, wht sides, bl roof ..$45.00

#AP-1 Airport Hanger, bl roof $25.00

#BB-9 Billboard, gr or wht ....$.50

#BK-1 Bank, gray sides, gr roof $30.00

#BL-2 Bridge & Pond..$8.00

#BN-1 Barn, red sides, wht roof..$12.00

#BR-2 Trestle Bridge $18.00

#BY-4 Barn Yard Animals $12.00

#C-18 Cathedral, wht sides, dk gray roof $25.00

#CC-7 Church, wht sides, gray roof $12.00

#CC-8 Country Church, wht sides, gray roof, lg door $12.00

#CC-9 Church, wht sides, lt gray roof................................$15.00

#CS-5 Chain Store/5 & 10¢..$18.00

#DE-7 Diner, gray sides, red roof $18.00

#DH-2 Hardware/Pharmacy $18.00

#FB-1 Frosty Bar, yel sides, wht roof................................$15.00

#FH-4 Fire House, wht sides, red roof $15.00

#FP-5 Flag Pole...$3.00

#FR-5 Fireplace, gray..$3.00

#GO-2 Gas Station (sm), wht sides, red roof, wht insert..$15.00

#GO-3 Gas Station (lg), w/Plasticville logo & pumps......$25.00

#HP-8 Cape Cod House, wht sides, red roof & trim $9.00

#HS-6 Hospital, no furniture..$18.00

#HS-6 Hospital, w/furniture...$25.00

#LC-2 Log Cabin, w/fence..$15.00

#LH-4 Two-Story Colonial House, wht sides, gr roof & trim ...$18.00

#LM-3 Station Platform..$8.00

#LP-9 Lamppost..$.50

#MH-2 New England Ranch House, tan sides, brn roof...$18.00

#ON-5 Outdoor Necessities..$15.00

#PB-5 Footbridge...$7.00

#PD-3 Police Station, dk gray..$25.00

#PD-3 Police Station, lt gray..$20.00

#PF-4 Citizens, w/pnts...$15.00

#PH-1 Town Hall, tan sides, red roof.................................$25.00

#PO-1 Post Office, gray front & roof..................................$18.00

#RH-1 Ranch House, wht sides, bl roof & trim.................$12.00

#RS-7 Suburban Station, gr roof & trim, brn platform.......$8.00

#SA-7 Outhouse, red sides, wht roof...................................$4.00

#SC-4 School, red sides, gray roof.....................................$15.00

#SG-2 Signal Bridge, blk..$8.00

#SL-1 Boulevard Light...$1.00

#SM-6 Super Market (sm)..$15.00

#SW-2 Switch Tower, brn sides, gray roof...........................$6.00

#WG-2 Crossing Gate, blk & wht..$.50

#WW-3 Wishing Well, brn..$3.00

#YW-4 Yard Pump, brn...$3.00

#0012-A Railroad & Street Signs...$8.00

#1090 Telephone Booth, wht sides, bl roof......................$10.00

#1302 Farm Implement Set, yel vehicles w/red trim........$30.00

#1304 Crossing Signal $10.00

#1305 Block Signal..$10.00

#1406 Playground Equipment, yel accessories & pool $25.00

#1407 Watchman Shanty, brn sides, gray roof..................$11.00

#1408 Windmill, lt gray..$40.00

#1503 Add-A-Floor $30.00

#1504 Mobile Home, wht sides, turq roof & trim.............$55.00

#1615 Water Tower, gray sides, brn roof............................$10.00

#1617 Farm Buildings & Animals $25.00

#1618 TV Station, wht sides, red roof & antenna $35.00

#1620 Loading Platform, brn shack, gray roof & platform..$8.00

#1621 Motel, w/3 autos, paper flowers $18.00

#1622 Dairy Barn, wht sides, red roof...............................$15.00

#1623 Cattle Loading Pen $45.00

#1624 House, under construction, lt gray..........................$45.00

#1625 Railroad Work Car...$15.00

#1626 Corner Store $45.00

#1627 Hobo Shack, gray sides, brn roof $135.00

#1629 Bungalow, wht sides, gr roof $28.00

#1703 Colonial Mansion, wht sides, red roof....................$25.00

#1803 Colonial Church $20.00

#1804 Greenhouse, w/flowers...$60.00

#1805 Covered Bridge..$18.00

#1806 Roadside Stand, w/pnt $30.00
#1853 Drug Store $25.00
#1900 Turnpike..$45.00
#1901 Union Station..$25.00
#1906 Factory, tan sides, gray roof..............................$35.00
#1907 Apartment House $65.00
#1908 Split-Level House, cream windows & trim $18.00
#1918 Park Assortment $15.00
#1957 Coaling Station..$35.00

Playsets

Louis Marx is given credit for developing the modern-age playset, and during the fifties and sixties produced hundreds of boxed sets, each with the buildings, figures and accessories that when combined with a child's imagination could bring any scenario alive, from the days of Ben Hur to medieval battles, through the cowboy and Indian era, and on up to Cape Canaveral. Marx's prices were kept low by mass marketing (through retail giants such as Sears and Montgomery Wards) and overseas production. But on today's market, playsets are anything but low-priced; some mint-in-box examples sell for upwards of $1,000.00. Just remember that a set that shows wear or has even a few minor pieces missing quickly drops in value.

Advisors: Mike and Kurt Fredericks (F4).

Air War, Marx, 1991, MIB, D4 ....$60.00
Alamo #3534, tin fort, 36 54mm Mexicans w/30 Texans,
    95% complete, photocopy instructions, 1961, EX+
    (VG box) $450.00
Alamo #3534, Marx, MIB $600.00
Alaska Frontier #3708, complete, unassembled, M (NM+
    box) $900.00
Army & Air Force Training Center #4158, Marx, MIB.$100.00
Army Combat Set #6017, complete, orig bags, orig instructions,
    NM (EX+ Sears Allstate box)..................................$375.00
Babes in Toyland, Disneykins Playset, Marx, 1961, M (EX box),
    M8 ....$95.00
Battle Action Mined Bridge, Ideal, complete, photocopy instruc-
    tions o/w MIB $65.00
Battle Action Sniper Post, Ideal, w/extra pcs, NM, J2 ..$185.00
Battle Front Playset, Multiple, 1960s, w/many figures & vehicles,
    EX (orig box), J5 ....$65.00
Battle of Navarone, 1992, 64 2" men w/4 tanks, MIB, S2...$30.00
Battle of the Blue & Gray, Marx #4745, 1959, MIB......$625.00
Battlefield, Timpo, NMIB $130.00
Battleground World War II Playset, missing pcs (orig box),
    H4..$90.00
Ben Hur Series 5000, Marx, 98% complete, NM (EX box),
    P3..$1,450.00
Big Inch Pipe Line, 95% complete, for 54mm figures, NMIB..$295.00
Blue & Gray Centennial #5929, Marx, MIB....................$85.00
Blue & Gray Civil War, Marx, miniature set, NM (NM
    box)..$275.00
Cape Canaveral #4526, Marx, assembled, few sm pc missing o/w
    EX (EX box) $200.00

Cape Canaveral #4526, Marx, scarce, missing saucer launcher,
    NM (EX box)..$300.00
Cape Canaveral #4535, Marx, orig instructions, NMIB.$170.00
Cape Kennedy #4625, Marx, 1968, litho tin carrying case, miss-
    ing 1 figure, EX+..$115.00
Captain Blood, Marx, 1991, MIB, D4 ....$60.00
Captain Space Solar Academy #7026, Marx, complete, NM (EX
    box)..$600.00
Chimp's Tea Party #4375, Britains, M (G box)..............$150.00
Civil War Centennial #5929, EX+ (VG+ box)..............$380.00
Coast Defense, Marx, 1925, military plane, cannons & soldiers
    on rnd base w/actions, 9" dia, no backdrop, NM (VG box),
    A..$1,550.00
Crop Duster Plane Set #0796, Marx, MIB $115.00
Daktari #5991, Marx, MIB $65.00
Daniel Boone Wilderness Scout #2640, NM (NM box)...$280.00
Davy Crockett Alamo #3544, Marx, NMIB $600.00
Desert Fort, Timpo, 85% complete, EX (orig box)........$130.00
Disney on Parade, Marx, miniature set, complete, MIB
    (sealed)..$450.00
Disneykin Play Set, EX (VG box w/circus background), M5...$76.00
Disneyland #5995, 98% complete, NM (NM box)........$625.00
Dragon Quest Castle, MPC, complete w/figures & accessories
    except sm pcs of castle, 85% complete, EX+ (orig box).$60.00
Early American Frontier Set, Auburn, ca 1958, complete w/figures,
    wild animals, horses, wagons, etc, unused, MIB, A......$95.00
Early American Transportation, Northwestern, 1950s, 10" tin
    wagons & horses w/cb cowboys & Indians, NM (VG+ box),
    A..$178.00
Farm #119, Built Rite, 52-pc, M (M box) $135.00
Farm Set #5942, Marx, NMIB....................................$45.00
Fire Chief, Topper, complete, NM (EX box) $80.00
Fire House, Arcade, 1941, red & wht, mk Engine Co No 99, com-
    plete w/CI ladder & pumper truck, 12½", EX, A ...$1,100.00
Fireball XL-5, MPC, scarce, NM................................$400.00
Foreign Legion, Lido, 1950s, plastic desert fort scene & figures,
    complete, unused, NM (EX box), A $45.00
Fort #16, Built Rite, M (M box)..................................$70.00

Fort Apache Set, Series 500, Marx, MIB, O1, $325.00.

Fort Apache, Marx, 1960s-70s, pnt figures, miniature sz, EX,
    J5 ....$25.00
Fort Apache, Marx, 1991, MIB, D4 ....$60.00
Fort Apache, Mego, M (EX box)..................................$60.00

Fort Apache #3681, Marx, unused, missing pc from barrel of cannon o/w MIB, H4...................$140.00

Fort Apache #4685, Marx, missing a few pcs & figures, VG (in tin case), H4 ....$60.00

Fort Apache Series 2000, Marx, complete w/60 54mm figures & accessories, NM (VG+ box)...................$245.00

Fort Apache Stockade #3612, Marx, 6 pioneers & 12 Indians, complete, NM (VG box)...................$200.00

Fort Apache Stockade #3616, Marx, 12 metallic bl 60mm cavalry & 2 Indians, complete, orig instructions, NM (VG box)..$350.00

Fort Apache Stockade #3678 Series 1000, Marx, complete w/accessories, 1958, M (EX+ box) $250.00

Fort Dearborn #3510, Marx, NMIB $300.00

Freedom Fighters, Lido, 1950s, plastic battle scene & figures, complete, EX+ (EX box), A $45.00

Futurematic Airport, Automatic Toy, 1950, tin base w/tower & station, controls work plane on rod, 15", NM (EX box), A...$300.00

Giant Martian Landing #4306, Marx, NMIB $30.00

Gunsmoke, Multiple, 1960s, complete, NM (EX box)...$225.00

Hamburger Hill Vietnam War #P-511, ESCI, 1980s, HO scale, MIB $25.00

Happytime Fort Apache #5962, Sears, NMIB $450.00

Heritage Alamo, Marx/Sears, NMIB...................$135.00

Heritage Fort Apache, Marx, buildings, cannon, cavalry & Indians, few sm pcs missing o/w NM (VG+ box)...........$120.00

Indian Village, AHI/Japan, contains 3 of 4 Tru-Size Metal Indian figures, tepee and campfire with utensils, EX (VG box), 45.00.

Knights & Vikings #4733, Marx, NMIB (photo box) $125.00

Medieval Castle Fort, litho tin castle, 20 knights w/6 horses, some sm parts missing, EX+ (EX+ box) $175.00

Model Farm, Crescent Toys/England, 19-pc lead set w/6 animals, 2 workers, other figures & accessories, MIB, A........$260.00

Modern Farm #3934, Marx, EX (orig box) $200.00

Motorific Alcan Highway Torture Track, Ideal, 1968, complete, EX (EX box), D9...................$49.00

Navarone #4302, Marx, MIB, from $30 to...................$40.00

Prehistoric Dinosaurs, Marx, 1978, MIB $85.00

Prehistoric Playset #3398, Marx, 1971, complete, EX (VG+ box), P3 ....$135.00

Prehistoric Times #3390, Marx, appears complete, EX (orig box), A...................$190.00

Prehistoric Times #3390, Marx, MIB...................$260.00

Revolutionary War Set, Marx, lithographed tin building and walls with plastic figures and accessories, M (EX box), from $375.00 to $575.00.

Richard Green as Robin Hood, Marx, EX+ (orig box)...$750.00

Rin-Tin-Tin #3657, complete w/54 mm figures & accessories, NM (EX box)...................$200.00

Robin Hood, 57 54mm figures w/accessories, complete, NMIB...................$295.00

Roy Rogers Rodeo Ranch #3985, Marx, NMIB.............$200.00

Star Station Seven #4115, Marx, some pcs missing o/w VG (VG box), J2...................$40.00

Steve Zodiac's XL-5 Space City, MPC, complete, M (EX+ box)...................$825.00

Superior Airport, 54mm figures, previously assembled, complete, no box, NM $175.00

Tom Corbett #7010, complete, some orig bags, photocopy instructions, NM (EX box), from $350 to...............$500.00

Tom Corbett #7012, Marx, NMIB...................$400.00

Untouchables, Marx, litho buildings, 17 figures, orig instructions, NM (NM box)...................$950.00

US Air Force, Marx, EX+..............................$120.00
US Army Training Center Playset, VG (orig box), H4....$95.00
US Naval Base #888, T Cohn Superior Toys, features revolving crane, scarce, missing torpedo, NM (EX box) $320.00
Wagon Train Covered Wagon Set, Marx, 1950s, w/wagon & cover, 2 horses, extra wheel, bucket & driver, VG (VG box), J5...$65.00
Walt Disney's Alamo #3540, Marx, lg set w/5 cannons, complete, NMIB...$685.00
Walt Disney's Davy Crockett at the Alamo #3530, Marx, sm set w/2 cannons, NM (VG box) $275.00
Walt Disney's Zorro #3758, Marx, complete except for cave & 5 shells for cannon, photocopy instructions, EX+ (VG+ box) $500.00
Western Town #4229, Marx, MIB.............................$350.00
White House, Marx, EX (orig box)..........................$100.00
WWII Ghurkas, Airfix, MIB....................................$25.00
7th Cavalry, Airfix, 29-pc set, MIB.......................$50.00

Political

As far back as the 19th century, children's toys with a political message were on the market. One of the most familiar was the Tammany Bank patented by J. & E. Stevens in 1873. The message was obvious — a coin placed in the man's hand was deposited in his pocket, representing the kickbacks William Tweed was suspected of pocketing when he was the head of Tammany Hall in New York during the 1860s.

Bush, George; squeeze doll, Santa w/Bush's face, rubber, EX, M11...$18.00
Carter, Amy; Amy Peanut, baby in peanut shell case, 3", MOC, H4...$12.00
Carter, Jimmy; walking peanut, w/up, EX, M11.............$28.00
Cleveland/Harrison, wooden block game, VG, M11......$240.00
Eisenhower, Dwight D; doll, Effanbee, 1987, from Presidents series, 16", M...$50.00
Eisenhower, Dwight D; Presidential Campaign Car, Lionel, 12", EX, M11..$150.00
Eisenhower, Dwight D; walking elephant, plush, battery-op, EX, M11...$125.00
Goldwater, Barry; doll, plastic, 5", MIB, M11...............$30.00
Harrison/Blaine Administration, puzzle, 4", VG, M11 ...$125.00
Hoover vs FD Roosevelt, puzzle, EX (orig box), M11.......$45.00
Johnson, Lyndon B; doll, Remco, plastic, 5", MIB, M11 ..$30.00
Johnson, Lyndon B; doll, Remco, 1964, 16", NM.............$35.00
Johnson, Lyndon B; flasher ring, Vari-Vue, LBJ for the USA, M...$12.50
Johnson, Lyndon B; Great Society Comic Book, 10", VG, M11...$20.00
Kennedy, John F, New Frontier, board game, NM, M11 ..$40.00
Kennedy, John F & Jackie; nodders, kissing, compo, 4", EX, M11...$200.00
Kennedy, John F; charm bracelet, 1963, MOC.................$50.00
Kennedy, John F; coloring book, Kanrom, 1962, caricature drawing by Mad artist Mort Drucker, unused, NM............$30.00

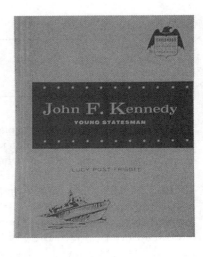

JFK, book, John F Kennedy, Young Statesman, Childhood of Famous Americans Series, Bobbs Merrill, 1964, EX, $6.00.

Kennedy, John F; flasher ring, Vari-Vue, 1960s, NM $18.00
Kennedy, John F; JFK in Rocking Chair, Kamar, 1963, vinyl & cloth figure in wood chair reading, w/up, 11", M (EX box), A...$390.00
Kennedy, John F; playing cards, Arco, 1963, box w/illus of Kennedy friends & famous people, NM.............................$22.00
Kennedy, John F; PT-109 boat, Japan, tin, 8½", EX, M11 ..$85.00
King, Martin Luther; flicker rings, 2 different, H4............$12.00
MacArthur, General Douglas; figure, compo, 5", EX, J5...$35.00
McGovern, George; top, plastic, McGovern Is Tops for America, EX, M1...$18.00
McKinley/Hobart, top, wood w/photos on paper label, G, M11...$175.00
Nixon, Richard; bubble gum cigars, 1960s, 24-pc, MIB (Win w/Dick slogan on box)..$50.00
Nixon, Richard; dart board, Stick Dick, 11½" sq, NM, M11 ..$25.00
Nixon, Richard; doll, Tricky Dick, rubber, 5", MOC, M11 ..$20.00
Nixon/Mao Tse-Tung, ping-pong paddles, MIP $35.00
Presidential Pencil Set, Pencil-Crafts, 1964, 35 illus pencils, 8x10" color photos of JFK, LBJ, etc, unused, EX+ $30.00
Reagan, Ronald; voodoo doll, MIP, M11 ....$25.00
Reagan Family, paper dolls, cut-out book, NM, M11 ....$10.00
Roosevelt, Franklin D; bank, Happy Days, barrel shape, 5", EX, M11...$15.00

Uncle Sam, balancing toy, jointed figure balances and pedals bike, new balance wire on wood base, 8¼" long, replaced weight, surface rust and scratches otherwise VG, A, $230.00.

Wilson, Woodrow; puzzle, diecut profile, w/envelope, VG, M11 ....$70.00

Premiums

Those of us from the pre-boomer era remember waiting in anticipation for our silver bullet ring, secret membership kit, decoder pin, coloring book, or whatever other wonderful item we'd seen advertised in our favorite comic book or heard about on the Tom Mix show. Tom wasn't the only one to have these exciting premiums, though, just about any top character-oriented show from the 1930s through the 1940s made similar offers, and even through the 1950s some were still being distributed. Often they could be had free for a cereal boxtop or an Ovaltine inner seal, and if any money was involved, it was usually only a dime. Not especially durable and often made in somewhat limited amounts, few have survived to the present. Today some of these are bringing fantastic prices, but the market at present is very volatile.

Advisor: Bill Campbell (C10).

Don Winslow, Secret Code Book, complete with magic slate and pencil, scarce, EX, $75.00.

Amos 'n Andy, Weber City map, Pepsodent, 1935, w/mailer picturing Amos & Andy, M, A $75.00
Buck Jones, ring, 1930s, C10 ....$75.00
Buck Rogers, book, Buck Rogers in the 25th Century, 1933, color illus, 32 pgs, EX+, A..$254.00
Buck Rogers, paper gun, 1930s, VG, J5 ....$35.00
Buck Rogers, rubber-band gun, Dille, 1940, gun lithoed on heavy paper to punch out, w/3 targets, unpunched, NM+, A .$135.00
Buck Rogers & Wilma Deering, photo, Cocomalt Cereal, 1934, Buck & Wilma in space gear w/spaceships zooming by, fr, NM, A $191.00
Buck Rogers/Tarzan, ice-cream cup lid book, C10 ....$125.00
Buffalo Bill, badge, Post Raisin Bran, J2 ....$20.00
Buffalo Bob, carrying case, Kagran, 1953, Welch's Grape Juice Doodyville series, cb, 5", EX+, A $234.00
Capt Franks, ring, Air Hawks, NM, C10.............................$75.00
Capt Marvel, Billy's Big Game giveaway, Double-Bubble gum, C10..$80.00
Capt Marvel, magic whistle, C10 ....$95.00
Capt Marvel, membership kit, 1941-42, C10 ....$300.00

Capt Marvel, paint book, C10...$75.00
Capt Marvel, photo, C10...$75.00
Capt Marvel, photo, glow-in-the-dark, C10 ....$115.00
Capt Marvel, tattoo transfers, Comic Hero, in envelope, C10 ....$180.00
Capt Marvel, tie clip, EX (on card), from $110 to..........$125.00
Capt Marvel & Mary Marvel, toss bags, C10, ea $27.00
Capt Marvel Jr, photo, glow-in-the-dark, C10.................$75.00
Capt Midnight, book, Trick & Riddle, VG $30.00
Capt Midnight, decoder, Silver Dart SQ, 1957, C10 .....$285.00
Capt Midnight, decoder, 1942, orig photo, C10............$130.00
Capt Midnight, decoder, 1946, EX, from $85 to..............$95.00
Capt Midnight, decoder, 1947, C10.................................$48.00
Capt Midnight, decoder, 1948, EX, C10..........................$150.00
Capt Midnight, decoder, 1955, C10.................................$140.00
Capt Midnight, game, Ringo-Jumpo Target Sheet, C10.....$4.00
Capt Midnight, manual, 1948, EX+, C10, from $130 to ..$140.00
Capt Midnight, manual & membership card, 1940, VG+, J2 ....$150.00
Capt Midnight, map, Flight Control Airline Services, NM, C10 ....$600.00
Capt Midnight, medallion, C10 ....$12.00
Capt Midnight, membership card, 1957, M, C10 ....$95.00
Capt Midnight, patch, Member, C10................................$145.00
Capt Midnight, patch, SQ, C10..$43.00
Capt Midnight, patch, w/letter, 1983, M (orig mailer), C10 ....$115.00
Capt Midnight, photo, Chuck Ramsey, C10......................$7.50
Capt Midnight, ring, Aztec, C10 ....$430.00
Capt Midnight, ring, Flight Commander, C10...............$245.00
Capt Midnight, ring, Mystic Sun God, NM, C10 ....$1,125.00
Capt Midnight, ring, Mystic Sun God, w/letter & instructions, M (orig mailer), C10...$2,400.00
Capt Midnight, ring, w/print top, C10............................$300.00
Capt Midnight, ring, w/secret compartment, C10..........$105.00
Capt Midnight, ring, Whirlwind Whistle, C10 ....$300.00
Capt Midnight, stamp album, w/unused stamps, C10......$48.00
Capt Midnight, wings, Mysto-Magic Weather, NM, J2....$35.00
Capt Midnight, wristwatch, Anniversary, M, C10 ....$28.00
Capt Video, ring, Secret Seal, rare, EX (EX box), A $350.00
Charlie McCarthy, Radio Party punch-out figures, 1938 Chase & Sanborn, cb, complete & unpunched, J5 ....$25.00
Cisco Kid, club membership card, 1950s, VG $25.00
Cisco Kid, paper gun, EX+, J2 ....$45.00
Daisy, handbook #2, C10..$75.00
Daniel Boone, patch, Trail Blazers' Club, D8 ....$18.00
Dick Darling, manual, New Bag of Tricks, 1934, VG+, J2..$25.00
Dick Tracy, badge, Girl's Division, EX, J2 ....$48.00
Dick Tracy, badge, Secret Service Patrol Lieutenant, 1938, 5-point star on rnd back, silver finish, G+, A $41.00
Dick Tracy, badge, Secret Service Patrol Sergeant, 1938, 5-point star over 3 bars, brass, 2¾", EX, A............................$56.00
Dick Tracy, comic book, Puffed Wheat giveaway, 1940s, NM, J5 ....$15.00
Dick Tracy, Crime Stopper Club Kit, John Henry Products, 1950s, w/handcuffs & badge, M (VG pkg), J5 ....$35.00
Dick Tracy, Crime Stopper Club Kit, 1961, mail-in offer, w/wallet, badge, flashlight, whistle, decoder, photo, etc, M, T2 ..$79.00

Dick Tracy, ring, Secret Service Patrol, features Tracy & Jr, scarce, NM, A...$55.00

Dick Tracy, tunic, mask & comic book w/Motorola brochure, 1953, unused, NM (NM envelope), A......................$47.00

Fireball Twin, ring, Explorers, NM.............................$75.00

Flash Gordon, pamphlet, World Battle Front, Macy's, 1943, fold-out map showing war theaters, EX, A.................$81.00

Gabby Hayes, Cannon ring, Quaker, 1951, brass or silver-tone base pictures Quaker man on one side and cereal being shot from cannon on the other, spring-loaded plunger intact, EX, $210.00.

G-Man, badge, Melvin Pervis Secret Operator, EX, J2.....$35.00

G-Man, fingerprint set, General Foods, 1936, complete & unused, NM (orig envelope), A $159.00

G-Man, Pursuit Rocket Ship, 1930s, orange, yel & bl 2-wheeled w/up vehicle, EX, A...$110.00

Gabby Hayes, Cannon ring, Quaker, 1951, brass tone, MIB, J2..$300.00

Gene Autry, face ring, C10 ....$55.00

Gene Autry, horseshoe nail ring, MOC..........................$200.00

Gene Autry, ring, gr plastic w/photo, EX $15.00

Gene Autry, 6-gun paper popper, advertises his TV show, T1..$6.00

General Custer, badge, NM, J2......................................$20.00

Green Hornet, ring, w/secret compartment, C10 ....$825.00

Helen Trent, radio show pin, C10...................................$48.00

Hopalong Cassidy, bank, Savings Club, 1950, bank promo, bronze-colored bust w/removable hat, 4", EX, A $65.00

Hopalong Cassidy, bank, Savings Club, 1950, bank promo, plastic bronze-colored bust w/removable hat, 4", M (VG box), A $132.00

Hopalong Cassidy, ring, face; NM, J2 ....$215.00

Hopalong Cassidy, ring, w/bust of Hoppy surrounded by horseshoe, ca 1950, scarce, NM, A...................................$80.00

Hoppy the Marvel Bunny, photo, glow-in-the-dark, C10 ....$75.00

Howdy Doody, badges, Kagran/Wonder Bread, 1950s, set of 6 featuring Howdy Doody characters, 2¾" dia, NM+, A $90.00

Howdy Doody, fan, Comic Circus Animals, Poll Parrot, 1954, turn hdl & make over 800 comic combinations, scarce, NM, A $160.00

Howdy Doody, ring, flasher; Poll Parrot, EX, J2..............$90.00

Howdy Doody, ring, plastic relief of Howdy's face lights up, Clarabell on brass band, battery-op, EX, A..............$160.00

Jack Armstrong, flashlight, Torpedo, EX $35.00

Jack Armstrong, Shooting Propeller Plane, w/both propellers, EX (orig box), C10..$110.00

Jack Armstrong, telescope, EX, J2 ....$55.00

Jack Armstrong, 3-D viewer, Novelart, ca 1938, w/Jack Armstrong in Africa blk & wht film, 4", NM (EX mailer box), A $205.00

Jimmy Allen, Flying Cadet Wings, EX+, J2 ....$25.00

Jimmy Allen, Official Secret Signal whistle, orig cord, w/secret signal code instruction sheet, NM, C10...................$100.00

Jr G-Man, badge, brass shield w/Junior G Man lettered on eagle shield bordered w/stars, 1½", M, A..........................$80.00

Jr G-Man, Equipment Manual, 2-sided flyer featuring Melvin Purvis & every premium offered, very scarce, NM, A $121.00

Jr G-Man, Instruction Manual, 20 pgs, EX, A $111.00

Little Orphan Annie, see also Radio Orphan Annie

Little Orphan Annie, tunic & mask w/Dick Tracy comic book & Motorola brochure, 1953, unused, NM (NM envelope), A $30.00

Lone Ranger, bracelet, silver-colored aluminum, 1930s, C10..$1,000.00

Lone Ranger, bullet, secret compartment w/compass, most silver finish is worn, J5 ....$20.00

Lone Ranger, bullet, silver plastic, Nestle Quik promo, w/orig papers, 1", cracked, M5...$12.00

Lone Ranger, club kit, Bond Bread, 1939, w/letter, membership card, envelope, badge & badge mailer, EX+, A.......$162.00

Lone Ranger, deputy kit, Cheerios, 1980, NM (in envelope), J2..$55.00

Lone Ranger, key chain, shaped like silver bullet, VG, J2 .$40.00

Lone Ranger, membership card, Merita Bakeries, 1940s, EX, C10..$48.00

Lone Ranger, pedometer, VG+, J2 ....$35.00

Lone Ranger, pin, Silver's Lucky Horseshoe, lg, C10 ....$55.00

Lone Ranger, pin, Silver's Lucky Horseshoe, sm, C10......$45.00

Lone Ranger, premium ad, TLR, 1955, shows all 8 character masks cut from Wheaties box, NM+, A...................$35.00

Lone Ranger, ring, face, C10......................................$250.00

Lone Ranger, ring, Filmstrip Saddle, no film, EX+ $50.00

Lone Ranger, ring, Filmstrip Saddle, w/films, M, C10....$125.00

Lone Ranger, ring, Six-Gun, C10................................$80.00

Lone Ranger, ring, w/flashlight on top, 1950s, gold-tone, NM, C1..$99.00

Lone Ranger, ring, w/secret compartment, no photo, C10..$185.00

Lone Ranger, ring, Weather, w/orig Weather-Detecting paper, C10..$85.00

Lone Ranger, Victory Corps tab, 1942, C10 ....$28.00

Mary Marvel, photo, glow-in-the-dark, C10.....................$75.00

Mary Marvel, pin, fiberboard, EX, C10.........................$185.00

Melvin Purvis, fingerprint set, Official Operator, unused, EX, J2 ....$85.00

Popeye, tunic and mask, complete with Dick Tracy comic book and Motorola brochure, 1954, EX, D10, $150.00.

Radio Orphan Annie, decoder badge, 1939, EX, J2 ....$48.00

Radio Orphan Annie, ring, Mystic Eye Look-Around, NM $125.00

Radio Orphan Annie, ring, w/bust of Annie, C10............$22.00

Radio Orphan Annie, Secret Society Code Book, 1935, EX (original mailer), $60.00.

Radio Orphan Annie, watch, Sundial, complete w/instructions, orig mailer, C10....................................$115.00

Rin-Tin-Tin, ring, w/Sgt Biff O'Hara, bl plastic, NM, C1 ..$24.00

Robin Hood, badge, 1950s, metal w/red jewel, EX, J5 ......$25.00

Roy Rogers, badge, Raisin Bran premium, 1950s, M (sealed), J5 ....$15.00

Roy Rogers, badge, w/whistle & secret compartment, C10..$45.00

Roy Rogers, ring, Branding Iron, w/cap, C10.................$175.00

Shadow, ink blotter, Blue Coal, NM, C10......................$30.00

Shadow, ring, Blue Coal, 1941, EX, A $402.00

Shadow, ring, Blue Coal, 1941, G, C10.........................$125.00

Shadow, ring, Blue Coal, 1941, NM, A $491.00

Sky King, Detecto-Scope, instructions, C10...................$130.00

Sky King, ring, Aztec, NM, C10 ....$625.00

Sky King, ring, Navajo Treasure, EX, C10.....................$150.00

Sky King, ring, Navajo Treasure, M, J2.........................$225.00

Sky King, ring, Radar, w/instructions, C10....................$150.00

Sky King, ring, TV, all 4 pictures, EX, C10 ....$190.00

Sky King, signal scope, complete w/whistle, magnifying glass, instructions & mailer, C10...............................$150.00

Space Patrol, belt & buckle, EX, C10 ....$190.00

Space Patrol, binoculars, Ralston Purina, 1950s, plastic rocket shape w/Space Patrol emb between lenses, NM (NM box), A $195.00

Space Patrol, cards, Ralston, set of 8, minor creasing o/w VG, J5 ....$45.00

Space Patrol, handbook, Ralston, features ad & premium offers w/information for Space Patrol members only, EX, J5 ..$45.00

Straight Arrow, card #21, NM, J2 ....$20.00

Straight Arrow, neckerchief, EX+, J2............................$75.00

Straight Arrow, ring, w/face, EX, C10...........................$63.00

Superman, Krypton Rockets, Kellogg's, 1950, 1 red & 1 bl plastic rocket w/launcher, M (G mailer), A..................$210.00

Superman, ring, Crusaders, silvered brass w/lg image of Superman in relief, slogan on band, NM, A $209.00

Superman, ring, Pep Airplane, Kellogg's, C10................$150.00

Ted Williams, ring, Nabisco, 1948, brass bands w/name, bat & ball designs, wht plastic figure on top, EX+, A........$420.00

Tom Mix, badge, Deputy Sheriff of Dobie County Siren, C10...$45.00

Tom Mix, badge, emb Ralston Straight Shooter on silver-tone metal, NM...$65.00

Tom Mix, badge, Wrangler, C10...................................$85.00

Tom Mix, jigsaw puzzle, Rexall, 1920s, shows Tom on horse, NM (EX advertising mailer), A $138.00

Tom Mix, mini comic, 1983, C10 ....$4.50

Tom Mix, premium ad, Ralston Cereal, 1937, depicts death-defying stories promoting his Lucky ring, scarce, EX, A....$60.00

Tom Mix, RCA w/film disc, C10 ....$45.00

Tom Mix, ring, Magnetic, EX, J2 ....$100.00

Tom Mix, ring, Mystery, NM, J2.................................$300.00

Tom Mix, ring, Siren, good lustre, C10...........................$90.00

Tom Mix, ring, Straight Shooters, C10...........................$36.00

Tom Mix, ring, whistle, NM, J2 ....$100.00

Tom Mix, rocket parachute, MIB (unopened), J2 ....$120.00

Tom Mix, rocket parachute, NM (EX box), A $106.00

Tom Mix, signal arrowhead, Lucite, C10.........................$28.00

Tom Mix, storybook, w/mailer, C10...............................$75.00

Tom Mix, telegraph set, Ralston Purina, 1940, litho cb w/metal key attached, NM (VG mailer), A..........................$85.00

Wild Bill Hickok, Treasure Map & Secret Treasure Guide, NM, (NM mailer), J2 ....$200.00

Pressed Steel

Many companies were involved in the manufacture of pressed steel automotive toys which were often faithfully modeled after actual vehicles in production at the time they were made. Because they were so sturdy, some made as early as the 1920s have survived to the present, and those that are still in good condition are bringing very respectable prices at toy auctions around the country. Some of the better-known manufacturers are listed in other sections.

See also Aeronautical; Buddy L; Keystone; Marx; Pedal Cars and Other Wheeled Goods; Smith-Miller; Structo; Tonka; Wyandotte.

CARS AND BUSSES

Airflow Sedan, Cor-Cor, red 4-door with rubber tires, battery-operated headlights, 17", paint chips otherwise VG, A, $1,400.00.

Airflow Sedan, Kingsbury, bl 4-door w/wht rubber tires, w/up, 14", non-working, G, A $100.00
Airflow Sedan, Kingsbury, red w/battery-op lights, w/up, 14½", G, A $160.00

Bus, Cor-Cor, 1920s, cream with red pinstripe, black tires with red hubs, restored, $250.00.

Graham Sedan, Cor-Cor, bl w/battery-op lights, 19½", VG, A $1,200.00
Inter-City Bus, Steelcraft, 1930s, battery-op lights, 24", EX, S9 ....$495.00
Lincoln, Turner, 1920, 28", G, M5 ....$2,500.00
Roadster, Kingsbury, red & tan w/up w/battery-op lights, 13", VG, A $375.00

Sedan & Travel Trailer, gr w/wood tires, trailer w/opening rear door, 10¾", G+, A $140.00
Sedan & Travel Trailer, Kingsbury, 1930s-style gr 2-door w/2-wheel trailer, w/up, 23½", EX, A $150.00
Sport Roadster, bl w/orange top, 18", G, A $200.00
Town Car, red & blk w/wood wheels, 6", G-, A $40.00

Coupe, Girard, yellow and orange with black tires, windup, 13½", EX, $250.00.

FIREFIGHTING

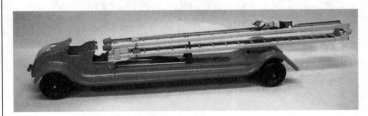

Ladder Truck, Kingsbury, 1930s, red and yellow with lithographed figure on ladder, 18", M, $600.00.

Fire Chief Car, Hoge, red & blk w/battery-op lights, siren, w/up, 13½", VG, A $400.00
Fire Chief Siren Coupe, Girard, red w/NP trim, battery-op, 14", non-working, G, A $140.00
Fire Engine, Kingsbury, red w/silver & gold boiler, w/up, 11½", VG+, A $500.00
Fire Engine, Sturditoy, American-La France, 26", no hoses, G, A $575.00
Fire Pumper, Kingsbury, w/up, 24", no hoses, G, A $900.00

Mack Ladder Truck, Turner, red with black tires, C-style cab, 26", EX, $650.00.

TRUCKS AND VANS

Army Truck, Son-ny, khaki w/canvas cover, division insignia on cab, 27", G, A $320.00

Auto Transport, red cab w/bl trailer loaded w/bl coupe & red roadster, battery-op lights, 21½", G+, A $160.00

Cargo Truck, Marklin, red & gr w/canvas top, battery-op lights, clockwork, 16", NM (EX box), A $650.00

Coal Truck, Sturditoy, orange & blk, 27", VG, A $1,300.00

CW Brand Coffee Delivery Truck, Metalcraft, 1930s, blk cab w/gr enclosed bed, 11", EX, A $250.00

CW Brand Coffee Tow Truck, Metalcraft, 1930s, blk cab & wench w/red truck bed, 11", EX, A $350.00

Dump Truck, red w/non-steering front, blk rubber tires w/red hubs, 19", G+, A $200.00

Dump Truck, Sturditoy, dk gr, blk & red w/open cab, 25", G, A $400.00

Dump Truck, Turner, red with green dump, black tires with red hubs, 26", NM, $850.00.

Express Truck, Sturditoy, gr, blk & red, 26", G, A $775.00

Heinz Pickles Truck, Metalcraft, 1930s, battery-operated lights, 12", EX, from $500.00 to $650.00.

Ice Truck, Marx, red w/Polar Ice ad on side of yel stake bed, w/orig glass ice blocks & tongs, 12", NM (EX box), A $545.00

Mack Van, Am National, gr & red, 26", G, A $450.00

Open Truck, Sturditoy, olive gr w/blk fr & fenders, 22½", P, A $120.00

Plee-Zing Quality Products Delivery Truck, Metalcraft, 1930s, blk cab w/gr enclosed bed, 11", EX, A $500.00

Shell Motor Oil Stake Truck, Metalcraft, red & yel, w/4 barrels, 12", worn pnt, A $275.00

Son-ny Parcel Post Truck, green and black with orange wheels, 26", G, A, $625.00.

Stake Truck, Banner, 1940s, red & yel w/Whelan's Drug Stores logo on side, 13¾", VG+, A $109.00

Stake Truck, bl & gr w/blk metal tires, NP grille, 20", pnt chips, VG, A $90.00

Stake Truck, Kingsbury, red & blk, w/up, 25", G, A ...$1,400.00

Telephone Truck, Lincoln Toys Canada, Patricia Contractors Ltd decal on top, side decals 60%, 11", VG+, M5 ...$170.00

Tow Truck, Metalcraft, red & wht, 3 spares, promotes Goodrich tires, 12", EX, A $250.00

Tractor Trailer, Sturditoy, fuel tanker, red, 33", G, A ...$1,900.00

Truck, mk Dayton OH, ca 1920, gr w/gold stripes & red fenders, 13", G, A $288.00

MISCELLANEOUS

Locomotive, US, 1-pc loco & tender, friction, 17", non-working, G, A $65.00

New York Central Tender, AC Gilbert, made for Erector Hudson locomotive, 19", EX, A $190.00

Pullman Car, Cor-Cor, 24", orig tracks rpl, VG, A $220.00

Road Roller, Wilkins, 1920s, rare, EX, $350.00.

Street Car, yel w/red roof & trim, new trolley pole, 24", rstr, EX, A $140.00
Trolley Car, gr & yel w/opening center doors, battery-op, rubber wheels, 19½", rpt, G, A $85.00
Trolley Car, red & yel, friction, 15½", VG, A $225.00

Trolley Car, 1920s, cast wheels, 22", missing steering wheel and top wires, minor dents, M5, $225.00.

Promotional Vehicles

Miniature Model T Fords were made by Tootsietoy during the 1920s, and though they were not actually licensed by Ford, a few of these were handed out by Ford dealers to promote the new models. In 1932 Tootsietoy was contacted by Graham-Paige to produce a model of their car. These 4" Grahams were sold in boxes as sales promotions by car dealerships, and some were sold through the toy company's catalog. But it wasn't until after WWII that distribution of 1/25 scale promotional models and kits became commonplace. Early models were of cast metal, but during the 1950s, manufacturers turned to plastic. Not only was the material less costly to use, but it could be molded in the color desired, thereby saving the time and expense previously involved in painting the metal. Though the early plastic cars were prone to warp easily when exposed to heat, by the mid-'50s, they had become more durable. Some were friction powered, and others held a battery-operated radio. Advertising extolling some of the model's features was often embossed on the underside. Among the toy manufacturers involved in making promotionals were National Products, Product Miniatures, AMT, MPC, and Jo-Han. Interest in '50s and '60s models is intense, and the muscle cars from the '60s and early '70s are especially collectible. The more popularity the life-size model attained, the more popular the promotional is with collectors.

Check the model for damage, warping, and amateur alterations. The original box can increase the value by as much as 30%. Jo-Han has reissued some of their 1950s and 1960s Mopar and Cadillac models as well as Chrysler's Turbine Car. These are usually priced between $20.00 and $30.00.

Advisor: Aquarius Antiques (A3).

Key:
u/c — undercarriage

1954 Pontiac, plastic w/metal u/c, blk, 2-door, no interior details, 7¾", VG, A $50.00

1954-55 Corvette, plastic w/metal u/c, wht w/red interior, decal on hood, friction, 6½", VG+, A $130.00
1955 Chevrolet, bank, 2-door hardtop, turq & wht, EX+ ..$125.00
1955-56 T-bird, AMT, Continental kit, plastic w/metal u/c, bl w/wht interior & red trim, friction, 7½", VG, A $35.00
1955-56 T-Bird, AMT, plastic w/metal u/c, blk w/red & wht interior, b/o remote control, 7¼" non-working o/w VG ...$60.00
1955-56 T-Bird, AMT, plastic w/metal u/c, gr w/gr & wht interior, b/o remote control, 7¼", non-working, G $60.00
1955-56 T-Bird, AMT, plastic w/metal u/c, red w/red & wht interior, cast metal bumpers, 7¼", VG $45.00
1955-56 T-Bird, plastic, turq w/wht top (unusual), silver seat panels, 8", G+ $75.00
1955-56 T-Bird, plastic w/metal u/c, bl-gray, friction, 7", some warping & discoloration, G, A $30.00
1955-56 T-Bird, plastic w/metal u/c, pale gr w/wht interior, red seat trim, 7", G, A...$30.00
1955-56 T-Bird, plastic w/metal u/c, red w/red & wht interior, friction, 7¼", VG, A...$65.00
1955-56 T-Bird, plastic w/metal u/c, red w/wht interior, friction, 7", G, A...$15.00
1956 Chevrolet, 4-door sedan, red & wht, VG.................$75.00
1957 Pontiac, plastic w/plain u/c, salmon colored w/wht top, 8¼", G, A..$35.00

1958 Chevrolet Impala, 2-tone blue, friction, $90.00.

1958 T-Bird, AMT, plastic w/metal u/c, turq w/wht top, gold seat panels, friction, 8", VG (VG display box), A $70.00
1958 T-Bird, AMT, plastic w/metal u/c, yel w/wht top, gold seat panels, friction, 8", VG, A..$30.00
1959 T-Bird, plastic w/metal u/c, bronze w/wht top, brn & gold interior, friction, 8", G, A..$35.00
1959 T-Bird Convertible, AMT, plastic w/metal u/c, bl & gray w/gold interior, friction, 8", G, A..............................$20.00
1959 T-Bird Convertible, plastic w/metal u/c, copper colored w/gold seat panels, 8", EX (VG display box), A.........$95.00
1959 T-Bird Convertible, plastic w/metal u/c, lt tan w/wht seat panels, friction, 8", VG, A..$70.00
1960 Corvair, 4-door sedan, M.......................................$75.00
1960 T-Bird, AMT, plastic w/detailed u/c, red w/red & silver interior, 8", EX (plain box), A $95.00
1960 T-Bird, AMT, plastic w/metal u/c, gr w/pale gr top, silver seat panels, friction, 8", G, A $25.00
1960 T-Bird, plastic w/metal u/c, yel w/silver seat trim, friction, 8", VG, A $75.00

1960 T-Bird Convertible, plastic w/detailed u/c, plum w/silver seat panels, 8", G, A $20.00

1960 T-Bird Convertible, plastic w/metal u/c, teal w/bl & silver interior, friction, 8", VG, A.................................$40.00

1960 T-Bird Coupe, AMT, plastic, red w/wht top, silver seat panels, 7½", NMIB, A $60.00

1961 T-Bird, plastic w/detailed u/c, gr w/tan interior, 8", few scratches, 8", VG (plain box), A $30.00

1961 T-Bird, plastic w/detailed u/c, tan w/red interior, 8", VG, A $35.00

1961 T-Bird Convertible, plastic w/metal u/c, pale bl, silver seat panels, friction, 8", VG $45.00

1961 T-Bird Coupe, plastic w/metal u/c, blk, silver seat panels, friction, 8", G+, A $40.00

1962 T-Bird, AMT, plastic w/detailed u/c, gr w/2-tone gray interior, 8¼", EX (plain box), A $55.00

1962 T-Bird, plastic w/detailed u/c listing features, cream, 8¼", VG, A $40.00

1962 T-Bird Convertible, plastic w/detailed u/c listing features, pale gr, Tonneau cap, friction, 8", VG+, A $65.00

1962 T-Bird Coupe, plastic w/detailed u/c listing features, burgundy w/silver seat trim, friction, 8", VG, A $90.00

1962 T-Bird Sport Roadster, plastic w/detailed u/c, blk w/silver silver seat panels/Tonneau cap, friction, 8", EX, A .$170.00

1962 T-Bird Sport Roadster, plastic w/detailed u/c listing features, dk gr w/silver seat panels, friction, 8¼", VG, A.........$150.00

1963 T-Bird, plastic w/detailed u/c, pale gr w/Tonneau cap, 8¼", spot on windshield, G, A $110.00

1963 T-Bird Convertible, plastic w/detailed u/c, red w/Tonneau cap, friction, 8", EX, A $160.00

1963 T-Bird Convertible, plastic w/detailed u/c, wht w/lift-out seat panels, 8", VG+, A $80.00

1963 T-Bird Coupe, plastic w/detailed u/c, plum, 8", VG, A..$55.00

1964 Chevrolet Chevelle Malibu, 2-door hardtop, M....$150.00

1964 Ford Falcon, red, $40.00.

1964 T-Bird, AMT, plastic w/detailed u/c, 8¼", EX (plain box), A $100.00

1964 T-Bird, plastic w/detailed u/c, bl hardtop, 8", VG, A..$40.00

1964 T-Bird, plastic w/detailed u/c, gold, VG, A.............$35.00

1964 T-Bird, radio, Philco, bl plastic, 8", non-working, G+, A $20.00

1964 T-Bird, radio, Philco, gold plastic, 8", non-working, VG, A $25.00

1964 T-Bird Convertible, plastic w/detailed u/c, wht, 8", EX (plain box), A $95.00

1964 T-Bird Coupe, plastic w/detailed u/c, avocado, 8", VG, A $30.00

1964 T-Bird Coupe, plastic w/detailed u/c, plum, 8", VG, A..$35.00

1965 Mustang Coupe, plastic w/detailed u/c, pale yel, 7¼", VG, A $35.00

1965 Mustang Coupe Pace Car, plastic, off-wht decal striping & lettering for Indy, wood base, brass plate, 7¼", VG, A $110.00

1965 Plymouth Barracuda, plastic w/detailed u/c, wht, A .$125.00

1965 T-Bird, plastic w/detailed u/c, burgundy hardtop, 8", EX (Jo-Han box), A $50.00

1965 T-Bird, plastic w/detailed u/c listing features, gold hardtop, 8", G+, A $40.00

1965 T-Bird, plastic w/detailed u/c listing features, red, 8", VG (P box), A $35.00

1965 T-Bird Convertible, plastic w/detailed u/c listing features, yel, 8", VG, A $130.00

1966 Chevrolet Impala, maroon, with working radio, $70.00.

1966 Lincoln Continental, plastic w/detailed u/c, M $95.00

1966 Mustang, plastic w/detailed u/c listing features, red, 7¼", VG+, A..$70.00

1966 Mustang Fastback, radio, tan, NM $125.00

1966 Pontiac GTO Convertible, M $200.00

1966 T-Bird, plastic w/detailed u/c listing features, gold, 8", VG, A $25.00

1967 Cadillac El Dorado, plastic w/detailed u/c, M $75.00

1967 T-Bird, plastic w/plain u/c, avocado, friction, 8¼", non-working o/w VG+, A $30.00

1967 T-Bird, radio, Philco, dk red, 8", G, from $15 to......$20.00

1967 T-Bird Coupe, plastic w/plain u/c, dk red, 8¼", EX, A.$45.00

1968 T-Bird Coupe, plastic, bl, 8¼", EX+ (VG box), A...$45.00

1968 T-Bird Coupe, plastic w/plain u/c, avocado, friction, 8", EX (VG box), A $45.00

1969 Camaro Convertible Indy Pace Car, M................$250.00

1969 T-Bird Coupe, plastic w/detailed u/c, olive, 8", G+, A..$30.00

1970 Camaro Coupe, plastic w/detailed u/c, gr, 7", VG, A..$75.00

1970 Oldsmobile 442 Coupe, plastic w/detailed u/c, yel, M...$95.00

1971 T-Bird, plastic w/detailed u/c, dk gr hardtop, 8½", VG, A $20.00

1972 Chevy Fleetside Pickup, orange, NM $125.00

1975 Corvette, plastic w/detailed u/c, orange flame, 7½", NMIB, A $100.00

1975 Corvette, plastic w/detailed u/c, silver, 7½", NMIB, A $90.00

1976 Corvette, plastic w/detailed u/c, Classic wht, 7½", MIB, A $70.00

1976 Corvette, plastic w/detailed u/c, metallic mahogany, 7½", NMIB, A..$110.00

1977 Corvette, plastic w/detailed u/c, red, 7½", NMIB $95.00

1977 Corvette, plastic w/detailed u/c, silver, 7½", NMIB.$95.00

1978 Corvette, plastic w/detailed u/c, rare 1-tone silver, 7½", VG+, A...$80.00

1978 Corvette, plastic w/detailed u/c, 2-tone silver & gray, 7", NMIB, A...$55.00

1979 Corvette, plastic w/detailed u/c, red, 7½", NMIB, A.$30.00

1980 Corvette, plastic w/detailed u/c, yel, 7½", NMIB, A..$20.00

1981 Corvette, plastic w/detailed u/c, dk bl, 7½", NMIB, A..$30.00

1981 Corvette, plastic w/detailed u/c, red-orange, 7½", MIB, A $30.00

1981 Corvette, plastic w/detailed u/c, silver (rare), 7½", NMIB..$75.00

1982 Corvette, plastic w/detailed u/c, burgundy, 7½", VG+..$25.00

1982 Corvette, plastic w/detailed u/c, claret, 7½", MIB ...$75.00

1984 Corvette, plastic w/detailed u/c, bronze, 7", MIB.....$25.00

1984 Corvette, plastic w/detailed u/c, gray, 7", NMIB, A.$25.00

1984 Corvette, plastic w/detailed u/c, red, 7", NMIB, A ..$20.00

1985 Corvette, plastic w/detailed u/c, metallic bl, 7", EX, A ..$15.00

1986 Corvette, plastic w/detailed u/c, brn, 7", NMIB, A..$20.00

1987 Corvette, plastic w/detailed u/c, metallic red (only 144 made), M $500.00

1987 Corvette, plastic w/detailed u/c, red, 7", NMIB, A..$20.00

1988 Corvette, plastic w/detailed u/c, dk red, 7", NMIB, A...$20.00

1990 Corvette Convertible, plastic w/detailed u/c, red, 6¾", EX, A $20.00

1990 Taurus SHO, plastic w/detailed u/c, wht, 7½", NMIB, A $15.00

1991 Corvette ZR-1, AMT, plastic, Quasar bl, 7", EX (orig box), A $25.00

Pull and Push Toys

Pull and push toys from the 1800s often were made of cast iron with bells that were activated as they moved along on wheeled platforms or frames. Hide and cloth animals with glass or shoe-button eyes were also popular, and some were made of wood.

See also specific companies such as Fisher-Price.

Bears on Cart, two painted cast-iron bears ring bells on steel frame with steel wheels, 10", some surface rust otherwise VG, A, $725.00.

Acrobats, Gong Bell, 2 dancing figures hold bells on swinging base attached to 4-wheeled platform, CI, 6½", EX, A........$460.00

Baby Quieter, J&E Stevens, father reads paper on wheeled couch while moving leg to amuse baby, CI, 8", EX, A.....$2,070.00

Bear Pulling Bell, compo bear on wheel pulls bell between 2 bl wheels, 7", EX (orig box), A....................................$160.00

Borden's Milk Wagon, Rich Toys, litho tin & pnt wood wagon pulled by pnt wood horse on wheels, w/driver, 18", VG, A $250.00

Carriage, Marklin, 1890s, 2 compo horses on wheeled platforms pull tin carriage w/lead wheels, sm pail, 16", EX, A.........$1,150.00

Carriage w/Galloping Horse, pulls ornate carriage w/lady in plumed hat, CI w/heart-shaped spoke wheels, 10", VG, A...$1,450.00

Cassie the Cow, Aladdin Plastics, ca 1950, pull cow & head moves, wooden hdl, 16", MIB, A $119.00

Cinderella's Chariot, ca 1890, CI w/bell, wht horse w/pk horse blanket, 9½", G, A $375.00

City Delivery Wagon, Converse, yel & red tin wagon pulled by dappled horse w/jtd legs, 11", G+, A........................$95.00

Clown & Poodle, clown guides poodle w/bell in mouth on 4-wheeled platform, pnt CI, 8", EX, A....................$1,150.00

Clown w/Horses, Hubley, 2 blk horses jump from platform causing clown to somersault & ring bells, CI, 6", EX, A .$805.00

Cow, Germany, early 20th century, blk & wht papier-mache w/glass eyes, wood platform w/steel wheels, 7", G, A .$230.00

Cow, Germany, early 20th century, hide-covered body w/glass eyes, head turns & moos, reservoir for milk, 11", VG+, A...$345.00

Dancing Bears, 2 pnt bears ring bells on steel fr w/steel wheels, 10", VG, A $725.00

Dog w/basket, brn-pnt tin dog w/gold basket on gr platform, iron wheels, 6¼", VG, A...$220.00

Eagle, red, wht & bl eagle w/bell in beak on platform w/fancy spoked wheels, CI, 5¾", eagle rpl, G, A...................$350.00

Egyptian Cart Pulled by Lion, ca 1910, painted cast iron, 7½", EX, D10, $450.00.

Goat, hide-covered w/nodding head & squeaker on pnt-wood platform w/iron wheels, 10½", G+, A $700.00

Goats (2), Am, tin goats pulling bell centering lg CI wheels, 6", EX, A $350.00

Goats w/Girl on Wheeled Platform, Am, pnt tin, 6", VG, A..$500.00

Grasshopper, Hubley, painted cast iron with clicker, rear legs go up and down when pulled, 12", EX, from $750.00 to $1,000.00.

Hobby Horse, Jaymar/WDP #1234, enamel on wood Babes-in-Toyland horse w/coiled wire neck, 8", unused, NM (VG+ box), A $195.00

Horse, blk-pnt tin horse w/red saddle on red platform, iron wheels, 7", G-, A $75.00

Horse, brn mohair w/leatherette & cloth tack, wooden platform w/steel wheels, 13½", A..$345.00

Horse, cloth covered, on 4-wheeled platform, 10½", G, A..$30.00

Horse, cloth covered w/hair mane & tail, 12½", EX, A .$275.00

Horse, George Brown, 1870s, fancy 4-wheeled platform, 6", EX, D10, $750.00.

Horse & Jockey, Globe, 1931, pnt CI, 7¼", VG, A $525.00

Horse & Jockey, Hull & Stafford, 1870s, pnt tin, 7", rpr, G- pnt, A $375.00

Horse Cart, Am, tin, single wht horse pulls fancy gr cart w/2 iron spoked wheels, 9", VG, A $325.00

Horse Cart, Am, tin, 2 emb flat horses pull bl wagon w/yel interior, 2 sm iron wheels, 10½", G-, A..............................$55.00

Horse on Platform, Germany, fabric-covered compo-mache horse on red-trimmed wooden platform, iron wheels, 12", G+, A $95.00

Horse-Drawn Fire Wagon, Germany, tin, cylindrical tank on 4-wheeled cart, w/driver & 1 horse, 12", G, A..............$75.00

Horse-Drawn Hay Wagon, red-pnt wagon w/yel wheels, cloth-covered horse on wooden platform, iron wheels, 26", EX, A..$350.00

Horse-Drawn Trolley, Germany, Tramway Co on banner, tin, advertising around upper deck, 12½", driver missing, G, A..$120.00

Horse-Drawn Wagon, Am, tin, single wht horse pulls orange Am Roadster wagon w/spoked wheels, 12½", G, A ...$55.00

Hospital Wagon, Marklin, 2 compo horses on wheeled platforms pull tin wagon w/lattice sections & 2 figures, 12", EX, A...$1,093.00

Lamb, Germany, early 20th century, lambskin w/glass eyes, wool twill face & legs, wood platform & wheels, 22½", EX, A ...$1,121.00

Lion Tamer in Wire Cage, French, tin & compo w/bsk head, molded tin lion, girl w/elaborate attire, glass eyes, 9", VG, A..$3,600.00

Little Nemo & Friend, 1905, figures sway causing 3 bells to ring on base w/heart-shaped spoke wheels, CI, 11", VG, A....$345.00

Man Riding Horse, Am, tin, 4-wheeled platform, 6½", EX, A..$550.00

Milk Wagon, Marklin, tin, dbl-decker w/2 mules on wheeled platforms, 2 figures & 6 milk cans, 15", EX, A $1,380.00

Monkey in Carriage, yel monkey in red 4-wheeled coach beats bell as coach moves, 7", EX+, A $1,150.00

Monkey on a Velocipede, J&E Stevens, jtd CI monkey in clothes on high 3-wheeled velocipede, 8¼", EX, A...........$3,680.00

Pacing Bob #20, Gibbs, paper litho horse pulls red-pnt cart, 13", EX+, A..$205.00

Pig w/Clown Rider, Gong Bell, clown on wht 3-wheeled pig w/bell attached to pig's snout, 6", VG, A $1,035.00

Pony Circus Wagon #53, Gibbs, 1920, 2 paper-lithoed horses pull wagon lithoed w/performers & animals, tin wheels, NM, A $985.00

Reindeer, Germany, litho tin, 4-wheel platform, 4", EX, A .$220.00

Rich's Little Milk Wagon, wooden horse w/litho tin milk wagon, pull cord, 20", NM (EX+ box that converts to barn), A $350.00

Rickshaw, ornate wheel & body design w/cloth top, soft metal & glass electric lanterns, spoke wheels, 11", VG+, A....$160.00

Rocky Mountain Express, Cass, 1946, vehicles travel on belts w/tunnels, lithoed wood on wheels, 19", NM (G box), A.....$135.00

Sandy Andy Trick Animals, Wolverine, 1930s, bear rings bell and seal balances ball, tin with rubber tread, 10", NM (G box), A, $775.00.

Sawing Watermelons, Gong Bell, 2 Black boys saw 3 watermelons on 4-wheeled platform, CI, 8½", EX, A $2,415.00

Sedan, Schieble, pnt sheet metal, bl w/blk tires, 17¼", VG, A $500.00

See-em Walk Dog, NOMA, molded compo, MIB............$65.00

Sheffield Farms Horse-Drawn Wagon, painted wood, complete with six milk bottles, 21", NM, D10, $850.00.

Snowflake & Swipes, Nifty/c Oscar Hitt, 1929, Snowflake & Swipes on wheeled platform run when pushed, 7", VG (VG box), A $1,650.00

Sunnyside Farm Milk Wagon, wood wagon w/stencil & CI wheels, pulled by 2 horses, 31", G-, A $200.00

Tabby Cat, gray & wht cloth-covered w/gr glass eyes & bow around neck, 4 tin wheels, 8", G+, A $130.00

Trailer, Holgate Toys #638, Auto Convoy wooden truck carries 2 cars w/passengers on trailer, 19¾", MIB, A...........$170.00

Trick Pony, Gong Bell, wht horse wearing red blanket swings on pedestal & rings bell on platform, CI, 8", EX, A $575.00

Turtle on Wheels, gr turtle w/lg bell on shell, CI, attached cord, 6¼", EX, A..$575.00

Wacky Duck, NOMA, molded compo, MIB $65.00

Whirly Tinker, Toy Tinkers, tin & wood, G $40.00

Windmill, Brio, wood, M (orig box) $24.00

Puppets

Though many collectible puppets and the smaller scale marionettes were made commercially, others were handmade and are today considered fine examples of folk art which sometimes sell for several hundred dollars. Some of the most collectible today are character-related puppets representing well-known television stars.

Advisor: Steven Meltzer (M9).

See also Advertising; Black Americana; Political.

FINGER PUPPETS

Addams Family, from cartoon series, set of 4 w/2-3 different characters on ea, store stock, M, H4 ....$15.00

Crypt Keeper, set of 3 different, rubber, store stock, M, H4..$12.00

Davy Jones (Monkees), Remco, 1970, NM, S2 ....$35.00

Devil, Clown or Skull, 1960s, cloth body w/celluloid head, MIP, S2, ea...$15.00

Donald Duck, Marx, finger marionette, plastic, EX, W5..$40.00

Mickey Dolenz (Monkees), Remco, 1970, NM, S2 ....$35.00

Pinocchio, Marx, finger marionette, plastic, EX, W5 ....$40.00

Raggedy Ann, Knickerbocker, 1972, 3¼", MOC, S2........$10.00

Roger Rabbit, figural foam head, MIP, S2 ....$15.00

Three Stooges, Applause, set of 3, M, S2 ....$25.00

HAND PUPPETS

Alf, Cookin' w/Alf, 1988, plush, 12", EX+, P3..................$8.00

Bamm-Bamm (Flintstones), VG, S2 ....$45.00

Batman, 1966, G, S2...$40.00

Batman, 1966, MIP, S2 ....$100.00

Bozo the Clown, plush body, EX, S2 ....$40.00

Brutus (Popeye), Gund, EX, S2 ....$55.00

Captain Hook, Gund, 1950s-early '60s, 2-pc cloth body w/checked design, vinyl head, 3½", D9..................$23.00

Car 54 Where Are You?, Officers Toddy & Muldoon, Eurolis, 1962, cloth bodies w/pnt soft vinyl heads, 9", EX+, pr $95.00

Cecil, talker, EX, S2...$95.00

Charlie Brown, foam body, NM, S2 ....$25.00

Charlie McCarthy, cb, 1938, M $65.00

Charlie McCarthy, Reliable Toy, 1950s, compo head, EX, S2 ....$150.00

Charlie McCarthy, 1930, compo head, VG+, J2 ....$125.00

Cinderella, Gund, VG+, J2 ....$33.00

Cinderella, plush body w/squeaker, EX+, S2 ....$55.00

Clarabell (Howdy Doody), Zany Toys, 1951, cloth w/vinyl head, 8½", EX (VG+ scarce box), A $193.00

Court Jester, w/big cheeks, nose & chin, NM, S2.............$20.00

Debbie Doll (Baby), Knickerbocker, 1965, EX, S2 ....$30.00

Dennis the Menace, HKK, 1958, lg head w/orig clothes, EX, S2 ....$65.00

Dennis the Menace's Mom Alice, very rare, EX, S2 ....$65.00

Dick Tracy, promo from Chicago Tribune & NY Daily News, 1961, cloth & vinyl, 3½", D9 ....$39.00

Dilly Dally (Howdy Doody), Zany Toys/Kagran, 1950s, vinyl & cloth, 8", EX+ (EX box), A.....................................$184.00

Dishonest John, Mattel, 1962, lg, EX, S2 ....$25.00

Donald Duck, Gund/WDP, 1950s, VG, I2 ....$19.00

Donald Duck, newer version, wht head, S2 ....$25.00

Dopey (Snow White & the Seven Dwarfs), Gund, w/squeaker, rare, VG, S2 ....$55.00

Dr Dolittle, Mattel, 1967, talker, working, EX, J2 ....$55.00

Dr Dolittle, talker, NM, M5, $110.00.

Dr Zauis (Planet of the Apes), plush w/hair on vinyl head, EX, S2 ....$65.00

Dumbo, Gund, w/squeaker, NM, S2....................$55.00

Ernie (Sesame Street), super-sz, EX, S2............................$20.00

European Man, w/gr cap, blk mustache & goatee, EX, S2 ..$10.00

Fred Flintstone & Barney Rubble, felt, MIP, S2, pr........$125.00

Fred Flintstone, Knickerbocker, 1962, VG, S2 ....$45.00

Gomez (Addams Family), 1960s, cloth body w/vinyl head, EX, J5 ....$45.00

Goofy, Gund, EX, J2 ....$23.00

Grandma, very detailed w/hair in scarf, EX, S2..................$15.00

Grandma, w/gray hair & bun, EX, S2....................$10.00

Grandpa Munster, 1960s, cloth body w/vinyl head, EX, J5..$45.00

Herman Munster, 1960s, cloth body w/vinyl head, EX, J5 ..$45.00

Howdy Doody, moving eyes, VG, S2 ....$75.00

Huckleberry Hound, Knickerbocker, 1959, VG, C1.........$21.00

Huckleberry Hound, Knickerbocker, 1965, plush body, EX, S2 ....$50.00

Huckleberry Hound, 1961, cloth body w/vinyl head, EX+, S2...$65.00

Incredible Hulk, 1970s, MIP, S2 ....$30.00

Jerry Mahoney, 1966, compo head, MIP, M9 ....$250.00

Jerry Mahoney & Knucklehead Smith, 1966, vinyl heads, MIP, pr...$200.00

Jiminy Cricket, EX, O1...$23.00

Kewpie Doll Look-Alike, 1960s, EX, S2 ....$35.00

King, crowned, wht or blk beard, EX, S2, ea......................$10.00

Lamb Chop or Hush Puppy, 1960s, J5, ea $32.00

Leo the Lion, Steiff, plush, w/tag & button, M, S2...........$85.00

Lily Munster, 1960s, cloth body w/vinyl head, VG, J5 .....$45.00

Magilla Gorilla, extremely rare, sm ink stain on back, EX, S2 ..$65.00

Manny Rabbit, Steiff w/button & tags, 4½", M $95.00

Mickey Mouse, pre-1939, stuffed velvet w/blk leather eyes & satiny 4-fingered hands, 9", NM, A $270.00

Minnie Mouse, Disney, bow in hair, VG, S2 ....$25.00

Minnie Mouse, Disney, older, G, S2 ....$25.00

Mister Ed, Mattel, 1962, talker, VG, S2 ....$100.00

Monkees, Mattel, 1966, w/4 vinyl heads, talker, working, EX+, J2 ....$160.00

Mr Ed, Mattel, 1962, talker, works, VG, S2....................$100.00

Myrtle, Mattel, 1969, EX+, J2 ....$125.00

Nurse, vinyl body, NM, S2 ....$15.00

Odd Job (Goldfinger movie), Gilbert, 12", unused, NMOC, M5 ....$440.00

Olive Oyl, Gund, 1957, EX, S2..$55.00

Olive Oyl, Gund, 1960s, vinyl head on cloth body, 10", G ..$25.00

Ossi Rabbit, orig ribbon, w/button & tags, 8", M.............$95.00

Pedro (Chihuahua), Disney, VG, S2.................................$50.00

Peter Pan, Gund, VG, S2 ....$55.00

Pig, pk, w/button & tag, 2", VG.......................................$135.00

Pinocchio, Gund, EX, S2 ....$55.00

Pinocchio, WDP, cloth and vinyl, EX, O1, $45.00.

Pluto, Gund, w/squeaker, NM, S2 ....$35.00

Pluto, Gund, 1955, M (EX+ window box), A...................$75.00

Pluto, Pedigree/England, 1950s-60s, plush, MIP, S2.........$55.00

Popeye, Gund, 1957, rare, VG, S2 ....$55.00

Popeye, Presents, 1987, lg head, EX, S2 ....$25.00

Popeye, talker, EX, S2 ....$125.00

Princess (Howdy Doody), 1970s, lg head w/rooted hair, VG, S2 ....$15.00

Punkin' Puss, Ideal, 1960s, EX, H4..................................$39.00

Raggedy Ann, EX, O1...$15.00

Ricochet Rabbit & Droopalong Coyote, EX, J2, pr $75.00

Road Runner, plastic & vinyl, EX, I2 ....$7.00

Scarecrow (Wizard of Oz), G, S2 ....$35.00

Scooby Doo, 1977, w/vinyl head, NM, S2 ....$40.00

Stingray Aquaphibian, Lakeside, 1965, M (in bag), H4 ...$45.00

Superman, Ideal, 1965, EX, J2 ....$40.00

Sylvester the Cat, Looney Toons, vinyl head & body, premium, NM, S2..$35.00

Talking DJ (Cecil & Beany), Mattel, 1962, pull string & DJ makes nasty comments, vinyl & cloth, MIB, A.......$225.00

Topo Gigio, EX...$50.00

Wimpy (Popeye), Gund, w/squeaker, VG, S2.................$40.00

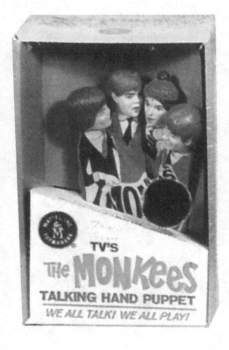

Monkees, Mattel/ Raybert, 1966, features each member, cloth with vinyl heads, talker, NM (NM box), A, $425.00.

Wing Ding, Ideal, 1960s, 9", M $25.00
Wizard of Oz, Proctor & Gamble premium, 1965-69, molded
    vinyl head on thin vinyl body, 10", M, A $52.00
Wolf, w/open mouth, EX, S2 ....$15.00
Yoda (Star Wars), NRFB, H4 ....$70.00
Yogi Bear, VG, S2 ....$55.00
Zebra, Steiff, w/button & tag, 6", M $75.00
Zorro, Gund/WDP, VG $70.00

**Superman, Ideal, 1965, realistic vinyl
face, MOC, A, $95.00.**

MARIONETTES

Alice, Hazelle's, talker, M, M9 ....$125.00
Angel, Pelham, MIB, M9 ....$95.00
Bengo the Dog, Pelham, MIB, M9 ....$65.00
Bimbo the Clown, Hazelle's, 800 Series, EX, M9 ....$75.00
Bimbo the Clown, Pelham, M, M9 ....$135.00
Boy, Pelham, talker, MIB, M9 ....$85.00
Buckaroo Bill, Hazelle's, talker, EX, M9 ....$175.00
Captain Hook, Disney/USA, 1930s, compo & cloth, 16", scarce,
    MIB, A $160.00
Captain Hook, Peter Puppet, 16½", M (rpr box), A $200.00
Chinese Girl, Pelham, 1950s, M $45.00
Clippo the Clown, Curtis Craft, MIB, M9 ....$65.00
Clippo the Clown, Effanbee/WWII, MIB, M9 ....$250.00
Clown, FAO Schwarz, 1960s, wood peg limbs, rubber head &
    cloth clothing, M, S2 ....$50.00
Clown, Pelham, talker, MIB, M9 ....$95.00
Cop, Pelham, talker, MIB, M9 ....$125.00
Creature From the Black Lagoon, 17", MIB, I2 ....$20.00
Dilly Dally (Howdy Doody), Peter Puppet, compo head, hands
    & feet, 14", M (rpr box), A $495.00
Donald Duck, Pelham, EX+ (orig box) $155.00
Dopey (Snow White & the Seven Dwarfs), 1950s, wood, compo
    & cloth, w/I am Dopey tag, 12", EX+ $250.00
Dutch Boy, Pelham, 1950s, M $45.00

**Dagwood, Hazelle,
1950s, MIB, $250.00.**

Emily Ann (Clippo's Girlfriend), Effanbee, M, M9 ....$125.00
Father, Mother & Son, Effanbee, set of 3, EX, M9 ....$425.00
Flub-A-Dub (Howdy Doody), Unitrol, Peter Puppet, 12", M (EX
    orig box), A $350.00
Freddy MC, Hazelle's, M, M9 ....$125.00
Gepetto (Pinocchio), Pelham, MIB, M9 ....$125.00
Girl, Pelham, talker, MIB, M9 ....$85.00
Hansel & Gretel, Hazelle's, M, M9, pr $175.00
Hillbilly, Hazelle's, 800 Series, M, M9 ....$95.00
Horse, Pelham, EX (EX box), M9 ....$75.00
Howdy Doody, Peter Puppet, 1950s, cloth body w/compo head,
    hands & feet, 15½", NMIB, A $249.00
Howdy Doody, Peter Puppet, 1950s, cloth body w/compo head,
    hands & feet, 15½", EX (EX box), A $161.00
Howdy Doody, 1970s, M, J2 ....$25.00
Indian, Peter Puppet, 14", NMIB, A $175.00
Jim-Bob & Suzy Pigtail, Curtis Craft, M, M9, pr $350.00
Jiminy Cricket, Gund, VG $50.00
Jiminy Cricket, Gund, NM $85.00
Little Boy Blue, Hazelle's, 800 Series, compo, M, M9 ....$135.00

**Mickey Mouse, Hestwood Stu-
dio, 1934, only 1,000 made,
12", controller not original otherwise NM, $2,500.00.**

Marilyn, Hazelle's, talker, EX, M9...................$155.00
Mickey Mouse, Pelham, M, M9.........................$95.00
Mother Dragon, Pelham, MIB, M9 ....$200.00
Mr Bluster (Howdy Doody), Peter Puppet, compo head, hands & feet, 14", EX (rpr box), A $450.00

Mr Turnip, Luntoy, cast metal, 6¾", EX (EX box), A, $240.00.

Nurse, Pelham, M, M9..$75.00
Old Lady, Pelham, MIB, M9 ....$125.00
Peter Pan, Peter Puppet, 14½", NM (rpr box), A...........$225.00
Pinky & Perky (Pigs), Pelham, MIB, M9, ea.....................$75.00
Pinocchio, Pelham, MIB, M9 ....$75.00
Pinocchio, Peter Puppet/WD, wood & compo w/cloth clothes, adjustable pull-out nose, 13", NM (VG box) $350.00
Pinocchio, 1960s, plastic head, G, S2 ....$20.00
Planet Flyer (Tom Corbett look-alike), Hazelle's, 1950s, NMIB..............................$250.00
Pop Singer, Pelham, gray suit, M, M9.................$250.00
Pop Singer, Pelham, Hawiian shirt, M, M9 ....$145.00
Popeye, Kohner, 1970, 5¼", MOC, S2....................$35.00
Prince & Princess, Hazelle's, talkers, M, M9, pr $250.00
Prince Charming, Pelham, MIB, M9 ....$125.00
Princess (Howdy Doody), EX, J2........................$240.00
Sailor, Hazelle's, talker, EX, M9.....................$125.00
Snake Charmer, Pelham, lg, MIB $200.00
Suzybell Clown, Hazelle's, talker, M, M9.........................$95.00
Teto the Clown, Hazelle's 700 series, compo, VG-EX, from $85 to..............................$125.00
Wendy (Peter Pan), Peter Puppet, 14", M (worn box), A $225.00
Witch, Hazelle's, talker, 14½", EX (orig box)................$225.00
Witch (Green Face), Pelham, M, M9 ....$145.00
Wolf, Pelham, G, M9 ....$250.00
Wombles (Furry Creatures from English TV), Pelham, MIB, M9, ea..............................$55.00

PUSH-BUTTON PUPPETS

Disney Pop Pals, Kohner, Mickey, Goofy, Donald & Pluto, 3" ea, set of 4, EX-NM, D9................$34.00
Donald Duck, Tricky Trapeze, NMOC, J2......................$35.00

Ernie (Sesame Street), side buttons, M, O1, $12.00; Superman Tricky Trapeze, Nat'l Periodical Publications, 1966, #4995, NM, O1, $75.00.

Fred Flintstone, Kohner, 1960s, EX..................$20.00
Hangover Pete, Kohner, #124, wood, w/label, EX+, I2 ......$35.00
Happy Hooligan, Empire Made, 1925, celluloid figure & donkey on cloth base, push base for action, 7", EX, A $167.00
Howdy Doody, Kohner, 1950s, Howdy w/NBC microphone, wood & plastic, 5½", NM (NM box), A..................$282.00
Incredible Hulk, Fleetwood, 1978, flips around on bar, 2½", H4.............................$29.00
Indian Chief w/tomahawk & shield, Kohner, 1950s, wood & plastic, 7", MIB, A.................$128.00
Lone Ranger on Silver, Kohner, 1950s, wood & plastic, 7", rare, MIB, A.............................$160.00

Magilla Gorilla, Kohner, Hanna-Barbera, M, O1, $35.00.

Mickey Mouse, Kohner, 5", EX, W5 ....$45.00
Mickey Mouse (Topo Gigio Circus), on trapeze, 1960s, rare,
    MIP, S2 ....$60.00

Mickey Mouse, Gabriel, No 78980, 4¼", NM, $20.00.

Olive Oyl, Kohner, EX, O1, $60.00.

Pluto, Kohner, WDP, 1960s, 4½", VG..............................$10.00
Princess Summerfall Winterspring, Kohner, 1950s, wood w/felt
    dress, red plastic base, 6", NMIB, A $212.00
Ricochet Rabbit, EX+, J2 ....$45.00
Robot, 5", EX+, M5 ....$25.00
Secret Squirrel, Kohner, 1960s, VG, H4.............................$30.00
Snoopy as Sheriff, Ideal, 4", NM, I2 ....$14.00
Superman, complete w/cape, 1960s, very rare, NM, S2..$100.00
Wilma Flintstone, Kohner/Hanna-Barbera, 1960s, Wilma in
    chair holding telephone, 7", scarce, EX, A $185.00
Wilma Flintstone & Pebbles, Kohner/Hanna-Barbera, 1962,
    NM (EX+ box), A $300.00

VENTRILOQUIST DOLLS

Billy Baloney (Pee Wee's Playhouse), 18", MIB, S2 ....$65.00
Boy, Pelham, M, M9...$125.00

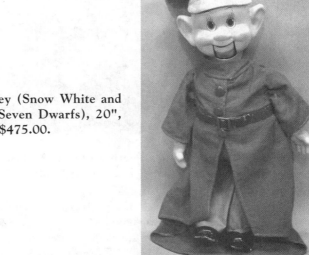

Dopey (Snow White and the Seven Dwarfs), 20", EX, $475.00.

Charlie McCarthy, Juros, unused, NMIB, J2 ....$125.00
Girl, Pelham, M, M9 ....$125.00
Jerry Mahoney, compo, 1950s, MIB, M9 ....$450.00
Jerry Mahoney, headstick, Juro, 32", MIB, M9 ....$350.00
Jerry Mahoney, headstick w/moving eyes, 32", MIB, M9 .$500.00
Knucklehead, 1950s, MIB, M9...$950.00
Moe (Three Stooges), Horsman, 1970s, M (in orig plain wht cb
    box w/label), H4..$160.00
Monk, Pelham, M, M9 ....$225.00
Mortimer Snerd, Juro, 1968, EX, S2...............................$75.00
Pee Wee Herman, 30", MIB, S2 ....$85.00
Rover, Pelham, M, M9..$95.00

Puzzles and Picture Blocks

    Jigsaw puzzles have been around almost as long as games. The first examples were handcrafted from wood, and they are extremely difficult to find. Most of the early examples featured moral subjects and offered insight into the social atmosphere of their time. By the 1890s jigsaw puzzles had become a major form of home entertainment. Cube puzzles or blocks were often made by the same companies as board games. Early examples display lithography of the finest quality. While all subjects are collectible, some (such as Santa blocks) often command prices higher than games of the same period.

    Because TV and personality-related puzzles have become so popular, they're now regarded as a field all their own apart from character collectibles in general, and these are listed here as well, under the subtitle Character.

Advisors: Bob Armstrong (A4); Norm Vigue (V1), Character. **See also Advertising.**

Alphabet of Country Scenes, picture blocks, McLoughlin Brothers, paper on wood, VG (G box), A, $825.00.

Arab Raiding Party, RW Bliss, 1930s, plywood, 153 semi-interlocking pcs, 1 pc rpl, G- (orig box), A4 ....$20.00

At the Fountain (peasant woman studying fountain inscription), 162 push-to-fit pcs, 12x9", 3 pcs rpl, EX (EX box), A4 ..$25.00

Begging Dog, 1910s, thick solid wood, 13x10", 183 semi-interlocking pcs, 1 pc rpl, EX (EX box), A4 ....$18.00

Birth of Home Sweet Home, artist P Moran, 1930s, plywood, 117 push-to-fit pcs, circular cut, 6x10", EX (candy box), A4 ....$12.00

Boating at Night (lady in boat under moon), att Ullman, 1910s, plywood, 72 push-to-fit pcs, 6x8", EX (rpl box), A4 ..$12.00

Boy & Girl Fishing From Rock, 1909, solid wood, 110 push-to-fit, color-line cut, 15x10", EX (w/box), A4 ....$20.00

Boy Chasing Cow w/Stick, artist Julien Dapel, 1930s, plywood, 75 push-to-fit pcs, EX (rpl box), A4 ....$6.00

Castle by a River, 1930s, plywood, 150 interlocking pcs, 7x9", EX (rpl box), A4 ....$12.00

Cherry Blossoms, artist Henry Smith, early 1900s, solid wood, 232 push-to-fit pcs, 12x17", G- (orig box), A4 ....$20.00

Circus Puzzle, Milton Bradley, 1900-1910, G, $75.00.

Child Holding Doll, 1930s, plywood, 70 interlocking pcs, EX (rpl box), A4..$10.00

Christ Among the Doctors, 1900s, solid wood, 280 push-to-fit pcs, 12x17", EX (rpl box), A4 ....$40.00

Church on the Hill, Atlantic/Kingsbridge, 1950-60, plywood, 300 interlocking pcs, strip cut, 13x10", EX (orig box), A4...$20.00

Clipper Ship, 1930s, plywood, 140 interlocking pcs, 10x9", EX (rpl box), A4..$15.00

Closeup of Flowers (from McCall's Homemaker), 1930s, masonite, 125 semi-interlocking pcs, EX (rpl box), A4...................$6.00

Country Scene, Atlantic/Kingsbridge, 1950-60, plywood, 350 interlocking pcs, strip cut, 12x16", EX (orig box), A4..$22.00

Dissected Map of the United States, jigsaw, McLoughlin Bros, litho paper, 9½", VG (orig box), A........................$110.00

Distance Lends Enchantment, RW Bliss, 1930s, plywood, 500 semi-interlocking pcs, 12x16", EX (orig box), A4 .....$60.00

Domestic Animals, jigsaw, Parker Bros, 1930, EX (orig box)...$40.00

Don Baltasar Carlos (Spanish boy rearing on horse), 1930s, plywood, 100 push-to-fit pcs, 9x7", EX (w/box), A4 ......$10.00

Dutch Mill, plywood, 172 interlocking pcs, 12x9", EX (rpl box), A4 ....$12.00

Echo Lake Colorado, artist Florence Hazeltine, plywood, 98 interlocking pcs, amateur cut, 8x9", EX (rpl box), A4.........$8.00

Eiffel Tower, Condor/Craftsman, plywood, 630 interlocking pcs, 16x20", EX (orig box), A4..$50.00

Family by Hearth, artist Murray, 1930s, plywood, 93 push-to-fit pcs, 8x7", EX (in old Christmas card box), A4 ....$13.00

Flemish Town, artist Henrie Marchal, 1930s, plywood, 75 push-to-fit pcs, 7x8", EX (rpl box), A4 ....$6.00

Flemish Town by River, 1930s, plywood, 200 semi-interlocking pcs, 9x12", EX (rpl box), A4 ....$20.00

Forest Rangers in Action, Straus, 1940s, artist Bellore Browac, plywood, 300 interlocking pcs, 12x16", EX (orig box), A4..$25.00

Four-Horse Carriage, William B Bean, 1930s, plywood, 350 edge interlocking pcs, 9x17", EX (orig box), A4................$45.00

French Coast Fishing Boat, plywood, 127 interlocking pcs, 8x9", G- (rpl box), A4..$8.00

Going Home, artist E Lamasure, 1909, solid wood, 248 push-to-fit pcs, color-line cut, 6 pcs rpl, EX (rpl box), A4......$30.00

Harbor Scene w/Freighter & Tugboat, artist Ellis Silas, plywood, 150 interlocking pcs, 8x12", EX (rpl box), A4...........$15.00

Haven (shepherd w/sheep), Schwabe print, 1910s, plywood, 296 push-to-fit pcs, color-line cut, 9x12", EX (orig box), A4..$38.00

Hill's Spelling Blocks, GL Hill & Son, 20 litho paper-covered wooden blocks w/scenes, numbers & alphabet, G+ (G+ box), A..$220.00

Hunt Is On (fox hunt), Straus, artist Gilbert Wright, 1930s, plywood, 300 interlocking pcs, strip cut, EX (orig box), A4.............$25.00

In the Sussex Weld, plywood, 500 interlocking pcs, strip cut, 16x20", 15 rpl pcs, EX (rpl box), A4..........................$45.00

Inaugural Ball (G Washington), artist R Moran, 1940s, plywood, 612 interlocking pcs, 16x20", 1 pc rpl, EX (orig box), A4......$75.00

Judgement of Paris, 1910, solid wood, 178 push-to-fit pcs, color-line cut, G- (SS Pierce box), A4 ....$25.00

Kanalfarden, ALGAS/Sweden, 1950s, plywood, 800 interlocking pcs, strip cut, 3 pcs rpl, EX (orig box), A4 ....$50.00

Lake Shore Photo, plywood, 300 push-to-fit pcs, 18x14", 1 pc rpl, EX (rpl box), A4 ....$35.00

Last Ray, 1930s, plywood (rough), 317 edge interlocking pcs, 12x16", some foxing, G- (w/box), A4 ....$20.00

Let's Get Going (master & dog prepare for walk), plywood, 468 interlocking pcs, 18x12", EX (rpl box), A4................$55.00

Man Fishing, Browning, 1960s, plywood, 210 interlocking pcs, 10x14", EX (orig box), A4..$30.00

Map of US, Madmar, 1926, wood, EX (orig box) $25.00

Map of US w/Information, Saalfield, 1932, NMIB $35.00

Photo courtesy of Bob Armstrong.

May Day (grazing sheep), early 1900s, solid wood, 564 push-to-fit pieces, 11x8", darkened (with box), $80.00.

Merry Chase (Fox Hunt), Straus, artist JS Sanderson, 1950s, plywood, 300 interlocking pcs, 16x12", EX (orig box), A4 ..$20.00

Michaelmas Daisies (in vase), Atlantic/Kingsbridge, 1950-60, plywood, 160 interlocking pcs, 11x8", EX (orig box), A4 ..$14.00

Mill Scene, artist Andel Kader, 1930s, plywood, 184 push-to-fit pcs, 11x8", darkened (w/box), A4................................$12.00

Model Ship Puzzle, Milton Bradley, paper on paperboard, framed, image: 17x23", EX (EX box), A, $330.00.

Mt Paradise, FAO Schwarz, 1950s, plywood, 300 interlocking pcs, 12x16", EX (orig box), A4.................................$30.00

Off for the Ride (winter scene), Straus, artist CJ Sternberg, 1950s, plywood, 300 interlocking pcs, EX (orig box), A4.......$25.00

Off to the Chase (fox hunt), Straus, artist G Wright, 1950s, 1,000 interlocking pcs, strip cut, 22x28", EX (orig box), A4 ....$75.00

Paddlewheel Boat City of Worcester, McLoughlin Bros, early, G, A $200.00

Passing Shower in Yellowstone, Straus, artist Moran, 1930s, plywood, 500 interlocking pcs, 16x20", EX (orig box), A4 ....$40.00

Pastoral Scene w/Cows, Parker, early 1900s, solid wood, 32 push-to-fit pcs, 6x8", EX (worn orig box), A4 ....$28.00

Prairie Fires of the Great West, 1920s, Currier & Ives print on masonite, 118 push-to-fit pcs, 11x16", EX (rpl box), A4..$20.00

Pride of Capture, Tuck, artist EM Bennett, 1930s, plywood, 530 interlocking pcs, 14x18", EX (orig box), A4...........$100.00

Racing Sailboats, 1920s, sepia-tone photo image on plywood, 100 interlocking pcs, strip cut, 7x9", EX (rpl box), A4 .....$10.00

Road by Stream, early 1900s, sepia-tone photo w/some coloring on solid wood, 164 push-to-fit pcs, EX (rpl box), A4 ....$22.00

Santa Claus, The Night Before Christmas, picture blocks, paper on wood, McLoughlin Brothers, includes six patterns, corners worn, G (G box), A, $1,100.00.

Scenic Countryside (pastoral), Browning, 1950-60, plywood, 488 interlocking pcs, EX (rpl box), A4 ....$65.00

Sea Captain's Children, Parker/Pastime, 1931, plywood, 155 semi-interlocking pcs, 11x8", EX (orig box), A4 ....$30.00

Serious Case, N Rockwell print, plywood, 250 interlocking pcs, tight cut, EX (rpl box), A4 ....$35.00

Serious Discussion, Parker/Pastime, 1930s, plywood, 202 interlocking pcs, color-line cut, 10x13", 2 pcs rpl, EX, A4 ....$35.00

Settling the Boundry, Ponda/England, 1960s, plywood, 1,000 interlocking pcs, strip cut (loose), 18x24", EX (orig box), A4 ....$60.00

Shadowland (Night Scene), 1920s, plywood (rough), 320 edge interlocking pcs, 16x12", EX (w/box), A4 ....$25.00

Shepherd Herding Sheep, Franz Dopinly print (?), early 1900s, solid wood, 222 push-to-fit pcs, A4...........................$30.00

Signing Mayflower Compact, 1920s, masonite, 80 push-to-fit pcs, 7x10", EX (RH Stearn mailing box), A4...........$15.00

Star of the Road (1849 N Currier print), 1920s, masonite, 142 edge-interlocking pcs, 1 pc rpl, G- (rpl box), A4.......$22.00

Summer Days at Mt Vernon, Straus, artist Ferris, 1940s, plywood, 500 interlocking pcs, 16x20", EX (orig box), A4........$35.00

Sunday Long Ago, early 1900s, solid wood, 207 push-to-fit pcs, color-line cut, 13x10", EX (orig box), A4..................$30.00

Sunny Mediterranean, Atlantic/Kingsbridge, 1950-60, plywood, 200 interlocking pcs, strip cut, 9x11", EX (orig box), A4......$12.00

Sunset in Venice, early 1900s, solid wood, 85 push-to-fit pcs, color-line cut, 5x10", EX (rpl box), A4......................$10.00

Tripoli Days (Maxfield Parrish-like scene), 1930s, plywood, 285 interlocking pcs, 9x12", EX (rpl box), A4.................$40.00

Photo courtesy of Bob Armstrong.

Unconquered Places, 1920s, plywood (rough), 324 interlocking pieces, 12x16", some foxing, G (with box), $20.00.

Venetian Revelers, artist P Moran, 1930s, plywood, 72 interlocking pcs, strip cut, 9x12", G color (rpl box), A4...$10.00

Village Blacksmith, artist WH Thompson, 1930s, plywood, 100 push-to-fit pcs, color-line cut, EX (w/box), A4 ....$13.00

Waikiki Beach, Straus, 1960s, photo image on plywood, 200 interlocking pcs, strip cut, 9x12", EX (orig box), A4..$12.00

Wild West Picture Puzzle, McLoughlin Brothers, 1890, EX, $375.00.

Washington DC, jigsaw, Saalfield, 1932, NMIB...............$35.00

Washington's Childhood Home, artist Hiebel, 1930s, plywood, 90 push-to-fit pcs, 8x6", w/box, A4............................$12.00

Welcoming the Guests (18th-century drawing-room scene), 1930s, plywood, 348 interlocking pcs, 14x18", EX (rpl box), A4 ....$55.00

Wild Animals, jigsaw, Parker Bros, 1930, EX (orig box) ..$40.00

Wild Turkeys on Fence at Night, early 1900s, solid wood, 121 push-to-fit pcs, 11x9", G- (w/box), A4 ....$10.00

Woman w/Horse Nibbling Bouquet, Parker, 1920s, plywood, 150 interlocking pcs, color-line cut, 13x9", 2 pcs rpl, EX, A4..$28.00

CHARACTER

Alf, jigsaw, Milton Bradley, 1987, 100 pcs, EX $4.00

Annie, jigsaw, Milton Bradley #4285, 1982, MIB (sealed) .$5.00

Baby Huey, jigsaw, Built-Rite, 1961, Baby Huey eating pies at fair, 70 pcs, MIB..$20.00

Bambi, fr-tray, Jaymar, 1950s, 11x14", EX, T2.................$20.00

Bambi, jigsaw, Jaymar, 1945, 2nd series, over 300 pcs, EX (EX box) $25.00

Barbie & Ken Little Theatre, jigsaw, #4004, 1963, MIB, D2..$50.00

Barbie & the Rockers, jigsaw, Golden #4815, 1987, NRFB..$5.00

Barbie's Rapunzel Little Theatre, fr-tray, Golden, 1984, MIP, D2..$6.00

Bat Masterson, jigsaw, Colorforms, 1960s, EX (VG box), J5 ..$65.00

Batman, jigsaw, Milton Bradley, M (EX box) $35.00

BattleStar Galactica, jigsaw, 1978, 140 pcs, EX $8.00

Beatles, jigsaw, Sgt Pepper's Band, Jaymar, 1968, EX $55.00

Beatles, jigsaw, shows Beatles performing, 340 pcs, complete, EX+ (EX box) $60.00

Beetle Bailey, jigsaw, Jaymar, 1963, 60 pcs, NM (EX+ box)..$16.00

Ben Casey, The Ordeal Is Over, jigsaw, Milton Bradley #4, 1962, operating room scene, M (EX+ box)...............$28.00

Black Hole, fr-tray, Whitman, 1979, shows astronaut facing Maximillian, NM, D9 ....$5.00

Black Hole, jigsaw, Whitman, 1979, shows Maximillian & Dr Reinhardt, 500 pcs, VG, H4 ....$5.00

Blondie, jigsaw, Jaymar, 1963, 100 pcs, NMIB, T2 ....$18.00

Buck Rogers, fr-tray, Milton Bradley/Dille, 1952, Buck & other figures in space, NM (EX+ dust jacket), A $65.00

Buck Rogers, jigsaw, Puzzle Craft, 1940s, set of 3, 1 incomplete, scarce, EX (VG box) $375.00

Bugs Bunny, fr-tray, Jaymar, 1950s, Elmer & other characters in garden scene, EX $30.00

Bugs Bunny & Porky Pig, jigsaw, Whitman Jr, 1960s, sack race w/Bugs, Porky & other characters, MIB $15.00

Buzzy the Crow, jigsaw, Built-Rite, 1961, Buzzy popping out of pie, 70 pcs, MIB, T2 ....$26.00

Captain Kangaroo, fr-tray, 1977, MOC............................$8.00

Charmin' Chatty, fr-tray, L6...$40.00

Chatty Baby, fr-tray, L6 ....$30.00

CHiPs, jigsaw, 1977, features Ponch, EX $15.00

Chitty-Chitty Bang-Bang, fr-tray, Whitman #4529, 1968, NM, C1 ....$20.00

Close Encounters of the Third Kind, jigsaw, Milton Bradley, 1977, 250 pcs, MIB (sealed), P3 ....$15.00

Creature From the Black Lagoon, jigsaw, 1990, 200 pcs, MIB.$15.00

Dick Tracy, jigsaw, Jaymar, Crime Does Not Pay Club, Dick Tracy w/friends & major villains, MIB......................$45.00

Disney Movie Classics #105, features Bambi, jigsaw puzzle, Jaymar, 100 pieces, EX (EX box)), $8.00.

Disney on Parade, jigsaw, Springbok, 1973, EX $7.00
Donald Duck, jigsaw, Whitman, 100 pcs, EX.....................$8.00
Dukes of Hazzard, jigsaw, 1982, 200 pcs, EX $10.00
Elvis, jigsaw, 1977, side view of Elvis w/microphone, 200 pcs, EX $10.00
Elvis, jigsaw, 1993, illus of postage stamp, limited edition, M, S2 ....$25.00
ET, jigsaw, Craft Master, 1982, EX.................................$6.00
Family Affair, jigsaw, Whitman, 1970, rnd, EX $25.00
Flash Gordon, fr-tray, Milton Bradley/KFS, 1951, Flash atop rocket trying to save heroine, NM (EX dust jacket)..$60.00
Flash Gordon, fr-tray, Milton Bradley/KFS, 1951, Flash shooting lg weapon into space, NM (EX dust jacket)...............$60.00
Flintstones, jigsaw, Whitman Jr, 1964, gruesome family w/Fred & Wilma in background, rare, EX, H4 ....$35.00
Flipper, fr-tray, Whitman #4546, 1966, G $12.00
Frankenstein, jigsaw, Jaymar, features Frankenstein, Doc & Igor, 100 jumbo pcs, MIB, A..$35.00
Gabby Gator, fr-tray, Preskool, 1963, Gabby conducting group of singing frogs, EX+, T2 ....$10.00
General Hospital, jigsaw, Tuco, 4 different puzzles featuring various characters, MIB (sealed), ea $5.00
Ghostbusters, floor puzzle w/49 extra-lg pcs featuring all of the characters, rare, M $20.00
Grasshopper & the Ants, jigsaw, Jaymar/Disney, 1943, 1st series, 300 pcs, EX (VG box), M8...................................$20.00
Green Hornet, fr-tray, Green Hornet & Kato in Black Beauty, 8x10", EX, J5...$25.00
Green Hornet, fr-tray, Whitman, 1960s, set of 4, 8x10", M (EX box)..$65.00
Gremlins, fr-tray, Golden, 1984, M (sealed) $10.00
Happy Days, jigsaw, 1976, features the Fonz, 250 pcs, EX...$15.00
Hardy Boys, jigsaw, Am Publishing #1515, 1978, features Shawn Cassidy, MIB (sealed) $18.00
Hopalong Cassidy, fr-tray, M, J2.....................................$50.00
Hopalong Cassidy, jigsaw, set of 3, EX (G box), O1 ....$90.00

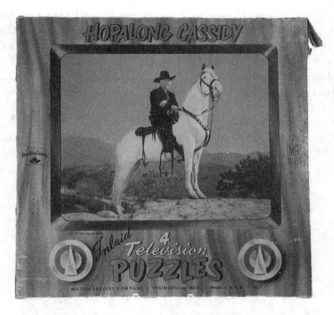

Hopalong Cassidy, Milton Bradley/W Boyd, 1950, set of four full-color puzzles in TV box, MIB, $125.00.

How the West Was Won, jigsaw, HG Toys #493-01, 1978, MIB (sealed)..$15.00
Howdy Doody, fr-tray, Whitman #4428, 1953, NM.........$35.00

Howdy Doody Puzzles, Milton Bradley/ Kagran, boxed set of three, NMIB, $50.00.

HR Pufnstuf, fr-tray, shows Witchipoo, Buzzard, Pufnstuf & Jimmy in Witch's Castle, EX, H4 ....$40.00
Johnny Appleseed & Davy Crockett, jigsaw, Playskool, boxed set of 2 w/bear-fighting scenes, 120 pcs, NM (EX+ box) .$85.00
King Leonardo, jigsaw, Jaymar, 1972, G (G box), S2 ....$10.00
Lassie, fr-tray, 1966, NM, J2 ....$18.00

Little Red Riding Hood Cut-Up Picture (A Puzzle To Put Together), diamond-shaped litho paper pcs, VG (G box), A $130.00

Lone Ranger, fr-tray, 1960s, NM, J2.................................$25.00

Love Boat, jigsaw, 1978, 150 pcs, EX $12.00

Magilla Gorilla, fr-tray, Whitman, 1964, 11x14", NM, T2..$30.00

Man From UNCLE, fr-tray, Jaymar, 1965, color scene w/Alexander Waverly at control panel, 11x14", NM.................$45.00

Mary Poppins, jigsaw, Jaymar, 1964, 100 pcs, EX $15.00

Maverick, fr-tray, Whitman #4427, 1960, NM.................$30.00

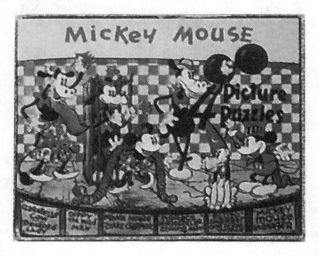

Mickey Mouse, Saalfield/WDE, 1933, contains three of four from original set, EX (VG+ box), A, $200.00.

Mickey Mouse, jigsaw, Parker Bros, 1950s, set of 4, EX (EX box), C1 ....$45.00

Mickey Mouse & Pluto, jigsaw, Chad Valley/England, plywood, set of 3, rare, EX+ (orig box), M8 ....$300.00

Mork & Mindy, jigsaw, Milton Bradley #2 or #3, 1978, 250 pcs, EX, ea $8.00

Mr I Magination, jigsaw, Jaymar, 1951, 400 pcs, EX+ (EX+ box) .$20.00

Mr Magoo, fr-tray, Warren, 1978, Mr Magoo looking at fish in aquarium, MIP (sealed) $12.00

Mr Magoo, fr-tray, 1967, Mr Magoo outside gym w/kangaroo, G $25.00

Mr Magoo, jigsaw, Jaymar, Beware of the Dog, 60 pcs, EX (rpr box), T2 ....$20.00

Munsters, jigsaw, Whitman, 1965, Lily playing organ, MIB ..$60.00

Munsters, jigsaw, Whitman, 1965, Munsters around cauldron w/Grandpa mixing potion, MIB $60.00

Munsters, jigsaw, Whitman, 1965, Munsters in car & Grandpa waving from house, MIB...$60.00

Muppets Christmas Party, jigsaw, Springbok, 1980, EX......$5.00

Our Gang, jigsaw, features Little Rascals in jalopy fire engine, NM, A $121.00

Our Gang, jigsaw, Wilder Mfg, features Spanky as Caesar & Buckwheat being fed to lion, NM, A $116.00

Pink Panther, jigsaw, 1979, Pink Panther playing violin for girl near Inspector, 125 pcs, G (G box)............................$10.00

Planet of the Apes, jigsaw, 1967, EX.................................$15.00

Raggedy Ann & Andy, fr-tray, 1980, EX, O1 ....$13.50

Road Runner the Big Beeper, jigsaw, Whitman, 1968, NM (NM box), C1 ....$36.00

Robin Hood, fr-tray, Built Rite, 1950s, EX, C1.................$20.00

Rocketeer, fr-tray, Rocketeer flying through barn, M (sealed) $10.00

Rocketeer, fr-tray, M, H10...$4.00

Rocketeer, jigsaw, autographed, MIB, H10 ....$15.00

Rocky & Bullwinkle, fr-tray, Roalex, 1960s, MOC, H4 ...$45.00

Roger Ramjet, fr-tray, Whitman, 1966, EX....................$28.00

Roy Rogers, fr-tray, Whitman, 1953, complete, EX+ $30.00

Secret of Nimh, fr-tray, Whitman, 1982, red or bl label, extra lg, MIB (sealed) $10.00

Simpsons, jigsaw, Milton Bradley, Bart riding bucking horse, 250 pcs, MIB $5.00

Simpsons, jigsaw, Milton Bradley, Bart skateboarding into Homer, 100 pcs, MIB...$5.00

Simpsons, jigsaw, Milton Bradley, Bart surfing, 250 pcs, MIB..$5.00

Six Million Dollar Man, jigsaw, shows Steve bursting through wall, M (sealed can).....................................$15.00

Six Million Dollar Man, jigsaw, shows Steve throwing drum, M (sealed can), S2...$20.00

Snow White and the Seven Dwarfs, frame tray, Jaymar, 11x14", M, $25.00.

Space Kidettes, fr-tray, Whitman, 1967, 11x14", EX........$25.00

Spiderman, jigsaw, Golden, 1988, shoots webs from lighthouse to SOS boat, 200 pcs, NMIB, S2...............................$10.00

Starsky & Hutch, jigsaw, HG Toys, 1976, 150 pcs, NMIB, T2..$20.00

Super Heroes, jigsaw, Jaymar, 1987, EX $10.00

Terrytoons, fr-tray, Jaymar, 1956, EX, T2 ....$30.00

Three Little Pigs, jigsaw, France, 1 w/Pigs outdoors & other w/Pigs & Red Riding Hood, rare, EX+ (no boxes), M8, ea.....$45.00

Three Stooges, jigsaw, Am Publishing Co, 1974, 200 pcs, EX (orig can) $25.00

Tiny Chatty Baby, fr-tray, L6...$35.00

Tom & Jerry, fr-tray, Whitman, 1953, as Sultans in India, 11x14", EX, T2 ....$18.00

Tom & Jerry, fr-tray, Whitman, 1959, beach scene, 11x14", EX, T2..$22.00

Tom & Jerry, fr-tray, Whitman, 1969, set of 4, VG (orig box), H4 ....$12.00

Tomorrowland, fr-tray, Whitman, 1957, Mickey, Goofy, Donald & his nephews at space center, NM, T2 ....$20.00

Tommy Tortoise & Moe Hare, jigsaw, Built-Rite, 1961, 70 pcs, MIB, T2 ....$26.00

Tortoise & the Hare, jigsaw, Jaymar, EX (EX box), J2 .....$35.00

Total Recall, jigsaw, features movie poster, 500 pcs, MIB (sealed)..$10.00

Twenty Thousand Leagues Under the Sea, Jaymar, 1960s, MIB, H4 ....$18.00

Universal Monsters, Dracula, fr-tray, Golden, 1980s, M (sealed), S2 ....$15.00

Universal Monsters, Frankenstein, fr-tray, Golden, 1980s, M (sealed), S2 ....$15.00

Wacky Races, jigsaw, Whitman, 1970, 100 pcs, EX+ (EX+ box), T2...$24.00

Welcome Back Kotter, fr-tray, Whitman, 1977, pictures all characters, EX+ $8.00

Woody Woodpecker, fr-tray, Walter Lantz, 1968, G, S2..$20.00

Woody Woodpecker, fr-tray, Whitman, 1954, Woody tied to helium balloons, 11x14", EX+, T2 ....$22.00

Woody Woodpecker, jigsaw, Whitman, 1960, 63 pcs, M (EX+ box), T2 ....$24.00

Zorro, fr-tray, Jaymar, 1960s, shows Guy Williams as Zorro & the bad guy on horses, VG, J5 ....$15.00

Zorro, jigsaw, Jaymar, 1950s, The Duel, NM (VG+ box) .$25.00

Radios, Novelty

Many novelty radios are made to resemble a commercial product box or can, and with the crossover interest into the advertising field, some of the more collectible, even though of recent vintage, are often seen carrying very respectible price tags. Likenesses of famous personalities such as Elvis or characters like Charlie Tuna house transistors in cases made of plastic that scarcely hint at their actual function. Others represent items ranging from baseball caps to Cadillacs. To learn more about this subject, we recommend *Collector's Guide to Transistor Radios* by Sue and Marty Bunis and *Collecting Transistor Novelty Radios, A Value Guide*, by Marty Bunis and Robert Breed.

Advisors: Sue and Marty Bunis (B11).

'57 Chevy, AM/FM radio & toilet paper holder, Beetland Tokyo, 6½" sq, EX $50.00

Avon's Skin-So-Soft Bottle, NMIB, J2 ....$33.00

Baseball Cap, Old Milwaukee, AM/FM, 2 ear plugs fit into bill of cap, EX...$35.00

Baseball Player, Sutton series, LA Dodgers, EX $42.00

Basketball, Chicago Bulls & Reebok/Sportmart, EX $42.00

Bass Fiddle, Radio Shack, transparent, EX.......................$52.00

Big Bird Face, S1...$20.00

Bike Light/Radio, Coca-Cola logo, Hong Kong, 4x6", NM..$45.00

Billy Beer, can form, NM..$90.00

Bird Cage, w/canary, metal & plastic cage, 4½x8", EX.....$80.00

Blabber Mouse, AM only, NM $35.00

Boeing 707, Hong Kong, 13¾" wingspan, 5½" high, EX...$110.00

Bowling Pin, early Japan, 12", EX $115.00

Bozo the Clown, plastic, 6x7", EX+, from $75.00 to $85.00.

Bullwinkle, PAT World Prod/Hong Kong, 3-D, plastic, EX..$210.00

Cable Car, CalTrade/Hong Kong, 4x8", EX.....................$68.00

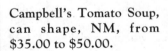

Campbell's Tomato Soup, can shape, NM, from $35.00 to $50.00.

Care Bears, Am Greeting Cards, 1985, 3-D rainbow on belly, 5½", EX $15.00

Champion Spark Plug, NM, T1 ....$125.00

Charlie Tuna, MIB $85.00

Chevy Impala SS, 1966, 8", NM $72.00

Coca-Cola Tote Bag, Randix, AM/FM, insulated, hdl & shoulder straps, NM...$30.00

Coffee Grinder, Nobility/Japan, wood & metal, NM........$45.00

Coke Vending Machine, AM/FM, plastic, NMIB, M5.....$35.00

Coronet Towels, S1 ....$40.00

Diner, Heartline Graphics Model NI 8712/China, 1988, chrome finish w/light-up windows, 11½", EX $85.00

Donald Duck, 1960s, plastic Donald figure, M (sealed), J5..$45.00

Duesenberg, 1934 Model J, Japan, EX $70.00

Eiffel Tower, 10", NM..$76.00

Elvis Presley, 1970s, full-figure doll in wht costume, 8¼", NMIB $65.00

Folgers Coffee, plastic can shape, 4", NM, from $60.00 to $75.00.

Photo courtesy of Sue and Marty Bunis.

Football (on tee), Japan, transistor, NM $45.00

Football Helmet, Dallas Cowboys emblem, Hong Kong, EX ..$42.00

Football Player, Sutton series, 1974, Hong Kong, 8½", NM ..$45.00

Ford T-Bird, Philco Model NT-11, ca 1964, EX $75.00

Fred Flintstone Head, S1 ....$60.00

Gas Pump, Marksman, 1940s replica w/light-up globe, AM/FM (?) cassette, 23½", EX $87.00

Ghostbusters' Marshmallow Man, figural w/night light, MIP ..$25.00

Ghostbusters' Slimer, Justin Toys/Columbia Pictures, 1984-88, FM only, EX $25.00

GI Joe, w/headset, EX $13.00

Golf ball (on tee), Ross Electronics Corp, Model PAR-72, EX..$90.00

Hamburger Helper, NM, J2 ....$40.00

He-Man/Skeletor, Nasta, 1984, figural, character from Masters of the Universe, MIB...$30.00

Highboy Horn Phonograph, S1 ....$45.00

Holly Hobbie, Vanity Fair Industries, 1978, Am Greeting Cards, 1976, shaped like jewelry box, EX.........................$42.00

Hopalong Cassidy, Arvin, blk w/face plate showing Hoppy on Topper w/name in script, scarce color, EX...............$350.00

Incredible Hulk, 1978, NM $65.00

Jukebox, Jr Collection, AM/FM, LED for bubble tubes, 5¾", NM..$33.00

Knight Rider, figural car radio, NMIB................................$25.00

Locomotive (1828), NM $60.00

Lone Ranger, Airline tube radio, wht molded plastic w/emb images of the Lone Ranger & Silver, lights up, 7½", EX........$750.00

Lunch Box, Lasersaurus, Fun Designs/Taiwan, 8", NM $27.00

Marlboro Cigarette Pack, Japan, NM..................................$90.00

Master Padlock, Hong Kong, premium, 4½", NM $65.00

McDonald's French Fries, 1977, EX, J2..............................$25.00

McDonald's French Fries, 1977, MIB, S2............................$50.00

Mercedes Benz Radiator Desk Set, Japan, NM $70.00

Michael Jackson, AM/FM, NM..$20.00

Mickey Mouse, Emerson tube radio, simulated wood w/emb images of Mickey playing different instruments, 7½", G, A...$200.00

Mickey Mouse, in chair, EX...$15.00

Mickey Mouse, transistor w/2-D face, MIP, S1 ....$20.00

Mickey Mouse, w/ear-shaped earphones, NMIB...............$30.00

Mickey Mouse, WD, lion tamer, NM...................................$42.00

Mickey Mouse, 3-D face, S1 ....$20.00

Mighty Mouse (flying on top of a pc of cheese), Vanity Fair Via Com/Hong Kong, 1978, 5x4¾", EX $135.00

Parking Meter, Thomas Model 131/China, AM/FM & cassette, 17", EX $68.00

Pepsi-Cola, Bakelite bottle tube radio, 24", EX $600.00

Pepsi-Cola, Bakelite bottle tube radio, 24", G, M5........$390.00

Playhouse, Radio Shack/China, 1992, AM/cassette, 7", EX .$30.00

Polaroid 600 Filmpack, battery-op, MIB $25.00

Pool Table, Japan, also a jewelry box, wood, w/3 balls, 7", NM..$55.00

Porsche Targa Police Car, Hong Kong, 7¾", NM.............$45.00

Pound Puppy, S1 ....$25.00

Riverboat, Robert E Lee on base, 16x9", NM $70.00

R2-D2 (Star Wars) #38530, Kenner/Hong Kong, EX.....$130.00

Safe, K-Mart/Hong Kong, radio & bank, 5", NM $45.00

Sailing Ship, Windsor/China, 11", NM $45.00

Slot Machine, Hong Kong, NM $70.00

Snap-On Tool Chest, Snap-On of Canada/China, AM/FM & cassette, EX $90.00

Sneaker Shoe, nylon & rubber sole, German-made earphones, 4½", EX $68.00

Superman in Phone Booth, marked Made in Hong Kong, plastic, 7", NM, from $150.00 to $175.00.

Photo courtesy of Sue and Marty Bunis.

Snoopy, Determined/United Features Syndicate, Hong Kong, 1965, 3-D on rnd base, 7", NM $42.00

Snoopy on Doghouse, S1 ....$30.00

Soccer Ball, ProSports Marketing/USA, 5½" dia, EX.......$42.00

Spam, 3¾", NM $48.00

Spiderman Wrist Radio, Janex/Hong Kong, EX...............$52.00

Stage Coach, Japan, Overland Stage Express, w/horses, NM..$95.00

Steam Engine, Waco/Japan, metal & plastic, EX $110.00

Sunkist Can, MIB $32.00

Superman, 1973, EX (EX box), J2 ....$60.00

Tiny Tim Crystal Radio Set, Remco, 1960s, unused, MIB, J2...$110.00

Tire, Japan, 5" dia, EX $68.00

Tony the Tiger, box only, EX..$32.00

Tony the Tiger, NM, S2 ....$50.00

Toy Soldier, General Electric/Hong Kong, 7", NM $68.00

Transformers Wrist Radio, Hasbro/Hong Kong, 1984, NM..$42.00

Trophy, Japan, also a jewelry box, features a bowler, EX ..$42.00

Tropicana Orange, M, J2 ....$22.00

TV set, Gold Star/Japan, EX...$68.00

Violin, Japan, detailed plastic, metal stand, EX.............$110.00

VW Rear End, Hong Kong, radio & toilet paper holder, EX.$68.00

V8, can shape, NM, from $35.00 to $50.00.

Photo courtesy of Sue and Marty Bunis.

Woolite, marked made in Hong Kong, 8", MIB, from $75.00 to $100.00.

Photo courtesy of Sue and Marty Bunis.

Winnie the Pooh, Hong Kong, figure on honey pot, 3¾x7", EX...$45.00

Wristwatch, lg, EX+, J2 ....$35.00

Wuzzel Butter Bear, S1 ....$25.00

7-Up Can, EX $25.00

7-Up Vending Machine, Markatron/Hong Kong, EX.......$85.00

Ramp Walkers

The concept of ramp-walking toys is not new, though nearly all you'll see on today's market are of fairly recent manufacture. They date back to the 1870s when the first cast-iron elephant walker was made by the Ives company. From the 1920s through the 1940s, wood and composition ramp walkers were made in the USA as well as Argentina and Czechoslovakia. One of the largest US producers was John Wilson of Pennsylvania. His Wilson Walkies are approximately 4½" tall, and most are 2-legged.

The Marx company made plastic ramp walkers from the '50s through the early '60s. Most were produced in Hong Kong and sold under the Marx logo, and some were sold by a subsidiary of Marx, the Charmore Co. Other examples of plastic walkers are known to have originated from England, Germany, Japan, Argentina and Poland.

Ramp walkers were made in three general sizes. The smaller ones measure about 1½" x 2" and are unpainted. The medium and larger size walkers are approximately 2¾" x 3" and 4" x 5" and may be either spray painted or painted by hand.

Advisor: Randy Welch (W4).

Donald Duck Pulling Nephews in Cart, $35.00; Donald and Goofy Riding a Cart, $40.00; Goofy Riding a Hippo, $40.00; Minnie Pushing a Baby Stroller, $40.00.

Ankylosaurus w/Clown, Marx, Animals w/Riders series ...$25.00

Asterix & Obelix, MOC $150.00

Baby Teen Toddler, Dolls Inc, plastic baby girl, lg $30.00
Baby Walk-a-Way, Marx, plastic, lg.................................$40.00
Band Drummers, European issue, NM...........................$200.00
Baseball Player, w/ball & bat $30.00
Bear, unmk, plastic..$15.00
Big Bad Wolf & 3 Pigs, plastic $150.00
Boy Walking Behind Girl, plastic, lg.............................$45.00
Buffalo, Marx, NM..$25.00
Bull, unmk, plastic $15.00
Captain Flint, Long John Silvers, 1989, gr, plastic coin weight,
     in series of 5 ....$10.00
Chicks & Easter Egg, unmk, plastic................................$30.00
Chinaman w/Duck in Basket, unmk, plastic $35.00
Choo-Choo Cherry, Kool-Aid, plastic coin weight..........$60.00
Clown w/Armadillo, Marx, NM $25.00
Cowboy, riding horse, plastic w/metal legs, sm $20.00
Dachshund, plastic..$15.00
Donald Duck, Marx, MIP, S2...$55.00
Donald Duck w/Wheelbarrow, Marx, NM.......................$20.00
Duck, NM $20.00
Dutch Boy & Girl, plastic..$30.00
Elephant, brn or gray, NM...$25.00
Eskimo, Wilson, wood & compo $70.00
Figaro the Cat, w/ball, plastic $25.00
Frontiersman w/Dog..$75.00
George Jetson & Astro, Marx/Hanna-Barbera, NM $75.00
Goofy Grape, Kool-Aid, plastic coin weight....................$60.00
Horse, plastic, lg...$25.00
House Painters, European issue, EX+ $150.00
Indian Chief, Wilson, wood & compo $45.00
Indian Mother w/Baby on Travois $75.00

Mother Goose, NM...$55.00
Native on Zebra, Marx, NM $25.00
Nurse, Wilson, wood & compo $30.00
Nursemaid Pushing Baby Buggy, EX...............................$20.00
Pig, NM $15.00
Pluto, Marx, MIP $15.00
Popeye, King Features, w/spinach can wheelbarrow, plastic,
     VG $25.00

Popeye and Wimpy, Marx, plastic, heads on springs, MIB, $80.00.

Reindeer $25.00
Santa w/Bag, EX...$28.00
Spark Plug (horse) $175.00
Three Little Pigs, NM...$50.00
Top Cat & Bennie, EX $42.00
Two Fireman, Marx, MIP $35.00
Two Sailors, Marx, MIP...$30.00
Wiz Walker Cow, Marx, NMOC, J2 ....$45.00

Jiminy Cricket with Cello, plastic, from $20.00 to $30.00.

Yogi Bear and Huckleberry Hound, marked Made in Hong Kong, plastic, minimum value $45.00.

Jolly Ollie Orange, Kool-Aid, plastic coin weight $60.00
Kangaroo w/Baby, Marx, extremely rare, MIP $25.00
Mad Hatter & Rabbit, NM...$65.00
Marty's Market Lady w/Shopping Cart $45.00

Records

Most of the records listed here are related to TV shows and movies, and all are specifically geared toward children. The more successful the show, the more collectible the record. But condition is critical as well, and unless the record is excellent or better, its value is lowered dramatically.

Adventures of the Lone Ranger, Deca, 1960s, 33⅓ rpm, radio stories, NM, T2 ....$8.00

Alice in Wonderland/Pinocchio, storyteller, VG, P3 ....$3.00

Allan Sherman My Son the Nut, Warner Bros, 1963, 33⅓ rpm, EX, T2 ....$10.00

Alvin & the Chipmunks Sing Chitty-Chitty Bang-Bang, 1960s, 5 45-rpm records, EX (w/sleeve & display box), J5 ....$45.00

Andy Griffith's Just for Laughs, Capitol Records, 1960s, 33⅓ rpm, G+ $12.50

Baa-Baa Black Sheep, 1976, 45 rpm, EX $8.00

Babes in Toyland, Little Golden Records, 1960s, VG (torn sleeve), S2 ....$5.00

Ballad of Davy Crockett, 1950, 45 rpm, EX $20.00

Batman, Power Records, 1975, 33⅓ rpm, H4 ....$5.00

Batman & Robin Record Set, USA, 1966, 45 rpm, set of 3, MIB, A $75.00

Belinda's Rainy Day, Little Golden Records, 1960s, NM (in sleeve), S2 ....$20.00

Bobby & Betty Go to the Moon, Happy House Records, 1960, 33⅓ rpm, EX+, T2 ....$15.00

Bozo & Magic Whistle, Little Golden Records, 1960s, NM (in sleeve), S2 ....$20.00

Bozo at the Circus, 1950, 78 rpm, EX..............................$25.00

Bozo's Christmas Singalong, 1973, EX $10.00

Brady Bunch Phonographic Album, LP, J6......................$55.00

Cinderella Work Song, Walt Disney Productions/ Golden Record, 1950s, 45 rpm, NM (original sleeve), $28.00.

Bugs Bunny & Yosemite Sam, Little Golden Records, 78 rpm, NM (EX color sleeve), T2 ....$10.00

Candid Camera's Allen Funk & Candid Kids, RCA, 1967, 33⅓ rpm, NM, T2......................................$20.00

Captain Kangaroo, CBS, 1956, 78 rpm, NM (blk & wht photo sleeve), T2 ....$10.00

Casper in a Musical Adventure Make-Believe Record Album, Peter Pan, 1965, 33⅓ rpm, VG+ (VG+ color sleeve), T2 ....$8.00

Casper the Friendly Ghost, Wonderland, 1965, 33⅓ rpm, EX, T2..$10.00

Catwoman's Revenge, 1975, w/cartoon image on cover, G, S2..$5.00

Curious George Takes a Job, Scholastic, 1969, 33⅓ rpm, w/ booklet, EX+..$10.00

Daffy Duck's Inn, Mel Blanc, 1948, 78 rpm, EX (no sleeve) .$12.00

Daniel Boone, Fess Parker, 1965, soundtrack, EX.............$35.00

Daniel Boone, Til Records, 1977, 33⅓ rpm, VG (in sleeve), I2..$15.00

Dark Shadows, Phillips, 1969, 33⅓ rpm, w/11x22" blk & wht poster, NM, C1..$31.00

Dick Tracy, Mercury Records, 1947, 2 records, unused, EX+ (sleeves w/cartoons inside on which to write story lines), A........$79.00

Disney Presents National Anthems #3931, 1965, 33⅓, stereo, M (sealed sleeve), J5 ....$15.00

Disney Presents Professor Wonderful #4 of Series DQ-1294, 1966, 33⅓, M, J5..$15.00

Disney Presents the Great Composers #1919, 1962, 33⅓, stereo, M (sealed sleeve), J5 ....$15.00

Disney Presents This Was the West #WDL-3033, 1950s, 33⅓, w/gatefold illus by Shirley Reed, M, J5..........................$15.00

Disney's Little Toot, 1952, 33⅓ rpm, EX (picture sleeve) $10.00

Disney's Nutcracker Suite #DQ-1243, music from Fantasia, 1963, 33⅓ rpm, mono, M, J5..$15.00

Donald Duck & His Friends, 45 rpm, 1-sided, scarce, in Disney-land mailer, M8..$25.00

Droid World, 45 rpm, w/booklet, M (sealed sleeve), P9 .....$9.00

Eddie Albert Album, Columbia, 78 rpm, features Green Acres Theme, Blowing in the Wind & more, EX (in sleeve), D9.............$14.00

Emmet Kelly — Clown & Kids, 1968, soundtrack, M (sealed sleeve) $20.00

Empire Strikes Back, 45 rpm, w/booklet, M (sealed sleeve), P9 ....$9.00

Ewoks Join the Fight, 45 rpm, w/booklet, M (sealed sleeve), P9 ....$9.00

Flintstones & Jose Jimenez, 1965, EX..............................$30.00

Flintstones Meet the Orchestra Family, Sunset, 1968, 33⅓ rpm, EX (VG sleeve), T2..$10.00

Frosty the Snowman, 1951, 45 rpm, EX $12.00

Godzilla vs Amphibian, 1977, 33⅓, M (sealed sleeve), S2 .....$30.00

Grease 2, 33⅓ rpm, 1982, EX (in sleeve) $10.00

Green Hornet, 1966, 45 rpm, EX (in sleeve) $30.00

Hanna-Barbera 3-On-1 Children's Record, Golden Records, 1961, 78 rpm, VG+ (EX+ color sleeve), T2..............$18.00

Heckle & Jeckle, Little Golden Records, 1958, 45 rpm, NM (NM sleeve), T2..$24.00

Heidi, 1972, 4 songs, 33⅓, EX (EX sleeve) $4.00

Home on the Range featuring Bing Crosby, Decca #DL8210, 1950s, EX (EX sleeve shows Bing in western garb), J5 ..$25.00

Hopalong Cassidy, Story of Topper, 45 rpm, G- (G sleeve), O1 ....$55.00

Hopalong Cassidy, Two-Legged Wolf, 45 rpm, EX (EX sleeve), O1 ....$70.00

Hopalong Cassidy & Legend of Phantom Pass, 78 rpm, EX (orig sleeve), D8 ....$35.00

Hopalong Cassidy & the Singing Bandit, w/booklet, 1950s, EX, D8..$75.00

Howdy Doody & Air-O-Doodle, 1949, 78 rpm, EX (EX sleeve) $40.00

Howdy Doody & You, RCA Little Nipper, 45 rpm, G, I2 ..$5.00

Howdy Doody's Crystal Ball, RCA, 45 rpm, G, I2 ....$6.00

Hucklebery Finn, 1974, M (sealed sleeve) $12.00

Jetsons First Family on the Moon, 1977, EX $15.00

Jiminy Cricket's Mouse Club Songs, Walt Disney Productions, 1975, 45 rpm, M (original sleeve), $20.00.

Joke Along With Jimmy Nelson Children's Record, Peter Pan, 1962, 45 rpm, M (NM sleeve), T2 ....$20.00

Last Starfighter, Buena Vista Records, 33⅓ rpm, w/24-pg read-along booklet, M (sealed sleeve), D9 ....$4.00

Leonard Nemoy Space Odyssey, Pickwick #SPC 3100, 33⅓ rpm, Star Trek Theme, Spock's Thoughts, etc, EX (EX sleeve) $30.00

Lone Ranger, He Helps the Colonel's Son, Decca, 1951, #4 of a series, EX, J5 ....$20.00

Man From UNCLE & Other TV Themes, Metro, 1966, 33⅓ rpm, color Robert Bond & David McCallahan photo sleeve, EX+, T2 ....$20.00

Masters of the Universe, 1983, M (sealed sleeve) $12.00

Mickey Mouse Club March, 1955, 45 rpm, EX $25.00

Mickey Mouse Newsreel Music Record, Official Mickey Mouse Club Records, 1950s, 78 rpm, M (NM illus sleeve), T2 .$12.00

Mickey Mouse Pledge, G, S2 ....$10.00

Muscle Beach Party, Annette, 45 rpm, EX......................$20.00

Old Man & the Sea, Columbia, 1950s, EX+ (color Spencer Tracy sleeve), T2 ....$32.00

Peter & the Wolf, 1949, 78 rpm, 2 records, EX (EX sleeve).$25.00

Peter Pan, 1979, 33⅓ rpm, w/4 stories, NM (in sleeve), P9 .....$8.00

Pinocchio, 45 rpm, 1961, EX (in sleeve)........................$12.00

Popeye the Sailor Man, Diplomat Records, 1960, 33⅓ rpm, EX, T2 ....$18.00

Puff the Magic Dragon, 1983, M (sealed sleeve) $8.00

Punch & Judy, Twinkle Records, 1950s, complete show, M, T2 ....$12.00

Quick Draw, Yogi, Cindy, Huckleberry Hound, Hokey Wolf & Snuffles, Golden Record, 1961, VG (VG sleeve), S2 ..$20.00

Quick Draw McGraw & Huckleberry Hound, Golden Record, 1959, 33⅓ rpm, VG+ (VG+ sleeve), T2...................$14.00

Quick Draw McGraw & Treasure of Sarah's Mattress, Colpix, 1961, 33⅓ rpm, VG (VG sleeve), T2 ....$14.00

Return of the Jedi, 33⅓ rpm, w/cassette & booklet, M (sealed sleeve), P9...$35.00

Return of the Jedi, 45 rpm, w/booklet, M (sealed sleeve), T2 .$9.00

Return of the Jedi Picture Disk Album, w/picture of Ewok on album disk, 1983, 33⅓ rpm, H4 ....$16.00

Robin Hood Starring Top Cat, 1965, EX.........................$25.00

Robin Hood Starring Top Cat, 1977, EX.........................$10.00

Roy Rogers' Thank You God, 45 rpm, D8.......................$22.00

Roy Rogers & Dale Evans, Bible Tells Me So, Golden Records, 1950s, EX (EX sleeve), J5 ....$25.00

Roy Rogers & Dale Evans Song Wagon, 7 records, EX (orig box) $55.00

Roy Rogers Rodeo Story Booklet, RCA Victor, 45 rpm, 2 records w/illus story, VG (sleeve w/Roy, Trigger & children) .$22.00

Ruff & Reddy Friends, 1959, 45 rpm, EX $25.00

Saturday Night Live, Arista, 1976, EX+ (color photo sleeve), T2 ....$22.00

Scooby Doo Christmas Stories, 1978, EX........................$15.00

Siamese Cat Song/Lady & the Tramp, Disney Little Gem Record, 1962, 45 rpm, M (NM sleeve), T2................$12.00

Silly Symphonies, England/RCA, 1930s, 33⅓ rpm, part 1 & 2 of Pied Piper, Mickey, Donald & Pig on label, EX+, A...$68.00

Snow White & the Seven Dwarfs' Whistle While You Work, 1958, 33⅓ rpm, EX (picture sleeve) $12.00

Spiderman, Power Records, 1974, 33⅓ rpm, G, H4...........$5.00

Spin & Mary, 1975, 33⅓ rpm, EX (photo sleeve).............$10.00

Star Trek (The Movie), Peter Pan Records, 1979, book & 33⅓ rpm record, EX, H4 ....$8.00

Star Wars, Planet of the Hoojibs, book & record set, EX (sealed sleeve), H4 ....$5.00

Star Wars Adventures in Colors & Shapes, record & book, M (sealed sleeve), P9...$9.00

Story of Star Wars, from the original motion picture, 1978, 33⅓ rpm, H4..$12.00

Story of Star Wars, 33⅓ rpm, w/booklet, M (sealed sleeve), D9..$40.00

Sword in the Stone, 1963, 45 rpm, EX............................$20.00

Tales of Wells Fargo, 1950s, 45 rpm, VG (in sleeve), J5 ..$25.00

Tales of Wells Fargo & Lonely Rider, Golden, EX (in sleeve), I2 ....$7.00

Three Little Kittens, 1960, 45 rpm, EX $8.00

Three Little Pigs, Peter Pan, 1960s, VG (in sleeve), S2 ...$15.00

Three Stooges Come to Your House & Make a Record, Golden Record/Maurer, ca 1959, 45 rpm, NM (in sleeve) **$18.00**

Three Stooges Nonsense Song Book, Coral, 1960, 33⅓ rpm, EX+ (VG+ sleeve), T2 ....$15.00

Top Cat, Dum-Dum, Lippy Lion, Hardy Har, Wally Gator & Touche Turtle, Golden Record, 1962, VG (VG sleeve), S2 ....$20.00

Top Cat Starring as Robin Hood, HER Records, 1962, 33⅓ rpm, VG+, T2 ....$20.00

Treasure Island Starring Sinbad Jr, EX (sealed sleeve) $35.00

TV Terrytoons Cartoontime Record Album, RCA, 1959, 33⅓ rpm, VG+ (VG+ sleeve), T2.....................................$15.00

Tweet Tweet Tweet, Mel Blanc, 1948, EX (no sleeve) $12.00

Twinkles & His Pals, Little Golden Records, 1961, 78 rpm, unused, M (EX+ color sleeve), T2............................$39.00

Walt Disney's Mickey Mouse Club, Robin Hood, 1950s, 45 rpm, NM (photo sleeve) $20.00

William Bendix Sings & Tells Famous Pirate Stories, Cricket Records, 1959, 45 rpm, M (M photo sleeve), T2.......$20.00

Wilma Flintstone Tells the Story of Bambi, Hanna-Barbera, 1965, VG...$6.00

Woody Woodpecker's Talent Show, 1975, EX $8.00

Yogi Bear Introduces Loope De Loope, Little Golden Records, 1960, unused, M, C1...$24.00

Zorro, 1958, w/dialogue, soundtrack, VG.........................$15.00

20,000 Leagues Under the Sea, Disneyland, 1971, w/booklet, VG, P3 ....$5.00

Reynolds Toys

Reynolds Toys began production in 1964, at first making large copies of early tin toys for window displays, though some were sold to collectors as well. These toys included trains, horse-drawn vehicles, boats, a steam toy and several sizes of Toonerville trolleys. In the early 1970s, they designed and produced six animated cap guns. Finding the market limited, by 1971 they had switched to a line of banks they call New Original Limited Numbered Editions (10-50) of Mechanical Penny Banks. Still banks were added to their line in 1980 and figural bottle openers in 1988. Each bank design is original; no reproductions are produced. Reynolds' banks are in the White House

and the Smithsonian as well as many of the country's major private collections. *The Penny Bank Book* by Andy and Susan Moore (Schiffer Publishing, 1984) shows and describes the first twelve still banks Reynolds produced. Values are given for mint-condition banks.

Advisor: Charlie Reynolds (R5).

MECHANICAL BANKS

01M, Train Man, 1971, edition of 30..............................$350.00
02M, Trolley Bank, 1971, edition of 30.........................$350.00
03M, Drive-In Bank, 1971, edition of 10.....................$750.00
04M, Pirate Bank, 1972, edition of 10 ....$725.00
05M, Blackbeard Bank, 1972, edition of 10.................$650.00
06M, Frog & the Fly Bank, 1972, edition of 10...........$1,200.00
07M, Toy Collector Bank, 1972, unlimited edition $550.00
08M, Balancing Bank, 1972, edition of 10....................$725.00
09M, Save the Girl Bank, 1972, edition of 10.............$1,200.00
10M, Father Christmas, 1 made ea year at Christmas.....$600.00
11M, Gump-on-a-Stump Bank, 1973, edition of 10....$1,100.00
12M, Trick Bank, 1973, edition of 10...........................$1,000.00
13M, Kid Savings Bank, 1973, edition of 10 ....$1,200.00
14M, Christmas Tree Bank, 1973, edition of 10.............$725.00
15M, Foxy Grandpa Bank, 1974, edition of 10..............$975.00
16M, Happy Hooligan Bank, 1974, edition of 10........$1,075.00
17M, Chester's Fishing Hole Bank, 1974, edition of 10 .$900.00
18M, Gloomy Gus Bank, 1974, edition of 10 ....$950.00
19M, Kids' Prank Bank, 1974, edition of 10...............$1,100.00
20M, Mary & the Little Lamb, 1974, edition of 20 ....$850.00
21M, Spook, 1974, edition of 10...................................$800.00

42M, Miss Liberty, 1986, edition of 36, $850.00.

Photo courtesy of Charlie Reynolds.

22M, Decoy, 1974, edition of 10..................................$600.00
23M, Decoy Hen, 1974, edition of 10.........................$600.00
24M, Comedy, 1974, edition of 10..............................$975.00
25M, Bozo, 1974, edition of 10 ....$825.00
26M, Reynolds Foundry, 1974, edition of 15...........$2,000.00
27M, Toonerville, 1974, edition of 10 ....$950.00
28M, Bank on Reynolds Toys, 1974, edition of 10........$425.00
29M, Simple Simon, 1975, edition of 10 ....$925.00
30M, Humpty Dumpty, 1975, edition of 20 ....$1,250.00
31M, Three Blind Mice, 1975, edition of 15 ....$1,100.00
32M, Clubhouse, 1975, edition of 10.........................$1,100.00
33M, Boat, 1975, edition of 10 ....$1,050.00
34M, St Nicholas, 1975, edition of 50 ....$525.00
35M, Forging America, 1976, edition of 13................$1,200.00
36M, Suitcase, 1979, edition of 22............................$725.00
37M, North Wind, 1980, edition of 23 ....$675.00
39M, Quarter Century, 25th Anniversary, 1982, edition of 25..$3,200.00
40M, Columbia, 1984, edition of 25 ....$950.00
41M, Whirligig, 1985, edition of 30............................$800.00
42M, Miss Liberty on a Pedestal, 1986, edition of 4....$1,400.00

Photo courtesy of Charlie Reynolds.

45M, Campaign '88, Bush Republican, Dukakis Democrat, 1988, edition of 50, $2,500.00.

43M, Auto Giant, 1987, edition of 30.......................$1,450.00
46M, Hollywood, 1989, edition of 35 ....$650.00
47M, Buffalo's Revenge, 1990, edition of 35 ....$600.00
48M, Williamsburg, 1991, edition of 35 ....$500.00
49M, Duel at the Dome, 1992, edition of 50 ....$550.00
50M, '92 Vote, 1992, edition of 50 ....$1,200.00
51M, Oregon Trail, 1993, edition of 50 ....$550.00
52M, Norway (Lillehammer), 1994, edition of 50.........$450.00
53M, Shoe House, 1994, edition of 50.......................$390.00

STILL BANKS

01S, Amish Man, 1980, edition of 50 ....$135.00
02S, Santa, 1980, edition of 50 ....$80.00
03S, Deco Dog, 1981, edition of 50...........................$70.00
04S, Jelly Bean King, 1981, edition of 100 ....$250.00
05S, Hag, 1981, edition of 50 ....$95.00
06S, Snowman, 1981, edition of 50............................$90.00
07S, Mark Twain, 1982, edition of 50 ....$110.00
08S, Santa, 1982, edition of 50 ....$125.00
10S, Redskins Hog, 1983, edition of 50 ....$95.00
11S, Lock-Up Savings, 1983, edition of 50.................$45.00
12S, Miniature Bank Building, 1983, edition of 50 ....$110.00
13S, Santa in Chimney, 1983, edition of 50 ....$80.00
14S, Santa w/Tree (bank & doorstop), 1983, edition of 25..$325.00
15S, Redskins NFC Champs, 1983, edition of 35...........$110.00
16S, Chick, 1984, edition of 50.................................$50.00
17S, Ty-Up (bank & stringholder), 1984, edition of 35..$140.00
18S, Tiniest Elephant, 1984, edition of 50.................$45.00
19S, Baltimore Town Crier, 1984, edition of 50..............$55.00
20S, Father Christmas Comes to America, July 4th, 1984, edition of 25 ....$290.00
21S, Campaign '84, 1984, edition of 100 ....$160.00
22S, Santa, 1984, edition of 50 ....$100.00
23S, Reagan '85, 1985, edition of 100.......................$200.00
24S, Columbus Ohio '85, 1985, edition of 50..............$55.00
25S, Austrian Santa (bank & doorstop), 1985, edition of 25.$280.00
26S, Halloween '85, 1985, edition of 50 ....$90.00
27S, 1893 Kriss Kringle (w/tree & candle decorations), 1985, edition of 20 ....$1,400.00
28S, Santa Coming to a Child, 1985, edition of 50........$165.00
29S, Halley's Comet '86, 1986, edition of 50..............$165.00
30S, 20th Anniversary, 1986, edition of 86 ....$155.00
31S, Father Christmas (bank & doorstop), gr, 1986, edition of 25 ....$280.00
32S, Santa & the Reindeer, 1986, edition of 50............$160.00
33S, Charlie O'Connor, 1987, edition of 50................$65.00
34S, Chocolate Rabbit, 1987, edition of 50................$65.00
35S, St Louis River Boat, 1987, edition of 60 ....$55.00
36S, German Santa (bank & doorstop), 1987, edition of 25..$255.00
38S, Old Stump Halloween, 1987, edition of 50 ....$75.00
39S, Santa in Race Car, 1987, edition of 100 ....$85.00
40S, Technology Education, 1988, edition of 88 ....$50.00
41S, Super Bowl XXII Redskins, 1988, edition of 50........$80.00
42S, Easter Rabbit, 1988, edition of 50 ....$45.00
43S, Florida Souvenir, 1988, edition of 75.................$90.00
44S, Father Christmas w/Lantern (bank & doorstop), edition of 35 ....$260.00
45S, Halloween Spook, 1988, edition of 50 ....$70.00
47S, Santa on Polar Bear, 1988, edition of 75 ....$90.00
48S, Bush-Quale, 1989, edition of 100 ....$150.00
50S, Pocket Pig (pr in trough), 1989, edition of 75........$125.00
51S, Regal Santa (bank & doorstop), 1989, edition of 35..$250.00
52S, Tiniest Snowman, 1989, edition of 75.................$50.00
53S, Santa on Motorcycle, 1989, edition of 75............$85.00
54S, Rabbit w/Mammy, 1990, edition of 75.................$90.00
55S, Antique Row Signpost, 1990, edition of 75.............$65.00
56S, Duck w/Puppy & Bee, 1990, edition of 75 ....$90.00

57S, 1865 Santa w/Wreath, 1990 edition of 35 ....$250.00
58S, Santa Coming on a Pig, 1990, edition of 75 ....$65.00
59S, St Louis Sally, 1991, edition of 55............................$60.00
60S, Santa w/Wassail Bowl, 1991, edition of 35.............$250.00
61S, Santa Express, 1991, edition of 55 ....$85.00
62S, Pig on Sled, 1992, edition of 55 ....$65.00
63S, Santa About To Leave, 1992, edition of 25...........$175.00
64S, Jack-O'-Lantern, 1992, edition of 75 ....$65.00
65S, Santa in Zeppelin, 1992, edition of 60.....................$65.00

66S, Clinton '93, edition of 100, $225.00.

67S, Windy City (Chicago Convention), 1993, edition of
    60 ....$65.00

68S, Santa and the Bad Boy (Summer Santa), 1993, edition of 50, $150.00.

69S, Arkansas President, 1994, edition of 100.................$95.00
70S, Santa & the Good Kids, 1994, edition of 35 ....$200.00
71S, Penny Santa, 1994, edition of 60 ....$75.00

Robots and Space Toys

Space is a genre that anyone who grew up in the sixties can relate to, but whether you're from that generation or not, chances are the fantastic robots, space vehicles and rocket launchers from that era are fascinating to you as well. Some emitted beams of colored light and eerie sounds and suggested technology the secrets of which were still locked away in the future. To a collector, the stranger, the better. Some were made of lithographed tin, but even plastic toys (Atom Robot, for example) are high on the want list of many serious buyers. Condition is extremely important, both in general appearance and internal workings. Mint-in-box examples may be worth twice as much as one mint-no-box, since the package art was often just as awesome as the toy itself.

Because of the high prices these toys now command, many have been reproduced. Beware!

See also Marx.

Acrobat Robot, Yonezawa, 1960s, movable arms & legs, light-up
    eyes, plastic, battery-op, 9¾", NM (NM box), A $286.00
Alpha 1 Ballistic Rocket Launching Kit, orig box, T1 .....$65.00
Answer Game Robot, battery-op, 15", EX, M5...............$285.00
Apollo Flasher Disc Set, plastic lifelike Vari-Vue flashers w/36 dif-
    ferent views of the Apollo mission, 16-pc, MOC, A.....$80.00
Apollo Lunar Module, DSK, bump-&-go w/spinning antenna,
    flashing lights & noise, United States, from $300 to..$350.00
Apollo Saucer, West Germany, 1950s, center dome w/stars & planets
    spins as saucer moves, tin, friction, 4" dia, MIB, A........$423.00

Astro-Scout, Yonezawa, lithographed tin with separate plate marked #3 on chest, friction, 9", EX (original box), A, $2,300.00.

Apollo Vehicle, TN, circling astronaut & flashing lights, plastic & litho tin, 9½", EX (VG box), A...........................$150.00

Apollo 11 Rocket, TN, advances, stops, underleg extends causing rocket to rise vertically, etc, plastic, 13½", MIB, A..$100.00

Apollo 15 Rocket Ship, KY, 1960s, astronaut pops in & out of cockpit, battery-op, 20", EX, A................................$100.00

Apollo-X Moon Challenger, TN, battery-op, 16", EX (EX box), O1 ....$150.00

Astro Base, Ideal, w/firing scout car, astro scope & space hoist, many actions, plastic, remote control, NMIB, A.....$294.00

Astro Base, Ideal, w/firing scout car, astro scope & space hoist, many actions, plastic, remote control, VG (VG box), A...$70.00

Astro Man, Dux, 4 different functions combine to pick up objects, light-up chest, battery-op, 12", EX+ (EX box), A..$1,400.00

Astro Mobile, Marubishi, travels w/noise & sparks, friction, 8½", EX+ (EX box), A......................................$275.00

Astro-Sound Satellite Talking Space Toy, EX (VG box), O1 ....$60.00

Astronaut, Irwin, 1950s, shakes in place w/blazing jtd guns, red plastic, w/up, 9", EX+, A $139.00

Astronaut, Y, walks w/siren noise as needle in radiation count meter in chest moves, crank action, 10", EX+, A ..$1,250.00

Atom Robot, KO, 1960s, bump-&-go action, 6½", EX+, M5..$380.00

Atom Rocket, Japan, 1960s, bump-&-go action w/flashing engine & rotating antenna, tin & plastic, battery-op, 13", MIB, A..$171.00

Atomic Robot Man, Japan, advances w/side-to-side action, litho tin w/pressed tin arms, w/up, 5", NM (EX+ box), A.......$1,700.00

Attacking Martian, Japan, advances as chest opens & gun fires, litho tin, battery-op, 11", NMIB, A $317.00

Attacking Martian, Japan, advances as chest opens & gun fires, litho tin, battery-op, 11", EX (VG box), O1 ....$225.00

Auto-Magic Picture Gun & Theater, Stephens, w/space viewer, theater & film, battery-op, rare, MIB, A...................$502.00

Billy Blastoff Space Base, Eldon, 1960s, VG (VG box), H4..$150.00

Cone Head Robot, Yonezawa, advances with sparking action behind plastic eyes, tin windup, 8¾", NMIB, A, $3,950.00.

Clown Robot, battery-op, 14", NM, M5 ....$240.00

Cone Head Robot, Yonezawa, advances w/sparking action behind plastic eyes, tin w/up, 8¾", EX, A.............$2,800.00

Cragstan Astronaut, Daiya, red, walks & raises gun w/flashing light & sound, plastic, battery-op, 14", NM (EX box), A $4,000.00

Cragstan Astronaut, Daiya, red, walks & raises gun w/flashing light & sound, plastic, battery-op, 14", VG (G box), A..$1,076.00

Chief Robot-man, KO, bump-and-go action with flashing lights and sound, tin, battery-operated, 12", NM (EX+ box), A, $1,800.00; EX (NM box), A, $1,200.00.

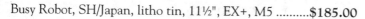

Busy Robot, SH/Japan, litho tin, 11½", EX+, M5 ....$185.00

Engine Robot, SH, advances with moving arms and spinning gears in chest, plastic, battery-operated, 9", NM (VG box), $200.00.

Cragstan Mr Robot, red w/blk arms & clear plastic head, bump-&-go w/spinning action, battery-op, 11", G, A $225.00

Cragstan Mr Robot, red w/blk arms & clear plastic head, bump-&-go w/spinning action, battery-op, 11", EX, A......$373.00

Cragstan Spaceman, 1950s, battery-op remote control, NM (torn box), A $847.00

Cragston Walking Lunar Lander, 1970, NMIB, W5 ......$185.00

Dalek (Dr Who), 1964, battery-op, NMIB, A $170.00

Ding-A-Ling Space Highway, EX (orig box), W5 ....$85.00

Dino the Robot, SH, head splits open to reveal Dino the Dinosaur w/growling noise, head lights up, 11", EX+ (EX box), A $1,020.00

Docking Robot, Daiya, Japan, revolving radar, rocket reels in satellite, litho tin, battery-op, EX (EX+ box), A $80.00

Docking Rocket, Daiya, revolving radar, reels in satellite, litho tin, battery-op, non-working light, 16", VG (EX box), A $45.00

Earth Man, TN, astronaut walks & raises his rifle w/sound & flashing lights, battery-op, remote control, 9", NM, A $800.00

Earth Man, TN, astronaut walks & raises his rifle w/sound & flashing lights, battery-op, remote control, 9", VG+, A $500.00

Fighting Robot, SH, swinging arms, moving antennas & spinning gears atop head, light-up chest, 11½", NM (EX+ box), A $440.00

Fighting Robot, swinging arms, moving antennas & spinning gears atop head, light-up chest, 12", EX+ , M5........$145.00

Fighting Spaceman, battery-op, 12", non-working light on gun, EX, M5 ....$170.00

Flash Space Patrol, TPS, bump-&-go action, lights flash, space noise, plastic prop spins, battery-op, 8", NM (EX box), A.......$350.00

Flashy Jim, SNK, 1950s, walks w/sparking action, gray tin w/red eyes, hands & trim, blk feet, w/up, 7½", EX+, A $550.00

Flying Saucer w/Space Pilot, Japan, litho tin w/plastic dome, battery-op, 7½" dia, EX (EX box), A $170.00

Flying Space Car, M, 1950s, wings pop out & retract, siren sound, litho tin, friction, EX, A $467.00

Flying Spaceman Super Cycle, Bandai, futuristic motorcycle w/rubber Superman, friction, 12", EX w/G man (G rpr box), A...$7,250.00

Forbidden Planet Robby the Robot, Masudaya, 1984, lighted mouth blinks, interchangeable hands, battery-op, 16", MIB, C1 ....$599.00

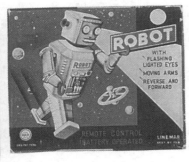

Gold Robot, Linemar, advances with swinging arms and flashing eyes, lithographed tin, remote control, 6", NM (NM box), A, $4,070.00.

Friendship-7 Rocket, SH, 1960s, litho tin w/revolving astronaut in cockpit, 9", NM, A.......................................$65.00

Gemini X-5, battery-op, 10", missing radar screen above dome, EX+, M5 ....$40.00

Giant Robot, battery-op, 17", EX+, M5 ....$340.00

Giant Robot (from Dr Who TV show), Denys-Fisher, 1976, jtd plastic, unused, NM (EX box), A $636.00

Golden Roto Robot, SH, walks & rotates, chest guns shoot w/lights & sound, battery-op, 9", NM (EX box), A.$285.00

Guided Missiles & Space Launcher, Empire, 1950s, plastic spring-loaded ray gun fires missiles, 7", rare, EX+ (EX box), A $121.00

Hopping Robot, w/up, 3", missing antenna, VG+, M5 .....$45.00

Hungarian Space Vehicle, blows ball on top of dome, EX+, M5 ....$65.00

Hysterical Robot, Japan, bump-&-go, head rises & arms swing, mouth opens & lights up, laughs hysterically, 14", EX, A..........$150.00

Johnny Astro Space Explorer, Toppers Toys, 1968, battery-op, EX (EX box), S2 ....$60.00

K-Robo, Toytown, performs forward & backward somersaults, red & bl plastic, 9", NM (VG+ box), A $230.00

King Flying Saucer, KO, 1960s, 180-X Space Patroller revolves, goes up & down at 45-degree angle, 8" dia, MIB, A ..$167.00

King Flying Saucer, KO, 1960s, 180-X Space Patroller revolves, goes up & down at 45-degree angle, 8", VG+ (VG box), A $65.00

Laughing Clown Robot, J, bump-&-go w/light-up face, opens mouth & sticks out tongue, laughs & swings arms, 14", NM, A $240.00

Laughing Robot, Yonezawa, mystery action, push button on head for laughing or space noise, plastic, battery-op, NMIB, A $120.00

Lavender Robot, Modern Toys, battery-op, rolls forward w/blinking eyes & mouth, 14¾", VG, A $3,500.00

Looping Space Tank, Japan, 1950s, battery-op, EX (EX box), A $308.00

Lost in Space Robot, AHI HK/20th-Century Fox, stop-&-go action w/blinking lights, plastic, 10", M (EX window box), A $300.00

Lost in Space Robot, AHI HK/20th-Century Fox, stop-&-go action w/blinking lights, plastic, battery-op, 10", EX, J2 ....$110.00

Lost in Space Robot, Remco, bl version, advances w/flashing lights, battery-op, MIB, A $966.00

Lost in Space YM-3, Masudaya, talking, 15", MIB, S2 ...$175.00

Lost in Space YM-3, Masudaya, 1985, w/up, 5", MIB, S2.$35.00

Lunar Hovercraft, battery-op, 8", EX (VG box), O1 ......$375.00

Lunar Landing, K/Japan, 2 Apollo 11 vehicles circle base lithoed w/astronauts & US flag, NM (EX box), A...............$210.00

Lunar Loop, Daiya, capsule revolves around spinning loop, NM (EX- box), M5 ....$160.00

Machine Gun Robot, Japan, machine gun pops out of chest, red tin & plastic, battery-op, 13", VG, A $65.00

Machine Robot, SH, swinging arms, moving antennas & see-thru chest plate w/spinning gears, 11½", EX+ (VG box), A.$535.00

Magic Color Moon Express, Daysran, mystery action w/lights & sound, tin & plastic, battery-op, 14", MIB, A..........$169.00

Magic Mike Talking Smoking Robot, 1980s, MIB, S2 .....$40.00

Man Made Satellite, Yonezawa, litho tin w/spring antennas, litho dog image in ea window, tin, 7", EX+ (G+ box), A..$222.00

Mars Explorer (Mars King Robot), SH, tin w/plastic arms, blk rubber tires, battery-op, 10", scarce, NM+ (EX box), A.$600.00

Mars Patrol Spacemobile, YM, 1950s, cockpit dome spins, litho tin, friction, 6", EX, A $182.00

Mercury Explorer, TPS, space vehicle travels w/bump-&-go action, makes noise & lights flash on dome, 8", MIB, A.........$258.00

Mercury ME-56 Space Rocket, Daiya, 1950s, litho tin, friction, 10", EX, A..$385.00

Mighty Robot, Daito, advances rapidly w/sparking in chest, litho tin w/plastic arms, 5", NM (M box), A....................$840.00

Mighty Robot, N, advances & chest sparks, litho tin, w/up, 5", unused, MIB, A $147.00

Missile Robot, SH, walks & rotates, hit lever to fire 4 rockets on head, plastic w/tin, battery-op, 9", MIB, A..............$100.00

Moon Astronaut, Daiya, walks while raising machine gun that fires w/noise, litho tin, 9", NM, A..........................$805.00

Moon Astronaut, Daiya, walks while raising machine gun that fires w/noise, litho tin, w/up, 9", EX, A...................$550.00

Moon Explorer, Japan, figure walks as antenna spins, red tin w/head in plastic bubble, crank action, 7", EX+, A.$413.00

Moon Explorer, MT, bump-&-go spacecraft w/flashing taillights, tin w/astronaut under clear dome, 14", EX (VG+ box), A.$650.00

Moon Explorer M-27, Yonezawa, 4-legged craft w/astronaut in plastic dome, rocket-shaped remote, 9", NM (EX+ box), A..$1,150.00

Moon Explorer Robot, Yoshiya, flywheel bump-&-go action, NM, M5 ....$445.00

Moon Globe Orbiter, Mego/Japan, moon under gr plastic cover on Earth-lithoed base, battery-op, 10", NM+ (EX box), A.$195.00

Moon Orbiter, Yonezawa, battery-op, plastic/tin, moves along Magnet Rail track, EX+ (orig 9x11" box), A.............$70.00

Moon Traveler Apollo-Z, TN, stop-and-go action with lights and sound, command ship extends and returns to capsule, lithographed tin and plastic, battery-operated, 12", NM (EX box), A, $165.00.

Moon Robot, Yonezawa, dk gray, spinning ribbons under dome, 10¾", EX- (VG+ box), A.....................................$3,000.00

Moon Rocket, Masuya, advances, rocket uprights w/other actions, battery-op, 15½", EX+ (G box), A.............$240.00

Moon Rocket, MT, yel & red litho tin w/astronaut at controls, mk #3, friction, 7", NM (NM box), A.....................$487.00

Moon Rocket, non-fall action w/rotating astronaut & periscope, lights & sound, litho tin, battery-op, 9½", MIB, A .$423.00

Morgan Talking Robot, Hong Kong, 1970, MIB, R7........$50.00

Mr Atom, Advance Toy, advances w/flashing lights & buzzing noise, plastic, battery-op, 18", EX+ (EX+ box), A ..$700.00

Mr Machine, 1977, see-through plastic, w/up, VG+, I2 ...$25.00

Mr Robot the Mechanical Brain, Alps, advances w/flashing light in ea hand & moving head, w/up, 8¼", EX (EX box), A..$900.00

Nando, Italy, air-powered, litho tin, 5", non-working mechanism, VG+ (rpr box), A $425.00

NASA Columbia Space Ship, Spain, bump-&-go, canopy opens, astronaut floats, tin & plastic, battery-op, 14", MIB, A...$100.00

NASA Space Shuttle Challenger, Tiawan, taxies, takes off, flies & lands, tin & plastic, battery-op, 16", M (EX box), A ..$175.00

New Astronaut, SH, walks & rotates as guns flash w/lights & make noise, plastic, battery-op, 9", M (EX+ box), A.$72.00

New Space Capsule, SH, bump-&-go w/several actions, plastic w/tin astronaut, battery-op, 9", VG (VG box), A......$75.00

New Space Capsule, SH, bump-&-go w/several actions, plastic w/tin astronaut, battery-op, 9", NMIB, M5..............$260.00

Nonstop Robot, MT, bump-&-go action w/blinking eyes, lavender, 14", battery cover missing o/w EX+, A.........$2,750.00

Orbit Explorer w/Airborne Satellite, KO, advances as figure in bubble rotates, ball floats above, 4¾", NM (EX box), A...$635.00

Outer Space Ape Man, Illco/Hong Kong, 1970, MIB, R7 ....$40.00

Outer Space Spider, Taiwan, mystery robot pops out of chest, head bobs, eyes glow, battery-op, 11", MIB, A $111.00

Pioneer PX-3 Robot Dog, litho tin, friction, 9", EX, O1...$475.00

Pioneer 3-Stage Rocket w/Launcher, Kraemer/Japan, tin, 11", rare, EX+ (G box), A $400.00

Piston Action Robot, TN, Robbie-type robot walks as lighted pistons in head move, remote control, 8¼", NM (EX box), A...$1,750.00

Piston Robot, STM, 1970, battery-op, MIB, R7 ....$100.00

Planet Explorer, MT, 1950s, non-fall action, flashing lights & sound, tin & plastic, battery-op, 9", EX (VG box), A.$207.00

Planet Explorer, MT, 1950s, non-fall action, flashing lights & sound, tin & plastic, battery-op, 9", NM (EX+ box), A...........$480.00

Planet Robot, KO, advances w/sparking action, blk w/red features, tin & plastic, w/up, 9", EX (NM box), A.......$288.00

Planet Robot, KO, advances w/sparking action, blk w/red features, tin & plastic, w/up, 9", MIB, A....................$350.00

Planet-Ship Mail Box, England, 1950s, cylinder shape w/space graphics, removable top, 4x2" dia, scarce, M, A......$100.00

Probe Force #2, friction, EX (EX box), O1 ....$45.00

Project Apollo, Parks, rocket launches, NMIB, T1..........$65.00

Prop Flying Robot Car, ATC, robot at steering wheel of red Mercedez mk Robot 3, friction, 8½", M (NM box), A.$4,150.00

QX-2 Space Model Walkie-Talkies, Remco, 1950s, electromagnetic 2-way phones, MIB, A $131.00

Radar Robot, battery-op, 12", EX (VG box), O1............$300.00

Radar Robot, SH, advances w/striding steps, rotating radar screen fitted w/3 missiles, plastic w/up, 7", NM (EX box), A..$237.00

Red Rosko Astronaut, TN, walks w/flashing helmet light, stops & lifts lighted walkie-talkies, battery-op, 13", NM, A .$1,100.00

Robbie the Roving Robot, Japan, advances in waddling motion, lithographed tin, windup, 7½", EX (EX rare box), A, $1,400.00.

Robbie, Japan, advances as multiple antennas spin on helmet, blk tin w/clear plastic bubble, crank action, 7", NM, A .$1,000.00

Robbie the Robot, replica of the original, silver, battery-op, 1 of 100, 9½", MIB, S2 ....$80.00

Robby Robot Bulldozer, San, robot waves flag as dozer advances, friction, 6½", EX, A...$240.00

Robby Space Patrol, TN/Japan, unauthorized Forbidden Planet design was removed from market, 12½", EX, A ...$5,750.00

Robby the Robot, Billiken, classic litho tin robot, w/up, 9", MIB, A $400.00

Robby the Robot, see also Forbidden Planet Robby the Robot

Robert the Robot, Ideal, plastic, 15", EX-, A.....................$50.00

Robert the Robot on His Bulldozer, Ideal, w/up w/trigger control for direction, plastic, 9", scarce, NM (EX+ box), A $1,900.00

Robo Tank TR-2, TN, bump-&-go action w/light-up guns & sound, litho tin & plastic, battery-op, 5½", NM, A..$127.00

Robot, Linemar, advances w/side-to-side motion, litho tin w/plastic claw hands, 6", EX+ (EX box), A $800.00

Robot, SY, advances w/engine noise, arms move, gray tin w/red & yel accents, w/up, 8", EX+, A $242.00

Robot, Yonezawa, bump-&-go action w/light-up dome top, litho tin, battery-op, 11", NM (EX+ box), A, from $1,200 to .$1,600.00

Robot (R-35), Linemar, walks w/side-to-side & arm-swinging motion, glass eyes light, remote control, 8", NM (EX+ box), A...$925.00

Robot A Resorte, Paya/Spain, 1960s, boy behind light-up helmet advances w/swinging arms, w/up, 11", EX (EX box), A..$584.00

Robot Bulldozer, Japan, 1950s, bump-&-go action w/light-up eyes & horn sound, battery-op, MIB, S9.................$695.00

Robot Lamp, 1950s, silver, blk & chrome Martian-type figure, light flashes from eyes & head, electric, 12", NM, A .$330.00

Robot Lilliput, KT, prewar Japan, mk NP 5357 on front, advances in primitive walking motion, 6½", scarce, EX+, A...$4,600.00

Robot St 1, West Germany, advances w/sparking action in chest, tin w/coil on head, w/up, 7½", VG (VG+ box), A...$500.00

Robot Tractor, TN, robot w/claw hands drives dozer-type tractor, pistons light up, battery-op, 9½", NM+ (EX box), A.$415.00

Robot-7, N, store display box complete w/12 claw-hand walking robots, litho tin, 4", MIB, A $300.00

Rocket Express, Linemar, spacecraft circle moon through a space station & mountain, 5½" sq, rare, M (EX+ box), A.$832.00

Rocket Race, TN, 1950s, Earth rotates as rockets & satellite orbit in opposite directions, w/up, 7", rare, NM+, A.........$303.00

Rocket Racer, MT, vinyl-headed pilot in tin rocket advances w/boing-boing noise, friction, 7", NM (EX+ box), A..$185.00

Rocket Racer, MT, vinyl-headed pilot in tin rocket advances w/boing-boing noise, friction, 7", VG, O1 ....$55.00

S-61 Space Explorer, Japan, friction, 13", VG, J2.............$70.00

Satellite in Orbit, Cragstan, blower suspends styrofoam satellite above Earth as they both spin, battery-op, MIB, A .$825.00

Satellite Launcher, Ideal, 1950s, futuristic vehicle launches flying rings, EX (EX+ box), D9 ....$45.00

Satellite Launching Truck, Y, astronaut at controls while saucers take off, w/radar screen, 12", EX+, A $251.00

Satellite X-107, Modern Toys, pnt tin w/astronaut under plastic dome, battery-op, 7½" dia, VG (worn box), A........$120.00

Saturn TV Robot, China, fires rockets from head, stop-&-go action w/light-up eyes & TV chest, battery-op, 13", MIB, A $76.00

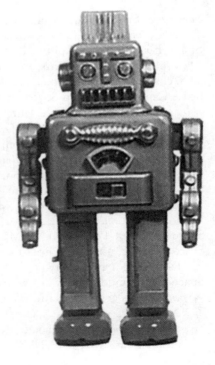

Smoking Spaceman, Linemar, advances with swinging arms and flashing eyes, mouth puffs smoke, gray with nickel-plated trim, 12", EX, A, $1,900.00.

Silver Warrior, CDI/Hong Kong, 1970, MIB, R7 ....$60.00

Sir Galaxy Robot, 1979, plastic, radio controlled, 18", VG+, A $50.00

Sky Patrol Flying Saucer, bump-&-go action w/rotating gears & flashing lights, litho tin, battery-op, 5" dia, MIB, A ..$319.00

Smoking Spaceman, Linemar, advances w/swinging arms & flashing eyes, mouth smokes, bl (rare) w/NP trim, 12½", EX, A................$2,250.00

Smoking Spaceman, Linemar, advances w/swinging arms & flashing eyes, mouth puffs smoke, gray w/NP trim, EX+ (EX box), A................$3,700.00

Solar-X Space Rocket, TN, wings deploy while rocket lifts upright w/lights & noise, battery-op, 16", NM (G box), A................$150.00

Sonar Space Patrol, Electro-Toy, blow whistle and spaceship changes direction, tin and plastic, 14", EX (VG box), A, $595.00.

Space Ace Space Phone Walkie-Talkie, 1950s, plastic, EX (EX box), A................$65.00

Space Bus, Usagayi, Robbie look-alike on roof, litho tin w/plastic window inserts, friction, 14½", EX+ (VG box), A................$1,450.00

Space Capsule, SH, bump-&-go action w/plastic astronaut flying around exterior of capsule, battery-op, 6", MIB, A..$160.00

Space Capsule w/Astronaut, Kanto/Japan, 1960s, astronaut rotates around capsule, litho tin, friction, 6", EX+, A...........$115.00

Space Capsule w/Astronaut, Kanto/Japan, 1960s, astronaut rotates around capsule, litho tin, friction, 6", VG, O1 ....$55.00

Space Capsule w/Floating Astronaut, MT, astronaut floats above capsule w/bump-&-go action, M (EX box), A, from $160 to................$220.00

Space Capsule X-17, 9" dia, EX+, M5 ....$98.00

Space Car, MT, astronaut's head turns in bump-&-go car, lights flash, space noise, battery-op, 9½", M (EX box), A .$281.00

Space Commando, TN, walks while holding space gun, gray w/red arms & blk feet, tin, w/up, 8", some flaking o/w VG, A................$575.00

Space Dog, KO, advances as mouth opens, ears flap & eyes roll, red tin w/blk ears, friction, 6", NM (scarce EX+ box), A ..$950.00

Space Dog, KO, advances as mouth opens, ears flap & eyes roll, red tin w/blk ears, friction, 6", EX, A $356.00

Space Explorer, astronaut w/parachute, throw in the air & parachute opens, plastic & rubber, MOC, A $45.00

Space Explorer, TN, train-type vehicle advances while 3 front-mounted guns move, friction, 13", scarce, NM (EX box), A................$590.00

Space Explorer, 1950s, advances w/siren sound, lithoed rockets & stars, friction, 4½", scarce, EX+, A $121.00

Space Fighter Robot, SH, 1960, battery-op, MIB, R7 ....$195.00

Space Helmet w/Radar Goggles, Banner Plastics, 1950s, rocket-ship atop helmet, unused, M (EX+ box), A.............$606.00

Space Man, SY/Japan, advances with arms moving in unison, lithographed tin, 8", NM (EX box), A, $525.00.

Space Missile Station, Linemar, generator revolves to blow up ball (missing), fires missiles, EX, M5........................$100.00

Space Patrol Super Cycle, futuristic cycle w/gr rubber figure, 14", EX+ w/G- man (G- box), A................$3,400.00

Space Patrol, MT, bump-&-go action w/Snoopy-type vinyl dog in tin & plastic spaceship, battery-op, 11", NM (EX box), A $260.00

Space Patrol Fire Bird 3, MT, advances w/mystery action & blinking light, litho tin, battery-op, 14", EX+ (VG box), A $585.00

Space Patrol Rocket Light, Ray-O-Vac, 1950s, chrome w/clear plastic nose cone, decals on fins, 12", NM (VG+ box), A ..$309.00

Space Patrol Tank, Japan, 1950-60s, 9", EX+ (VG box), M5.$200.00

Space Patrol Tank, Yonezawa, non-fall action w/lights & sound, litho tin, 8", scarce, NM (EX box), A......................$399.00

Space Patrol w/Astronaut, Asahi, space jet travels w/bump-&-go action, noise & lights, 7", NM (EX box), A $351.00

Space Patrol Walkie-Talkies, J&L Randall, plastic, NMIB, A $125.00

Space Patroller X-081, KO, 1960, battery-op, NM, R7 ....$95.00

Space Pioneer, Bandi, litho tin & plastic, orange, battery-op, scratches, non-working, VG (G box), A....................$85.00

Space Port, Superior, complete, w/flying saucer, MIB $345.00

Space Port, T Cohn, litho tin w/plastic figures, 11", NM (EX+ box), A...$534.00

Space Port & Planetary Cruiser Patrol, Pyro, 1950s, litho tin hangar w/plastic spaceship & figures, 10", EX+ (EX box), A..$400.00

Space Rocket, Masudaya, battery-op, 12", EX+ (VG+ box), M5..$275.00

Space Rocket Patrol, Courtland, futuristic tin car w/plastic roof, blk rubber tires, friction, 7¼", EX, A $111.00

Space Satellite, W Germany, mk #562, advances as inner circle w/3 antennas spins, friction, 4" dia, NM (NM box), A......$150.00

Space Saucer Mercury, Mego, mystery action w/revolving radar, light-up engine & sound, litho tin, battery-op, 8", MIB, A...$218.00

Space Ship X-711, HC/Hong Kong, 1970, EX, R7 ....$50.00

Space Ship X-711, HC/Hong Kong, 1970, MIB, R7 ......$100.00

Space Station, SH/Japan, early red tin version, mystery action, 5 rooms w/3-D people, NASA mks, 11½", EX (G box), A...$1,350.00

Space Tank, Japan, 1960s, non-stop action, battery-op, NMIB, A...$327.00

Space Tank, Modern Toys, bump-&-go, battery-op, 8½", air to blow ball not working, no ball, EX+, M5 ....$90.00

Space Tank w/Spinning Ball Cockpit, MY, Mars Patrol No 17, astronaut disappears in action, friction, 6", EX (VG+ box), A...$221.00

Space Trip, MT, cars travel down ramp into revolving space station w/flashing lights, battery-op, NM (EX box), A ..$525.00

Space Trip Station, Electro Toy, revolving dome, TV screen, 3 satellites, battery-op, 14", EX (VG box), M5 ....$250.00

Space Viewer, Stephens, 1950s, Space Viewer gun w/7 space films, box converts to theater, M (EX+ box), A......$200.00

Space Walk Man, China, advances w/stop-&-go blinking lights & gun sound, body rotates, battery-op, 12", MIB, A .$85.00

Space Wars, HG Toys, late 1970s, space station, ships & aliens, MIB (sealed) $40.00

Spacecraft Jupiter, w/up, 5", EX (EX box), O1 ....$125.00

Spaceman, TN, carries gun & flashlight, headlight works as arms move, battery-op, remote control, 9", NM, A $750.00

Spaceship, England, 1950, gold & red tin w/passengers lithoed in portholes, plastic fins, friction, 9½", EX+, A...........$285.00

Spaceship X-5, Taiwan, 1970, battery-op, MIB, R7..........$75.00

Spacey Spider, Talbot, 1985, 10", NM (shelf-worn box), S2 ..$75.00

Sparkling Rachet Robot, TN, 1950s, walks while holding wrench & sparks fly from chest, battery-op, 8", MIB, A $1,745.00

Sparkling Space Tank, KO, 1950s, engine sparks, litho tin w/astronaut in cockpit, friction, 6", EX (EX box), A $147.00

Sparky Robot, Japan, 1950s, advances w/lights & sound, w/up, EX+ (NM box), A..$236.00

Sputnick, W Germany, 1950s, dog inside clear capsule revolves around Earth, 4½", scarce, MIB, A $300.00

Star Strider Robot, battery-op, 13", NM (EX box), O1 ....$95.00

Strolling Space Station, w/up, 4", EX (VG box), O1........$85.00

Super Astronaut, SH/Japan, battery-op, 12", NM+ (EX+ box), M5..$200.00

Super Giant Robot, SH, walks, stops & rotates, doors open & he fires gun w/lights & sounds, 16", NM (EX box), A .$275.00

Super Sonic Speedster Rocket Racer, Modern Toys, tin friction, non-working spark, 6½", VG- (EX box), A $300.00

Super Space Capsule, SH/Japan, moves around, doors open to emit spaceman w/camera, NM, M5......................$105.00

Television Spaceman, Alps, robot walks w/noise as TV screen in chest shows space scenes, etc, battery-op, 13", MIB, A..$725.00

Thunder Robot, Asakusa Toy, stop-and-go action with light-up features, shoots weapon, plastic, battery-operated, 11", scarce, NM (VG box), $2,000.00.

USA-NASA Apollo, MT, figure on wire circles bump-&-go spacecraft w/flashing lights & noise, 9", NM (EX window box), A..$186.00

Venus Robot, KO, plastic, battery-op, remote control, 5½", MIB, A..$170.00

Sparkling Space Ranger, Elvin, advances and sparks, lithographed tin, friction, 7" long, NM (EX box), A, $400.00.

Video Robot, SH, advances w/light-up space scenes in chest, litho tin & plastic, battery-op, 9½", NM (EX box), A.......$135.00

Video Robot w/Dinosaur, SH, advances w/light-up dinosaur scenes in chest, tin & plastic, 11", rare, NM (EX box), A...$675.00

Walking Robot, SY, gray litho tin w/swinging arms, battery-op, 7½", tabs missing on head, motor sticks, G-, A.........$25.00

Walking Space Man, Tomiyama, advances w/high-stepping motion & swinging arms, hard plastic, 5½", EX+ (EX+ box), A...$1,200.00

Walking Spaceman, SY, advances w/swinging arms & twirling antennas, litho tin w/plastic claw hands, 8", EX+ (EX+ box), A..$660.00

White Chief Robot Man, KO, bump-&-go action w/flashing lights & sound, tin, 12", scarce, EX, A.................$1,200.00

X-16 Space Control Saucer, Japan, 1950s, satellite ball floats over craft w/lights & sound, non-fall action, rare, MIB....$321.00

X-5 Flying Saucer Spaceship, tin, battery-op, EX, J2........$75.00

X-7 Flying Saucer, Modern Toys, pnt tin, battery-op, 7½" dia, VG (VG box), A...$110.00

X-27 Explorer, Yonezawa, advances with crank lever, blue and red lithographed tin, 9", NM (EX box), A, $2,300.00.

X-80 Planet Explorer, box only, EX-, M5 ....$30.00

X-80 Planet Explorer, Modern Toys, pnt tin w/plastic dome, battery-op, 7½" dia, VG (G box), A $95.00

XZ-7 Space Ship, ST/Japan, advances w/spinning blade, litho, tin, friction, 7", MIB, A...$250.00

XZ-7 Space Ship, ST/Japan, advances w/spinning blade, litho tin, friction, 7", VG (EX box), A $50.00

MISCELLANEOUS

Bank, Saturn Guided Missile Savings Bank, litho tin, shoots coins into rocket top, 11", EX+ (orig box), A $200.00

Bank, Space King nodder, Lego, 1950s, comical spaceman sitting on planetary base, pnt compo, 7½", EX+ $85.00

Figure, Zoltan the Android, Tootsietoy, plastic, gr w/chrome chest plate, clear helmet, EX, H4 ....$12.00

Finger Puppet w/Space Vehicle, Adventure Boy in His Skymobile, Remco, 1970s, MIB, H4 ....$25.00

Flasher Ring, Apollo II, flashes from Armstrong climbing down ladder to his famous saying "One Small Step...," S2 ..$35.00

Flasher Ring, Apollo II, flashes from Neil Armstrong to Moon, S2 ....$35.00

Flashlight & Whistle, Space Boy, litho tin, NM, W5.......$85.00

Game, Spaceman Jiggle Puzzle, Am, 1957, try to balance satellites in outer space, litho paper, MIB, A $55.00

Kite, Alox Mfg, 1950s, paper w/space graphics, wooden supports, 22x28", unused, EX+ $18.00

Pencil Case, ICBM missile, vinyl, 1960s, T1 ....$35.00

Poster, Historic Moon Landing, Rand McNally, 24x28", M (orig wrapper), H4 ....$5.00

Sci-Fi Monster Glove, detergent promotion, 1960s, thin plastic as reptilian skin w/snake crawling out, NM, scarce, T2 ....$30.00

Space Pilot Wings w/Compass, 1952, MOC $45.00

Rock 'n Roll

From the '50s on, Rock 'n Roll music has been an enjoyable part of many of our lives, and the performers themselves have often been venerated as icons. Today some of the all-time great artists such as Elvis, the Beatles, Kiss, and the Monkees, for instance, have fans that not only continue to appreciate their music but actively search for the ticket stubs, concert posters, photographs, and autographs of their favorites. More easily found, through, are the items that sold through retail stores at the height of their careers — dolls, games, toys, books, magazines, etc. In recent years, some of the larger auction galleries have sold personal items such as guitars, jewelry, costumes, automobiles, contracts, and other one-of-a-kind items that realized astronomical prices. If you're an Elvis fan, we recommend *Elvis Collectibles* and *Best of Elvis Collectibles* by Rosalind Cranor (Overmountain Press).

Advisors: Bob Gottuso (B3), Beatles; Rosalind Cranor (C15), Elvis.

See also Action Figures; Bubble Bath Containers; Celebrity Dolls; Coloring, Activity and Paint Books; Paper Dolls; Pin-Back Buttons; Puppets.

Andy Gibb, flip book, Shadow Dancing, EX, B3 ....$24.00

Beatles, balloon, United Industries, yel w/group silhouette image, blk & wht photo on pkg, MIP (sealed), A......$65.00

Beatles, bank, waist-length bust of George from Yellow Submarine, compo, 8", EX, B3 ....$375.00

Beatles, beach towel, Cannon, VG, R2 ....$125.00

Beatles, Beatlemaniac Fan Club Kit, complete w/photographs, cards, sticker & puzzle, EX+ (EX envelope), A $173.00

Beatles, blanket, Whitney, cream & red w/bust portraits, signatures & instruments, 80", EX................................$450.00

Beatles, book, Beatles Forever, Schaffner, 1978, hardbound, w/dust jacket, VG, R2......................................$15.00

Beatles, book, Beatles Quiz Book, United Kingdom, 1964, paperback, VG+, R2..$40.00

Beatles, book, Complete Beatles Quiz Book, 1982, hardbound, w/dust jacket, VG+, J2.......................................$6.00

Beatles, book, Lennon Play: In His Own Write, 1968, hardbound, EX, R2..$65.00

Beatles, book, We Love You Beatles, 1971, hardbound, w/dust jacket, VG, R2 ....$30.00

Beatles, brush, NMIP $40.00

Beatles, carry-all bag, off-wht, vinyl pouch w/cord strap, NM, M5...$279.00

Beatles, cartoon statues, Paul & Ringo, artist-made, 1985, hand-painted cold-cast resin, 6", M $60.00

Beatles, diary, Scotland, 1965, VG, R2 ....$20.00

Beatles, dolls, inflatable cartoon image of ea member, set of 4, EX+ $100.00

Beatles, drum, New Beat by Selco, facsimile portrait & signature of Ringo, orig stand, 13", NM, A $550.00

Beatles, figure, Paul, bendable, 10", VG+, B3.................$280.00

Beatles, flasher rings, bl, set of 4, S2...............................$65.00

Beatles, flasher rings, silver, set of 4 ....$70.00

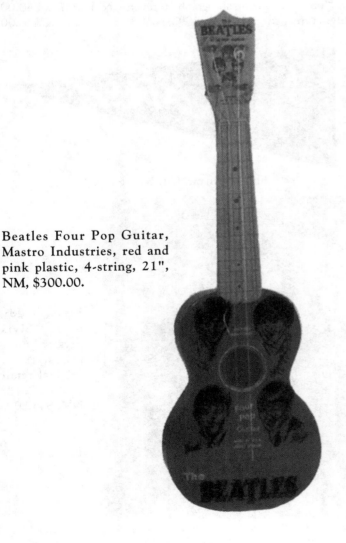

Beatles Four Pop Guitar, Mastro Industries, red and pink plastic, 4-string, 21", NM, $300.00.

Beatles, guitar, New Beat by Selcol, orange & maroon 4-string w/signatures, 33", EX+ (EX box), A.......................$500.00

Beatles, guitar, New Sound by Selcol, orange & cream plastic 4-string w/facsimile signatures, 23", EX, A.................$240.00

Beatles, hair bow, Burlington/NEMS, 1960, bl w/facsimile signatures, Official... & photos on card, rare, NM (EX card), A...$193.00

Beatles, handbag, 1960s, group picture & facsimile sgn, vinyl w/built-in brass handles, cloth lining, 10", EX, A....$250.00

Beatles, handkerchief, United Kingdom, group photo & With Love From Me to You in center, 8½", VG+, R2........$35.00

Beatles, magazine, Official Beatles Yellow Submarine, 1968, VG, R2..$25.00

Beatles, magazine, Teen Screen Life Story of Ringo, 1964, VG, R2..$18.00

Beatles, mobile, Sunshine Art Studios, punch-out characters & string to hang, MIP (sealed), B3 ....$160.00

Beatles, necklace, US Ceramic, features color drawing of George, Paul or Ringo, VG+, R2, ea....................$60.00

Beatles, nodder, Paul McCartney, 8", sm crack in back of head o/w VG, R2 ....$60.00

Beatles, nodders, by Carmascots, ca 1964, composition, set of 4, NM, A, $368.00. (Beware of reproductions!)

Beatles, notebook, group photo in Paladium door, top-bound or side-bound, EX, B3, ea...........................$60.00

Beatles, paint set, Paint Your Own Beatle, Artistic Creations, w/George Harrison, M (VG+ partially sealed box), B3.$800.00

Beatles, pencil case, yel vinyl w/group image & autographs, zip closure, EX, B3...$140.00

Beatles, pennant, 1964, red w/picture of group, 29", NM, S2 .$55.00

Beatles, pillow, waist-up photos w/instruments on bl, EX..$120.00

Beatles, pin, classic pose in porcelain surrounded by gold metal fr w/names in script, 1¾" dia, M, A $80.00

Beatles, pin, 1964, guitar shape w/blk & wht picture of group, MOC...$35.00

Beatles, playing cards, pictures Beatles standing in doorway, complete, VG, R2 ....$90.00

Beatles, punch-out portraits, complete w/4 unpunched portraits, coloring & fun book attached inside, rare, VG+, B3..$230.00

Beatles, Puzzle in a Puzzle, Lyrics, includes envelope w/answers, VG (VG box), R2 ....$150.00

Beatles, record carrier, rnd plastic w/angled hdl atop, features 4 head portraits w/signatures, yel or bl, EX, B3, ea $135.00

Beatles, record carrier, rnd plastic w/angled hdl atop, features 4 head portraits & signatures, red, EX, B3 ....$150.00

Beatles, record carrier, Seagull Entertainment, standing pose on bl background, 7½" sq, EX, B3 ....$220.00

Beatles, record holder, Pyx, United Kingdom, 1964, vinyl with color portraits on both sides, EX, $150.00; Rug, full-color image, 21½x33½", NM+, M5, $335.00.

Beatles, ring, gold metal w/group photo disk, minor discoloration o/w VG..$40.00

Beatles, rub-on sheets, 1968, cereal premium, colorful Yellow Submarine litho on waxed paper, 2½x3½", unused, M $25.00

Beatles, scrapbook, Whitman, stickers in right upper corner, G, R2 ....$35.00

Beatles, stamps, 1960s, blk & wht, 5 of ea member & 5 of group, EX $12.00

Beatles, stationery, Yellow Submarine, 1968, 4 sheets & envelopes w/different member on ea, EX+, R2 ....$12.00

Beatles, store display for Beatles Diary, 1965, yel & wht cb w/photo on diecut record at top, w/4 diaries, EX, A ..$200.00

Beatles, wallet, beige-gr vinyl w/photos on front, autographs on back, VG, B3 ....$65.00

Beatles, wallet, wht vinyl w/group pictured on front & Florida on back, w/rare metal edge, EX, B3........................$210.00

Beatles, watercolor set, complete w/4 6x8" unpnt pictures & paints, VG+, B3 ....$135.00

Beatles, wig, 1964, MIP $65.00

Beatles, Yellow Submarine, resin reproduction of the Corgi Yellow Submarine w/base, figures & octopus, EX, B3 .....$70.00

Beatles, 8mm film, Beatle Medal Story, blk & wht, 200 ft, EX, R2..$40.00

Beatles, 8mm film, Live at Shea Stadium, blk & wht, 100 ft, EX, R2..$30.00

Bee Gees, guitar, 1979, plastic, 29½", EX $60.00

Bee Gees, puffy stickers, 1979, 4 different sets w/6 stickers ea, M, B3, ea set $5.00

Blondie, scarf, promotional for Parallel Lines album, 48", M.$25.00

Def Leppard, pencil holder, Pyromania '84, metal, EX, B3.$18.00

Donnie & Marie Osmond, Colorforms Dress-Up Kit, 1977, complete, EX $25.00

Donnie & Marie Osmond, Disco Amplifier, 1970s, EX (damaged box), J5 ....$15.00

Donnie Osmond, bobbin' head, Japan, 1972, 7", EX, H4.$125.00

Doors, concert ticket, 1967, unused, M............................$60.00

Elvis, balloon, advertises Kid Galahad movie, cb feet, unused, M..$50.00

Elvis, book, Meet Elvis Presley, Scholastic, 1971, softbound, VG+, from $7 to $10.00

Elvis, bracelet, Elvis Presley Enterprises, lady's dog tag on card, M..$28.00

Elvis, bracelet, Elvis Presley Enterprises, 1977, w/color head shot, M, B3..$14.00

Elvis, charm bracelet, 1950s, w/guitar, photo, broken heart & hound dog, EX (orig card) $100.00

Elvis, guitar, Emenee, w/hound dog on 1 side & Elvis on the other, EX, B3 ....$375.00

Elvis, guitar, Lapin Productions, 1984, plastic, EX, H4 ....$60.00

Elvis, guitar, Selcol, 1959, rare, EX, B3..........................$700.00

Elvis, key chain, flasher type w/full-figure Elvis on yel background, M, B3 ....$18.00

Elvis, key chain, 1960s, record shape w/silver portrait image of Elvis, Holsum Bread ad on back, 3" dia, EX...............$20.00

Elvis, music box, late 1970s, plastic guitar shape, plays Love Me Tender, 10", MIB..$35.00

Elvis, music box w/sm pull-out jewelry drawer, plays Hound Dog as Elvis dances, 8", scarce, EX, A $105.00

Elvis, necklace, 1976 Midwest Tour, medallion w/Elvis pictured on 1 side & emb autograph on reverse, NM $40.00

Elvis, ornament, Hallmark, 1992, NRFB..........................$20.00

Elvis, pennant, felt, NM, $45.00.

Elvis, teddy bear, Elvis Presley Enterprises, 1957, original retail $3.98, 24", NM, $450.00.

Elvis, pin, color flasher, Vari-Vue, 3", NM $25.00

Elvis, playing cards, 1991, Best of Elvis, MIB, S2..............$15.00

Elvis, poster, Coloring Contest, 1962, NM $6.00

Elvis, poster, youthful portrait, RCA, blk & wht, 8x10", EX $60.00

Elvis, scrapbook, Solid Gold Memories, Ballantine Books, 1977, EX $16.00

Elvis, toy guitar, 1980s, MIP, S2................................$95.00

Humble Pie, flip book, Roach Card, EX, B3 ....$24.00

Kinks, concert ticket, 1969, unused, M........................$35.00

Kiss, ballpoint pen, features Ace, MOC, B3 ....$50.00

Kiss, bracelet, gold chain & logo w/red inset, w/backing card, B3 ....$35.00

Kiss, Colorforms, MIB (sealed)................................$65.00

Kiss, makeup kit, Remco, Kiss Your Face, MOC (sealed) .$95.00

Kiss, necklace, gold letters, from gum machine, M, B3 ....$4.00

Kiss, necklace, 78" gold autograph style featuring Peter, MIP, B3 ....$32.00

Kiss, notebook, Stewart Hall, spiral bound, M................$45.00

Kiss, patch, band portrait, Dynasty promotion, 4x3", NM..$8.00

Kiss, pencils, set of 4, MIP, B3 ....$45.00

Kiss, pendant, heavy silver-tone V-shape metal featuring Gene & logo, M, B3 ....$35.00

Kiss, puffy stickers, Rockstics, set of 4, MOC (sealed) $60.00

Kiss, sheet music book, w/photos, M $15.00

Kiss, sticker, 1970s, 8x10", NM $5.00

Led Zeppelin, patch, Song Remains the Same, 4x3½", NM...$8.00

Lita Ford, wristband, blk leather studded w/metal Lita, EX, B3 ....$15.00

Madonna, earrings, MOC, S2....................................$20.00

Madonna, pillow cases, w/printed picture, 1 pr, standard sz, MIP, S2 ....$30.00

Madonna, removable tattoos, Just Toys, 1991, MOC, S2.$15.00

Michael Jackson, Colorforms, 1984, MIB (sealed), C1.....$21.00

Michael Jackson, jacket (Thriller), red & blk leather, adult-sz, NM, D2..$225.00

Monkees, book, Monkees Go Mod, 1967, fully illus, softbound, EX, P3..$5.00

Monkees, bracelet, 4 color head shots in brass-colored disk, MIB, B3..$30.00

Monkees, candy cigarette box, Monkees Sweet Cigarettes, 1967, 3-D box features Davy on front & group photo on bk, NM, A $52.00

Monkees, flasher ring, flashes from 2 to the other 2, chrome, VG, B3..$20.00

Monkees, flip books, M, B3, ea................................$14.00

Monkees, full-color photos in plastic disc, Kellogg's premium, 1960s, set of 12, NM, M5 ....$60.00

Monkees, guitar, Mattel, 1960s, 20", VG+, B3 ....$95.00

Monkees, magazine, Teen Life, May 1978, NM................$18.00

Monkees, Monkeemobile, ASC, red tin & plastic GTO convertible w/figures, advances & plays song, 12", EX+ (EX box), A..$637.00

Monkees, record carrier for 45-rpm records, Mattel/Canadian, vinyl, EX+ $80.00

Monkees, stickers from gum machine, 1960s, uncut, VG, J5..$25.00

Monkees, sunglasses, M (w/orig tag), B3 ....$8.00

Monkees, tablet, photo cover, unused, M, B3 ....$40.00

Pat Boone, pin, 1950s, gold-tone metal, blk & wht insert photo & gold & wht charms of his shows dangle below, EX, J5 ....$25.00

Paul McCartney & Wings, book, Paul McCartney & Wings, Jeremy Pascall, hardbound, w/dust jacket, VG, R2....$15.00

Police, puffy stickers, set of 5, EX, B3 ....$5.00

Ricky Nelson, photo, w/facsimile autograph, studio issue, dtd Aug 1958, 5x7", NM, C1................................$25.00

Rolling Stones, belt buckle, 1970s, enameled silver-toned metal, NM..$25.00

Rolling Stones, key ring, 1983, photo of group, M (sealed), B3..$10.00

Rolling Stones, puffy stickers, 1983, 4 different sets w/6 stickers ea, B3, ea set..$4.00

Rolling Stones, wall clock, 1980s, quartz, 3-D, M (VG pkg), J5..$15.00

Sex Pistols, patch, 1976, 3x2", NM $8.00

Shawn Cassidy, see Hardy Boys in Character, TV and Movies category

Van Halen, binoculars, w/logo, B3.............................$15.00

Van Halen, key chain, brass, M $8.00

Van Halen, puffy stickers, 3 different sets w/David Lee Roth, B3, ea set..$5.00

Van Halen, 1980 Concert Tour Program, w/orig ticket, unused, EX, H4 ....$35.00

Rubber Toys

Toys listed here are made of rubber or a rubber-like vinyl. Some of the largest producers of this type of toy were Auburn Rubber (Indiana), Sun Rubber (Ohio), Rempel (also Ohio) and Seiberling. Because of the very nature of the material, most rubber toys soon cracked, collapsed or otherwise disintegrated, so they're scarce today. Character-related rubber toys are listed in Character, Movie and TV Collectibles.

Telephone Truck, Auburn Rubber, turquoise with bright yellow tires, 7", EX, $35.00.

Army Truck, Made in USA, gr rubber w/canvas-look top, 5½", EX, I2 ....$14.00

Calf, Auburn Rubber, late version, sm, scarce, 98% pnt, A1.**$9.00**
Collie, Auburn Rubber, lg, 99% pnt, A1 ....**$14.00**
Collie, Auburn Rubber, sm, scarce, 99% pnt, A1 ....**$12.00**
Colt, Auburn Rubber, brn, 95% pnt, A1 ....**$7.00**
Cow, Auburn Rubber, blk & wht, slight warp to base, 97% pnt, A1 ....**$8.00**
Girl, Ruth B Newton, Sun Rubber, 1950s-60s, in pk dress w/wht polka dots, 8", EX, S2 ....**$25.00**
Horse, Auburn Rubber, 96% pnt, A1.............................**$10.00**
Pig, Auburn Rubber, late version, sm, scarce, 99% pnt, A1..**$9.00**
Sheep, Auburn Rubber, late version, sm, scarce, 98% pnt, A1 ....**$9.00**
Tractor, Auburn Rubber, Graham-Bradley w/farmer, both hooks intact on hitch (rare), 4½", NM, A1 ....**$48.00**
Turkey, Auburn Rubber, M, A1 ....**$8.00**

Russian Toys

Many types of collectible toys continue to be made in Russia. Some are typical novelty windups such as walking turtles and pecking birds, but they have also made robots, wooden puzzles, and trains. In addition, they've produced cars, trucks and military vehicles that are exact copies of those once used in Russia and its Republics, formerly known as the Soviet Union. These replicas were made prior to June 1991 and are marked Made in the USSR/CCCP. They're constructed of metal and are very detailed, often with doors, hoods and trunks that open.

Advisors: Natural Way (N1); David Riddle (R6).

REPLICAS OF CIVILIAN VEHICLES

Aeroflot (Russian Airline) Service Station Wagon, 1/43 scale, MIB, $18.00.

Belarus Farm Tractor, 1/43 scale, MIB, R6 ....**$20.00**
KamA3 Model #5320 Flat bed Truck, cab tilts forward, 1/43 scale, MIB, R6...**$35.00**
KamA3 Model #53213 Airport Fire Truck, 1/43 scale, MIB, R6...**$40.00**
KamA3 Model #5410 Truck Cab, 1/43 scale, MIB, R6 ....**$40.00**
Kamaz Model #53212 Cargo Truck, 1/43 scale, MIB, R6 .**$40.00**
Kamaz Model #5511 Dump Truck, 1/43 scale, MIB, R6...**$40.00**

Gorbi Limo, 1/43 scale, metal, MIB, $25.00.

KamA3-53213 Oil Truck, 1/43 scale, MIB, $40.00.

Lada #2121 4x4, trunk, doors & hood open, 1/43 scale, MIB, R6...**$15.00**
Lada #2121 4x4 w/Trailer, trunk, doors & hood open, 1/43 scale, MIB, R6...**$18.00**
Lada Auto Service Station Wagon, trunk & hood open, 1/43, MIB, R6 ....**$15.00**
Lada Sedan, trunk & hood open, 1/43 scale, MIB, R6......**$15.00**
Lada Station Wagon, trunk & hood open, 1/43 scale, MIB, R6...**$15.00**
Moskvitch Aeroflot (Soviet Airline) Station Wagon, hood opens, 1/43 scale, MIB, R6 ....**$15.00**
Moskvitch Auto Service Station Wagon, hood opens, 1/43 scale, MIB, R6...**$15.00**

Moskvitch Medical Services Sedan, 1/43 scale, MIB, $15.00.

Moskvitch Panel Station Wagon, hood opens, 1/43 scale, R6...**$15.00**
Moskvitch Sedan, hood opens, 1/43 scale, MIB, R6.........**$15.00**

Moskvitch Slant-Back Sedan, trunk & doors open, 1/43 scale, MIB, R6 ....**$15.00**

Moskvitch Soviet Traffic Sedan, hood opens, 1/43 scale, MIB, R6 ....**$15.00**

Moskvitch Station Wagon, hood opens, 1/43 scale, MIB, R6 ..**$15.00**

Moskvitch Taxi Sedan, hood opens, 1/43 scale, MIB, R6 ..**$15.00**

OMO 1937 Fire Truck, #1 in series of 6, 1/43 scale, MIB, R6 ....**$40.00**

OMO 1937 Fire Truck, #2 in series of 6, 1/43 scale, MIB, R6.**$40.00**

RAF Ambulance Van, back & 3 doors open, 1/43 scale, MIB, R6 ....**$20.00**

RAF Traffic Police Van, 1/43 scale, MIB, $20.00.

Volga Ambulance Station Wagon, back & 3 doors open, 1/43 scale, MIB, R6 ....**$22.00**

Volga Sedan, trunk, hood & doors open, 1/43 scale, MIB, R6 ....**$20.00**

Volga Taxi Sedan, trunk, hood & doors open, 1/43 scale, MIB, R6 ....**$20.00**

Volga Taxi Station Wagon, trunk, hood & doors open, 1/43 scale, MIB, R6 ....**$20.00**

Volga Traffic Police Sedan, trunk, hood & doors open, 1/43 scale, MIB, R6 ....**$22.00**

REPLICAS OF MILITARY VEHICLES

T-34-85 Tank, metal, rarest of the set of 6, MIB, $25.00.

Armored Car, 1/43 scale, MIB, R6 ....**$10.00**

Armored Personnel Carrier, 1/43 scale, MIB, R6.............**$15.00**

Armored Troop Carrier, 1/86 scale, MIB, R6..............**$15.00**

Cannon, 1/86 scale, MIB, R6 ....**$15.00**

Command Car, 1/86 scale, MIB, R6......................**$15.00**

N-153 Biplane Fighter, 1/72 scale, MIB, R6 ....**$40.00**

N-16 Fighter, 1/72 scale, MIB, R6......................**$40.00**

Rocket Launcher Armored Truck, 1/86 scale, MIB, R6 ...**$15.00**

Rocket Launcher Truck, 1/86 scale, MIB, R6............**$15.00**

Self-Propelled Cannon, 1/86, MIB, R6 ....**$15.00**

SU-100 Self-Propelled Cannon, 1/43 scale, MIB, R6.......**$15.00**

Tank, battery-op, 1/72, MIB, R6 ....**$45.00**

Tank, 1/86, MIB, R6......................**$12.00**

Troop Truck, 1/86 scale, MIB, R6......................**$15.00**

100mm Cannon, 1/43 scale, MIB, R6 ....**$15.00**

76 mm Cannon, 1/43 scale, metal, MIB, $12.00.

MISCELLANEOUS

Cast Metal, 1917 Revolution Soldiers Pulling Cannon, set of 10, MIB, N1 ....**$25.00**

Cast Metal, 1917 Russian Revolution Soldiers w/Rifles, set of 10, MIB, NI **$25.00**

Metal, bird, w/up, MIB, N1......................**$5.00**

Metal, car set, 6-pc set, MIB, N1 ....**$12.00**

Metal, car track, w/up, MIB, N1 ....**$20.00**

Metal, chicken, MIB, N1 ....**$5.00**

Metal, dancing snow girl, MIB, N1 ....**$12.50**

Metal, doll, Matryoshki, w/up, MIB, N1 ....**$18.00**

Metal, hen, w/up, MIB, R6 ....**$8.00**

Metal, monster beetle, MIB, N1 ....**$8.00**

Metal, parking garage, MIB, N1 ....**$15.00**

Metal, pedal car, lg, N1 ....**$295.00**

Metal, rooster, w/up, MIB, R6 ....**$8.00**

Metal, train track, w/up, MIB, N1 ....**$20.00**

Plastic, car on garage lift, MIB, N1 ....**$8.00**

Plastic, chicken inside egg, w/up, MIB, N1 ....**$5.00**

Plastic, fighter jet, bl, MIB, N1 ....**$5.00**

Plastic, missile carrier, MIB, N1 ....**$5.00**

Plastic, tank, MIB, N1 ....**$5.00**

Plastic, woodpecker on a tree, w/up, MIB, N1 ....**$30.00**

Plastic & Metal, doll swing, MIB, N1 ....**$12.50**

Plastic & Metal, moon buggy w/2 cosmonauts, w/up, MIB, F1 ....$12.00
Plastic & Metal, motorcycle & sidecar, in display case, MIB, N1 ....$20.00
Wood, doll set, Lenin, Stalin, Kruschev, Brezhnev & Gorbachev, Matryoshki, made in China, MIB, N1 ....$30.00
Wood doll set, various sets of 5 or more, Matryoshki, made in Russia, MIB, N1, from $75 to................................$195.00

Sand Toys

Included here are not only beach toys but also early toy dioramas enclosed in wood or paperboard boxes that became animated as the weight of the sand they contained shifted when they were tilted.

George Brown, 1870s, 8", $1,800.00.

Dutch Mill #26, McDowell Mfg, ca 1920, litho tin, 12", EX (VG orig box), A $230.00
Organ Grinder, France, mid-19th century, litho paper w/glass front, man cranks, monkey plays violin, VG, tape rpr, A $518.00
Picture, Black soldier, shifting weight of sand causes him to move, L5 ....$825.00
Seesaw, Chein, 1925, pour sand in top to activate boy & girl on horses, 11", EX+, A $178.00
Wheelbarrow Loader, Wolverine, 1948, loader travels down ramp & dumps sand into tray, litho tin, MIB, A $187.00

Santa Claus

Christmas is a magical time for young children; visions of Santa and his sleigh are mirrored in their faces, and their eyes are wide with the wonder of the Santa fantasy. There are many who collect ornaments, bulbs, trees, etc., but the focus of our listings is Santa himself.

See also Battery Operated; Books; Reynolds Toys; Windups, Friction and Other Mechanicals; and other specific categories.

Bank, HTC/Japan, 1960, plush Santa sits atop tin house, 4 actions, battery-op, 11", M (EX box), A $285.00
Bank, Santa Claus in easy chair, pnt wht metal, savings institution premium, 7", NMIB, A $110.00
Bisque Figure, German, Santa in sleigh w/reindeer, 3", EX, A..$110.00
Bisque Figure, German (?), Santa w/horse, 3", EX, A.....$200.00
Bisque Figure, Japan, Santa Claus at child's bed, 3", EX, A..$110.00
Bisque Figure, Santa driving train, waving, w/passenger, 3", EX, A $120.00
Candy Container, cb Santa w/clay face, cloth attire, crepe paper sack, bark & cb base, 10½", VG, A...........................$220.00
Candy Container, chenille-type Santa w/papier-mache face, wire arms, fur beard, 7", EX-, A..............................$250.00
Candy Container, cotton batting Santa, scrap face, tissue paper hat, gold braid belt, 5½", EX-, A...........................$130.00
Candy Container, German, Santa w/long coat & basket, papier-mache & cb body, mk base, 11", VG, A $800.00
Candy Container, Santa, stapled cb, 'fur' trim on jacket & hood, 10", VG, A..$250.00
Candy Container, Santa dressed in cotton 'fur' coat & hood, papier-mache & pressed cb, 11½", EX, A $220.00
Candy Container, Santa in sleigh w/log, papier-mache & wire, cloth dressed, bl collar & pants, 14", NM-, A $700.00
Candy Container, Santa on wood pile, papier-mache & wire, cloth attire, cb base opens, mica decoration, 5", VG, A......$230.00
Candy Container, Santa w/bird on sleeve, papier-mache & cb, 10", EX-, A $600.00
Candy Container, Santa w/bl pants, papier-mache & cb, opens at waist, 8½", VG, A $185.00
Candy Container, Santa w/snow on coat, papier-mache & cb, well-pnt face, opens at feet, 10", EX, A $1,150.00
Cube Puzzle, McLoughlin, 1897, litho paper on wood, 13", G- (w/box), A $875.00
Diecut, Santa in airplane, emb cb pnt w/mica decorations, 11", EX, A $265.00
Doll, stuffed cloth w/pressed cloth face, blk velvet boots, 21", EX, A $185.00
Lamp, Ungers Fibre Cell-U-Pon Products, molded paper Santa figure, early bulb, 18", EX, A................................$230.00
Life-Size Santa Claus, pleated papier-mache w/full-color cb hands, feet & head, 60", EX (orig envelope torn), A............$185.00
Mask, German, very early, papier-mache full head w/applied cotton beard, very rare, 20", EX-, A $300.00
Nodder, German, 1920s, papier-mache head & hands, bl pants, molded boots, w/up, 27", VG, A $1,700.00
Nodder, Japan, celluloid on tin base, rubber-band action, 7", EX, A $130.00
Nodder, mk Made in Japan, celluloid Santa holding gift sack on tin base, pendulum-type lever, 7", EX+, A $350.00
Nodder, papier-mache & cb w/wire arms, felt hat, 26", EX, A $685.00

Rolly Dolly, see Schoenhut category

Roly Poly, Santa w/gray hat, pnt papier-mache, 8½", EX, A ..$465.00

Santa, Belsnickle, bl 'fur' trim on hood, mica decoration on jacket, 9¾", EX-, A..$350.00

Santa, Belsnickle, papier-mache, wht coat w/mica, blk base, 11", EX, A $635.00

Santa, Belsnickle, papier-mache w/gold-flecks & mica, yel, 14", EX-, A..$1,760.00

Santa, Belsnickle, wht mica-decorated coat, 6½", EX, A..$450.00

Santa, cloth-wrapped wire figure w/bsk face, crepe paper clothing, basket on back, rare, 7", VG, A $300.00

Santa, crepe paper-wrapped wire figure w/compo face, basket on back, 7", VG, A $495.00

Santa, European, early, cloth-dressed papier-mache w/up walking figure, 9½", EX, A $1,300.00

Santa, German, post-WWII, solid compo w/yel plush coat, basket on back, 10½", EX, A $165.00

Santa, German, 1910-20, papier-mache & cb w/felt suit, w/up, 21", VG, A $1,100.00

Santa, papier-mache & cb, gold pnt decor on coat, w/toy, 8½", VG, A $1,000.00

Santa, Pennsylvania (?), chalkware w/dk purple-brn coat, gold & wht trim, 18", EX-, A $990.00

Santa, stapled cb w/high-gloss pnt, no base closure, 11", EX, A $100.00

Santa, 1930s, molded head & hat, jtd shoulders & hips, red flannel & simulated fur outfit, blk patent boots, 19", EX, A ..$230.00

Santa in Moss Car, German, papier-mache figure driving moss car w/tin wheels, felt attire, 7", EX, A $1,265.00

Santa in Sleigh, celluloid, spun cotton Santa w/5 reindeer, cb base, 24", G, A...$60.00

Santa in Sleigh, Japan, celluloid, 2 reindeer w/glass eyes, 18", VG, A $45.00

Santa in Sleigh, wood sleigh w/clay-face Santa & 6 celluloid reindeer on rnd base as if flying over snow, 16", G, A...$70.00

Santa on Elephant, German, papier-mache, elephant's head nods, rollers in feet, 10½", VG, A..........................$750.00

Squeaker Toy, compo & wood, push down & Santa stretches open pack, 7½", silent but working, EX-, A.............$110.00

Schoenhut

Albert Schoenhut & Co. was located in Philadelphia, Pennsylvania. From as early as 1872 they produced toys of many types including dolls, pianos and other musical instruments, games and a good assortment of roly polys (which they called Rolly Dollys). Around the turn of the century, they designed a line they called the Humpty Dumpty Circus. It was made up of circus animals, ringmasters, acrobats, lion tamers and the like, and the concept proved to be so successful that it continued in production until the company closed in 1935. During the nearly thirty-five years they were made, the figures were continually altered either in size or by construction methods, and these variations can greatly affect their values today. Besides the figures themselves, many accessories were produced to go along with the circus theme — tents, cages, tubs, ladders and wagons, just to mention a few. Teddy Roosevelt's African hunting adventures inspired the company to design a line that included not only Teddy and the animals he was apt to encounter in Africa but native tribesmen as well. A third line featured comic characters of the day, all with the same type of jointed wood construction, many dressed in cotton and felt clothing. There were several, among them were Felix the Cat, Maggie and Jiggs, Barney Google and Spark Plug, and Happy Hooligan.

Several factors come into play when evaluating Schoenhut figures. Foremost is condition. Since most found on the market today show signs of heavy wear, anything above a very good rating commands a premium price. Missing parts and retouched paint sharply reduce a figure's value, though a well-done restoration is usually acceptable. The earlier examples had glass eyes; by 1920, eyes were painted on. Soon after that, the company began to make their animals in a reduced size. While some of the earlier figures had bisque heads or carved wooden heads, by the twenties, pressed wood heads were the norm. Full-size examples with glass eyes and bisque or carved heads are generally more desirable and more valuable, though rarity must be considered as well.

During the 1950s, some of the figures and animals were produced by the Delvan company, who had purchased the manufacturing rights.

Consult the index for Schoenhut toys that may be listed in other categories. Our values reflect prices realized at auction.

ANIMALS

Alligator, pnt eyes & teeth w/leather feet, 12½", G, A ..$150.00

Bactrain Camel, Style II, pnt eyes, neck & head, 6¾", VG, A $260.00

Squeaker toy, Rempel, rubber, 11½", $10.00; Squeaker toy, Sanitoy, rubber, 8½", $8.00.

Bactrian Camel, Style I, glass eyes, leather ears, cord tail, 7¼", EX, A, $700.00; Zebu, painted eyes, leather ears and horns, 8", VG+, A, $900.00.

Buffalo, dk brn, leather horns, swivel neck, jtd legs, rope tail, 8", EX, A $225.00
Burrow, pnt eyes, leather ears, pnt teeth, molded & pnt mane, rope tail, 4½x7", VG A $160.00
Elephant, pnt eyes, swivel neck, jtd trunk, legs & ankles, leather ears & tusk, rope tail, 7", EX, A $60.00
Felix the Cat, Pat Sullivan, 1924, blk-pnt jtd wood w/compo head, leather ears, Felix decal on chest, 8¼", EX, A $515.00

Gorilla, Style II, painted eyes, carved ears, 8", VG, A, $1,800.00.

Hippopotamus, glass eyes, open nostrils, open mouth w/teeth, leather ears, swivel neck, jtd legs, 5½", EX, A $275.00
Horse, Style I, wht dappled w/glass eyes, leather ears & cloth mane, 9½", G, A...$180.00
Lion, glass eyes, fur mane, rope tail, 5x8", VG, A...........$185.00

Lion, pnt eyes, open/closed mouth w/pnt teeth, swivel neck, jtd legs, rope tail, 6¼", EX, A $170.00
Ostrich, pnt eyes, 8", VG, A $175.00

Polar Bear, Style I, glass eyes, leather ears, cord tail, 8", EX, A, $1,300.00.

Poodle, pnt eyes, wht enamel finish, swivel neck, jtd legs, rope tail, 6", EX, A $125.00
Poodle, Style III, molded head w/intaglio eyes, 7½", G-, A..$55.00

Speedy Felix Car, missing steering wheel and headlights, A, $200.00.

PEOPLE

Batting Clown, pnt papier-mache head w/wooden arms & legs, wire hook moves right arm when pulled, 8", VG, A..$75.00
Big Game Hunter, #270/4, ca 1916, w/orig gun, belt & bullets, NMIB, A $1,093.00
Clown, 2-part head w/leather ears, 8¼", orig costume discolored, VG, A $90.00

China Man, jointed wood with painted features, original white pants and blue jacket with gold felt, 8", VG, A, $300.00; Monkey, joined wood with painted features, brown rope tail, original red felt body suit and hat, 8", VG, A, $425.00; Hobo, jointed wood with painted features, white shirt with blue dots and brown pants and jacket, 8", EX, A, $215.00.

Gent Acrobat, Style II, bsk head w/blk hair, 7¾", G+, A .$225.00
Lady Circus Rider, Style V, bsk head w/brn hair, 8", G, A.$225.00
Negro Dude, wht top hat w/blk coat & checked pants, yel vest,
     9", EX+, A $590.00
Ringmaster, pnt eyes, closed mouth, molded mustache & goatee,
     6", G, A..$55.00
Ringmaster, pnt eyes & hair, molded mustache & goatee, VG,
     7", A...$115.00

MISCELLANEOUS

Advertising Poster, illus circus scene w/Black ringmaster selling
     Schoenhut circus pcs, matted, 11x8", M, A..............$90.00
Circus Cage Wagon, orange & gray bars & wheels w/yel sten-
     ciled lettering, 9¾", G+, A......................................$225.00
Doll, girl w/carved hair & bl bow, closed mouth, 20" (rare sz),
     EX, A...$1,500.00
Fan-Tel, 1937, 48 wooden blades in cb container, ea w/numbers
     & symbols, tells fortunes, unused, A $40.00
George Washington's Private Carriage, 2-horse team, 23", rpl
     coach lamps, minor rpt, A $1,700.00
Hobby Horse on a Stick, w/reins, carved mane & cloth saddle,
     25", G, A...$55.00
Humpty Dumpty Circus, pnt wood, chairs, barrel, stand, clown,
     donkey & 2 ladder sections, 15", VG (VG box), A.$210.00
Piano, wht keys have pnt-on blk keys, dark finish, top lifts to show
     xylophone-type keys & hammers, 16x10x9", VG, A .$185.00
Piano, wht upright w/gold highlights, exposed works, w/stool,
     24x16", EX, A $80.00
Piano, 8 wht keys w/blk keys pnt on, litho of cupids & girls
     above keys, 7x9", EX, A $200.00
Pick-Up Sticks, ca 1930, NMIB $75.00
Railroad Station, red roof lifts off, gray block facade, metal office
     cages, 10x17x13", VG, A $475.00
Railroad Station, simulated buff brick w/red tile roof, Telegraph
     & Ticket office above windows, 17x11x13", EX, A...$600.00
Rolly Dolly, Santa, papier-mache, 14" (rare sz), VG, A..$2,000.00
Rolly Dolly, Santa, papier-mache, 8", G, A...................$400.00

Skiddles Nine Pins (three shown), paper lithograph on wood figures, lacquered hardwood base, 10", VG, A, $700.00.

Rolly Dolly, 1910, 4½", EX, D10, $325.00.

Slot Cars

Slot cars first became popular in the early 1960s. Electric raceways set up in retail storefront windows were commonplace. Huge commercial tracks with eight and ten lanes were located in hobby stores and raceways throughout the United States. Large corporations such as Aurora, Revell, Monogram, and Cox, many of which were already manufacturing toys and hobby items, jumped on the bandwagon to produce slot cars and race sets. By the end of the early 1970s, people were loosing interest in slot racing, and its popularity diminished. Today the same baby boomers that raced slot cars in earlier days are revitalizing the sport. Vintage slot cars are making a comeback as one of the hottest automobile collectibles of the 1990s. Want ads for slot cars appear more and more frequently in newspapers and publications geared toward the collector. As you would expect from their popularity, slot cars were generally well used, so finding vintage cars and race sets in like-new or mint condition is difficult. Slot cars replicating the 'muscle' cars from the sixties and seventies are extremely sought after, and clubs and organizations devoted to these collectibles are becoming more and more commonplace. Large toy companies such as Tomy and Tyco still produce some slots today, but not in the quality, quantity or variety of years past.

Aurora produced several types of slots: Screachers (5700 and 5800 number series, valued at $5.00 to $20.00); the AC-powered Vibrators (1500 number series, valued at $20.00 to $150.00); DC-powered Thunderjets (1300 and 1400 number series, valued at $20.00 to $150.00); and the last-made AMX SP1000 (1900 number series, valued at $15.00 to $75.00.)

Advisor: Gary Pollastro (P5).

COMPLETE SETS

AC Gilbert, #19080, Autorama Figure 8 Corvette, missing A/F power supply & 1 car, orig box, G............................$100.00

AMT, 1/24 scale, #TR-190, AMT Turnpike Set, orig box, G...$150.00

Aurora, HO scale, #2071, Jackie Stewart Oval 8, orig box, VG...$85.00

Aurora, HO scale, #2323, Golden Gate Bridge Set, orig box, G...$65.00

Aurora, HO scale, #2703, Mario Andretti GP International Challenge, orig box, G...........................$55.00

Elden, 1/32 scale, #3581, Power Pack Set, orig box, G.....$50.00

Elden, 1/32 scale, #745110, Power Pack 8, orig box, G-...$40.00

Marx, 1/32 scale, #22635, Grand Prix Set, orig box, G....$65.00

Strombecker, 1/32 scale, #9945, American Road Race, orig box, VG...$140.00

Strombecker, 1/32 scale, #9950, International Road Race Set, orig box, G...$150.00

Strombecker, 1/32 scale, #9959, 4 Lane Mark IV Race Set, orig box, VG...$250.00

Strombecker, 1/32 scale, #9975, Indianapolis 5/1, orig box, G...$125.00

Strombecker, 1/32 scale, #9930, Highway Patrol, VG (original box), $195.00.

Strombecker, 1/32 scale, #9945, American Road Race, VG (original box), $140.00.

Strombecker Road Racing Set, complete with track, NM (box torn otherwise EX), $160.00.

Tyco, HO scale, #8105, Tyco Pro International Pro Racing, orig box, G $75.00

SLOT CARS ONLY

AFX, '57 Corvette Convertible, yel, EX+ $60.00

AFX, '57 Nomad, lime gr, EX...$45.00

AFX, Rebel Charger, orange, EX+ $85.00

AMT, 1/24 scale, 1962 Ford T-Bird, 2-door hardtop, ivory, EX+ $110.00

AMT, 1/24 scale, 1962 Pontiac Bonneville, 2-door hardtop, powder bl, steering unit, NM (illus box).................$170.00

Aurora, HO scale, #1359, Indy Racer, tan, 4 slicks, NM, A3 ....$40.00

Aurora, HO scale, #1541, Jaguar, yel, M, A3 ....$65.00

Aurora, Thunderjet, #1356, 1963 Corvette Stingray, bl, VG $85.00

Aurora, Thunderjet, #1366, Hot Rod Coupe, red & tan, VG $60.00

Aurora, Thunderjet, #1368, Ferrari 250, turq & blk, VG $40.00

Aurora, Thunderjet, #1384, Green Hornet, w/sticker, VG $150.00

Aurora, Thunderjet, #1403, Cheetah, gr, VG.................$30.00

Cox, 1/24 scale, #16, Classic Industries' Manta Ray, orange, MIB, $125.00.

Cox, 1/24 scale, #9400, Ferrari, red, EX, $75.00.

Aurora, Vibrator, #1542, Mercedes, yel, EX, A3 ....$50.00

Aurora, Vibrator, #1542, Mercedes Benz 300 SL Convertible, wht, VG $55.00

Aurora, Vibrator, #1553, Hot Rod Roadster, bl, yel or gr, VG, ea $75.00

Aurora, Vibrator, #1580, International Pickup Truck, dk gray & blk, EX $150.00

Aurora, Vibrator, #1586, Van Body Trailer, dk gray, VG ...$15.00

Dynamic, 1/24 scale, Dubro (body only), MIB.................$44.00

Lionel, HO scale, Corvette, tan, NM+, A3 ....$25.00

Marklin, 1/32 scale, #1302, Porsche Carrera 6, wht, NM (EX box)...$130.00

Marklin, 1/32 scale, #1306, BMW Formula 2, bl & wht, NM+ (EX box) $125.00

Marklin, 1/32 scale, #1317, Porsche Carrera Sportswagon, red, NM (EX box)...$120.00

Marklin, 1/32 scale, #7, Chaparral 2-E, wht w/bl spoiler, NM.$165.00

Marklin, 1/32 scale, Lola Formula 2, red, NM+ (VG box).$125.00

Revell, 1/24 scale, #R-3262, Ford Cobra Racer, body only, plastic, burgundy, M (NM sealed box) $95.00

Scalextric, 1/32 scale, #C7, Rally Mini Cooper, gr w/wht roof, drivers have red helmets, #1 on sides, NM+ (EX box).............$185.00

Strombecker, 1/32 scale, Ford GT40, yel, MIB................$24.00

Strombecker (Canadian), 1/32 scale, #109525, Ford J, yellow, MIB; Strombecker (Canadian), 1/32 scale, #109596, Formula I, red, MIB; Strombecker (Canadian), 1/32 scale, #9561, Old's Powered Special, blue, MIB, $35.00 each.

Triang, HO scale, Bentley, blk, brass base, rare, NM+ ...$120.00

ACCESSORIES

AMT, 1/24 scale, steering wheel control unit, NM $30.00

Aurora, #1462-100, Hop-Up-Kit, EX................................$20.00

Aurora, 1/24 scale, #1804, Sebring Chaparral, Challenger Sidewinder motor, decals, display card & paperwork, NMIB..$140.00

Gilbert, 1/32 scale, #19224, Railway-Highway Crossing, MIB $22.50

Strombecker, #9120, fence, EX..$1.00

Strombecker, #9130, 24 half-tires, EX.............................$15.00

Strombecker, #9135, 12 barrels, EX.................................$7.00

Strombecker, #9140, 12 bales of hay, EX $7.00
Strombecker, #9150, track customizer, EX $2.00
Strombecker, #9160, Deluxe Overpass Support Set, EX $2.00
Strombecker, #9175, curved track road shoulder, EX $3.00
Strombecker, #9180, straight track road shoulder, EX $2.00
Strombecker, #9185, 30-degree add-on curved track, EX ...$4.00
Strombecker, #9190, curved track, EX $3.00
Strombecker, #9195, straight track, EX $3.00
Strombecker, #9198, pit garage, EX $15.00
Strombecker, #9199, utility building, EX $15.00
Strombecker, #9250, obstacle strip, EX $5.00
Strombecker, #9290, Pagoda Control Tower, EX $20.00
Strombecker, #9298, hump w/bridge, EX $20.00
Strombecker, #9388, lane-changing track, EX, pr $15.00
Strombecker, #9399, grandstand, EX $20.00
Strombecker, #9695, lap counter w/track, EX...................$25.00
Strombecker, #9730, lap counter, EX..............................$20.00

Smith-Miller

Smith-Miller (Los Angeles, California) made toy trucks from 1944 until 1955. During that time they used four basic cab designs, and most of their trucks sold for about $15.00 each. Over the past several years, these toys have become very popular, especially the Mack trucks which today sell at premium prices. The company made a few other types of toys as well, such as the train toy box and the 'Long, Long Trailer.'

Advisor: Doug Dezso (D6).

COE Chevy Coke Truck, red, EX $550.00
Ford Coke Truck, red, G $550.00
GMC Bank of America, EX $475.00
GMC Bekins Moving Van, VG $495.00
GMC L-Mack Mobile Oil Tanker & Pup, VG $895.00
GMC Lyons Moving Van, EX $475.00
GMC Rack Truck, red, EX $400.00
GMC Silver Streak, EX $450.00
GMC Union Oil w/Barrels, VG $495.00

Ladder truck, No 3, red with gold lettering outlined in black, silver ladders, ca 1950s, VG+, $800.00.

L-Mack Bekins Van, EX..$1,450.00
L-Mack Blue Diamond, G $900.00
L-Mack Fire Truck w/Ladder, VG $600.00
L-Mack PIE, VG $800.00
Lincoln & Long Long Trailer, EX..............................$1,350.00
Mack Lumber Truck & Trailer, EX...............................$895.00

MIC Wrecker, EX..$900.00
Orange Blue Diamond Dump, VG.............................$1,750.00
PIE Truck (First), M...$1,500.00
Toy Box, train boxcar, 34", EX....................................$1,000.00
West Coast Fast Freight, EX $1,000.00

Snow Domes

Snow domes are water-filled paperweights that come in several different styles. The earliest type was made in two pieces and consisted of a glass globe on a separate base. First made in the middle of the 19th century, they were revived during the thirties and forties by companies in America and Italy. Similar weights are being imported into the country today from the Orient. The most common snow dome on today's market is the plastic half-moon shape made as souvenirs or Christmas toys, a style that originated in West Germany during the 1950s. Other shapes were made as well, including round and square bottles, short and tall rectangles, cubes and other simple shapes.

During the 1970s, figural plastic snow domes were especially popular. There are two types — large animate shapes themselves containing the snow scene, or dome shapes that have figures draped over the top. Today's collectors buy them all, old or new. For further information we recommend *Collector's Guide to Snow Domes* by Helene Guarnaccia, published by Collector Books.

ADVERTISING

Air Canada, airplane flying over city in dome, yel footed base, EX..$16.00
American Express Vacations, wht image of plane on bl sky above advertising, 800 phone number on wht footed base, EX..$16.00
Flamingo Productions, 2 pk flamingos against advertising & palm trees, wht footed base, EX+ $15.00
IBM, computer against lt bl European map in dome, footed base, EX..$25.00
Texaco, tanker truck against cityscape in rnd globe, trapezoid base w/dealer advertising, EX $65.00
Universal Studios, New York skyline w/King Kong in background in dome, wht base, EX..................................$10.00

CHARACTER

Bugs Bunny, Bugs seated w/globe between legs, w/Elmer Fudd & Sylvester, EX...$90.00
Bugs Bunny, wood w/glass dome, plays Singing in the Rain, MIB, S2...$85.00
Charlie Chaplin, Enesco, 1989, MIB, S2 ....$25.00
Donald Duck, Schmid, 1989, Donald w/single-wheeled riding toy in tall dome, rnd bl base w/name in wht, M $10.00
Flintstones, Hanna-Barbera 1975, Fred, Pebbles, Bamm-Bamm & Dino against bl ground, plastic dome on footed base, NM, S2..$95.00
Happy Face, Germany, yel Happy Face w/legs & arms in tall dome w/glitter, rnd blk base, EX...............................$15.00

Lone Ranger Round-Up, Drier, 1940s, lassoing cow in glass dome on rnd base, M $125.00

Mickey Mouse, Bully, 1977, blk & wht striding Mickey in dome, EX................................$18.00

Mickey Mouse, Monogram Products, 1980, Mickey in space suit in oval dome, red plastic base, M................................$8.00

Teenage Mutant Ninja Turtles, dome w/different characters, M, ea................................$8.00

Yosemite Sam, wood w/glass dome, plays Home on the Range, MIB, S2 ....$85.00

HOLIDAYS AND SPECIAL OCCASIONS

Birth Announcement, stork perched on seesaw w/2 newborns on bl ground in plastic dome, wht footed base, EX $8.00

Birthday, It's Down Hill From Here, Enesco, 1991, features Garfield w/floating numbers, MIB, S2........................$20.00

Christmas, boy skier & tree in red lantern w/4 clear plastic sides, M................................$18.00

Christmas, Driss, Rudolph in glass dome, paper label on plastic base, EX................................$40.00

Christmas, Oscar the Grouch and Cookie Monster from Sesame Street Muppets, marked Jim Henson Productions, M, $10.00 each.

Christmas, Santa figure w/deer on shoulders, dome tummy w/Santa & deer scene, EX $18.00

Christmas, Santa on rocket, lg, S2 ....$20.00

Christmas, snowman & trees in clear plastic gift box w/red bow, wht sq base, M $15.00

Christmas, 1988, features Snoopy, musical, M, S2............$40.00

Christmas, 1990, Ninja Turtles, 4 different in Christmas pose in tall dome, rnd gr base w/name, EX, ea........................$15.00

Halloween, owl, ghost & pumpkin perched on sign reading Best Witches in globe body of witch w/broom & crow, M ..$18.00

SOUVENIRS AND COMMEMORATIVES

Arizona Memorial, depicts memorial in 2-tone water in lg squat dome, rnd wood base w/gold 50th Anniversary label, M..$60.00

Calgary Zoo, name plaque & 2 resting tigers in grass against blk in dome, blk rnd base, EX $12.00

End of the Berlin Wall, 1989, oval dome w/symbolic scene, wht footed dome, M................................$25.00

Europe, dome containing 12 flags of the Common Market countries, Europe mk on wht footed base, M $14.00

Florida, gr frog w/hands clasped atop globe belly, 3 frogs & Florida label inside, M $15.00

Galveston Island, dolphin atop rnd globe, beach scene w/dolphins on seesaw inside w/label, M $15.00

Grand Canyon National Park, name plaque, pack mule & canyon scene in plastic dome, wht base, EX $15.00

Kansas, buffalo w/name plaque in front of pine trees in dome, wht base, EX $10.00

Key West Florida, gr alligator in bottle w/bl cap, EX $7.00

Moon Landing, German, silver-tone landing scene in tall dome on rnd silver-tone base, M................................$22.00

New York City, red apple w/city scene in center, wht rnd base, EX................................$15.00

Ozarks, cabin scene with hunter and deer on seesaw, white footed base, $8.00; Amish Farm and House, Lancaster PA, red calendar base, $9.00.

Sea World of Florida, name plaque & penguins against arctic scene in globe, EX................................$10.00

Soldiers

'Dimestore soldiers' were made from the 1920s until sometime in the 1960s. Some of the better-known companies who made these small-scale figures and accessories were Barclay, Manoil, and Jones (hollow cast lead); Gray Iron (cast iron); and Auburn (rubber). They're about 3" to 3½" high. They were sold in Woolworth's and Kresge's 5 & 10 Stores (most for just five cents), hence the name 'Dimestore.' Marx made tin soldiers for use in target gun games; these sell for about $8.00. Condition is most important as these soldiers saw lots of action. They're most often found with much of the paint worn off and with some serious 'battle wounds' such as missing arms or legs. Nearly 2,000 different figures were made by the major manufacturers, plus a number of others by minor makers such as Tommy Toy and All-Nu. Serious collectors should refer to *Collecting Toys* (1993) or *Toy Soldiers (1992)*, both by Richard O'Brien, Books Americana.

Another very popular line of toy soldiers has been made by Britains of England since 1893. They are smaller and usually more detailed than 'Dimestores,' and variants number in the thousands. O'Brien's book has over 200 pages devoted to Britains and other foreign makers.

You'll notice that in addition to the soldiers, many of our descriptions and values are for the vehicles, cannons, animals, and cowboys and Indians made and sold by the same manufacturers. Note: Percentages in the description lines refer to the amount of original paint remaining, a most important evaluation factor.

Advisors: Sally and Stan Alekna (A1).

See also Plastic Figures.

Key:
ROAN — Regiments of All Nations

Barclay, cowboy, with tin brimmed hat, VG, $22.00.

Auburn Rubber, bugler, early version, 98%, A1 ....$25.00
Auburn Rubber, Marmon-Harrington tank, 3¼", NM, A1 ..$38.00
Auburn Rubber, soldier, gun tip intact (rare), early version, NM, A1 ....$49.00
Auburn Rubber, soldier, plane shooter; scarce, 94%, A1 .$55.00
Auburn Rubber, soldier marching, port arms, early version, NM, A1 ....$19.00
Barclay, #1 cannon, very scarce (1st Barclay toy made), 99%, A1 ....$68.00
Barclay, AA gunner, blk tires, diecast, 98%, A1................$24.00
Barclay, AA gunner, brn, 98%, A1 ....$14.00
Barclay, AA gunner, cast helmet, 98%, A1 ....$25.00
Barclay, AA gunner (podfoot), red, very scarce, 93%, A1 .$98.00
Barclay, aircraft carrier, 2 orig planes, very scarce, 90-95%, A1 ....$135.00
Barclay, Army truck, open bed, no decals, ca 1960, 99%, A1 ....$15.00
Barclay, Austin Coupe, metal wheels, ca 1931, 97%, A1.$39.00
Barclay, aviator (podfoot), brn, 96%, A1 ....$19.00
Barclay, beer truck, red & wht tires, no barrels, mk Barclay #376, ca 1940, 98%, A1 ....$45.00
Barclay, boy, red & tan, M, A1 ....$17.00
Barclay, boy, 99%, A1 ....$15.00
Barclay, boy skater, 98%, A1 ....$12.00
Barclay, brakeman, 97%, A1 ....$7.00
Barclay, bride, scarce, 97%, A1 ....$19.00
Barclay, bugler, brn, 98%, A1...$18.00
Barclay, bugler, gr, 99%, A1 ....$21.00
Barclay, bugler, rare wht helmet (podfoot), 98%, A1 ....$29.00
Barclay, bull, brn & blk, 98%, A1.....................................$15.00
Barclay, cadet, short stride, tiny casting flaw on shoulder, 95%, A1 ....$18.00
Barclay, cadet officer in wht, short stride, 98%, A1..........$28.00
Barclay, cavalryman, mounted on brn horse, 1930, 96%, A1 .$32.00
Barclay, chinese soldier, no pocket, scarce, 94%, A1 .....$180.00
Barclay, conductor, 98%, A1 ....$9.00
Barclay, cow, grazing, tan, 99%, A1 ....$14.00
Barclay, cow, lying down, M, A1.......................................$15.00
Barclay, cowboy, mounted, colored outfit, 93%, A1........$27.00
Barclay, cowboy w/lasso, gray, M, A1..............................$22.00
Barclay, cowboy w/no lasso, gray, 98%, A1......................$20.00

Barclay, cowboy w/pistol on horse, 97%, A1 ....$29.00
Barclay, delivery van, gr & wht tires, 96%, A1................$29.00
Barclay, dirigible, very scarce, 96%, A1 ....$150.00
Barclay, dispatcher w/dog, scarce, 93%, A1 ....$72.00
Barclay, drummer, rusty helmet, short stride, 96%, A1 ....$24.00
Barclay, dump truck, red & bl, ca 1960, M, A1 ....$15.00
Barclay, engineer, 99%, A1 ....$9.00

Barclay, Indian with bow and arrow, EX/NM, $18.00.

Barclay, fireman w/hose, 98%, A1 ....$28.00

Barclay, flagbearer, brn, 98%, A1 ....$19.00

Barclay, flagbearer, long stride, 93%, A1 ....$19.00

Barclay, girl, scarce, 99%, A1 ....$16.00

Barclay, girl in red, 98%, A1 ....$14.00

Barclay, girl in rocker, 98%, A1 ....$19.00

Barclay, girl on sled, 99%, A1 ....$21.00

Barclay, girl skater, bl, M, A1 ....$21.00

Barclay, girl skater, wht w/red trim, 98%, A1 ....$12.00

Barclay, groom, scarce, 99%, A1 ....$21.00

Barclay, hobo, 99%, A1 ....$9.00

Barclay, Indian chief w/tomahawk & shield, flat base, 97%, A1 ....$17.00

Barclay, Indian on horse, bare legged, 97%, A1 ...$30.00

Barclay, Indian on horse, yel buckskins, 97%, A1 ....$30.00

Barclay, Indian on horse, 99%, A1 ....$36.00

Barclay, Indian w/tomahawk & shield, M, A1 .....$16.00

Barclay, knight w/shield, M, A1 ....$20.00

Barclay, long-range cannon, w/rubber tires, lg, NM, A1 ..$35.00

Barclay, machine gunner, brn, 98%, A1 ....$16.00

Barclay, machine gunner, gr, 97%, A1 ....$17.00

Barclay, male passenger, 98%, A1 ....$12.00

Barclay, male skier in bl, 99%, A1 ....$20.00

Barclay, mailman, green with brown mail bag, $15.00.

Barclay, male speed skater, rare brn pnt, 98%, A1 ....$12.00

Barclay, man, 99%, A1 ....$7.00

Barclay, man on sled, yel sled, 98%, A1 ....$20.00

Barclay, marine, 98%, A1 ....$20.00

Barclay, marine marching, oval base, 95%, A1 ......$18.00

Barclay, marine officer, oval base, 93%, A1 ....$16.00

Barclay, marine officer, tin hat, short stride, scarce, 97%, A1 ....$36.00

Barclay, marksman, gr, 97%, A1 ....$19.00

Barclay, milk delivery van, bottles on side of van, wht tires, 2⅞", scarce, 94%, A1 ....$35.00

Barclay, minister in hat, walking, very scarce, 99%, A1 ...$62.00

Barclay, monoplane, single engine, very scarce, 98%, A1 .$99.00

Barclay, moving truck, gr & silver, no decals, ca 1960, 99%, A1 ....$14.00

Barclay, naval officer, wht, long stride, 98%, A1 ....$21.00

Barclay, naval officer, wht, short stride, 88%, A1 ....$15.00

Barclay, newsboy, 99%, A1 ....$9.00

Barclay, nurse, hand on hip, blonde, bl case, red cross on cap, 98%, A1 ....$25.00

Barclay, nurse, hand on hip, brunette, brn case, bl cross on cap, 98%, A1 ....$25.00

Barclay, officer, brn, M , A1 ....$21.00

Barclay, officer w/sword, tin hat, long stride, 97%, A1 .....$27.00

Barclay, oil truck, red cab, bl tank, no decals, 97%, A1 ...$13.00

Barclay, old man w/cane, 98%, A1 ....$16.00

Barclay, pigeons dispatcher, 97%, A1 ....$30.00

Barclay, plane (sm Lindy-type), tin prop, metal wheels, very scarce, 93%, A1 ....$85.00

Barclay, policeman, 99%, A1 ....$9.00

Barclay, policeman w/figure-8 base, M, A1 ....$25.00

Barclay, porter w/wisk broom, NM, A1 ....$20.00

Barclay, ram, yel w/blk horns, M , A1 ....$15.00

Barclay, redcap, 99%, A1 ....$9.00

Barclay, sailor, bl, scarce, NM, A1 ....$42.00

Barclay, sailor, bl, short stride, 98%, A1 ....$27.00

Barclay, sailor, flagbearer, long stride, 97%, A1 ....$38.00

Barclay, sailor, wht, short stride, 88%, A1 ....$15.00

Barclay, sailor, wht, 98%, A1 ....$20.00

Barclay, Santa (sm) on red sled, 96%, A1 ....$39.00

Barclay, Santa on lead skis, 98%, A1 ....$51.00

Barclay, soldier at searchlight, smooth lens variation, scarce, M, $350.00.

Barclay, sedan (sm), metal wheels, 98%, A1 ....$7.00

Barclay, sheep, lying, NM, A1...$12.00

Barclay, side-dump truck, yel & bl, ca 1960, MIP, A1......$25.00

Barclay, signalman flags, 96%, A1....................................$33.00

Barclay, sniper kneeling, brn, 95%, A1.............................$13.00

Barclay, soldier, bomb thrower; brn, 98%, A1..................$16.00

Barclay, soldier, bomb thrower; gr, 99%, A1....................$20.00

Barclay, soldier, gray, long stride, 98%, A1......................$25.00

Barclay, soldier charging, gr, M, A1 ....$22.00

Barclay, soldier charging w/tommy gun, gr, 98%, A1 ....$19.00

Barclay, soldier crawling w/rifle, 97%, A1.......................$28.00

Barclay, soldier eating, scarce, 98%, A1 ....$46.00

Barclay, soldier lying wounded w/blanket, tin hat, 98%, A1 ....$28.00

Barclay, soldier marching, cast hat, 90%, A1...................$17.00

Barclay, soldier marching, tin hat, long stride, 99%, A1 ..$23.00

Barclay, soldier marching, tin hat, short stride, 98%, A1 .$24.00

Barclay, soldier marching at slope, gr helmet, M, A1 ....$24.00

Barclay, soldier marching w/slung rifle, brn, 99%, A1 ......$16.00

Barclay, soldier marching w/slung rifle, gr helmet, 98%, A1 ....$20.00

Barclay, soldier running looking up, brn, M, A1..............$18.00

Barclay, soldier sitting w/rifle, 98%, A1 ....$31.00

Barclay, soldier under marching orders, brn, M, A1 ....$17.00

Barclay, soldier w/telephone, rusty helmet, 94%, A1 ......$19.00

Barclay, tank (#4562), 2 men in turret, 98%, A1 ....$39.00

Barclay, tommy gunner, gr helmet, 95%, A1 ....$22.00

Barclay, tractor-trailer, orange, Allied Van Lines decal, ca 1960, 97%, A1 ....$24.00

Barclay, transport set, w/2 cars, ca 1960, 98%, A1...........$49.00

Barclay, typist, at mess, 85-88%, A1 ....$14.00

Barclay, typist w/typewriter, no table, 98%, A1 ....$48.00

Barclay, US Army pursuit plane, red, 98%, A1 ....$34.00

Barclay, winter figures, made in Japan for Sears, plastic, 10-pc, M, A1..$48.00

Barclay, woman in red, no dog, M, A1............................$10.00

Barclay, woman w/baby, lt bl, scarce, 99%, A1.................$16.00

Barclay, 2-man crew at searchlight, 99%, A1 ....$32.00

Barclay, 2-man rocket team, 97%, A1...............................$39.00

Britains, #1, Life Guards, mounted at walk, officer on rearing horse, EX (G box), A $160.00

Britains, #2, Royal Horse Guards, mounted at walk, officer on rearing horse, 1935, 5-pc, VG (P Whisstock box), A $170.00

Britains, #8, 4th Queen's Own Hussars, mounted at gallop in review order, w/trumpeter, VG (G box), A $110.00

Britains, #24, Queen's Royal Lancers, mounted at halt, w/officer, 1935, 5-pc, EX (G box), A $300.00

Britains, #24, 9th Queen's Royal Lancers, mounted w/lances, officer turned in saddle, 5-pc, NM (VG box), A $200.00

Britains, #32, Royal Scots Greys, mounted w/officer, 1902, 15-pc, G (G- early printers box w/battle honors), A $190.00

Britains, #33, 16th/5th Lancers, mounted in review order, officer turned in saddle, 5-pc, EX (VG box), A $140.00

Britains, #35, Royal Marines, marching at slope w/officer, 1940, 8-pc, EX (EX Whisstock box), A $200.00

Britains, #37, Band of Coldstream Guards, marching w/full instru-mentation & drum major, 21-pc, VG (G box), A.....$425.00

Britains, #39, Royal Horse Artillery, 6-horse team, gun, limber, mounted outriders & officer, EX (P British Army box), A $850.00

Britains, #47, Skinner's Horse, mounted in review order, w/trumpeter, 5-pc, EX (G box), A $180.00

Britains, #50, Life Guards & 4th Hussars, mounted guards, offi-cers, mounted Hussars w/trumpeter, 10-pc, M (EX box), A $300.00

Britains, #60, 1st Bombay Lancers, troopers w/lances, trum-peter & officer, 1910, 15-pc, G (P box w/blk & wht label), A $850.00

Britains, #69, Pipers of Scots Guards, marching in feather bon-nets, 1940, VG (G Whisstock box), A $275.00

Britains, #77, Gordon Highlanders, marching at slope w/piper, 1935, 8-pc, EX (EX Whisstock box), A $180.00

Britains, #101, Band of the Life Guards in State Dress, kettle drum-mer & director of music, 12-pc, NM (VG box), A $475.00

Britains, #115, Egyptian Cavalry, mounted w/lances, w/officer, M (EX box), A...$250.00

Britains, #123, Bikanir Camel Corps, 1935, G (EX box), A, $510.00.

Britains, #134, Japanese Infantry (2nd version), charging in review order, 1900, VG (G- printers box), A $700.00

Britains, #147, Africa's Savage Warriors, Zulus, 8 running figures with spears and shields, EX (G box), A, $230.00.

Britains, #136, Russian Cossacks, mounted at gallop, w/officer, EX (EX box), A $200.00

Britains, #155, Railway Station Staff, station master, ticket taker, porters, trolleys & assorted luggage, G (G box), A....$650.00

Britains, #167, Turkish Infantry, standing on guard position, 1935, 5-pc, EX (EX Whisstock box), A $475.00

Britains, #168, Civilians, passengers, yachtsman, chauffer & policeman, G, A $900.00

Britains, #196, Greek Evzones, marching at slope, 1940s, EX (EX Types of Greek Army box), A.................................$180.00

Britains, #197, Gurkha Rifles, marching at trail, 1945, EX (VG Whisstock box), A $140.00

Britains, #201, Officers of the General Staff, field marshall, general officer & 2 aides-de-camp, 4-pc, M (EX box), A........$275.00

Britians, #205, Coldstream Guards, at present arms, officer holding sword at salute, 8-pc, EX (EX Whisstock box), A $250.00

Britains, #217, Argentine Cavalry, mounted w/lances, w/officer, NM (EX box), A $250.00

Britains, #226, West Point Cadets, marching in winter dress, 1930, 8-pc, EX (VG Whisstock box), A..................$180.00

Britains, #228, US Marines, marching in winter dress blues w/sergeant, 1935, 8-pc, VG+ (VG+ Types of USA Forces box), A......................................$300.00

Britains, #255, Green Howards (2nd version), flag bearer, drummer & officer, 9-pc, EX (G Types of World Armies box), A $900.00

Britains, #312, Grenadier Guards, marching at slope w/winter coats, w/officer, 8-pc, NM (EX box), A $180.00

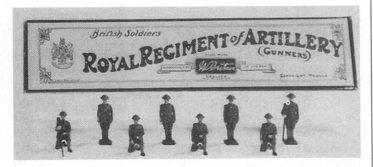

Britains, #313, Royal Regiment of Artillery, 1940-41, kneeling and standing gunners, rare, EX (EX box), A, $650.00.

Britains, #1283, Grenadier Guards, 3 positions, 1935, 9-pc, EX (EX Armies of the World box), A $170.00

Britains, #1290, British Army Band of Line, marching, service dress, instruments, drum major, 1935, 12-pc, G, A .$475.00

Britains, #1301, US Army Military band, in active service dress & peak caps, 1940, 12-pc, EX (EX Armies of World box), A $550.00

Britains, #1349, Royal Canadian Mounted Police, mounted at gallop in summer dress, w/officer, 5-pc, M (EX box), A $250.00

Britains, #1389, Belgian Infantry, marching, service dress, steel helmets, 1935, 8-pc, VG (G Armies of World box), A....$250.00

Britains, #1510, Royal Navy Sailors, marching empty-handed in regulation dress, 1940s, 8-pc, VG (VG box), A $170.00

Britains, #1515, Coldstream Guards, marching at slope w/officer, 8-pc, M (EX box), A $160.00

Britains, #1527, Royal Air Force Band, w/instruments, drum major, VG (G- box), A $400.00

Britains, #1730, Royal Artillery Gun Detachment, gunners in service dress, steel helmet, w/ & w/o shells, officer, NM, A $150.00

Britains, #1911, Officers & Petty Officers of the Royal Navy, 3 in wht, 2 in bl, VG (G Types of Royal Navy box), A...$140.00

Britains, #2067, Sovereign's Standard of the Life Guards & Escort, trumpeter, bearer, corporals & farriers, 7-pc, EX, A $300.00

Britains, #2073, Royal Air Force, marching at slope w/officer, 8-pc, EX (G box), A $120.00

Britains, #2074, 1st King's Dragoon Guards, mounted in review order, w/officer, 5-pc, M (VG box), A $160.00

Britains, #2075, 7th Queen's Own Hussars, mounted in review order, w/officer, 5-pc, NM (EX box), A $180.00

Britains, #2076, 12th Royal Lancers, mounted in review order on trotting horses, w/officer, 5-pc, NM (EX box), A $225.00

Britains, #2079, Royal Company of Archers, w/officer, 13-pc, EX, A $275.00

Britains, #2084, Colour Party of the Scots Guards, w/ensigns carrying colours & 4 sergeants, 6-pc, NM (VG box), A.....$500.00

Britians, #2062, Seaforth Highlanders, mounted officer & 2 pipers, 17-pc, M (G box), A.................................$400.00

Charbens, #5550, American Soldiers, w/US GI's in action, 12-pc, NM (G box), A $120.00

Courtenay, Archbishop of Sens, position 4, falling wounded, mace in right hand, signed, EX, A $375.00

Courtenay, Castillan of Amposta, position 6, sword in hand, mk, EX, A $425.00

Courtenay, John Welles, Squire of the Black Prince, position H-2, signed, A, $850.00.

Courtenay, Duke of Brittany, position H1, on galloping horse, lance in moveable arm, moveable visor, EX, A $550.00

Courtenay, Edward, The Black Prince, position H6, mounted w/mace, VG, A....................$750.00

Courtenay, John Pateshull, position 7, w/battle-ax, mk, sm chip on nose o/w EX, A....................$275.00

Courtenay, King Edward III, mounted on Joan of Arc horse, jtd hand, G, A....................$325.00

Courtenay, King Edward III, position 6, sword in right hand, gold armor & crown, signed, EX, A $550.00

Courtenay, King Henry V, golden armor & crown, sword in moveable right arm, mounted w/full trappings, EX (few chips), A....................$950.00

Courtenay, King John of France, position 1, fighting w/knife & broken sword, signed, EX, A $400.00

Courtenay, Sir Edward Fitz Alan, position 18, battle-ax & moveable visor, EX, A....................$425.00

Courtenay, Sir John Chandos, mounted w/trappings, jtd arm, helmet moves, EX (VG Morrell of Burlington Arcade box), A $850.00

Courtenay, Sir Richard Talbot, H6 variation of position 18 head, mounted, w/battle-ax, helmet w/visor, EX, A....................$800.00

Courtenay, Sir Robert Holland, position 15, advancing w/sword in upright arm, moveable visor, signed, EX, A $425.00

Courtenay, Sir Sanchet D'Ambreticourt, mounted, full tournament trappings, lance & great helmet, EX, A....................$850.00

Courtenay, Thierry D'Auffay 'Le Hardi,' position Z5, w/sword in arm, moveable visor, mk, EX, A....................$375.00

Courtenay, Tournament Knight of Sir Hugh Courtenay, KG, on horse w/trappings, lance in moveable arm, EX (EX box), A....................$130.00

Courtenay, Vicomte Rochechouart, position 12, falling w/arrow imbedded in side, VG, A....................$400.00

Courtenay, Wounded Knight, modified position 3, lying wounded, G, A....................$650.00

Courtenay, 15th Century English Archer, firing bow, outstretched right arm, mk, EX, A $900.00

Courtenay-Greenhill, Sir Walter Woodland, position Z5, sword in right hand & banner in left, moveable visor, mk, EX, A....................$700.00

Dinky, #148, 30HM, Daimler ambulance, NM, F2 ....$125.00

Dinky, #150A, officer w/binoculars, EX, F2....................$18.00

Dinky, #150B, private, seated, NM, F2....................$30.00

Dinky, #150C, private, standing, NM+, F2....................$22.00

Dinky, #150D, driver, NM, F2....................$28.00

Dinky, #150E, NCO, walking, EX, F2....................$20.00

Dinky, #152A, light tank, EX+, F2....................$50.00

Dinky, #152B, reconaissance car, EX, F2....................$85.00

Dinky, #152C, Austin Seven Military, M, F2....................$35.00

Dinky, #153A, US Army Jeep, NM, F2 ....$65.00

Dinky, #160A, officer w/binoculars, NM+, F2....................$25.00

Dinky, #160B, gunner, seated, NM+, F2....................$22.00

Dinky, #160B, gunner, seated, VG, F2....................$10.00

Dinky, #161A, searchlight lorry, rpt, M, F2....................$150.00

Dinky, #161B, antiaircraft gun, NM, F2....................$75.00

Dinky, #162, Dragon Tractor set, hook rpl, blast shield on gun missing, EX, F2....................$75.00

Dinky, #162C, 18-pounder cannon, EX, F2 ....$30.00

Dinky, #22S, searchlight lorry, rare, EX, F2....................$650.00

Dinky, #341, trailer (military version), rpt military gr, M, F2 .$45.00

Dinky, #602, armored command car, MIB, F2....................$75.00

Dinky, #603, army private, NM+, F2....................$13.00

Dinky, #603, driver, EX, F2....................$10.00

Dinky, #604, bomb disposal unit, orig plastic robot (unassembled), MIB, F2....................$75.00

Dinky, #609, US howitzer w/3-man crew, MIB, F2 ....$75.00

Dinky, #612, commando jeep, all metal, MIB, F2....................$55.00

Dinky, #615, US jeep & 105mm howitzer, M, F2....................$95.00

Dinky, #616, AEC transporter w/tank, MIB, F2 ....$160.00

Dinky, #617, VW KDF w/pak gun, MIB, F2....................$115.00

Dinky, #618, AEC transporter w/helicopter, MIB, F2....$160.00

Dinky, #620, Berliet missle launcher, rare gray color, orig insert, MIB, F2....................$250.00

Dinky, #621, 3-ton Army wagon, M, F2....................$65.00

Dinky, #622, Bren gun carrier, orig decal sheet, MIB, F2 .$65.00

Dinky, #622, 10-ton Army truck, NMIB, F2....................$100.00

Dinky, #623, Army covered wagon, NM, F2....................$40.00

Dinky, #625, 6-pounder anti-tank gun, MIB, F2....................$45.00

Dinky, #626, military ambulance, EX, F2....................$55.00

Dinky, #641, 1-ton cargo truck, M, F2....................$65.00

Dinky, #642, pressure refueler, EX, F2....................$75.00

Dinky, #651, Centurion tank, M, F2....................$65.00

Dinky, #654, 155mm mobile gun, MIB, F2....................$75.00

Dinky, #660, Antar tank transporter, MIB, F2....................$150.00

Dinky, #661, recovery tractor, MIB, F2....................$165.00

Dinky, #666, Corporal missile, MIB, F2....................$450.00

Dinky, #667, armored patrol car, MIB, F2....................$55.00

Dinky, #667, missile-servicing platform, MIB, F2....................$325.00

Dinky, #668, Foden Army truck, MIB, F2....................$80.00

Dinky, #670, armored car, EX, F2....................$35.00

Dinky, #673, scout car, w/o driver (early version), EX, F2..$35.00

Dinky, #674, Austin Champ, NM, F2....................$30.00

Dinky, #674, Coast Guard missile launcher, MIB, F2....................$35.00

Dinky, #675, US Army staff car, EX, F2....................$70.00

Dinky, #676, armored personnel carrier, M, F2....................$50.00

Dinky, #676, Daimler armored car, MIB, F2....................$60.00

Dinky, #677, armored command vehicle, EX, F2....................$80.00

Dinky, #680, Ferret scout car, MIB, F2....................$40.00

Dinky, #681, DUKW, MIB, F2....................$40.00

Dinky, #682, Stalwart load carrier, MIB, F2....................$40.00

Dinky, #686, 25-pounder field gun, plastic wheels, nylon tires, MIB, F2....................$65.00

Dinky, #687, convoy Army truck, MIB, F2....................$40.00

Dinky, #687, limber (trailer), EX+, F2....................$30.00

Dinky, #690, Scorpion tank, NM, F2....................$50.00

Dinky, #691, Striker anti-tank vehicle, MIB, F2....................$85.00

Dinky, #692, Leopard tank, MIB, F2....................$80.00

Dinky, #692, 5.5" med gun, M, F2....................$35.00

Dinky, #693, 7.2" howitzer, M, F2....................$60.00

Dinky, #697, 25-pounder field gun set, NM, F2....................$95.00

Dinky, #699, Leopard recovery vehicle, MIB, F2....................$90.00

Dinky, #731, Sepcat Jaguar aircraft, MIB (sealed), F2 ......$90.00

Dinky, #734, Swift fighter, MIB, F2....................$80.00

Dinky, #736, Hawker Hunter fighter, M (VG box), F2....$75.00

Dinky, #80A, EBR panhard, MIB (sealed), F2....................$85.00

Dinky, #80B, military Jeep, w/driver, M, F2....................$80.00

Dinky, #80C, AMX 13T tank, M, F2 ....$80.00
Dinky, #80D, Berliet 6x6, blk baseplate, MIB, F2 ....$140.00
Dinky, #80F, Renault ambulance, MIB, F2.....................$125.00
Dinky, #804, Mercedes Unimog, MIB, F2 ....$135.00
Dinky, #808, GMC wrecker, gr, MIB, F2........................$425.00
Dinky, #810, Dodge command car, w/camo net, MIB, F2 .$210.00
Dinky, #813, 155mm cannon automoteur, MIB, F2 ....$210.00
Dinky, #817, AMX 13T tank, M, F2 ....$80.00
Dinky, #818, Berliet 6x6, M, F2 ....$110.00
Dinky, #820, Renault ambulance, M, F2 ....$100.00
Dinky, #821, Mercedes Unimog, M, F2 ....$95.00
Dinky, #822, M-3 halftrack, NM, F2...............................$75.00
Dinky, #823, Cuisine Roulante, MIB, F2 ....$85.00
Dinky, #824, Berliet Gazelle, MIB, F2............................$245.00
Dinky, #825, DUKW, MIB, F2 ....$250.00
Dinky, #826, Berliet wrecker, M, F2 ....$175.00
Dinky, #827, EBR panhard FL-10, MIB, F2 ....$125.00
Dinky, #828, Jeep w/rockets, MIB, F2 ....$110.00
Dinky, #883, AMX bridgelayer, NM, F2.........................$175.00
Dinky, #884, Brockway bridgelayer, MIB, F2..................$425.00
Dinky, #890, Berliet tank transporter, M, F2 ....$200.00
Grey Iron, boy in wht summer suit, very scarce, 94%, A1 ..$29.00
Grey Iron, cannon, red wheels, nickel barrel, NM, A1 ....$31.00
Grey Iron, colt, for ranch scene, scarce, 96%, A1............$39.00
Grey Iron, cowboy, NM, A1...$26.00
Grey Iron, Ethiopian chief, scarce, 95%, A1....................$77.00
Grey Iron, fence gate, 99%, A1....................................$28.00
Grey Iron, flagbearer, 94%, A1....................................$26.00
Grey Iron, Greek Evzone, very scarce, 95%, A1 ....$110.00
Grey Iron, gray slip cannon (Battery F), EX, A1 ....$12.00
Grey Iron, gunner, EX, A1...$9.00
Grey Iron, hold-up man in blk (Hoppy), 99%, A1 ....$24.00
Grey Iron, Indian chief w/knife, 98%, A1.......................$28.00
Grey Iron, knight in armor, 96%, A1..............................$18.00
Grey Iron, lady skater, ca 1920s, very scarce, orig pnt 95%,
    A1 ....$145.00
Grey Iron, Legion bugler, 97%, A1 ....$22.00
Grey Iron, pilot, very scarce, EX, A1..............................$12.00
Grey Iron, pirate boy 'Jim,' 96%, A1 ....$34.00
Grey Iron, pirate w/dagger, bl outfit, 93%, A1 ....$23.00
Grey Iron, pirate w/hook, orange outfit, 97%, A1 ....$30.00
Grey Iron, pirate w/sword, gr outfit, 94%, A1 ....$27.00
Grey Iron, rifleman, EX, A1 ....$4.00
Grey Iron, shell loader bending, EX, A1 ....$9.00
Grey Iron, US Doughboy, bomber crawling, brn pistol, 97%,
    A1 ....$29.00
Grey Iron, US Doughboy charging, early version, 95%, A1 ...$19.00
Grey Iron, US Doughboy, shoulder arms, 97%, A1 ....$16.00
Grey Iron, US Infantry charging, early version, 90%, A1 ...$12.00
Grey Iron, US Infantry, officer, prewar, 96%, A1.............$20.00
Grey Iron, US Infantry, port arms, 98%, A1....................$23.00
Grey Iron, US Infantry, shoulder arms, 97%, A1.............$17.00
Grey Iron, US machine gunner, prewar, 99%, A1 ....$21.00
Grey Iron, US Naval officer in wht, prewar, 94%, A1......$20.00
Grey Iron, 3 ducks on single base, for ranch scene, very scarce,
    98%, A1 ....$80.00
Heinrichsen (28 mm), Prussian Troops & Austrian Troops
    (depicting battle), 1925, VG (VG box), A $130.00

Heyde, US Army Ambulance Unit, WWI, horse-drawn ambu-
    lance, hospital tent, stretcher teams, wounded, medics, 18-
    pc, VG, A $350.00
Heyde, US Infantry, in dress blues, marching w/mounted & foot
    officers & drummer, 20-pc, 1930s, VG (P box), A ..$450.00
Jones, calf, #236, 95%, A1 ....$10.00
Jones, farmer, 99%, A1..$19.00
Jones, farmer's wife, 97%, A1......................................$17.00
Jones, hen, M, A1...$10.00

Photo courtesy of Sally and Stan Alekna.

Jones, painted as Germans in green/gray, scarce, from $400.00 to $475.00.

Lucotte, French Napoleonic Artillery Gun Team, 6-horse team,
    3 drivers w/whips, limber & cannon, G, A $325.00
Lucotte, French Napoleonic Horse-Drawn Artillery Caisson, six-
    horse team, 3 drivers, G-, A $300.00
Manoil, aviator carrying bombsight, wide base, 97%, A1 ...$41.00
Manoil, blacksmith making horseshoes, 92%, A1 ....$19.00
Manoil, blacksmith w/wheel, 99%, A1 ....$28.00
Manoil, bomb thrower w/2 grenades in pouch, 98%, A1 ...$28.00
Manoil, boy carrying wood, 99%, A1 ....$27.00
Manoil, bugler, 2nd version, 93%, A1 ....$19.00
Manoil, cadet, 99%, A1...$28.00
Manoil, caisson w/v-loop, 96%, A1...............................$27.00
Manoil, cannon, spoke wheels, hitch on bottom, 96%, A1.$18.00
Manoil, cannon loader, 98%, A1...................................$26.00
Manoil, carpenter carrying door, scarce, 98%, A1 ....$65.00
Manoil, carpenter sawing lumber, 99%, A1.....................$37.00
Manoil, coastal defense cannon, inner brace to support halves,
    early version, 98%, A1 ....$35.00
Manoil, colt, maroon, scarce, 99%, A1 ....$27.00
Manoil, cow grazing, 99%, A1......................................$15.00
Manoil, cowboy, 2nd version, 95%, A1 ....$16.00
Manoil, cowgirl, yel & red, no horse, 97%, A1................$28.00
Manoil, doctor in wht, 97%, A1 ....$29.00
Manoil, ensign, 96%, A1..$21.00
Manoil, farmer at water pump, 99%, A1 ....$24.00
Manoil, farmer carrying pumpkin, 98%, A1 ....$28.00
Manoil, farmer cutting corn, 99%, A1............................$26.00
Manoil, farmer pitching sheaves, 98%, A1 ....$27.00
Manoil, farmer sharpening scythe, 98%, A1 ....$26.00

Manoil, farmer sowing grain, 99%, A1 ....$24.00
Manoil, flagbearer, skinny, 97%, A1 ....$32.00
Manoil, girl watering flowers, 98%, A1 ....$26.00
Manoil, hound, 98%, A1 ....$24.00
Manoil, lady w/churn, 97%, A1 ....$23.00
Manoil, lady w/pie, 98%, A1 ....$31.00
Manoil, machine gunner, motorized, scarce, 98%, A1 .....$74.00
Manoil, machine gunner sitting, 93%, A1 ....$33.00
Manoil, man carrying sack on back, 98%, A1..................$24.00
Manoil, man dumping wheelbarrow, 98%, A1 ....$26.00
Manoil, marine, 2nd version, 98%, A1 ....$30.00
Manoil, mason laying bricks, 93%, A1 ....$29.00
Manoil, nurse, red bowl, 97%, A1 ....$19.00
Manoil, observer, 95%, A1...$34.00
Manoil, officer, 2nd version, 96%, A1 ....$26.00
Manoil, old man fixing shoe, scarce, 97%, A1.................$32.00
Manoil, parachutist, 98%, A1 ....$53.00
Manoil, parade, 5th version, M, A1 ....$23.00
Manoil, sailor marching, wht, casting flaw in base, 96%, A1..$22.00
Manoil, scarecrow w/straw hat, 97%, A1 ....$23.00
Manoil, scarecrow w/top hat, 98%, A1 ....$25.00
Manoil, shepherd w/flute, scarce, 96%, A1 ....$49.00
Manoil, signalman (sailor), 2nd version, 93%, A1 ....$27.00
Manoil, soldier charging w/bayonet, scarce, 91%, A1 .....$38.00
Manoil, soldier marching w/rifle & pack, 99%, A1 ....$23.00

Manoil, soldiers writing letters, one smoking cigarette, rare, ea, $145.00.

Manoil, tommy gunner, 2nd version, 92%, A1................$23.00
Manoil, tommy gunner, 97%, A1......................................$28.00
Manoil, tractor, plain front, 99%, A1 ....$23.00
Manoil, water wagon, lg #72, rarest variation, 96%, A1...$31.00
Marx, Soldiers of Fortune, 36-pc, 1930s, NMIB, S9.......$360.00
Mignot, Ancient Franks, marching w/spears & battle-axes, M (EX box), A $190.00
Mignot, Austrian Hussars, mounted w/sabers, gr & red uniforms, shakos, standard bearer, 1813, 5-pc, M (VG box), A $225.00
Mignot, Band of Paris Guards, full instrumentation, director in bl uniform, plumed caps, 1890-1914, 12-pc, EX (G box), A $325.00

Mignot, British Infantry of the Line, advancing w/bayonets, w/officer, drummer & bearer, 1812, 12-pc, NM (EX box), A $275.00
Mignot, English Life Guards, in review order, officer, trumpeter & bearer, 6-pc, M (EX box), A $250.00
Mignot, French Army Work Party, soldiers in fatigues w/tools & implements, officer, 12-pc, EX (EX box), A $225.00
Mignot, French Colonial Infantry, bl & wht uniforms w/wht helmets, officer, bugler & bearer, 1890-1910, EX (EX box), A $250.00
Mignot, French Foreign Legion, 3 positions, khaki service uniforms, 1930, EX (EX box), A $180.00
Mignot, French Infantry of Line Band, instruments, kepis, band leader, 1890-1914, 12-pc, EX (EX box), A $190.00
Mignot, French Napoleonic Camel Corps, 2 troopers w/rifles, officer, trumpeter & bearer, VG+ (G box), A $300.00
Mignot, French Napoleonic Mamelukes, 2 mounted w/sabers, 1 bearer, 1813, VG+ (G Mignot box), A....................$120.00
Mignot, French Navy Band, 1914, full instruments, summer wht uniforms, 12-pc, EX (EX box), A $275.00
Mignot, limited edition, Trumpeters of the Empire, mounted French Napoleonic trumpeters, 10-pc, M (EX box), A $550.00
Mignot, Medieval English Archers, long bows, crossbows, swords & bills, 12-pc, M (EX box), A $275.00
Mignot, Paris Fire Department Command Car, driver, fire chief & lieutenant, 1910, VG (EX box), A $160.00
Mignot, Paris Fire Department Command Car, w/pompier driver, 1910, NM (EX box), A...............................$250.00
Mignot, Paris Fire Department Motorized Boiler Wagon, w/pompier driver, 1910, NM (EX box), A........................$250.00
Mignot, Polish Lancers, mounted w/slung lances, red & bl uniforms, officer, trumpeter, bearer, 1812, 6-pc, M (EX box), A $300.00
Mignot, Spanish Infantry, marching at slope, dk bl uniforms, officer, 2 drummers & bearer, 1808, 12-pc, M (EX box)..$300.00
Mignot, Vignette of French Fire Fighters (Pompiers), w/safety net, ca 1900, set of 4, M (EX box), A $140.00
Mignot, 14th Century Knights, mounted w/lances in full armor, EX (EX box), A $190.00
Potsdamer Zinnsoldaten, Indian Tiger Hunt, hunters, lady, natives, steward, tiger, wild boar, 1890, 29-pc, M (EX box), A $300.00
Soljertoy, marine, very scarce, 99%, A1...........................$28.00
Soljertoy, officer on horse, scarce, 98%, A1.....................$45.00
Soljertoy, officer w/sword, scarce, 98%, A1 ....$27.00
Soljertoy, soldier marching left shoulders arms, scarce, 98%, A1 ....$18.00
Soljertoy, soldier on guard w/bayonet, scarce, 98%, A1 ...$18.00
Timpo, #770, West Point Cadets, band w/instruments, drum major & flag bearer, 19-pc, NM (VG illus box), A .$300.00
Trophy 1st, West India Regiment, marching in review order, 6-pc, EX (VG box), A..$60.00
Wollner, Austrian Foot Guard, guardsman, mounted & foot officers, bearer, 1900s, 15-pc, VG, A $200.00
Wollner, Band of 1st Bosnian Infantry Regiment, full instrumentation, drum major & bass drum on donkey cart, 1900, G, A $300.00

Sporting Collectibles

Baseball — the great American Pastime — has given us hundreds of real-life sports heroes plus a great amount of collectible memorabilia. Baseball gloves, bats, game-worn uniforms, ephemera of many types, even games and character watches are among the many items being sought out today. And there are fans of basketball, football, and hockey that are just as avid in their collecting.

As you can see, many of our listings describe Kenner's Starting Lineup figures. These small plastic likenesses of famous sports greats were first produced in 1988. New they can be purchased for $5.00 to $8.00 (though some may go a little higher), but they have wonderful potential to appreciate. For instance, Nolan Ryan (card #94) is worth about $275.00 or so (MIB), John Stockton (card #72), even more — about $400.00. These are two of the top-prized figures, but on the average most from 1988 run from $25.00 to $50.00. In addition to basketball and baseball series, a football series has been made as well, and in 1993 Kenner added hockey. If you're going to collect them, be critical of the condition of the packaging.

Bobbin' head dolls made of papier-mache were made in Japan during the 1960s up until about 1972, and we've listed some of these as well. They were about 7" high or so, hand-painted and then varnished. Some of them represent sports teams and their mascots. Depending on scarcity and condition, they'll run from as low as $35.00 up to $100.00, though there are some that sell for $300.00 or so. A few were modeled in the likeness of a particular sports star; these are rare and when they can be found sell in the $500.00 to $1,000.00 range. For more information we recommend *Bobbin' Head Dolls* by Patrick Flynn (MinneMemories).

See also Cereal Boxes; Character Clocks and Watches; Games; Pin-Back Buttons.

Detroit Tigers, doll, 1977, stuffed cloth, 12", EX, $35.00.

Dodgers, scarf, 1951, silk, illustrates scoreboard, Ebbets Field and map of Brooklyn, scarce, EX, from $900.00 to $1,200.00.

All-Stars Baseball Statuettes, Robert Gould Inc, boxed group of 7 players, scarce, NM (VG box), from $350.00 to $400.00.

Babe Ruth, statue, Esso, 17", M $60.00
Bo Jackson, autographed football, M.............................$175.00
Brooklyn Dodgers, pin, 1955 World Champions enameled on metal pennant, tie-tac back, 1¾", M.........................$15.00
Cincinnati Reds, pennant, felt, 1940s, 28", EX...............$75.00
Duke Snider, autographed baseball, M............................$22.00

Enos Slaughter, autographed baseball, w/authenticity certificate, M..$25.00
Frank Thomas, poster, Donruss, 1994, 24x34", M...........$40.00
Gaylord Perry, pin, Chevron Oil, M (M photo card w/stats) .$3.00
Hank Aaron, card & pin set, Atlanta Stadium, 1968, commemorate of 500th home run game, M.............................$10.00
Harry Carey, book, Holy Cow!, 1989, EX $20.00
Joe Garagiola, book, Baseball Is a Funny Game, 1960, w/autograph, EX $25.00
Ken Griffey Jr, pennant, 1992, M.....................................$12.50
Kirby Puckett, autographed baseball, NM.......................$30.00
Marcel Dionne, hockey puck, Detroit Red Wings, signed, M.$10.00

Joe DiMaggio Baseball Shoes, D10, $400.00.

Mario Lemieux, yearbook, Hockey News, 1986, NM $25.00

Michael Jordan, autographed baseball, w/authenticity certificate, MIB $75.00

Michael Jordan, Chicago Bulls cap, signed on bill, M $120.00

Michael Jordan, Chicago White Sox jersey, signed, M ..$300.00

Mickey Mantle, baseball glove, Cambridge, 1950s, pro model, EX $200.00

Mickey Mantle, pen, bat form, 1960s, MIP (sealed), I2....$26.00

Mickey Mantle, stadium program, June 8, 1969, 8x10", M..$17.50

Mike Ditka, helmet, signed, authentic, M $350.00

Mike Tyson, figure, vinyl & plush, w/jail uniform, 12", M, S2 ....$25.00

New York Yankees, book, An Informal History of the New York Yankees, Van Rees Press, 1948, EX (VG dust jacket)..$25.00

New York Yankees, pennant, blk felt, 1950s, EX............$75.00

Oakland A's, program & scorecard, 1984, VG...................$4.00

Red Sox, official team magazine, Diehard, July 1991, M $5.00

Sandy Koufax, autographed baseball, w/authenticity certificate, M...$60.00

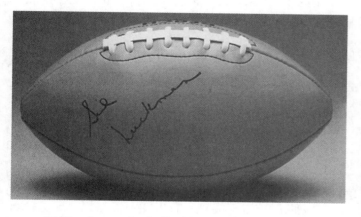

Sid Luckman, football with signature, $450.00.

Scottie Pippin, color photo, signed, 8x10", M $30.00

Spokane Indians, program, Minor League, 1979, M $3.50

Spud Webb, poster, Slam-Dunk King, full-color, 23x35", M .$3.00

Ted Williams, baseball bat, Sears, 1950s, EX $90.00

Ted Williams, fishing reel, 1950s, facsimile autograph, EX+ ..$95.00

Ted Williams, key chain, Moxie bottle, 2", M, from $4 to .$8.00

Ty Cobb, newspaper sports section, dated 1905, EX+ $25.00

Wayne Gretzky, jersey, LA Kings, signed, authentic, M...$600.00

Wilson Tennis Balls glasses, set of 5, $65.00.

BOBBIN' HEAD DOLLS

Atlanta Falcons, 1960s, M (NM box), H4 ....$85.00

Baltimore Colts, 1961-62, bl sq base, from $30 to $40.00

Baltimore Colts, 1966-68, realistic face, gold rnd base $45.00

Baltimore Orioles, Type I, gr diamond-shaped base, M, from $150 to..$200.00

Boston Bruins, boy's face, sq base, from $150 to $250.00

Chicago Cubs, blue square base, rare, $200.00.

Boston Patriots, Type VI, lg shoulder pads, from $300 to..**$400.00**
Chicago Bears, 1961, Type II, blk base, from $60 to.........**$80.00**
Chicago Cubs Mascot, 1961-62, emb team name, wht sq base, rare **$325.00**
Cleveland Indians Mascot, 1961-62, emb team name, wht sq base, rare **$285.00**
Detroit Redwings, boy's face, sq base, from $50 to...........**$70.00**
Harlem Globetrotters, gr & bl sq base, minimum value .**$150.00**
Houston Oilers, 1966-67, gold rnd base, rare **$75.00**
Little League Baseball Boy, Type VIII, gr rnd base, miniature, minimum value..**$100.00**
Los Angeles Dodgers, 1961-62, emb team name, wht sq base, rare **$125.00**
Los Angeles Rams, 1966-68, gold rnd base **$45.00**
New Orleans Saints, 1960s, M (NM box), H4.................**$75.00**
New York Mets, 1960-61, bl sq base, rare **$200.00**
Philadelphia Eagles, 1961-62, 1960 Champions emb on gr rnd base, scarce..**$80.00**
San Diego Chargers, 1960s, M (NM box), H4.................**$85.00**

St Louis Cardinals Mascot, gold base, $85.00.

St Louis Cardinals, 1960s, M (NM box), H4 ....**$75.00**
Washington Redskins, Merger series, gold rnd base, rare .**$80.00**
Washington Senators, Type VI, boy's face, gold rnd base, from $70 to **$90.00**

KENNER STARTING LINEUP FIGURES

Andre Dawson, 1990, MIP..**$12.00**
Andy Van Slyke, 1989, MIP..**$16.00**
Bo Jackson, 1990, MIP..**$18.00**
Bobby Bonilla, 1988, MIP..**$25.00**
Brett Saberhagen, 1988, MIP **$18.00**

Cal Ripken, 1989, MIP...**$25.00**
Carlos Baerga, 1993, MIP **$20.00**
Darryl Strawberry, 1991, MIP..**$12.00**
Dave Winfield, 1990, MIP..**$12.00**
David Robinson, 1991, MIP...**$15.00**
Dwight Gooden, 1991, MIP...**$15.00**
Ed Belfour, 1993, MIP...**$95.00**
Eric Lindros, 1994, MIP...**$18.00**
Glenn Davis, 1989, MIP...**$12.00**
Jaromir Jagr, 1993, MIP, from $15 to **$20.00**
Jeremy Roenick, 1993, MIP, from $15 to **$20.00**
Jim Abbott, 1990, MIP...**$22.00**
Joe Montana, 1994, MIP, from $20 to..............................**$25.00**
Kareem Abdul-Jabbar, 1988, MIP **$30.00**
Ken Griffey Sr, 1988, MIP..**$40.00**
Ken Oberkfell, 1988, MIP..**$16.00**
Kirby Puckett, 1989, MIP...**$12.00**
Larry Bird, 1992, MIP **$25.00**
Mark Davis, 1989, MIP..**$18.00**
Orel Hershiser, 1989, MIP...**$25.00**
Patrick Ewing, 1990, MIP..**$35.00**
Ray Bourque, 1993, MIP..**$18.00**
Roberto Kelly, 1990, MIP...**$20.00**
Ryne Sandberg, 1990, MIP, from $20 to **$30.00**
Shane Rawley, 1988, MIP...**$16.00**
Steve Sax, 1988, MIP **$16.00**
Steve Yzerman, 1993, MIP **$18.00**
Tom Seaver, 1992, MIP..**$30.00**
Troy Aikman, 1990, MIP, from $35 to...............................**$40.00**
Will Clark, 1989, MIP **$20.00**
Willie Hernandez, 1988, MIP...**$18.00**
Wilt Chamberlain, 1989, MIP...**$20.00**

Star Trek

The Star Trek concept was introduced to the public in the mid-1960s via a TV series which continued for many years in syndication. The impact it had on American culture has spaned two generations of loyal fans through its animated TV cartoon series (1977), six major motion pictures, and Fox network's 1987 TV show, 'Star Trek, The Next Generation.' As a result of its success, vast amounts of merchandise, both licensed and unlicensed, have been marketed including jewelry, clothing, calendars, collector plates, comics, costumes, games, greeting and gum cards, party goods, magazines, model kits, posters, puzzles, records and tapes, school supplies, and a wide assortment of toys. Packaging is very important; an item mint and in its original box is generally worth 75% to 100% more than one rated excellent.

Advisor: Craig Reid (R9).

See also Character and Promotional Drinking Glasses; Coloring, Activity and Paint Books; Fast-Food Collectibles; Halloween Costumes; Lunch Boxes; Model Kits.

FIGURES

Antican, Galoob, STNG, 3¾", MOC, D8 ....**$45.00**

Arcturian, Mego, 1979, 12", MIB, $85.00.

Captain Kirk, Mego, 1974, 8", NMOC, D9 ....$48.00
Chief Miles O'Brien, Deep Space 9, MOC, T1 ....$10.00
Commander Data, Galoob, STNG, 2nd issue, speckled face, MOC, H4...$40.00
Commander Data, Galoob, STNG, 3rd issue, flesh face, MOC, H4 ....$20.00
Commander Riker, Galoob, STNG, 1988, 3¾", M (M card), from $12 to $15.00

Decker, Mego, The Motion Picture, 3¾", EX, from $10 to..$15.00
Ferengi, Playmates, STNG, MOC, D8............................$18.00
Ferengi (no blk on boots variation), Playmates, STNG, 1st issue, MOC, D8...$35.00
Gorn, Mego, 1972-74, w/Neptunian outfit, 8", EX, I2......$65.00
Gowron, Playmates, STNG, 1992, MOC $35.00
Ilia, Mego, 3¾", MOC, from $30 to $40.00
Kirk, Mego, The Motion Picture, 3¾", EX, H4.................$8.00
Kirk, Mego, 8", EX, from $15 to $25.00
Kirk, Mego, 8", MOC, S2 ....$45.00
Kirk, Scotty, Spock or Klingon, Ertl, Star Trek III, MOC, ea, $20 to $30.00
Klingon, Mego, 1974, 8", NMOC, D9 ....$45.00
LaForge, Galoob, STNG, 3¾", MOC, D8........................$12.00
LaForge, Playmates, STNG, w/removable visor, MOC, D8..$40.00
McCoy, Mego, The Motion Picture, 3¾", EX, H4...........$12.00
Picard, Galoob, STNG, 3¾", MOC, D8, from $12 to.......$18.00
Picard, Playmates, STNG, 1st issue, MOC, from $12 to ..$18.00
Q, Deep Space 9, MOC, from $8 to $12.00
Quark, Deep Space 9, MOC, from $8 to $12.00
Riker, Galoob, STNG, 1988, 3¾", NM (VG card), from $8 to...$10.00
Romulan, Playmates, STNG, MOC, from $25 to.............$35.00
Scotty, Ertl, Star Trek III, 1984, 3¾", M (NM card), from $20 to...$30.00
Scotty, Mego, 1974, 8", NM, from $40 to.......................$50.00
Selay, Galoob, STNG, 3¾", MOC, D8.............................$45.00
Sisko, Deep Space 9, MOC, D8......................................$10.00
Spock, Mego, 1974, 8", EX, from $15 to $25.00
Spock, Mego, 1974, 8", MOC, D8, from $45 to................$55.00

Neptunian, Mego, 8", M, $150.00.

Spock, Mego, 1979, 12½", missing phaser otherwise NMIB, $75.00.

Tasha Yar, Galoob, STNG, 1988, MOC, from $20 to......$30.00
Troi, Playmates, STNG, 1st issue, MOC, D8...................$25.00

PLAYSETS

Ferengi Fighter, Galoob, STNG, 1988, MIB, from $35 to.**$50.00**

Mission to Gamma VI, Mego, complete, very rare, MIB, from $700 to..**$950.00**

Star Trek Command Communication Console, Mego, 1976, M (EX+ box) from $70 to...**$80.00**

Star Trek USS Enterprise Bridge, Mego, 1975, vinyl fold-out, w/chair, control panel, cb views, VG.........................**$30.00**

Star Trek USS Enterprise Bridge, Mego, 1975, vinyl fold-out, NRFB (sealed), from $150 to **$175.00**

Star Trek USS Enterprise Bridge, Mego, 1975, vinyl fold-out, for 8" figures, M (EX box) from $120 to.......................**$160.00**

Star Trek USS Enterprise Bridge, Mego, 1980, The Motion Picture, molded wht plastic, for 3¾"/4" figures, NRFB, from $100 to **$135.00**

VEHICLES

Klingon Cruiser, Dinky, 1978, NM (VG card) **$20.00**

Klingon Warship, Corgi, Star Trek II, 1982, diecast, #149, NMOC, H4..**$18.00**

Shuttlecraft Galileo, Galoob, STNG, MIP, D8 ....**$55.00**

Shuttlecraft Galileo, Galoob, STNG, NM (VG box), from $40 to..**$50.00**

USS Enterprise, cb, 36", VG, O1 ....**$50.00**

USS Enterprise, Dinky, The Motion Picture, 1978, 8", NM (G card) **$20.00**

USS Enterprise, Ertl, Star Trek V, M (NM pkg), O1.........**$20.00**

USS Enterprise, Galoob, 1988, diecast, STNG, MOC.....**$25.00**

MISCELLANEOUS

Autographed Picture, Quark, D8.....................................**$25.00**

Book and Record Set, Star Trek the Motion Picture, 33⅓ rpm, MIP, from $10.00 to $15.00.

Belt Buckle, 1979, copper color w/3-D bust of Kirk & Spock, EX, from $10 to..**$20.00**

Book, 1977 Annual, World Distributors/England, color cover of Spock, hardbound, 77 pgs, NM pgs w/VG cover, from $15 to...**$20.00**

Book w/48 Postcards, 1977, postcards are detachable, NM..**$25.00**

Calendar, 1984, pictures throughout, M, from $15 to **$20.00**

Chest Patch, Star Fleet, NM (EX card), from $5 to.........**$10.00**

Colorforms Set, 1975, MIB, from $20 to.........................**$40.00**

Decanter, figural Spock bust, ceramic, MIB, from $40 to.**$60.00**

Doll, Kirk, Knickerbocker, stuffed w/vinyl head, 12", M (shelf-worn box), S2 ....**$45.00**

Doll, Spock, Knickerbocker, stuffed w/vinyl head, 12", M (shelf-worn box), MIB, S2 ....**$45.00**

Figure, Checkov, porcelain, Ernst, 1988, limited ed, w/orig clothes & brass weapons, MIB, S2 ....**$300.00**

Figurine Paint Set, Whiting, 1979, w/4¼" Spock figure, M (G card), S2..**$25.00**

Game, Star Trek III, West End, 1985, M (EX box) **$20.00**

Game, Star Trek Motion Picture Game, Milton Bradley, 1979, incomplete (EX box), D9 ....**$20.00**

Game, Star Trek Pinball, plastic, 14", VG, from $30 to ...**$35.00**

Game, Super Phaser Target Game, Mego/Taiwan, 1975, blk plastic w/gray rim around light, 6", VG (G box), from $15 to...**$25.00**

Inter-Space Communicator, Lone Star/England, 1974, Kirk & Spock on box, NMIB...**$35.00**

Manual, Technical Star Fleet, 1st edition w/letter, from $50 to...**$75.00**

Marshmallow Dispenser, Star Trek V, Kraft promo, EX, S2.**$25.00**

Movie Viewer w/Film Strips, 1960s, MOC, from $25 to ..**$35.00**

Official ID Set, Larami, The Motion Picture, vinyl wallet-like pc, MOC, H4 ....**$15.00**

Oil Paintings-By-Number #2109, Hasbro, 1974, MIB (sealed), from $60 to..**$70.00**

Ornament, Enterprise, Hallmark, lights up, MIB, from $350 to...**$450.00**

Ornament, Galileo, Hallmark, NRFB, from $15 to **$30.00**

Phaser Ray Gun, AHI, 1976, M (EX card) **$25.00**

Plate, Ernst, features entire crew, 1 of series, MIB, S2 ......**$75.00**

Plate, Ernst, Spock, limited edition, Leonard Nemoy signature, MIB, S2...**$135.00**

Pocket Flix Cassette, Ideal, NM (G pkg), from $35 to **$45.00**

Program, International 1974 Convention, 40-pg w/full-pg photos, Spock on cover, NM, C1 ....**$17.00**

Silly Putty, 1979, The Motion Picture, MOC, S2 ....**$20.00**

Snow Dome, Willits, 1993, STNG, limited edition, musical, plays theme from movie, MIB, S2 ....**$100.00**

Snow Dome, 1992, lights up w/Enterprise inside, MIB, S2...**$125.00**

Store Display, Galileo Shuttlecraft, from Hallmark, EX, H4...**$130.00**

Tablet, 1960s, color shot of Kirk & Enterprise, 8x10", M, S2...**$20.00**

Tracer Gun, 1966, w/MOC box of tracers, VG.................**$40.00**

Tricorder, Mego, 1978, w/tape of sounds & voices from series, NM (worn box), from $150 to **$180.00**

Vulcan Ears, 1976, MIP, S2...**$20.00**

Water Pistol, Aviva, 1979, gray plastic w/classic hand phaser
    design, 7", MOC $35.00
Yo-Yo, Data, STNG, Spectra Star, MOC, P9 ....$4.00
Yo-Yo, Picard, STNG, Spectra Star, MOC, P9.................$4.00

Star Wars

The original 'Star Wars' movie was a phenomenal box office hit of the late 1970s, no doubt due to its ever-popular space travel theme and fantastic special effects. A sequel called 'Empire Strikes Back' (1980) and a third hit called 'Return of the Jedi' (1983) did just as well. As a result, an enormous amount of related merchandise was released — most of which was made by the Kenner Company. Palitoy of London supplied England and other overseas countries with Kenner's products and also made some toys that were never distributed in America. Until 1980 the logo of the 20th Century Fox studios (under whom the toys were licensed) appeared on each item; just before the second movie, 'Star Wars' creator, George Lucas, regained control of the merchandise rights, and items inspired by the last two films can be identified by his own Lucasfilm logo. Since 1987 Lucasfilm, Ltd., has operated shops in conjunction with the Star Tours at Disneyland theme parks.

In all, more than ninety action figures were designed. The last figures to be issued were the 'Power of the Force' series (1985), which though of more recent vintage are steadily climbing in value. A collector coin was included on each 'Power of the Force' card.

Original packaging is very important in assessing a toy's worth. As each movie was released, packaging was updated, making approximate dating relatively simple. A figure on an original 'Star Wars' card is worth more than the same character on an 'Empire Strikes Back' card, etc.; and the same 'Star Wars' figure valued at $50.00 in mint-on-card condition might be worth as little as $5.00 'loose.' For more information we recommend *Modern Toys, American Toys, 1930 to 1980*, by Linda Baker.

Advisor: George Downes (D8).

See also Character and Promotional Drinking Glasses; Coloring, Activity and Paint Books; Fast-Food Collectibles; Halloween Costumes; Model Kits.

Key:
ESB — Empire Strikes Back
POTF — Power of the Force
ROTJ — Return of the Jedi

FIGURES

A-Wing Pilot, Kenner, POTF, 3¾", MOC, from $75 to ..$95.00
A-Wing Pilot, Kenner, 3¾", M (EX tri-logo card), O1 ....$75.00
Admiral Ackabar, Kenner, ROTJ, 3¾", M (EX card), H4/O1,
    from $9 to...$12.00
Anakin Skywalker, Kenner, 3¾", MOC (tri-logo card), S2/
    D4...$45.00

Amanaman, Kenner, Power of the Force, 3¾", M (EX card), O1, $95.00.

Anakin Skywalker, Kenner, 3¾", NM, H4 ....$25.00
AT-AT Commander, Kenner, ESB, 3¾", M (VG card), O1,
    from $15 to..$20.00
AT-AT Commander, Kenner, ROTJ, 3¾", MOC, from $18
    to $25.00
AT-AT Driver, Kenner, ESB, 3¾", M (G card), O1, from $15
    to $22.00
AT-ST Driver, Kenner, ROTJ, 3¾", M (VG card), O1/H4 .$15.00
AT-ST Driver, Kenner, 3¾", MOC (tri-logo card), H4 ...$16.00
B-Wing Pilot, Kenner, POTF, 3¾", MOC, from $15 to ...$20.00
B-Wing Pilot, Kenner, ROTJ, 3¾", M (VG card), O1 .....$12.00
Barada, Kenner, POTF, 3¾", M (EX card), from $40 to...$60.00

Ben Obi-Wan Kenobi, Kenner, 3¾", M, $12.00.

Ben Obi-Wan Kenobi, Kenner, ESB, 3¾", M (VG card), O1 .**$30.00**

Ben Obi-Wan Kenobi, Kenner, ROTJ, 3¾", MOC, H4 ...**$30.00**

Ben Obi-Wan Kenobi, Kenner, 12", EX, H4 ....**$95.00**

Bespin Security Guard, Kenner, ESB, Black, 3¾", M (VG card), O1 ....**$25.00**

Bespin Security Guard, Kenner, ESB, Black or Caucasian, 3¾", w/accessories, NM, H4, ea **$8.00**

Bib Fortuna, Kenner, ROTJ, 3¾", M (VG card), O1 ....**$22.00**

Biker Scout, Kenner, ROTJ, 3¾", w/accessories & orig backing card, H4 ....**$10.00**

Boba Fett, Kenner, ROTJ, 3¾", MOC, from $60 to **$68.00**

Boba Fett, Kenner, 13", complete (G box), J5, from $175 to **$225.00**

Bossk, Kenner, bounty hunter, ESB, 3¾", M (VG card), O1.**$25.00**

Bossk, Kenner, bounty hunter, 3¾", w/accessories, NM, H4 .**$10.00**

C-3PO, Kenner, Power of the Force, 3¾", M (VG card), O1, from $60.00 to $80.00.

C-3PO, Kenner, ESB, removable limbs, 3¾", w/accessories & orig backing card, H4 ....**$10.00**

C-3PO, Kenner, ROTJ, removable arms, 3¾", M (VG card), O1 ....**$20.00**

C-3PO, Kenner, 12", EX, O1...**$25.00**

C-3PO, Kenner, 12", NM (VG box), O1 ....**$135.00**

Chewbacca, Bendee, MOC, P9 ....**$10.00**

Chewbacca, Kenner, ROTJ, 3¾", MOC, D4 ....**$30.00**

Chewbacca, Kenner, 12", EX+, H4 ....**$90.00**

Chewbacca, Kenner, 12", NM (VG box), O1 ....**$145.00**

Chewbacca, Kenner, 3¾", M (P tri-logo card), O1...........**$19.00**

Chewbacca, Kenner, 3¾", w/accessories, NM, H4............**$10.00**

Chief Chirpa, Kenner, ROTJ, 3¾", M (VG card), O1 .....**$15.00**

Chief Chirpa, Kenner, ROTJ, 3¾", w/accessories & orig backing card, H4..**$8.00**

Cloud Car Pilot (Twin Pod), Kenner, ESB, 3¾", M (VG card), O1, from $20 to **$25.00**

Darth Vader, Bendee, MOC, P9 ....**$10.00**

Darth Vader, Kenner, early bird certificate version, vary rare, w/accessories, NM, H4 ....**$125.00**

Darth Vader, Kenner, Power of the Force, 3¾", MOC, O1, $65.00.

Darth Vader, Kenner, 12", complete, NM, P9/H4............**$90.00**

Darth Vader, Kenner, 12", MIB **$200.00**

Darth Vader, Kenner, 12", VG, O1/S2 ....**$45.00**

Darth Vader, Kenner, 3¾", w/accessories, NM, H4 ....**$12.00**

Death Star Droid, Kenner, Star Wars, 3¾", M (NM card), O1 ....**$75.00**

Death Star Droid, Kenner, 3¾", w/accessories, NM, H4.....**$8.00**

Dengar, Kenner, ESB, 3¾", M (P card), O1.....................**$20.00**

Dengar, Kenner, 3¾", w/accessories, NM, H4.....................**$8.00**

Emperor's Royal Guard, Kenner, Return of the Jedi, MOC, $40.00.

Emperor's Royal Guard, Kenner, 3¾", w/accessories & orig backing card, H4 ....$10.00

EV-9D9, Kenner, POTF, 3¾", M (EX card), O1 ....$100.00

EV-9D9, Kenner, 3¾", M (EX tri-logo card), O1 ....$75.00

Ewok Action Figures, Kenner, 1984, Lucasfilm logo, set of 3, M (EX box), from $50 to..$60.00

FX-7, Kenner, ESB, 3¾", M (VG card), O1....................$28.00

FX-7, Kenner, 3¾", w/accessories, NM, H4 ....$10.00

Gamorrean Guard, Kenner, ESB, 3¾", M (G+ card), D9...$7.00

Gamorrean Guard, Kenner, POTF, MOC, from $100 to..$150.00

Gamorrean Guard, Kenner, ROTJ, M (EX card), O1, from $15 to..$20.00

General Madine, Kenner, ROTJ, 3¾", MOC, H4, from $12 to..$15.00

Greedo, Kenner, ROTJ, 3¾", M (G card), O1.................$20.00

Greedo, Kenner, Star Wars, 3¾", M (NM card), O1........$85.00

Greedo, Kenner, 3¾", M (factory bag), H4.....................$10.00

Hammerhead, Kenner, ROTJ, 3¾", M (G card), O1........$24.00

Hammerhead, Kenner, 3¾", M (factory bag), H4.............$10.00

Han Solo, Kenner, Bespin outfit, 3¾", w/accessories, NM, H4..$12.00

Han Solo, Kenner, Carbonite Chamber outfit, 3¾", M (NM tri-logo card), O1...$125.00

Han Solo, Kenner, trench coat, 3¾", M (G tri-logo card), O1 ....$35.00

Han Solo, Kenner, w/pants, shirt & vest, 12", NM, S2 ..$125.00

Han Solo, Kenner, 12", MIB, S2 ....$475.00

IG-88, Kenner, 12", NM, O1 ....$275.00

IG-88, Kenner, 15", rare, MIB, from $450 to.................$600.00

IG-88, Kenner, 3¾", w/accessories & orig backing card, H4...$14.00

Imperial Commander, Kenner, ESB, 3¾", M (VG card), O1 ....$25.00

Imperial Commander, Kenner, ROTJ, 3¾", M (VG card), O1 ....$17.00

Imperial Dignitary, Kenner, POTF, 3¾", M (NM card), H4 .$60.00

Imperial Dignitary, Kenner, 3¾", M (EX tri-logo card), O1 .$45.00

Imperial Gunner, Kenner, POTF, 3¾", MOC, from $65 to..$95.00

Imperial Stormtrooper, Kenner, ESB, 3¾", M (VG card), O1, from $40 to $50.00

Imperial Stormtrooper, Kenner, Hoth gear, 3¾", w/accessories, NM, H4...$12.00

Jawa, Kenner, ROTJ, 3¾", M (EX card), O1 ....$30.00

Jawa, Kenner, 12", complete, NM, P9/H4 ....$100.00

Jawa, Kenner, 12", M (EX+ box), O1 ....$195.00

Jord Dusat, Droid, Kenner, 1985, MOC, H4...................$10.00

King Gorneesh, Kenner, NM (NM tri-logo card), M5 .....$10.00

Klaatu, Kenner, ROTJ, 3¾", M (NM card), O1/D4 ....$15.00

Klaatu, Kenner, ROTJ, 3¾", w/accessories & orig backing card, H4...$6.00

Lando Calrissian, Kenner, POTF, General Pilot outfit, 3¾", M (EX card), O1, from $75 to.......................................$95.00

Lando Calrissian, Kenner, ROTJ, Skiff Guard outfit, MOC, D4/H4...$20.00

Lando Calrissian, Kenner, Skiff Guard outfit, 3¾", w/accessories, NM, H4...$10.00

Leia Organa, Bendee, MOC, P9 ....$20.00

Leia Organa, Kenner, ESB, Bespin gown, 3¾", M (EX card), O1 ....$120.00

Leia Organa, Kenner, POTF, combat poncho, 3¾", M (EX card), H4..$45.00

Leia Organa, Kenner, POTF, combat poncho, 3¾", MOC, D4/O1..$65.00

Leia Organa, Kenner, ROTJ, battle poncho, MOC, S2....$40.00

Leia Organa, Kenner, ROTJ, Bespin gown, 3¾", MOC, D4, from $40 to...$50.00

Leia Organa, Kenner, 12", MIB, from $200 to...............$275.00

Leia Organa, Kenner, 12", VG, H4 ....$50.00

Lobot, Kenner, ESB, 3¾", MOC, O1 ....$28.00

Lobot, Kenner, ESB, 3¾", w/accessories & orig backing card, H4..$8.00

Logray, Kenner, ROTJ, 3¾", w/accessories & orig backing card, H4..$8.00

Luke, Bendee, MOC, P9..$10.00

Luke Skywalker, Kenner, early bird certificate version w/extendable light sabre tip, very rare, w/accessories, NM, H4 ....$125.00

Luke Skywalker, Kenner, POTF, battle poncho, 3¾", MOC, from $60 to...$75.00

Luke Skywalker, Kenner, POTF, Imperial Stormtrooper outfit, 3¾", MOC, O1, from $170 to $225.00

Luke Skywalker, Kenner, POTF, Jedi Knight outfit, 3¾", MOC, O1..$125.00

Luke Skywalker, Kenner, shirt, belt & boots, 12", VG, S2..$85.00

Luke Skywalker, Kenner, X-Wing Pilot, 3¾", w/accessories, NM, H4..$12.00

Luke Skywalker, Kenner, 12", EX, from $100 to............$150.00

Luke Skywalker, Kenner, 12", NM (EX sealed box), O1, from $235 to...$275.00

Lumat, POTF, 3¾", MOC, D4 ....$25.00

Nein Nunb, Kenner, 3¾", M (orig Kenner bag), H4 ....$8.00

Nikto, Kenner, ROTJ, 3¾", M (VG card), from $10 to ...$15.00

Paploo, Kenner, POTF, NMOC, M5, from $10 to $20.00

Patrol Dewback, Kenner, complete, harness broken o/w NM, P9 ....$18.00

Patrol Dewback, Kenner, Star Wars, EX, O1 ....$10.00

Power Droid, Kenner, ROTJ, 3¾", M (EX card), O1........$20.00

Prune Face, Kenner, ROTJ, 3¾", MOC, from $12 to.......$15.00

Prune Face, Kenner, ROTJ, 3¾", w/accessories & orig backing card, H4..$8.00

Rancor Keeper, Kenner, ROTJ, 3¾", M (VG card), O1/D4.$12.00

Rancor Keeper, Kenner, ROTJ, 3¾", w/accessories & orig backing card, H4..$6.00

Rancor Monster, Kenner, ROTJ, 10", EX $30.00

Rancor Monster, Kenner, ROTJ, 10", NM (EX box) $45.00

Rebel Commander, Kenner, ESB, 3¾", M (G card), O1 ..$27.00

Rebel Soldier, Kenner, ESB, 3¾", M (VG card), O1........$15.00

Ree-Yees, Kenner, ESB, 3¾", M (EX+ card), D9 ....$20.00

Ree-Yees, Kenner, ROTJ, 3¾", MOC, H4, from $12 to...$18.00

Ree-Yees, Kenner, 3¾", w/accessories, NM, H4.................$6.00

Ree-Yees, ROTJ, Kenner, 1983, 3¾", M (G card), D9 .....$14.00

Romba, Kenner, POTF, 3¾", M (NM card), O1 ....$42.00

Romba, Kenner, 3¾", M (EX tri-logo card), O1 ....$42.00

R2-D2, Bendee, MOC, P9...$10.00

R2-D2, Kenner, ESB, w/sensorscope, 3¾", M (EX card), O1.$40.00

R2-D2, Kenner, remote control, NMIB, S2 ....$150.00

R2-D2, Kenner, ROTJ, w/sensorscope, 3¾", MOC, from $35 to..$50.00

R2-D2, silver and blue; R5-D4, orange and white, both by Kenner, $12.00 each.

R2-D2, Kenner, 12", M (EX+ sealed box), O1 ....$150.00
R2-D2, Kenner, w/sensorscope, 3¾", M (NM tri-logo card)...$35.00
R2-D2, Takara/Japan, remote control figure, MIB, S2 ...$500.00
R5-D4, Kenner, 3¾", w/accessories, NM, H4................$8.00
Sand People, Kenner, ESB, 3¾", w/accessories & orig backing card, H4................$8.00
Sand People, Kenner, Star Wars, 3¾", M (EX card) $150.00
Snaggletooth, Kenner, Star Wars, 3¾", M (NM card), O1 .$95.00
Snaggletooth, Kenner, 3¾", w/accessories, NM, H4 ....$8.00
Squid Head, Kenner, ESB, 3¾", M (EX card), D9, from $15 to................$20.00
Squid Head, Kenner, ROTJ, 3¾", MOC, from $15 to......$20.00
Star Destroyer Commander, Kenner, 3¾", w/accessories, NM, H4................$10.00

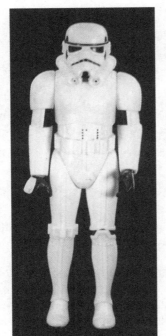

Stormtrooper, Kenner, 12", EX, from $100.00 to $125.00.

Stormtrooper, Bendee, MOC, P9 ....$10.00
Stormtrooper, Kenner, POTF, MOC, S2/01 ....$185.00
Stormtrooper, Kenner, ROTJ, 3¾", M (VG card), O1, from $18 to..$25.00
Stormtrooper, Kenner, ROTJ, 3¾", MOC, from $30 to ...$40.00
Stormtrooper, Kenner, 12", no accessories, light fading, VG, S2 ....$50.00
Tauntaun, Kenner, ESB, open belly, NRFB (sealed), H4/S2..$38.00
Teebo, Kenner, ROTJ, 3¾", M (VG card), O1...............$20.00
Teebo, Kenner, 3¾", MOC (tri-logo card), H4 ....$10.00
Trash Compactor Monster, Kenner, w/accessories, NM, H4..$25.00
Tusken Raider, Kenner, 3¾", w/accessories, NM, H4.......$10.00
Ugnaught, Kenner, 3¾", w/accessories, NM, H4 ....$8.00
Walrus Man, Kenner, 3¾", w/accessories, NM, H4 ....$10.00
Wampa Snow Creature, Kenner, NM (VG box), O1.......$20.00
Warok, Kenner, POTF, 3¾", MOC, from $30 to.............$40.00
Weequay, Kenner, ROTJ, MOC, D4 ....$15.00
Weequay, Kenner, ROTJ, 3¾", w/accessories & orig backing card, H4................$8.00
Wicket W Warrick, Kenner, ROTJ, 3¾", NMOC, M5....$10.00
Yoda, Kenner, ESB, 3¾", M (VG card), O1 ....$40.00
Zuckuss, Kenner, 3¾", w/acessories, NM, H4...................$8.00
2-1 B, Kenner, 3¾", w/accessories, NM, H4.....................$10.00
4-Lom, Kenner, ESB, 3¾", w/accessories & orig backing card, H4 ....$12.00
4-Lom, Kenner, ROTJ, 3¾", M (P card), O1 ....$20.00
4-Lom, Kenner, 3¾", w/accessories, NM, H4.....................$6.00
8D8, Kenner, ROTJ, 3¾", M (VG card), O1, from $20 to...$30.00

Playsets

Bespin Control Room, Kenner, Micro Collection, NRFB, H4................$55.00
Bespin Freeze Chamber, Kenner, Micro Collection, MIB...$40.00
Bespin Gantry, Kenner, Micro Collection, MIB (sealed), J2 ..$40.00
Bespin World, Kenner, NMIB (sealed), J2 ....$150.00
Cantina Adventure, Kenner, Star Wars, Sears promo, NMIB, O1................$450.00
Cloud City, Kenner, ESB, EX, O1 ....$120.00
Creature Cantina, Kenner, NMIB, O1 ....$110.00

Creature Cantina, Kenner, 1979, EX (VG box), I2, from $45.00 to $65.00.

Death Star Space Station, Kenner, Star Wars, VG, O1 ...$55.00

Death Star World, Kenner, NMIB (sealed), J2...............$175.00

Degobah, Kenner, ESB, EX (EX box), O1 ....$45.00

Droid Factory, Kenner, label sheet used & missing 6 connector pins (EX box), D9...$15.00

Droid Factory, Kenner, Star Wars, EX (VG box), O1, from $40 to $65.00

Ewok Assault Catapult, ROTJ, MIB, S2 ....$25.00

Ewok Combat Glider, ROTJ, MIB, S2..............................$40.00

Ewok Village, Kenner, ROTJ, M (EX sealed box), O1 .....$95.00

Ewok Village, Kenner, ROTJ, 1983, no accessories, G, P9 ....$15.00

Hoth Generator Attack, Kenner, Micro Collection, MIB (sealed), from $50 to...$75.00

Hoth Ice Planet, Kenner, NMIB, S2..............................$100.00

Hoth Turret Defense, Kenner, Micro Collection, NRFB, H4 ....$45.00

Hoth Wampa Cave, Kenner, 1982, Micro Collection, MIB, from $20 to $35.00

Hoth World, Kenner, Micro Collection, unused, NMIB, J2 ....$165.00

Imperial Attack Base, Kenner, ESB, VG (G box), O1 .....$45.00

Imperial Attack Base, Kenner, ESB, 1980, MIB, S2 ....$125.00

Imperial Attack Base, Kenner, 1981, complete, NM, C1 .$36.00

Jabba the Hut, Kenner, ROTJ, 1970s, complete, 9" figure, EX, D9...$15.00

Jabba the Hutt, Kenner, MIB (limited edition wht picture box), D4, from $30 to $45.00

Land of the Jawas, Kenner, Star Wars, EX (VG box), O1 ..$65.00

VEHICLES

AST-5, Kenner, Mini-Rigs, EX (G box), O1, from $18 to...$25.00

AT-AT, Kenner, ROTJ, complete, EX, O1 ....$75.00

AT-AT, Kenner, ROTJ, EX (VG box), O1..................$150.00

AT-AT, Kenner, ROTJ, MIB, from $225 to................$275.00

B-Wing Fighter, Kenner, ROTJ, NM (EX box), O1, from $60 to $85.00

B-Wing Fighter, Kenner, ROTJ, 22", EX, from $12 to $18.00

CAP-2 Captivator, Kenner, Mini-Rigs, EX (G box), O1 .$20.00

Darth Vader Star Destroyer, Kenner, ESB, EX (VG box), O1 ....$70.00

Darth Vader TIE Fighter, Kenner, EX, H4.....................$30.00

Darth Vader TIE Fighter, Kenner, Star Wars, VG (VG box), O1 ....$40.00

Desert Sail Skiff, Kenner, Mini-Rigs, EX (EX box), O1 ...$25.00

Endor Forest Ranger, Kenner, Mini-Rigs, NM (NM box), O1 ....$25.00

Ewok Battle Wagon, Kenner, ROTJ, EX (VG box), O1 ..$85.00

Imperial Cruiser, Kenner, diecast, M (bubble cut away o/w NM box), H4...$99.00

Imperial Shuttle, box only, Kenner, 1984, VG, I2............$20.00

Imperial Shuttle, Kenner, ROTJ, NMIB, O1, from $165 to..$225.00

Imperial Star Destroyer w/Drop Ship, Kenner, diecast, VG, O1 ....$30.00

Imperial TIE Fighter, Kenner, Star Wars, EX (EX box), O1...$70.00

INT-4 Interceptor, Kenner, Mini-Rigs, NM (VG box), O1 ..$20.00

Jawa Sandcrawler, remote controlled, EX, J6.................$375.00

Landspeeder, Kenner, lg, M (EX box), J6 ....$165.00

Landspeeder, Kenner, MIB, S2.......................................$100.00

Rebel Command Center, Empire Strikes Back, Kenner, NM (EX box), $160.00.

Rebel Command Center, Kenner, ESB, MIB, from $200 to $250.00

Rebel Command Center, Kenner, Star Wars, Sears promo, EX (VG box), O1 ....$175.00

Turret & Probot, Kenner, ESB, EX (VG box), O1 ....$65.00

Landspeeder, Kenner, 1978, diecast, with C-3PO and Luke Skywalker, 5" long, M, $35.00.

Landspeeder, Kenner, Star Wars, diecast, NM (VG card), O1 ....$65.00

Millennium Falcon, Kenner, diecast, EX, H4 ....$30.00

Millennium Falcon, Kenner, diecast, NM (bubble cut away o/w NM box), H4 ....$99.00

Mobile Laser Cannon MLC-3, Mini-Rigs, EX $10.00

One-Man Sand Skimmer, Kenner, POTF, 1984, very rare, M (lt worn/creased card), H4...$110.00

PDT-8, Kenner, Mini-Rigs, EX (EX box), O1, from $12 to..$18.00

Rebel Transport, Kenner, ESB, EX, O1 ....$40.00

Rebel Transport, Kenner, missing front windshield o/w VG, H4 ....$15.00

Scout Walker, Kenner, 1982, ESB, complete, 11", EX, D9 .$15.00

Slave I, Kenner, diecast, EX, from $35 to..........................$50.00

Slave I, Kenner, ESB, NM (G box), O1.............................$98.00

Slave I, Kenner, ESB, w/Han Solo, MIB, S2...................$150.00

Snowspeeder, Kenner, diecast, NM (EX card), O1 ....$65.00

Speeder Bike, Kenner, ROTJ, NMIB, from $20 to $35.00

Speeder Bike, Kenner, ROTJ, 1983, complete w/instruction sheet & booklet, M (EX box), D9 ....$19.00

TIE Fighter, Kenner, diecast, NM (EX card), O1, from $50.$65.00

Twin-Pod Cloud Car, Kenner, diecast, EX, H4/O1 ....$25.00

Twin-Pod Cloud Car, Kenner, diecast, NM (VG card), O1.$50.00

Vehicle Maintenance, Energizer, Kenner, Mini-Rigs, EX (G box), O1..$12.00

X-Wing Fighter, Kenner, diecast, battle damaged, NM (VG box), O1..$75.00

X-Wing Fighter, Kenner, diecast, EX, O1 ....$55.00

X-Wing Fighter, Kenner, diecast, MOC, J5...................$125.00

X-Wing Fighter, Kenner, ESB, MIB, from $90 to...........$120.00

X-Wing Fighter, Kenner, Micro Collection, plastic, EX+, J2 $42.00

Y-Wing Fighter, Kenner, diecast, VG, O1 ....$45.00

Y-Wing Fighter, Kenner, MIB, S2 ....$125.00

MISCELLANEOUS

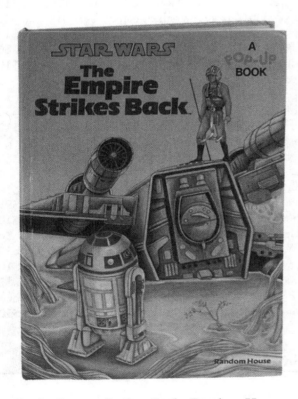

Book, Empire Strikes Back, Random House,
1980, 13 pop-ups, EX, from $10.00 to $15.00.

Bandolier Strap, Chewbacca, Kenner, MIB, J5 ....$25.00

Bank, C-3PO, ceramic, gold, 7½", EX+, M5.....................$30.00

Bank, Darth Vader, 1977 20th Century Fox Film Corp on bottom, ceramic, missing stopper o/w M (NM box), P9.$175.00

Bank, Emperor's Royal Guard, EX, O1.............................$15.00

Bank, Emperor's Royal Guard, NM (VG box), O1...........$28.00

Bank, Princess Kneesha figure, MIB, from $25 to $30.00

Bank, R2-D2, 20th Century Fox, 8", M $60.00

Bank, Wicket figure, vinyl, MIB, from $25 to...................$30.00

Beauty Bag, for shampoo & soap, Princess Leia, VG, O1 .$45.00

Belt, C-3PO & R2-D2 buckle, EX, O1..............................$12.00

Belt, Darth Vader, leather, w/orig price tag, NM, P9........$30.00

Book, ESB, Journal of the Making, paperback, EX, P9 ....$5.00

Book, ROTJ, Ewok Joins the Fight, Random House, 1984, EX, P9 ....$3.00

Book, ROTJ, hardbound, M, from $8 to $12.00

Book, Star Wars, The Making of the Movie, Step-Up Books, color photos of the movie being made, EX, D9 ....$4.00

Bubble Bath Container, Princess Leia, full, EX, O1..........$20.00

Bubble Bath Container, R2-D2, EX, I2 ....$12.00

Cake Pan, Darth Vader, pressed aluminum w/paper insert, 1980, M, I2 ....$12.00

Case, C-3PO, EX, O1 ....$25.00

Case, C-3PO, NM (sealed), O1, from $40 to.....................$55.00

Case, Chewbacca, bandolier strap, holds figures, EX, O1 .$12.00

Case, Chewbacca, bandolier strap, holds figures, NM (VG box), O1..$25.00

Case, Darth Vader, VG, O1..$7.00

Case, Laser Rifle; NM, O1 ....$25.00

Case, Laser Rifle; NM (EX box), O1 ....$45.00

Case, Star Wars, holds 24 figures, EX, O1 ....$15.00

Cassette & Book, Ewoks Join the Fight, M (sealed), P9 .....$9.00

Cassette & Book, Planet of the Hoojibs, M (sealed), P9 ....$7.00

Cassette & Book, Star Wars, 1977, sealed, H4...................$8.00

Cassette & Book, Star Wars Adventures in ABC's, M (sealed), P9 ....$9.00

Cassette & Tape, ROTJ, Read Along, EX (VG pkg), O1...$5.00

Clock, see Character Clocks and Watches

Coat Tree, Ewoks, EX, O1 ....$75.00

Cookie Jar, R2-D2, from $150 to $185.00

Cookies, Star Wars, Pepperidge Farm, 1983, MIB, H4 .....$15.00

Cup, Coca-Cola, plastic, 1977, H4....................................$5.00

Cup & Bowl, ESB, O1, set..$12.00

Curtains, Star Wars, EX, from $25 to................................$35.00

Doodle Pad, 1983, Rebo Band graphics, M, S2 ....$15.00

Eraser, Darth Vader, MOC, from $3 to $5.00

Figure, Boba Fett, Sigma, ceramic, MIB, $40 to...............$55.00

Figure, Han Solo, Sigma, ceramic, MIB, from $40 to $55.00

Figure, Klaatu, Sigma, ceramic, MIB, from $40 to $55.00

Figure, Lando Clarissian, Sigma, ceramic, MIB, from $40 to.$55.00

Figure, Leia Organa, Sigma, ceramic, MIB, from $40 to...$55.00

Figure, Wicket, Sigma, ceramic, MIB, from $40 to...........$55.00

Figurine Painting Kit, Craft Master, Luke figure, M (EX card), H4...$9.00

Game, Battle at Sarlacc's Pit, ROTJ, EX (VG box), O1, from $10 to $15.00

Game, Escape From Death Star, Star Wars, VG, O1........$15.00

Game, Ewoks Save the Trees, NM (P box), O1...............$15.00

Game, Play-For-Power Card Game, ROTJ, NM (VG box), O1 ....$9.00

Game, Ultimate Space Adventure, Star Wars, NM (G box), O1 ....$15.00

Game, Wicket the Ewok, MIB (sealed), O1 ....$15.00

Game, Wicket the Ewok, NM (G box), O1 ....$5.00

Game, Yoda the Jedi Master, EX (G box), O1 ....$15.00

Give-a-Show ESB Projector Set, 1977, w/15 of 16 strips, EX (G box), S2 ....$35.00

Intergalactic Passport, Ballantine, 1983, H4 ....$18.00

Iron-On Transfer, R2-D2 or C-3PO, M, D4, ea $5.00

Jacket, Star Wars, youth size, NM, O1 ....$38.00

Key Chain, Yoda, brn plastic, M, P9 ....$5.00

Kite, Spectra, 1983, MIP, H4 ....$18.00

Light Saber, Darth Vader, 43" long, EX, J2/O1 ....$38.00

Magnets, set of 4, D4 ....$10.00

Mug, ROTJ, plastic, 1983, H4 ....$6.00

Night Light, C-3PO, 2½", NM (VG card), P9 ....$5.00

Night Light, Darth Vader, 2½", NM, S2 ....$5.00

Night Light, Yoda figure, 1983, MOC, S2, from $10 to ...$15.00

Notebook, Stormtrooper, 1977, NM, P9 ....$5.00

Paint-By-Number Set, C-3PO & R2-D2, MIB, J5 ....$15.00

Paint-By-Number Set, Jabba the Hutt, Craft Master, 1983, M, S2 ....$10.00

Paint-By-Number Set, Lando & Boushh, MIB, J5 ....$15.00

Party Invitations, R2-D2, set of 8, MIP (sealed), D4, from $3 to $5.00

Patch, ROTJ or Lucasfilm Fan Club, M, D4, ea $5.00

Pencil Case, ROTJ, EX, O1 ....$7.00

Pencil Pouch, 1983, Luke Fighting Vader graphics, vinyl, NM, S2 ....$15.00

Pendant w/Chain, 1983, 3-D figures of R2-D2, Darth Vader or Yoda, MOC, S2, ea $20.00

Photos, ROTJ, 1983, 5 full-color photos of various scenes, 14½", NM, D9 ....$9.00

Picture Frame, C-3PO, Sigma, ceramic, 5x3", MIB, from $40 to $60.00

Picture Frame, R2-D2, Sigma, ceramic, 5x5", MIB, from $40 to $60.00

Pillow, Darth Vader & Boba Fett, ESB, EX, O1 ....$15.00

Pitcher, ROTJ, plastic, Coke promo, EX, O1 ....$12.00

Placemats, R2-D2 & C-3PO, 2-pc set, NM (NM pkg), O1 ....$25.00

Play-Doh Set, Jabba, EX (G- box), D9 ....$18.00

Plush Toy, Chewbacca, w/bandolier, 21", rare, NM, S2 ..$55.00

Plush Toy, R2-D2, w/tags, NM, O1 ....$55.00

Plush Toy, Wicket W Warrick, Kenner, EX, O1 ....$18.00

Plush Toy, Wicket W Warrick, Kenner, ROTJ, MIB, S2 ..$40.00

Poster, ESB, Han & Leia kissing, rolled, D4 ....$10.00

Poster Art, Star Wars, w/markers, EX, O1 ....$25.00

Puppet, Yoda, Kenner, 1981, hollow vinyl w/simulated strands of hair, 7½", VG, D9 ....$9.00

Puzzle, Han Solo & Star Wars, series 1, NM (G box), O1 ..$5.00

Puzzle, Leia & Wicket, ROTJ, NM (EX pkg), O1 ....$6.00

Puzzle, R2-D2 & C-3PO, Star Wars, jigsaw, NM (G box), O1 ....$5.00

Rain Poncho, 1977, vinyl, NM, S2, from $5 to $10.00

Record, Story of ROTJ, O1 ....$15.00

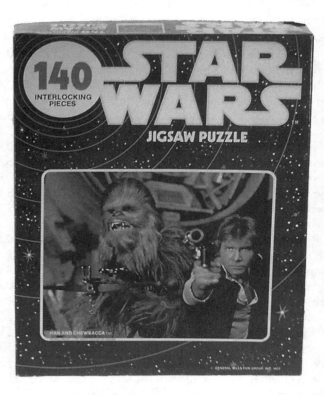

Puzzle, jigsaw; Star Wars, General Mills Fun Group Inc, 1977, 140 pieces, MIB, $12.50.

Record Tote, features Yoda, C-3PO & R2-D2, M, P9/S2 .$28.00

Record Tote, Star Wars, EX, O1 ....$12.00

Scissors, ROTJ, w/1¾" dia flasher scene, MOC, C1 ....$18.00

Shampoo Bottle, Luke Skywalker, empty, VG, O1 ....$15.00

Sheet, Star Wars, EX, O1 ....$15.00

Soap Bar, w/cvd figures, MIB, H4, any $6.00

Soundtrack, w/posters, VG+, P3 ....$10.00

Stained Glass Set, ESB, J5 ....$15.00

Stamp Kit, 1977, Intergalactic seals w/cantina scenes or spaceship, M (sealed), S2 ....$30.00

T-Shirt, Admiral Akbar, youth's size, EX, O1 ....$12.00

Tablecloth, Star Wars, Luke Skywalker & Darth Vader, NM (NM box), O1 ....$3.00

Tablet, ROTJ, 1983, R2-D2 & Wicket cover graphics, NM, S2 ....$10.00

Telephone, Darth Vader, EX, O1 ....$95.00

Toothbrushes, Oral-B, NRFB, H4 ....$10.00

Tumbler, Han Solo & Chewbacca, plastic, VG, O1 ....$6.00

Vase, Yoda, Sigma, MIB, J5, from $25 to $50.00

Wallet, Yoda, ROTJ, red, EX (orig card) $10.00

Watercolor Paint Set, Ewok, unused, NM, P9 ....$5.00

Yoda Fortune Teller, turn him upside down & look at your fortune, 5", H4 ....$50.00

Steam Powered

During the early part of the century until about 1930, though not employed to any great extent, live steam power was used to

activate toys such as large boats, novelty toys and model engines.
See also **Boats.**

Fire Pumper, Marklin, ca 1896, red and black with cream piping and copper-colored boiler, 19" long, EX, A, $2,400.00.

Model Engine, Weeden #32, A $75.00
Model Plant, DC, flywheels, pistons, pressure gauges & valves, 15", VG/EX, A..$500.00
Model Plant, Falk, ca 1920-30, 14", 11x10" base, no cord, EX+, M5..$390.00

Portable Steam Engine, Bing, painted steel and iron, 7" long, G+, A, $225.00.

Steam Plant, German, mounted on wood base, w/blacksmith & anvil, windmill, stamping mill, etc, on individual bases, EX, A...$4,600.00

Steam Plant, Marklin, early 1900s, horizontal boiler on burner w/smokestack, Dynamo motor, beveled base, 21x21", EX, A..$5,175.00
Steam Plant, Marklin (?), 1930s, horizontal boiler on burner stand w/smokestack & flywheel, footed base, 11x13", EX, A..$1,035.00

Steiff

Margaret Steiff made the first of her felt toys in 1880, stuffing them with lamb's wool. Later followed toys of velvet, plush and wool, and in addition to the lamb's wool stuffing, she used felt scraps, excelsior and kapok. In 1897 and '98 her trademark was a paper label printed with an elephant; from 1900 to 1905 her toys carried a circular tag with an elephant logo that was different than the one she had previously used. The most famous 'button in ear' trademark was registered on December 20, 1904. 1904 and 1905 saw the use of the button with an elephant (extremely rare) and the blank button. The button with Steiff and the underscored or trailing 'F' was used until 1948. For more information about Steiff's buttons, chest tags and stock tags as well as the inspirational life of Margaret Steiff and the fascinating history of Steiff toys we recommend *Button in Ear Book* and *The Steiff Book of Teddy Bears*, both by Jurgen and Marianne Cieslik; *Teddy Bears and Steiff Animals*, 2nd and 3rd series, by Margaret Fox Mandel; *4th Teddy Bear and Friends Price Guide* by Linda Mullins; and *Collectible German Animals Value Guide* by Dee Hockenberry.

Advisor: Cynthia Brintnall (C14).

See also Clubs, Newsletters and Other Publications under Cynthia's Country Store.

Cockie Spaniel, brown and white mohair with glass eyes, 4", M with all identification, $200.00.

Bear, #0203/26, w/3 tags & button, 9", M, I2....................$95.00

Bear on Wheels, beige mohair w/gold shaved muzzle, glass eyes, floss nose & mouth, unjtd, rubber tires, late, 15x19", G $450.00

Bear on Wheels, gold plush, blk button eyes, blk stiched nose & claws, felt pads, ca 1910, 9", EX+, A $1,100.00

Bessy the Cow, w/udders, orig collar & bell, 1950s, 9", M..$265.00

Boar, plastic tusks, no ID, 1950s, 8", VG $160.00

Camel on Wheels, felt & mohair, blk eyes, ear button, 1913, 9¾", VG, A $1,200.00

Cat Hand Puppet, plush w/glass eyes, 1950s, 8½", EX, A.$75.00

Cocker Spaniel, standing, blk & wht, raised script button, stock tag, chest tag, 1950s, 4½", M...................................$185.00

Cocker Spaniel, standing, reddish brn, raised script button, stock tag & chest tag, 13", M...$500.00

Cockie Spaniel Hand Puppet, plush, w/tag, 1950s, M....$165.00

Dally Dalmatian, sitting, raised script button, stock tag & chest tag, 1950s, 12", M..$985.00

Diggey Badger, standing, raised script tag, stock tag, chest tag, 4", M...$125.00

Dinosaur Stegosauras, mohair with glass eyes, original tag and raised button, 13", minimum value $1,250.00.

Duck, w/button & tag, 1950s, 5", M.................................$85.00

Floppy Kitty, sleeping, raised script button, stock tag & chest tag, 1950s, 6", M...$150.00

Foxy Terrier Hand Puppet, plush, w/tag, 1950s, M.........$155.00

Froggy Hand Puppet, plush, w/tag & button, 1950s, M..$125.00

Lady Bug on Wheels, 1950s, mohair, 19" long, $495.00.

Gaty Alligator Hand Puppet, plush, w/tag, 1950s, M $165.00

Golden Age of the Circus Set, 2 bears, tiger, giraffe, lion & elephant, ear button, EX, A $950.00

Golden Age of the Circus Set, 2 bears, tiger, giraffe, lion & elephant, ear button, MIB $3,000.00

Llama, 1964, plush with glass eyes, original tag and incised button in ear, 6", $95.00.

Goose, w/button & tag, 4½", M $145.00
Horse, felt w/glass eyes, leather tack, ear button, wheeled base, 1930s, 14x15", EX, A $700.00
Jocko, raised script button, stock tag & chest tag, 1950s, 12", M...$295.00
Leo the Lion Hand Puppet, plush w/tag & button, M....$185.00
Leopard, standing, raised script button, stock tag & chest tag, 1950s, 6", M...$195.00
Lion, recumbent, mohair w/glass eyes, ear button, 1950s, 15", EX $250.00
Lion, standing, w/button, 4", EX $125.00
Lion on Wheels, ca 1920, 26", G+, from $1,450 to.....$1,800.00
Mimic Dally Dalmatian Arm Puppet, plush, w/tag, 1950s, M..$395.00
Mockie Hippo, raised script button, stock tag & chest tag, 1950s, 5", M...$150.00
Molly Dog, sitting, raised script button, stock tag & chest tag, 1950s, 10½", M..$950.00
Nagy Beaver, raised script button, stock tag & chest tag, 1950s, 4", M..$145.00
Niki Rabbit, raised script button, stock tag & chest tag, 1950s, 7", M..$496.00
Nosy Rhino, raised script button, stock tag & chest tag, 1950s, 5", M..$150.00
Paddy Walrus, raised script button, chest tag, 1950s, 5", M.$250.00
Parrot Hand Puppet, w/button & tag, 1950s, M $250.00
Polar Bear, wht plush w/blk boot button eyes, underscored Steiff button, stitched nose & claws, 1920s, 13", EX, A ..$1,380.00
Pomeranian on Wheels, long mohair & felt, blk boot-button eyes, elephant button, 1908, 8", EX+, A $1,150.00
Racy Raccoon, standing, raised script button, stock tag & chest tag, 1950s, 4", M..$145.00
Raudi the Dog, orig collar & tag, VG $145.00

Rhinosaurus Nosy, mohair with braided tail, original stock tag and button, 5½" long, $135.00.

Squirrel w/Nut, standing, red, raised script button, stock tag & chest tag, 1950s, 7", M $135.00
Teddy Baby Hand Puppet, plush, w/tag, M....................$450.00

Spidey, 1960s, mohair with glass eyes, raised script button and stock tag, 5", $595.00.

Teddy Bear, apricot w/blk button, blk boot-button eyes, swivel head, jtd arms, stitched claws, rpl arm pads, 20", G, A.......$3,450.00
Teddy Bear, blond mohair w/blk steel eyes, brn embroidered features, fully jtd, excelsior stuffing, 16", EX, A........$2,760.00
Teddy Bear, brn w/blk plastic eyes, swivel head, jtd limbs, stitched nose, 4 stitched paws, sqeaker, 12", G, A...$575.00

Teddy Bear, 1904-10, yellow mohair with black button eyes, embroidered nose and mouth, felt pads, fully jointed, 29", EX/NM, from $8,000.00 to $12,000.00 (depending on condition).

Teddy Bear, curly hair w/glass eyes, script button, stitched nose & claws, cream pads, growler, 30", M, A $2,530.00

Teddy Bear, gold mohair, blk boot-button eyes, stitched nose, 5 stitched claws w/felt pads, swivel head, jtd, 12", G, A .$1,495.00

Teddy Bear, gold mohair w/blk steel eyes, early 1900s, fully jtd, embroidered features, excelsior stuffing, 15", EX, A ..$460.00

Teddy Bear, gold mohair w/glass eyes, embroidered nose, mouth & claws, fully jtd, excelsior stuffing, 1910, 12", EX, A ...$690.00

Teddy Bear, gold w/blk boot-button eyes, blank button, stitched nose & paws, swivel head, jtd limbs, ca 1905, 14", EX, A.................$2,070.00

Teddy Bear, gold w/glass eyes, printed button, swivel head, jtd limbs, blk stitched paws, 1920s, 19", G, A $2,300.00

Teddy Bear, mohair, blk steel eyes, embroidered nose & mouth, fully jtd, excelsior stuffing, new pads, 12", VG-, A..$144.00

Teddy Bear, mohair w/blk shoe-button eyes, blk embroidered features, fully jtd, pk & yel clown outfit, 1904, 14", VG+, A.................$805.00

Teddy Bear, mohair w/excelsior stuffing, glass eyes, floss nose & mouth, jtd shoulders & hips, 20", VG, A $2,300.00

Teddy Bear, wht w/blk boot-button eyes, blank button, jtd elongated limbs, hump, swivel head, ca 1905, 20", NM, A $5,520.00

Teddy Bear, wht w/glass eyes, brn stitched nose, 4 stitched claws, swivel head, jtd limbs, felt pads, 1920s, 14", M, A..$4,600.00

Teddy Bear, yel mohair w/button eyes, fully jtd, ear button, 1904-10, 29", moth damage to pads, some fiber loss, A...$5,400.00

Tessie Schnauzer, standing, raised script button, stock tag & chest tag, 1950s, 10", M.............$395.00

Tiger, recumbent, raised script button, stock tag & chest tag, 1950s, 12", M.................$285.00

Zebra, standing, velvet, raised script button, stock tag, 1950s, 5", M.................$150.00

Strauss

Imaginative, high-quality tin windup toys were made by Ferdinand Strauss (New York, later New Jersey) from the onset of World War I until the 1940s. For about fifteen years prior to his becoming a toymaker, he was a distributor of toys he imported from Germany. Though hard to find in good working order, his toys are highly prized by today's collectors, and when found in even very good to excellent condition, many are in the $500.00 and up range.

Advisor: Scott Smiles (S10).

Alabama Coon Jigger (Tombo), 1910, litho tin figure dances on stage, 10", G, S10.................$600.00

Alabama Coon Jigger (Tombo), 1910, litho tin figure dances on stage, 10", M (NM box), from $1,400 to $1,500.00

Bus Deluxe, #105, chaffeur, dbl row of seats, 13½", G (G- box), from $1,000 to.................$1,100.00

Chek-A-Cab, mk 69, full-figure driver, 4 lithoed doors, 8½", EX, A.................$1,100.00

Dandy Jim Clown Dancer, 1921, does jig & plays cymbals atop circus tent, litho tin, 10", NM, S10 ....$950.00

Dandy Jim Clown Dancer, 1921, does jig & plays cymbals atop circus tent, litho tin, 10", VG $550.00

Dizzie Lizzie, touring car w/colloquial sayings shakes, bounces & rattles, litho tin, 8", NM (worn box), A $375.00

Flying Zeppelin, 1920, hung from string, spinning prop propels zeppelin, aluminum mk Graf...GZ-2017, 16", NM (EX box), A.................$1,100.00

Ham and Sam, Black banjo player standing beside piano player, lithographed tin, 5½", MIB, from $1,500.00 to $1,750.00.

Ham & Sam, Black banjo player standing by piano player, litho tin, 5½", G, A.................$250.00

Ham & Sam, Black banjo player standing by piano player, litho tin, 5½", NM, S10.................$1,200.00

Handcar, workmen pump yel hand car w/2 yel wheels, EX+, from $250 to $300.00

Inter-State Double-Decker Bus, gr & yel, working, 10½", VG, S10, from $700 to $800.00

Jackie the Hornpipe Dancer, ca 1930, sailor dances on boat deck as it advances, 9", NM (rare EX+ box), from $1,500 to $1,600.00

Jackie the Hornpipe Dancer, ca 1930, sailor dances on deck of boat as it advances, glossy, 9", EX, S10.................$1,000.00

Jitney Bus #66, 1920s, gr w/yel trim, wht balloon tires, full-figure driver at wheel, 10", rare, VG, A $575.00

Leaping Lena Car, 1930, blk & wht litho tin w/driver, clockwork mechanism, 8", EX, from $500 to.................$600.00

Air Devil Plane, 1926, lithographed tin, 9¾" wingspan, EX, from $500.00 to $750.00.

Jazzbo Jim, 1920s, Jazzbo holds banjo and dances on cabin roof, Black depictions lithoed on cabin, 10", EX, S10, $800.00.

Photo courtesy of Scott Smiles.

Jenny the Balky Mule, 1920s, farmer moves back and forth in cart while mule balks, 9", EX, from $450.00 to $550.00.

Lux-a-Cab, mk 58, full-figure driver, 4 lithoed doors, 8½", EX, A...$1,050.00
Play Golf 'Just Like Daddy,' litho tin, 5" golfer on 21" base, MIB, from $750 to $850.00
Racer #21, w/driver, yel & red w/gr tires, bullet-shaped back, pnt side louvers, raised side trim, 9", VG+, from $350 to ..$400.00
Rollo-Chair, litho tin, G, A $650.00

Santa Claus Sleigh, Santa jumps up & down as 2 reindeer gallop, 12", EX, S10, from $1,000 to $1,200.00
Santee Claus, 1923, St Nick moves in sleigh as reindeer move back & forth while advancing in circle, 12", NM (EX box) $2,000.00
Speedboat Ferdinand, red tin floor-type w/driver, 10", G, from $200 to..$250.00
Thrifty Tom's Jigger Bank, 1918, insert coin & Tom does the jig on box, litho tin, w/up, 10", NM (EX box), A $4,750.00
Tourist Car, 33 on front grille, litho tin w/full-figure chauffer, raised designs on doors & louvers, 10", VG+, A......$580.00
Travelchiks, 4 chicks atop railroad car bend & peck for food, litho tin chicks as passengers, 8", VG+, from $400 to........$450.00
Trikauto, early tin auto w/driver travels forward & reverse, circles w/crazy-car action, 7½", scarce, NM (G box), A......$575.00
Twin Trolleys, litho tin trolley w/unpowered trailer, 6½", trolley pole missing, non-working, VG, from $150 to.........$200.00
Yell-O-Taxi, #59, full-figure driver, 4 lithoed doors, 8½", EX, from $500 to $600.00

Structo

Pressed steel vehicles were made by Structo (Illinois) as early as 1920. They continued in business well into the 1960s, producing several army toys, trucks of all types, and firefighting and construction equipment.

Dump Truck, 1930s, red and black with spoke wheels, 18", EX, D10, $575.00.

Dump Truck, red-pnt heavy gauge tin w/orange metal wheels, open cab, 17½", rear wheel hubs missing, scratches, G, A $160.00
Fire Truck, red & blk, mk CFO, complete w/hose & 4 ladders, 21⅜", NM, A...$1,050.00
Ladder Truck, w/2 ladders, pnt heavy gauge tin mk City Fire Dept, wht metal tires w/red wheels, rstr, 18", EX, A.............$275.00
Mobile Crane #810, gr & yel w/blk plastic tires, 19", NM (EX box), A..$225.00
Sanitation Truck, 1960, 18½", NM, R7........................$200.00
Tank Truck, blk truck w/gray tank, 26", rstr, EX, A.......$275.00
Transport Tractor-Trailer, bl pnt cast aluminum cab pulls red pressed-steel trailer, rubber tires, 22", G, A $35.00

Ready Mix Cement Mixer, #700, metallic enamel with black tires, NM (EX+ box), P3, $230.00.

Rigger and Hauler, 1950s, green with black rubber tires, 20", EX, D10, $175.00.

US Army Missile Launcher #410, gr w/blk rubber tires & plastic weapon, complete w/3 dart missiles, 17", NM (EX box), A $165.00

Teddy Bears

Early bears have long snouts, jointed limbs, large feet and felt paws, long curving arms, and glass or shoe-button eyes. Most have a humped back and are made of mohair stuffed with straw or excelsior. Some of the most desirable were made early in the century by the Steiff company (see Steiff), but they don't necessarily have to be old to be collectible. Many collectors choose to include toys, blocks, buttons, books, and other items dealing with teddies in their collections as well as the bears themselves.

Our advice on this category comes from Cynthia's Country Store (C14).

3½", Schuco, dk golden mohair over metal fr, tummy opens to reveal oval mirror & powder puff tray, 1920s, G, A .$325.00
4", Schuco, brn mohair, metal eyes, fully jtd, orig ribbon, M $385.00
5", wht mohair, plastic brads on outside, EX $65.00
9", sleeping on tummy, glass eyes, red collar, M.............$195.00
10", gray mohair w/cotton print body, glass eyes, EX......$250.00

8", US Zone Germany/Schuco, skating bear with keywind action, mohair with glass eyes, $1,500.00.

11", Am, beige mohair, glass eyes, long snout, early, EX .$345.00
11", celluloid shoulder-head doll face on 5-pc mohair bear body, VG, A $200.00
11", Germany/US Zone, mohair swivel head, glass eyes, floss nose & mouth, 5-pc body, hump, non-working squeaker, EX, A $475.00

11", bottle warmer, plush with glass eyes, zipper closure, rare, $395.00.

12", Knickerbocker, long blond & gold mohair, glass eyes, EX $250.00

12", Schuco, yes/no, mohair swivel head, shoe-button eyes, floss nose & mouth, jtd body, G, A $450.00

12", Zotty, brn mohair, swivel head, gold shaved mohair muzzle, glass eyes, open/closed mouth w/tongue, EX, A.......$130.00

13", Hermann, lt gold mohair, swivel head, glass eyes, jtd arms & legs, growler, NM, A $95.00

13", mohair swivel head, shoe-button eyes, floss nose, jtd shoulders & hips, floss claws on pads, very worn, fragile, A...$425.00

13x21", riding toy, brn plush, straw stuffed, glass eyes, floss nose & mouth, gr metal wheels, 1950s, A.........................$350.00

14", Alpha Farnell, long mohair, glass eyes, 1920s, NM..$1,950.00

14", Chad Valley, gold mohair, rexine pads, M $375.00

15", German, brn mohair, glass eyes, pnt details, 1927, EX $350.00

16", Schuco, yes/no, golden mohair, glass eyes, floss nose, jtd shoulders & hips, EX, A $925.00

17", vanilla mohair, long snout, button eyes, 1904, NM.$2,750.00

18", Am, lt brn mohair, modified hump, fully jtd, glass eyes, straw stuffed, 1920s, rpl nose, A $485.00

18", English, blond mohair, fully jtd, glass eyes, 1930s, A..$230.00

19", Hermann, Zotty, shaggy brn mohair w/bl tips, swivel head, glass eyes, gold shaved muzzle, squeaker, unused, EX, A $200.00

20", Ideal, gold mohair, twill nose, button eyes, 1910, M ..$400.00

21", frosted mohair, open mouth, 1940s, NM $265.00

22", mohair, excelsior stuffed, swivel head, glass eyes, cloth nose, floss mouth, hump, EX, A $1,450.00

28", possibly Knickerbocker, 1940s, grayish-black mohair with glass eyes, fully jointed, two growlers (front and back), from $500.00 to $550.00.

Tekno

The Tekno company was formed in Denmark during the late 1920s. The toy vehices they made were of the highest quality, fully able to compete with the German-made Marklin toys then dominating the market. The earliest Tekno vehicles were made of tinplate, and though some were not marked at all, others were stamped with a number. The factory continued to expand until WWII broke out and restrictions made further building impossible. In 1940 the government prohibited the use of tinplate for toy production, and the company began instead to manufacture diecast vehicles in a smaller (1/43) scale. These were exported worldwide in great volume. Collectors regard them as the finest diecasts ever made. Due to climbing production costs and the resulting increases in retail prices that inevitably hurt their sales, the company closed in 1972. Tekno dies were purchased by Mercury Kirk Joal who used them to produce toys identical to the originals except for the mark.

#0 ASG Transport-Spedition, dk bl & yel, NMIB, C6.....$30.00

#00 Transport-Spedition Truck, wht w/bl cover, MIB, C6 ....$40.00

#142 Scania Truck w/Long Wheel Base Trailer, bl & red body, silver trailer cover, NM, C6............................$50.00

#321 Falck Utility Truck, red, tinplate, G $195.00

#341 Falck Fire Engine, red, G $225.00

#361 Falck Searchlight Truck, red w/blk fenders, G.......$225.00

#401 Flying Fortress, silver, US, VG $75.00

#415 Ford Taurus Transit, 'Zonen,' blk & wht, MIB $60.00

#421 Ford Taurus 1000 Pickup, bl & red, MIB $120.00

#423 Ford V8 Garbage Truck, gr & red, G $45.00

#428 Ford V8 Wrecking Truck, red & blk, metal tires, rare, G $175.00

#434 Volvo BP Tanker, gr, M, L1 ....$150.00

#445 Scania Vabis Ladder Truck, red, EX......................$100.00

#451 Scania Truck & Trailer, red bodies, wht covers, M (EX separate boxes), C6.......................................$100.00

#452W Transport Trailer, wht w/bl cover, MIB, C6 ....$14.00

#452Y Covered Trailer, Tekno Transport, yel w/bl cover, M (VG box), C6 ....$14.00

#480 Ford V8 Tipping Truck, 'Zonen,' red, VG $35.00

#727 DKW Junior Coupe, metallic bl, M, L1 ....$85.00

#731 Mercedes Benz 220 SE Ambulance, red & blk, EX (orig box)..$150.00

#736 Dodge Beer Truck, wht w/red 'Tuborg,' VG+..........$95.00

#739 Dodge Truck, w/topper, yel & red, VG+ $125.00

#740 Dodge Milk & Cream Truck, bl & wht, NM, L1...$175.00

#775 Small Utility Trailer, MIB, C6 ....$30.00

#785 Hawker-Hunter Jet-Fighter, RAF, silver, EX.........$125.00

#812 Cooper Norton #1, silver, EX $60.00

#814K US Army Cannon, MIB, C6, from $30 to.............$45.00

#815 Sprite Musketeer Camping Trailer, ivory & lt gr, VG+..$50.00

#824 MGA Coupe 1600, lt bl, EX (orig box) $170.00

#832 MG1100, wht, MIB, C6.....................................$55.00

#833 Ford Mustang, metallic bl, MIB...........................$145.00

#834K 1967 Ford Mustang Kit, MIP (sealed), C6.............$30.00
#834RH 1967 Ford Mustang, blk hardtop & blk interior, MIB, C6...$70.00
#834WC 1967 Ford Mustang Convertible, wht, MIB, C6.$70.00
#834WH 1967 Ford Mustang Hardtop, wht w/blk hardtop, MIB, C6...$70.00
#837 SAAB 99, wht, MIB, C6 ....$40.00
#914 Ford D800 Tipping Truck, red side panels, MIB......$45.00
#917 Ford D800 Lumber Truck, MIB............................$120.00
#926 Jaguar XKE Roadster, red, M, L1 ....$75.00
#929 Mercedes Benz 280SL, red, blk roof, MIB, G3.......$110.00
#930S Corvair Monza Coupe, chrome, M, L1 ....$45.00
#931 Monza Spyder, wht, MIB, C6 ....$65.00
#934TM Toyota 2000 GT, mustard body, MIB, C6 ....$40.00
#950 Mercedes Benz 0302 Bus, Ostrerreische Post, MIB, C6 ....$40.00

Telephones

Novelty phones representing a well-known advertising or cartoon character are proving to be the focus of lots of collector activity — the more recognizable the character the better. Telephones modeled after a product container are collectible too, and with the intense interest currently being shown in anything advertising related, competition is sometimes stiff and values are rising.

Advisor: Jon Thurmond (T1).

Alf, made in Hong Kong, NM, $75.00.

Alvin (Chipmunks), figural, 16", VG $50.00
Bart Simpson, figural, MIB, S2 ....$35.00

Baseball Bat, T1 ....$75.00
Batmobile (First Movie), MIB...................................$60.00
Beetle Bailey, figural, EX+ $65.00
Bozo the Clown, Telemania, MIB, T1 ....$75.00
Budweiser Beer Can, T1 ....$25.00
Cabbage Patch Girl, Coleco, 1980s, EX $95.00
Charlie Tuna, 1987, 9", MIB, H4 ....$50.00
Crest Man (Sparkle), 1980s, plastic, 11", M $45.00
Garfield, eyes open & close, 1980s, EX, T1 ....$35.00
Ghostbusters' No Ghost, video promotion, NMIB, S2...$155.00

Gumby, Perma Toys, 1985, MIB, $65.00.

Heinz Ketchup Bottle, plastic, MIB................................$65.00
Inspector Gadget, 1984, figural, MIB $60.00
Little Sprout, figural, T1 ....$75.00
Mario Brothers, 1980s, figural, MIB, T1.......................$45.00
Mickey Mouse, ATC, NM, I2 ....$99.00
Mickey Mouse, Unisonic, NM, O1 ....$65.00
Pizza Hut Pete, 1980s, figural, EX+, R3 ....$50.00
Raid Bug, MIB from $125 to $150.00
Snoopy as Joe Cool, 1980s, MIB, T1 ....$55.00
Star Trek Enterprise Spaceship, MIB, T1.......................$75.00
Tyrannasarus Rex, MIB, T1.......................................$75.00
Woody Woodpecker, hand-painted prototype, 14", NM, A $429.00
Ziggy, 1989, MIB, T1 ....$75.00
7-Up Can, EX+ $30.00

Tonka

Since the mid-forties, the Tonka Company (Minnesota) has produced an extensive variety of high-quality painted metal trucks, heavy equipment, tractors and vans.

Advisor: Doug Dezso (D6).

Airport Tractor, orange, MIB.....................................$225.00
Allied Van Lines Semi #400, 1951, 23½", M $350.00
Army Truck w/Topper, 1965, olive gr, VG $75.00

Boating Set, 1961, pontoon and V-bottom boat with pickup truck, red and white, M, $525.00.

Boat Transport Semi #41, 1959, 5-pc, 28", EX $550.00
Camper #70, 1964, 9½", M $175.00
Carnation Milk Truck, 1955, 12", NM, A $668.00

Carnation Milk Truck, 1955, white pressed steel with black rubber tires, chrome-like bumpers, original decals on sides and front, 12", EX, $425.00.

CAT Dumpster, yel, M $25.00
Chevron Semi, limited edition, MIB................................$90.00
Dump Truck, 1961, red, VG+ $135.00
Dump Truck & Sand Loader #616, red & yel, EX $120.00
Dune Buggy, 1970, VG $50.00
Fire Engine, aerial ladder, 1960, MIB............................$575.00
Fisherman Pickup #110, 1960, 14", M $150.00
Ford Pickup, 1956, bl, VG...$175.00
Forklift #2970, MIB $65.00
Hydraulic Dump Truck #20, 1959, wht, VG....................$50.00
Jeep Dispatcher #200, fold-down windshield, 9½", EX+ (VG+ box), A...$60.00
Jeep Gladiator Hi-Way Patrol Wagon #64, M $90.00
Jeep Gladiator Wrecker #68, wht & blk, EX.....................$90.00
Jeep Universal #249, 1962, 9¾", EX................................$60.00
Jeep Wrecker, 1964, wht & blk, EX $90.00
Jeepster Stump Jumper, EX (EX box) $90.00
Jet Delivery #410, 1962, 14", M $275.00
Log Hauler w/Logs, 1960, VG $90.00
Logger Semi Tractor-Trailer, 1960, EX...........................$225.00
Lumber Truck #998, 1956, 18¾", M $185.00

Military Jeep #251, 1963, 10½", M.....................................$65.00
Minute Maid Delivery Van #725, 1954, 14½", G...........$300.00
Nationwide Moving Semi, 1958, 24¼", M $240.00
Parcel Delivery Van, 1957, 12", EX $350.00
Pickup, 1961, red, NM...$120.00
Pickup & Trailer, 1959, metallic sand, EX......................$195.00
Pumper & Accessories, 1957, VG $200.00
Pumper & Accessories, 1963, EX $165.00
Ser-Vi-Car, EX..$75.00
Steam Shovel #50, 1947, 20¾", M...................................$125.00
Suburban Pumper #990, 1956, 17", M $300.00
Surrey Jeep, pk, NMIB..$110.00
Terminal Train #720, 4-pc, 33⅜", EX..............................$175.00
Tractor-Carry-All Trailer #130, 1949, 30½", G...............$90.00
VW Beetle, bl w/wht interior, pnt 90%, VG+, P3...........$27.00
VW Bug, 1960s, orange, 8⅝", EX $22.50
Winnebago, 1970s, wht, EX $75.00
Wrecker, 1959, VG $185.00
Wrecker #518, 1963, red & wht, EX................................$160.00

Wrecker, 1961, white pressed steel with whitewall rubber tires, original decals, M, $400.00.

Toothbrush Holders

Figural ceramic toothbrush holders have become very popular collectibles, especially those modeled after well-known cartoon characters. Disney's Mickey Mouse, Donald Duck, and the Three Little Pigs are among the most desirable, and some of the harder-to-find examples in mint condition sell for upwards of $200.00. Many were made in Japan before WWII. Because the paint was not fired on, it is often beginning to flake off. Be sure to consider the condition of the paint as well as the bisque when evaluating your holdings. For more information we recommend *Pictorial Guide to Toothbrush Holders* by Marilyn Cooper.

Advisor Marilyn Cooper (C9).

Boy in Nickers Next to Mailbox, Japan, 4¼", EX $60.00
Boy Playing Violin w/Dog, Japan, 5", EX $70.00
Boy w/Flowers & Picnic Basket, Japan, 4½", VG.............$60.00
Cat Seated, unmk, Art Deco style, 4", EX, A $185.00
Cat w/Bass Fiddle, Japan, 6", EX, C9 ....$150.00

Clown, Germany, w/open arms standing behind dish, 4⅜", EX,
A $230.00
Clown Holding Mask, Japan, 5½", EX, C9 ....$100.00
Dalmatian, Germany, 4", EX, C9..................................$150.00
Doc, Maw of England, Disney, 1937, figural, glazed china, 3½",
EX+, A...$120.00
Dog (Seated), Germany, 4¾", EX, A $130.00
Donald Duck, Maw of England, 1930s, Donald holding ear of
corn, 4", NM, A...$605.00
Donald Duck, prewar Japan, 2 long-billed Donalds w/arms
entwined, 4½", scarce, NM $400.00
Donald Duck, prewar Japan, 3-D long-billed head in profile
w/emb body on sq container, 5¼", EX, A $165.00
Donkey, Goldcastle/Japan, 5¾", G, C9.............................$85.00
Dopey, prewar English, 4", scarce, M, A $248.00
Duck w/Bucket, Germany, 3¼", EX, A............................$120.00
Dutch Boy w/Open Pockets, unmk, 5", EX, A $70.00
Dutch Children Kissing, Japan, 5½", EX..........................$55.00
Frog, Germany, sitting on haunches, dk gr w/off-wht belly &
throat, 4⅜", EX, A..$230.00
Frog w/Mandolin, Goldcastle/Japan, 6", G-, C9 ....$85.00
Goggled Kids, Japan, 2 behind wheel of auto w/goggles, 5",
EX $70.00
Happy, British, w/winking expression, 3½", rare, NM, A..$150.00
Jiminy Cricket, plastic figure holds brush in his hand, 1960s,
MOC, M5 ....$30.00
Little Girl (Dressed Up) & Dog, Japan, 6", EX, A............$80.00
Mickey Mouse, classic image of Mickey w/hands on hips, mk
WD, 4½", EX+, A $580.00
Mickey Mouse, prewar Japan, w/lg smile, movable arms & cloth
tail, red pants & tan shoes, 5¼", 75% pnt $300.00
Mickey Mouse, prewar Japan, w/thinner face, movable arms &
tail, gr pants & dk brn shoes, 5¼", 98% pnt $400.00

Mickey and Minnie, bisque, 4", $425.00 each.

Penguin, Japan, 5½", VG+ $85.00
Practical Pig, Maw of England, Disney, 1933, figural, 4¼", NM,
A $140.00
Soldier At Attention, unmk, 5", EX, A $75.00

Three Little Pigs, prewar Japan, playing flute, drum & violin, 4",
NM, A $195.00
Three Little Pigs, prewar Japan, playing flute, drum & violin, 4",
G, A $130.00

Penguin, painted and glazed bisque, 5½", EX, A,
$130.00; Boy, with open arms, painted and glazed
bisque, 6", EX, A, $75.00; Soldier, standing at attention,
painted and glazed bisque, 6⅝", EX, A, $75.00.

Tootsietoys

The first diecast Tootsietoys were made by the Samuel
Dowst company in 1906 when they reproduced the Model T
Ford in miniature. Dowst merged with Cosmo Manufacturing in
1926 to form the Dowst Manufacturing Company and continued
to turn out replicas of the full-scale vehicles in actual use at the
time. After another merger in 1961, the company became
known as the Stombecker Corporation. Over the years, many
types of wheels and hubs were utilized, varying in both style and
material. The last all-metal car was made in 1969; recent Tootsietoys mix plastic components with the metal and have soft plas-

tic wheels. Early prewar mint-in-box toys are scarce and command high prices on today's market. For more information we recommend the *Collector's Guide to Tootsietoys* and the new second edition which will be coming out in Fall 1995, featuring Tootsietoys from 1910-79 with over 700 color photos, both by David E. Richter.

Advisor: David E. Richter (R1).

Airport, 1930s, with two trimotor Ford airplanes, tin hangar and flag, box doubles as lithographed airport scene, NM (EX box), A, $745.00.

Aerial Hook & Ladder Truck #489, red w/silver ladder, blk tires, 9", unused, MIB..$145.00
Aeroplanes, pot-metal helicopter, mail plane, passenger plane, crusader & 1 TWA, 3¾" average, EX (G box), A...$500.00
Andy Gump Car #5101X, 1932-33, EX............................$300.00
Andy Gump Car #5101X, 1932-33, M............................$457.00
Andy Gump Roadster #348, pnt cast metal w/articulated figure, 2¾", G, A..$130.00

Auto Gyro Plane, #4659, 1930s, green and yellow, M, $120.00.

Auto Transport #207, 1950s, red cab w/yel removable ramp, 3 cars, tin, unused, MIB, A..$150.00
Bluebird Racer #4666, 1932-33, 4", M............................$55.00
Buck Rogers Battle Cruiser #1031, 1937, yel w/red, M (EX+ box), A..$250.00
Buck Rogers Battle Cruiser #1031, 1937, 5", EX............$125.00
Buck Rogers Destroyer #1032, 1937, cream w/bl, 5", NM (EX+ box), A..$250.00
Chevy Monza, 1980s, purple, 2⅛", VG+............................$1.00

Chrysler Thunderbolt, 1942, red, 6", M, $50.00.

Contractor Set w/3 Side Dumper Cars #0191, 1933-41, lime gr truck pulling 3 side dumpers, 13", EX+............$150.00
Crusader Plane #719, NM, M11............................$100.00

Domaco Gasoline and Oil Truck, green and red with white rubber tires, 5½"; Express Truck, orange with white rubber tires, 5½"; Dairy Truck, yellow with white rubber tires, 5½", all 1930s, M, from $100.00 to $175.00 each.

Doodle Bug #716, 1930s, NM, S9............................$100.00
Federal Store Van, Boggs & Buhl, 1920s, bl, 4", rare, NM .$600.00
Fiat Abarth, 1974, metallic bl, 2½", NM............................$1.50
Fire Department, 4 red & silver pnt cast-metal trucks & engines w/wht rubber tires, 3" ea, EX (VG box), A............$400.00
Flash Gordon Star Ship, 1978, MOC............................$25.00
Ford GT Race Car, 1960s, metallic bl, 2⅛", EX, W1..........$2.00
Ford Model A, 1930s, MIB (New Ford on box)............$145.00
Ford w/Travel Trailer #1043, 1937-41, 2-pc, NM............$90.00
Greyhound Bus, pnt worn, 8", VG+, P3............................$20.00
Greyhound Bus #769, 1955-69, 7", M (VG box)............$100.00
Gyro-Plane #4659, 1930s, diecast, cream w/bl rotor & prop, balloon tires, 4", NM..$115.00
HO Sports Set #4110, 1960, 6-pc set, about 2-2½" ea, EX+ (EX box), A..$125.00
Interchangeable Truck Set, 1950-58, 2 1940 International truck cabs, trailer, van & machine hauler, 5-pc, M (EX+ box)..$350.00
Interchangeable Truck Set #4900, 1958, 2 1947 Mack tractor cabs, trailer & machinery, 6-pc, NMIB............$350.00
Jaguar Race Car, 1960s, purple, 2⅜"............................$1.50
Jeep Truck, 1960s, purple, blk plastic tires, 2⅜"............$1.50

Jumbo Torpedo 1937 Greyhound Bus #1045, bl & silver, closed fenders, blk rubber tires, M..$65.00

Jumbo Torpedo 1937 Greyhound Bus #1045, lt bl, open front fenders, wht rubber tires, tin undercarriage, EX, A....$80.00

Lincoln Zephyr #6015, 1936, gr w/wht rubber tires, w/up, 4", scarce, G, A $400.00

MG Sports Car, 1960s, brn, w/tow hook, 2⅛".....................$2.00

Oil Tanker #669, 9", NM (VG+ box), A........................$135.00

Oil Tanker #669, 9", unused, MIB, A $160.00

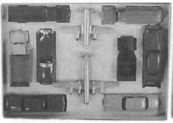

Playtime Set, #7000, complete with two planes and eight vehicles, NM (EX box), A, $600.00.

Porsche, 1960s, red, blk plastic tires, 2⅜" $2.00

Tow Truck, 1950s, gr, 4½", missing boom, W1..................$4.50

Triumph TR3, 1950s, gr, blk plastic tires, 3", M..............$20.00

USN Los Angeles Zeppelin #1030, 1930s, silver w/emb letters, 5", NM (EX box) $200.00

Utility Truck #869, gr w/blk tires, complete, 9", unused, MIB $125.00

Waco Bomber Bi-Wing Plane #718, red & silver or bl & silver, M, ea...$125.00

Waco Dive Bomber #718, M...$140.00

Wrigley's Spearmint Gum Truck, #1010, green with colorful logo on side, white rubber tires, M, $105.00.

Trading Cards

Modern collector cards are really just an extension of a hobby that began well before the turn of the century. Advertising cards put out by the food and tobacco companies of that era sometimes featured cute children, their pets, stage stars, battle scenes, presidential candidates, and so forth. Collectors gathered them up and pasted them in scrapbooks.

In the twentieth century, candy and bubble gum companies came to the forefront. The cards they issue with their products carry the likenesses of sports figures, fictional heroes, TV and movie stars, Disney characters, Barbie dolls and country singers!

Distinguishing a collectible trading card from other cards may be a bit confusing. Remember, trading cards are released in only two ways: 1) in a wax or foil pack, generally in multiples of 12 — 24, 36, or 48; or 2) as a premium with another product. The only exception to this rule are sets issued as limited editions, with each set individually numbered. Cards issued as factory sets are not trading cards and have no collector value unless they cross over into another collecting area, for example, the Tuff Stuff Norma Jean (Marilyn Monroe) series. For more information we recommend *Collector's Guide to Trading Cards* by Robert Reed.

Advisors: Mark and Val Macaluso (M1).

A-Team, Monty Gum, 1983, set of 100 ....$15.00

Addams Family, Topps, 1991, set of 99 w/11 stickers.......$11.00

Alf, Topps, 1987, 1st series, set of 47 w/22 stickers...........$12.00

Alien, Topps, 1979, set of 84...$35.00

Alien Nation, FTCC, 1990, set of 60................................$15.00

American G-Men, 1930s, 6 of 48, VG+, A $80.00

Americana, Starline, 1992, set of 250 ....$30.00

Andy Griffith, Pacific, 1990, 1st series, set of 110 ....$25.00

Andy Griffith, Pacific, 1991, 2nd series, set of 110..........$12.50

Avengers, Cornerstone, 1993, 1st series, set of 99 ....$18.00

Baby, Topps, 1984, set of 66 w/11 stickers........................$8.00

Babysitter's Club, Topps, 1992, set of 55..........................$15.00

Barbie 1986, Action/Panini, 1992, set of 196, $25.00.

Batman (from movie), Topps, 1989, 1st series, set of 132 w/22 stickers $18.00

Batman Returns, Topps, 1992, set of 88 w/10 stickers $12.50

Battlestar Galactica, Wonder Bread, 1978, set of 36 ....$10.00

Beetlejuice, Dart, 1990, set of 100 w/20 stickers $18.00

Bernard & Bianca, Panini, set of 360 ....$35.00

Best of Cracked Magazine, Fleer, 1978, set of 55 ....$18.00

Black Hole, Topps, 1979, set of 88 w/22 stickers $15.00

Bozo, Lime Rock, 1994, set of 50..................................$10.00

Buck Rogers, Topps, 1979, set of 88 w/22 stickers $25.00

Buck Rogers Cartoon Adventure Series #433, John Dille, 1936, 1 of 24, VG+, A.................................$46.00

Buck Rogers Cartoon Adventure Series #437, John Dille, 1936, 1 of 24, VG+, A.................................$43.00

Buck Rogers Cartoon Adventure Series #440, John Dille, 1936, 1 of 24, VG+, A.................................$41.00

California Raisins, Diamond, 1988, set of 25 ....$6.00

CB Convoy Code, Donruss, set of 44 ....$28.00

Charlie's Angels, Topps, 1977, 1st series, set of 66 w/11 stickers..$28.00

Close Encounters, Topps, 1978, set of 66 w/11 stickers $18.00

Close Encounters, Wonder Bread, 1978, set of 24 ....$9.00

Country Classics, Collect-a-Card, 1992, set of 100 ....$20.00

Creature Feature, Topps, 1980, set of 88 w/22 stickers $39.00

Dallas, Donruss, 1981, set of 56 ....$12.00

Dark Crystal, Donruss, 1982, set of 78 ....$10.00

Dark Shadows, Imagine, 1993, set of 62.......................$18.00

Deathmate, Upper Deck, 1993, set of 110 ....$25.00

Deathwatch, Classic, 1993, set of 100 ....$12.00

Desert Storm, Pro Set, 1991, set of 260 ....$20.00

Desert Storm, Topps, 1991, 1st series, set of 88 w/22 stickers..$12.00

Dick Tracy, Johnson Candy, ca 1940, #121 thru #144, last 24 in set of 144, ea illus part of story w/story lines, M, A....$97.00

Dick Tracy, Topps, 1993, set of 88 w/22 stickers $10.00

Dinamation Dinosaurs, Star Pics, 1992, set of 80 ....$16.00

Dinosaurs, Canada, 1993, set of 24 ....$5.00

Dinosaurs, Nu-Card, 1962, set of 80 ....$400.00

Disgusting Disguises, Topps, set of 24 w/27 stickers........$250.00

Disney, Skybox, 1993, 2nd series, set of 200 ....$22.00

Dollman, Full Moon, 1991, set of 6 ....$2.50

Dracula, Topps, 1992, set of 66 ....$30.00

Dragon's Lair, Fleer, 1984, set of 30 w/63 stickers.............$54.00

Dream Machines, Champs, 1992, 2nd series, set of 55 .....$12.50

Dune, Fleer, 1984, set of 132 ....$25.00

Duran Duran, Topps, 1985, set of 33 w/33 stickers $9.50

Elvis, Donruss, 1978, set of 66 ....$25.00

Elvis Collector Series, Donruss, 1978, 36 packs w/1 extra in orig display box, M, H4 ....$130.00

Empire Strikes Back, Topps, 1980, 1st series, set of 132 ...$40.00

Empire Strikes Back, Topps, 1980, 3rd series, set of 88 w/22 stickers..$27.00

ET, Topps, 1982, set of 88 ....$12.00

Excalibur, Comic Image, 1990, set of 45 ....$29.00

Exotic Dreams, All Sports Cars, 1992, set of 100.............$20.00

Fantastic Odd Rods, Donruss, 1973, set of 66 ....$45.00

Fantasy Girls, Imagine, 1994, 2nd series, set of 60 ....$12.00

Ferngully, the Last Rainforest, Dart Flipcard, 1992, set of 100 ....$18.00

Fievel, an American Tail II, Impel, 1991, set of 90 ....$15.00

Firefighters, KFB Enterprises, 1st, 2nd or 4th series, complete, ea..$12.50

Flaming Carrot, Comic Image, 1988, set of 50................$60.00

Flash Gordon, MV Jasinski, 1990, set of 36 ....$30.00

Flintstones, Cardz, 1993, set of 100 ....$28.00

Flying Things, Topps, set of 8......................................$24.00

Football Superfreaks, Donruss, 1974, set of 44 ....$20.00

Forty To Fear Murders, Pizz Sad Otis Link, 1 set of 1,000 printed, numbered & signed, rare, M (in orig sealed box), H4 ....$40.00

Freddie & the Dreamers, Donruss, 1965, set of 66 ....$95.00

G-Men Heroes of the Law, Gum Inc, 1936, 5 from set of 168, EX, A..$62.00

Garbage Pail Kids, Topps, 1985, 1st series, set of 88.......$150.00

Ghost Rider, Comic Image, 1990, set of 45......................$25.00

Ghostbusters II, Topps, 1989, set of 88 w/11 stickers........$10.00

GI Joe, Diamond, 1987, set of 225 ....$20.00

GI Joe, Milton Bradley, 1986, set of 192 w/12 stickers $55.00

Gong Show, Fleer, 1979, set of 66................................$22.00

Goonies, Topps, 1986, set of 86 w/22 stickers...................$15.00

Grease II, OPC, 1978, set of 66 ....$10.00

Gremlins, Topps, 1984, set of 82 w/11 stickers $16.00

Growing Pains, Topps, 1988, set of 66 w/11 stickers $18.00

Happy Days, Topps, 1976, set of 44 w/11 stickers............$25.00

Harlem Globetrotters, Comic Image, 1992, set of 90 ....$15.00

Harley-Davidson, Collect-a-Card, 1992, 1st series, set of 100 ....$35.00

Harry & the Hendersons, Topps, 1987, set of 77 w/22 stickers..$12.00

Heavy Metal, Comic Image, 1991, set of 90 ....$12.00

High Chaparral, Monty Gum, 1970, set of 124.................$75.00

Hildebrandt, Comic Image, 1992, set of 90.....................$18.00

Hocky Freaks, Dart, 1992, set of 100 ....$15.00

Hollywood Walk of Fame, Starline, 1991, set of 250........$20.00

Home Alone II, Topps, 1992, set of 66 w/11 stickers $12.00

Home Improvement, Skybox, 1994, set of 80 w/10 stickers...$22.00

Honeymooners, Comic Image, 1988, set of 51.................$60.00

Hook, Topps, 1991, set of 99 w/11 stickers $12.00

Howard the Duck, Topps, 1986, set of 77 w/22 stickers ...$18.00

Hulk, Drakes, 1978, set of 24......................................$150.00

I Love Lucy, Pacific, 1991, set of 110, pk or silver border.$15.00

Iditarod (Alaskan dog sled race), Motor Art, 1992, set of 110 ....$30.00

In Living Color, Topps, 1992, set of 88 w/11 stickers.......$15.00

James Bond, Monty Gum, 1986, 1st series, set of 100 ....$125.00

James Bond, Monty Gum, 1987, set of 100....................$100.00

Jason Goes to Hell, Eclipse, 1993, set of 110 ....$18.00

Jaws II, Topps, 1978, set of 59 w/11 stickers.....................$9.50

John Kennedy, Rosan, set of 64 ....$60.00

Jungle Book, Topps, 1993, set of 88 w/11 stickers.............$15.00

King Kong, Topps, 1976, set of 55 w/11 stickers $35.00

Kiss I, Donruss, 1978, set of 66 ....$45.00

Kitchen Sink Cards, Kitchen Sink, set of 36, issued in comic stores..$7.50

Kojak Playing Cards, Monty Gum, set of 52 ....$18.00

Kung Fu, Topps, set of 55 ....$100.00

Lady Death, Chaos, 1994, set of 100 ....$8.00

Last Action Hero, Topps, 1993, set of 88 w/11 stickers....$18.00

Leave It to Beaver, Pacific, 1984, set of 60.......................$75.00

Legend of Bigfoot, Leesley, 1989, set of 100....................$12.00

Lion King, Skybox, 1994, set of 90.................................$20.00
Lone Ranger, WTW Reprint, set of 48.........................$45.00
M*A*S*H, Donruss, 1982, set of 66.............................$29.00
Mad Magazine, Lime Rock, 1992, 1st series, set of 50......$10.00
Magnum PI, Donruss, 1983, set of 66...........................$12.00
Marilyn Monroe, European, 1990, set of 8....................$10.00
Marilyn Monroe, Sports Time Cards, 1993, set of 100.....$30.00
Marvel Masterpiece, Skybox, 1993, 1st series, set of 90....$40.00
Marvel Super Heroes, FTCC, 1984, set of 60.................$22.00
Marvel Universe, Impel Market, 1990, set of 162.............$45.00
Masters of the Universe Movie, Panini, 1987, set of 240.$32.00
Max Headroom Test, Topps, 1988, set of 33 stickers w/11 foils,
    rare..$75.00
Michael Jackson, OPC, 1984, set of 33 w/33 stickers.......$10.00
Michael Jackson, Topps, 1984, set of 33 w/33 stickers........$8.50
Mickey Mouse, Americana, set of 360...........................$150.00
Mike Zeck, Comic Image, 1989, set of 45.....................$25.00
Minnie & Me, Impel, 1991, set of 160...........................$22.00
Monkees, British, 1967, complete set of 54 blk & wht cards
    w/puzzle on back, NM, J5......................................$45.00
Monster Laffs, Topps, 1966, set of 66............................$75.00
Moon Mars, Space Ventures, 1991, set of 36....................$65.00

**Mork and Mindy, Paramount Pictures
Corporation, 1978, MIP, $15.00.**

Movie Giant Pinups, Topps, 1981, set of 12.....................$12.50
Munudo, Topps, 1983, set of 66 w/22 stickers..................$12.00
Muppets NFL, Cardz, 1994, set of 80.............................$15.00
National Lampoon, 21st Century, 1993, set of 100..........$20.00
New Kids on the Block, Topps, 1990, set of 88 w/22 stick-
    ers...$12.00
Nightmare, Kilian, 1991, set of 25.................................$12.50
Nintendo, Topps, 1990, set of 55 w/33 stickers................$6.50
Peanuts, Pro Sport, 1992, set of 200.............................$25.00
Petty Girls, 21st Century, 1994, set of 50.......................$12.00

Planet of the Apes TV, Topps, 1975, set of 66.................$55.00
Pro Cheerleaders Basketball, Lime Rock, 1992, set of 41.$12.00
Puppetmaster III, Full Moon, 1991, set of 6....................$2.50
Raiders of the Lost Ark, OPC, 1981, set of 88.................$12.00
Rambo, Panini, 1987, set of 240..................................$40.00
Rat Patrol, Topps, 1966, complete set of 66 color, NM, J5..$65.00
Ren & Stimpy, Topps, 1994, set of 50...........................$15.00
Return of the Jedi, Monty Gum, 1983, set of 100.............$55.00
Return of the Jedi, Topps, 1983, 1st series, set of 132 w/66 stick-
    ers...$25.00
Rhonda Shear, Imagine, 1993, set of 60.........................$15.00
Richard Petty, Traks, 1991, set of 25..............................$5.00
Robin Hood, Topps, 1991, set of 88 w/9 stickers.............$12.50
RoboCop II, Topps, 1990, set of 88 w/11 stickers............$11.00
Rock Stars, AGI, 1982, set of 108 w/12 stickers..............$45.00
Rock Stars, Donruss, 1979, set of 66.............................$16.00
Rocketeer, Topps, 1991, set of 99 w/11 stickers..............$10.00
Rocky II, Topps, 1979, set of 99 w/22 stickers.................$14.00
Roger Rabbit, Topps, 1988, set of 132 w/22 stickers.........$18.00
Royal Canadian Mounted Police, OPC, set of 55.............$50.00
San Diego Zoo, Cardz, 1993, set of 110.........................$30.00
Santa Around the World, TCM, 1994, set of 72...............$10.00
Saturday Night Live, Star Pics, 1992, set of 150..............$16.00
Saturday Serials, Epic, 1988, set of 40..........................$25.00
Scream Queen, Imagine, 1993, 3rd series, set of 60..........$15.00
Seedpeople, Full Moon, 1991, set of 6............................$2.50
She-Ra, Panini, 1987, set of 216..................................$35.00
Simpsons, Topps, 1990, set of 88 w/22 stickers...............$17.00
Six Million Dollar Man, Monty Gum, 1975, set of 72........$75.00
Snow White, Panini, 1987, set of 225............................$40.00
Snow White, Skybox, 1994, 2nd series, set of 90.............$18.00
Space Art, Lime Rock, 1993, set of 55...........................$12.00
Space Scenes, Bowman, 1951, 7 of 108-card series: #s 1-2 & 4-8,
    EX, A...$150.00
Space Scenes, Bowman, 1951, 7 of 108-card series: #s 11-14 &
    17-19, EX, A..$150.00
Space: 1999, Donruss, 1976, unopened box & 24 wax packs of
    cards w/box featuring show's stars, M (EX+ box).......$42.00
Space: 1999, Panini, 1st series, set of 400......................$65.00
Spiderman, Comic Image, 1992, 1st series, set of 90.........$20.00
Spiderman, French, 1975, set of 300.............................$50.00
Spoofy Tunes, Butthedz, 1994, set of 55........................$15.00
Spy Vs Spy, Lime Rock, 1993, set of 55...........................$7.50
Star Trek, Impel, 1991, 2nd series, set of 160..................$20.00
Star Trek, Morris National, 1975, set of 30 puzzle cards...$25.00
Star Trek IV, FTCC, 1987, set of 60..............................$22.00
Star Trek Next Generation, Panini, 1989, set of 240.........$55.00
Star Trek Next Generation Behind the Scenes, Skybox, 1993,
    set of 40...$20.00
Star Trek The Motion Picture, Topps, 1979, set of 88.......$32.00
Star Wars, Panini, 1978, set of 256..............................$150.00
Star Wars, Topps, 1977, 1st series, set of 66...................$49.00
Star Wars, Topps, 1977, 3rd series, set of 66...................$18.00
Star Wars, Wonder Bread, 1978, set of 16......................$18.00
Street Fighter II, Topps, 1994, set of 88 w/11 stickers.......$14.00
Stupid Smiles, OPC, 1990, unopened box......................$50.00
Superman, Drakes, 1979, set of 24...............................$15.00
Superman I, English, 1979, 1st series, set of 66................$30.00

Superman the Movie, Topps, 1978, 1st series, set of 77....$18.00

Swap 'Em Cards, Comic Stars Inc, 1949, complete set of 10 featuring Pug, Superman, Robin, Dinny, etc, M (EX box), A $125.00

Tales From the Crypt, Cardz, 1993, set of 110 ....$29.00

Teenage Mutant Ninja Turtles, Diamond, 1989, set of 180..$17.50

Teenage Mutant Ninja Turtles, OPC, 1990, set of 88 ....$8.50

Terminator 2, Impel, 1991, set of 192 ....$15.00

Terminator 2, Topps, 1991, set of 44.............................$6.00

Terrorist Attacks, Piedmont Candy, 1987, set of 35.........$16.00

Three's Company, Topps, 1978, set of 16 w/44 stickers....$22.00

Three Stooges, FTCC, 1985, set of 60 ....$75.00

Thunderbirds, Pro Set, 1992, set of 100 ....$35.00

Tiny Toons, Topps, 1991, set of 77 w/11 stickers $20.00

Tom & Jerry, Cardz, 1993, set of 60 ....$15.00

Toxic High, Topps, 1992, set of 88...............................$8.00

Trading Card Treats, Impel, 1991, 6 sets of 6 ea $9.00

Traks '91, Traks, 1991, set of 200 ....$30.00

Transformers, Milton Bradley, 1985, set of 192 w/24 stickers...$60.00

Trivia Battle, Topps, 1984, set of 132 w/11 stickers..........$18.00

Trolls, Topps, 1992, set of 66 w/11 stickers.....................$10.00

Trolls (Norfin), Collect-a-Card, 1992, set of 50 ....$9.00

Tron, Donruss, 1982, set of 66 w/8 stickers $16.00

TSR '92, TSR, 1992, 1st or 2nd series, ea $25.00

TV Smelly Awards, Fleer, 1970s, set of 64 ....$18.00

Twin Peaks, 1992, factory set of 76 ....$20.00

Universal Monsters, Topps, 1994, set of 100 ....$30.00

Untraverse, Skybox, 1993, set of 100 ....$22.00

Valiant, Upper Deck, 1993, set of 120 ....$15.00

Vietnam War, Dart Cards, 1988, set of 66 ....$33.00

Vote, Donruss, 1972, set of 44 ....$18.00

Wacko-Saurs, Diamond, 1987, set of 48 ....$10.00

Wacky Packages, Topps, 1979, 1st series, set of 66 reprints ..$30.00

Web of Spiderman, Comic Image, 1991, set of 75 w/album $85.00

Welcome Back Kotter, Topps, 1976, MIP, $20.00.

Where's Waldo, Mattel, 1991, set of 128 ....$15.00

Wildlife America, Bon Air, 1991, factory set of 50.............$4.50

Wildlife in Danger, Dart/Panini, 1992, set of 100.............$20.00

Wings of Fire, Dart/Action, 1992, set of 100 ....$16.00

Winston Cup, Pro Set, 1991, set of 200 ....$39.00

Wizard of Oz, Pacific, 1990, set of 110 ....$20.00

Wolverine-Marvel Cards III, Comic Image, 1988, set of 50 ....$60.00

Wrestlemania III, Topps, 1987, set of 75 w/22 stickers.....$15.00

Wrestling, Topps, 1985, 1st series, set of 66 w/11 stickers...$20.00

X-Men, Comic Image, 1989, 1st series, set of 90.............$75.00

Yo Raps, Pro Set, 1991, set of 100 ....$15.00

Youngblood, Comic Image, 1992, set of 90 ....$12.00

Zero Heros, Donruss, set of 66 ....$15.00

21 Jump Street, Topps, 1988, set of 44 ....$8.50

BOXES

Addams Family, Topps, 1991.....................................$4.00

Avengers, Cornerstone, 1993 ....$5.00

Barbie, Dart/Pani, 1992..$4.00

Batman Photo Series, Topps, 1960s, EX, J5 ....$75.00

Beauty & the Beast, Upper Deck, 1993 ....$4.00

Beverly Hillbillies, Eclipse, 1993 ....$5.00

California Raisins, Diamond, 1988 ....$4.00

Coneheads, Topps, 1993...$4.00

Dark Shadows Giant Pinups Cards, 1960s, purple & gr, VG, J5 ....$45.00

Deep Space 9, Skybox, 1994......................................$4.00

Elvis, Donruss, 1978..$8.00

Flying Nun, Donruss, 1968, EX, J5 ....$45.00

Garrison's Gorilla's, Leaf, 1967, EX, J5 ....$45.00

Gomer Pyle USMC, Fleer, 1965, EX, J5 ....$95.00

Gruesome Greeting, Topps, 1993 ....$4.00

Hook, Topps, 1991...$5.00

Indiana Jones & the Temple of Doom, Topps, 1984...........$6.00

Laugh-In, Topps, 1968, graphics of the cast, VG, J5 ....$65.00

M*A*S*H, Donruss, 1982...$4.00

Magnum PI, Donruss, 1983.......................................$5.00

McHale's Navy, Fleer, 1965, EX, J5 ....$65.00

Munsters, Leaf, 1964, cartoon illus of cast, VG, J5 ....$65.00

Pagemaster, Skybox, 1994..$4.00

Return of Superman, Skybox, 1993 ....$5.00

Robot Wars, Fleer, 1985 ....$4.00

Saturday Night Fever, Donruss, 1978 ....$6.00

Star Trek, Morris National, 1975 ....$25.00

Superman II, Topps, 1981...$6.00

Three Stooges, 1960s, EX, J5.....................................$45.00

Tiny Toons, Cardz, 1994..$4.00

Tune in for Terror, Playhouse, 1993 ....$6.00

Ultraverse Master, Skybox, 1994.................................$5.00

Vietnam War, Dart Cards, 1988...................................$3.00

Voyage to the Bottom of the Sea, Donruss, 1964, blk & wht photos of the Seaview heading towards an octopus, EX, J5 ....$95.00

Wildlife in Danger, Dart/Panini, 1992 ....$4.00

Yo Raps, Pro Set, 1991...$3.00

You Slay Me, Imagine, 1992 ....$5.00

WRAPPERS

Bad Channels, Full Moon, 1991 ....$2.50
Batman Returns Stadium Club, Topps, 1992 ....$.75
Bay City Rollers, Topps, 1977 ....$7.50
Beverly Hillbillies, Topps, 1963, 5¢, yel, EX, J5.................$85.00
Bill & Ted's Adventure, Pro Set, 1991 ....$.50
Buck Rogers, Scanlens, 1979 ....$4.00
Close Encounters, Topps, 1978..$.75
Dallas Cowboy Cheerleaders, Topps, 1981.......................$.50
Disney Tattoos, Denmark $1.00
Dracula, Topps, 1992 ....$1.00
Evel Knievel, Topps, 1974 ....$6.00
Flying Nun, Donruss, 1968 ....$8.00
Harry & the Hendersons, Topps, 1987 ....$.50
In Living Color, Topps, 1992 ....$.50
Kiss I, Donruss, 1978..$2.00
Little Shop of Horror, Topps, 1987.....................................$.50
Lost in Space, Topps, 1966...$90.00
Monster in My Pocket, Source Group, 1991 ....$.50
Moonraker, OPC, 1979...$1.00
Pee Wee's Playhouse, Topps, 1989 ....$.50
Raiders of the Lost Ark, Topps, 1981 ....$.75
Rocky IV, Topps, 1985..$.50
Saturday Night Live, Star Pics, 1992 ....$.50
Soupy Sales, Topps, 1960s, red w/Soupy in blk & wht, EX,
    J5 ....$15.00
Tales From the Crypt, Cardz, 1993 ....$.75
Teenage Mutant Ninja Turtles Secret of the Ooze, Topps,
    1991..$.50
Three Stooges, FTCC, 1989 ....$.75
Transformers, Milton Bradley, 1985 ....$1.00
Tron, Donruss, 1982...$.75
Wacko-Saurs, Diamond, 1987 ....$.50
Wacky Packages, Topps, 1970s, red or bl, EX, J5, ea $15.00
Welcome Back Kotter, Topps, 1976 ....$1.50
Wizard of Oz, Pacific, 1990..$1.00

Trains

Some of the earliest trains (from ca 1860) were made of tin or cast iron, smaller versions of the full-scale steam-powered trains that transversed America from the East to the West. Most were made to simply be pushed or pulled along, though some had clockwork motors. Electric trains were produced as early as the late 19th century. Three of the largest manufacturers were Lionel, Ives, and American Flyer.

Lionel trains have been made since 1900. Until 1915 they produced only standard gauge models (measuring 2½" between the rails). The smaller O gauge (1¼") they introduced at that time proved to be highly successful, and the company grew until by 1955 it had become the largest producer of toys in the world. Until discontinued in 1940, standard gauge trains were produced on a limited scale, but O and 027 gauge models dominated the

market. Production dwindled and nearly stopped in the mid-1960s, but the company was purchased by General Mills in 1969, and they continue to produce a very limited number of trains today.

The Ives company had been a major producer of toys since 1896. They were the first to initiate manufacture of the O gauge train and at first used only clockwork motors to propel them. Their first electric trains (in both O and #1 gauge) were made in 1910, but because electricity was not yet a common commodity in many areas, clockwork production continued for several years. By 1920, #1 gauge was phased out in favor of standard gauge. The company continued to prosper until the late 1920s when it floundered and was bought jointly by American Flyer and Lionel. American Flyer soon turned their interest over to Lionel, who continued to make Ives trains until 1933.

The American Flyer company had produced trains for several years, but it wasn't until it was bought by AC Gilbert in 1937 that it became successful enough to be considered a competitor of Lionel. They're best noted for their conversion from the standard (wide gauge) 3-rail system to the 2-rail S gauge (⅞") and the high-quality locomotives, passenger and freight cars they produced in the 1950s. Interest in toy trains waned during the space-age decade of the 1960s. As a result, sales declined, and in 1966 the company was purchased by Lionel. Today both American Flyer and Lionel trains are being made from the original dies by Lionel Trains Inc., privately owned.

Because of limited space, the only time we will use the number sign will be to indicate a set number. Numbers of individual pieces will not be preceded by the sign. For more information we recommend *Collecting Toy Trains, An Identification and Value Guide*, by Richard O'Brien.

Advisor: Richard Trautwein (T3).

See also Buddy L for that company's Outdoor Railroad.

Key:
b/c — boxcar	obv/c — observation car
bg/c — baggage car	st/c — stock car
fl/c — flat bed car	tk/c — tank car
loco — locomotive	/c — car

CARS

American Flyer, O ga, 506 B&O b/c, diecast, VG (rough display
    box), A..$55.00
American Flyer, S ga, 24323 Bakers Chocolate tk/c, wht ends,
    Knuckle coupler, NM-, A $1,200.00
American Flyer, S ga, 636 reel/c, depressed center, pressed wood
    fr, brake wheels intact, EX- $325.00
American Flyer, S ga, 767 Branford diner, complete, smokestack
    loose, some pnt chips, EX (orig box), A $100.00
American Flyer, wide ga, 4006 hopper, red, fixed trucks, EX-,
    A..$500.00
American Flyer, wide ga, 4010 tk/c, yel & bl, rstr, A $375.00
American Flyer, wide ga, 4017 gondolas (2), gr, fixed trucks, EX,
    A..$130.00
American Flyer, wide ga, 4018 b/c, buff & gr, gray flex trucks,
    EX-, A $110.00

American Flyer, wide ga, 4020 st/c, 2-tone bl, trucks & journals pnt blk, EX-, A $160.00

Bing, coal/c, EX, A $150.00

Bing, O ga, Reichsbahn covered goodswagon, red & blk litho, EX, A $10.00

Bing, petroleum tanker, dk gray mk w/Bavaria diamond trademark, EX, A $161.00

Bing, 1 ga, Wasserwagon, HP, missing figure & 1 buffer, faucet hdl grips broken, VG, A $250.00

Elektoy, 1 ga, 906 dump/c, red tipple, blk fr, rust on 1 corner, EX, A $270.00

Ives, O ga, 124 merchandise transport/c, red roof, MIB, A $100.00

Ives, O ga, 125 MK & T b/c, red roof, some oxidation on fr, chips on roof, EX (orig box) $475.00

Ives, O ga, 125 Union Lines reefer, red roof, NMIB, A ..$325.00

Ives, O ga, 125-85 Chicago Great Western b/c, red roof, EX $750.00

Ives, O ga, 128 gondolas (3), gray, red litho, journal trucks, EX, A $85.00

Ives, O ga, 131 bg/c, 129 Saratoga Pullman, pnt 70%, EX, A $950.00

Ives, O ga, 64 b/c, yel litho, gray roof, oxidated spot on roof, EX+, A $210.00

Ives, O ga, 7546 caboose, EX, A $184.00

Ives, O ga, 7648 coal/c, dk gr, mk Pennsylvania Coal & Coke Co, some pnt flaking, G, A $58.00

Lionel, O ga, Erie-Lack caboose, blk & wht, MIB, G1 .....$65.00

Lionel, O ga, 17605 Reading caboose, NMIB, G1 ....$60.00

Lionel, O ga, 1866 general mail/c, M, M4 ....$95.00

Lionel, O ga, 2257 SP-type freight/c, M, M4 ....$50.00

Lionel, O ga, 2420 searchlight wrecker caboose, MIB, M4 ....$125.00

Lionel, O ga, 2530 bg/cs (2), 1 lg-door version, EX (orig boxes), A $550.00

Lionel, O ga, 2534 Pullman/c, Silver Bluff, NMIB, M4..$250.00

Lionel, O ga, 2814R reefer, wht, tuscan roof, blk rubber stamping & trim, 1941 high box coupler, NMIB, A......$2,300.00

Lionel, O ga, 2816 hopper, blk, heat stamping, blk trim, EX+, A $450.00

Lionel, O ga, 3276 operating giraffe/c, M, M4 ....$225.00

Lionel, O ga, 3359 operating dump/c, MIB, M4 ....$225.00

Lionel, O ga, 3360 operating burro/c, MIB, M4 ....$600.00

Lionel, O ga, 3361 operating fl/c, M, M4 ....$150.00

Lionel, O ga, 3361 operating lumber/c, MIB, M4 ....$135.00

Lionel, O ga, 3362 operating helium/c, M, M4 ....$395.00

Lionel, O ga, 3364 NYC operating b/c, M, M4 ....$175.00

Lionel, O ga, 3364 operating log dump/c, MIB, M4 ....$85.00

Lionel, O ga, 3444 cop & hobo/c, MIB, M4 ....$300.00

Lionel, O ga, 3459 coal dump/c, aluminum, bl letters, EX+ (orig box), A...$240.00

Lionel, O ga, 3461 operating log/c, blk, NMIB, M4 ....$225.00

Lionel, O ga, 3461 operating log/c, gr, NMIB, M4 ....$250.00

Lionel, O ga, 3462 operating milk/c, NMIB, M4............$175.00

Lionel, O ga, 3464 San Francisco operating b/c, MIB, M4 .$145.00

Lionel, O ga, 3469 operating b/c, NMIB, M4 ....$175.00

Lionel, O ga, 3472 operating milk/c, NMIB, M4............$175.00

Lionel, O ga, 3530 generator/c, MIB, M4 ....$500.00

Lionel, O ga, 3545 TV monitoring/c, rod for camera missing, EX (orig box taped), A $120.00

Lionel, O ga, 3559 operating dump/c, M, M4 ....$195.00

Lionel, O ga, 3562-50 operating barrel/c, M, M4 ....$225.00

Lionel, O ga, 3619 copter launcher, yel, EX, G1 ....$175.00

Lionel, O ga, 3650 extension searchlight/c, MIB, M4 ....$250.00

Lionel, O ga, 3656 operating cattle/c/corral, MIB, M4...$350.00

Lionel, O ga, 3662 operating milk/c, NMIB, M4............$350.00

Lionel, O ga, 3665 minuteman launcher, EX, G1 ....$125.00

Lionel, O ga, 3665 minuteman launcher, NMIB, M4.$150.00

Lionel, O ga, 400 Budd/c, NMIB, A $375.00

Lionel, O ga, 6356 NYC st/c, EX (orig box), G1 ....$65.00

Lionel, O ga, 6362 truck/c, MIB, M4 ....$175.00

Lionel, O ga, 6415 3-dome tanker, MIB, M4 ....$195.00

Lionel, O ga, 6427 Virginian caboose, EX+, A $330.00

Lionel, O ga, 6427-500, girl's caboose, NMIB $350.00

Lionel, O ga, 6430 piggyback/c, MIB, M4 ....$300.00

Lionel, O ga, 6434 poultry dispatch/c, MIB, M4 ....$325.00

Lionel, O ga, 6436-25 hopper/c, MIB, M4 ....$225.00

Lionel, O ga, 6445 Fort Knox Gold/c, MIB, M4 ....$350.00

Lionel, O ga, 6454 Erie b/c, M, M4 ....$125.00

Lionel, O ga, 6460 wrecker crane, M, M4 ....$200.00

Lionel, O ga, 6462-500, girl's canister/c, NMIB $200.00

Lionel, O ga, 6464-1 Western Pacific b/c, M, M4 ....$325.00

Lionel, O ga, 6464-1971 Mickey Mouse TCA, 1971, M, M4 ....$450.00

Lionel, O ga, 6464-200 PA b/c, metal trucks, EX+ (handwritten Hagerstown box) $150.00

Lionel, O ga, 6464-225 Southern Pacific b/c, M, M4 .....$400.00

Lionel, O ga, 6464-325 Baltimore & Ohio sentinel b/c, NMIB $650.00

Lionel, O ga, 6464-375 Central of Georgia, 1966, M, M4...$375.00

Lionel, O ga, 6464-400 Baltimore & Ohio, 1957, M, M4 .$195.00

Lionel, O ga, 6464-400 Baltimore & Ohio b/c, EX+ (orig box) $150.00

Lionel, O ga, 6464-425 New Haven b/c, 1969, M, M4...$150.00

Lionel, O ga, 6464-450 Great Northern b/c, M, M4 ......$175.00

Lionel, O ga, 6464-475 Boston & Maine b/c, M, M4.....$175.00

Lionel, O ga, 6464-515 girl's MKT b/c, rare, NM, A......$550.00

Lionel, O ga, 6464-650 Rio Grande b/c, metal trucks, VG, A $160.00

Lionel, O ga, 6464-725 New Haven b/c, 1969, M, M4.$350.00

Lionel, O ga, 6464-75 Rock Island b/c, M, M4..............$135.00

Lionel, O ga, 6464-900 New York Central b/c, M, M4 ..$400.00

Lionel, O ga, 6465 2-dome tanker, M, M4 ....$75.00

Lionel, O ga, 6470 explosives/c, EX, G1 ....$25.00

Lionel, O ga, 6500 Bonanza transport/c, red over wht airplane, wht prop, NMIB, A $575.00

Lionel, O ga, 6517-175 Erie bay-window caboose, EX+ .$400.00

Lionel, O ga, 6517-175 Erie bay-window caboose, NMIB.$500.00

Lionel, O ga, 6519 Allis Chalmers freight/c, M, M4 ......$225.00

Lionel, O ga, 6520 searchlight/c, NMIB, M4 ....$175.00

Lionel, O ga, 6556 MKT 2-level st/c, EX+ (orig box worn), A $275.00

Lionel, O ga, 6651 USMC cannon fl/c, 2 wooden missiles, working baffle, EX+, A $120.00

Lionel, O ga, 6656 cattle/c, M, M4 ....$75.00

Lionel, O ga, 6672 San Francisco reefer, bl or blk, M, M4, ea $225.00

Lionel, O ga, 6805 atomic disposal/c, M, M4..................$395.00

Lionel, O ga, 6807 duck fl/c, NMIB, A..........................$230.00

Lionel, O ga, 9276 Peabody hopper/c, MIB, G1 ....$40.00

Lionel, O ga, 9308 aquarium/c, MIB, G1......................$275.00

Lionel, std ga, 1766 Pullmans (2), red & maroon, VG, A .$350.00

Lionel, std ga, 184 bungalows (2), red litho roof, 1 w/lt fading, dirty, EX+, A $160.00

Lionel, std ga, 213 st/c, Mojave & maroon, VG, A $175.00

Lionel, std ga, 213 st/c, terra cotta & pea gr, VG+, A....$140.00

Lionel, std ga, 214 b/c, yel & orange, EX (orig box), A..$250.00

Lionel, std ga, 214R reefer, wht, peacock roof, EX+ (orig box), from $650 to $750.00

Lionel, 215 tanker, 1926-40, standard gauge, green tank, brass trim, 12½", NMIB, A, $430.00; Lionel, 217 Caboose, 1926-40, standard gauge, red with peacock roof, 17½", NMIB, A, $315.00.

Lionel, std ga, 216 hoppers (3), brass trim, VG, A $350.00

Lionel, std ga, 219 derrick, early colors, EX, A $210.00

Lionel, std ga, 219 derrick, early colors, VG (orig box)..$160.00

Lionel, 219 crane car, 1926-40, standard gauge, peacock cab, dark green roof, red boom, 22½", NMIB, A, $690.00; Lionel, 214 boxcar, 1926-40, standard gauge, terra cotta body, dark green roof, 12½", broken door glide otherwise EX (original box), A, $285.00.

Lionel, std ga, 220 searchlight/c, early colors, EX (orig box), A...$225.00

Lionel, std ga, 220 searchlight/c, terra cotta & brass, EX+, A...$270.00

Lionel, std ga, 419 combine, Mojave, maroon & wood-grain trim, EX, A $170.00

Lionel, std ga, 513 st/c, cream & maroon, EX, A............$750.00

Lionel, std ga, 514 b/c, yel & orange, EX+, A.................$140.00

Lionel, std ga, 515 tk/c, ivory, EX, A $180.00

Lionel, std ga, 520 searchlight/c, gr & nickel, sm chips, EX, A...$210.00

Lionel, 027 ga, 069 track maintenance/c, hairline crack on handrail, EX, A..$200.00

Marklin, caboose, tin, pnt red, PRR on sides, door hdls rpl, 7¼", VG, A..$325.00

Marklin, logging/c, fl/c w/set of logs, EX, A...................$138.00

Marklin, O ga, 1687 Mineralwassur wagon, litho, EX+, A.$150.00

Marklin, O ga, 1688N Gambrinus beer wagon, litho, EX, A $175.00

Marx, Pullman obv/c, tin, 6", NM, M5 ....$35.00

LOCOMOTIVES AND TENDERS

American Flyer, S ga, 21205 B&M Alco F9, sm chip in truck sideplate, EX+, A..$200.00

American Flyer, S ga, 21831 T&P GP7, diecast fr, EX+, A..$525.00

American Flyer, S ga, 234 C&O GP7, diecast fr w/bell, EX, A $300.00

American Flyer, S ga, 282 C&NW, 1952, complete, NM.$120.00

American Flyer, S ga, 322 Hudson & smoking tender, VG (orig box), A $140.00

American Flyer, S ga, 336 Northern loco & tender, 1 broken rear step, EX-, A $300.00

American Flyer, S ga, 370 GP7, EX-, A............................$150.00

American Flyer, S ga, 372 UP GP7, diecast fr, EX- $170.00

American Flyer, S ga, 372 UP GP7, VG, A.....................$120.00

American Flyer, S ga, 474 & 475 Rocket PA Alco AA, chrome & gr, yel lettering, broken horns, orig loco wraps, EX+, A...$725.00

American Flyer, S ga, 494 & 495 NH PA Alco AA diesels, EX+ $900.00

American Flyer, S ga, 499 NH EP5, hairline crack in 1 side, EX-, A $210.00

American Flyer, std ga, 4692 loco, 4671 tender w/40% peacock stripe & gray fixed trucks, EX- $675.00

American Flyer, std ga, 4692 loco, 4693 tender w/gray fixed trucks, rstr $550.00

American Flyer, std ga, 4692X loco, 4693 tender, rstr, A $325.00

AMT, B&O F7 diesel, bl & gray, yel letters (incomplete), VG (orig box), A $325.00

Beggs, live steam, blk pnt & nickel w/gold & red trim, VG+, A $425.00

Bing, O ga, trolley & trailer, clockwork, brn & yel litho, orange trim & wheels, circle of track, EX+ (orig box), A ...$650.00

Hornby, O ga, Princess Elizabeth, no tender, electric, pnt tin, pony & guide wheels pnt blk, EX-, A $625.00

Ives, 11 loco, clockwork, blk plates, wht letters, gold & red trim; 11 tender, gold rubber stamped; VG, A $350.00

Ives, 17 loco, clockwork, blk, red & gold trim, blk plate, gold trim, EX; 17 tender, rubber stamped, G; A..............$325.00

Ives, 20 loco, clockwork, blk plates, wht letters; LVE tender, 1915 motor, rpl coupler on tender; EX, A $350.00

Ives, 20 loco, 1914 motor, clockwork, reverse; 25 tender, both w/rubber stamping, EX+, A....................................$450.00

Ives, 3200 loco, blk, no # version, red trim, EX-, A........$140.00

Ives, 3200 loco, blk, red, cast-in #, roof pnt chipped, EX-, A $250.00

Ives, 3200 loco, olive, red & gold, solid wheels, embossed #s, some roof pnt flaking, EX, A......................................$460.00

Ives, 3238 loco, blk, red trim, AC/DC version, EX, A ...$400.00

Lionel, O ga, 003-5342 Scale Hudson, steam, w/tender, NM, M4......$1,475.00

Lionel, O ga, 68 Executive/c, M, M4 ......$500.00

Lionel, O ga, 203 loco, 1941-style high box coupler, NMIB, A......$525.00

Lionel, O ga, 226 B&M Alco AB, EX (orig box), A......$160.00

Lionel, O ga, 226E loco, 226W tender, 1938 couplers, VG, A......$350.00

Lionel, O ga, 228 Semiscale switcher & 2228B tender, 1941-style couplers, EX+, A......$1,300.00

Lionel, O ga, 238E PRR Torpedo, steam, w/tender, VG, M4 ......$350.00

Lionel, O ga, 253 loco, dk gr & brass, VG, A $160.00

Lionel, O ga, 254E loco, pea gr, orange hatches & stripes, slight fatiguing to lights, EX+, A......$250.00

Lionel, O ga, 255 locomotive, 263W tender, gun metal, bulkhead fatigued, VG+, A $700.00

Lionel, O ga, 624 C&O switcher, no decal cracks, EX+ (orig box), A......$750.00

Lionel, O ga, 671 PRR turbine, steam, w/tender, NMIB, M4......$650.00

Lionel, O ga, 671 RR turbine, 2046-50 PA tender, lt touch-up on loco, EX+, A......$300.00

Lionel, O ga, 675 PRR Prairie 2-6-4, steam, w/tender, NMIB, M4......$375.00

Lionel, O ga, 726 Berkshire (orig box), 242W tender, VG, A......$550.00

Lionel, O ga, 726 loco (orig box), 2426W tender, 1946 version w/smoke bulb (missing), VG+, A $250.00

Lionel, O ga, 746 N&W loco & tender, short stripe, EX, A......$550.00

Lionel, O ga, 773LTS Hudson, steam, w/tender, 1950, NMIB, M4 ......$4,500.00

Lionel, O ga, 773LTS Hudson, steam, w/tender, 1966, spoked wheels, NMIB, M4......$2,300.00

Lionel, O ga, 2321 Lackawanna FM, gray top, screw cracks, VG, A......$300.00

Lionel, O ga, 2330 PA GGI, dk gr, 5 stripe (90%), EX (orig box), A......$625.00

Lionel, O ga, 2331 Virginian FM, NRFB......$1,400.00

Lionel, O ga, 2332 GG-1 PRR Electric, NMIB, M4 ...$2,400.00

Lionel, O ga, 2340 GG1, 5 stripes (50%), tuscan, 1 insulator gone, orig instructions, VG, A $400.00

Lionel, O ga, 2341 Jersey Central, EX, M4......$3,500.00

Lionel, O ga, 2341 Jersey Central, VG, A $1,500.00

Lionel, 2350 New Haven EP-5, minor battery damage otherwise NMIB (not shown), $1,200.00.

Lionel, O ga, 2343 San Francisco AA, NMIB, M4 .....$1,750.00

Lionel, O ga, 2344 NYC AA, NMIB, M4 ......$1,750.00

Lionel, O ga, 2350 NH EP5, 2 chips on 1 decal, orig box, VG, A......$270.00

Lionel, O ga, 2354 NYC F-3 AA, NMIB, M4......$1,650.00

Lionel, 2355 Western Pacific F-3AA, NM, A, $800.00.

Lionel, O ga, 2356 Southern F-3 ABA, NMIB, M4....$3,800.00

Lionel, O ga, 2358 Great Northern EP5, nose decal chipped, G, A......$300.00

Lionel, O ga, 2378 Milwaukee Road F3 AA, repro tops, fr rstr, battery damage, A......$65.00

Lionel, std ga, 10E loco, peacock, rewheeled, VG, A $120.00

Lionel, std ga, 42 loco, single motor, thick rims, gray, minor dings, VG, A......$400.00

Lionel, std ga, 318 loco, gray, wheels fatigued, 1 coupler unattached, VG, A......$200.00

Lionel, std ga, 380 loco, maroon, VG+, A......$450.00

Lionel, std ga, 381E loco, wheels blown, rstr, pnt flaking on roofs, missing some trim, oxidation under rstr, A....$525.00

Lionel, std ga, 385E loco, w/384T tender, gun metal, VG (orig boxes), A $400.00

Lionel, std ga, 390E loco, w/390T tender, loco rewheeled & rstr, tender restriped, VG, A......$275.00

Lionel, std ga, 392E loco, w/390T tender, blk, brass & copper trim, orange stripe on tender, EX, A $475.00

Lionel, std ga, 402 loco, Mojave, rewheeled, VG, A $425.00

Lionel, std ga, 402E loco, Mojave, rstr, A......$350.00

Lionel, std ga, 408E loco, apple gr, repro lights, no whistles, lt fatiguing to wheels, G, A......$525.00

Lionel, 027 ga, 50 gang/c, center horn, M, M4......$275.00

Lionel, 027 ga, 50 gang/c, side horn, M, M4......$225.00

Lionel, 027 ga, 60 trolley, M, M4......$500.00

Lionel, 027 ga, 205 MOPAC Alco AA, has cowl supports, EX-, A $85.00

Lionel, 027 ga, 213 M&StL Alco AA w/6059 M&StL caboose in orig box, pnt version, EX+, A $230.00

Lionel, 027 ga, 221 SF Alco, khaki, made for JC Penney, VG, A......$275.00

Lionel, 027 ga, 221E NYC Steamline, gray, w/tender, M, M4 ......$1,680.00

Lionel, 027 ga, 1615 0-4-0 switcher, NMIB, M4......$1,250.00

Lionel, 027 ga, 1656 loco, w/6403B tender, VG (orig boxes), A $325.00

Lionel, 027 ga, 2023 Alco AA loco, silver & grey, NMIB, M4 ......$1,450.00

Lionel, 027 ga, 2023 Alco loco, yel w/gray trucks, NMIB, M4......$1,850.00

Lionel, 736 Berkshire, 1952, smokes and whistles, EX, $350.00.

Lionel, 027 ga, 2025 PRR K-4 2-6-4, steam, w/tender, NMIB, M4......$475.00

Lionel, 027 ga, 2025RR PRR K-4 2-6-4, steam, w/tender, NMIB, M4......$675.00

Lionel, 027 ga, 2037-500 girl's loco, w/1130T-500 tender, 1043-500 transformer, NMIB, A......$2,800.00

Lionel, 027 ga, 2065 loco, 6026W tender, minor bend on 1 loco step, bottle of smoke pellets, EX+ (orig boxes), A...$275.00

Lionel, 027 ga, 2240 Wabash F3 AB, minor battery damage, EX, A......$1,350.00

Lionel, 027 ga, 2242 NH F3 AB, B unit has sm chip in corner of cab, EX (orig box), A......$950.00

Lionel, 027 ga, 2245 Texas Special F3 AB, NMIB, M4 .$2,900.00

Lionel, 027 ga, 2245 Texas Special F3 AB, porthole version, VG (orig box), A......$375.00

Lionel, 027 ga, 2322 VGN FM Diesel, NMIB, M4 .....$1,375.00

Lionel, 027 ga, 2338 Milwaukee GP9, orange stripe, NRFB......$1,100.00

Lionel, 027 ga, 2338 Milwaukee Road GP, orange stripe, VG-, M4......$975.00

Lionel, 027 ga, 2348 Missouri & St Louis GP-9, NMIB, M4 ......$850.00

Lionel, 027 ga, 6220 San Francisco NW-2 Switcher, NMIB, M4......$875.00

Lionel, 027 ga, 726LTS Berkshire, steam, w/2426W tender, NMIB, M4......$1,900.00

LTI, 18006 Reading T1, 4-8-4, 042 ga, NMIB, A $525.00

LTI, 8406 NYC Hudson & tender, NMIB, A......$700.00

Marklin, HO ga, DL800, red-brn, silver trim, VG+ (orig box), A......$1,500.00

Marklin, O ga, St E V 20 snowplow, HP, iron wheels, missing dummy headlight & figures, EX, A $950.00

Marx, UP F9 Sear's Special, missing horns & engine plate mounting plugs, steps intact, EX-, A......$45.00

Marx, 4000 Penn Central F9 AA, steps intact, EX+, A.$200.00

Marx, 99 RI F3 diesels AA, scissor coupler broken on A dummy, EX+, A......$85.00

Right-Of-Way Industries, SF Alco PA ABA, 3-rail, NMIB, A......$300.00

Weaver, Highrail RS-3 diesels (2), 5508 SF, NMIB, A..$200.00

Weaver, PA M1a Mountain, 3-rail, 4-8-2, NMIB, A.....$450.00

Weaver, Penn RR GG1, 3-rail, tuscan, 5 stripes, NMIB, A..$600.00

Weaver, UP FEF 4-8-4 Northern, 3-rail, NMIB, A........$425.00

Williams, NYC Niagara, 5602 loco, 4-8-4, NMIB, A.....$400.00

Williams, PA Trainmaster, gr, NM (torn box), A..........$150.00

Williams, PA Trainmaster, tuscan, NMIB, A......$150.00

Williams, UNDEC, lettered UP 410, NM- (shipping carton), A......$100.00

Williams, 381E loco, gr, no motor, NM, A......$475.00

Williams, 5200 PRR B65b switcher, 0-6-0, NMIB, A....$350.00

Williams, 5300 PRR E6S, 4-4-2, NMIB, A......$350.00

Williams, 9E loco, gray, w/display board, no motor, EX+ (orig box), A......$200.00

SETS

American Flyer, Panama Limited Model 19, complete with metal track and clips, VG (original box), A, $325.00.

American Flyer, #48-T, 342 NPR switcher, 631 gondola, 633 B&O b/c, 625 st/c, 630 cabooses (2), NMIB........$1,100.00

American Flyer, #50-T, Royal Blue Freight, 350 loco, 631 gondola, 642 b/c, 638 caboose, NMIB $600.00

American Flyer, #20015-5615-T, 303 loco, 801 hopper, 970 b/c, 804 gondola, 806 caboose & track, EX (orig box), A......$300.00

American Flyer, blk CI loco, clockwork not working; 120 litho tender (VG+); 1205 bag/c; 1103 coach; EX+, A.....$190.00

American Flyer, IC streamliner, gr w/yel trim (missing stacks); coaches (3); obv/c; G, A......$210.00

American Flyer, S ga, 282 loco, w/smoke & coal pusher, missing 1 front step, 651 bg/c, 650 Pullmans (2), gr, EX, A .$100.00

American Flyer, S ga, 300AC Atlantic loco; AFL Reading tender; 633 B&O, 637 MKT, 622 GAEX b/cs; 607 caboose; EX-, A......$80.00

American Flyer, std ga, Pocahontas, 4637 Shasta loco, 4340 combine, 4341 Pullman, 4343 obv/c (diner), 4342 obv/c, EX, A......$3,700.00

American Flyer, 1681 Hudson loco, streamline tender, 1621 coaches (3), 1622 obv/c, loco & tender G, cars EX, A......$1,000.00

American Flyer, 21925 & 21925-1 PA Alco AA, 24837 combine, 24883 coach, 24839 vista dome, 24847 obv/c, EX-, A......$2,100.00

American Flyer, 234 Defender USMC, b/c w/rocket, search-light/c, caboose, EX (orig boxes), W5 ....$1,000.00

Aurora, N scale, Postage Stamp Train, Penn Central freight, 1973, made by Trix, W Germany, complete, MIB, A3 ....$45.00

Aurora, N scale, Postage Stamp Train, Sante Fe AA freight, 1967, made by Trix, W Germany, complete, MIB, A3 ....$45.00

Bing, CI loco, clockwork, blk w/red trim; tender; 2395 NYC combine; 205 Pullman; 250 obv/c; G, A..................$275.00

Bing, steam engine 2990, tender, express car w/restaurant/c & sleeping/c (both w/interior lighting), EX, A.........$5,175.00

Classic Model Trains, Southern loco & tender, 4-6-0, 2 coaches, obv/c, EX, A $650.00

Elektoy, 1 ga, brass & nickel; 911 b/c & 090 gondola (both yel litho); 912 caboose, sm rust spot; VG, A..............$2,500.00

Elektoy, 1 ga, 904 loco, rubber-stamped PRR 237, nickel cowcatcher, solid red wheels; 914 bg/c; 913 coach; EX-, A...$2,900.00

Hoge, #881 Tom Thumb electric loco, 881 Pullmans (2), 881 obv/c w/powerhouse, no cord, VG, A $110.00

Hubley, floor train, 5 PRR loco, 44 Washington coaches (2), Narcissus obv/c, all olive w/gold trim, complete, EX+, A $450.00

Ives, O ga, Black Diamond, 3255 loco, diecast cowcatchers; 141 Pullmans (2); 142 obv/c; blk, red roof, brass trim, G, A..$1,100.00

Ives, std ga, 3236R loco; 185 parlor/c, plated; 171 parlor/c; 172 obv/c, rubber stamped, lt brn, pnt flaking; VG, A $80.00

Ives, 11 loco, motor incomplete (EX); 11 tender; 54 gondola; 53 PA b/c; 57 lumber/c; 56 caboose; VG, A $210.00

Ives, 25 loco, clockwork, silver windows; 25 tender, rpt; 130 combine; 129 Saratoga, high Marklin-type trucks; G, A $525.00

Ives, 25 loco, clockwork; FE tender, coupler missing; 60 LVE bg/c, missing 1 door; 61 LVE Yale Pullman; VG, A $1,000.00

Ives, 257 loco, 257T tender, 1707 gondola, 1708 st/c, 1709 b/c, 1712 caboose, cars VG, loco & tender EX, A..........$230.00

Ives, 3216 loco, 65 st/c, 66 Standard Oil tk/c, 67 caboose, VG, A..$110.00

Ives, 3218 loco, blk-pnt CI w/red trim; 60 bg/c, 61 chair/c, 52 parlor/c; gr litho, gray roofs, G, A $150.00

Ives, 5 loco, clockwork, pnt CI, motor dated 1928; 11 tender; 50 bg/c, 51 chair/c, 52 parlor/c, orange litho; EX-, A ...$150.00

Joyline, loco, pnt tin, electric; 357 coaches (3); 458 obv/c, 1 tab off obv/c railing; EX-, A $120.00

Katz, #5:15 LTD, loco, coaches (2), loco missing coupler, some loco rivets rpl w/screws, 521 Dynamo transformer, EX, A $40.00

LGB, 2051S electric loco, 4069 container fl/c, 4063 goodswagon (broken), 4040S tk/c, 4031 goodswagon, 5065 gate, EX, A $400.00

LGB, 2073D tk/loco (rpr), 3040 coach, 3061 coach, VG (orig boxes), A $200.00

Lionel, O ga, #507, 623 SF NW2 switcher, 6511 fl/c (G), 6520 searchlight/c, 6257 caboose, VG+ (orig set boxes), A $250.00

Lionel, O ga, #751E City of Portland, 752E power/c, 753 coach, 754 obv/c (all silver), NMIB, A $4,100.00

Lionel, O ga, #1612 General set, 1862LT, 1866 mail-bag/c, 1865 passenger/c, plus accessories, MIB (w/set box), M4 ....$1,200.00

Lionel, O ga, City of Portland, 752E loco, 753 coach, 754 yel & brn obv/car, EX.......................................$350.00

Lionel, O ga, 221 Rio Grande Alco A w/custom 221 Alco A dummy, 6315 chemical tk/c, 6476 hopper, 6017 caboose, VG, A...$85.00

Lionel, O ga, 224E loco, 2225W tender, 2655 b/c, 2653 hopper, 2654 tk/c, 2657 caboose, 1941 couplers, stamped, EX+, A...$150.00

Lionel, O ga, 228E loco, 265W tender, 602 bg/c, 600 Pullman, 601 obv/c, EX, A $525.00

Lionel, O ga, 248 loco, 629 Pullman, 630 obv/c, orange, VG, A..$160.00

Lionel, O ga, 248 loco, 630 obv/c, both orange & peacock; 629 coaches (2); VG, A..$120.00

Lionel, O ga, 262 loco, brass & copper trim; 262T tender, diecast; 607 coaches (2); 608 obv/c, peacock & orange; EX, A..$375.00

Lionel, 296, O gauge, features peacock engine 253, pullman car 607, observation car 608 and a transformer, VG (original box), A, $520.00.

Lionel, O ga, 1119, 1110, 1001T, 1002, 1004 & 1007; 1951, NMIB (w/set box), M4 ....$375.00

Lionel, O ga, 1441WS Deluxe Work Train, 2020, 2020W, 2461, 3451 & 2419; 1947, NMIB, M4..........................$1,575.00

Lionel, O ga, 1449WS, 2020, 6020W, 3472, 6465, 6411 & 6357; 1948, NMIB, M4......................................$1,650.00

Lionel, O ga, 1457B, 6220, 6462, 3464, 6520 & 6419; 1949-50, NMIB, M4...$1,650.00

Lionel, O ga, 1464W, 2023, UP AA 2421, silver & grey; 2422 & 2423; 1951, M (orig boxes), M4 ....$3,800.00

Lionel, O ga, 1475WS, 2046, 2046W, 3656, 3461, 6472, 3469 & 6419; 1950, NMIB, M4..................................$1,800.00

Lionel, O ga, 1485WS, 2025, 6466W, 6462, 6465, 6257; 1952, MIB (w/set box), M4...................................$1,250.00

Lionel, O ga, 2125WS, 671, 671W, 2411, 2454, 2452 & 2457; 1947, NMIB, M4..**$1,450.00**

Lionel, O ga, 2163WS.736, 2671WX, 6472, 6462, 6555 & 6457, test run, MIB (w/set box), M4 ....**$4,000.00**

Lionel, O ga, 2235W-A-20, 2338 Milwaukee GP, 6436 hopper, 6362 truck/c, 6560 crane, 6419 wrecker, MIB (w/set box), M4..**$2,950.00**

Lionel, O ga, 2379 Rio Grande F3 AB, repro shells, VG, A.**$230.00**

Lionel, OO ga, 003 loco, 003W tender, 0045 Shell tk/c, 0044 PA b/c, 0046 SP hopper, 0047 NYC caboose, VG, A...**$650.00**

Lionel, std ga, #347, 8 loco, Mojave, rstr; 337 Pullman; 338 obv/c, olive & maroon; VG (orig boxes, set box taped), A...**$150.00**

Lionel, std ga, #352E, 10E loco, sm ding in roof; 332 bg/c, 1 broken coupler; 339 coach; 341 obv/c; EX (orig boxes), A...**$475.00**

Lionel, std ga, 33 loco, U fr; 35 Pullman; 36 obv/c; EX, A...**$180.00**

Lionel, std ga, 402E loco (G), 429 combine, 428 coach, 430 obv/c, EX, A..**$450.00**

Lionel, std ga, 408E loco, Mojave; 419 combine, 418 parlor/c & 490 obv/c in Mojave w/orange trim; EX **$2,000.00**

Lionel, 027 ga, Jr Streamline, 1700E loco, 1701 Pullmans (2), 1702 obv/c, red & chrome, VG, A..........................**$160.00**

Lionel, 027 ga, 1015 loco, electric; 1016 tender, 1011 Pullmans (3), 1012 Winnertown station, empty, EX-, A........**$130.00**

Lionel, 027 ga, 1688 loco, 1689T tender, 1680 Shell tk/c, blk; 1679 b/c; 1682 caboose; G, A **$110.00**

Marklin, HO ga, ST800R loco w/coach & obv/c, cream & red; ST800MT BL coach, bl w/vestabule; EX+, A **$2,800.00**

Marklin, 1030 loco, clockwork, no tender, 2945 combine, 2944 coaches (2), EX, A **$900.00**

Marx, Comm Vanderbilt electric loco, NYC tender, 1678 hopper, 552 gondola, 553 tk/c, 59 st/c, 556 caboose, VG, A...**$100.00**

Marx, Santa Fe Streamliner, 5-pc set, J6.........................**$175.00**

Marx, Sound-O-Power, EX (orig box), J6.......................**$145.00**

Marx, Tronic Electric Train System, 1950s, red, blk & yel plastic, battery-op, 12-ft track, MIB, A........................**$135.00**

Marx, UP Streamline electric, #M10005, 8 cars, 424 Radio Train control, electrical switches (2), 2-tone whistle, NMIB, A...**$625.00**

Marx, William Crooks, loco, tender, St Paul & Pacific b/c & coach, NMIB, A...**$650.00**

Marx, 21 SF F3 AA, litho tin, 3 horns missing; C&O gondola; Shell tk/c; GAEX b/c; AT&SF caboose; VG+, A **$25.00**

Marx, 3000 loco, red, chrome trim; electric tender; Montclair cars (4); 1 Bogata; 1 obv/c, red litho; VG, A...........**$350.00**

McCoy, std ga, Wells Fargo Express, 2-4-0, General loco, Cascade tender, bg/c, combine/c, coach, NMIB (except loco), A...**$125.00**

Pride Lines Hiawatha, 250E loco w/tender & 4 cars, EX+, A...**$450.00**

Williams, O ga, 2381 SF Trainmaster, bl & yel; bg/c; vista/c; coaches (2); obv/c; aluminum streamliner/c; NMIB, A...**$325.00**

Williams, TCA, 1979 GG1 w/Pullmans (2), obv/c, MIB (shipping boxes also), A...**$400.00**

Williams, 799 brass freight, hopper/c, tk/c, b/c, caboose, MIB, A...**$275.00**

Williams American Flyer, President Special Reproduction, std ga, loco w/4 cars in bl, NMIB, A **$1,800.00**

ACCESSORIES

American Flyer, S ga, 23787 log loader, missing man, EX+, A...**$180.00**

American Flyer, service station clock, lights up, 12x24", EX, A...**$1,100.00**

American Flyer, 102 Central Station, orange base, chimneys, EX, A..**$250.00**

American Flyer, 2206 flashing signal, bl light, orange base, 4206 highway flasher, EX-..**$100.00**

American Flyer, 2210 lampposts (2), no bulbs, EX..........**$90.00**

American Flyer, 2230 crossing signal, EX- **$40.00**

American Flyer, 23780 Gabe the Lamplighter, pnt silver, w/controller, dk gr plastic, EX, A......................................**$500.00**

American Flyer, 23789 station & baggage smasher w/controller, EX+, A...**$275.00**

American Flyer, 24569 wrecking cranes (2), S ga, Pikemaster couplers, NMIB (boxes taped), A **$65.00**

American Flyer, 270 News & Frank stand, missing 1 man, hanging magazines torn, VG, A.......................................**$120.00**

American Flyer, 271 whistle-stop, S ga, dirty, EX, A **$140.00**

American Flyer, 273 Glendale station, EX (orig box), A...**$160.00**

American Flyer, 274 freight stations (2), 1 missing hanging scale, o/w complete, EX (1 w/orig box), A................**$170.00**

American Flyer, 275 Eureka Diner, EX+, A **$220.00**

American Flyer, 342AC switcher, VG, A......................**$210.00**

Marx, Union Pacific Streamline, complete, VG (original box), A, $250.00.

American Flyer, 596 water tank, NRFB..................$250.00

American Flyer, 596 water towers, (2), 1 rstr, other has top decal chipped, EX-, A $85.00

American Flyer, 731 Pike Planning kit, 759 bell danger signal, 706 uncoupler, 769A beacon w/house, NMIB.........$170.00

American Flyer, 751A log loader, complete, VG (orig box), A $200.00

American Flyer, 768 oil supply depot, no chimney, EX (orig box), A..................$120.00

American Flyer, 785 coal loader, complete, NMIB, A ...$350.00

American Flyer, 785 Seaboard coaler, 3-button version, 23 bags of coal, EX+, A $275.00

American Flyer, 792 RR terminal, NMIB (w/inserts), A..................$450.00

American Flyer, 92 switch towers (2) w/bells, EX (1 w/orig box), A..................$160.00

American Flyer, 97 freight station, yel chimney, tank base, EX, A..................$220.00

Bing, chalet, litho tin, dirty, EX+, A $120.00

Bing, destination board (in English), rubber-stamped signs, EX-, A $220.00

Bing, Grand Central Railroad Station, litho tin, CI window & door fr, 21", G, A..................$750.00

Bing, Rico-style passenger station & freight station, both pnt & litho tin, VG+, A..................$130.00

Carlisle & Finch, elevated uprights (5), pnt CI, 3 have wooden ties, VG+, A..................$750.00

Dorfan, 410 3-pc bridge, gr & tan, EX-, A..................$140.00

Dorfan, 421 electric crossing gate, some pnt flaking on base & cross arm, dirty, EX-, A $175.00

Germany, train station, red & wht tin 'brick' building w/center walk-through flanked by arched canopies, 19", EX, A..................$805.00

Germany, train station, tin 2-story building flanked by canopies on rectangular base, 16½", G+, A..................$400.00

Goelring/Germany, train station, archway under dual staircases leading to canopied platform w/fancy railing, 16", EX, A..................$2,185.00

Ives, Gravel Central Station, pnt & litho tin single-story w/lg CI & glass canopy on wood columns, 2 benches, 23", G+, A..................$600.00

Ives, std ga, 3-pc bridge, railing unattached, G, A $10.00

Ives, 113 station, litho over silver pnt CI trim & chimney, EX-, A..................$625.00

Ives, 333 ringing signal, CI base, 302 dbl arm semaphore, dirty, VG+, A..................$310.00

Lionel, HO ga, 301 yard sign, NMIB, M4 ....$10.00

Lionel, O ga, #022 remote switches (3 pr), no controls, VG (orig boxes), W5..................$80.00

Lionel, O ga, 110 trestle set, NMIB, G1..................$25.00

Lionel, O ga, 154 auto highway signal, EX, G1..................$25.00

Lionel, O ga, 156 station platforms (2), gray uprights, vermillion roofs, some layout pnt on base, VG (orig boxes), A..................$210.00

Lionel, O ga, 164 lumber loader, EX+ (orig box taped), A..................$275.00

Lionel, O ga, 175 rocket launcher, NMIB, M4..................$600.00

Lionel, O ga, 252 crossing gate, EX, G1 ....$25.00

Lionel, O ga, 282 Portal Gantry crane, rewired, cracked controller, VG (orig box), A..................$170.00

Lionel, O ga, 310 billboard, NMIB, M4 ....$50.00

Lionel, O ga, 313 Bascule bridge, rstr..................$220.00

Lionel, O ga, 315 trestle bridge & 316 trestle bridge, both silver, oxidation on bottom, EX (orig boxes), A $75.00

Lionel, O ga, 352 ice depot, brn structure, NMIB $250.00

Lionel, std ga, 0440 signal bridge, silver & red; 440C panel board, red w/switches; VG, A..................$325.00

Lionel, std ga, 101 3-pc bridge, gr & yel, G, A..................$65.00

Lionel, std ga, 113 station, late colors, some touch-up, VG, A..................$300.00

Lionel, std ga, 115 Lionel City station, EX, M4..................$750.00

Lionel, std ga, 116 station, dbl window, late colors, VG, A..................$1,050.00

Lionel, std ga, 155 freight station (2), 1 late color, minor oxidation on base; 1 early color, touched-up roof, EX, A..$600.00

Lionel, std ga, 184 bungalows (3), 2 have gr litho roofs, 1 has a pea gr roof w/pnt chimney, VG, A..................$130.00

Lionel, std ga, 189 villa, ivory, peacock roof, terra cotta base, G-, A..................$250.00

Lionel, std ga, 192 RR control tower, EX+ (VG orig box), A..................$180.00

Lionel, std ga, 199 microwave relay towers (2), 1 w/silver antenna, 1 w/wht, EX+ (G orig boxes), A..................$160.00

Lionel, std ga, 300 Hellsgate bridge, early colors, EX ..$1,500.00

Lionel, std ga, 397 coal elevator, EX, G1 ....$115.00

Lionel, std ga, 397 coal elevator, no coal, orig box, EX+, A..................$180.00

Lionel, std ga, 415 diesel fueling station, missing 1 window insert & 1 terminal, EX+ (orig box), A $170.00

Lionel, std ga, 437 switch tower, early colors, EX+, A ...$600.00

Lionel, std ga, 45 operating gateman, VG, G1..................$25.00

Lionel, std ga, 455 oil derrick, gr on gr, missing 1 drum & sign, EX+ (orig box)..................$300.00

Lionel, std ga, 462, derrick platform set, 1 handle broken, 3 cracked, EX (orig box), A $325.00

Lionel, std ga, 464 lumber mill, M, M4..................$450.00

Lionel, std ga, 494 rotating beacon, silver, EX, G1 ....$45.00

Lionel, std ga, 497 coal station, missing coal bag, dk gr roof, EX+ (orig box), A..................$270.00

Lionel, std ga, 89 villa, cream, pea gr & gray, EX $240.00

Lionel, Super O ga, 38 pumping water tower, orig finial, repro spout, EX, A..................$350.00

Lionel, type R transformer, 110 watt, VG+, P3 ....$70.00

Lionel, 027 ga, 54 ballast tamper, minor oxidation on handrail, EX, A..................$240.00

Lionel, 027 ga, 56 lampposts (4), EX, A $350.00

Lionel, 1033 transformer, 90 watts, EX, G1 ....$45.00

Lionel, 1044 transformer, 90 watt, EX (EX box), P3 ....$50.00

Marklin, grade crossing w/operating gate, ringing bell, hand-operated semaphores, 9½x14", G, A..................$130.00

Marklin, 2002B station, pnt tin, EX, A..................$75.00

Marx, RR station, automatic gate, litho tin, EX (orig set box), A $75.00

MTH, Hellsgate bridge, late colors, NMIB, A..................$900.00

MTH, 444 roundhouse sections (2), NMIB, A..................$600.00

MTH, 840 powerstation, NMIB, A..................$550.00

Transformers

Made by the Hasbro Company, Transformers were introduced in the United States in 1984. Originally there were twenty-eight figures — eighteen cars known as Autobots and ten Decepticons, evil robots capable of becoming such things as a jet or a handgun. Eventually the line was expanded to more than two hundred different models. Some were remakes of earlier Japanese robots that had been produced by Takara in the 1970s. (These can be identified through color differences and in the case of the Diaclone series, the absence of the small driver or pilot figures.)

The story of the Transformers and their epic adventures were told through several different comic books and animated series as well as a highly successful movie. Their popularity was reflected internationally and eventually made its way back to Japan. There the American Transformer animated series was translated into Japanese and soon inspired several parallel series of the toys which were again produced by Takara. These new Transformers were sold in the U.S. until the line was discontinued in 1990.

A few years ago, Hasbro announced their plans to reintroduce the line with Transformers: Generation 2. Transformers once again had their own comic book, and the old animated series was brought back in a revamped format. So far, several new Transformers as well as recolored versions of the older ones have been released by Hasbro, and the size of the series continues to grow. Sustained interest in them has spawned a number of fan clubs with chapters worldwide.

Because Transformers came in a number of sizes, you'll find a wide range of pricing. Our values are for Transformers in unopened original boxes. One that has been opened or used is worth much less — about 25% to 75%, depending on whether it has all its parts (weapons, instruction book, tech specks, etc.) and what its condition is — whether decals are applied well or if it is worn.

Advisor: David Kolodny-Nagy (K2).

SERIES 1, 1984

Autobot Car, #TF1021, Ironside, red van $30.00
Autobot Car, #TF1025, Bluestreak, silver Datsun Z.........$40.00
Autobot Car, #TF1027, Jazz, Porsche..............................$30.00
Autobot Car, #TF1031, Trailbreaker, camper $30.00
Autobot Car, #TF1035, Hound, Jeep................................$30.00
Autobot Car, #TF1039, Prowl, police car $30.00
Autobot Car, #TF1055, Camshaft, silver car, mail-in $15.00
Autobot Car, #TF1059, Overdrive, red car, mail-in.........$15.00
Autobot Car, #TF1063, Powerdasher #2, car, mail-in $10.00
Autobot Car, #TF1163, Skids, Le Car...............................$25.00
Autobot Car, #TF1167, Grapple, crane $25.00
Autobot Commander, #TF1053, Optimus Prime w/Roller, tractor trailer, scout vehicle..............................$150.00
Case, #TF1069, Collector's Case, briefcase $15.00
Case, #TF1071, Collector's Case, rnd 3-D case $25.00
Cassette, #TF1017, Ravage & Rumble...............................$20.00
Cassette, #TF1019, Frenzy & Laserbeak............................$20.00

Decepticon Communicator, #TF1049, Soundwave & Buzzsaw, tape player & gold condor $50.00
Decepticon Jet, #TF1043, Starscream, gray jet $40.00
Decepticon Jet, #TF1045, Thundercracker, bl jet............$35.00
Decepticon Leader, #TF1051, Megatron, Walther P-38 ....$100.00
Minicar, #TF 1008, Bumblejumper, yel...........................$40.00
Minicar, #TF1001, Bumblebee, yel VW bug.....................$35.00
Minicar, #TF1003, Cliffjumper, red race car....................$25.00
Minicar, #TF1011, Windcharger, red Firebird..................$15.00
Minicar, #TF1015, Gears, bl truck $15.00
Watch, #TF1067, Time Warrior, transforming watch, Autobot insignia, mail-in...$80.00

SERIES 2, 1985

Autobot Air Guardian, #TF1201, Jetfire, F-14 jet.........$120.00
Autobot Car, #TF1171, Smokescreen, red, wht & bl Datsun Z $30.00
Autobot Car, #TF1173, Inferno, fire engine $30.00
Autobot Communicator, #TF1199, radio/tape player.......$30.00
Autobot Scientist, #TF1197, Perceptor, microscope $40.00
Constructicon, #TF1127, Bonecrusher (1), bulldozer.......$15.00
Constructicon, #TF1131, Scrapper (3), front-end loader .$15.00
Constructicon, #TF1135, Long Haul (5), dump truck......$15.00
Constructicon, #TF1139, Devastator, construction gift set $90.00
Decepticon Jet, #TF1187, Ramjet, wht jet.......................$25.00

Decepticon Operations, Shockwave, #TF1203, MIB, $70.00.

Deluxe Insecticon, #TF1155, Chop Shop, beetle $45.00
Deluxe Insecticon, #TF1159, Benom, bee $45.00
Deluxe Insecticon, #TF1161, Ransack, grasshopper $45.00
Deluxe Vehicle, #TF1193, Whirl, lt bl helicopter $40.00
Deluxe Vehicle, #TF1195, Roadbuster, off-road vehicle ..$40.00
Dinobot, #TF1177, Grimlock, Tyrannosaurus $40.00
Dinobot, #TF1179, Slag, Triceratops $35.00
Dinobot, #TF1183, Stegosaurus..$35.00
Insecticon, #TF1143, Shrapnel, beetle..............................$20.00
Insecticon, #TF1145, Bombshell, boll weevil $20.00

Insecticon, #TF1141, Kickback, grasshopper $20.00
Jumpstarter, #TF1147, Twin Twist, drill tank..................$15.00
Jumpstarter, #TF1149, Topspin, spaceship.......................$15.00
Minicar, #TF1101, Bumblebee, yel VW bug.....................$25.00
Minicar, #TF1105, Cliffjumper, red race car....................$15.00
Minicar, #TF1107, Cliffjumper, yel race car.....................$15.00
Minicar, #TF1113, Brawn, gr Jeep.......................................$15.00
Minicar, #TF1114, Brawn, w/minispy $25.00
Minicar, #TF1116, Gears, w/minispy $25.00
Minicar, #TF1119, Powerglide, plane $15.00
Minicar, #TF1123, Beachcomber, dune buggy.................$15.00
Motorized Autobot Defense Base, #TF1205, Omega Supreme,
    rocket launcher base $85.00
Triple Changer, #TF1151, Blitzwing, tank/plane $30.00
Triple Changer, #TF1153, Astrotrain, shuttle/train.........$30.00
Watch, #TF1207, Autoceptor, Kronoform watch car.......$20.00
Watch, #TF1209, Deceptor, Kronoform watch jet...........$20.00
Watch, #TF1213, Listen 'n Fun w/tape & yel Cliff-
    jumper...$25.00

SERIES 3, 1986

Aerialbot, #TF1263, Air Raid (1), F-14...........................$15.00
Aerialbot, #TF1265, Skydive (2), F-15 ....$15.00
Aerialbot, #TF1269, Slingshot (4), Harrier $15.00
Aerialbot, #TF1273, Superion, Aerialbot gift set $100.00
Autobot Car, #TF1333, Blurr, futuristic car.....................$30.00
Autobot Car, #TF1337, Hot Rod, red race car $40.00

Autobot City Commander, Ultra Magnus, #TF1365, MIB, $50.00.

Autobot City Commander, #TF1369, STARS Control Center,
    action cb, mail-in..$60.00
Autobot City/Battle Station, #TF1359, Metroplex, robot city
    w/Scamper, blk minicar, Slammer, tank, Six-Gun, tower &
    guns $75.00
Battlecharger, #TF1311, Runamuch, Corvette $13.00
Battlecharger, #TF1313, Runabout, Trans Am..................$13.00
Cassette, #TF1315, Ratbat & Frenzy, bat & bl robot..........$8.00

Cassette, #TF1318, Rewind & Steeljaw, silver weapons, blk
    robot & lion $8.00
Cassette, #TF1320, Ramhorn & Eject, gold weapons, rhino &
    gray robot $8.00
Combaticon, #TF1289, Brawl (1), tank $12.00
Combaticon, #TF1291, Blast Off (3), shuttle $12.00
Combaticon, #TF1295, Onslaught (5), missile transport .$30.00

Decepticon City Commander, Galvatron, #TF1363, MIB, $60.00.

Heroes, #TF1329, Wreck-Gar, futuristic motorcycle........$35.00
Heroes, #TF1331, Rodimus Prime, futuristic RV $35.00
Jet, #TF1353, Scourge, hovercraft $25.00
Jet, #TF1355, Cyclonus, space jet.....................................$35.00
Minicar, #TF1251, Wheelie, futuristic car $20.00
Minicar, #TF1255, Tailgate, wht Firebird.........................$15.00
Minicar, #TF1259, Pipes, bl semi cab...............................$15.00
Motorized Autobot Space Shuttle Robot, #TF1359, Sky Lynz,
    shuttle $75.00
Motorized Decepticon City/Battle Station, #TF1357, Trypticon,
    dinosaur w/Brunt, robor tank & Full-Tilt, buggy.....$100.00
Predacon, #TF1339, Razorclaw (1), lion $25.00
Predacon, #TF1343, Divebomb (2), vulture $25.00
Predacon, #TF1347, Headstrong (5), rhino $25.00
Sharkticon, #TF1351, Gnaw, futuristic shark $30.00
Stunticon, #TF1275, Dead End (1), Porsche $10.00
Stunticon, #TF1279, Wildrider (3), Ferrari $10.00
Stunticon, #TF1283, Motormaster (5), tractor trailer $30.00
Stunticon, #TF1285, Menasor, Stunticon gift set.............$70.00
Triple Changer, #TF1321, Springer, armoured car/heli-
    copter $25.00
Triple Changer, #TF1325, Broadside, aircraft carrier/
    plane..$25.00

SERIES 4, 1987

Cassette, #TF1441, Slugfest & Overkill, Stegosaurus & Tyran-
    nosaurus...$9.00
Clone, #TF1443, Pounce & Wingspan, puma & eagle.....$40.00
Double Spy, #TF1447, Punch-Counterpunch, Fiero $40.00
Duocon, #TF1437, Battletrap, Jeep/helicopter $20.00

Headmaster Autobot, #TF1477, Chromedome w/Stylor, futuristic car $55.00

Headmaster Autobot, #TF1481, Highbrow w/Gort, helicopter...$35.00

Headmaster Autobot, #TF1483, Brainstorm w/Arcana, jet...$35.00

Headmaster Base, #TF1497, Scorponok w/Lord Zarak & Fasttrack, scorpion, mini-tank $80.00

Headmaster Decepticon, #TF1485, Skullcruncher w/Grax, alligator $30.00

Headmaster Decepticon, #TF1489, Weirdwolf w/Monzo, wolf $30.00

Headmaster Horrorcon, #TF1491, Apeface w/Spasma, jet/ape $40.00

Headmaster Horrorcon, #TF1493, Snapdragon w/Krunk, jet/dinosaur $40.00

Monsterbot, #TF1461, Grotusque, tiger.....................$25.00

Monsterbot, #TF1465, Repugnus, insect......................$25.00

Sixchanger, #TF1495, Sixshot, starfighter jet, winged wolf, lazer pistol, armoured carrier, tank...........$60.00

Targetmaster Autobot, #TF1449, Pointblank w/Peacemaker, race car & gun..$30.00

Targetmaster Autobot, #TF1451, Sureshot w/Spoilsport, off-road buggy & gun...$30.00

Targetmaster Autobot, #TF1457, Kup w/Recoil, pickup truck & gun $35.00

Targetmaster Autobot, #TF1459, Blurr w/Haywire, futuristic car & gun $45.00

Targetmaster Decepticon, #TF1467, Triggerhappy w/Blowpipe, dk bl jet & gun..$30.00

Targetmaster Decepticon, #TF1471, Slugslinger w/Caliburst, twin jet & gun...$30.00

Targetmaster Decepticon, #TF1475, Scourge w/Fracas, hovercraft & gun $35.00

Technobot, #TF 1429, Stafe (3), fighter plane $10.00

Technobot, #TF1425, Afterburner (1), motorcycle..........$10.00

Technobot, #TF1427, Nosecone (2), drill tank...............$10.00

Technobot, #TF1432, Lightspeed w/decoy $15.00

Technobot, #TF1433, Scattershot (5), spaceship $30.00

Terrocon, #TF1413, Rippersnapper (1), lizard.................$10.00

Terrocon, #TF1415, Sinnertwin (2), 2-headed dog..........$10.00

Terrocon, #TF1418, Cutthroat w/decoy...........................$15.00

Terrocon, #TF1419, Blot (4), monster............................$10.00

Terrocon, #TF1421, Hun-grrr (5), 2-headed dragon $30.00

Throttlebot, #TF1401, Goldbug, VW bug.......................$10.00

Throttlebot, #TF1403, Freeway, Corvette $10.00

Throttlebot, #TF1405, Chase, Ferrari $10.00

Throttlebot, #TF1409, Rollbar, Jeep $10.00

Throttlebot, #TF1411, Searchlight, race car...................$10.00

Throttlebot, #TF1412, Searchlight w/decoy....................$15.00

Throttlebot, Wideload, dump truck $10.00

SERIES 5, 1988

Autobot Sixchanger, #TF1615, Quickswitch, jet, flying puma, lazer pistol, drill tank, hovercraft................................$35.00

Cassette, #TF1539, Squalktalk & Beastbox, hawk & gorilla $8.00

Firecon, #TF1509, Flamefeather, monster bird $7.00

Headmaster Autobot, #TF 1555, Hosehead w/Lug, fire engine $25.00

Headmaster Autobot, #TF1559, Nightbeat w/Muzzle, race car $25.00

Headmaster Decepticon, #TF1563, Fangry w/Brisko, winged wolf...$25.00

Powermaster Autobot, #TF1567, Getaway w/Rev, MR2..$35.00

Powermaster Autobot, #TF1571, Slapdash w/Lube, Indy car $35.00

Powermaster Autobot Leader, #TF1617, Optimus Prime w/HiQ, tractor trailer..$80.00

Powermaster Decepticon, #TF1573, Darkwing w/Throttle, dk gray jet $30.00

Powermaster Mercenary, #TF1613, Doubledealer w/Knok (robot) & Skar (bat), missile launcher.....................$45.00

Pretender, #TF1491, Sky High, jet w/shell $25.00

Pretender, #TF1577, Landmine, race car w/shell $25.00

Pretender, #TF1581, Waverider, submarine w/shell $25.00

Pretender, #TF1585, Bomb-Burst, spaceship w/shell $25.00

Pretender, #TF1587, Submarauder, submarine w/shell.....$25.00

Pretender, #TF1595, Iguanus, motorcycle w/shell $25.00

Pretender, #TF1599, Finback, sea skimmer w/shell $25.00

Pretender Beast, #TF1601, Chainclaw, bear w/shell........$15.00

Pretender Beast, #TF1603, Catilla, sabertooth tiger w/shell..$15.00

Pretender Beast, #TF1605, Carnivac, wolf w/shell $15.00

Pretender Vehicle, #TF1609, Gunrunner, red jet w/vehicle shell...$30.00

Seacon, #TF1513, Overbite (1), shark............................$10.00

Seacon, #TF1517, Nautilator (3), lobster $10.00

Seacon, #TF1521, Tentakil (5), squid.............................$10.00

Seacon, #TF1525, Piranacon, Seacon gift set $75.00

Sparkbot, #TF1501, Fizzle, off-road buggy....................$7.00

Sparkbot, #TF1505, Guzzle, tank.................................$7.00

Targetmaster Autobot, #TF1543, Scoop w/Tracer & Holepunch, front end loader & 2 guns...............................$12.00

Targetmaster Autobot, #TF1547, Quickmix w/Boomer & Ricochet, cement mixer & 2 guns $15.00

Targetmaster Decepticon, #TF 1549, Quake w/Tiptop & Heater, tank & 2 guns $15.00

Targetmaster Decepticon, #TF1551, Spinster w/Singe & Hairsplitter, helicopter & 2 guns.............................$15.00

Tiggerbot, #TF1527, Backstreet, race car.......................$15.00

Tiggerbot, #TF1531, Dogfight, plane.............................$15.00

Triggercon, #TF1533, Ruckus, dune buggy $15.00

Triggercon, #TF1537, Crankcase, Jeep $15.00

SERIES 6, 1989

Legends, K-Mart Exclusive, #TF1731, Grimlock, dinosaur $40.00

Legends, K-Mart Exclusives, #TF1727, Bumblebee, VW bug $30.00

Mega Pretender, #TF1717, Vroom, dragster w/shell.........$25.00

Mega Pretender, #TF1721, Crossblades, helicopter w/shell..$25.00

Micromaster, #TF1667, Roughstuff, military transport.....$15.00

Micromaster Base, #TF1679, Skyhopper, helicopter; Micromaster, F-15...$35.00

Micromaster Base, #TF1735, Skystalker, Space Shuttle Base & Micromaster Porsche $45.00

Micromaster Patrol, #TF1651, Off-Road Patrol, Powertrain (semi cab), Mudslinger & Highjump (4x4 trucks), Tote (van), ea..$10.00

Micromaster Station, #TF1671, Greasepit, pickup w/gas station $20.00

Micromaster Station, #TF1673, Hot House, plane w/fire station..$20.00

Micromaster Station, #TF1675, Ironworks, semi w/construction site $20.00

Micromaster Station, #TF1677, Airwave, jet w/airport....$20.00

Micromaster Transport, #TF1663, Overload, car carrier ..$15.00

Micromaster Transport, #TF1665, Flattop, aircraft carrier..$15.00

Micromaster Transport, #TF1669, Erector, construction crane $15.00

Pretender, #TF1697, Pincher, scorpion w/shell $20.00

Pretender, #TF1701, Stranglehold, rhino w/shell $20.00

Pretender, #TF1707, Double-Header, twin jet w/shell $20.00

Pretender, #TF1713, Starscream, jet w/shell....................$30.00

Pretender Classic, #TF1709, Bumblebee, VW bug w/shell.$30.00

Pretender Monster, #TF1683, Icepick (1)........................$12.00

Pretender Monster, #TF1687, Wildfly (3) $12.00

Pretender Monster, #TF1691, Birdbrain (5) $12.00

Ultra Pretender, #TF1727, Skyhammer, race car w/figure & vehicle...$30.00

Series 7, 1990

Action Master, #TF1781, Soundwave: Soundwave (bat), Wingthing...$15.00

Action Master, #TF1785, Grimlock: Grimlock Anti-tank cannon (tank gun)...$15.00

Action Master, #TF1789, Rad: Rad, Lionizer (lion).........$15.00

Action Master, #TF1791, Rollout: Rollout, Glitch (mini-robot)...$20.00

Action Master, #TF1795, Krok: Krok, Gatoraider (alligator)...$10.00

Action Master, #TF1799, Blaster: Blaster, Flight-Pack (jet pack) $15.00

Action Master, #TF1803, Mainframe: Mainframe, Push-Button (mini-robot)..$15.00

Action Master, #TF1807, Banzai-Tron: Banzai-Tron, Razor-Sharp (crab) $10.00

Action Master, #TF1823, Starscream: Starscream, Turbo Jet ....'.....$35.00

Action Master, #TF1833, Optimus Prime: Optimus Prime, Armored Convoy...$65.00

Micromaster Combiner, #TF1763, Battle Squad: Meltdown, Half-Track, Direct-Hit, Power Punch, Fireshot, Vanquish $15.00

Micromaster Combiner, #TF1765, Constructor Squad: Stonecrusher, Excavator, Sledge, Hammer, Grit, Knock-out $15.00

Micromaster Combiner, #TF1767, Metro Squad: Wheel Blaze, Road Runner, Oiler, Slide, Power Run, Strikedown..$15.00

Micromaster Combiner, #TF1769, Astro Squad: Phaser, Blast Master, Moonrock, Missile Master, Barrage, Heave ..$15.00

Micromaster Combiner, #TF1773, Cannon Transport: Cement Head, Terror Head..$15.00

Micromaster Combiner, #TF1777, Anti-Aircraft Base: Blackout, Spaceshot...$15.00

Micromaster Patrol, #TF1751, Race Track Patrol: Barricade, Roller Force, Ground Hog, Motorhead $7.00

Micromaster Patrol, #TF1753, Construction Patrol: Takedown, Neutro, Groundpounder, Crumble............................$7.00

Micromaster Patrol, #TF1757, Monster Truck Patrol: Hydraulic, Slow Poke, Hauler, Heavy Tread............................$7.00

Micromaster Patrol, #TF1761, Military Patrol: Bombshock, Tracer, Dropshot, Growl..$7.00

Generation 2, Series 1, 1992-93

Autobot Car, #TF1863, Jazz, Porsche.............................$20.00

Autobot Car, #TF1867, Inferno, fire truck $20.00

Autobot Leader, #TF1879, Optimus Prime w/Roller, tractor trailer w/sound-effect box..$35.00

Autobot Minicar, #TF1883, Hubcap, metallic minicar $10.00

Autobot Minicar, #TF1887, Seaspray, metallic hovercraft..$10.00

Color Change Transformer, #TF1905, Deluge.................$10.00

Color Change Transformer, #TF1909, Drench.................$10.00

Constructicon (orange version), #TF1853, Scavenger (2), steam shovel $7.00

Constructicon (orange version), #TF1857, Hook (4), crane .$7.00

Constructicon (orange version), cement truck $7.00

Constructicon (yel version), #TF1851, Bonecrusher (1), bulldozer $6.00

Constructicon (yel version), #TF1855, Scrapper (3), front-end loader $6.00

Constructicon (yel version), #TF1859, Long Haul (5), dump truck $6.00

Decepticon Jet, #TF1877, Ramjet, purple jet w/electronic light & sound effect box...$25.00

Decepticon Leader, #TF1913, Megatron, gr tank w/electronic sound-effect treads $35.00

Dinobot (new colors), #TF1871, Slag, Green Triceratops.$25.00

Dinobot (orig gray color), #TF1869, Grimlock, Tyrannosaurus..$30.00

Dinobot (orig gray color), #TF1873, Snarl, Stegosaurus.......$30.00

Small Autobot Car, #TF1897, Rapido..............................$7.00

Small Autobot Car, #TF1901, Windbreaker.....................$7.00

Small Decepticon Jet, #TF1895, Windrazor.....................$7.00

Small Decepticon Jet, #TF1889, Afterburner $7.00

Generation 2, Series 2, 1994

Aerialbot, #TF 1917, Air Raid (2), F-14 ....$7.00

Aerialbot, #TF1915, Skydive (1), F-15 ....$7.00

Aerialbot, #TF1919, Fireflight (3), Phantom....................$7.00

Aerialbot, #TF1923, Silverbolt (5), Concorde $18.00

Combaticon, #TF1929, Swindle (2), Jeep $7.00

Combaticon, #TF1933, Vortex (4), helicopter $7.00

Heroes, #TF1953, Autobot Hero Optimus Prime.............$15.00

Heroes, #TF1955, Decepticon Hero Megatron.................$15.00

Laser Rod Transformer, #TF1937, Electro, 1993 ....$15.00
Laser Rod Transformer, #TF1941, Jolt, 1993 ....$15.00
Rotor Force, #TF1847, Manta Ray $7.00
Rotor Force, #TF1949, Powerdrive.....................................$7.00
Stunticon, #TF1925, Breakdown (2), Countach $30.00
Tramsformer Watches, #TF1961, Ultra Magnus $12.00
Transformer Watches, #TF1957, Superion $12.00
Transformer Watches, #TF1959, Galvatron.....................$12.00
Transformer Watches, #TF1963, Autobot.........................$12.00
Transformer Watches, #TF1965, Scorpia $12.00

Trolls

The first trolls to come to the United States were molded after a 1952 design by Marti and Helena Kuuskoski of Tampere, Finland. The first trolls to be mass produced in America were molded from wood carvings made by Thomas Dam of Denmark. As the demand for these trolls increased, several US manufacturers were licensed to produce them. The most noteworthy of these were Uneeda Doll Company's Wishnik line and Inga Scandia House True Trolls. Thomas Dam continued to import his Dam Things line. Today trolls are enjoying a renaissance as baby boomers try to recapture their childhood. As a result, values are rising.

The troll craze from the '60s spawned many items other than just dolls such as wall plaques, salt and pepper shakers, pins, squirt guns, rings, clay trolls, lamps, Halloween costumes, animals, lawn ornaments, coat racks, notebooks, folders and even a car.

In the '70s, '80s and '90s new trolls were produced. While these trolls are collectible to some, the avid troll collector still prefers those produced in the '60s. Remember, trolls must be in mint condition to receive top dollar.

Advisor: Roger Inouye (I1).

Boy Bank, Dam, felt jumper, any eye or hair color, 6", G, I1 ....$20.00

Clown, marked Dam Things, 1965, painted-on clothes, yellow eyes and red nose, 5½", I1, from $175.00 to $250.00.

Cow, Dam, 1964, vinyl, sm, M, I1 ....$45.00
Cow, flesh tone & amber eyes, w/bell, I2 ....$175.00
Donkey, Dam, w/wht hair on mane & tail, lg amber eyes, 9", G, I1 ....$50.00
Elephant, Dam, 1964, wrinkled flesh-tone skin & orange hair, w/bell, 5½", I1...$175.00
Giraffe, Dam, amber eyes, gray hair, 12", G, I1..............$125.00

Batman, blond hair, felt clothing, 3", $25.00.

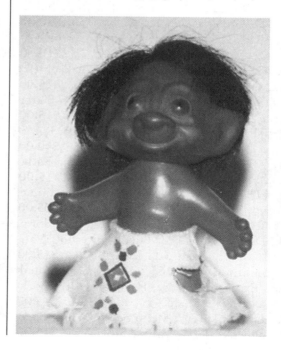

Indian Dress, Wishnik, Black with black rooted hair, black painted eyes, 3½", I1, $75.00.

Judge, Uneeda Wishnik, gray hair, orange eyes, 5½", I1 ...$30.00
Lion, Dam, lg, M, I1 ....$125.00

Monkey, Shekter, 1966, vinyl with jointed neck, original clothes, $40.00.

Moonitik, Uneeda Wishnik, mohair body w/rubber feet & shake eyes, 18", extremely rare, I1......................................$100.00
Neanderthal Man, Bijou Toy, 1963, pnt eyes, 7½", I1......$32.00
Nude, Dam, any eye or hair color, 3", G, I1 ....$8.00
True Troll, Scandia House Ent, 1965, in felt swimsuit w/heart tag around neck, orange hair & gr spiral eyes, 3", M, I2 ...$25.00
Viking, wht hair, bl eyes, unmarked, 3½", I1 ....$35.00
Weird Creature, 1960s, real animal hair, 3", MIP, I1 ....$30.00
Werewolf Monster, 1960s, 3", I1 ....$40.00

MISCELLANEOUS

Bank, Silvestre Bros, 1964, glazed ceramic, 18", M, I1 ...$150.00
Carrying Case, Ideal, w/molded waterfall, M, I1 ....$25.00
Carrying Case, Ideal, Wishnik w/inside labeled Niks & Naks, any color, I1 ....$20.00
Coloring Book, Wishnik Color & Play, Whitman/Uneeda, 1966, uncolored, rare, M, I1 ....$100.00
Cookie Cutter, Mills, 3½", extremely rare, M, I1 ....$50.00
Greeting Card, Am Greeting Corp, 1965, w/3" troll tied on card, rare, I1...$100.00
Halloween Costume, Wishnik, Uneeda, MIB, I1 ....$100.00
Handlebar Grips, Sears, figural plastic, I1, pr.................$100.00
Lamp, Wishnik, complete, 18", rare, I1 ....$250.00
Night Light, troll sitting on crescent moon, MOC, S2.....$10.00
Paper Dolls Book, Wishnik, Whitman, 1964, M, I1 ....$65.00
Pencil Topper, astronaut troll, Scandia House Ent, 1½", MIP, I1 ....$45.00

Salt & Pepper Shakers, ceramic boy & girl w/pnt-on clothes, 3½", I1, pr..$150.00
Troll Clothes, any make, MIP, I1, ea $15.00
Troll House, pnt wood mk Troll House w/'S' backwards, unmk, 9x5½", rare, I1 ....$85.00
Troll House, Standard Plastics Products, cave-like w/molded furnishings, 12x8½", I2....................................$20.00
Troll Travelling Bag, Bunallan Inc, plastic, 5x7", G, I1 ...$25.00
Troll Village, Marx, MIB, I2 ....$300.00

View-Master and Tru-Vue

View-Master, the invention of William Gruber, was introduced to the public at the 1939-1940 New York World's Fair and the Golden Gate Exposition in California. Since then, View-Master reels, packets, and viewers have been produced by five different companies — the original Sawyers Company, G.A.F (1966), View-Master International (1981), Ideal Toys, and Tyco Toys (the present owners). Because none of the non-cartoon single reels and three-reel packets have been made since 1980, these have become collectors' items. Also highly sought after are the 3-reel sets featuring popular TV and cartoon characters. The market is divided between those who simply collect View-Master as a field all its own and collectors of character-related memorabilia who will often pay much higher prices for reels about Barbie, Batman, The Addams Family, etc. Our values tend to follow the more conservative approach.

The first single reels were dark blue with a gold sticker and came in attractive gold-colored envelopes. They appeared to have handwritten letters. These were followed by tan reels with a blue circular stamp. Because these were produced for the most part after 1945 and paper supplies were short during WWII, they came in a variety of front and back color combinations, tan with blue, tan with white, and some were marbleized. Since print runs were low during the war, these early singles are much more desirable than the printed white ones that were produced by the millions from 1946 until 1957. Three-reel packets, many containing story books, were introduced in 1955, and single reels were phased out. Nearly all viewers are very common and have little value except for the very early ones, such as the Model A and Model B. Blue and brown versions of the Model B are especially rare. Another desirable viewer, unique in that it is the only focusing model ever made, is the Model D. For more information we recommend *View-Master Single Reels, Volume I*, by Roger Nazeley.

Advisor: Roger Nazeley (N4).

Adventures of GI Joe, B-585, MIP $15.00
Airplanes of the World, B-773, MIP, D8, from $20 to $25.00
Alaska the 49th State, A-101, MIP, D8, from $14 to.......$18.00
America's Man in Space, John Glenn...; B-657, MIP, D8, from $18 to $25.00
American Indian, B-725, MIP..$10.00
Annapolis Naval Academy, A-783, MIP, D8 ....$18.00
Apollo Moon Landing, July 20th, 1969; B-663, MIP, D8, from $18 to $20.00

Apple's Way, B-558, MIP $19.00
Aristocats, B-365, MIP, J5, from $8 to $10.00
Bad News Bears Breaking Training, H-77, MIP, C1, from $15
    to $19.00
Bahamas, B-027, MIP, D8 ....$12.00
Bambi, B-400, MIP, J5 ....$10.00
Batman, B-492, MIP $32.00
Beautiful Washington DC, A-800, MIP, D8, from $8 to ..$12.00
Bedknobs & Broomsticks, B-366, MIP, D8, from $19 to ..$25.00
Beep, Beep, The Road Runner; B-538, MIP $12.00
Berlin (Germany), B-192, MIP........................$28.00
Bible Heroes, B-852, MIP, D8, from $10 to $15.00
Birth of Jesus, B-875, MIP.............................$8.00
Black Hole, K-35, MIP $11.00
Blondie & Dagwood, B-537, NMIP, T2 ....$29.00
Bonanza, B-471, MIP $29.00
Buck Rogers, L-15, MIP $19.00
Buck Rogers in the 25th Century, J-1, MIP $10.00
Buffalo Bill Jr, B-464, MIP $25.00
Butterflies of North America, B-610, MIP, D8 ..$12.00
Car & Carriage Caravan, A-830, MIP, D8 ....$75.00
Casper the Friendly Ghost, B-533, MIP $4.00
Cat From Outer Space, J-22, MIP, C1, from $13 to.........$15.00
CHiPs, L-14, MIP, C1, from $15 to.................$18.00
Colonial Williamsburg Virginia, A-813, MIP, D8, from $8
    to $12.00
Colorado Ski Country USA, A-331, MIP, D8.....$11.00
Conquest of Space: Astronautics, B-681, MIP, D8, from $18
    to $20.00
Daktari, B-498, MIP......................................$28.00
Daniel Boone, B-479, MIP, D8.......................$35.00
Dark Shadows, B-503, MIP............................$97.00
Dennis the Menace, B-539, MIP $12.00
Doctor Strange, K-22, MIP............................$10.00
Dracula, B-324, MIP $15.00

Dukes of Hazzard, L-17, NM (EX+ pkg), C1.....................$21.00
Eight Is Enough, K-76, MIP, D8.......................$22.00

Electra Woman and Dyna Girl, Krofft Supershow, GAF, 1977, MIP, $20.00.

Emergency, B-597, NMIP, C1, from $18 to $20.00
England, B-156, MIP, D8, from $18 to.............$20.00
Exploring the Universe, Astronomy; B-687, MIP, D8, from $26
    to $30.00
Fat Albert & the Cosby Kids, B-554, MIP $4.00
Flintstones, B-514, MIP, C1, from $10 to $15.00
Flipper, B-485, MIP $15.00
Frankenstein, B-323, MIP.............................$16.00
Germany, B-193, MIP, D8, from $12 to.........$15.00
Grand Canyon, A-361, MIP..........................$10.00
Grand Canyon II, A-362, MIP, D8 ....$12.00

Dr Shrinker and Wonderbug, #31163, Krofft Supershow, GAF, 1977, MIP, from $18.00 to $23.00.

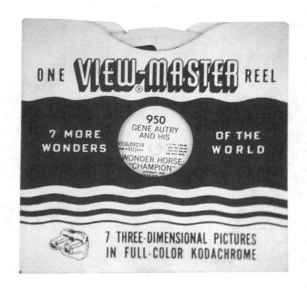

Gene Autry & His Wonder Horse Champion, 7 More Wonders of the World, Sawyers #950, $5.00.

Great Smokies National Park, A-889, MIP......................$9.00

Greater Miami, A-963, MIP, D8, from $12 to $14.00

Greece, B-205, MIP, D8, from $12 to $14.00

Hardy Boys, B-547, MIP $15.00

Harlem Globetrotters, H-69, MIP, D8 ....$19.00

Hawaii, The 50th State, A-120, MIP, D8, from $10 to $12.00

Holland, B-190, MIP, D8, from $10 to.........................$18.00

Hollywood California, A-194, MIP...............................$11.00

Hong Kong, B-251, MIP, D8 ....$12.00

Insect World, Entomology, B-688, MIP, D8, from $40 to .$45.00

Inspector Gadget, BD-232, MIP $8.00

Ireland, B-160, MIP, D8 ....$18.00

Iron Man in Spell of Black Widow, H-44, MIP $8.00

Isis, T-100, MIP, C1, from $16 to $19.00

Italy, B180, MIP..$11.00

Jamaica, B-032, MIP, D8, from $20 to $25.00

Jetsons, L-27, MIP $4.00

Joe Forrester, BB-454, MIP $19.00

Jungle Book, B-363, NMIP, T2, from $18 to $20.00

Knight Rider, #4054, MIP, C1, from $13 to....................$15.00

Lancelot Link & Secret Chimp, B-504, NMIP, C1, from $27
to $35.00

Lassie Look Homeward, B-480, NM (EX pkg), C1 ....$18.50

London (England), B-157, MIP....................................$11.00

London (England), C-277, MIP, D8 ....$12.00

Mannix, Enter Tami Okada, BB-450, MIP, C1, from $25
to $29.00

Marineland of Florida, A-964, MIP, D8, from $15 to.......$20.00

Marineland of the Pacific, A-188, MIP..........................$11.00

Matter & Energy (Physics), B-682E, MIP, D8 ....$25.00

Michigan, A-580, MIP, D8..$12.00

Mickey Mouse Club Mouseketeers, B-524, MIP.............$42.00

Mister Magoo, H-56, MIP..$7.00

Mod Squad, B-478, MIP, D8 ....$25.00

Modern Israel, B-224, MIP, D8, from $15 to $18.00

Mork & Mindy, K-67, MIP, C1, from $13 to..................$16.00

Mount Rushmore National Memorial, A-487, MIP, D8, from $7
to $12.00

Nassau in the Bahamas, B-026, MIP, D8 ....$18.00

Nation's Capitol, US Capitol Building...; A-794, MIP, D8 ..$12.00

New York City, Famous City Series, A-649, MIP.............$23.00

New York City at Night, A-647, MIP, D8 ....$12.00

Niagara Falls, A-655, MIP, D8 ....$12.00

Pan Am's 747, B-747, MIP $52.00

Parrot Jungle, Miami FL, A-965, MIP, D8 ....$12.00

Parrot Jungle, Miami FL, Bird Performance; A-970, MIP,
D8 ....$12.00

Partridge Family, B-569, MIP, D8 ....$35.00

Pee Wee's Playhouse, #4074, MIP $8.00

Pink Panther, J-12, MIP...$8.00

Plant Kingdom, Botany; B-680, MIP, D8, from $20 to.....$25.00

Popeye, B-516, MIP $6.00

Raggedy Ann & Andy, B-406, MIP, T2, from $8 to.........$10.00

Rin-Tin-Tin, B-467, MIP, D8, from $12 to $18.00

Robin Hood, B-371, MIP (sealed), C1 ....$27.00

Robinson Crusoe, B-438, MIP, C1 ....$24.00

Rockefeller Center, New York City; A-652, MIP, D8, from $18
to $25.00

Rocks & Minerals, Mineralogy; B-677, MIP, D8, from $18
to $21.00

Rocky Mountain National Park, A-322, MIP, D8, from $9
to $12.00

Rome (Italy), B-182, MIP...$12.00

Rookies, BB-452, MIP, C1, from $19 to.........................$21.00

Rowan & Martin's Laugh-In, B-497, MIP......................$35.00

Scenic USA, A-996, MIP..$12.00

Scooby & Scrappy Doo, B-553, MIP.............................$20.00

Search, B-591, M (NM pkg), C1 ....$29.00

Six Million Dollar Man, AVB-559, MIP, S2 ....$35.00

Sleeping Beauty (Disney), B-308, MIP..........................$7.00

Smithsonian Institution, A-792, MIP, D8 ....$15.00

Smithsonian Institution, Washington DC, A-799, MIP,
D8 ....$28.00

Spain, B-171, MIP, D8...$12.00

Spiderwoman, The Enforcer Strikes, L-7, MIP, D8, from $10
to $12.00

Star Trek, Mr Spock's Time Trek; B-555, NM (EX+ pkg),
T2 ....$12.00

Star Trek, The Motion Picture; K-57, MIP.....................$23.00

Superman Meets Computer Crook, AVB-584, MIP.........$95.00

Superman Meets Computer Crook, B-584, MIP..............$14.00

SWAT, BB-453, MIP, C1 from $22 to............................$27.00

Switzerland, B-185, MIP, D8, from $15 to $18.00

Texas, A-410, MIP, D8...$12.00

View-Master Personal Stereo Camera, MIB, $100.00; View-Master Stereo-Matic 500 Projector, M, $200.00; as shown in vintage ad.

Time Tunnel, B-491, MIP $49.00

Tom Corbett, Space Cadet; B-581, MIP $25.00

Twenty-Thousand Leagues Under the Sea, B-370, MIP.....$7.00

Universal Studios Scenic Tour, Packet #1, A-241, MIP...$21.00

US Air Force Academy, A-326, MIP $9.00

US Spaceport, B-662, MIP, D8, from $11 to $15.00

Virgin Islands, B-036, MIP, D8 ....$25.00

Washington DC, A-790, MIP, D8, from $10 to...............$15.00

Weeki Wachee, Spring of Live Mermaids, FL; A-991, MIP $28.00

Welcome Back Kotter, MIP, D2/D8/C1, from $15 to.......$18.00

White House, A-793, MIP, D8...........................$22.00

Wizard of Oz, 1978, MIP (sealed), C1...................$23.00

Wonders of the Deep, B-612, MIP, D8 ....$12.00

Yellowstone, A-306, MIP, D8 ....$12.00

101 Dalmatians, MIP $6.00

Western

No friend was ever more true, no brother more faithful, no acquaintance more real to us than our favorite cowboys of radio, TV, and the siver screen. They were upright, strictly moral, extrememly polite, and tireless in their pursuit of law and order in the American West. How unfortunate that such role models are practically extinct nowadays.

This is an area of strong collector interest right now, and prices are escalating. For more information and some wonderful pictures, we recommend *Character Toys and Collectibles, First* and *Second Series,* by David Longest and *Guide to Cowboy Character Collectibles* by Ted Hake.

Advisors: Donna and Ron Donnelly.

See also Books; Cereal Boxes; Character and Promotional Drinking Glasses; Character Clocks and Watches; Coloring, Activity and Paint Books; Guns; Lunch Boxes; Premiums; Windups, Friction and Other Mechanicals; and other specific categories.

Andy Devine as Jingles, note pad, 1950s, color photo of Jingles on cover, minor creases o/w VG, J5 ....$25.00

Annie Oakley, hat, 1950s, red felt, faded logo, VG, J5.....$15.00

Annie Oakley, outfit, Iskin-Oakley Ent, ca 1950, skirt, vest & neckerchief, Annie illus on pockets, NM+ (EX box) $165.00

Annie Oakley, outfit, Pla-Master, 1950s, cotton vest & skirt w/plastic fringe, images of Gail Davis on ea, EX+ (EX+ box) $135.00

Annie Oakley, sewing set, Pressman, complete w/7" plastic doll, EX+ (EX+ box), A...............................$55.00

Bonanza, filmstrip viewer, 1961, w/films, NM, J2 ....$20.00

Brave Eagle, outfit, EX+ (EX box), M5.....................$140.00

Cisco Kid, neckerchief slide, 1950s, EX $25.00

Dale Evans, decal, Star Cal, 1950s, M (orig envelope).....$20.00

Dale Evans, jewelry set, MOC, D8 ....$28.00

Dale Evans, outfit, vest & skirt, EX, J2 ....$130.00

Dale Evans, skirt, EX, M5 ....$65.00

Dale Evans, washcloth puppet, 1950s, 8", EX $35.00

Dale Evans, Western Dress-Up Kit, Colorforms, 1969, NMIB, J2 ....$60.00

Daniel Boone, inflatable canoe, 1960s, vinyl w/head of Fess Parker as Daniel Boone, 18" long, EX $35.00

Davy Crockett, bank, bronze torso of Davy holding rifle & knife, name on base, 6", NM, A $70.00

Davy Crockett, bank, Frontier Dime, Davy w/rifle in prairie scene, tin, 2½", scarce, EX, A $285.00

Davy Crockett, belt & buckle, mk Made in France/WDP, brn w/emb rifle & powder horn on metal buckle, M (EX card), A $45.00

Davy Crockett, braces, brn w/western images, attached photo mk Walt Disney's Official Davy Crockett, NMOC...$95.00

Davy Crockett, charm bracelet, WD/Fess Parker, Davy on horse, sgn & fr photo, Bowie knife, etc, 6", scarce, MOC, A $70.00

Davy Crockett, cup & bowl, Fire-King, 1950s, milk glass w/images of Davy in western scenes, M.................$65.00

Davy Crockett, doll, Indian Fighter, rubber in brn cloth outfit & coonskin cap, 17", NM (VG window box), A.........$115.00

Davy Crockett, doll, Uneeda, 1950s, w/coonskin cap, 14", EX $85.00

Davy Crockett, iron-on transfer set, NM $40.00

Davy Crockett, Jailer's Keys & Handcuffs, complete w/sheriff's badge, handcuffs & keys, scarce, MOC, A $80.00

Davy Crockett, knife, Auburn Rubber, red & silver, 8", VG, I2 ....$30.00

Davy Crockett, Old West Model Train, Plasticraft, 1950s, 13", NM (EX+ box), A $70.00

Davy Crockett, outfit, complete w/powder horn, belt, key chain w/compass & mirror, MOC, A $70.00

Davy Crockett, paper plate, Walt Disney, 1950s, EX, J5 ..$15.00

Davy Crockett, party invitation & game, Punch-In-Vite Enterprises, 1955, scarce, unused, NM (EX+ box), A $80.00

Davy Crockett, patch, yel & red, 4½ x6", D8 ....$12.00

Davy Crockett, Pencil Craft Painting Set, Hassenfeld/WDP, mk Special Edition, complete, NM (EX+ box), A $235.00

Davy Crockett, Play Box, 1950s, w/wallet, story book, coloring book, puzzle, dot-to-dot, etc, NM (EX+ box), A $195.00

Davy Crockett, powder horn, Daisy/WDP, 1955, 7" plastic horn in fringed leather holder, MIB, A...............................$78.00

Davy Crockett, shirt, pioneer style, EX, J2 ....$80.00

Davy Crockett, stamp book, 1955, King of the Wild Frontier, stamps applied, EX, M8 ....$25.00

Davy Crockett, wallet, WD, 1955, vinyl w/Davy's image in plush coonskin hat, M (EX+ box), A $45.00

Deputy, marshal's badge, Top Gun Co/20th Century Fox, NMOC (card features Henry Fonda as Marshal Simon Fry)...............................$35.00

Gabby Hayes, Carry-All Fishing Outfit, Nassau, ca 1950, complete in 24" tube featuring Gabby, EX $195.00

Gabby Hayes, Sheriff's Set, 1950s, unused, NMOC, J2 ....$80.00

Gene Autry, braces w/attached Sheriff's badge, gr elastic w/wht stripes, EX+ (EX card), A...............................$125.00

Gene Autry, guitar, Emenee, ca 1950, tan plastic w/emb image of Gene & other western scenes, 31", M (EX+ box) $225.00

Gene Autry, Official Ranch Outfit, MA Henry, 1941, chaps w/plaid shirt, tie, hat, lasso & holster, EX+ (G box) .$265.00

Gene Autry, guitar, Emenee, ca 1950, tan plastic with embossed image of Gene and other western scenes, 31", M (EX+ box), A, $225.00.

Gene Autry, slippers, ca 1950, white patches on bl w/bl stars on red cuffs, gun whistle on chain, NM (EX box), A...$225.00

Hopalong Cassidy, badge display card, Lone Star, illustrated card with metal Sheriff's badge and Special Agent badge, EX, A, $200.00.

Hopalong Cassidy, bank, bronze-tone bust, NM, J2 ....$75.00
Hopalong Cassidy, Birthday Club card, NM, O1..............$15.00
Hopalong Cassidy, box camera & flash reflector, Galter, 1940, NM (separate VG boxes), A $475.00
Hopalong Cassidy, canasta tray, Hoppy's saddle, Pacific Playing Card Co/W Boyd, 1950, blk plastic, NM (EX box), A..$235.00

Hopalong Cassidy, charm, William Boyd, 1950, silver-tone metal bust form, M..$16.50
Hopalong Cassidy, charm bracelet, ca 1950, charm w/emb head of Hoppy on orig bracelet, 1½" dia charm, NM, A....$75.00
Hopalong Cassidy, crayon & stencil set, Transogram, 1950, complete, EX+ (EX box) $195.00
Hopalong Cassidy, Dr West's Dental Kit, Weco, ca 1950, complete, EX+ (EX box) $295.00
Hopalong Cassidy, drinking straws, Regal Products, 1 cutout from Hoppy series on back, contains 38 of 50 straws, EX $125.00
Hopalong Cassidy, field glasses, VG (EX box)...............$225.00
Hopalong Cassidy, flashlight, Topper Toys, 1950, tin w/red decal, needs new bulb o/w EX $150.00
Hopalong Cassidy, Hair Trainer, NM, O1 ....$35.00
Hopalong Cassidy, hat, Bailey Hollywood, red felt w/silkscreened name, leather slider string, EX+, A....$90.00
Hopalong Cassidy, Hoppy's Bar 20 Chow Set, Anchor Hocking, 1950, milk glass tumbler, bowl & plate w/blk images, MIB, A...$350.00
Hopalong Cassidy, Junior Chow Set, box only, Imperial Knife Co, 1950, 8", NM..$100.00
Hopalong Cassidy, knife, ca 1950, blk miniature jackknife w/decals, 2", scarce, VG, A..$78.00
Hopalong Cassidy, knife, w/key chain, EX, O1..............$125.00
Hopalong Cassidy, lamp, Aladdin, ca 1950, upright bullet shape w/decal, milk glass, 8", rare, NM $650.00
Hopalong Cassidy, movie viewer, Acme-Shapiro, 1950, plastic viewer w/2 Heart of the West films, NM (VG box), A..$200.00
Hopalong Cassidy, napkin, 1950s, paper, dinner-sz, NM..$10.00
Hopalong Cassidy, night light, 1950, plastic cylinder w/red top & bottom, revolving litho shade, 9½", NM...........$550.00
Hopalong Cassidy, outfit, girl's, Iskin, 1950, fringed skirt, neckerchief, blouse & belt, M (EX+ box) $245.00
Hopalong Cassidy, paint & crayon set, EX (VG box), O1 ....$290.00
Hopalong Cassidy, paint set, Laurel Ann Arts, complete w/3 figures & paints, EX+ (EX box) $500.00
Hopalong Cassidy, paper plates, cups & tablecloth, EX (orig pkg), O1 ....$300.00
Hopalong Cassidy, pencil case, Hasbro, ca 1950, name flanks bust portrait of Hoppy, slide-out drawer, 5x9", NM, A...$100.00
Hopalong Cassidy, pennant, original, 18", NM $65.00
Hopalong Cassidy, photo album, 1950, emb leather strap w/graphics of Hoppy & Topper, name in script, 14", EX $115.00
Hopalong Cassidy, picture, ca 1950, signature fr w/Hoppy & Topper around picture of Hoppy, 9x7", EX+ $65.00
Hopalong Cassidy, Picture Gun & Theatre, Automagic, 1939, w/gun & 2 boxed films, Hoppy photo, cb theatre, M (EX+ box), A..$340.00
Hopalong Cassidy, pin, metal in shape of Hoppy's gun w/pearly inset grip, 2½", M, A..$75.00
Hopalong Cassidy, Secret Gun Pin, W Boyd, 1950, metal gun w/movable barrel, simulated pearl hdl, 2⅜", MOC, A..$200.00

Hopalong Cassidy, Siren Flashlight, HJ Ashe/Hong Kong, 1950s, w/Hoppy secret code pamphlet, 7", rare, NM (VG box)..$300.00

Hopalong Cassidy, sweater, cream color w/red bust of Hoppy on front & Topper on back, acrylic, Made in California, M, A..$175.00

Hopalong Cassidy, wall plaque wishing good luck, NM, J2 .$50.00

John Wayne, calendar, Western Legends Calendar, 1986, blk & wht illus of famous Western stars, 11x17", M $6.00

Kit Carson, Golden Stamp Book, M, J2............................$35.00

Lone Ranger, brush set, TLR, 1939, wood brush w/decal of Lone Ranger on Silver, 4¼", EX+ (VG box) $85.00

Lone Ranger and Tonto, squirt guns, plastic, 5", EX, O1, $40.00 each.

Lone Ranger, tattoos, Philadelphia Gum Corp, 1966, Lone Ranger throwing frogman on wrapper, NM, T2 ....$32.00

Lone Ranger, De-Luxe Cine-Vue Films and Camera, Acme, 1940, has three boxed films, M (EX+ box), A, $245.00.

Lone Ranger, figure, chalkware, S1 ....$80.00

Lone Ranger, mask, 1950s, cut from back of Wheaties cereal box, EX, J5 ....$35.00

Lone Ranger, outfit, Pla-Master/Iskin-Lone Ranger Inc, 1955, brn w/graphics, Tonto & Silver in script, MIB, A...$120.00

Lone Ranger, outfit, Pla-Master/Iskin-Lone Ranger Inc, 1955, fringe & graphics, Tonto lettered vertically, MIB, A..$105.00

Lone Ranger, paint box, Milton Bradley, red background, NM, A $28.00

Lone Ranger, pedometer, VG+, D8 ....$35.00

Lone Ranger, pencil box, Am Pencil, 1949, heavy cb w/simulated blk leather, emb illus, 9", NM, T2....................$80.00

Lone Ranger, picture printing set, StamperKraft/c 1939 TLR, complete, EX (NM box), A....................................$135.00

Lone Ranger, record player, wood, no needle & hums loud o/w EX, I2 ....$330.00

Lone Ranger, scrapbook, Whitman, unused, M, J2...........$60.00

Lone Ranger, signal siren & flashlight, litho tin & plastic, complete w/scarce Silver Bullet Secret Code book, MIB, A...$152.00

Lone Ranger, squirt gun, Lido, 1970s, w/Butch Cavendish figure, MIP, H4 ....$40.00

Lone Ranger, wallet, Hidecraft, 1948, EX, O1, $125.00.

Lone Ranger, Western Gun Collection, Am Cast/Lone Ranger, 1950, set of 6 miniature CI guns, NM (EX 8x10" paper fr), A...$150.00

Lone Ranger, whistle, tin, 3", VG+, M5 ....$10.00

Lone Ranger on Silver, figure, Barclay (?), 1930s, Lone Ranger waving & Silver prancing, hand-painted lead, 3", VG+, A...$130.00

Maverick, Paint-By-Number Set, Hasbro, 1950s, NM, J5 .$35.00

Rin-Tin-Tin, Coloring Fun Set, Transogram, 1956, EX (EX box), T2 ....$100.00

Rin-Tin-Tin, magic slate, Whitman, M, J2 ....$45.00

Rin-Tin-Tin, outfit, Corporal Rusty 101st Cavalry, Pla-Master, 1955, shirt, neckerchief, holster & gun, NM (EX box), A $95.00

Rin-Tin-Tin, Paint-By-Number Set, Transogram, 1956, 6 pictures w/watercolors, 4 neatly pnt, EX+......................$35.00

Roy Rogers, balloons, King of the Cowboys, Oak Rubber, 5 balloons w/depictions of Roy, scarce, NMOC (sealed), A..$350.00

Roy Rogers, bedspread, woven gray w/continued designs featuring Roy, subtle red & gr highlights, 95", EX, A.......$185.00

Roy Rogers, binoculars, Roy & Trigger inscriptions & designs, metal & plastic w/vinyl strap, NM (NM box), A...$175.00

Roy Rogers, chaps, 1950s, vinyl w/1 picturing Trigger & 1 picturing Roy, used for kids' rain gear, EX, J5.........$65.00

Roy Rogers, Cowboy Branding Set, Knox Resse, 1950, includes ink pad & rubber stamp w/Double R Ranch insignia, MIB, A..$500.00

Roy Rogers, cowboy hat, 1950s, tan wool felt w/band of western motif, orig photograph tag of Roy & Dale, M, A.......$95.00

Roy Rogers, Fix-It Stagecoach, Ideal, VG (EX box), A....$90.00

Roy Rogers, scarf and cowboy hat slide set, #N367/USA, EX+ (EX box), A, $400.00.

Roy Rogers, wood-burning set, 1950s, complete in cb case w/plastic hdl & metal lock, unused, NM, A............$175.00

Roy Rogers & Dale Evans, school bag, Pall Mall, simulated leather, mk King of the Cowboys & Queen of the West, VG, A...$92.00

Roy Rogers & Dale Evans, Song Wagon, Simon/Schuster, record holder containing 7 of 8 45-rpm records, EX (EX+ box), A...$120.00

Tales of Wells Fargo, Marshal's badge, Overland/20th Century Studios, 1959, NMOC (card features Dale Robertson)...$35.00

Tales of Wells Fargo, Paint-By-Number Set, Transogram, 1959, 6 drawings w/8 watercolors, MIB..............................$75.00

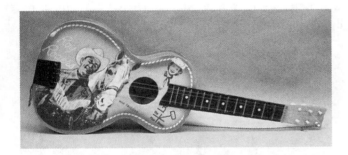

Roy Rogers, guitar, 28", EX, D10, $85.00.

Roy Rogers, harmonica, T1 ....$45.00

Roy Rogers, hobby horse, Trigger, Dartmore/Roy Rogers Ent, 1950s, inflatable, red, yel & bl, 18", NM (VG box), A............$160.00

Roy Rogers, Horse Trailer & Jeep, Ideal, 1950s, plastic w/Roy, Pat Brady & Trigger w/saddle, 13", NM+ (VG+ box), A..$207.00

Roy Rogers, horseshoe, blk rubber, NM $20.00

Roy Rogers, neckerchief, 1950s, gold & maroon, features Roy & Trigger, EX, J5...$25.00

Roy Rogers, pajama top, Rob Roy, EX, J2......................$90.00

Roy Rogers, postcard, w/picture & signature, T1 ....$22.00

Roy Rogers, postcard, 1950s, glossy blk & wht close-up of Roy & Trigger, NM, C1..$15.00

Roy Rogers, raincoat, Buchsbaum, yel & blk vinyl w/signature, diecut tag w/'Roy's Pledge to Parents' on back, NM, A...$215.00

Roy Rogers, saddle, child's, 1950s, VG+.........................$400.00

Roy Rogers, signal siren & flashlight, litho tin & plastic w/ranch scene, complete w/scarce code book, MIB, A..........$160.00

Roy Rogers, stagecoach w/horses & driver, Ideal, plastic, EX...$75.00

Roy Rogers, toy phone, Ideal, 1957, crank side lever for electric bell sound, plastic, 9", NM (EX box), A..................$285.00

Roy Rogers, wallet, 1950s, emb design of Roy on rearing Trigger, unused, NM, A...$50.00

Roy Rogers, wood-burning set, Burn-Rite/Rapaport, 1950s, incomplete o/w VG $50.00

Texas Ranger, spurs and gloves, Toy Town, 1950s, MIB, D10, $35.00.

Tom Mix, handkerchief, 16" sq, EX, J2..............................$75.00

Wagon Train, TV projector & films, 1960s, battery-op, NMIB, A $80.00

Wyatt Earp, handcuffs & badge, 20th C Toys, 1950s, Hugh O'Brian pictured on card, EX, A $78.00

Wyatt Earp, Marshal's Outfit, Iskin, 1950s, w/vest, shirt, tie & pants, tin star badge, gun & holster, M (EX box), A $275.00

Wyatt Earp, outfit, Pla-Master, sz 2, MIB.........................$60.00

Wyatt Earp, Yankiboy, shirt, vest & pants w/2-gun leather holster & belt, plastic guns, etc, EX+ (EX box) $95.00

Zorro, Dominoes, Halsam/WDP, 1950s, ea domino features Zorro on Toronado, complete, M (EX+ box)...........$75.00

Zorro, gloves, 1960s, blk, wht & red, NM, S2..................$30.00

Zorro, gum ball machine display card, 1958, ring offer, Zorro w/Toronado & logo, M, T2 ....$40.00

Zorro, Magic Erasable Pictures Book, WD, 1950s, hardbound w/12 color & wipe-off pictures, w/boxed crayons, EX.$35.00

Zorro, magic slate, Strathmore, 1958, w/orig wood stylus, NM...$30.00

Zorro, pinwheel, WDP, 1950s-60s, 4 red fins w/Z logo & 4 blk & silver fins w/Zorro graphics, w/bell sound, 18", EX, D9...$30.00

Zorro, sword & mask, Lone Star, blk plastic sword & vinyl mask, NMOC, A..$140.00

Zorro, television & film, Lido/WD, 1950s, plastic TV w/4 boxed films & 1 in TV, NMOC, A...................................$80.00

MISCELLANEOUS

Belt, western style w/studs, child-sz, NM...........................$8.00
Cowgirl Outfit, red skirt & vest, EX+.............................$60.00
Cuffs, jewelled & studded leather, child-sz, NM..............$35.00
Flashlight, tin w/cowboy design, NM, J2.........................$30.00
Indian Outfit, buckskin, 3-pc, child-sz, VG+...................$85.00
Seventh Cavalry Glove & Neckerchief Set, Riegel, 1950s, MIP (sealed), J2..$60.00
Spurs, England, solid nickel, EX...................................$25.00

Windups, Friction and Other Mechanicals

Windup toys represent a fun and exciting field of collecting — our fascination with them stems from their simplistic but exciting actions and brightly colored lithography, and especially the comic character or personality-related examples are greatly in demand by collectors today. Though most were made through the years of the thirties through the fifties, they carry their own weight against much earlier toys and are considered very worthwhile investments. Various types of mechanisms were used — some are key wound while others depend on lever action to tighten the mainspring and release the action of the toy. Tin and celluloid were used in their production, and although it is sometimes possible to repair a tin windup, experts advise against investing in a celluloid toy whose mechanism is not working, since the material is usually too fragile to withstand the repair.

Many of the boxes that these toys came in are almost as attractive as the toys themselves and can add considerably to their value.

Advisors: Richard Trautwein (T3); Scott Smiles (S10).

See also Aeronautical; Automobiles and Other Vehicle Replicas; Boats; Chein; Lehmann; Marx; Robots and Space Toys; Strauss.

AMERICAN

Alpine Cable Car Ride, Ohio Art, 2 cable cars travel up & down 3-level slope, litho tin, NM, A.................................$115.00

Ambulance, Wyandotte, 1940s, features removable stretcher, plastic, friction, 9", NM, S9.....................................$150.00

American Railway Express w/Trailer, Lindstrom, tandem trailer w/hinged roof, litho tin, 16", EX, A.........................$675.00

Artie Car, Unique Art, smiling clown in dunce-type hat rides in crazy car w/dog on hood, 7", VG, from $200 to.......$250.00

Betty, Lindstrom, 1930s, litho tin girl in pants & apron holding purse & wearing hat vibrates around, 8", EX+.........$150.00

Ace Indianapolis Racer, Nasco, 1950s, red with yellow driver, plastic, 8", MIB, D10, $150.00.

Photo courtesy of Scott Smiles.

Billiard Players, Ranger Steel, 1930s, EX, from $300.00 to $325.00.

Clown on Velocipede, Ives, 1870s, clockwork mechanism, EX, D10, $11,000.00.

Bombo the Monk, Unique Art, monkey tumbles from palm tree, litho tin, 10", EX, S10 ....$225.00

Bugs Bunny & Porky Pig, Talking Toy/Warner Bros, 1949, litho tin figures on plastic base, crank activates sound, EX+, A $250.00

Capitol Hill Racer, Unique Art, 1930, spring lever action, litho tin, 16", EX, S10 ....$225.00

Checker Cab, Courtland, gr & yel w/rubber tires, lithoed driver & passenger, 7", VG, A $90.00

City Cab, Lupor, litho tin w/rubber tires, NMIB, A $170.00

Climbing Monkey, Lindstrom, monkey goes up & down rope, G (G box), A $55.00

Coney Island Giant Dip, H Katz, 1920, roller coaster w/8 lithoed figures on car, 4 planes on towers, 19", EX+ (G box), A $3,300.00

Crane, Wolverine, 1947, turn crank to manuever in circle or lower bucket, litho tin, 18", NM (G box), A $180.00

Crane Truck, Courtland, ca 1950, tin w/plastic cab roof, crane operator lithoed in window, crank, 13", NM (EX box) $150.00

Dancing Dude & Music Box, Mattel, cowboy does the jig on lithoed stage, hand crank, NM (box rprs), A $130.00

Dancing Dutch Boy, Lindstrom, 1930s, litho tin boy w/concertina vibrates around, 8", NM (EX box), A..........$300.00

Dancing Katrinka, 1930s, litho tin ethnic girl vibrates around, 8", EX+, A $200.00

Dancing Lassie, Lindstrom, litho tin girl in plaid vibrates around, 8", EX+, A $155.00

Diving Submarine, Wolverine, 1940, w/litho guns, EX, R7..$150.00

Diving Submarine, Wolverine, 1940, w/2 3-D guns, EX, R7 ....$180.00

Doin' the Howdy Doody, Unique Art, Howdy dances while Buffalo Bob plays piano, litho tin, EX (G box), S10 .$1,400.00

Donald Duck Carousel, Borgfeldt, Donald balances spinning umbrella w/balls, celluloid & pressed steel, 4", rare, NMIB, A...$6,800.00

Donald Duck Rail Car, Pride Lines, Donald & Pluto on house car w/track, pnt steel, O gauge, electric, 10", NMIB, A $170.00

Drum Major, Wolverine, yel & blk w/wht highlights, 13½", VG, S10...$150.00

Elgin Street Sweeper, Nylint, yel litho metal w/plastic driver, turning brushes, rubber wheels, 8½", EX, from $160 to $175.00

Ferryboat, Lindstrom, red, yel & gr side-wheeler w/passengers lithoed in windows, single stack, 7", G, A $120.00

Finnegan, Unique Art, bump-&-go, cb figure on front of luggage cart w/uncut cb luggage pcs, 14", NM (EX box), A.$250.00

Photo courtesy of Scott Smiles.

Flasho the Mechanical Grinder, Girard, 1920s, G, from $150.00 to $200.00.

Gertie the Galloping Goose, Unique Art, 1930s, pecks & bounces, litho tin, MIB, A $300.00

Donald Duck Rail Car, Lionel, 1935-36, EX, D10, $875.00.

Donald Duck Rail Car, Lionel #1107, compo Donald & Pluto on tin house car, Pluto's head moves, 9½", EX (EX+ box), A $1,600.00

GI Joe and His Jouncing Jeep, Unique Art, 1941, marked CR 5-4065, forward and reverse action, 8", EX, S10, $250.00.

GI Joe & His K-9 Pups, Unique Art, walks while carrying lithoed pups in cages, 9", EX, S10, from $250 to $350.00

Girl on Velocipede, Brown & Stevens, ca 1875, hand-painted tin & CI, girl has compo head & cloth dress, 10", EX, A $1,600.00

Golden Arrow, Kingsbury, sleek bronze-colored tin racer w/driver, 20", EX, A $925.00

Greatest Show on Earth, Lindstrom, 1930, elephant pulls circus wagon, other animals trailing behind, EX, A $1,700.00

Photo courtesy of Scott Smiles

Hee Haw, Unique Art, 1930s, VG, from $225.00 to $275.00.

Hen Laying Egg, Baldwin, 1950, hand crank, NM, R7.....$75.00

Hillclimber Fire Engine, Dayton, pnt sheet metal w/CI figures, 14½", VG, A..............................$625.00

Hillclimber Locomotive & Tender, pnt sheet metal, red & gold, friction, 26", VG, A..............................$250.00

Hoky Poky, Wyandotte, 2 clowns in polka-dot suits & cone hats work red & yel handcar, litho tin, 6", EX, from $275 to..............................$325.00

Photo courtesy of Scott Smiles

Home Run King, Selrite, 1930s, VG, from $750.00 to $825.00.

Horse & Chariot, Mason & Parker, horse w/jtd legs pulls chariot, 14", no figure, ears or tail, VG, A $65.00

Hot Rod #7, Saunders, ca 1950, red plastic w/driver, blk rubber tires, friction, 7", NM, A $70.00

Hot Rod Racer, Nosco, ca 1950, red plastic w/driver & passenger, blk rubber tires w/yel hubs, 7½", NM, A..........$350.00

Humphrey Mobile, Wyandotte, 1950, pulling house on 3-wheeled cycle, litho tin, 8½", EX, S10....................$550.00

Injun Chief, Ohio Art, crawling Indian w/tomahawk, 7½", NM (EX box), A $150.00

Jazzbo Jim, Unique Art, 1920s, Jim dances and plays banjo atop cabin, 10", NM (EX box) $1,000.00.

Johnny the Clown, Lindstrom, 1930s, red & yel litho tin clown w/hands behind back vibrates around, 8", EX+, A ..$200.00

Kiddy Cyclist, Unique Art, blond-haired boy pedals trike w/erratic action & ringing bell, EX, S10..................$325.00

Krazy Kar, Unique Art, 1920s, soapbox racer style w/balloon design, yel wheels, farmer driver, EX+ (G box), from $575 to........................$700.00

Li'l Abner & His Dogpatch Band, Unique Art, characters around piano, 7", EX (EX box), S10, from $750 to .$900.00

Lincoln Tunnel, Unique Art, vehicles travel road out of tunnels, cop in center, 24", NM (EX box), from $575 to......$700.00

Loop De Loop, Wolverine, car performs loop-the-loop, lithoed carnival scenes on base, MIB, A $575.00

Mammy, Lindstrom, 1930s, litho tin Black lady in red wearing wht apron & hat w/red bow vibrates around, 8", EX+, A $250.00

Man on the Flying Trapeze #516, Wyandotte, athlete swings & turns on trapeze, 9", EX+ (orig box), S10 ....$225.00

Mechanical Billiard Table, Ranger Steel, 2 men shooting pool, EX (G box), S10, from $300 to $375.00

Mechanical Playground, Lee/USA, tin playground base w/6 magnetized kids, swings, seesaw, etc, NM (EX box)........$280.00

Merry-Go-Round, Wolverine, w/horses & airplanes, plinker noise, spring lever, 11" dia, missing flags o/w G+, A $160.00

Mickey Mouse Car, 1930s, Mickey in racer w/wht rubber tires, 4", EX, A..$575.00

Mickey Mouse Circus Train, Lionel, engine, coal tender & 3 circus cars, compo Mickey figure, 40", non-working, VG, A..$1,900.00

Mickey Mouse Hand Car, Lionel, 1930s, Mickey & Minnie work hdl on rare orange car, 8", NM (EX box), A........$1,600.00

Mickey Mouse Washing Machine, Ohio Art, 1930s, shows Mickey & Minnie washing clothes, 7½", NM (VG rare box), A..$1,100.00

Monkey Shines, Emporium, 1950, monkey goes up & down palm tree w/paper leaves, tin, 18", NM (EX box), from $175 to..$225.00

Mr Machine, Ideal, 1960s (later version), 16", D10, from $50.00 to $60.00; Mr Machine, Ideal (early version), 16", D10, from $200.00 to $300.00.

Musical Kiddie-Go-Round, Unique Art, boats & horses w/riders go in circular motion, litho tin, 11", EX+ (G+ box), A..$325.00

Musical Sail Away, Unique Art, kids in 3 plastic boats attached to canopy fly out & circle lighthouse, 9", EX (G box), A..$265.00

Mystery Alpine Express, Automatic Toy, train cars navigate track, w/tunnel & station, litho tin, 20", EX+ (EX box), A..$230.00

Mystery Car, Wolverine, press down on rear bumper & car advances, red litho tin w/wood wheels, 13½", VG, A..$175.00

Mystery Car & Trailer, Wolverine, 1950s, press down on roof of car to activate, bl & red litho tin, 27", NM (G box), A..$310.00

Neck & Neck, Wolverine, turn crank & 4 horses w/jockeys race down track, litho tin, NM (G box), from $200 to...$225.00

Negro Peacher, Ives, head turns from side to side as upper body moves up & down, right arm pounds podium, 10½", EX, A..$5,200.00

Oreo Tailspin Pup, Orianna Metal Products, 1940s, spinning action, 5", MIB, S10..$100.00

Panama Truck, Kingsbury, dumps from bottom of truck, sheet metal w/CI driver & rubber wheels, clockwork, 13", EX, A..$525.00

Parcel-Carrying Deliverall, Nylint, bl & yel w/full-figure driver, tin w/clear plastic windshield, 10", EX (VG box), A..$285.00

Peter Rabbit Chick-Mobile, Lionel, 1930, Peter pumps handcar, pnt compo & steel, w/track, 10", EX (G box).........$900.00

Police Cycle, Unique Art, litho tin, tan w/metal wheels, 8", drive wheel loose, G-, A..$145.00

Pool Table w/Players, Ranger Steel Products Corp, litho tin, 14", EX (EX orig box), A..$260.00

Pump-Mobile, Nylint, litho tin full-figure cowboy pumps lever in pressed steel cart, 8½", EX+ (EX+ box), A.........$528.00

Pure Milk Co Delivery Truck, Kingsbury, sheet metal, wht w/blk rubber tires, complete w/carrier & 4 bottles, 9", M, A..$375.00

Racer #5, tin boat-tail racer w/balloon tires, tin steering wheel, 10½", A..$156.00

Ranger Truck & Trailer Fleet, 1950, Ranger Motor Line, Ranger Oil & Stake Trailer, litho tin, 6", NM+ (EX box), A..$300.00

Red Ranger Ride 'Em Cowboy, Wyandotte, cowboy on horse mounted on rocking platform, litho tin, 7", EX, A....$95.00

Rodeo Joe in His Yipee-I-Aaay Jouncing Jeep, Unique Art, car rocks back & forth, EX, S10..$250.00

Santa Claus, Lindstrom, litho tin, advances & vibrates, 8", G, A..$120.00

Santa Car, Lionel, features Mickey Mouse in Santa's gift bag, MIB, $1,500.00.

Santa Hand Car, Pride Lines, Santa works car w/trees on trailers, w/track, O gauge, electric, 9½", EX (EX box), A.....$170.00

Scooter-Girl, Buffalo Toys, 1925, girl in swimsuit drives golf cart-type scooter w/figure-8 action, 7", NM (EX+ box), A..$515.00

Sheriff Sam Whoopee Car, forward & reverse action, head turns, litho tin & plastic, 7", VG+, A..$155.00

Photo courtesy of Scott Smiles.

See-Saw Circus, Lewco Products, 1940s, VG, from $150.00 to $200.00.

Silver Dash, Buffalo, 1925, early tin race car w/driver & passenger, pull out rod & car advances, 14", scarce, VG, A $450.00

Skeeter Duck #55, Lindstrom, advances in 'S' pattern, head moves, rubber bumper, 9½", NM (EX box), A $135.00

Ski Jumper, Wolverine, 1930s, skier rolls down track & somersaults over obstacle, litho tin, EX+ (VG box), A $250.00

Sky Rangers, Unique Art, 1930s, litho tin monoplane circles lighthouse, EX+ (EX box), from $350 to $450.00

Sky Rangers, Unique Art, 1930s, litho tin monoplane circles lighthouse, EX, S10, from $300 to $350.00

Spiral Speedway, Automatic Toy, 1950s, 2 buses travel on track that loops on an overpass, MIB, A $200.00

Sunny Andy Kiddie Kampers, Wolverine, 1930s, w/active semaphore scout, litho tin, 14", rare, EX+, A $350.00

Sunny Andy Tank, Wolverine, 1930s, advances w/tank noise, heavy tin w/blk & yel litho, 15", EX (VG box), A..$380.00

Super Racing Car, Irwin, ca 1950, yel & red plastic w/blk rubber tires, NM+ (EX box), A $180.00

Taxi Cab, John C Turner, 1920s, blk & yel w/lithoed passengers, tin, friction, 10", VG, A $700.00

Turbo-Jet Car, Ideal, 1950s, red & yel plastic rocket shape w/wheels on horizontal tin launch pad, 11", NM (EX box), A $250.00

Whistling Boy, Irwin, plastic, NMIB, S9 ....$125.00

White Mustang Dump Truck #37, Wolverine, litho tin w/lever-action dumping, friction, 12½", NM (EX+ box), A .$160.00

XP-1960 Dream Car, Mattel, futuristic style, yel plastic w/blk rubber tires, friction, 8", EX+ (EX+ box), A............$175.00

Zilotone, Wolverine, figure plays tunes on xylophone w/3 interchangeable disks, M, S10 ....$900.00

Zilotone, Wolverine, figure plays tunes on xylophone w/3 interchangable disks, EX, S10...$700.00

ENGLISH

Breakdown Lorry, Minic, separate w/up activates hook assembly, red & blk tin, NM (EX box), A $500.00

Broderick Crawford Highway Patrol Car, Welsotoy, shows Dan Mathews on box, friction, 11", scarce, NM (NM box) $350.00

Dairy Truck, Minic, blk cab, wht tanker w/Minic Dairies 3.150 Gallons decals, 7", EX+, A......................................$235.00

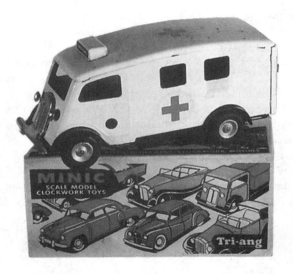

Ambulance, Minic/Tri-ang, white tin with red medical decals, rear door opens, 5", NM (EX+ box), A, $225.00.

Fire Engine, Minic, prewar, red tin with hose, ladder and bell, compartment doors open, NM (EX box), $400.00.

Ford Saloon, Minic, bl tin, 3½", NM (EX+ box), A.......$150.00

Gyro Cycle, Tri-Ang, plastic boy w/cloth arms pedals metal cycle, gyroscope & reduction gear in front wheel, 8", EX, A $270.00

Inverted Clown, Wells, stars & crescent moons on pants, litho tin, clockwork, EX (EX box), S10, from $200 to.....$225.00

Mickey Mouse Hand Car, Wells, 1948, Mickey & Donald work car, Pluto & Goofy lithoed on sides, EX+ (EX+ box), A...$1,525.00

Minic Tri-Ang Garage, for Minic vehicles, litho cb w/tin trim, plastic windows, string-operated ramps, 19", EX, A..$500.00

Moto-Police, SFA, 1930s, policeman in sidecar w/sparking machine gun, balloon tires, 4", EX (EX box), S10...$450.00

Nautilus Submarine, 20,000 Leagues Under the Sea, Sutcliffe, MIB, S10, from $325 to..$375.00

Pendine Super Racer #7, Toby Toy, ca 1950, aluminum racer runs w/crank action using rubber bands, EX+ (G box), A.$100.00

Racer #6, early litho tin racer w/balloon tires, adjustable front wheels, molded driver, 7", EX+, A $95.00

Royal Mail Van, Minic, red tin w/decals, 3½", EX, A $110.00

Santa Claus, 2 dolls peek out of sack while Santa waddles around, litho tin, 4½", NM (EX box), A $300.00

Searchlight Lorry, Minic, w/electric searchlight, Shell gas can, blk tin w/rpl wht rubber tires, NM (EX box), A $585.00

Short Nose Tipper Truck, wire-activated dump action w/opening gate, gr tin, 4½", NM (G box), A $250.00

Stake Truck, Wells, litho tin w/tin driver & balloon tires, crank-activated dumping action, 10½", EX+, A $275.00

Taxi, Minic, blk tin complete w/meter & spare on rear, 4", NM (EX box), A $275.00

Tractor, Mettoy, tin, gr, 7½", NM (EX box), M5 ....$100.00

Train Engine, Mettoy, ca 1950, tin, friction, 6", NM, S9.$115.00

Transport Express Van, Minic, bl tin w/decals, 3½", NM, A...$80.00

Transport Van, Minic, red tin w/Minic Transport Road-Rail Sea-Air Express Service decals, 5", NM (EX+ box), A ...$225.00

Vauxhall Cabriolet, Minic, lt bl tin, rpl wht rubber tires, 5", EX, A $130.00

Vauxhall Tourer Convertible, Minic, gr & blk tin, 5", NM (EX box), A...$180.00

FRENCH

Bellvue, 2 cars travel through tunnels & stations on 3-D base lithoed w/country scenes, 13" base, NM (EX box), A .$230.00

Citroen Wagon, Joustra, pnt & litho tin 1960s style, bl & wht, opening tailgate, friction, 8", VG (orig box), A $120.00

Delivery Boy, Victor Bonnet, boy pushing 2-wheeled flat-bed cart, hand-painted & litho tin, cloth clothes, 8", EX, A...$800.00

El Diablo, Fernand Martin, cloth-dressed man on red base, hand-painted tin body, 8", EX, A $1,900.00

Le Pochard, Martin, ca 1900, walking drunk, hand-painted tin w/orig clothes, 8", EX+ (orig box), A $975.00

Man Pushing Barrels, hand-painted & litho tin cloth-dressed body, tin barrels, 7½", NM , A..............................$1,900.00

Miracle Car, stop-and-go action, hood opens along w/driver's door showing chauffer attached to door, 6", EX (EX box), A...$175.00

Motorcycle w/Sidecar, SFA, 1930s, bl driver & passenger on silver & red cycle w/wht spoked tires, 4", EX, from $250 to..$275.00

Ruban Bleu Speedboat, JEP, wht tin boat w/compo driver, prop spins, lever-activated steering, 13", NM (EX+ box), A...$440.00

Stock Car, Joustra, 1950, 3 litho tin cars line up against grandstand, push levers & cars go, scarce, NM (EX box), A...$400.00

Swimming Fish, CIJ, tail moves, pnt & stenciled tin fish on wooden base, crank on mouth, 17", EX (EX box), A $1,400.00

GERMAN

Amusement Park Airplane Ride, WK, litho tin, celluloid props, battery-op lights, 12", EX, A $1,000.00

Andy Sparkler (Amos 'n Andy), tin face in derby hat w/glass eyes smoking cigar, still sparks, 6¾", EX, A $750.00

Angel, Schuco, tin w/pk cloth robe & yel wings, 5", some moth damage, VG+, A $1,485.00

Arabian Trotter, West Germany, 1955, horse trots in circle, compo & tin, 6", NM (EX box), A $180.00

Baker Street Railroad, trolley-type cars travel up & down tracks w/buildings, 30", EX (G box), A $625.00

Balloon Vendor, 1940s, holding Mickey Mouse and animals on string in one hand and balloons in the other, green base, EX, $1,200.00.

Barney Google & Spark Plug, Nifty, 1920s, Barney riding Spark Plug, 7", VG, from $850 to......................................$950.00

Barrel Clown, Erco/US Zone, clown balances on barrel as it rolls, 8", rare, EX (EX box), A.................................$825.00

Beatrix Cart, lady driving 3-wheeler, 1920s, missing 1 gear, EX, M5...$350.00

Bicycle, Gunthermann, litho tin w/pnt tin figure, as rider pedals, steering wheel changes position, 8", EX, A $1,650.00

BOBY, US Zone, circus monkey peddles trike in circular motion, litho tin, 4", NM (EX box), A.....................$225.00

Boy on Sled, Hess, boy on belly w/jtd arms steers sled w/cast wheels, litho tin, 6¾", VG, A $450.00

Boy on Steer, Gunthermann, ca 1920, figure rocks while steer's head moves, litho tin, 6½", G-, A $550.00

Buick Convertible, Gunthermann, turns around when bumpers hit solid object, bl & cream, tin w/compo driver, 11", EX, A..$345.00

Carnival Airplane Carousel, 1950s, 4 litho tin airplanes w/celluloid propellers circle around tower, 9", NM (EX box), A ..$380.00

Carnival Bell Ringer, G Levy, 1930s, flat tin figure swings mallet, clowns face shoots up & bell rings, EX, from $230 to...$375.00

Cat Chasing Mouse, 1930s, litho tin cat & mouse on wires attached to rnd base chase each other, 10", EX+ (EX box), A...$365.00

Charlie Chaplin, Schuco, tin w/cloth outfit, 6½", EX (EX box), A..$1,700.00

Circus Elephant on Tricycle, US Zone, umbrella spins from trunk as he moves in circle, tin, 8", NM, S10, from $175 to...$225.00

Clown in Crazy Car, prewar, advances in erratic motion, litho tin w/oversized wheels, 6½", EX, A.........................$600.00

Clown Juggler, Schuco, litho tin, 4¾", EX, from $120 to ...$200.00

Clown Musicians, EHN/West Germany, 1940s, two seated clowns playing drums and cymbals, lithographed tin with circus animals on base, 8½" long, EX, from $500.00 to $600.00.

Clown w/Boy, Schuco, tin, cloth dressed, clown lifts celluloid boy, 5", VG, A...$660.00

Clown w/Mouse, Schuco, litho tin w/fabric coverings, red & blk, lifting action, 4½", VG, A..................................$180.00

Command Car 2000, Schuco, press lever or blow whistle for action, bl tin streamlined body, 5½", NM (VG box), A $250.00

Cowboy on Horse, GNK/US Zone, tin, MIB, S10..........$200.00

Crazy Car, Distler, ca 1930, googly-eyed driver in open car w/crazy actions, 7½", EX, A $700.00

Dancers, Schuco, mother rabbit holds & swings plastic baby w/floppy ears & pipe-stem legs, 4¼", EX, A.............$168.00

Donald Duck, Schuco, vibrates around as beak opens & closes, earlier version w/orange beak, 6", EX, from $280 to..$425.00

Donald Duck, Schuco, vibrates around as beak opens & closes, earlier version w/orange beak, 6", MIB, A $650.00

Drinking Mouse, Schuco, tin, cloth dressed, raises ceramic beer mug, 4", EX, A..$175.00

Examico 4007, Schuco, bl w/red interior, gearshift & lever controls movement, tin, friction, 5½", NM (VG box), A $135.00

Express Boy Porter, compo porter pushes tin trunk, leans forward to push harder while legs kick, 3", NM (EX box), A...$275.00

Felix the Cat on Scooter, Nifty, litho tin, 7½", VG, A ..$750.00

Ferris Wheel, B&S, press plunger for spinning motion, 6 litho tin gondolas w/2 riders in ea, 10½", EX+ (EX box), A...$275.00

Ferry, Nifty, 1920s, forward & reverse action, pump assembly goes up & down, tin, 8", rare, EX, from $275 to......$400.00

Ford Model T Phaeton, Bing, litho tin, lady driver, 6½", EX, A...$465.00

Ford Model T Sedan, Bing, ca 1925, w/driver, blk tin w/metal spoked tires, 6½", EX, A....................................$425.00

Format Coupe 2900, Arnold, lt gauge steel, 2 compo figures, steers, 10", NM (damaged box), A.........................$300.00

Gama 501 Dump Truck, red, blue and yellow metal, removable top and opening doors, 15½" long, VG+, A, $175.00.

Garage w/Autos, Orobr, orange 2-door garage w/gr tourer & orange & blk sedan, 6" autos, G+, A....................$2,000.00

George Washington Bridge, Bueschel/Borgfeldt, 1930s, Greyhound Lines bus travels bridge, 25", scarce, EX+ (EX box), A..$1,500.00

German Submarine, Arnold, red & gr tin w/swivel deck gun, fences, conning tower & Nazi flag, prop spins, EX, A.$495.00

Girl on Scooter, gr, orange & blk, litho tin, changes direction, 8¾", non-working, VG, A $75.00

Grand Prix Race Set, Technoflex/US Zone, 1950, w/2 cars, VG+, R7 ....$135.00

Grand Prix Racer, Schuco, bl w/red interior, lug wrench removes tires, Schuco key, on-off lever, NM+ (VG box), A.$475.00

Hand-Standing Clown, US Zone, balances on hands, moves back & forth, well detailed, 5", NM, S10 ....$350.00

Hopsa Monkey w/Mouse, Schuco, clothed plush monkey twirls lifting skirted mouse up & down, 5", NM (EX box), A...$300.00

Horse & Jockey, US Zone, jockey on horse that walks on all 4's, 5", litho tin, EX+ (VG box) $200.00

Howdy Doody the Live Acrobat, Arnold/Kagran, Howdy Doody performing tricks on trapeze, lever action, 15", NM (EX box), A...$1,000.00

Hurricane Motor Launch, West Germany, litho tin, gr, red & wht, 7", VG+ (VG box), A $25.00

Indian Motorcycle, litho tin, w/driver & sidecar, 4¼", non-working, EX, A $1,100.00

Jack Sprat, Gunthermann, early 20th century, pnt tin Jack & his wife dance, 6½", rpt, A $460.00

Jumbo the Elephant, US Zone, olive gr, orange & yel, working, VG, S10 ....$150.00

Krazy Kat on Skooter, Nifty, 1920s, tin, EX, D10, $950.00.

Lasso Cowboy, US Zone, cowboy spins lasso overhead as horse spins around on base, litho tin, 6", EX+ (EX box), A $195.00

Limousine, Carette, litho tin, wht w/pnt tin driver, opening doors, hand brake, 9", rpt driver, EX-, A $1,975.00

Limousine, Moko, early sedan w/butler driver & spoked wheels, engine parts move as car advances, 8", NM+, A ..$1,250.00

Photo courtesy of Scott Smiles.

Mac 700 Motorcycle, Arnold, black cycle, lithographed tin, two levers control action, 7½", NM, $1,000.00.

Mac 700 Motorcycle, Arnold, red cycle, litho tin, 2 levers control action, EX+, S10 ....$1,250.00

Maggie & Jiggs, figures fight on wheeled platforms joined by spring, 7", scratches, dk finish o/w VG, A $850.00

Magic Arithmetical Dog w/Clown Trainer, 1950s, dog nods head to solve math problem, plastic & tin, 7½", EX, A $140.00

Manrovier Tank, Gescha, lever activated left & right movements, sparking guns, 8", NM (G box), A $165.00

Mercedes Benz, Schuco #1225, EX (orig box), W5 ....$120.00

Micro-Jet #1030 Thunderjet, Schuco, red tin, w/orig Schuco key, 5½", EX+, A $110.00

Mini Race Car, Technofix/US Zone, 1950, w/2 Porsche cars, MIB, R7 ....$450.00

Mirakocar 1001, Schuco, non-fall action, red tin streamlined body, 4½", EX+ (EX box), A $150.00

Photo courtesy of Scott Smiles.

Moko Sedan, 1920s, with driver, NM, $1,050.00.

Monkey on Trike, Arnold/US Zone, highly detailed monkey pedals & steers tricycle, 3½", VG, from $200 to......$250.00

Motorcycle, Technofix, litho tin, red cycle, rider in bl pants, wht shirt, 7", NM, M5, from $190 to $300.00

Mountain Express Train, Technofix/US Zone, litho tin mountain scene w/cable car bus, extends to 44", NM (EX box), A $240.00

Mouse in Convertible, Schuco, Sonny 2005, bl car w/gray fabric mouse, tin, 5¾", G, A $220.00

MP Police Car, Arnold/US Zone, 1949, compo MP soldier & passenger in wht & blk tin car, 10", scarce, EX+ (G box), A $225.00

Musical Carousel, prewar, circles as music plays, 2 motorcycles w/drivers & 2 fire trucks, litho tin, scarce, VG, A...$450.00

Mystery Car & Garage, PN #900, enters & exits garage in circular motion, litho tin, EX+ (EX+ box), A $391.00

Noli Snails, EPL #915/Lehmann, 1957-81, 3 litho tin snails w/rubber antennae, friction, 2½", NM (EX+ box), A $50.00

Paak-Paak Ducklings, EPL #903/Lehmann, 1955-81, 6 litho tin ducklings, friction, ea 3", NM (EX+ box), A $60.00

Packard (1952), Distler/US Zone, forward & reverse lever action w/3 speeds, 10", EX, from $265 to $400.00

Peacock, Eberl, 10", minor rstr to pnt, M5 ....$240.00

Police Cycles, PN, attached side-by-side cycles w/policemen advance in figure-8 pattern, 7", EX (EX box), from $470 to $600.00

Police Varianto 3040, Fernlenk Auto, Schuco, 2-tone VW w/adjustable gearing for speed, litho tin, 4", MIB, A.**$300.00**

Policeman, ca 1925, lever attached to policeman's hand activates the stop-&-go sign, 6", NM, A.........................**$630.00**

Porsche Formel II Micro-Racer, Schuco #1037, red, lever control, friction, 4¼", NM (EX+ box), A......................**$100.00**

Pot Ball Clown, George Levy, 1935, clown w/parasol & duck atop chute, many actions, litho tin, 9½", EX+, A...**$1,025.00**

Powerful Katrinka, Fontaine Fox, 1923, Katrinka advances as she lifts Jimmy up & down in wheelbarrow, 6½", VG, A...**$1,400.00**

Rabbit, Schuco, tin & plush, cloth dressed, jtd swiveling hands & arms, unmarked, 6½", EX, A................................**$110.00**

Rabbit w/Cymbals, Gunthermann, 9½", EX, A.............**$375.00**

Race Car Loop, Arnold/US Zone, car shoots around loop & automatically stops, litho tin, M (EX plain box), A.**$200.00**

Racer, 1925, goggled driver in brn & blk racer w/running boards, JN-47 on license plate, 7", EX, from $300 to..........**$400.00**

Racer #8, Schuco, 1950s, 5½" long, D10, $125.00.

Racer #32, Tipp, litho tin w/molded driver, 16", EX, A.**$2,900.00**

Racing Cycle, Technofix, litho tin, rider in red & bl w/#2 tag, metal front wheel turns, 7", VG, A...........................**$140.00**

Rowboat Carnival Ride, US Zone, child in ea of 4 rowboats that swing as melody plays, striped canopy overhead, 9", NM, A...**$400.00**

Silver Mine Express #314, Technofix/West Germany, car travels around mine & returns, 23", unused, MIB, A..........**$150.00**

Smitty Scooter, Nifty, 1920s, 8", G, A...........................**$600.00**

Solisto Clown Drummer, Schuco/US Zone, vibrates while beating snare drum, tin w/cloth clothes, 4½", NM, A....**$195.00**

Solisto Clown Drummer, Schuco/US Zone, vibrates while beating snare drum, tin w/cloth clothes, 4½", NM+ (EX box), A **$365.00**

Solisto Clown Drummer, Schuco/US Zone, vibrates while beating snare drum, tin w/cloth clothes, 4½", EX (EX box), A **$280.00**

Solisto Clown Violinist, Schuco/US Zone, vibrates while playing, tin w/cloth clothes, 4½", MIB, A......................**$350.00**

Solisto Monkey Violinist, Schuco/US Zone, vibrates while playing, tin w/cloth clothes, 4½", MIB, A......................**$218.00**

Speedboat 2050, litho tin w/full-figure driver, 9", EX.....**$175.00**

Strawbridge & Clothier Van, Tipp, litho tin, w/driver & opening rear door, 7¾", VG+, A **$1,980.00**

Studio 1050, the Steerable Driving School Car, Schuco, steering wheel controls direction, tin, 5½", NM (EX box), A..**$260.00**

Super Constellation Lufthansa Plane, Tipp, friction, litho tin, 4-prop, battery-op wing lights, 18½", EX **$250.00**

Thunderbird, PN, bl & silver litho tin w/compo driver, working horn & windshield wipers, friction, 13", NM (VG+ box), A...**$150.00**

Tick-Tack Express, US Zone, 2 buses travel back & forth into tunnels & station house, 18", EX (G box), A..........**$225.00**

Tipp Co Sedan, 1930s, cream & brn litho tin, 9¼", missing seat o/w G, A...**$375.00**

Tipping Hat Clown, 1950s, advances in vibrating motion while tipping hat, litho tin, 6", scarce, EX, A...................**$540.00**

Toonerville Trolley, Nifty, ca 1922, red and yellow lithographed tin, 5", NM, $950.00.

Toonerville Trolley, Nifty, ca 1922, red & yel litho tin, 5", EX, S10...**$750.00**

Town Car, Bing, litho tin, w/driver, 7", EX, A.............**$795.00**

Toy Vendor, 1930s, man raises toys on string & eyes shift as monkeys swings under box, 6½", VG, S10...............**$500.00**

Tractor, Distler, w/driver, gr litho tin w/red wheels, 7", EX, M5...**$370.00**

Traffic Crossing, Technofix, 2 cars travel base lithoed w/traffic scenes & cop figure directing traffic, 19", MIB, A...**$300.00**

Traveler, Schuco, 1940s, clown w/suitcase, broken spring o/w EX, S9 ....**$150.00**

Triumphator, flat tin pnt horse & rider on gyroscope, tin base, 4", EX (VG box), A...**$180.00**

Twin Racers, RN, 2 litho tin racers attached to rod advance & change positions, 5", NM (EX box), from $125 to ..**$200.00**

Uncle Wiggily Car, crazy-quilt pattern, fading on 1 side, arm w/cane & ears rpl by Joe Freeman's Tin Toy Works, M12 ....$2,500.00

Varianto-3010 Auto Set, Schuco, 1930s, complete with track and buildings (not shown), D10, $750.00.

Wright Bros Type Airplane, Gunthermann, celluloid prop, litho tin pilot, 7", EX, A $1,000.00
XK 120 Jaguar, Prameta/British Zone, travels w/3 speeds, chrome-plated, rubber whitewalls, cop-shaped key, 6", EX+, A $235.00
Zeppelin Go Round, Mueller Kadeder, pnt tin, 10½", VG, A $770.00
Zeppelin w/Gondola, pnt tin w/paper props, early, 8", EX (orig box & instructions), A $685.00
Zeppelin w/Man in Gondola, Muller Kadeder, pnt tin, 10", missing parachute & man that climbs string underneath, VG, A $1,100.00
100 Sedan, mk GAMA Patent/Schuco License, bl tin, 6¼", scarce, non-working o/w NM, (VG+ box), A $210.00

JAPANESE

Acrobat & Clown on Highbar, CK, tin w/celluloid figures, 12", G (G box), A $65.00
AHA, #550, 5½", EX+, M5 ....$385.00
Air Carousel, ATC, 3 planes w/child riders swing away from tower, lever action, celluloid & litho tin, 6", EX, A.$118.00
Allied Van Truck, gray, red, gr & silver horse transport van, litho tin, friction, 9", MIB, A $150.00
American Circus Truck, litho tin truck pulling 2 circus wagons w/a tiger & elephant, friction, 19", NM, A $315.00
Amphibious Nautilus Y-10 Submarine, Yonezawa, advances on wheels w/crank lever on deck, litho tin, 15", EX (EX+ box), A $200.00
Amusement Park Rocket Ride, Yone, 2 rockets circle tower w/bell, litho tin, 8" base, EX (VG box), A $218.00
Apache Rider, Haji, litho tin, 7", G (orig box), A $40.00
Arty the Trapeze Artist, Toyland Toys, tumbles & sommersaults on trapeze, celluloid, 12", scarce, MIB, A $150.00

Atom Motorcycle, TN, litho tin cycle w/rider that dismounts, 11½", VG, A..............$250.00
Atom Speedboat, Sankyo Toys, NMIB, W5 ....$210.00
Atomboat, Sajo, pilot in red tin boat w/rear fins, Harbor Command lettered on roof, 11", NM (EX box) $200.00
Auto Cycle, KT, prewar, Japanese soldier on advancing camouflaged cycle w/sparking machine gun, 5¾", NM (VG+ box), A $305.00
Auto Dockyard Crane, Linemar, 1950, VG+, R7 ....$75.00
Automatic Racing Game, Haji, red, gr & yel cars race out of garage w/driveway, plunger action lever, EX+ (EX+ box), A .$250.00

Babes in Toyland Soldier, Linemar/WDP, 1961, lithographed tin, 7", EX, from $325.00 to $375.00.

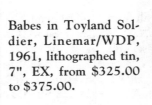

Ball-Playing Giraffe, TPS, litho tin w/rubber ears, clockwork mechanism, 8½", EX-NM, S10, from $400 to $450.00
Banjo Bunny, Alps, wht celluloid bunny sitting on red tree trunk playing banjo, 8", NM (G box), A $225.00
Bar-B-Que Bear, Alps, plush bear pours sauce on hamburger & takes a bite, 7", EX+ (EX box), A $145.00
Barney on Dino, advances in waddling motion w/sound, litho tin & vinyl, 8½", EX+ (EX+ box), A $535.00
Batman, Billiken/DC, 1989, walks, arms swing, litho tin w/vinyl cape, 9", MIB, A $145.00
Battleship Destroyer, TN, litho tin, 8", G, from $30 to $60.00
Big League Hockey Player, TPS, red, yel & bl litho tin, aluminum stick & puck, clockwork mechanism, EX $325.00
Billy Boy the Porter, porter pushes labeled steamer trunk, litho tin & celluloid, 4", scarce, NM+, A $310.00
Bleating Pig, CM, moves w/vibration & nodding head, celluloid w/hand-painted features, 5½", EX+ (EX box), A $135.00
Bob Sleigh, jtd figure seated on sled, friction, 6", MIB, A .$45.00
Bobby's Crazy Car, KO, early 1950s, tin clown w/vinyl head & moving arms in red litho tin bumper car, 8", NM (EX box), A $350.00

Bear Golfer, TPS, twists and hits ball across ramp into hole, lithographed tin with rubber ears, 7¼", from $160.00 to $300.00.

Bobo the Strong Man, TPS, bounces ball from hand to hand, 6", EX, A $450.00

Boxing Boys, 2 figures on wheeled base, celluloid & litho tin, 5¼", VG (VG box), A.............................$55.00

Boxing Dog, Y, staggers from side to side & boxes in erratic motion, litho tin & plush, 6", MIB, A $85.00

Boy on Tricycle, prewar, celluloid boy on trike w/bell, 5¼", NM (EX box), A.......................................$215.00

Boy on Wagon, pnt celluloid boy rides litho tin wagon w/Indian graphics, 3", EX, A......................................$85.00

Bubbling Boy, San, lowers head, blower dips into pan & he blows bubbles, litho tin, 8", NM (NM box), S10, from $175 to...$225.00

Bucking Bronco, 1950s, cowboy bounces up & down on bucking horse, celluloid & litho tin, 5½", MIB, A...............$115.00

Bump-&-Go FD Car, mystery action as fire chief moves arms & steers, litho tin, hand-crank friction, 6½", MIB, A .$100.00

Busy Mouse, TPS, litho tin mouse on 6x9" base, EX (orig box), S9 ....$125.00

Butterfield Stagecoach, Alps, litho tin stage & horses, no driver, scratches, works but wheels don't turn, 13", G, A $50.00

Calypso Joe, Linemar, native in grass skirt beats tune on tom-tom, rocking platform, 6", EX, A $125.00

Camera Shooting (Cine) Bear, Linemar, clothed bear lifts camera to lighted eyes, worms shoot out of camera, 11", MIB, A..$1,100.00

Camouflage Soldier Cycle, Usagayi, mk C-7 Combat, advances w/siren sound, litho tin, friction, 8", EX, A $225.00

Candy Loving Canine, TPS, flips candy in mouth, litho tin, 6", NM, S10, from $200 to $225.00

Car & House Trailer, red car pulls silver-colored trailer w/port-hole-type windows & doors, friction, 11", VG, A......$90.00

Carousel Truck, TN, truck advances as carousel w/3 figures on horses spin in truck bed, friction, 8½", EX, A..........$145.00

Cary the Crow, hopping tin crow lithoed w/blk suit, checked vest & red bow tie & hat, MIB, from $150 to..........$175.00

Cary the Crow, Linemar, litho tin, EX, S10 ....$100.00

Cat w/Vacuum Cleaner, Linemar, 1950s, advances in vibrating motion w/twirling tail, litho tin, 3½", NM (NM box), A...$150.00

Central Express Car, TT, mk Super Express, litho tin, friction, 6", MIB, A $105.00

Central RR Train, wheels & connectors move, siren sound, litho tin, friction, 8½", MIB, A.............................$95.00

Champ on Ice Bear Skater Trio, TPS, three bears dressed in winter outfits, 9", EX (EX box), $600.00.

Champion Indy Racer #33, 1950s, litho tin w/rubber wheels, friction, 4", NM, A $110.00

Cheery Cook, pnt celluloid boy w/plate moves erratically, 4½", EX (EX box), A $40.00

Child Indian in War Paint, Y, 1950, MIB, R7..............$130.00

Circus Boat, KO, clown driver rocks as boat moves w/mystery action, litho tin & vinyl, friction, 7", NM (EX box), A..$140.00

Circus Boy, rings bell while moving head side to side & shifts sign, litho tin in 1950s colors, 6½", EX, A..............$220.00

Circus Clown, MT, does antics from the highbar, litho tin w/cloth limbs & rubber hands, 5", scarce, NM (EX+ box), A...$300.00

Circus Clown Robot in Mercedes, ATC/Cragstan, mk Circus 8, driver catapults from seat, siren sound, 8 ", NM (NM box), A...$2,300.00

Circus Cyclist, TPS, clown in cloth outfit advances as bell rings, litho tin, 6½", NM (NM box), A..........................$900.00

Circus Elephant, advances on hind wheels as she pushes plastic ball & parasol spins, 7", NM (EX box), A $100.00

Circus Parade, TPS, 1950s, 11", EX, from $325.00 to $375.00.

Circus Parade, TPS, 11", MIB, S10, from $400 to $500.00

Circus Plane, Yone, litho tin clown pilot in plane that advances & flips over, 3¼", NM (EX+ box), A $140.00

Circus Seal, TPS, waddles while balancing ball on his nose, plush w/tin feet, 6½", EX (VG+ box), A $80.00

Circus Trailer, K, elephant & tiger sway in cages as cab advances, litho tin, 18", NM (NM box), A $625.00

Circus Train, SKK, as train advances tiger's body spins, clown faces at both ends, friction, 15", NM (EX+ box), A ..$90.00

Circus Tricycle, advances in erratic circular motion, litho tin w/celluloid figure, 5", scarce, MIB, A.......................$120.00

Circus Truck w/Animals & Voice, TN, mk World Circus, litho tin, friction, 10", NM (NM box), A.........................$300.00

Cleo Clown Training the Dog, TPS, litho tin clown holds felt hoop while dog circles & jumps through, NM (EX+ box) $350.00

Climbing Pirate, TPS, climbs up & down string pulled by finger loops, litho tin, 7", scarce, NM (EX box), A $290.00

Climbing Pirate, TPS, climbs up & down string pulled by finger loops, litho tin, 7", scarce, VG, S10........................$100.00

Climbo the Climbing Clown, TPS, moves w/jtd arms & legs up & down string, litho tin, 7", NM (EX box), A $425.00

Clown, TN, tips hat & wiggles red nose, moves cane as body rises & lowers, clothed tin w/vinyl head, 8", NM (EX box), A $135.00

Clown Jalopy Cycle, TPS, clown's head bobs as cycle goes, breaks apart when it hits object, friction, 9", NM (EX box), A $725.00

Clown Magician, TN, clown stands behind pedestal, lifts hat & rabbit appears, litho tin & cloth, 7", EX+ (EX+ box) $600.00

Clown Musician, moves w/trumpet in mouth, cloth body w/vinyl head & wooden shoes, 10", EX (EX box), A $60.00

Clown on Roller Skates, TPS, swings leg, leans forward & skates around, tin w/bl cloth pants, VG-EX, S10...............$325.00

Clown w/Lion, TPS, lion jumps through red felt hoop, litho tin, 6", NM (EX+ box), S10 ....$350.00

Comet DH 106 Airplane, Modern Toys, litho tin, friction, 6½", G, A $60.00

Consolidated Freightways Tractor Trailer, silver & gr w/opening rear doors, friction, 15½", EX, A $110.00

Continental Trailways Silver Eagle Bus, wht silver & red tin w/plastic tires & windows, NM (EX box), A $60.00

Convertible Ship, friction, litho tin, changes from warship to steamship by lever control, 12", missing gun (rpr box), A $75.00

Convertible w/Boy & Dog, friction, pnt & litho tin, red, driver's head turns as car moves, 8", EX (orig box) $400.00

Convertible w/Donald Duck Driver, Linemar/WDP, litho tin w/celluloid figure, friction, 5", NM (EX box), A $600.00

Covered Wagon, K, litho tin wagon, driver & horses w/Indian graphics, friction, 9", VG, A.......................................$60.00

Cowboy, Occupied Japan, celluloid child, red hat & shirt, yel neckerchief, guns move up & down, 5", EX, A $150.00

Cowboy Riding Horse, prewar, horse realistically prances, celluloid, 8", rare, NM, A...$150.00

Cowboy w/Lariat, spins rope & sways, celluloid head w/cloth pants & hat, 8¼", EX, A $100.00

Crazy Car, Yone, clown's head spins as car advances, gr w/red plastic spoked wheels, 5", MIB, A............................$112.00

Dancing Couple, Occupied Japan, MIB, S10..................$125.00

Dancing Sam, litho tin figure dances on revolving base, working, 8¾", EX (orig box), S10 ....$200.00

Dandy, man walks as front of shoes move, tips hat & rolls eyes, litho hand, 10", NM (EX+ box)...............................$250.00

Daredevil-Acrobatic Stunt-Motorcycle, Alps, goggled driver moves body as motorcycle tumbles, 5½", EX+ (EX box), A $150.00

Delicious Ice Cream Truck, HTC, 1950s, travels w/bell noise, canopy roof, rear door opens, 8", EX+ (EX box), A .$500.00

Delivery Cycle, KO, boy on cycle w/delivery box on rear, friction, NM+ (EX+ box), A $225.00

Dino Ferrari, YM, red tin w/plastic front & rear windows & steering wheel, friction, 11", EX+, A $275.00

Dino the Dinosaur, Linemar/Hanna-Barbera, 1961, walks as he opens & closes his mouth, litho tin, 8", NM+ (M box), A..$1,040.00

Disney Airplane, Linemar/WDP, lithoed Disney characters w/Mickey as pilot, friction, 8" wingspan, EX+ (EX box), A..$1,425.00

Donald Duck Dipsy Car, Linemar/WDP, advances w/erratic action, litho tin w/plastic figure, 6", EX+ (NM box), A, from $725 to $925.00

Donald Duck Drummer, Linemar, advances & rocks while beating drum, litho tin, NM (EX+ box), A $675.00

Donald Duck Drummer, Linemar, advances & rocks while beating drum, litho tin, 6", VG, A..................................$375.00

Donald Duck Flivver, Linemar/WDP, push down on Donald's head for movement, characters lithoed on car, 5", EX+, A ..$255.00

Donald Duck Flivver, Linemar/WDP, push down on Donald's head for movement, characters lithoed on car, 5", NM (NM box), A..$795.00

Donald Duck Motorcyclist, Linemar/WDP, friction, 3½", EX+, A $250.00

Donald Duck on Rocking Horse, mk Made in Japan, early, rocks, celluloid on pressed steel base, 4½", EX+, A $1,400.00

Donald Duck Dipsy Doodle, Linemar, 1950s, Donald on tractor-type vehicle, metal body, 6" long, EX, D10, $675.00.

Donald Duck on Tricycle, Linemar/WDP, advances w/ringing bell, litho tin w/celluloid figure, 4", NM (NM box), A $725.00

Donald Duck the Acrobat, Linemar, Donald performs on trapeze, celluloid, 9", scarce, MIB, A $545.00

Donald Duck w/Huey & Voice, Linemar/WDP, pull rope for action & sound, litho tin, 5½", EX+ (EX+ box), A .$965.00

Driveway & Greyhound Bus, Fine Toys, 1950s, bus navigates rnd truck, litho tin, 8" dia, EX (VG box), A $175.00

Driving Pet #1, 1950s, moves back & forth as dog passenger barks, litho tin, friction, 7", MIB, A $150.00

Driving Pet #3, Ichiko, advances w/engine noise as dog in passenger seat moves & barks, friction, 7", NM (EX box), A..$150.00

Drummer Boy, prewar, boy in uniform advances & sways while beating drum, celluloid head & arms, 7½", EX (EX box), A..$205.00

Drummer Boy, prewar, boy in uniform advances & sways while beating drum, celluloid head & arms, 7½", EX, A...$140.00

Duckmobile, duck pops in & out of car, litho tin w/celluloid figure, friction, 6½", scarce, M (VG box), A $390.00

Dugan's Bakery Truck, wht & olive gr litho tin Divco truck, friction, 7", G+, A $110.00

Easter on Parade, MM, celluloid rabbit pulls sled w/3 chicks in basket on pressed steel base, 8", NM (NM box) $250.00

Educational Pet Pooch, TPS, turn dial & dog will nod head number of times the dial indicates, 4½", litho tin, MIB, A...$75.00

Elephant w/Road Roller, KO, litho tin, NMIB, A $68.00

Elf on Donkey, tin, 6", NM, A $25.00

Emergency Fire Chief Helicopter, advances w/spinning prop, litho tin, 6", MIB, A $85.00

Emergency Police Helicopter, advances w/spinning prop, litho tin, MIB, A $85.00

Fairy Land Taxi, TPS, beetle pulls leaf w/monkey driver & 2 squirrels that turn, litho tin, 12", NM (EX box), A.$200.00

Fast Freight Semi, friction, 13", EX+, M5 ....$70.00

FD Fire Engine, TN, fireman raises & lowers flag as bell rings, adjustable ladder, friction, 11", MIB, A $200.00

Ferdinand the Bull, Linemar/WDP, 1950s, advances w/twirling tail & head movement, litho tin, 5½", scarce, EX...$250.00

Ferris Wheel Truck, TN, children spin in Ferris wheel as truck advances, litho tin, 8½", NM (NM box), A $415.00

Fire Chief Car, Ichiko, mk FD 176 on hood, advances w/siren & warning light, litho tin, friction, 8", G (G box), A ...$85.00

Fire Engine w/Siren & Bell, Y, 1950s, push button & fireman goes up ladder, w/sound, friction, 11", EX (G box), A $160.00

Fishing Bear, TPS, litho tin bear w/rubber ears bounces fish in & out of net, 7", NM (EX+ box) $375.00

Fishing Boy, Linemar, boy spins & fish wraps around pole, litho tin, 4", MIB...$225.00

Fishing Monkey on Whale, TPS, whale moves & rocks as fish move & fins flap, litho tin, 9", EX+ (G box), A......$495.00

Flag Fire Engine No 4, TN, advances w/sound & spinning extension ladder, litho tin, friction, 6", NM (VG box), A....$150.00

Flintstone Turnover Tank, Linemar, 1961, advances as Fred forces tank to flip over, 4", NM (scarce VG box), A...........**$650.00**

Flower Delivery Sedan, Bandai, friction, Ford Lasts Longer on panels, litho tin, bl, 12", non-working, G, A...........**$200.00**

Flying Birds, TPS, 2 birds fly & chirp above 4½" dia base w/farmhouse, litho tin, NM (EX+ box) **$200.00**

Flying Fish Boat, Asahi, friction, litho tin racing boat, red & gr hull, 11", VG, A **$50.00**

Flying Jeep, Daiya, mk US Army X3, advances w/visible spinning engines, litho tin, friction, 9", NM (EX+ box), A **$150.00**

Four-Alarm Firehouse & Car, Alps, NMIB, W5 ....**$300.00**

Fox the Magician, NGT, fox behind stand lifts hat to reveal rabbit, tin & plush, 6½", NM (EX+ box), A **$335.00**

Fred Flintstone on Dino, Linemar, 1962, tin Dino moves w/growling noise, Fred w/vinyl head, NM (scarce EX+ box), A **$750.00**

Fred Flintstone on Dino, Linemar, 8", non-working, EX+, M5 ....**$200.00**

Fred Flintstone Tricycle, Linemar, celluloid figure on tin trike w/bell, 4¼", M (EX+ box), A **$600.00**

Funny Tiger, plays drum, 6½", NM+ (EX box), M5 ....**$95.00**

Future Car, Meiko, advances w/siren, bubble dome top & bullet-shaped lights, friction, 9", scarce, NM (EX box), A .**$575.00**

Gay Cabellero, Alps, Mexican in sombrero on vibrating donkey w/spinning tail, celluloid, 6", NM (EX box), A **$200.00**

Girl on Motorcycle, Haji, friction, red cycle, girl w/vinyl head, synthetic ponytail, 8", EX-, A **$50.00**

Girl w/Chickens, TPS, girl simulates throwing feed to chickens as she nods her head, litho tin, 5", EX (EX box), A.**$365.00**

Go-Go Chimpee, Alps, 1960, MIB, R7..............................**$75.00**

Godzilla Egg, Takara, 1988, bursts out of egg & walks, MIP, S2 ....**$85.00**

Good Humor Ice Cream Truck, friction, sliding red & wht canopy, ringing bells, 11", non-working, G-, A **$55.00**

Good Time Charlie, Alps, clown moves up & down & circles while twirling cane & blowing party horn, 10", NM (EX box), A...**$392.00**

Goofy, see also Whirling Tail Goofy w/Turtle

Goofy's #3 Disneyland Stock Car, Linemar, 1955, red & yel tin w/lithoed characters, 6", EX+, A..............................**$275.00**

Graham Paige No 3, CK, features automatic stopper, bl & silver, tin w/spare tire mounted on trunk, 6", EX (EX box), A..**$245.00**

Greyhound Scenicruiser Bus, Daiya, 1950s, blk, silver & wht w/blk rubber tires, friction, 8½", NM (EX box), A **$80.00**

Greyhound Scenicruiser Bus, Stone, 1950s, center scenic roof & luggage rack, friction, 10½", EX (EX box), A..........**$100.00**

Greyhound Sightseeing Bus, New York marquee, roof windows, whitewall tires, friction, 9", EX, A **$50.00**

Guardsman on Parade, Mikuni, soldier on horse advances as 2 trailing soldiers bob around, 9", NM (EX box), from $150 to..**$200.00**

Gull Speedboat, ATC, NMIB, W5 ....**$150.00**

Gyron, futuristic style, press button & dome flips up, red w/blk top, friction, 8½", EX (VG box), A **$270.00**

Ham 'N Sam, Linemar, Sam dances as Ham plays piano, words to 'Solid Jackson' lithoed on piano, 5½", EX+ **$1,000.00**

Gay '90s Cyclist, TPS, 1950s, lithographed tin, 7", EX, from $275.00 to $325.00.

Happy the Violinist, TPS, clown with stilt legs sways as he plays violin, lithographed tin and plush, 8½", MIB, $350.00.

Happy Hippo, TPS, bump-&-go action as Hippo tries to eat bananas, litho tin, 6", NM..................................$325.00

Happy Mr Penguin, San, advances in waddling motion w/quacking sound, litho tin, 6", M (rpr box), A $135.00

Happy Pig, prewar Japan, celluloid pig stands on bellows while pushing tin cart w/4 celluloid chicks, 7", EX, A $450.00

Happy Pup Car, pup opens mouth as car advances, red & bl litho tin, 8", G+, A..$40.00

Happy Skaters, TPS/Cragstan, rabbit skates in realistic motion, 6", NM (EX+ box), A..$650.00

Happy Speed Car, Hadson, prewar, litho tin trolley, EX+, A..$30.00

Happy-Go-Lucky (Bobo) Magician, TN, lifts top hat & rabbit & chick appear, litho tin, 9", EX+ (NM box), from $650 to...$750.00

Harley-Davidson Motorcycle, TN, 3 moving pistons, blk tin w/rubber tires, wheels turn, friction, 9", VG, A.......$150.00

Henry Eating Ice-Cream Cone, Linemar, vibrates while head moves as if eating cone, tin w/cloth tongue, 5½", EX+, A..$725.00

Henry on Elephant, Borgfeldt, turbaned boy on vibrating elephant w/ears wiggling & Henry on trunk, 8", EX+ (G box), A..$1,450.00

Highway Patrol Car, SY, late 1950s, blk & wht Plymouth w/roof light, friction, 8½", VG (VG+ box), A....................$165.00

Honey Bear, Alps, blk plush bear licks bees' nest while bee flies overhead, 7", EX+ (EX box), A $200.00

Honeymoon Cottage, Linemar, train goes in circle under 3 tunnels, gate rises & lowers, cottage in center, 7" sq, EX+, A..$150.00

Honeymoon Express, Linemar, NMIB, S10....................$275.00

Honk-Along Children Bus, Kanto Toys, music plays as bus advances, litho tin, friction, 8½", EX+ (EX box), A..$130.00

Hot Rod w/Dog Driver, MS, mk Hot Dog Rod, advances as full-figure dog barks & rocks, friction, 8", EX+ (EX box), A...$205.00

House Trailer, AN, red tin sedan pulls trailer, friction, non-working o/w VG+ (G+ box), A $75.00

House Trailer, SSS, 1950s, car pulls trailer, porthole windows w/adjustable awnings, opening door, 11", M (EX box), A..$270.00

Howdy Doody's Pal Clarabell, Linemar/Kagran, 1950s, cable control, 7", NM (EX+ box)....................................$750.00

Hula-Hoop Monkey, Plaything, 1950s, monkey stands on barrel & hula-hoops, litho tin, 10", NM (EX box), A.......$100.00

Hurricane Racer, Midoriya Tokyo/Occupied, tin racer w/celluloid driver, tin balloon tires, friction, 5", M (EX box), A..$200.00

Hustling Bulldozer, KO, mystery bump-&-go action, driver steers, litho tin, hand-crank friction, 6", MIB, A $120.00

Ice Cream Vendor, Occupied Japan, boy rides cycle behind cart mk Ice Cream, celluloid, 4", pnt chips, VG (EX box), A..$125.00

Indians in Canoe, litho tin canoe, 2 Indians drumming & paddling, friction, 9½", VG..$175.00

Infants Bus 305, SN, lithoed animals & people, friction, 8½", MIB, A..$100.00

Jalopy Stock Car #3, NGS, mk 30 HP on hood, red & blk, litho tin w/plastic underside, friction, 6¼", NM (NM box), A..$170.00

Jet Speedboat, K Toys, NMIB, W5 ....$210.00

JFK Rocking Chair, see Political category

Jimmy the Clown, 6", NMIB, A....................................$450.00

Joe the Acrobat, TPS, clown w/cloth pants rolls forward on ball, litho tin, 6", scarce, EX (EX box), A......................$800.00

John the Naughty, bald-headed toddler tries to run as dog bites his behind, celluloid, 6", scarce, NM+ (EX box), A.$455.00

Joker (Batman), Billiken/DC, 1989, walks & swings arms, litho tin, 9", MIB..$100.00

Jolly Pig, advances w/clown pulling his tail, celluloid, 7", MIB, A..$165.00

Jolly Snake, TPS, wiggles as head turns side to side, litho tin, 7½", NM (EX box), A..$165.00

Juggling Clown, Linemar, swivels & spins arms while balancing plate of fruit on his nose, 8½", NM (EX+ box), A .$1,300.00

Juggling Clown, TN, sways while balancing plates on rods overhead, tin body w/vinyl head, 8½", MIB, from $300 to..$400.00

Juggling Duck & His Friends, TPS, duck balances implements on his nose & pulls 3 squirrels, tin, 9", NM (EX box), A.$284.00

Jumbo Bubble Blowing Elephant, Y, plush elephant on tin base puts trunk into cup & blows bubbles, 7", NM (EX box), A..$105.00

Jumping Clown, Mikuni, clown holding felt cloth & metal cane jumps, dances & tips his hat, 6½", NM (EX+ box) .$200.00

Jumping Rocket, SY, primitive robot rides in rocket w/legs that jump, litho tin, 6", NM (EX+ box), A....................$275.00

Jungle Constructor Elephant, KO, pulls drum & bell rings, head nods & ears flap, litho tin, 7½", MIB, A..................$200.00

Jungle Monkey, TE, monkey swings & circles sm tree while the other climbs lg fruit tree, 12", EX+ (EX box), A $135.00

Huckleberry Aeroplane, Linemar/Hanna-Barbera, 1961, lithographed tin with vinyl figure, friction, 10" long, NMIB, A, $675.00.

K-360 3-Wheel Delivery Truck, Bandai, pnt & litho tin, red & wht, tan bed & interior, 7½", EX, A $375.00

Katnip Bobbin' Head, Linemar, litho tin figure vibrates w/spring bobbing head, EX, A $195.00

Knitting Cat, TN, wht plush cat w/glasses realistically knits, litho tin base, 6", NM (EX+ box), A $125.00

Knitting Minnie, Linemar, mc litho tin & cloth w/rubber ears, clockwork mechanism, 7½", VG-EX, S10 ....$800.00

KO-KO Sandwich Man, TN, tin clown w/vinyl head & wearing sign tips hat & wiggles nose, moves up & down, NM (EX+ box)..$250.00

Lady Bug Family, TPS, mother bug pulls 3 kids behind her as they turn & zigzag, litho tin, 12", M (EX box) $100.00

Liberty Ferry, Y, bus & ferry travel around New York Harbor, 26", MIB, A...$800.00

Lighted Pom-Pom Guns, Linemar, friction truck w/battery-op lighted pom-pom guns manned by soldier, 16", NM (EX box), A..$180.00

Lincoln Wagon, Boat & Trailer, Olympic, friction, NMIB, W5...$270.00

Little Shoemaker, Alps, shoemaker hammers nail in shoe, litho tin w/cloth shirt & orig hat, 6", EX+ (EX+ box), A.$175.00

Long Haulage Truck, TPS, orange & gr litho tin open panel truck w/full-figure driver, tin wheels, 10", G, A $120.00

Louie in His Dream Car, Linemar/WDP, litho tin w/celluloid figure, friction, 4¾", NM (EX+ box), A $575.00

Lucky Baby Sewing Machine, Marusan/Japan, celluloid seamstress, 5", NMIB, A..$475.00

Magic Circus, TPS, monkey & seal dance & shake w/magnetic action on platform, litho tin & plastic, 6", NM (NM box), A...$195.00

Magic Tunnel & Dream Land Bus, TPS, bus travels around carnival base, litho tin, NM (EX+ box), A $175.00

Mammal of the Seas, J, fish on string held in front of whale who opens mouth to gobble up fish, NM+ (EX box), A .$230.00

Mary & Her Little Lamb, CK, prewar, Mary advances while pulling lamb behind her, celluloid, 4", M (EX box), A $275.00

McDonnell Demon Navy Jet, Bandai, lithoed pilot, wht w/navy & red trim, friction, 7", NM (M box), A.................$145.00

Merry Ball Blowing Circus Car, KO, advances while balancing Styrofoam ball above in stream of air, friction, 5", EX+, A..$60.00

Merry Christmas Santa Claus, TN, tin Santa w/celluloid head & arms holds sign & rings bell, 5", G (VG box), A.......$75.00

Merry Christmas Santa Claus, TN, tin Santa w/celluloid head & arms holds sign & rings bell, 5", M (EX box), A $125.00

Merry Gondola, Alps, lithoed carnival ride on sq base travels up & down on undulating sides w/bell noise, NM+ (M box), A..$460.00

Merry-Go-Round, Alps, 4 gondolas w/child riders circle above base, litho tin w/celluloid balloons, 10", EX (VG+ box), A..$250.00

Merry-Go-Round Truck, TN, Country Fair Series, advances & spins w/3 kids on horses, friction, scarce, EX (EX box), A......$300.00

Mickey Driver, Linemar, advances w/non-fall action as Mickey waves & nods head, litho tin, 6½", rare, NM (EX box), A..$865.00

Mickey Mouse Dipsy Car, Linemar/WDP, advances w/erratic action, litho tin w/plastic figure, 6", EX (NM box), A...$725.00

Mickey Mouse Dipsy Car, Linemar/WDP, advances w/erratic action, litho tin car & figure, 6", NM (EX+ box), A .$1,225.00

Mickey Mouse Motorcyclist, Linemar/WDP, litho tin, friction, 3⅝", EX+ $400.00

Mickey Mouse on Trapeze, Borgfeldt, celluloid Mickey flies up & over wire bar, 8", EX+ (G box), A......................$660.00

Mickey Mouse on Tricycle, prewar, rides in circles, litho tin & celluloid, 4", scarce, NM+, A $1,118.00

Mickey Mouse Roller Skater, Linemar, 7", NM (EX box), A..$600.00

Mickey Mouse the Unicyclist, Linemar, litho tin w/cloth outfit & rubber ears, 5½", NM (NM box), A................$1,850.00

Mickey Mouse Xylophone Player, Linemar, Mickey plays xylophone w/metal sticks, litho tin, 6½", EX, A $565.00

Mighty Aircraft Carrier & Helicopter, Cragstan, plane sparks & helicopter blade spins, friction, 9½", NM (EX+ box), A..$160.00

Military Motorcycle, TYDY, celluloid Japanese soldier on camouflaged cycle w/sparking machine gun, 7", EX, from $445 to..$600.00

Minnie Mouse in Rocking Chair, Linemar, 1950s, chair rocks as Minnie knits, 7", NM, $575.00.

Monkey Banana Vender (sic), Yone, 1950s, tin monkey pulls cart w/2 lg yel plastic bananas, 8", NM (EX box), A $150.00

Monkey Basketball Player, TPS, monkey bends over & shoots underhand into basket, litho tin, 8", NM (EX box), S10..$375.00

Monkey Batter, AAA, bat raises, head turns & tail spins while moving about, litho tin, 7", NM (EX box), A $515.00

Monkey Cycle, Bandai, driver rings bell & eyes pop in & out of his head, 'Comic Circus' on flag, 5", NM (EX+ box), A ..$222.00

Monkey Dean, KSK, advances in crouched position, plush w/celluloid face, 6", EX+ (EX box), A $110.00

Monkey Machine Gun, MM, plush monkey dressed in western attire vibrates while shooting gun, 7½", MIB, A $85.00

Monkey on Seal, Japan, 4", EX, A.....................................$30.00

Monkey Rider, Kanto Toys, monkey slides off & on rear wheel, full-figure driver, 6", EX+ (EX box), A $485.00

Motorcycle Racer #27, 1960s, litho tin w/full-figure driver, friction, 3½", NM, A...$90.00

Motorcycle Racer #3, Linemar, litho tin w/driver, friction, 3¼", NM+, A...$155.00

MP Motorcycle, w/driver, MT, litho tin w/siren, rear plate mk USA 165, friction, 7", NM (EX+ box), A $350.00

Mr Dan Coffee-Drinking Man, TN, 1960s, litho tin, working, MIB, S10, from $125 to..$200.00

Mr Dan Hot Dog Eating Man, TN, lifts hot dog to mouth, chews & wipes mouth, 7", M (NM box), S10, from $125 to..$225.00

Mule & Elephant Rocking Horse, litho tin animals on rocking base lithoed w/stars & angels, 7¼", VG, A $150.00

Musical Bunny, TN, 1950, MIB, R7.............................$75.00

NBC Television Car, Asahitoy, mk Cragston Broadcasting Co Inc, cameras on roof, friction, 6", EX (EX box), from $200 to..$250.00

New Mode Wagon Bus, Marusan, friction, 12", non-working, EX-, M5 ....$140.00

New Sports Car, 1962, ATC, experimental Toyota, red tin w/NP trim, 10", G (orig box), A $50.00

Ocean Speedboat, Bandai, NMIB, W5 ....$250.00

Old Jalopy, Linemar, litho tin, red w/blk fenders, printed slogans, friction, 9", VG, A..$145.00

Old Timer Delivery Truck, SSS, flip-down windshield, turn crank in front, friction, 10½", NM (EX box), A......$100.00

Old Timer Locomotive, K/Japan, friction, litho tin, NM (VG+ box), M5 ....$45.00

Pango-Pango, TPS, brn-skinned native vibrates around as head & neck stretches back & forth, 6", EX, S10 ....$175.00

Pango-Pango, TPS, brown-skinned native vibrates around as head and neck stretches back and forth, 6", MIB, from $325.00 to $375.00.

Pegasus I Air Car, Toy Master, futuristic style w/4 circular engines, bl w/yel-tinted dome, friction, 9", EX (EX box), A $245.00

Pet Shop Truck, Cragstan, bl & yel litho tin w/swivel bed doors, friction, 11", EX+ (EX+ box), A $115.00

Peter Clown, KK, prewar, celluloid clown w/cloth clothes does somersaults, 6", EX+ (EX box) $280.00

Pigeon Scooter, litho tin sparking motor, friction, 6", non-working, VG, A $320.00

Pilot Harbor Boat, Bandai, NMIB, W5 ....$215.00

Playful Animal Swing, SY, bear & dog swing as their arms move, 6", M (EX box), A $165.00

Playful Pluto & Goofy, Linemar, figures vibrate around as rubber tails spin, 5¼", EX+ (EX box), A..........................$1,350.00

Playful Puppy, TPS, puppy on rectangular base chases butterfly, non-fall action, litho tin, 9" base, MIP, A $155.00

Pluto the Unicyclist, Linemar, 1950s, lithographed tin, 6", EX, from $600.00 to $800.00.

Olive Oyl Mechanical Tricycle with Revolving Bell, Linemar, 1950s, lithographed tin, MIB, from $1,500.00 to $1,800.00.

Playing Family Dach's Hund, S&E, mother dog advances in erratic action w/2 babies on her back, 11", EX+ (EX+ box), A $120.00

Pleasure Goose, Daiya, advances w/flapping wings & clicking sound, beak opens & closes, friction, 6", NM (EX box), A $125.00

Pluto, Linemar/WDP, walks & moves his head from side to side, wags tail, cloth over tin, 6", NM.........................$250.00

Pluto, see also Walking Pluto and Playful Pluto and Goofy

Pluto Delivery Wagon, Linemar/WDP, Pluto petals 'Mickey's Delivery Cart,' friction, 6", EX+, A $388.00

Pluto on Motorcycle, Linemar/WDP, litho tin, friction, 3½", EX+, A...$250.00

Pluto the Drum Major, Linemar/WDP, rocks while tooting horn & shaking bell & cane, litho tin, 6", EX+ (EX+ box), A $550.00

Poor Pete, bald-headed Black toddler w/melon tries to run as dog bites his behind, celluloid, 6", scarce, M, A.............$540.00

Popeye on High Wheel Bike, Linemar/KFS, circular motion w/ringing bell, litho tin, 6½", VG+, A $840.00

Popeye on Tricycle, Linemar, peddles trike as bell rings, litho tin w/celluloid arms & legs, 4", EX+, A $1,150.00

Popeye Pilot, lithographed tin, 8½" long, EX, $600.00.

Popeye Transit Co Moving Van, Linemar, 1950s, lithographed tin, friction, 14", NM, $950.00.

Popeye Turnover Tank, Linemar, flat Popeye figure underneath springs open to flip tank, 4", NM (EX+ box), A $750.00

Popeye Turnover Tank, Linemar, 4", EX+, M5 ....$325.00

Power Boat (Whiz), CK, prewar Japan, pnt tin, red & wht, sterno heater, w/pilot & sailor, 13", rare, EX+ (EX box), A .$600.00

Prehistoric Animal (dinosaur), Linemar, yel & gr, clockwork mechanism w/sound, 8", EX (orig box), S10, from $550 to...$600.00

Professor Ludwig Von Drake Go-Mobile, Linemar/WDP, 1961, litho tin w/vinyl head, friction, 6", NM+ (EX box), A.$270.00

Race Car, Sanyo, litho tin w/tin driver, much chrome trim, blk tin balloon tires, friction, 4½", NM (EX+ box), A..$200.00

Racer #8, YM, litho tin w/driver, yel, 8½", G, A $180.00

Racer #12, XM, litho tin, 8", VG (EX box), A................$325.00

Reading Santa Claus, Alps, 1950s, turns pages of book, 7", MIB, S9, from $225 to...$325.00

Record Racer, Bandai, litho tin sleek futuristic style, friction, 13", EX+, A...$400.00

Riding Cowboy, TN, mk Occupied Japan, horse gallops in awkward motion as cowboy holds on, celluloid, NM (NM box), A...$175.00

Roaring Lion, Alps/Occupied Japan, 1950, MIB, R7......$150.00

Rocket Racer #5, Hadson, w/helmeted driver, makes engine noise, lg blk rubber tires, friction, 6¼", EX+ (VG+ box), A...$155.00

Rocky Mountain Express, SE, 1950, MIB, R7.............$115.00

Rodeo Cowboy, Alps, twirls lasso over head & around waist as upper body moves, celluloid, tin, cloth, 9", NM (EX box), A...$135.00

S-1011 Police Car, 1952, litho tin, friction, 5", scarce, M (EX box), A...$110.00

Safety First Police Officer, Alps, stop-&-go action on litho tin platform w/bell, celluloid officer, 7½", NM, A $775.00

Sam the Strolling Skeleton, Mikuni, rocks while strolling, arms move, litho tin, 5½", EX+, from $125 to.................$150.00

Sam the Strolling Skeleton, Mikuni, rocks while strolling, arms move, litho tin, 5½", NM+ (EX+ box), from $200 to...$225.00

Sandwich Man, TN, advances while ringing bell & swinging sign, Eat At Joe's Diner, litho tin, 6½", scarce, EX..$350.00

Santa Claus, TN, Santa holds sign & rings bell, head sways, litho tin, 6", EX, S10 ....$150.00

Santa Claus Christmas Eve, reindeer pulls Santa, bell rings, celluloid on pressed steel base, EX+ (VG+ box), from $75 to $110.00

Santa Claus Cycle, 1950s, advances in circular motion w/ringing bell, litho tin & celluloid, 4½", M, A $105.00

Santa Claus on Sled, MM/Tokyo, 1940s, Santa travels in sleigh pulled by single deer, celluloid & tin, 8", NM (EX box), A...$105.00

Santa on Tricycle, Suzuki, 1940, NM, R7.....................$50.00

Satellite Launcher, TN, 1950, plastic disk spins off army truck, soldiers lithoed on windows, friction, NM (EX box), A...$200.00

Sea Queen Cabin Cruiser, Alps, NMIB, W5 ....$235.00

Sea Wolf, Alps, peg-legged pirate circles while eyes open & close, litho tin, 7", EX+, A $165.00

Seesaw, prewar, tin seesaw travels back & forth as celluloid boy & girl go up & down, 7", MIB, A..............................$300.00

Silver Jet Racer, litho tin w/tin driver, plastic tires, makes engine noise, friction, 10", NM (G box), A................$70.00

Silver Pigeon Cycle, female rider holding onto male driver, litho tin w/windshield & spare tire, friction, 5", EX, A....$435.00

Skating Chef, TPS, skates while holding plate, litho tin w/cloth pants, 6¾", VG (G- box) $225.00

Skating Hobo Clown, TPS, realistic skating motion w/push-off leg action, litho tin, 6", VG+.................................$200.00

Skip Rope Animals, TPS, sm bear skips rope twirled by dog & squirrel, litho tin, 8", EX+ (EX box), from $175 to .$200.00

Skip Rope Animals, TPS, sm bear skips rope twirled by dog & squirrel, litho tin, 8", M (EX box), from $225 to.....$250.00

Soldier, Yone, 1960s, EX, from $150.00 to $175.00; Chef, Yone, 1960s, EX, from $125.00 to $150.00; Pirate, Yone, 1960s, EX, from $175.00 to $200.00.

Skipping Puppy, TN, dog dressed as a young boy skips rope and nods head, lithographed tin, 6", NM (NM box), A, $110.00.

Stagecoach, 1950s, lithographed tin, complete with two horses and driver, friction, 9" long, M, $150.00.

Skippy the Tricky Cyclist, TPS, clown in cloth outfit rides unicycle, litho tin, 6", EX (EX box), S10, from $275 to....$350.00

Snapping Alligator, S&E, twists & snaps jaws w/sound as he tries to catch bee in front of him, tin, 12", NM (EX box), A $95.00

Snow Crop Frozen Foods Truck, H, bl & wht litho tin w/blk rubber tires, friction, 8½", NM (EX+ box), A..............$140.00

Soldier on Motorcycle, KT, tin w/camouflage design, 5½", G, A $175.00

Space Whale, KO, mk Pioneer, advances w/opening & closing mouth, rolling eyeballs & flapping ears, 9½", EX, A $495.00

Sparking Destroyer, TN, friction, NMIB, W5 ....$175.00

Sparkling Tank, prewar, mk US 385, head pops up & down, gun sounds & sparks, litho tin, 5", scarce, NMIB, A $138.00

Speedo Speedboat, Haji, red, wht & gr outboard runabout, litho tin, friction, 8½", VG, A $30.00

Standard Coffee Delivery Sedan, yel & blk Ford w/lift-up rear window, 12", G, A...$1,100.00

Star of the Day Clown, Cragstan, car advances as clown tips hat, turns head & waves, litho tin, friction, 6½", VG, A...$182.00

Starfire #52 Race Car, Marusan, silver, yel & red tin w/tin driver, blk rubber tires w/red hubs, friction, 12", EX+, A $165.00

Strutting Parade Bear, Alps, turns & twirls cane, mouth opens & closes w/sound, litho tin & cellulloid, 7", MIB, A...$120.00

Strutting Parade Duck, Alps, turns & twirls cane, bill opens & closes w/quacking sound, tin & celluloid, 7", NMIB, A $120.00

Strutting Sam, Linemar, Black man performs realistic tap dance on rnd drum-like lithoed stage, 11", NM (EX box), A $650.00

Suitcase Traveler, CK, prewar, celluloid man advances w/tin suitcase lithoed w/cities of the world, 4½", EX+, A.$175.00

Suketo Ningyo, roller skating couple w/bird between them, celluloid, friction, NM (EX+ box), A...........................$155.00

Super Electric Train, K, mk Super Express, advances w/ringing bell, litho tin, friction, 14", MIB, A........................$116.00

Super Rocket Ride, Yone, 2 litho tin rockets w/vinyl-headed boy riders perform loop-de-loop, 9", EX (EX box), A.....$235.00

Surprise Santa Claus, cloth Santa w/vinyl head pulls present from bag as he rings bell, 9", NM (EX box), A........$110.00

Suzy Bouncing Ball, TPS, Suzy bounces ball while arms move, vinyl head on tin body, 5", NM+ (EX box), A........$100.00

Swing Time Clock, B, baby swinging below clock, celluloid & litho tin, 9¼", G, A...$45.00

Tabby the Cat & Her Pet Canary, Alps, advances & shakes cage while trying to catch her bird, 10½", EX (VG box), A $275.00

Talking Police Car, Y, 1970, friction, MIB, R7.................$60.00

Tambourine Teddy, NGT, clothed plush bear sways as bells hit tambourines, 7", MIB, A $139.00

Tap Dancer, Occupied Japan, Black man in cloth clothes dances under Harlem street sign, 8", NM (orig box), from $420 to $600.00

Teacup Merry-Go-Round, MM, 3 plush bears spin in plastic teacups on ride w/umbrella, 8", NM (EX box), from $250 to $300.00

Photo courtesy of Scott Smiles.

Teddy's Cycle, Occupied Japan, 1950s, tin with celluloid figure, MIB, from $150.00 to $175.00.

Telephone Santa Claus, Alps, vinyl-headed Santa answers ringing phone & nods head as if to talk, 7", MIB, A $135.00

Television M889 Jeep, M, w/driver & 2 soldiers in back watching TV, tin w/blk rubber tires, friction, 17", NM (EX+ box), A...$320.00

Three Little Pigs & Big Bad Wolf, Linemar, hoppers, ea has box that converts into house, EX (NM boxes)............$2,000.00

Thunderbolt Cap Firing Tank, Frankonia, 1950s, automatic cap shooting & smoke effect, friction, 8", scarce, MIB, A..$120.00

Tigger Plane, S&E, pull trigger & plastic props spins, press lever to shoot wing rockets, tin, 7½", NM (EX box), A...$110.00

Tita the Hopping Monkey, Alps, holds banana & hops around, litho tin & plush, 6", MIB, A..................................$120.00

Tom & Dick Hand Car, Exelo, men working handlebars propel car as pistons move inside, friction, 6", MIB, A $125.00

Tom Tom Canoe, MS, 2 Indian chiefs in canoe that moves along as 1 Indian rows & 1 beats drum, 9½", NM (EX box), A...$630.00

Town to Town, CK, prewar, circus boy balances lg block on his nose, litho tin & pressed steel, 6½", EX (EX box), A...$224.00

Trick Seal, Alps, red celluloid seal twirls ball on nose as he advances, 5½", M (EX+ box), A.........................$115.00

Trigger Action Plane, S&E, mk N38434 on wing, prop spins & shoots 2 rockets from under wings, friction, 8", NMIB, A...$105.00

Photo courtesy of Scott Smiles.

Touchdown Pete, TPS, 1950s, football player in red and blue uniform, lithographed tin, 5", scarce, NM, from $375.00 to $425.00.

Triksie the Magician Dog, plush dog barks & drops hat over chick then lifts it to reveal an egg, 8", EX, A $435.00

Photo courtesy of Scott Smiles.

Trombone Player, Linemar, 1950s, lithographed tin, 5½", EX, from $350.00 to $400.00.

Tumbling Chimp, TPS, advances & somersaults in circular motion, litho tin, 4½", NM (EX+ box) $450.00

Tumbling Monkey, Occupied Japan, plastic, 4", NM (VG box), M5.................$45.00

Tumbling Peter Clown, KK, prewar, performs somersaults, celluloid w/cloth outfit, 6", EX+ (EX box), A.................$165.00

Turkey, Alps, brn, yel & gr, litho tin, clockwork mechanism, 7", EX (orig box), S10, from $125 to.................$150.00

Turnpike Speeder, Linemar, car goes in circle, 3 bridges & tunnel w/traffic & motorcycle cop, 7" sq base, NM (EX box), A.................$575.00

Turntable Railway, TM, litho tin, engine pushes coach then returns to pick it up, 12", EX (P box), M5 ....$65.00

Upsy Down Clown, Alps, clown on motocycle, lithographed tin, friction, 6½" long, NM (EX box), A, $775.00.

US Army Jeep, KO, friction, tin w/2 soldiers, radio & TV screen lithoed on back, 11", non-working o/w EX (G+ box), A $85.00

Vacation Land Airplane Ride, boats & planes revolve around tower, litho tin, clockwork, 5¼", EX, S10, from $125 to $150.00

Venus Auto Cycle, TN, piston action, clear plastic piston covering w/colored ball in ea cylinder, 8½", NM (NM box), A $260.00

Venus Speedboat, Sans Toys, NMIB, W5 ....$150.00

Wagon Fantasyland, TPS, beetle pulls lg leaf w/monkey driver & 2 spinning squirrels, 12", NM (EX box), A.................$170.00

Walking Bear w/Grasscutter, advances w/realistic strides pushing lawnmower, litho tin, 7", NM (EX+ box), A $275.00

Walking Drummer, Fukada, litho tin w/celluloid head, 8¾", G+, A.................$95.00

Walking Drummer Clown, I, walks while playing drum & holding trumpet, tin head w/fancy cloth suit, NM+ (EX box), A $325.00

Walking Pluto, Linemar/WDP, advances w/nodding head, litho tin w/rubber nose & tail, 7", EX, A.................$214.00

Walking Rabbit, 1960, EX, R7 ....$30.00

Walt Disney Delivery Wagon, Linemar/WDP, Donald on bicycle pulling 'Mickey's Delivery Wagon,' 6", NM (EX+ box), A.................$525.00

Western Ranger (Lone Ranger-type), K, wht horse bounces along w/figure holding gun, rubber tail, 5", NM (M box) $300.00

Whaling Ship, TN, red & wht tin ship named Penguin, gun on front deck, prop spins, friction, 12", NM (EX box), A.................$225.00

Whirling Tail Goofy w/Turtle, Linemar, Goofy vibrates around as turtle bites twirling tail, NM+ (VG box), A $825.00

Wild Roaring Bull & Boy, Mikuni, bull advances as boy is dragged behind, 9", NM (EX box), S10.................$250.00

Wonder MG Car, Marusan, travels back & forth on track w/twirling umbrella, 2 passengers, litho tin, 12", EX+ (EX+ box), A.................$400.00

Xylophone Clown, Linemar, litho tin w/brn cloth jacket, clockwork, 5", VG, S10, from $200 to.................$225.00

Yellow Cab, SSS Toys, yel w/red & wht checked design, Taxi roof plate, friction, 5", non-working o/w EX+ (EX box), A $65.00

Yo-Yo Playing Bunny, MM, moves head side to side as he rolls yo-yo on string, plush & litho tin, 7½", NM (EX+ box), A.................$75.00

101 Dalmatians Bus, MT/WDP, red & yel w/lithoed Dalmatian in ea window, tin, friction, 16", NM (EX box), A...$575.00

SPANISH

Bugatti Racer I-970, Paya, reissue, blue racer with driver in olive green, 19", EX (EX box), $250.00.

Boat w/Planes, Paya, 2 planes on rod above ship w/3 toothed wheels, litho tin, 9", EX, A $210.00

Donald Duck Walking Car, Geyper/WD, 1965, bl w/Donald's nephew & Ludwig Von Drake on sides, 5½", EX+ (EX+ box), A $175.00

Donald Duck Walking Car, Geyper/WD, 1965, red w/Pinocchio & Jiminy Cricket on sides, 5½", EX (EX+ box), A .$140.00

Motorcyclist, Rico, 1930s, #10 cyclist advances on balloon tires, 6¼", EX $500.00

Rodeo Joe, Rico, 1950s, cowboy in crazy car, 4½", EX, S10 ....$350.00

Vaquero Mareado (Rodeo Joe), Rico, jeep travels in circular motion as vaquero jumps up & down, 5", EX+ (EX+ box), A $250.00

Wyandotte

Though the Wyandotte Company (Michigan) produced toys of all types, included here are only the heavy-gauge pressed-steel cars, trucks, and other vehicles they made through the 1930s and 1940s.

See also Aeronautical; Boats; Character, TV and Movie Collectibles; Windups, Friction, and Other Mechanicals.

Ambulance, NP grille, operating rear door, 11", VG, A ..$120.00

Army Truck, 1939, marked Army Supply No 42 Corps, tin with cloth truck bed top, tin balloon tires, EX (NM box), A, $395.00.

Boat-tail Racer, red & wht w/rubber tires, electric lights, 8½", G+, A $100.00

Cabriolet Sedan, red & wht w/wooden wheels, NP grille, 5⅞", NM, A $160.00

Chrysler Airflow Coupe, 1924, gr & blk, EX $125.00

Coupe, 1936, red sheet metal w/tin wheels, 9", VG, A ..$325.00

Flash Strat-O-Wagon, ca 1940, red, wht & bl futuristic wagon w/fins, lithoed rocket ship, 6", NM+ (VG box), A .$175.00

La Salle, red w/silver grille, wood wheels, 15", VG+, M5 ....$240.00

Cord Auto and House Trailer, blue, replaced wooden trailer wheels, 24", VG, $350.00.

Igloo Ice Company Truck, blue and white, black balloon tires with white hubcaps, 2 plastic ice cubes in truck bed, 10", EX+, A, $220.00.

La Salle Sedan w/House Trailer, lt bl w/wht rubber tires, 26", NM, A $650.00

Moving Van, red, wht & bl w/Wyandotte advertising, 8", NM (G box), A $152.00

Nationwide Air Rail Service Truck, red & cream litho tin w/blk rubber tires, 12", EX, A $198.00

Rocket Ship, VG, J2 ....$90.00

Sedan, red & blk 4-door w/wht rubber tires, 6½", G+, A $55.00

Sedan w/Trailer, pnt, gr, 17½", VG, A $450.00

Soft-Top Coupe, red & yel w/rubber tires, articulated soft top, 12½", EX, A $275.00

Stake Truck, gr w/blk trim, wht rubber tires w/wood hubs, homemade headlights, w/6 wooden milk cans, 12", G, A $110.00

Stake Truck, 1930s, red & gr w/bl grille, pressed steel w/wooden wheels, 12½", VG+ $160.00

Streamline Sedan & Travel Trailer, red w/opening door on trailer, rpl wht rubber tires, 25", G+, A $210.00

Toytown Estate Wagon, litho tin w/simulated wood side panels, features opening passenger doors, 21", G+, A..........$145.00

Woodie Coupe, red w/lithoed 'wood' panels, trunk opens, roof slides back to change to convertible, 12½", VG+, A $275.00

Woody Station Wagon, Toytown Estate, 20", EX $300.00

Yo-Yos

Yo-Yos are starting to attract toy collectors, especially those with special features such as Hasbro's 'Glow-Action' and Duncan's 'Whistler.'

Advisor: Lucky Meisenheimer (M3).

Alox Mfg, Flying Disc, wood, ca 1950s, 2⅛", M, M3........$15.00

Duncan, Cattle Brand, late 1970s, MOC, M3.....................$8.00

Duncan, Glow Imperial, orange letters, MIP, M3............$10.00

Duncan, Glow Imperial, red letters, early 1970s, MIP, M3.$5.00

Festival, Be a Sport Series, 1970s, M (M pkg), M3...........$20.00

Festival, Disney (Goofy), 1970s, MOC, M3....................$15.00

Festival, Disney Characters (Mickey, Pluto or Donald), 1970s, MOC, M3, ea..$10.00

Hasbro, Glow Action, 1968, MOC, M3, from $10 to.......$15.00

Spectra Star, Freddy Krueger, 1980s, MOC, M3.................$5.00

Spectra Star, Ghostbusters, 1980s, MOC, M3....................$5.00

Spectra Star, Pee Wee Herman, 1980s, MOC, M3.............$5.00

Dealer Codes

Most of our description lines contain a letter/number code just before the suggested price. They correspond with the names of the following collectors and dealers who sent us their current selling list to be included in this addition. If you're interested in buying an item in question, don't hesitate to call or write them. We only ask that you consider the differences in time zones, and try to call at a convenient time. If you're corresponding, please send a self-addressed, stamped envelope for their repy. **Because our data was entered several months ago, many of the coded items will have already sold,** but our dealers tell us that they are often able to restock some of the same merchandise over and over. Some said that they had connections with other dealers around the country and might be able to locate a particular toy for you. But please bear in mind that because they may have had to pay more to restock their shelves, they may also have to charge a little more than the price quoted in their original sales list.

If you have lists of toys for sale that you would like for us to use in the next edition, please send them to us at the address below no later than February 1, 1996. We will process incoming lists as they arrive and because our space is limited, even by then we may have no room left, so the earlier you send it, the better. Please do not ask us to include you in our Categories of Special Interest unless you contribute useable information. Not only are we limited on available space, it isn't fair to those who do. If you would like to advertise with us but cannot contribute listings, display ads are available (see page 479 for rates). We will hold a previously assigned dealer code over for you who are our contributors/advisors from year to year as long as we know you are interested in keeping it, but if we haven't heard from you by February 1, we will reassign that code to someone else.

Direct your correspondence to:

Huxford Enterprises, Inc.
1202 7th St.
Covington, IN 47932

(A1)
Stan and Sally Alekna
4724 Kernan Mill Lane East
Jacksonville, FL 32224
904-992-9525

(A2)
Jane Anderson
Rt. 1, Box 1030
Saylorsburg, PA 18353

(A3)
Aquarius Antiques
Jim and Nancy Schaut
P.O. Box 10781
Glendale AZ 85318-0781
602-878-4293

(A4)
Bob Armstrong
15 Monadnock Rd.
Worcester, MA 01609

(A5)
Geneva Addy
P.O. Box 124
Winterset, IA 50273
515-462-3027

(B1)
Richard Belyski
P.O. Box 124
Sea Cliff, NY 11579
516-676-1183

(B2)
Larry Blodget
Box 753
Rancho Mirage, CA 92270

(B3)
Bojo
Bob Gottuso
P.O. Box 1203
Cranberry Twp., PA 16033-2203
Phone or FAX 412-776-0621

(B4)
Dick Borgerding
RJB Toys
720 E Main
Flushing, MI 48433
810-659-9859

(B6)
Jim Buskirk
175 Cornell St.
Windsor, CA 95492
707-837-9949

(B7)
Danny Bynum
12311 Wedgehill Ln.
Houston, TX 77077-4805
713-972-4421 or 713-531-5711

(B8)
Stanley A. and Robert S. Block
P.O. Box 51
Trumbull, CT 06611
203-261-3223 or 203-775-0138

(B9)
Marlis Bean
3525 Glen Oak Dr.
Eugene, OR 97405
503-683-3855

(B11)
Sue and Marty Bunis
RR 1, Box 36
Bradford, NH 03221-9102

(C1)
Casey's Collectible Corner
HCR Box 31, Rt. 3
N Blenheim, NY 12131
607-588-6464

(C2)
Mark E. Chase and Michael Kelley
Collector Glass News
P.O. Box 308
Slippery Rock, PA 16057
412-946-2838

(C3)
Ken Clee
Box 11142
Philadelphia, PA 19111
215-722-1979

(C4)
Arlan Coffman
1223 Wilshire Blvd., Ste. 275
Santa Monica, CA 90403
310-453-2507

(C5)
Joe Corea
New Jersey Nostalgia Hobby
401 Park Ave.
Scotch Plains, NJ 07076
908-322-2676; FAX 908-322-4079

(C6)
Cotswold Collectibles
P.O. Box 249
Clinton, WA 98236
206-579-1223; FAX 206-579-1287

(C9)
Marilyn Cooper
8408 Lofland Dr.
Houston, TX 77055; 713-465-7773
Author of *The Pictorial Guide to Tooth-brush Holders*

(C10)
Bill Campbell
1221 Littlebrook Lane
Birmingham, AL 35235
205-853-8227; FAX 405-658-6986

(C11)
Jim Christoffel
409 Maple
Elburn, IL 60119
708-365-2914

(C12)
Joel J. Cohen
Cohen Books and Collectibles
P.O. Box 810310
Boca Raton, FL 33481
407-487-7888; FAX 407-487-3117

(C13)
Brad Cassidy
1350 Stanwix
Toledo, OH 43614
419-385-9910

(C14)
Cynthia's Country Store
11496 Pierson Rd., #C1
Commerce Park - Wellington
West Palm Beach, FL 33414
407-793-0554
FAX 407-795-4222 (24 hours)

(C15)
Rosalind Cranor
P.O. Box 859
Blacksburg, VA 24063

(D1)
Allen Day
Yesterday's Toys
P.O. Box 525
Monroe, NC 28810

(D2)
Marl Davidson (Marl & Barbie)
5705 39th St. Circle East
Bradenton, FL 34203
813-751-6275; FAX 813-751-5463

(D3)
Larry DeAngelo
516 King Arthur Dr.
Virginia Beach, VA 23464
804-424-1691

(D4)
John DeCicco
57 Bay View Dr.
Shrewsbury, MA 01545
508-797-0023

(D5)
Day-Old Antiques
76 Bowers St.
Newtonville, MA 02160
617-527-1881; FAX 617-527-1899

(D6)
Doug Dezso
864 Patterson Ave.
Maywood, NJ 07607
201-488-1311

(D7)
Ron and Donna Donnelly
Saturday Heroes
P.O. Box 7047
Panama City Beach, FL 32413
904-234-7944

(D8)
George Downes
Box 572
Nutley, NJ 07110
201-661-3358

(D9)
Gordy Dutt
P.O. Box 201
Sharon Center, OH 44274-0201
216-239-1657; FAX 216-239-2991

(D10)
Dunbar's Gallery
Leila and Howard Dunbar
76 Haven St.
Milford, MA 01757
508-634-8697; FAX 508-634-8696

(E3)
Alan Edwards
Toys From the Crypt
P.O. Box 3294
Shawnee, KS 66203
913-383-1242

(F1)
Figures
Anthony Balasco
P.O. Box 19482
Johnston, RI 02919
401-946-5720; FAX 401-942-7980

(F2)
Paul Fideler
20 Shadow Oak Dr., Apt. #18
Sudbury, MA 01776
617-386-0228 (24 hours)

(F3)
Paul Fink's Fun and Games
P.O. Box 488
59 S Kent Rd.
Kent, CT 06757
203-927-4001

(F4)
Mike and Kurt Fredericks
145 Bayline Cir.
Folsom, CA 95630
916-985-7986

(F5)
Fun House Toy Co.
G.F. Ridenour
P.O. Box 343
Bradfordwoods, PA 15015-0343
412-935-1392 (FAX capable)

(F7)
Finisher's Touch Antiques
Steve Fisch, proprietor
10 W Main St.
Wappingers Falls, NY 12590
914-298-8882; FAX 914-298-8945

(G1)
Gary's Trains
R.D. #2, Box 147
Boswell, PA 15531
814-629-9277

(G2)
Mark Giles
510 E Third St.
Ogalala, NE 69153
308-284-4360

(G3)
Robert Goforth
4061 E Castro Vly. Blvd.
Ste. 224
Castro Valley, CA 94552
510-889-6676; FAX 510-581-0397

(G5)
John F. Green Inc.
1821 W. Jacaranda Pl.
Fullerton, CA 92633-USA
714-526-5467; 800-807-4759

(G6)
Carol Karbowiak Gilbert
2193 14 Mile Rd. 206
Sterling Height, MI 48310

(G7)
Charles Gookin
Remember When
18 W Prospect St.
Waldwick, NJ 07463
291-652-5437

(H1)
The Hamburgs
Happy Memories Antique Toy Co.
P.O. Box 1305
Woodland Hills, CA 91365
818-346-9884 or 818-346-1269
FAX 818-346-0215

(H3)
George Hardy
1670 Hawkwood Ct.
Charlottesville, VA 22901
804-295-4863; FAX 804-295-4898

(H4)
Jerry and Ellen L. Harnish
110 Main St.
Bellville, OH 44813
Phone or FAX 419-886-4782

(H6)
Phil Helley
Old Kilbourne Antiques
629 Indiana Ave.
Wisconsin Dells, WI 53965
608-254-8770

(H7)
Jacquie and Bob Henry
Antique Treasures and Toys
Box 17
Walworth, NY 14568
315-986-1424

(H8)
Homestead Collectibles
Art and Judy Turner
R.D. 2, Rte. 150
P.O. Box 173-E
Mill Hall, PA 17751
717-726-3597; FAX 717-726-4488

(H9)
Pamela E. Apkarian-Russell,
the Halloween Queen
C.J. Russell & the Halloween Queen Antiques
P.O. Box 499
Winchester, NH 03470
603-239-8875

(H10)
Don Hamm
712 N. Townsend St.
Syracuse, NY 13203
315-478-7035

(I1)
Roger Inouye
765 E. Franklin
Pomona, CA 91766

(I2)
Terri Ivers
Terri's Toys and Nostalgia
419 S 1st St.
Ponca City, OK 74601
405-762-8697; FAX 405-765-5101

(J1)
Bill Jackameit
200 Victoria Dr.
Bridgewater, VA 22812
703-828-4359 (Monday-Thursday, 7 pm-
9 pm EST)

(J2)
Ed Janey
2920 Meadowbrook Dr. SE
Cedar Rapids, IA 52403
319-362-5213

(J3)
Dana Johnson Enterprises
1347 NW Albany Ave.
Bend, OR 97701-3160
503-382-8410

(J5)
Just Kids Nostalgia
310 New York Avenue
Huntington, NY 11743
516-423-8449; FAX 516-423-4326

(J6)
June Moon
245 N Northwest Hwy.
Park Ridge, IL 60068
708-825-1411 (24 hr phone)
FAX 708-825-6090

(K1)
K-3 Inc.
Bendees Only; Simpson Mania
2335 NW Thurman
Portland, OR 97210
503-222-2713

(K2)
David Kolodny-Nagy
May through Jan:
3701 Connecticut Ave. NW #500
Washington, DC 20008
Jan through May:
MB 845 Brandeis University
P.O. Box 9110
Waltham, MA 02251-9110
202-364-8753

(K3)
Ilene Kayne
1308 S Charles St.
Baltimore, MD 21230
410-685-3923

(L1)
Jean-Claude H. Lanau
740 Thicket Ln.
Houston, TX 77079
713-497-6034 (after 7:00 pm, CST)

(L2)
John and Eleanor Larsen
523 Third St.
Colusa, CA 95932
916-458-4769 (after 4 pm)

(L4)
Tom Lastrapes
P.O. Box 2444
Pinellas Park, FL 34664
813-545-2586

(L5)
Stephen Leonard
Box 127
Albertson, LI, NY 11507
516-742-0979

(L6)
Kathy Lewis
Chatty Cathy's Haven
187 N Marcello Ave
Thousand Oaks, CA 91360
805-499-7932

(L7)
Terry and Joyce Losonsky
7506 Summer Leave Ln.
Columbia, MD 21046-2455
301-381-3358

(L8)
Mary Jane Lamphier
577 Main St.
Arlington, IA 50606
319-633-5885

(M1)
Mark and Val Macaluso
3603 Newark Rd.
Marion, NY 14505
315-926-4349; FAX 315-926-4853

(M2)
John McKenna
801-803 W Cucharres
Colorado Springs, CO 80918
719-630-8732

(M3)
Lucky Meisenheimer
7300 Sand Lake Commons Blvd.
Orlando, FL 32819
407-354-0478

(M4)
Bill Mekalian
550 E Chesapeake Cir.
Fresno, CA 93720
209-434-3247

(M5)
Mike's General Store
52 St. Annes Rd.
Winnipeg, Manitoba, Canada R2M-2Y3
204-255-3463; FAX 204-253-4124

(M6)
Paul David Morrow
13550 Foothill Blvd. #28
Sylmar, CA 91342
818-898-9592

(M7)
Judith A. Mosholder
R.D. #2, Box 147
Boswell, PA 15531
814-629-9277

(M8)
The Mouse Man Ink
P.O. Box 3195
Wakefield, MA 01880
phone or FAX 617-246-3876

(M9)
Steven Meltzer
670 San Juan Ave. #B
Venice, CA 90291
310-396-6007

(M10)
Gary Metz
4803 Lange Ln. SW
Roanoke, VA 24018
703-989-0475

(M11)
Michael and Polly McQuillen
McQuillen's Collectibles
P.O. Box 1141
Indianapolis, IN 46201
317-322-8518

(M12)
Martin McCaw
1124 School Ave.
Walla Walla, WA 99362
800-451-9755

(N1)
Natural Way/DBA Russian Toy Co.
820 Massachusetts
Lawrence, KS 66044
913-841-0100

(N2)
Norman's Olde & New Store
Philip Norman
126 W Main St.
Washington, NC 27889-4944
919-946-3448

(N3)
Neil's Wheels, Inc.
Box 354
Old Bethpage, NY 11804
516-293-9659; FAX 516-420-0483

(N4)
Roger Nazeley
4921 Castor Ave.
Philadelphia, PA 19124
FAX 215-288-8030

(O1)
Olde Tyme Toy Mall
105 S Main St.
Fairmount, IN 46928
317-948-3150

(P1)
Parkway Furniture & Gift Shop
603 Volunteer Parkway
Bristol, TN 37602
615-968-1541

(P2)
Dawn Parrish
9931 Gaynor Ave.
Granada Hills, CA 91343-1604
818-894-8964

(P3)
The Toy Cellar
John and Sheri Pavone
29 Sullivan Rd.
Peru, NY 12972

(P4)
Plymouth Rock Toy Co.
P.O. Box 1202
Plymouth, MA 02362
508-746-2842; FAX 508-830-1880

(P5)
Gary Pollastro
5047 84th Ave. SE
Mercer, WA 98040
206-232-3199

(P6)
Judy Posner
R.D. 1, Box 273
Effort, PA 18330
717-629-6583

(P7)
Greg Plonski
93 Beaver Dr.
Kings Park, NY 11754-2209

(P8)
Diane Patalano
P.O. Box 144
Saddle River, NJ 07458
201-327-2499

(P9)
Pak-Rat
Andrew Galbus
1608 4th Ave. NW
Austin, MN 55912-1416
507-437-1784 (5 pm to 10 pm Central)

(P10)
Poe-pourri
Bill and Pat Poe
220 Dominica Circle E
Niceville, FL 32578-4068
904-897-4163; FAX 904-897-2606

(R1)
David Richter
6817 Sutherland Dr.
Mentor, OH 44060-3917

(R2)
Rick Rann, Beatlelist
P.O. Box 877
Oak Park, IL 60303
708-442-7907

(R3)
Jim Rash
135 Alder Ave.
Pleasantville, NJ 08232
609-646-4125

(R4)
Robert Reeves
104 Azalea Dr.
St. Mathews, SC 29135
803-578-5939 (leave message)

(R5)
Reynolds Toys
Charlie Reynolds
2836 Monroe St.
Falls Church, VA 22042
703-533-1322

(R6)
David E. Riddle
P.O. Box 13141
Tallahassee, FL 32308
904-877-7207

(R7)
Leo E. Rishty, Toy Doctor
77 Alan Loop
Staten Island, NY 10304
718-727-9477; FAX 718-727-2151

(R9)
Craig Reid
P.O. Box 100
Post Falls, ID 83854
509-536-3278 (6-10 pm PST)

(S1)
Sam Samuelian, Jr.
700 Llanfair Rd.
Upper Darby, PA 19082
215-566-7248

(S2)
Steve's Lost Land of Toys
Steve Reed
3572 Turner Ct.
Fremont, CA 94536
510-795-0598; FAX 510-795-7717

(S3)
Irwin Stern
20032 Water's Edge Lane, Unit 1402
Boca Raton, FL 33434
407-483-1440
or
4 Deer Run
Watchung, NJ 07060
908-561-4880

(S4)
SLX Toys
7233 Michael Rd., Apt. #1
Orchard Park, NY 14127-1406
716-674-0432

(S5)
Son's a Poppin' Ranch
John Rammacher
1610 Park Ave.
Orange City, FL 32763-8869
904-775-2891

(S6)
Bill Stillman
Scarfone & Stillman Vintage Oz
P.O. Box 167
Hummelstown, PA 17036
717-566-5538

(S7)
Nate Stoller
960 Reynolds Ave.
Ripon, CA 95366
209-599-5933

(S8)
Steve Santi
19626 Ricardo Ave.
Hayward, CA 94541
510-481-2586

(S9)
Bob Stevens
529 N. Water St.
Masontown, PA 15461
412-583-8234

(S10)
Scott Smiles
848 SE Atlantic Dr.
Lantana, FL 33462-4702
407-582-4947

(S11)
Starspace
55 Sylvan
Pleasant Ridge, MI 48069
810-543-5175

(S12)
Nancy Stewart Books
1188 NW Weybridge Way
Beaverton, OR 97006
503-645-9779

(S13)
Marian Schmuhl
7 Revolutionary Ridge Rd.
Bedford, MA 01730-2057
617-275-2156

(S14)
Cindy Sabulis
3 Stowe Dr.
Shelton, CT 06484
203-926-0176

(T1)
Jon Thurmond
Collector Holics
15006 Fuller
Grandview, MO 64030
816-322-0906

(T2)
Toy Scouts, Inc.
Bill Bruegman
137 Casterton Ave.
Akron, OH 44303
216-836-0668; FAX 216-869-8686

(T3)
Richard Trautwein
Toys N Such
437 Dawson St.
Sault Ste. Marie, MI 49783
906-635-0356

(T4)
Toy Talk
2509 Brookside Drive
Lancaster, PA 17601
717-898-2932

(T5)
Bob and Marcie Tubbs
31 Westwood Rd.
Fairfield, CT 06432-1658
203-367-7499

(T6)
TV Collector
P.O. Box 1088
Easton, MA 02334
508-238-1179 or FAX by pre-set agreement

(V1)
Norm Vigue
62 Bailey St.
Stoughton, MA 02072
617-344-5441

(V2)
Marci Van Ausdall
P.O. Box 946
Quincy, CA 95971

(W1)
Dan Wells Antique Toys
P.O. Box 6751
Louisville, KY 40206
502-897-1598 (before 9:00 pm EST)

(W4)
Randy Welch
1100 Hambrooks Blvd.
Cambridge, MD 21613
410-228-5390

(W5)
Linda and Paul Woodward
14 Argo Drive
Sewell, NJ 08080-1908
609-582-1253

(Y1)
Henri Yunes
971 Main St., Apt. 2
Hackensack, NJ 07601
201-488-2236

Categories of Special Interest

If you would like to be included in this section, send us a list of your 'for sale' merchandise. These listings are complimentary to those who participate in the preparation of this guide. Read the paragraph under the title *Dealers Codes* for more information. If you have no catalogs or lists but would like to advertise with us, see the display ad rate sheet on page 479.

Action Figures
Also GI Joe, Star Wars and Super Heroes
John DiCicco
57 Bay View Dr.
Shrewsbury, MA 01545
508-797-0023

Captain Action, Star Wars, Secret Wars and other character-related Western, TV, movie, comic or paperback tie-ins
George Downes
Box 572
Nutley, NJ 07110
201-935-3388

Figures
Anthony Balasco
P.O. Box 19482
Johnston, RI 02919
401-946-5720; FAX 401-942-7980

GI Joe, Captain Action and other character-related TV, advertising, Marx and Mego figures; send $2 for sales catalog
Jerry and Ellen Harnish
110 Main St.
Bellville, OH 44813
Phone or FAX 419-886-4782

Advertising
Author of book on advertising characters
Mary Jane Lamphier
577 Main St.
Arlington, IA 50606
319-633-5885

Gary Metz
4803 Lange Ln. SW
Roanoke, VA 24018
703-989-0475

Also general line
Mike's General Store
52 St. Annes Rd.
Winnipeg, Manitoba, Canada R2M 2Y3
204-255-3463; FAX 204-253-4124

Banks
Ertl; sales lists available
Homestead Collectibles
Art and Judy Turner
R.D. 2, Rte. 150
P.O. Box 173-E
Mill Hall, PA 17751
717-726-3597; FAX 717-726-4488

Also children's sadirons, Black Americana dolls and memorabilia
Diane Patalano
Country Girls Appraisal and Liquidation Service
P.O. Box 144
Saddle River, NJ 07458
201-327-2499

Parkway Furniture and Gift Shop
603 Volunteer Pky.
Bristol, TN 37602
615-968-1541

Penny banks (limited editions): new, original, mechanical, still or figural; also bottle openers
Reynolds Toys
Charlie Reynolds
2836 Monroe St.
Falls Church, VA 22042
703-533-1322

Ertl; First Gear
toy talk
2509 Brookside Dr.
Lancaster, PA 17601
717-898-2932

Barbie and Friends
Also wanted: Mackies, holiday and porcelain as well as vintage Barbies; buying and selling ca 1959 dolls to present issues
Marl Davidson (Marl & Barbie)
5705 39th St., Circle East
Bradenton, FL 34203
813-751-6275; FAX 813-751-5463

Battery Operated
Tom Lastrapes
P.O. Box 2444
Pinellas Park, FL 34664
813-545-2586

Also Windups, Friction, Japan, Marx, etc.; broken is OK. Buy or trade
Leo E. Rishty
Toy Doctor
77 Alan Loop
Staten Island, NY 10304

Also general line
Mike Roscoe
3351 Lagrange
Toledo, OH 43608
419-244-6935

Boats and Toy Motors
Also Japanese wood toys
Dick Borgerding
RJB Toys
720 E Main St.
Flushing, MI 48433
810-659-9859

Books
Little Golden Books, Wonder Books, many others; 20-page list available
Ilene Kayne
1308 S Charles St.
Baltimore, MD 21230
410-685-3923

Specializing in Little Golden Books and look-alikes
Steve Santi
19626 Ricardo Ave.
Hayward, CA 94541; 510-481-2586.
Author of *Collecting Little Golden Books, Volumes I and II*. Also publishes newsletter, *Poky Gazette*, primarily for Little Golden Book collectors

Children's Books
Nancy Stewart Books
1188 NW Weybridge Way
Beaverton, OR 97006
503-645-9779

Breyer
Carol Karbowiak Gilbert
2193 14 Mile Rd. 206
Sterling Height, MI 48310

Building Blocks and Construction Toys
Arlan Coffman
1223 Wilshire Blvd., Ste. 275
Santa Monica, CA 90403
310-453-2507

Richter's Anchor (Union) Stone Building Blocks
George Hardy
1670 Hawkwood Ct.
Charlottesville, VA 22901
804-295-4863; FAX 804-295-4898

Candy Containers
Jeff Bradfield
Corner of Rt. 42 and Rt. 257
Dayton, VA 22821
703-879-9961

Also Tonka, Smith-Miller, Shafford black cats, German nodders
Doug Dezso
864 Patterson Ave.
Maywood, NJ 07607
201-488-1311

Cast Iron
Pre-war, large-scale cast-iron toys and early American tinplate toys
John McKenna
801-803 W Cucharres
Colorado Springs, CO 80918
719-630-8732

Any taxi cab item
Nathan Willensky
5 E 22nd St., Ste. 24C
New York, NY 10010
212-982-2156; FAX 212-995-1065

Character and Promotional Glasses
Especially fast-foods and sports glasses; publishers of Collector Glass News
Mark Chase and Michael Kelly
P.O. Box 308
Slippery Rock, PA 16057
412-946-2838

Character Clocks and Watches
Also radio premiums and decoders, P-38 airplane-related items from World War II, Captain Marvel and Hoppy items, Lone Ranger books with jackets, selected old comic books, toys and cap guns; buys and sells Hoppy and Roy items
Bill Campbell
Kirschner Medical Corp.
1221 Littlebrook Ln.
Birmingham, AL 35235
205-853-8227; FAX 405-658-6986

Character Collectibles
Dolls, rock 'n roll personalities (especially the Beatles), related character items and miscellaneous toys
BOJO
Bob Gottuso
P.O. Box 1203
Cranberry Twp., PA 16033-2203
Phone or FAX 412-776-0621

1940s-'60s character items such as super heroes, TV and cartoon items, games, playsets, lunch boxes, model kits, comic books and premium rings
Bill Bruegman
Toy Scouts, Inc.
137 Casterton Ave.
Akron, OH 44303
216-836-0668; FAX 216-869-8686

TV, radio and comic collectibles; sports and non-sports cards; silver and golden age comics
Casey's Collectible Corner
HCR Box 31, Rt. 3
N Blenheim, NY 12131
607-588-6464

Mark E. Chase
P.O. Box 308
Slippery Rock, PA 16057
412-946-2838

Disney, especially books and animation art
Cohen Books and Collectibles
Joel J. Cohen
P.O. Box 810310
Boca Raton, FL 33481
407-487-7888; FAX 407-487-3117

California Raisins (PVC); buying collections, old store stock and closeouts
Larry DeAngelo
516 King Arthur Dr.
Virginia Beach, VA 23464
804-424-1691

Early Disney, Western heroes, premiums
and other related collectibles
Ron and Donna Donnelly
Saturday Heroes
P.O. Box 7047
Panama City Beach, FL 32413
904-234-7944

Rocketeer memorabilia
Don Hamm
712 N. Townsend St.
Syracuse, NY 13203
315-478-7035

Disneyana, toys, tools, glassware, etc.
Lynn Marie Hughes
DBA The Mouse House
10521 Second St. Box 2340
Shasta, CA 96087

Any and all, also sports, political and
advertising
Hunter's Vault
P.O. Box 657
Cicero, IN 46034
317-984-2194

Any and all; general line
Dave Hutzley
407 S Washington
Royal Oak, MI 48067

Any and all, also Hartland figures
Terry-Mardis Ivers
Terri's Toys
419 S 1st St.
Ponca City, OK 74601
405-762-8697; FAX 405-765-5101

TV, Western, Space, Beatles; auction as
well as set-price catalogs available
Just Kids Nostalgia
310 New York Ave.
Huntington, NY 11743
516-423-8449; FAX 516-423-4326

Especially bendee figures and the Simpsons
K-3 Inc.
Bendees Only; Simpson Mania
2335 NW Thurman
Portland, OR 97210
503-222-2713

Disney and other character collectibles
Kathy and Skip Matthews
Second Childhood Antiques & Collectibles
1154 Grand Ave.
Astoria, OR 97103
503-325-6543

Uncle Wiggily toys; buy and sell
Martin McCaw
1124 School Ave.
Walla Walla, WA 99362
800-451-9755

Especially Disney; send $5 for annual sub-
scription (6 issues) for sale catalogs
The Mouse Man Ink
P.O. Box 3195
Wakefield, MA 01880
Phone or FAX 617-246-3876

General line
Olde Tyme Toy Mall
105 S Main St.
Fairmount, IN 46928
317-948-3150

Especially pottery, china, ceramics, salt and
pepper shakers, cookie jars, tea sets and children's china; with special interest in Black
Americana and Disneyana; illustrated sale
lists available
Judy Posner
R.D. #1, Box 273
Effort, PA 18330
717-629-6583

Buying, selling and trading original Beatles
memorabilia
Rick Rann, Beatlelist
P.O. Box 877
Oak Park, IL 60303
708-442-7907

Special interest in Star Trek and Aurora slot cars
Craig Reid
P.O. Box 100
Post Falls, ID 83835
509-536-3278 (6-10 pm PST)

Also Star Wars, Pez, Ramp Walkers, Push-
up Puppets
James and Brenda Roush
739 W 5th St.
Marion, IN 46953
317-662-6126

Also battery-ops, character clocks and novelties
Sam Samuelian, Jr.
700 Llanfair Rd.
Upper Darby, PA 19082
215-566-7248

Especially Star Wars, Star Trek, Marvel,
cartoon, also robots
Starspace
Barbara Troy
55 Sylvan
Pleasant Ridge, MI 48069
810-543-5175

All characters, A to Z; 20,000 items in
stock, $3 for 43-pg catalog
Steve's Lost Land of Toys
3572 Turner Ct.
Fremont, CA 94536
510-795-0598; FAX 510-795-7717

Wizard of Oz memorabilia; quarterly mail/phone
bid auctions available for $2; always buying Oz
Bill Stillman
Scarfone & Stillman Vintage Oz
P.O. Box 167
Hummelstown, PA 17036
717-566-5538

General line
Jon Thurmond
Collector Holics
15006 Fuller
Grandview, MO 64030
816-322-0906

Especially tinplate toys and cars, battery-op
toys and toy trains
Richard Trautwein
Toys N Such
437 Dawson St.
Sault Ste. Marie, MI 49783
906-635-0356

TV, movie, rock 'n roll, comic character, commercials, radio, theater, etc., memorabilia of all
kinds; Send $4 for sale catalog. We are not
interested in buying items. All inquiries must
include SASE for reply unless ordering catalog
TV Collector
P.O. Box 1088
Easton, MA 02334
508-238-1179 or FAX by pre-set agreement

Games, premiums, cartoon personalities, Dick Tracy, Popeye, Buck Rogers, Flash Gordon, Tarzan, Lone Ranger and others
Norm Vigue
62 Bailey St.
Stoughton, MA 02072
617-344-5441

Especially Hopalong Cassidy
Lloyd White
515 Joe Martin Rd.
Lowell, IN 46356

Especially Disneyana and Roger Rabbit
Yesterday's Toys
Allen Day
P.O. Box 525
Monroe, NC 28810

Chinese Tin Toys
Also buying and selling antiques, old toys and collectibles; custom refinishing and quality repairing
Finisher's Touch Antiques
Steve Fisch, proprietor
10 W Main St.
Wappingers Falls, NY 12590
914-298-8882; FAX 914-298-8945

Dakins
Jim Rash
135 Alder Ave.
Pleasantville, NJ 08232

Diecast
Also pressed steel trucks and comic character toys
Aquarius Antiques
Jim and Nancy Schaut
P.O. Box 10781
Glendale, AZ 85318-0781
602-878-4293

Especially banks; also Lionel trains, action figures, Star Trek, lunch boxes, and Flintstones
Roderick Duck
Roderick's Relics
1302 E. Main St.
Shawnee, OK 74801
405-273-5337

Especially Dinky; also selling inexpensive restorable diecast as well as reproduction parts and decals for many diecast brands
Paul Fideler
20 Shadow Oak Dr., Apt. #18
Sudbury, MA 01776
617-386-0228 (24 hours)

Especially English-made toy vehicles
Mark Giles
510 E Third St.
Ogalala, NE 69153
308-284-4360

Hot Wheels, Matchbox, Dinky and Corgi
Robert Goforth
4061 E Castro Vly. Blvd.
Ste. 224
Castro Valley, CA 94552
510-889-6676; FAX 510-581-0397

Especially Matchbox and other small-scale cars and trucks
Bill Jackameit
200 Victoria Dr.
Bridgewater, VA 22812
703-828-4359 (Monday-Thursday, 7 pm-9 pm EST)

Especially Matchbox, Hot Wheels, Majorette
Dana Johnson Enterprises
1347 NW Albany Ave.
Bend, OR 97701-3160
503-382-8410
Author/publisher of *Matchbox Blue Book, Hot Wheels Blue Book* and *Collecting Majorette Toys* (prices updated yearly)

Especially Dinky; also obsolete French, German, Italian and English-made vehicles
Jean-Claude Lanau
740 Thicket Ln.
Houston, TX 77079
713-4971-6034

Matchbox of all types including Dinky, Commando, Convoys, Harley-Davidson, Indy/Formula 1, and Looney Toons; also Corgi, Hartoy, Hot Wheels, Tomica, and Tyco slot cars
Neil's Wheels, Inc.
Box 354
Old Bethpage, NY 11804
516-293-9659; FAX 516-420-0483

Ertl, banks, farm, trucks and construction
Son's a Poppin' Ranch
John Rammacher
1610 Park Ave.
Orange City, FL 32763-8869
904-775-2891

All types; also action figures such as GI Joe, Johnny West, Matt Mason and others
Robert Reeves
104 Azalea Dr.
St. Mathews, SC 29135
803-578-5939 (leave message)

Especially Soviet-made toys (marked USSR or CCCP)
David E. Riddle
P.O. Box 13141
Tallahassee, FL 32308
905-877-7207

All diecast cars and trucks, especially Matchbox and Hot Wheels
S&E Sales
P.O. Box 572
Russels Point, OH 43348

Especially Corgi and Dinky
Irwin Stern
20032 Water's Edge Lane, Unit 1402
Boca Raton, FL 33434
407-483-1440 or
4 Deer Run
Watchung, NJ 07060
908-561-4880

Hot Wheels, Matchbox and all obsolete toy cars, trucks and airplanes
Dan Wells Antiques Toys
P.O. Box 6751
Louisville, KY 40206
502-896-0740

Dolls
Chatty Cathy and Mattel; has repair service
Kathy Lewis
Chatty Cathy's Haven
187 N Marcello Ave.
Thousand Oaks, CA 91360
805-499-7932
Author of book: *Chatty Cathy Dolls, An Identification and Value Guide*

Betsy McCall
Marci Van Ausdall
P.O. Box 946
Quincy, CA 95971

Liddle Kiddles and other small dolls from the late '60s and early '70s
Dawn Parrish
9931 Gaynor Ave.
Granada Hills, CA 91343-1604
818-894-8964

Black dolls, many makers, types, prices
Barb's Ethnic Dolls
Barbara M. Rogers
15097 NE County Rd. #314
Silver Springs, FL 34488-2939
904-625-2180

Dolls from the 1960s-'70s such as Barbie, Tammy, Tressy, and Little Kiddles
Cindy Sabulis
3 Stowe Dr.
Shelton, CT 06484
203-926-0176

Strawberry Shortcake dolls, accessories and related items
Geneva Addy
P.O. Box 124
Winterset, IA 50273
515-462-3027

Celebrity and character dolls
Henri Yunes
971 Main St., Apt. 2
Hackensack, NJ 07601
201-488-2236

Dollhouse Furniture
Especially Tootsietoy
Charles Gookin
18 W Prospect St.
Waldwick, NJ 07463
201-652-5437

Renwal, Ideal, Marx, etc.
Judith A. Mosholder
R.D. #2, Box 147
Boswell, PA 15531
814-629-9277

Renwal, Plasco, Marx, etc.
Marian Schmuhl
Revolutionary Ridge Rd.
Bedford, MA 01730-2057
617-275-2156

Dollhouses
Tin and fiberboard dollhouses and plastic furniture from all eras
Bob and Marcie Tubbs
31 Westwood Rd.
Fairfield, CT 06432-1658
203-367-7499

Elvis Presley Collectibles
Rosalind Cranor
P.O. Box 859
Blacksburg, VA 24063
Author of books: *Elvis Collectibles, Best of Elvis Collectibles*

Ertl
Also Tonka, construction and logging toys, pressed steel, diecast toy trucks, Smokey Bear items
Glen Brady
P.O. Box 3933
Central Point, OR 97502
503-772-0350

Fast Food
All restaurants
Jim Christoffel
409 Maple
Elburn, IL 60119
708-365-2914

All restaurants and California Raisins
Ken Clee
Box 11412
Philadelphia, PA 19111
215-722-1979

McDonald's only, especially older or unusual items
John and Eleanor Larsen
523 Third St.
Colusa, CA 95932
916-458-4769

McDonald's
Terry and Joyce Losonsky
7506 Summer Leave Lane
Columbia, MD 21046-2455
410-381-3358
Author of *Illustrated Collector's Guide to Mcdonald's® Happy Meals® Boxes, Premiums, and Promotionals* ($9.50 postpaid)

All restaurants
Poe-pourri
Bill and Pat Poe
220 Dominica Circle E
Niceville, FL 32578-4068
904-897-4163; FAX 904-897-2606
Send $3.00 for catalog; see Clubs, Newsletters and Other Publications for information on McDonald's club

Fisher-Price
Brad Cassidy
1350 Stanwix
Toledo, OH 43614
419-385-9910

Games
Victorian, cartoon, comic, TV and nostalgic themes
Paul Fink's Fun & Games
P.O. Box 488
59 S Kent Rd.
Kent, CT 06757
203-927-4001

Paul David Morrow
13550 Foothill Blvd. #28
Sylmar, CA 91342
818-898-9592

Gas-Powered Toys
Airplanes, cars and boats
Danny Bynum
12311 Wedgehill Ln.
Houston, TX 77077-4805
713-972-4421 or 713-531-5711

General Line
Kim Bordner
408 W South
Angola, IN 46703

GI Joe
Also diecast and Star Wars
Cotswold Collectibles
P.O. Box 249
Clinton, WA 98236
206-579-1223; FAX 206-579-1287

Guns
Pre-WWII American spring-air BB guns, all Red Ryder BB guns, cap guns with emphasis on Western six-shooters; especially wanted are pre-WWII cast iron six-guns
Jim Buskirk
175 Cornell St.
Windsor, CA 95492
707-837-9949

Specializing in cap guns
Happy Memories Antique Toy Co.
The Hamburgs
P.O. Box 1305
Woodland Hills, CA 91365
818-346-9884 or 818-346-1269
FAX 818-346-0215

Also model kits, toy soldiers and character toys and watches; character watch service available
Plymouth Rock Toy Co.
P.O. Box 1202
Plymouth, MA 02362
508-746-2842; FAX 508-830-1880

Hartland Plastics, Inc.
Issues price guide
Gail Finch
1733 N. Cambridge Ave.
Milwaukee, WI 53202

Halloween Collectibles
Also postcards
Pamela E. Apkarian-Russell
C.J. Russell & The Halloween Queen
Antiques
P.O. Box 499
Winchester, NH 03470
603-239-8875

Japanese Sci-Fi Vinyl Figures
Also robots and space toys, other tin windups, Godzilla, model kits
Day-Old Antiques
76 Bowers St.
Newtonville, MA 02160
617-527- 1881; FAX 617-527-1899

Lunch Boxes
Norman's Olde and New Store
Philip Norman
126 W Main St.
Washington, NC 27889-4944
919-946-3448

Also characters such as cowboys, TV shows, cartoons and more
Terri's Toys
Terri Ivers
1104 Shirlee Ave.
Ponca City, OK 74601
405-762-8697 or 405-762-5174
FAX 405-765-5101

Marionettes and Puppets
Steven Meltzer
670 San Juan Ave. #B
Venice, CA 90281
310-396-6007

Marx
Figures, playsets and character toys
G.F. Ridenour
Fun House Toy Co.
P.O. Box 343
Bradfordwoods, PA 15015-0343
412-935-1392 (FAX capable)

Model Kits
Specializing in figures and science fiction
Gordy Dutt
P.O. Box 201
Sharon Center, OH 44274-0201
216-239-1657 or 216-239-2991

Also action figures, monsters (especially Godzilla and Japan automated toys), Star Trek and non-sports cards
Alan Edwards
Toys From the Crypt
P.O. Box 3294
Shawnee, KS 66203
913-383-1242

From and of science fiction, TV, movies, figures, space, missiles, comics, etc.
John F. Green Inc.
1821 W. Jacaranda Pl
Fullerton, CA 92633
714-526-5467

Character, space, monster, Western, radio and cereal premiums and toys; GI Joe, Captain Action, tin toys and windups
Ed Janey
2920 Meadowbrook Dr. SE
Cedar Rapids, IA 52403
319-362-5213

Also plastic toys and radio, movie or TV tie-ins, movie posters
The Toy Cellar
John and Sheri Pavone
29 Sullivan Rd.
Peru, NY 12972

Non-Sport Trading Cards
Send $1 for our 40-page catalog of non-sport cards ca 1970 to date; dealers send large SASE for our 10-page wholesale and close-out list
Mark and Val Macaluso
3603 Newark Rd.
Marion, NY 14505
315-926-4349; FAX 315-926-4853

Also promotional and model cars
Greg Plonski
93 Beaver Dr.
Kings Park, NY 11754-2209

Pedal Cars
Also specializing in Maytag collectibles
Nate Stoller
960 Reynolds Ave.
Ripon, CA 95366
510-481-2586

Penny Toys
Jane Anderson
Rt. 1, Box 1030
Saylorsburg, PA 18353

Also Tootsietoys, buy and sell
Bob Stevens
529 N. Water St.
Masontown, PA 15461
412-583-8234

Pez Candy Dispensers
Marlis Bean
3525 Glen Oak Dr.
Eugene, OR 97405
503-683-3855

Richard Belyski
P.O. Box 124
Sea Cliff, NY 11579

Trading, buying and selling since 1991
SLX Toys
7233 Michael Rd., Apt. #1
Orchard Park, NY 14127-1406
716-674-0432

Plastic Figures
Also Dakins, cartoon and advertising figures, and character squeeze toys
Jim Rash
135 Alder Ave.
Pleasantville, NJ 08232
609-649-4125

Playsets
Also GI Joe, Star Trek and Dinosaurs
Mike and Kurt Fredericks
145 Bayline Circle
Folsom, CA 95630-8077

Political Toys
Michael and Polly McQuillen
McQuillen's Collectibles
P.O. Box 1141
Indianapolis, IN 46201
317-322-8518

Promotional Vehicles
'50s and '60s models (especially Ford); also F&F Post Cereal cars
Larry Blodget
Box 753
Rancho Mirage, CA 92270

Puzzles
Wood jigsaw type, from before 1950
Bob Armstrong
15 Monadnock Rd.
Worcester, MA 01609

Radios
Authors of several books on antique, novelty, and transistor radios
Sue and Marty Bunis
RR 1, Box 36
Bradford, NH 03221-9102

Ramp Walkers
Specializing in walkers, ramp-walking figures, and tin windups
Randy Welch
1100 Hambrooks Blvd.
Cambridge, MD 20783
410-228-5390

Russian and East European Toys
Wooden Matrioskha dolls, toys of tin, plastic, diecast metal; military theme and windups
Natural Way/DBA Russian Toy Co.
820 Massachusetts
Lawrence, KS 66044
913-841-0100

Specializing in Russian Toys
Vofka Gorokhowsky
2492 No. Murray #110
Milwaukee, WI 53211

Sand Toys
Jane Anderson
Rt. 1, Box 1030
Saylorsburg, PA 18353

Slot Cars
Especially HO scale from the 1960s to the present; also vintage diecast
Joe Corea
New Jersey Nostalgia Hobby
401 Park Ave.
Scotch Plains, NJ 07076
908-322-2676; FAX 908-322-4079

Specializing in slots and model racing from the '60s-'70s; especially complete race sets in original boxes
Gary Pollastro
5047 84th Ave. SE
Mercer, WA, 98040
206-232-3199

Soldiers
Barclay, Manoil, Grey Iron, Jones, dimestore types and others; also Sirrocco figures
Stan and Sally Alekna
4724 Kernan Mill Lane E
Jacksonville, FL 32224
904-992-9525

Star Wars
Also other toys, advertising, antiques, and fine art
June Moon
245 N Northwest Hwy
Park Ridge, IL 60068
708-825-1411 (24-hr phone)
FAX 708-825-6090

Star Wars, Star Trek
Also picture records, Little House on the Prairie, Wallace and Berrie figurines
Pak-Rat
Andrew Galbus
1608 4th Ave. NW
Austin, MN 55912-1416
507-437-1784 (5 pm to 10 pm Central)

Steiff
Especially limited editions
Cynthia's Country Store
11496 Pierson Rd., #C1
Commerce Park - Wellington
West Palm Beach, FL 33414
407-793-0554; FAX 407-795-4222

Particularly bears; also Schucos and dolls
Bunny Walker
Box 502
Bucyrus, OH 44820
419-562-8355

Taxi Cabs
Anything Taxicab; buy, sell and trade
Nathan Willensky
5 E 22nd St. #24C
New York, NY 10010
212-982-2156

Tonka
Also candy containers and German nodders
Doug Dezso
864 Patterson Ave.
Maywood, NJ 07607
201-488-1311

Toothbrush Holders
Also Pez
Marilyn Cooper
8408 Lofland Dr.
Houston, TX 77055

Tootsietoys
David Richter
6817 Sutherland Dr.
Mentor, OH 44060-3917
Author of Collector's Guide to Tootsietoys

Tractors
Ertl, John Deere, any and all
Gary Haisley
542 Circle Dr.
Fairmount, IN 46928

Trains
Lionel, American Flyer and Plasticville
Gary's Trains
R.D. #2, Box 147
Boswell, PA 15531
814-629-9277

Also Fisher Price, Tonka toys and diecast vehicles
Bill Mekalian
550 E Chesapeake Cir.
Fresno, CA 93720
209-434-3247

Buying American Flyer S gauge. Toys of all types for sale. Satisfaction guaranteed; color photos with SASE; shipping extra. No return calls on sold items; phone until midnight
Linda and Paul Woodward
14 Argo Drive
Sewell, NJ 08080-1908
609-582-1253

Toy Mall; general line (toys on second floor)
Bo-Jo's Antique Mall
3400 Summer Avenue
Memphis, TN 38122
901-323-2050

Transformers
Specializing in Transformers, Robotech, Shogun Warriors, Gadaikins, and any other robots; want to buy these MIP — also selling similar items
David Kolodny-Nagy
May through Jan:
3701 Connecticut Ave. NW #500
Washington, DC 20008
Jan through May:
MB 845 Brandeis University
P.O. Box 9110
Waltham, MA 02251-9110
202-364-8753
For copy of BotCon Transformer Comic Book, *Comic Smorgasbord Special*, send $3 + $1.50 for single issues, $2.50 each for 10 or more + $2. Also available: *Transformers: BotCon '94 Ten-Year Retrospective* (130+ pages) at $15 + $2

Trolls
Roger Inouye
765 E. Franklin Ave.
Pomona, CA 91766

View-Master
Roger Nazeley
4921 Castor Ave.
Phil., PA 19124
FAX 215-288-8030

Windups
Especially German and Japan tin toys,
Cracker Jack, toothbrush holders, radio pre-
miums, pencil sharpeners and comic strip toys
Phil Helley
Old Kilbourne Antiques
629 Indiana Ave.
Wisconsin Dells, WI 53965
608-254-8770

Also pressed steel toys, battery-ops, candy
containers, dolls and children's things, games,
soldiers, Noah's ark, space, robots, etc.
Jacquie and Bob Henry
Antique Treasures and Toys
Box 17
Walworth, NY 14568-0017
315-986-1424

Also battery-operated toys; cast-iron cars
and other vehicles; vintage toys
Kent Comstock
507 Vine St.
Ashland, OH 44805

Fine character windups; also Black Americana
Stephen Leonard
Box 127
Albertson, LI, NY 11507
516-742-0979

Also friction and battery operated; Fast-food
toys, displays
Scott Smiles
848 SE Atlantic Dr.
Lantana, FL 33462-4702
407-582-4947

Yo-Yos
Lucky Meisenheimer
7300 Sand Lake Commons Blvd.
Orlando, FL 32819
407-354-0478

Clubs, Newsletters and Other Publications

There are hundreds of clubs, newsletters and magazines available to toy collectors today. Listed here are some devoted to specific areas of interest. You can obtain a copy of many newsletters simply by requesting a sample.

Action Figure News & Toy Review
James Tomlinson, Editor
556 Monroe Turnpike
Monroe, CT 06458
203-452-7286; FAX 203-452-0410

Action Toys Newsletter
P.O. Box 31551, Billings, MT 59107
406-248-4121

The Antique Trader Weekly
Kyle D. Husfloen, Editor
P.O. Box 1050
Dubuque, IA 52004

American Game Collectors Assn.
49 Brooks Ave.
Lewiston, MA 04240

American International Matchbox Collectors
& Exchange Club News-Monthly
Dottie Colpitts
532 Chestnut St.
Lynn, MA 01904
617-595-4135

Anchor Block Foundation
908 Plymouth St.
Pelham, NY 10303
914-738-2935

Antique Advertising Association
P.O. Box 1121
Morton Grove, IL 60053
708-446-0904

Antique & Collectors Reproduction News
Mark Cherenka
Circulation Department
P.O. Box 71174
Des Moines, IA 50325
800-227-5531
Monthly newsletter showing differences
between old originals and new reproduc-
tions; subscription: $32 per year

Antique Trader Weekly
Kyle D. Husfloen, Editor
P.O. Box 1050
Dubuque, IA 52004
Subscription $32 (52 issues) per year

The Autograph Review (newsletter)
Jeffrey Morey
305 Carlton Rd.
Syracuse, NY 13207
315-474-3516

Autographs & Memorabilia
P.O. Box 224
Coffeyville, KS 67337
316-251-5308
6 issues per year on movie and sports
memorabilia

Barbie Bazaar (magazine)
5617 Sixth Ave., Dept NY593
Kenosha, WI 53140
414-658-1004; FAX 414-658-0433
6 issues for $25.95

Barbie Talks Some More!
Jacqueline Horning
7501 School Rd.
Cincinnati, OH 45249

The Baum Bugle
The International Wizard of Oz Club
Fred M. Meyer
220 N 11th St.
Escanaba, MI 49829

Berry-Bits
Strawberry Shortcake Collectors' Club
Peggy Jimenez
1409 72nd St.
N Bergen, NJ 07047

Beyond the Rainbow Collector's Exchange
P.O. Box 31672
St. Louis, MO 63131

Big Little Times
Big Little Book Collectors Club of America
Larry Lowery
P.O. Box 1242
Danville, CA 94526
415-837-2086

Bojo
P.O. Box 1203
Cranberry Township, PA 16033-2203
412-776-0621 (9 am to 9 pm EST)
Issues fixed-price catalog containing Beatles and rock 'n' roll memorabilia

Buckeye Marble Collectors Club
Betty Barnard
472 Meadowbrook Dr.
Newark, Oh 43055
614-366-7002

Bulletin
Doll Collectors of America
14 Chestnut Rd.
Westford, MA 01886
617-692-8392

Bulletin of the NAWCC
National Assn. of Watch and Clock Collectors, Inc.
Thomas J. Bartels, Executive Director
514 Poplar St.
Columbia, PA 17512-2130
717-684-8621; FAX 717-684-0878

Canadian Toy Collectors Society
Gary A. Fry
P.O. Box 636
Maple, Ontario, Canada L6A 1S5

Candy Container Collectors of America
P.O. Box 352
Chelmsford, MA 01824-0352
or
Jeff Bradfield
90 Main St.
Dayton, VA 22821

The Candy Gram newsletter
Candy Container Collectors of America
Douglas Dezso
864 Paterson, Ave.
Maywood, NJ 07607
201-845-7707

Captain Action Collectors Club
P.O. Box 2095
Halesite, NY 11743
516-423-1801
Send SASE for newsletter information

Cast Iron Toy Collectors of America
Paul McGinnis
1340 Market St.
Long Beach, CA 90805

Cat Collectors Club
33161 Wendy Dr.
Sterling Heights, MI 48310
Subscription: $18 per year

Cat Talk
Marilyn Dipboye
31311 Blair Dr.
Warren, MI 48092
313-264-0285

Century Limited
Toy Train Collectors Society
160 Dexter Terrace
Tonawanda, NY 14150
716-694-3771

Coca-Cola Collectors Club International
P.O. Box 49166
Atlanta, GA 30359
Annual dues: $25

Collecting Tips Newsletter
% Meredith Williams
P.O. Box 633
Joplin, MO 64802
417-781-3855 or 417-624-2518
12 issues per year focusing on fast-food collectibles

Collector Glass News
P.O. Box 308
Slippery Rock, PA 16057
412-946-9012; FAX 412-946-2838
6 issues per year focusing on character glasses, $15 per year

The Cookie Jar Collector's Club News
Louise Messina Daking
595 Cross River Rd.
Katonah, NY 10536
914-232-0383; FAX 914-232-0384

Cookie Jarrin' with Joyce: The Cookie Jar Newsletter
R.R. 2, Box 504
Walterboro, SC 29488

Cynthia's Country Store
Wellington Mall #15A
12794 West Forest Hill Blvd.
West Palm Beach, FL 33414
FAX or phone 407-793-0554
Specializing in Steiff new, discontinued and antique. Publishes quarterly Steiff and bear-related newsletter and limited edition yearly price guide. $15 per year for both. Call or FAX for information or if you have any questions. Also specializes in pieces by R. John Wright, other bear manufacturers, toy soldiers and some old toys. Many Steiff color catalogs and books available.

Dark Shadows Collectibles Classified
Sue Ellen Wilson
6173 Iroquois Trail
Mentor, OH 44060
216-946-6348
For collectors of both old and new series

Dionne Quint Collectors Club (see also *Quint News*)
Jimmy Rodolfos
P.O. Box 2527
Woburn, MA 01888
617-933-2219

Doll Investment Newsletter
P.O. Box 1982
Centerville, MA 02632

Doll News
United Federation of Doll Clubs
P.O. Box 14146
Parkville, MO 64152

Dollhouse & Miniature Collectors Quarterly
Sharon Unger, Editor
P.O. Box 16
Bellaire, MI 49615
$20.00 for 4 issues per year, 45-50 pages of information, buy & sell ads, pricing information.

Dunbar's Gallery
76 Haven St.
Milford, MA 01757
508-634-8697; FAX 508-634-8698
Specializing in quality advertising, Halloween, toys, coin-operated machines; holding cataloged auctions occasionally, lists available

Ephemera News
The Ephemera Society of America, Inc.
P.O. Box 37, Schoharie, NY 12157
518-295-7978

The Ertl Replica
Ertl Collectors Club
Mike Meyer, Editor
Hwys 136 & 20
Dyersville, IA 52040
319-875-2000

The Fisher-Price Collector's Club
This club issues a monthly newsletter
packed with information and ads for toys.
For more information write to:
Fisher-Price Club, CC Jeanne Kennedy
1442 N. Ogden
Mesa, AZ 85205

FLAKE, The Breakfast Nostalgia Magazine
P.O. Box 481
Cambridge, MA 02140
617-492-5004
Bimonthly illustrated issue devoted to
one hot collecting area such as Disney,
etc., with letters, discoveries, new
releases, and ads; single issue: $4 ($6 foreign); annual: $20 ($28 foreign); free 25-
word ad with new subscription

Friends of Hoppy Club and Newsletter
Laura Bates
6310 Friendship Dr.
New Concord, OH 43762-9708
614-826-4850

Game Times
American Game Collectors Assn.
Joe Angiolillo, Pres.
4628 Barlow Dr.
Bartlesville, OK 74006

Garfield Collectors Society Newsletter
% David L. Abrams, Editor
744 Foster Ridge Rd.
Germantown, TN 38138-7036
901-753-1026

Gene Autry Star Telegram
Gene Autry Development Assn.
Chamber of Commerce
P.O. Box 158
Gene Autry, OK 73436

Ginny Doll Club News
Jeanne Niswonger
305 W Beacon Rd.
Lakeland, FL 33803
813-687-8015

Gone With the Wind Collectors Club Newsletter
8105 Woodview Rd.
Ellicot City, MD 21043
301-465-4632

Good Bears of the World
Terri Stong
P.O. Box 13097
Toledo, OH 43613

Grandma's Trunk
P.O. Box 404
Northport, MI 49670
Subscription: $8 per year for 1st class or
$5 per year for bulk rate

Hartland Newsletter
Gail Fitch
1733 N. Cambridge Ave., #109
Milwaukee, WI 53202
Subscription: $8 for 6 issues or $4.50 for 3
issues. Classified ads are $2 for 50 words.

Headquarters Quarterly, for GI Joe
Collectors
Joe Bodnarchuk
62 McKinley Ave.
Kenmore, NY 14217-2414

Hello Again, Old-Time Radio Show
Collector
Jay A. Hickerson
P.O. Box 4321
Hamden, CT 06514
203-248-2887; FAX 203-281-1322
Sample copy upon request with SASE

Highballer for Toy Train collectors
% Lou Bohn
109 Howedale Dr.
Rochester, NY 14616-1543

Hobby News
J.L.C. Publications
Box 258
Ozone Park, NY 11416

Holly Hobbie Newsletter
Helen McCale
Route 3, Box 35
Butler, MO 64730

Hopalong Cassidy Newsletter
Hopalong Cassidy Fan Club
P.O. Box 1361
Boyes Hot Springs, CA 95416

Ideal Doll & Toy Collectors Club
P.O. Box 623
Lexington, MA 02173
617-862-2994

International Figure Kit Club
Gordy's
P.O. Box 201
Sharon Center, OH 44274-0201
216-239-1657; FAX 216-239-2991

International Wizard of Oz Club Inc.
P.O. Box 95
Kinderhook, IL 62345

Kit Builders Magazine
Gordy's
P.O. Box 201
Sharon Center, OH 44274-0201
216-239-1657; FAX 216-239-2991

Madame Alexander Fan Club Newsletter
Earl Meisinger
11 S 767 Book Rd.
Naperville, IL 60564

Marble Mania
Marble Collectors Society of America
Stanley Block
P.O. Box 222
Trumbull, CT 06611
203-261-3223

Martha's Kidlit Newsletter
Box 1488A
Ames, IA 50010
A bimonthly publication for children's
books collectors. Subscription: $25 per
year

Matchbox USA
Charles Mack
62 Saw Mill Rd.
Durham, CT 06422
203-349-1655

McDonald's Collecting Tips
Meredith Williams
Box 633
Joplin, MO 64802
Send SASE for information

McDonald's Collector Club
Joyce & Terry Losonsky
7506 Summer Leave Ln.
Columbia, MD 21046-2455
301-381-3358
Authors of *Illustrated Collector's Guide to
McDonald's® Happy Meal® Boxes, Premiums, & Promotions©* with updated 1994
values; available for $9.50 (includes
postage)

McDonald's Collector Club 'Sunshine Chapter'
Bill and Pat Poe, founders
c/o Dominica Circle. E.
Niceville, FL 32578-4068
904-897-4163; FAX 904-897-2606

McDonald's Collector Club Newsletter
% Tenna Greenberg
5400 Waterbury Rd.
Des Moines, IA 50312
515-279-0741

Model & Toy Collector Magazine
Toy Scouts, Inc.
137 Casterton Ave.
Akron, OH 44303
216-836-0668; FAX 216-869-8668

Modern Doll Club Journal
Jeanne Niswonger
305 W Beacon Rd.
Lakeland, FL 33803

The Mouse Club East (Disney collectors)
P.O. Box 3195
Wakefield, MA 01880
Family membership: $25 (includes
newsletters and 2 shows per year)

The Mouse Club (newsletter)
Kim and Julie McEuen
2056 Cirone Way
San Jose, CA 95124
408-377-2590; FAX 408-379-6903

Movie Advertising Collector (magazine)
George Reed
P.O. Box 28587
Philadelphia, PA 19149

NAOLH Newsletter
National Assn. for Outlaw & Lawman History
Hank Clark
P.O. Box 812
Waterford, CA 95386
209-874-2640

NAPAC Newsletter
National Assn. of Paper and Advertising
Collectors
P.O. Box 500
Mt. Joy, PA 17552
717-653-4300

National Fantasy Fan Club (Disney collectors)
Dept. AC, Box 19212
Irvine, CA 92713
Membership: $20 per year, includes newsletters, free ads, chapters, conventions, etc.

National Headquarters News
Train Collectors Assn.
300 Paradise Ln.
Strasburg, PA 17579

Novelty Salt and Pepper Club
% Irene Thornburg, Membership Coordinator
581 Joy Rd.
Battle Creek, MI 49017
Publishes quarterly newsletter & annual roster. Annual dues: $20 in USA, Canada, and Mexico; $25 for all other countries

Paper Collectors' Marketplace
470 Main St., P.O. Box 128
Scandinavia, WI 54977
715-467-2379
Subscription: $17.95 (12 issues) per year in USA; Canada and Mexico add $15 per year

Paper Doll News
Ema Terry
P.O. Box 807
Vivian, LA 71082

Paper Pile Quarterly
P.O. Box 337
San Anselmo, CA 94979-0337
415-454-5552
Subscription: $12.50 per year in US and Canada

Peanuts Collector Club Newsletter
Peanuts Collector Club
Andrea C. Podley
P.O. Box 94
N Hollywood, CA 91603

The Pencil Collector
American Pencil Collectors Soc.
Robert J. Romey, Pres.
2222 S Millwood
Wichita, KS 67213
316-263-8419

Pepsi-Cola Collectors Club Newsletter
Pepsi-Cola Collectors Club
Bob Stoddard
P.O. Box 1275
Covina, CA 91722
714-593-8750
Membership: $15

Pez Collector's News
Richard and Marianne Belyski, Editors
P.O. Box 124
Sea Cliff, NY 11579
516-676-1183
First issue due to be released October 1995; call for information

Plastic Figure & Playset Collector
5894 Lakeview Ct. E
Onalaska, WI 54650

The Pokey Gazette, A Little Golden Book collector newsletter
Steve Santi
19626 Ricardo Ave.
Hayward, CA 94541
510-481-2586

Positively PEZ
Crystal and Larry LaFoe
3851 Gable Lane Dr., Apt. 513
Indianapolis, IN 46208

The Prehistoric Times
Mike and Kurt Fredericks
145 Bayline Circle
Folsom, CA 95630
916-985-7986
For collectors of dinosaur toys; 6 issues (1 yr), $19

Quint News (see also Dionne Quint Collectors Club)
Dionne Quint Collectors
P.O. Box 2527
Woburn, MA 01888
617-933-2219

Record Collectors Monthly (newspaper)
P.O. Box 75
Mendham, NJ 07945
201-543-9520; FAX 201-543-6033

Roy Rogers-Dale Evans Collectors Assn.
Nancy Horsley
P.O. Box 1166
Portsmouth, OH 45662

Schoenhut Newsletter
Schoenhut Collectors Club
Robert Zimmerman
45 Louis Ave.
W Seneca, NY 14224

The Shirley Temple Collectors News
8811 Colonial Rd.
Brooklyn, NY 11209
Dues: $20 per year; checks paybable to Rita Dubas

The Silent Film Newsletter
Gene Vazzana
140 7th Ave.
New York, NY 10011
Subscription $18, send $2.50 for sample copy

The Silver Bullet
Terry and Kay Klepey
P.O. Box 553
Forks, WA 98331
206-327-3726
Subscription $10 per year, sample issue
$4; also licensed mail-order seller of mem-
orabilia and appraiser

Smurf Collectors Club
24ACH, Cabot Rd. W
Massapequa, NY 11758
Membership includes newsletters. LSASE
for information

Steiff Life
Steiff Collectors Club
Beth Savino
% The Toy Store
7856 Hill Ave.
Holland, OH 43528
419-865-3899 or 800-862-8697

The Television History Magazine
William J. Flechner
700 E Macoupin St.
Staunton, IL 62088
618-635-2712

Toy Collector Club of America (for Ertl toys)
P.O. Box 302
Dyersdille, IA 52040
800-452-3303

Toy Dish Collectors
Abbie Kelly
P.O. Box 351
Camillus, NY 13031
315-487-7415

Toy Gun Collectors of America Newsletter
Jim Buskirk, Editor & Publisher
175 Cornell St.
Windsor CA 95492
707-837-9949
Published quarterly, covers cap guns,
spring air BB guns and other toy guns.
Dues: $15 per year; SASE for information

Toy Shop
700 E State St.
Iola, WI 54990
715-445-2214
Subscription (3rd class) $23.95 for 26 issues

Toy Trader
100 Bryant St.
Dubuque, Iowa 52003
1-800-364-5593
subscription in US $24 for 12 issues

Toychest
Antique Toy Collectors of America, Inc.
2 Wall St., 13th Floor
New York, NY 10005
212-238-8803

Toys & Prices (magazine)
700 E State St.
Iola, WI 54990-0001
715-445-2214; FAX 715-445-4087
Subscription: $14.95 per year

Transformer Club
Liane Elliot
6202 34th St., NW
Gig Harbor, WA 98335

The Trade Card Journal
Kit Barry
86 High St.
Brattleboro, VT 05301
802-254-2195
A quarterly publication on the social and
historical use of trade cards

The Trick or Treat Trader
CJ Russell and the Halloween Queen
Antiques
P.O. Box 499, 4 Lawrence St. and Rt. 10
Winchester, NH, 03470
Subscription is $15 a year for 4 issues or
$4 for a sample.

Trainmaster (newsletter)
P.O. Box 1499
Gainesville, FL 32602
904-377-7439 or 904-373-4908
FAX 904-374-6616

Troll Monthly
5858 Washington St.
Whitman, MA 02382
800-858-7655 or 800-85-Troll

Turtle River Farm Toys
Rt. 1, Box 44
Manvel, ND 58256-9763

The TV Collector
Diane L. Albert
P.O. Box 1088
Easton, MA 02334-1088
508-238-1179
Send $4 for sample copy

View-Master Reel Collector
Roger Nazeley
4921 Castor Ave.
Philadelphia, PA 19124
215-743-8999

Western & Serials Club
Rt. 1, Box 103
Vernon Center, NM 56090
507-549-3677

The Working Class Hero (Beatles newsletter)
3311 Niagara St.
Pittsburgh, PA 15213-4223
Published 3 times per year; send SASE for
information

The Wrapper
Bubble Gum & Candy Wrapper Collectors
P.O. Box 573
St. Charles, IL 60174
708-377-7921

The Yellow Brick Road Fantasy Museum
& Gift Shop
Rt. 49 & Yellow Brick Rd.
Chesterton, IN 46304
219-926-7048

NOEL BARRETT
ANTIQUES & AUCTIONS

Box 1001 • Carversville, PA 18913
215-297-5109 • Fax 297-0457

PERSONALIZED SERVICE
QUALITY CATALOGING
FIRST RATE PROMOTION

BACK ISSUE CATALOGS WITH PRICES REALIZED FOR SALE

We are known for the quality of our catalogs, many of which have become price and identification guides in their fields. We have a limited supply of back numbers for sale. All are supplied with post-sale price-keys as well as pre-sale estimates.

THE TOM ANDERSON COLLECTION: APRIL 1991 The finest collection of American clockwork toys ever sold at auction. More than 60 classic toy are pictured in full color, plus American tin toys, Christmas items, folk art and country store fixtures. More than 20 pages of color. Issue price $20. now $12.00

SIEGEL COLLECTION OF GAMES & TOYS: JUNE 1992 The definitive game auction - more than 700 items described - over 200 games pictured in color plus numerous lithographed toys, blocks and puzzles also pictured in color - plus optical toys, Christmas toys, penny toys, etc. -- 32 pages of color plus full color covers. Price: $22.00

SPILHAUS COLLECTION: MECHANICAL TOYS: JULY 1993
500 toys from this renowned collection: mechanicals,
Schoenhut, automata, etc. 8 pages color, -- $12.00

HAROLD WILLIAMS COLLECTION OF PRESSED STEEL:
NOVEMBER 1992 - near definitive collection of large
pressed steel toys: Buddy L, Keystone, Steelcraft,
Kingsbury, etc. plus 120 windups. --- $22.00

PRESSED STEEL PLAYTHINGS - RALSTON COLLECTION:
NOVEMBER 1993 - 450 pressed steel toys large and
small all pictured in color. -- $25.00

PRESSED STEEL COMBO: order both for $37.00

Send orders to:
BARRETT AUCTION CATALOGS • PO BOX 1001
CARVERSVILLE, PA 18913

THE GOTTSCHALK COLLECTIONS

AUTOMOTIVE TOYS AT AUCTION: APRIL 6 & 7 1990 - The classic book on Automotive toys by Lillian Gottschalk is Out of Print. But the entire book is reproduced in this catalog together with many toys not in book. 700 items pictured in black and white: cast iron, tin, and steel. Price $20.00

STEAM TOYS & OTHER TOYS: JUNE 2, 1990 - 500 items: comprehensive collection of steam engines and accessories, plus American tin, clockwork toys, & aeronautical toys. Issue price: $20 -- now $12.00

AUTOMOBILIA AT AUCTION: OCTOBER 3, 1989 - 400 items: auto mascots, gas globes, pedal cars, signs, ceramics., etc. issue price: $18.00, now $10
Buy set and get illustrated sales list : GOTTSCHALK IV - OCTOBER 1990 - automotive toys, Steelcraft Trucks, etc., - 530 lots - 100 items pictured.

COMPLETE GOTTSCHALK SET: $40.

Please include $3.00 for postage and handling.

Antique Toys and Collectibles

Auctions held in our galleries at Christie's East,
219 East 67th Street, New York, New York 10021.
For further information, please contact the Collectibles
Department at 212 606 0543. For auction catalogues,
please telephone Christie's Publications at
800 395 6300.

A rare tinplate Marklin Ferris Wheel, circa 1890s, 21 in. high.
Sold at Christie's New York, June 1994, for $55,200.

Principal auctioneer: Kathleen Guzman #762176

CHRISTIE'S
EAST

Before you consign to any auction company, be certain you are *making the right choice.*
Ask the questions that could mean the difference between a *successful* return on your investment
or another *horror story to pass along to your friends.*

QUESTIONS	others	McMasters
• Do they have *years of experience and specialized knowledge?*	?	yes
• Are their policies and professional fees provided in *writing?*	?	yes
• Are they *members of UFDC?*	?	yes
• Are they *members of the National and State Auctioneer Association?*	?	yes
• Do they *personally pick-up and pack* your collection?	?	yes
• Do you receive a *complete list* at the time of pick-up?	?	yes
• Are catalog *descriptions complete enough* to encourage absentee bidding?	?	yes
• Are your items sold *without reserve* to assure larger auction attendance?	?	yes
• Are your items sold with *no buyer's premium* to promote higher prices?	?	yes
• Do you receive *payment after each sale* (not after the entire collection is sold)?	?	yes
• Have their catalogues *won National and State awards for excellence?*	?	yes

Let's be honest . . . . we have heard "horror" stories of other auction companies. At McMasters, we pride ourselves
in genuinely caring about our customers and their collection. We have 18 years of experience and have built our
business on being honest and fair with our customers. When you decide to sell your collection or estate,
we encourage you to "shop around" . . . . *then come to us for peace of mind.*

SIGN OF CONFIDENCE

McMasters

Since 1976

5855 Glenn Highway • P.O. Box 1755 • Cambridge, Ohio 43725

James E. McMasters, Auctioneer, Member OAA, PAA, NAA • Shari McMasters, Member UFDC

Office: 614-432-4419 • Fax: 614-432-3191

    McMasters . . . . the difference . . . . Integrity.

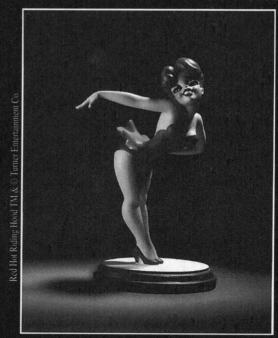

Index to Advertisers